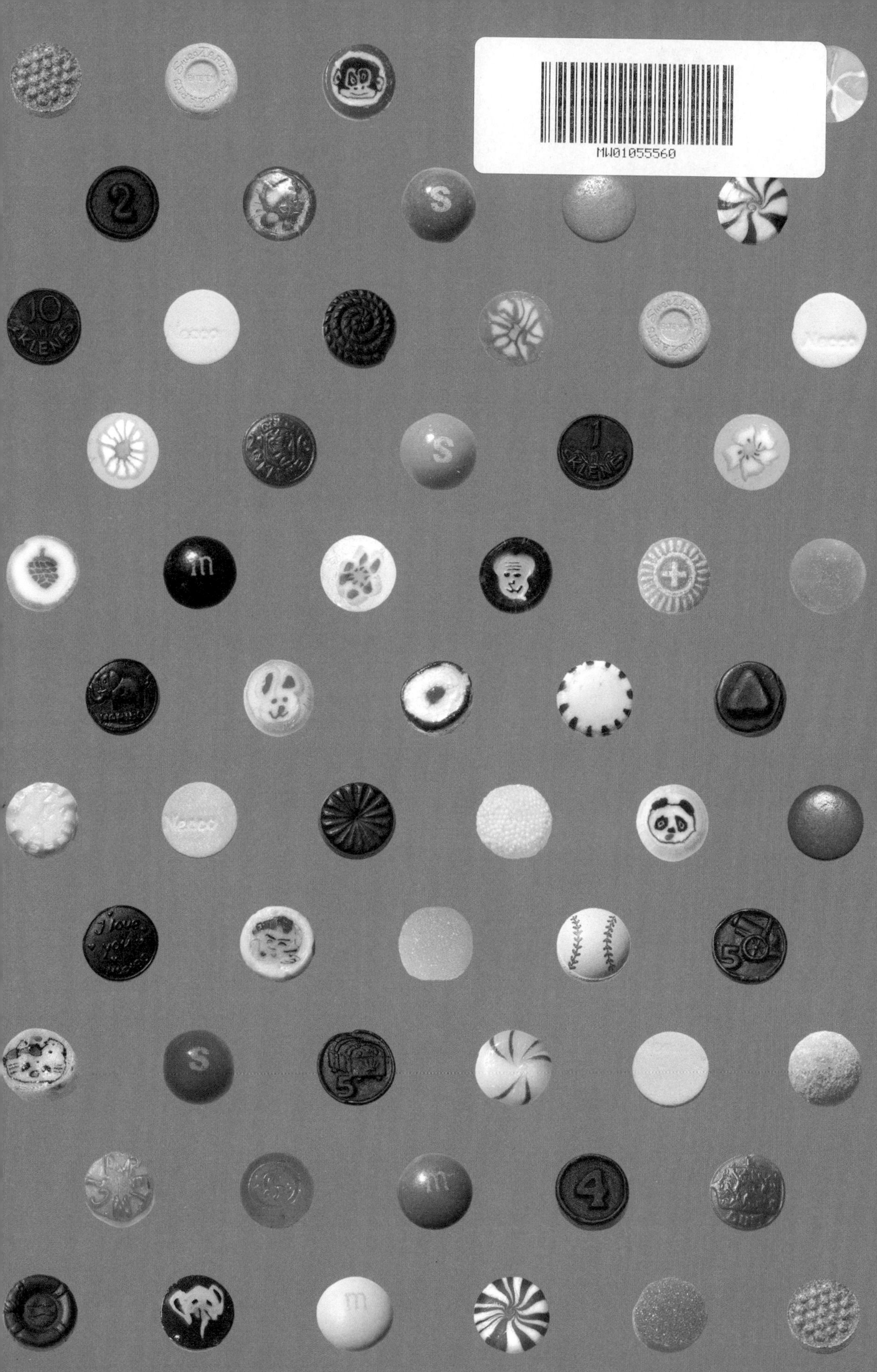
MW01055560

THE OXFORD COMPANION TO SUGAR AND SWEETS

OXFORD
UNIVERSITY PRESS

OXFORD
UNIVERSITY PRESS

Oxford University Press is a department of the University of Oxford. It furthers the University's objective of excellence in research, scholarship, and education by publishing worldwide.

Oxford New York
Auckland Cape Town Dar es Salaam Hong Kong Karachi
Kuala Lumpur Madrid Melbourne Mexico City Nairobi
New Delhi Shanghai Taipei Toronto

With offices in
Argentina Austria Brazil Chile Czech Republic France Greece
Guatemala Hungary Italy Japan Poland Portugal Singapore
South Korea Switzerland Thailand Turkey Ukraine Vietnam

Published in the United States of America by
Oxford University Press
198 Madison Avenue, New York, NY 10016
www.oup.com

Library of Congress Cataloging-in-Publication Data
Goldstein, Darra.
The Oxford companion to sugar and sweets / edited by Darra Goldstein.
pages cm
Includes bibliographical references and index.
ISBN 978-0-19-931339-6 (alk. paper)
1. Sweeteners—Encyclopedias. I. Title.
TP421.G65 2015
664'.1003—dc23 2015000402

1 3 5 7 9 8 6 4 2

Printed in the United States of America
on acid-free paper

CONTENTS

FOREWORD

I can remember easily the first time I stood deep in a field of sugarcane in full bloom, a field already marked for harvesting. It was the spring of 1948, and I had just begun fieldwork in Puerto Rico. The field lay in a rural barrio on the south coast of the island, only about a hundred yards inland from the beach. The well-irrigated soil in which the cane was growing was clayey, black in color. It looked cool under a blinding sun, but the air in the field was intensely hot.

The cane was the kind called *gran cultura* (literally, "big growth"), a term that means only that it was left to grow for 15 months or even more before being cut. Topped by the pale, wheat-like, lavender sugarcane blossoms they call *guajana*, the cane was thicker than a man's wrist. Standing more than 12 feet tall, these plants are bred to be one of the most substantial and important economic grasses in the world. They were full to bursting of their intensely sweet green sap, *guarapo*, which is drunk by the cupful nearly everywhere that cane is grown.

That sap is not won easily from the cane. Once it is cut and stripped of its leaves, it must be delivered to the mill as soon as possible to be crushed, ground, and soaked to extract its juice, before it begins to dry out or to sour. When freshly extracted, *guarapo* is definitely an acquired taste, even among sweet-crazed humans. Gray-green in color, lukewarm and cloying, and, if not strained, full of bits of cane fiber and other even less pleasant stuff, it also brims over with calories. The cane on a single acre of good tropical land can supply about 8 million calories. To get that many calories in wheat requires 9 to 12 acres. (And how many acres to get that many calories in beef? Don't even ask.)

There is a great deal aesthetically pleasing about sugarcane. Each stalk is a tiny living photosynthetic factory, transformed by human effort to maximize its yield. But the history of these beautiful grasses, and of the people who have looked after them during these last 2,000 years or so, is not so much beautiful as profoundly tragic.

After 30 years' study of sugar and the countries that grow sugarcane and sugar beet and produce sugar in the New World, I started to write a book about it. I aimed to uncover the part that sugar played in world history during the first chapter of the economic system called capitalism. I knew something about the history of sugar. I realized that I would have to do what I could with this one thin thread, of sweetness and violence, embedded in the thick fabric of the past and stretching far back, long before anything like capitalism could even have been dreamed of. I found unexpected masses of data, much of it fascinating. What kept me afloat in a sea of alluring description was the simple hunch that sugarcane was not merely a "dessert crop," as scholars of tea, coffee, chocolate, and sugar were wont to describe it. Far more than desserts, I thought, the history of sugar's production and consumption might shed a bright light on the everyday unfolding of the capitalistic system.

Since it was linked for at least five centuries to the pain and suffering of millions of human beings, I have long thought of sugar's sweet thread as red in color—the color of blood. During the long struggle against the slave trade and slavery, blood was in fact the liquid the abolitionists came to invoke to depict the terrible work of men and women in chains: a teaspoonful of sugar for so many drops of blood.

This essay is not the place to examine that link at length. One aspect of it should be pointed out, however. North Americans in particular associate slavery with cotton, not sugar, because of the American Civil War. But the crop that benefited the slave owners in the Americas most, and the one that used the largest number of slaves, was sugarcane. Plantation slavery in the New World lasted more than three and a half centuries, and it was involved with the killing or enslavement of an estimated 13.5 million Africans and African Americans. These people, and their descendants, were the victims of this institution during 375 years of profit-taking by some, and weighty discussions of the ethics of enslavement by others. During the first half of those 375 years, the West's much-touted admiration for the idea of universal human freedom remained a terrible mockery. New World slavery simply grew more customary, and more important.

It has been sugar's singular virtue for humans that the taste of sweetness can seem almost timelessly exciting, by which I mean that its taste is so intense it can nearly drown our senses. That taste, unlike salt, sour, or bitter, seems, when experienced, to evoke a desire for more of the same in nearly everyone. And the memory of sweet is easily awakened; the desire can become patterned, habitual. One thoughtful scholar has wondered whether our memories of food are qualitatively different from the rest of human memory (Sutton, 2001), and he may be on to something. But I'd claim for sweetness a memory that may be qualitatively different from all other food. Sweetness is unlike any other taste to the tongue, and as sweet as mother's milk.

Sugar's easy acceptance into nearly all cuisines occurred because its taste was so singularly pure. I want to contemplate that taste, and its uses and manifold meanings, from a perspective I never had before: 65 years of looking at what today is a cheap and banal food, but was once unimaginably rare and costly. Behold the substance that would one day overcome the sweetness that permeates the Bible, that other ancient sweetness we all know as honey.

Honey

Eight thousand years ago, a Mesolithic artist painted a scene that imparts drama to an inveterate human greed. The painting is still there, on the wall of a cave in northern Spain. It portrays a human figure in a tree, enveloped in a cloud of insects. The insects are bees. This ancient evidence of our species-wide love of intense sweetness probably attests to what must have been a practice or custom among those people who depicted their experience on a cave wall. Such quests for sweetness are characteristic of members of our species. Chimpanzees and bonobos, primate relatives with whom we share nearly 98 percent of our DNA, also rob beehives. So far as can be told, wherever humans coexisted with bees, they went to great lengths to obtain the sweet gooey syrup. Many, including this writer, are persuaded that this lust has been part of primate nature for countless millennia.

Honey is the sweetness of the Bible. Samson's riddle (Judges 14) turns on bees' honey. There is no sugar in the Bible. But today all the honey on earth amounts to a figurative spoonful when compared to the world's sucrose, or "table sugar," as it is generally known. While honey has always been treasured for its great variety of distinctive tastes and odors, refined sugar, for so long now honey's greatest rival, tastes of nothing—that is, of nothing beyond sweetness itself. All artisanal honeys have distinctive tastes. They are justly prized for those differences, as are wines, hams, and coffees, among other food products. But because of sugar, the history of sweetness became a history of the so-called democratization of taste, a gigantic broadening of access to the mass production of factory food that has marked the emergence of the modern world. Sugar's triumph was not that it was sweet, or even that it became so cheap. Beyond these facts, and unlike all its rivals, sugar was nothing but sweet. It could be made pure white; it could be used in any dish, any beverage, any cake, pudding, or candy (and at one time any prescription)—while providing a taste of sweetness alone, to which any other taste could be added.

Honey has not disappeared. But cane and beet sugar, which, for culinary purposes, are the same, have gradually pushed aside the many other caloric sweeteners, such as maple syrup, palm sugar, sorghum syrup, carob, and so on. These sweeteners have not disappeared; each has its own taste, and most of them enjoy specialty markets. But sugar's market is the world, and for that market it is one product. The specialty markets of these other sweet foods are measured only against each other, not against sugar.

An epitome of sugar's conquest was the manufacture of a semi-refined sugar syrup and its subsequent naming as "golden syrup," thus reducing before the consumer's eyes the apparent differences between honey made by bees and a cane sugar derivative processed by men. The crowning touch was to display on its label a dead lion surrounded by bees, along with the answer to Samson's riddle—a biblical touch, courtesy of modern advertising. Though there is manifestly no honey in it, Golden Syrup has been eaten by generations of Englishmen as if they were eating honey. Golden Syrup is touted as England's first brand, a sugar syrup that replaced—and for most users, supplanted—the taste of honey. It was cheap; it came in two "flavors," light and dark; and it always tasted exactly the same. As noted earlier honeys are different from each other. The virtue of manufactured products is that they always taste the same, unlike the tastes of nature.

The Nature of Sugar, Culturally Speaking

Several characteristics of sugar stand out, the most important being that it is sweet. (Saying so is not quite so vacuous as it sounds.) Our species' diligent quest for sweetness appears to be universal, or nearly so. Though in some interesting cases, sugar has been tabooed, there is no evidence of any human group wholly uninterested in foods that taste sweet. Food taboos on the eating of a specific plant, animal, or other food (e.g., salt, eggs, blood) are common, but there is no taboo for sweetness. Nor has it been proven that a predisposition toward sweetness in humans and other primates is only determined genetically. Yet the evidence pointing to just such a structurally determined, species-wide, inborn liking for sweet is powerful. Many humans worldwide react positively to sweetness, and human infants everywhere exhibit signs of pleasure when given sweet-tasting liquids. The Eskimo and Inuit people of Alaska and Canada liked sucrose the first time they were given it, and they apparently chose to continue eating it even though it caused them digestive discomfort (Bell et al., 1973; Jerome, 1977). If this liking is indeed structurally determined, it may have evolved in relation to the sweetness of ripe fruit—a sign of edibility, as some writers have suggested.

But there are significant differences in worldwide consumption of sucrose (and other sweeteners). Whatever the role played by genes and sweet tooths, economic and social factors profoundly affect sugar consumption. Where sugar does become significant, governments are disposed to treat it as politically relevant, similar to the ways that they had long treated alcohol and then tobacco. Fondness for sugar, on the one hand, and the rich (but cheap) harvest of calories from tropical lands, on the other, help us understand why sweet things please not only consumers, but also governments and corporations. Sweet calories from sugar (not honey), then, are cheap and versatile calories, deliverable in many forms. Those of us who were around during World War II may remember how a nation accustomed to plentiful alcohol, tobacco, coffee, and sugar (not to mention beef) would turn uneasy and sullen when confronted with food rationing.

Sugar did not begin to be treated as an everyday pleasure before about 1800. For the poor, sugar became a necessity in popular European taste mostly as a companion to the novel hot stimulant beverages—coffee, tea, and chocolate. Tea and coffee reached Europe as drinks; sweetening them with sugar was a European addition. Before the nineteenth century, chocolate was also known in Europe only as a drink, and it became a sweetened drink as well. Only after the invention of conching in 1879, which made possible the even distribution of the cocoa butter in the chocolate, was it possible to begin mass-producing chocolate candy bars. In a later era, it would be flavored soda, notably Coca-Cola, that became a vehicle for sugar and caffeine. Such foods may become so popular that a scarcity of sugar could prove to be as urgent politically as a shortage of caffeine or alcohol. Like those others, and maybe more so, sugar is good to keep plentiful, and good to control. Internationally, the United States discovered, sugar is also a good tool to control other nations with, by using quotas and tariffs to reward and to punish.

Our affinity for sweetness permeates our language. Sweet words become loving words: honey, honeybunch, sweetie, muffin, sweetie pie, lollipop, sugar daddy, sweetheart. But there is more to this than terms of endearment. An engine runs sweetly. A tenor sings sweetly. Sweets for the sweet. Think of the running back Walter "Sweetness" Payton, or of the boxers Sugar Ray Leonard and, earlier, Sugar Ray Robinson. Money can be "sugar," too. We do not ask how come; it seems too obvious. "It mus' be jelly 'cause jam don' shake like dat" is notably suggestive about what sweetness can stand for. Both symbolically and metaphorically, sweetness is easily transferred to bodily activities beyond digestion.

Perhaps no other concept associated with the human sensory system has been so thoroughly worked over, sifted through, or squeezed as fondly for figures of speech as sweetness.

The idea of sweetness is close to our hearts, and probably even close to our awareness of our own bodies. Most of us learn it first as a taste at a tender age, and often in the arms of those who love us. Once we are old enough to take note, it is likely to settle into our consciousness, often with enduring affective associations. Bitterness, sourness, and saltiness—all tastes that are powerful stimuli to our sensory system—are patently different from sweetness. Like sweet, salt lies close to our particular—mammalian and primate—nature. Yet these tastes are never confused, and they can never replace each other. The gentle, insistently alluring nature of sweetness, however, has its own assertiveness. Anyone who has been interrupted by an urgent request while eating chocolate may be able to recall a faint but genuine irritation aroused by the need to reply before swallowing. That is because chewing sweet things while speaking are acts in conflict with each other. To articulate properly means having to swallow the bolus of semi-melted chocolate in one's mouth, and thus losing forever the fleeting sweet sensation that particular mouthful promised—a sacrifice the brain was already anticipating.

A remarkable feature of sugar is the ways in which, over the course of time, it has been employed aesthetically. When thoroughly mixed together, sugar and ground almonds with a bit of oil becomes a kind of modeling clay. When heated, refined white sugar liquefies. Properly handled as it dries, it can be dyed, spun, blown, artistically cast, or painted. Its uses in these ways have long existed in China, India, and the Middle East. Once sugar spread from the Old World to the New, its production expanded explosively, and it was put to such uses in many other places. Hence, there is no single center of origin for the artistic uses of sugar, even though the baker-sculptors of Egypt, Italy, Germany, and the United Kingdom, and the candy makers of Mexico and Indonesia, among others, are justly famous. Spun and sculpted sugar figures—some classic, some comical—seem to have become popular wherever artistic individuals happened to work in or near kitchens.

Using techniques probably borrowed from the Middle East, the sixteenth-century European sugar artists produced replicas of famous sculptures called *trionfi*, or "triumphs," for display at grand banquets in Italian centers of trade and luxury. In Great Britain and France, large sugar sculptures depicting cathedrals and castles, some emblazoned with messages, became a vogue among royalty and the high clergy. In England they were called "subtleties." Such artful play with sugar depended not only upon the confectioner's skill, but also upon an early post-Columbian drop in the price of sugar. When production was moved to the rich, ample lowlands of the Caribbean and intensive mass production became possible, the price began to fall. Lower prices put the purchase of large quantities of sugar within the easy reach of the wealthy and powerful, but not the poor. It would be another three centuries before sugar would become an everyday necessity of the European wage earner.

Like its shapes, sugar's colors also became an experimental arena. But the process for producing a granular white or powdered sugar was long paramount. When it can be fully refined, sugar becomes white, and it can then be further whitened chemically. If not fully refined, it will be some shade of brown. The molasses drained from semi-crystalline sugar varies in color from brown to nearly black; the final molasses (used commonly for animal feed) is called "blackstrap," and black is its color. The world is full of local sugars that come in various shades of brown and in various shapes, depending on local processing methods. Crystalline sugar almost certainly was made for the first time in India, and Sanskrit textual references to sugar are the world's most ancient; sugar there figures frequently in religious ritual. But in India, for sugar to be ritually pure, it must not be white. At one time most sugar was not white, because it was incompletely refined, and hence brown. Such incompletely refined sugars have distinctive tastes, and for this reason might be called "unmodern."

At some point the whiteness of sugar probably became an ideal, because white—at least in some places—suggested purity. Long before it had become ordinary, fine white sugar was made into a costly and desirable medicine by lengthy, labor-intensive processing. Every medicine for the Black Death (bubonic plague) contained powdered white sugar, which was also a favored item for treating eye ailments. Unfortunately, when mixed with gold dust and ground pearl and blown into the eyes, this remedy had nothing to recommend it beyond its cost and the fact that it was unavailable to the poor. One famous eighteenth-century English doctor touted sugar as a dentifrice, explaining to his patients how children more eagerly drank milk and other liquids if they had been sweetened beforehand. It is slightly humbling to notice that, only a few decades ago, Coca-Cola was being advertised as a health drink for the young.

Whiteness, medicine, and sugar reappear together in the Spanish *manjar blanco* and the French *blanc manger*, dishes composed of breast of chicken, almond milk or ground almonds, white bread, milk, ginger, and sugar. These were dishes intended for invalids, and the idea that what is pure can purify may have been embodied in them. Sugar did not disappear from the Western pharmacopeia until well into the twentieth century, while the association between whiteness and purity has still not lost its pull upon Western thinking.

Problems with a Future

People have been eating sucrose in its seemingly infinite incarnations for nearly two millennia. Touted and damned for centuries, all that seems certain is that the human craving for it is unimpaired. Even a glance at its world tonnage over the last couple of centuries suggests as much. Yet, over the course of the last half-century or so, sugar's position as the world's greatest sweetener has been challenged, and some of those challenges may raise questions about its future success as a food for human beings. Foremost among these challenges is sugar's increasingly unfavorable press, inspired mostly by the role imputed to it in the higher rates of obesity, hypertension, diabetes, and other ailments in the United States and elsewhere. The industry has fought back fiercely, and it has held its ground with some success, at least in the United States. But the campaigns against processed foods and for healthier diets, organic foods, and sustainable agriculture, though still only blips on the sugar industry's screens, have refused to go away. While establishing a scientifically solid case against sucrose alone has turned out to be more difficult than it might seem, a large number of reputable food scholars, physicians, and nutritionists are convinced that sucrose is at the very least one of a number of guilty parties, especially in relation to young consumers.

The rise of noncaloric sweeteners has continued, and can, I believe, be expected to spread. At this point there are some new contenders among them, including Stevia. Though long used in other countries, glucosides of the plant *Stevia rebaudiana* are relatively new in the United States. While such sweeteners are mostly used by persons who cannot eat sucrose for medical reasons, or by those who are seeking to limit or control weight gain, the continued pressure such substances are putting on the sugar industry cannot be ignored.

A third challenge has been the growing importance of high-fructose corn syrup (HFCS), a contender for sugar's place since at least the 1970s. This rivalry is complicated, however, by evidence that *Stevia rebaudiana* may be a healthful substitute for both table sugar and HFCS (Jeppesen, 2013).

Lastly, there is the old rivalry between cane and beet sugar. This debate deserves mention because the two crops have always represented two different climatic zones: tropical and temperate. In the light of global climate change—and even though beet sugar currently constitutes only about a fifth of the annual globally marketed sucrose—change may be coming.

Though any specific link of sugar to obesity is disputed or denied by the sugar industry, the growing obesity pandemic worries health authorities everywhere. Obesity in the young is particularly worrisome, and it has grown in many so-called less developed countries, providing the disturbing image of overlapping populations composed of the obese and the malnourished. Similar images are also seen in the West, leading to campaigns to improve school lunches, change the contents of food-dispensing machines, intensify physical education programs in schools, and invest in other ameliorative or preventive measures. But whether any—or indeed all—of these changes are having any significant effect on the eating habits of Americans or others is not really known at this time.

Politics played an indirect role in HFCS's first success in the American market, when President Eisenhower and the U.S. Congress placed an embargo on Cuban sugar in 1960. As a result, commercial demand for an alternative sweetener rocketed. Once in the market, HFCS began to supplant the sugar used in prepared and processed foods, such as cookies, breakfast cereals, frozen dinners, and, most of all, soft drinks. Though no one knew it at the time, HFCS's first significant entry into the soft drink field with Coca-Cola was a flop, but it proved a triumph for its predecessor, the "classic" Coke made with sucrose, which it was intended to replace. Because HFCS is cheaper than sucrose when used for ready-to-eat foods, it is consumed more in the United States and Western Europe and by the middle classes in the world's cities, but far less in lands where packaged foods matter little. In the United States, HFCS may now constitute one-third of the total sugars consumed. Much of the negative publicity for it rests on the way that the fructose in HFCS is metabolized, and on the effects of that metabolism on the liver.

Cane sugar became the world's sweetener around the start of the nineteenth century. Three decades or so later, beet sugar began to compete with cane sugar, a rivalry that subsequently became global. That was the first time that a temperate-zone product threatened to become the effective rival of an important tropical commodity. Though the United States was able to produce beet sugar, and still does so, it solved many of its own sugar problems, intentionally or not, through war, when it scooped up Spain's old sugar colonies in the Caribbean and Pacific regions during the Spanish-American War (1898–1899).

Epilogue

At best, a personal view is only that, a view encased in the flow of time. As moments in time become past moments, it is the flow of time that lets us see the personal for what it is. My parents came from Eastern Europe to the United States more than a century ago. My mother would complain for the rest of her life about American sugar cubes, which melted in her mouth before she could finish drinking her tea. The sugar that she remembered eating in Belarus was broken off a sugar loaf with a hammer; one could hold it under the tongue while drinking a cup of tea, and it would not melt entirely until the last swallow. (In Iran in 1966 we sampled loaf beet sugar produced for export to North Africa, where up until recently sugar loaves were preferred in the countryside. We brought back samples, to my mother's delight.)

But my mother also told me about her first sugary treat, long before she had ever tasted processed sugar: parsnips (*pasternak*), dug out of the frozen earth, peeled, and then grated. "Almost like ice cream," she recounted.

I recall my own saccharose epiphany. It was around 1930, as the world Depression settled not only into the minds of people across America, but into their bones as well. I got to eat my first candy, and it was the most delicious food I had ever tasted. A waitress named Rosie gave me a taste: chocolate creams. They came from Woolworth's, my hometown's first five-and-ten, and they cost ten cents a pound. Those chocolate creams, I now think, had few mysteries. A glob of the cheapest sort of fondant—no egg white, butter, or cream in *that* stuff—thinly coated with inferior chocolate. Yet I found the taste of the sugar inside so intoxicating that I wanted to scrape the chocolate off with my teeth.

These memories are dated, and a far cry from Claude Lévi-Strauss writing about the honey of the stingless bees of South America. His memories of its taste reach back, perhaps, to our primate nature: "A delight more piercing than any normally afforded by taste or smell breaks down the boundaries of sensibility, and blurs its registers, so much so that the eater of honey wonders whether he is savoring a delicacy or burning with the fire of love" (Lévi-Strauss, 1973, p. 52).

Sugar has been part of New World history for half a millennium, and for at least four times that in the Old World. It is a food that has meant much to humans, one that supplanted its predecessor worldwide, and that is a metaphor for so much, its history brimming over with the cruelty of man to man, but also with thoughts of sweetness and all of the pleasures that taste connotes.

The author warmly thanks Jackie Mintz and Katherine Magruder for their invaluable editorial and research assistance.

Bell, R. R., H. H. Draper, and J. G. Bergman. "Sucrose, Lactose and Glucose Tolerance in Northern Alaskan Eskimos." *American Journal of Clinical Nutrition* 26 (1973): 1185–1190.

Jeppesen, Per Bendix. "Is There a Correlation between High Sugar Consumption and the Increase in Health Problems in Latin America?" In *Sugar and Modernity in Latin America*, edited by V. de Carvalho, S. Hojlund, P. B. Jeppesen, and K.-M. Simonsen, pp. 25–54. Aarhus, Denmark: Aarhus University Press, 2014.

Jerome, Norge W. "Taste Experience and the Development of a Dietary Preference for Sweet in Humans: Ethnic and Cultural Variations in Early Taste Experience." In *Taste and Development: The Genesis of Sweet Preference*, edited by James Weiffenbach, pp. 235–248. Fogarty International Proceedings No. 32. Washington, D.C.: Government Printing Office, 1977.

Lévi-Strauss, Claude. *From Honey to Ashes.* New York: Harper & Row, 1973.
Mintz, Sidney. "Sweet, Salt and the Language of Love." *Modern Language Notes* 106, no. 4 (1991): 852–860.
Mintz, Sidney. *Tasting Food, Tasting Freedom: Excursions into Eating, Culture and the Past.* Boston: Beacon, 1996.
Mintz, Sidney. "Quenching Homologous Thirsts." In *Anthropology, History, and American Indians: Essays in Honor of William Curtis Sturtevant,* edited by William Merrill and Ives Goddard, pp. 349–357. Smithsonian Contributions to Anthropology 44. Washington, D.C.: Smithsonian Institution Press, 2002.
Sutton, David E. *Remembrance of Repasts: An Anthology of Food and Memory.* Oxford: Berg, 2001.

Sidney Mintz

INTRODUCTION

My sweet tooth defined my childhood. Yellow watermelon so sugary it made my teeth ache. Snow cones dripping neon blue at the pool. Cinnamon rugelach made by my grandmother's hand, the pastry meltingly tender. I can still remember the frisson of frozen Sugar Babies popped lazily into my mouth, as though summer—life itself—would never end, and the first lemon meringue pie I made for my father, glorious even though it wept. Apples and honey and honey cake at the Jewish New Year; macaroons (my madeleines!) and fruit jellies at Passover. Taste is a locus of memory that helps us recapture our past and connect us to the stories of others. While tasting occurs entirely in our heads—in our mouths, our noses, and brains—it is also part heart. And when the taste is sweet, it triggers a powerful, positive response in nearly all mammals (cats being the notable exception).

The Human Condition

Sweet memories, however, don't really explain the degree to which humans crave sugar, or the way sweetness holds us in its thrall. To understand this captivation, we need to look deeper into the past, when a taste for sweets was more advantageous and calorie sources were far less abundant than they are for most of us today. Our ancestors needed to differentiate between sweet foods that promised a high dose of energy—fast calories for survival—and foods that tasted bitter, and were more likely toxic. And so we adapted accordingly. Our positive response to sugar is thus hard wired: when given a sugar solution, newborns put on a happy face (see the photo accompanying the "Sweetness Preference" article). Gazing deep inside the brain, as today's technology enables us to do, we can actually see our reaction to sugar: the same parts of the brain light up for sugar that light up for cocaine. No wonder craving feels addictive! We are hardwired for pleasure, too, a characteristic that inevitably inclines us toward excess and extravagance.

In earlier times, succumbing to excess, or giving in to temptation, was either held in check by scarcity or regulated by agricultural cycles and religious calendars. The ripe, sweet fruits of the harvest; the candied-fruit-studded cakes of Christmas; the myriad doughnuts and other fried foods of Carnival—all were special treats to be anticipated and savored only periodically, typically once a year. But excess today is quotidian, and most of us quite literally enjoy too much of a good thing. Where sugar was once rare, prized not only for its sweetness but also for its preservative properties, it is now ubiquitous. Yet our craving has only intensified. And so we are faced with an array of health problems, such as tooth decay, diabetes, obesity, and a predisposition to certain cancers. Recent studies show that nearly 70 percent of the added sugars in the U.S. food supply come from processed foods. Western consumers, especially Americans, have been conditioned to seek out ever-sweeter tastes. Even condiments like ketchup, once pungent and vinegary, are increasingly cloying on the palate. These changing tastes reflect sugar's changing meanings. As a luxury substance that provided energy and beneficial heat (in the humoral system of medicine), sugar represented wealth and offered a promise of health. Today, both of these associations are reversed. Though sugar still marks social class, it is no longer the delight of the elite, but rather the scourge of the poor.

Our Sense of Excess

Only in the late nineteenth century was sugar fully democratized, thanks to the affordable technology of extracting it from beets. The fine white crystals seem utterly mundane now, but a tour of an old-fashioned bakery with its sugar figurines allows us to glimpse the grand role sugar had in the past. Idols were made of sugar, and the miniature plastic models of brides and grooms that perch atop modern-day wedding cakes barely hint at the fantastic sugar sculptures that once symbolized power and wealth. The eleventh-century court of the Fatimid caliph delighted in table ornaments crafted of sugar, as did the Byzantine emperors, whose confectioners were renowned. Spectacular statues of sugar, pastry, and marzipan dazzled the eye at fifteenth-century European feasts. So towering and finely wrought were these constructions that the French chef Marie-Antoine Carême, famous in the nineteenth century for his elaborate *pièces montées*, declared architecture "the first among the fine arts," with confectionery its principal branch.

Both architecture and immoderate excess characterized the royal dessert table set on 29 June 1672 to celebrate the baptism of the future Russian tsar Peter the Great. As described by A. V. Tereshchenko in his *Byt russkago naroda* (1848), the conceits included

> a cinnamon spice cake (*kovrizhka*) made with sugar in the shape of the Muscovy coat of arms; a large, cone-shaped cinnamon spice cake decorated with colors, weighing 2 *puds* 20 pounds [92 pounds]; large, molded sugar confections shaped like eagles with the royal orb, one white and the other red, each weighing 1½ *puds*; a 2-*pud* swan of molded sugar; a half-*pud* sugar duck; a 10-*pud* sugar parrot and an 8-*pud* sugar dove; a sugar Kremlin with infantry, cavalry and two towers, with eagles soaring above them, and the city molded into a square surrounded by cannons; two large 15-pound horns made of sugar and flavored with cinnamon, one red and the other white; two large marzipan cakes made with sugar, one on 5 rounds, the other made with hard candies; two candy spires, one red and one white, each weighing 12 pounds; 40 dishes of sugar decorations depicting infantry and cavalry and other figures, half a pound on each plate . . . in all there were 120 dishes on the table.

We marvel at such staggering extravagance, particularly in a land of widespread hunger. But sensorial wonder quickly yields to other, more practical, questions: How was sugar transported from the tropics to Moscow? Did the Russian masses know the taste of sugar? How was it colored red, and why was red such an important color? The histories of trade, commerce, dyeing, status, culinary technique, and spices are all hidden in this display, begging revelation, not unlike Blake's world in a grain of sand. It is such histories that this *Companion* aims to expose.

The Dark Side

No matter where sugar was introduced, it became an object of desire, enthralling. Yet beneath the idea of allure lies the core meaning of "thrall," which points to the darker sides of sugar. Because even as sugar pleases, it subjugates. Though sugar can be cast into marvelous forms, it has historically cast people into thralldom—not only addiction, that bondage to excess, but also slavery. The once pure notion of sweetness, considered the most perfect of virtues (Matthew Arnold's "sweetness and light"), has been forever tainted by the triangular trade of slaves, sugar, and rum; by the punishing labor in the sugarcane fields and the sugar plantations themselves; and by the exorbitant riches of the sugar barons. Sugar's associations with the brutalities of the slave trade have been powerfully explored by artists like Vik Muniz (in his "Sugar Children" series, 1996), Maria Campos-Pons (*Sugar/Bittersweet*, 2010), and Kara Walker (*A Subtlety, or the Marvelous Sugar Baby*, 2014).

Such cruelties are not ensconced in the past, however. The damage continues in the child labor used in harvesting cacao beans, in the sugar-heavy diet that undermines health in African American communities, and in the stereotypes still associated with certain forms of sweets. Although many cultures have abandoned disparaging names for candies and overtly racist imagery on packaging, negative connotations persist in the popular imagination, especially in the United States. Indeed, the very essence of sugar—its refinement from molasses brown into pure white—suggests a prevailing attitude about purity and goodness that is not easily overcome. Since these histories cannot be overlooked, they, too, are part of this volume.

The Project

So, how to create a compendium that would bring all this together, to celebrate the allure of things sweet while recognizing the despicable aspects of human activity; to laud sugar's ability to inspire creativity and technological innovation while also acknowledging its detrimental effects? How to marvel at the symbolism of the sweet in ritual and art while at the same time confronting the menace of addiction and the cynical manipulations of sugar lobbies whose sole purpose is to ensure that sugar remains a profitable force in the world economy? The notion of the sweet has brought richness to language and art, and of course to the realm of gastronomy. But is it possible to exalt pleasure without trivializing its costs? Such questions concerned me as I began to conceptualize what an encyclopedic companion to all things sweet could be. With the help of the project's brilliant editorial director, Max Sinsheimer, and of our inspired editorial board, the *Companion* grew to nearly 600 entries that explore the human predilection for the sweet from every possible angle. These entries reveal how the desire for sugar has, over the ages, led to great changes in culture, society, and technology—for better and for worse.

Food historians, neuroscientists, chemists, philosophers, art historians, cookbook writers, and pastry chefs have contributed entries, each writing in a distinctive style and voice. The volume's geographical scope and chronological sweep begin in prehistory with the human proclivity for the sweet, and then move through centuries of culinary and industrial developments into the present day, when sweeteners both natural and artificial define our diets. Along the way, aesthetics, agriculture, technology, and trade are examined in relation to human desire and endeavor.

In addition to covering topics that one might expect in a book about sweets (the history of candy, the evolution of the dessert course, the production of chocolate), the *Companion* includes less well-known material that I hope will offer a sense of discovery and delight. Readers will learn about "sugar of lead" (lead acetate), prescribed for stomach troubles in the nineteenth century, and about beaver extract, beloved by the modern food industry for the sweet taste it imparts. Did you know that the silent-screen star Zasu Pitts wrote a charming cookbook, *Candy Hits by Zasu Pitts*, or that the bakery manager William Russell Frisbie has been immortalized in the popular sport to which his pie plates lent their name? Such unexpected facts abound.

Taste is often dependent on culture, and the ultimate definition of "sweet" remains elusive. There are no fixed rules about when sweet foods should be eaten, and fashions continually change. In Tudor England, dessert tables were sometimes laid in separate "banqueting houses" to create a visually ravishing end to a fine dinner; in contemporary American life, breakfast might be the sweetest meal of the day, with its sugar-laden cereals and syrup-soaked pancakes. European traditions of special daytime breaks with sweet foods—the *fika*, the Kaffeeklatsch, the *Jause*—continue, if in diminished form, probably because they are as much about sharing friendship as about sharing food. Even the distinction between sweet and savory remains slippery. Just as these flavors comingled in medieval feasts, desserts at high-end Western restaurants today subdue the sensation of sweet with ingredients like rosemary and bacon. No volume, then, can claim absolute definitiveness. But this one comes close. *The Oxford Companion to Sugar and Sweets* will carry you across many thousands of years and around the globe many times, affording glimpses deep into the brain as well as stratospheric flights into the world of sugar-crafted fantasies. Like a kid in a sweet shop, you may wish to marvel at the variety before you choose from among the offerings. Let the taste of one sweet thing lead you to another, and then return for more.

*****

The enormity of this project calls for enormous thanks. At the top of the list is Max Sinsheimer, editor extraordinaire, who oversaw the project from inception to completion with grace, efficiency, insight, and humor; he has been wonderful to work with. Associate editor Michael Krondl brought exceptional knowledge of food history to the project, and he labored above and beyond expectation. His irreverent wit kept our spirits light in moments of heavy lifting. Area editors Ursula Heinzelmann, Laura Mason, Jeri Quinzio, and Eric Rath were invaluable to this volume—their erudition, attentiveness, and devotion are reflected in the pages of this book. I'm also grateful to the staff at Oxford University Press: Damon Zucca, whose enthusiasm for the project was crucial; Brady McNamara, who brought visual delight to the *Companion*; Brad Rosenkrantz for coordinating production with such professionalism; and Emily Wordsman for her adept, cheerful labors. And, of course, I can't fail to mention the contributors who are the heart of this book—all 265 of them! It has been both thrilling and educational to work with them, none more so than my husband, Dean Crawford, who deserves special thanks.

Darra Goldstein

TOPICAL OUTLINE OF ENTRIES

Entries in the body of *The Oxford Companion to Sugar and Sweets* are organized alphabetically. This outline offers an overview of the *Companion*, with entries listed in the following categories:

Beverages
Biography
Breads and Dough
Cakes
Candy
Chocolate
Companies and Brands
Confections
Cookies
Culture
Dessert
Equipment
Fruits and Preserves
Health and the Body
History
Holidays and Celebrations
Ice Cream and Ices
Industry and Profession
Ingredients
Language and Terminology
Pastries and Pies
Politics
Presentation and Decoration
Puddings and Custards
Regions
Religion
Sugar

Beverages

Alkermes, confection of
bubble tea
egg drinks
fortified wine
hippocras
horchata
kombucha
lemonade
liqueur
mead
milkshakes
mulled wine
Orange Julius
punch
rum
soda
sweet wine
syllabub
tea

Biography

Athenaeus
Beeton, Isabella
Carême, Marie-Antoine
Chase, Oliver
Emy, M.
Escoffier, Georges Auguste
Farmer, Fannie
Fourier, Charles
Gilliers, Joseph
Havemeyer, Henry Osborne
Hermé, Pierre
Hershey, Milton S.
Hines, Duncan
Jarrin, William Alexis
Latini, Antonio
Lenôtre, Gaston
Lindt, Rodolphe
Maillard, Henri
Marshall, Agnes Bertha
Médici, Catherine de
Nobin Chandra Das
Nostradamus
Peter, Daniel
Pitts, ZaSu
Plat, Sir Hugh
Rombauer, Irma Starkloff
Sri Ramkrishna
Stohrer, Nicolas
van Houten, Coenraad Johannes
Weber, Johannes Martin Erich

Breads and Dough

breads, sweet
buchty
dango
dumplings
filo
fried dough
fritters
laminated doughs
manjū
pancakes
pastry, choux
pastry, puff
pie dough
stollen

Cakes

angel food cake
Appalachian stack cake
baba au rhum
Baumkuchen
Black Forest cake
Boston cream pie
bûche de Noël
cake
cannelé
cassata
cheesecake
chiffon cake
coffee cake
cupcakes
Dobos torte
Dolly Varden cake
fruitcake
galette
gingerbread
Gugelhupf
icebox cake
kuchen
layer cake
Linzer Torte
madeleine
muffins
pavlova
placenta
pound cake
Rigó Jancsi
Sachertorte
shortcake
small cakes
sponge cake
tiramisù
torte
tres leches cake
trifle
upside-down cake
vinarterta
whoopie pie
zuppa inglese

Candy

barley sugar
bird's milk
bonbons
brittle
butterscotch
candy
candy bar
candy canes
caramels
chewing gum
children's candy
cotton candy
extreme candy
gag candy
gummies
hard candy
jelly beans
licorice
Life Savers
lollipops
marshmallows
penny candy
popping sugar
rock
sherbet powder
taffy
toffee

Chocolate

brownies
chocolate, luxury
chocolate, post-Columbian
chocolate, pre-Columbian
chocolate, single origin
chocolates, boxed
chocolates, filled
cocoa
fudge
gelt
kisses
truffles

Companies and Brands

American Sugar Refining Company
Aunt Jemima
Baker's
Baskin-Robbins
Ben & Jerry's
Betty Crocker
Cadbury
Cool Whip
Cracker Jack
Dairy Queen
Dunkin' Donuts

Confections

Cookies

Culture

Dessert

dessert
dessert design
desserts, chilled
desserts, flambéed
desserts, frozen
Mehlspeise
plated desserts
sweet meals

Equipment

chocolate pots and cups
confectionery equipment
cookie cutters
cookie jars
cookie molds and stamps
cooking irons
Frisbie pie tins
gumball machines
ice cream makers
molds, jelly and ice cream
pans
pastry tools
saccharimeter
whisks and beaters

Fruits and Preserves

candied flowers
candied fruit
dates
dried fruit
fruit
fruit desserts, baked
fruit pastes
fruit preserves
grape must
marmalade
miracle berry
mostarda
pastila
soup
suckets
sugarplums
tutti frutti

Health and the Body

addiction
animals and sweetness
aphrodisiacs
dental caries
medicinal uses of sugar
neuroscience
olfaction
pharmacology
psychoanalysis
shape
sound
sugar and health
sweetness preference
sweets in human evolution
Vipeholm experiment
vision

History

ancient world
banqueting houses
Boston Molasses Disaster
breakfast cereal
colonialism
court confectioners
guilds
military
slavery
Spanish-American War
street food, ancient
sugar barons
sugar rationing
sugar riots

Holidays and Celebrations

birth
Carnival
celebration cakes
Chinese New Year
Christmas
Day of the Dead
Diwali
Easter
fairs
festivals
funerals
Halloween
Hanukkah
holiday sweets
honeymoon
ice cream socials
Passover
piñatas
Ramadan
Rosh Hashanah
Twelfth Night cake
Valentine's Day
wedding
wedding cake

Ice Cream and Ices

akutuq
Baked Alaska
Eskimo Pie
ice cream
ice cream cones
Italian ice
Popsicle
shave ice
sherbet
soda fountain
sundae

Industry and Profession

adulteration
advertising, American
candy packaging
confectionery manuals
pastry chef
pastry schools
publications, trade
refrigeration
sugar refineries
sugar refining
sugarcane agriculture

Ingredients

ambergris
angelica
azuki beans
butter
buttermilk
cake mix
cassava
castoreum
cheese, fresh
chemical leaveners
chestnuts
coconut
cream
dulce de leche
eggs
evaporated milk
extracts and flavorings
flour
flower waters
food colorings
frangipane
gelatin
honey
insects
mastic
milk
nutmeg
nuts
pandanus
pekmez
poppy seed
salt
sauce
shortening
sour cream
spices
starch
sweetened condensed milk
tapioca
tragacanth
vanilla
vegetables and herbs
wheat berries
yeast
yogurt

Language and Terminology

baker's dozen
Brix
measurement
munchies
proverbs
sexual innuendo
slang
sports nicknames
sweet and sour

Pastries and Pies

baklava
cannoli
chiffon pie
cream pie
crescent
croissant
croquembouche
dariole
doughnuts
flan (tart)
Japanese baked goods
lauzinaj
mince pies
mooncake
mud pie
pie
qaṭā'if
strudel
tart
tarte Tatin
turnovers
zalabiya

Politics

child labor
legislation, historical
plantations, sugar
politics of sugar
race
sugar lobbies
sugar trade
Sugar Trust

Presentation and Decoration

à la mode
aroma
cake and confectionery stands
cake decorating
candy dishes
entremets
epergnes
fondant
icing
leaf, gold and silver
pastillage
servers, ice cream
servers, sugar
serving pieces
sprinkles
sucket fork
sugar sculpture
trompe l'oeil
verrine

Puddings and Custards

blancmange
charlotte
clafoutis
crème brûlée
custard
flan (pudím)
fools
gelatin desserts
Guriev kasha
Huguenot Torte
junket
pastel de nata
payasam
pudding
sanguinaccio
sticky toffee pudding
summer pudding
zabaglione

Regions

Australia and New Zealand
Austria-Hungary
Baghdad
Belgium
Brazil
Budapest
Canada
China
East Asia
France
Germany
Greece and Cyprus
India
Istanbul
Italy
Japan
Kolkata
Korea
Kyoto
Latin America
Mexico
Middle East
Midwest (U.S.)
Netherlands
New England (U.S.)
New Orleans
New York City
North Africa
Pacific Northwest (U.S.)
Paris
Persia
Philadelphia
Philippines
Portugal
Portugal's influence in Asia
Russia
Scandinavia
South (U.S.)
South Asia
Southeast Asia
Southwest (U.S.)
Spain
sub-Saharan Africa
Switzerland
Thailand
Turkey
United Kingdom
United States
Venice
Vienna
West (U.S.)

Religion

Buddhism
Christianity
convent sweets
Hinduism
Islam
Judaism
manna
Priapus
spirituality
temple sweets

Sugar

agave nectar
artificial sweeteners
biofuel
cane syrup
corn syrup
fermentation
fructose
glucose
golden syrup
isomalt
lead, sugar of
malt syrup
maple sugaring
maple syrup
molasses
palm sugar
panning
pulled sugar
sap
sorbitol
sorghum syrup
stages of sugar syrup
Stevia
Sucanat
sugar
sugar, biochemistry of
sugar, unusual uses of
sugar beet
sugar cubes
sugar in experimental cuisine
sugarcane
sugars, unrefined
wasanbon
xylitol

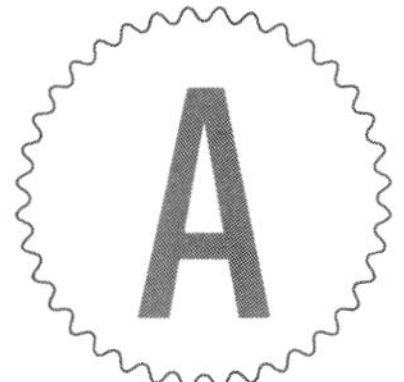

à la mode is a French phrase that translates to "in the current fashion." In the realm of sweets, it turns out to be even *more* American than apple pie (whose roots, in fact, lie elsewhere), because in the United States "à la mode" refers to a scoop of vanilla ice cream served with a piping hot slice of pie. See ICE CREAM and PIE.

The *New York Times* credits the spread of this term to Charles Watson Townsend. His 1936 obituary reported that after ordering ice cream with his pie at the Cambridge Hotel, in the village of Cambridge, New York, around 1896, a neighboring diner asked him what this wonder was called. "Pie à la mode," Townsend replied. When Townsend subsequently requested this dessert at the famous Delmonico's restaurant in New York City, the staff had no idea what it was. Townsend inquired why such a fashionable venue had never heard of pie à la mode. *Bien sûr,* the dessert found its way onto Delmonico's menu and requests for it soon spread.

Not long thereafter several midwestern newspapers provided evidence that John Gieriet of Switzerland had previously invented the dessert in 1885 while proprietor of the Hotel La Perl in Duluth, Minnesota, where he served the ice cream with warm blueberry pie.

The term "à la mode" has become so established in the United States that it now extends to a variety of flavors added to all sorts of desserts. The phrase has also come to be used metaphorically, most recently by the musical group *Destiny's Child* that in 2001 recorded a hit song titled "Apple Pie à la Mode," to refer to a beyond-fabulous lover.

In France, however, *à la mode,* in a culinary context, refers to a traditional recipe for braised beef, which at one time was considered a new fashion.

"Charles W. Townsend." *New York Times,* 21 May 1936, p. 23.

Carolin C. Young

addiction, in relation to sweets, refers to the hypothesis that sugar (in certain forms) may be capable of triggering an addictive-like process in vulnerable individuals. Changes in the food environment and the manner in which sugar is incorporated into food may be related to neurobiological and behavioral changes in our eating that resemble addiction. If sugar can be addictive, this may speak to why our relationship with food is so difficult to change, and why sugary products are a major contributor to the obesity epidemic.

The food environment that we live in has changed dramatically over the last 30 years. Ultra-processed, highly palatable foods are cheap, easily accessible, and heavily marketed. The addition of higher levels of sugar has been one of the major drivers of this change, along with increased levels of fat, salt, refined flours, and food additives. Hyper-palatable foods (like ice cream, cakes, and candy) surpass the level of reward associated with more natural, minimally processed foods such as vegetables, fruits, and nuts. The rising rates of obesity and binge eating that have accompanied the influx of these types of foods have led to the hypothesis that hyper-palatable foods may be capable of triggering an addictive process.

Sugar is not inherently addictive. In fact, sugar (along with fat and salt) is important for our survival. The high-calorie content associated with sugar and fat ensures that we do not starve in times of food scarcity, and sodium derived from salt is essential for a number of important bodily functions (e.g., fluid balance, nerve function). Humans may even have evolved a greater reward response to these life-sustaining nutrients to ensure that we were motivated to seek out and consume them. See SWEETS IN HUMAN EVOLUTION.

Nevertheless, the way sugar exists in our current food environment is significantly different from the naturally occurring foods our brains may have evolved to expect. In fact, many high-sugar foods have been altered in a manner analogous to the way in which drugs of abuse are created. Both the elevated potency of a substance and its rapid absorption into the bloodstream increase its addictive potential. Many drugs of abuse derive from plant materials that are refined into highly concentrated substances (e.g., grapes into wine) to become more potent, and to allow the active ingredient to be more quickly absorbed into the bloodstream. For example, when the coca leaf is chewed or brewed as tea, it produces only mild stimulation and is thought to have little addictive potential. Yet, when the leaves are refined into a powder form, such as cocaine, they become a very potent, quickly absorbed, and highly addictive substance. An analogous process has occurred with many high-sugar foods.

In many of the processed foods available today, sugar comes in higher doses and is coupled with other rewarding ingredients (e.g., salt, fat). For instance, one of the greatest sources of naturally occurring sugar is fruit. See FRUIT. A banana (a relatively high-sugar fruit) has approximately 16 grams of sugar. In contrast, modern candy bars can have up to 40 grams of sugar—over double the dose of sugar in the banana. Moreover, many candy bars combine sugar with high levels of fat, whereas most fruits have little to no fat. See CANDY BAR. In fact, very few naturally occurring foods contain high levels of both sugar and fat (e.g., avocados and nuts have fat, but little sugar). Furthermore, many of these ultra-processed foods have been stripped of fiber, water, protein, and other components that would slow absorption of ingredients like sugar into the system, so their consumption leads to a bigger blood sugar spike and likely increases the brain's reward response. Thus, in comparison with the food environment humans evolved in, our foodscape is composed largely of foods with unnaturally high levels of rewarding ingredients that are combined to increase palatability, to have a greater impact on the body.

Sugar-Addicted Rats

Much of the initial research on food and addiction emerged from animal models of eating behavior. Rats given intermittent access to sugar (in addition to standard rat chow) binge on progressively larger quantities of sugar, exhibit signs of withdrawal when sugar is removed, and display greater motivation for traditionally addictive substances (e.g., alcohol). Animals consuming sweets (like Oreos and cheesecake) are more likely to binge on these foods when stressed and will continue to seek out these sugary foods despite receiving electric shocks. Not only do these animals exhibit extreme behaviors, but also their consumption of these highly palatable foods is related to changes in their brains that have been linked with addiction, such as a reduction in dopamine receptors.

Sugar Addiction in Humans

Neuroimaging and behavioral research in humans also provide evidence of the addictive potential of sweet foods. Palatable foods (including high-sugar foods) and drugs of abuse activate similar brain systems (e.g., dopamine and opioid systems). Obese and substance-dependent participants exhibit similar patterns of neural response to cues (i.e., increased activation in motivation and reward areas) and consumption (i.e., decreased activation in control and reward areas) of palatable foods and drugs, respectively. Furthermore, healthy-weight individuals who consume ice cream more frequently display in the fMRI scanner a lower reward-related response in the brain when consuming a milkshake. This may reflect the development of tolerance to the hedonic effects of ice cream analogous to the way that people develop tolerance to the rewarding effects of drugs of abuse.

The Yale Food Addiction Scale (YFAS) was developed to measure addictive-like eating in humans by translating the diagnostic criteria for substance dependence (e.g., withdrawal, loss of control) to evaluate food consumption. Sugary foods, such as chocolate, are often identified as problem foods on the YFAS. The prevalence of YFAS food addiction may be around 5.4 percent in the general population; addictive-like eating is associated with severe obesity and a higher percentage of body fat. Individuals exhibiting more symptoms of food addiction on the

YFAS (regardless of body mass index [BMI]) showed a pattern of neural activation in response to cues and consumption that is implicated in other types of addiction; they also have genetic indicators associated with elevated risk for addiction. The similarities identified in the neural system converge with behavioral overlap between addiction and problematic eating. For example, diminished control over consumption, continued use despite negative consequences, elevated levels of craving, and repeated relapse to problematic behavior are key constructs for both problematic substance use and eating behavior.

If sugar is addictive, it would not affect adults alone. Children naturally prefer high levels of sugar and are motivated to eat sweet things (like sugar-sweetened cereals). Children are also more vulnerable to the negative effects of addictive substances, because their brains and psychological coping strategies are developing. Research in this area is just beginning, but children who report more food addiction symptoms on the YFAS have higher BMIs and are more likely to overeat due to emotions. Thus, addictive-like eating may start in childhood for some individuals, which could contribute to lifelong eating-related problems.

Sugar Addiction and Public Health

In summary, the research suggests that for certain people sweets (and other ultra-processed foods) may be capable of triggering an addictive process that results in compulsive food consumption. Yet, there are still more questions than answers in this burgeoning line of research. For instance, there have been almost no studies examining what might be the active ingredient in foods that would make them more addictive, although high levels of sugar are a likely possibility. Identifying which foods may be addictive is especially important when we consider the huge public health costs incurred by addictive substances. Although a significant proportion of people develop full-blown addictions, the number of people who develop "subclinical" problems with addictive substances is far greater. Take the example of alcohol. Around 5 to 10 percent of people develop an addiction to alcohol, but it is the third leading cause of preventable death in the United States. This statistic is driven in large part by individuals who exhibit enough of a subclinical addictive response to alcohol (e.g., binge drinking) that they overconsume it in a way that threatens their health and safety.

Like alcohol, addictive foods may have a huge public health cost that will be driven in large part by the group of adults and children who exhibit a subclinical response. This may be especially true in the case of hyper-palatable, high-calorie foods, as only a few extra hundred calories a day can lead to obesity. Thus, if someone is showing a subclinical-addictive response to these foods, such as struggling to control their level of consumption, that person could face elevated food intake and increased weight gain. Given that highly processed foods are cheap, legal, and more accessible than alcohol and tobacco, the public health costs associated with potentially addictive foods could be significant.

Greater understanding of addiction should suggest possible avenues to reduce negative consequences. Encouraging people to make behavioral changes and providing treatment for individuals with addictions are important, but it is also necessary to focus beyond personal responsibility or clinical disorders to reduce the public health costs of addictive substances. In the case of cigarettes, public policy has been an important tool. Specifically, policies focusing on changing the availability, marketing, and costs of tobacco products have resulted in huge public health gains. Similar environmental interventions may be needed to reduce the consequences of potentially addictive ingredients like sugar.

See also SODA and SUGAR AND HEALTH.

Avena, Nicole M., Pedro Rada, and Barley G. Hoebel. "Evidence for Sugar Addiction: Behavioral and Neurochemical Effects of Intermittent, Excessive Sugar Intake." *Neuroscience & Biobehavioral Reviews* 32 (2008): 20–39.

Burger, Kyle S., and Eric Stice. "Frequent Ice Cream Consumption Is Associated with Reduced Striatal Response to Receipt of an Ice Cream–Based Milkshake." *American Journal of Clinical Nutrition* 95 (2012): 810–817.

Davis, Caroline, Natalie J. Loxton, Robert D. Levitan, Allan S. Kaplan, Jacqueline C. Carter, and James L. Kennedy. "'Food Addiction' and Its Association with a Dopaminergic Multilocus Genetic Profile." *Physiology & Behavior* 118 (2013): 63–69.

Gearhardt, Ashley N., William R. Corbin, and Kelly D. Brownell. "Preliminary Validation of the Yale Food Addiction Scale." *Appetite* 52 (2009): 430–436.

Gearhardt, Ashley N., Sonja Yokum, Patrick T. Orr, Eric Stice, William R. Corbin, and Kelly D. Brownell.

"Neural Correlates of Food Addiction." *Archives of General Psychiatry* 68 (2011): 808–816.
Johnson, Paul M., and Paul J. Kenny. "Dopamine D2 Receptors in Addiction-Like Reward Dysfunction and Compulsive Eating in Obese Rats." *Nature Neuroscience* 13 (2010): 635–641.
Pedram, Pardis, et al. "Food Addiction: Its Prevalence and Significant Association with Obesity in the General Population." *PloS One* 8 (2013): e74832.

Ashley Gearhardt

adulteration is the process by which foods are debased with extraneous, weaker, cheaper, harmful, or inferior ingredients. In terms of sweeteners, honey, fruit juice, jams, and agave nectar have been adulterated with cheaper additives made from cane sugar, beet sugar, rice, corn syrup (including high-fructose corn syrup), and other ingredients. Producers of "maple syrup" have added less expensive sweeteners or injected air into the syrup to increase bulk.

Most added sugars are not usually harmful to health. National and regional food agencies have developed tests to determine whether natural sweeteners have been adulterated with other products, but government agencies cannot test every product and often only do so when a complaint has been lodged.

There are less common cases, however, in which antibiotics, heavy metals, and other harmful impurities have ended up in natural sweeteners. This adulteration has been associated with honey imported from Asia, particularly China. Honey imported from these sources has been banned in Europe. In the United States, it is common to filter out the pollen from the honey in food processors. Often processors also infuse honey with hot water, which thins the honey, adds bulk, and makes it easier to process and less difficult for customers to remove from containers. Such tampering is neither illegal nor unsafe, but critics claim that honey without pollen or with added water is not natural honey. Filtering out pollen removes impurities, extends honey's shelf life, and makes for a more consistent liquid product, which appeals to American consumers who generally dislike honey crystallization.

Critics have called for changes in the definition of processed sweeteners. They have also called for improved labeling that indicates whether natural sugars are processed or in their raw form, whether sugars and water have been added, and whether natural ingredients have been filtered out.

See also HONEY.

Bishop, Holley. *Robbing the Bees: A Biography of Honey, the Sweet Liquid Gold That Seduced the World.* New York: Free Press, 2005.

Andrew F. Smith

advertising, American is older than the United States itself; European colonists had brought the idea of advertising with them to the New World. In the early American colonies, most advertising was local and resembled current-day classified ads. In 1705 the first known ad for the chocolate trade appeared in the *Boston Newsletter*, offering cocoa, chocolate, and molasses among other commodities for sale. Twenty-five years later, the *New York Gazette* carried the first ad for an American sugar factory selling all sorts of "sugar and sugar candy."

By the mid-1800s machines were mass-producing goods with uniform quality, and large companies had increased production. For the first time, it cost people less to buy a product than to make it themselves. In the Victorian era, factories also started to manufacture sweets, including individual hard candies, chocolate bars, the modern marshmallow, chewing gum, and toffee.

Post–Civil War to 1920s

Between 1870 and 1900 the price of sugar dropped, causing the commodity to lose its luxury status. Jam became an important product for the working class, and dessert gradually became standard as a sweet course after dinner. As more mass-produced consumer products became available, manufacturers looked for ways to tell people about them.

Brand Name Advantage

The key to a product's success lay in the national advertising of a memorable brand name, attractive packaging, and a trademark that could differentiate one product from others on the market. For example, printed labels on pottery jars enhanced the appeal of Keiller's Dundee marmalades, whereas a collection of "Choice Mixed Sugar Plums" from Stephen F. Whitman became the first packaged

The Franco-American Food Company, founded in 1887 by the French immigrant Alphonse Biardot, skillfully adopted early advertising practices to build its brands, which initially included sweet products. This late-nineteenth-century chromolithograph is from a set of advertising trade cards. PRIVATE COLLECTION © LOOK AND LEARN / BARBARA LOE COLLECTION / BRIDGEMAN IMAGES

confection in a trademarked box. See CHOCOLATES, BOXED. A change in packaging could also reposition a product. While other grocers were filling cheap containers, P. J. Towle filled a miniature, log-cabin-shaped tin with his blended table syrup. Customers willingly paid extra for the novelty.

Sales also soared for Cracker Jack, mostly due to the advertising of an appealing package. Street-food vendors Frederick and Louis Rueckheim first sold the new confection of popcorn, molasses, and peanuts at amusement parks. In 1896 they registered the name Cracker Jack, common slang for "first rate." They then packaged their snack in a wax-sealed box, which kept it fresh for a long time, and marketed it to professional vendors at baseball parks. The slogan "The More You Eat, the More You Want" summed the product's appeal. See CRACKER JACK.

As companies moved from a production to sales orientation, they packaged and branded their products, and engaged in heavy national advertising. Among the early brands of this era, the image of the smiling Aunt Jemima first appeared on boxes of a self-rising pancake mix in the 1890s. The Davis Milling Company hired Nancy Greene, a black cook, to serve as a living trademark for the product. In this persona she traveled around the country and cooked thousands of pancakes at fairs, inspiring the ad line "I's in Town, Honey." See AUNT JEMIMA.

National Advertising Campaigns

By 1900 the majority of the revenue for newspapers came from advertising, and national brands appeared in regional and local papers. National magazines also became part of everyday life. Advertisers gradually began to turn their campaigns over to advertising agencies to be integrated into sound marketing strategies.

The National Biscuit Company (later Nabisco) set the standard for the well-coordinated advertising plan with the introduction of Uneeda Biscuit, a flaky soda cracker. With a brand name chosen, it created an airtight, wax-lined package that looked different from anything else but would ship well. Next it conceived a distinct image and then spent an unprecedented amount on advertising. This trademark identity theory essentially passed through Nabisco's whole product line of cookies, including Fig Newtons, Oreos, and Animal Crackers. See ANIMAL CRACKERS; FIG NEWTONS; and OREOS.

Early brands of this era included Jell-O gelatin, Domino sugar, and Wrigley's spearmint gum. See CHEWING GUM; GELATIN DESSERTS; and AMERICAN SUGAR REFINING COMPANY. The manufacturers of Jell-O embarked on a massive advertising campaign, calling the unheard-of packaged good "America's Most Favorite Dessert." They also reached the public with recipe booklets and promotional items, and hired artists like Norman Rockwell and Maxfield Parrish to contribute illustrations for lavish ads. Similarly, the American Sugar Refining Company began labeling the company's sugar products "Domino" after the sugar cube, to convince grocers to purchase its product in packages rather than in bulk.

Entirely new products like Crisco also joined the list of nationally advertised brands. When Procter & Gamble began processing its own oil, a key ingredient in soaps, the company also began to develop a vegetable shortening that would remain solid year round. One of the first Crisco ads appeared in the 1912 *Ladies Home Journal*, announcing "An absolutely new product. A scientific discovery that will affect every kitchen in America." In addition to national advertising, P&G also sponsored cooking schools to promote its product's benefits over animal fats. See SHORTENING.

1920 to World War II

For the first time, more than half of the nation lived in urban areas, providing marketers with a ready-made mass market. Whatever they had to sell, most advertisers aimed their message at the American woman. For decades, statisticians estimated that women accounted for 80 percent of all household purchases.

Betty Crocker

By the 1920s there were well-developed advertising vehicles to reach the women's market. When General Mills ran an ad in national magazines with a puzzle for its Gold Medal brand flour in 1921, the contest generated thousands of responses, many of which included questions on food preparation. Since the company could not personally respond to every letter, it decided to send recipes collected from its employees and sign them with the friendly but fictitious name of Betty Crocker. Betty Crocker served as a valuable persona. Actresses representing her ran regional cooking schools and, beginning in 1924, regional radio programs. See BETTY CROCKER.

One of the early products that came under the Betty Crocker brand was Bisquick. In 1931 the package appeared with the slogan, "Makes Everyone a Perfect Biscuit Maker." While Betty's name continued to be used, her picture did not appear in print ads until 1936. Despite the promises of convenience, biscuit, cake, pie crust, and muffin mixes were not associated with good eating until the 1950s.

Craze for Sweets

Sugar demand and consumption exploded in the 1920s and 1930s. The postwar crash in sugar prices allowed candy makers to sell chocolate bars at lower prices, and solid chocolate surpassed drinking chocolate in popularity. But the familiar wrapped candy bars did not appear widely until merchants put them adjacent to cash registers in grocery stores, drugstores, newsstands, and cigar stores. See CANDY BAR.

The arrival of modern refrigeration led to affordable frozen novelties. In 1919 Christian Nelson, an ice cream parlor owner, found a way to dip blocks of frozen ice cream in chocolate. He called them "Temptation I-Scream Bars." They were so popular that, with entrepreneur Russell Stover, he began to mass-produce them, wrapping each one in aluminum foil and changing the name to Eskimo Pie. However, Good Humor is credited as the first company to put ice cream on a stick, with the slogan "The New Clean Convenient Way to Eat Ice Cream." See ESKIMO PIE and GOOD HUMOR MAN.

Americans also enjoyed frozen ice on a stick in fruit flavors that had the same appeal as soft drinks. In 1923 Frank Epperson introduced frozen pop on a stick at amusement parks and beaches. See POPSICLE. The first ads for the product, which sold for a nickel, explained what it was by calling the popsicle (initially named "the Epsicle ice pop") "the Frozen Drink on a Stick." At the height of the Depression, when the company was looking for ways to make the treat more affordable, it produced a splittable popsicle with two sticks so that children could share it.

Small, packaged desserts also became popular with both children and adults. In 1914 the Tasty Baking Company produced individually wrapped snack cakes with the catchy name Tastykake. Baked and delivered fresh daily, each boxed mini-cake sold for a dime. Five years later, Continental Baking introduced its first snack cake—a devil's food frosted cupcake. Persuasive advertising contributed to the success of this new product line, called Hostess: "Now baking cake at home is needless . . . these famous cakes will eliminate all that drudgery." See HOSTESS.

After the Wall Street crash of 1929, the economy hit hard times. So did advertising. But radio surged ahead to become the nation's first free entertainment medium, and advertisers could quickly reach a national audience. During this time Jell-O sponsored the *Jack Benny Comedy-Variety Hour*. The comic skillfully mentioned the sponsor's name in the script both at the start and the end of the program ("Jell-O again. This is Jack Benny").

While daytime soap operas were largely aimed at housewives, the roster of shows extended to adventure series and westerns targeted at children. The malted chocolate drink mix Ovaltine sponsored one of the most well-known of these programs, *Little Orphan Annie*. By redeeming box tops and a small amount of cash for "postage and handling," young fans could receive such premiums as a whistling ring, mug, or secret decoder that could decipher the daily clues given at the end of the broadcast.

To improve its effectiveness, the National Confectioners Association decided not only to advertise its member companies' products but also to market the industry as a whole. It commissioned a study to assess the amount of money the candy industry spent on advertising compared to the amount other groups spent on promoting their respective products. After discovering that candy was "the least advertised food product," the confectioners launched the "Candy Is Delicious Food—Eat Some Every Day" campaign in 1938. A series of ads touted the message "Candy Is an Energizing Food" as part of the "Candy as a Wholesome Food" campaign.

When chocolate was promoted as nutritious, World War II soldiers found Hershey bars, Mars candy-coated chocolates, and Tootsie Rolls in their survival rations. See MILITARY. To support the war effort, the Kellogg Company also supplied packaged products. In 1941 it added the Rice Krispies Treats recipe to the back of the Rice Krispies cereal box and trademarked the simple dessert. This crispy yet gooey snack became a popular item to mail to soldiers serving overseas. However, since the consumption of butter, sugar, and chocolate among other staples was limited on the home front during the war years, few other new snacks were introduced until later in the decade.

1950 to 1990

The postwar economy recovered quickly. As more and more imitative products showed up in the marketplace, advertising's emphasis shifted from product features to brand image to align brands with the most profitable market segments based on class, race, gender, and age. The emerging marketing concepts placed even more emphasis on research.

Elaboration of Target Markets

Where goods for the home were concerned, women represented a crucial market for frozen foods, precooked meals, and dry mixes. In 1947 Pillsbury hired the Leo Burnett Company to launch a new line of ready-to-use cake mixes aimed at this group. See CAKE MIX. The ads repeated a simple message: just drop this mix in a bowl, add water, mix, and bake. But sales were slow. Motivational research revealed that the problem lay in the powdered eggs used in the mixes. So the manufacturers changed the package directions: "You add fresh eggs" or "You add fresh eggs and milk," allowing women to feel more involved in baking, and the sale of cake mixes took off.

The ultimate in convenience came with Sara Lee's cakes, which perfected a process in which cakes could be baked, frozen, and then shipped, a first in the food industry. In 1951 Sara Lee's marketing strategy focused on the taste and quality of its ingredients, such as the number of pecans in its All Butter Pecan Coffee Cake. Later the emphasis shifted from product features to emphasis on the product as an everyday treat, using the memorable line "Nobody Doesn't Like Sara Lee." See SARA LEE.

Children also represented an enormous demographic to food manufacturers, and the new medium of television provided a way to quickly reach a national audience. Howdy Doody, Miss Frances of Ding Dong School, and Captain Midnight all sold Ovaltine. The producers carefully worked the product into songs and ads. As the 1960s unfolded, advertising to children and youth began in earnest. In 1962 McDonald's introduced advertising campaigns with cartoonlike characters to appeal to children. By 1970 the bulk of advertising on children's TV programs pitched sugared foods. Among them, Nestlé Quik introduced the animated cartoon bunny wearing a "Q" on his shirt for its flavored milk mix. The bunny reminded young viewers: "It's so rich and thick and choco-lick! But you can't drink it slow if it's Quik!"

The large volume of television advertising directed at children elicited concern from many parents, consumers, and legislators. As a result, the Children's Advertising Review Unit (CAU) was founded in 1974. The self-regulatory organization set high standards for the industry to assure that national advertising directed at the child audience was not deceptive, unfair, or inappropriate. When CARU found violations, it sought changes through voluntary cooperation.

By 1970 greater emphasis on the consumer began to take place, as the idea of market segmentation took hold in most companies. Recognizing social trends and increased income potential, advertisers began to segment and target more specific groups. They also tied their products to distinct lifestyles, immediate gratification, youth, and sexuality.

Yuppies—young urban professionals—were one of the earliest lifestyle target groups to receive attention. In the 1980s they exhibited an unlimited appetite for consuming premium goods. Häagen-Dazs offered luxury ice cream, making it exclusive, sophisticated, even sexy. Godiva chocolate ads presented classic images of prestige, luxury, and refinement. Pepsi then showed what money could buy, trotting out a list of celebrities from Michael Jackson to Madonna to get their message across: Pepsi was "The Choice of a New Generation." See GODIVA and HÄAGEN-DAZS.

The New World for Advertising

As the 1990s unfolded, the internet had a dramatic effect on the advertising industry. Within a very short time, new media options based on new technologies reinvented the very process of advertising. Sales messages once clearly labeled were now subtly woven into movies and TV shows, or made into their own entertainment. Other promotions involved play, like video games with brand messages embedded in colorful, fun adventures. Meanwhile, the M&M characters went "virtual Hollywood" across the internet. See M&M's.

Within a very short time, computer technology had a huge impact. Advertising is no longer just advertising; it now involves consumers by soliciting their experiences and engaging them in conversation. An excellent example is one of the most talked about viral videos, the sublime "Cadbury Gorilla" playing the drums to a Phil Collins hit. Released in 2007, it has since been enjoyed by millions. There is no talk of chocolate at all; rather, the 90-second spot aims to make people smile, subliminally suggesting the same pleasure provided by a bar of Cadbury Dairy Milk Chocolate.

American advertising has come a long way since its first simple announcement for sugar candy. Sweets are now sold as an undeniable pleasure. They are fantastic, fun, and a sign of love. Over the years sweets have been promoted as a sinful indulgence while simultaneously being marketed as wholesome energy-dense snacks, at times even to help you keep slim. Through such associations, ads for sweets offer a connection with the product and a promise of guiltless pleasure.

See also CADBURY; CANDY; CHILDREN'S CANDY; CONFECTION; ICE CREAM; NESTLÉ; RACE; SUGARPLUMS; TWINKIE; and UNITED STATES.

Goodrum, Charles, and Helen Dalrymple. *Advertising in America: 200 Years.* New York: Harry N. Abrams, 1990.

McDonough, John, and Karen Egoff, eds. *The Ad Age Encyclopedia of Advertising.* Chicago: Fitzroy Dearborn, 2002.

Pincas, Stephen, and Mark Loiseau. *A History of American Advertising.* New York: Taschen, 2008.

Sivulka, Juliann. *Soap, Sex, and Cigarettes: A Cultural History of American Advertising.* Boston: Cengage Learning, 2011.

Juliann Sivulka

agave nectar (or syrup) is a sweetener made from agaves. The agaves are a genus of succulent plants, native to the Americas, with most species concentrated in Mexico. In the United States they are best known as ornamental garden plants and the source of tequila, which is made by expressing the liquid from the cooked core, *piña*, of *Agave tequilana*, fermenting the solution, and distilling it.

Patents for commercial production of agave sweeteners date from the 1980s. In the mid-1990s entrepreneurs began marketing agave nectar as an ancient, natural, raw health food, high in fructose and with a low glycemic index. Consumers seeking a less refined, less glucose-dense sweetener than cane or beet sugar, particularly those who adhered to a "Paleolithic" diet, enthusiastically adopted the syrup. Agave syrup's aura declined as scientists and physicians argued that it is neither ancient nor significantly different from other calorific sweeteners in its chemical and dietary properties. See SUGAR AND HEALTH. Various brands of agave nectar continue to be widely available in health food stores and supermarkets.

The traditional Mesoamerican way of extracting sweet liquid from agaves involves cutting an opening in the core of the mature plant. Using a long hollow tube, collectors could daily suck out 3 to 6 liters of sweetish sap, gathering 500 to 1,000 liters from each plant. After some processing, the sap is either drunk as *aguamiel* ("honey water"), widely and correctly believed to be nourishing and healthful, or fermented into pulque, the traditional mildly alcoholic drink of Mexico. By contrast, commercial production appears to involve chopping and centrifuging the starchy core of the plant, something not always obvious from labeling and promotional material. The resulting liquid is treated with chemicals to create the agave nectar.

See also FRUCTOSE; GLUCOSE; and MEXICO.

Soto, José Luis Montañez, José Venegas González, Aurea Benardino Nicanor, and Emma Gloria Ramos Ramiréz. "Enzymatic Production of High Fructose Syrup from *Agave tequilana* Fructans and Its Physicochemical Characterization." *African Journal of Biotechnology* 10 (2011): 19137–19143.

Rachel Laudan

akutuq is known by outsiders as Eskimo ice cream. Pronounced auk-goo-duck, the word "akutuq" means "to stir." This indigenous dish (1 part hard fat, 1 part polyunsaturated oil, and 4 parts protein or plant material) has been the culinary lifeblood of Natives in North America's Arctic for 600 generations, nourishing families and traveling hunters. In its savory form, akutuq is considered analogous to the Indian pemmican bar. In its sweet berry-filled form, akutuq remains a favorite dessert.

Although precise ingredients may differ, Inupiaq elders still adhere to a basic method of preparation. Traditionally, the best hard white caribou fat (from the area surrounding the small intestines) is softened and whipped until fluffy. Then seal oil, rendered until clear and golden, is slowly beaten into the mass. After 45 minutes of beating with splayed fingers, tablespoons of water are whisked in, lightening it further and making it fluffy. In appearance and texture aqutuq resembles a classic French buttercream stabilized with sugar syrup. But after icy flavoring ingredients from the permafrost cellar or freezer are added, the silky-smooth consistency "breaks." The mass instantly loses volume, appearing curdled. No one minds. It is a classic texture and has always looked that way.

Classic flavorings include salmonberries and blueberries, which are folded into the whipped mass. The labor-intensive dish used to be kept in permafrost cold cellars, ready for impromptu get-togethers. Until the early 1900s, yearly trade fairs featured raucous akutuq cooking contests, with husbands cheering wives on to create new flavors with fermented fish eggs or seal flippers—the more outrageous, the better. Today, southern Native Alaskans prepare akutuq by whipping Crisco shortening with sugar in lieu of the original, indigenous ingredients that are low in saturated fat. Schoolteachers (whether Native or not) do the same, to the detriment of a healthy Native lifestyle and the culinary traditions of the Inupiaq.

Spray, Zona. "Arctic Foodways and Contemporary Cuisine," *Gastronomica: The Journal of Food and Culture* 7, no. 1: 41–49.

Zona Spray Starks

Alkermes, confection of, is a sweet medicinal syrup of Arab origin, a cordial made with kermes or cochineal, two bitter red dyes derived from insects. The first recorded recipe, written by the Persian physician Yūhannā Ibn Māsawaih (777–857 C.E.), calls for kermes-dyed silk, apple juice, rosewater, sugar, gold leaf, cinnamon, ambergris, musk, white pearls, aloes, and lapis lazuli. This expensive concoction was prescribed to strengthen the heart and to cure melancholy and madness. Translators and practitioners brought the recipe to medieval Europe, where "confectio alchermes" became a valued remedy. During the Renaissance, variations on the confection appeared in many European medical treatises and handbooks, with spices replacing some of the more expensive original ingredients. By the early 1600s the defining ingredient of the confection, kermes (*Kermes vermilio*), had been largely supplanted by cochineal (*Dactylopius coccus*), a more intense red dye produced by a Mexican insect. Despite alterations, the confection's reputation continued to grow, and it was prescribed not only for weak hearts and depression but also for plague, poisoning, and childbirth. Casanova used it as an ingredient in sugared comfits that also contained his paramour's ground-up hair, and when made up in "Aromaticum Lozenges," the confection was said to sweeten the breath. Often the confection was combined with alcohol before it was administered. This development reached its zenith in Florence in 1743, when the Dominican monks of Santa Maria Novella created an Alkermes liqueur. In the 1800s physicians increasingly questioned the efficacy of the confection, and it disappeared from the pharmacopeia, although Alkermes is still sold as a liqueur.

Greenfield, Amy Butler. "Alkermes: 'A Liqueur of Prodigious Strength.'" *Gastronomica* 7 (2007): 25–30.

Amy Butler Greenfield

ambergris is a waxy calculus that is created in the digestive tracts of sperm whales in response to irritation caused by the sharp, indigestible beaks of ingested squid. It is usually found washed up on beaches or floating in the ocean. It turns up all over the world, but it is most commonly encountered on the coasts of the Indian Ocean, Australia, and New Zealand. This enormously variable substance occurs in irregular or round lumps ranging in weight from a few grams to many kilos. A piece weighing 336 pounds was sold in London in 1913. Ambergris is a brown, black, gray, or white grainy substance and has a faint odor that ranges from mildly fecal when relatively fresh, to "musky" or "earthy" when mature. It is thought to improve from spending a good deal of time in the ocean, but the quality of its scent varies from sample to sample. That of gray ambergris is said to be the best.

Ambergris was an important flavoring in high-status renaissance and baroque confectionery and cookery. It was frequently used in the production of dragées and biscuits, often in combination with musk. To perfume these items, most professional confectioners used a tincture or essence of ambergris, which was made by macerating the ambergris in alcohol in a closed vessel exposed to the heat of the sun or in a stopped glass immersed in hot dung. Lady Anne Fanshawe (1625–1680) included ambergris in combination with rosewater in a circa 1664 ice cream recipe. Sir Edward Viscount Conway (1564–1630), Principal Secretary of State to Charles I, gave his name to a sweet ambergris pudding, recipes for which were published in a number of seventeenth-century cookery texts.

Kemp, Christopher. *Floating Gold: A Natural (and Unnatural) History of Ambergris.* Chicago: University of Chicago Press, 2012.

Ivan Day

ambrosia is "the food of the Gods" in Greek mythology, but in the earthly realm it is a cross between a salad and a dessert. In the seventeenth and eighteenth centuries, the word "ambrosia" referred to a drink; the *Oxford English Dictionary* describes it as "a mixture of water, oil, and various fruits anciently used as a libation; also a perfumed draught or flavored beverage." It is uncertain exactly when the leap from cup to plate occurred, but published American recipes for ambrosia date to the late 1800s. The earliest, such as the one in Woods Wilcox's *Buckeye Cookery* (1877), call for sprinkling sugar between layers of peeled, sliced oranges and grated "cocoanut." By the early twentieth century cut-up pineapple found its way into the recipe. Mid-twentieth-century versions included whipped cream, marshmallows, bananas, nuts, and raisins.

The growing popularity of ambrosia throughout the United States followed the widespread distribution of citrus fruits from Florida. Ambrosia took hold especially in the American South, most likely due to the South's fondness for sweets. Sparkling cut-glass bowls adorn groaning sideboards during the winter holiday season, when serving ambrosia is traditional, and family feuds are fought over dried versus freshly grated coconut. Although ambrosia is classified under "salads" in most Southern cookbooks, it can be eaten after the meal as well as along with it.

Davidson, Alan. "Ambrosia." In *Oxford Companion to Food*, edited by Alan Davidson, p. 14. New York and Oxford: Oxford University Press, 1999.

Mariani, John F. "Ambrosia." In *Encyclopedia of American Food and Drink*, p. 5. New York: Lebhar-Friedman, 1999.

Wilcox, Estelle Wood. *Buckeye Cookery*, p. 135. Minneapolis: Buckeye, 1877.

Cynthia Graubart

American Sugar Refining Company is the world's largest refined cane-sugar producer and the maker of Domino Sugar, among other major brands. Trademarked in 1906, the name Domino was derived from the fact that the rectangular shape of the company's sugar cubes resembles the pieces used in the namesake game.

The company traces its roots to the so-called Sugar Trust, known as the Sugar Refineries' Company when "Sugar King" Henry Osborne Havemeyer organized it in New York in 1887. See HAVEMEYER, HENRY OSBORNE and SUGAR TRUST. Modeled on the nation's first trust, John D. Rockefeller's Standard Oil Company, this then-new form of industrial entity was created by a merger of many separate refineries in several eastern seaboard cities. A near-perfect monopoly, fully legal at inception, it was designed to fix prices, limit supply, keep down labor costs, and discourage competition.

In 1890, however, the company was confounded by passage of the Sherman Antitrust Act. Havemeyer was not deterred. After a New York State court forced the company's dissolution, he simply tweaked its name, reorganized it as a holding company, and chartered the American Sugar Refining Company—the American, for short—in New Jersey. "From being illegal as we were, we are now legal as we are: change enough, isn't it?" Havemeyer remarked.

Havemeyers & Elder was the company's flagship—a half-dozen massive structures situated on a quarter-mile parcel along the Brooklyn waterfront. Almost completely destroyed by an 1882 fire, the site was rebuilt two years later to become the largest sugar refinery on the planet. In 1905 the company was selling about 1.5 billion pounds of sugar a year. Havemeyer once remarked that he had the capacity to supply the sugar demand of the entire country, plus 20 percent.

As the company forged linkages between its refineries and banks, retailers, coal companies, railroads, and the like, legal tangles and government scrutinies were never far behind. In 1911 a special committee of the U.S. House of Representatives began a major investigation. A prolonged affair interrupted by World War I, it was finally concluded with a 1922 decision stating that although the firm had once violated antitrust laws, it was no longer doing so.

The judgment was fair enough, not because the company's philosophy or tactics had changed but because the sugar business itself had. Factors such as increasing competition from high-fructose corn syrup and other sweeteners, artificial and otherwise, were diminishing the company's share of the market. See ARTIFICIAL SWEETENERS and CORN SYRUP. Also, the leaders who took over after Havemeyer's death in 1907—Havemeyer's son Horace being among them—intensified the company's focus on its already existing interests in Caribbean sugar plantations, where it was more difficult for the U.S. government to intervene.

The 1920s brought the so-called Dance of the Millions to Cuba, when that country's sugar prices soared, due to World War I's destruction of the beet industry in Europe. The American profited, until the crash. What hurt the American even more badly than the Great Depression was World War II. First came disruption of unrefined sugar deliveries from the Caribbean and Central America, then the double whammy: sugar rationing. See SUGAR RATIONING.

A slow decline in the industry occurred over the next several decades as high-fructose corn syrup rose to the ascendancy and health advocates condemned refined white sugar as nothing less than "White Death." See SUGAR AND HEALTH. In 1970 the American became the Amstar Corporation, the name change reflecting a growth in its activities beyond sugar refining. In 1984, still struggling, the company was bought at a bargain price by the private investment banking firm of Kohlberg, Kravis, Roberts & Company and, after almost 100 years, ceased to be publicly traded. (The American had been among the original 12 Dow Jones stocks to be traded when the index debuted on 26 May 1896.) Merrill Lynch owned Amstar for one year (1986–1987). The following year the large English sugar company Tate & Lyle acquired Amstar's American Sugar Division. See TATE & LYLE. Tate & Lyle renamed it the Domino Sugar Corporation in 1991.

In 2001 the company was sold to the Florida Crystals Corporation, headed by Alfonso "Alfy" and José Pepe Fanjul Sr., whose family founded vast sugarcane plantations and sugar mills in Cuba in the nineteenth century—all of it lost when Castro assumed power in 1959. See PLANTATIONS, SUGAR and SUGAR BARONS. Their former mansion in Havana is now a museum. After immigrating to the United States, the Fanjuls began anew, establishing plantations and mills in the Florida Everglades, Dominican Republic, and elsewhere. In recent years, the Fanjuls have been excoriated in the media for their labor practices, treatment of the environment, ties to politicians from both parties, and a gilded lifestyle that rivals Havemeyer's. But what the Sugar King wrought can no longer be ascribed to any individual's might. Big Sugar is what this bittersweet empire is aptly called today. See SUGAR LOBBIES.

See also FRUCTOSE; SUGAR CUBES; SUGAR REFINERIES; SUGAR REFINING; and SUGARCANE.

Ayala, César J. *American Sugar Kingdom: The Plantation Economy of the Spanish Caribbean, 1898–1934.* Chapel Hill and London: University of North Carolina Press, 1999.

Catlin, Daniel, Jr. *Good Work Well Done: The Sugar Business Career of Horace Havemeyer, 1903–1956.* New York: D. Catlin, 1988.

Havemeyer, Harry W. *Merchants of Williamsburgh: Frederick C. Havemeyer, Jr., William Dick, John Mollenhauer, Henry O. Havemeyer.* Brooklyn, N.Y.: H. W. Havemeyer, 1989.

Jeanne Schinto

ammonia

See CHEMICAL LEAVENERS.

ancient world is a general term for the classical Greek and Roman civilizations that flourished in southern Europe from about the seventh century B.C.E. to the fifth century C.E. Greeks developed a high culture in gastronomy, as they did in many other aspects of life. Romans, imitating and at the same time despising the Greeks, transformed this culture and spread it, along with their empire, from end to end of the Mediterranean.

For Greeks and Romans, "sweet" was merely one taste quality among many. To dieticians in particular, who based their prescriptions on humoral theory, sweet substances and ingredients were in general classed as "hot" and were to be taken sparingly or avoided by those with hot constitutions. Since alcoholic drinks were also hot, as were most spices, honeyed and spiced wines were extremely hot and were taken before the meal: their heating effect would be mitigated by the "cold" foods to be served later. See MEDICINAL USES OF SUGAR.

If sweets are now almost defined by their inclusion of sugar, sugar as we know it had no part in ancient dining. The Greeks and Romans knew of cane sugar, a rare spice imported from distant India by way of Alexandria, but it was so expensive that it was used only as a medicine: sugar is not called for in any surviving food recipe from the ancient world. Instead of sugar, the sweets of the ancient world were sweetened with dried fruits, or grape syrup, or honey. See HONEY and PEKMEZ.

Sweets came last in ancient Greek and Roman meals, as they do in modern Europe. They formed a separate, smaller course and were prepared by specialized pastry cooks; hence, there is no section on sweets in the Roman cookbook *Apicius*. Yet these were the flavors that lingered in the mouth when the earlier course had already slipped from the diner's memory. In ancient dining the frontier between "first tables" and "second tables" was, as the very names suggest, an almost physical thing. Tables being small and portable, the first tables, smeared with the remains of the meat and fish dishes, the beans, and soups and stews, were taken away to be replaced by the second, laden with sweet foods. Music and dancing intervened to make the break even clearer.

Greek and Roman writings, when they describe dinner at all, are sadly unspecific about second tables. We fall back on a few rare, specialized sources that supply names and (in rare cases) brief recipes for cakes and sweets. Unexpectedly useful is the earliest of all Latin prose texts, Cato the Elder's short work *On Farming* from about 150 B.C.E., which includes a dozen recipes for cakes. A few similar recipes survive from Greek textbooks on baking and patisserie. These sources say little or nothing about the occasions on which sweets were eaten. For example, whether Cato's cakes were intended as religious offerings or as a commercial sideline has been a matter of guesswork.

The earliest Greek texts, up to early fifth century B.C.E., suggest that second tables consisted simply of *tragemata*—"things to be chewed"—raisins, dried figs, dates, hazelnuts, and walnuts. See DRIED FRUIT and NUTS. This is not the full picture, however. Contemporary vase paintings of feasts show conical or pyramidal cakes on the tables as frequently as they show meat. Thus, coming to the late fifth century, it is no surprise that the comic poet Aristophanes mentions among others a cake named *pyramous*, which ought, from its name, to be pyramidal. Mentioned about this time are *oinoutta*, a cake that incorporated must (grape juice) as flavoring and raising agent; *melitoutta*, which must have been honey soaked; and *sesamis*, a cake or sweetmeat in which sesame evidently contributed taste and texture.

The next cake of note, first mentioned about 350 B.C.E. by two Greek poets, is *plakous*. See PLACENTA. At last, we have recipes and a context to go with the name. *Plakous* is listed as a delicacy for second tables, alongside dried fruits and nuts, by the gastronomic poet Archestratos. He praises the *plakous* made in Athens because it was soaked in Attic honey from the thyme-covered slopes of Mount Hymettos. His contemporary, the comic poet Antiphanes, tells us the other main ingredients, goat's cheese and wheat flour. Two centuries later, in Italy, Cato gives an elaborate recipe for *placenta* (the same name transcribed into Latin), redolent of honey and cheese. The modern Romanian *plăcintă* and the Viennese *Palatschinke,* though now quite different from their ancient Greek and Roman ancestor, still bear the same name.

Some of the other cakes for which Cato gives recipes have significant histories, though no others survive under their ancient names. *Encytus* was unusual in shape and method. It was made by injecting a narrow stream of cheesy batter into hot fat. Already in the fifth century B.C.E. the satirical Greek poet Hipponax noticed, and played on, the analogy between this procedure and the sexual act. *Encytus* was not in itself sweet, but Cato instructs that it is to be served with honey or with *mulsum,* the honeyed wine that Romans often drank as an aperitif. The names of Cato's cakes are all originally Greek, with the single exception of *globi,* which may have resembled modern zeppole. They were deep-fried in oil or fat and soaked in honey. See FRIED DOUGH. Their Latin name is shared with that of a geometrical form, from which we know their typical shape: they were spherical or globular. *Globi* clearly resemble a Greek cake with a quite different name, *enkris,* mentioned in the sixth century B.C.E. by the archaic poet Stesichoros, perhaps the earliest Greek author to have named any sweet or cake.

Another cake known to Romans and Greeks under different names deserves mention, although Cato omits it—perhaps it was too simple for him. But Galen, a second-century C.E. author on diet and medicine, had watched the frying of pancakes and describes the process carefully. Pancakes (*lucunculi* in Latin, *tagenitai* in Greek) recur regularly in ancient writings. Not in themselves sweet, pancakes were served with honey and—as early as Hipponax—sprinkled with sesame seeds. See PANCAKES.

Cakes were often ritually offered to Greek gods, a gentler form of worship than the slaughtering of a sacrificial animal. Probably people ate the cakes when the ritual was over (but not the *pankarpia,* an offering of "every kind of fruit" in the form of a honey-soaked cake: herbalists buried this in the ground as thanks giving for rare medicinal plants). We have the names of offertory cakes, but few of the details. *Amphiphon* was a cheesecake decorated with lighted candles, offered to Artemis the huntress on the full moon of the month Mounychion. *Basynias,* honey cake garnished with a dried fig and three walnuts, was offered to Iris, the rainbow goddess, on the island of Delos. *Myllos,* shaped like female genitalia, was offered by the Greeks of Sicily to the goddess Demeter and her lost daughter, abducted from a Sicilian meadow by the underworld god Pluto. There are others: the *hebdomos bous* or "seventh ox" was offered alongside six *phthoeis,* but what form did it take? At least the *phthoeis* can be described: also called *selene* or "moon," they were round and white, made with wheat flour, cheese, and honey, and eaten alongside the entrails of a sacrificial animal.

Romans, too, offered cakes to the gods. The commonest Roman offertory cake was a *libum,* and Cato supplies a recipe for it: cheese, wheat or durum wheat flour, and an egg, all mixed, formed into a large cake, and then placed on bay leaves to bake. There was more than one kind, however: the poet Ovid, in his religious poem *Fasti,* tells us that millet was an ingredient in the *libum* offered to Vesta, the goddess of the hearth.

From the fourth century B.C.E. onward, a few narratives of dinners mention the cakes, sweets, and other delicacies that were served at second tables. The oldest is the *Dinner* of Philoxenos, probably describing an entertainment among the Greeks of fourth-century B.C.E. Sicily. Philoxenos noted sesame cakes and sweets of several kinds (sesame remains a favorite flavor in modern Greek sweets). Then, in early-third-century B.C.E. Macedonia, comes the wedding feast of Karanos, enthusiastically described in a letter by Hippolochos, one of the guests at this lavish—perhaps royal—entertainment. Hippolochos mentions sweets that were local specialities of Greek cities, Cretan, Samian, and Athenian. One of those Cretan sweets might have been *gastris,* for which a recipe survives in a different source. See GASTRIS.

Fictional narratives of Roman meals give an impression of lavish disorder. Second tables at the overly elaborate "Feast of Trimalchio" in Petronius's *Satyricon* were served at least twice, and on both occasions were savory rather than sweet, but they had been preceded by a *pompa* or set piece, presided over by a pastry Priapus and featuring sweets made to look like fruits and filled with saffron sauce. See PRIAPUS. At the meal at Scissa's, described as an aside in the same episode, a cold *scriblita* or "cheesecake" was served with hot honey sauce: a good idea, but it arrived among the meats at first tables.

Returning to history, the poet Statius gives us the fullest menu for Roman second tables. In this case, admittedly, there are no tables. Around the year 95 C.E. the emperor Domitian entertained the citizens of Rome to a Saturnalia feast in the Colosseum. Meats were served in hampers; then, as a battle among Amazons was staged in the arena, sweets descended from the skies, including hazelnuts, Syrian dates, Egyptian dates, Damascus prunes, *lucunculi*, and little Amerine cheeses. Domitian, surely the most generous of imperial hosts, was murdered at his wife's instigation a year later.

See also CHEESECAKE; DATES; DESSERT; HIPPOCRAS; and MEAD.

Dalby, Andrew. "Cakes." In *Food in the Ancient World, from A to Z*, pp. 69–71. London: Routledge, 2003.
Dalby, Andrew, and Sally Grainger. *The Classical Cookbook*. 2d ed. London: British Museum Press, 2012.
Grant, Mark. *Roman Cookery: Ancient Recipes for Modern Kitchens*. London: Serif, 1999.
Leon, E. F. "Cato's Cakes." *Classical Journal* 38 (1943): 213–221.
Newlands, Carole Elizabeth. "The Emperor's Saturnalia: Statius, Silvae 1.6." In *Flavian Rome: Culture, Image, Text*, edited by A. J. Boyle and William J. Dominik, pp. 499–522. Leiden, The Netherlands: Brill, 2003.

Andrew Dalby

angel food cake, one of the sweetest and lightest of all cakes, gets its name from its whiteness and cloud-like texture. According to two authoritative sources, the *Confectioners' Journal* of April 1883 and Jessup Whitehead's *The American Pastry Cook* (1894), angel food cake was created by a St. Louis baker. They do not agree, however, on who this baker was.

Confectioners' Journal identifies him as Mr. George S. Beers, a frequent contributor to the *Journal*. *The American Pastry Cook* simply credits S. Sides. Both sources report that the recipe was for sale. A few months after the April *Confectioners' Journal* article, the *Journal* published an angel food cake recipe without attributing it to anyone.

It turns out that the angel food cake has an earlier beginning than that reported in *Confectioners' Journal*. Culinary historian Pat Reber has found mention of a cake called "Angel's Food" in *The Home Messenger Book of Tested Receipts* (1878), although that recipe is imprecise. It was not until 1884, when a detailed recipe called Angel Cake appeared in the now-classic *Boston Cooking School Cook Book*, that angel food cake gained immortality.

Aside from egg whites, flour, sugar, and flavoring, the key to the success of an angel food cake is cream of tartar, an acidic powder derived from sediment produced during wine fermentation; it stabilizes egg whites and contributes to the cake's volume and whiteness.

By the 1930s the method of making angel food cake and the ratio of ingredients that went into it were firmly established. What had not been determined was the science behind why the cake was such a success.

In 1936 M. A. Barmore approached the topic in a highly technical way. He chose angel food cake because it had few ingredients, and he conducted his experiments in Colorado in a room pressure-adjusted for altitude to over 10,000 feet. He decided to measure the specific gravity of egg whites to determine the optimum for cake volume, the tensile strength of cakes baked at different altitudes, and the effect of oven temperature on the volume and texture of the cakes. He also tested different mixing methods to see which gave the tenderest results.

Barmore found that cream of tartar produced cakes with the finest texture, much better than citric and acetic acids. Baking cakes at different temperatures had minimal effects on texture and volume because the temperature of the cake itself remains fairly constant. For tenderness and cakes with a tight crumb, fresh egg whites proved to be superior to those a few days old. Cakes baked at 10,000 feet were more tender but had less tensile strength than cakes baked at sea level, because of the reduced air pressure.

Another investigator, E. J. Pyler, showed that baking an angel food cake at 450°F (232°C) for 21 minutes produced a cake that rose significantly more than the same batter baked at 325°F (163°C) for 45 minutes. The air cells expand so quickly that the protein meshwork around them is shocked into setting as soon as the cake gains maximum volume.

Other studies revealed that cakes rise best if put into a cold oven before turning it on. Gradual heating allows the air cells to expand less rapidly and slows the setting of the proteins around them, ensuring that the cake will not collapse.

Hanging the baked cake upside down maintains the structure of the air cells as the cake cools. Do not be afraid, though. It will not fall out of the pan while your back is turned.

See also CAKE.

Barmore, M. A. *The Influence of Various Factors, Including Altitude, in the Production of Angel Food Cake.*

Technical Bulletin 15. Fort Collins: Colorado State College, Colorado Experiment Station, 1936.
Patent, Greg. "Angel Food Cake: Just Heavenly!" *Gastronomica: The Journal of Food and Culture* 13, no. 2 (2013): 9–12.

Greg Patent

angelica is the common name for *Angelica archangelica*, a stout, umbelliferous plant that starts out as a rosette of large (30–70 cm in length), compound leaves with hollow, tubular leaf stalks. In its first year or two (occasionally longer), it will accumulate nutrients in a thick taproot. Then it will flower, set seeds, and die. The green, occasionally purplish, flower stem may grow to a height of 2 m or more. The small, greenish flowers are set in spherical umbels, 10–15 cm or more across. When bruised, the whole plant has a strong aromatic scent, often described as musky.

Angelica is widely cultivated, mainly for its root, in several European countries, including Germany, Belgium, Holland, Poland, and France. Its main uses are in herbal medicine. It was once considered a panacea and used as a remedy for just about every imaginable ailment. Extracts of the roots are utilized in the production of various alcoholic beverages, such as vermouth, Benedictine, Chartreuse, and gin.

Fifty tons of angelica are harvested annually in the marshlands of Marais Poitevin, in the French region of Poitou-Charentes. When grown and prepared here, it may be labeled *angélique de Niort*. The most common use is to candy the stalks, as *confiture d'angélique*, for inclusion in cakes and confectionery. The stalks are cut into short pieces and cooked in a sugar syrup several times until saturated. Pure candied angelica is a somewhat dull green. Today it is often artificially colored to make it a gaudy, metallic green. Sulfur dioxide may be added for a longer shelf life. The English trifle is frequently decorated with pieces of candied angelica.

See also CANDIED FRUIT and TRIFLE.

Fosså, Ove. "Angelica: From Norwegian Mountains to the English Trifle." In *Wild Food: Proceedings of the Oxford Symposium on Food and Cookery 2004*, edited by Richard Hosking, pp. 131–142. Totnes, U.K.: Prospect Books, 2006.

Ove Fosså

animal crackers refer to sweet-tasting crackers molded into the shapes of various circus animals. In the late 1800s animal-shaped cookies (or "biscuits," in British terminology), called simply "animals," were introduced from England to the United States. The earliest recipe for "animals" was published on 1 April 1883 by J. D. Hounihan in *Secrets of the Bakers and Confectioners' Trade*. It called for "1 bbl [barrel] flour, 40 lbs sugar, 16 lbs lard, 12 oz soda, 8 ozs ammonia, 6¾ gals milk."

The demand for these cookies grew to the point that commercial American bakers began to produce them. In 1902 the National Biscuit Company officially introduced the most popular brand still known today, Barnum's Animal Crackers, named after P. T. Barnum (1810–1891), the famous circus owner and showman. The packaging was part of the treat—the box looked like a colorful circus train with animals. Initially designed as a Christmas tree ornament, the string holding the box was soon put to use as a handle by which small children could carry the box around. Although a number of other manufacturers presently make animal crackers, Barnum's remain the most famous.

Over the years, 37 different animals have been included in Barnum's Animal Crackers, but the only ones to have survived the product's entire lifetime are bears, elephants, lions, and tigers. Although child actress Shirley Temple sang "Animal crackers in my soup / Monkeys and rabbits loop the loop" in *Curly Top* (1935), rabbits never found their way into a box of Barnum's Animal Crackers. Today, each box contains 22 crackers with 19 different animal shapes: 2 bears (one sitting and one standing), a bison, a camel, a cougar, an elephant, a giraffe, a gorilla, a hippo, a hyena, a kangaroo, a koala, a lion, a monkey, a rhinoceros, a seal, a sheep, a tiger, and a zebra. For the one-hundredth anniversary of the brand, the koala was added on the basis of consumer surveys, beating out the penguin, walrus, and cobra.

Today's Barnum's Animal Crackers are baked in a 300-foot-long traveling band oven in a Fair Lawn, New Jersey, bakery belonging to Nabisco Brands. More than 40 million packages of animal crackers are sold each year, both in the United States and in 17 countries abroad. These fun-to-eat treats have remained popular with children and adults, partly because of the many references to animal crackers in popular culture. In addition to Shirley Temple's song, used in many Nabisco commercials, *Animal Crackers* was the name of a 1930 Marx Brothers' musical and film.

See also ANTHROPOMORPHIC AND ZOOMORPHIC SWEETS.

Cahn, William. *Out of the Cracker Barrel: The Nabisco Story, From Animal Crackers to ZuZus.* New York: Simon & Schuster, 1969.

Frey, Jennifer. "The Modern History of Animal Crackers." *Washington Post,* 31 December 2001.

John-Bryan Hopkins

animals and sweetness is a subject that has not received much systematic attention. Little is known about why and how human animals evolved their sweet tooth from nonhuman animals. Nonetheless, existing data reveal some surprising and very interesting discoveries for the relatively few animals that have been studied, and it turns out that the ability to discriminate sweets is phylogenetically old. For example, chemotaxic responsiveness (orientation or movement toward or away from certain chemicals along a concentration gradient) to sugars and sweetness has been discovered in motile bacteria such as *E. coli.*

Evolutionary biologist Jason Cryan notes that humans have evolutionarily and physiologically "associated a sweet taste with high-energy foods which would have helped our earliest ancestors survive better in their environment" (Bramen, 2010). On the other hand, our perception of bitter tastes was important in identifying and avoiding toxic plants. It is possible that one could make the same argument for nonhumans.

Research shows that much variation exists among other animals in terms of their ability to taste sweets. Cats, including lions, tigers, cheetahs, and jaguars, and some other carnivores do not taste sweets and do not show preferences for them. Neither do dolphins, sea lions, or Asian otters. It has been suggested that animals that mainly eat meat do not benefit from eating sweets and have lost their ability to taste sweet foods as a result of genetic mutations. According to Gary Beauchamp, director of the Monell Chemical Senses Center in Philadelphia, when the data for cats were first published, people claimed that their cats did, in fact, like sweets. However, Beauchamp goes on to explain that the cats' preference for sweets was really a preference for fat and other components of the sweet items.

Beauchamp further notes that the loss of a taste for sweets occurred independently in different species. An animal's diet seems to determine whether a mutation will be effective and retained over subsequent generations. Thus, we need to be careful about generalizations across species because domestic dogs, nonhuman primates, spectacled bears, and many other animals prefer natural sugars; and the taste preferences of a large number of species have never been rigorously studied. It is also widely accepted that although domestic dogs do like sweets, the sweets are not good for them.

Interestingly, bees play a significant role in the understanding of human sweet perception and metabolic disorders. Researchers at Arizona State University discovered connections between sugar sensitivity, diabetic physiology and carbohydrate metabolism, and that bees and humans may partially share these connections ("Bees Shed Light," 2012). By inactivating two genes that control food-related behaviors in the bees' "master regulator" module, researchers uncovered a possible molecular link between sweet taste perception and the state of internal energy. One of the researchers, Ying Wang, noted that the same bees resembled people with Type 1 diabetes in that both showed high levels of blood sugar and low levels of insulin. Clearly, more research is needed, but the relationship between taste perception in bees and human disease is intriguing. See SUGAR AND HEALTH.

It is also known that the brain is not needed to perceive sweetness. Taste scientist Robert Magolskee notes that when researchers put sugar directly into the stomach or small intestine of mice, the mice "know that that's something good and something positive, and they will seek more of that stimulus" ("Getting a Sense," 2011).

Data also exist showing that German cockroaches are losing their sweet tooth because the traps used to catch them utilize sugared poisons. The mutant cockroaches have neurons, activated by glucose; some say, "Sweet!" while others say, "Yuck!" The "Yuck!" neurons lessen the signal transmitted from other neurons, so the message "this taste is awful" gets sent to the brain. It takes about 25 generations or 5 years for such a change to occur. This discovery is a compelling example of evolution at work and shows that taste preferences in nonhumans are evolutionarily labile. The rapid emergence of this highly adaptive behavior underscores the plasticity of the sensory system to adapt to rapid environmental change.

There still is much to learn about taste perception and preferences in animals. Existing data offer some unanticipated results among carnivores and other species. Nobel Prize–winning ethologist Niko Tinbergen has suggested that researchers consider four general questions when studying animal behavior: evolution, adaptation, causation, and ontogeny (development). Because eating sweets is enjoyable, psychologist Gordon Burghardt has proposed adding "subjective experience" to Tinbergen's scheme. Applying Tinbergen's and Burghardt's ideas will surely contribute to the database for research on taste preferences and place these sorts of studies in a more naturalistic and comparative evolutionary framework.

See also SWEETS IN HUMAN EVOLUTION.

"Bees Shed Light on Human Sweet Perception and Metabolic Disorders." 2012. http://www.sciencedaily.com/releases/2012/06/120629211804.htm.

"Bitter-Sweet Truth about Cockroach Survival Skills." 2013. http://www.dailymail.co.uk/sciencetech/article-2329911/Cockroaches-quickly-lose-sweet-tooth-survive-study-shows-Roaches-evolve-aversion-glucose-commonly-traps.html. The abstract for the original research paper can be accessed at http://www.sciencemag.org/content/340/6135/972.

Bramen, Lisa. 2010. "The Evolution of the Sweet Tooth." http://blogs.smithsonianmag.com/food/2010/02/the-evolution-of-the-sweet-tooth.

Magolskee, Robert. 2011. "Getting a Sense of How We Taste Sweetness." http://www.npr.org/2011/03/11/134459338/Getting-a-Sense-of-How-We-Taste-Sweetness.

Sohn, Emily. "Why Cats, Other Carnivores Don't Taste Sweets." *Discovery News*, 2010. http://news.discovery.com/animals/zoo-animals/carnivores-taste-sweet-120312.htm.

Marc Bekoff

anthropomorphic and zoomorphic sweets have, over the centuries, been prepared, bought, and exchanged as presents that add significance to convivial, pagan, and religious celebrations. A wealth of creatures, or parts of their bodies, convey symbolism from the most remote, even pretotemic times. These sweets are highly aesthetic, as well as delicious and diverse in their ingredients, techniques, intentionality, and meanings. Often they are employed as messengers of mythological beliefs, pagan legends, or episodes of biblical origin, shared through oral tradition and now embedded in updated imagery and practices. Their methods of production and consumption were often recorded in medieval texts. In Spain, writers such as Lope de Vega and Cervantes described them, and the secrets of their production were standardized in treatises on the art of sweet making, such as those by Diego Granado, Martinez Montiño, and Juan de la Mata.

Zoomorphic and anthropomorphic sweets remind us who we are and where we come from. These edible metaphors, vestigial markers of identity often closely tied to festivities, combine tradition with innovation and encourage collective indulgence, as if to prove the truth of the adage "You become what you eat and survive from what you sell." Whether homemade or bought from convents, stalls in fairs and markets, or from bakeries and cake shops, these ritual sweets offer an opportunity for families and friends to gather and celebrate.

Some anthropomorphic sweets betray the pagan traditions that underlie Christian celebrations, such as Easter sweets that evoke spring fertility rituals. Kulich, the Russian Easter bread replete with candied fruits and drizzled with white icing, is unmistakably phallic, although it is never acknowledged as such. See RUSSIA. In Amarante, Portugal, *doces fálicos* (phallic sweets) are exchanged by men and women during the Festes de Sao Gonçalo in the first week of June, in a sort of fertility rite marking the name day of the patron saint of spinsters. See PORTUGAL.

Other anthropomorphic sweets made for particular celebrations include *san martino a cavallo* cookies with their highly decorative depictions of Saint Martin on horseback, which are baked in Venice on Saint Martin's Day. Hamantaschen, the triangular filled cookies baked for the Jewish holiday of Purim, are formed in the shape of the Persian vizier Haman's three-cornered hat. By eating this symbolic hat, the evil Haman is destroyed. See HAMANTASCHEN.

Gingerbread men, springerle, Lebkuchen, and speculaas are Central European examples of anthropomorphic cookies, representing figures ranging from Saint Nicholas to an individual family member who inscribes her name in icing on the human shape. Alsatian Gugelhupf is made in various human and animal shapes for different occasions, including that of a swaddled Christ child at Christmas. In pre-Revolutionary Russia during the Christmas season, particularly in the north, decoratively iced animal-shaped cookies made of gingerbread or honey cake were an important part of the caroling ritual. Groups of gaily dressed mummers would proceed from house to house, singing for the cookies as their reward. The most common shapes of these *kozuli* were deer, eagles, goats, and horses, as well as the sun and human figures. The cookies were also hung on Christmas trees and distributed to children. In the spring, lark-shaped buns (*zhavoronki*) were baked as harbingers of the new growing season. See CHRISTMAS; GINGERBREAD; GUGELHUPF; RUSSIA; SPECULAAS; and SPRINGERLE.

Specific Examples

Anthropomorphic sweets rely on the specific requirements for each type of dough. Some malleable consistencies allow for realistic pieces like *orejas de fraile* (friar's ears)—thin, fragile ear shapes. Others, like the *brazo de gitano/reina/venus* (gypsy's/queen's/Venus's arm), have many layers: the skin, flesh, and blood. Some have protruding parts, such as *tetas de novicia* (novice's tits), which are airy with brown meringue on top, or *barrigas de fraile* (friar's bellies).

Zoomorphic sweets, on the other hand, require a certain intentionality to produce recognizable figures, whether flat or three-dimensional, like marzipan figures and *monas de Pascua* (Easter figures) in the shape of swans, dragons, bears, crocodiles, or camels. The *monas* are made from chocolate in Cataluña. Three-dimensional cakes in the shape of lambs are popular at Easter time in a number of countries across Central Europe; they are baked in special two-part molds. Other types of dough are hand-shaped into two-dimensional figures, traditionally in the shape of snails, oysters, mussels, clams, anchovies, shrimps, crayfish, seahorses, insects, worms, doves, chickens, and swans. Cookie dough has long been popular for making two-dimensional figures, whether imprinted with molds, such as springerle, or formed with cookie cutters, such as gingerbread men. See COOKIE CUTTERS and COOKIE MOLDS AND STAMPS. Boiled sugar sweets on sticks, mainly in the shape of roosters but also other animals, have been handmade in Turkey since the sixteenth century. They are often hollow and can be blown as whistles. These confections may have inspired the German *roter Zuckerhase* (red sugar hares), three-dimensional, bright red rabbit sugar figurines that represent the triumph of life and love at Easter. The many industrially produced sweets made from gelling agents, such as Gummi Bears, are more recent iterations of zoomorphic forms. See GUMMIES and HARIBO.

In Spain, many sweets are nominally anthropomorphic, their names referring to states of mind. These can be categorized as follows:

- Signs of melancholy: *lágrimas* (tears); *suspiros de novicia* (novice's sighs), light airy meringues; very tiny *paciencias* (patiences)
- States of mind: *melindres* (apprehension), *picardías* (cunning), *alegrías* (joy), *regañadas* (scolding), *fanfarrona* (boastful)
- Natural states: *dormidos* (asleep), *tontas* (silly), *listas* (clever)
- Addictive attitudes: *borrachos* (drunks)

Other Spanish sweets are more or less realistic reproductions of bodies or body parts, such as *cabello de ángel* (angel hair), *trenzas* (braids), *orejas* (ears), *bocas* (mouths), *dentaduras* (false teeth), *bigotes* (mustaches), *labios* (lips), *lenguas* (tongues), *gargantas* (throats), *corazones* (hearts), *brazos de gitano* (gypsy's arms), *dedos* (fingers), *tetas de novicia* (novice's tits), *barrigas de fraile* (friar's bellies), *tripas de monja* (nun's innards), *chochos de vieja* (old lady's vulvas), *penes* (penises), and *huesos de santo* (saint's bones).

The most beautiful and delicious of these is *cabello de angel* (angel hair) that also features as a filling in many other sweets. One seventeenth-century version, made from transparent candied citron, was known as *diacitron*. Another version is made by pouring liquid egg yolks through a colander with five tiny spouts into boiling syrup, so that the threads of yolk resemble blonde hair. Angel hair is used to adorn trays of luxury cured meats.

Transforming the Fantastic into the Real

Through culinary artistry and the names they give their confections, sweet makers establish a territory of fertile imagination, seduction, and invention. Each edible creature broadens reality, expands the realm of fiction, and embodies the past in the present. The artisans combine the old and the modern, paying tribute to both canonical tradition and heresy, to the local and the universal, to the system of language, to the realm of chance and creativity, and to necessity and survival.

Some historical examples in Spain include *animas del purgatorio* (souls in purgatory), a version of floating island for which meringues are set onto custard cream colored red with beet juice, and *orejones* (big ears), a favorite seventeenth-century delicacy that consisted of peaches modeled to resemble ears and then air-dried. The contemporary *orejas* or *orelletes* found throughout Spain are very thin, delicate fried sweets in the shape of ears.

Even today, when home cooks bake round loaves of ancient simplicity based on the Roman *panis candius,* they give a piece of dough to children for them to create their own edible amulets, thereby accentuating the magical and religious dimension of bread as a sacred element offered in social and religious celebrations. The children's doves, lizards, and snails are drizzled with olive oil and sprinkled with sugar before being baked until brown and crunchy.

Mysteriously, two very old zoomorphic sweets from distant regions in Spain, the Majorcan *ensaimada* and the *anguila de mazapán* (marzipan eel) from Toledo, share the same snail shape of coiled dough. The Majorcan pastry is of Christian origin, because its *hojaldre* dough is made with pork fat; the Toledan *anguila* has Semitic roots. We must suspect that its name is a euphemism to avoid mentioning a taboo: the serpent. Magnificently stuffed with sweet potato, almond paste, and egg yolk with syrup, and ornamented in the style of Toledan filigree, the expensive *anguila* symbolizes power and wealth. It appears at Christmas surrounded by marzipan figurines and *turrón* (nougat candy), heralding a dense calendar of festive opportunities to cultivate the idiosyncratic Spanish passion for embellishing everyday life, to exchange gifts with peers, reward moral authorities, show appreciation to donors, and request intercession from the spheres of sanctity and deity. See NOUGAT and SPAIN.

The Emergence of Thematic Sweets in Spain

The immensely contrasting regions of Spain have been enriched by a convivial crush of various ethnicities. Native Tartessians and Iberians saw the arrival and challenge of Celts, Greeks, Romans, Jews, Visigoths, Moors, other Europeans, and Americans, all exchanging material culture such as ingredients, instruments, and techniques, as well as the wealth of their conceptual imagery. Primal sobriety, isolation and poverty, then classicism, followed in 711 by the sudden impact of the Arabic sense of refined luxury, established a culinary wisdom reflecting the synthesis of three cultures: Moorish, Jewish, and Christian. Marzipan and zoomorphic marzipan figures are Semitic in origin. See MARZIPAN. From the fifteenth to eighteenth centuries, symbols of political and economic power were imported from Italy and found their way into kitchen and dining room. The tables of nobles and kings were invaded by monumental scenes of heroic animals and humans at leisure or in combat, cast of sugar, pastry, or marzipan and decorated with arabesques and *pan de oro* (gold foil), and colored with fancy substances such as cochineal and sandalwood, as described in the literature of the period. See FOOD COLORINGS and SUGAR SCULPTURE.

Everyday Spanish life is still marked by festive conviviality featuring music and food. Spaniards are prepared to invest time, energy, and money in celebrating rites of passage from birth to death, as well as the sequence of religious festivals aimed to incur the favor of God and the saints. The public is also given the opportunity to spend and celebrate at regular commercial events, such as local fairs and markets, during which ancestral traditions of producing and eating certain sweets are revived as an excuse for commerce and socializing. The bone-shaped sweets that appear in the streets and markets on All Saints Day are one example. *Huesos de santo* are made of marzipan with different fillings; *huesos de San Expedito* are fried; and other "bones" look broken because they are *reliquias* (relics). See DAY OF THE DEAD; FAIRS; and FESTIVALS.

Why, where, and how these sweets survive depend on the producers. Their champions are to be found in the home—the mothers and grandmothers and the children who learn from them—and at the closed convents where the *monjas de clausura* sell their divine specialties. See CONVENT SWEETS. Professional bakers also deserve special mention for their perseverance, mindful as they are of their role as the keepers of sweet-making traditions, and tied up as they are in their own means of survival. The true enemies of the fantastic tradition of anthropomorphic and zoomorphic sweets are the changes in the availability and quality of basic ingredients, and the contemporary panic over diet and nutrition.

See also ANIMAL CRACKERS; EASTER; FRIED DOUGH; and HOLIDAY SWEETS.

Armengaud, Christine. *Le diable sucré: Gâteaux, cannibalisme, mort et fécondité*, pp. 84, 138. Paris: Editions de La Martinière, 2000.

Alicia Rios

aphrodisiacs are substances, often edible, that are used to enhance the desire for and enjoyment of sex. In earlier times they were also used to increase fertility and longevity by attempting to strengthen and increase life-containing bodily fluids and overall life force. The word "aphrodisiac" is derived from the Greek *aphrodisiakon*, "pertaining to Aphrodite," the ancient Greek goddess of love and sexuality.

We associate love and sex with sweetness; we have sweethearts, sweeties, honeys, and sugar pies. See SLANG. We go on honeymoons, during which love and lovemaking are supposed to be the most idealized. See HONEYMOON. We give boxes of candy to our sweethearts, especially on Valentine's Day. See CHOCOLATES, BOXED and VALENTINE'S DAY. Many sweet foods have long been considered to have aphrodisiac properties.

Some of the most ancient aphrodisiacs recorded are from India. All but one of the *Kama Sutra*'s aphrodisiac recipes contain sugar, milk, or honey. The text makes extravagant claims for a sweet-potato cookie:

> Crush sweet potatoes in cow's milk, together with swayamgupta seeds [*Mukunia pruriens*], sugar, honey and clarified butter. Use it to make biscuits with wheat flour.... By constantly eating these biscuits, one's sperm acquires such force that it is possible to sleep with thousands of women who, in the end, will ask for pity.

Vajikarana (*vaji* meaning "stallion") was a branch of Ayurveda (India's ancient medical system) devoted to promoting fertility, virility, and sexual pleasure. Its primary text, the *Charaka Samhita*, states that "whatever is sweet...is known as an aphrodisiac" and that "the edibles prepared with raw sugar, sesame, milk, honey, and sugar are aphrodisiac...." *Panchamritam*, "five immortalities," a mixture of milk, yogurt, sugar, honey, and clarified butter, is still prescribed to increase fertility, restore vitality, and promote longevity. See INDIA.

Licorice was used as an aphrodisiac in ancient India, Egypt, and China. The root indeed contains traces of the hormone estrogen. The *Kama Sutra* contains this formula: "Mix garlic root with white pepper and licorice. When drunk with sugared milk, it enhances virility." See LICORICE.

The obsession with aphrodisiacs in China to this day originally reflected Confucianism's emphasis on

Chocolates have long been considered to have aphrodisiac properties, one reason they are so popular on Valentine's Day.

male heirs and the Taoist pursuit of longevity. Rather than targeting specific symptoms and organs, Chinese aphrodisiacs address *yang-shen*, "life-nurture," or long-term vitality, which in turn supports potency and sexual desire. One ancient prescription was a mixture of ground walnuts, peanuts, almonds, and dates, to be taken twice daily for virility and immortality.

Sharbat, an icy liquid from which sherbet originates, was considered a love potion from the Middle East to India. In Sir Richard Burton's commentaries on his translations of *The Arabian Nights* and of India's *Ananda Ranga*, he says that "no Persian will drink sherbet in the presence of his future Mother in-law" because of its aphrodisiac qualities, and that Hindu men imbibe it during sex to prolong the act. See SHERBET.

The Islamic sex manual *The Perfumed Garden*, ca. 1410–1434, contains many aphrodisiac recipes for use by married men. The text advises, "If a man will passionately give himself up to the enjoyment of coition without undergoing great fatigue, he must live upon strengthening foods.... The quality of the sperm depends directly on the food you take." One prescription was to eat 20 almonds and 100 pine nuts, chased by a glassful of thick honey for three successive days.

Majoon, a traditional aphrodisiac sweet still found today in countries ranging from Morocco to India, consists of honey, fruits, nuts, spices, and marijuana, to which cantharides (Spanish fly) was occasionally added in the past. In Morocco it was said that "this dessert will make all women want to cast off their clothes and run naked through the streets and cause all men to cry, 'Allah be praised!'"

Breads and pastries shaped like genitalia were utilized in European sex magic. Romans employed *heterae*, sacred prostitutes, to bake phallic-shaped breads. (*Forno*, Latin for "oven," is the derivation of "fornicate.") Similarly shaped loaves are described in old Teutonic histories. See ANTHROPOMORPHIC AND ZOOMORPHIC SWEETS.

Sex magic was also practiced by anointing a cake with body secretions and feeding it to a lover. One such practice was graphically described by an outraged Buchard, Bishop of Worms in his 1023 *Decretum*, a 20-volume canon law of the Holy Roman Empire: "Have you done what certain women are in the habit of doing? They prostrate themselves face downwards, rump upward and uncovered, and have a loaf of bread kneaded upon their nude nates; when it has been baked, they invite their husbands to come and eat it; this they do in order to inflame their men with a greater love for them."

Seventeenth-century English diarist John Aubrey recorded that women would press pieces of dough against their vulvas, bake them, and offer them to the men they desired. Scientists today point out that the "magic" might have been powerful sex-attractant pheromones in body secretions that were transferred to the baked goods.

Gingerbread men were originally prepared by crones for lovesick women. They laced dough with ginger, believed to have aphrodisiac properties, then sculpted it to resemble the man for whom the lady lusted. When her beloved ate the cookie, his heart, and parts further south, would be enslaved to the damsel forever. See GINGERBREAD.

Alcoholic beverages have long been used to enhance, if not encourage, sexual encounters. Cakes dipped in alcohol were eaten by eighteenth-century French newlyweds to lower their inhibitions on their wedding nights. Rum cakes and alcohol-laced fruitcakes are part of the culinary tradition, if not the belief.

Although Mesoamericans had aphrodisiacs aplenty, usually in the form of herbs and herbal mixtures, we do not know whether chocolate was one of them. The only information we have comes from records of Spanish conquistadores, whose interpretations of Aztec life were colored by their own beliefs. Bernal Díaz del Castillo, a foot soldier who traveled with Cortés and chronicled his Mesoamerican conquest, started the titillating trend by reporting, "From time to time, gold cups were brought to him [Montezuma] containing a beverage made from cacao. He was said to drink it before going to his women, but," del Castillo added piously, "we did not pay any attention to this detail." *Atextli*, an aphrodisiac chocolate and herb beverage, was described in an Aztec *Materia Medica* compiled and written by the Spanish royal physician Francisco Hernández. Its erotic effects are believed to have come from an herb that modern botanists have yet to identify. Hernández classified chocolate as being able to "excite the venereal appetite"—and leaving us ignorant of what the Aztecs themselves thought about it. See CHOCOLATE, PRE-COLUMBIAN.

When chocolate reached Europe, scientists were swift to label it a botanical slut. In 1651 Spaniard

Antonio Colmenero claimed in *A Curious Treatise of the Nature of Chocolate* that it "vehemently incites to Venus, and causeth conception in women." British Royal Physician Henry Stubbes published *The Indian Nectar, or a Discourse Concerning Chocolata* in 1662. He wrote, "As chocolate provokes other evacuations through the several Emunctories of the body, so doth that of seed, and becomes provocative to lust upon no other account than that it begets good blood." Another Englishman, the aptly named James Wadsworth (1768–1844), optimistically observed in *A History of the Nature and Quality of Chocolate*:

> Twill make Old women Young and Fresh;
> Create New Motions of the Flesh,
> And cause them to long for you know what,
> If they but taste of chocolate.

A medical theory in which Renaissance and baroque physicians put great stock was the doctrine of signatures. Its premise was that after Adam and Eve were expelled from the Garden of Eden and humankind began to experience diseases, God mercifully gave each plant a visible sign, usually in the form of a resemblance to the part of the human body it could be used to treat. Some herbs and plants were labeled aphrodisiacs because they resembled genitalia. Vanilla, the long, slender pods of a Mexican orchid, reminded Spanish physicians of a sheath, which encompassed the idea of a vagina. They named the plant *vaina* or *vainillo*, from "vagina"—never mind that *orchis*, the Greek root of "orchid," means "testicles"! Vanilla thus became known as an erotic stimulant in Europe. See VANILLA.

Modern physiologists believe that eating delicious food triggers the brain to release a flood of endorphins, causing people to feel more relaxed, happy, and, at times, more sexy. The endorphin system can also be stimulated by opiates in foods, and there is evidence that high-fat and sweet foods can trigger the release of endorphins. Phenylethylamine, a neurostimulant that works similarly to cocaine and amphetamines to produce exhilaration and heightened sensitivity, is found in chocolate. Honey contains boron, a mineral that increases testosterone and helps metabolize estrogen. However, it is not yet known whether a reasonable portion of any food contains enough of these chemicals, and whether they can be metabolized in a way that reliably trips the sex switches in the brain.

The way foods send sensory signals to the brain through appearance, taste, and smell is also being examined by psychologists and physiologists. It may be that a whiff of a food odor containing a sex pheromone, or the sight of a dish that reminds an individual of a memorable erotic tryst, may stimulate that giant sex organ, the brain, more powerfully than eating a platter of the delicacy. However, at heart, such inquiries reinforce the ancient premise that certain foods positively affect sexuality.

See also MEDICINAL USES OF SUGAR and SWEETNESS PREFERENCE.

Allport, Susan. *The Primal Feast: Food, Sex, Foraging, and Love.* New York: Harmony, 2000.
Hendrickson, Robert. *Lewd Food: The Complete Guide to Aphrodisiac Edibles.* Radnor, Pa.: Chilton, 1974.

Miriam Kasin Hospodar

Appalachian stack cake is a traditional autumn harvest dessert unique to the Appalachian mountain region in the southern United States; it is made from sun-dried apples and sorghum syrup. This inexpensive cake was especially valued during hard times; cut thinly, a dried apple stack cake can yield upwards of 50 slices.

Although the cake's precise origins are murky, the thinness and number of its layers, as well as its use of a fruit filling, clearly relate it to German tortes, and the large German immigrant population of Appalachia supports this theory. A typical dried apple stack cake consists of seven thin layers, each about half an inch thick. In between each layer is a filling of dried apples that have been reconstituted by boiling in water for several hours, then puréed. The preferred apple is the Winesap, prized for its tartness that counterbalances the sweetness of the cake. Spicing can be nonexistent or any combination of cinnamon, cloves, and nutmeg added to the cake batter, to the apples, or both. Apple butter and applesauce are commonly used if no dried apples are on hand.

The cake batter consists of items readily found on the farm or at the country store: flour, eggs, buttermilk, sorghum syrup, and shortening. See SHORTENING and SORGHUM SYRUP. Cast-iron skillets, turned upside down, were often used to bake the cake layers. Because the layers are so thin, baking time is a mere six or seven minutes. After the cake has been baked and assembled, it must season for two or three days for the flavors to blend and the layers to become moist. Stories abound in Appalachia about children who could not wait that long and got into trouble for cutting into the cake too early. Often the cake's only adornments are scalloped edges (if the dough has been cut with a tin pie pan or tart pan) and a pattern of scattered sugar on top. Carefully spaced fork prickings not only keep the layers from rising but also add to the cake's simple design.

For many mountain people, dried apple stack cake now exists only in memory, having fallen victim to the pressures of quick cooking and the shortcuts of convenience cuisine. Rarely is dried apple stack cake offered on restaurant menus.

See also LAYER CAKE; SOUTH (U.S.); and TORTE.

Sauceman, Fred W. *The Place Setting: Timeless Tastes of the Mountain South, from Bright Hope to Frog Level—First Course.* Macon, Ga.: Mercer University Press, 2006.

Fred Sauceman and Jill Sauceman

aroma has long been used by chefs to determine "doneness," to teach apprentices about the stages of cooking, and to beguile diners with rapturous smells. The aroma of baking bread triggers a visceral, and pleasurable, reaction in most people, and the sense of smell is crucial to the ability to taste. Our olfactory sense couples with our taste buds to communicate flavors to the brain. In an evolutionary sense, aroma developed as a litmus test for the environment. The ability to smell allows us to evaluate danger and distinguish predators from prey. In regard to the foods we eat, aroma is essential for seeking the nutritious while rejecting the toxic or spoiled. See OLFACTION; SWEETNESS PREFERENCE; and SWEETS IN HUMAN EVOLUTION.

Historically, Western tradition has maintained a hierarchy of the senses in which sight and hearing are considered the most refined. Because mind is privileged over body, the "chemical senses" of smell and taste have been relegated to the lowest categories. Japanese culture, however, recognizes the importance of the sense of smell. *Kōdō*, the appreciation of incense, is considered one of the three classical Japanese arts of refinement (the others being *kadō* or *ikebana* [flower arrangement] and *chado* [tea ceremony]).

The mind-body division means that taste and smell are often disparaged because they do not easily lend themselves to intellectual abstraction. How can the fragrance of vanilla be described accurately without mentioning the vanilla bean itself? Yet the ephemeral and complex properties of aromas found in food can be a means of communicating or an avenue of learning. The response to any given aroma may be subjective, but the power of smell is undeniable, as evidenced by the $30 billion perfume industry. Some chefs have marketed perfumes inspired by edibles—a logical step for Jordi Roca of El Celler de Can Roca in Girona, Spain, who has used natural essential-oil perfumes in his restaurant. He created the fragrance "Núvol di Llimona" (Lemon Cloud) based on one of his innovative desserts. The American celebrity chef Roblé Ali is launching a women's perfume rumored to smell like his dessert French Toast Crunch.

The biologists Linda Buck and David Axel received the Nobel Prize in 2004 for discovering that the olfactory genes comprise 3 percent of the mammalian genome connected to the amygdala, the seat of memory in the brain. Yet almost a hundred years earlier, in *Remembrance of Things Past*, the French novelist Marcel Proust wrote, "When nothing else subsists from the past, after the people are dead, after the things are broken and scattered... the smell and taste of things remain poised a long time, like souls... bearing resiliently, on tiny and almost impalpable drops of their essence, the immense edifice of memory."

Aroma triggered memories and emotions for Proust, and it is used by chefs today in the same fashion. Modern chefs, in particular, have diffused smoke, steam, and perfumes at the table to achieve these effects. Perhaps the best example of this kind of "edible perfume" is found once again in the desserts of Jordi Roca, who has riffed on such perfumes as Calvin Klein's "Eternity" and Dior's "Hypnotic Poison." His "Trésor of Lancôme," inspired by the perfume, consists of a warm peach cream, loquat syrup, vanilla, apricot sorbet, and honey caramel rose petals, served with a small swatch of the original fragrance so that the two may be compared.

The mysterious nature of aroma makes it a compelling subject of study for chefs and neuroscientists today. Indeed, the high-order cognitive implications of smell are just beginning to be understood by chefs and scientists alike, and chefs are increasingly focusing on specific olfactory events to enhance the diner's experience. To emphasize the interplay of scent and memory, Heston Blumenthal of The Fat Duck sent scented letters of confirmation to a series of guests and then released the same scent at the entrance to the restaurant upon their arrival. Daniel Patterson, an accomplished San Francisco chef, and Mandy Aftel, the foremost natural perfumer, collaborated on the book *Aroma*, in which they pursue the culinary benefits of using essential oils.

The smells of home cooking elicit some of our strongest involuntary memories. Thanksgiving dinner and Grandma's chocolate chip cookies are the subjects of serious study by the Monell Chemical Senses Center in Philadelphia, whose chemists, neuroscientists, and psychologists produce an astounding body of work on the connections among odors, memory, and emotion. Combined with taste these are the real ingredients of fine desserts.

See also SUGAR IN EXPERIMENTAL CUISINE.

Drewnowski, Adam, Julia A. Mennella, Susan L. Johnson, and France Bellisle. "Sweetness and Food Preference." *Journal of Nutrition* 142 (2012): 1142S–1148S.
Mainland, Joel D., Jason R. Willer, Hiroaki Matsunami, and Nicholas Katsanis. "Next-Generation Sequencing of the Human Olfactory Receptors." *Methods in Molecular Biology* 1003 (2013): 133–147.
Patterson, Daniel, and Mandy Aftel. *Aroma.* New York: Artisan Press, 2004.
Shigemura, Noriatsu, Shusuke Iwata, Keiko Yasumatsu, et al. "Angiotensin II Modulates Salty and Sweet Taste Sensitivities." *Journal of Neuroscience* 33 (2013): 6267–6277.

Bill Yosses

art depicting sweets has flourished for as long as sugar has had a steady presence on our tables. Sweets—sugar, chocolate, and the treats that can be made or baked with them—first appear as a recurring subject in Northern European still life painting, and their debut notably correlates with the rise of sugar production and trading. While sugar had long been cultivated in tropical climates and traded in small quantities as a luxury good, it was not until the early sixteenth century that large-scale sugar production was launched in the New World by European colonists. Built on African slave labor and plantation system production methods, sugar cultivation was a highly profitable colonial enterprise that, over time, transformed sugar and the goods it sweetened from aristocratic and patrician luxuries into staples enjoyed throughout society. Artists have been keen observers of this evolution, and the following brief overview shows how their work offers important ideas about the production, consumption, and social meaning of sweets.

Still Life Painting

Commensurate with the rise of Antwerp and, later, Amsterdam as thriving centers of sugar refinement, sugar and its progeny, sweets, began to appear with prominence and frequency in Northern still life painting around 1600. The Flemish painters Clara Peeters and Osias Beert, and their German contemporary Georg Flegel, were among the earliest to devote panels to scrupulously realistic still lifes that included such sweets as ragged comfits (nuts, seeds, or spices coated in sugar), sweetmeats, pastries, letter cookies, and even loaves of crisp, raw sugar. See COMFIT. Many of these early Northern still lifes contain Christian references such as wine, symbolizing the blood of Christ, or sweets arranged in the shape of a cross. See CHRISTIANITY. Such paintings show sugar replacing honey as a traditional symbol of spiritual sweetness, God's abundance, and eternal life. These depictions of luxurious sweets were also intended to display wealth and status and, as such, reflected rising affluence (not unrelated to colonial ventures), and a newly emerging cultural focus on trade, consumption, and living prosperously.

Some Northern still lifes have further layers of meaning. Georg Flegel's ca. 1630 *Large Food Display*, for example, portrays a buffet resplendent with fruit, nuts, pastries, and, at the center, sweetmeats and ragged comfits in a silver compote. A contemporary viewer would have understood this painting as a statement of wealth and cultivation, while also recognizing symbols of Christian faith, such as the parrot (which can be interpreted as the word of God), walnuts (representing the wood of the cross on which Christ was crucified), and an open pomegranate (a symbol of Christ's resurrection), all of which temper the picture's earthly, sweet abundance with higher spiritual principles. In an added twist, though, these same elements—especially the open walnut and pomegranate—had sexual connotations, too, and a contemporary viewer would have recognized this sly nod to lust. See SEXUAL INNUENDO. A 1640 painting by

The sweets depicted in *Still Life with Candle, Sweets, and Wine* (1607) by the Dutch artist Clara Peeters carry multiple messages, both religious and secular. The cookies and comfits represent ephemeral pleasure, as they so easily crumble and decay. The edible letterform "P" could reference Saint Peter but more likely suggests the artist's pride in her painterly achievement.

the Antwerp painter Jan Davidsz. de Heem, *A Table of Desserts*, layers the cautionary message of a *vanitas* into a still life of a sumptuous buffet. Here, the teetering, spoiling leftovers of a grand feast, a half-eaten pie at the center, allude to the trappings of excessive indulgence and the certainty of decay and death.

In Spain, Juan van der Hamen y León painted still lifes with confectionery that reflected the extravagant hospitality practiced among the aristocracy and the affluent. His *Still Life with Sweets and Pottery* (1627), for example, shows a carefully staged and chromatically harmonious arrangement of delicate cookies, sugared fruit, and boxes of marzipan. Antonio de Pereda exhibited Spain's colonial gains—chocolate, raw sugar, and baked goods—in the exquisitely rendered *Still Life with an Ebony Chest* of 1652. A century later, the French painter Jean-Baptiste-Siméon Chardin studied the seventeenth-century Dutch and Flemish masters, but, like van der Hamen y León, was drawn to form more than symbolism. His 1763 *La Brioche* shows a splendidly risen pastry flanked by a sugar bowl and macarons that reveal his mastery of form, color, and texture. See BREADS, SWEET. When *La Brioche* went on view at the Louvre in 1869, it inspired the French painter Édouard Manet to paint an homage of the same title. Like Chardin's masterpiece, Manet's study is a display of formalistic and painterly brilliance.

In American still life painting prior to the Civil War, sweets were not a frequent subject, but the work of Raphaelle Peale is a notable exception. Peale returned numerous times to a still life composition that included a petite iced raisin cake. His small, spare paintings, such as *Still Life with Cake* (1818), show both Dutch and French affinities, but Peale's work is most like Chardin's with its quiet restraint and hovering sense that the sweets presented are not about to be enjoyed but are instead a study of form. In the later nineteenth century Joseph Decker and John Peto expanded the repertoire of still life subject matter with compositions of diverse, colorful hard candy that reflect the widening availability of such confections. See HARD CANDY. Though sweets do not factor prominently in earlier twentieth-century art, after 1960 a new and lively profusion of sweets appears in art.

Contemporary Variations on the Still Life

In the early 1960s the California artist Wayne Thiebaud began painting cakes, pies, and slices of American food culture to create an iconic and widely loved body of work. Well aware of predecessors like

Chardin, Cézanne, and Manet, Thiebaud reinvigorated the still life with spare arrangements of desserts that were lushly described, with thick impasto mimicking frosting. Thiebaud was drawn to the simple geometries of commercial baked goods and the patterns created when these attractive sweets were offered up for sale in rows or grids at a bakery counter. Like Chardin, he was also following an interest in the everyday—here, distinctly American confections from his childhood, painted from memory—while also imparting a nobility, tinged with longing, to his commonplace subject. Thiebaud's influential work, exemplified by his 1963 *Cakes*, speaks to the abundance and formal beauty of expanding American consumer culture and the desire it stoked.

Forty years later the American artist Sharon Core found herself spellbound by Thiebaud's paintings and sought to reconstruct them. Her *Thiebauds* series of 2003–2004 is composed of glossy photographs that she took of meticulously constructed stagings of Thiebaud paintings (Core baked all the sweets herself). Working from reproductions in books and catalogs, Core's appropriations playfully engage Walter Benjamin's ideas about the role that technological reproduction plays in shaping aesthetic experience. Core's beautifully rendered photographs succeed because viewers recognize the cakes: Thiebaud's delectable images are affectionately embedded in our collective visual memory through contact with originals and reproductions alike.

Like Thiebaud, Pop artists were drawn to everyday objects of mass production, including appealing but standardized sweets like pies, cakes, and candy. But unlike Thiebaud's restrained nostalgia, Pop art appropriated popular-culture imagery with irony, humor, and whimsy. Foremost among Pop artists in depicting sweets was Claes Oldenburg, who challenged the convention that sculpture must be serious, rigid, and permanent. Oldenburg's oversized, soft sculptures from the early 1960s, such as *Floor Cake* and *Soft Fur Good Humors* (ice cream bars rendered in colorful animal prints), can be read as playful, outsized three-dimensional still lifes. Oldenburg's sculpture also foregrounded commercially produced sweets from everyday American life, in an era when this was still novel, to draw our attention to how much of what we ingest and enjoy is industrially produced. Four decades later Jeff Koons, continuing an interest of Pop artists, makes flawless, oversized replicas of common objects of consumption. His *Sacred Heart (Red/Gold)* (1994–2007) emphasizes the shiny, enticing cellophane wrapping of a chocolate heart while calling attention to the workings of a mature consumer economy: slick packaging that stimulates desire but may not deliver satisfaction. See CANDY PACKAGING.

The Photorealist movement that emerged in the late 1960s was, like Pop, fascinated with the commonplace. Working from photographs of everyday objects to render precise, large-scale reproductions, Photorealists asked viewers how their perception of reality is influenced by photographic technology. Desserts and candy were, and continue to be, a frequent Photorealist subject for their brilliant, often unnatural colors, their rich capacity to reflect light, and the complex way they engage the eye. A viewer studying Audrey Flack's superbly painted 1974 *Strawberry Tart Supreme*, for example, knows how the whipped cream will gently give way to a spoon, or how the brightly flavored strawberry filling might zing the tongue. See TART. Likewise, Ralph Goings's 1995 *Donut* could prompt a wave of pleasurable memories of glazed doughnuts enjoyed with coffee. See DOUGHNUTS. These outsized copycat sweets activate multiple senses and involuntary memories, not unlike Marcel Proust's madeleines. See MADELEINE. More recently, the Italian artist Roberto Bernardi paints stunningly faithful candy still lifes, such as *Caramelle di Cristallo* (2010), which suggest that the commonplace sweets we savor primarily through one sense—taste—are worthy of another, our studied gaze. The British artist Sarah Graham paints extra-vivid, hyper-real desserts and candies, set against brightly colored backgrounds, that read less as actual sweets than as nostalgic memories of sweets.

The American painter Emily Eveleth shares Wayne Thiebaud's abiding interest in monumentalizing a beloved, ordinary American sweet—for her, the jelly doughnut. But unlike Thiebaud's more visually cheerful work, Eveleth's large, luminous canvases, like *Pact* of 1996, shimmer with tension. In Eveleth's hands, a common glazed doughnut is lusciously painted and pregnant with sweet, cherry-red filling, but is simultaneously an oozing, possibly sinister corporeal mass. This duality triggers contradictory feelings of anticipation and comfort, disgust and anxiety, all of which are common to contemporary discourse around sweets. The California photographer Jo Ann Callis also explored a menacing aspect to sweets in her 1993 series *Forbidden Pleasures*. Her still life subjects—éclairs and strawberry tarts, for example—are staged on shiny, sensuous textiles to emphasize desire, temptation, and the guilt associated with the consumption of sweets. Here, the Christian concern about confectionery abundance seen in Northern seventeenth-century painting has morphed into a self-centered guilt about the personal consequences of succumbing to the seduction of now ubiquitous sweets. More recently, the Canadian photographer Laura Letinsky, in her 2004 *Hardly More Than Ever* series, makes quiet still lifes of staged leftovers and messy, postrevelry tables to challenge images of domestic perfection published in popular magazines. Like Jan Davidsz. de Heem's still life, Letinsky's partially eaten desserts and soiled dishes suggest a narrative of conviviality and consumption, but Letinsky introduces notes of alienation and melancholy.

Social, Economic, and Political Critiques

Thanks to advertising, the sugar and chocolate proffered today, and so strongly associated with pleasure and even luxury, have been detached from their past and present systems of production. See ADVERTISING, AMERICAN. The work of Cuban-born María Magdalena Campos-Pons brings critical attention to this gap by highlighting the role of slavery in the Cuban sugar industry. Her 2010 installation *Sugar/Bittersweet* takes the form of a sugarcane field with rows of erect African spears balanced on African and Chinese stools and encircled by disks of raw sugar like those exported on the triangular trade. Alluding to the enslaved African and indentured Chinese laborers upon whose backs the Cuban sugar industry was built, Campos-Pons opens up a backstory to Antonio de Pereda's lavish display of Spanish wealth. More recently, the American artist Kara Walker pointed to the historical entwinement of race, power, and exploitation in sugar production with her 2014 site-specific installation in a former Domino Sugar warehouse in Brooklyn. See RACE. *A Subtlety, or the Marvelous Sugar Baby* centers on a 90-foot-long African American female sphinx coated in white sugar. Inspired by the "subtlety," a small, clever, edible sculpture often made of sugar paste that appeared on wealthy medieval banquet tables, Walker created a commanding sphinx with the knotted kerchief of a mammy, exaggerated breasts, and fully exposed genitalia. See SUGAR SCULPTURE. Both a tribute to sugar workers of African origin and a wider indictment of the historical production systems in which they worked, Walker's work impels viewers to recognize that enslaved and disempowered female sugar workers also endured both sexual stereotyping and exploitation.

The Brazilian artist Vik Muniz focused on the offspring of contemporary sugar plantation workers on the island of Saint Kitts in his 1990s series *The Sugar Children*. See PLANTATIONS, SUGAR. He saw that years of backbreaking work left the parents embittered and broken, and understood that their sweet and carefree children faced the same dire future. Muniz took Polaroid photographs of the children; back in his New York studio, he meticulously copied these photographic portraits by sprinkling granulated white sugar on black paper. He then photographed the sugar "drawing" before destroying it, echoing the impermanence of the children's sweet nature. Muniz's use of sugar in his artistic production references the legacy of colonialism, slavery, and present-day exploitation. See POLITICS OF SUGAR.

Chocolate production has received similar scrutiny from artists. The American conceptual artist April Banks spent three months in West Africa, the historical locus of the Atlantic slave trade and a region that today supplies the majority of the world's cacao. Her study of cacao cultivation in West Africa, and the global economy in chocolate, informed her 2006 installation *Free Chocolate*. Combining photography, video, and text, Banks's work reveals how much our pleasure in chocolate is "guilty," predicated on the oppression of cacao farmers and the inequitable profit margins of the chocolate industry. The Kenyan-born photographer James Mollison also brings attention to invisible workers in the chain of chocolate production. With his large-scale color portraits of cacao farmers in the Ivory Coast, viewers engage with the direct gazes of the hardworking, disenfranchised people who pick the cacao beans that beget their luxurious sweet. The German conceptual artist Hans Haacke, known for mapping social systems of patronage and enrichment, deconstructed the empire of the wealthy German chocolate manufacturer and art collector Peter Ludwig. Haacke's 1982 exhibition and artist book *Der Pralinenmeister* (The Chocolate Master) exposed underpaid immigrant labor, female workers living in locked compounds, government tax breaks, and back-room business and art deals. Haacke's work calls attention to the complicity of politicians, taxpayers, and chocolate consumers that enabled Ludwig to profit excessively and at a huge human cost.

Consumerism and scripted consumption have been rich areas of inquiry for artists. In 1959 Andy Warhol published *Wild Raspberries,* an artist's book that charmingly satirized the French cookbooks so popular in the 1950s. Readers are treated to haute cuisine dishes, including elaborate desserts, that are illustrated by Warhol and accompanied by fancy instructions and humorous shortcuts, like calling the Royal Pastry Shop to request delivery of half-inch chocolate balls. The British photographer Martin Parr vividly chronicled everyday working- and middle-class British cuisine in his 1995 series *British Food.* Among sandwiches, sausages, and fried foods, he showcases sweets such as cakes and cupcakes crowned with artificially colored frosting, waxy sprinkles, and British flags. These brilliantly colored, flash-saturated images indict blind consumption and excess.

More recently, the American painter Julia Jacquette combines sweets with text to bring attention to the way advertisers and magazine editors manufacture consumer desire by provoking a primal longing for human connection. Will Cotton, another American painter, explores this well of human desire that fuels our pleasure-seeking consumer society. His saccharine-sweet confectionery landscapes, many featuring cotton-candy clouds and nude women awaiting the viewer's pleasured gaze, are a momentarily seductive fantasy world, but this vision of utopia is a place where desire is sated to gluttonous, nauseating extremes. Perhaps a modern-day *vanitas,* Cotton's paintings caution the viewer about fulfilled wishes.

Cindy Sherman's *Untitled #175* (1987) is a particularly graphic image of out-of-control consumption. A staged close-up photograph of a chaotic, sandy scene with suntan lotion and sunglasses (showing Sherman's posed reflection), partially consumed cupcakes and Pop-Tarts, and strewn vomit, Sherman pulls back the curtain on binging and its repulsive consequences. Sweets amplify the grotesque aspect of her scene since they normally engage the senses and stimulate desire, not disgust. See PSYCHOANALYSIS. With this work Sherman was also critiquing trend-oriented 1980s art collectors: "... let's see if they put this above their couch," she explained to Kenneth Baker in a 2012 interview published in the *San Francisco Chronicle.* Focusing on the private world of disordered eating, the American realist painter Lee Price, in works like *Jelly Doughnuts,* creates aerial-view images of women binging on doughnuts, cakes, ice cream, and junk food. These intimate paintings call attention to cultural attitudes toward women and their cravings, especially for the guilty pleasure of sweets. See GENDER.

Use of Sweets as a Medium

Chocolate, a widely loved sweet with rich sensory engagement, is a potent medium for artists. Though not the first, the Swiss German artist Dieter Roth was a pioneer in exploring chocolate as a medium starting in the 1960s. Roth was intrigued with the organic properties of chocolate and its inevitable dissolution. In works like *Chocolate Lion (Self-Portrait as a Lion)* (1971) and, later, *Schokoladeturm (Chocolate Tower)* (1994/2013), Roth's vertical assemblage of neatly arranged trays of self-portraits, sphinxes, and lion heads, all cast in chocolate, the artist foregrounded physical decay as an essential, natural element of life—a modern take on the *vanitas.* In an era when museums were mandated to preserve everything that entered the collection, Roth's chocolate-based works were also subversive—they naturally attracted bugs and mold—and challenged museum-based notions of permanence. A decade later, the German artist Sonja Alhäuser invited museum viewers to become active participants in the process of destruction. For *Exhibition Basics* (2001), she fabricated sculptures and pedestals out of dark and white chocolate and marzipan, and instructed visitors to eat them, eventually erasing the work completely. Alhäuser called into question conventions of museum visitor behavior—do not touch, much less destroy, the art—and used sweets to conflate art with everyday acts of pleasurable food consumption. Alhäuser's work formed an antipodal point to Ed Ruscha's 1971 *Chocolate Room,* where visitors entered an enclosed space covered with sheets of paper coated with silky, fragrant chocolate. Viewers were enveloped by the rich, aromatic chocolate but could not consummate their desire to consume it.

In the 1980s the American performance artist Karen Finley famously smeared herself in chocolate in a visceral act that outraged critics of the National Endowment for the Arts, which funded her work. By slathering her nude body in melted chocolate, she decried women being treated like excrement and consumable commodities. A few years later, in 1992, the Bahamas-born performance artist Janine

Antoni debuted *Gnaw*, based on two 600-pound minimalist cubes—one chocolate, the other lard. Over a period of six weeks Antoni gnawed at the cubes and spit out bites that she ultimately fashioned into colorful lipsticks and molded into appealing chocolate candies. Antoni chose chocolate for the way it stirs desire; its partner, lard, represented the consequences of succumbing. She drew attention to the contiguity of desire and disgust; one can be overcome with desire for chocolate but also disgusted by the lard, which, in turn, is a common ingredient in lipstick, which, she said, women use to make themselves more desirable.

Sugar has also been employed by artists as a medium, though not as frequently as the more alluring chocolate. Dieter Roth built *Zuckerturm (Sugar Tower)*, a companion to his chocolate tower that was populated with colorful sugar casts. In 2000 the American artist Shimon Attie created the installation *White Nights, Sugar Dreams*, which included video projections that surrounded the viewer with a haunting, mountainous landscape of white sugar. A diabetic, Attie chose sugar for its dual nature—both "nutrition and poison." The surreal landscape that he created and filmed is a metaphor for the diabetic's experience of low blood sugar and the careful calibration of insulin in response to the body's sugar levels. See SUGAR AND HEALTH.

Some artists, such as the Taiwanese YaYa Chou, have, like Chardin, created art in response to the simple, formal beauty of sweets. Her 2005 *Chandelier*, for example, is made up of hundreds of colorful Gummi Bears strung together to imitate a sparkling Venetian glass chandelier, transforming a beloved common candy into an object of splendor. Decades earlier the American artist Sandy Skoglund identified patterns found in certain commercial cookies and playfully extended them by placing the cookies in similarly patterned contexts and photographing them.

The Cuban American artist Felix Gonzales-Torres created "candy spills," large singular piles of wrapped hard candy carefully placed on the floor of a gallery. One of these spills, *Untitled (Portrait of Ross in L.A.)* of 1991, was a poignant installation that was at once political and deeply personal. *Ross* was created from 175 pounds of colorfully wrapped candy that referenced the healthy weight of Gonzales-Torres's former partner Ross, who had died of AIDS-related illness. Viewers were invited to take away candies, gradually depleting the mound until it was replenished by the museum, thereby sustaining the cycle of life and death. Consuming the candies, which represented the body of Ross, was both an act of communion and an act of complicity that made viewers agents in the symbolic demise of Ross. In this way Gonzales-Torres alluded to the destruction of the gay community, one by one, during the AIDS epidemic, while many people and governments stood by idly.

For the past four centuries artists have borne witness to the remarkable rise of sweets. They have traced the arc of their expanding presence in society with attention to their form and allure, as well as to their underbelly. Just as our relationship with sweets is ongoing and evolving, artists will continue to be drawn to them and offer visually engaging, critical insights about our passion for sugary things, our history, and ourselves.

Bendiner, Kenneth. *Food in Painting: From the Renaissance to the Present.* London: Reaktion, 2004.

Bland, Bartholomew F. *I WANT Candy: The Sweet Stuff in American Art.* Yonkers, N.Y.: Hudson River Museum, 2007.

Hochstrasser, Julie Berger. *Still Life and Trade in the Dutch Golden Age.* New Haven, Conn., and London: Yale University Press, 2007.

Nash, Steven A., with Adam Gopnik. *Wayne Thiebaud: A Paintings Retrospective.* New York: Thames & Hudson, 2000.

Schneider, Norbert. *Still Life: Still Life Painting in the Early Modern Period.* Cologne and Los Angeles: Taschen, 2009.

Stefanie S. Jandl

artificial sweeteners are industrially produced substitutes for sugar, intended for those who want or need to curtail their intake of sucrose. One could argue that the taste of sweet "discovered" artificial sweeteners. Saccharin, the first artificial sweetener, was identified in the 1870s when a scientist at Johns Hopkins University licked his finger and found it shockingly sweet. Sodium cyclamate, the second sweetener to be discovered, emerged as marketable in the 1930s when a graduate student at the University of Illinois placed his lit cigarette on a lab bench (where a bit of the substance had landed), only to find the next puff unexpectedly sweet. Aspartame, better known as NutraSweet, came to market only after a pharmaceutical chemist licked his finger mid-experiment and tasted sweetness. And sucralose, or

Splenda, first appeared in the 1970s when a research chemist, while working with sucrose (table sugar), told a colleague to "test" one of the resulting compounds. Hearing "taste" rather than "test," the scientist did so and found it intensely sweet.

Such stories of discovery suggest that lab safety left much to be desired well into the twentieth century. They also reveal that these products were sweet accidents, tastes inadvertently discovered by scientists who were researching something else. That artificial sweeteners have become such key ingredients in our lives tells us much about the modern American desire for sweets without caloric consequence.

How Sweet Are Sweeteners?

All artificial sweeteners on the market today are much sweeter per part than is sucrose. Aspartame is roughly 200 times sweeter, saccharin about 300 times sweeter, and sucralose—the sweetest of all—nearly 600 times sweeter. Sodium cyclamate was the least sweet, at 30 to 50 times the intensity of sugar, and many of its advocates believe that with its less sweet taste, stability when heated, and nonbitter aftertaste, it remains a superior option for sweetening. However, it was removed from the U.S. market in 1969 by the Food and Drug Administration after fears surfaced that it was carcinogenic. Of the artificial sweeteners remaining, only sucralose (branded as Splenda) can be heated, making it the choice for bakers who avoid sugar (although complaints about dryness in the results abound). The key distinction between sucrose and artificial sweeteners, in addition to the intensity of sweetness, is the fact that while sucrose provides food energy and is always absorbed by the body, artificial sweeteners provide no food energy (calories) and can pass through the body without being absorbed.

Changing Perceptions of Artificial Sweeteners

Ideas about artificial sweeteners and health have changed dramatically over the last century. Much of this change can be attributed to how the United States has thought about sugar. In the early twentieth century, when mothers were advised to feed their children sugar because of its high calorie (energy) content and low cost, artificial sweeteners were soundly rejected. "It ought to be a penal offense," declared one *New York Times* reader when he discovered that manufacturers had been secretly replacing the more expensive "cane syrups" with cheaper saccharin in carbonated beverages. Only Teddy Roosevelt's personal use of saccharin kept it on the market during the Progressive Era, and even then it was deemed a medicine suitable only for diabetics or those on calorie-restricted diets.

The 1950s saw the rehabilitation of artificial sweeteners' reputation. Not coincidentally, this movement coincided with national concerns about obesity and sugar. Advertised in newspapers across the country, Tillie Lewis's "Diet With Sweets" was one of the first campaigns to link artificial sweeteners explicitly with weight loss, a tactic that contributed greatly to its success. The 21-day plan provided menus heavy in the company's Tasti-Diet products and claimed that, without any change in lifestyle, weight loss could be achieved merely by replacing sugar with artificial sweetener. In the early 1970s Jean Nidetch promoted a similar message when introducing her line of artificially sweetened foods and sodas, core components of Weight Watchers' efforts to draw new participants into its weight-loss community. Advertisements promoted chocolate sodas or desserts, all sweetened with saccharin, as appropriate indulgences for times when eaters simply could not resist cravings for sweets.

At the same time that food manufacturers and diet companies promoted saccharin, antisugar sentiments were on the rise in American popular culture. John Yudkin's *Sweet and Dangerous* (1972), along with similarly themed articles in the popular press, invited Americans to see their excess sugar consumption as the cause of ailments from ulcers and heart disease to diabetes, as well as tooth decay, hyperactivity, and obesity. See DENTAL CARIES and SUGAR AND HEALTH. Doubts about sugar, then, helped fuel experimentation with saccharin. In 1977, when the Food and Drug Administration sought to ban saccharin after correlations between high use and cancer risk were found in rats, the majority of consumers protested.

NutraSweet Nation and the Mainstreaming of Artificial Sweeteners

By 1980 artificially sweetened sodas and desserts could be found throughout supermarket aisles. See SODA. These products, however, remained choices for dieters or people watching their weight. The situation changed with the introduction of aspartame, under the brand name NutraSweet. Using a technique known as supplier-initiated ingredient branding, Searle Pharmaceutical sent 5 million American households a small package of brightly colored gumballs attached to a flyer. While consumers tasted the newly approved sweetener NutraSweet, they read pages of testimonials from customers who found it "the best thing since the invention of food." This combination of sending a sample associated with fun and pleasure rather than with diets and deprivation, and instructing consumers to go look for (and demand) this new ingredient, revolutionized the place of artificial sweeteners in the U.S. marketplace. No longer a substitute, aspartame became the most modern, healthful option for indulging in sweets. And, according to advertising material, it was not artificial. "If you've had bananas and milk, you've eaten what's in NutraSweet," explained one early advertisement. A methyl ester of aspartic acid and phenylalanine, aspartame did have things in common with bananas and milk. But it was not derived from milk or bananas, nor was it produced in a way that would have been considered "natural" to most consumers. By successfully presenting NutraSweet as both modern and natural, and by turning consumers into advocates, NutraSweet's promoters converted the nation to artificial sweetener consumers. Only five years after its introduction, the red-and-white swirl denoting a product's use of 100 percent NutraSweet had become ubiquitous, and product sales reached over $700 million worldwide. In the 1980s alone, NutraSweet replaced roughly a billion pounds of sugar in American diets. By 1990 three-quarters of the U.S. population had tried NutraSweet. Many of these new consumers were children. With NutraSweet's superior taste to saccharin and new fears of childhood obesity on the rise, an artificial sweetener was for the first time perceived as the most healthful sweetening option for the family.

Splenda and Doubts about Artificial Sweeteners' Healthfulness

Introduced in 1999, Splenda, the brand name for sucralose, is the latest artificial sweetener on the market, and it is now the most frequently consumed. Splenda's ability to withstand heat enabled it to serve as a replacement for sugar not only in prepared foods and beverages but also in home baking. Its sugarlike taste and flexibility, combined with an early campaign message that it was "made from sugar, so it tastes like sugar," encouraged consumers to make the switch from NutraSweet. One study in the mid-2000s found that while Splenda sales rose 90 percent in a single year, sales for saccharin and NutraSweet dropped 12 percent and 90 percent, respectively. Consumers may also have been motivated by a low-level yet persistent unease about NutraSweet's health effects. For the small percentage of consumers who suffer from phenalynine syndrome, aspartame consumption can be life threatening. Moreover, in websites and books, and through word of mouth, former NutraSweet users had since the 1990s complained that their headaches, seizures, and memory loss came as a result of consuming large quantities of aspartame. Splenda likely benefited from these rumblings, but unease about all artificial sweeteners remains. Recent marketing studies find over half of Americans who use artificial sweeteners are concerned about these products' safety. Add to this recent studies suggesting that artificial sweetener use, over time, may lead more often to weight gain then weight loss, and space for a new alternative appears.

The Future of "Artificial" Sweetness

Today, an increasing number of Americans desire local, whole, and organic foods. Artificial sweeteners are, by definition, none of these things. Assuming this trend continues, a strong market will exist for alternatives to artificial sweetener that can provide sweet taste with reduced caloric intake. One of these will certainly be Stevia, an increasingly popular natural sweetener formed by crushing the leaves of the stevia plant. See STEVIA. And new research avenues into taste may enable us to become our own artificial sweeteners. In one study, researchers are exploring whether our own taste receptors can be altered so as to make our experience of sweetness more intense. Such a twist, while currently more science fiction than fact, would enable our bodies to draw more sweet pleasure from naturally occurring sugar, and to consume less.

See also SUGAR.

de la Peña, Carolyn. *Empty Pleasures: The Story of Artificial Sweetener from Saccharin to Splenda.* Chapel Hill: University of North Carolina Press, 2011.

Fowler, S. P., K. Wiliams, R. G. Resendez, et al. "Fueling the Obesity Epidemic? Artificially Sweetened Beverage Use and Long-Term Weight Gain." *Obesity* 16, no. 8 (August 2008): 1894–1900.

Severson, Kim. "Showdown at the Coffee Shop." *New York Times*, 4 April 2009. http://www.nytimes.com/2009/04/15/dining/15sweet.html?pagewanted=all (accessed 28 June 2013).

Yudkin, John. *Sweet and Dangerous.* New York: P. H. Wyden, 1972.

Carolyn Thomas

Athenaeus, formally Athenaeus of Naucratis, a Greek city in Egypt, produced his massive *Deipnosophists* (Learned Banqueters) in 15 books sometime around 200 C.E. Nominally an account of the food and wine consumed and the topics discussed at a series of elaborate dinner parties in Rome, this work is, in fact, an antiquarian history of luxury, and it is among the most important sources for ancient banqueting and culinary practices, as well as for otherwise lost Greek literary material of every sort. The overall structure of the *Deipnosophists* imitates that of an individual dinner (*deipnon*) and the drinking party (*symposion*) that followed it. Baked bread (*artos*) and unbaked barley cakes (*maza*), which were consumed as part of the main meal, are accordingly discussed early on, whereas cakes and specialty sweets are treated toward the end of the work.

Culinary history was already a topic of academic discussion by the mid-third century B.C.E., and Athenaeus reports that at least four now lost treatises on cake making (by Aegimus, Hegesippus, Metrobius, and Phaestus) were included in Callimachus's catalog of the holdings of the Ptolemaic library in Alexandria. Athenaeus himself appears to have had at least secondhand access to other similar works, including Chrysippus of Tyana's *Breadmaking*, Heracleides of Syracuse's *Art of Cooking*, and Iatrocles's *On Cakes*, from all of which he preserves scattered, brief quotations. Athenaeus additionally draws on various lexicographers, local historians, and the like, who cited rare terms (including names of cakes) and preserved literary passages—many from otherwise vanished lyric poems and comedies—in which they occurred.

Some of the cakes described in Book 14 or in passing in Book 3 are ritual offerings, often with their own local names and shapes, such as the *mulloi* formed out of sesame seeds and honey to resemble female genitalia that were carried in processions in honor of Demeter and Kore in Sicily. Most of the others are *tragêmata* (snacks), which were served on the so-called second tables as something approaching a dessert course after the main meal had ended and the drinking had begun, along with boiled eggs, almonds, hare meat, and roasted birds. Some of these cakes are fried in olive oil, such as the Syracusan *staititas* ("Moist spelt-flour dough is poured out into a frying pan, and honey, sesame-seeds, and cheese are added on top of it," according to Iatrocles), but others appear simply to be kneaded together and served cold. The most common extra ingredients in the descriptions offered by Athenaeus are honey (also poured over fried items), cheese, sesame seeds, milk, grape must, and wine. See GRAPE MUST. In the early and most emphatically Greek cakes, neither herbs and seasonings (such as anise, cardamom, and garlic) nor fruit (including raisins) plays a role. Some of the handful of Roman-era recipes offered by Chrysippus of Tyana are more elaborate, such as that for a Cretan *gastris* (glutton cake):

> Thasian nuts, Pontic nuts, and almonds, along with some poppy seed; toast them, keeping a close eye on them as you do, and mash them fine in a clean mortar; mix the fruit in and work it smooth along with some reduced honey; add a considerable amount of pepper; and work it smooth. It turns out black because of the poppy seed. Flatten it out into a square. Next, grate white sesame seed; work it into a paste with reduced honey; press it into two sheets, putting one on the bottom, and the other on top of it, so that the black mixture can go in the middle; and assemble it nicely.

See also ANCIENT WORLD; GASTRIS; PRIAPUS; and SYMBOLIC MEANINGS.

Braund, David, and John Wilkins, eds. *Athenaeus and His World: Reading Greek Culture in the Roman Empire.* Exeter, U.K.: University of Exeter Press, 2000.

Olson, S. Douglas, ed. and trans. *Athenaeus: The Learned Banqueters.* 8 vols. Cambridge, Mass., and London: Harvard University Press, 2006–2012.

S. Douglas Olson

Aunt Jemima is the brand name and fictional spokeswoman for a line of processed food products, most notably ready-mix pancake flour. She was depicted as a loyal slave with a magical touch in the kitchen; her creation was actually inspired by a stage tune, "Old Aunt Jemima," based on an American slave song. Upon hearing a performance of that tune in a St. Joseph, Missouri, minstrel hall in 1889, Christopher Rutt, in collaboration with Charles Underwood, adopted the title character of

Aunt Jemima pancake flour, one of the earliest American products to be marketed through advertisements featuring its namesake, played on popular but racially problematic nostalgia for the antebellum South. © BUSY BEAVER BUTTON MUSEUM

the song as the name of their new pancake batter. See PANCAKES.

The image of Aunt Jemima, a large, dark-skinned woman wearing a bandanna, was later popularized in a live performance by a former slave who played Aunt Jemima in a display at the 1893 Chicago World's Fair. Nancy Green was the first of a series of African American women who depicted Aunt Jemima in print, radio, and television advertisements through the 1960s. The fictional slave's life and times were embellished in a series of advertisements created by adman James Webb Young and illustrator N. C. Wyeth that ran in American women's magazines such as the *Ladies' Home Journal* during the 1920s and 1930s. They depicted Aunt Jemima solving domestic problems on the antebellum plantation by whipping up a batch of the best pancakes anybody had ever eaten and then heading to the North after a Chicago-based milling company "bought" her imaginary pancake recipe and mass-produced it. The tagline for these ads was "I'se in town, honey," a statement that was backed by a succession of actresses who fanned across the United States to give demonstrations on pancake preparation and dispense folksy if inarticulate wisdom. A caramel-colored syrup bearing Aunt Jemima's name was first marketed in the 1960s. See CORN SYRUP.

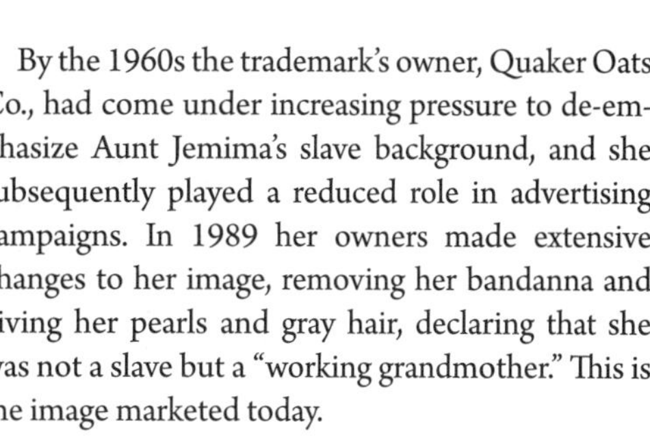
By the 1960s the trademark's owner, Quaker Oats Co., had come under increasing pressure to de-emphasize Aunt Jemima's slave background, and she subsequently played a reduced role in advertising campaigns. In 1989 her owners made extensive changes to her image, removing her bandanna and giving her pearls and gray hair, declaring that she was not a slave but a "working grandmother." This is the image marketed today.

See also RACE and SLAVERY.

Manring, M. M. *Slave in a Box: The Strange Career of Aunt Jemima*. Charlottesville: University Press of Virginia, 1998.

M. M. Manring

Australia and New Zealand, two countries in the southern hemisphere known collectively as the Antipodes, were colonized separately by the British—a heritage that produced a predilection for confectionery in both places. Sociologist Allison James has asserted that "sweets . . . are an entirely British phenomenon. There is no equivalent abroad and the British sweet industry, in its production of a very extensive range of confectionery, seems to be unique" (1986, p. 296). James was, however, unaware that Australia and New Zealand boast equally rich, although different, cultural and industrial confectionery histories. Children in both places have a voracious appetite for what they call "lollies," rather than sweets or candy. For them, confectionery is a topsy-turvy wonderland of gustatory adventure that offers also a means of exercising consumer authority and subverting adult norms. Little wonder that when they reminisce about childhood "Down Under," adults recall buying and consuming sweets in terms of power and enchantment.

The Magic of Lollies

When confectionery historian Laura Mason observed in *Sugar-Plums and Sherbet* that "sugar is fantasy land" (1998, p. 19), she could have had in mind Antipodean lolly counters, where a seemingly infinite range of shapes enables parents to turn children's birthday cakes into oceans, jungles, moonscapes, and almost anything else. Perhaps a marker of difference for Australian confectionery is the prevalence of animals; if it flies, crawls, slithers, or runs, it may be found in miniature form at the lolly counter. The candy manufacturer A. W. Allen's starch jellies, especially, have come in every shape imaginable: rats, cats, snakes, sharks, frogs, witchetty grubs, and so on. To this dazzling array add Allen's Freckles and Steam Rollers; Hoadley's Violet Crumbles and PollyWaffles; Mastercraft's Golden Roughs, Redskins, and Bobbies; Plaistowe's Choo Choo Bars; Riviera's Fags; Scanlen's Blackjack; Griffiths's Kool Mints; and Lagoon's Sherbet Bombs. A similar spectacle awaits children at New Zealand lolly counters, which offer Pineapple Lumps, Cola Rollers, Whittaker's Peanut Slab, Chocolate Fish, Jet Planes for re-enacting scenes from *Top Gun*, and Fruit Puffs for making the ubiquitous Lolly Cake.

Life's a Ball with Jaffas

When a lolly defines an era and becomes a national icon, it has as much to do with cultural ritual as gustatory pleasure. From the myriad backyard confectioners operating in Australia in the early twentieth century, Stedman's became one of the industry giants during the 1920s and 1930s, alongside Allen's, MacRobertson's, Hoadley's, Small's, Plaistowe, Mastercraft, Dollar Sweets, and Darrell Lea. James Stedman (1840–1913) was the son of a convict. Apprenticed in 1854, this currency lad (a term denoting boys of the first generation to be born in the colony) founded Sweetacres, the makers of Minties (wrappers with Moments Like These cartoons), Fantales (wrappers with film-star biographies), Cobbers, Marella Jubes, Throaties, and the lollies Australians recall most often, Jaffas.

Developed in Sydney in 1931, Jaffas are chocolate balls panned with bright red, orange-flavored sugar. See PANNING. Hard and heavy, like marbles, they make ideal missiles. In postwar suburban movie theaters, organists were often pelted with Jaffas at the beginning of children's matinees. Another barrage was unleashed if the film started late or if the reel broke. Best of all, a Jaffa rolling down the bare, sloped wooden floor of a darkened cinema during a tense moment provoked mirth and mayhem. The carnivalesque ritual of Jaffa-rolling epitomizes Australia's anti-authoritarian identity and exposes larrikinism, for which Australians are renowned, as the province of girls and boys alike. New Zealanders have taken the sport of Jaffa-rolling to another level. Since 2002 an annual charity event involves millions of Jaffas racing down Baldwin Street in Dunedin, the steepest street in the world.

Making a "Chocolate King"

Equally legendary is the tale of pauper Macpherson Robertson (1860–1945), who converted an old nail can into a furnace, procured a secondhand pannikin for boiling sugar and began making lollies in the family bathroom. Outfitted for 9 pence as a teenager, he would boast an annual turnover of 2 million pounds and a staff of 2,500 by 1925. His company MacRobertson's Chocolates became self-contained, encompassing a 1,000-acre cacao plantation in New Guinea along with subsidiary industries—maize, milk, timber, cask-making, and engineering—spread over a 35-acre Melbourne property dubbed "the Great White City." By 1935 "the young man with the nail can" had become Australia's "Chocolate King," the highest taxpayer in the country. MacRobertson's was renowned for exquisite packaging and for products like Cherry Ripe, Old Gold Chocolate, Snack, Freddo Frog, Columbine Caramels, and Clinkers.

An audacious entrepreneur, Robertson contributed 10,000 pounds to Antarctic expeditions in 1929–1930, prompting explorer Sir Douglas Mawson to name part of the territory MacRobertson Land. To celebrate Melbourne's centenary, Robertson put up 15,000 pounds in prize money for a London-to-Melbourne air race, an enterprise that stimulated the development of aviation. Robertson was knighted in 1932.

Cakes, Desserts, and Biscuits

While "lollies" means confectionery, "sweets" refers to the sweet course served at the end of meals. Traditionally, this meant tinned fruit and ice cream or jelly and custard, and while plum pudding dominates Christmas, trifle and Pavlova are enduring wedding favorites. Pavlova, ANZAC biscuits, fairy bread (birthday fare), and Peach Melba are culinary icons, even if Australians and New Zealanders disagree over who owns what. See PAVLOVA. Named for Queensland Governor Lord Lamington (in office from 1896 to 1901), lamingtons are cubes of day-old sponge cake coated in thin chocolate icing and dipped in coconut. They were created around the time of Federation (1901), when coconut was not widely used in European cooking. Biscuits ("bikkies," not cookies) such as Iced Vovos, Tim Tams, and Milk Arrowroot, made by Arnott's Biscuits (established in 1888), are traditional companions of the mid-morning "cuppa."

Sweets foods are also found among the "bush tucker" eaten for centuries by Australia's indigenous people, including acacia gum, lerps (honeydew), and honey ants.

See also CHILDREN'S CANDY.

Clark, Pamela, ed. *Australian Women's Weekly Children's Birthday Cake Book.* Sydney: Australian Consolidated Press, 1980.

James, Allison. "Confections, Concoctions and Conceptions." In *Popular Culture: Past and Present,* edited by Bernard Waites, Tony Bennett, and Graham Martin, pp. 294–307. London: Routledge, 1986.

Robertson Jill. *MacRobertson: The Chocolate King.* Melbourne: Lothian, 2004.

Robertson, Macpherson. *A Young Man and a Nail Can: An Industrial Romance.* Melbourne: McRobertson's, 1921.

Toni Risson

Austria-Hungary, the former Hapsburg Empire and the political units that have succeeded it, has one of the richest sweet food traditions anywhere. Much of this has to do with its location at the heart of Europe. Every cuisine emerges from a juncture of geography, history, and culture. Nowhere is this more obvious than in the countries that once made up the Central European Hapsburg Empire, officially renamed Austria-Hungary in 1867 and finally disbanded in 1918. Today, Austria, Bosnia and Herzegovina, Croatia, Czech Republic, Hungary, Slovakia, Slovenia, and parts of Italy, Poland, Romania, Serbia, and Ukraine all share the imperial heritage.

The Empire

The old empire extended from the Alps to the south and west to the broad range of the Carpathian Mountains to the east. From the baker's perspective, the region's southern reaches are good for grapes, cherries, apricots, and wheat, while the north is better for apples, pears, plums, and sugar beets. Berries of every description grow in the forests, and walnuts, hazelnuts, and chestnuts are ubiquitous. Pigs provide lard, and cows butter and cream.

Following the Counter-Reformation, the region was militantly Catholic. The church's liturgical calendar specified what one could eat and when it could be eaten. With all the fast days, meat was forbidden almost one day in three. In the strictest interpretation of the rules, eggs and dairy were also forbidden, though in practice this level of abstemiousness was not always observed. On meatless days Central European cooks often turned to flour-based foods: noodles, dumplings, pancakes, and leavened baked goods. Many of these were sweetened initially with fruit, fresh or preserved, and later with beet sugar as it became affordable. Out of this

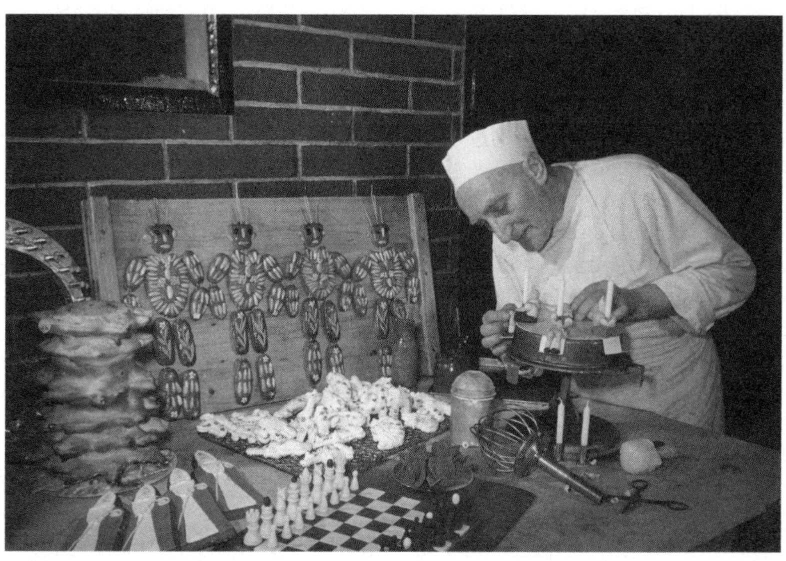

A pastry chef decorates a cake near other edible sculptural creations. Vienna, Austria, 1951. NGS IMAGE COLLECTION / THE ART ARCHIVE AT ART RESOURCE, N.Y.

practice came the vast repertoire of Mehlspeisen, a term that now translates as "pastry" but once encompassed any flour-based dish, whether sweet or savory. See MEHLSPEISE.

Both the geographic proximity and the liturgical connection to Italy meant that culinary trends and ingredients flowed continually, mostly from south to north. Bohemian silver paid for the spices and sugar shipped across the Alps by the Venetians. By the baroque era, Italian cookie bakers and ice cream makers were also peddling their wares in the northern capitals. Echoes of the southern influence are found in a scattering of food loan words, most notably in *torte/dorte* (from the Italian *torta*) for which Austria is famous. See TORTE.

Proximity to the Ottoman Empire in the east also left its mark. In Hungarian, the word for apricot is *kajszi* or *kajszibarack*, both deriving from the Turkish *kayısı*. From a culinary standpoint the Ottoman influence is less obvious. Facts are few, even if legends abound. Perhaps the most famous concerns Vienna's Kipferl, the crescent-shaped sweet roll associated with Vienna's coffeehouses. During the 1683 Turkish siege of Vienna, the early-rising bakers supposedly heard noises beneath the ground, which turned out to be the attackers tunneling under the walls. Alerted, the city was saved, and the bakers created a crescent-shaped pastry in imitation of the crescent on the Turkish flag. Other stories specify a baker named Peter Wendler as the inventor. In Budapest they tell a similar tale, theirs dating back to the 1686 siege of that city. However, as medieval sources attest, these crescent- or horn-shaped pastries (the terms are occasionally used interchangeably) date back hundreds of years earlier. See CRESCENT.

Another commonly held assumption, that the hand-stretched dough used to make strudel was imported from the Turks, is probably also incorrect. A Venetian source mentions something called a *Torta ungaresca* (Hungarian pie) made with layers of stretched dough as early as the fourteenth century, long before the Ottomans had made any inroads into Hungary. See STRUDEL. Where the Turks undoubtedly had influence was in introducing the coffee habit, both in the territories they ruled directly but also within the empire itself. Certainly, when the Ottoman ambassador Kara Mahmud Pasha visited Vienna in 1665, his opulent train of 300 attendants, including the coffeemakers Mehmed and Ibrahim, made an impression.

Hapsburg politics and the whims of culinary fashion introduced Central European sweet makers to flavors and techniques from far beyond the empire's borders. The Hapsburgs may trace their origin to an obscure Alpine cul-de-sac, but by the 1500s their astute marriages had raised them to the top rank of European aristocracy. Nuptial alliances with Spain and France were especially common. As a result, Viennese courtiers early on picked up the Spanish habit of drinking chocolate. Matthias de Voss, the earliest recorded court sugar refiner ("Zuckerbäcker bei Hof," 1563), was from the Netherlands, another Hapsburg possession at the time.

As the court at Versailles and all things French became à la mode in the eighteenth and nineteenth centuries, courtiers in Central Europe demanded that their own dessert tables be decorated with recherché *biscuits*, *crèmes*, and *petits choux*. When Maria Theresa (1717–1780) married Francis Steven, the Duke of Lorraine, the imperial household largely converted to French-style dining. For the upwardly mobile, serving tea, or at least a mostly sweet meal called by that name, became a symbol of sophistication. See SWEET MEALS.

After the French Revolution, numerous French chefs found employment in the aristocratic households of the empire. Franz Sacher, for example, trained under a certain *maître* Chambellier, so it is not surprising that his eponymous torte is based on a decidedly French *biscuit*. See SACHERTORTE. Even the great French pastry chef Antonin Carême worked in Vienna for a time, in the employ of the English ambassador. See CARÊME, MARIE-ANTOINE. This Gallic influence is evident in numerous dessert recipes, such as the Biscuiten, Bonbons, and Rouladen in Katharina Prato's best-selling *Die süddeutsche Küche* (first published in 1858 and still in print). The legendary Budapest culinary impresario József Dobos was so steeped in French cooking that he published a French-Hungarian cookbook (*Magyar-franczia szakácskönyv*) in 1881. Central European pastry chefs both adapted and elaborated on French techniques. Beloved cakes such as the *Panamatorte* came to be frosted with *Pariser crème* (a whipped ganache), while countless others came to depend on buttercream, a frosting first used to embellish the decidedly French *le gâteau moka*. See ICING.

Within the empire itself, techniques and recipes were freely traded from one region to the next. Czechs have their version of *linecké těsto* (named after the Austrian town of Linz), a buttery dough enriched with hazelnuts or almonds used to make cookies and tarts; Hungarians make *szilvásgombóc,* plum-filled dumplings dusted with toasted breadcrumbs, which their neighbors would recognize as *švestkové knedlíky* (Czech) or *slivkové knedle* (Slovak). Strudel has been part of the Austrian repertoire so long that it is difficult to recall its Hungarian origins.

City

The sweet specialties for which the countries of the former empire are renowned often resulted from the rivalries among both pastry cooks and their patrons in nineteenth-century Vienna and the provincial capitals. Elite confectionery was a highly urban phenomenon that depended on costly ingredients such as eggs, sugar, fresh butter, cream, and, in later years, chocolate, as well as a highly skilled, rigorously regulated, yet fiercely competitive workforce of pastry cooks and confectioners. In Vienna, the court was long the arbiter of taste, yet unlike Versailles, it never had the staff to be self-sufficient and therefore depended on town confectioners for its catering needs. See COURT CONFECTIONERS. As the bourgeois population of the cities swelled during the Biedermeier period (1815–1848), the sweetshops' customers were increasingly middle-class women who used pastry as a tool for social advancement. Occasionally, this phenomenon was made explicit, as in *Der Zuckerbäcker für Frauen mittlerer Stände* (1824), in which F. G. Zenker, one-time chef to the princely Schwarzenbergs, explains in great detail how to throw pastry-rich tea parties just like the aristocrats do.

Whereas these sorts of get-togethers were formerly held late in the night by the titled set, the more puritanical bourgeoisie shifted the social event to the middle of the afternoon, eventually leading to the Austrian institution of *Jause,* which now mostly features coffee and a sugary or savory snack. The social demands of the *Jause* led to the invention and elaboration of an enormous repertoire of sweet tidbits. By 1900 the trend of taking tea in the English fashion gave further incentive to confectioners and home bakers alike. The 1906 edition of Katharina Prato's *Die Süddeutsche Küche* included more than 120 recipes for Theegebäck (as these cookies and petits fours came to be known), as well as some 70 for hors d'oeuvres–type snacks appropriate for the afternoon meal. In the twentieth century many Theegebäck were adapted for Christmas. Perhaps the most ubiquitous of these holiday treats are Vanillekipferl, crescent-shaped almond cookies, and Linzer Augen, jam-filled sandwich cookies made with Linzer dough.

Up until the late nineteenth century the highly bureaucratic nature of the Hapsburg realm forbade cafés to sell confectionery, and confectioners to sell coffee. When this regulation was finally relaxed in the 1890s, the hybrid *Café-Konditorei* (café-confectioner's) emerged, giving women a respectable public gathering spot. See CAFÉ. Some of Vienna's most famous confectioners belong to this category, including Demel (founded 1786), Heiner (1840), and Gerstner (1847).

Although confectioners in the regional capitals were more alike than different, certain cities became associated with specific desserts: Vienna for its Sachertorte, Bratislava for its *rožky* (poppy seed–filled crescents, *Pressburger Kipferln* in German), Budapest for Rigó Jancsi and Dobos torte, and Salzburg for its Nockerl (a sort of soufflé or *Auflauf* as it is known in Austria). See DOBOS TORTE and RIGÓ JANCSI. In Fred Raymond's 1938 operetta *Saison in Salzburg (Salzburger Nockerln),* the last of these edible urban icons is praised as *Süß wie die Liebe und zart wie ein Kuss* ("sweet as love and tender as a kiss").

Country

If the aristocracy and bourgeoisie of the Hapsburg cities sipped tea, coffee, and chocolate, consulted cookbooks that told them how to cook in the latest Italian or French fashion, and could avail themselves of pastry shops selling ice cream, bonbons, and every other fantasy that expensive cane sugar could elicit, the country folk lived in a very different world of sweetness. Up until the industrialization of sugar beet production in the second half of the nineteenth century, and even a generation or two beyond that, sweetness came from two primary sources: honey and fruit. See FRUIT and HONEY.

As elsewhere in Europe, apiculture was established as early as the Middle Ages—though honey was still being gathered in the wild well into the 1800s. In an effort to encourage this locally produced sweetener, Empress Maria Theresa even established a school for beekeeping. In 1775, by imperial decree, beekeeping instructors were sent to the provinces and honey was excluded from taxes. Whatever honey was not sold (or given in tithe under feudalism) found its way into

Lebkuchen (gingerbread), sweetened the porridges and gruels that formed one of the main staples of the peasantry, or was fermented into mead. See GINGERBREAD and MEAD. Honey-sweetened gingerbread itself became a sweetener (as well as a binding agent), grated over dumplings, pancakes, and porridge or added to poppy seed and other sweet pastry fillings.

The imperial palace also recognized the importance of fruit to its subjects. Maria Theresa's son Joseph II (1741–1790) went so far as to award farmers a silver medal when they planted more than 100 fruit trees, and he required that several fruit trees be planted prior to obtaining a wedding license. According to the imperial land register, in 1800 there were close to 8 million fruit trees in Bohemia alone, or almost three trees for each person. Naturally, much of this fruit was eaten fresh, and some was distilled into brandy, but a great deal was also preserved either by drying or cooking it down into fruit butters: *lekvár* (Slovak, Hungarian), *povidle* (Czech), *Powidl* (South German). While today these fruit preserves are almost always made with damson plums, earlier sources speak of apples, pears, cornelian cherries (from a tree in the dogwood family), bilberries (European blueberries), strawberries, rose hips, and others. See FRUIT PRESERVES. These fruit butters were spread on pancakes or used as fillings for various yeast-based pastries such as *koláče* (round tarts made with an enriched yeast dough) or buchty. See BUCHTY. In Hungary and Slovakia, cornmeal was formerly made into *görhe* or *görhő*, a sort of baked johnnycake, sweetened with prune butter or sometimes just carrots. In fact, carrots were often used like a fruit, utilized to make a syrup or dried and pulverized into a sweet powder. Desiccated apples and pears were given a similar treatment and sprinkled on sweet foods in much the same way the wealthy used confectioner's sugar. Just about every fruit that could be dried, was. See DRIED FRUIT.

Fruit both dry and fresh has long been transformed into dumplings. An early recipe for plum dumplings appears in a sixteenth-century manuscript, and today versions filled with apricots and other fruit are widespread. See DUMPLINGS. Fresh and dried fruit has been used to make soups, compotes, and a sort of fruit porridge cooked with milk and thickened with flour. None of these dishes would have been considered dessert. Rather, they would have been a meal unto themselves, possibly accompanied with bread in the case of the more liquid preparations. See SOUP.

The region's noodles are also often served sweet. *Mohnnudeln*, thick noodles made with potato dough, are served with butter, ground poppy seeds, and sprinkled with sugar. The similar Czech *škubánky* look more like gnocchi. In *Bröselnudeln* the poppy seeds are replaced with breadcrumbs. Hungarian *rakott tészta* layers more conventional egg noodles with cottage cheese and is baked like a pudding.

At least three types of pancakes have been commonly eaten as a main course. Perhaps the oldest are yeast-raised *lívance*, pancakes cooked in a special pan with flat, round indentations. Austria has various forms of *Schmarrn*, a thick pancake chopped up after cooking. The best known is the upscale *Kaiserschmarrn*, made by folding beaten egg whites and raisins into the batter prior to cooking and shredding. *Palatschinken* (or the Slavic or Hungarian equivalent) is the local name for crepes, which are typically smeared with jam or fruit butter. See PANCAKES.

Holidays

Among the oldest of the festive sweet foods for holidays, weddings, and christenings are the many variations of Lebkuchen (gingerbread). Not only are they traditional for Christmas, they are a familiar sight at the numerous saint's day fairs. Carnival brings jelly doughnuts (*Faschingskrapfen*), whether in Transylvania or the Tyrol. See DOUGHNUTS. Enriched yeast breads crop up across the festive calendar in multiple forms: as the braided Czech *vánočka* for Christmas, or the similar Austrian *Osterzopf* for Easter. To make *Reindling*, a Carinthian Easter specialty, the baker rolls an enriched yeast dough, strudel-like, around a filling of raisins and walnuts and bakes it in a Bundt cake tin, while Czechs form a similar dough into round loaves and stud it with almonds to make *mazanec* for the holiday. Weddings have long been celebrated with a Gugelhupf in the German-speaking regions, a role mostly played by *koláče* north of the Danube. See GUGELHUPF. George Lang describes a Transylvania wedding confection called a *menyasszonykalácsfa* (bridal cake tree) or *eletfa* (life tree), made by dipping a stripped branch in batter before frying it and setting it in a cake base. This "tree" was then decorated with ribbons, small cakes, and edible figures.

Industrialization

As in England and Germany, the nineteenth century brought industrialization and urbanization to the Hapsburg realms. It also brought the sugar beet, which first transformed the diets of city dwellers and eventually the foodways of everyone See SUGAR BEET. Starting in the 1830s, the vast majority of the empire's sugar beets were produced in Bohemia, which by 1863 was producing 12 percent of the world's beet sugar, much of it destined for export. Enough was left over, though, to add increasing amounts of sugar to flour-based foods that had once been barely sweet or sweetened only with fruit.

Industrially refined sugar also paved the way for sweet foods produced on an industrial scale. Formerly artisanally made wafers long popular at spas like Karlovy vary (Karlsbad) were commoditized by Karl Bayer in 1867 into a nationally marketed product. In 1898 Joseph Manner's Vienna company made its name by sandwiching a similar wafer with hazelnut cream. *Mozartkugeln* were developed in Salzburg by Paul Fürst in 1890; however, since he never patented these pistachio marzipan-filled chocolates, several companies (including Fürst) now produce billions of the foil-wrapped candies each year. In Hungary, Bonbonetti was founded in 1868 and by 1883 was mass-producing chocolates in its steam-powered Pest factory. The company was acquired in 2012 by the Ukranian Roshen Confectionary Corporation. In Bohemia, the Orion brand was registered in 1914 by František Maršner's two-decades-old "oriental sweets" and chocolate company. The brand survived both World War II and years of communism; it is now owned by Nestlé. Worldwide, the best-known brand to emerge from old Hapsburg realms is PEZ candy, developed originally in Vienna in 1927 by Eduard Haas III. See PEZ.

After the Empire

The collapse of the Hapsburg Empire in 1918 initially had little impact on the sweet repertoire of the newly independent nations of Czechoslovakia, Hungary, Austria, and Yugoslavia. However, economics and politics soon created fissures in the common culinary heritage. Rapid urbanization, increased availability of processed food, and the gradual erasure of religious dietary observance sidelined the habit of sweet, flour-based meals. The shortages of eggs and butter during the Depression and World War II and then the imposition of communism in Hungary (1947) and Czechoslovakia (1948) lowered the standards of both home and professional bakers. In communist Czechoslovakia all private enterprise was banned (in Hungary the regime was less draconian), including bakeries, pastry shops, cafés, and restaurants. Under the command economy many of the goods sold at these food-service operations were now produced in central factory-like commissaries to state-mandated norms that left little room for quality. Artisanal production ceased for two generations.

Thanks to the revival of individual enterprise following communism's demise in 1989, the craft of pastry has slowly been returning to standards that had never been abandoned in next-door Austria. Whether in Linz or Bratislava, today's pastry chefs look for inspiration both to the region's deep confectionery tradition and to trendy French and American models. The old empire's prodigious sweet tooth endures.

See also BREADS, SWEET; BUDAPEST; CARNIVAL; CHOCOLATE, POST-COLUMBIAN; CROISSANT; FAIRS; FRANCE; LINZER TORTE; NESTLÉ; SMALL CAKES; and VIENNA.

Krondl, Michael. *Sweet Invention: A History of Dessert.* Chicago: Chicago Review Press, 2011.

Lang, George. *The Cuisine of Hungary.* New York: Atheneum, 1971.

Leitich, Ann Tizia, and Maria Franchy. *Wiener Zuckerbäcker: Eine süsse Kulturgeschichte.* Vienna: Amalthea, 1980.

Maier-Bruck, Franz. *Das grosse Sacher-Kochbuch: Die österr. Küche.* Munich: Schuler, 1975.

Úlehlová-Tilschová, Marie. *Česká strava lidová.* Prague: Družstevní práce, 1945.

Michael Krondl

azuki beans (*Vigna angularis,* also romanized as *adzuki*) have been cultivated in Japan since the prehistoric period. High in protein, B1, and iron, they are indispensable to Japanese confectionery and even find their way into Western-style baked goods in Japan. Although the color of red azuki is considered auspicious, the English translation "red beans" is a misnomer because there are also white azuki.

Cooked with glutinous rice, the beans provide color and flavor to the celebratory dish Red Rice (*sekihan*); they can also be cooked in a rice porridge, or mashed up to make a sweet soup called *shiruko,* to which dango or rice cakes (mochi) may be added—when whole azuki are used, the soup is called *zenzai.* Azuki, however, truly shine in confectionery. Mashed azuki sweetened with sugar make *an,* often translated as "bean jam," the most frequently used filling for sweets like manjū or mochi; *an* is also used as a topping in traditional confections such as dango. See DANGO; MANJŪ; and MOCHI. In recipes for traditional sweets, the consistency of the beans can take two forms: *tsubuan* retains some of the original shape of azuki in the bean paste, whereas *koshian* is a smooth paste with the remaining lumps strained away. The confection called *yōkan,* which entered the diet of Zen monks in the Kamakura period (1185–1333), was originally a vegetarian substitute for mutton. It is made from steamed *an*, sugar, flour, kudzu starch, and flavorings. The version of the recipe that developed by the nineteenth century substituted agar agar (*kanten*) for the flour and kudzu starch to create more gelatinous versions, a texture much prized by the Japanese: softer *mizuyōkan* and firmer *neriyōkan*. Because *yōkan* is troublesome to make at home, it is sold at traditional confectioners in long cakes that can be sliced into servings.

Kan Sanmi. *Anko no hon: Nando demo tabetai*. Osaka: Keihanshin Erumagajinsha, 2010.

Eric C. Rath

baba au rhum is a rum-saturated, yeast-leavened cake that is as soaked in legend as it is in boozy syrup. The name comes from the Slavic term for "old lady" and has been used by Czechs and Poles for a variety of sweet, mold-baked preparations since at least the Middle Ages. At some point before the eighteenth century, the term also became a synonym for Gugelhupf. See GUGELHUPF. The *Nouveau grand dictionnaire françois, latin et polonois et sa place dans la lexicographie polonaise* (1743) defines a "baba ciasta" (dough baba) as a yellow cake (*gâteau*). In France, the word was adopted for just such a saffron-tinted pastry sometime in the eighteenth century, presumably due to the influence of exiled Polish king Stanisław Leszczyński or his daughter Marie Leszczyńska, the queen consort of Louis XV.

Numerous fanciful tales recount Leszczyński's participation in the genesis of the yeasty cake. Some credit him personally with inventing it while in residence in Lorraine in the 1710s, whereas others assign the innovation to his pastry chef Nicolas Stohrer. See STOHRER, NICOLAS. According to one story, the king was reading the newly translated *One Thousand and One Nights* and spilled some fortified wine on his slice of Gugelhupf. He is supposed to have named this new creation "baba" after the Ali Baba of one of the tales. According to another story, it was Leszczyński's young pastry cook who came up with the idea of soaking the cake in a rum syrup. The trouble with both tales is that soaking the pastry was not part of the recipe until the nineteenth century. As late as 1808, the French food writer Grimod de La Reynière noted that "the principal flavoring of the baba is saffron and Corinth raisins [dry currants]." Contemporary cookbooks confirm that the cake was little different from a Gugelhupf at this point.

Although Leszczyński most certainly did not invent the Gugelhupf—a common enough pastry throughout Central Europe—it is highly plausible that either he or his daughter popularized the idea of snacking on the yeasty cake at Versailles when the 22-year-old princess married the 15-year-old French king in 1725. Certainly, the Polish name would have been easier than its German counterpart for the French courtiers to pronounce.

Just when the rum syrup was added is a little unclear. References to "baba au rhum" begin to crop up only in the 1840s. Ever since, the ring-shaped, rum-syrup-soaked cake has become firmly rooted in the French pastry repertoire.

Curiously, it was in Naples rather than in France that the baba became a regional icon. As in the rest of Europe, French cooking was all the rage in nineteenth-century Naples, and no self-respecting aristocratic kitchen was complete without its *monsù* or French chef. Consequently all sorts of French tarts, crèmes, and gâteaux were commonly served in the palazzi, and many French techniques came to be adopted by Neapolitan *pasticcieri*. Of all the sweet Gallic imports, none came to be as loved as the baba, now often presented in the form of a mushroom-shaped single serving, split and filled with pastry cream. Today, the baba is vastly more popular in Naples (and in Italian American pastry shops in the United States) than in France. Neapolitans are so fond of the dessert that the name is used as a term of endearment. "Si nu' baba" (you are a baba) roughly means "you're the real deal." It can also mean "you're hot stuff," if your intentions are less platonic.

Krondl, Michael. *Sweet Invention: A History of Dessert.* Chicago: Chicago Review Press, 2011.

Liénard, Pierre, François Duthu, and Claire Hauguel. *Moi, Nicolas Stohrer, pâtissier du roi, rue montorgueil, au pied de Saint-Eustache, à Paris.* Paris: Lattès, 1999.

Michael Krondl

Baghdad, today's capital of Iraq, was founded by the Abbasids in 762 C.E. Built on the ruins of an ancient Mesopotamian city dating back to around 2000 B.C.E., Baghdad was a thriving trade center strategically located at the crossroads of the Eastern and Western cultures of Persia, Greece, and Rome.

Baghdad rapidly flourished under Abbasid rule. To meet an increasing demand for spices and other luxury merchandise, traders ventured to places as distant as China. Between the eighth and thirteenth centuries, Baghdad grew into the hub of a medieval Islamic world renowned for a remarkably diverse culinary repertoire. It drew directly on the Arabs' native heritage and on Iraq's indigenous foodways, and indirectly on Persian practice, which had refined these traditions throughout several centuries of dominance. Active international trade introduced foreign elements, and slave girls proficient in the art of cooking were in high demand.

The Evolution of Baghdad's Medieval Sweets

The cultivation of ingredients such as sesame, wheat, and dates from ancient times helped nurture a sweets-loving culture in the region well before the foundation of Abbasid Baghdad. Fragments of cuneiform tablets of fruitcake recipes and other records show that making pastries and confections was already a thriving business in the region, and desserts were consumed in large amounts during the religious festivals. Among these sweets were date-filled, rosewater-infused cookies (*qullupu*), date halvah (*mirsu*), and *muttaqu*, a flour-based pudding. See HALVAH.

The only culinary source surviving from the following era of Persian presence in the region, the fourth-century Sassanian book *King Khosrau and His Page*, mentions almond and walnut candy (*lauzenak* and *guzenak*) as well as *faludhaj*, a starch pudding made with fruit juice, butter, and honey. The Arabs themselves were familiar from pre-Islamic times with sweetmeats of dates mashed with toasted flour and clarified butter, and the affluent relished the translucent *faludhaj*.

The cultivation and processing of sugarcane, begun in the southern regions of Iraq and Persia by the sixth century C.E., contributed to the creativity of cooks to meet the demands of the newly wealthy leisure class of the Abbasid era. Islam was not against such indulgences, since sensual delight in eating was considered legitimate. Good food, after all, was one of the promised pleasures of Paradise. Moreover, dessert, with its hot properties, was believed to aid digestion when consumed after meals. Still, in the heat of summer, connoisseurs preferred to have their crêpe-like *qatayif*, fresh dates, and honeycomb served on crushed ice.

Dignitaries of all ranks joined professional cooks and poets in creating gourmet dishes and writing about food, both in cookbooks and in gastronomic poetry. The caliphs loved participating in cooking contests and delighted in listening to poems about food, such as one by the famous poet Kushajim (d. 961), who described lusciously made *nāṭif* (nougat): "like solid silver it looks, but soft and sweet as lips it tastes." See NOUGAT. The story of "The Porter and the Three Ladies of Baghdad" from *The Arabian Nights* details a "shopping list" with more than 20 sweet items, imported and local, including Lebanese *malban* (chewy starch candy), sultanas from Yemen, and all kinds of cookies and sticky fried pastries. This was by no means fictitious fodder; a repertoire of over 100 dessert recipes has survived in al-Warraq's and al-Baghdadi's tenth- and thirteenth-century cookbooks, respectively, both titled *Kitāb al-Ṭabīkh*.

Baghdadi cooks were spoiled as to the varieties of sugar at their disposal. The best all-purpose white sugar was *sukkar ṭabarzad* (chiseled sugar-cone). Less-refined *qand* was shaped into small balls and sticks, a delicacy to nibble at the table. Powdered sugar was generously sprinkled on desserts, while unrefined crystallized brown sugar was used only for baking cookies like *kaʿk*. The purest sugar was crystal-clear *sukkar nabat* (rock candy), eaten as candy but also crushed to decorate desserts. *Sukkar Sulaymāni* was a hard candy made from white sugar boiled into a thick syrup, then beaten until crystallized and shaped into discs, rings, or fingers. See CANDY. Molasses was also produced, though it was deemed inferior to honey. Fried pastries were commonly submerged in honey or *jullab*, a rosewater-infused sugar syrup.

Honey was more extensively used than sugar for making jams (*murabbayat*) and pastes. See FRUIT PRESERVES and HONEY. Although the main purpose of these preserves was to aid digestion, cure simple aches and pains, or invigorate coitus, they were often enjoyed as sweets. Most were locally made from rose petals, citron peel, quince, apple, dates, dried ginger root, and even celery, carrots, and radish, though mango jam imported from India was very popular.

Light milk-puddings (*muhallabiyyat*) were thickened with wheat starch, rice flour, or *itriya* (fine noodles). Thicker puddings like *khabīs* and *faludhaj* were made with wheat starch, rice flour, or crushed almonds, and sometimes with pureed carrots, melon, apples, or quince. Sweetened with honey, they were spread on flat platters and copiously sprinkled with powdered sugar; for festive events, they were often decorated with elaborate domes of honey taffy, colored almonds, and sugar candy. Hospitality was gauged by how much *faludhaj* was served for dessert, and no wedding was deemed complete without it.

The latticed fritters *zalabiya mushabbak*, fried in sesame oil and drenched in honey, were a Baghdad specialty, beautifully described by the Abbasid poet Ibn al-Rumi (d. 896):

> I saw him at the crack of dawn frying *zalabiya*,
> Tubes of reed, delicate, and thin. The oil I saw
> Boiling in his pan was like hitherto elusive alchemy.
> The batter he threw into the pan looking like silver,
> Would instantly transform into lattices of gold.

See ZALABIYA. An unusual sweet called *barad* (hailstones) was made by binding tiny balls of crisp fried pastry with cooked honey, not unlike today's Rice Krispies squares. Spongy, delicate cakes with and without eggs, called *furniyya* and *safanj*, were baked in the *tannour*, a clay oven, or steamed in special pots. Milk and clarified butter were poured over the inverted cakes, which were given a final sprinkle of powdered sugar and black pepper. The brittle double-crusted honey pie *basīsa* was baked in the commercial oven for controlled heat. Basketfuls of *kaʿk* (delicate cookies), luxuriously perfumed with rosewater, ambergris, camphor, mastic, and musk, were sent as favors and distributed during religious festivals. The nut- and date-filled cookies called *khushkananaj* marked the end of religious festivals.

A popular street food was sweet-savory *judhaba*—many thin layers of bread spread in a shallow pan, sprinkled with sugar and nuts, drenched in syrup and sesame oil or chicken fat, then baked in the *tannour* with a chunk of meat suspended above it. The bread was served with the thinly sliced meat, with the sweet component deemed necessary to aid digestion of the meat. Quite possibly this complex dish was an early inspiration for the Ottoman *baklava* and Moroccan *bistilla*.

Although Baghdad had much to indulge in, food was not cheap. Making desserts was labor intensive and expensive, so people with limited means satisfied their cravings by purchasing a handful of *fanīd* (pulled taffy) from hawkers or buying sweets at the confectioners' market, where they were not always of top quality (people with deceptive appearances were often compared to second-rate *faludhaj* purchased from the marketplace). From extant market inspection books we learn that it was common to adulterate honey with grape molasses, to make cookies with flour debased with ground lentil or sesame hull, or to drench *zalabiya* in cane-sugar syrup rather than the more desirable bees' honey. See ADULTERATION. While the poor ate cheap dates and date syrup, the affluent enjoyed refined sugars and honey, sucked on crystal-clear rock candy, and chewed on small sticks of peeled sugarcane infused with rosewater. Only a few times a year were the have-nots given a taste of luxury—mainly on grand occasions like religious or public feasts.

The Heritage of Baghdad's Medieval Sweets

The sweet legacy of medieval Baghdad spread far in place and time, to the medieval Levant, Egypt, Morocco, and Andalusia, and even beyond Muslim territories. But the Mongol invasion of 1258 eclipsed Baghdad's star, and with the rise of the Ottoman Empire the limelight shifted to Istanbul. Even so, many Abbasid desserts were incorporated into Ottoman kitchens, for which Arab cooks were often hired. The first Turkish cookbook, Muhammed Shirvani's fifteenth-century *Kitabu't-Tabīh*, was based on his translation of al-Baghdadi's thirteenth-century *Kitāb al- ṭabīkh*.

By the fall of the Ottoman Empire in 1918, life in Baghdad was characterized by religious and ethnic diversity. Most of the traditional desserts persisted, especially at social gatherings and dinner parties.

Today, a small box of baklava and *zalabiya* makes a handsome gift for a birthday party or circumcision, and trays full of them are served at weddings. In the heat of summer, Baghdadis enjoy chilled puddings, drinks, and ice cream. A typically Baghdadi sweet breakfast treat is *kahi,* thin sheets of dough generously brushed with oil, folded into squares, and baked. *Kahi* is served warm with light syrup and a scoop of clotted cream.

Various candies, such as *ḥalqūm* (Turkish delight), *simsimiyya* (a chewy candy of date syrup and tahini encrusted with toasted sesame seeds), and diamond-shaped *lauzīna,* are displayed in small bazaar shops and sold by hawkers. A distinctly Iraqi candy is the exotic *mann il-sima* (heaven-sent manna), whose main ingredient, manna, is harvested in the north of Iraq. See MANNA. It is enjoyed all year round, but the Chaldean Christians particularly offer it for their spring festival Khidr Elias. Up until the 1950s when there was still a thriving Jewish community in Baghdad, the confectioners among them were considered the best at making it. Also favored by Baghdad Jews for Purim was an unusual candy called *khirret,* made with pollen of cattail (*Typha* spp.) in the southern marshes of Iraq. See JUDAISM. A common scene at Muslim holy shrines is that of women whose prayers have been answered showering visitors with an assortment of hard candies as they ululate shrilly.

Since the early 1990s, Iraq has been going through very harsh times, and the difficult economic conditions have made sweets a luxury beyond the reach of most people. Prices have skyrocketed and good-quality ingredients are hard to find. But sweets are so deeply ingrained in Iraqi culture that they are hard to abandon. An Iraqi newspaper interview about festive Muslim customs quoted one man as saying, "But can any of us husbands persuade the wife not to make *kleicha* [date and nut cookies] in these difficult times? I doubt it!"

See also DATES; FLOWER WATERS; MIDDLE EAST; PUDDING; PULLED SUGAR; and RAMADAN.

Baghdadi, Muhammad bin Kareem al-Katib al-. *A Baghdad Cookery Book.* Translated by Charles Perry. Totnes, U.K.: Prospect, 2005.

Nasrallah, Nawal. *Delights from the Garden of Eden: A Cookbook and History of the Iraqi Cuisine.* 2d ed. Sheffield, U.K.: Equinox, 2013.

Nasrallah, Nawal. "The Iraqi Cookie, *Kleicha,* and the Search for Identity." *Repast* 24, no. 4 (Fall 2008): 4–7. https://cooks.aadl.org/files/cooks/repast/2008_Fall.pdf (accessed 22 October 2014).

Warraq, Ibn Sayyar al-. *Annals of the Caliphs' Kitchens.* English translation, with introduction and glossary by Nawal Nasrallah. Leiden, The Netherlands: Brill, 2007.

Nawal Nasrallah

Baked Alaska is a trick dessert that consists of frozen ice cream on a sponge cake base, encased by hot meringue. See MERINGUE and SPONGE CAKE. The insulating properties of the air in the sponge cake and the meringue make it possible to deliver hot and cold temperatures in the same dish.

The origins of Baked Alaska are obscure. Baron Brisse (Léon Brisse), in his daily food column for the French newspaper *La Liberté* in 1866, told readers of a visit by the Chinese emperor to Paris, during which his chefs demonstrated for their French counterparts a dessert known in China "since time immemorial." It consisted of ginger-accented vanilla ice cream baked in a pastry crust. The ice cream and meringue dessert known as *omelette norvégienne,* or Norwegian omelet, entered the French culinary repertoire in the 1890s.

In the United States, the dessert is associated with Delmonico's restaurant in New York City, where Charles Ranhofer created a hot frozen dish called "Alaska Florida." Many sources state it as fact, but without evidence, that he created the dessert in 1867 to celebrate the American government's purchase of Alaska that year.

In *America Revisited* (1882), the British journalist Charles Augustus Sala described eating an "Alaska" at Delmonico's, with more enthusiasm than accuracy—he mistook the meringue for whipped cream. "The nucleus or core of the *entremet* is an ice cream," he wrote. "This is surrounded by an envelope of carefully whipped cream [*sic*], which, just before the dainty dish is served, is popped into the oven, or is brought under the scorching influence of a red hot salamander; so that its surface is covered with a light brown crust. So you go on discussing the warm cream *soufflé* till you come, with somewhat painful suddenness, on the row of ice" (Vol. 1, p. 90).

Ranhofer included his dessert in his massive cookbook *The Epicurean* (1894). The recipe calls for vanilla and banana ice cream and for the sponge base to be filled with apricot marmalade. Baked

Alaska first appeared under that name in the first edition of *The Boston Cooking-School Cook Book* by Fannie Merritt Farmer in 1896. Constantly rediscovered, it reached peak popularity in the 1950s, enjoyed a revival in the 1970s, and, after the turn of the millennium, began attracting a fresh wave of admirers in search of a showpiece dessert.

See also ICE CREAM.

Lang, Joan. "Fire and Ice: Pastry Chefs Are Rediscovering the Cold Comfort of Baked Alaska and Dessert Lovers Are Responding Warmly." *Restaurant Business*, 15 February 2003, pp. 58–59.

Ranhofer, Charles. *The Epicurean*. New York: C. Ranhofer, 1894, p. 1007.

William Grimes

Baker's is an American brand of chocolate primarily associated with home baking. The modest place it occupies in today's supermarket with its semisweet, unsweetened, and German's line of baking chocolate belies the company's pivotal role in inspiring Americans to make chocolate desserts in the first place. Originally, Baker's chocolate was not made for baking. The company was established by James Baker in Dorchester, Massachusetts, in 1765. At first, the Walter Baker Company, as it came to be known after the founder's grandson, manufactured tablets of drinking chocolate. They sold it locally, subsequently expanding their market across the East Coast and then nationally when, in 1869, the Transcontinental Railroad made it possible to ship the chocolate to every major American city. Prior to 1865, Baker's sold three grades of drinking chocolate: "Best Chocolate," "Common Chocolate," and a low-quality "Inferior Chocolate" supplied mainly to American and West Indian slaves.

Baker's vastly expanded its market share under the leadership of Henry Pierce (1825–1896), who assumed control of the company in 1854. Having briefly worked at a midwestern newspaper, Pierce knew the power of advertising firsthand. Consequently, once the Civil War was over, he invested heavily in promoting the brand, often using images of an attractive European waitress known as "La Belle Chocolatière," based on a pastel by Jean-Étienne Liotard. By 1872 Baker's was running ads in over 150 regional papers; a decade later this number had increased to over 530, and by 1896 Baker's was reaching readers in some 8,000 newspapers nationwide. In an early version of saturation marketing, Pierce also bought full-page ads in the back of some 6 million novels and placed posters in streetcars, billboards along train routes, and cards and signs in grocery stores. At first, the company's chocolate was touted as a wholesome, family beverage, but eventually Baker's started promoting the idea of chocolate as a dessert ingredient.

Since women were not accustomed to baking with chocolate, they needed instruction. This tutelage came first in the form of recipe booklets and then in full-fledged cookbooks. In 1893 the company hired celebrity cooking instructor Maria Parloa of the famed Boston Cooking School to write several Baker's cookbooks. In 1898, when Parloa protégé Fannie Farmer penned the *Boston Cooking School Cookbook*, it contained 16 chocolate desserts—specifying Baker's brand chocolate in every one.

By 1897 the recently incorporated company was sold to a conglomerate of Boston capitalists headed by John Malcolm Forbes. It changed hands once again in 1927, when it was acquired by Postum (later named General Foods). Phillip Morris bought the company in 1985, and it finally spun off as a division of Mondelēz International in 2012. In 1965 the storied New England company moved to Dover, Delaware. The old Baker's buildings in Dorchester have been converted to luxury apartments.

See also COCOA.

"Sweet History: Dorchester and the Chocolate Factory." Boston: The Bostonian Society, 2005. http://www.bostonhistory.org/sub/bakerschocolate/SWEET_HISTORY_2005.pdf.

Michael Krondl

baker's dozen, a phrase that denotes a cluster of 13 items, was first recorded in a pamphlet titled *Have with You to Saffron-Walden*, published by Thomas Nashe in 1596. According to John Hotten's *Slang Dictionary* of 1864, the phrase arose from bakers' practice of providing an additional free loaf whenever a customer bought 12 loaves, in case the loaves were underweight. The penalties for selling underweight bread were indeed severe (ranging from fines, to the destruction of the baker's oven, to the pillory), and in England they dated back to a thirteenth-century statute known as the Assize of Bread and Ale. However, Hotten's commonly cited explanation is probably incorrect.

Instead, the phrase "baker's dozen" likely arose from the practice of bakers giving extra loaves to "hucksters," that is, to peddlers who sold the bread in the street. Because the price of a loaf was fixed by the Assize of Bread and Ale, the hucksters could not charge more for the loaves than what they had paid the bakers. This meant that they could make a profit only if the bakers gave them a free loaf; the bakers were happy to comply, because they could sell more bread to the hucksters who roamed the streets than they could by remaining at their stalls to sell their own bread. This free thirteenth loaf was called the "vantage loaf" (first recorded in 1612, and so named because it gave the huckster an advantage) or "in-bread" (first recorded in 1639, and so named because the extra loaf was "thrown in" by the baker). In the early nineteenth century, a baker's dozen also came to be known as a "devil's dozen" because of the sinister associations of the number 13.

Hotten, J. C. *The Slang Dictionary*. London: John Camden Hotten, 1872, p. 69. Available online via Google Books.

Simpson, J. A., and E. S. C. Weiner, eds. *Oxford English Dictionary*. 2d ed. 20 vols. Oxford: Clarendon, 1989. Also available at http://www.oed.com.

Mark Morton

baklava is a many-layered pastry, soaked in syrup, that is made in central and western Asia and parts of the Balkans, in countries ranging from Greece to Uzbekistan and Turkey to Egypt. The most common type of baklava consists of 40 to 80 layers of tissue-thin filo, moistened with melted butter before baking, and soaked with hot syrup after baking. See FILO. It is usually filled with nuts, the most common being walnuts or almonds. In Turkey, fillings also include fresh cheese and a custard made of milk thickened with starch or semolina. Other examples of regional variations are cinnamon added to the nuts in Greece, and cardamom or rosewater to the syrup in Iran. See FLOWER WATERS. Baklava is usually cut into small lozenges. Variations are made by rolling or folding the pastry sheets into diverse shapes, known in Turkey as *dilberdudağı* (beauty's lips), *sarığıburma* (twisted turban), *bülbülyuvası* (nightingale's nest), *vezirparmağı* (vizier's finger), and *gül baklava* (rose baklava). Sugar syrup is used in Turkey and the Middle East, although honey syrup and boiled grape juice were common in the past when sugar was a luxury for ordinary people. See PEKMEZ. In Greece, honey is sometimes added to the syrup. To make the filo sheets, dough is either rolled in individual pieces or first rolled into small circles, next stacked 10 at a time, with starch sprinkled between each layer; then the whole pile is rolled out simultaneously. The latter method is often used by both professional and home cooks and is easier for the inexperienced baker. Although few city dwellers make their own baklava today, homemade baklava is still widely produced in provincial Turkish towns.

Baklava filled with fresh cheese is always eaten hot (like the cheese-filled *kunāfa* of the Levant). In the past, cheese was a common baklava filling in Istanbul, but it survives today only in the provincial cuisines of Urfa, Çorum, and Isparta. *Kuru baklava* ("dry baklava") is a type made for sending long distances or taking on journeys. So that the syrup does not seep out of the packaging or drip when eaten, the lemon juice that ordinarily prevents the syrup from crystallizing is omitted, giving the baklava a dry and crunchy texture. Damascus has long been famed for its *kuru baklava*, which visitors to the city traditionally buy to take home.

Baklava, first recorded in Ottoman Turkey in the early fifteenth century, originated in pastries made of layered and folded filo that have been known in Central Asian Turkic cuisines since the eleventh century. Such dishes appear to have then joined forces with the Arab culinary tradition of soaking pastries in syrup, giving rise to baklava. A thirteenth-century Arabic cookbook *Kitāb al-Wuslaila al-Habib* describes a sweet pastry very similar to baklava with the Turkish name *karnıyarık* ("split belly") and uses the Turkish term *tutmaç* for the thin pastry sheets. In this recipe each sheet of filo is rolled around a slender rolling pin, gathered into a concertina, and formed into circles, much like the baklava types known today as *sarığıburma* or *bülbülyuvası*.

An early-fifteenth-century poem by the mystic Kaygusuz Abdal mentions baklava filled with either almonds or lentils, fillings specified in two early-sixteenth-century Persian recipes. Other fillings mentioned in historical Turkish sources are clotted cream and puréed melon. Ottoman pastry cooks working for the palace or wealthy patrons sought to make baklava with an increasing number of ever-thinner layers. An account of the circumcision feast for the son of Murad III mentions "trays of many-layered baklava," and in the mid-seventeenth century one writer refers to baklava consisting of a thousand layers, clearly an exaggeration but revealing how the number of layers had become a culinary status symbol. Moreover, the baklava had to be so delicate that a coin dropped from a height of about 2 feet pierced each layer and struck the bottom of the baking tray.

Baklava is a festive dish, associated above all with Ramazan (Ramadan in Arabic-speaking nations). Until 1826, every year on the 15th of Ramazan, janissary soldiers marched to the palace in the Baklava Procession to collect hundreds of trays of the sweet, which had been baked in the palace kitchens. One tray was shared by 10 janissaries, 2 of whom would carry the tray back to the barracks. A popular Ramazan poem about this event begins with the following verse:

As the sun and moon revolve
May divine aid be your company
The sultan gave baklava
To his loyal janissaries.

For centuries baklava has been a feature of meals on religious feast days, or at weddings and other celebrations; it also once was the custom to present baklava as a gift to neighbors and acquaintances on special occasions. Turkish novelist Aziz Nesin (1915—1995) recalled that when he was a child of five, his mother had become inconsolable because she could not afford the sugar and nuts needed to bake a tray of baklava as a gift for his schoolteacher. Today, baklava still retains this festive character in many countries and is often made or bought for family gatherings on days and nights of celebration and thanksgiving.

See also GREECE AND CYPRUS; ISLAM; MIDDLE EAST; PERSIA; and TURKEY.

Işın, Mary. "Baklava." In *Sherbet and Spice: The Complete Story of Turkish Sweets and Desserts*, pp. 178–190. London: I.B. Tauris, 2013.

Perry, Charles."Early Turkish Influence on Arab and Iranian Cuisine." In *Dördüncü Milletlerarası Yemek Kongresi, Türkiye 3–6 Eylül 1992*, edited by Feyzi Halıcı, pp. 242–243. Konya, Turkey: Kültür ve Turizm Vakfı Yayını, 1993.

Priscilla Mary Işın

banqueting houses were small garden buildings in Tudor and Stuart England, so called because "banqueting" was the primary activity enjoyed in them. The Tudor "banquet" was not the sumptuous feast that we now associate with the word, but a delectable, intimate repast of marzipans, jellies, quince cakes, meringues, gingerbread, and other treats, washed down with *ipocras*, a form of mulled wine flavored with cinnamon, cloves, ginger, peppercorns, nutmeg, and rosemary, all steeped in sugar. See HIPPOCRAS. Gervase Markham described the banquet in *The English Housewife* (first published in 1615), giving specific orders for the "making of Banquetting stuffe and conceited dishes, with other pretty and curious secrets." The order in which the food was presented was precisely detailed, beginning with "a dish made for shew only, as Beast, Bird, Fish or Fowl," followed by the sweets listed above, as well as marmalade, not a jam but oranges filled with sugar paste, then sliced. The elegant and decorative little delicacies were eaten off special plates or roundels, approximately the same size as dessert plates today, often decorated with witty pictures, inscriptions, and puzzles. Fine examples in embossed and painted leather survive (at the Victoria & Albert Museum, London), but the most magnificent are the set of eight silver plates, hallmarked 1586, depicting the life of the Prodigal Son (part of the Collection of the Duke of Bucchleuch). The banquet was offered to intimate friends of the host, invited into a banqueting house in the garden or sometimes on the roof. At some houses, there was a choice of going to the garden or onto the roof.

The origins of the banqueting house appear to be medieval, as in the early sixteenth century the antiquary John Leland noted that Henry VIII had moved a "praty baketynge house of tymber," originally erected in the early fifteenth century by Henry V, from the "Pleasance" at Kenilworth into the court of the castle. Henry VIII himself built numerous little banqueting houses in his garden at Hampton Court, all carefully recorded in Wyngaerde's drawings of ca. 1560 (at the Ashmolean Museum, Oxford). Each of Henry's banqueting houses was different in plan (some square, some polygonal) but each had an upper room, brilliantly glazed on all sides and accessible via a stair turret that rose to a platform on the "leads" or flat roof. Clearly, the banquet was meant to be consumed while appreciating the glories of the landscape. Nowhere is this better illustrated

Banqueting houses were small garden buildings where hosts entertained guests at the end of a formal meal and served delicacies such as marzipan, gingerbread, meringues, and hippocras, a mulled wine. This drawing by the British artist Thomas Forster (1672–1722) depicts the royal banqueting house in Whitehall, London. YALE CENTER FOR BRITISH ART, PAUL MELLON COLLECTION

than at Lacock Abbey (Wiltshire), where ca. 1550 Sir William Sharington built a three-story octagonal tower with a banqueting room in the upper story with expansive windows and, at its center, a splendidly carved Purbeck marble table. Shell-headed niches in the base contain figures of Bacchus, Ceres, and the Roman epicure Apicius, wonderfully apposite banqueting companions. After enjoying their banquet, the more energetic banqueters could climb the winding stair up to the balustraded roof of the tower for splendid views over the gardens and medieval fishponds.

Later Elizabethan houses, such as Hardwick Hall (Derbyshire), had banqueting houses on both the roof and in the garden. At Hardwick, the great south tower room is approached via a long walk across the roof and entered through a door, above which looms a ferocious gorgon's head, an apotropaic device to discourage evil spirits from destroying the joyful mood. On roof level, one can also look down on Bess of Hardwick's two lozenge-shaped banqueting houses: one in the corner of the south garden and the other in the orchard, to the north of the house.

Because of their relatively small size, banqueting houses were inexpensive to build, so they were perfect for architectural experimentation. Just like banqueting food, they were meant to be "curious" and "artificiall," according to Markham again, who wrote that they "lustre to the Orchard." The octagonal form was particularly popular in the Tudor period and remained an option well into the seventeenth century. Even Elizabeth I, who rarely spent money on her palaces or gardens, erected an octagonal banqueting house at the end of the long terrace at Windsor in 1576 for which plans survive in the National Archives (London). Later banqueting houses were built on more unusual plans: rectangular; oval; lozenge-shaped (as at Hardwick); or in the shape of a cross superimposed on a square, as at Montacute (Somerset). When Sir Francis Drake's ship "The Golden Hind" became unfit, he removed the cabin from its deck and turned it into a banqueting house in his garden in Deptford. William Cecil, Lord Burghley, had banqueting houses at all of his houses: sketches in his own hand survive for those he built in his London garden (dated 1565; preserved at Burghley House, Northamptonshire). At his grandest house, Theobalds (Hertfordshire), visitors commented on a semicircular banqueting house with statues of 12 Roman emperors and, on the roof, lead cisterns that could be used for bathing in the summer.

Such exuberance did not please everyone, and at the turn of the century, John Stow wrote grumpily in his *Survey of London* (1598) that banqueting houses bear "great shew and little worth." Although the practice of building them continued through the early Stuart period, the practice gradually died out. Those few banqueting houses that survive today generally stand empty and unused, evidence of changes in fashion that not only affected gardens but also spelled the doom of the little banquet itself.

See also DESSERT and SWEET MEALS.

Henderson, Paula. *The Tudor House and Garden: Architecture and Landscape in the 16th and 17th Centuries.* New Haven, Conn., and London: Yale University Press, 2005.

Markham, Gervase: *The English Huswife, Containing the Inward and Outward Virtues Which Ought to Be in a Complete Woman.* London, 1615.

Paula Henderson

bar cookies are made by pouring, spreading, or pressing batter into a square or rectangular pan (sometimes in several layers) and cutting the finished product into individual pieces after baking. This type of cookie is more cake-like than are drop cookies and rolled cookies, due to the addition of more eggs or shortening to the batter. See DROP COOKIES and ROLLED COOKIES. Bar cookies are also known as pan cookies, squares, bars, and, in Britain, tray bakes.

These cookies were not invented at a single moment in time, but rather represent a natural evolution from cakes and sweet breads cooked in a single pan. They are a style of bakery item particularly suitable for families and informal events, and because they are more quickly made than individually formed cookies, and also pack and transport well in the pan, they are popular with the busy home cook. The best known, and arguably the most popular form, are brownies. See BROWNIES.

References to "bar cookies" appear in grocers' advertisements in the 1890s, but their exact nature is not certain. Most of these references apply to Kennedy's Fig Bar Cookies (later called Fig Newtons), but these are formed from extruded dough with a filling. See FIG NEWTONS. Other references to fruit and date squares at this time are clearly for a confectionery product. The first known recipe for a baked item that unequivocally fits the concept of a bar cookie appears in the *Indianapolis Star* on 3 July 1924 for a peanut bar cookie with a peanut frosting.

Bar cookies are still popular today, and are likely to remain so, because of their ease of preparation and great range of ingredients, flavors, and textures.

See also SMALL CAKES.

"Cookies, Crackers & Biscuits." http://www.foodtimeline.org/foodcookies.html.

"History of Cookies." http://whatscookingamerica.net/History/CookieHistory.htm.

Janet Clarkson

barfi (also spelled burfi), from the Persian and Urdu word for snow, is a sweet with a fudge-like consistency that is especially popular in northern India. It seems to be a relatively recent invention. The classic barfi is made from finely granulated sugar and khoa/khoya, milk solids produced by slowly boiling milk until it becomes thick, stirring constantly to prevent caramelization. These two ingredients are cooked together and, when thick, spread over a greased plate. Once cooled, the mixture is cut into squares, diamonds, or circles. At this stage it resembles snow, hence its name. According to Mrs. Balbir Singh in her classic *Indian Cookery*, a sugar to khoa ratio of 1 to 4 is the preferred base for barfi.

Varying proportions of other ingredients may be added, including melon seeds, guava, grated carrot, or grated coconut. Flavorings include saffron, rosewater, kewra water (an extract made from padanus flowers), vanilla, orange, mango, and especially cardamom powder. Some varieties, notably those made with pistachios and almonds, do not contain khoa; instead, ground nuts (peanuts) are boiled in a sugary syrup. Barfi is a favorite sweet at Diwali, the Hindu festival of lights. When distributed to guests at weddings and other festivities, barfi is often decorated with finely beaten and edible silver leaf (vark).

A variant is Mysore pak, a popular South Indian sweet with a granular texture. It is made by roasting chickpea flour with ghee, then cooking it with sugar syrup, adding more ghee, and cutting it into squares when cool.

Singh, Mrs. Balbir. *Indian Cookery.* London: Mills & Boon, 1961.

Colleen Taylor Sen

barley sugar is a hard, clear sugar confection with a golden color, formed in round or oval drops or long twisted sticks. It is made in the United Kingdom, Australia, and North America ("barley sugar candy"), and also in France, where it is known as *sucre d'orge*.

Traditionally, barley sugar is made by boiling sugar to hard crack or the start of caramel at 328° to 346°F (150° to 160°C) and adding an acid to prevent recrystallization on cooling. See STAGES OF SUGAR SYRUP. Craft production employed lemon juice or vinegar, but mass-produced barley sugar in the United Kingdom is now often made with a mixture of sugar and glucose, which has the same effect. See GLUCOSE. Lemon essence is generally used as a flavoring in the British tradition of sugar boiling.

In *Les friandises et leurs secrets* (1986), Annie Perrier Roberts notes how in France, *sucre d'orge* is a speciality of various spa towns, as well as the city of Tours, and as Sucre d'Orge des Religieuses de Moret it has an association with convent sweets and the town of Moret sur Loing. See CONVENT SWEETS.

Originally, the sweets contained a decoction of barley, but this disappeared from recipes around the start of the eighteenth century. Barley sweets were regarded in some way as medicinal; even today in Britain, sucking barley sugar is sometimes recommended as a treatment for overcoming motion sickness. In the United States, the Food and Drug Administration, after discovering the complete lack of barley in modern barley sugar, has discouraged the use of this traditional name.

Mason, Laura. *Sugar Plums and Sherbet*. Totnes, U.K.: Prospect Books, 2004.

Perrier-Robert, Annie. *Les friandises et leurs secrets*. Paris: Larousse, 1986.

Laura Mason

Baskin-Robbins, an American chain of ice cream shops, was the brainchild of brothers-in-law Burton "Burt" Baskin and Irvine "Irv" Robbins. Today, every ice cream shop in the United States seems to churn out a host of exotic flavors, from olive oil and lavender to honey jalapeño and sweet corn. But when Baskin-Robbins was launched in the early 1950s, its notion of serving 31 flavors was novel.

Burt and Irv had started out as small-time ice cream shop owners with separate businesses in Southern California. In 1945 Robbins opened Snowbird Ice Cream in Glendale, California, where he offered 21 flavors. A year later Baskin opened Burton's Ice Cream Shop in Pasadena. By 1948 the two ice cream entrepreneurs boasted half a dozen shops in Southern California. A year later the number had jumped to more than 40. In 1953 the brothers-in-law took a leap and joined forces to create Baskin-Robbins, which became the international ice cream juggernaut we know today. They also began to franchise their operation.

For years, Americans had been fiercely loyal to the classic ice cream triumvirate of vanilla, chocolate, and strawberry. Even Howard Johnson, who marketed 28 flavors in its famous orange-roofed restaurants dotting America in the 1950s and 1960s, could not quite manage to tear customers away from the tried-and-true ice cream standards. Baskin and Robbins changed all that. Believing that Americans were ready for a more sophisticated menu of flavors, they rolled out 31. Black Walnut, Cherry Macaroon, Chocolate Mint, Coffee Candy, and Date Nut were among the original flavors.

Not only were the men bent on expanding Americans' palate for ice cream, they wanted their shops to project an aura of fun. The advertising firm they hired recommended that the company adopt a "31" logo, to represent Baskin-Robbins's strategy of offering a different flavor of ice cream for each day of the month. They also created a shop décor that instantly invited customers to have a good time, with its riot of smiling clowns and pink and brown polka dots. (Today, the dots are pink and blue.)

Baskin-Robbins, believing that people should be allowed to try a range of flavors to discover the one they most wanted to buy, also introduced a now-iconic small plastic spoon with which to sample ice cream flavors. Thus was born the famous little pink spoon that spawned millions of progeny in ice cream shops around the world.

Despite Howard Johnson's conviction that Americans would never stray from their preference for plain old vanilla, ice cream devotees flocked to Baskin-Robbins stores. At their factory in Burbank, Baskin and Robbins invented hundreds of ice cream flavors each year, including classics like Blueberry Cheesecake and Jamoca Almond Fudge. Flavors rotated through the stores so that customers would be greeted with something new whenever they stopped by for ice cream. Since 1945 the company has rolled out more than 1,000 flavors. Some, however, never made it to the ice cream shops, such as Ketchup, Lox and Bagels, and Grape Britain. More successful were flavors celebrating popular culture or special events, such as the popular Lunar Cheesecake (a nod to Neil Armstrong's moon landing), Cocoa a Go-Go (a tribute to the go-go dancing craze), and Beatle Nut, to honor the Fab Four as they were about to embark on their first American tour.

In 1967 the Baskin-Robbins ice cream empire was sold to United Fruit Company for an estimated $12 million. Six months later Baskin died of a heart attack at age 54. In the 1970s the company expanded into the global market, unveiling outlets in Japan, Saudi Arabia, Korea, and Australia. In many countries, Baskin-Robbins has introduced flavors designed to appeal to local tastes. For example, in Japan, Matcha (green tea) ice cream shares freezer space with Strawberry Shortcake. Today, Baskin-Robbins, with over 7,000 stores in nearly 50 countries, is part of Dunkin' Brands, owner of another global snack icon, Dunkin' Donuts. See DUNKIN' DONUTS.

In a 1976 interview in the *New York Times,* Irv Robbins took credit for Americans' newfound delight in exotic ice cream flavors. "They're not embarrassed to ask for some of these wild flavors," the bespectacled ice cream man said. "I think we've had a little bit to do with making it acceptable."

See also ICE CREAM.

"Baskin-Robbins Company History." http://www.baskinrobbins.com/content/baskinrobbins/en/aboutus/history.html.

Hevesi, Dennis. "Irvine Robbins, Ice Cream Entrepreneur and a Maestro of 31 Flavors, Dies at 90." *New York Times,* 7 May 2006. http://www.nytimes.com/2008/05/07/business/07robbins.html.

Nelson, Valerie J. "Irvine Robbins, 90: Co-founder of the Baskin-Robbins Ice Cream Empire." *Los Angeles Times,* 7 May 2008. http://www.latimes.com/local/obituaries/la-me-robbins7-2008may07-story.html.

Weiss, Laura B. *Ice Cream: A Global History,* pp. 106–107. London: Reaktion, 2011.

Laura B. Weiss

Baumkuchen means "tree cake," and a glance at one of these German specialties explains the name. In its uncut form, a Baumkuchen is a 3- to 5-foot-tall cylindrical column, hollow on the inside and patterned in ridged rings on the outside. The result surely suggests a tree trunk, albeit one glazed with a sheer white icing or, for more modern tastes, a chocolate frosting. To be served, it is cut horizontally in curved shavings and slices to show a series of rings much like the age rings of tree trunks. Those rings are a result of the baking process. Baumkuchen is one of a long line of spit cakes, some dating back to medieval times. These cakes are baked—or perhaps more correctly, grilled or toasted—on rotisserie spits over or in front of wood fires or, commercially today, electric grill-ovens. The spits are fitted with cone-shaped or elongated sleeves covered in layers of wet parchment. The batter for Baumkuchen is a rich, foamy, custard-like mixture that includes eggs, butter, flour, and possible flavorings of lemon, almond, or vanilla. When the spit is hot enough, portions of batter are poured over the parchment (or the spit is lowered into a trough of batter), and the thick liquid wraps around the revolving spit as it bakes. When one layer has turned pale golden brown, another is poured over and so on, accounting for the rings and often adding up to between 16 and 35 layers, depending on the width desired.

Baumkuchen is the most famous spit cake but not the only one. Lithuanians love their *šakotis,* Poles their *sękacz,* Hungarians their *kürtőskalács,* and Swedes their *spettekaka.* The French cherish the petite, cone-shaped *gâteaux à la brioche* still baked by artisans in the southwest part of the country. In Hampton Court, the palace of Henry VIII, one can watch Tudor-period cooking demonstrations during the Christmas season that often include the spit cake trayne roste. Oddly, Baumkuchen enjoys a loyal following in Japan, where in about 1919 a German baker, Karl Juchheim, who had been imprisoned by the Japanese, went to Kobe upon his release and opened a Baumkuchen bakery that not only survives but also has inspired many others throughout the country. Baumkuchen today is baked in the United States, especially in Chicago and in Huntington Beach, California.

Sheraton, Mimi. *The German Cookbook.* New York: Random House, 1965.

Sheraton, Mimi. "How to Bake Spit Cake." *The New Yorker,* 23 November 2009.

Mimi Sheraton

Bavarian cream

See DESSERTS, CHILLED.

bean paste sweets are a group of popular Asian confections filled or composed of a sweetened bean paste. Bean paste made from azuki beans is the quintessential sweet filling used in numerous Japanese, Chinese, and Korean pastries. See AZUKI BEANS. It is prepared by boiling azuki beans, pounding or chopping them, and combining and cooking the paste with sugar, and lard in some countries. For a more refined version, the paste is pressed through a sieve to remove the skins. Red azuki beans, because of their auspicious color, have meant good fortune since the Han dynasty (206 B.C.E to 220 C.E.) and are eaten on holidays, birthdays, and other festive occasions in pastries, puddings, soups, and other sweet confections.

Typical azuki desserts in Japan include *anmitsu*, for which *an*, small cubes of agar-agar jelly, and pieces of fruit are served in a syrup. *Anpan* is a sweet bun filled with red bean paste. (This is also a popular dim sum or sweet in China.) *An* is also used as a stuffing for mochi and as a topping for dango. See DANGO; JAPANESE BAKED GOODS; and MOCHI.

In China, the most popular azuki-bean confections include *tang yuan*, glutinous rice balls filled with red azuki, ground sesame, or date paste that are served at banquets for festive occasions as well as on the Lantern Festival, a holiday observed 10 days after Chinese New Year. *Zong-zi* are conical-shaped dumplings made with glutinous rice stuffed with sweet and savory fillings and wrapped in bamboo leaves and served during the Dragon Boat Festival in the spring. Mooncakes are the traditional holiday pastry served on the Festival of the Harvest Moon. See MOONCAKES. *Baozi* or *do sha bao* is a steamed bun filled with sweet azuki or date paste.

Korean azuki-paste desserts are equally celebrated. The most prominent are *chalboribbang*, "sweet" rice pancakes consisting of two glutinous barley-flour pancakes stuffed with sweet bean paste, and *patjuk*, an azuki-bean porridge traditionally served during the Winter Solstice Festival.

See also CHINA; JAPAN; and KOREA.

Simonds, Nina, Leslie Swartz, and the Children's Museum of Boston. *Moonbeams, Dumplings & Dragon Boats.* San Diego, Calif.: Harcourt, 2002.

Cost, Bruce. *Bruce Cost's Asian Ingredients: Buying and Cooking the Staple Foods of China, Japan, and Southeast Asia.* New York: William Morrow, 1988.

Tsuji, Shizuo. *Japanese Cooking: A Simple Art.* Tokyo: Kodansha International, 1980.

Nina Simonds

Beeton, Isabella (1836–1865) was a writer, cook, and author of *Mrs Beeton's Book of Household Management* (1861), arguably the most famous English domestic manual ever published. As an icon of Victorian culture, both during and after her lifetime, Beeton bridged the transition from tradition to modernism, typifying an era in the throes of industrialization and advancing knowledge.

Originally commissioned as a series of articles by her publisher husband Samuel Beeton, *Mrs Beeton's Book of Household Management* was a compilation of essays and recipes, ranging from medicinal tonics to pineapple ice cream. In addition to recipes for kitchen classics such as boiled carrots and mashed potatoes, four extensive chapters were dedicated to cakes, confectionery, and sweet dishes—a dessert panorama showcasing traditional English recipes like Bakewell Tart alongside dishes with a more colonial twist, such as "Delhi Pudding."

Although the publication celebrated traditionally feminine domestic skill, acknowledging the real expertise that had perhaps gone unappreciated in the past, it also strongly implied that a woman's place was in the home, a space somewhat isolated from the public jurisdictions of men. While Beeton may not be considered a feminist by today's standards, her work unified the domestic experience, becoming a ubiquitous title in bookshelves across the country. Her legacy lies in her unique talent for digesting and communicating information, making it accessible to the world beyond the kitchen walls.

Though it may be a surprise to most, Isabella Beeton was not the matronly or middle-aged mother that we often presume her to be; she died at the age of 28, a day after giving birth to her fourth child. Her books, however, lived on beyond her years, a timeless comment on domestic prowess and an embodiment of the nineteenth-century feminine ideal. So powerful was her influence that her subsequent publishers kept the news of her death quiet in order to give gravitas to future installments of *Household Management*, and even published full titles under her name.

This lithograph depicting fashionable pastries and puddings appeared in the 1888 edition of *Mrs Beeton's Book of Household Management*, England's most famous domestic manual. The volume was popularly called *Mrs Beeton's Cookbook* because more than 900 of its 1,112 pages contained recipes. BRITISH LIBRARY, LONDON © BRITISH LIBRARY BOARD. ALL RIGHTS RESERVED / BRIDGEMAN IMAGES

See also UNITED KINGDOM.

Beeton, Isabella. *Mrs Beeton's Book of Household Management.* Abridged ed. Edited by Nicola Humble. Oxford: Oxford World's Classics, 2008.

Hughes, Kathryn. *The Short Life and Long Times of Mrs. Beeton.* London: Harper Perennial, 2006.

Tasha Marks

beignets

See DOUGHNUTS.

Belgium, a small kingdom in Western Europe, has been internationally famous for its chocolate and waffles only since the 1970s. The country's reputation for sweets can be explained by its long history of culinary influences and its many eras of opulence. Before Belgium became an independent nation in 1830, the region had been part of various monarchies that introduced French, Spanish, and Austrian influences, and with them Italian, Arabic, and Near-Eastern ones. With regard to foreign influences, it is telling that in the late fifteenth century the Canary Islands were known as the Flemish Isles because of the large population of Flemings who grew sugarcane there to ship to the Low Countries. As a result of their activity, the price of sugar fell by almost 60 percent within several years. See SUGAR TRADE.

Despite—or because of—foreign domination, this part of Europe flourished: agricultural output was high; international trade enriched the ports of Bruges, Ghent, and Antwerp; and manufacture brought prosperity to Brussels, Liège, and Mons. Even during harsh years when prices were high, Flemish laborers ate fruit pies, sugared compotes, and pancakes with honey at fairs, harvest feasts, and weddings. See FAIRS. Jacques Jordaens has depicted Belgium's sweet tooth in various versions of his painting *The King Drinks* (ca. 1640), which shows a celebration of the children's feast Drie Koningen (Three Kings Day, 6 January), when a special cake containing an almond was baked. Whoever found the almond became king for a day. Jordaens's holiday table is laden with waffles, pastries, beer, and wine. See TWELFTH NIGHT CAKE.

By the end of the eighteenth century, however, austere times had arrived, and abundant sweets were for most of the population a thing of the past. Average annual sugar consumption at that time barely reached 5 kilos per capita. Very slowly, sugar intake rose to 15 kilos before World War I. In the 1930s the League of Nations estimated Belgium's average sugar consumption to be 28 kilos, higher than the European average (22 kilos) but significantly lower than the annual intake in, for example, Great Britain (49 kilos). Belgian nutritionists encouraged higher sugar consumption because of sugar's energy value. One way to achieve this was by promoting tea drinking (which was unpopular in Belgium) with plenty of sugar, "as in England," to increase the number of calories consumed by the elderly. Moreover, housewives were instructed to convince their husbands and children to consume more sugar in any way possible. The campaign worked. In the 1970s average yearly sugar consumption rose to 35 kilos per capita; it is 45 kilos today.

The nineteenth century's low intake can be explained by both the high price of sugar and the subsequently close link between sugar and higher social class. For a long time, pastries, viennoiseries, cakes, puddings, ice creams, chocolates, marmalades, cookies, and various friandises found in French haute cuisine were available exclusively to rich Belgians. Harsh living conditions caused working-class men to consider a sweet tooth a feminine trait, so they hardly even used sugar in their daily cups of coffee. Nonetheless, relatively simple pastries such as *mattentaart* (a small round cheesecake), *pain à la grecque* (crisp, thin bread that has no connection with Greece, but with the Flemish word for "ditch"), *peperkoek* (gingerbread), speculaas (a shortbread biscuit with cinnamon), or *vlaai* (a solid flan with brown sugar) were produced locally, becoming more widespread in the 1900s. See GINGERBREAD and SPECULAAS.

By that time, the situation had irrevocably begun to change as a result of technological and organizational innovations in the production, transportation, and retailing of sugar and candy; the lowering of taxes on sugar; and promotional campaigns by manufacturers, nutritionists, and public authorities. The price of sugar fell, and gradually more people ate it in very diverse forms, including the "invisible" sugar added to lemonade, canned vegetables, and bread. Moreover, the large biscuit and chocolate factories that had appeared in the 1880s manufactured individually wrapped products that could be advertised easily (among which was Côte d'Or, which produced individually sized chocolate bars).

Several developments illustrate the diffusion of sugar within Belgian society between the late 1880s and early 1930s. Especially telling is the story of the *gâteau du dimanche*, the "Sunday cake" that the governor of the province of Hainault in southern Belgium advocated in 1886: he favored establishing home economics schools for young girls, where they could learn how to prepare a sweet pie that might be used as a reward for good children (and to keep husbands away from the tavern). Significant, too, was the fact that school manuals for household education gradually included a larger number of recipes for sweets: between 1900 and 1930, desserts barely accounted for 10 percent of the total recipes in these books, but their numbers rose to 30 percent in the late 1930s to 1950s. Furthermore, the amount of sugar called for in pastries, biscuits, and other desserts in these manuals increased between 1900 and 1950. Waffles are a good example: the ratio of sugar to flour was 1 to 3 around 1900, but it rose to 1 to 1 in the 1930s to 1950s.

It was during the latter part of this sweet zenith that warnings against too much sugar consumption appeared: sugar, especially for young children, was considered bad for the health. See SUGAR AND HEALTH. In 1956, for example, a dietician cited sugar's energy as very harmful; he warned particularly against processed white sugar, preferring by far the unrefined cane sugar that he saw as natural. Such a view appeared increasingly in cookbooks, women's magazines, and television programs, and it influenced the perception and usage of sugar. Since the 1970s the number of desserts in cookbooks has diminished somewhat, and the amount of sugar (for example, for making waffles) has declined significantly. Although the use of visible sugar (as added to coffee, for instance) has fallen, the use of "invisible" sugar has only grown.

The trends toward healthier and so-called authentic desserts have necessitated the upgrading of many ordinary sweets like speculaas, which nowadays appears as a flavor in honey and ice cream and as a spread for bread, as well as in numerous forms on the menus of fancy restaurants. Many of Belgium's old, ordinary sweets have now been transformed into culinary heritage, thereby giving them a second life. This upgrading of ordinary sweets has been accompanied by the gradual trickling down of luxury sweets to the masses, leading to a great variety of chocolates, ice creams, and pastries that can be enjoyed by the Belgian population at large. Baba au rhum, bavarois, and savarin have descended from haute cuisine, while éclairs and waffles from popular cooking have gained new status.

See also CHOCOLATE, LUXURY and GODIVA.

De Vooght, D., S. Onghena, and P. Scholliers, eds. *Van pièce montée tot pêche melba: Een geschiedenis van het betere (nagerecht)*. Brussels: VUB, 2008.

Scholliers, P. *Food Culture in Belgium*. Westport, Conn.: Greenwood, 2009.

Peter Scholliers

Ben & Jerry's is now an internationally recognized ice cream business, but that was not part of Ben Cohen and Jerry Greenfield's career plan when they were growing up on Long Island, New York. In fact, they had no career plan. After college, each considered different options before deciding to go into business together. Starting a bagel company was their first choice. They planned to deliver fresh bagels, lox, cream cheese, and the *New York Times* to customers every Sunday morning. However, after they learned how steep the start-up costs would be, they opted for ice cream.

They took a $5 correspondence course in ice cream making from Penn State University and began visiting homemade ice cream shops, tasting and taking notes. In 1978, with $12,000 they had scraped together, they renovated a gas station in Burlington, Vermont, and opened Ben & Jerry's Homemade Ice Cream and Crepes. They chose Burlington, despite its cold winters, because it was a college town and had no homemade ice cream shop. The crepes were intended as a hedge against the slow winter ice cream business. The partners stopped making crepes when their ice cream became popular enough to weather the winter.

Cohen and Greenfield created an ice cream that was richer and creamier than most because it contained more butterfat and was mixed with less air. Since Cohen did not have a strong sense of taste, they flavored the ice cream more intensely as well. Best of all, taking their cue from the mix-ins Steve Herrell had made famous in his eponymous Somerville, Massachusetts, ice cream parlor, they mixed extra-large chunks of chocolate, nuts, cookies, or candy into the ice cream. Customers flocked to the small shop.

Soon, the partners began selling ice cream to local restaurants and grocery stores. They continued to expand the business, adding shops, distributing to more stores, and franchising scoop shops. In 1984, needing capital, they sold shares in the company to Vermont residents, thereby strengthening the company's local image as well as raising cash. The stock was priced at $10.50 a share, with a minimum purchase of 12 shares. The offering sold out quickly.

Cohen and Greenfield believed in supporting the Vermont community. In addition to selling stock only to Vermonters, they used local, non-bovine-growth-hormone milk in their ice cream. They hired a local artist to design the company graphics. They also thought work should be a pleasure. "If It Isn't Fun, Why Do It?" was a company credo. They gave their flavors funky names like Whirled Peace, Chubby Hubby, and Chunky Monkey. They held a free ice cream cone day every year and gave pregnant women two free cones, all of which created a strong brand identity.

Values before Profits

From the beginning, the men applied their countercultural values to the enterprise. They believed that no one in the company should earn more than five times the entry-level staff's salary. They put a profit-sharing plan in place almost before there were profits. One of the more popular company benefits was free ice cream. Each employee could have up to three pints a day.

The business was thriving and competitors noticed. When the Pillsbury corporation tried to freeze Ben & Jerry's out of some supermarkets to protect its

Häagen-Dazs brand in 1984, the company fought back with a successful "What's the Doughboy Afraid Of?" campaign. Cohen and Greenfield were seen as young entrepreneurs standing up to a corporate giant. The case, which was settled out of court, was a public relations triumph for Ben & Jerry's. See HÄAGEN-DAZS.

In 1985 the men established the Ben & Jerry's Foundation with gifts from Cohen and Greenfield and an annual company contribution of 7.5 percent of pretax profits. Ben & Jerry's was recognized as a progressive company with a strong social conscience. In 1993 the partners received the James Beard Humanitarians of the Year Award.

The company's sales had reached $48 million by 1988, the year President Ronald Reagan presented Cohen and Greenfield with the National Small Business Persons of the Year Award in a White House ceremony. Ironically, at the time they were developing Peace Pops, a chocolate-covered ice cream bar that promoted reducing the military budget. They hardly expected an invitation to the White House.

The company continued to grow, expanding into Canada in 1988, to Russia in 1992, the United Kingdom in 1994, and Japan in 1998. To raise capital for continued growth, Cohen and Greenfield took the company public. In April 2000 the board accepted a $325 million offer, and Ben & Jerry's became a wholly owned subsidiary of Unilever.

Although no longer involved in the operation of the company, Cohen and Greenfield are active in its foundation as well as other philanthropic enterprises. Ben & Jerry's ice cream remains a popular global brand and an inspiration to entrepreneurs.

See also ICE CREAM.

Funderburg, Anne Cooper. *Chocolate, Strawberry, and Vanilla*. Bowling Green, Ohio: Bowling Green State University Press, 1995.

Lager, Fred. *Ben & Jerry's: The Inside Scoop*. New York: Crown, 1994.

Quinzio, Jeri. *Of Sugar & Snow: A History of Ice Cream Making*. Berkeley: University of California Press, 2009.

Weiss, Laura B. *Ice Cream: A Global History*. London: Reaktion, 2011.

Jeri Quinzio

benne seed wafers, crisp and delicate sweet wafers dotted with benne (sesame) seeds, have been a favorite cookie attributed to the Lowcountry of South Carolina and Georgia since the 1940s, both in general American cookbooks and local Charleston ones. They are typically served at weddings, funerals, and similar catered affairs, and it has been said that if benne seed wafers were not served at a Charleston wedding, the couple would not be legally married. Approximately the size of a U.S. quarter, but with the thickness and crispness of a Communion wafer, benne seed wafers are sold both in bulk and retail, usually in small packages or cookie tins in gift stores.

The typical benne seed wafer recipe calls for butter beaten until light with brown sugar; egg whites or whole eggs, flour, and benne seeds are added to make a batter thin enough to drop or pipe in rounds before baking. The wafers' small size and quick baking time make them laborious to bake at home without specialized equipment.

Benne seeds, *Sesamum indicum*, were originally brought to the American colonies from Africa as a source of oil and to feed West African slaves. They grow in rows in an okra-like pod with a fuzzy green exterior that is attached to the slender stalk of a flowering plant. The word for "sesame" in the Wolof language of Senegal is *benne*, which came to be used in the American South; Thomas Jefferson refers to the seed with a variety of spellings, including Bene, benne, and beni.

It is likely that the original cookie was made from a drop batter in which sesame seeds were substituted for nuts. See DROP COOKIES. Several bakeries, primarily Old Colony Bakery in Mount Pleasant, South Carolina, are known for their benne seed wafers, but no compelling evidence exists for attributing the recipe to a specific bakery or creator.

See also SOUTH (U.S.).

Brown, Cora, Rose Brown, and Bob Brown. *America Cooks: Recipes from the 48 States*. New York: Norton, 1940.

Fowler, Damon Lee. *Damon Lee Fowler's New Southern Baking: Classic Flavors for Today's Cook*. New York: Simon & Schuster, 2005.

Harris, Jessica B. *Iron Pots and Wooden Spoons: Africa's Gifts to New World Cooking*. New York: Simon & Schuster, 1999.

Mount Pleasant School Parent Teacher Association. *Mount Pleasant's Famous Recipes*. Mount Pleasant, S.C., 1941.

Nathalie Dupree

betty

See FRUIT DESSERTS, BAKED.

Betty Crocker began as a simple feminine signature on the bottom of a letter from a Minneapolis flour company in 1921 and grew into a name so recognizable that, in 1945, *Fortune* magazine called her the second best-known woman in America—superseded only by First Lady Eleanor Roosevelt. The ranking was especially impressive, considering that Betty never actually existed.

Betty Crocker was created out of the belief that homemakers did not want to correspond with a man when they sent letters with baking questions to the Washburn Crosby Company (the forerunner to General Mills, which was incorporated in 1928). Samuel Gale, working in the company's in-house advertising department, believed that women wanted replies from another woman on domestic matters. The surname "Crocker" was chosen in honor of William G. Crocker, a recently retired director of the company, and "Betty" for its all-American wholesomeness.

In the first few years of Betty's existence, a dialogue of sorts blossomed between the flour company and its customers through letters and text-heavy magazine ads. Women had questions, and Betty had answers. The need for a baking expert was understandable, since new technology was making mother's traditional kitchen advice increasingly obsolete. More and more homes had running water and electricity. Refrigerators were replacing iceboxes, while gas and electric stoves replaced coal-burning stoves. Food was changing, too—new convenience products began to line grocery shelves, and flour was increasingly processed. To complicate matters, units of measurement were not standardized. A cup might mean either 8 fluid ounces or the teacup from the cupboard. Baking pans came in all shapes and sizes, making it difficult to plan for baking success.

To help spread the gospel of good baking advice, the Washburn Crosby Company gave Betty Crocker her own radio show, with several different members of the company's home service staff voicing the part of Betty. The powerful combination of love and baking quickly emerged as a popular theme in Betty's radio broadcasts, recipe booklets, and advertisements. Cake, more than any other baked good, came to embody all that was Betty Crocker. Birthdays, graduations, retirement parties, and other holidays and family gatherings, she assured listeners, would not be the same without cake. Her Old-Fashioned Jelly Roll Cake, Pineapple Upside Down Cake, and Favorite Fudge Cake signified something extra, something special—a treat equal parts presentation and taste. It is no surprise that a flour company should promote recipes

The wholesome image of Betty Crocker, an icon of modern American convenience baking, has changed over the years to make her persona more up to date. Here she appears in advertising from 1955, 1965, and 1996.

that used as much flour as possible, and Betty's followers proved all too eager to "bake someone happy."

An early recipe pamphlet series titled *Foods Men Hurry Home For!* included recipes for Honey Chocolate Cake with Marshmallow Filling and Almond Roca Frosting, as well as recipes for Chocolate Coconut Ribbon Cake and Kaffee Klatsch Cake (Orange Coffee Cake). Betty's team was so serious about cakes that they introduced the finely milled Gold Medal Special Cake Flour (later renamed Softasilk). Betty devoted an entire 1935 radio broadcast "Cake Clinics" to curing "sick" cakes:

> This morning I am going to talk about the food that strikes the highest note in the entire meal—the cake you serve for dessert. I think among all the foods served at your table, this is one where your reputation as a hostess and as a good provider for your family is most at stake.

For better or worse, Betty's take on cake as one of the tenets of feminine achievement resonated with homemakers as they scrambled for Betty's latest Pink Azalea Cake; Lord, Lady, and Baby Baltimore Cakes; Cherry Angel Food Cake; and Creole Devil's Food Cake recipes. One woman wrote to Betty, "I don't make your fudge cake, because I like white cake, but my neighbor does. Is there any danger of her capturing my husband?" Another wrote, "I derive so much from your lessons. Before I started listening to your talks on WCCO, I made such wretched cakes that my husband used to throw them down to the furnace to burn them. But now I am really proud of the ones I make."

Cake continued to be big business for General Mills when it paid a large, undisclosed amount to a notorious Hollywood cake baker, the aptly named Harry Baker, for his Chiffon Cake recipe. See CHIFFON CAKE. In 1948 Betty Crocker announced her latest cake, "The Cake Discovery of the Century," combining the richness of butter cake with the lightness of sponge cake. The secret ingredient of vegetable oil helped catapult Betty's Chiffon Cake into sweets stardom, to become the most popular cake of the mid-century.

At around the same time, Betty Crocker's cake mixes advertising "You Add the Eggs Yourself" eclipsed all other cake-mix brands, including Pillsbury, Swans Down, and Duff. Betty's cake mixes still dominate grocery-store baking aisles, as if echoing her reassuring message, "I guarantee a perfect cake every time you bake... cake... after... cake... after... cake."

See also ANGEL FOOD CAKE; CAKE; CAKE MIX; HINES, DUNCAN; and UPSIDE-DOWN CAKE.

Betty Crocker's 15 Prize Recipes, Favorites of Each Year 1921–1936. Minneapolis: General Mills, 1936.

Foods Men Hurry Home For! By Betty Crocker. Series no. 2 and 3. Minneapolis: General Mills, n.d.

Marks, Susan. *Finding Betty Crocker: The Secret Life of America's First Lady of Food*. New York: Simon & Schuster, 2005.

Susan Marks

biofuel, unlike the fossil fuels extracted from decomposed material, is made from living plants. Sugarcane (*Saccharum officinarum*) is the source of two major fuels: solid-based (bagasse—the fiber left over after crushing the cane—and the cane's tops and leaves) and liquid-based (ethanol, obtained from the fermentation of sugars). Approximately 26 million hectares of sugarcane are planted worldwide (a small area compared to all major crops), of which about 5 million are currently dedicated to ethanol fuel, primarily in Brazil. Sugarcane is produced in more than 100 countries, though a handful, including Brazil, India, China, Pakistan, and Thailand, represent three-quarters of the total production.

Solid Fuel

Sugarcane is one of the most efficient energy crops. Bagasse has historically been used around the world to power sugar and ethanol mills. A well-run mill (for example, with efficient boilers) can be self-sufficient in heat and power, and also generate a large surplus that may be sold to the grid.

The potential for co-generation from sugarcane biomass has long been recognized, and many studies have investigated this vast and highly underutilized fuel. Conservative estimates from 2009 put worldwide potential at 425 million tons, equivalent to 662.4 million barrels of crude oil, located primarily in Asia (China, India, Pakistan, and Thailand) and South America (Brazil and Colombia) but also in Australia, Mexico, and Guatemala. In 2012 Brazil, for example, generated 1400 million watts from bagasse, though the potential would be 10 to 15 times greater if tops and leaves were included. Currently, a major limiting factor is the low price paid to sugarcane producers for their surplus electricity due to competition from hydropower.

Liquid Fuel: Ethanol

Ethanol can be produced from many feedstocks, but sugarcane remains king. Brazil provides the world's leading example of ethanol from sugarcane. In 2012 about 85 billion liters were produced worldwide (approximately 536 M bbl, or million barrels oil equivalent), of which about 45 percent were from sugarcane. Fermentable sugars represent 6 to 16 percent of the sugarcane weight, making it the best feedstock for ethanol. Consequently, many sugarcane-producing countries in addition to Brazil are considering the ethanol option, primarily as a blend with gasoline in different proportions. These include China, Colombia, Central America, India (where cane is also used as feedstock in the chemical industry), Kenya, Malawi, Mozambique, South Africa, Tanzania, and Thailand.

The use of ethanol as transport fuel goes back to the origin of the automobile industry. In 1826 Samuel Morey ran the prototype engine on ethanol; Nikaulos Otto in 1860 burned ethanol in his engines; and Henry Ford's 1908 Model T, called the Quadricycle, also used ethanol. The use of ethanol fuel was so widespread that in 1902 an exhibition was held in Paris dedicated to its uses for vehicles, farm machinery, cookers, and heaters.

Sugarcane fuel ethanol has been used in Brazil since the early twentieth century (the first tests took place in 1907), but dramatic expansion began with the creation of Brazil's National Alcohol Program in 1975. In its 2013–2014 harvest, Brazil produced about 25 billion liters of ethanol. There are currently 17 million cars with flex fuel engines (engines modified to use hydrated ethanol and gasoline in different blends), a number that could reach 49 million by 2020. In 2013 demand was estimated at 22 billion liters, of which 10 billion were anhydrous (almost pure ethanol used in a fixed blend of 20 to 25 percent with gasoline) and 12 billion hydrous. It is predicted that in 2020 demand in Brazil will reach 34.6 billion liters (16.6 billion anhydrous and 17.8 billion hydrous ethanol). This represents 60 percent of the estimated 840 million tons of raw cane production in 2020. The average productivity of ethanol is currently 6,000 to 7,000 liters per hectare (lha), but various studies indicate that with efficient management and money spent on research and development, the amount could increase to 15,000 lha.

Combining Solid and Liquid Fuels

Sugarcane stalks contain approximately 14 to 16 percent sucrose and 12 to 14 percent bagasse with other residues (for example, tops and leaves), which are increasingly used as fuel. The sugar contents represent 2.54 gigajoules per ton and 4.65 gigajoules per ton for residues. Based on an average yield of 82.4 tons per hectare in southeast Brazil, this represents 383 gigajoules per hectare. Considering a co-generation efficiency of 69 percent, about 287 gigajoules per hectare are available per ton of sugarcane. With the progressive introduction of more efficient boilers (currently 20 to 100 kilowatt hours and up to 200 kilowatt hours), and of greater amounts of sugarcane processed, huge surpluses of electricity can be generated. A modern sugarcane plantation could generate up to 15 times more energy than it consumes. In addition, current productivity is considered low compared to its agronomic potential of up to 340 tons per hectare.

Since many countries run a very inefficient sugar industry, sugarcane fuel has great potential for improvement with modest investment and hence will continue to play a key role in the future, despite the potential advances of second-generation biofuels.

A drawback of ethanol fuel is that it requires land. As the world's population exceeds 7 billion, competition for food crops continues to increase, which has generated heated debate. However, in the case of sugarcane, the potential impact would be minimal, because it is one of the best feedstocks for ethanol production, both from an agronomic and an economic standpoint, and the total area is very small compared to what is needed for major crops such as wheat, corn, or soybean.

See also SUGAR REFINING; SUGARCANE; and SUGARCANE AGRICULTURE.

Cortez, Luís Augusto Barbosa, ed. *Sugarcane Bioethanol: R&D for Productivity and Sustainability*. São Paulo, Brazil: Blucher, 2010.

Horta Nogeira, L. A., J. R. Moreira, U. Schuchardt, and J. Goldemberg. "The Rationality of Biofuels." *Energy Policy* 61 (2013): 595–598.

Rocha, L. B. "Brazil's Sugar and Ethanol in 2013 and Beyond." *International Sugar Journal* 115, no. 1374 (2013): 392–398.
Rosillo-Calle, Frank, and Francis X. Johnson, eds. *Food versus Debate: An Informed Introduction to Biofuels.* London: Zed, 2010.

Frank Rosillo-Calle

bird's milk is the stuff of fantasy, and the name of this beloved Eastern European sweet reflects its mythical qualities and physical scarcity. The candies are indeed ethereal: small, chocolate-enrobed bars with a soft, marshmallow-like interior, colored white for vanilla or egg-yolk yellow for lemon. Bird's milk candies were first produced in Poland by the famous E. Wedel company in the mid-1930s; in 2010 the company received a trademark for them from the European Union. From Poland the candy spread in popularity throughout Eastern Europe, especially Russia, where during the Soviet era of food deficits, obtaining a box of bird's milk candies was considered a coup, nearly as unlikely as milking a bird.

Bird's milk torte, a sponge cake with a soft, mousse-like filling and a chocolate glaze, is a purely Soviet invention from 1978, dreamed up by Vladimir Guralnik, the pastry chef at Moscow's once-chic Praga restaurant. The cake soon became a cult item, almost as unattainable as its name suggests. Within a few years a factory was built to accommodate Muscovites' yearning for this dessert, yet even the production of 2,000 tortes a day could not satisfy demand, and the cake remained a deficit item.

Still, whenever it could be obtained, bird's milk was enjoyed by all segments of Soviet society. "As Guralnik later recalled in an interview for the *Moscow Times*, "I remember making a 15-kilogram sponge cake for Brezhnev's 70th birthday. I don't know if he really liked sponge cake, but that's all he could eat with his constantly slipping dentures." In the United States, bird's milk cake is still popular among Russian émigrés, who use gelatin and Cool Whip to achieve the desired consistency.

Viktoriya Mitlyng. "Cake Weighs Heavily in Russian Life." *Moscow Times*, 22 May 1997. http://www.themoscowtimes.com/print/article/cake-weighs-heavily-in-russian-life/306849.html (accessed 8 August 2013).

Darra Goldstein

birth is a life event associated with sweet foods that appear in various rituals, among which baptism, christening, or other formal presentation of a new child to a community are public events, while the actual birth, attended by women only (at least historically), is private. The foods served vary according to religion, culture, and personal beliefs, but sweetness fulfills various symbolic and practical roles, including bestowing good fortune on the child and wishing the mother well to recover her strength. Sweets form part of gift exchanges within a community and can symbolize joy and fertility, prosperity, and also provide visitors with refreshment.

In contemporary Britain, North America, and former English colonies in the southern hemisphere, a formal christening party provides the principal example of sweetness in a christening cake covered in icing and decorated with a pastillage plaque of an infant, or a model of a crib or baby, or possibly a more overtly religious symbol, such as a bible or religious text. Fruitcakes have been used to celebrate births in British culture since at least the seventeenth century, when a "groaning cake" (along with a cheese known as a groaning cheese) was provided for female supporters waiting to be allowed into the birth chamber. See FRUITCAKE. These women were known as "God's sibs" (siblings in God, hence "gossip"), and were also provided with drinks, as mentioned by Shakespeare in *A Midsummer Night's Dream*, where Puck talks of a gossip's bowl containing ale and a roasted crab[apple]. Rum butter (a solid mixture of butter, sugar, and rum) was provided in the English Lake District for visitors, who left coins for the baby in the bowl it was served in.

In Continental Europe, comfits or confetti are some of the most important sweet items associated with births. See COMFIT and CONFETTI. Today, countries around the northern Mediterranean use these as favors, now mostly in the form of sugared almonds. Packed in bags or boxes with colors and trimmings considered appropriate, a few are presented to each guest. Favors, essentially tokens in exchange for gifts given to mother and child, are also found in North American baby showers and christening showers. In Dutch tradition, the arrival of a child is celebrated with *musjies* ("little mice"), tiny pink and white anise comfits, served on top of buttered rusks. Further afield, *noql* (sugared almonds with an irregular, bobbly surface) are served with tea and sweet biscuits at Afghan naming celebrations.

The association of comfits with birth ritual goes back many centuries. Renaissance Italian practice included various sweetmeats provided in the birth chamber for visitors, and images on special birth trays often include depictions of attendants carrying round sweetmeat boxes; records occasionally detail items including almond or pine nut sweetmeats, cakes (*pane biancho*, or white cake, probably like a sponge cake), and confetti as a general term. Some items were purchased from apothecaries; others were homemade.

In the sixteenth-century poem *Batchelar's Banquet*, a satirical translation of the French *Quinze Joies de Mariage*, the author bemoans the "cost and trouble" of laying in sweets, including various comfits, only to see female guests carry away as much as they pleased. This poem also mentions sugar for the midwife. Both sugared almonds as celebratory foods and the custom of paying the midwife partly with sweet foods appears to have been more widespread. In *Sherbet and Spice* (2013), food historian Mary Işın reveals that during the late Ottoman period in Turkey, at six days after the birth of a child the potty under the cradle was filled with sugar almonds, which were given to the midwife.

Informal practices are poorly recorded. Some cultures say that a child's first taste should be sweet. In the Muslim world, this sweetness takes the form of date juice rubbed on the child's gums, a practice carried out by the Prophet Muhammad. See ISLAM. Madhur Jaffrey, in *Madhur Jaffrey's Indian Cookery* (1982), relates that when she was newborn, her grandmother "wrote the sacred syllable 'Om' ('I am') on my tongue with a finger dipped in fresh honey." A Turkish custom, as recorded by Işın, was to smear sugar or honey on the newborn's mouth in the hope that the child would be sweet-spoken.

Another custom discussed by Işın is the use of large squares of grained sugar, colored red and flavored with cloves "used to make lohusa şerbeti, hot spiced sherbet traditionally made after the birth of a child to give the new mother energy and improve her supply of milk" (2013, p. 80). The color symbolized happiness, and jugs of the sherbet were sent to other households to announce the birth. Sustaining food for the mother was considered important in many cultures—for instance, as *shola-e-holba*, Afghanistan's sweet rice with fenugreek, mentioned by Helen Saberi in *Noshe Djan* (2000)—but these foods are generally underrecorded because of the essentially female, private nature of birth.

Rituals surrounding birth may extend for several weeks, although the use of sweet foods seems to diminish as time elapses from the actual birth. However, in Chinese culture, sweetness seems to creep into the "red egg and ginger" party marking the end of the first month of a child's life. Red symbolizes happiness, but real eggs are now sometimes replaced by chocolate ones; the warmth of ginger, sometimes candied, balances the depleted yin of the mother.

Işın, Mary. *Sherbet and Spice: The Complete Story of Turkish Sweets and Desserts*. London: I. B. Tauris, 2013.

Musacchio, Jacqueline Marie. *The Art and Ritual of Childbirth in Renaissance Italy*. London and New Haven, Conn.: Yale University Press, 1999.

Swinburne, Layinka, and Laura Mason. " 'She Came from a Groaning Very Cheerful . . .': Food in Pregnancy, Childbirth, and Christening Ritual." In *Food and the Rites of Passage*, edited by Laura Mason, pp. 62–86. Totnes, U.K.: Prospect, 2002.

Laura Mason

birthday cake

See CELEBRATION CAKES.

biscotti cover a very wide range of sweetened baked goods with many regional variations, seasonal and religious significance. Recently, the Italian term has become popular in most English-speaking countries. Biscotti is derived from the medieval Latin *biscoctus*, a bread or cracker baked twice to dry out the moisture and prolong storing time. Pliny the Elder mentions that baked goods like *panis militaris* could last very long; hence, they were among the staple foods vital for the Roman Legion's diet. The ancient Romans consumed a very dry biscuit made solely of grape must and flour known as *mustaceus*, and Cato included the first recipe for it baked on a laurel leaf in *De re rustica*; the name was eventually transmuted to *mostaccioli*. In Calabria, this enriched biscotto assumes a significant role with many symbolic shapes, and a guild of *mostaccioli* makers still endures today. *Mostaccioli* have evolved considerably and they now sometimes have a softer, spongy consistency, with the frequent addition of chopped nuts and dried fruit. This specialty is generally diamond- or oval-shaped, often coated with dark or white chocolate, and is available in many regions.

Perhaps the earliest recipe for these twice-cooked cookies comes from Bartolomeo Scappi's *Opera* of 1570. It calls for slicing up a cooked *pan di Spagna* (sponge cake) and baking the slices a second time. See SPONGE CAKE. Just how far back this practice goes is unclear, but presumably it did not predate the introduction of sponge cake in Italy, which may have occurred as late as the sixteenth century. Various kinds of small cakes that Italians would now call biscotti were frequently found in banquets from the Middle Ages to the baroque era, frequently served with sugared strawberries or clotted cream to begin the repast. From the sixteenth century onward *mostaccioli* became a popular ingredient, in crumbled form, for preparing other dishes, especially as a sauce thickener.

Today, biscotti abound in every region of Italy, sometimes as variations of the same type, like *bocconotti* (almond-filled pastry pockets), and sometimes typical of a region, like *zaleti* (crunchy yellow corn biscuits) from Veneto. Most of these are no longer baked twice, unlike their American counterparts, which are mostly derived from the *biscotti di Prato* variety. From north to south we find *amaretti* made of sweet and bitter almonds, chopped or pulverized, varying in shape, size, and consistency: those from Sassello, soft and spongy, individually wrapped in fringed paper; from Chivasso, minuscule round *nocciolini*; from Lazio, larger soft-centered sweetmeats; from Saronno, industrially produced crisp biscuits and an Amaretto liqueur.

In Sicily, the early medieval Arab presence influenced the monastic traditions of almond paste confectionery (*frutta martorana*), begun at the convent of Martorana and appreciated starting in the fourteenth century by princes and prelates alike. *Viscotto da monaca* (nun's biscuit) is a popular S-shaped biscotto, also pulverized in milk for baby food. *Nzuddi* (St. Vincent) too was made by the nuns with honey and orange peel.

Many biscotti celebrate religious festivities and patron saints. *Fave di morti* (for the day of the dead) are bone-shaped or ovals of sweetened chopped almonds found in many regions. A range of biscuits dedicated to St. Anthony are made in an innovative artisanal confectionery factory in the Padua prison and include *il glglio* (the lily) and *la corona del santo* (crown of the saint) made with barley flour and fig jam, and "cavaliers" flavored with cardamom and hippocras. A special biscuit feast for Sant' Anselmo is held at Bomarzo on 23 April every year. Christmas is the time for *susamelle* (dark spicy sliced biscuits) and *rococo* (rock-hard biscuits) from Campania; *panesapa* (must-sweetened cookies) from Sardinia; and *ricciarelli* made of almond paste dusted with sugar from Tuscany.

One of the most renowned types of biscotti is *biscotto di Prato,* first documented by Amadio Baldanzi in the eighteenth century and prepared by a local baker named Antonio Mattei, who garnered special mention in the 1867 Exposition Universelle in Paris. A characteristic of this traditional biscuit is the absence of butter, liquids, yeast, fat, or oil. The recipe requires only flour, sugar, eggs, pine nuts, and unskinned almonds. The damp dough is shaped into a slab and baked, then cut into slices diagonally, and baked again. Known generally as *cantucci* (a term of Tuscan origin, but widely found in other distant cuisines), these are typically dipped into Vin Santo or another dessert wine for a traditional after-dinner treat. Modern mass-manufactured biscotti similar to *biscotti di Prato* show regional deviations, including the use of yeasts or milk to make them moist, and flavorings like cinnamon, almond essence, and anise to enhance the aroma. The basic dough is often enriched with olive oil or margarine, while cheaper hazelnuts substitute for almonds.

Carquinyolis are the Catalan version of these biscotti, made with whole or sliced almonds associated with other regions such as Aragon, Batea, Prat de Comte. They are also found in Valencia, where they are called *rosegons* or *rosegós*. In Minorca, *carquinyols* are a simple square-shaped biscotto without whole almonds.

Among the numerous traditional Tuscan biscotti, one may count: *berlingozzi* and *befanini* (fun shapes for children); *brigidini* (a wafer-thin specialty often prepared at fairs); and *bruttiboni* (ugly but good), crunchy mounds of chopped nuts, sugar, and egg whites found especially in central Italy. *Ciambelle* (doughnut-shaped) are present in all regions, in many sizes, with some identifiable as biscotti, others more cake-like. The typical Lazio variety is *ciambelle al vino* with olive oil, sugar, flour, and white wine in equal proportions. Passover specialties include anise-flavored *ciambelette* prepared in the Roman Jewish ghetto. Among the many regional versions today, a variety of additions exist: nuts, raisins, chocolate, coconut, and sugar glaze.

With the increased popularity of Italian food worldwide in the 1980s, biscotti came to be absorbed into the repertoire of bakers everywhere, but especially in the United States. There, they were frequently associated with the spread of high-end coffee chains such as Starbucks and occasionally promoted as being a "healthier" choice (that is, lower in fat) than more traditional American cookies. By 2014 the English-language books published on the subject easily outpaced the Italian.

Chovancova, Ilona. *Biscotti*. Lodi, Italy: Bibliotheca Culinaria, 2006.
Krondl, Michael. *Sweet Invention: A History of Dessert*. Chicago: Chicago Review Press, 2011.
Talbott, Mona, and Mirella Misenti. *Biscotti: Recipes from the Kitchen of the American Academy in Rome*. New York: The Little Bookroom, 2011.

June di Schino

biscuit de Savoie

See SPONGE CAKE.

biscuits, British, describes a vast range of small baked items, mostly sweet and usually crunchy, not dissimilar to some types of North American cookies. Britain is notable for its obsession with sweet biscuits and for pioneering their industrial production. Yet despite a rich baking heritage and a revival of home baking, many traditional biscuits, such as the wafers that were popular across Europe for centuries, are nearly obsolete. Today, when most Britons think of biscuits, the endless mass-market varieties come first to mind: chocolate-covered digestives, bourbon creams, and garibaldis (irreverently nicknamed "squashed fly biscuits" because of the currants they contain). These biscuits are based on a relatively narrow range of ingredients and rely as much on shape and appearance for identity as on flavor or texture.

Biscuit eating—in adulthood, most often with a cup of tea—is a marker of Britishness but also an act of comfort and reassurance, a tiny, sanctioned dose of sugar to raise energy levels and brighten the day. The wide variety of biscuits available from the largest supermarket to the smallest grocery creates an illusion of luxurious choice at a modest price, and having a favorite is de rigueur. When, in 2009, incumbent prime minister Gordon Brown refused to disclose his favorite biscuit during a live online interview, *The Observer* newspaper quipped that "this raises serious questions regarding his suitability to remain in office."

The British affection for biscuits explains the cult following of Nice Cup of Tea and a Sit Down, a website and book by "Nicey," who analyzes scores of British biscuits with a mixture of enthused intellect and irony. Of the ever-popular custard cream, a sandwich biscuit with a vanilla-flavored filling, he writes:

> This biscuit, perhaps more than any other, has the ability to warp the fabric of space-time and transport us effortlessly back to days gone by.... With

Two women package Wright's Biscuits in this 1947 photograph. Wright's Biscuits was a well-known company in South Tyneside, England, that started out by supplying ships in 1790 but later turned to producing more upscale biscuits. The factory closed in 1973. TYNE & WEAR ARCHIVES & MUSEUMS its baroque detailing, the Custard Cream defies us to pin it down to any particular period of history. It is tempting to think that it was knocking around in the sixteenth century, its ornate swirls providing the muse for such great artists as Rubens or Caravaggio, as they nibbled on one over a late morning cuppa.

The quotidian custard cream—whatever its graphic niceties—has more in common with commodities such as toothpaste than it does with Dutch or Italian high art, and Nicey knows this. His anachronistic riffs underpin the importance of British biscuit-eating as an act of nostalgia, both for one's own childhood and for the perceived simplicity of a pre-industrial era.

The association of biscuits with nostalgia was deliberately forged by the biscuit manufacturers of the Victorian era, whose packaging and marketing materials featured images of children at play, often in rural settings. Chief among these manufacturers was Huntley & Palmers, and every industrial biscuit produced today, in any part of the world, is somewhat in their debt. The company's rise roughly parallels the trajectory of Queen Victoria's reign from 1837 to 1901, a period during which British society completed a seismic shift from an agricultural way of life to an urban one. It all began in 1822, when Joseph Huntley opened a shop at 72 London Street in Reading. It was only 18 feet wide and straddled a large underground bakehouse. By 1898 Huntley & Palmers was worth £2.4 million and was producing more than 400 varieties of biscuit. Several key innovations had radically reduced manpower and boosted output, including a revolving oven that enabled biscuits to be baked in a continuous flow. This oven was based on one used for manufacturing ship's biscuit (hardtack), the plain, hard mixture of flour and water baked so dry that it could be kept months at sea during exploration and war, and was thus an unsung hero of the British Empire.

The new biscuits were considered so important that the British newspaper *The Morning Star* devoted a whole article to the phenomenon in 1860, explaining the difference between hardtack and the new biscuits:

> Closely allied to our old friend the bread baker... is his more modernised relative, the manufacturer of that nutritious, sweet, toothsome little condiment known as a biscuit. Of course we don't mean for a moment to pay a compliment to the great, hulky, ill-conditioned article which serves as one of the bases of England's naval greatness. We have to write about a different genus altogether—of picnics, Osborne's, Queen's, caraways, lunch, coffee and wine biscuits, of cracknels, and nonsuches, and all those little creations which form a part, and a distinguished part, in our social economy, and bear as much relation to the hard-baked compound of flour and water on which sailors feed as does the full-grown intellectual man to the polypus, from which, if modern theorists speak truly, he first derived the power of existence, and launched himself upon the sliding-scale of creation.

Social Darwinism and biscuits? In Victorian England, biscuits were indeed a symptom and an enabler of a new social order. A vast proportion of British society was now laboring in large factories, making everything from widgets to biscuits. A casualty of this transition was mealtimes. Before the 1860s large breakfasts were eaten as late as 10 A.M., and the evening meal between 4 and 5 P.M. After 1860 breakfasts tended to be smaller and earlier, and the evening meal later. As lunch and tea rose in prominence, biscuits proved an efficient addition to these meals, as they do to this day.

Corley, T. A. B. "Nutrition, Technology, and the Growth of the British Biscuit Industry 1820–1900." In *The Making of the Modern British Diet*, edited by Derek J. Oddy and Derek S. Miller, pp. 2–35. London: Croon Helm, 1976.

Corley, T. A. B. *Quaker Enterprise in Biscuits: Huntley and Palmers of Reading, 1822–1972*. London: Hutchinson, 1972.

Payne, Stuart. *Nice Cup of Tea and a Sit Down*. London: Time-Warner, 2004.

Anastasia Edwards

black and white cookies, slightly mounded drop cakes frosted half in chocolate and half in white icing, are a fixture in New York City bakeries and delis. How these cookies traveled from a sturdy industrial city in the southern Adirondacks to the Big Apple remains a mystery. Perhaps a transplanted Upstate New Yorker missed the local treat and introduced a larger, two-fisted version to the city. In any case, New York City–style black and white cookies have a slightly lemony base, rather than chocolate, and they are often individually wrapped because they quickly turn stale.

Food historians trace the cookie's origin to the 1920s and the now-closed Hemstrought's Bakery of Utica. Locally called "half-moons," these cookies are still featured in a number of Upstate New York bakeries and are popular in New England and even in the Midwest, where they are generally somewhat smaller than the New York City version. Hemstrought's signature half-moon had a chocolate cake base with chocolate fudge icing on one side and thick vanilla buttercream on the other. Coconut and vanilla versions were also available.

Both city and upstate fans hold strong opinions about how best to consume the cookies: Do you eat the vanilla or the chocolate side first, or start from the middle? Opinions are also strong regarding the cookie's best version. In a famous episode of the American TV sitcom *Seinfeld*, as Elaine and Jerry scour the city bakeries and corner delis for the best black and white, the cookie comes to symbolize ideal race relations. "Look to the cookie!" Jerry exclaims. In a January 2011 *New York Times Magazine* article, Molly O'Neill asserted that some consider the cookies an "icon of balance."

Black and white cookies are related to other soft cake cookies, such as MoonPies, scooter pies, and whoopie pies, popularized during the same period. However, while these other treats are cream-filled sandwich cookies, black and whites are frosted only on top.

See also MOONPIES and WHOOPIE PIE.

"Halfmoon Cookies." http://www.saveur.com/article/Recipes/Halfmoon-Cookies (accessed 2 September 2013).

Judith Hausman

black bun

See FRUITCAKE.

Black Forest cake, or *Schwarzwälder Kirschtorte,* is a glorious combination of a thin chocolate shortcrust base, chocolate sponge cake, sour cherries, generous amounts of kirschwasser (cherry brandy), freshly whipped cream, and dark chocolate shavings. It is without doubt the most famous German torte, at its best a marvelous combination of richness and lightness. However, the better and more widely a recipe is known, the more distorted it tends to become, and all too frequently Black Forest cake appears as a poor imitation, with cheap (but longer-lasting) buttercream, artificial chocolate sprinkles, and, worst of all, glacéed cherries.

The moment and place of birth of the Black Forest cake are difficult to pin down, and its origin is much discussed. The credit most often goes to pastry chef Josef Keller (1887–1981), a native of Radolfzell on Lake Constance, who is said to have invented the cake in 1915 while working at the Café Agner in Bad Godesberg. The first written recipe appeared in 1927. Other sources date the cake to 1930 and attribute it to a pastry chef in Tübingen.

The cake's name may come from its resemblance to the traditional black, white, and red costume of the Black Forest region. Certainly that region claims the cake today as part of its culinary tradition, since cherry trees have long been cultivated in the Black Forest and the fruit has been distilled there into brandy. Nevertheless, because it took quite a long time for popular cookbooks to include the recipe (it appeared in Dr. Oetker's *Backen macht Freude* only in 1951, for example), it seems safe to assume that Black Forest cake was a professional recipe that trickled down into private households. In the second half of the twentieth century, the cake traveled around the globe, even topping dessert charts in such unlikely places as the United Kingdom. Today, the Black Forest theme is used generally by the food industry to denote the combination of chocolate and dark cherries, omitting any link to cake and brandy.

See also GERMANY; SPONGE CAKE; and TORTE.

Oetker, Doktor August. *Backen macht Freude*. Bielefeld, Germany: Ceres-Verlag, 1963.

Weber, Johannes Martin Erich. *250 Konditorei-Spezialitäten und wie sie entstehen. Der praktische Unterricht in 580 Bildern von Werdegängen aus 24 Fachabteilungen bei kleinster Massenberechnung*. Radebeul, Germany: J. M. E. Weber, 1934.

Ursula Heinzelmann

blancmange is a pudding made of milk, cornstarch (cornflour in the United Kingdom), and sugar in Western cuisines today, although this version only appeared in the second half of the nineteenth century.

The much-altered recipe evolved from medieval Arab cuisine. By the thirteenth century, the predecessor to blancmange—known either as *maʾmûniyya* or *muhallabiyya* (names that were also used for a variety

The once-fashionable sweet milk pudding known as blancmange was originally made with shredded chicken. Meatless versions appeared in the early eighteenth century; by the twentieth century the dessert was largely relegated to the nursery or sickroom. This plate showing a blancmange mold is from *Mrs Beeton's Book of Household Management* (1861).

of other dishes made with meat and rice)—was prepared from shredded chicken breast, pounded rice, milk, and sugar. A recipe for *muhallabiyya* in a thirteenth-century Andalusian cook book begins with the following story, suggesting that the dish originated in Sassanid Persia: "It is reported that a cook of Persia had his residence next to that of Muhallab b. Abi Safra and that he presented himself to prepare for him a good dish and so that he could test him; he prepared it and offered it to him; he was pleased and called it *Muhallabiyya*."

The earliest surviving recipe for *muhallabiyya* made with chicken breast, rice, milk, and sugar is recorded by Ibn Sayyār al-Warrāq, writing in Baghdad in the tenth century. In Europe the dish became known as blancmange, meaning "white food" (*blanc-manger* in French, *biancomangiare* in Italian, and *manjarblanco* in Spanish), or as *mammonia, mawmenny, mamony,* and various other terms deriving from the Arabic original. The two earliest European recipes, dating from the late thirteenth or early fourteenth centuries, are a recipe called *blancmengier* (in *Traité de cuisine écritvers 1300*) made with chicken, rice, sugar, and optionally milk or almond milk, and another called *mammoniam* (in *Liber de Coquina*) made of pounded capon meat, rice, almond milk, spices, and honey. In fourteenth-century France, blancmange prepared for banquets was sometimes tinted in different colors and arranged in patterns. At a state banquet given during his visit to France in 1377, the Holy Roman Emperor Charles IV was served blancmange with green and white stripes.

Recipes for blancmange made with shredded chicken continued to appear in European cookery books through the seventeenth century, but thereafter Europeans replaced the minced chicken and rice with breadcrumbs, then with isinglass in the early eighteenth century, and arrowroot and gelatin in the nineteenth century. See GELATIN. In Britain and the United States, cornstarch took over after 1850 or so, while the French stuck to gelatin, as illustrated by Escoffier's recipes in *Le Guide Culinaire* (1903), where blancmange made with gelatin is titled *blanc-manger à la française,* while that made with cornstarch is *blanc-manger à l'anglaise.* In Italy, too, *bianco mangiare* came to be made with isinglass and later gelatin.

Blancmange made with shredded chicken, rice, and milk entered Turkish cuisine under the name *muhallebi* and was frequently prepared for the Ottoman sultan Mehmed II (1451–1481). Sixteenth-century records mention meatless versions of blancmange flavored with rosewater or musk. Today, Turkey is the only country where the original blancmange made with shredded chicken and ground rice remains popular. Known as *tavukgöğüsü* ("chicken breast") to distinguish it from the meatless *muhallebi,* it is rarely made at home but is sold in Istanbul's pudding shops (*muhallebici*). Since the chicken is boiled and then soaked at length in water before shredding, it has no discernible chicken flavor, only a slightly chewy texture and richer taste that distinguishes it from ordinary blancmange made with rice flour. A caramelized version of this, called *kazandibi* ("cauldron bottom"), evolved in nineteenth-century Istanbul to become one of Turkey's best-loved milk puddings. Another popular type of blancmange is *su muhallebisi*, a light version made of wheat starch and water served sprinkled with powdered sugar and rosewater. This was originally a cheap substitute sold only by street vendors, but its light and delicate flavor gradually won *su muhallebisi* a place in mainstream Turkish cuisine.

Blancmange also found its way into Indian Moghul cuisine. At a banquet given by Asaf Khan in Delhi in the early seventeenth century, two versions of blancmange appeared on the menu: one meatless, made of ground rice, sugar, and rosewater, and the other made of chicken, described at length by one of the guests, the Reverend Edward Terry:

> The flour of rice, mingled with sweet almonds, made as small as they could, and with some of the most fleshy parts of hens, stewed with it, and after, the flesh so beaten into pieces, that it could not be discerned, all made sweet with rose-water and sugar-candy, and scented with Ambergrease; this was another of our dishes, and a most luscious one, which the Portuguese call *mangee real* [*manjar real*], food for a King. (Terry, 1777, p. 197)

No longer does blancmange in its modern forms deserve such praise, and certainly no one would serve it at a banquet. In France, this dish has virtually died out, despite Escoffier's praise of both the French version with almonds and, surprisingly, of the bland English version made with cornstarch. Today in England, blancmange has become a pudding eaten mainly by children, quickly prepared from a packet in vanilla, banana, chocolate, or strawberry flavors—a sad end for a pudding once fit for gourmets. The Italian version made with gelatin, cream, and milk has been more fortunate; garnished with fruit coulis and various sauces, it is today enjoying a wave of popularity under the new name panna cotta.

See also FLOWER WATERS; INDIA; PERSIA; PUDDING; STARCH; and TURKEY.

Escoffier, Auguste. *A Guide to Modern Cookery*, pp. 759–760. London: Heinemann, 1952. First published 1907, translated from Escoffier's *Guide Culinaire* (1903).

Gouffé, Jules. *Le livre de cuisine*, p. 723. Paris:Librairie de L. Hachette et Cie, 1867.

Işın, Mary. *Sherbet and Spice: The Complete Story of Turkish Sweets and Desserts*, pp. 91–100. London: I. B. Tauris, 2013.

Krondl, Michael. *Sweet Invention: A History of Dessert*, pp. 45–46, 97, 130, 178. Chicago: Chicago Review Press, 2011.

Perry, Charles, trans. *An Anonymous Andalusian Cookbook of the Thirteenth Century*. http://daviddfriedman.com/Medieval/Cookbooks/Andalusian/andalusian_contents.htm.

Rodinson, Maxine, A. J. Arberry, and Charles Perry, eds. *Medieval Arab Cookery*, pp. 190–191, 264. Totnes, U.K.: Prospect, 2001.

Terry, Edward. A Voyage to East-India. Salisbury, U.K.: Printed for W. Cater, S. Hayes, J. Wilkie, and E. Easton, 1777. Reprinted from 1655 edition.

Warrāq, Ibn Sayyār al-. *Annals of the Caliphs' Kitchens: Ibn Sayyr al-Warrâq's Tenth-Century Baghdadi Cookbook*. Translated by Nawal Nasrallah, pp. 258, 407–408, 535. Leiden, The Netherlands, and Boston: Brill, 2007.

Priscilla Mary Işın

blown sugar

See SUGAR SCULPTURE.

boardwalks in American coastal resort towns are promenades running parallel to the beach, with shops and amusements fronting them along their landward sides. The first boardwalk was built in Atlantic City, New Jersey, in 1870 (although Cape May, New Jersey, claims an 1868 boardwalk). Railroad officials and hotel owners proposed a planked walkway on the beach to prevent coach and lobby floors from getting covered with sand when resort patrons returned from the beach. The resulting boardwalk was a hit, and commercial establishments catering to thronging promenaders soon positioned themselves accordingly.

Spaces for strolling and carriage riding had been set aside at earlier leisure sites, such as the spas, seaside resorts, and pleasure gardens of eighteenth- and nineteenth-century Britain, and their facsimiles in the early United States. Though American (and Continental) coastal leisure venues were based on British models, the boardwalk itself was an American innovation. In Britain, promenading and its accompanying entertainments were brought closer to the sea not by walkways parallel to the coastline but by piers extending into the water. American resorts usually built boardwalks first, then added British-style piers. One aspect of British practice among many replicated in the United States was the architectural prominence of "oriental" motifs.

Boardwalks facilitated leisure locales' long-established function of self-display. Well-dressed middle-class Americans on the twentieth-century Atlantic City boardwalk were engaged in the same ritual as their elite American predecessors had been in Newport, Rhode Island's "carriage parade," and their even earlier fashionable British counterparts on the Steine in Brighton. In all cases, the aim was to confirm, or to announce attainment of, high social position. This project by definition entailed identification of those who remained below. In 1837 in New York, it was thought undesirable "to be seen walking the same [pleasure garden] grounds with mechanics, house servants, and laboring people" (Asa Greene, *Glance at New York,* quoted in Conlin, 2013, pp. 144–145). In 1937 in Atlantic City, newly prosperous white Americans in rented rolling chairs ("democratized" versions of upper-class carriages) were propelled along the boardwalk by low-wage African Americans.

In 1895 at Britain's Blackpool, about one-third of all shops in the prime beachfront district were sweets shops, and half of these shops sold ice cream. See ICE CREAM. In early-nineteenth-century American pleasure gardens, ice cream constituted such a major attraction that "ice cream garden" became a synonym for "pleasure garden," and in some advertisements an image of a glass of ice cream typified the delights awaiting visitors. Pleasure-garden patrons enjoyed their ice cream sitting down, in refined ice cream "parlors." On the twentieth-century American boardwalk, ice cream was for sale, but it was not fully adapted to the strolling boardwalk milieu until the ice cream cone came into widespread use and the dress code was relaxed. See ICE CREAM CONES. A perambulator licking a cone filled with soft ice cream arrayed in a swirling pattern ascending and narrowing to a peak was consuming with his tongue the same "Moorish" exoticism that he could take in with his eyes when gazing up at the hotels along his path. A comparable aura of romance enveloped the cotton candy to which he treated his children. See COTTON CANDY.

Fudge, funnel cakes, and other items were sold on the boardwalk, as they still are today, but the signature boardwalk sweet food is saltwater taffy, allegedly created by chance in Atlantic City in 1883 when a vendor's premises were flooded with seawater while the taffy was being prepared. See FUDGE and TAFFY. Instead of throwing the batch away, the vendor offered it for sale as even more tasty.

This story is doubtless apocryphal, but it contains the kernel of truth that "saltwater" taffy is a marketing gimmick—a sophisticated version of what a budding Coney Island entrepreneur did in 1876: fill medicine bottles with seawater and sell them to midwestern tourists. This huckster's medicine bottles hint at the link between saltwater taffy and the origins of seaside resorts, the emergence of which in the eighteenth century was founded on claims of the therapeutic value of sea air and sea bathing. Richard Russell (credited with launching Brighton, England, into seaside preeminence) and other eighteenth-century physicians prescribed not only bathing in seawater but also drinking it. In Brighton and elsewhere, the quest for health was superseded almost immediately by the pursuit of pleasure. A century later, Atlantic City and other American boardwalk resorts at first promised good health as the reward of a visit, but like their English counterparts, they soon were devoted almost exclusively to pleasure. So when saltwater became a crucial part of what was to be ingested when enjoying a boardwalk sweet, the purportedly healthful dimension of the seaside holiday was neatly merged with the pleasurable dimension. In the words of the advertising copy for one Atlantic City saltwater taffy vendor, "Sea Air and Sunshine Sealed in Every Box."

Conlin, Jonathan, ed. *The Pleasure Garden, from Vauxhall to Coney Island.* Philadelphia: University of Pennsylvania Press, 2013.

Lilliefors, James. *America's Boardwalks: From Coney Island to California.* New Brunswick, N.J.: Rutgers University Press, 2006.

Simon, Bryant. *Boardwalk of Dreams: Atlantic City and the Fate of Urban America.* New York: Oxford University Press, 2004.

Walton, John K. *The English Seaside Resort: A Social History, 1750–1914.* Leicester, U.K.: Leicester University Press, 1983.

Keith Stavely and Kathleen Fitzgerald

boiled sweets

See HARD CANDY.

bombe

See DESSERTS, CHILLED.

bonbons,

bonbons, or bon-bons, are small candies. The name is French, a duplication of the word *bon,* meaning "good." Spanish uses *bombon* and Portuguese, *bombom.*

The term "bonbon" originated at the French royal court in the seventeenth century. The earliest bonbons may have been seventeenth-century Jordan (sugar-coated) almonds and small candies based on fruits. By the eighteenth century, the use of the term "bonbon" had spread to other European countries. *Bonbonnières* or *drageoirs,* ornate boxes or dishes for serving the morsels made of porcelain, glass, or metal, began to appear in Europe by mid-century. See SERVING PIECES. At first they came in pairs. In France, a particularly popular *bonbonnière* was in the form of a pair of fancy shoes. Bonbons would be presented as gifts in such containers on holidays and at festivals, particularly on New Year's Day.

By the nineteenth century, bonbons that could be contained in individual wrappers were being marketed. In 1827 the London confectioner William Jarrin wrote of bonbons, "The various envelopes in which they are put up, display the ingenuity of this gay and versatile people: fables, historical subjects, songs, enigmas, jeux des mots, and various little gallantries, are all inscribed upon the papers in which the bon-bons are enclosed, and which the gentlemen present to females of their acquaintance." See JARRIN, WILLIAM ALEXIS. In 1866 Johann Strauss II composed the waltz *Wiener Bonbons* for an event to raise money to construct German hospitals in Paris. On the title page, the composition's name was spelled out in twisted bonbon wrappers.

Today in France, bonbons generally are based on fruits and fruit essences including candied fruits, nuts including brittles and nougats, boiled sugar sweets such as dragées and caramels, and chocolate-based morsels. The nineteenth-century invention of solid chocolate that could be melted and used to coat sweets before drying to form a hard shell promoted the proliferation of chocolate truffles with chocolate ganache centers and other small, chocolate-covered bonbons. In Belgium, ubiquitous chocolate bonbons with soft fondant or ganache centers are known as pralines. See BELGIUM and FONDANT.

In the United States, Bon Bon is the Hershey Company's trademarked name for a frozen sweet consisting of a dome of vanilla ice cream with a hard chocolate coating. They are sold in elongated rectangular boxes in movie theaters, and they also come in buckets elsewhere. However, in the United States as elsewhere throughout the Western world, "bonbon" continues to refer to small candies, which at their best can be produced in small lots by artisan confectioners. Some feature regional ingredients and flavors and iconic shapes and appearances, such as the whole candied fruits of Provence and Louisiana pralines. See CANDIED FRUIT. The bite-sized morsels also present opportunities for confectioners' most creative flights of imagination, offering a never-ending range of flavors, ingredients, shapes, and decorations.

See also BRITTLE; CARAMELS; CHOCOLATES, BOXED; NOUGAT; and PRALINE.

Hopkins, Kate. *Sweet Tooth: The Bittersweet History of Candy*. New York: St. Martin's, 2012.
Mason, Laura. "Bonbon." In *The Oxford Companion to Food*, 2d ed., edited by Alan Davidson, pp. 93–94. Oxford: Oxford University Press, 2014.

Miriam Kasin Hospodar

Boston cream pie

Boston cream pie is a two-layer sponge cake filled with a rich pastry cream and topped with a chocolate glaze. This icon of American cookery was proclaimed the official Massachusetts State Dessert on 12 December 1996. Boston's Parker House (today's Omni Parker House hotel) claims to be the birthplace of Boston cream pie, but what the hotel restaurant serves is a completely different creation.

When the Parker House opened in 1856, an Armenian French chef by the name of Sanzian is said to have created a dessert called Parker House Chocolate Cream Pie, a two-layer butter sponge cake brushed with rum syrup and filled with a classic crème patissière. More crème patissière was spread on the sides of the cake, which were then coated with toasted sliced almonds. The cake's top was decorated with a layer of chocolate fondant and squiggles of white fondant. The recipe is classically French.

The Boston cream pie that Massachusetts celebrates is a far less complicated dessert, one that likely descends from the simple Washington pie, a two-layer yellow cake filled with jam and dusted with confectioner's sugar. Over time, the jam was replaced with pastry cream, and a chocolate glaze replaced the confectioner's sugar, giving us today's Boston cream pie.

These "pies" are actually cakes. The terminology is confusing because many cakes in the nineteenth century were baked in shallow, straight-sided pans called Washington pie plates or jelly-cake tins. Pie tins and cake tins were the same thing. See PANS. Furthermore, the cakes themselves were referred to as "crusts," since that word was used for both cake layers and pie crusts.

Washington pies existed long before Harvey Parker built his famous hotel in 1856. What we call a Boston cream pie today was possibly an attempt to Americanize a glorious French cake by morphing the humble Washington pie into it. The name "Boston cream pie" appeared in print for the first time in the *Granite Iron Ware Cookbook,* an 1878 piece of ephemera. The pie is essentially a Washington pie with a custard filling and an unadorned top layer. *The Kansas Home Cook* (1879) contained a recipe for Chocolate Cake, a four-layer yellow cake filled with vanilla custard and frosted on the top and sides with chocolate icing. In essence, this was a double Boston cream pie. *Miss Parloa's Kitchen Companion* (1887), published in 1887, offered a recipe called Chocolate Cream Pie, essentially a Boston cream pie as we know it but with a thin layer of the chocolate glaze also spread over the custard.

These findings suggest that two origins exist for Boston cream pie. The first can be traced back to Washington pie. Over time, as stoves became more reliable and cooks gained more confidence, a vanilla custard became the preferred filling, replacing jam. As chocolate became more affordable, home cooks began using it in cakes and in glazes, and some inventive home cook decided to gild her Washington pie with it.

The second origin lies in the Parker House Chocolate Cream Pie, a complicated creation best left to professional pastry chefs. It is a magnificent cake, French to the core, and not American like the Washington pie.

Patent, Greg. "Origins: Boston Cream Pie." *Gastronomica: The Journal of Food and Culture* 1, no. 4 (2001): 82–87.

Greg Patent

The **Boston Molasses Disaster** occurred in 1919 when a molasses storage tank located in a congested city neighborhood ruptured. A flood of viscous molasses estimated to be 20 feet high and

The Boston Molasses Disaster of 1919 occurred when a 50-foot-tall steel tank burst, sending a flood of molasses 20 feet high and nearly 200 feet wide into Boston's North End neighborhood. This photograph captures the resulting devastation, in which 21 people died and many more were injured. PHOTOGRAPH COURTESY OF BILL NOONAN

160 feet wide tore through the streets at nearly 35 miles an hour. The disaster took the lives of 21 men, women, and children; injured 150; and demolished everything in its path.

Long after the triangle trade of molasses, rum, and slaves had ended, molasses continued to be an important commodity in Massachusetts. In addition to sweetening gingerbread, baked beans, and cookies, it was used to make industrial alcohol for munitions manufacture during World War I. After the war, molasses was sought for rum production in anticipation of strong pre-Prohibition sales.

In 1915 the United States Industrial Alcohol Company (USIA) built a 50-foot-high steel molasses storage tank with a capacity of 2.3 million gallons at the edge of Boston's inner harbor. The location, known as the North End, was convenient to the ships that brought molasses from the Caribbean and the railroad that transported it to distilleries. The North End was also a bustling Italian immigrant neighborhood, but on 15 January 1919 at midday, it was devastated.

USIA blamed anarchists' bombs. However, legal proceedings that spanned several years proved that the tank was built hastily, poorly constructed, and never tested. In fact, the tank had leaked so much that local children routinely collected the molasses that spilled from its sides. In 1925 the USIA was declared culpable.

Today, children play tranquilly where the tank once stood, and an inconspicuous plaque commemorates the tragedy.

See also MOLASSES.

Puleo, Stephen. *Dark Tide: The Great Boston Molasses Flood of 1919*. Boston: Beacon, 2003.

Jeri Quinzio

Brazil has a tradition of eating sweets that arrived with the Portuguese. Indigenous Brazilians had used honey from native bees to flavor raw hearts of palm or smoked fish, and they consumed abundant amounts of fruit. But "dessert" as it is known today developed only after the Portuguese colonized Brazil, bringing a taste for sweet—in fact, *very* sweet. The Portuguese had developed the practice of using sugarcane when North African Muslims occupied the Iberian Peninsula in the eighth century. Before contact with Arabic culture, the Portuguese, too, had sweetened their food with honey.

Sugar

The first sugar plantations were planted in Brazil in the second half of the sixteenth century. The Portuguese brought sugarcane from the island of Madeira, and the plant adapted easily to the climate and soil of Brazil. Before long, the new colony had become a major producer of sugar and was exporting it via Portugal's extensive trade routes.

Sugar production, built on the backs of African slave labor, generated great wealth for plantation owners in Brazil. The sugar mills provided an abundance of raw material for Brazil's national sweets, many of which stem from the Portuguese tradition. They included sweets made with molasses and brown sugar (*rapadura* in Portuguese), which was also eaten alongside many foods, particularly *farinha de mandioca* (cassava flour), a tradition that continues to this day.

Among the native population, molasses quickly came to replace wild honey and was used to sweeten tubers and tuberous roots like yam, cassava, and sweet potato, all of which are served in indigenous communities not as dessert, but as breakfast or afternoon snacks.

A Mix of Influences

The amalgam of cultures that came together in Brazil adapted Old World culinary techniques to the myriad Brazilian fruits that previously had only been eaten fresh, in season. With European techniques of preservation, fruits could be dried, candied, preserved into jam, or turned into pastes and bars. Guava, which grows abundantly in Brazil, is a prime example. Fragrant and delicious, it easily took the place of quince in traditional Portuguese *membrillo*. The guava paste *goiabada* was wrapped in banana leaves and packed in cans and wooden boxes. Today, *goiabada* is often eaten with cheese much as the Spanish eat *membrillo*. This combination, dubbed "Romeo and Juliet," is considered Brazil's national dessert.

In addition to fruit desserts, Portuguese cooks found ways to use other abundant indigenous ingredients, such as cashew nuts, cassava, maize, and peanuts. These foods were incorporated into preparations with milk, eggs, and sugar by means of primarily European techniques, but mostly cooked by

Africans. African customs also filtered down through the kitchens of Brazil, and culinary traditions from Senegal, Benin, Angola, and Mozambique can be discerned in the local desserts today. Once the coconut—Asian by origin, but easily adapted to Brazil's climate and diet—was introduced (the earliest accounts date to the sixteenth century), the repertoire of Brazil's popular desserts expanded greatly. *Cocada* is a dense sweet made of grated coconut and cane sugar that is served both crystallized and as a sweet paste; *manjar* is a delicate and often molded pudding made of milk, sugar, and grated coconut, thickened with a bit of cornstarch and served with a sauce of prunes in caramel; *quebra-queixo* (literally, "jigsaw chin") is a chewy, syrupy street sweet made of coconut, sugar, ginger, and lime; *queijadinha* is a tart made with a thin pastry crust and filled with coconut egg custard; and the ever-popular *quindim* made with egg yolks, sugar, and eggs and often molded into a ring is a favorite party dessert.

The spices brought by the Portuguese also played an important role in the development of Brazilian sweets. Cinnamon was sprinkled on rice pudding, on sweet potatoes, and over *canjica*, a pudding of white maize (or hominy) and roasted banana. Whole cloves were used to flavor sweet pumpkin and grated green papaya, and anise was mixed into the batter of sweet corn cakes.

Finally, although Brazil had indigenous varieties of cacao in the Amazon region, use of the bean as a cultural practice did not take hold until the Portuguese, who had developed a taste for sweetened chocolate, introduced chocolate as a dessert in the seventeenth century. See COCOA.

Sweets in Regional Cultures

In the seventeenth century, the custom of selling cakes, sweets, and biscuits on the streets emerged in Brazil's northeastern and midwestern regions, the hubs of the colonial agricultural empire. A set of goodies was often laid out in trays and dubbed *quitanda*, or grocery—a name that is still used to designate this manner of selling candy and sweet snacks today in these parts of the country.

In the northeast of Brazil, coconut and sugar are commonly combined to make coconut sweets of various kinds: creamed coconut, coconut ribbon, white coconut, burnt coconut, or coconut mixed with cassava or cassava meal for making cakes, puddings, porridges, and *beijus* (crepe-like wafers) of tapioca (a derivative of cassava). See TAPIOCA. In the midwest, most sweets are made from fruit, which is also candied and made into jams and preserves. Corn, milk, eggs, and fresh cheese also find their way into desserts there. In the south, with its colder climate, wheat-based sweets introduced from Italy and Germany dominate, including apple tarts, grape cakes, and fried or baked cookies.

Sweets, especially those made from corn and peanuts, play an important role in the June festivals celebrated throughout Brazil. The most common ones include *curau* (corn porridge with milk, sugar, and cinnamon), *canjica* (for which white corn is slow-cooked with milk, sugar, cloves, and cinnamon after its germ has been removed), and various children's sweets.

Sweets in Contemporary Brazil

In the late nineteenth century the introduction of sweetened condensed milk began to influence various recipes, particularly puddings. In the twentieth century this type of milk became wildly popular as an ingredient for party sweets, including bonbons like *brigadeiros* (balls of condensed milk and chocolate with chocolate sprinkles), *cajuzinho* (made from cashews or peanuts and condensed milk), *beijinho* (condensed milk and coconut), and *olho de sogra* (prunes stuffed with a sweet coconut and condensed milk mixture).

More recently, as Brazil has globalized and become home to diverse groups of immigrants, desserts from European and American traditions have been introduced into the national repertoire, including mousses, ice creams, puddings, pies, and custards.

Cascudo, Luis da Câmara. *Historia da alimentação no Brasil.* 3d ed. São Paulo, Brazil: Global Editora e Distribuidora, 2007.

Rigo, Neide. "Come-Se." http://come-se.blogspot.com.

Zappi, Lucrecia. *Mil-folhas: História ilustrada do doce.* São Paulo, Brazil: Cosca Naify, 2011.

Sara B. Franklin and Neide Rigo

breads, sweet, belong to one of three major categories within the greater bread kingdom, the other two being lean bread (little or no fat and sugar, as in French bread) and enriched breads (moderate amounts of sugars and fats, each typically less than 10 percent of the flour weight, as in sandwich breads, challah, soft rolls, and the like). Sweet breads are also known as rich breads, meaning that the ratio of sugar to total flour weight is anywhere from 1:10 to 1:4, and the ratio of butter or other fats to total flour weight is from 1:10 to 9:10. For this reason this category is referred to more properly as "sweet rich breads."

Historically, sweet rich breads have tended to exist primarily for the elite, who could afford large amounts of butter, eggs, milk, and sugar or honey. Many of these ingredients were scarce but still available to earlier civilizations, such as the ancient Romans, who were known to make a honey-sweetened bread, which was very similar to modern-day sweet rich breads, primarily for the wealthy class. See ANCIENT WORLD. Whether ancient or modern, sweet rich breads have often served as social and political signifiers, and they have sometimes even been referred to as "royal bread," exemplified by products such as brioche and its buttery European cousins like pan d'oro (literally, "golden bread") or crown- or turban-shaped gugelhupfs. See GUGELHUPF.

However, sweet rich breads also became important, and even essential, for the less affluent masses, especially during various religious, commemorative, or celebratory events. For this reason, the category of sweet rich breads is best understood through both a cultural and a religious lens.

Brioche

Brioche is noted more for its butteriness than its sweetness, containing a ratio of anywhere from 1:4 to 9:10 parts butter to flour with most versions around 1:2. It is often included in the Viennoiserie family of doughs because of its use in many applications, including loaf bread, pastry crust, and morning pastries. See LAMINATED DOUGHS. But its best-known version is as a small roll, baked in a flared and fluted pan, with a small topknot, known as brioche à tête ("with a head"). Between the fifteenth and eighteenth centuries, brioche gradually evolved from an everyday loaf containing only small amounts of enrichments to a highly buttered dough. It found its richest expressions during the reign of King Louis XIV and onward, when it was considered as much a cake as a bread. The process of perfecting this rich dough, through the skills of bakers from Vienna and Italy, and later from Paris, has established brioche as the benchmark against which many international sweet rich breads are compared.

Celebration Breads

It is a truism that every major world religion regards bread as a theological or cosmological symbol as well as an essential food. In many culturally specific breads, the ingredients and methodology are similar, sometimes nearly identical, to breads from other regions, and the differences may be as simple as a twist, a chosen braid, a garnish, or a particular spice, fruit, or nut. Unlike "everyday" breads, consumed primarily as a foodstuff and less for commemorative or symbolic meaning, celebration breads fulfill synchronous cultural functions regardless of their geographical context. Such breads are often used as vehicles through which stories are told and knowledge is passed from generation to generation via rituals, music, and festivities. The ample use of eggs, for example, is both symbolic and practical, as many of these breads are made after long fasting periods in which eggs, universal symbols of life and birth, are collected but not used until the actual day of festivity, when the fast is finally broken.

Celebration breads reveal both the functionality and cultural import of the sweet rich bread category. For example, Italian panettone, while clearly rooted in the Milanese region of Italy, and often baked in a tall, round, turban-like form, is not all that different from the Veronese pan d'oro that is baked in a tall, star-shaped pan. Each is made with ample quantities of butter, eggs, sugar, and various dried fruits. Both breads were originally associated with Christmas but are now available year round, and each has a similar formulation to brioche, Dresden stollen, and nearly every other sweet, rich celebration bread. See STOLLEN. Whether baked in the shape of a star, a turban, or a folded blanket, and regardless of which nuts and spices are used or which fruit colors are chosen (usually red ones, such as cherries, for Christmas), the symbolism is embedded in each bread and not only allows for pleasant eating but also affords an opportunity for local celebratory customs. While not an exhaustive list, other international celebration breads include:

- *Barmbrack* ("speckled yeast bread") is of Irish origin and is associated with both St. Bridgid's Day and also with All Hallow's Eve (a.k.a. Halloween). The "speckles" refer to raisins.
- *Bo lo bao* ("pineapple bread") is a Cantonese and Hong Kong sweet bread with surface designs

that resemble a pineapple; it is used to commemorate many occasions.

- *Colomba di Pasqua*, a Milanese Easter loaf shaped to resemble a dove, is now made in many countries.
- Hot cross buns, of English origin, are most closely associated with the celebration of Good Friday. They are, essentially, sweet spice rolls with a commemorative cross made of dough or icing on top.
- *Julekake* and *julekage* are two variations of Scandinavian Christmas breads, made with nuts, candied fruits, and cardamom, and often braided into a wreath.
- *Kulich* is a Russian Easter bread, usually baked in a can or tall mold, with the Cyrillic letters XB, signifying "Christ is Risen," piped onto the side or added decoratively with candied fruits or nuts.
- *Lussekatter*, originating in Sweden, celebrate Santa Lucia Day. They are baked in the shape of either crowns or rolls called "cats"—coiled dough with a raisin dotting the center to symbolize the blinding of the martyr St. Lucy by her Roman captors.
- Moroccan holiday bread, made with cornmeal, pumpkin, and sesame seeds, is used in various celebrations.
- *Pääsiäisleipä* is a Finnish Easter bread, traditionally baked in large milking pails and filled with yellow raisins, almonds, cardamom, and citrus peel.
- Sugar plum bread is an English Christmas loaf filled with large quantities of dried and candied fruits and peels, and spiced with nutmeg.
- Scottish black bun is a traditional New Year's bread, densely packed with dried and candied fruits that have been soaked in Scotch whisky. It is not unlike an American Christmas fruit cake.

Tsoureki (or *choureki*) is the general name for Greek holiday breads, with specific versions designated for particular celebrations: *Christopsomo*, a round Christmas loaf with a cross made from the same dough embossed on top; *lampropsomo*, a braided Paschal (Easter) loaf with dyed eggs tucked into the braids; and *Vasilopita*, a large, round loaf baked with a good-luck coin hidden inside, baked to commemorate St. Basil's Day, which is also the New Year's Day celebration.

Vánočka is a similar Czech braided bread, enriched with raisins and almonds. There is a round Easter variation called *mazanec*.

Other Sweet Rich Breads

Babka has its origins in Eastern Europe, especially Poland, Bulgaria, Macedonia, and Albania, where it is often baked in cylindrical, fluted pans. In Romanian tradition, babka serves as a Christmas and general holiday bread, but in the United States and Europe it is mainly associated with Eastern European Jewish communities, where the dough is typically spread with chocolate or poppy-seed fillings and then coiled into a loaf. In more contemporary versions, babkas are often made much like a baking-powder-leavened Bundt cake.

Cinnamon buns are associated with Germany, where they were known as *Schnecken*, or "snails," for their coiled shape. Although recipes for these buns can be found in early German cookbooks from the 1500s, they may originally have been introduced from Byzantium. The buns soon spread to many places, including Scandinavia, where various forms of kanelbullar are typically served with coffee. In the early eighteenth century, many Germans moved to Pennsylvania, bringing with them their sweet pastries and other food traditions. See PENNSYLVANIA DUTCH and PHILADELPHIA. Cinnamon buns eventually spread to other parts of the United States, where they took on regional variations, such as pecan rolls and honey buns. Philadelphia sticky buns, for which coiled rolls filled with cinnamon sugar are baked on a glaze of sugar or honey that transforms into a gooey, caramelized topping when the rolls are inverted after baking, derive from English Chelsea buns.

Pan dulce is a large subcategory of Mexican and Latin American sweet breads whose origins lie in both Spanish and French influences over the past 500 years. These breads are made into unique shapes and embellished with designs and colorful glazes. Three of the most well-known types include *conchas* (shells), *campechanas*, and *cuernos* (horns); there are also religious breads such as *pan de muerto* (bread of the dead) and *roscón de reyes* (king's cake).

Portuguese sweet bread, also known as Hawaiian bread, is a good example of a sweet holiday bread that became so popular in New England and Hawaii—thanks to the large population of Portuguese immigrants—that it is now consumed as an everyday bread.

Quick breads are leavened without yeast fermentation, either by chemical leavening (such as baking powder and baking soda) or physical leavening (by air and steam). Many popular sweet breads fall into this large subcategory, including banana bread, zucchini bread, and gingerbread. Steamed Boston brown bread, Irish soda bread, breakfast muffins, biscuits, and scones are other types of quick breads. See CHEMICAL LEAVENERS and MUFFINS.

Clayton, Bernard, Jr. *Bernard Clayton's New Complete Book of Breads*. Rev. ed. New York: Simon & Schuster, 2003.

Ingram, Christine, and Jennie Shapter. *The World Encyclopedia of Bread and Bread Making*. New York: Lorenz, 1999.

Jones, Judith, and Evan Jones. *The Book of Bread*. New York: Harper & Row, 1982.

Oppenneer, Betsy. *Celebration Breads*. New York: Simon & Schuster, 2003.

Rubel, William. *Bread: A Global History*. London: Reaktion, 2011.

Peter Reinhart

breakfast cereal is an American food whose dramatic evolution in form and function has rendered it nearly unrecognizable as the same product that took hold of the American imagination in the early 1900s.

The origins of breakfast cereal can be traced back to the mid-nineteenth century when religious leaders such as Sylvester Graham (1794–1851), father of the graham cracker, began advocating for dietary reforms. Advances in farming and milling technology allowed for the industrialization of food production, which in turn provoked a reaction against processed foods such as white bread and mass-produced meat. What began as a fringe belief gained currency as some Americans grew increasingly tired of their predominantly meat-and-simple-starch diets. Breakfast, before the advent of breakfast cereal, consisted of griddlecakes, beefsteak, potatoes, buckwheat breads, eggs, sausages, and porridges—a diet many considered to cause nationwide dyspepsia.

Capitalizing on the desire for a curative lifestyle, doctors and enterprising businessmen opened sanitariums across the country. In Battle Creek, Michigan, Dr. John Harvey Kellogg (1852–1943) fed patients dry, crumbled bricks of toasted cereal grains, which became popular enough with sanitarium guests that Kellogg began to market them. Soon Charles Williams Post (1854–1914), a former patient at Battle Creek, introduced his own version of cereal: "Brains are Built on Grape Nuts" read the 1898 slogan. By 1899 Kellogg's was a multimillion-dollar business, with Post providing the biggest competition.

Scientists joined the stampede toward toasted grains, looking to make the starch molecule more readily digestible. In 1901 a young American biochemist named Alexander P. Anderson successfully puffed rice in a test tube. Once he realized that any vessel could puff grains given enough heat and pressure, he began adapting cannons for the large-scale manufacture of puffed wheat and rice. The Quaker Oats Company quickly brought Anderson and his puffing technique into their business. At the 1904 World's Fair in St. Louis, Missouri, Quaker Oats featured eight bronze cannons that explosively puffed grains using Anderson's technique. Despite the cereal's spectacular debut, sales lagged until Claude Hopkins, a renowned adman, energized sales with the slogan "The Food Shot from Guns."

Advertising proved necessary for cereal sales and was central in shaping the identity of this new breakfast food. Consumers needed to be convinced that cereal was a requisite staple in a nutritious diet; thus, early cereal companies advertised medical testimonies and nutritional facts to boost sales. As advertising media changed, the target audience of cereal advertising shifted from mothers to children. When the nutritional value of cereal failed to appeal to a young consumer base, the health benefits of cereal were dropped in favor of flashier marketing techniques. In 1926 the first singing commercial for Wheaties aired on the radio, and by the late 1950s cereal companies were sponsoring television cartoon shows. General Mills created personalities such as Trix the Rabbit and the Lucky Charms Leprechaun, while Kellogg's featured the Rice Krispies trio—Snap, Crackle, and Pop—as well as Tony the Tiger for Frosted Flakes.

When breakfast cereal and the technology of its production evolved to fit the changing advertising environment, the cereal underwent a simultaneous transformation in taste. Brands cast off the image of cereal as "found in nature" and began to feature products that were artificially sweetened. In 1939 the first presweetened breakfast cereal was introduced to the market: Range Joe Popped Wheat Honnies. Presweetened cereal quickly established itself as the dominant form of breakfast cereal in the United States.

Sugar content in cereals continued to increase for the next several decades. Post's Sugar Crisp and Kellogg's Sugar Smacks, which lead the contemporary cereal market in sugar content (51 percent and 55 percent sugar weight, respectively), arrived on the market within four years of each other in the early 1950s. As sugar content levels increased, the counterculture movement of the late 1960s began advocating for a return to whole grains. Manufacturers, sensing the shift in public opinion, toned down their products by tweaking the cereal names. In the 1980s Sugar Smacks became Honey Smacks, and Sugar Crisp became Golden Crisp. When preferences for natural and organic foods became mainstream, big cereal companies diversified by creating product lines geared toward the health-conscious consumer. Products such as Cascadian Farms and Great Grains emphasized high fiber and protein content but suffered for their high sugar levels. Meanwhile, sugary cereal brands worked to decrease sugar and sodium content in order to appeal to an increasingly health-minded demographic. In 2005 General Mills announced that all of its "Big G" cereals would be made with whole grains. However, as cereal brands adjusted the nutritional content of their products, they also struggled with providing the taste their customers have grown accustomed to. Cheerios became free of genetically modified organisms in 2014, yet despite the publicity surrounding the announcement, sales remained unchanged. The same year, Post launched a GMO-free version of Grape-Nuts without the cereal's much-vaunted vitamin benefits. Breakfast cereal will always

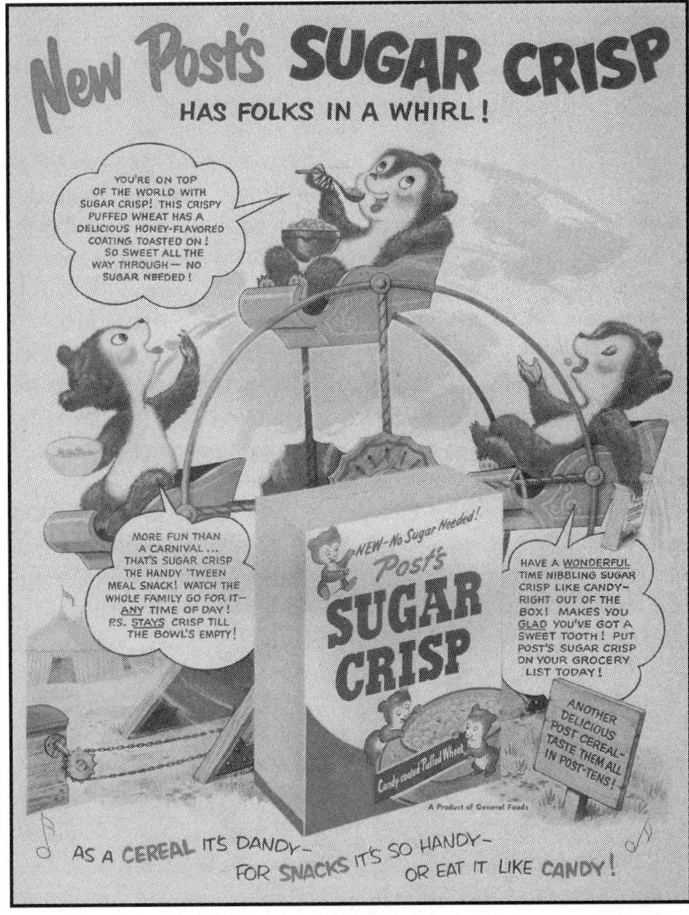

The first presweetened breakfast cereal dates to 1939. Packaged to appeal to children, artificially sweetened cereals soon dominated the U.S. market. In the early 1950s, General Foods introduced Post's Sugar Crisp, with an astonishing sugar content of 51 percent. This advertisement appeared in the 3 September 1951, issue of *LIFE* magazine. GALLERY OF GRAPHIC DESIGN adapt to both technological advances and trends in taste, and because of its elasticity, this century-old American invention has grown to become an industry worth $10 billion in annual revenue.

Ashraf, Hea-Ran L. "Diets, Fad." In *The Oxford Companion to American Food and Drink*, edited by Andrew F. Smith, pp. 189–190. New York: Oxford University Press, 2007.

Krondl, Michael. "Advertising." In *The Oxford Companion to American Food and Drink*, edited by Andrew F. Smith, pp. 2–7. New York: Oxford University Press, 2007.

Lovegren, Sylvia. "The Pure Food Act of 1906." In *The Oxford Companion to American Food and Drink*, edited by Andrew F. Smith, pp. 484–485. New York: Oxford University Press, 2007.

Thomas, Robin G., Pamela R. Pehrsson, Jaspreet K. C. Ahuga, Erin Smieja, and Kevin B. Miller. "Recent Trends in Ready-to-Eat Breakfast Cereals in the U.S." *Procedia Food Science* 2 (2013): 20–26.

Visser, Margaret. *Much Depends on Dinner: The Extraordinary History and Mythology, Allure and Obsessions, Perils and Taboos, of an Ordinary Meal.* Toronto: McClelland and Stewarts, 1986.

Hannah Smith-Drelich

brittle is an English term for sugar, and sometimes other ingredients, boiled to the light caramel stage 345.6°F (160°C) and poured over nuts or seeds. The delicious mass is smoothed into a sheet and allowed to set before being broken or cut into pieces. Alternately, it is dropped in small lumps while still warm.

Any nut or seed can be used. Peanuts are a favorite in the United States, almonds or sesame around the Mediterranean, and pistachios in the Middle East. Chinese versions include a sesame brittle flavored with salt and pepper. As with the nuts and seeds, sugar types also vary. They include molasses (especially popular in South America) and jaggery (on the Indian subcontinent); honey is also frequently added to Middle Eastern and Mediterranean brittles.

The French term *croquant* and Italian *croccante* are quite widely used to refer to confections similar to brittle that are eaten as candy or used for decoration. Greek *pasteli*, Sicilian *cubbaita*, and *chikki* from Pakistan and India can also be classified as brittles. *Sohan asali* is a saffron-flavored mixture of sugar, honey, butter, and almonds from Iran that is formed into small pieces and sprinkled with chopped pistachios. In *Noshe Djan: Afghan Food and Cookery* (2012), Helen Saberi remarks that *khasta-e-shireen*, large "plates" of caramelized nuts or apricot kernels, are associated with festivities such as New Year and Eid al-Fitr and have been a common sight in the bazaars for as long as anyone can remember.

Brittle-type candies were almost certainly honey-based to begin with. They are so widespread, and the ingredients so widely available—especially in southwest Asia and the Mediterranean—that the confection must be an ancient one. In the English-speaking world, their history is obscure, although almond brittle was apparently known as almond hardbake in nineteenth-century London.

Caramel and almonds, ground to a powder and used for flavoring other confections, are known to the French as praline. Brittle-type confections are closely related to nougat, torrone, and Spanish turrón. See NOUGAT.

Leon, Simon I. *An Encyclopedia of Candy Making.* New York: Chemical Publishing, 1959.

Laura Mason

Brix (or °Brix or °Bx) is a measurement of dissolved solids in an aqueous solution. Each degree of Brix corresponds to 1 gram of dissolved solids in 100 grams of solution. Brix is usually measured via hydrometry or refractometry. Measuring devices are calibrated using a sucrose standard. Temperature influences both types of measurement and must be taken into account if the tools used are not self-correcting.

The Brix scale was developed by Adolf Brix in the mid-1800s. The scale is essentially a recalibration of a similar scale developed by Karl Balling in 1843. Brix recalibrated the scale from a reference of 63.5° to 59.0°F (17.5° to 15.5°C). Today, most Brix tables are calibrated to 68°F (20°C).

Although newer methods of measuring Brix have been developed, such as infrared spectroscopy, the hydrometer and refractometer remain the principal Brix-measuring tools. Hydrometry determines Brix by directly measuring the density of a liquid. The hydrometer is allowed to float in the liquid; the depth at which it floats indicates the density and thus the Brix of the liquid, assuming the solution is sucrose in water. Because ethanol is less dense than water, the final Brix reading of a wine with no residual sugar will be less than zero. The measured Brix of a fermenting or fermented liquid will not accurately represent the sugar content of that liquid, but it is nevertheless a useful tool for monitoring the progress of a fermentation.

Refractometers measure the refractive index of a liquid. Brix refractometers are calibrated based on the known refractive index of sucrose–water solutions of various strengths. Since alcohol has a higher refractive index than water, its presence in solution makes refractometry unreliable. Brix is used in wine production to assess the ripeness of grapes, predict the potential ethanol content of the wine, and to monitor the fermentation. Brix is also measured to determine the water content of honey; the sugar content of maple syrup; and the optimal time to pick sugarcane, tomatoes, and some fruits. In addition, it is used as a quality-control measure for products such as ketchup, soft drinks, and fruit juices. Brix can also be utilized to measure sugar content in urine, especially in monitoring or testing for diabetes.

It is rarely the case that the measured liquid is a sucrose in water solution, so the measured Brix is only an approximation of the actual sugar content of the liquid. Nevertheless, the measurement is useful for comparison and is often sufficiently close to the actual percent-by-weight of sugar to make the measurement acceptable.

Refractometry and hydrometry are relatively simple and inexpensive techniques for measuring Brix. As a fermentation nears completion, however, these tools are of little use. The light- and/or density-altering effects of alcohol, and the differences between a pure sucrose–water solution and a wine containing fructose, glucose, dissolved acids and other dissolved solids, and ethanol, are too great to overcome. More advanced and expensive techniques such as enzymatic analysis with UV spectroscopy, or infrared spectroscopy, give the wine producer a better understanding of the amount of unfermented, residual sugar in the wine.

See also FERMENTATION; HONEY; MAPLE SYRUP; SACCHARIMETER; SUGAR AND HEALTH; SUGARCANE; and SWEET WINE.

Ashurst, P. R., ed. *Chemistry and Technology of Soft Drinks and Fruit Juices.* 2d ed. Oxford: Blackwell, 2005.

Boulton, R. B., V. L. Singleton, L. F. Bisson, and R. E. Kunkee. *Principles and Practices of Winemaking.* New York: Chapman & Hall, 1998.

Matt Reid

brownies, small squares of rich chocolate cake, originally contained no chocolate. Molasses-based recipes for individual cakes called brownies appeared in both *The Boston Cooking School Cook Book* (1896) and *The Sears, Roebuck Catalogue* (1897). In 1893 the Palmer House Hotel in Chicago featured a chocolate bar cookie with apricot glaze for the Columbian Exposition, and it is this cookie that the Palmer House claims was the first chocolate brownie. This brownie was envisioned as a smaller, lighter dessert to appeal to women; it is still served at the Palmer House today. Little evidence exists for the folklore that brownies were a culinary accident, resulting from missing baking powder in a fudge cake recipe. The origin of the cake's name is similarly uncertain, though the color of the bars may account for it, or they may have been named after a popular 1887 children's book about elves (aka brownies).

In 1904 and 1905 versions of the recipe using chocolate appeared in a number of community cookbooks in both the Midwest and New England, including a recipe for Bangor Brownies in cookbooks published in New Hampshire, Boston, and Chicago. Between 1904 and 1910, the amount of chocolate called for in recipes increased although molasses-flavored recipes called "brownies" still appeared as late as 1926. Blondies—vanilla or butterscotch brownies—made their debut in the 1950s, sometimes frosted with chocolate or studded with chocolate chips. British tray bakes (when chocolate) bear a distant resemblance to brownies, as do the no-bake Canadian Nanaimo bars. In the United States, 8 December is National Brownie Day.

See also BAR COOKIES; MOLASSES; NANAIMO BAR; and SMALL CAKES.

Zanger, Mark H. "Brownies." In *Oxford Encyclopedia of Food and Drink in America*, 2d ed., edited by Andrew F. Smith, pp. 220–222. New York: Oxford University Press, 2013.

Judith Hausman

bubble gum

See CHEWING GUM.

bubble tea is a popular cassava-based beverage believed to have been created, or at least touted, in the early 1980s by Taiwanese entrepreneurs Liu Han Chieh, Tu Tsong-He, and/or Lin Hsui Hui. The tea relies on the starch of *Manihot esculenta*, which had been introduced to Taiwan from Java and the Philippines. See CASSAVA. To make bubble tea, this tuber is cut, dried, ground, and mixed with similarly prepared sweet potato and brown sugar and shaped into balls that resemble tapioca but are larger. See TAPIOCA. The balls are boiled for about an hour, after which they turn black, gelatinous, and somewhat translucent; they are then cooled in water. They can also be made in various other colors by means of certain proprietary processes.

Modern bubble tea recalls an earlier Taiwanese beverage that included brewed black tea, condensed milk, and ice. When the innovators added cassava balls to the tea mixture along with any number of sweet, flavored syrups and, on occasion, honey, sugar, and fruit pulp, the resulting beverage was dubbed "bubble tea"—called *boba* in Taiwan and by Taiwanese expats in the United States. It has also been called McBubble Beverage, pearl tea, and tapioca tea; in Chinese, the drink's full name is *zhen shou nai chai* (pearl boba tea).

Bubble tea is served in dome-topped or flat-topped clear plastic containers so that the bubbles are clearly visible. Because they are heavy, the bubbles sink to the bottom of the container. The bubbles and their liquid are imbibed through a wide, often brightly colored plastic straw. Bubble tea can be served plain or as a carbonated beverage, with or without tea. The most popular flavors are lychee, peach, pear, papaya, lemon coke, and a half-tea half-coffee mixture called *yuan yang*. Most people enjoy bubble tea with sweet or savory snacks and drink it in places similar to coffeehouses. Adored by the young and the young at heart, bubble tea is an inexpensive, versatile, and nonalcoholic drink.

Martin, Laura C. *Tea: The Drink That Changed the World.* Rutland, Vt.: Tuttle, 2007.

Newman, Jacqueline M. "Bubble Tea." *Flavor and Fortune* 6, no. 4 (1999): 5–6.

Jacqueline M. Newman

bûche de Noël, a fanciful dessert of the Christmas season, translates from the French as "yule log," which it is made to resemble. A sheet of genoise or light sponge cake is spread with a filling such as buttercream and rolled up lengthwise, then spread with chocolate icing or ganache striated with the tines of a fork to imitate bark. Often the ends are cut off and put on the trunk, like stumps of a limb, with tree rings piped on the cut surface. Meringue mushrooms, spun-sugar spider webs, crushed pistachio moss, confectioner's sugar snow, red berries, and angelica leaves can contribute to the visual illusion—but best not all at once! The flavors of vanilla, coffee, chestnut, chocolate, and rum can combine in this delicious gastronomic conceit.

The actual yule log of pre-Christian northern Europe, which was brought in for the winter solstice season, burned in the open hearth during the festivities, providing warmth and light. This ritual faded, along with the pagan symbols of mistletoe, holly, and ivy, as hearths grew smaller and social patterns changed. The origins of the dessert bûche de Noël are obscure, but in the nineteenth century patisseries flourished in Paris and offered elaborate pastries made by professional chefs who earlier had worked for the aristocracy. During the last century, bûche de Noël has grown in popularity, abroad as well as in France, and is increasingly prepared by cooks at home who can indulge their fantasies to share with family and friends over the holidays.

See also ANGELICA; ICING; MERINGUE; and SPONGE CAKE.

Gershenson, Gabriella. "A Slice of Christmas." *Saveur,* 10 November 2011.

Elizabeth Gawthrop Riely

buchty, sweet buns made with an enriched yeast dough, have the most iconic resonance of any sweet food in the Czech repertoire. During the nineteenth-century period of national revival, they featured in folk songs and tales as a culinary avatar for honest rural virtue, and to some degree they still do. To make buchty, the farmwife (neither men nor city folk could possibly have the right knack) fills pockets of butter- or lard-enriched yeast dough with sweetened farmer's cheese, ground poppy seeds, or fruit (both fresh and fruit butters were once popular though now prune butter is most common). These pockets are arranged side by side on a generously buttered pan so that they rise into square or rectangular pastries. Buchty were typically eaten as a meal, perhaps preceded by a bowl of soup, or as a substantial snack. Cookbooks prior to the mid-nineteenth century sometimes give recipes for boiled buchty that are almost indistinguishable from dumplings, but this type is now almost unheard of.

In the Czech imagination, the homey pastry is often linked to Hloupý Honza ("Foolish John"), the folk personification of the good-hearted Czech peasant boy. When Honza leaves his simple home to make his fortune, it is inevitably with a satchel of buchty. During the nineteenth-century struggle by Czechs to forge an identity distinct from that of their German-speaking neighbors, Honza with his buchty transparently represented the antithesis of what was seen as an urban, aristocratic, and exploitative German-speaking ruling class. Not that this prevented the Austrians from adopting the recipe under the name of Buchteln. Today, you find the buttery pastry on both sides of the Danube, and as Ofen- or Rohrnudeln in Bavaria and the Palatinate.

See also BREADS, SWEET and SWEET MEALS.

Úlehlová-Tilschová, Marie. *Česká strava lidová*. Prague: Družstevní práce, 1945.

Michael Krondl

buckle

See FRUIT DESSERTS, BAKED.

Budapest is the capital of Hungary, a nation of sweet-lovers with one of Europe's great baking traditions. The city offers an array of sweets from *kürtőskalács* (chimney cake) sold by street vendors and *rétes* (strudel) sold from tiny shop windows, to fairy-tale creations sold at *cukrászdas* (patisseries) that have been honing their skills for generations. Sweets are omnipresent in Budapest, found at elegant cafés (perfect for lingering over espresso and cake), hectic bakeries (where tables are standing-only and to-go orders are plentiful), elegant chocolate shops, and kiosks on the street. Before cane sugar was introduced in the fourteenth century, honey was the sweetener used to produce a wide range of *mézeskalács* (honey cake). See HONEY. This fondness for honey-sweetened cakes remains, particularly at festivals and fairs when vendors sell brightly iced honey cakes in various shapes. See FAIRS. Sugar appeared on the menus of royal feasts in the fifteenth century, a time of rigid division among craftsmen. As George Lang explains in *The Cuisine of Hungary* (1971), confectionery "was the exclusive privilege of the guild of pharmacists, as was the making of spiced drinks and perfumes" (p. 12).

King Matthias I, who ruled from 1458 to 1490, and his Italian wife Beatrice loved to eat and significantly elevated the country's cuisine by bringing back chefs, pastry chefs, ingredients, and recipes from Italy. The subsequent Ottoman occupation resulted in much suffering but also some lasting culinary influences. Right after the Ottoman army was defeated in 1686 at the siege of Buda, the Habsburgs assumed power and attempted to dominate all aspects of life, including cuisine.

During the seventeenth century, the production of sweets became its own profession, no longer the exclusive domain of the pharmacists' guild, though at first they were made only in aristocratic homes. By the end of the eighteenth century, delicacies such as fruit syrups, candied fruit, preserves, marzipan, and sweet liqueurs became available to the general public. See CANDIED FRUIT; FRUIT PRESERVES; and MARZIPAN. The first pastry shop in Pest opened in 1770, and by 1805 there were four such shops in Buda and nine in Pest. In 1827 the shop that would later be known as Ruszwurm (when Vilmos Ruszwurm married into the family) opened in the Buda Castle. In the nineteenth century, regulars included members of the nobility and the royal family, including Queen Elisabeth. The Ruszwurm sweetshop still retains its Biedermeier atmosphere, although today it is sought out by tourists rather than royalty.

With the rise of industrial sugar production in the mid-1800s, the honey cake industry started to decline, and this is when the story of Budapest's sweets, as we still know them today, begins. At this time, coffeehouses were opening all over town, becoming second homes to poets, politicians, journalists, and artists who spent their days working and socializing in them. For women, pastry shops (which had previously been places to only buy sweets) played a similar role when their owners added tables, music, and elegant décor.

When the Austro-Hungarian dual monarchy was born with the 1867 Compromise, Austria and Hungary became almost equal partners, ushering in a golden age for not only sweets but also the city itself (in 1873 Pest, Buda, and Óbuda united to form Budapest). In 1868 Frigyes Stühmer, a pastry chef from Hamburg, founded Budapest's, and Hungary's, first chocolate factory. Stühmer played a major role in industrializing chocolate and candy production and is considered the founder of the Hungarian chocolate industry. His brand was known for its quality and attractive packaging, and was widely exported. By 1900 there would be 60 chocolate factories in Hungary.

In 1870 confectioner Henrik Kugler relocated his elegant pastry shop to what is today's Vörösmárty tér, where it remains the city's most opulent *cukrászda*. Kugler came from a family of confectioners. He was inspired by the time he spent training in France, and when he opened his first patisserie in 1858, he wanted to provide a Parisian experience to his customers. Even before he moved to Vörösmárty tér, in the center of Pest, Kugler and his shop had gained a reputation as one of Budapest's best. Kugler's was by far the most luxurious patisserie in Budapest; it later even added a separate salon for the royal family who were frequent guests, as was the composer Franz Liszt. Kugler was famous for his bonbons, and he introduced French mignons, or petit fours (now called mignon or *minyon* in Hungarian), which he called Kuglers. See BONBONS and SMALL CAKES. In 1875 Kugler became confectioner to the Imperial Royal Court. Having no heirs, he tapped Swiss confectioner Emil Gerbeaud to take over his business in 1884. Gerbeaud expanded the scale of the shop, bringing it to an even higher level. He opened a chocolate factory, focused on mechanization, and expanded the product line. The shop was immensely popular (and still is), and its style and quality greatly influenced Budapest's pastry scene. Gerbeaud's "biggest value was that he did not conceal his recipes," writes Miklós Niszács in *The Gerbeaud* (2008). "Consequently, the novelties introduced by him became well known throughout Hungary" (p. 12).

The year 1884 was significant. Not only did Emil Gerbeaud arrive in Hungary, but József Dobos also invented his six-layer Dobos torta. See DOBOS TORTE. This cake became a sensation, which patisseries throughout Budapest tried to imitate. By then 60 pastry shops existed in Budapest; even industrial factories opened salons with elegant shop windows. Afternoon tea and cakes had become a ritual for ladies.

World War I brought high food prices and shortages. Even opulent Gerbeaud was turned into a stable for 133 days, and similar disruptions occurred throughout the city. Some level of normalcy returned during the interwar period, but World War II and subsequent Communist rule from 1949 to 1989 devastated the country and its cuisine. Businesses were nationalized during this period, and although agriculture had long been a strength of Hungary, it was neglected, and cooperatives became the norm. Food shortages arose, and many culinary traditions, products, and recipes were lost.

Today, once again, Budapest is a city of thriving bakeries, cafés, and patisseries in styles ranging from traditional to contemporary. Pastry chefs still respect the traditional recipes, and classics such as Dobos torta, *krémes*, and *Eszterházy torta* are widely available. However, today's pastry chefs increasingly seek inspiration from beyond Hungary's borders while still building on the city's illustrious past. They are crafting sweets that are familiar yet novel. Chefs such as József Dobos and Emil Gerbeaud would surely have approved.

Éliás, Tibor, and Katalin Csapó. *Dobos and 19th Century Confectionery in Hungary*. Budapest: Hungarian Museum of Trade and Tourism, 2010.

Lang, George. *The Cuisine of Hungary*. London: Atheneum, 1971.

Niszács, Miklós. *The Gerbeaud*. Budapest: Gerbeaud Gasztronómia Kft., 2008.

Carolyn Bánfalvi

Buddhism has been practiced across most of the Asian continent for over 2,500 years, with clergy and laity in different regions embracing a range of sacred teachings, scriptural languages, liturgical calendars, and moral precepts. Given this variety, it is unsurprising that the food cultures of Buddhist institutional and lay practice should also vary widely, as these cultures naturally include the preparation, offering, and consumption of sweets.

Specific foods appear as offerings of nourishment at key junctures of influential versions of the life of the Buddha: shortly before his awakening, when he ended his ascetic trials by accepting milk gruel from a cowherd girl; and shortly before his death, when he accepted a final meal (either of pork or of mushrooms) from a metalworker. Sweet foods also appear in some biographical traditions. The first meal offered to the Buddha after his awakening, given by two merchants who became his first lay disciples, was reportedly of wheat and honey. In later Indian Buddhism, the pilgrimage center of Vaiśāli was famed as the site of a monkey's gift of honey to the Buddha, one of the "Eight Great Events" in late accounts of his life. Another sweet appears in an episode from the monastic code of the Mūlasarvāstivāda school of Buddhism. After renouncing the world and awakening, the Buddha returned to his home kingdom. There, his former consort Yaśodharā offered him an aphrodisiac sweetmeat (*vaśīkaraṇamodaka*) in an effort to entice him to return to his life as a ruler and husband. Yaśodharā sent their son Rāhula to deliver it to the Buddha, but the Buddha merely returned it to Rāhula, who ate it and became so intoxicated with his father that he decided to abandon his mother to follow the Buddha. The euphemistic translation of the name of the sweet into Chinese as "balls of joy" (*huanxituan*) may reflect discomfort with the erotic implications of the Sanskrit name, which specifically refers to the manipulation of bewitching another person.

The preparation and offering of "balls of joy" or "buns of bliss" represent one rare example of a sweet whose use is long established within Japanese Buddhist ritual practice and has clearly Indian origins. This sweet is descended from the modaka dumpling, beloved of the Hindu deity Gaṇeśa. See MODAKA. In India, the modaka is subject to some variation, but it is typically made with jaggery (unrefined sugar) and coconut, in a dumpling of rice flour. As Gaṇeśa entered the pantheon of esoteric Buddhist deities as the god of joy (in Japanese, *Kangiten*), the rituals surrounding him were also adapted and brought to China and then to Japan. The modaka seems to have been among the earliest "foreign sweets" (*kara kudamono*, aka *tōgashi*) to reach Japan, where its name appears in a dictionary dating back to the early tenth century. Today known commercially as *seijō kankidan*, these "balls of joy" are on offer from just one shop among the many selling traditional sweets (wagashi) in Kyoto: Kameya Kiyonaga, founded in 1617, whose early progenitors reputedly learned to make them from a high-ranking cleric from the nearby Buddhist temple complex on Mount Hiei.

The composition of these dumplings has varied over the centuries, but the current version is made with seven different spices: sandalwood, clove, peppermint, licorice, pepper, cinnamon from the stem of the plant, and cinnamon from the trunk of the plant. These are mixed in a base of strained sweet azuki bean paste (*an*); wrapped in a dough of rice flour, wheat, and other spices; shaped into small pouches; and then deep-fried in sesame oil. See AZUKI BEANS. The final dumpling has eight "petals" on its top, representing an eight-lobed lotus blossom. Although these "buns of bliss" are now available for sale to the public, they still play an important role in ritual offerings to the god of joy held at Japanese Buddhist temples of the Shingon or Tendai denominations. Often represented as a "hidden image" (*hibutsu*) of two figures twining in an erotic embrace, the god of joy is worshipped in Japan at these temples for success in business (often by workers in Japan's nighttime entertainment industry), the removal of obstacles, marital harmony, and the restoration of sexual potency. In this sense, too, the "ball of joy" is a faithful descendant of the sweet described in the story from the Mūlasarvāstivāda monastic code.

More generally, any celebrated Buddhist institution in Japan may be associated with a specific wagashi, used in its altar offerings and made near its precincts, adding up to a bewildering variety; most of these sweets originated in the seventeenth century. See WAGASHI. On special occasions, home Buddhist altars in Japan are still adorned with *rakugan*, pressed and dried sweets made from rice flour and Japanese

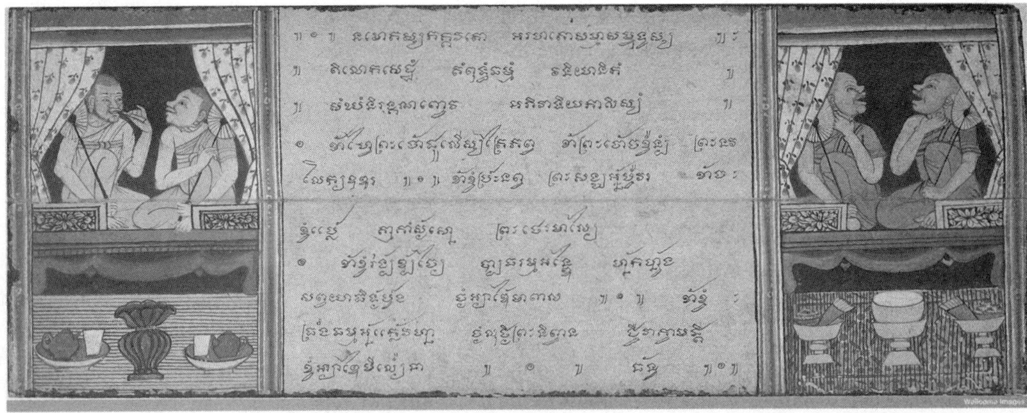

This watercolor depicts tea and sweets laid out in front of Buddhist monks. The monk on the left holds a cheroot in his mouth; those on the right are holding their throats, a reference to vocal fatigue from long periods of chanting or recitation. WELLCOME LIBRARY, LONDON

refined sugar (wasanbon), and molded into colorful shapes (fruit, vegetables, money, etc.) as offerings to the buddhas and ancestors. See WASANBON. Thus, sweets still serve a role in the "economy of merit," as introduced in the biography of the Buddha himself.

See also APHRODISIACS; JAPAN; and KYOTO.

Deeg, Max. "Chips from a Biographical Workshop: Early Chinese Biographies of the Buddha." In *Lives Lived, Lives Imagined: Biography in the Buddhist Traditions*, edited by Linda Covill, Ulrike Roesler, and Sarah Shaw, pp. 49–87. Somerville, Mass.: Wisdom Publications, 2010.

Fujimoto, Josen. *Nihon no kashi*. Nihon no bi to kyōyō 19. Kyoto: Kawara Shoten, 1968.

Kamei, Chihoko. *Nihon no kashi: Inori to kansha to yakuyoke to*. Tokyo: Tōkyō Shoseki, 1996.

Strong, John S. "A Family Quest: The Buddha, Yaśodharā, and Rāhula in the Mūlasarvāstivāda Vinaya." In *Sacred Biography in the Buddhist Traditions of South and Southeast Asia*, edited by Juliane Schober, pp. 113–128. Honolulu: University of Hawai'i Press, 1997.

Suzuki, Shin'ichi, and Fumio Tanai. *Wagashi fudoki*. Bessatsu Taiyō: Nihon no kokoro 135. Tokyo: Heibonsha, 2005.

Micah Auerback

buñuelo

See FRIED DOUGH; SPAIN; and SOUTHWEST (U.S.).

burnt sugar

See CARAMELS.

butter is the fat element of liquid milk coalesced by agitation during the churning process. A product of ancient origin and of great importance in Eurasia and countries influenced by northern European foodways, it is an essential ingredient in many sweet foods, to which it gives structure and flavor. Butter is also boiled with sugar for certain confections, such as English toffee, in which sugar and the residual milk proteins contained in the butter combine in the Maillard reaction to produce delicious aromas and tastes.

The importance of good butter for baking and pastry is often underestimated. It is the preferred fat because of its delicate, sweet, fresh cream flavor and pleasing aroma, which are very compatible with other ingredients and make a good canvas for other flavors. Many sweet baked recipes combine butter with sugar and wheat flour to give a variety of textures—short and crisp or crumbly, as in some types of cookie and short pastries, or delicately layered, as in puff pastry and Danish pastries. See PASTRY, PUFF. In these recipes, butter shortens the gluten and gives flavor. Adding eggs allows for a whole range of cakes. Here, in addition to having a shortening effect, butter helps to hold air in the cake batter. Butter is also essential to many yeast-leavened baked goods. The mouthfeel of butter is a smooth coating of richness, compared to the more flavorful and heavy mouth coating of lard, or shortening's naked, bland taste and greasy mouthfeel. See SHORTENING.

The best butter contains only cream; annatto is added seasonally to create a little more color when the cows are not eating fresh grasses. Much depends on what the cows are fed, and they should be humanely treated, which means pasturing or keeping them in a clean, well-ventilated, and sanitary barn. Cows are social and complex animals that experience pain, fear, and anxiety. A stressed cow will produce inferior milk and cream. The finest butter is organic, which is best used for finer pastries. A higher fat content does not mean better flavor.

It takes 10 quarts of milk to produce 1 pound of regular butter. Regular U.S. butter is between 80 and 82 percent butterfat; the average is 81 percent. European-style butter is 82 to 86 percent butterfat; its average is 84 percent. High-fat, low-moisture butter, made by churning cream more slowly and for a longer time and often marketed as European butter, is preferred. Low moisture means a denser, firmer, and silkier texture that will hold more air when creamed or whipped. The other advantage is that it will cream faster, provide more volume, and create a stronger structure, because it is not holding extra moisture. This quality is especially noticeable in buttercreams and creamed cake recipes, such as pound cakes and cupcakes. See CUPCAKES; ICING; and POUND CAKE. High-fat, low-moisture butter is denser and firmer, which means it is preferable for pie and tart dough because it makes them easier to form and roll out. See PIE DOUGH. When used in puff pastry, the firmer low-moisture butter is much easier to roll and fold because it is denser and therefore remains cooler longer.

Unsalted butter (sometimes erroneously called "sweet" butter) should always be used in dessert recipes. Salt is not always needed, for instance, in buttercreams and mousses. There is no industry standard as to how much salt is added to butter; it can vary from 0.4 to 4 percent, depending on the manufacturer. Salt is added as a preservative to extend the shelf life of butter, but it affects its delicate, fresh flavor. Too much salt in dough causes the flour to overdevelop gluten structure and become tough.

Storing and Using Butter

Butter, like all fats, is a vehicle for flavor and will easily pick up other odors. It can also quickly become rancid. Butter should always be stored away from highly aromatic foods. Heat and light can also cause undesirable chemical and physical changes in butter. Leaving butter unrefrigerated can result in flavor changes, rancidity, and mold growth, which affect the texture and can give the butter a distinctive smell—stale, cheesy, or decomposed. Bring out only the amount of butter that you plan to use for each recipe. After measuring what you need, any remaining butter should be covered or rewrapped and returned to the refrigerator immediately.

Store butter in its original container or an odor-free covered container in the coldest part of the refrigerator, at 32° to 38°F (0° to 3°C). Butter can also be frozen: when properly stored between 20° and 30°F (–7 to –1°C), the shelf life is between four to six weeks. Freezing will cause gradual flavor and texture changes the longer butter is held. Never wrap it in plastic wrap, which can release unpleasant odors that the butter will absorb.

Recipes such as buttercreams or pound cakes require butter at room temperature for creaming. Allow chilled butter to stand, wrapped and away from heat or direct sunlight, for about 1 to 1½ hours, until it reaches a plastic state. When squeezed, the wrapped butter should still be cool.

For pie, tart, or puff pastry, butter should be kept refrigerated until just before use. The coldness will allow the butter to be cut into the flour more evenly and prevent it from becoming prematurely soft.

Butter, usually clarified in the form of ghee, is also important in Indian sweets, and has spiritual significance as a food.

See also CAKE; CREAM; INDIA; MAILLARD, HENRI; MITHAI; MOUSSE; and TOFFEE.

Corriher, Shirley O. *Bake Wise*. New York: Scribner, 2008.
Dodge, Jim, with Elaine Ratner. *The American Baker*. New York: Simon & Schuster, 1987.

Jim Dodge

buttercream

See ICING.

buttermilk is a term surrounded by much historical confusion. It originally referred to the liquid that drains away from butter after churning. This buttermilk was highly unstandardized in both appearance and flavor. It could be scanty and almost as thin as whey if made from rich cream, but plentiful and creamy if made from whole unhomogenized milk. (This counterintuitive result reflects the fact that cream contains more butterfat and less of everything else than milk.) Buttermilk can be almost flavorless if the milk is "sweet" (unfermented), or pleasantly sour if the milk has undergone some lactic acid fermentation, or "ripening."

Yet another variable is the kind of lactic acid bacteria that predominate in ripened buttermilk. In northwestern Europe and most of North America, they are usually "mesophilic" species that thrive at temperatures between about 75° and 85°F (24° to 30°C). These organisms produce a mild, delicate acidity similar to that of cultured sour cream. See SOUR CREAM. In the hotter dairying regions of western Asia and India, "thermophilic" species that thrive in temperatures between about 105° and 118°F (40° to 48°C) flourish. These happen to be the organisms used for making yogurt; in effect, Indian butter and buttermilk are churned from yogurt, and the buttermilk naturally retains more of a yogurt flavor than the Western counterpart. See YOGURT.

Until the late nineteenth century, buttermilk was a humble byproduct of butter-making in many American households. Most often it had undergone some degree of ripening, since housewives usually skimmed off the cream from several days' milking and set it aside until enough had accumulated to be practical for churning. Especially in summer, cream could be noticeably sour by the time it was churned.

Having this source of lactic acid on hand most of the time proved to be useful when alkaline leavenings such as potash and sodium bicarbonate achieved wide use in baking after about 1840. See CHEMICAL LEAVENERS. Though the word "buttermilk" rarely crops up in recipe titles in cookbooks of the era, the ingredient itself certainly began to figure widely for starting the necessary chemical reaction with alkali in batters for quick breads, pancakes, and many quick-raised cakes. So did naturally soured milk, with which it was more or less interchangeable.

Both buttermilk and sour milk stopped being produced at home when specialized commercial dairy manufacturing triumphed in the early twentieth century. After about 1920, both were replaced by low-fat milk inoculated with laboratory-grown strains of mesophilic cultures and fermented until lightly soured and thickened. It is this cultured product that most consumers now equate with the term "buttermilk," though it is quite unconnected with butter making.

Cultured buttermilk is still as useful as its churned or home-soured predecessors in reacting with baking soda in cake, doughnut, and muffin batters. During the twentieth century it also acquired popularity in a few desserts such as buttermilk pie (a member of the southern-style "chess pie" family) as well as ice creams and sherbets. It is also processed on an industrial scale to produce dried buttermilk powder, an important ingredient in commercial bakery and confectionery products.

See also BUTTER; CREAM; and MILK.

Mendelson, Anne. *Milk: The Surprising Story of Milk through the Ages*. New York: Knopf, 2008.

Selitzer, Ralph. *The Dairy Industry in America*. New York: Dairy & Ice Cream Field and Books for Industry, 1976.

Anne Mendelson

butterscotch refers to both a type of candy and the flavor associated with it. The basic recipe involves cooking together sugar, butter, and sometimes other ingredients such as glucose and flavorings until they reach a temperature of 294°F (146°C), between soft and hard crack. The texture of the finished sweet is hard but easily broken, and the combination of sugar and dairy creates a characteristic and appealing flavor that has become popular in sweet sauces and syrups, especially in North America, where butterscotch is used in numerous desserts, drinks, and other confectionery items, such as icing.

Although brown sugar is sometimes specified for the recipe, white sugar can be used. Cream is sometimes added, along with additional flavors: vanilla is used in North America, while lemon oil and salt are standard in British recipes. The origin of the name "butterscotch" remains a mystery. It may relate to the habit of cutting the confection into small squares, an action for which the word "scotching" was sometimes used; this style of presentation was a distinctive feature of the confection in the late nineteenth century. Butterscotch has been made in Britain since at least the mid-nineteenth century, when a company called Parkinson's became famous for its production in the northern English town of Doncaster. The Dutch confection known as *boterbabbelaars* also has a similar texture and flavor.

Mason, Laura. *Sugar-Plums and Sherbet*. Totnes, U.K.: Prospect, 2004.

Laura Mason

cacao

See COCOA.

Cadbury is the trademark representing the large manufacturers who dominated chocolate production in the twentieth century in the United Kingdom and a range of countries formerly part of the British Empire. In 1824 a Birmingham-based Quaker, John Cadbury, opened a shop selling tea, coffee, and "Cocoa Nibs, prepared by himself, an article affording a most nutritious beverage for breakfast," as he proclaimed in his first advertisement. Cadbury would have remained an obscure retailer had he not seen the potential for expansion afforded by the government slashing the then-crippling import duties on cacao beans, an opportunity he seized in 1831 when he switched to manufacturing and opened his first factory.

Although Cadbury's timing had been ideal, his range of generic cocoas offered nothing new or different than those provided by Britain's leading cocoa firm, J. S. Fry & Sons. By the early 1860s, when Cadbury handed over control to his two sons, Richard and George, trade had withered away, losses had mounted, and the end seemed inevitable.

The company was saved by an attribute of George's that became one of the company's leading characteristics: a willingness to borrow and exploit a good idea when he saw one. "It was no use studying failure. I wanted to know how men succeeded, and it was their methods I examined and, if I thought them good, applied" (Gardiner, 1923, p. 24), he explained later in his life. The success in question was a much-improved cocoa produced in Holland by Coenraad Johannes van Houten using a hydraulic press, one of which George Cadbury purchased to produce a new brand, Cadbury's Cocoa Essence. See COCOA and VAN HOUTEN, COENRAAD JOHANNES.

Cocoa Essence would become Britain's leading brand of cocoa thanks largely to Cadbury's most un-Quaker-like competitive streak: George Cadbury lobbied the British parliament to ensure that only his Cocoa Essence brand could be labeled "cocoa." His rationale was that the competition's cocoas contained fillers such as flour, sago, or tapioca, whereas the hydraulically pressed Cocoa Essence was "100% Pure, Therefore Best," an advertising slogan the firm hammered away at for 40 years. While Cadbury's legal bid failed, the message seeped through to the public's consciousness.

By the 1900s, the company was being run by the next generation of family members: Edward, William, George Jr., and Barrow Cadbury, all of whom had inherited the borrow-with-pride philosophy. Following the invention of the milk chocolate bar, Cadbury decided which of the versions turned out by a host of Swiss firms was the best, and then copied those milky characteristics to launch its own version, Cadbury's Dairy Milk, in 1905. See CANDY BAR.

Much impressed by a visit to Henry Ford's production lines in Detroit, the company revolutionized the British chocolate market between the two World Wars by investing heavily in mass-production technology. It then ploughed the cost savings into a series of price reductions that, when applied against Dairy Milk and a range of new brands such as Fruit & Nut and Wholenut, gave Cadbury a dominant position in the British market. Between 1920 and 1938, Cadbury cut its prices by 70 percent, making chocolate an affordable everyday treat for all, a strategy that increased sales fivefold. During this same period, Cadbury absorbed its great rival, J. S. Fry & Sons, makers of Fry's Turkish Delight and Fry's Chocolate Cream (the world's oldest brand of chocolate bar), and drove another competitor, Rowntree, to the brink of extinction.

This stunning success funded Cadbury's next great initiative. To protect its export markets threatened by rising import tariffs, Cadbury built factories in Australia, Canada, New Zealand, Ireland, South Africa, and India, the running of which they left largely to local management, who built commanding market positions while Cadbury's major international competitors remained largely excluded.

Following World War II, Cadbury's U.K. business went into relative decline as its competitors adopted strategies that avoided head-on competition with Cadbury, creating new market segments in which Cadbury held no inherent advantage. Coupled with an increasingly conservative management style, this shift would result in Cadbury losing its market leadership in Britain by the late 1970s.

In 1969 Cadbury, having become a takeover target, merged with the similarly threatened soft drinks firm Schweppes. The growth strategy for both categories was acquisition to fill glaring geographic gaps in the company's global presence—the chocolate side had barely expanded beyond its interwar markets, while the soft drinks side was missing out on the vast American market.

The drinks gap was plugged by the acquisitions of Dr Pepper and the U.S. rights to 7Up, but no such blockbuster moves occurred in chocolate. Instead, the company accumulated a large number of local and regional companies, such as France's Poulain and Poland's Wedel. Lacking big chocolate takeover targets, the company moved into candy with the acquisitions of Trebor and Bassett's and subsequently chewing gum with its 2002 purchase of Adams Brands, which temporarily made Cadbury the world's largest confectionery company.

This moment was to be its high-water mark. In the early years of the twenty-first century, the company came under pressure from activist shareholders calling for the confectionery and beverages businesses to be separated. Cadbury succumbed to the pressure, progressively selling and spinning off its soft drinks businesses. This action left the remaining confectionery business more vulnerable to takeover, a fate that befell Cadbury in 2010, when Kraft Foods gained control of the company.

Kraft subsequently reorganized, forming a new company based on its confectionery and snack brands, Mondelēz International Inc., where Cadbury now resides alongside two of its fiercest competitors from a century ago, Suchard and Tobler.

Bradley, John. *Cadbury's Purple Reign: The Story Behind Chocolate's Best-Loved Brand.* Chichester, U.K.: Wiley, 2008.

Gardiner, A.G. *Life of George Cadbury.* London: Cassell and Co., 1923.

Williams, Iolo A. *The Firm of Cadbury 1831–1931.* London: Constable, 1931.

Witzel, Morgen. *Fifty Key Figures in Management*, pp. 43–48. London: Routledge, 2003.

John Bradley

café means more or less the same thing virtually anywhere in the world: a place to drink coffee or another hot beverage, or perhaps even a cold drink—sometimes alcoholic, sometimes not. Most cafés offer snacks, if not full menus. The original idea, however, was subtly different.

The distant origins of the café lie in the coffeehouse and the coffee craze that gripped Europe in the seventeenth century, a fact reflected in French and Italian, whose individual words for "coffee," "coffeehouse," and "café" are identical. The late Henri Enjalbert, an eminent French geographer and oenologist, was perhaps the first to speak of a "drinks revolution" in the seventeenth century, which led not only to the refinement of claret, cognac, and champagne as we now know them but also to the discovery of coffee, tea, and chocolate by Europeans. See CHOCOLATE, POST-COLUMBIAN and TEA.

In Vienna, anecdotal history dates the city's passion for coffee to 1683 and the Turkish siege. See VIENNA. As the story goes, the Ottomans abandoned their sacks of coffee in their retreat, and a Serb called Kolschitzky brewed up the beans and addicted the Viennese to coffee at the sign of the Blue Bottle. In fact, the first recorded coffeehouse had opened a generation earlier: in Oxford, England, in 1652. That same year another was opened by the Armenian Pasqua Rosée in the City of London. Another ethnic Armenian, Johannes Diodato, was a pioneer in Vienna, too, after emigrating from the Ottoman Empire.

At the restoration of the English monarchy in 1660, coffee's popularity increased, and the coffeehouse became a center of social life. It may be that, unlike the taverns of the time, a more sober atmosphere was bred by the absence of alcohol on the premises, although this changed when some coffeehouses began to double up as emporia and "punch-houses." See PUNCH. In Queen Anne's time there were as many as 500 coffeehouses; from Ned Ward's *Wealthy Shopkeeper* (1706) we know that "every respectable Londoner had his favourite house, where his friends or clients could seek him out at known hours."

In London, coffeehouses were above all meeting places, as the *Wealthy Shopkeeper* reveals:

> Remember John,
> If any ask, to th' Coffee House I'm gone.
> Then at Lloyd's Coffee House he never fails
> To read the letters and attend the sales.

The maritime insurance market Lloyds started out as Lloyd's Coffee House in Tower Street around 1680, moving to Abchurch Lane in 1682. Coffeehouses also fathered gentlemen's clubs. The most exclusive and aristocratic club, Whites, was founded in 1693 as White's Chocolate House. It is the sole survivor of a seventeenth-century coffeehouse. Three centuries ago the political coffeehouses—Cocoa Tree, St James's (with its inner room for political discussions), Will's, the clerical Truby's or Child's, the scholarly Grecian, and so on—were just as well known. The coffeehouse was not just a place to consume coffee, tea, or chocolate (all heavily sweetened) and talk; it was a place to play card games like piquet and basset.

In the United Kingdom, coffeehouses metamorphosed into clubs or were replaced by pubs. The last native British institution was the Domino Room in the old Café Royal, which closed in 1923. Until recently, Dublin could offer a genuine coffeehouse in the form of Bewleys, where you might run into le tout Dublin, but it has been deserted by its regulars and is now just a tourist trap. There are plenty of continental-style cafés in London, but the contemporary iteration of the native British café, or "caff," has distorted the original meaning of the place: these informal eating houses serve a variant on breakfast throughout the day. There is seldom wine, and most people drink tea from mugs. The Parisian coffeehouse or café is nearly as old as its London counterpart. Le Procope at 13 rue de l'Ancienne Comédie was founded in 1670 by the 20-year-old Sicilian nobleman Francesco Procopio dei Coltelli, who sold coffee imported by two Armenians called Pascal and Maliban. At the time, the preferred term for the Parisian purveyors was *limonadier*, since they sold both cold and hot sweetened beverages. Sweet snacks were also on offer. Until 1675 Le Procope was in the rue de Tournon, where it was a signal success. The café moved to its present location in 1686 to be opposite the original Comédie-Française and henceforth attracted a crowd of theatergoers. In the eighteenth century Procope was frequented by wits and became the veritable "oral newspaper of Paris." Later, the Encyclopédistes—Voltaire, Diderot, d'Alembert—made it a home away from home. Procope was popular with Revolutionaries, too, but by then most had gravitated toward the Palais Royal, the Café de Foy, and the Café Anglais (the latter became the restaurant Beauvilliers). The famous lawyer and gastronome Brillat-Savarin met his friends at the Bonapartist Café Lemblin, while habitués fought pitched battles with royalists in the Café de Valois next door. Procope was closed from 1890 to 1940 and is now chiefly frequented by bus parties. Most Parisian cafés, however, had already departed from the original idea of a coffeehouse and begun to serve an extensive menu. The original idea can still be found, however: cafés such as the Flore or the Deux Magots in Saint-Germain-des-Prés are still true cafés, even if their coterie is now diluted by tourists. Some lovely cafés have also survived in the French regions, notably the Empire-style Deux Garçons in Aix-en-Provence.

Italy, too, has its famous cafés, such as the Caffè Florian in Venice, dating from 1720, or the Caffè Greco in Rome, founded in 1760, which still looks the part and is a magnet to artists and writers even if they are generally outnumbered by tourists.

The list of notable cafés is endless: Madrid's Gran Café de Gijón, Oporto's Majestic, and the now sadly mothballed Café A Brasileira.

The coffee craze was slow to cross the Rhine, but the most famous coffee music of all time was composed to commemorate Zimmermann's Coffee House in Leipzig 80 years after the first cafés surfaced in London. Johann Sebastian Bach wrote his *Coffee Cantata* to words by Picander (Christian Friedrich Henrici) about a young girl's coffee addiction:

> Ei wie schmeckt der Coffee süße,
> Lieblicher als tausend Küsse,
> Milder als Muskatwein.
>
> [Oh how nice this coffee is,
> Better than a thousand kisses,
> Sweeter than Muscat wine.]

Today, opposite Bach's Thomaskirche in Leipzig, a café commemorates one of the composer's few lighthearted works.

In the 1840s, Karl Marx's friend Ernst Dronke made a study of Berlin cafés: he thought Kranzler, which then served only chocolate, the best. After the war Kranzler moved to the Kurfürstendamm and became quite the dullest café in Berlin, if not in Germany. The Romanische was the café of reference for a later generation, taking over as the city's bohemian haunt from the Café des Westens with its artists' table. The café, called "Romanesque" because it was part of the architectural scheme around the Memorial Church to Emperor William, was big enough to divide down the middle with "swimmers" and "nonswimmers" "pools" (rooms)—the former for the artists, the latter for the gawkers. Habitués had their own language: *auf Pump* (keeping a tab); *Nassauerei* (staying all day on the strength of one coffee); and *Ausweis* (banishment). The Romanische was destroyed by Allied bombing in 1943. The enormous Café Luitpold in Munich was the place to be seen before it suffered the same fate as the Romanische. Hitler favored the intimate Café Heck, where he would sit surrounded by his thugs. The building is still there, even if it denies previous association with the Führer.

Sometimes the lure of particular cakes has assured the fame of a café, like Gerbeaud in Budapest or Kreutzkamm on the Altmarkt in Dresden, which still makes the best stollen. See STOLLEN. The real guardian of the café concept is Vienna, however, for only in Vienna do the Kaffeehäuser (coffeehouses) remain true to the original idea of an "extended drawing room." In Britain, the place for locals to gather is the pub; in Germany, the Kneipe; in France, the bistrot. In Vienna, people seek admission to the *Stammtisch* or regulars' table at their chosen café or *Stammcafé*. Admission requires a good relationship with the owner, but also with the waiters, who wield considerable power. If the waiter (*Ober*) does not know you, you can wait a long time for your Mokka (black coffee) or Melange (half and half), which always comes on a shiny metal salver with a glass of water and sugar cubes. Most drink their coffee sweet. Once the waiter knows you, however, the coffee arrives before you have even ordered it.

You can have a beer or a glass of wine in a Viennese café, too, and most offer some sort of food—particularly cakes—even if serious food is generally found elsewhere. Once you have something to eat, the coffeehouse world is yours: a warm place to sit, free newspapers, somewhere to meet your friends—and all for the price of a coffee.

All Viennese cafés have seen better times, and many have gone into inexorable decline. Too polished an appearance is generally a sign that the coffeehouse is no longer frequented by locals and has become the province of Zuagraste—outsiders—as have the Central, Schwarzenberg, Landtmann, and Mozart, to name just a few. To get the feel of a Viennese coffeehouse today, you must try Hawelka, Bräunerhof, or Prückel. This is a sad fate for the Central in particular: not only is it visually perhaps the most extraordinary café in the world, but it also has a distinguished history as a literary haunt, like the Procope in Paris or the Café Royal in London. Writers, however, vote with their feet: men like Karl Kraus and Peter Altenberg (who wrote a list of 10 pretexts for going to the café) deserted the Central for the Herrenhof, where they were joined by Robert Musil, Franz Werfel, and Joseph Roth. The Herrenhof closed in 1960, and what was left of bohemia moved on to the Hawelka.

Emigrants from the coffee-drinking capitals brought the café idea to wherever they settled, whether in New York, Havana, or Rio de Janeiro. One of the loveliest of the New World café's is perhaps Café Tortoni in Buenos Aires, originally opened by a French settler in 1858. In the United States, New Orleans's Café des Artistes (founded in 1862) is primarily known for its chicory-laced coffee and beignets (square doughnuts).

Prior to the coffee bar explosion of the 1980s, cafés in the United States tended to cater to specific ethnic groups (Cubans in Havana, Italians in New York) but also to beatniks, hippies, and other bohemians. Greenwich Village spots such as the San Remo Café (as a much a bar as a café) was a gathering spot for Beat writers such as Allen Ginsberg, William S. Burroughs, and Jack Kerouac in the 1950s.

Since the 1980s the European café has been reinvented by chains such as Starbucks, as well as by local cafés and coffee bars that often fetishize the coffee-making process. In modern American usage, "café" refers to a casual restaurant where sandwiches or more substantial meals can be ordered. The spirit of the original café is found in what are called coffee shops, which have proliferated across the United States. Drinking coffee has again become so chic that there are now training courses for the baristas, who make specialty coffees according to methods ranging from drip to siphon. Like their European predecessors, the best coffee shops serve as gathering places, although today's patrons are more likely to remain focused on their wireless devices than to engage in conversation with others.

See also LEMONADE.

Enjalbert, Henri. *L'Histoire de la vigne et du vin: l'Avènement de la qualité.* Paris: Bordas, 1975.
Hillairet, Jacques. *Dictionnaire historique des rues de Paris.* Vol. 1. Paris: Editions de Minuit, 1963.
Neumann, Petra, ed. *Wien und seine Kaffeehäuser: Ein literarischer Streifzug durch die berühmtesten Cafés der Donaumetropole.* Munich: William Heyne, 1997.
Trevelyan, George Macaulay. *English Social History: A Survey of Six Centuries, Chaucer to Queen Victoria.* Harmondsworth, U.K.: Penguin, 1967.
Turberville, Arthur Stanley. *English Men and Manners in the Eighteenth Century.* Oxford: Oxford University Press, 1929.

Giles MacDonogh

cake is a sweet food, most often baked, that usually contains flour, sugar, eggs, and frequently butter or another fat. It comes in various flavors, shapes, and sizes and is often chemically leavened with baking powder or baking soda. Derived from the Old Norse *kaka,* the word "cake" entered Middle English spelled as it is today, though it was probably first pronounced KAH-keh.

Cakes in the Ancient World

Ancient cakes—made from bread dough or similarly dense mixtures; sweetened with honey; enriched with eggs, fresh cheese, or oil; and flavored with nuts, dried fruits, herbs, and seeds—likely evolved from early breads. They are thought to have been made with rye, barley, and oat flours as well as wheat flour. Sumerian texts from some 4,000 years ago mention these sorts of baked goods, and Cato describes a similar kind of cake in *De Agri Cultura* (second century B.C.E) that was wrapped in leaves before baking and served at weddings and fertility rites. See ANCIENT WORLD.

Sixteenth- to Nineteenth-Century Cakes

Heavy, bread-like cakes made from dense mixtures and often still leavened with yeast continued to be made well into the eighteenth century in England. In France, lighter cakes were developing simultaneously, beginning in the sixteenth century with brioche, perceived at the time as more of a sweet product than a bread. Yeast-risen cakes such as the Gugelhupf, sweeter and richer than brioche, and the baba, originally similar to a Gugelhupf (now lighter) and soaked with rum syrup, remained popular. See BABA AU RHUM and GUGELHUPF. During the eighteenth century in France and Italy, meringues, sponge cakes made with whole or separated eggs, and cake batters based on soft butter or

This "slice" of cake is actually a 36 × 24-inch layer cake made for the chef's own birthday party. The cake is covered and decorated with sugar paste, while the "plate" is made of pastillage. PHOTO © RON BEN-ISRAEL CAKES

with melted butter added to sponge mixtures became widespread. See MERINGUE and SPONGE CAKE. By the mid-nineteenth century, both baking soda and baking powder ushered in an era of American creativity in the development of cake recipes, and chemically leavened butter cakes, devil's food cake, and many others began to appear. See CHEMICAL LEAVENERS. Angel food, a cake of American origin made from only whipped egg whites, sugar, and flour, is the symbol of the nineteenth century's search for lightness and delicacy in cakes. See ANGEL FOOD CAKE.

Cake Terminology

In American baking terminology, a cake is anything, large or small, filled or unfilled, made from a sweet batter, whether dense or light. In most other Western baking traditions, "cake" is not the general term that it is in American English. In the United Kingdom, a cake is what Americans might call a "plain cake" and usually refers to a dense baked good such as Madeira cake, similar to what Americans might call a pound cake, or to a fruit-laden Christmas cake (U.S. fruitcake). See FRUITCAKE and POUND CAKE. In the United Kingdom, a layer cake is referred to as a "sandwich sponge," "sandwich," or by the French term *gâteau*. See LAYER CAKE.

In France, *le cake* is a loaf-shaped pound cake often enriched with dried or candied fruits. Lately, the French have begun to apply the term to any loaf-shaped, flour-based baked goods; one result is *le cake salé* (salted cake), a dense savory cake. A layer cake can be a *gâteau* in France as well as in the United Kingdom, though the same term may also refer to desserts made from pastry doughs, such as the almond-filled *gâteau des rois* (kings cake or Twelfth Night cake) made from puff pastry, the *gâteau Basque* made from a sweet pastry dough, or the *gâteau Saint Honoré* made from unsweetened pastry dough or puff pastry and *pâte à choux* (cream puff pastry). See PASTRY, CHOUX and PASTRY, PUFF. Delicate layer cakes with rich or soft fillings are also referred to as *entremets* (desserts).

In German-speaking countries, terminology mostly follows classic South German nomenclature. Plain cakes, those embellished with fresh fruit, or those made from yeast-leavened doughs are referred to as *Kuchen*. See KUCHEN. Layer cakes and some rich cakes made from pastry doughs are referred to as *Torten*, as in *Punschtorte*, layers of sponge cake moistened with rum punch and filled with apricot jam; *Sachertorte*, a rich chocolate cake; and *Linzertorte*, a dense, jam-filled cake that lies halfway between a cake and a pastry. See LINZER TORTE; SACHERTORTE; and TORTE. A Torte is sometimes mistakenly thought to be a cake or cake layer made without flour, probably because the Viennese baking tradition often uses ground nuts either alone or combined with flour or dry breadcrumbs for *Tortenboden* or cake layers.

Italian bakers solve the problem by referring to most cakes, as well as to pies and tarts, as *torte*. An Italian *torta* may be either a layer cake, as in *torta bignè* (a cream-filled layer cake covered with tiny unfilled cream puffs or *bignè*), or an unfilled, denser cake such as an almond pound cake (*torta di mandorle*). It can refer to a savory pie (*torta rustica*) or to a sweet one (*torta di mele*).

Cake Baking Equipment

Straight-sided cake pans meant for baking round cakes and cake layers came into common use during the nineteenth century. See PANS. American and British professional and home bakers still use them today; American pans are usually 1½ to 2 inches deep, whereas British ones are deeper owing to the British preference for taller plain cakes. French closed cake pans, about 2 inches deep, have sloped sides and are referred to as *moules à manqué* (molds for ruined [cake]). The term is said to have originated with a baker who, on removing his butter-enriched sponge cake from the oven, found that the cake had not risen as much as he had hoped and cried, "Le gâteau est manqué!" ("The cake is ruined!") Recipes for *gâteau manqué* appear in many French baking collections to this day.

The use of a bottomless hoop for baking cake layers destined to be sliced horizontally and made into layer cakes, as well as for some denser mixtures, persists throughout Europe. Widespread use of the cake hoop, renamed *cercle à entremets* (dessert circle or ring), occurred during the emergence in the 1960s of *la pâtisserie moderne* (modern pastry making) spearheaded by the Normandy-born Parisian dessert mogul Gaston Lenôtre. Stainless-steel rings became available in a variety of diameters and depths and were used for molding layer cakes with liquid mousse fillings, as well as for constructing layer cakes finished with denser mixtures such as buttercream or ganache. Use of the rings enabled less skilled finishers to produce cakes that emerged perfectly symmetrical from the oven.

See also BREADS, SWEET; CUPCAKES; DESSERT; ENTREMETS; FRANCE; GERMANY; ITALY; SMALL CAKES; TWELFTH NIGHT CAKE; WEDDING; and WEDDING CAKE.

David, Elizabeth. *English Bread and Yeast Cookery.* New York: Viking, 1980.

Montagné, Prosper. *Larousse gastronomique.* New York: Crown, 1961.

Sender, S. G., and Marcel Derrien. *La grande histoire de la pâtisserie-confiserie Française.* Geneva, Switzerland: Éditions Minerva, 2003.

Nick Malgieri

cake and confectionery stands for the presentation of these items on the sideboard, dining table, or in a retail environment usually take the form of a circular dish elevated above the surface of the table or display case by a flaring central foot. The form is essentially that of a tazza, a versatile stem vessel with a shallow bowl that functioned from ancient times as a drinking cup, food dish, and display piece. Examples in delicate glass and precious metal, holding biscuits and sweets, may be found in Dutch still-life paintings and Italian frescoes. Another form of confectionery stand is the pyramidal étagère, composed of circular glass, metal, or porcelain dishes of diminishing diameter fixed by a central rod emanating in a handle. Commonly employed for English high tea, étagères were, and still are, made by every porcelain manufacturer in Europe, even if the market for them is not obvious.

Most popular cookbooks illustrate cakes on stands, though the authors do not comment on how to display or serve a cake. Lifestyle gurus, on the other hand, love cake stands. "Our prop house shelves are overflowing with cake stands of every imaginable size, design, color, and material," writes Kevin Sharkey of *Martha Stewart Living.* "We love cake stands for not just cakes but to display flowers, votive candles, even Easter eggs. Nothing makes a delicious pie or cake better than a great cake stand." The cake stand collection of Food Network television star Ina Garten, the Barefoot Contessa, is apparently legendary and has pride of place on the open shelving in her kitchen.

Like cake knives, the modern-day cake stand is probably a Victorian invention. "A party without cake is just a meeting," once asserted Julia Child. The cake plate or confectionery stand is a superb accessory for celebrating and protecting many forms of sweetness.

See also EPERGNES and SERVING PIECES.

"All About Cake Stands." http://www.marthastewart.com/1061823/cake-stands

Maureen Cassidy-Geiger

cake decorating, the art of making cakes attractive with sugar icing, gilding, and other materials, came into its own in the late 1800s, due largely to new technology and societal changes. Decorative confections originated from Renaissance *trionfi di tavola,* sugar sculptures made to adorn feasts of the wealthy. These sculptures survived alongside ornate cakes on affluent dinner tables into the early 1800s and are used

This rosette, or floral decoration, was made around 1975 by Hans Strzyso, the chief baker at Madsens Supermarket in New Ulm, Minnesota. Strzyso specialized in lavishly decorated cakes and German baked goods. PHOTO BY FLIP SCHULKE / U.S. NATIONAL ARCHIVES

for commercial purposes to this day. See SUGAR SCULPTURE. However, over the course of the nineteenth century, the growth of a large middle class in Europe and America, along with more reliable ovens and affordable ingredients, led to standardized cake recipes. Some special cakes, such as those made in England for weddings and Twelfth Night, were decorated with sugar paste figures from the late eighteenth century onward. See TWELFTH NIGHT CAKE; WEDDING; and WEDDING CAKE. It was not long before the cakes' appearance became as important as their taste, as evidenced by the chromolithographs of decorated cakes in the 1892 edition of *Mrs Beeton's Book of Household Management.* See BEETON, ISABELLA.

Piping and Icing

For a century, however, cake decoration would remain a mostly professional matter, made possible by the 1840s French invention of piping. First extruded from paper cones, then later from metal tubes (also called tips), piped icing made elaborate cake decorating possible for all levels of bakers. With practice—and the help of colored icing and pastry school courses or printed instruction—bakers could now apply elaborate trims directly to the cake itself or attach them when they were dry. Unlike other sugar ornamentation, most piping did not have to be removed before eating.

With the use of metal "nails," piped flowers blossomed on cakes. Piped letters and numbers produced names and messages on both holiday and personal celebration cakes. Piped "weaves" made two-dimensional or stand-alone baskets possible. Intricate piping created the look of fine lace, especially when it was done on net for added strength.

Originally a German specialty, network became the rage in Edwardian England when émigré confectioners Herr Willy, Ernest Schulbe, and R. Gommez produced publications detailing the method. At one English trade show, a wedding cake covered in piped network was even lit with "small electric lamps" ("a troublesome piece of work," admitted its creator, Ernest Schulbe). By the 1920s Joseph Lambeth, an English émigré to America, had popularized his interwar variation, overpiping, with its multiple layers of thin stringwork. However, single-layer tortes, piped in vivid colors, had replaced much of the white lace multi-tier look, except for weddings. In the 1930s, when some wedding gowns were colored, all-color wedding cakes became a fad, too. After World War II, Nirvana (the pen name of Ernest Arthur Cardnell) brought the run-out technique of piping to 1950s Britain. This technique literally flooded geometric shapes with icing. Piping was also used to create animal forms (including circus animals) and figures (including dancers and acrobats).

With cake recipes appearing in newspapers and magazines and the introduction of supermarket cake mixes, suburban housewives, especially in the United States, became major practitioners of cake decorating. See CAKE MIX. American firms like Wilton advertised that "every homemaker can learn to decorate cakes—even the most inartistic or unskilled." Although 1950s plastic ornaments might have been a godsend to some women, so many others practiced true cake decorating that even an independent baking-school owner like Richard Snyder devoted four books to floral piping between 1957 and 1963; the fourteenth printing of his original 1953 manual for amateurs appeared in 1976. See PUBLICATIONS, TRADE.

Meanwhile, Wilton's books illustrated the company's own 8-foot-tall cake for the San Francisco Association of Retail Bakers Convention and official seven-tier cake for the Chicago International Trade Fair. For the 1962 Seattle World's Fair, a sugar company, baking company, baking school, and restaurant chain joined forces to produce and promote the "World's Largest Birthday Cake," which weighed 25,000 pounds and stood 23 feet high. The cake was sold as boxed slices to fair attendees.

True creativity stagnated until the 1990s cake-decorating revival that pitted trained professional pastry chefs against amateurs, often art directors or crafts enthusiasts. See COMPETITIONS. Professionals increasingly concentrated on geometric fantasies—usually inedible and meant as showpieces. Cake decorators increasingly looked to Australia, South America, and Asia for invention. Australian housewives developed the fashion for fondant covering, whereas wildly intricate yet innovative piping was practiced by Indonesians, Filipinos, and Central Americans, whose wedding cakes often occupied an entire table, just when the craze for tiers of cupcakes took Anglo-American cake decorating by storm. See CUPCAKES and FONDANT.

Showpieces

Although piping became the dominant cake-decorating method, molded and modeled ornaments, made by professionals from gum paste or marzipan, were highly desirable on sugar showpieces that required longer shelf lives. See MARZIPAN and TRAGACANTH. In the nineteenth century foods of all kinds, not just desserts, were subject to sculpting and molding. Sometimes the ingredients were artificial so that the finished item—while looking good enough to eat—could withstand the wear of display. Instead of being made exclusively for private parties, these showpieces began to appear in professional competitions, at trade shows and public exhibitions, and in shop windows. Despite the change of venue and audience, some continued to have classical shapes—temples, plinths, even a Venus de Milo carved in beet sugar—but their purpose was to promote bakers' skills. Faux vases, baskets, and pillows became mainstays of shop-window showpieces, but wedding cakes remained the most effective vehicle for cake decoration. A 1923 article in *Bakers' Helper* magazine, "Show Pieces That Attract Custom," featured an enormous five-tier wedding cake that had "been used more than once in the Kunze (bakery) windows." As time went on, professionals attracted wider attention to their showpieces. W. C. Baker, for example, created a heavily publicized cake for the 1939 Golden Gate International Exposition, weighing 1,000 pounds and with tiny models of San Francisco landmarks. Today's decorating professionals often find television shows the best way to feature their art.

See also DOLLY VARDEN CAKE; ICING; and PASTILLAGE.

Lambeth, Joseph A. *Lambeth Method of Cake Decoration.* Chicago: Bakers' Helper, 1934.
Nirvana. *Advanced Piping and Cake Designs.* London: Maclaren, 1950.
Schulbe, Ernest. *Advanced Piping and Modeling.* Manchester, U.K.: Sherratt and Hughes, 1906.
Zenker, John J. *Artistic Cake Decorating from A to Z.* Chicago: Clissold, 1951.

Francine Kirsch

cake mix is an icon of American home cooking, a product so deeply rooted in the nation's culinary culture that when U.S. homemakers say they baked a cake from scratch, most often they mean they used a mix. See CAKE.

The first cake mix on the market was Duff's Ginger Bread Mix, which appeared in 1929 and contained dried, powdered molasses as well as flour, sugar, leavenings, and spices. It was developed by P. Duff and Sons, Inc., a molasses company in Pittsburgh, Pennsylvania, that hoped to boost the sales of molasses. See GINGERBREAD and MOLASSES. The initial response to Duff's was so positive that the company quickly introduced white, spice, and devil's food cake mixes. During the 1930s other small companies began producing cake mixes, until wartime shortages of sugar and fat halted production.

Research and development continued, nevertheless, especially at the nation's major flour companies, and after the war, industry giants such as General Mills and Pillsbury moved directly into the cake-mix business. Sales of flour for home baking had been dropping for years, as fewer and fewer women made their own bread. Here was an excellent way to reinvent flour and charge more for it. General Mills introduced a fine-textured gingerbread it called "Ginger*cake*" (italics in the original) in 1947. A year later Pillsbury introduced a white cake mix and a chocolate fudge cake mix, and by the 1950s some 200 manufacturers were turning out cake mixes. Sales more than tripled from 1949 to 1955. The industry was exuberant and so was the food press. As early as 1949, the popular weekly magazine *Collier's*

Sales of cake mixes tripled in the post–World War II United States, redefining home baking and spawning an industry of brand-driven cookbooks as Betty Crocker, Duncan Hines, and Pillsbury became household names.

declared that "most housewives" had switched to mixes.

"Most housewives," however, had done no such thing. True, the early cake-mix business had ballooned rapidly, but according to a U.S. Department of Agriculture study, by 1955 only 4 out of 10 families were using "flour mixes," a category that included long-established pancake and biscuit mixes, as well as cake mix. Ten years later a food-industry study concluded that "per capita consumption of cake mixes has been virtually stable since 1956."

Industry experts were puzzled by the slowdown, but an apt assessment of the product appeared in *Hilltop Housewife Cookbook*, compiled by the New England food journalist Hazel B. Corliss. She had no objection to short-cut cookery on principle, but when it came to cake mixes, she balked. "My late husband, 'Pop,' couldn't abide cake mixes," she wrote. "I used one once and he insisted that it was only fit for the hens to eat! Prepared mixes usually do not have the good 'home' flavor, and they don't have that most precious ingredient, a wife and mother's love for her family" (p. 5).

Evidently, the symbolic power of a homemade cake—long seen as the epitome of feminine love and skill—posed a threat to the expansion of the cake-mix market. According to many journalistic accounts of how this problem was solved, manufacturers simply decided to reformulate the packaged mix. They eliminated the dried eggs and required the homemaker to add her own fresh eggs, thus persuading her she was indeed engaged in traditional baking.

This solution, often attributed to studies for General Mills conducted by the consumer-psychology expert Ernest Dichter, is apocryphal. Manufacturers had been pondering the question of whether to use fresh or dried eggs since the early years of cake-mix research. They knew that adding fresh eggs gave the cake better flavor and texture; they also knew that including dried eggs in the mix made it faster and easier to do the work. Surveys showed that consumers were divided as to which approach they preferred. By 1948 General Mills had chosen fresh eggs, Pillsbury had chosen dried eggs, and both companies were market leaders—until the sales of both companies sagged after 1955.

The larger issue suggested by the egg anecdote, however, was significant. Dichter's research clearly indicated that homemakers were reluctant to forfeit a sense of personal involvement in cake baking. Hence, an emphasis on "creativity" became prominent in advertising: women were encouraged to add oil, pudding mix, spices, and other ingredients to make their cakes more personal. (This also helped to counter the taste of artificial flavorings that often identified a cake-mix cake.) Even more powerful was the new role assigned to decorating. According to innumerable magazine stories, a "creative cook" could transform a cake-mix cake into an elaborate fantasy by deploying frosting, food coloring, candies, and the like. See CAKE DECORATING.

These changes in technology and marketing brought about new standards for home baking. Traditionally prepared cakes came to seem inferior to cake-mix cakes, which were invariably light, sweet, and flawless. Today, most American home cooks prefer cake mixes not only for their speed but also for their factory-bred taste and texture, reliably achieved by following the directions on the box.

Dichter, Ernest. "A Psychological Research Study on the Sales and Advertising Problems of Bisquick." Personal papers, Box 7, folder 148C (Accession 2407). Wilmington, Del.: Hagley Museum and Library.

Gerot, Paul S. "Convenience, Ease and Success from the Oven: The Story of Prepared Cake Mixes." In *Business Decisions That Changed Our Lives*, edited by Sidney Furst and Milton Sherman, pp. 187–199. New York: Random House, 1964.

Park, Michael Y. "A History of the Cake Mix, the Invention That Redefined 'Baking.'" http://www.bonappetit.com/entertaining-style/pop-culture/article/cake-mix-history (posted 26 September 2013).

Shapiro, Laura. *Something from the Oven: Reinventing Dinner in 1950s America*, pp. 68–80. New York: Viking, 2004.

Laura Shapiro

Canada, in its early history, was a country where sweets tended to be regional, dependent on local ingredients and the origins of new arrivals. By the end of the nineteenth century, the huge nation was largely settled, and the increasing availability of cookbooks influenced the range of sweets that make up what we now call dessert—cakes, small cakes and cookies, pastries, pies, tarts, and puddings. Most recently, new twentieth- and twenty-first-century technologies and the arrival of new Canadians from around the world have further expanded its ever-bountiful sweet table.

When European settlers arrived in the early seventeenth century, they found an already established taste for sweets. In the St. Lawrence River basin and eastern Canada, for example, where maple trees flourish, the Sugar Moon was a time of tribal gatherings and celebrations involving maple products. Members of the First Nations collected sap, then boiled it down using a succession of heated stones. With metal pots the process was sped up. Maple became a distinguishing Canadian flavor. See MAPLE SUGARING; MAPLE SYRUP; and NATIVE AMERICAN.

Maple syrup production grew in the provinces of Ontario, Nova Scotia, Prince Edward Island, and New Brunswick, but especially in Quebec, which now accounts for almost three-quarters of the world's supply. Maple syrup and sugar remain important ingredients in such traditional recipes as *grand pères au sirop d'érable* (dumplings in maple syrup), *tourlouche* (maple syrup upside-down cake), and *tarte au sirop d'érable* (pie with custardy maple syrup, egg, and cream filling). One of the best loved is *tarte au sucre* (sugar pie), with a cream, butter, and maple sugar filling. An instant maple treat is *tartine à l'érable*—a slice of homemade bread, with a sprinkle of grated maple sugar and a drizzle of cream. *Pouding au chômeur* (poor man's pudding), a famous twentieth-century, two-layer indulgence consisting of cake on top, custardy brown sugar, and often maple syrup underneath, has emerged as the definitive Quebec dessert. In other parts of eastern Canada, backwoods pie (again a maple custard filling), maple cottage pudding, maple fudge, and maple ice cream are old-time favorites.

Another swath of sweetness encompassed much of Atlantic Canada, notably Newfoundland and Labrador. Here, molasses from the Caribbean—traded for salt cod—became the sweetener of choice. See MOLASSES. Molasses buns, made with salt pork, molasses, cloves, allspice, ginger, and raisins, used to be a noon-hour meal for men fishing or cutting firewood in winter. *Toutons*, pieces of bread dough, were fried and sauced with hot molasses and butter. See FRIED DOUGH. Molasses was combined with dried fruit and spices in fruitcakes for Christmas and weddings and was also integral to gingerbread cakes. See FRUITCAKE and GINGERBREAD. A Newfoundland specialty, lassy tarts have a molasses, egg, and breadcrumb filling. The most famous Newfoundland sweet is figgy duff with molasses coady. This is a boiled pudding (duff) with raisins or currants (figgy) with a hot molasses and salt pork or butter sauce (coady). Molasses still enjoys prominence in the pantries of eastern Canada, in gingerbread cakes and spiced cookies. Examples are soft drop cookies such as cry babies, or others rolled thick and cut, such as Fat Archies. In Canada's west, honey is often the choice of sweetener.

Everywhere in Canada, wild berries have figured prominently in sweets. Berries differ from east to west, south to north. Many of Canada's heritage sweets are based on whichever berry is local and free for the picking. In Newfoundland and Labrador, there are cloudberries, known locally as bake apples, and tart partridgeberries, also known as lingonberries. From the Atlantic to northern Ontario, wild low-bush blueberries are harvested. The land has also provided wild elderberries, strawberries, raspberries, gooseberries, currants, and blackberries for desserts and preserves. In the prairie provinces of Manitoba, Saskatchewan, and Alberta, Saskatoon berries, high-bush cranberries, and various wild cherries are the starting point for sweets. British Columbia is lush with such wild berries as blackberries. Not as well known is the Canadian buffalo berry, also known as soap berry or soopolallieis, which is crushed, sweetened, and whipped to make a frothy treat known as "Indian ice cream." See AKUTUQ. In the north, foraging for wild berries such as cranberries, Saskatoons, and bake apples is a way of life. Berries found their way into a variety of English- and American-influenced puddings, buckles, grunts, cobblers, and the roly-poly, with the fruit combined in some way with biscuit dough. See FRUIT DESSERTS, BAKED.

In the nineteenth and twentieth centuries, cookbooks helped define and popularize sweets. The first English-language cookbook *The Cook Not Mad* was published in 1831 in Kingston, Ontario. A book of the same title, published a year earlier in Watertown, New York, introduced North American ingredients, including pumpkins, squash, cranberries, and cornmeal, to a largely English repertoire. *La cuisinière canadienne* (1840) first defined Canadian, or more precisely, French Canadian cooking. Sweet recipes of French and English origin called for ingredients such as pumpkin and cranberries, and included a generous selection of puddings, among them plum pudding and bread pudding. See PUDDING. "Canada is the land of cakes," wrote Catharine Parr Trail in 1854 in her book *The Female Emigrant's Guide*, an encouraging and practical guide for newcomers. For example, in addition to offering a recipe for apple pie, Traill provides instructions on selecting suitable apple trees, planting, grafting, harvesting, storing, even drying a bumper crop. As for cakes, she wrote, "I have limited myself to such cakes as are in common use in the farm houses" and continues, "A tea-table is generally furnished with several varieties of cakes and preserves." As evidence, Trail provides a variety of mostly chemically leavened cakes that would have been familiar to cooks across settled North America. See CAKE and CHEMICAL LEAVENERS. Traill put her stamp on the kinds of cakes newly arrived Canadians embraced.

The best-selling English-language cookbook of the nineteenth century was the 1877 *Home Cook Book*, Canada's first community cookbook. By 1885, 100,000 copies of it had been sold to a population of 4.5 million. According to culinary historian Liz Driver, the *Home Cook Book* followed a pattern of community cookbooks recently established in the United States. The *Home Cook Book* provided a model for women in English-speaking Canada to use their own recipes, and to support good causes such as hospitals, charities, churches, and organizations like the Women's Institute, a tradition that continues to this day. Its emphasis on sweets set a precedent for subsequent community cookbooks. As in the United States, cookbooks and booklets were created by manufacturers of new products such as baking powder, corn syrup, and cocoa, as well as of established ingredients, such as flour. These publications encouraged the sweet side of cooking. A prominent example is *The Five Roses Cookbook*, the 1915 edition of which had enormous influence, with sales of 950,000 copies, enough for one in every second Canadian home. The recipes were devoted almost entirely to sweet baked goods and breads, again favoring cakes over puddings, pies, and cookies, but including a small chapter on doughnuts, described as "dainty goodies." The recipes indicate that Canadian pantries stocked bananas, dates, canned pineapple, shredded "cocoanut," chocolate, and gelatin in addition to familiar molasses, maple syrup, apples, cranberries (mock cherries), mincemeat, dried apples, rolled oats, raisins, currants, and candied fruit. See CANDIED FRUIT.

Among the book's treasures is a recipe for Butter Tarts, admittedly not the first for what some consider the only created-in-Canada dish. That honor, according to culinary historian and researcher Mary Williamson, goes to the recipe in the 1900 cookbook published by the Women's Auxiliary of the Royal Victoria Hospital in Barrie, Ontario, which contains a recipe called "Filling for a Tart." Over the next few years the recipe, now named Butter Tarts, reappeared in other cookbooks, such as the *Canadian Farm Cookbook* in 1911, where six versions exist as collected from Ontario home bakers.

Since Canada's population was mainly rural at the beginning of the twentieth century, it produced much of its own food, notably baking ingredients—butter, cream, milk, lard, eggs, and fruit. Canadian wheat was considered the finest in the world, as the gold medals it won at the St. Louis World's Fair in 1904 demonstrated. By the mid-nineteenth century, cook stoves began to replace hearths and bake ovens. In the twentieth century, in turn, electric and gas ranges made cook stoves obsolete and baking easier. With these new resources Canadians could afford to have dessert every day. And they did, even pie for breakfast. When company was coming, hostesses rose to the challenge by offering generous dessert spreads: a choice of pies, a pudding, a cake, cookies, and preserved fruit. One's reputation was made when company called; at fall fair baking competitions; in the desserts provided for threshers; and in the pies the ladies brought to community suppers. See FAIRS.

A significant change in sweets took place with the development of domestic science in the late nineteenth century. Celebrated in this movement was Fannie Farmer. Her influential *The Boston Cooking-School Cook Book* (1896) was widely distributed in Canada. See FARMER, FANNIE. Notable in Canada for disseminating a similarly rational approach to cooking and baking was Nellie Lyle Pattinson's *Canadian Cookbook* (1923), originally a university textbook but later a very consumer cookbook that went through many editions. Pattinson's use of the word "Canadian" helped define Canadian desserts.

It would be hard to find a country anywhere in the world with a more varied populace than Canada's, or a richer collection of sweets that reflect former homelands. In southwestern Ontario, the Mennonite and Amish communities are celebrated for Dutch apple pie. See PENNSYLVANIA DUTCH. The Mennonites who settled in the west came from Russia. At their afternoon break, *faspa*, the table often holds a rhubarb, plum, or apple platz—a tender cakey crust with fruit and sweet crumbs on the top. Icelandic settlers in Manitoba retain homeland memories with vinarterta, layers of cake and cardamom-spiced prune filling. See VINARTERTA. Jewish bakers have added rugelach and hamantaschen filled with lekvar (thick prune or apricot jam) to the sweet table; the Portuguese contributed custard tarts; the Italians gelati and biscotti; South Asians mango kulfi (ice cream) and cashew barfi (fudge). See BARFI; BISCOTTI; HAMANTASCHEN; and RUGELACH. Eastern Europeans provided richly decorated Easter breads, honey cakes, buttery crescents, strudels, and tortes; Greeks baklava and sugar-dusted *kourabiethes*; and Latin Americans tres leches cake and dulce de leche. See BAKLAVA; DULCE DE LECHE; and TRES LECHES CAKE. These top picks represent a much wider repertoire, filtered to appeal to already established Canadian ingredients, tastes, and techniques. Baklava appears, but no Greek custard pie, *galaktoboureko*; Chinese fortune or almond cookies win out over traditionally sweet red bean soup. Just as the sweets of earlier immigrant communities evolved to include pumpkin, Saskatoon berries, cornmeal, cranberries, carrots in Christmas pudding, and maple, so did the sweets of recent arrivals, who add blueberries to their coffee cakes and sauce their panna cotta with rhubarb compote.

Although home baking was widely practiced, Canadians long satisfied their sweet tooth at local bakeries where cinnamon rolls, fruity Chelsea buns, sugar-coated jam doughnuts, and raisin bread augmented everyday fruit and nut loaves, pumpkin pies, raisin oatmeal cookies, and layer cakes. On a larger scale, the Quebec bakery Vachon grew into a national chain, along the way giving the world the snack cakes May West (vanilla sponge-cake layers) and Jos Louis (chocolate layers), both filled with cream and coated with hard chocolate. Prominent also in the sweet snack line is the Whippet, originally Montreal-produced, a vanilla cookie base topped with a round pillow of marshmallow and coated with hard chocolate. Equally part of Canada's sweet snack repertoire is the doughnut as sold by the very popular Tim Hortons chain, Canada's largest food-service operator. There, you can buy a Canadian maple-honey cruller and double chocolate doughnut to go with your double double coffee (coffee with two sugars and two creams). See DOUGHNUTS.

Today, there are dessert cookbooks to respond to any interest, whether in French or Middle Eastern sweets, shortbread or cake pops, or simply the latest food fashion from the United Kingdom, France, Italy, or the United States. Celebrity pastry chefs and bakeries share their secrets on television shows and blogs. An emerging interest in low-fat and sugar-, gluten-, dairy-, egg- or nut-free products is driving new developments in sweets. Homemade is now simpler—fewer pies and more puddings, squares, and muffins are created. See MUFFINS.

The Canadian love of the dessert course, and especially of baking, lives on. Certain desserts are classics: date squares, self-saucing lemon or rhubarb puddings, blueberry muffins, flapper pie (a meringue-topped custard pie with a graham cracker crust), apple pie, Queen Elizabeth cakes (date slab cake with a broiled coconut topping), oatmeal cookies, Nanaimo bars, banana bread, sugar pie (*tarte au sucre*), and gingerbread houses. See NANAIMO BAR. To paraphrase Catharine Parr Traill, Canada is truly the land of sweets.

See also BREADS, SWEET; DROP COOKIES; FLOUR; FRUIT; PACIFIC NORTHWEST (U.S.); PORTUGAL; ROLLED COOKIES; and UNITED STATES.

Benoit, Jehane. *My Grandmother's Kitchen*. Toronto: McGraw-Hill Ryerson, 1981.

Driver, Elizabeth. *Culinary Landmarks: A Bibliography of Canadian Cookbooks, 1825–1949*. Toronto: University of Toronto Press, 2008.

Ferguson, Carol, and Margaret Fraser. *A Century of Canadian Home Cooking: 1900 through the '90s*. Scarborough, Ont.: Prentice-Hall Canada, 1992.

Jesperson, Ivan F. *Fat-Back & Molasses: A Collection of Favourite Old Recipes from Newfoundland & Labrador*. St. John's, Nfld.: Jesperson Press, 1977.

Traill, Mrs. C. P. (Catherine Parr). *The Female Emigrant's Guide and Hints on Canadian Housekeeping*. Toronto: Maclear and Co., 1854.

Elizabeth Baird

candied flowers are produced by several different methods, depending on whether the whole flower or only its petals are used. For candied petals, what is technically a real "candying" process—the osmotic penetration of sugar, similar to that used for candied fruits—is most common. See CANDIED FRUIT. For the whole flower, which is too difficult to candy, a crystallization technique, called *praliner* in French, is used. A third method, sometimes used at home, is to paint flowers or petals with egg white and dust them with sugar.

The use of flowers in confectionery dates back to the medieval Arab world. The flowers were mostly used as ingredients in syrups and sherbets (from the Arabic *sharab*), as well as in many kinds of perfumed waters, mainly rosewater and orange flower water. See FLOWER WATERS and SHERBET. The origin of candied fruit techniques is definitely Middle Eastern, with candied flowers given the distinctive name of *murrabayat*, preserves made of pulverized flowers mixed with sugar. In the Western world, the use of flowers in confectionery is first mentioned in the eleventh century, as rose and violet waters for use in fruit preserves and jams. See FRUIT PRESERVES.

Flowers, in the form of "fake" sugar flowers perfumed with flower essences, featured prominently in the extravagant sugar compositions of the seventeenth and eighteenth centuries. See SUGAR SCULPTURE. Around the same time, though, a renewed interest arose in the use of "real" flowers in confectionery. In *Delightes for Ladies*, the English writer and inventor Sir Hugh Plat wrote:

> Dip a rose that is neither in the bud, nor overblowne, in a sirup, consisting of sugar, double refined, and Rose-water boiled to his full height, then open the leaves one by one with a fine smooth bodkin either of bone or wood; and presently if it be a hot sunny day, and whilest the sunne is in some good height, lay them on papers in the sunne, or else dry them with some gentle heat in a close roome.

Plat also offered a more extravagant recipe that describes how to candy rose petals on the bush by pouring syrup over them and letting the petals dry in the sun.

Among the flowers most frequently mentioned as fit for candying are violet, rose, orange flower, marigold, lilac, acacia, mimosa, chrysanthemum, carnation, daffodil, lemon and jasmine, borage, and rosemary. However, only roses, violets, and to a lesser extent orange flowers had historically broad use, becoming part of a candied flower industry that still produces them commercially. Because flowers must be harvested during the night or at dawn to preserve their freshness, and sugared within a few hours, the candied flower artisans (and, later, a few industries) were located very close to flower-growing areas, mostly in Spain, southern France, and the northwestern Italian region of Liguria.

Pietro Romanengo fu Stefano, the famous Italian confectionery company based in Genoa and founded in 1780, still makes candied fruits and flowers in the traditional way, using a proprietary handwritten manual from 1906 that describes the candying of rose and violet petals as follows:

> Pick the largest and thickest petals. Bring a sugar syrup to 86°F (30°C). Dip the petals in it and take them out when the syrup starts boiling. Press the petals. Put them back in a 86°F (30°C) syrup and let them rest for 24 hours. Change the syrup and let the petals rest up to one week. Spread the petals to dry and grain them twice with colored sugar.

All nineteenth- and twentieth-century recipes for candied flowers include some tinting of the flowers with natural or artificial colors because flowers when boiled tend to lose their colors (and some of their aroma), which need to be manually restored. See FOOD COLORINGS.

The only flower still commercially candied or crystallized whole is the violet. This flower, usually *Viola odorata* (known also as *Viola di Parma*), is preserved by coating it in egg white and crystallized sugar. Alternatively, hot syrup is poured over the fresh flower, or the flower is immersed in the syrup and stirred until the sugar recrystallizes. Violets were formerly an important part of the economy of the southern French city of Toulouse. Originally brought from Italy, the violet-growing business became so widespread in the Toulouse region that in 1907 there were some 400 farms producing 600,000 bouquets a year. The candied violet industry commenced in the nineteenth century to absorb the excess production of flowers. Today, whole candied violets, known as *violettes de Toulouse*, are made commercially by only one company in Toulouse: Candiflor.

Candied or crystallized flowers are used mainly to decorate desserts. Confiserie Florian, a traditional confectionery company based in a small village above Nice, produces candied flowers but is also expanding the use of candied fruits by creating new recipes. Pietro Romanengo fu Stefano puts whole candied violets in boxes of *marrons glacés*. Orange flowers in many countries are associated with weddings. Candied orange flowers were once used in Italy as wedding favors, associated with confetti or sugared almonds, but they have been replaced by sugar pastilles flavored with orange flower water. See CONFETTI.

See also CAKE DECORATING; CHESTNUTS; PASTILLAGE; and WEDDING.

Blumenfeld, Zoé. *La cuisine de la fleur sucrée*. Tourrettes sur Loup, France: ROM Edition, 2006.

Richardson, Tim. *Sweets: A History of Temptation*. London: Bantam, 2003.

Andrea Rocco

candied fruit is whole fruit or pieces of fruit preserved with sugar through a series of operations in which the natural liquid of the fruit is replaced by sugar. To some extent, candied fruit has affinities with fruit pastes, marmalades, and jams, but differs from these products in that candying requires a sequence of operations over a week or more. Candied fruit is alternatively known as crystallized fruit or glacé (or glacéed) fruit, depending on the product, the country, and the type of finish, but the process is basically the same: steeping cooked fruit in increasingly concentrated sugar solutions so that, by osmosis, the sugar permeates the fruit and reaches a concentration that will ensure the stability of the final product. Candied fruit is "dry"; it might be sticky, but it does not need to be submerged in sugar syrup for storage, although the earliest forms of candied fruit probably were.

The Romans recognized that fruits could be preserved in sweet syrups; Book 1 of *Apicius* (a compilation of early Roman recipes) includes recipes for whole quinces stored in honey and defrutum (thick, concentrated grape juice), and for preserving fresh figs, apples, plums, pears, and cherries by covering them in honey, making sure that none of the fruits touched. Although these preparations might have been precursors, candied fruit as we know it today dates from the medieval era, evolving more or less in tandem with progress in sugar technology and with the availability and affordability of sugar.

Arab culture introduced the art of sugar refining to Mediterranean Europe, and probably also culinary techniques using sugar. A thirteenth-century Arab recipe manuscript includes a recipe for candied citron peel using equal quantities of sugar and honey and flavoring it with ginger, long pepper, Chinese cinnamon, and mastic. It is not clear whether the peel was stored in syrup or dried.

Sweet and therefore prestigious, candied fruit was one component of the final course of a medieval banquet. At a reception given by Pope Clement VI in mid-fourteenth-century Avignon, the dessert featured a multicolored array of candied fruits. At this time, when sugar was still relatively scarce and expensive, honey or concentrated grape must could be substituted for sugar; Clement VI and his successor received an annual gift from the town of Apt of "fruits confits avec du raisiné" (reduced must). In his 1552 book of preserves, Nostradamus similarly recognized the interchangeability of sugar, honey, and concentrated must, though he believed that sugar yielded the best results. See GRAPE MUST and NOSTRADAMUS.

Fifteenth Century

Possibly the earliest recipe collection devoted entirely to confectionery, the fifteenth-century Catalan

Candied pineapple, dates, and cherries create a colorful still life. The process of candying, or glacéeing, fruit is an old one. It involves steeping cooked fruit in increasingly strong sugar solutions until the sugar permeates the fruit and thereby preserves it. © NUTROASTERS

manuscript *Libre de Totes Maneres de Confits*, gives recipes for candied fruits and sweetmeats made with honey and alternative versions of the same using sugar. Significantly, the recipes call for successive boilings of the syrup, whether honey or sugar, before pouring it over the fruit, repeating this process until done: "fins que conegau que sien fets" (literally, "until you know that they are done"). Unfortunately, the recipes do not specify whether the fruits—a great variety, including citrons, oranges, lemons, peaches, apples, quinces, melon, and cherries—are to be stored in the concentrated syrup that, in the final step, is reduced to the "thread" stage, or whether they are allowed to dry. See STAGES OF SUGAR SYRUP. In one recipe for candied citron peel (with sugar), however, the final step calls for dipping the peel in a reduced rosewater-flavored syrup and then transferring it to sheets of paper; this process might have produced a thin, brittle sugar shell around the strips of peel.

In fifteenth-century England, according to C. Anne Wilson, "banquetting stuffe"—the sweetmeats, creams, jellies, and other sweet dishes presented for the final service of a feast—included candied fruit and peel, called "wet sucket" when they were stored in syrup and "sucket candy" when dry. See SUCKET FORK and SUCKETS. Early recipes are not always specific as to whether the product is "wet" or "dry," but it seems likely that until about the seventeenth century, the former was more common. In the sixteenth century Nostradamus indicates that preserves of citrus peel were stored in jars in syrup, whereas candied slices of edible gourd were coated in spiced sugar and stored with sugar in alternate layers. The recipes for candied citrus peel in both Scappi's *Opera* (1570) and Bradley's *The Country Housewife and Lady's Director* (1736) are for "wet" variants, though La Varenne, in his *Le confiturier françois* (1660), expressly states that his candied whole oranges and lemons, orange slices, and orange peel are to be dried on a layer of straw. Massialot, at the end of the seventeenth century, gives instructions "à confire toute sorte de fruits, tant au sec qu'au liquide," at the same time noting that some fruits, such as berries and grapes, are best preserved in syrup. Nevertheless, even fruit stored in dense syrup could be subsequently extracted from the syrup and dried on slate in a drying oven.

Citrus fruits seem to have been the popular choice for candying, although other fruits could also be used. At the end of the seventeenth century Massialot proposed a month-by-month calendar, starting with green apricots in May and cherries in July, chestnuts in November and December, then oranges and other citrus fruit, often imported, in January and February. Angelica could be harvested for candying in spring, summer, and autumn. See ANGELICA. The range of candidates was broader in the warmer climates of Italy, Provence, Spain, and Portugal. *Le cuisinier méridional*, published in Avignon in 1839, gives very detailed instructions for candying green apricots, apricot quarters, peaches, plums, figs, pears, quarters of quince, cherries, walnuts, chestnuts, and oranges. The process is very delicate, the author notes, as the fruit has to be at the correct stage of maturity (slightly less than perfectly ripe) and the sugar must be cooked to the right degree. If the syrup is too concentrated, the sugar cannot penetrate the fruit. Furthermore, Indian sugar is preferred to sugar from the West Indies.

Until the nineteenth century, the candying of fruit was mainly a domestic process, often the task of the mistress of the household or, in noble dwellings, the "officier de bouche," but its production gradually shifted to the domain of the professional, with manuals for professional confectioners becoming more common in the nineteenth century. In France this could well have been a consequence of the Revolution. One of the earliest works outlining the process is *Le confiseur moderne*, first published in Paris in 1803, the same year that Grimod de la Reynière published the first of his *Almanachs des gourmands*. Grimod describes in detail the delights of the *confiseurs* of the rue des Lombards in Paris, with their "confitures sèches et liquides, fruits au candi," though he makes no explicit reference to "fruits confits."

Contemporary Production

Candied fruit production today is most often associated with Mediterranean countries, including Portugal, and countries colonized by them. Certain regions have a reputation for the excellent quality of their candied fruits, including Sicily and the town of Apt in southern France. While stone fruit, citrus fruit, figs, and melons are most commonly represented in European manufactures, tropical fruit such as pineapple, papaya, mango, and guava are candied in Mexico, Brazil, and the Philippines.

Many Asian countries also use the candying process to preserve fruit; China, where the history of candied fruit dates back to the Sung period (960–1279), produces candied ginger, kumquats, pineapple, and even candied kiwi in slices. In the Moluccas, once known as the Spice Islands, the fruit of the nutmeg—the flesh surrounding the mace-covered nutmeg—is candied and dried.

The commercial process, as practiced at Apt, begins with sorting the fruit to eliminate bruised, imperfect specimens. Next, stones or seeds are removed, and any fruits damaged in this process are discarded. The fruit might then go into a sulfur solution to facilitate the absorption of sugar; this solution can also serve for temporary storage. Any traces of sulfur are removed in the subsequent blanching, followed by several rinses in fresh water. The candying proper starts with immersion in a light sugar syrup that is slowly brought to a boil, followed by cooling in the syrup. This process of immersion, bringing to the boil, and cooling is repeated as many as 15 times, with the concentration of sugar (or sugar plus glucose) in the syrup gradually increased each time until the fruit reaches a sugar content of about 65–70 percent. Because the sugar interacts with hemicelluloses and pectins in the cell walls, candied fruit retains its shape. The fruit is dried on racks, after which it might be glazed to enhance appearance and preserve flavor and texture.

Unsurprisingly, given the labor-intensiveness of the process, candied fruit is a luxury product generally reserved for gift giving and special occasions, typically Christmas in the Western world, New Year in Chinese cultures. In Sicily, the traditional Easter cassata is decorated with candied fruits—cherries, oranges, and, in particular, *zuccata*, candied squash. This product dates back at least as far as the fourteenth century and was originally made with zucca or edible gourd, an elongated, white-fleshed fruit with pale green skin, the "carabassat" of the *Libre de totes maneres de confits*. A Sicilian specialty, *zuccata* today uses squash or yellow pumpkins.

The cost of candied fruit generally restricts their culinary use to garnish or decoration, and few recipes call for candied fruit as a principal ingredient. One of these, variously known as American fruit cake, Brazil nut fruit cake, festive fruit and nut cake, or gourmet fruitcake, is essentially a multicolored mix of candied fruit and nuts held together by a small amount of batter. See FRUITCAKE. Diced candied fruit features in the classic French dessert *riz à l'impératrice*, while candied citrus peel goes into a variety of cakes and desserts and can also be coated in chocolate.

See also CANDIED FLOWERS; FRUIT; and MOSTARDA.

Le cuisinier méridional. Avignon, France: Imprimerie Laffont, 1984. First published 1839 by Pierre Chaillot.

Faraudo de Saint-Germain, Luis. "*Libre de totes maneres de confits:* Un tratado manual cuatrocentista de arte de dulceria." *Boletín de la Real Academia de Buenas Letras de Barcelona* 19 (1946): 97–134.

Massialot, François. *Nouvelle instruction pour les confitures, les liqueurs et les fruits*. Paris: Claude Prudhomme, 1716. http://mdc.cbuc.cat/cdm/singleitem/collection/fonsgrewe/id/18/rec/1.

Nostradamus, Michel. *Le traité des fardements et des confitures*. Lyon, 1552. http://www.oldcook.com/doc/nostradamus.pdf.

Scully, Terence, trans. *La Varenne's Cookery: The French Cook; the French Pastry Chef; the French Confectioner*. Totnes, U.K.: Prospect, 2006.

Wilson, C. Anne, ed. *Banquetting Stuffe: The Fare and Social Background of the Tudor and Stuart Banquet*. Edinburgh, U.K.: Edinburgh University Press, 1991.

Barbara Santich

candy, strictly speaking, refers to sweets that are made from sugar or acquire their solid texture mainly from sugar, as opposed to pastries, jellies, puddings, and the like. However, the lines are a little vague. Many people would consider gumdrops to be candies, and to Americans, chocolates are candy. In the United States, a box of candy usually means a box of chocolates.

Indian Beginnings

The history of candy begins in India, where sugar was first refined from cane sap. By 100 C.E. *śarkarā* ("pebbles") was the Sanskrit word for hard sugar crystals drained from syrup. At this stage, *khaṇḍa* or *khaṇḍaka* ("broken piece") meant a cruder product, soft brown crystalline sugar. These words would travel to Europe by way of Persian (*shakar*, *qand*) and Arabic (*sukkar*, *qand*). See SUGAR.

It took centuries for "candy" to come to mean a product made from sugar. The earliest candy was, in effect, *śarkarā* allowed to develop particularly large crystals. In Arabic it was called *sukkar al-nabāt* ("plant sugar") because the crystals "grow" in dense syrup as it cools. This type of large crystal is referred to as rock candy. Although no longer a very important category today, it still appears at the end of a wooden stick for stirring cocktails. And it is still beloved by children, until they discover candies that are not literally rock-hard crystals.

Back in India, the refining process started with a crude syrup made by boiling cane sap so that coarse plant material would rise to the surface, where it could be skimmed off. See SUGAR REFINING. This was called *phāṇita* (in Sanskrit, "skimmed"). In sixth-century Iran, *pānīd* had surprisingly become the name of the first candy made by dissolving refined sugar and then boiling down the syrup. When the syrup became so thick it was chewy, the syrup would be repeatedly stretched on a peg pounded into a wall to make what is called pulled taffy. See TAFFY. Boiling the syrup might have started out as a quasi-alchemical attempt to create a super-refined sugar; on the other hand, the taffy-pulling technique might have been known already, because a similar medieval candy was made by boiling down honey. Both kinds of taffy were often kneaded with nuts.

The Arab Period

For the next few centuries, candy innovation moved to the Arab world. The most important discovery of this period was hard candy (called "boiled sweets" in England). See HARD CANDY. This process requires syrup to be boiled to the hard-crack stage, when it is only about 1 percent water. See STAGES OF SUGAR SYRUP. If this syrup is cooled quickly, it has no crystalline structure and is technically just a super-cooled liquid, like glass. In fact, molten hard-crack syrup can be worked using the same tools and techniques that a glassblower utilizes.

Like glass, hard candy has a pleasant, smooth texture and is easily broken, so it can be crunched comfortably between the teeth. However, as boiling syrup approaches the hard-crack stage, it may suddenly "seize up" or crystallize. This probably explains a peculiar medieval Arabic name for hard candy, *aqrāṣ līmūn*, "lemon cakes." The surviving recipes do not actually call for any lemon juice; they simply instruct the cook to boil syrup until it is about to crystallize, and then to drip it into chilled molds or onto a greased tray.

That might have been enough of a recipe for a professional confectioner, but the term *aqrāṣ līmūn* suggests cooks had already discovered that adding an acid ingredient such as lemon juice—not necessarily enough to taste but enough to split some of the sucrose molecules into fructose and glucose—interferes with crystallization. (Adding an "invert sugar" such as honey or corn syrup also works for the same reason. One thirteenth-century recipe from Moorish Spain says to add honey so that the syrup "retains its moistness and doesn't break up.") The fact that hard candies were called *aqrāṣ līmūn* makes one suspect that adding some lemon juice for luck was a nearly universal practice. It is by no means an accident that so many hard candies in modern times have a sweet-sour fruit flavor, like lemon drops and Life Savers. See LIFE SAVERS. And like today's Life Savers, *aqrāṣ līmūn* were often colored red, yellow, or green. Brightly colored candy is a medieval heritage.

It is known that these confections had reached Europe by the twelfth century because recipes exist for *penidias*, hard candy, and even a pulled honey sweet in *Mappae Clavicula*, a collection of metallurgical and glass-making formulas.

Medieval Arab confectioners also made a sort of *pralin* or perhaps nougatine (*lauzīnaj yābis*) by melting sugar crystals in a pan and tossing ground almonds into it; in addition, they created a kind of nougat (*al-danaf, nāṭif*) by beating egg whites with boiling syrup. See NOUGAT. Finally, they practiced candying, though not with fruits because of the Middle Eastern distaste for fruits' acidity in sweets. A thirteenth-century Syrian book offers a recipe for candying gourd by treating the pieces with lye and then boiling them in syrup until "if you take a piece into the light of the sun, it looks like amber in translucency and color." See CANDIED FRUIT and VEGETABLES AND HERBS.

Candy Goes West

During the Renaissance, candy innovation moved to Europe. By the fifteenth century, candy-coating was a known practice. Tossing a small item such as a nut in a pan of syrup still makes a host of candies—comfits, Jordan almonds, jelly beans, and M&M's. See COMFIT and PANNING.

European confectioners began to experiment with the use of dairy products in candy. In the late eighteenth century, butterscotch was created by adding butter to sugar syrup, which prevented "seizing up" by making the sugar crystals slide past each other rather than linking up. See BUTTERSCOTCH. This use of fat became so common in the nineteenth century that English confectioners referred to the medieval technique of adding lemon juice as "greasing" the syrup. Around this time dairy products such as milk and cream were added to syrup to make soft, rich candies such as caramels and New Orleans praline. See CARAMELS and PRALINE.

Modern technology has created an endless variety of candies, but such is the human sweet tooth that most of the techniques were already known 800 years ago.

See also CORN SYRUP; FRUCTOSE; GLUCOSE; and HONEY.

Mason, Laura. *Sugar-Plums and Sherbet: The Prehistory of Sweets.* Totnes, U.K.: Prospect, 2004.

Toussaint-Samat, Maguelonne. *A History of Food.* 2d ed. Oxford: Wiley-Blackwell, 2009.

Charles Perry

candy bar, an iconic confectionery form consisting of chocolate and other ingredients, is the sweet by-product of two intertwined and indomitable forces: the Industrial Revolution and capitalism. For most of its history, chocolate was prohibitively expensive, mostly consumed in a liquid form and almost exclusively by the aristocracy. But several European innovations of the mid-nineteenth century changed all that. In 1847 the English confectioner Joseph Fry came up with the idea of creating a moldable paste of cocoa powder, sugar, and cacao butter. His discovery was followed by Henri Nestlé's creation of the first bar of milk chocolate and Rodolphe Lindt's invention of conching, a process that makes chocolate creamier. See COCOA; LINDT, RODOLPHE; and NESTLÉ. In 1893 American confectioner Milton Hershey saw a conching machine on display and immediately purchased it. Following in the footsteps of Cadbury and other European pioneers, Hershey—considered by Americans the godfather of the candy bar—began to mass-produce and distribute milk chocolate bars in 1905. See CADBURY; HERSHEY, MILTON S.; and HERSHEY'S.

The American market for candy bars was accelerated a decade later by the United States military, which asked Hershey's and other companies to produce a single-serving portion of chocolate for the ration kits given to soldiers. The doughboys returned home with an appetite for chocolate bars, soon to be called "candy bars," which quickly spread to the general population. See MILITARY.

Ray Broekel, widely considered the world's leading authority on candy bars, estimates that regional confectioners manufactured tens of thousands of different brands in the "golden age" of candy bars between the World Wars. Most were made of the same suite of ingredients—chocolate, caramel, fudge, and nuts—though locally grown fruits such as cherries, figs, or even pineapple, were sometimes included. The health craze of the 1920s spawned a bar known as the Vegetable Sandwich, consisting of dehydrated vegetables enrobed in chocolate and including the ill-advised tagline "Will Not Constipate." A decade later, during the Great Depression, candy bars such as the Chicken Dinner and the Club Sandwich—which featured mostly chocolate, nuts, and caramel—sold for a nickel and were advertised as a protean form of fast food, promising the consumer quick energy on the cheap. This emphasis on caloric heft led to the introduction of whipped nougat and marshmallow, which made bars appear larger and therefore more filling. See MARSHMALLOWS and NOUGAT. All these additions also made the bars cheaper, since the quantity of expensive chocolate was minimized.

Because of the similar ingredients included in most candy bars, manufacturers sought to distinguish their brands through marketing. Some were linked to cultural icons such as Charles Lindbergh, Clara Bow, or Babe Ruth. Other bars celebrated popular expressions (Boo Lah, Dipsy Doodle), exotic locales (Cocoanut Grove, Nob Hill, Fifth Avenue), dance crazes (Tangos, Charleston Chew), local delicacies (Baby Lobster), hit songs (Red Sails), carnival attractions (Sky Ride), even quiz shows (Dr. IQ). During Prohibition, the Marvel Company of Chicago made an Eighteenth Amendment Bar, which boasted "the prewar flavor" and pictured a bottle of rum on the label. World War II ushered in a battalion of militaristic bars: Flying Fortress, Jeep, Chevron, Buck Private, Big Yank, and Commando.

As documented by Joël Brenner in *The Emperors of Chocolate*, Milton Hershey and his chief rival, Forrest Mars, quickly came to dominate the U.S. market by automating their factories, establishing a national distribution system, buying out competitors, and stockpiling raw ingredients. See MARS. As a result, by the 1980s more than 90 percent of the bars that appeared on domestic candy racks were made by one of three multinational corporations: Hershey's,

Mars, or the European giant Nestlé. (On the world market, Mondelez, which owns Cadbury, is second only to Mars.) Because so much of their equity resides in the production techniques used to manufacture different bars, the confectionery companies are highly secretive. They have been known to blindfold noncompany workers brought in to repair particular machines, and they rarely allow nonemployees inside their plants.

The number of candy bars produced by smaller American companies has continued to dwindle as the retail landscape has consolidated. Large retail chains such as Walmart charge often prohibitive "slotting fees" to place candy bars in desirable locations in its stores, such as near the cash registers, where many shoppers make impulse buys.

In order to increase the variety of candy bars offered, the so-called Big Three have embraced the concept of brand extensions, introducing new versions of leading bars such as Snicker's, Milky Way, and Kit Kat. In this way, they are able to capitalize on recent confectionery trends, such as the popularity of dark chocolate. The Big Three have also experimented with different sizes. The standard candy bar weighs roughly 2 ounces. Mars has introduced bars nearly twice that size, as well as "fun size" and "bite size" bars that are well under an ounce.

The cost of candy bars has risen roughly in correspondence with inflation (although the Hershey's Bar stayed at a nickel for nearly half a century, until 1969). Nevertheless, candy bars remain relatively cheap compared to gourmet chocolates, which are usually sold in boxed sets or by the piece. See CHOCOLATE, LUXURY and CHOCOLATES, BOXED.

Many of the most popular varieties of candy bar, however, do not actually take the form of a bar. Two brands that consistently rank in the top five are Reese's Peanut Butter Cups and M&M's, small pods of candy-coated chocolate. See M&M's and REESE'S PIECES.

See also ADVERTISING, AMERICAN and CHOCOLATE, POST-COLUMBIAN.

Almond, Steve. *Candyfreak: A Journey through the Chocolate Underbelly of America*. Chapel Hill, N.C.: Algonquin, 2004.

Brenner, Joël. *The Emperors of Chocolate*. New York: Broadway, 2000.

Broekel, Ray. *The Great American Candy Bar Book*. Boston: Houghton Mifflin, 1982.

Steve Almond

candy canes are hard candies, or "boiled sweets," that evoke the sights, sounds, and smells of Christmastide with their brilliant red and white stripes and sweet, peppermint, hard candy crunch.

The manufacturing process begins with the boiling of granulated sugar and water to the "hard crack" stage, around 300°F (142°C). See STAGES OF SUGAR SYRUP. The resulting liquid takes on a straw-like color and molten consistency before being poured onto a table for cooling. When the sugar cools sufficiently to handle, it is pulled repeatedly on a taffy hook to incorporate air into the mass. While the candy is being stretched and pulled, it turns brighter and whiter, reflecting and refracting light. Flavoring, usually peppermint oil in liquid form, is now added. The batch is then rolled on the table and divided, with the candy maker sectioning off by knife or scissors a small portion of it to form the red striping.

A boy eagerly peers at a candy cane in a store window in Bangor, New York, in this early-twentieth-century promotional card. Candy canes were made by hand until the Bunte Bros. of Chicago began mass-producing them in the late 1920s.

Red or another color is now kneaded into this portion of the batch, which is then left to rest while still warm. This colored portion will not be worked on the hook as long, in order to obtain a glassy translucence against the white opaque body. See FOOD COLORINGS.

The main batch is then further hooked by hand or pulled on a machine until the kneaded sugar attains a pearly white color. Then it is formed into an oblong loaf. At this point, the colored section is drawn out and rolled by hand to form a red rope, which is carefully twisted around the white loaf. Soon the familiar striping begins to emerge. Usually, this work is done either in front of "batch warmers" to keep the sugar pliable or, ideally, on a "batch roller," large steel cylinders that rotate the batch mechanically while simultaneously keeping it warm. The mass is then extruded by hand to the desired thickness and cut into uniform lengths using candy shears. As one candy maker is working to maintain the consistency of the stripe during extrusion, a fellow candy maker is "crooking" the sticks while they are still warm to achieve the familiar cane shape. The hard candy quickly cools and will be packaged in paper or cellophane.

Although the process of making candy canes has not changed much over the centuries, the symbolism and traditions originally associated with them have. Popular competing myths surround the origin of the candy cane. Regardless of which tale (if any) is true, it is safe to say that candy canes are closely associated with the story of the Nativity and the ensuing Christian holidays.

The most enduring story takes us to Cologne, Germany, around 1670. The choirmaster of the imposing Dom cathedral there attempted to quell the noisy chatter of children during holiday services, when a live Nativity scene or *Putz* was taking place. Hard candy sticks were a common confection in seventeenth-century Germany, available in apothecaries and sweetshops. See HARD CANDY. The choirmaster at Cologne engaged a local confectioner to make a special hard candy stick, with a hook on the end to resemble a cane or, more specifically, a shepherd's crook. This confection was intended to remind the young churchgoers to observe the Nativity with quiet reverence as "shepherds abiding in the field, keeping watch over their flock by night." Owing to the Christian nature of the confection, it has also been suggested that the inverted candy cane was intended to form a "J" for Jesus. Symbolism aside, the sugar clearly helped satiate the children during the long and often uncomfortable liturgies.

Some religious commentators believe that the candy canes of old were white to reflect the purity of Christ. Actually, the first candy canes would have been a cream color at best, depending on the refined state of the sugar available to the confectioner. A story from seventeenth-century England posits that the white "body" of the candy cane refers to Christ's flesh, while the thick red stripe references his blood; the three tiny red stripes symbolize the Father, the Son, and the Holy Ghost. In any case, by the second half of the nineteenth century, candy canes had taken on the red and white striped pattern as highly refined white sugar and commercial red food dyes became readily available.

Prior to World War I, candy canes were handmade and produced in modest quantities by local confectioners throughout the Western world. The colors of the stripes varied by confectionery to denote flavor, with green for spearmint, black for anise, and brown for clove or sassafras. In 1921 the Bunte Bros. of Chicago applied for a patent for a machine to manufacture candy canes. By the late 1920s, Bunte was mass-producing the confection wholesale, distributing candy canes to candy shops and druggists all over the United States. Currently, 1.7 billion candy canes are sold each year. They are now made in every imaginable flavor and color combination, although the traditional peppermint red and white canes predominate. Their convenient shape and festive colors adorn Christmas trees, garlands, and stocking tops in both religious and secular traditions. By hook or by crook, candy canes are here to stay.

See also CHRISTMAS.

Bellis, Mary. "History of Candy Canes." http://inventors.about.com/od/foodrelatedinventions/a/candy_canes.htm.

Collins, Ace. *Stories Behind the Great Traditions of Christmas.* Grand Rapids, Mich.: Zondervan, 2003.

Ryan Berley

candy corn

See HALLOWEEN.

candy dishes, like ashtrays and cookie jars, are specialty containers that serve modern consumer habits. Usually of low, shallow form, possibly circular or square, candy dishes tend to be lidless (and unsanitary), while candy jars have lids. Some candy dishes could be confused for ashtrays and vice versa; in a nonsmoking household, an ashtray might be deployed as a candy dish. By extension, almost any vessel could function as a candy dish. Wrapped or unwrapped, candy apparently shows best in glass, according to the great number of dishes in evidence in this medium.

Candy dishes have their roots in Renaissance sugar-paste containers for biscuits and sweets that were arrayed around the princely table during the dessert course. Eighteenth-century inventories of royal court pantries indicate that hundreds of small glass containers were on hand for displaying and serving *dragées*, nonpareils, and drops. One German inventory from 1733 indicates small glass *Confect-Bechergen* (candy cups) and larger *Confect-Schällgen* (candy bowls). Figural examples in Meissen or Du-Paquier porcelain superseded their ephemeral prototypes and were termed "sweetmeat dishes." Emily Post, in *Etiquette in Society, in Business, in Politics and at Home* (1922), used the terms "candy dish" and "compotier" interchangeably.

Novelty or seasonal containers for sweets have a place in American culture. For instance, President John F. Kennedy presented guests on Air Force One with souvenir candy dishes. Open dishes with wrapped or unwrapped candies are a leitmotif in the American workplace, inviting snacking and chance conversation away from the watercooler. Holiday-themed M&M's and ribbon candy are especially popular. President Ronald Reagan kept jars of Jelly Belly jellybeans on his desk at the White House and on Air Force One.

See also CANDY; COMFIT; HARD CANDY; and SERVING PIECES.

Brown, Peter, and Ivan Day. *Pleasures of the Table/Ritual and Display in the European Dining Room 1600–1900.* York, U.K.: Fairfax House, 1997.

Chilton, Meredith, et al., eds. *The Theater of Dessert, Fired by Passion: Vienna Baroque Porcelain of Claudius Innocentius Du Paquier*, pp. 848–911. Stuttgart: Arnoldsche, 2009.

Maureen Cassidy-Geiger

candy hearts

See VALENTINE'S DAY.

Candy Land, a board game, is for many Americans synonymous with childhood. The allure of being transported to a magical world where sweets grow by the roadside is exciting to any child; combine that with brightly colored squares and lovable characters, and it is no wonder that the game, introduced in 1949, remains popular today.

Eleanor Abbott, a retired schoolteacher, developed Candy Land while recovering from polio in the 1940s. She sold the idea to the Milton Bradley Company, which used the marketing slogan "a sweet little game for sweet little folks." The game's promise of plenty—all the sweets you can eat, without a tummyache—immediately caught on with children emerging from the deprivations of World War II.

There have been nine editions of Candy Land. In 1984, when Milton Bradley merged with the toy company Hasbro, specific characters and a narrative—"The Legend of the Lost Castle"—were introduced onto what had been a plotless board. Players now had an incentive to finish the game, not just meander, as they searched for King Kandy's lost castle. This new quest was populated by characters like Plumpy the local sugarplum purveyor, Mr. Mint the candy-cane man, a giant gumdrop called Jolly, Gramma Nutt, Princess Lolly, Queen Frostine, Gloppy the chocolate monster, and the fearsome Lord Licorice. Pulling a character's card could either help or hinder each player's progress, determining how far he or she would travel on that turn. The first player to reach King Kandy's castle is the winner. Players pull cards with either colors (corresponding to the colored squares) or characters. If a player pulls a card with two yellow squares, for example, she would jump ahead two yellow squares on the board; if she were to pull Queen Frostine, however, she would jump ahead to the queen's square. It is entirely a game of luck rather than skill: players can also pull Gloppy's card, which effectively sends them back to the beginning of the board.

In 2010, in response to changing tastes, Hasbro released "Candy Land: The World of Sweets." This latest version eliminates Plumpy, Mr. Mint, and Jolly. Gramma Nutt, who was famous for her peanut brittle, becomes Gramma Gooey, famous for her fudge. And the game no longer seems so innocent: both Lolly and Frostine have been sexualized to reflect new cultural perceptions of female beauty.

First introduced in 1949, the American board game Candy Land has gone through nine editions, with a changing cast of characters that reflect shifting tastes and evolving notions of female beauty and health. © HASBRO

Kawash, Samira. "Polio Comes Home: Pleasure and Paralysis in Candy Land." *American Journal of Play* 3, no. 2 (Fall 2010): 187–220.

Leila Crawford

candy packaging is a twentieth-century innovation. Candy manufactured and sold through the nineteenth century was typically packed in wooden barrels (later cardboard boxes) and shipped to the retailer. Retailers might serve the candy to their customers out of the manufacturer's container, or they might transfer the goods to more attractive glass jars or counter displays. There was little sense of product differentiation or brand identity.

The rise of consumer advertising and brand awareness in the early twentieth century drove manufactures to begin to use packaging to identify and differentiate their product. A growing consumer awareness of hygiene and fear of "germs" in the 1910s also put pressure on candy makers to begin wrapping their goods. Wrappers were a sign that candy was clean and germ-free (although the conditions in factories where the candy was produced would sometimes suggest otherwise).

The trend toward selling candy in factory packages was also accelerated by developments in packaging technology. In the second decade of the 1900s, machines that could efficiently and cheaply wrap small candies such as kisses and drops as well as larger bars became widely available. Advances in wrapping materials also created new possibilities for candy packaging.

Paper and cardboard were the first materials used to wrap candies. The results were not always satisfactory: the porous material did not preserve freshness or flavor, and glues could react with the candy to mar the taste. Paper, however, could be printed, which allowed candy manufacturers to identify their product.

Hershey's was one of the first manufactures to use packaging to develop a brand identity. As early as

1905, the wrappers for Hershey's Bars had a consistent look and always featured the Hershey name prominently. A few other manufacturers successfully branded their goods prior to World War I, but the use of the label to secure a consistent brand did not become common practice until the 1920s. See HERSHEY'S.

Cost was a factor in whether a candy would be sold wrapped. Around 1900, five- and ten-cent candy boxes and paper-wrapped bars began to appear, but it was not economical to wrap cheap "penny candies." Tootsie Roll, introduced in 1908, is believed to be the first individually packaged candy, priced at one cent. The candy cylinders were wrapped in printed paper and packed in boxes that could be used as counter displays. The wrapper featured both the Tootsie logo and patent claims, and was intended to fend off imitators as much as to promote the product. See TOOTSIE ROLL.

Tin foil was better than paper at preserving and protecting the candy, but it could not be printed. This created copycat problems. Many chocolate manufactures put out goods resembling the popular foil-wrapped chocolate morsel Wilbur Buds (1894). H. O. Wilbur spent heavily in the early 1910s on advertising, admonishing consumers to demand authentic Wilbur Buds. Life Savers Pep-O-Mint gained success in 1913, with a printed paper label wrapped around the tin foil tube to create a package that simultaneously protected and advertised the goods. See LIFE SAVERS.

Visual appeal was an important aspect of candy selling. Both paper and foil wrappers had the disadvantage of concealing the contents. Candy makers quickly adopted transparent wrapping materials when they became available in the late 1910s. The first, glassine, was a semi-transparent paper that could be printed and wrapped around bars or made into pouches or envelopes.

Better than glassine was cellophane, a fully transparent wrapping material that revolutionized candy packaging. Cellophane was manufactured in France in the 1910s, but it was not until DuPont began producing it in the United States in 1923 that cellophane became widely adopted for wrapping individual candies, making transparent bags for bulk candies, creating windows in cardboard boxes, and sealing fancy boxed candies to guarantee hygienic freshness.

By the 1940s, many Americans were buying groceries in self-service supermarkets. After World War II, candy packaging changed to reflect this new shopping style. "Penny candies" that had previously been sold in bulk were now packaged in 1- or 2-pound bags. Candy bars were also packaged into 6- or 12-bar units See CANDY BAR. This "family" packaging encouraged shoppers to view candy as similar to other groceries that one might stock regularly. It also gave the shopping parent—typically, the mother—greater control over the candy consumed by her children.

Twenty-first-century innovations in candy packaging emphasize convenience and portioning. Resealable pouches and cupholder-shaped tubs encourage consumers to take candy with them wherever they go. Candy bars today come in a wide range of sizes to accommodate a variety of eating occasions, from the small, snack-sized bars to the extra-large multipiece bar packages that are supposed to encourage saving some for a later occasion or sharing (formerly called "king size"). In response to mounting concerns about the links between diet and health, candy manufacturers are also changing their packaging to give increasing prominence to nutritional and calorie information.

See also CHILDREN'S CANDY and CHOCOLATES, BOXED.

Kawash, Samira. "The Candy Prophylactic: Danger, Disease, and Children's Candy around 1916." *Journal of American Culture* 33, no. 3 (September 2010): 167–182.

Kawash, Samira. *Candy: A Century of Panic and Pleasure.* New York: Faber & Faber, 2013.

McMahon, James D., Jr. *Built on Chocolate: The Story of the Hershey Chocolate Company.* Santa Monica, Calif.: General Publishing Group, 1998.

Samira Kawash

cane syrup is made by peeling and mashing sugarcane (*Saccharum officinarum*), then reducing its juices to produce a toasty, caramelized syrup with slightly bitter notes. Though it is common worldwide wherever the perennial grass grows in tropical and subtropical climates, cane syrup was once particularly loved in the American South—a place where weather demanded an early harvest. Unripe cane would not yield a large quantity of refined sugar—the important commodity—but it was suitable for cane syrup production. On small southern farms cane syrup became a common sweetener, requiring little equipment to make. Cajun Louisianans used the syrup in *gâteau de sirop* (spice

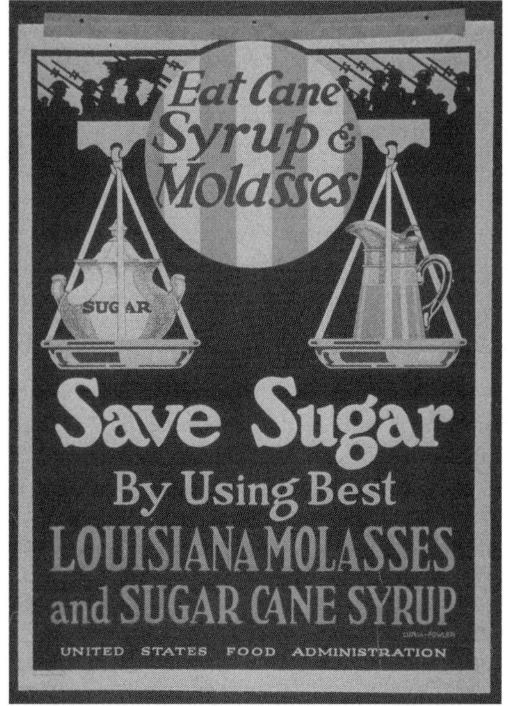

During World War I the U.S. government urged citizens to voluntarily reduce their sugar intake to conserve refined sugar for the war effort. This 1918 poster shows a scale weighing a bowl of sugar against a pitcher of syrup, implying that cane syrup or molasses were the more patriotic options. LIBRARY OF CONGRESS

cake) and *pain perdu* (French toast), or as "syrup soppin," drizzled on a plate at the end of a meal and eaten with bread.

In the early 1900s cane syrup production proliferated in several southern towns, including Cairo, Georgia, which dubbed itself "Syrup City." The real hub, however, was balmy New Orleans, which sold all manner of the sugarcane that grew nearby, in the processed forms of crystallized sugar, dark molasses, and cane syrup—once more commonly called "New Orleans syrup." See NEW ORLEANS. The production of cane syrup was partially spurred by members of the Interstate Sugar Cane Growers Association, as well as by the sugar rationing implemented during World Wars I and II. See SUGAR RATIONING. Nevertheless, it remained largely a small, home-based practice and was eventually eclipsed by falling sugar prices and the prevalence of other syrups, especially Karo corn syrup. See CORN SYRUP. Today, few traditional cane syrup mills remain; the industry is centered in Abbeville, Louisiana—150 miles from New Orleans, and home of Steen's 100 percent Pure Cane Syrup since 1910.

See also GOLDEN SYRUP; MAPLE SYRUP; MOLASSES; and SOUTH (U.S.).

Agee, Hamilton P. *Cane Syrup Making*. Baton Rouge, La.: Ramires-Jones, 1911.
Warner, Deborah Jean. *Sweet Stuff: An American History of Sweeteners from Sugar to Sucralose*. Washington, D.C.: Smithsonian Institution Scholarly Press, 2011.

Emily Wallace

cannelé, a little cake made of a crêpe-like batter and baked in a small cylindrical fluted copper mold, is said to have a 300-year history, although cannelé recipes have only recently begun to appear in cookbooks. A cannelé comes out of the oven rich and moist on the inside, while the outside is deep brown from the thick coating of caramelized sugar. The cakes are named after the shape of the molds in which they are made, *cannelé* meaning "fluted." Such molds are depicted in an early-twentieth-century restaurant supply catalog from J. Jacquotot in Paris, in which the word "cannelé" describes the appearance of several molds and does not indicate a particular cake by that name. Paula Wolfert, who includes a recipe for cannelés in her cookbook *The Slow Mediterranean Kitchen* (2003), writes that when she worked in Bordeaux in the 1970s, cannelés were unknown: "No local guide or notable cookbook published since the start of the twentieth century even mentioned them." Wolfert says that several Bordeaux bakers revived this former local specialty in the 1980s. Cannelés became so popular that they were made all over France, provoking a group of Bordeaux patissiers to lobby for a protected status for their special recipe and method of making the cakes. Today, the cannelé is the "official cake" of the city of Bordeaux. City officials changed the spelling to *canelé de Bordeaux*, whereas the old spelling is used for the "generic" or unofficial version of *cannelé bordelais* (cannelés in the style of Bordeaux).

See also FRANCE and SMALL CAKES.

"Canelé de Bordeaux." http://www.paula-wolfert.com/recipes/canele.html (accessed 24 August 2013).
Fabricant, Florence. "Temptation: A French Morsel with Its Own Memories." *New York Times*, 25 February 1998.

Kyri W. Claflin

cannoli, one of the best-known Sicilian pastries, originated in Palermo to celebrate Carnival but is now a year-round favorite. The name derives from *canna*, a noduled cane reed (*Arundodonax*) cut into sections and then used as a mold to fry the pastry shell. The batter is prepared with flour, eggs, sugar, aromatic wine, and suet, and then fried in hot oil until golden brown. The filling consists of sweetened sheep's ricotta cheese, which is thoroughly sieved to make it creamy. Sometimes the cheese is flavored with chocolate or pistachio, or with small cubes of candied citrus peel, *zuccata* (candied pumpkin), or chocolate chips. Ideally, the creamy filling should be added just before eating to maintain its contrast with the crisp outer layer.

In Sicily cannoli come in various sizes, ranging from minute *cannulicchi* (5 cm) to the enormous ones (20 cm) made at Pianadegli Albanesi. Cannoli have always been a highly appreciated gift, and an old tradition was to offer *la testadelturcu* ("Turk's head"), a large pastry base in the shape of a Turk's turban filled with several rows of cannoli.

Contemporary variations include cannoli that are baked instead of fried, and industrially produced shells are now sold vacuum-packed. Some small Italian *pasticcerie* still use the canes for frying, although they have been replaced for the most part by metal cylinders. Outside Italy, various fillings are substituted for the original recipe; they include custard, mascarpone, whipped cream, and other ingredients.

See also CARNIVAL and ITALY.

Coria, Giuseppe. *Profumi di Sicilia: Il libro della cucina siciliana*. Palermo, Italy: Vito Cavalotto, 2006

Taylor Simeti, Mary. *Pomp and Sustenance: Twenty-five Centuries of Sicilian Food*. New York: Knopf, 1989.

June di Schino

caramels or caramel candies are small sweets created by cooking glucose, sugar, and milk or cream together with butter and flavoring to yield a confection that is opaque, medium brown in color, and with a texture that ranges from soft to medium-hard and chewy. Once cooked, the mixture is usually cut into small squares that are wrapped individually to prevent the pieces from sticking together. A softer version is made for filling chocolates and chocolate bars. This type of caramel is also used in cakes or cookies, such as the layered combination of soft caramel and chocolate topping set upon a shortbread base, known as caramel squares, or sometimes as millionaire's shortbread. Very soft caramel mixtures with a velvety texture are popular in North America and elsewhere, swirled through ice creams, as cake fillings, sweet sauces, flavors for puddings and syrups, and as a coating for caramel corn or sweetened popcorn.

Confusingly, the word "caramel" (singular) has a technical meaning in English, referring to one of the stages of boiled sugar created by cooking sugar syrup to temperatures of 320°F (160°C) or above when it browns and acquires a burnt flavor. See STAGES OF SUGAR SYRUP. To complicate matters, this is a relatively modern usage of the word. In previous centuries caramel indicated the stage now known as hard crack, when the sugar cools to a hard but uncolored mass. This helps to explain why in some languages, for instance, Spanish and Russian, *caramelo* or *karamel* indicates clear hard sugar sweets or hard candy, not the milky, chewy type of confection purchased in the sweetshops of the Anglophone world.

The notion of caramelized sugar is not helpful in understanding the chewy caramel candies popular in the English-speaking world. The distinctive flavor of this sweet is provided by caramelization of the milk in the presence of sugar. The mixture is cooked at 257° to 266°F (125° to 130°C), at which temperature a small amount of moisture (about 7 percent) remains, which enables the texture to be malleable. Recipes are carefully balanced to optimize this characteristic; as Charles Appel explained in *Twentieth Century Candy Teacher* (1912), "When people are eating a caramel they want something they can chew." In industry, condensed milk is preferred to cut down on cooking time, and glucose syrup is used in addition to brown sugar. Flavors added to the candies include vanilla, fruit essences, maple syrup, and chocolate. Fat is also important; industrial producers have experimented with substitutes for the traditional butter, and vegetable fats are frequently used in place of dairy ones.

In their ingredients and flavor, caramels are related to butterscotch and toffee and, like these sweets, have a slightly mysterious history, emerging as formalized recipes only at the end of the nineteenth century. Although it is impossible to identify the exact moment when caramels diverged from these other confections, the British clearly saw them as an American innovation, calling them "American caramels" and regarding them as a much-sought-after novelty; E. Skuse commented on this in *The Confectioner's Handbook* (ca. 1892). A French caramel sweet, *negus de Nevers*, also originated around this time, but Dutch *hopjies*, with a caramel coffee flavor, claim a much older pedigree, dating back to the late eighteenth century.

Lees, R., and E. B. Jackson. *Sugar Confectionery and Chocolate Manufacture*. Aylesbury, U.K.: Leonard Hill, 1973.

Mason, Laura. *Sugar-Plums and Sherbet*. Totnes, U.K.: Prospect, 2004.

Laura Mason

cardamom

See SPICES.

Carême, Marie-Antoine

Carême, Marie-Antoine (1783/4–1833), christened Marie-Antoine but nearly always known as Antonin, styled himself the "Palladio of patisserie" and has some claim to be the father of modern French confectionery. He was pastry chef to Charles-Maurice Talleyrand, Napoleon's foreign minister, and his fame spread first via the diplomatic corps as a result of his skill as a sculptor and scenic artist working with sugar as his medium. In truth his primary gift may have been as a self-publicist as much as confectioner, which is why he is also known as the first "celebrity" chef. Carême exploited his connections to forge a successful publishing career, arguably the first chef to find mass market appeal during the gastronomic publishing boom of the early nineteenth century, itself connected to the era's obsession with decorative confectionery.

Carême illustrated his own cookbooks and had a signal interest in the visual impact of food served in the courtly service à la française style. This required elaborate sculptural center pieces (*pièces montées*) frequently made partially or entirely of spun sugar. See SUGAR SCULPTURE. Carême's books described and illustrated semi-edible ships in sail, turning globes, and architectural follies. They rarely featured clear recipes, but he is nevertheless credited with coining the phrase "you can try this yourself at home." Carême's greatest gifts to confectionery history therefore were as both a food-chronicler and a cook. He spun gold out of sugar via publishing, helping to create the cult of the chef as well as positing sugar as the key ingredient in glamorous cuisine. He claimed to be the originator, variously, of choux pastry, soufflés, the toque or iconic chef's hat, the vol-au-vent, and the definitions of the boiling points of sugar. Little of this was properly his invention. See PASTRY, CHOUX; SOUFFLÉ; and STAGES OF SUGAR SYRUP.

Born in the slums of Paris's Left Bank in 1783, Carême may have had as many as 23 siblings. He went on to cook for Napoleon, the Russian tsar Alexander I, and the British prince regent, but his self-aggrandizing legend as "the Napoleon of the kitchen" began during the French Revolution. Carême was abandoned as a nine-year-old at the height of The Terror (1792) and began cooking at a *gargotier* (chophouse) near the site of the guillotine. He was apprenticed at Bailly's patisserie on the rue Vivienne before being talent-spotted by Talleyrand, probably around 1797. Certainly by the end of the eighteenth century, Carême's skill as a patissier and sugar sculptor had caught the attention of

Marie-Antoine Carême was arguably the first celebrity chef, known especially for his elaborate sculptural centerpieces (*pièces montées*), which were frequently constructed of spun sugar. He is also remembered for several masterly cookbooks. This engraving is from an 1854 edition of *Le pâtissier royal parisien*, first published in 1815.

Paris. His first written work, *Le pâtissier royal parisien* (1815), makes it certain that he studied in the print room of the Bibliothèque Nationale and there began a lifetime's fascination with architecture and the decorative arts, which in turn closely informed his work. His style of sugar craft, featuring hermitages and ruined temples, may be regarded as the confectionery analog to English garden follies of the neoclassical and Gothic period. Carême's fame therefore rests on his obsession with the architectural and plastic properties of the increasingly refined sugars of his era. His definitions of the boiling points of sugar stand to this day, and his description of the means of testing temperature (with bare hands and iced water nearby) is still a rite of passage for patissiers.

The tumultuous politics of Carême's era—the rise and fall of Napoleon, the invasion of the Russian army, and the restoration of the Bourbon monarchy under Louis XVIII—offered occasions for grand court and regimental dining featuring elaborate desserts and *pièces montées*. These banquets gave both reason and budget for Carême's increasingly lavish deployment of spun sugar, and he was one of the star chefs involved in the gargantuan Champs Elysées feast for 10,000 veterans in 1815, as well as in the Allies' victory banquets in Champagne. It is for this work, beyond confectionery, that he is often remembered.

Following these military banquets Carême's cooking, and his career, moved increasingly toward publishing. *Le pâtissier royal parisien* (1815) was followed by *Le pâtissier pittoresque* (1816), *Le maître d'hôtel français* (1822), *Le cuisinier parisien,* (1828), and his masterwork, *L'art de la cuisine française au XIXe siècle,* in five volumes (1833). Although Carême took commissions from time to time—with the British prince regent (catering one Brighton banquet featuring 137 dishes and 8 separate sugar *pièces montées*), for the British ambassador and his wife in Vienna and the marquis and marchioness of Londonderry, and in Russia for the dowager empress Maria Feodorovna—his desire to cook "below stairs" palled along with his need to do so. The patronage of Betty Rothschild in the late 1820s brought Carême into close contact with Chopin, Paganini, and Victor Hugo, and he became particularly friendly with Heinrich Heine and Rossini, who dedicated compositions to him just as Carême dedicated dishes to Rossini. Such attention marks a certain ascendancy for the profession of confectioner, treated as an equal among the great artists of the era, but Carême's professional triumphs were bought at the expense of his health, and he died in 1833, aged less than fifty.

See also FRANCE and PARIS.

Bernier, Georges. *Antonin Carême: La Sensualite gourmande en Europe*. Paris: Grasset, 1989.

Dumas, Alexandre. *Le Grand Dictionaniare de cuisine.* Edited, abridged, and translated by Louis Colman. London: W. H. Allen, 1959.

Kelly, Ian. *Cooking for Kings: The Life of Antonin Carême, the First Celebrity Chef.* New York: Walker, 2004.

Rodil, Louis. *Antonin Carême.* Marseilles, France: Éditions Jeanne Laffitte, 1980.

Ian Kelly

Carnival is a secular holiday celebrated in many places where Catholicism is or was the dominant religion. Despite its inherently secular nature, Carnival is intimately tied to the Christian calendar. Specifically, it is a time of revelry and feasting that immediately precedes the liturgically somber period of Lent, which was traditionally marked by strict fasting for the approximately six weeks preceding Easter. The name "Carnival" itself reflects this relationship to fasting, as it derives from the medieval Latin *carnem levare,* "the setting aside of meat."

The length of the Carnival celebration has been variably interpreted: in some cases, it has focused largely on the Tuesday immediately preceding Ash Wednesday, known traditionally in English as Shrove Tuesday but now also as Fat Tuesday, a calque of the French Mardi Gras. Even more extended interpretations of Carnival season exist, however, as in modern New Orleans, where Mardi Gras celebrations take place over the course of the two weeks preceding Lent, and the broader Carnival season begins with or immediately after the Epiphany (6 January, the end of the Christmas season).

Although it is widely believed that some of the core traditions associated with Carnival celebrations have pre-Christian origins (e.g., in the Roman *Saturnalia*), the modern manifestations clearly go back to medieval or early modern practices. Carnival traditions have survived most strongly in the western Mediterranean lands of Italy, southern France, and Iberia. With European colonial expansion, Carnival celebrations also became firmly entrenched in various parts of the Americas, most famously in areas formerly belonging to France (New Orleans,

Mobile, Guadaloupe) and Portugal (Rio and generally in Brazil).

Two basic aspects of the holiday have directly influenced the foods associated with it. The first is Carnival's juxtaposition to the period of Lenten fasting. Originally, the fast involved abstinence from all animal products, including lard, butter, cheese, and eggs, and there was a general expectation that food consumption during Lent would be restrained, so that lavish use of any expensive and especially tasty preparations, including those not involving animal products, would also be avoided on fast days. The impending sobriety of Lent brought about a natural intensification of the opposition of fat and lean and a particular inclination to consume fatty and fried dishes during the Carnival period, but also more generally to indulge in festive preparations that involved costly ingredients, such as highly refined wheat flour, sweeteners, and spices.

The other aspect of Carnival that strongly influenced its culinary traditions was the importance of the communal celebratory gatherings it featured, with widespread traditions of parades, competitions, musical performances, and plays carried out on the streets of cities, towns, and villages throughout Europe in which all elements of society, including the poor, participated. Simple but festive foods that are quintessential "street foods" have therefore always been a central part of Carnival celebrations, including, among sweet offerings, all kinds of deep-fried dough preparations. See FRIED DOUGH. The geographical and cultural splits between northern Protestant and southern Catholic lands are reflected to a degree in surviving culinary practices: whereas the tradition of fried sweets, especially doughnuts, was apparently once extremely widespread throughout Europe, it is now less strongly represented in northern, Protestant Europe but continues to flourish in the Catholic south.

Some traditional carnival sweets include the following:

- England and the British Isles: Shrove Tuesday traditionally calls for eating pancakes; the holiday itself is in some places called "Pancake Day." See PANCAKES.
- Low Countries: In Dutch Limburg, one finds *nonnevotte*, a member of the fried dough family with a particularly handsome, bow-like form.
- Scandinavia: In Sweden, the main Carnival sweet is the *semla* (pl. *semlor*), also called *fastlagsbulle* or *fettisdagsbulle*. It is a bun made with enriched dough flavored with cardamom and filled with almond paste and whipped cream; variants are also consumed in Finland and Estonia. In Denmark and Norway, a similar baked sweet, the *fastelavnsbolle*, serves the same function, though it is made of Danish-style puff pastry and typically filled with jam or vanilla custard.
- Poland and Roman Catholic Eastern Europe: Three types of sweets are widely enjoyed: doughnuts (plain or filled); simple bits of crisply fried, shaped dough dusted with sugar; and pancakes served most often with fruit preserves or sweetened cottage cheese. The most famous are the Polish doughnuts known as *pączki*, which have close analogs in the Czech *koblihy* and the Hungarian *farsangi fánk*. See DOUGHNUTS. In Lithuania, the main Carnival sweet is pancakes, *blynai*; other forms of pancakes are part of the pre-Lenten celebrations in the Czech Republic (*palačinky*), Hungary (*palacsinta*), and Croatia (*palačinke*). Polish *faworki*, Hungarian *csöröge fánk*, and Croatian *krostule* are examples of simple fried doughs.
- Germany and Austria: Fried sweetened yeast-dough products, often filled with fruit preserves or jam, are popular in virtually all regions and often bear the name *Krapfen* (*Fastnachtskrapfen, Faschingskrapfen*). As a Carnival prank, one doughnut in a batch filled with fruit preserves or jam might contain a filling of mustard. Fritters are also widely consumed. See FRITTERS. Note, too, the North German *Berliner Pfannkuchen*, which are in fact doughnuts and not pancakes.
- Italy: The two most widespread forms of Carnival sweets are doughnuts and simple shaped bits of fried dough, with great variation in the details of preparation and their local names. In the doughnut realm, there are *ciambelle di Carnevale* and zeppole; *chiacchiere, cenci*, and *crostole* are only a few types of fried dough. Small balls of fried dough dressed with honey (*cicerchiata*) are also traditional in some regions.

In addition to the aforementioned, a few other notable Carnival sweets are the southern Italian sausage sanguinaccio; *schiacciata alla fiorentina* (a sort of cake made with lard and flavored with orange); and *berlingozzo* (a ring-shaped cake flavored with anise). See SANGUINACCIO. *Castagnole*, originally from the region of Romagna, are lemon-flavored fritters that resemble chestnuts. Sicilian cannoli, with their fried tubular shells and ricotta-based filling, are also strongly associated with Carnival celebrations in their home region. See CANNOLI.

- France: As elsewhere, fried sweets are especially important throughout the country, especially beignets, with many regional variants of recipes and names, such as the Lyonnais *bugnes*, the *beugnons* of Berry and Sologne, *faverolles*, *roussettes*, and *merveilles*; they can be plain or include fruit. Also widely consumed are pancakes (crêpes), which are particularly associated with the Carnival season holiday of La Chandeleur (2 February). In the north of France, waffles (*gaufres*) are also an important part of the celebrations.
- Spain: Like France's beignets, the *buñuelos* of Spain have many local variations. In southern Spain, *pestiños* are a sweet dough flavored with sesame, cinnamon, white wine, and citrus peel; folded into a distinctive shape; and then fried. In some areas, they are flavored with bay leaf and anise and are finished with confectioner's sugar or honey.
- United States: In the United States, where so many immigrant groups have brought their holiday traditions, we find king cakes and beignets in New Orleans, *pączki* in places like Chicago with large Polish populations, *fasnachts* (doughnuts) in areas where a German influence is strong, and *malasadas* in Hawaii, reflecting a Portuguese influence.

See also FESTIVALS and HOLIDAY SWEETS.

Aris, Pepita. *The Complete Spanish Cookbook.* London: Hermes House, 2004.

Burke, Peter. *Popular Culture in Early Modern Europe.* Aldershot, U.K.: Ashgate, 1996.

Mosesson, Anna, Janet Laurence, and Judith H. Dern. *The Food and Cooking of Scandinavia: Sweden, Norway, Denmark.* Wigston, U.K.: Lorenz, 2011.

Saint-Ange, E. *La bonne cuisine de Madame Saint-Ange.* Translated by Paul Aratow. Berkeley, Calif.: Ten Speed, 2005.

Scharfenberg, Horst. *The Cuisines of Germany: Regional Specialties and Traditional Home Cooking.* New York: Poseidon, 1989.

Anthony F. Buccini

cassata is a lavish cake from Sicily, a complex concoction of layered liqueur-soaked sponge cake interspersed with sweetened ricotta cheese, fruit preserves, and jellies surrounded by marzipan and decorated with baroque garnishes and flourishes of marzipan fruits, rosettes, flowers, and curlicues. Cassata probably originated as a simple egg, sugar, and ricotta cheese cake. See CHEESE, FRESH and CHEESECAKE. Cassata also refers to a contemporary ice cream inspired by the cake.

Although the etymological derivation of "cassata," and therefore clues as to its origins, is not yet a settled matter, the notion that cassata comes from the Latin *caseus*, the word for cheese, because it can be made with cheese, was called "far-fetched" by the famous early-twentieth-century etymologists da Aleppo and Calvaruso. The Latin derivation is not as far-fetched as they make out, though, because even in the fourteenth century, Angelo Senisio, a Sicilian abbot who wrote a dictionary of Sicilian vernacular in 1348, defines cassata as a *torta* (cake) derived from the Sicilian *casu*, that is, *cacio* (cheese), a food of bread and cheese (*vivanda di pane e cacio*). The history in verse *La vita di lo Beato Corrado* composed by the nobleman Andriotta Rapi of Noto, probably in the fifteenth century, also records the word "cassata," which C. Avolio in *Introduzione allo studio del dialetto siciliano* (1888) defines as "a cake with a base of cheese (*caseata*)."

However, the Latin etymologies for the Sicilian cassata might be tenuous because the various words used to describe a cheese cake might refer either to a cake with cheese unrelated gastronomically to the Sicilian cassata, or to something completely other than cheese. For example, in both Michele Pasqualino's eighteenth-century Sicilian-Italian dictionary and Vincenzo Mortillaro's nineteenth-century Sicilian-Italian dictionary, the definition of "cassata" also means, besides a kind of cheesecake, a sweet-box where sweets are kept, derived from *casseta*, a kind of small box.

However, cassata is, more than anything, born of a fascination with sugar, not cheese, and sugar was not cultivated in Sicily during the Roman era. It was only when the Arabs brought sugar to Sicily and an energetic sugar industry took root in the tenth century that sweet inventions using this product appeared. The more likely derivation is from the word for the baking tray or earthenware bowl in which the primitive cassata was cooked, the Arabic *qasʿat*. Thus, the genesis of the Sicilian cassata may very well be traced to the Arab era, or shortly afterwards to the Arab-influenced kitchens of Norman-Sicilian monasteries, as a very simple concoction of eggs and flour. Cassata was early on a springtime cake traditionally made as an Easter specialty by the monastery nuns or for Purim by Sicilian Jews. Cassata was so delicious and seductive that as late as 1574, the diocese of Mazara del Vallo had to prohibit its making at the monastery during the holy week because the nuns preferred to bake and eat it than pray. Documents show that large purchases of ricotta were made in Sicily before the end of Lent.

Cassata seems related to not only Lent but also Passover. A document referring to Sicilian Jews, an old community in Sicily who spoke Arabic in the eleventh century, contains an explicit reference to *festum Judeorum nuncupatum di li Cassati* (for the Jewish festival, it is called *cassati*), which must be Passover. It is contrasted to Easter, which is what the reference to *festum Azimorum* in the documents must mean (*azimorum* translates to "unleavened"). The earliest and clearest reference to cassata as a specifically Sicilian cake made with ricotta cheese, as it is today, dates to a delivery contract of 1409 to a Jew named Sadon Misoc. However, the first mention of a possible ancestor of cassata appears in the Paris manuscript of the *Riyād an-nufūs*, a tenth-century description attributed to Abū Bakr al-Mālikī, about whom we otherwise know nothing. He reports that Abū al-Fadl, an orthodox jurist from the Aghlabid capital in Tunisia, refused to eat a sweet cake called a *kaʿk* because it was made with sugar from Sicily, then ruled by unorthodox Shiites. In the twelfth-century diet book of Abū Marwān ibn Zuhr, *Kitāb al-aghdhiya* (Book of Diet), a *kaʿk* is described as a kind of twisted ring-shaped bread or cake fried in oil and finished with pistachios, pine nuts or almonds, rosewater, and honey. This certainly sounds like a precursor of cassata.

Another manuscript from the Middle Ages, dated to 1428, is the *Al-kalām ʿala al-aghdhiya* of al-Arbūlī, a scholar working during the Nasrid reign in Granada. Al-Arbūlī mentions the word *kaʿk*, a kind of cake that is originally Egyptian, and not Persian, which may be the ancestor of the Sicilian cassata. In Andalusia, it referred to as a kind of round or twisted bread loaf or cake with a hole in the middle. Michele Amari, the preeminent historian of the Arabs in Sicily, was the first to note, in his monumental study *Storia dei musulmani di sicilia* (History of the Muslims in Sicily, 1868), that vestigial Arabisms permeated the Sicilian language most especially in the areas of sweet making, agriculture, and hydrology. It seems quite possible that cassata was part of this Arab-influenced repertoire of Sicilian cooks.

See also FRUIT PRESERVES; MARZIPAN; MIDDLE EAST; PERSIA; SPONGE CAKE; SUGAR; and TORTE.

Wright, Clifford. *A Mediterranean Feast: The Story of the Birth of the Celebrated Cuisines of the Mediterranean from the Merchants of Venice to the Barbary Corsairs.* New York: William Morrow, 1999.

Clifford A. Wright

cassava (*Manihot esculenta* Crantz), also called mandioca, manioc, aipim, and yuca, is an Amerindian staple food native to Brazil. By the time the Europeans arrived in the New World, it had already spread throughout South America and the Caribbean basin. Through programs of plant exchange cassava was introduced into the tropics, reaching Africa and Asia in the seventeenth century. Early Brazilian documents refer to the root as "bread," and the flour processed from it soon came to be used as a wheat substitute in baking when combined with sugar or molasses. See MOLASSES and SUGAR. Because cassava is often planted on small farms, it plays an important role in preserving local cultures. Today, Nigeria is the world's largest producer of cassava.

When peeled, cassava can vary in color from white to mustard yellow. All types of cassava contain a poisonous substance, hydrocyanic acid. Bitter cassava, with its higher poison content, is fit for consumption only after having been processed into flour. The roots must be laboriously peeled, washed, grated, compressed, and slowly heated to produce different kinds of flour, depending on the intended use. The finer the flour, the more elegant the resulting cakes and porridges will be. Grainier flours are mainly boiled for use as a starchy accompaniment to savory dishes.

Starchy cassava, or manioc, root is an important tropical staple that is processed into flour or made into tapioca to thicken puddings and sauces. The Dutch painter Albert Eckhout captured the plant's beauty in his *Still Life with Manioc* (1640).

Sweet cassava is less poisonous and is therefore appropriate for home cooking; it has to be peeled and well washed before being used raw, cooked, or fermented for a couple of days in water. As the leftover water from washing the cassava roots evaporates, it results in a very fine powder, the starch, used as a thickener in puddings and sauces and also to make tapioca. See TAPIOCA.

Thanks to cassava's high starch content, desserts made from it typically have a soft texture midway between that of a cake and a pudding. Sweet and golden, they were originally based on Portuguese and Spanish recipes that include a generous amount of sugar and eggs. See EGG YOLK SWEETS; PORTUGAL; and SPAIN. Examples are Filipino cassava cake, Brazilian *bolo de aipim,* and Vietnamese sticky coconut cassava cake, which incorporates mung bean purée in the batter.

See also BRAZIL.

Coe, Sophie D. *America's First Cuisines.* Austin: University of Texas Press, 1994.

Freyre, Gilberto. *Assucar: Algumas recitas de doces e bolos dos engenhos do Nordeste.* Rio de Janeiro, Brazil: Livraria José Olympio Editora, 1939.

Schiebinger, Londa. *Plants and Empire: Colonial Bioprospecting in the Atlantic World.* Cambridge, Mass.: Harvard University Press, 2007.

Marcia Zoladz

caster sugar

See SUGAR.

castoreum is a fragrant food additive harvested from castor sacs at the base of a beaver's tail. Beavers discharge castoreum, a yellowish, viscous fluid, from their cloacal opening to mark their territories. In high concentrations, the substance can be quite pungent; diluted, it exudes a musky, leathery smell.

The unique scent is derived from the beaver's diet. Scientists believe that antifeedants (predator-repelling chemicals) found in many trees are distilled by the beaver's body into castoreum's rich blend of phenolic and neutral compounds.

Castoreum can be extracted either by milking a live beaver or excising the castor sacs from a dead one. The conjoined castor sacs (historically, often misidentified as testicles) are then dried, transforming the castoreum within into a hard, brown, resin-like substance that can be diluted into an extract or oil.

Castoreum has been used in perfumes and medicines for millennia, but its use in food appears to be a more recent phenomenon. Since at least the 1920s, beaver extract has been used as an occasional flavoring ingredient in baked goods, candies, puddings, beverages, and gum—commonly as a vanilla substitute. Castoreum has also been used to flavor cigarettes and is the featured ingredient of the Swedish schnapps BVR HJT.

The additive rarely appears in mass-produced foods, since beaver posterior is a limited, and elusive, resource. The U.S. Food and Drug Administration classifies castoreum as safe for consumption and does not require its explicit identification on nutrition labels. Instead, the rodent secretion is listed as "natural flavoring."

Doucleff, Michaeleen. "Does Beaver Tush Flavor Your Strawberry Shortcake? We Go Myth-Busting." *The Salt,* NPR, 26 March 2014. http://www.npr.org/blogs/thesalt/2014/03/26/293406191/does-beaver-tush-flavor-your-strawberry-shortcake-we-go-myth-busting (accessed 5 July 2014).

Müller-Schwarze, Dietland. *The Beaver: Its Life and Impact.* 2d ed. Ithaca, N.Y.: Cornell University Press, 2011.

Katie Liesener

cavities

See DENTAL CARIES.

celebration cakes mark special occasions, from birthdays to religious holidays to family and civic gatherings. In the late summer of 1598, a German lawyer touring the English countryside passed a wooden cart piled high with a flower-strewn load of wheat, in which a group of people shouted as they waved a "richly dressed" effigy. This tourist was glimpsing the celebration of an ongoing harvest festival, one of many communitarian festivities staged in early modern England under the auspices of local manors or Anglican churches. Variously celebrating agricultural events (sheep washing or shearing), saints' days and religious holidays, and ancient calendar days like May Day and Midsummer, these festivals featured music, dancing, games, mumming, and Maypole frolicking, as well as plenty of drink and special foods, including, if the hosts were generous, a great cake baked in the capacious oven of the manor house or rectory. The private celebrations of the privileged, too, were highlighted by great cakes—manorial court day, commencement day at Oxford and Cambridge, Christmas and Twelfth Night, funerals, and, above all, weddings. See CHRISTMAS; FUNERALS; TWELFTH NIGHT CAKE; and WEDDING.

A great cake was typically compounded of a peck, or 14 pounds, of the finest, whitest wheat flour and enriched with butter, cream, eggs, spices, and a touch of costly sugar. And it was always stuffed with masses of the small raisins called currants, which the English imported from Corinth (hence the name) in such huge quantities that an English travel writer remarked, in 1617, that the Greeks must think that the English used the fruits to dye cloth or feed hogs. Thus, the cake weighed some 35 pounds and stretched 3 or 4 feet across, making it, indeed, a great—or large—cake, and when slicked with a hard white "ice" or "frost" of egg whites and sugar, as it often was, it made a spectacular climax to the celebration. See ICING. The Elizabethan great cake was raised with the yeasty froth skimmed from fermenting ale, and to us it would taste like nothing more than good raisin bread. But to Tudor farm folk, inured to the coarsest black bread eked out with rye, oats, and peas, it was a tremendous treat.

Celebration Cakes Come to America

The English great cake came to America with the earliest English colonists, but many of its original occasions did not. In place of the loathed religious red-letter days of the Anglican Church, as well as the ancient calendar days like May Day, which the Puritans deprecated as pagan, the New England Puritans promulgated various secular holidays, the earliest of which was Connecticut's Election Day, whose boisterous celebration of drink and great cake at the

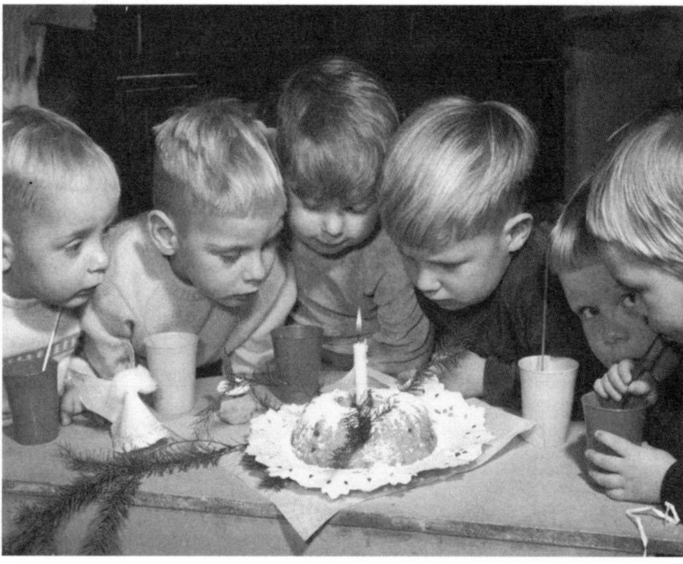

Special cakes baked to mark religious and secular occasions have been around for millennia. In this 1960 photograph, little boys in the Netherlands gather around a yuletide cake dusted with powdered sugar and festively decorated with pine branches. NATIONAL ARCHIVES OF THE NETHERLANDS

colonial court in Hartford was already renowned throughout English North America by 1700. Amelia Simmons, America's first cookbook author, installed Election Cake into enduring memory when she printed a recipe for a great Election Cake weighing close to 100 pounds. Several other American secular holidays also came to be celebrated with great cakes: university commencement days (originally celebrated in connection with Harvard and Yale), Thanksgiving Day, and, to a lesser extent, Independence Day. And early American weddings—and funerals, too—often featured great cakes. Samuel Sewall, one of the judges who condemned the witches of Salem, made several references in his diary to enjoying wedding and funeral great cakes, sometimes with cheese and sometimes with the hot sherry-spiked custard drink called posset, a favorite English cake accompaniment.

American cookbook authors continued to outline modernized (and usually batch-baked, in large quantity) recipes for yeasted, fruited election, Thanksgiving, and commencement cakes into the late nineteenth century. The survival of these cakes was partly nostalgic, but, especially in the case of wedding cakes, it was also practical. These cakes were far cheaper and easier to make than their more modern—and fancier—counterpart, the plum cake. This cake emerged in England around 1700 and took its name from its trove of raisins and currants, which the English came to call "plums" around 1660. Plum cake was not raised by yeast but rather by beating air into roughly equal weights of flour, sugar, butter, and eggs. When made with a pound each of the basic materials and 4 to 5 pounds of fruit, as was typical, the cake filled a pan 14 inches across and 2 to 3 inches deep—not as gargantuan as the great cakes of yore but still an impressive cake, especially if meringue-frosted, and plenty for at least 50 people, as the cake is rich. Plum cake—often called black cake or fruitcake after 1830—reigned as the standard American celebration cake through the time of the Civil War. As cookbook author Eliza Leslie told her readers, "at the close of the evening," it was "usual to send round a large plum-cake" to cap the festivities. Families who celebrated Christmas and Twelfth Night did so with a fine plum cake, and fruitcake was the only genteel choice for a wedding cake, not that everyone could afford one. Birthday and anniversary fruitcakes were still featured in cookbooks published into the 1930s, and wedding fruitcakes, which became tiered and acquired soft icings in the early twentieth century, remained commonplace into the 1960s. Christmas fruitcakes are still treasured by many today. See FRUITCAKE and WEDDING CAKE.

Celebration Cakes after the Civil War

During the last quarter of the nineteenth century, ever more Americans came to celebrate an ever-greater range of occasions, and in more varied and generally more lavish ways. Americans of the more privileged half were becoming wealthier, and their lives easier, due to innumerable technological advances, and they found all sorts of new excuses to party—birthdays, wedding anniversaries, high school graduations, job promotions, retirements, and even whimsical non-occasions, like the change of seasons, a favorite theme of ladies' luncheons. Instructions, often detailed, for luncheons, afternoon tea parties, dinner parties, and evening parties honoring such events appear in not only cookbooks but also etiquette and entertainment books. And many of the plans entail a special cake.

There were reasons for this. By the time of the Civil War, nearly all American households had given up cooking at the hearth in favor of cooking at the enclosed iron stove, whose easily reheated oven made cake baking a much simpler affair than formerly, especially since American women by this time had embraced much cheaper, quicker, more surefire recipes for cake, the linchpin of which was chemical leavening. See CHEMICAL LEAVENERS. Meanwhile, technology had gifted the kitchen with cheaper cake ingredients in more convenient forms—whiter flour, granulated sugar, vegetable shortening, and innumerable flavoring extracts and food colorings—as well as the Dover egg beater, mass-manufactured cake pans in myriad sizes and shapes, and, for the ambitious, pastry bags and tips. Inevitably, American women went on a cake-baking spree. See PANS; PASTRY TOOLS; and WHISKS AND BEATERS.

One stunning consequence of the new enthusiasm for parties and party cakes was the rise of the children's birthday party, with its attendant cake. Before the Civil War, people simply did not throw birthday parties for children, and while they might prepare something special for the little ones on their birthdays, they did not bake cakes for them. (Catharine Beecher, in her influential cookbook of 1845, suggests an apple bread pudding as a children's birthday treat.) But in her cookbook of 1912, Fannie Farmer unveiled for her upper-middling readers "Birthday Cake for a Three-Year-Old." See FARMER, FANNIE. Shown in a full-page photograph, the cake is quite a project: a fashionable new angel cake covered with smooth white icing and decorated in stunning art nouveau style, with daisies made from small non-pareil candies, roses assembled from candied rose petals, and foliage carved from thinly sliced citron. The cake is to be crowned with "three small candles placed in rose cups" made of hard sugar paste, which Farmer helpfully adds "may be bought of first-class city grocers." The early twentieth century seems to have marked the zenith of American women's cake-decorating ambitions. See CAKE DECORATING. In later cookbooks, celebration cakes, birthday and otherwise, are typically festooned only with a few squiggles and rosettes of colored icing and a few artfully placed candied cherries or nutmeats.

It is not possible to speak of a standard American celebration cake after the Civil War because all fashionable cakes were dragooned for celebration purposes—and fashions in cakes were ever changing. Yet there were, perhaps, some usual choices. In 1872 southern cookbook author Mrs. Porter unveiled the White Mountain Cake, a five-layer yellow cake filled and covered with meringue frosting, which, Porter enthused, was "very nice indeed, particularly for weddings and parties." Shortly after the advent of the White Mountain Cake there emerged various red-on-white butter cakes, some layer and others loaf. See LAYER CAKE. The most popular of these cakes for receptions and other large parties was the watermelon cake, a tube cake featuring a white outer layer and a deep-red, currant-flecked core—and sometimes a green icing to complete the conceit. In the mid-twentieth century the reddened-cake idea somehow coalesced into the red velvet cake, which lay low for decades before recently becoming a mega-celebration cake, favored these days even for weddings.

During the mid-twentieth century the angel cake and the white butter cake were frequently pressed into celebratory service. See ANGEL FOOD CAKE. Angel cake was prized for its ethereal softness and towering height, and the white butter cake was loved for its delicate crumb and richness. But what really made both cakes special was their stark white color, which had exerted a peculiar fascination over American women since the invention, in the 1830s, of the white butter cake's grand predecessor, the lady cake, a white pound cake flavored with bitter almonds and rosewater. See POUND CAKE. In her cookbook of 1857, Eliza Leslie wrote that a lady cake, when iced "entirely with white" and decorated with "white flowers," was "now much in use at weddings, and if well made, and quite fresh, there is no cake better liked." Leslie meant "in use" as the so-called bride's cake, not the wedding cake proper, which would have been a fruitcake, of course. But, by the 1940s, lady cake had indeed trumped fruitcake as the standard wedding cake, at least according to *Joy of Cooking* author Irma Rombauer, who wrote that her lady cake "tastes and looks like a traditional wedding cake, that is, traditional since fruit cake fell from grace."

As Irma Rombauer clearly foresaw, another cake would soon enough replace the white cakes and all other cakes as America's favorite celebration cake for all occasions—and would become America's favorite cake, period. In the same edition of *Joy*, trailing a weary resignation, she wrote, "After entertaining I often wonder whether it is worthwhile to bake anything but chocolate cake." Rombauer was flummoxed by the cake's "overwhelming popularity" and could only declare, "Undoubtedly, chocolate cake has 'it.'"

See also CAKE; CHIFFON CAKE; CHOCOLATE, POST-COLUMBIAN; FLOUR; and ROMBAUER, IRMA STARKLOFF.

Farmer, Fannie Merritt. *A New Book of Cookery*. Boston: Little, Brown, 1912.

The Good Housekeeping Hostess: Entertainments for all Seasons and Occasions, Described in Detail by a Group of Accomplished Entertainers. New York: Phelps Publishing, 1904. Facsimile ed., Whitstable, U.K.: Pryor, n.d.

Leslie, Eliza. *Lady's Receipt-Book*. Philadelphia: Carey & Hart, 1847.

Leslie, Eliza. *Miss Leslie's New Cookery Book*. Philadelphia: T. B. Peterson, 1857.

Porter, Mrs. M. E. *Mrs. Porter's New Southern Cookery Book*. Philadelphia: John E. Potter, 1871. Facsimile ed., with introduction by Louis Szathmáry. New York: Promontory Press, 1974.

Rombauer, Irma S. *Joy of Cooking*. New York: Bobbs-Merrill, 1943.

Rye, William Brenchley. *England as Seen by Foreigners in the Days of Elizabeth and James the First*. London: John Russell Smith, 1865.

Stephen Schmidt

charlotte designates two types of dessert, one baked, the other not. The types are represented in two of the most famous charlotte recipes: the first, *charlotte aux pommes,* or apple charlotte, is formed in a charlotte mold lined with buttered bread or brioche, filled with cooked fruit, then baked; the second is for charlotte russe, for which the mold is lined with ladyfingers, filled with flavored cream or bavarois (Bavarian cream), and chilled. Both types of charlotte are deftly flipped upside down and unmolded before serving, making for an elegant presentation.

Viard's *Cuisinier impérial* (1806) has what appears to be the first published apple charlotte recipe. The apples are peeled and cored, cut into small pieces, and cooked with sugar and cinnamon. Viard describes the texture of the cooked apples as a marmalade (or compote), which gives an idea of how thick the fruit filling must be so that the dessert will not collapse when it is turned out of the mold. While the apples cool, bread is cut into thin slices of equal size. They are dipped into warm melted butter and then arranged snugly and symmetrically around the mold. The filling is poured in, a hole is made in the middle of the apple filling to hold thick apricot purée, more buttered bread slices are symmetrically arranged around the top, and then the whole concoction is baked. In later recipes, the bottom of the mold is lined with buttered bread, as that becomes the top of the charlotte when served.

One of the most popular British cookbooks of the early nineteenth century, Maria Rundell's *A New System of Domestic Cookery,* included a recipe for apple charlotte in the 1808 revised edition published in London by John Murray, two years after the first edition of the book appeared. The origins of the charlotte are quite murky, some claiming it to be a late-eighteenth-century English confection named for the wife of King George III, Queen Charlotte. Others claim it is French.

French chef Marie-Antoine Carême took credit for the creation of the cold *charlotte à la parisienne,* or charlotte russe. See CARÊME, MARIE-ANTOINE. He offered several cold charlotte recipes in his first book, *Le pâtissier royal parisien* (1815). Carême writes that while he had designated this charlotte *à la parisienne,* others named it *à la russe* ("in the Russian style"). The bottom of the mold is lined with ladyfingers cut into a decorative design—a star in Carême's case—or simply triangles. The sides are lined with upright ladyfingers, which can be frosted (as Carême instructs) or soaked in liqueur-flavored sugar syrup. Carême instructs the cook to fill the charlotte with vanilla Bavarian cream and cover the cream with more ladyfingers. The charlotte is chilled until it is firm enough to keep its shape when unmolded. The first edition of *Le pâtissier royal parisien* includes Carême's own drawing of *charlotte à la parisienne,* but it lacks the star design he specifies in the recipe.

Apple charlotte is equally good made with pears, peaches, plums, or any fruit that can keep a stiff consistency after cooking. Instead of Bavarian cream of any flavor, a cold charlotte can be made with Chantilly cream (*charlotte à la Chantilly*), a delicate almond cream (*charlotte Malakoff*), chocolate mousse, or even ice cream (filled immediately before serving). The addition of gelatin to either a fruit or cream filling helps to ensure that the filling is firm enough to keep the bread or ladyfingers from collapsing after unmolding. See GELATIN.

The classic charlotte mold is deep, made of metal with high sides; it flares out slightly from bottom to top. Two flat metal handles near the top help with the unmolding. The extra width at the top of the mold creates a more stable bottom when the dessert is turned upside down on the serving plate. Exactly when the mold came into use is an open question. Many nineteenth-century cookbook illustrations show the unmolded charlotte with perfectly straight sides. Jules Gouffé's *Livre de pâtisserie* (1873) includes an illustration of a "dessert mold" (*moule d'entremets*) that differs from the one we use today only in having straight, not flared, sides. Urban-Dubois's *Pâtisserie d'aujourd'hui* (1894) illustrates a straight-sided mold accompanying the recipe for cooked apple charlotte, and a flared mold next to the cold charlotte russe. The early-twentieth-century catalog of the restaurant supply company J. Jacquotot in Paris indicates that both straight-sided and flared molds were called charlotte molds at that time.

See also CONFECTIONERY EQUIPMENT and PUBLICATIONS, TRADE.

Child, Julia. *Mastering the Art of French Cooking.* New York: Knopf, 1979.

Montagné, Prosper. *The New Larousse gastronomique.* American ed. Edited by Charlotte Turgeon and Nina Froud; translated by Nina Froud. New York: Crown, 1977.

Viard, André. *Le cuisinier impérial.* Paris: Chez Barba, 1806. Facsimile ed. Nîmes, France: Lacour, 1993.

Kyri W. Claflin

Chase, Oliver (1821–1902) set up an apothecary business in Boston, Massachusetts, as a young English immigrant in 1847. His trade involved cutting out medicinal lozenges by hand from a mixture of sugar paste and bitter medicines. See MEDICINAL USES OF SUGAR. Soon he began making candy lozenges from a basic recipe of sugar, gelatin, and flavorings. To improve the process, he patented the first American candy-making machine, a lozenge cutter. Chase's wafers were round to distinguish them from other lozenges that were generally diamond shaped.

His machine looked like a clothes wringer. A sheet of candy paste was fed into one end and circular wafers emerged as brass dies on the roller stamped out the candy disks. Chase and his brother Silas Edwin founded Chase and Company that same year, setting up a small factory in South Boston. Their first product was "Chase Lozenges," the forerunner of the now-famous NECCO Wafer. Other successful candies they later made include Canada Mints and Sweethearts.

Chase's wafers were about the size of a quarter and came wrapped in glassine paper. See CANDY PACKAGING. This durable candy with a long shelf life was the first candy sold in multipiece rolls. Chase's NECCO Wafers (1840s), Hershey Bars (1880s), and Tootsie Rolls (1890s) are probably the three oldest candies sold today in their original form. See HERSHEY'S and TOOTSIE ROLL.

Two other candy companies competed with the Chase company: Daniel Fobes's Hayward and Co., founded in 1848, and Bird, Wright and Co. (later known as Wright and Moody), which began production in 1856. The three companies combined in 1901 to form the New England Confectionery Company (NECCO). NECCO is one of the oldest candy companies in the United States.

See also NECCO.

Brokel, Ray. *The Great American Candy Bar Book*, pp. 75–77. Boston: Houghton Mifflin, 1982.

Costello, Irene. "Candy Land: History of Candy in the Bay State." *Edible Boston*, Spring 2012, 90–94. http://edibleboston.com/candy-land-history-of-candy-in-the-bay-state/.

Mote, Dave. "New England Confectionery Co. NECCO." In *International Directory of Company Histories*, Vol. 15, edited by Tina Grant, pp. 323–325. Detroit: St. James, 1996.

Joseph M. Carlin

cheese, fresh, meaning cheese that is eaten without a period of ripening, can be made from any dairy animal's milk. Since prehistoric times, cow's, goat's, and sheep's milk have been the basis of most kinds of fresh cheese. Either whole milk, skim milk, or cream can be used.

Before pasteurization, the milk was left to sour through the natural action of lactic acid bacteria; today, it is usually inoculated with bacterial cultures of the "mesophilic" type (suited for growth at temperatures between about 75° and 90°F [24° to 32°C]). Rennet or another source of enzymes may be added to further promote coagulation. Once the casein sets into a curd, it is drained and pressed to expel more whey. Renneted curd may be gently heated to firm up the texture and cut into pieces so as to present a larger surface area for efficient whey drainage. Rennetless cheeses generally omit heating or curd-cutting. The fat content of the milk or cream, the mixture of different bacterial species, the pH of the cultured milk, the strength of the enzyme solution, and the temperature to which the curd is heated are the chief variables affecting the flavor and texture of the finished cheese. Sometimes a little cream is worked back into skim-milk cheese for added richness.

Before refrigeration, fresh cheeses were simple farm products, slightly less perishable than milk but too short-lived to travel far to market. They predate modern manufacturing technology and tend to have an unsystematic array of names. In English, these include clabber (now obsolete), cottage cheese, pot cheese, farmer cheese, and (in the United Kingdom) curd cheese. French *fromage blanc*, German *Quark* or *Topfen*, and Russian *tvorog* are other members of the family. American commercial cream cheese and its reduced-fat cousin Neufchatel (unrelated to the Neufchatel cheese of Normandy) require special description (see below). The popular versions of Italian ricotta and Indian *panir* made by adding lemon juice or other acidulants to boiling milk are not true cheeses produced by culturing or renneting, but in a pinch they are roughly interchangeable with some kinds of fresh cheese.

When fresh cheeses are used without further cooking, their freshness is their charm. The simplest presentations are lightly sugared and eaten with fresh cream and a few "sweet" spices, or paired with berries or other fruits. Clabber was long served this way in the American South until pasteurization became universal after World War II. Farmstead fresh cheeses had begun declining much earlier in the North, though large influxes of Eastern European immigrants (especially

Ashkenazic Jews) revived the idea in major American cities late in the nineteenth century.

This immigrant wave helped fuel a comeback for fresh cheeses during a great early-twentieth-century expansion of the dairy industry. Commercial versions of cottage cheese, promoted during World War I as a patriotic meat substitute, were soon advertised as a low-calorie dieter's aid. Cream cheese, previously a generic name for various sorts of fresh cheese made by draining ripened cream, became synonymous with cheese cultured and packaged by a special "hot-pack" process involving gum stabilizers, developed at the Geneva Experiment Station in New York State in the late 1920s and also used for Neufchatel. Other versions of fresh cheese arrived after the 1980s along with new waves of immigrants from the old Soviet bloc.

Fresh cheeses—preferably dry, close-textured farmer cheese, pot cheese, or Russian *tvorog*—are popular fillings in strudels and other pastries. Ordinary cottage cheese is too wet and coarse-textured for the purpose without prior draining, pressing, and sieving. The same is true of Russian *syrniki* or *tvorozhniki* (lightly sweetened cheese fritters) and *paskha*, the celebrated Easter dish made by combining *tvorog*, butter, cream, sugar, and egg yolks and letting the smoothly beaten mixture drain in a special mold (or in a pinch, a flowerpot). See RUSSIA.

The most famous American fresh-cheese dessert is cheesecake. The name has historically been applied to several different sweets but during the twentieth century came to mean either a sort of custard of smoothly combined fresh cheese, sugar, cream, and eggs baked in a shortbread-like or regular pie pastry crust, or a similar dessert with a crust of zwieback or graham cracker crumbs, sometimes chilled without baking. The preferred cheese was farmer or drained cottage cheese until the late 1920s, when Kraft Foods acquired an upstate New York company then making cream cheese under the brand name "Philadelphia" (a city formerly renowned for excellent cream cheeses). At this time, "hot pack" manufacturing was boosting nationwide cream cheese sales. Kraft developed a cheesecake recipe using its packaged cream cheese just as two New York City restaurants (Lindy's and Reuben's) began touting cheesecakes based on a similar formula. See CHEESECAKE and NEW YORK CITY. Today, most commercial as well as homemade cheesecakes employ cream cheese, sometimes with other ingredients such as pumpkin purée or chocolate (which may be swirled in for a marbled effect). Sweet fruit toppings, usually glazed, are popular.

See also CREAM and MILK.

Kindstedt, Paul S. *Cheese and Culture: A History of Cheese and Its Place in Western Civilization*. White River Junction, Vt.: Chelsea Green, 2012.

Kosikowski, Frank V., and Vikram V. Mistry. *Cheese and Fermented Milk Foods*. 3d ed. 2 vols. Great Falls, Va.: Kosikowski, 1997.

Mendelson, Anne. *Milk: The Surprising Story of Milk through the Ages*. New York: Knopf, 2008.

Selitzer, Ralph. *The Dairy Industry in America*. New York: Dairy & Ice Cream Field/Books for Industry, 1976.

Anne Mendelson

cheesecake, originally a cooked pastry tart with a filling of soft cheese, eggs, spices, and sometimes honey, has evolved over the centuries into a nearly infinite variety of cakes whose creamy filling may be baked or unbaked on a sponge, cookie, or pastry base. The precise origin of cheesecakes remains unknown, but cakes containing cheese were served to athletes in Greece at the first Olympic Games in 776 B.C.E. The ancient Greeks enjoyed a layered pastry of goat's cheese and honey called *plakous*; Athenaeus lists a wide range of cheese-enriched cakes in the *Deipnosophists*. See ANCIENT WORLD; ATHENAEUS; and PLACENTA.

Early Cheesecakes

Although cheesecakes were recorded in England as early as 1265, when "cheese for tarts" was listed in the account books of the countess of Leicester, the earliest cheesecake recipe in England appeared in 1390 in *Forme of Cury*, the first English cookery book. It was a pastry shell baked with a filling of cheese, egg yolks, ginger, saffron, sugar, and salt. Medieval luxury fare was characterized by the use of expensive spices, sugar, and imported dried fruits, ingredients that became status symbols for the self-indulgent elite. Thus, cheesecakes were regarded as luxury foods.

Early French cookbooks, such as *Le ménagier de Paris* (a medieval manuscript from around 1393), included recipes for tarts and cakes made with fresh cheese. A modern version, *gâteau au fromage blanc*, consists of fresh cheese, crème fraîche, sugar, eggs, flour, lemon zest, and vanilla baked in a dish or tin until golden.

The cheese mentioned in English medieval recipes for tarts was usually a soft, rich cheese known as "ruayn" or "rewain." The seventeenth-century diarist John Evelyn wrote that the best time to make the cheese is when the "cows go in Ravens." This term is a variant of the word "rowan" or "rewain," the second crop of rough grass or hay that provided autumn and winter fodder for cows. The soft cheese was mixed with egg yolks, sugar, and spices and baked in a pastry "coffyn." See PIE. Other ingredients were frequently added, such as saffron, spices, and dried fruits. Green cheese, a moist, soft cheese named for its newness, was also used. This fresh, young "gren" cheese was pounded and sieved, then mixed with egg whites, ground almonds, and sugar and baked in a pastry case. New cheese was also made from "beestings"—the first thick yellow milk (colostrum) from a newly calved cow.

Brie imported from France was familiar in medieval England. "Tart de Bry," mentioned in the *Forme of Cury*, included egg yolks, sugar, ginger, and saffron. Another similar recipe called for "nessh" (a soft, fresh curd cheese), butter, and whole eggs, but no ginger or saffron.

Medieval cheese tarts survived virtually unchanged into the Elizabethan era; small cheese tarts, known today as Maid of Honor tarts, were reputed to be a favorite of Anne Boleyn. Soft cheeses and curds were also used to make boiled and baked puddings at this time. Their popularity may have led to the omission of the pastry case altogether in some recipes; by the seventeenth century, such dishes were commonly known as cheesecakes. Intriguingly, several recipes omitted the cheese entirely. These "cheesecakes" contained ground almonds or flour, but no cheese. A clue to their name comes from a recipe in Richard Bradley's *The Country Housewife and Lady's Director* (1728), where he instructs that the filling of lemon peel, hard-boiled egg yolks, cream, orange flower water, sugar, and butter be beaten "as will render it of the Consistence of Cheescake-meat."

Modern Cheesecakes

Cheesecakes are popular throughout the world, made with whatever soft cheese is available. For over a thousand years, young white cheeses have been employed in making cheesecakes. Examples include Anari in Cyprus (made from sheep's milk or a mixture of sheep's, goat's, and cow's milk), Lor in Turkey (sheep's or cow's whey), Manouri or Myzithra in Greece (sheep's, goat's, or cow's milk), ricotta in Italy (cow's, sheep's, goat's, or water buffalo's whey), Brocciu in Corsica (sheep's or goat's whey and milk), Urdă in Romania (sheep's or goat's whey), Quark in Germany and the Netherlands (cow's milk), and *tvorog* in Russia and Poland (cow's milk). Cheesecakes are prevalent throughout Eastern Europe: the glory of the Russian Easter table is the pyramidal *paskha,* rich with *tvorog,* sour cream, heavy cream, and butter; and *sernik* (cheesecake) is so popular in Poland that it is regarded as a national dish. *Sernik* may be baked or unbaked with the addition of poppy seeds or raisins, and it is sometimes topped with fruit and jam, poppy seeds, or chocolate. Jews who emigrated from Central and Eastern Europe to the United States, Western Europe, and Great Britain retained a particular affection for cheesecakes, which are traditional for the festival of Shavuot that celebrates the giving of the Torah to the Jews on Mount Sinai. See JUDAISM.

Tarts filled with fresh cheese, often sweetened and spiced, are common in medieval and Renaissance Italian sources. The seventeenth-century Tuscan writer Antonio Frugoli, in his 1631 *Pratica e Scalcaria,* wrote at length about the uses of ricotta in cooking, including in tarts and as a filling. The traditional Easter tart of Naples, *la pastiera,* is made with ricotta, spices, and candied fruit baked in a pastry case. See HOLIDAY SWEETS. The nineteenth-century cookbook author Pellegrino Artusi described *budino alla ricotta,* made with sugar, eggs, almonds, and lemons, as well as a similar tart that was a favorite wedding dish of peasants in Emilia-Romagna. Even Sicilian cassata could be described as a sort of cheesecake. See CASSATA.

Many modern cheesecakes, particularly in the United States and Canada, use cream cheese and may be baked or unbaked; the latter have a cookie crumb base and an uncooked filling of rich cream cheese, sometimes set with gelatin. In 1872 William Lawrence, a New York dairy farmer, made an especially cream-rich cheese in the style of French Neufchatel. It was eventually branded as "Philadelphia Cream Cheese," after the then-fashionable city, and became the popular choice for cheesecakes. Lawrence's company was eventually acquired by Kraft, and the formula changed entirely in the 1920s. Today's foil-wrapped bricks of soft cheese get much of their texture from the gums added to stabilize the mixture during processing.

North America has several different types of cheesecake, but New York Cheesecake—especially the recipe made famous by Lindy's Restaurant—has become an American classic. Dense with cream cheese, cream, eggs, and sugar and flavored with orange and lemon rind, it has a buttery short crust. Philadelphia-style cheesecake is lighter in texture; Chicago-style cheesecake is firm on the outside, and soft and creamy inside; and Pennsylvania Dutch cheesecake uses pot or farmer's cheese, which has large curds and a lower water content than cream cheese.

See also CHEESE, FRESH; ITALY; NEW YORK CITY; and PENNSYLVANIA DUTCH.

Artusi, Pellegrino. *The Science of Cooking and the Art of Eating Well.* Translated by Murtha Baca and Stephen Sartarelli. New York: Marsilio, 1997.
Bradley, Richard. *The Country Housewife and Lady's Director.* 3d ed. London: Woodman and Lyon, 1728.
Cookery Book II., Harleian ms 4016. ca. 1450.
Craig, Elizabeth. *Court Favourites*, pp. 109–110. London: Andre Deutsch, 1953.
Giacosa, Ilaria Gozzini. *A Taste of Ancient Rome*, p. 163. Chicago: University of Chicago Press, 1992.
Maher, Barbara. *Cakes.* London: Norman & Hobhouse, 1982.
Pettigrew, Jane. *The Festive Table.* London: Pavilion 1990.
Roden, Claudia. *The Book of Jewish Food: An Odyssey from Samarkand to New York.* New York: Knopf, 1996.

Carol Wilson

chemical leaveners reduce the density of baked goods by introducing carbon dioxide (CO_2) into doughs and batters through in situ chemical reactions. The source of the carbon dioxide is bicarbonate ion, a negatively charged ion with the chemical formula HCO_3^-. When mixed with an acid in a wet dough or batter, the mildly alkaline bicarbonate reacts to form gaseous carbon dioxide and water in the form of steam. As with yeast leavening, the resulting gas bubbles create cavities in the batter, which are preserved when the batter sets up during baking, creating a less dense material. See YEAST.

Compared to leavening with yeast, chemical leavening is a recent development, first employed in the early nineteenth century. It was initially considered a poor substitute for yeast leavening, despite being a faster and more reliable method than the yeast leavenings available at the time. Quick breads are leavened with chemical leaveners, not yeast, taking their name from the speed of the rising, minutes instead of hours.

The usual culinary source of bicarbonate ion is baking soda, which has the chemical name sodium bicarbonate ($NaHCO_3$). The positively charged sodium ion does not participate in the reaction between bicarbonate and acids; chemists classify it as a spectator ion. As sodium's only role is to serve as an electrical counterbalance to the negatively charged bicarbonate ion, many other positively charged counter ions can and are used without affecting the leavening reaction. Historically, both potassium and sodium bicarbonates have been used in baked goods. Saleratus (from the Latin for "aerated salts"), an early commercial chemical leavener, was a mixture of both potassium and sodium bicarbonate. Hartshorn, or ammonium carbonate $(NH_4)_2CO_3$, can be used as a leavening agent, producing ammonia in addition to carbon dioxide and water. Ammonium carbonate decomposes to produce ammonia gas and bicarbonate with an ammonium (NH_4^+) counter ion at low temperatures. While the ammonia gas adds leavening power, hartshorn can be used only in doughs and batters where the gas can escape upon baking; otherwise, the final product will smell and taste of ammonia. Hartshorn was, and occasionally still is, called for in traditional Scandinavian and German baking to produce crisp, well-formed cookies.

Regardless of its source, each bicarbonate ion produces one molecule of carbon dioxide upon reaction with acid. A teaspoon of sodium bicarbonate will release almost 5 liters of carbon dioxide at 350°F (177°C), enough to inflate a balloon about 8 inches in diameter, or acceptably leaven one cup of flour.

Not every dough or batter contains enough acid to convert all of the bicarbonate into carbon dioxide. Early chemically leavened recipes called for the addition of sour milk, a source of lactic acid. See MILK. Subsequently, baking powders were developed. These powders contain an acid in dry form, along with a source of bicarbonate (usually baking soda). Carriers, such as cornstarch, are added to keep the acid and bicarbonate separate and dry, preventing a premature reaction. When baking powder is mixed with wet ingredients the reaction proceeds, releasing carbon dioxide and water.

Common dry baking acids include calcium monophosphate ($Ca(H_2PO_4)_2$), sodium acid pyrophosphate ($Na_4P_2O_7$), sodium aluminum sulfate

($NaAl(SO_4)_2$), and cream of tartar (potassium bitartrate, $K(HC_4H_4O_6)$). Once the powder comes into contact with water, the speed of the reaction with bicarbonate depends on the identity and form of the dry acid. Calcium monophosphate reacts quickly, liberating two-thirds of bicarbonate's load of carbon dioxide in less than two minutes at room temperature. Sodium aluminum sulfate triggers the reaction only when heated. The rate of release can be controlled by altering the physical form of the powder. Coating the grains of calcium monophosphate slows the reaction, as does increasing the size of the sodium acid pyrophosphate granules.

Single-acting baking powders produce a single release of carbon dioxide, while double-acting powders have two waves of carbon dioxide production, achieved by blending two or more forms of dry baking acids. The first, rapid rise is usually provided by calcium monophosphate. Sodium aluminum sulfate is an ideal second-stage leavening agent, as it is not activated until heated and thus produces a consistent "spring" (the extra rise achieved during baking). Those concerned about aluminum in the diet can find double-acting powder that uses a blend of uncoated and coated calcium monophosphate to provide the two stages. Sodium acid pyrophosphate is used commercially for the second rise, as it has a long shelf life, though it is limited to sweet goods that can mask its unpalatable aftertaste.

A simple home replacement for commercial baking powder can be made by blending cream of tartar and baking soda in a 2 to 1 volume ratio. An equal amount of cornstarch or arrowroot can be added to prolong the storage life of the mixture. Self-rising flour is flour that has baking powder added to it, and instant biscuit mixes also contain baking powder. Adding water to either triggers the leavening reaction.

See also BREADS, SWEET; FLOUR; and STARCH.

Brodie, John, and John Godber. "Bakery Processes, Chemical Leavening Agents." In *Encyclopedia of Chemical Technology*, 4th ed., edited by Raymond E. Kirk and Donald F. Othmer, pp. 892–901. Hoboken, N.J., and Chichester, U.K.: Wiley, 1992.

Michelle M. Francl

chess pie

See PIE.

chestnuts, once a savior for poorer communities lacking sufficient food, continue to be treasured in the form of desserts, particularly at Christmas, New Year, christenings, weddings, and feasts. Thanks to their natural sweetness, these nutritious nuts are aptly named "sweet chestnuts."

In 1780 Antoine Parmentier, the French apothecary who taught the French to eat potatoes, discovered he could extract sugar from the chestnut. He formed this sugar into an impressively large cone weighing several pounds and sent it to the Academy at Lyon for consideration as a sugar source in place of regular cane sugar. Although chestnut sugar made transparent crystals that tasted similar to cane and beet sugar, Napoleon decided that France should prepare its own sugar from beets, whose processing was cheaper, so chestnut sugar fell by the wayside. See SUGAR BEET. Nevertheless, the sweetness of the chestnuts themselves makes them perfect for inclusion in all kinds of confectionery, puddings, and sweet baked desserts.

Chestnut trees can grow to massive proportions. A favorite one near Mount Etna in Sicily is reputed to have sheltered 100 horsemen in a storm. The main edible varieties are the *Castanea sativa* of southern Europe, the Caucasus, and North Africa; China's *Castanea mollissima*; and Japan's *Castanea crenata.* Until the nineteenth century, *Castanea dentata* were found in huge quantities in the United States, but up to 3 billion of these trees fell victim to chestnut blight. The trees all but disappeared, and the habit of eating chestnuts dwindled to a minor role at Thanksgiving.

Chestnuts are highly nutritious, and few other foods are as healthy. They have saved many lives in hard times; in eighteenth-century Périgord, the local peasants ate little else but boiled chestnuts and bread, polenta, or cakes made from chestnut flour for six months of the year or more. Although the main reputation of chestnuts has been as "the bread of the poor" (in southern France, the tree is nicknamed *l'arbre à pain* or "bread tree"), they have also, for centuries, been eaten for pleasure. Hot roasted chestnuts perfume the streets in China, the Balkans, Europe, and the Mediterranean in the autumn, and chestnut flour is still much liked in cakes, biscuits, and fritters. Roasted or boiled chestnuts were enjoyed by nuns and monks and at the tables of noblemen, often paired with fresh fruit for dessert. They were served at a banquet held in Périgueux in 1773 for Comte Arlot de la Roque, at which 38 main courses and eight desserts were presented, including two dishes of waffles, four compotes, two iced cheeses, pralines, marzipan, macarons, and chestnuts.

Chestnut Products

Marrons glacés, chestnuts candied in sugar syrup, are decidedly *bonbons de luxe*. See CANDIED FRUIT. Said to have originated in the time of Louis XIV, they were probably known in Piedmont as early as 1450 and were once a "must" at any high-class wedding.

In 1882 Clément Faugier in the Ardéche invented the invaluable *crème de marrons* using broken pieces of *marrons glacés*; this spread can still be obtained in tins and tubes and is ideal for cooking desserts and sweets. While commercially made *crème de marrons* is light and delicate, manufactured chestnut products can vary considerably in quality. *Purée de marrons* in a tin is often dull, and tinned chestnuts are usually tasteless. Vacuum-packed chestnuts can be very good for use in savory dishes, whereas dried chestnuts are mainly used for puréed soup or polenta or ground into flour. However, fresh chestnuts are always best.

Sweets and Desserts

Chestnuts combine perfectly with chocolate, cinnamon, cream, rum, vanilla, and orange. Maltese chestnut tartlets, *pastizotti tal-qastan*, are flavored with marmalade, orange, tangerine, or lemon rind, rum, and chocolate—only one teaspoon of sugar is needed to sweeten the filling. Christmas breakfast in Malta consists of chestnut soup, *imbuljuta*, eaten after midnight mass. It is made with dried chestnuts, cocoa, sugar, and tangerine peel cooked with the chestnut soaking water.

In Corsica the chestnut was once an essential part of life, dried in the upper stories of the house by the smoke of the open chimney (*fucone*) and ground into flour to make a variety of sweet dishes. *Nicci* were little cakes cooked on chestnut leaves. At weddings, guests enjoyed up to 22 different chestnut desserts, flavored with wild fennel, walnuts, vanilla, honey, rum, eau-de-vie, or curd cheese.

Although chestnuts are no longer a food of necessity in Europe, they remain culturally important. In southern France and certain regions of Italy, chestnuts are still part of the 13 desserts offered to the Christ child on Christmas Eve and at christenings. *Castagnaccio*, a flat cake made with chestnut flour flavored with rosemary, pine nuts, and raisins or sultanas, is an Italian classic. *Marrons Mont Blanc*, glossy, sweetened chestnut purée piped into a cone shape to resemble a mountain, then covered with *crème Chantilly* to resemble snow, remains a celebratory French dessert.

Iced Nesselrode Pudding, popular in the nineteenth century and named after the Russian foreign minister Count Karl Nesselrode, contains chestnut purée, vanilla, maraschino, egg yolks, thick cream, and brandied dried fruits. An offspring of Nesselrode Pudding, Nesselrode Pie, with a filling of chestnuts, cream, eggs, gelatin, rum, and candied fruits and a topping of grated chocolate, became a favorite American sweet of the 1950s. Peking Dust, mashed chestnuts studded with glacé fruits, particularly cherries, and eaten at Chinese New Year, might be considered a relative of Nesselrode Pudding. (Westernized versions include cream and brandy.) In Japan, New Year is celebrated with *Kuri Kinton*, a classic dish of mashed sweet potato with chestnuts in chestnut syrup and mirin. The beautiful golden color of the dish symbolizes wealth.

See also NUTS.

Avanzato, Damiano. "Italy." In *Following Chestnut Footprints*, edited by Damiano Avanzato. Leuven, Belgium: International Society for Horticultural Science, 2009.

Bruneton-Governatori, Ariane. *Le pain de bois: Ethnohistoire de la châtaigne et du châtaignier*. Toulouse, France: Eché, with Centre National de la Recherche Scientifique, 1984.

Lavialle, Jean-Baptiste. *Le châtaignier*. Paris: Vigot Frères, 1906.

Caroline Conran

chewing gum is made of any number of cohesive and sticky substances that people chew but do not swallow. It can be as simple as the naturally flavored sap of a tree or as complex as artificially flavored hydrocarbon polymers like styrene butadiene rubber.

Early History

Black lumps of birch bark tar with well-defined human tooth impressions dating back to 7000 B.C.E., the Early Mesolithic era, have been found in Germany, Scandinavia, and elsewhere in Northern Europe.

No one knows for certain whether prehistoric people chewed tar for purposes of pleasure, stimulation, medicine, and/or ritual. Studies of the tooth impressions indicate that the majority of chewers were children of the age when baby teeth fall out, so it may be that tar was chewed to reduce oral discomfort. Exactly how the tar was produced is also a mystery, as it can only be derived from bark under extreme heat (well over 1472°F [800°C]) and in air-free conditions, a technology known only since the Neolithic Era, beginning around 10,000 B.C.E. Sealed pots were unknown in the Early Mesolithic—perhaps the tar was formed during natural conflagrations.

There is ample evidence from around 1000 C.E. that Mayans in the Yucatan chewed on chicle, the sap of wild sapodilla trees, and that during the same era Greeks chewed on mastiche, the resin of mastic trees. Rosin from the large variety of pine trees native to the northern hemisphere, spruce in particular, has been chewed for ages. In 1848 John Curtis used spruce sap to make the world's first commercial gum. Other natural resins and latexes that can be chewed directly from trees include the latex of jelutong trees from Borneo, Malaysia, Sumatra, and southern Thailand; and sorva, the sweet sap of the Central and South American Couma Macrocarpa tree. Today, sorva is cultivated in the Peruvian Amazon for use as rubber, plastic, medicine, and waterproofing, and is chewed by monkeys and people alike.

Modern Chewing Gum

Many people also chew on naturally occurring waxes, including paraffin, a by-product of petroleum, and it was a penny piece of paraffin chew named White Mountain that was serendipitously responsible for the creation of modern chewing gum. In the 1860s Antonio Lopez de Santa Anna, who was several times president of Mexico and conqueror of the Alamo, had 1 ton of chicle sent from Mexico to his friend Thomas Adams Sr. in Manhattan. The plan was that the inventive Adams might discover a way to combine chicle with the sap of the rubber tree to create a less expensive blend for the making of carriage bumpers and tires. After a year of experimentation, Adams and his eldest son Thomas Jr. deemed the experiments a failure and were ready to discard the chicle when Adams Sr. happened upon a young girl asking a druggist for a penny's worth of chewing gum—the aforementioned White Mountain—and he was struck with an idea for salvaging his chicle. The Adamses began offering chicle gumballs on consignment and met success. They expanded quickly, renting a building in Jersey City, New Jersey, where they employed a few dozen young women to hand-wrap pure, unflavored chicle in colored tissue paper and package it in boxes bearing a color picture of New York's City Hall and environs. The new commercial product was named Adams New York No. 1 Chewing Gum, and the machine they devised to make it was awarded a patent on 14 February 1871. In 1879 William White created the first flavored chicle chewing gum by adding peppermint.

Manufacture

Chewing gum is hard to make and takes a good deal of time and care. Most twenty-first-century gum is made with three basic ingredients: gum base, softener, and flavoring. These are heated, cooled, kneaded, formed, coated, and conditioned. Chewing gum comes in stick, tablet, flake, nugget, powder, and paste form. Masticating merriment ensues when it is fancifully packaged to resemble everyday articles like checkbooks, tubs of sidewalk chalk, combination locks, and laundry soap. Artists like Betty Ruth Curtiss, Hannah Wilke, and Ben Wilson use chewing gum as their medium, and Angela Lorenz has published a book made of chewing gum titled *Chewing Tzu, The Rumination Book.*

In the 1990s, distressed by the plastic, rubber, and other inedible additives used by industrial gum manufacturers, boutique manufacturers like Mexico-based Chicza began producing gum in the simpler, more natural style of precommercial gum. Verve, Inc., the makers of Glee Gum, became the first fair-trade chewing gum company by employing thousands of *chicleros* (professional gum tree farmers) who work in a sustainable manner in the rainforests of the Peten region of Mexico and Guatemala.

Bubblegum

In 1905 twenty-three-year-old Walter Diemer, an accountant for Fleers Chewing Gum Company, tried to improve on his boss's 1906 Blibber Blubber, a failed attempt to make bubblegum. Diemer hit on the perfect formula by accident, and distinguished the lucky batch with the last drops of food coloring in his house. Red turned pink in the test batch and thus was established the traditional soft pink color of bubblegum. Diemer summed up the importance of his work: "I've done something with my life. I've made kids happy around the world." The Guinness Record for the world's largest bubblegum bubble was set in 2004 at a remarkable 20 inches in diameter.

Marketing

The most famous name in chewing gum is William Wrigley Jr., who created iconic brands including Doublemint and Juicy Fruit in the factory he started in Chicago in 1898. Wrigley understood the power of marketing and once mailed free gum to over 1.5 million people listed in the U.S. phone book. His fame and fortune speak as much of gum as they do of advertising in general, and Wrigley spawned innovations like those of Topps, which began wrapping gum in comics just after World War II, and added baseball cards to gum packs in 1952.

Gum around the World

In *Chewing Gum*, Michael Redclift remarked, "The history of chewing gum is, at one level, an example of the globalization of taste; at another level it can be explained as the outcome of globalization." Gum made in the United States is exported around the world and its international popularity is due in part to U.S. soldiers, who carry it wherever they go. As a result, American gum brands are often imitated with look-a-like packages and sound-a-like names such as Balonka (Yugoslavija), Wribson (Jordan), and Heart Juicy (Korea).

International tastes differ widely, and Wrigley's has made strawberry Juicy Fruit for Spaniards and cherry-mint Orbit for Poles. Chiclets come in violet flavor in Mexico (where customers are sometimes offered candy-coated gum in lieu of small change); lemon in Thailand; and banana, peach, and apricot in Lebanon. Gum can be transnational: for example, Roma brand cardamom-flavor tablets from Guatemala are popular throughout the Arab-speaking world. Turkey is the nation with the largest number of gum manufacturers; with a few exceptions, the importation into Singapore of any chewing gum is prohibited; and Japan may be the home of gum's most innovative styles. The Japanese are partial to the products of Korean gum manufacturer Lotte, which sells uncommon flavors like jasmine, plum, and mangosteen, as well as gums targeted at young ladies like Glamatic, which comes in a holographic blue and silver wrapper with rainbows, seahorses, and kissing angel fish. Japanese competitor Kanebo Ltd. launched "Otoko Kaoru" (male scent) in 2006, a chewing gum that contains a chemical which claims to block body odor by helping sweat glands release the gum's menthol-rose scent. In southern Africa, xakuxaku is the onomatopoetic name of the noise made by chewers and egestors of the fruit of the *Thespesia garckeana* tree, a sweet, glutinous fruit known to some by the inaccurate nickname "African chewing gum."

Medical Uses

The Greek physician, pharmacologist, and botanist Pedanius Dioscorides first used powdered mastiche as dental and intestinal medicine on the Isle of Chios around 50 C.E. In 1882 Ohio physician Edward Beeman, at the suggestion of his bookkeeper Nellie Horton, added to chewing gum the pepsin powder he had compounded as an aid to digestion. In 1899 druggist Franklin V. Canning created a gum designed to clean teeth and breath. He combined the words "dental" and "hygiene" to arrive at the name Dentyne. Over the ensuing years other medicines like penicillin and acetaminophen have been added to gum in the belief that gum maintains the potency of medicaments and that the long-chewing product slowly and evenly distributes remedies throughout the body. It is commonly believed that chewing gum helps humans relax, relieves inner ear pressure, and may also stimulate saliva and digestion. Twenty-first-century research suggests that chewing sugarless gum after colon cancer surgery can speed recovery and shorten hospital stays by as much as one-third. The connection between gum and health is complicated and should be considered on a case-by-case basis—after all, gums come in astounding variety, from candied gum that looks like real cigarettes and cigars complete with powdered sugar "smoke," to nicotine-laced gum that counteracts the urge to smoke.

Pros and Cons

Gum is a lifestyle product that has always had issues of image. For over 25 years, Emily Post refused to mention chewing gum in her etiquette books. On the other hand, there are block-long brick walls in

Seattle, Washington, and San Luis Obispo, California, where gum lovers happily stick their chewed cud for posterity. For over a hundred years, "gum chewing has been viewed as a terrible habit that Americans were imposing around the world" (Mathews, 2009). Gum makers address such problems with politeness campaigns like the one that urged consumers to be respectful and "Save This Wrapper to Dispose of Your Gum." The Hong Kong subway system features gum "targets," so commuters can spit their expended wads into the garbage instead of marring the floor. The *New York Times* summarized gum's image by calling it a "badge of insouciance" and adding "just ask Jack Nicholson." Regardless of individual opinion, chewing gum has long carried important commercial, environmental, and social implications the world over.

See also MASTIC.

Lundy, Rocky. "The History of Chewing Gum." http://usmintindustry.org/Portals/1/The%20History%20of%20Chewing%20Gum.pdf.

Mathews, Jennifer P. *Chicle: The Chewing Gum of the Americas, from the Ancient Maya to William Wrigley*. Tucson: University of Arizona Press, 2009.

Redclift, Michael. *Chewing Gum: The Fortunes of Taste*. New York and London: Routledge, 2004.

Harley Spiller

chiffon cake made a sensation in 1948, when General Mills published a recipe pamphlet proclaiming it "the biggest kitchen news in 100 years." Two years later, *Betty Crocker's Picture Cook Book* described chiffon cake as being "light as angel food, rich as butter cake."

For many decades, three basic foam cakes—sponge, angel food, and genoise—had held sway in the kitchen. See ANGEL FOOD CAKE and SPONGE CAKE. Foam cakes depend on the aeration of eggs, either beaten whole or separately as yolks and whites for the magnificent heights they attain in the oven. The newfangled chiffon cake was the brainchild of Harry Baker, a Los Angeles insurance salesman, baking hobbyist, and caterer. In the 1920s, he became a celebrity by baking his invention for many Hollywood personalities, as well as for the Brown Derby restaurant chain. Despite many pleas for the recipe, he refused to divulge it until General Mills paid him for the recipe in 1947. The mystery ingredient turned out to be vegetable oil.

Not much was known about Harry Baker until the writer Joseph Hart did some sleuthing and uncovered little known facts from Baker's past. Baker had arrived in Hollywood in 1923, having been forced to leave his wife and two children back in Ohio after he was discovered *in flagrante delicto* with another man. His insurance business had gone south so, desperate for cash, he turned to his lifelong hobby, making fudge. Baker was able to make a living manufacturing fudge, but he decided to turn his attention to cakes. His quest was to create a moister and sweeter angel food cake. He spent years testing hundreds of different formulas, but nothing satisfied him until, as he told a reporter at the *Minneapolis Tribune*, a "sixth sense—something cosmic" revealed salad oil as the secret ingredient.

At about the same time, a Brown Derby restaurant opened on Wilshire Boulevard and became a magnet for Hollywood celebrities. Baker brought a sample of his chiffon cake to the restaurant, where it became a signature dessert. One of the most popular flavors of the cake was grapefruit, created especially for the famous (and overweight) gossip columnist Louella Parsons, who had told the restaurant owner, "Put grapefruit on something—everyone knows that grapefruit is less fattening."

Although people clamored for the original recipe, Baker refused, taking pains to dispose of his garbage away from home to prevent the discovery of empty bottles of salad oil. Throughout the 1930s he baked his cakes for Hollywood royalty, charging $2.00 apiece. At the height of his business, he produced 42 cakes in an 18-hour day—the batter for each prepared individually and baked in 1 of his 12 tin hot-plate ovens set up in a spare bedroom. In today's dollars, the resulting income adds up to something like $1,000 a day.

Today, despite its wonderfully light and moist texture, chiffon cake is overshadowed by angel food cake and sponge cake.

Hart, Joseph. "When Harry Met Betty." *The Rake*, 29 January 2007. http://www.rakemag.com/2007/01/when-harry-met-betty/.

Greg Patent

chiffon pie is a single-crust pie with a light, fluffy filling. This filling is generally a custard mixture lightened with beaten egg whites and/or whipped cream, with or without gelatin, and flavored with an almost infinite variety of ingredients. See CUSTARD and GELATIN. The pie shell was originally made from pastry, but crumb crusts are now popular.

There is much overlap among recipes for chiffon pies, gelatin pies, and soufflé pies, all of which appeared virtually simultaneously between 1919 and 1921. The first recipe found to date that fits the concept was Coffee Soufflé Pie. It appeared in *Good Housekeeping* magazine in June 1919 and called for egg whites, cream, and gelatin in addition to coffee.

The first known mention of a chiffon pie by that name appears in the *Emporia Gazette* on 6 January 1921, in an article suggesting that this type of pie was then in vogue. In November of the same year, *Good Housekeeping* included a recipe for a chiffon pie as "a delicious novelty." This pie was citrus-flavored and lightened with egg whites, but interestingly, it was baked, not simply chilled, as is more typical. As an example of the variability within the concept, the chiffon pie that appeared in Crisco advertisements in 1924 was prepared in the style of a baked lemon meringue pie.

Chiffon pies fell briefly out of favor in the 1980s due to concerns about the risk of salmonella poisoning from the consumption of raw egg whites. Pasteurized egg products are now recommended in unbaked pies.

See also CHIFFON CAKE.

"Food Timeline FAQs: Pie & Pastry." http://www.foodtimeline.org/foodpies.html.

Janet Clarkson

child labor is presumed to be older than recorded history, but the connection between child labor and the sweets industry is a phenomenon of the Industrial Revolution.

As factories started to replace America's farm-driven economy in the late 1700s and early 1800s, children began to be pressed into the industrial work force in large numbers—working up to 70 hours a week in often dirty, damp, and dangerous conditions. By 1810 more than 2 million school-age children were employed in factory work in the United States and England alone, earning wages that could be as low as 40 cents a day.

Most child laborers were employed in textile-making facilities, but a small number worked in the candy business. Cracker Jack, begun in Chicago in 1896 by a German immigrant, found itself among several sweets makers being investigated by Hull House, an early activist organization, for poor working conditions for their youthful employees. See CRACKER JACK.

Penny candy entered the sweets lexicon in the late 1890s and was the first confection children could afford to buy with money they had earned themselves. Unfortunately, the work they did was often rendered in factories that exploited them. See PENNY CANDY.

In 1913 the sociologist and photographer Lewis Hine, as he traveled around the United States documenting child labor abuses for the National Child Labor Committee, produced an iconic photograph of child workers on the loading dock of the now-defunct Hughes Brothers Candy Factory on South Ervay Street in Dallas, Texas. Hine wrote of the encounter: "One girl told me that she is 13 years old, 'but we have to tell them we're 15. I run a chocolate machine'" (1998).

Hine's work is widely credited with raising awareness that prompted many states and the federal government to pass a series of laws severely curbing child labor, most notably the national 1938 Fair Labor Standards Act. Britain acted much earlier, passing a number of factory acts and a compulsory school bill that abolished most child labor by 1900.

Worldwide, however, child labor remains the norm in many developing countries and no more so than in the agricultural sector—and the chocolate industry in particular. UNICEF estimates that as many as 500,000 children work on farms in the West African nation of Ivory Coast, producer of about 40 percent of the world's cocoa. A smaller but still substantial number work the cacao fields of Ghana. Worldwide, according to the United Nations, as many as 168 million children toil as child laborers—half of them involved in hazardous work that "endangers their health, safety and moral development." See COCOA.

Children's rights activists have made some strides in pressuring multinational chocolate makers to reach agreements aimed at eliminating child labor in cacao growing and harvesting. A series of damaging press accounts and documentaries revealing that a subset of cocoa child laborers were actually enslaved led to the passage in 2001of the Harkin-Engel Protocol, a voluntary global cocoa industry agreement to eliminate the worst forms of West African child labor. Out of that came the formation in 2002 of the International Cocoa Initiative representing nongovernmental organizations, trade unions, and the chocolate industry to press for the reforms advocated by Harken-Engel.

The going has been slow, however, and the matter has turned litigious. Hershey Co., which controls more than 40 percent of the U.S. chocolate market, issued a press release in October 2012 declaring that it would "source 100 percent certified cocoa for its global chocolate product lines by 2020 and accelerate its programs to help eliminate child labor in the cocoa regions of West Africa." A month later, activist shareholders filed suit in Delaware Chancery Court, seeking to force Hershey to disclose the names of its Ghana and Ivory Coast growers on the grounds that the chocolate maker "has knowingly failed to fulfill its promises" to stop the practice.

Meanwhile, Nestlé SA, maker of Nestlé Crunch, remains locked in a federal lawsuit alleging that it violated the 1789 U.S. Alien Torts Statute by allowing its Ivory Coast cacao growers to employ child slave labor—a charge it denies.

See also HERSHEY'S and NESTLÉ.

"Child Labour." http://www.un.org/en/events/childlabourday/background.shtml (accessed 16 January 2014).
Freedman, Russell, and Lewis Hine. *Kids at Work: Lewis Hine and the Crusade Against Child Labor*. New York: Houghton Mifflin, 1998.

Ken Wells

children's candy was once a rarity. Because sugar was expensive, few children could expect much more than the occasional "sugarplum" at Christmas. See SUGARPLUMS. However, new sources and lower prices for sugar in the latter part of the nineteenth century, as well as the introduction of new machine production techniques and new packaging, storage, and transportation technologies, transformed candy from a local and handmade product to a regional, mass-produced commodity.

In the United States, the lowest end of the manufactured candy trade came to be known as "penny candy." It was cheap, plentiful, and made to appeal to a child's eye. Licorice, marshmallows, suckers, kisses, caramels, jellies, and more could be had at the candy shops found around every corner, several pieces to the penny. In the golden age of penny candy, from about 1880 to the early 1930s, children were significant buyers of candy for their own immediate consumption, and penny candies made for and sold directly to children were a significant portion of the candy market. See PENNY CANDY.

Once candy became cheap and plentiful enough to be within the grasp of even children and their pennies, children had a new opportunity to fashion themselves as shoppers. Candy was children's entry point into a newly emerging culture of consumption. In the late nineteenth and early twentieth centuries, children as young as four or five had the freedom to travel to candy shops and make purchases independently. In the candy shop, a child could learn the value of the penny and the importance of discrimination.

Many reformers worried about children's independent access to sweets and called on mothers to protect their children from the putative dangers of candy. Moral reformers attacked children's candy eating, on the grounds that it would lead to more pernicious vices, including smoking, gambling, drinking, and masturbation. Food reformers also singled out candy for special abuse. The "pure food" movement of the 1890s and 1910s drew attention to the questionable ingredients and processes of new forms of industrial food processing. Alarmists alleged that cheap penny candies were liable to be dangerous, even poisonous, because of the use of artificial colors and flavors as well as degraded ingredients. Neither federal nor state food inspectors ever succeeded in locating any of the alleged "poisons" said to be lurking in cheap penny candies. On closer inspection, the frequent stories of candy poisoning turned out to be the result of simple overeating, or sickness due to other causes.

Early candy manufacturers understood the importance of visual appeal above all in enticing the child customer. This was one of the reasons reformers became so suspicious of children's candies: they were brightly colored with new kinds of artificial dyes that were highly suspect. Novel shapes also were important, especially shapes that mimicked toys or suggested play. Nineteenth-century candy makers were skilled in the production of clear toy candy using intricate handmade metal molds, a German tradition that was brought to Pennsylvania in the eighteenth century. This laborious craft was transformed by the introduction of drop machines to mold hard candy, and starch molds for soft candies, which allowed for much faster and cheaper production. See GUMMIES and HARD CANDY. Licorice, chewing gum, and hard and soft molded candies could be made in an infinite array of shapes and colors. Children purchasing their own candy typically had limited means and sought out candies that, by virtue of low price or longevity, offered the best value. Jawbreakers, taffies, and lollipops (aka "all-day suckers") were long-lasting candies that would stretch a penny's worth of candy into an afternoon of pleasure. See CHEWING GUM; LICORICE; and LOLLIPOPS.

"Better" candy stores avoided penny candy sales, viewing the children's trade as an inconvenience and a distraction. Profit margins on penny goods were razor-thin, and the penny candy merchant had to spend more on labor to serve the demanding but small-spending customers making numerous small purchases. Nevertheless, the children's trade was significant. In 1932–1933, it was estimated that nearly 18 percent of total U.S. candy production corresponded to the juvenile penny candy market.

The children's penny candy scene changed dramatically during World War II. U.S. entry into the war in 1941 brought with it the rationing of sugar and other candy ingredients. Although the candy industry was still able to secure access to needed supplies, prices rose significantly. During the war years, about half the nation's candy production went into provisioning the military, thereby reducing the amount of candy that could be sold domestically. The result of these forces was to drive out the penny candy trade. Bulk and box candies were far more profitable, and for manufacturers, even those with nostalgic ties to the candy past, penny lines no longer made economic sense. By 1947 the portion of total candy output that was produced for the penny market had fallen to less than 4 percent. Few of the little shops that had sold penny goods and catered to the children's trade were able to survive, and the corner candy store largely disappeared after the war.

In the 1950s and 1960s, candy for children's consumption was increasingly purchased at large self-service grocery stores, where it was packaged in cellophane bags or other "family-size" packs rather than offered as individual pieces. Many other forms of highly sweetened food were developed and promoted as special foods to appeal to children's appetites, and these began to compete with more established kinds of candy. Frosted Flakes, Sugar Pops, and Trix cereals were born in the 1950s. See BREAKFAST CEREAL. Sweet snack cakes, already popular, became sweeter: Hostess added crème filling to its popular cupcakes after World War II, while the coconut- and marshmallow-covered Sno Balls debuted in 1947 and by 1950 had been amped up with a crème filling. See HOSTESS.

Advertising for candy and other sweet foods in the 1950s was primarily aimed at mothers who were encouraged to see these products as a wholesome way to please their children. In the 1960s, manufacturers for sweet cereals, candy, and snack foods began to target children directly with advertising during the Saturday morning block of television cartoons and kiddie shows. See ADVERTISING, AMERICAN. A new movement of antisugar food reformers and antiadvertising media activists in the 1970s put pressure on candy, soda, and cereal manufacturers to curtail their efforts to hook children on what many were coming to view as sugar-laden junk food, but that movement had little lasting effect.

Most of today's well-known branded candies first appeared in the decades before World War II, when the American candy industry was ascendant and the pace of innovation was dazzling. Today, chocolate candy bars appeal equally to children and adults, as did nonchocolate candies in the prewar era. However, since the 1950s, sugar-based candies—ranging from early 1900s classics like NECCO Wafers, Tootsie Rolls, and Chuckles to more recent brands like Jolly Ranchers, Starburst, and Skittles—have come to be seen as appealing primarily to children and teens, although some adults also like them. See CANDY BAR; TOOTSIE ROLL; and NECCO.

Candy marketed exclusively to children continues to emphasize visual appeal and play value, as in Ring Pops, Fun Dip, and pressed candy novelties such as candy necklaces and interlocking blocks. Whereas mainstream candies are moving toward natural colors and flavorings, vivid and surprising colors achieved with artificial food dyes distinguish the juvenile lines. The most notable candy innovations in the postwar era have incorporated surprising or extreme tastes and textures to appeal to the youth market. Zotz (1968) brought the fizz of baking soda plus acid to the inside of a hard candy (same idea as those science club "volcanos"). Razzles (1966) started out like a candy and morphed into gum. Pop Rocks (1975) unleashed the power of carbon dioxide to explode between the teeth. Super-sour candies coated in edible acids first began to appear in the 1980s and continue to grow in popularity. See EXTREME CANDY.

Children's candy consumption today accounts for only a small portion of added sugar in the diet (about 6 to 8 percent, with the portion being higher for younger children). However, many other significant sources of added sugar might be termed "invisible candy," including breakfast cereals, fruit snacks, snack bars, and sweetened drinks. It is the ubiquity and popularity of these products, soda in particular, that has led to the rapid rise in children's sugar consumption. Significantly, opponents have targeted sugar in drinks by renaming these beverages "liquid candy." Although candy itself may not be the problem, reformers today invoke candy as shorthand for danger and dietary woe, just as they did more than a century ago. See SODA.

See also GAG CANDY.

Kawash, Samira. "Polio Comes Home: Pleasure and Danger in CANDY LAND." *American Journal of Play* 3, no. 2 (Fall 2010): 186–229.

Kawash, Samira Kawash. *Candy: A Century of Panic and Pleasure*. London: Faber and Faber, 2013.

Woloson, Wendy. *Refined Tastes: Sugar, Confectionery, and Consumers in Nineteenth Century America*. Baltimore: Johns Hopkins University Press, 2002.

Samira Kawash

children's literature has a direct relationship with sweets: the text is not just sweet but is itself a sweet. "A is an apple pie," reads one alphabet verse—a seventeenth-century ditty that continues to be re-illustrated up to the present, the drama of which is founded on the consumption of "A Apple Pie." In *Giles Gingerbread* (1820), the whole alphabet is a confection: Giles learns to read with letters made of cake, studying his "gingerbread book" until "he gets it by heart, And then he eats it up, As we eat up a tart." In some seventeenth-century Jewish teaching methods, new students are invited to lick honey from the alphabet. In these and other tales of edible alphabets, children's literature and learning are presented as mouthwateringly enticing: sweet letters draw children in and children, in turn, draw those letters into themselves, where literature and literacy become part of their very formation, bodily and intellectually.

Many eighteenth-century titles advertise wholesome children's stories as sweets—such as John Newbery's *The Twelfth Day Gift*, with its dedication "to all good Little Masters and Misses who have a true relish for the sweet-meats of learning, this Sugar-Plumb is most humbly inscribed by their obedient servant, the author" (1767), or the Glasgow publication *The Sugar-Plumb, or Sweet Amusement for Leisure Hours: being an entertaining and instructive collection of stories* (1786). In these titles, "sweet" suggests a valuable and licit pleasure: something desirable and good to desire, promising pleasure for the moment and fortification for the future. The song "Just a Spoonful of Sugar" in Disney's *Mary Poppins* (not in P. L. Travers's original story) is only one example in centuries of positive temptations reflecting Newbery's marketing, summed up in his motto *delectando monemus* (instruction with delight). Indeed, the efficacy of sweetness in attracting the young to educational experience—whether as readers or as characters in stories—goes virtually unchallenged throughout the history of children's books.

And no wonder: breast milk itself is sweet, designed for (or creating) a taste for sweets in the newborn.

In the Grimm Brothers' story "Hansel and Gretel" two children find a witch's house "with walls of bread, a roof made of cake, and windows of transparent sugar." This lithograph by Robert Ambrose Dudley appeared in *Once Upon a Time*, a collection of fairy tales published by Ernest Mister around 1900. PRIVATE COLLECTION / BRIDGEMAN IMAGES

Writers and illustrators play on this early taste, and incidents involving cakes, cookies, candy, and pie are pervasive in children's stories. Indeed, stories that dwell happily on the sheer pleasure of eating sweets show the rationale for more complex tales that illustrate the moral and social pressures generated by powerful desire—within the fictional context of the stories and also in the "real" world, where over time, the increasing availability of sweets, both literal and literary, affects the texts of children's stories and our ideas about children's literature itself.

The sheer pleasure of eating sweets often marks moments of well-earned indulgence—triumphant ends to communal adventures in which the pleasure of company, sweets, and a completed adventure merge. Hence, Captain Flint's declaration in Arthur Ransome's *Swallows and Amazons* (1930): "All the best sea fights end with a banquet" and the subsequent strawberry ices, parkins, bath buns, rock cakes, ginger nuts, chocolate biscuits, and cake with "a picture of two little ships done in pink and white icing." So, too, the splendid conclusion in *Mr Gumpy's Outing* (1970): "It's time for tea." Cherries and cherry cake are resplendent in John Burningham's picture of wordless, culminating conviviality—as is "plum pie in the sun: I spy everyone!" in the last image of Janet and Allan Ahlberg's classic *Each Peach Pear Plum* (1978). Pleasure, sweets, and adventure merge in personal feasts as well, as we see in *Winnie-the-Pooh* (1926) and *The Adventures of Paddington Bear* (1958). Here, sweets consumption and sweetness of disposition are linked: the heroes' taste for sweets endears them to their friends, and Pooh's overindulgence in honey gets him into a "tight place," but the worst said to or about him is a loving endearment: "silly old bear!" See WINNIE-THE-POOH. In both communal and personal contexts, then, sweets associate unalloyed pleasure and fulfilled desire.

Conflicting Messages

However, that very pleasure and desire provide the rationale for why, more often than not, sweets in children's stories bear complex, conflicting messages—of abundance and scarcity, desire and restraint, obedience and disobedience. In *Little House on the Prairie*, when Mr. Edwards swims the Verdigris River to bring Laura and Mary candy and cakes from Santa Claus, the sweets highlight scarcity. The awed pleasure with which Laura tastes her one stick of candy, or notices the pure white flour and sugar of her tiny cake, is born of their rarity. She tastes her candy right away, "just one lick." But that is not enough for Wilder's story; she goes on to comment, "But Mary was not so greedy. She didn't take even one lick of her stick." Even in the context of scarcity, she implies, where there is pleasure, there can be sin; indeed, the possibility for reprehensible self-indulgence in relation to sweets is a theme that is thoroughly mined throughout children's literature.

Nowhere are conflicting messages more iconically present than in Jakob and Wilhelm Grimm's *Hansel and Gretel*, when the starved children find a witch's house "with walls of bread, a roof made of cakes [Küchen], and windows of transparent sugar." Their enthusiastic consumption of the house alerts the cannibalistic witch to their presence; the sweet house functions as temptation and deceit, a sign of the children's own edibility and a concealment of the witch's unsweet (and unsavory) nature. For psychoanalytic interpreter Bruno Bettelheim, "The house stands for oral greediness and how attractive it is to give in to it" (1976, p. 161); for literary scholar Maria Tatar (1992), however, this is not a cautionary tale about greed but a therapeutic story empowering readers with the example of Gretel's resourceful self-rescue. The house's very energy as an icon comes from its paradoxical double value as a focal point for both scarcity and luxury, and the contradictory impulses of need and desire, dependency and self-reliance.

Generally, a surfeit of sweets provides a simple forum for testing self-control, as it does in Roald Dahl's *Charlie and the Chocolate Factory* (1964). For Charlie, whose family barely subsists, the chocolate factory offers a dream ending to basic hunger; but for the over-indulged children on the tour, the candy gives occasion for disobedience and punishment in a manner reminiscent of Hilaire Belloc's or Heinrich Hoffman's punitively cautionary tales. Self-restraint and obedience are rewarded; self-indulgence inevitably leads to physical humiliation.

C. S. Lewis focuses an even more complex self-indulgence on candy in *The Lion, the Witch and the Wardrobe* (1950) when Edmund, already morally weak, accepts Turkish Delight from Narnia's evil usurping Queen. Having consumed it, Edmund only wants more: "The Queen knew... that this was enchanted Turkish Delight and that anyone who once tasted it would want more and more of it, and would even, if they were allowed, go on eating it until they killed themselves." Edmund's subsequent actions are governed by an addictive desire that erodes his sense of family loyalty, justice, and every virtue the story values. Through plot and imagery, Lewis links this complicated Turkish Delight to Christian interpretations of the fall of Adam and Eve. He makes clear that there are bad sweets (addictive candy offered by a usurping, dominant female) and good sweets (the wholesome "great and gloriously sticky marmalade roll, steaming hot," which sates the siblings at the home of Mr. and Mrs. Beaver); they are differentiated by the moral qualities of both host and consumer. So, too, does the chocolate in Robert Cormier's young adult novel, *The Chocolate War* (1974), carry a freight of moral compromise: when Jerry Renault refuses to join his Catholic school's chocolate sale fundraiser, he is beaten down by a hierarchy of bullies, from priest to schoolmates. The chocolate here is an arbitrary commodity, ironically signifying a marked absence of literal and figurative sweetness—polluted with human sin by its very provenance.

Desire for sweets thus provides the engine for many fictional stories, but it reflects a desire that operates prodigiously in our world and brings with it "real-world" ethical issues. The less poetic, more factual aspects of sweets-related moral choices have long had a place in children's texts. Responding to criticisms concerning racism, Dahl revised his original description of Willy Wonka's factory workers, the African Oompa-Loompas, "tiny, miniature pygmies" with "almost black" skin that makes Charlie think they are made "out of chocolate"; in the revision, they are notable for their "funny long hair," hail from fictional Loompaland, and do not remind Charlie of chocolate.

The controversy over Dahl's text evokes an earlier explicit connection between labor, sweets, and children's literature: Amelia Opie's moving poem for children, *The Black Man's Lament or How to Make Sugar* (1826). "Oh! that good Englishmen could know / how Negroes suffer for their pleasure!" laments the protagonist of this abolitionist story, stirring young readers to political action. See SUGAR CANE. A century or so later, however, in the children's pamphlet *The Romance of Chocolate* (1934), the William Nielson Ltd. chocolate company admitted no qualms about enjoying the aesthetic aspects of "native" labor in cacao harvesting:

> Only natives can stand the hard work, and their crude methods require white overseers.... There is no more picturesque sight than the variegated patches of colour due to the brilliant hues of the pods... the coloured native men cutting them...; the women, in showy garments, scooping out the glistening pulp....

See COCOA. Political and social attitudes are thus variously embedded in children's stories about sweets, moving from the personal "guilt" associated with self-control to the broader scope of social awareness.

Inflation

Stories relating to labor illustrate the shifting valuation of sweets and sweets making in factual and fictional contexts. In domestic fiction, the making of cakes measures girls' skill and maturity: in *Anne of Green Gables* (1908), Anne's liniment-flavored cake cures her of "carelessness in cooking"; in *Emily of New Moon* (1925), Emily's successful production of a cake causes her aunt to concede Emily's identity as a competent family member. In recent years, however, comic culinary ineptitude is celebrated: "Puffy popcorn chocolate soufflé or carbonated exploding swamp?" Saffron asks of a burned cake she and her friend Sarah bake in Hilary McKay's *Permanent Rose* (2005). The hilariously disastrous cake is a sign that like Saffron's mother, a successful artist and kitchen incompetent par excellence, the girls are interesting, creative people. After two failed attempts, they resort to a prepared cake mix, and the resulting confection is received with as much enthusiasm and respect as one "made from scratch."

The casual way McKay's girls dump two failed cakes suggests easy access to sugar and chocolate—a long way from Laura Ingalls Wilder's awe at the white sugar in her tiny cake—but the changing valuation of sweets in children's books is most clearly apparent in descriptions of the witch's house in the various retellings of *Hansel and Gretel*. The original bread, cake, and spun-sugar house grows increasingly sugary as it moves through and beyond the twentieth century, and sweets become easily available.

"Its walls were made of gingerbread, its roof was made of cake. It was trimmed with cookies and candy, and its window-panes were of pure transparent sugar," writes Wanda Gág (1936); for Michael Morpurgo, "Amazingly, it was built of sugar-coated gingerbread! And the roof was made of icing. The chimney was a stick of licorice! As for the window-panes, they were marzipan, and the panes of glass were of purest sugar. The front door was made entirely of shortbread..." (2008). Illustrations reflect this fantastic glut—with peppermint cane pilasters, candy hearts, raspberry jellies, gumdrops, gingerbread men, hundreds-and-thousands, and lashings of icing in Susan Jeffers's version (1980); or pinwheel cookies, tarts, madeleines, macarons, profiteroles, candied cherries, icing, nuts, and the glistening buttery brown gloss of sweet pastries in Pauline Ellison's (1981). See CHILDREN'S CANDY and PENNY CANDY.

In the Grimms' text, the now seemingly modest house of bread, cake, and sugar was a luxurious remedy for starvation; today, only a superabundance of candy evokes a suitably ecstatic desirability for a young audience. Or perhaps *Harry Potter*'s success shows that ordinary candy is not enough: literary taste now demands "Special Effects" sweets such as those sold in Honeydukes in *Harry Potter and the Prisoner of Azkaban* (1999): "Tiny black Pepper Imps ('breathe fire for your friends!'), Ice Mice ('hear your teeth chatter and squeak!'), peppermint creams shaped like toads ('hop realistically in the stomach')..." and, of course, the famous (now produced in our "real" world) Bertie Bott's Every Flavour Beans.

In children's books, sweets are a dependable fulcrum for moral, political, and social messages. That children desire sweets is accepted as an unassailable fact fundamental to the stories, and this desire is what provides leverage for the stories' points—a desire rooted in the child's physical being, and understood by its very bodily force to exercise heart, mind, and soul. Children's writers and illustrators manipulate this desire to convey taste as well as intellectual and moral nourishment; it also operates in the very experience of children's reading. Giles Gingerbread's cake letters are meant to attract the young, but they show also that children's literature is itself a confection designed to whet desire.

Never has this been more apparent than at the launches of the *Harry Potter* books in the first decade of the twenty-first century: in the early morning of the release day of *Harry Potter and the Goblet of Fire*, a boy squeezed himself into a shopping cart in a supermarket. Not content to put his book down even for a minute, he sat among the family groceries enjoying the biggest treat of all. He was deliciously, compulsively reading the 636-page *Goblet of Fire* in the context in which he understood it: as a sweet comestible, a *Sugar-plumb* beyond the imaginings of even John Newbery.

See also CANDY LAND and LITERATURE.

Aronson, Marc, and Marina Budhos. *Sugar Changed the World: A Story of Magic, Spice, Slavery, Freedom, and Science.* New York: Clarion, 2010.
Bettelheim, Bruno. *The Uses of Enchantment.* New York: Knopf, 1976.
Keeling, Kara K., and Scott Pollard, eds. *Critical Approaches to Food in Children's Literature.* New York: Routledge, 2009.
Tatar, Maria. *Off with Their Heads! Fairy Tales and the Culture of Childhood.* Princeton, N.J.: Princeton University Press, 1992.

Deirdre F. Baker

chimney cake

See BAUMKUCHEN.

China. Chinese food encompasses a wealth of sweet dishes and sweet snacks, but no dessert course is served at the end of a typical meal, and the conceptual boundary between sweet and savory foods is much less strict than it is in Western cultures. Most meals in most parts of the country consist solely of savory dishes, and if a separate course is served at the end of a repast, it will normally be fresh fruit, either whole or, on more formal occasions, cut into elegant pieces. Sweetness is just one of the traditional "five flavors" (sweet, salty, sour, bitter, and pungent) that must be combined harmoniously in a meal, in no predetermined order. Cookery books, with occasional exceptions, tend not to include sections on desserts or sweet dishes: sweet foods are normally subsumed into other categories, such as *dian xin* (otherwise known as "dim sum": dainty snacks or refreshments that are eaten between meals), or cold appetizers.

Mostly, sweet foods are eaten as snacks between main meals, and on special occasions such as the

Chinese New Year, when they symbolize the sweetness of life, but they may also be incorporated into a menu at any point. See CHINESE NEW YEAR. In the southern Yangtze region, the set of appetizers served at the start of a feast might include cold kumquats in syrup (*bing tang jin ju*) or fried peanuts and seaweed with a sprinkling of sugar (*tai cai hua sheng mi*). In Sichuan, a sweet dish such as *ba bao guo zheng*, a stir-fried pudding of cooked wheat flour, lard, sugar, nuts, and candied fruits, might occasionally be served toward the end of a banquet, but it is classed as a "hot dish" rather than a separate sweet.

Though some Chinese dishes and snacks might accord with a Western conception of dessert, like the toffee bananas (*ba si xiang jiao*, literally "bananas trailing silken threads") and red bean pancakes served in place of dessert in Chinatown restaurants abroad, countless others straddle the supposed borders of "sweet" and "savory" dishes. For example, the old-fashioned Sichuanese dish *tian shao bai*, a favorite at rural celebrations, consists of slices of pork belly laid in a bowl, topped with sweet black sesame paste and glutinous rice mixed with lard and sugar, and steamed. No one would call such a dish a "dessert," but it is undoubtedly sweet.

Sweetness and Sweeteners

In general, sweetness in China carries similar connotations to sweetness in other cultures. The oldest Chinese character for "sweet," *gan* (甘), also means "pleasant" and "willingly"; it appears in compounds meaning "contented," "delicious," and "smooth-tongued." Both *gan* and the character that later largely replaced it, *tian* (甜), symbolize the happier side of life: "sweetness and bitterness" is a common metaphor for life's ups and downs.

The character for "honey" (*mi* 蜜) appears among the oldest extant examples of the Chinese script, the characters engraved on excavated "oracle bones," while the earliest manmade sugar was malt sugar or maltose (*yi*), mentioned in the ancient *Book of Songs*. Sugarcane juice was known very early on, but it was not until the Tang dynasty (618–907 C.E.) that the production of cane sugar became widespread. In modern China, honey may be stirred into hot water and drunk as a tonic. Malt sugar is still widely used in pastries and confectionery, and to lend gorgeous color to roasted and barbecued foods. Rock or crystal sugar, known in Chinese as "ice sugar" (*bing tang*), is often favored as a sweetener for tonic foods, such as a comforting soup of silver ear fungus and goji berries (*yin er geng*). Brown sugar, known in Chinese as "red sugar" (*hong tang*), is used to lend flavor and color to various sweetmeats and sweet–savory dishes, while regular white sugar made from cane or beets is mostly widely used in all aspects of the culinary arts.

Key Ingredients of Sweet Foods

One of the most striking differences between Chinese and European sweet food traditions is the general absence in China of the dairy foods and chocolate that are so important in European sweets and desserts. In traditional Chinese sweet pastries and cakes, lard or pork fat often plays the part of butter in other cuisines. Chocolate has so far made few inroads into Chinese cooking. There are some exceptions when it comes to the use of dairy, including the delicate milk custards of the Cantonese south and the imperial palace sweetmeats of Beijing. In the old neighborhood around the Drum and Bell Towers in Beijing, there are small shops specializing in imperial dairy foods, including gently baked junkets seasoned with fermented glutinous rice wine (*nai lao*), and "dried junket" (*nai lao gan*), a caramel-dark, fudgy mass of sweetened, dehydrated junket. See JUNKET.

In European cuisines, the plant ingredients used in sweets are predominantly fruits, nuts, and spices; the Chinese additionally make liberal use of root vegetables such as taro and sweet potato, and pulses, including mung, azuki, and occasionally haricot beans. This open-mindedness toward the creative possibilities of all ingredients leads to creations that would be regarded as eccentric in the West, such as a warm, sweet wood ear fungus smoothie in Taiwan, and stir-fried fava bean paste with lard and sugar (*can dou ni*) in Sichuan.

Certain ingredients used in sweet foods stand out as distinctively Chinese. Among fruits, jujubes or "Chinese dates," persimmons, and haw fruits are favored in northern China; lychees, longans, and Chinese apricot (*mei*) in the south. Lotus seeds, a traditional symbol of fertility, are often made into a sweet paste to fill dumplings and buns. Mung and azuki beans are commonly used in sweet or savory soups and congees: azuki are the main ingredient in "red bean paste" (*dou sha*), one of the most common stuffings for buns and pastries. See AZUKI BEANS.

Potatoes and sweet potatoes can be mashed, mixed with sugar and lard, and then deep-fried into *bing* (the generic word for round, flattened foods from pancakes to patties). When it comes to nuts, sesame seeds, walnuts, and peanuts are most widely used. Peanut brittle (*hua sheng su*) is made in many parts of the country, and shoppers can sometimes watch muscled men crush the nuts by hammering the warm toffee with enormous wooden mallets.

In autumn in the southern Yangtze region, the scent of tiny yellow osmanthus flowers fills the air like honey; the flowers provide one of the most delightful Chinese sweet flavors. Osmanthus flowers are brined and sugared to preserve them, and then mixed with lard and cooked flour to make stuffings for dainty snacks; they are also used in sweet soups, sauces, and jellies. Rose petals, bruised with white sugar to make a preserve, are another sweet flavoring.

Notable Sweet Foods

There are some distinctive major categories of Chinese sweet foods. Round mooncakes (*yue bing*), commonly but not exclusively sweet, are eaten at the Mid-Autumn Festival on the fifteenth day of the eighth lunar month, when people traditionally gather to admire the fullness of the autumn moon. See MOONCAKES. Another festival food found across the country is *tang yuan* or *yuan xiao*, the boiled glutinous rice spheres eaten at the Lantern Festival on the fifteenth day of the first lunar month, symbolizing the sweetness of family reunion and marking an end to the Chinese New Year holiday. They are often stuffed with a sweet black sesame paste made glossy with lard.

Traditionally, baking ovens were a rarity in most parts of China, which may explain the greater reliance on steaming as a method for cooking cakes and breads. For the Double Ninth Festival on the ninth day of the ninth lunar month, you may see crowds of people queueing in Shanghai to buy the appropriate seasonal sweetmeat, steamed *chong yang gao*, a colorful sandwich of green- and pink-colored glutinous rice paste layered with red bean paste. Peach-shaped, pink-tinted steamed buns with sweet fillings are a traditional birthday food, particularly for elderly people, because peaches are a symbol of immortality. Sweetened, leavened doughs made from corn or rice may be wrapped in maize husks or other fragrant leaves for a rustic snack—a kind of Chinese tamale.

Another whole genre of Chinese sweet snacks are flaky pastries made from wheat flour pastry layered with lard. Pieces of raw pastry may be cleverly shaped so that, after a gentle deep-frying, they puff out into fantastical forms such as water lilies, straw hats, or hedgehogs. A more dramatic variation is the "rippled-silk oil-cake" (*bo si you gao*), a small dumpling with a sweet filling that flowers up into crisp, fragile waves in the cooking oil.

Warm, sweetened creams made from nuts or seeds, such as apricot kernels or walnuts, mixed with ground rice, are a favorite belly-warmer, and just one type of the liquid sweets that are an important aspect of Chinese food culture. Another soupy sweet is "oil tea" or "fried flour gruel" (*you cha*), a food beverage made by mixing toasty fried wheat flour, chopped nuts, and sugar with piping hot water. *Jiu niang yuan zi*, small glutinous rice dumplings in a broth seasoned with sugar, osmanthus flowers, and fermented glutinous rice, is a popular snack in eastern China. Other delicacies are neither solid nor liquid, like *san he ni*, the sweet, lardy paste of ground rice studded with candied fruits that is an old-fashioned Sichuan street snack.

Regional Variations

Although many kinds of sweet foods can be found in different forms across China, there are striking regional variations. In Hunan, savory main dishes are rarely sweetened, while the people of Suzhou and Wuxi in eastern China are notorious in other parts of the country for adding sugar to almost everything. Local specialties include Wuxi sweet-and-sour ribs (*wu xi rou gu tou*), Suzhou cherry-red pork (*ying tao rou*), Suzhou "squirrel" fish (*song shu yu*), and Suzhou "boat snacks" (*chuan dian*): the little steamed dumplings ingeniously colored and sculpted to resemble fruits, nuts, and animals that were once served on the pleasure boats that thronged Tai Hu Lake. This local predilection for sweetness is also felt in nearby Shanghai, a melting pot of culinary influences from its surrounding region.

In the Cantonese south of China, the Chiuchow region, a center of sugarcane production, is known not only for seafood and savory street snacks but also for sweetmeats, including rich taro paste, sautéed water chestnut cake, and candied chestnuts and pumpkin with Chinese dates. See CHESTNUTS. And in Hong Kong, the territory's colonial history and status as an international port is reflected in the European-derived sweetmeats such as custard tarts that are served in dim sum restaurants alongside Chinese preparations. Notable Beijing sweets include *wan dou huang*, a cool jelly made from dried peas that was beloved by the Dowager Empress Cixi; *sa qi ma*, a Manchu nibble made from strips of rich, soft, deep-fried dough mixed with syrup and compressed into a cake; and "sugared ears" (*tang er duo*), deep-fried dough twists drenched in syrup that recall the sweetmeats of the Middle East.

Candy and Confectionery

The Chinese also enjoy what Americans call "candy": confectionery that is eaten between meals, for pleasure rather than nutrition. Some street vendors specialize in sugar-blowing (*chui tang*), handling thick malt sugar syrup like Venetian glass, blowing it into animal shapes to the delight of watching children. In Chengdu, peddlers make pictures by drizzling molten caramel onto a board, and picking the flat image up with a wooden stick to make a marvelous lollipop. See SUGAR PAINTING. Also in Chengdu, itinerant street traders sell "Ding Ding" malt sugar toffee (*ding ding tang*), announcing their arrival with metal clappers that make the sounds "ding ding dang!"—hence the name. Another spectacle of a sweetmeat is Dragon's Beard toffee (*long xu tang*), made like a miniature version of hand-pulled noodles by pulling toffee into hair-thin threads. In Beijing, childhood is often associated with the local equivalent of toffee apples, skewers of red haw fruits dipped in toffee (*bing tang hu lu*). See TOFFEE. Since the 1950s White Rabbit creamy candies, in their distinctive red, white, and blue packaging, have been the most instantly recognizable commercial Chinese sweet.

As of the early 1990s, sales of sugary confectionery have steadily grown. Mars Foods (China) has successfully promoted Dove chocolate bars, M&M's, and Snickers, which have become familiar sights in convenience stores across the country: in 2013 Mars had a 40 percent share of the Chinese chocolate market. See MARS and M&M'S. Although Western confectionery is making significant inroads in the Chinese market, consumers also enjoy modern manufactured sweets that are more suited to local tastes, such as individually wrapped sweetcorn gums in the shape of tiny ears of corn. Demand for sugar-free sweets is rising alongside a general growth in demand for candy, as more sophisticated consumers try to make healthier food choices in the face of soaring rates of obesity and type-2 diabetes. See SUGAR AND HEALTH.

See also FRIED DOUGH; HONEY; MALT SYRUP; STICKY RICE SWEETS; SUGAR; and SUGARCANE.

Anderson, E. N. *The Food of China*. New Haven, Conn.: Yale University Press, 1988.

Chang, Kwang-chih, ed. *Food in Chinese Culture: Anthropological and Historical Perspectives*. New Haven, Conn.: Yale University Press, 1977.

Ren Baizun, ed. *Zhongguo shi jing*. Shanghai: Shanghai wenhua chubanshe, 1999.

So, Yan-Kit. *Classic Food of China*. London: Macmillan, 1992.

Fuchsia Dunlop

Chinese New Year, the precise date of which is determined each year on the lunar calendar, is the most important of nine major holidays celebrated by most Chinese. Called *Chunjie* or *Nongli Nian* in Chinese, its practices vary by location and by the Chinese population celebrating it both in China and abroad. Each year is named sequentially after the 12 animals that came to see Buddha (for instance, the Year of the Horse began on 31 January 2014 and the Year of the Sheep on 18 February 2015; the year of the Monkey will commence on 8 February 2016). New Year traditions are practiced by almost all Chinese, whether they actually believe in them or not, because they offer a sense of identity and a touchstone to the past.

On the eighth day of the twelfth month of the old year, to signal the imminence of the New Year, people traditionally eat *laba* porridge made from sweet rice, in addition to other propitious foods like millet, berries, seeds, beans, and special sweets such as sugared coconut pieces and sugared dried fruits.

Before New Year's Day, homes are cleaned of every speck of dust so as not to sweep out good fortune once the holiday begins. People also purchase new clothes, often in red—the color of blood, health, strength, and happiness—along with other special items in preparation for this event. It is their most important annual festival.

On the twenty-fourth day of the twelfth month of the old year, families use a sweet, sticky substance such as maltose or corn syrup to smear the lips of the image of the Kitchen God that usually hangs above their hearth. See CORN SYRUP and MALT SYRUP. They then light firecrackers and burn the image to send off the god to the Jade Emperor in heaven, where he will report sweet, good things about them and their extended family. Many families prepare or purchase sticky rice cakes or other sweets to send off with the Kitchen God, such as Eight-Treasure Pudding made with nuts, sweets, seeds, candied fruits, and honey. See STICKY RICE SWEETS. The god will return on the last day of the old year when families hang a new picture of him above their hearth.

During the last week of the old year, business owners host a banquet for their employees and hand out red envelopes with even amounts of cash to help their workers attend the traditional family reunion dinners held on the eve of the New Year. Chinese New Year celebrations once lasted for 15 days, with festivities beginning on the first day of the first month of the lunar calendar, sometime between 21 January and 19 February. Today, the holiday is also called Spring Festival, and the government gives workers seven days of vacation. Homes are decorated for the holiday with peach branches and other symbols of longevity and happiness. Before New Year's Day, all debts are settled, and throughout the holiday people eat honey to purify their systems for health in the year to come. Families paste couplets on their front door for blessings and happiness, and light incense before the reunion dinner, which is attended by all generations of the extended family. This is a time to kowtow to photographs of the ancestors and pay respects to all elders. The special reunion dinner includes many vegetable dishes; noodle dishes made with long noodles to symbolize a long life; a whole fish for prosperity; and sweet sticky rice to ensure a sweet year. Some Chinese families exchange gifts, with southerners giving flowers and northerners offering sweet pastries and wine. All families give red envelopes called *laisze* filled with even amounts of cash to children, elders, the infirm, and the poor.

Days before this dinner, many families make hundreds of dumplings called *jiaozi* to bid farewell to the old year and welcome in the new. These dumplings are said to be shaped like gold ingots to wish everyone treasure in the coming year. Other families make *niangao*, or New Year cakes, with glutinous rice flour to symbolize going "higher and higher." These special foods are eaten both at dinner and at other times throughout the holiday. When families share holiday foods and sweets, they never use knives so as not to symbolically cut their luck. Many also abstain from eating animals during all or part of this holiday, to show respect and enhance their own longevity. On New Year's Day, no garbage is taken out so as not to cast out any family fortune, and no hair is cut for the same reason. On the fifth day of the New Year, everyone stays home to welcome the God of Wealth. Businesses close for the first three to five days of the New Year and reopen with a ceremony to this god.

Every Chinese person's birthday is customarily celebrated on New Year's Day, since the Chinese believe that at birth every child is already 1 year old and thus will turn a year older each time the New Year comes around. Throughout the holiday, guests are welcomed with tea and sweets from an eight-section round or octagonal dish called the "tray of togetherness," which is supposed to bring luck and sweetness to all who share it. The contents, which vary according to region and ethnic group, often include red melon and lotus seeds for happiness and many children; kumquats for prosperity; sweetened coconut for togetherness; dried bamboo shoots so that all will go well; candied melon for good health; and so on. Some families have a nine-sectioned tray, to include wishes for wealth. Guests are expected to bring oranges or tangerines as wishes for their hosts' prosperity; their edible gifts are reciprocated with items from the host's tray of togetherness.

See also CHINA.

Hu, William C. *Chinese New Year: Fact & Folklore.* Ann Arbor, Mich.: Ars Ceramica, 1991.
Newman, Jacqueline M. *Food Culture in China,* pp. 156–162. Westport, Conn.: Greenwood, 2004.
Xiang Wei, Benjamin Cheng, and Lingque Hu. *Chinese Customs.* New York: Better Link Press, 2008.
Yan Liao. *Food and Festivals of China.* Philadelphia: Mason Crest, 2006.

Jacqueline M. Newman

chocolate, luxury, refers to high-quality chocolates and chocolate confections that are lushly packaged and often sold in elegant specialty shops. The cachet of specialty brands and confectioners, and of course price, figure into what are now considered luxury chocolates. However, the distinction between high-end and ordinary chocolate scarcely existed until the early twentieth century, when chocolate was first mass-produced from inexpensive materials. Before then, chocolate was always a luxury good.

In Aztec society, where Europeans first encountered it in 1519, chocolate was served as a beverage that only the highest classes were allowed to consume—the royalty, the military, and long-distance traders. Beginning in the mid-1500s, when conquistadors brought it to the court of King Philip II of Spain, chocolate became a luxurious imported good available only to royalty and nobility, and to Catholic clergy because of their foothold in the New World. Served almost exclusively as a beverage, chocolate spread to European royal courts through marriages and alliances.

Chocolate became available to other social classes through the proliferation of coffeehouses and chocolate houses in the 1600s. See CAFÉ. However, it was more expensive than coffee and remained a luxury drink. After the French Revolution, artisan chocolatiers began setting up shop in Paris. In 1807 Grimod de la Reynière's *L'Almanach des gourmands*, a publication with food reviews, praised a shop for its "exquisite chocolate prepared with cacao selected with uncommon care."

In the nineteenth century, technologies invented in Europe transformed chocolate into a substance that could be made into bars and confections. Entrepreneurs gradually realized the profits to be made by bringing such products affordably to the general public.

Some of those who mass-produced chocolate confections marketed them with an aura of luxury. Festive packaging, often with themes of holidays and romance, symbolized luxury even when the chocolate was less expensive. In England in 1861, Cadbury created elegant packaging called "The Fancy Box" for its filled chocolate candies. Over the years the boxes became more elaborately decorated. The candies were given French names to make them sound more elegant. Overall, luxury chocolates took the form of beautifully presented candies. See BONBONS; CHOCOLATES, BOXED; and CHOCOLATES, FILLED.

By the early 1900s, especially with the rise of Hershey's in the United States, chocolate became affordable for almost everyone. See HERSHEY'S. However, the quality of chocolate suffered. Manufacturers used inexpensive Forastero cacao beans and substituted cheaper fats for cocoa butter. Such material was used ubiquitously in chocolate candies, including those represented as luxury chocolates, until the late 1980s. The difference between what was sold as a luxury good and what was marketed as inexpensive chocolate often lay in the presentation and the marketing.

Some of the first chocolate candies presented as luxury goods in the United States were Sherry's, founded by Louis Sherry, whose name was associated with New York's Sherry-Netherland Hotel even though he died in 1926, a year before it opened. From 1881 to 1919, Sherry sold expensive chocolate confections made from ingredients "of the highest quality" to wealthy customers such as J. P. Morgan and the Vanderbilts in his upscale candy shop. He packaged his chocolate candies in signature ribbon-festooned boxes.

Almond Roca, founded in 1912, consisted of chocolate-covered toffees sold in supermarkets throughout the United States. But they were individually wrapped in gold-colored aluminum foil and packaged in beautiful pink cans that gave the candy an air of luxury.

Around 1985, with France leading the way, a few small companies such as Valrhona began to make chocolate from high-quality beans from specific regions. See CHOCOLATE, SINGLE ORIGIN and VALRHONA. The rare, prized Criollo variety was sought out and employed (and more trees were planted as demand increased), followed by Trinitario, a cross between Criollo and Forastero beans. In 2003 Domori, an artisanal Italian company, produced the first 100 percent Criollo bar. As high-quality chocolate became available, artisan confectioners sprang up to create chocolate candies with fillings or additions made with quality ingredients to match the chocolate.

The concept of luxury chocolate begins with the quality of the chocolate itself, emphasizing single-origin chocolates and the concept of terroir, or the skillful blending of high-quality beans. Truly excellent chocolate will also contain cocoa butter as its fat and pure vanilla. See VANILLA. The packaging may list the percentage of cocoa solids (ground cacao beans) contained in the bar. Such chocolate is mostly produced by small companies, making quality chocolates rare and exclusive. They are usually carried in high-end retail stores and through exclusive websites. Wine pairings with specific chocolate bars add to the perception of luxury.

Some artisan confectioners began experimenting with unusual flavors such as tea, wasabi, bacon, mushrooms, beer, basil, and fennel pollen. Others feature regional ingredients. Handmade candies are often miniature works of art, and some artisan shops have become destinations for people seeking the finest foods. With ever more innovations in agriculture, manufacture, and confections, the concept of luxury chocolate will continue to evolve.

See also CAFÉ; CHOCOLATE, POST-COLUMBIAN; CHOCOLATE, PRE-COLUMBIAN; COCOA; CONFECTION; and TOFFEE.

Doutre-Roussel, Chloé. *The Chocolate Connoisseur*. New York: Tarcher, 2005.

Rosenblum, Mort. *Chocolate: A Bittersweet Saga of Dark and Light*. New York: North Point, 2005.

Miriam Kasin Hospodar

chocolate, post-Columbian, refers to the culture of cacao after Spanish explorers brought New World cacao beans to Europe, beginning in the sixteenth century. Unlike the very wary reception of two other New World crops, potatoes and tomatoes, cacao was much more readily embraced by Europeans, thanks to its similarity—once roasted, ground, and prepared as a beverage—to two other popular, nonalcoholic drinks, tea and coffee. See COCOA.

Although it would take a few hundred years for some of the New World crops to be incorporated into Old World dietary systems, cacao's trajectory was much shorter. Still, there was nothing inevitable about chocolate's reception in Europe when Spanish conquistadors returned with those first cacao beans, which they referred to as "almonds." (Hernán Cortés and not Christopher Columbus is generally believed to have been the first European to introduce cacao to the Old World, although no proof of this exists.) See CHOCOLATE, PRE-COLUMBIAN.

The bitter, murky, and undersweetened (by Spanish standards) beverage was not appreciated by all. Furthermore, the Galenic theory of medicine frightened off potential takers of the exotic new beverage, as its hot and dry (according to some) or cold and humid (according to others) properties were considered dangerous. These initial health concerns did not prove a deterrent for long, however, as some medical practitioners claimed that when roasted, ground, and properly prepared, hot chocolate was nutritious and would make one happy and strong.

One theory as to why this drink spread rapidly in Catholic Spain was that it could be consumed on fast days. As a beverage, it did not break the fast, and unlike coffee and tea, it provided sustenance due to its high fat content. On an empty stomach, theobromine (chocolate's caffeine-like compound) increased the drink's stimulating effects.

Naturally, the Spanish colonists living in New Spain developed the same appreciation for chocolate as did their confrères back home, and the steady interchange between Spain and New Spain fostered the creation of different preparations for hot chocolate that were better suited to European taste buds. The more familiar spices such as cinnamon and nutmeg, anise, cloves, mace, and cardamom replaced earflowers, chili peppers, achiote, and other New World ingredients. It was, therefore, a creolized culture of cacao developed after the Conquest that was exported back to Spain and subsequently to the rest of Europe. These hot chocolate recipes would continue to evolve (both black and white pepper would be substituted, and chili pepper would subsequently be reintroduced) as chocolate traveled between Europe and the New World.

Beginning in the seventeenth century, a number of treatises and monographs on chocolate and its medicinal uses were published first in Spanish and soon thereafter in English, French, and Italian; many were translations of earlier Spanish works. Some of these volumes were published by priests, others by medical doctors; in some instances, the writers had lived for long periods of time among the Native populations of the New World. In addition to their firsthand observations of traditional ways with cacao, and analyses of "cacao nuts" and their effects on the human body, these books featured a number of hot chocolate recipes, all initially water-based, as there had been no cows in the New World until the Europeans introduced them. A hot chocolate preparation containing milk was, therefore, a significant development.

One of the earliest such preparations combining milk with water may be found in Englishman John Chamberlaine's translation of Sylvestre Dufour's treatise on coffee, tea, and chocolate, published in London in 1685 as a translation of the Spaniard Antonio Colmenero de Ledesma's much earlier monograph from 1631. One of Chamberlaine's hot chocolate recipes calls for adding milk to the water along with one egg yolk for every ounce of milk used. Whether it was the Spanish, English, or French who first began adding milk to hot chocolate preparations is difficult to establish. What is known, however, is that the addition of milk to chocolate dramatically reshaped the history of cacao.

By the second half of the seventeenth century, chocolate had joined coffee and tea in London coffeehouses as an Enlightenment beverage: one that, unlike alcoholic drinks, promoted clear thinking. See CAFÉ. One could sip chocolate all day long and remain clearheaded and productive. Fashionable, delicious, and nutritious, chocolate was all the rage among the affluent on the Continent and across the Channel.

Colonial Americans, in particular seafaring ones, quickly recognized the nutritional aspects of chocolate as well as its portability. And cacao beans, like rum and sugar from the Caribbean, were much-sought-after imports in the seventeenth and eighteenth centuries. Hot chocolate preparations joined coffee and tea as nonalcoholic alternatives to cider and beer. (The passage of the Townsend Acts beginning in 1767 made chocolate or coffee drinking a patriotic act, as tea was heavily taxed under these new measures.) Hot chocolate could be enjoyed outside the home, or unsweetened, coarsely ground chocolate cakes could be purchased at an apothecary or dry goods shop and prepared in one's own kitchen. The cakes would either be dissolved into the liquid first and then warmed, or shaved into a pot in which the liquid had already boiled.

The chocolate breakfast (ideally while one was still in bed or even in the bath) came into vogue in Italy and France in the eighteenth century, and in response porcelain manufacturers like Meissen (and later Sèvres) expanded their coffee and tea service offerings to include double-handled chocolate cups (often with lids) set on deep saucers, known as *trembleuses,* and chocolate pots that were designed expressly for the new beverage. See CHOCOLATE POTS AND CUPS. French and Italian Rococo artists like Nicolas Lancret and Pietro Longhi depicted world-weary lords and ladies sipping hot chocolate in their private chambers. Chocolate, served in such surroundings, was deemed the antithesis of coffee, as the latter symbolized work and industriousness. Chocolate, on the other hand, represented studied leisure and idleness.

The Spread of Cacao

Besides the (drinkable) chocolate breakfast, desserts in Italy and France at this time began to feature chocolate as a flavoring in custards and creams. Across the Channel, the 1726 edition of Patrick Lamb's cookbook *Royal Cookery* featured a French-inspired, meringue-topped chocolate tart. Such tarts and especially meringues were also popular in colonial America. See MERINGUE.

The increased consumption of chocolate among Europeans was made possible by the spread of cacao plantations throughout the Caribbean. Following its introduction in the Caribbean by the Spanish, the English, French, and Dutch were soon experimenting with cacao in Brazil, Curaçao, Guadalupe, Hispaniola, Jamaica (which soon became England's main source of cacao), Suriname, the West Indies, and Venezuela (and later in Africa and Indonesia). With cacao's increased importance in the colonies came increased production, which led to the founding of two early chocolate factories, the first in Providence, Rhode Island (Brown Brothers in 1752), and the second in Dorchester, Massachusetts (Walter Baker and Co. in 1765). The founding of Baker's Chocolate (by a chocolatier and a physician), the year after a smallpox epidemic in Boston, is perhaps not coincidental. Chocolate was frequently recommended for those afflicted with smallpox. See BAKER'S.

With the growing demand for chocolate on both sides of the Atlantic, it is not surprising that improved means of processing cacao beans would be developed. The nineteenth-century inventions of a small handful of Dutch, Swiss, and English chemists revolutionized the processing of cacao beans and reshaped an entire industry. As production capabilities increased due to mechanized grinding, so did the demand for an ever-greater supply of cacao beans. African countries like Ghana and Ivory Coast (with no history of cacao) were planted with the New World trees in the nineteenth century, and by the twentieth century had become the most important producers on the world stage.

Coenraad Van Houten's mechanized grinding of cacao beans allowed for the separation of the fat (cocoa butter) from the solid (cocoa mass) and made possible the mass production and marketing of a powdered drinking chocolate. See VAN HOUTEN, COENRAAD JOHANNES. The hydraulic press he invented with his father in 1828 proved inspirational to Roger Fry in England, who had been searching for a way to produce a paste of chocolate that would be thin enough to pour into molds for bars.

Henri Nestlé's invention of powdered milk in 1867 made possible chocolatier Daniel Peter's winning creation: milk chocolate. In 1879 the first milk chocolate bar was produced by adding (dry) milk solids to cocoa mass. See NESTLÉ and PETER, DANIEL.

The next great Swiss innovation, also dating from 1879, was Rodolphe Lindt's invention of "conching," a refining process that causes the cocoa liquor, or paste, to be ground into a micron size so small that no solids can be detected on the tongue. Although most foods do not benefit from mechanized processing, cacao is an exception. Without the refining and conching stages, perfectly smooth chocolate with a clean melt would be unknown. See LINDT, RODOLPHE.

Tempering, too, invented around this time, greatly advanced the culture of chocolate. It remains a vital step in chocolate making today, as untempered chocolate does not have the same sheen and snap. By raising and lowering the temperature of the melted chocolate, the molecular structures of the fat and sugar crystals are aligned and become stable, thus maintaining the shine associated with well-made chocolate.

By the close of the nineteenth century, chocolate was already a popular flavoring ingredient for desserts in the United States. The 1896 edition of Fannie Merritt Farmer's *Boston Cooking School Cookbook* features almost 20 recipes for cakes, frostings, puddings, cookies, and ice cream, some of which specifically called for Baker's chocolate. As the twentieth century dawned, milk chocolate in confectionery reigned supreme. Milton Hershey introduced the Kiss in 1907 and a year later a milk chocolate almond candy bar. See FARMER, FANNIE; HERSHEY'S; and KISSES.

Chocolate as Candy

The decades of the 1920s and 1930s saw the creation of such iconic American candy bars as Mr. Goodbar, Snickers, Baby Ruth, Three Musketeers, Butterfinger, and Milky Way bars. See CANDY BAR. These candy bars, more caramel, nuts, and nougat than chocolate, came to define what most Americans considered chocolate to be. It was only with the arrival of Valrhona chocolate in the United States in 1984 (initially only for pastry and chocolate professionals, not the general public) that perceptions about chocolate began to change. Dark chocolate became an important ingredient on its own, not just a supporting actor to nuts, ice cream, milk, coconut, or caramel. In well-made flourless chocolate cakes, mousses, tarts, and sculpture-like plated desserts, chocolate had the starring role. Soon the public began to make a distinction between milk and dark chocolate. Origins and cocoa percentages began to matter. One of the first new-wave American barsmiths (as bean-to-bar producers are known) was Napa Valley winemaker John Scharffenberger, who founded Scharffenberger Chocolate with Robert Steinberg in 1996. The company was sold to Hershey's in 2005. America's oldest bean-to-bar chocolate company still in family hands is Guittard, begun in San Francisco by Frenchman Etienne Guittard at the time of the Gold Rush. See GUITTARD and VALRHONA.

With the increased public awareness of food around the turn of the twenty-first century, a great number of sustainable-minded bean-to-bar companies were established in the United States and abroad. Socially and environmentally conscious, these chocolate artisans shunned beans from countries where farmers or children were exploited. See CHILD LABOR. Working in small batches, often on nineteenth-century equipment, with fine, flavorful beans (frequently without vanilla or lecithin), these producers redefined the taste of chocolate.

As a means of reconfiguring the first-world or third-world economic model of chocolate making, cacao-growing countries have now become chocolate-producing countries. Despite the challenges of producing chocolate in a tropical country, companies in Grenada, Ecuador, and Madagascar are currently doing so and maximizing profits for cacao farmers. The revolution set in motion by these vanguard producers was quickly noted by the Lindts, Mars, and Hersheys of the world. Soon these industrial producers were adding single-origin and high cocoa content bars to their portfolios. See CHOCOLATE, SINGLE ORIGIN and MARS.

Fine Chocolate

In recent years, as producers large and small, in the United States and abroad, began to worry about the world supply of cacao beans, Mars and Hershey's undertook the genetic sequencing of the cacao bean in order to ensure a sustainable future for cacao. Their findings, published in 2010, have helped to identify the most flavorful, disease-resistant plants that are robust producers. Concern over the plight of cacao farmers, among the world's most impoverished workers, has increased as public awareness about chocolate in general has grown. Seeking to shorten the food chain, many barsmiths are traveling the world, forging direct connections with cacao collectives rather than sourcing beans from brokers. This practice ensures that the premiums they pay for superior beans actually end up in the farmers' pockets. In many ways, the traditional model of chocolate making has been turned on its head, with cacao-growing countries now becoming chocolate-making nations.

As the worldwide demand for chocolate increases and global production flattens, countries with no history of cacao cultivation are beginning to plant trees, with varying degrees of success. At the same time, countries that were once producers are revitalizing their industries. And so the history of chocolate continues to unfold in much the same way as it always has. Just as cacao was once taken from its New World home clear across the world, traveling as seedlings aboard wooden sailing ships, so it is with cacao today that is planted in Thailand, India, and Australia, miles from its origins in the Americas.

With the public's appetite for chocolate growing ever more voracious as media outlets tout the health benefits of dark chocolate, and with tasting classes, festivals, and chocolate-centered ecotravel itineraries further tempting consumers, the world of chocolate is also becoming ever more niche. In 2014 an important chapter in chocolate's history was ushered in with the creation of the Heirloom Cacao Preservation Initiative, dedicated to identifying, preserving, and propagating the finest-flavor cacao, and at the same time recognizing and rewarding the growers who cultivate it.

Drinkable, spreadable, enjoyable in many forms, *Theobroma cacao*, the food of the gods, remains a favorite food among mortals throughout the world.

See also CHOCOLATE, LUXURY; CHOCOLATES, BOXED; CHOCOLATES, FILLED; PLATED DESSERTS; and SPAIN.

Coe, Sophie., and Michael D. Coe. *The True History of Chocolate*. New York: Thames and Hudson, 1996.

Gordon, Clay. *Discover Chocolate*. New York: Gotham, 2007.

Grivetti, Louis Evan, and Yana Shapiro. *Chocolate: History, Culture, and Heritage*. Hoboken, N.J.: Wiley, 2009.

Presilla, Maricel. *The New Taste of Chocolate: A Natural and Cultural History of Chocolate with Recipes*. Berkeley, Calif.: Ten Speed, 2001.

Rosenbloom, Mort. *Chocolate: A Bittersweet Saga of Dark and Light*. New York: North Point, 2005.

Schivelbusch, Wolfgang. *Tastes of Paradise: A Social History of Spices, Stimulants, and Intoxicants*. New York: Vintage, 1993.

Alexandra Leaf

chocolate, pre-Columbian, was the New World's most dazzling gift. Made from cacao seeds, or "beans," enclosed in thick-skinned pods that sprout straight from both the trunk and branches of the slender, evergreen cacao tree (*Theobroma cacao*), chocolate is one of the most complex foods on earth. Nourishing, stimulating, packed with more than 400 chemical compounds that produce nuanced flavors and can heal and even alter mood, chocolate also has a mystical aspect. It is the stuff of desire and obsession, and has been a marker of class and status through the ages.

When you cut open a cacao pod, you find beans enveloped in ivory-colored, mucilaginous pulp with a sweet-tart flavor reminiscent of litchis. Attached to their central "placenta," the beans, with their white, purple, lavender, or pinkish cotyledons, are often bitter and astringent in raw form, tasting nothing like chocolate until they have been fermented, dried, roasted, and ground. How did the people of tropical America stumble upon these processes? Where did cacao originate, and who first domesticated it? These questions have puzzled scholars for centuries.

If the history of chocolate were a 24-hour cycle, glossy chocolate bars and confections would represent a few seconds, while cacao and chocolate beverages would account for the vast majority of a long saga that began in South America 56 centuries ago, at least 1,670 years before the Egyptians built their first step pyramid. In 2010, research to decode the cacao genome established that the species originated in the Upper Amazon region. This pioneering project, launched with funding from Mars, Inc., was carried out mainly at the Subtropical Horticultural Research Station of the U.S. Department of Agriculture's Agricultural Research Division, in Miami, Florida. There, the Venezuelan-born geneticist Juan Carlos Motamayor also broke the long-established paradigm of two main types of domesticated cacao—Forastero (bitter and astringent, with purple cotyledons) and Criollo (nutty, nuanced, and sweet-tasting, with white cotyledons), plus a hybrid of the two called Trinitario—and shed new light on the complexity of genotypes within the species. Motamayor

Cacao was essential to Maya and Aztec culture. The beans were dried and ground into a paste that was dissolved in hot water for a savory and nourishing drink. This illustration of a cacao tree is from the Tudela Codex, a sixteenth-century Aztec cultural encyclopedia. ALBUM / ART RESOURCE, N.Y.

announced in 2008 that there were 10 distinct genetic clusters, a number that has grown to 15 as scientists have continued to examine samples of cacao gathered in Bolivia, Ecuador, and Peru, and this number has continued to rise.

While the genome sequencing project helped clarify the origins of cacao as well as the relationships among the types, it also raised questions about the absence of anything resembling chocolate in the plant's native territory. At the time, no pre-Columbian ceramic or stone vessel containing traces of the alkaloid theobromine, the key chemical marker of cacao, had been found in the species' Amazonian cradle, nor did there seem to be a tradition of chocolate making among contemporary Amazonian people. The consensus was that cacao was domesticated further north, in Mesoamerica, where it had arrived from South America in pre-Columbian times, and that it was in Mesoamerica that it had been first turned into chocolate.

A scene painted on a Late Classic Maya vase from Guatemala, now at the Princeton Art Museum, shows a woman pouring a chocolate drink from one vessel to another, the first held high above the second to create a head of foam, the most valued part of the beverage. This scene is the first known painted representation of a timeless ritual passed down to the Aztecs and then to Spanish colonists (who added their own twist, the *molinillo,* a wooden stick ending in a knob or rings used to agitate the liquid). It was also the first to show the crucial role of women in the making of chocolate beverages among the Maya.

The women spread the beans on a flat surface to dry, most likely after using the pulp for drinks. They roasted and shelled the dried beans before grinding them into a sticky paste that could be dissolved in hot water straight from the three-legged grinding stone called a *metate*; or, once dried, in cold water to make nourishing beverages.

Pre-Classic Maya pottery vessels dating from 500 C.E. found at Río Azul in the Petén region of Guatemala in 1987 offered tantalizing clues as to the antiquity of such chocolate drinks. Scrapings from their interior walls and bottoms analyzed by W. Jeffrey Hurst, senior scientist at the Hershey Foods Technical Center, yielded traces of theobromine. Even more thrilling, the Maya epigraphy expert David Stuart decoded two fish-shaped glyphs painted on one of the beautiful, stirrup-handled vessels as "kakawa," or cacao. These findings led to other momentous discoveries that kept pushing back the date of the first Mesoamerican chocolate. Spouted pots from Colha, Belize, dating to 500 B.C.E., were found to contain residues of cacao, as were sherds from narrow-necked pottery dating to 1400–1100 B.C.E. excavated at the Puerto Escondido site in the Lower Ulúa River Valley in Honduras. The oldest milestone in the Mesoamerican chocolate saga came from traces of cacao on a single pottery sherd dating to 1900–1500 B.C.E. found at Paso de la Amada, a village on the Pacific coast of today's Chiapas State in Mexico occupied by the Mokaya, a farming and fishing community.

Did the Moyaka or the people of the Ulúa River Valley consume chocolate or were they drinking fresh cacao juice or fermented cacao pulp drinks? Some scholars argue that the spouted, narrow-necked shape of the vessels points to the latter use, but it is incontrovertible that cacao had been domesticated and was consumed as a food by some of the earliest ceramic-using peoples of Mesoamerica.

There have been challenges to the Mesoamerican claim to chocolate primacy, however. Archaeological work at Santa Ana-La Florida, a pre-Columbian site near the town of Palanda in the Ecuadorian province of Zamora Chinchipe, 3,040 feet up the eastern slopes of the Andes, have brought cacao's center of origin into revised focus. In 2003, a Franco-Ecuadorian team led by the Ecuadorian archaeologist Francisco Valdez excavated tombs and funerary offerings, a small ceremonial center, and domestic structures in this river valley by the Valladolid, a headwater stream of the Mayo Chinchipe River, which is a tributary of the mighty Peruvian Marañón. Their findings reveal an upper Amazonian culture of the early formative period now called Mayo Chinchipe-Marañón that had spread throughout the basin of the Chinchipe River. They practiced sedentary agriculture in a transitional cloud forest zone called *ceja de montaña* (eyebrow of the mountain) known for high plant diversity, and had a fairly advanced material culture of stone carvings and ceramics. Most important, residues contained in two beautiful, intact, anthropomorphic, stirrup-spout vessels, stone bowls, and a ceramic vessel recovered from tombs dating to 3500–3350 B.C.E. tested positive for cacao. That conclusion was based on analysis of cacao starch granules, which are less perishable than theobromine, by the archaeologist Sonia Zarrillo at Calgary University.

Thus, it seems that cacao not only had been grown in the *ceja de montaña* for millennia, but also that it had made the leap into drinks of ceremonial importance at least 1,450 years earlier than in Mesoamerica. In her doctoral dissertation Zarrillo (2012) writes, "It is interesting that starch granules of maize, especially, and chili peppers, reminiscent of the Mesoamerican chocolate recipes, were recovered from the same context as the possible *T. cacao* starch granules." The starch granules of plant species identified at Santa Ana-La Florida—peppers, yuca, sweet potato, arrowroot, and cacao—date from the first formative period, and are the earliest evidence of the use of cacao to date.

Meanwhile, researchers from Ecuador's Instituto Nacional Autónomo de Investigaciones Agropecuarias (INIAP) and France's Centre de Coopération Internationale en Recherche Agronomique pour le Développement (CIRAD) determined that trees growing at the Mayo Chinchipe-Marañón site were direct ancestors of Ecuador's prized Nacional cacao strain. The tombs and ceremonial space excavated there also contained marine shells, most important Spondylus, from today's coastal provinces. In other words, by 3300 B.C.E. trade routes across the double Andean mountain range connected the Amazonian region and the Pacific coast, showing that the lands that later became a part of Ecuador had developed a vertically integrated agricultural economy—the same system perfected by sixteenth-century Inca rulers that allowed the exchange of products from various altitudes and ecosystems.

The Aztecs, and the Maya before them, may not have been the first to experiment with cacao, but there is general agreement that they brought drinking chocolate to a high degree of sophistication, often combining roasted ground cacao beans with *masa* made from fresh or boiled lime-treated dried corn and a number of aromatic flavorings. The glyphs arranged around the rims of the tall, straight-sided polychrome vessels used for drinking chocolate show that the Maya colored, spiced, and perfumed the beverage with flavorings such as achiote, chiles, vanilla, honey, maguey sap, and flowers. The glyphs also spell out the names of green cacao drinks, meaning that fresh cacao pulp, unsweetened "bitter cacao," "honeyed cacao," and "foamy cacao" were drunk from these vessels.

Ethereal, foamy toppings were created by pouring chocolate drinks from a height from one cylindrical container to another, as depicted in the Princeton vase, but the survival of ceremonial recipes in some contemporary Maya communities of Guatemala suggests that by beating a *masa* made with ground cacao and its relative *Theobroma bicolor* (*pataxte*) together with a *masa* of lime-treated corn while adding hot corn gruel (*atole*), the cocoa butter and some of the corn float to the top as a firmer white topping.

Commissioned from local artists, chocolate-drinking vases were part of an elaborate gift-giving system that cemented social relations and alliances among the Maya nobility. On some bright ceramic paintings of the Classic Period (250–550 C.E.), nobles are shown seated on low platforms next to tall vases brimming with chocolate drinks topped with a reddish foam, a clear reference to achiote-colored drinks, and squatter vessels containing thicker corn-enriched *atoles*, more likely combined with chocolate.

The pairing of cacao and corn is a constant in the Mesoamerican history of chocolate to this day, as is a predilection for achiote as a coloring for chocolate. Achiote (known as annatto in English) is an important edible dye obtained from small, hard seeds enclosed in the red pods of a small tropical shrub. When ground with cacao beans, achiote imparts an intense brick-red color to chocolate drinks that the Maya equated to the blood of sacrificial victims, a central theme of Maya religious beliefs and rituals. While the color red was a favorite, the preferred flavoring for chocolate was the woody flower of an *annonaceae*, known today as ear flower (*orejuela*). On a beautiful Maya vase, two courtiers are shown bringing bouquets of ear flowers to a Maya chieftain seated on a low platform. When toasted, as most flavorings for chocolate are to this day, ear flowers taste like white pepper.

The cacao-growing regions that sustained the flowering of chocolate in pre-Hispanic Mesoamerica were few. Information coming from the early colonial period shows that the most intensive production occurred in a few scattered spots in a rather narrow region of the tropical lowlands, including points on the Pacific coast of today's Guatemala and the state of Chiapas in Mexico, Tabasco State on the Gulf coast of Mexico, and Honduras. Not coincidentally, they overlap with the spots where archaeologists have discovered the earliest evidence of cacao used as food or drink: Paso de la Amada, El Manatí (an Olmec site), and Ulúa. Isolated areas of lesser production were found further north and south on both the Pacific and Gulf coasts (Colima and Tuxpan, respectively) of Mexico.

Recent discoveries of pottery containing traces of cacao in pre-Colombian sites in the Midwest, Southeast, and Southwest of the United States reveal the far-reaching influence of the Mesoamerican chocolate culture. In 2009 the archaeologist Patricia Crown reported that shards from tall, cylindrical clay jars dating from between 1100 and 1125 C.E., found at the Pueblo Bonito site in the Chaco Canyon, New Mexico, had tested positive for theobromine and caffeine, two chemical markers of cacao. More recently, the archaeologist Dorothy K. Washburn has found traces of cacao in older ceramics from the eighth-century Alkali Ridge site in southeastern Utah and from Mississippian platform mounds, dating from 1050 and 1250 C.E., respectively. There is still ongoing debate about whether the biomarkers found in the Mississippian pieces belong to *Theobroma cacao* or to Yaupon holly (*Ilex vomitoria*), used to make a stimulant brew that archaeologists call Black Drink, but the latest evidence seems to point to cacao.

Given the towering importance of cacao in the value systems of the Maya and their contemporaries, it was inevitable that people living outside of cacao-producing regions would take up arms to gain control over to the prized crop. Cacao wars were fought among various powerful, bellicose peoples of the Guatemalan highlands, where cacao would not grow. Before the Spanish conquest, the Quiché Maya had repeatedly invaded areas of the coastal Pacific plains in order to get their hands on land suitable for cacao orchards. The food historian Sophie Coe and her husband, the archaeologist Michael Coe, report that the subjugated peoples were required to pay tribute in cacao to the overlords, the same demand imposed by the Aztecs when they conquered the cacao-growing areas the Maya had fought over. The most important of these regions was Soconusco in today's Chiapas State.

By the time the Aztecs conquered Soconusco and other parts of Mexico in the late fourteenth century, they had already developed a complex chocolate culture based on tributes in the form of cacao and cacao flavorings from the subject tropical lands where it grew. As in other parts of Mesoamerica, cacao was highly valued and used as a form of currency among the Aztecs. We know that the Aztecs hungered for cacao without being able to grow it in their own cities. It reached Tenochtitlan, their cold capital on the highlands, from the subject tropical regions on the shoulders of porters (*tlamemes*), who walked for thousands of miles with bundles of the precious cargo fastened to their foreheads with straps.

From Spanish eyewitnesses of the early colonial period, including the Dominican friar Bernardino de Sahagún, author of the monumental *Historia general de las cosas de la Nueva España* (General History of the Things of New Spain), we get a detailed picture of the place of cacao and chocolate drinks among the Aztecs. All histories of chocolate among the Aztec begin with the classic story of the fifteenth-century emperor Motecuhzoma II (Moctezuma II) imbibing cacao drinks daily from cups that looked as if they were made of gold. Upper-class families served chocolate at the naming ceremonies of their children, and the powerful merchant class incorporated it into banquets to celebrate successful trading journeys. It was an essential element of ceremonies where slaves were sacrificed and their flesh eaten. The paraphernalia of chocolate serving, such as decorated gourds and tortoise-shell stirrers, were among the gifts given to special guests.

A marker of class, chocolate drinks in colors ranging from white to red and black, and flavored variously with peppery ear flowers, sweet honey, and aromatic vanilla, came to the tables of the nobility at the conclusion of lavish banquets. As tokens of conspicuous wealth, even servants were handed gourdfuls of the precious brew. Bernal Díaz del Castillo comments that about 2,000 gourds of chocolate were doled out to the servants and staff at Motecuhzoma's court after the emperor had consumed about 50 *jicaras* (gourdfuls) of the brew.

At the time of the Spanish conquest, cacao beans were available for purchase at the great market of Tlatelolco, where retailers displayed them by quality and provenance. In pre-Columbian times, the peoples of Mesoamerica learned to cultivate a particularly fine strain of cacao originally native to a region of Venezuela between Lake Maracaibo and the Andes. Other strains were known throughout the South American tropics, but the multiple pieces of the genetic puzzle had to await modern genomic sequencing. What the Maya, the Aztecs, and the Spanish colonizers all recognized was the superiority of the cacao that came to be called Criollo, now identified as one of the genetic clusters of the *Theobroma* cacao species. In the rich, well-watered volcanic Maya lands stretching along the Pacific coastal plain from Soconusco to parts of Guatemala and El Salvador, Criollo was valuable enough to make fortunes both before and after the Spanish conquest. What made Criollo special were its white cotyledons and its mild, nutty flavor, laced with herbal notes in some cultivars. When lightly toasted and ground, it made a honey-colored chocolate light enough to showcase colorings such as achiote.

The same merchants dealing cacao at the market sold the main flavorings for chocolate: *tlilxochitl* (vanilla), *ueinacaztli* (ear flower), and *mecaxochitl* (the thin, elongated flower stalk of *Piper aurantium*, or *hoja santa*). See VANILLA. Prized by the Aztecs, these flavorings came to Tenochtitlan, like cacao, from warmer lands in the empire. The Spanish historian Diego Durán, in his *Historia de las Indias* (History of the Indies), tells us that late in the reign of Motecuhzoma I, a fifteenth-century predecessor of the last emperor, the ruler's brother and chief advisor suggested an ambitious plan "that would bring him glory and praise after his days were done"—nothing less than a botanical garden near Tenochtitlan, warm and well-watered enough to raise hopes that plants from other regions might survive.

The chosen spot was Huaxtepec near Cuautla in today's Morelos State (still the site of famous gardens). Here Motecuhzoma commanded that cacao trees and other plants bearing sweet-scented flowers be brought from the southern lands that supplied some of the most treasured goods in the imperial storehouses and the Tenochtitlan market. The task was undertaken with the most solemn sacrifices and rituals, and thanks to the care of skilled gardeners, every plant bloomed luxuriantly within three years—a result that Durán is careful to ascribe to the Devil's cunning snares. The emperor and his brother wept with joy at being able to "bequeath to Mexico-Tenochtitlan and all the nations in the provinces associated with the Aztecs the refreshment and the delights of the flowers they had lacked until then."

Besides vanilla and intensely fragrant flowers like the *rosita de cacao*, the Aztecs added corn in varying proportions to most chocolate drinks. Women ground the cacao beans on a *metate* several times with boiled, nixtamalized corn to achieve the right texture. The resulting paste was dissolved in water to make drinks on the spot. The amount of water and corn added to the cacao mixture were important variables determining quality (the more water or corn, the less desirable the drink). Even more important was the amount and beauty of the froth on the top of the drink, not unlike the head of foam on a contemporary cup of cappuccino.

Startled at first by the inordinate importance given to chocolate by the Aztecs, the conquering Spaniards succumbed to its charms and made it their own, absorbing the millennial technology that had transformed a tropical fruit into a dark brew of desire, and changing its flavor with Old World spices like cinnamon and sugar. Enthroned as the beverage of the upper classes and imbued with an aura of prestige, chocolate drinks traveled with colonial officials, merchants, sailors, nuns, and friars to Spain and capitals of the Spanish colonial empire from Mexico to the Philippines. The indispensable grinding stone, the *metate*, the gourds from which chocolate was drunk, and many of the recipes that had been created in the Americas also made the journey. What ensued was a new, transcontinental chocolate empire, a fluid world built on a Mesoamerican chocolate culture, which gave rise to new rituals and recipes that would flow back and forth across the Atlantic.

In the Americas, where it had all begun, two worlds of chocolate coexisted during the colonial period and beyond, one based on the elite drinks transformed by the Spaniards, which gradually lost their flavor complexity, and another fiercely clinging to ancient pre-Columbian traditions that never died, particularly in Mexico and Central America. Wherever one travels in the old lands of cacao, women still roast beans on clay *comales* and grind beans on *metates*. They make chocolate drinks like the *bupu* of Oaxaca, with its crown of froth, and the *tejate* of Oaxaca, with its firm white topping, redolent of *rosita de cacao*. At the same time, artisanal producers throughout Central America and microbatch chocolate makers in North America are experimenting with flavorings so old that they seem new again.

See also CHOCOLATE, POST-COLUMBIAN; CHOCOLATE, SINGLE ORIGIN; COCOA; LATIN AMERICA; MEXICO; and SPAIN.

Coe, Sophie D., and Michael D. Coe. *The True History of Chocolate*. Rev. ed. London: Thames and Hudson, 2007.

Loor Solorzano, Ray Gaston, Oliver Fouet, et al. "Insight into the Wild Origin, Migration, and Domestication History of the Fine Flavour Nacional *Theobroma cacao* L. Variety from Ecuador." *PLoS ONE* 7, no.11 (2012): e48438. http://www.plosone.org/article/info%3Adoi%2F10.1371%2Fjournal.pone.0048438 (accessed September 17, 2014).

McNeil, Cameron L., ed. *Chocolate in Mesoamerica: A Cultural History of Cacao*. Gainsville: University Press of Florida, 2006.

Motamayor, Juan C., et al. "Geographic and Genetic Population Differentiation of the Amazonian Chocolate Tree (*Theobroma cacao* L)" *PloS ONE* 3, no. 10 (October 2008): e3311. http://www.plosone.org/article/info%3Adoi%2F10.1371%2Fjournal.pone.0003311 (accessed September 17, 2014).

Presilla, Maricel E. *The New Taste of Chocolate: A Natural and Cultural History of Cacao with Recipes*. Rev. ed. Berkeley, Calif.: Ten Speed, 2009.

Sahagún, Fray Bernardino de. *Historia general de las cosas de Nueva España*. Mexico City: Editorial Porrúa, 1992.

Valdez, Francisco. *Primeras Sociedades de la Alta Amazonía La cultura Mayo-Chinchipe-Marañón*. Quito, Ecuador: Impresora Flores, 2013.

Valdez, Francisco, Jean Guffroy, Geoffroy de Saulieu, et al. "Découverte d'un site cérémoniel formatif sur le versant oriental des Andes." *Comptes Rendus Palevol* 4, no. 4 (2005): 369–374.

Zarrillo, Sonia. "Human Adaptation, Food Production, and Cultural Interaction during the Formative Period in Highland Ecuador." Ph.D. diss., University of Calgary, 2012.

Maricel E. Presilla

chocolate, single origin, is a buzzword of today's fine-chocolate industry. "Single origin" is perceived as a mark of distinction, even quality, promising consumers chocolate made with cacao beans from a verifiable source, not an anonymous blend. Use of the term is not standardized or regulated, however, and chocolate manufacturers have applied it in various ways, some of which are more meaningful than others.

One of the least meaningful is to label a chocolate made of beans sourced in a single country as "single origin." While it can be generalized, for example, that Ecuadorian cacao has recognizable delicate and elegant flavor notes, each cacao-growing region of the country—Esmeraldas, Manabí, Guayas, Los Ríos, El Oro, Amazonia—has a distinct flavor profile determined by genetics and terroir. Even cacaos from a single plantation might be a mixed bag of hybrids and clones, not necessarily of excellent quality, and few plantations can prove claims of growing pure, single cultivars of rare, fine beans, such as the prized Criollos of Venezuela. Nevertheless, single-origin chocolates, when produced by conscientious chocolate makers who source their beans directly from reputable farmers, can deliver a luscious lesson in how genetics and terroir in its broadest sense—geography, growing conditions, and post-harvest practices—conspire to determine flavor.

For much of the twentieth century, American chocolate makers produced mild, sweet candies from hardy beans grown in Brazil and West Africa, while Switzerland's Lindt and other European brands owned the fine-chocolate market, with little focus on the origin of the cacao. Beginning in the late 1970s, American consumers began to show interest in darker chocolate, often from Belgium or France, and in the 1990s, Valrhona began marketing its line of "grand crus," chocolates with high percentages of cacao bearing romantic names like Manjari, Guanaja, and Pur Caraïbe that were loosely associated with particular cacao-growing regions. See CHOCOLATE, POST-COLUMBIAN; and VALRHONA.

Venezuela is South America's premier producer of quality cacao, and its venerable Chocolates El Rey, founded in 1929, played a key role in advancing this trend. In 1984 the company launched traceable, single-origin couvertures (tempered chocolate with a high cocoa-butter content) using complex Carenero beans, a commercial blend of cacao strains that have grown in the Barlovento region northeast of Caracas since colonial times. Following Valrhona's lead, El Rey also made chocolates with varying cacao content, displaying the percentages on the packaging. El Rey became the most progressive chocolate maker in Latin America, with a state-of-the-art facility dedicated to the production of chocolates with premium Venezuelan cacao. Its first export market was the United States, where in the 1980s, El Rey sponsored lectures on the concept of single-origin chocolates that attracted chocolate professionals. El Ray also created a program called La Ruta del Cacao (The Cacao Road) to take leading chocolatiers, pastry chefs, and journalists on trips to Venezuela's cacao farms and El Rey's factory in Barquisimeto. Motivated by the success of Valrhona and El Rey, artisanal American chocolate makers began producing chocolate from carefully selected beans with high cacao content and without the alkalis, fillers, and artificial flavors common in mass-produced chocolate. They found an eager audience among chefs and sophisticated consumers. Food lovers who had learned to distinguish between Robusta and Arabica coffees and to appreciate nuances of wine varietals were beginning to approach chocolate in the same critical fashion.

One of these American pioneers was Robert Steinberg, who interned with the Lyon chocolate maker Bernarchon. In 1996 Steinberg opened a small chocolate company with the former champagne maker John Scharffenberger, blending beans, as was the practice in France. Scharffen Berger Chocolate debuted with two couvertures with varying percentages of cacao and composed of at least seven beans. In the early 2000s Steinberg began experimenting with single beans, developing two outstanding couvertures with beans from Cuyagua, an isolated plantation on the Caribbean coast of Venezuela, and Hacienda La Concepción, a progressive plantation in the Barlovento region northeast of Caracas. These were followed by El Carmen, a single-plantation chocolate with a whopping 75 percent cacao from fermented beans sourced from a small sector of La Concepción. With its amazing complexity, intense fruitiness, and remarkable smoothness, El Carmen was a perfect example of the excellence the best American chocolate companies were beginning to achieve.

The San Francisco company Guittard, founded in 1868 by Frenchman Etienne Guittard, soon followed with blends of high cacao percentage and single-origin couvertures. One of Guittard's early single-origin chocolates was Sur del Lago, made with a blend of premium beans from the area south of Lake Maracaibo, the cradle of the fine Venezuelan Criollo cacao known as porcelana. See GUITTARD.

The success of these companies, along with the innovations of European manufacturers like France's Michel Cluizel and Italy's Amedei and Domori, inspired micro-batch chocolate producers in the United States. Large manufacturers have also gotten into the action, among them Hershey, which in 2006 acquired Scharffen Berger, keeping that company's line of fine chocolates and introducing its own line of single-origin chocolates.

While Latin America is still known primarily for the raw material rather than the finished product, a few small firms have joined El Rey in producing premium chocolates. In Quito, Ecuador, tiny Pacari Chocolate is successfully competing with the world's best brands. Working only with sustainable organic and biodynamic cacao sourced from genetically diverse old farms, Pacari has created bars that capture the distinctive flavor of various Ecuadorian and Peruvian regions. Its single-source Pacari Piura Quemazón, with complex notes of citrus, dried fruit, and a lingering dairy tinge, was named the world's best dark bar at the International Chocolate Awards in London in October 2013, followed by another major victory in 2014 for a bar made with heirloom Nacional cacao.

As our chocolate choices increase, the selection process can seem bewildering. To the rescue come chocolate tastings, which have become as commonplace as wine, cheese, or olive oil tastings, as well as chocolate blogs, chocolate shops where one can sample the wares, and a growing number of chocolate guides that take you by the hand as you navigate the brave new world of single-origin chocolate.

See also COCOA; CHOCOLATE, PRE-COLUMBIAN; LATIN AMERICA; and LINDT, RODOLPHE.

Presilla, Maricel E. *The New Taste of Chocolate: A Cultural and Natural History of Cacao with Recipes*. Rev. ed. Berkeley, Calif.: Ten Speed, 2009.

Maricel E. Presilla

chocolate pots and cups are used to prepare and serve drinking chocolate. Chocolate was consumed primarily as a beverage before the nineteenth century, and material objects contributed significantly to its sensory impact and cultural meaning. Among the Maya and Aztecs, the fruit of the cacao tree could express religious beliefs, elite status, and the power of rulers. Between the thirteenth century B.C.E. and the Spanish conquest of the 1500s, various cacao-based liquids figured in rituals related to warfare, diplomacy, marriage, and burial. Artfully designed containers cast this symbolic potency in permanent form. They included cylindrical jars, footed vases, and spouted bottles made of clay, as well as round cups fashioned from calabash gourds. Decoration ranged from rhythmic patterns to detailed scenes of cacao consumption. An inscription might identify a specific type of concoction or an owner's name and title. Preparation could be a dramatic performance as a beverage was poured from one vessel to another to produce a delectable layer of foam.

Recipes and values changed during the seventeenth and eighteenth centuries as native Mesoamerican and Spanish foodways influenced one another and chocolate became available throughout Europe and colonial North America. People debated the merits of a drink that now incorporated the sugar and spices of Old World cuisine. Many embraced it as a cure for numerous ailments or a luxurious treat at social gatherings, but others worried about harmful side effects. Preparation involved multiple steps. Prepared chocolate (cacao beans that had been

European chocolate pots, designed to serve the fashionable new beverage in style, had a short spout set high on a cylindrical, conical, or pear-shaped body, and an opening in the lid through which a stirring rod was inserted to emulsify and froth the chocolate. This silver and wood chocolate jug was crafted by Henry Louis Le Gaigneur around 1740. IMAGE © STERLING AND FRANCINE CLARK ART INSTITUTE, WILLIAMSTOWN, MASSACHUSETTS (PHOTO BY MICHAEL AGEE)

fermented, roasted, husked, ground, and sometimes seasoned) was grated and dissolved in simmering water or milk. Sweetness and spice were adjusted, and enriching ingredients like eggs or ground nuts were sometimes added. The thick, potent mixture required vigorous beating to incorporate a fat content of around 50 percent.

Euro-American chocolate was served from many types of containers, including modest earthenware jugs and copper beakers. For wealthy consumers, especially during the eighteenth century, chocolate's appeal was enhanced by specialized pots crafted from expensive silver or porcelain. Porcelain was a novel medium, imported in large quantities from China and commercially produced in the West only after 1710. Some chocolate pots belonged to larger services for coffee and tea—two other imports gaining favor during the same period—or to travel kits equipped for grooming and letter writing. Many resembled and probably doubled as coffee pots. Shared elements could include a short spout set high on a cylindrical, conical, or pear-shaped body; a curved or horizontal handle placed at a right angle to the spout; and three slender feet that raised some vessels above the tabletop like dancers on tiptoe. Certain features contributed to functionality as well as elegance. Wooden handles remained cool to the touch. Some designs addressed chocolate's oily consistency with longer, lower spouts that kept separated fat from escaping into cups, or with heating stands to optimize temperature and viscosity.

The only feature that definitively marked a vessel as a chocolate pot was an aperture in the lid, often covered by a finial or sliding disk. Found on both modest and ornate models, the opening accommodated a stirring rod, usually made of turned or carved wood with a bulbous end rather like that of a modern honey dipper. Rolling this implement briskly between the palms lightened the drink's texture by emulsifying fat and creating a frothy head. Invented in Mesoamerica sometime before or during the Spanish conquest, the device became known by various names, including *molinillo*, *moulinet*, or mill, and is still used in parts of Latin America today.

Blended to unctuous perfection, chocolate was served in very small portions. Elites often enjoyed theirs from delicate porcelain cups with matching saucers. Generally taller and narrower than tea cups and purchased in sets, chocolate cups could also be used for coffee and were available in a wide range of designs. Most had a single handle, but there were also tulip-shaped tumblers without handles, and two-handled models with lids to keep the beverage warm. Their smoothly glazed exteriors might be painted with delicate bouquets, flirtatious couples, or exotic Asian landscapes.

Luxury chocolate wares were fundamentally social objects. During morning *toilettes*, afternoons in the garden, and candlelit balls, one was expected to appreciate containers as much as their contents. Pots and cups expressed an owner's taste and status through precious materials, fine workmanship, fashionable style, and sometimes a monogram or coat of arms. Decorative motifs stimulated conversation; sipping daintily from tiny cups demonstrated refined comportment. The frothing process, whether undertaken by masters or servants, provided moments of entertaining adult play. The implications of design could be quite tantalizing. In the ongoing debate over chocolate's physiological effects, some claimed it was an aphrodisiac, while others considered it a balm for delicate constitutions. Both possibilities were engaged by special saucers with indentations or mounts that prevented cups from spilling in the trembling hands of over-exerted drinkers. And in a society that appreciated erotic innuendo, the brisk action of a phallic stirring rod inside a curvaceous vessel may have inspired witty remarks. Chocolate paraphernalia also facilitated a sense of cultural control over a substance still associated with foreignness. Virtuoso containers materialized colonial conquest, literally enclosing chocolate in evidence of Euro-American aesthetics and consumer power.

The use of chocolate pots diminished during the nineteenth and twentieth centuries. Coffee and tea became far more ubiquitous and consumers favored chocolate in the newer forms of solid confections and hot cocoa. Milder, less fatty, and easier to mix than the beverage of previous centuries, cocoa was also better suited to middle-class conceptions of good health and family life. Currently, chocolate pots are enjoying a modest comeback inspired by interest in novelty tableware, historical recipes, and premium bittersweet chocolate laced with spices. Some contemporary models feature transverse handles, splayed feet, or frothing devices that recall traditional designs. Yet even if chocolate beverages have regained a certain allure, aficionados can only begin to imagine what it once meant to whirl an exotic substance inside an elegant pot and savor it slowly, one precious sip at a time.

Grivetti, Louis Evan, and Howard-Yana Shapiro, eds. *Chocolate: History, Culture, and Heritage*. Hoboken, N.J.: Wiley, 2009. See chapters 8, 10–13, 25, 31, 43–44, 54.

Hellman, Mimi. "Of Water and Chocolate." *Gastronomica: The Journal of Food and Culture* 4 (Fall 2004): 9–11.

McNeil, Cameron L., ed. *Chocolate in Mesoamerica: A Cultural History of Cacao*. Gainesville: University Press of Florida, 2006. See chapters 7, 9, 10, 11.

Mimi Hellman

chocolates, boxed, traditionally include various individual chocolate-covered confections or bonbons, placed next to one another in single-portion cups within a tin or cardboard box. The term "bonbon" encompasses creams, fruits, nuts, caramels, jellies, and other bite-sized confections enrobed with chocolate. See BONBONS. It is generally accepted that the French are responsible for elevating chocolate to new gastronomic heights with the creation and ascendant popularity of bonbons beginning in the seventeenth century. Due to their costly processing, exotic ingredients, and delicate nature, only royalty and the privileged elite enjoyed bonbons at this time.

Bonbons were safely packaged and presented in beautiful handmade boxes that came to be known as *bonbonnières.* These were presented at weddings, religious events, and celebrations, their contents infused with symbolic meaning. One of the earliest recorded mentions of a chocolate *boette* (box) comes from 1659, when King Louis XIV of France granted a royal patent to the queen's confectioner David Chaliou, allowing him the exclusive privilege "for twenty-nine years to manufacture and sell chocolate liquor, pastilles, boxes and in other ways that please him." As chocolate and sugar became more readily available in the late eighteenth century, French chocolatiers marketed bonbons in fancy paper boxes adorned with paintings and rococo embellishments. Consuming delicate boxed chocolates represented exactly the sort of elite pastime that democratic French revolutionaries aimed to destroy in 1789.

A different sort of revolution made the transport and processing of cocoa and sugar increasingly cheaper and more accessible during the early nineteenth century. See COCOA. Industrial Britain saw the rise of competitor firms Fry and Cadbury, each vying for dominance of the burgeoning chocolate market. See CADBURY. In order to compete with Fry's popular Chocolate Cream Sticks, Richard Cadbury looked to France for inspiration of a new product line: the Fancy Box, introduced in 1861. Brilliant chromolithographed pictures decorated the box's exterior, many designed by Cadbury himself. Inside, lacy doilies caressed colorful, assorted chocolates tempting the beholder with their silky texture. Many of the bonbons were given French names like *chocolat du Mexique* and *chocolat des delices aux fruits,* adding to their exotic appeal. Cadbury's boxed chocolates were all the rage in Britain and Europe during the 1860s and 1870s. Assortments often emphasized a particular category of palate: Fruit & Nut, Double Milk, and Extra Superfine Chocolate Creams.

As the turn of the century neared, the popularity and variety of chocolate boxes exploded, with competitors Fry and Rowntree featuring dozens of different assortments, each housed in a specially designed box. The public eagerly anticipated the arrival of the Christmas- and Easter-themed assortments, and especially the chocolates commemorating the coronation of King George V. So popular were specialty and limited-run assortments that many chocolate makers began to produce commemorative metal tin boxes for their chocolates, capitalizing on the collectible nature of the boxes themselves.

Despite the early market saturation of the British chocolate boxes, it was an American who takes honors for the earliest recorded commercial chocolate box, one that remains famous today. Stephen Whitman opened his confectionery shop in Philadelphia in 1842, when he was only nineteen. By 1854, with his modern steam-powered confectionery producing chocolates in high volume, Whitman introduced his Choice Mixed Sugar Plums packaged in an "elegant box, pink and gilt, lavishly decorated with designs of rosebuds and curlicues." From the start, Whitman understood the effectiveness of magazine advertising and began to market his packaged chocolates to a national audience. In 1888 his son Horace became the first to incorporate cellophane in boxes of chocolate to preserve the freshness of the bonbons. Yet real genius struck in 1912 when company president Walter Sharp found inspiration in an old needlework sampler on the wall of his home. With the help of a Philadelphia artist,

Sharp designed and marketed the Whitman's Sampler, the first-ever box of chocolates with a printed key revealing the contents of the chocolates. Housed in a now-iconic yellow box with a needlework design, the Sampler by 1915 had become the top-selling boxed assortment of chocolates in the United States. Since then, the Sampler has remained king of chocolate boxes worldwide; the company estimates that a box is sold every 1.5 seconds.

No article on chocolate boxes would be complete, however, without a certain heartfelt mention. Ever since it was introduced to Europe, chocolate has been associated with temptation and imagined to have aphrodisiacal properties. See APHRODISIACS. Both Casanova and the Marquis de Sade extolled the virtues of chocolate in their pursuit of love. Cupid struck Richard Cadbury in 1868, when he introduced the first heart-shaped chocolate box. Today, over 35 million heart-shaped boxes are sold worldwide each year for Valentine's Day. See VALENTINE'S DAY. As much as they symbolize love, however, boxed chocolates are also a metaphor for uncertainty. As Forrest Gump famously said in the eponymous 1994 film, "My momma always said, 'Life was like a box of chocolates. You never know what you're gonna get.'"

See also CHOCOLATE, LUXURY; CHOCOLATE, POST-COLUMBIAN; CHOCOLATE, PRE-COLUMBIAN; and CHOCOLATES, FILLED.

Cadbury, Deborah. *Chocolate Wars: The 150-Year Rivalry Between the World's Greatest Chocolate Makers*. New York: Public Affairs, 2010.

Chrystal, Paul. *Cadbury & Fry Through Time*. Gloucestershire, U.K.: Amberley, 2012.

Gordon, Bertram M. "Chocolate in France: Evolution of a Luxury Product." In *Chocolate: History, Culture and Heritage*, edited by Louis Evan Grivetti and Howard-Yana Shapiro, pp. 569–582. Hoboken, N.J.: Wiley, 2009.

Kimmerle, Beth. *Chocolate: The Sweet History*. Portland, Ore.: Collectors Press, 2005.

Ryan Berley

chocolates, filled, consist of a hard chocolate coating around a center, usually made of nougat, ganache, toffee, fruit, or nuts. They originated with the nineteenth-century invention of conching, which emulsified the chocolate and made it smooth. Previously, chocolate had been drunk as a beverage, or used as a gritty, oily paste to flavor pastries and sweets.

The first solid chocolate bar was produced in 1847 by Roger Fry in England. His company, Fry's, also invented the first filled chocolate candy, Cream Sticks, in 1853. These were essentially sticks of mint-flavored boiled and hardened sugar dipped into melted chocolate. To produce the sweet on a larger scale, Fry's created molds into which the mint sticks were placed, and melted chocolate was poured over them and allowed to set. In 1866 these candies were mass-produced as Fry's Chocolate Creams.

In 1861 the English firm Cadbury offered the Fancy Box, a decorated box of chocolate candies filled with marzipan, orange, chocolate ganache, and fruit-flavored crèmes. Richard Cadbury imported a Parisian chocolatier to develop recipes for the fillings. The confections were christened with elegant French names, such as *Chocolat des delices aux fruits*.

In 1868 Cadbury created one of the Fancy Boxes in the shape of a heart for Valentine's Day. Boxes of filled chocolates, heart-shaped and otherwise, quickly became widely associated with the holiday. See CHOCOLATES, BOXED and VALENTINE'S DAY. After the 1880s Swiss innovation of milk chocolate for eating (milk chocolate for drinking had been invented a few years earlier), Cadbury began to employ milk chocolate as a candy coating, calling it Dairy Milk. By 1910 the company had created Dairy Milk–coated candy Easter eggs. Whitman's of the United States offered its Sampler box in 1912 and provided the first pictorial guides within the boxes to the fillings inside each chocolate.

A major step toward mass production took place in 1913, when Jules Sechaud of Montreux, Switzerland, invented machinery for filling chocolates. Two main methods of mechanically filling chocolate confections are used today:

- *Enrobing* is the mechanized version of hand dipping. Hard-candy centers are placed on a wire mesh conveyor belt, or in containers with drain holes on the conveyor belt. The belt passes through liquid chocolate, kept at a controlled temperature, that completely coats the centers. The coating's thickness is controlled by how fast the centers pass through the coating, and how much coating is applied. Another wire mesh conveyor belt propels the filled chocolates through a cooling tunnel or to a cooling area for the coatings to harden.

- *Shell molding*, a process common in Europe, can be accomplished by hand or mechanically. Melted chocolate is poured into individual molds. The mold is then turned upside down to allow most of the chocolate to run out. The layer of chocolate left behind and now coating the mold cools and hardens. It is filled with a center, and then a layer of melted chocolate is applied over the top. After cooling, the filled candy is taken out of the mold. Alternatively, the filling is left uncovered, and identically shaped candies are sealed together with a little melted chocolate around the edges of the chocolate coating to form a rounded morsel, such as a three-dimensional ball or seashell. Shell molding presents the opportunity for a variety of intricately beautiful shapes as well as novelty gag forms.

The best filled chocolates are covered with *couverture*, meaning "covering." Couverture contains at least 32 percent cocoa solids and has cocoa butter for its fat. Sugar and vanilla, plus a small amount of soy lecithin to keep the fat and chocolate from separating, are the remaining ingredients. The chocolate is then tempered, an exacting process of heating it to a specific temperature and cooling it down. Tempering imparts to chocolate coating a glossy appearance and a crisper texture. Tempering also gives coatings a longer shelf life and helps avoid "bloom," when the cocoa butter and chocolate separate and white blotches appear on the finished product. Compound chocolate or compound coating, made with a smaller percentage of chocolate and vegetable fats instead of cocoa butter, is used in the production of lesser-quality filled candies.

One of the most universal and well-loved filled chocolates is the truffle, a spherical confection in which a chocolate coating surrounds a center of creamy chocolate ganache. The most common coatings are couverture or cocoa powder, sometimes with finely chopped nuts added. The ganache centers may be flavored with liqueurs and other additions. The best chocolate truffles are handmade, and can be concocted by home cooks with a fair amount of ease. See TRUFFLES.

Boxes of assorted filled chocolates with a variety of fillings remain ubiquitous in the United States and Europe. They are mass-produced by large companies in varying qualities. Small artisan businesses offer boxes of handmade assortments created from high-quality ingredients.

See also CHOCOLATE, LUXURY; CHOCOLATE, POST-COLUMBIAN; and CHOCOLATE, PRE-COLUMBIAN.

Cadbury, Deborah. *Chocolate Wars: The 150-Year Rivalry between the World's Greatest Chocolate Makers.* London: Harper, 2010.

Coe, Sophie D., and Michael D. Coe. *The True History of Chocolate.* 2d ed. New York and London: Thames and Hudson, 2007.

Hopkins, Kate. *Sweet Tooth: The Bittersweet History of Candy.* New York: St. Martin's, 2012.

Miriam Kasin Hospodar

Christianity and sweets present us with a paradox. Jesus's Last Supper with his disciples centered on bread and wine, and throughout Christian churches the Eucharist commemorating his life, death, and resurrection is identified with these staples of a frugal meal. The commonest alternatives then and now are bread (leavened or not) and unfermented grape juice, or water, or bread alone. Yet Christians have created and adopted an ever-expanding array of sweet treats—from fig cakes and St. Lucia's Eyes to Trappistine creamy caramels—as ways of celebrating their spirituality in everyday life. See SPIRITUALITY. These treats also draw their vitality from biblical scriptures, perhaps above all from the paradox that sweetness in Christianity is inseparable from bitterness.

Christianity emerged in Roman Palestine some 2,000 years ago among Jews who considered Jesus of Nazareth to be the *mashíakh* ("anointed [one]"), translated into Greek as Khristós, whence "Jesus Christ" in the letters of the 50s C.E. attributed to the apostle Paul. To the "Old" scriptures they shared with other Jewish sectarians, Christians added scriptures canonized as "New" over the next 300 years. In 380 C.E. Emperor Theodosius proclaimed Christianity as defined at the Council of Nicaea (325 C.E.) the official religion of the Roman Empire, but Christianity has kept diversifying in keeping with centuries-long tensions between priestly and populist strains. Theodosius's partition in 395 C.E. of his eastern and western domains between his two sons contributed over later centuries to distinctions among Eastern Orthodox and Western Christianities, Roman Catholicism, and eventually Protestantism.

Sweets in Christianity are thus rooted in biblical ideas and practices of food and eating shared with Judaism—above all, the conviction that food, articulated in meals, expresses God's Word, divine Wisdom. See JUDAISM. Throughout the world, who feeds or eats what with whom, when, where, and how, speaks directly to people's closest social relations. Biblical meals express the covenant binding people and God. Jewish sectarians, including early Christians, used the language of meals to state their understanding of the divine covenant. "O taste and see that the Lord is good; happy are those who take refuge in him" (Psalms 34:8), echoed in the New Testament (Hebrews 6:5, I Peter 2:3). The sweetest of all sweets in the Bible is the "law of the Lord... the decrees... the precepts... the commandment... the ordinances of the Lord.... More to be desired are they than gold, even much fine gold; sweeter also than honey, and drippings of the honeycomb" (Psalms 19:7–10, echoed in Psalm 119:103).

Hearing with the Mouth

How did such sweet words taste to Christians in Roman Palestine and the growing diaspora? The biblical land "flowing with milk and honey"—the favored description of the fertile promised land of Canaan in Exodus, Leviticus, Numbers, and Deuteronomy—actually flowed with *dvash* in Hebrew (*dibs* in Arabic), translated as *méli* in the Greek Septuagint and New Testament, a term having the same broad meaning. These sweet, thick substances ("sticky" is the root meaning of *dvash*) included fruit syrups made from figs, dates, grapes, pomegranates, and carob pods, as well as wild and domesticated honey. See DATES and HONEY. The common feature of these early honeys—and the syrups, cordials, jams, pastes, compotes, and comfits made from them—is the intensity of their sweetness, the result of time- and labor-intensive practices we still celebrate in bees and in the occupational language and practices of confectioners: chopping, boiling, straining, concentrating, and compounding. Sugarcane, introduced from India, was grown in the seventh and eighth centuries C.E., but did not become a significant cash crop until the tenth century. See SUGARCANE.

Thus, to feel the visceral impact of the words "sweeter than honey" to early Christians—indeed, all Christians into the late nineteenth century—twenty-first-century readers in the United States would have to forgo the roughly 76 pounds of sugar consumed per person per year. The ancient sweets were rare and precious. Furthermore, they were crucial to life. According to the humoral theory of Galen (129–216 C.E.), prevalent among Jews, Christians, and Muslims for over a thousand years, their warm and moist qualities contributed to the vitality of the body in health and its restoration in sickness. The antiseptic and healing properties of bees' honey were used to treat wounds as well as preserve foods, medicines, and (in Egypt) bodies.

Above all, words sweeter than honey had a bitter aftertaste. Early Christians drew on the complexity of sweetness in the Hebrew Scriptures. The Revelation to John (10:8–11) echoes Ezekiel (2:10–3:6) in describing the angel's command to prophesy God's word made flesh—Jesus Christ—to the world: " 'Go, take the scroll that is open in the hand of the angel.... Take it, and eat; it will be bitter to your stomach, but sweet as honey in your mouth.' So I took the little scroll from the hand of the angel and ate it; it was sweet as honey in my mouth, but when I had eaten it, my stomach was made bitter. Then they said to me, 'You must prophesy....' " The sweet scroll in Ezekiel's stomach was filled with the bitter "words of lamentation and mourning and woe" he must prophesy to the "rebellious house" of Israel. John's sweet–bitter revelation is the "good news" (*euangélion*, whence "Godspel" or "gospel" in English) that Christians' salvation is born of Jesus Christ's suffering and death.

Sweet Offerings in Everyday Life

Sweets thus have a complicated history in Christianity. They remain central to the meals and words with which Christians have celebrated their faith over the past two millennia. Yet they prevail not in the formal rituals of Christian churches, but in ceremonies at homes, graveyards, and neighborhoods. They accompany births, baptisms, and marriages as festive treats. See BIRTH; FUNERALS; and WEDDING. But their spiritual significance emerges mainly in funerals and ancestral commemorations in which the dead are made present again among the living. The table or grave becomes an altar, and the sweet offerings take on Eucharistic dimensions; they are often shaped like the body of the dead and may be inscribed with his or her name. Women are the cooks and main officiants, especially where church rituals remain in men's hands. Fertility, growth, and love are among the life-and-death issues with which they are concerned, surely entwined with longing as in the biblical Song of Solomon, but this aspect of Christian sweets remains veiled.

Among Eastern Orthodox Christians, All Saints' and All Souls' Days from the Levant to Siberia center on a dish of boiled grains (usually wheat berries), honey, nuts, and spices, made in many local varieties: *ameh masslouk* or *snuniye* (Lebanon, Palestine, and Jordan); *sliha* (Syria) or *burbara* (for *Eid il-Burbara,* St. Barbara's Feast throughout the Middle East); *cuccia* (Sicily); *koliva* (Greece); *koljivo* (Serbia); *colivă* (Romania); *kolivo* (Bulgaria); and *kutia* (in eastern Poland, Ukraine, Belarus, and Russia). The mound of porridge, likened to the grave, is decorated with the initials or full name of the dead spelled out in fruits, nuts, or candies, and in some cases a portrait. See WHEAT BERRIES.

Except for the *koliva* made by monks at some monasteries on Mount Athos, grandmothers, mothers, wives, and daughters make these dishes. On All Souls' Day in Greece, the women take their delicacies to the church where the priest blesses them in the names of all the dead, but each woman takes her *koliva* to the grave of the deceased, after which they are shared among all. The *koliva,* called *makario* ("that which is blessed"), is identified symbolically with the body of the deceased, called *makaritis* ("she or he who is blessed"), described in one funeral lament as "My little ear of wheat husked and reaped before your time." Among Lebanese Christians, wheat berries (seeds) are symbols of rebirth.

Future research may clarify whether these dishes spreading north and east from the Mediterranean are related historically to the *bsisa* still made by women in Arab-speaking Sephardic Jewish families in mid-twentieth-century Jerba (Tunisia) and Tripoli (Libya). The porridge of grains (wheat, barley, and sorghum), ground into flour and combined with sugar, herbs, and spices, crowns the festive meal celebrating the first day of the three weeks culminating in Passover. See PASSOVER. The *bsisa* presages fertility and sweetness for the family in the coming year.

From Honey to Sugar

Sweets in eastern Christianity are still based on honey, its taste, consistency, and color being tied to the particular flowers and fields that went into bees' making, even though it may be covered with cane-sugar frostings or decorations. In Western Christianity, cane sugar imported from around the Mediterranean began to replace honey beginning in the tenth century because it was seen as more delicate and refined, whiter, and healthier. See MEDICINAL USES OF SUGAR. In the wedding banquets depicted in Sandro Botticelli's series "The Story of Nastagio degli Onesti" (1483), said to show the marriage of Giannozzo Pucci and Lucrezia Bini in Florence, cane sugar sweets cover the tables and fill the trays that servants offer to the viewer. The costly sweets—assorted comfits (sugar-coated nuts, seeds, and spices), pine-nut cakes, marzipan, and candied fruits—mark the high status of the alliance as much as the familial emblems, silver and gold vessels, lavish clothing, and jewelry adorning the guests. See CANDIED FRUIT; COMFIT; and MARZIPAN. Sweets were significant gifts between families and individuals in health and illness because of their festive-nutritional-medicinal properties, suitable to every age and temperament.

In contemporary Sicily and in the Sicilian diaspora, the feast Day of St. Lucia of Syracuse (13 December) is still celebrated with *cuccia*, but also with St. Lucia's Eyes (*Occhi di Santa Lucia*): sweets of cane sugar, flour, eggs, milk, and flavorings, shaped like eyes. The dough may be rolled, sliced, deep-fried, and dusted with sugar, or shaped into little doughnuts and frosted, or into little round cookies topped with curls of candied fruit. Research in Renaissance Italy and colonial Peru shows that many Saints' and All Souls' sweets originated as the creations of elite women who became nuns when their marriage prospects failed. Sweet making may have been a form of spiritual expression, but giving sweets also kept them in touch with their families, even at the expense of their order. Only later did "convent sweets" become a source of income. See CONVENT SWEETS. Suor Maria Celeste, who was not wealthy, wrote to her father Galileo in 1629 from the Convent of San Matteo, Arcetri: "I also want to know how you feel, Sire, . . . and, not having anything better to send you, I offer a little poor man's candied quince, by which I mean that I prepared it with honey instead of sugar."

Sweets such as St. Lucia's Eyes, St. Agatha's Breasts, Bones of the Dead, St. Joseph's Staff, and St. Anne's Book replicate the long-prevailing iconography of the saints and saints' relics in paintings, sculptures, and prayer cards. Even saints' sweets that are not shaped like sensitive body parts are intensely personal because they are one with their cooks: nuns in convents; women in families; families over generations, neighborhoods, regions. St. Agatha's Breasts are miniatures of the cassata identified with Palermo and its Monastero delle Vergini: round sponge cakes soaked in fruit juice or liqueur, filled with a custard of ricotta and candied fruits, covered in marzipan (green and white since the eighteenth century), coated with frosting, and decorated with candied fruit. See CASSATA. St. Agatha's *cassatelle*—also called *Minni di Vergine* ("virgins' breasts")—are adorned with cherry-nipples and sold in pairs.

St. Agatha and St. Lucia, named in the Canon of the Latin Mass, are now found among Catholics worldwide, but domestically they speak local culinary dialects. Sicilian migrants treasure their families' recipes for St. Lucia's Eyes. So do Catholics in Scandinavia who celebrate Sankta Lucia by eating *Lussekatter* ("Lucia cats"): yeasted sweet buns flavored with saffron (and sometimes other spices) and raisins (or currants or sultanas). Some are eye-shaped, like S-shaped St. Lucia's Breads in Sicily with a raisin in each center, but they also take other forms. In Swedish families, the eldest daughter is their cook. Dressed as Saint Lucia in a white gown and a leafy candle-lit crown, she serves them to her parents on St. Lucia's Day to celebrate the morning of the first day of Advent. Or, she buys them premixed or frozen from the Swedish company IKEA through the Internet.

Sweetness and Sin

Following the Protestant Reformation in the sixteenth century, sumptuary laws barred excess in sweets as in other luxuries among Catholics and Protestants alike. Changing theologies of divinity and humanity were associated with changing theories of the human body in health and illness, expressed in efforts to separate the "Greek" elements of Galenic theory from its "Arab" elements. Sugar and sweets were redefined as burning, corrosive, and hard to digest. The "burial cakes" (*Beerdigungskuchen*, usually *Blechkuchen*, or sheet cakes), "death cakes" (*doodkoecks*), and *avral* (or *avril*) bread or funeral biscuits of German, Dutch, and English Protestants still found in Europe and among their migrant communities in the United States in the nineteenth and early twentieth centuries reflect these changes in theology, medicine, sociality, and food. Like Catholics' sweets, Protestants' sweets also speak in the vernacular. The avral breads in nineteenth-century Yorkshire's North Riding were small, round "crisp sponge" cakes "slightly sprinkled with sugar," but large round "Scotch short-cakes" in the West Riding. In Leicestershire, Lincolnshire, and Shropshire, they were oblong "sponge biscuits" or "sponge fingers," but pieces of "rich cake" in Cumbria and "hot plum-cake fresh from the oven" in Radnorshire in Wales.

The cakes, biscuits, or cookies might be dipped in wine at the funeral, but they were also taken home as mementoes of the dead to be shared or saved uneaten. The practice among some Protestant sectarians of marking "funeral tokens" (as they were also called) with the initials of the deceased suggests that they might have developed historically from sweets more explicitly shaped like human bodies. Yet Protestants would have heeded their preachers' debates over whether the bread and wine in the Eucharist were the trans- or consubstantial body and blood of Christ, or simply emblems thereof. Perhaps owing to such concerns, Protestant funeral tokens were also decorated with generic Christian images like crosses and doves, or even motifs drawn from commercial funeral paraphernalia. Sweets served in contemporary Protestant rites of passage from births to funerals are indistinguishable from the everyday fare of all-too-human beings.

"Do this in remembrance of me" (Luke 22:19)

Multisensory meals are memorable everywhere. In Christian meals, living people commemorate the dead, and in remembering their generations in the face of death, they consider the foundations of their existence. The prominence of sweets outside church services is a sign that Christianity in its many forms is reproduced by clergy in universalizing terms and also by congregants who create their sweet–bitter confections out of their everyday experiences of living and dying.

See also DAY OF THE DEAD; EASTER; ISLAM; and MANNA.

Albala, Ken, and Trudy Eden, eds. *Food and Faith in Christian Culture*. New York: Columbia University Press, 2011.

Bentley, Jeanine, and Jean C. Buzby. "Loss-Adjusted Food Availability—Sugar and Sweeteners (Added)."

http://www.ers.usda.gov/data-products/food-availability-(per-capita)-data-system.aspx (accessed 19 November 2014).
Coogan, Michael D., Marc Z. Brettler, Carol A. Newsom, and Pheme Perkins, eds. *The New Oxford Annotated Bible with Apocrypha*. New Revised Standard Version, 4th ed. New York: Oxford University Press, 2010.
Danforth, Loring M. *The Death Rituals of Rural Greece*. Princeton, N.J.: Princeton University Press, 1982.
Feeley-Harnik, Gillian. *Eucharist and Passover in Early Christianity*. 2d ed. Washington, D.C.: Smithsonian Institution Press, 1991.
McGowan, Andrew. *Ascetic Eucharists: Food and Drink in Early Christian Ritual Meals*. Oxford: Clarendon, 1999.
Shaw, James, and Evelyn Welch. *Making and Marketing Medicine in Renaissance Florence*. New York: Rodopi, 2010.
Sobel, Dava. *Galileo's Daughter: A Historical Memoir of Science, Faith and Love*. New York: Walker, 1999.
Udovitch, Abraham, and Lucette Valensi. *The Last Arab Jews: The Communities of Jerba, Tunisia*. New York: Harwood Academic, 1984.

Gillian Feeley-Harnik

Christmas is a major, month-long Christian festival that coincides with the midwinter solstice in the northern hemisphere. Doctrinally, Christmas is a feast celebrating the birth of Christ, yet it has absorbed so many pagan and non-Christian practices that one need not be an observant Christian to enjoy the bounty. The season opens with Advent, starting on the Sunday four weeks prior to Christmas Day. Originally a fasting period, it is now a whirlwind of socializing, with different festivities that vary by country and culture. In areas with Roman Catholic and Protestant heritage, Christmas Eve (24 December), Christmas Day (25 December), New Year's Eve and Day (31 December–1 January), and Twelfth Night (6 January) are the most commonly celebrated; less widespread are the Dutch St. Nicholas's Day (6 December) and the Swedish St. Lucy's Day (13 December). Eastern Orthodox Christians observe Christmas Day on or about 7 January.

Sacred and pagan symbols mingle throughout the holidays. For example, the 13 desserts (*lei tretze dessèrts*) of Provence—an unpredictable assortment of fresh and dried fruits, nuts, nougat, biscuits, and cakes that appears for several days in France—are said to represent Christ and His Apostles, while the bûche de noël, a log-shaped cake decorated with a forest's worth of meringue mushrooms, pays homage to the Old Norse *jól* festival, marking the winter solstice. See BÛCHE DE NOËL and HOLIDAY SWEETS. Other sweets allude to a darker side of folk celebrations, often linked to the unruly Roman Saturnalia. The tiny comfits that noisily erupt from Christmas crackers conjure charivaris, rowdy parades where participants loudly went door-to-door extorting food, drink, and money from their economic betters until this public carousing was domesticated in the nineteenth century; caroling now replaces the marauding. Yet the unsettling origins lurk in the words of one popular carol, when singers demand figgy pudding, threatening, "We won't go until we get some."

Specific sweets became Christmas specialties only in the late Middle Ages. Early Christmas confections used expensive sugar, spices, dried and candied fruits, and nuts, making them suitable for gift giving. These were not newly invented dishes, but ones retrofitted with symbolism. What distinguished them was their appearance: they evoked religious and cultural emblems, whether through the design of the cook or the attribution of pointed meanings by opinion makers. Gingerbread men, bûche de noël, and candy canes shaped like a bishop's crozier appear only at Christmas, notwithstanding that gingersnaps, rolled cakes, and peppermint hard candies are found year round. Color coding with red and green foodstuffs, dyes, and packaging also helped turn standard sweets into Christmas specialties in the late nineteenth century.

Dried Fruit Hashes, Puddings, and Cakes

Mincemeat pies and plum puddings originated as hashes of meats, offal, suet, spices, fresh and dried fruits, and sugar or honey before evolving into their modern, usually meatless dessert versions in the second half of the nineteenth century. In the seventeenth through nineteenth centuries, Puritans and other strict Protestant sects in England and especially America freighted mincemeat pies with religious disapproval, equating the expensive spices with the Magi's frankincense and the oblong pie crusts with Jesus's crèche, calling this "food of the Papists" and "idolatrie in a crust." See MINCE PIES. The closely related plum pudding, with its traditional 13 ingredients, was identified with Christ and the Apostles: those who still celebrated Christmas ritually stirred the pudding from east to west in the belief that emulating the direction of the Magi's journey would bring good luck. By the nineteenth century the religious food fight subsided, and plum pudding became an iconic conclusion to many Anglophone Christmas dinners, set ablaze with spirits and marched into the dining room with confident pomp, or fretted over by the literary likes of poor Mrs. Cratchit in Charles Dickens's *A Christmas Carol.*

Rich and boozy fruitcakes are eagerly anticipated treats in the United Kingdom and most of its former colonies, although they have never found favor in the United States, notwithstanding their ubiquity. See FRUITCAKE. Garishly studded with cherries candied in the unnatural, if Christmasy, hues of emerald and vermillion, they are the butt of jokes: urban legend holds that they are never eaten but given to unlucky recipients, who regift them the following year. More appealing is the Scottish black bun, an exceptionally dense dried fruit mélange wrapped in pastry and served on Hogmanay, the Scottish name for New Year's Eve. The Italian panforte, literally "strong bread," a specialty of Siena, is nowadays a dense mash of candied fruit and nuts, piquantly spiced.

Panettone is a Lombardian specialty that legend attributes to a poor fifteenth-century baker named Tonio with a beautiful daughter adored by the scion of a wealthy family: only after Tonio became rich by adding sultanas and candied citrus rind to the standard Christmas bread could the couple marry. This fable's nexus of Christmas to marriage resonated on grounds theological and customary: Christian dogma analogizes the love of Christ at Christmas to that of spouses, and in pre-industrial Europe and America, the period between Christmas and Epiphany, when larders were fat from the winter slaughter, was a popular wedding season.

The Veronese *pan d'oro*, essentially a panettone minus the fruits, is baked in a tall, star-shaped mold said to evoke the Star of Bethlehem; it is especially popular on New Year's morning, falling at the midpoint of the Magi's journey. When the identical recipe is baked instead in a dove-shaped mold and garnished with almonds it becomes the Easter *colomba*. Stollen is a German culinary cousin; at Christmas, it is baked in a tapering pan with a central ridge. When dusted with powdered sugar, it becomes Christollen, for the swaddled Christ Child. These cakes, requiring special pans, are beyond the ken of all but the most intrepid home bakers, making them popular commercial products, primed for gift giving in beribboned packages. See BREADS, SWEET and STOLLEN.

In Sweden, St. Lucy's bread, a saffron- or orange-flavored leavened bread, is served on 13 December, most frequently bedecked with lighted candles. Other gift cakes are the French *gâteau de roi*, a round or ring-shaped yeasted sweet bread, the Iberian *roscón de reyes*, and the now-rare Twelfth Night cake, all served on Epiphany. These cakes traditionally include a bean and a few other small trinkets, and the people finding the trinkets have special privileges or obligations. Twelfth Night cakes, the most visually dazzling member of this culinary family, faded in the nineteenth century as the Christmas tree became the holiday decoration of choice. See TWELFTH NIGHT CAKE.

Decorative Cookies and Candies

The modern Christmas tree started as a vehicle for displaying Christmas confections. Cookies, especially gingerbread men, and paper cones cradling old-fashioned comfits, were among the most common nineteenth-century ornaments. Candy canes still festoon trees; although likely first appearing in the 1840s as a handmade confection, they became the emblematic Christmas candy in the 1950s, when production was successfully mechanized. See CANDY CANES.

The gingerbread men trace their roots to ancient confections, with archival documents from the thirteenth century describing a bread made with honey and black pepper. Similar pepper, ginger, and other sweet spice-flavored hard biscuits are found throughout Northern Europe: a brief catalog includes Norwegian *pepperkaker,* Swedish *pepparkakor,* Danish *brunkager,* the Dutch *speculoos* (a specialty for St. Nicholas's Day), and the German *Lebkuchen.* See GINGERBREAD and SPECULAAS. The cities of Nuremberg and Dijon were famous for their dry gingerbreads, with guilds of gingerbread makers established in the fifteenth and sixteenth centuries; although made year round, holiday versions were crafted in ornate molds carved with the image of Father Christmas. Gingerbread houses remain a German specialty that spread with German emigration patterns to the United States. Another beautiful German cookie is the springerle, distinctively flavored with anise or caraway and embossed with designs, often on the theme of love and marriage. See SPRINGERLE. Similar treats generically called "cookeys" show up in

America as the first confections specifically labeled for "Christmas" in late eighteenth-century cookbooks. New cookies, incorporating such nontraditional ingredients as chocolate and coconut, swell the ranks of American cookie exchanges. These parties, taking place in early December and at which each attendee brings dozens of cookies to trade, are a modern riff on the gluttonous feasting that has historically marked Christmas.

See also CANDIED FRUIT; CHRISTIANITY; COMFIT; DRIED FRUIT; EGG DRINKS; FESTIVALS; MARZIPAN; MULLED WINE; NOUGAT; PUDDING; and SCANDINAVIA.

"Christmas Food." http://www.foodtimeline.org/christmasfood.html (accessed 13 October 2013).
Henisch, Bridget Ann. *Cakes and Characters: An English Christmas Tradition.* London: Prospect, 1984.
Nissenbaum, Stephen. *The Battle for Christmas.* New York: Random House, 1996.
Sheraton, Mimi. *Visions of Sugarplums: A Cookbook of Cakes, Cookies, Candies and Confections from All the Countries That Celebrate Christmas.* New York: Random House, 1968.
Weaver, William Woys. *The Christmas Cook: Three Centuries of American Yuletide Sweets.* New York: HarperPerennial, 1990.

Cathy K. Kaufman

churros

See FRIED DOUGH.

cinnamon

See SPICES.

clafoutis designates a rustic cherry flan or tart. See FLAN (TART). *Larousse gastronomique* describes clafoutis as a thick fruit pancake. It is a specialty of the Limousin region in central and southwest France and features the region's black cherries. In the Occitan language, the old language of the south of France, the word "clafotis" means "to fill"; this may be the origin of "clafoutis." A clafoutis is made by putting the cherries directly on the bottom of a buttered, sugared tart dish and pouring a thick crêpe or pancake batter over them. When the clafoutis is baked, the batter browns and the tops of the cherries are just visible as dark red dots on the surface. The top can be dusted with confectioner's sugar once the flan cools slightly. It is served warm or cold. Some cooks insist that for a true clafoutis the cherries must not be pitted, but few recipes advise this.

The prolific cookbook author Henri-Paul Pellaprat (1869–1954) noted that like many local specialties, clafoutis is not an elegant dessert. However, he adds, "It is certainly pleasant in the countryside, which is without the resources of the Parisian pastry shops" (1927, p. 51). Clafoutis are made all over France, and cooks use a variety of different fruits, including peaches and apricots. Many add a dash of liqueur to the batter. Susan Herrmann Loomis, in her *French Farmhouse Cookbook* (1996), writes that this "is a dessert that all French farm women have at their fingertips" (p. 363) for a frequent afternoon snack, with no need for a recipe. In fact, Loomis says that no single formula exists for making a proper clafoutis. For a more refined appearance, some cooks make clafoutis in a tart dish or flan mold lined with a short crust.

See also FRANCE.

Pellaprat, Henri. *Le pâtisserie pratique.* Paris: Bibliothèque du journal "Le Cordon Bleu," 1927.

Kyri W. Claflin

cobbler

See FRUIT DESSERTS, BAKED.

cocoa technically refers to cocoa powder, although the term "cacao" has been Anglicized to "cocoa" over the years. By the time the Europeans discovered cacao in the New World in the beginning of the sixteenth century, it had been used to produce chocolate in the Americas for over 2,500 years. See CHOCOLATE, PRE-COLUMBIAN. Mesoamerican societies referred to the tree or fruit of the tree as cacao, or *kakaw*, as part of their spoken or written languages. Today, the term "cacao" refers to the cacao tree, pod, or bean.

Chocolate as a Drink

Until eating chocolate was developed in the late 1800s, drinking chocolate was the primary form of chocolate consumption. Chocolate drink recipes included chocolate liquor (roasted, ground cacao),

The process by which cocoa butter is removed from chocolate to create cocoa powder was pioneered by the Dutchman Coenraad van Houten in the early nineteenth century. This poster advertising cocoa was commissioned by the Amsterdam chocolate manufacturer F. Korff & Co. around 1900, most likely for the French market.

sugar, and a variety of spices that produced an enticing aroma and a rich flavor and mouthfeel. Drinking chocolate was prepared by melting chocolate in a liquid such as water, milk, or brandy; it was consumed at or after mealtimes. The chocolate drink had an intense chocolate flavor and aroma and a thick, satiating mouthfeel. When someone drinks hot chocolate today, it is usually hot cocoa, a beverage made with cocoa powder, milk powder, sugar, and water. Although this is a pleasant drink, particularly in the wintertime, hot cocoa does not have the flavor, texture, or mouthfeel of real hot chocolate.

Creation of Cocoa

One of the inherent problems with regularly drinking chocolate was the high cocoa butter content of the cacao beans that, when overconsumed, resulted in excessive weight gain and digestion issues. To reduce the cocoa butter content of the chocolate drink, various processes were developed to extract and separate the cocoa butter from the cacao solids. Cocoa butter was a by-product of these processes and found utility elsewhere as a fat in other foods or in cosmetics. Coenraad van Houten, an early-nineteenth-century chocolate maker from Amsterdam, developed an industrial-scale cocoa press to extract butter from the chocolate liquor. See VAN HOUTEN, COENRAAD JOHANNES. It took many years for the butter press to become a standard process in the chocolate industry. By the 1860s, the Englishman George Cadbury, searching for a way to differentiate his chocolate from the competition, added cocoa presses from van Houten. See CADBURY. The resulting product, named Cadbury's Cocoa Essence, was the first reduced-fat cocoa powder available in England at the time, and it launched the long-term success of the Cadbury business. By the end of the 1800s, the pressing process was commonplace throughout the industry.

Cocoa Process

To produce cocoa, the cacao beans are roasted, the shells removed, and the nibs ground into chocolate liquor. The liquor is pumped into pots in a hydraulic press and squeezed to separate the butter from the solids. The defatted liquor is compressed into disks called cocoa cakes, which are milled to produce cocoa. The cocoa attributes are affected by the type of cacao beans, the roast level of the beans, and the residual fat content of the cocoa. Cocoas are typically pressed to produce high-fat cocoa (22 to 24 percent fat), medium fat cocoa (10 to 12 percent fat), or defatted cocoa (less than1 percent fat). The nibs, liquor, cake, or cocoa can also be alkalized to modify the pH, color, and flavor. Because cacao beans are naturally acidic, chocolate makers have developed methods to reduce the acidity. The Aztecs reduced the acidity by mixing wood ashes into the chocolate. Because of the lack of sophistication of the Aztec wood ash addition, European chocolate manufacturers did not appreciate the potential of this alkalizing process until years later. In the 1860s, the Dutch company van Houten was the first to industrialize the alkalization process for cocoa. Because of its origins, the alkalization process is also referred to as "dutching," or the "Dutch process." Treating cocoa with alkali can produce various flavors and colors, ranging from brown to red to black.

Uses of Cocoa

Cocoa consists of finely ground cacao cells of the deshelled and partly defatted cacao bean. The two most important features of cocoa are flavor and color, but the cocoa also influences the mouthfeel, shelf life, stability, and structure of the end product. Natural, or nonalkalized, cocoa typically has a yellowish-brown color and an acidy cocoa flavor. Natural cocoas are suited for cream fillings for wafers, chocolate truffles, compound coatings, icings, and fat-based syrups and pastes. Alkalized, or dutched cocoa, is available in colors ranging from light brown and red to deep dark brown, red, and black. Alkalized cocoas are used with dairy products, instant products, bakery products, cake mixes, desserts, ice cream, syrups, and coatings. Because product colors can create taste expectations and consumers can detect very slight differences in color, the choice of cocoa type is critical. See VISION.

The color of the cocoa in its dry form is referred to as its external color and is strongly influenced by the light absorption of the residual fat in the cocoa. The external color of the cocoa is important when it is sold as a retail product or used in dry blends. When cocoa is used in a water- or fat-based product, the external color disappears, and only its intrinsic color plays a role. The interchangeability of natural and alkalized (dutched) cocoa is dependent on the flavor, color, and pH requirements of the finished product. To avoid unintended changes to the finished product, alternate cocoas should be tested before the product recipe is altered.

See also CHOCOLATE, PRE-COLUMBIAN and CHOCOLATE POTS AND CUPS.

Cadbury, Richard. *Cocoa: All About It.* 2d ed. London: Sampson Low, Marston and Co., 1896.
Gardiner, A. G. *Life of George Cadbury*. London: Cassell and Co., 1923.
Grivetti, Louis, and Howard-Yana Shapiro. *Chocolate: History, Culture and Heritage*. Hoboken, N.J.: Wiley, 2009.
Lees, Ron. *A History of Sweet and Chocolate Manufacture.* Surbiton, U.K.: Specialised Publications, 1988.

Rodney Snyder

coconut, the fruit of the coconut palm *Cocos nucifera,* has multifarious food applications. The principal products used for sweet goods are the fresh grated or shaved mature flesh of the nut, coconut milk and cream extracted from this flesh, and desiccated coconut flesh, usually marketed in grated form. Coconut flesh has a high percentage of fat but does not contain trans fats or cholesterol and has a low sugar content. Because of the laborious process of extracting the fresh flesh, coconut is most often processed and combined with other ingredients for use in sweet foods, although it is also sold at street markets in cities as diverse as Honolulu and Venice. It is the desiccated form of coconut that is used primarily in American and European sweets, particularly in famous confectionery brands such as Bounty Bars and Tunnock's Snowballs. It also finds use in baked goods such as coconut cream pie, coconut macaroons, and coconut cakes, although the freshly grated form makes these desserts even more delectable. In cakes the coconut is not only incorporated into the sponge mix but also used for external decoration.

In Asia coconut milk and cream are key components of a wide range of sweet foods. Coconut is made into custard to be baked in hollowed-out pumpkin shells in the Thai dish *sankaya.* In Indonesia the coconut milk is used to cook a black rice pudding that is consumed with extra coconut cream and palm sugar for breakfast. See PALM SUGAR.

Vietnamese cuisine offers a range of puddings and cakes that combine coconut milk and cream with a selection of ingredients including banana, cassava, tapioca, and beans. Some mimic French foods, such as crème caramel, whereas others include tropical ingredients that yield dairy- and gluten-free sweets.

Thailand has a dazzling array of *khanom* (puddings) that rely on coconut and are often cooked and presented in intricate banana-leaf packaging. They are convenient street food as well as a welcome conclusion to a spicy meal. In *tako* coconut cream is set on top of a sweet jelly seeded with chips of fresh coconut flesh. *Khanom sai sai* wraps the banana leaf around a coconut cream and rice-flour paste, which in turn shrouds a core of more coconut, banana, or taro.

See also CAKE; NUTS; PIE; and PUDDING.

Davidson, Alan. "Coconut." In *The Oxford Companion to Food,* 3d ed., edited by Tom Jaine. Oxford: Oxford University Press, 2014.
Harries, Hugh C. "Coconut." In *The Cambridge World History of Food,* Vol. 1, edited by Kenneth F. Kiple and Kriemhild Coneè Ornelas. Cambridge, U.K.: Cambridge University Press, 2000.

Phil Iddison

coffee

See CAFÉ and COFFEE CAKE.

coffee cake, as Americans know it today, descends from ancient honey cakes, yeasty French galettes, medieval enriched breads, and seventeenth-century German kuchen. The practice of pairing sweet cakes with exotic hot beverages is of long standing. Nearly as soon as coffee, tea, and chocolate were introduced into Europe in the seventeenth century, patissiers and confectioners began making sweet foods to accompany them.

In Germany, Henriette Davidis's popular nineteenth-century middle-class German cookbook *Praktisches Kochbuch* (Practical Cookbook, 1879) offered recipes for cakes (*Kuchen*) especially suited for serving with coffee. See KUCHEN. These included Westphalian Butter, or Coffee or Sugar Cake, a yeast-based warm-milk kuchen topped with coarsely chopped almonds, cinnamon, and butter cut into thick strips; and American Cake, which she advised eating with coffee or tea or for dessert. Davidis carefully explained how to serve coffee and "small friendly" cakes, providing a long list of baked goods appropriate for such occasions. Although the book's 1904 American edition, *German National Cookery for American Kitchens,* offered many of the same recipes, Davidis's notes on coffee service were eliminated, and the single recipe titled Coffee Cake featured coffee as an actual ingredient—not at all a traditional *Kaffeekuchen.*

The Oxford English Dictionary defines "coffee cake" as a "U.S. breakfast bread," deferring to American dictionaries for descriptions and dating. Stuart Berg Flexner's *Listening to America* (1982) confirms that the term "coffee cake" came into common usage in the 1870s, which historic American cookbooks bear out. However, the meaning differed from our current understanding: the earliest American "coffee cake" recipes listed coffee as an ingredient, with no reference to a specific meal or beverage pairing. Estelle Woods Wilcox's *Buckeye Cookery* (1877) is typical: "Coffee Cake. Two cups brown sugar, one of butter, one of molasses, one of strong coffee as prepared for the table, four eggs, one tea-spoon saleratus, two of cinnamon, two of cloves, one of grated nutmeg, pound raisins, one of currants, four cups flour."

Early American print references connecting coffee cake and coffee drinking are scant, although one newspaper circa 1876 mentioned dunking coffee cake in coffee. Cookbooks grouped recipes for coffee cake in the bread and/or cake sections, depending on the specific formula. An early Philadelphia source recommended shaping coffee cake into pretzels, perhaps hinting at a connection with Pennsylvania Dutch (German) heritage. See PENNSYLVANIA DUTCH. The more likely connection lies with German Jewish immigrants who brought German baking traditions to the United States in the second half of the nineteenth century. In her history of Jewish life on New York City's Lower East Side, Jane Ziegelman (2010) writes that their yeast-based cakes "came in an assortment of shapes and with a variety of toppings and fillings. There were chopped nuts or poppy seeds, pretzel-shaped cakes, and cakes that were rolled up like snails then brushed with butter and sprinkled with cinnamon, sugar and currants.... The Germans called then *kuchen,* but we know them as coffee cake." Over the ensuing decades, recipes for German-style coffee cake proliferated, and by the 1920s the kuchen-style coffee cake familiar to us today had achieved distinct genre status, meriting separate index headings and chapters in cookbooks. In 2013 the Library of Congress "coffee cake" subject heading listed nine books published on the subject since 1967.

Preserved fruit, cheese, yogurt, and other creamy fillings, similar to those used in Danish pastry, are often called for in today's American coffee cake recipes. Crumb and streusel toppings are not uncommon; icing is rarely used, and then only as a drizzle. American coffee cakes may be yeast-raised or chemically leavened; sizes, shapes, and packaging vary. While generally consumed with morning coffee, coffee cake is a welcome snack throughout the day. Not as sweet as doughnuts, nor as plain as bread, this type of cake offers appealing balance.

See also BREADS, SWEET; CHEMICAL LEAVENERS; and STREUSEL.

Jones, Evan. *American Food: The Gastronomic Story.* 2d ed. New York: Vintage, 1981.

Ziegelman, Jane. *97 Orchard: An Edible History of Five Immigrant Families in One New York Tenement.* New York: Smithsonian Books/HarperCollins, 2010.

Lynne M. Olver

colonialism entails the occupation, exploitation, and continued repression of peoples in one territory by another more powerful nation-state through both material and human forms of exploitation. The opening up of the New World was a result of colonial prowess and dominance punctuated by violence in virtually every domain, including the political, economic, social, and cultural spheres. The demand for sugar profoundly affected not only the New World but also the balance of European imperial power, as exemplified by the rise of the British Empire in the seventeenth century and the rapid increase in sugar consumption, which grew in proportion to Britain's influence. The virtually complete transformation of nations such as Barbados into massive sugar plantations was accompanied by simultaneous changes in European habits of consumption and domestic culture that fundamentally altered the world.

The insatiable demand for sugar in Europe in the seventeenth century necessitated the development of large agricultural-industrial complexes requiring extensive commitments of capital and labor. At the same time, the production of sugar, a heavily labor-intensive crop, became increasingly racialized, with slavery an integral and indispensable part of the commodity production process. The linkages between black history and white sugar are widely acknowledged. The dislocation and displacement caused by plantation slavery not only led to new configurations in the New World but also changed the very manner in which Africa came to be incorporated into the global system. See PLANTATIONS, SUGAR; SLAVERY; and SUGARCANE AGRICULTURE.

Although a trade in slaves preceded plantation slavery, it was the intensity and scale of this latter form of slavery that transformed the way in which Africa was treated within European discourse. The slave trade ensured that Africa was constructed as not having its own history, of not belonging to the world, and this idea of Africa became deeply embedded in the European imagination.

While colonialism was linked inextricably to the development of the New World by plantation slavery, Africa remained on the margins of the European-constructed world. This absence pervades every analysis of the seventeenth- and eighteenth-century trade triangle that connected Europe, Africa, and the New World. In this configuration, manufactured goods were shipped from Europe to Africa, African slaves were shipped to the Americas, and produce from the New World was shipped to Europe. See SUGAR TRADE.

This collectors' card from around 1900, from the French chocolate company Chocolat Guerin-Boutron, shows a dark-skinned boy picking cacao beans while a light-skinned schoolboy enjoys chocolate, the fruit of his labors. Western chocolate consumption increased dramatically in the eighteenth and nineteenth centuries, made possible by the spread of cacao plantations throughout the Caribbean. MUSÉE NATIONAL DES ARTS ET TRADITIONS POPULAIRES, PARIS / ARCHIVES CHARMET / BRIDGEMAN IMAGES

The development of the trade triangle and the narrative of plantation slavery parallel the manner in which Africa was dealt with in European discourse. As its people were denigrated and the continent's very history denied, Africa became the logical place to pilfer in order to populate the New World.

Africa was initially the location from which slaves were taken to the New World. The slave trade was the single most important factor in the depopulation and diminishment of the African continent. The slave trade, begun well before Columbus's famous voyage, was introduced into the New World with considerable zeal. The growth of the slave trade corresponded to Britain's and Europe's insatiable demand for sugar, which not only necessitated the extension of empire but also fundamentally altered taste and domestic patterns of consumption.

The abolition and emancipation of slaves in the New World in 1863 did not signal an end to the plantation. Rather, the end of slavery produced new dislocations through the use of indentured labor, which was essential in not only the New World plantations but also newly developed sugar-producing areas such as Natal, Mauritius, and Fiji. The movement of indentured labor across the globe to work on sugar plantations was one of the most significant demographic forces in world history.

The Dutch introduced sugarcane into the African island countries of Mauritius and Reunion in the eighteenth century, and by the nineteenth century it had become the basis of their export-oriented economies. However, sugarcane was not introduced onto the mainland until early in the twentieth century, at which time sugar production developed along the lines of the New World plantation system. The adoption of the plantation in Africa exemplifies the manner in which the process of transculturation between the New World, Europe, and Africa produced new organizational forms considered to be the best systems of production. These interactions, however, were underpinned by the colonizers' assertion of unquestioned superiority, as the civilizing mission upon which colonialism was legitimated had become imbued deeply within Western culture.

See also RACE and SUGARCANE.

Ahluwalia, D. P. S., Bill Ashcroft, and Roger Knight, eds. *White and Deadly: Sugar and Colonialism*. Commack, N.Y.: Nova Science, 1999.

Ahluwalia, D. Pal, and Paul Nursey-Bray, eds. *Post-colonialism Culture and Identity in Africa*. Commack, N.Y.: Nova Science, 1997.

Blackburn, Robin. *The Making of New World Slavery: From the Baroque to the Modern, 1492–1800*. London: Verso, 1997.

Mintz, Sidney. "The Plantation as a Sociocultural Type." In *Plantation Systems of the New World*, edited by Research Institute for the Study of Man and Pan American Union, pp. 42–50. Social Science Monographs 7. Washington, D.C.: Pan American Union, 1959.

Mintz, Sidney. *Sweetness and Power: The Place of Sugar in Modern History*. New York: Viking, 1985.

Pal Ahluwalia

comfit is an archaic word for spices or nuts repeatedly coated with thin layers of sugar syrup that form a shell around the center. Important types include sugared almonds and various spice-based confections, including caraway comfits.

Like the word "confetti," comfit originates from *conficere*, meaning "to put together"—the same Latin linguistic root as confection; but comfit, along with sugarplum (which had roughly the same meaning), has almost vanished from English usage. The contemporary industry name, panned sweets, refers to panning, the process of making them.

Comfits originated as spices and other items dredged with sugar. This may have aided preservation, but, perhaps more significantly, was thought to enhance medicinal qualities of various items. In the Middle Ages, they were served at the end of a meal and considered to aid digestion. They may have developed from honey-based versions made in the classical Mediterranean world. Comfits eventually became important in European social rituals as part of dessert and developed strong associations with Carnival and other festive events; those made with almonds are still used as wedding and christening favors in Continental Europe. Still-life paintings from the sixteenth and seventeenth centuries show comfits, emphasizing their interesting shapes and textures: small irregular balls or long comfits that used matchstick-like slivers cut from cinnamon sticks as their centers. As recorded by Sir Hugh Plat in *Delightes for Ladies* (1609), making items such as "ragged comfits," which had a rough, heavily textured surface, was part of the special skill of the comfit maker.

British aniseed balls belong to the comfit tradition; so, more tenuously, do North American cinnamon hots, although both have lost the actual nucleus of spice. Comfits based around pieces of licorice are still made in the United Kingdom, and French confectioners continue to make various types, such as *anis de Flavigny*. Although comfits are still well known in the English-speaking world, no collective term has emerged to replace this word in common usage, and these confections now tend to be known under individual names.

Richardson, Tim. *Sweets: A History of Temptation.* London: Bantam, 2002.

Laura Mason

competitions belong to a lengthy tradition of professional cooking contests. The earliest may have taken place in the seventh century B.C.E., when the Assyrian king Sardanapalus, who was known for his love of feasting, organized a contest that rewarded the winner with money and honor. In 1882 the first *concours culinaire* was held in Paris. This cooking competition quickly became an annual event, with pastry and confections featuring so prominently that by 1894 a critic complained that they dominated the offerings. Similar tests of culinary prowess were organized over the next decades in Vienna, London, Brussels, and New York. The Internationale Kochkunst Ausstellung, or "Culinary Olympics," is the oldest international competition, its title picking up on an enduring kinship between cooking and spectator sports. Four nations participated in the original IKA, which took place in Frankfurt, Germany, in 1896 with the goal of promoting tourism via the exchange of culinary techniques and ideas. Today, the Culinary Olympics—which includes pastry as both a team and individual event—takes place every four years and features more than 750 professional chefs from 31 countries.

A growing number of international competitions are devoted exclusively to pastry, including the Coupe du Monde de la Boulangerie, World Pastry Championship, StarChefs International Pastry, and the World Dessert Championships. In keeping with its long tradition of elite competitive cooking, France is home to the Meilleurs Ouvriers (crafts competition) in pastry and candy making, where a highly select group of patissiers competes for the exclusive title of M.O.F. (best craftsperson in France) awarded by the French Ministry of Labor. The drama of training and competing in the Meilleurs Ouvriers was captured in the 2009 film *Kings of Pastry*, which shows the exclusive (and all male) makeup of the competitors and judges.

The United States has demonstrated a more democratic bent in baking, pastry, and confectionery competitions, which are traditionally associated with such populist venues as fairs, local festivals, cook-offs, and bake-offs. In keeping with more general patterns in the culinary world, elite, professional competitions (typically designated by the more lofty term "pastry" rather than the homier categories of "baking" or "candy") tend to be dominated by men, whereas the reverse is true of amateur dessert contests. In the United States, the first of these was the brainchild of Elkanah Watson, who sought to attract women to his 1813 agricultural fair in Pittsfield, Massachusetts, by holding contests for domestic products, needlework, and jams. The concept soon caught on with newspapers, which used recipe contests to attract readers and glean materials for cookbooks. Food manufacturers such as Knox Gelatin, Perfect Baking Powder, and Pillsbury seized on the cooking competition as a way to gain name recognition and promote their products. Today, the Pillsbury Bake-Off, which started in 1949, continues to be among the most prominent of such contests.

Although televised baking and pastry competitions are a relatively recent phenomenon, cooking shows have been a part of television programming since James Beard's *I Love to Eat* premiered in 1946. The most famous early TV chef was Julia Child, who delighted viewers with her ebullient personality and charming approach to the occasional on-air culinary disaster. Following the success of her series *Cooking with the Master Chefs*, Child created a spin-off called *Baking with Julia* that featured one pastry chef or baker per episode and aired from 1996 to 2001. Competitive cooking became part of the U.S. television repertoire with the unexpected success of the campy Japanese import *Iron Chef* in 1999, and an American spin-off that first aired in 2005. Although *Iron Chef* tended to feature a range of courses—savory and sweet—organized around the surprise "ingredient of the day," cable television soon began to feature programs devoted exclusively to dessert. Citing the rising popularity of such televised dessert competitions, *Food and Wine Magazine* declared 2010 "The Year of the Pastry Chef." These shows include *The American Baking Competition,*

Cupcake Wars, Sweet Genius, Next Great Baker, Ultimate Cake Off, Top Chef Just Desserts, and *Last Cake Standing,* as well as special segments of *Food Network Challenge.* Airing in the evening, they steer away from the more how-to nature of daytime cooking shows. Instead, they treat dessert making as a sport practiced largely by professionals, accompanied by play-by-play commentary and emphasizing speed, precision, and spectacle.

The popularity of these programs suggests that television viewers are less interested in making their own desserts than in watching others do so under ever more sensational circumstances. At the same time, the rising numbers of actual dessert contests indicate an equally powerful desire among both amateurs and professionals to be not just spectators but to enter the ring as competitors in their own right.

Adams, Rachel. "My Adventures in Sugar." *Gastronomica* 11, no. 1 (Spring 2011): 71–76.

Mercuri, Becky. "Cooking Contests." In *The Oxford Encyclopedia of Food and Drink in America,* edited by Andrew F. Smith, pp. 521–524. New York: Oxford University Press, 2005.

Sutherland, Amy. *Cookoff: Recipe Fever in America: Heartbreak, Glory, and Big Money on the Competitive Cooking Circuit.* New York: Viking, 2003.

Rachel Adams

conching

See LINDT, RODOLPHE.

confection denotes any type of sweetmeat, especially candy and sugary items. By extension, "confectionery" has become a collective noun for these goods, and a "confectioner" is one who makes them, especially for commercial sale. Sugar plays a prominent role in all confections, but chocolate and flour also have important functions.

The word "confection" derives from the Latin *conficiere,* meaning "to make up." Closely related words are found in several European languages. In Italian, *confettiere* is one who makes sweets, and confetti is a general term for the product. This latter term is related to the English word "comfit" for items made by panning. See COMFIT; CONFETTI; and PANNING. *Conficiere* transformed into *confiseur* and *confiserie* in French, and *confiteria* in Spanish. (Confusingly, in French, *un confection* is made up of cloth, such as a dress for a special occasion, as is *una confección* in Spanish.) The German word *Konditor,* and various similar words in European languages, come from a different Latin term, *conditus,* meaning to have "stored" or "preserved" something.

The idea of a confection as a noun for sweet foods requiring special skill with sugar is a Western one, although Middle Eastern languages contain the word "halvah," a general term for all sorts of sweet foods, from sweet desserts of semolina and nuts to more specifically sugar-based items. See HALVAH. Of all the countries that use the word, Turkey has a particularly strong tradition of working with sugar, including a special guild of sugar workers, as explored by Mary Işın in *Sugar and Spice* (2013). See TURKEY.

In English, the idea of confectionery now tends to be one of industry, and it is often used in relation to companies such as Hershey's or Cadbury and their products. "Confection" carries overtones of technical formality, professionalism, and artifice, and now seems mildly archaic. Numerous more colloquial expressions are used for confections made primarily of sugar, bought as treats and consumed casually, especially by children. These include "candy" in North American English, bonbon in French, and "sweets" in the United Kingdom. See BONBONS. The latter is a contraction of the term "sweetmeat," meaning any sweet food, but it also applies to items for dessert, as does the word *dulces* in Spanish. None of these diminutives fully encompass the range covered by the idea of a confection, and numerous other terms exist in European languages for sweet items and the craft of making them. Some languages make clear distinctions between sugar workers and pastry cooks (for whom sugar is one ingredient among many); in French, they are *confiseurs* and patissiers, respectively, while in other languages, such as British English, a "confectioner" was historically responsible for many sweetened foods, including cakes and desserts.

"Confection" is an important word whose history illuminates much about the early roles of sugar in special mixtures. It was first recorded in English during the late Middle Ages and refers to a wide range of recipes, not always sweet, and not necessarily edible. It had overtones of subtlety and secret knowledge, and was particularly associated with compounding drugs and medicines. It is through this aspect that sugar confections developed such prominence. See PHARMACOLOGY.

The Ancient and Essential Role of Sugar

Sugar was vital to the development of confections. Originally, Europeans sweetened foods with honey (which is still used in nougat), or in grape juice boiled down until thick and syrupy, but these products have distinctive flavors and tend to be colored. When sugar first reached medieval Europe from the East during the period of the Crusades, it must have seemed magical, with its ability to be refined into limpid syrups, crystals of sparkling transparency, or worked until pure white in color. Using special knowledge of the "secrets" of working sugar as a material, craftsmen could make it up into various confections with interesting textures that snap and crunch and crumble when eaten.

Apothecaries were the first European confectioners, because sugar was thought to be an aid to good health. See MEDICINAL USES OF SUGAR. Ideas about health and techniques for working with sugar were both taken from Arabic practice. In *Sweets: A History of Temptation* (2002), Tim Richardson explains how sugar was perceived by medieval physicians. Adhering to the Galenic theory of the four elements—an abstract notion of hot, cold, moist, and dry elements that permeated all things—they considered sugar to be hot and moist. It was suitable for making up confections intended to maintain an ideal temperament in the human body, and for counteracting diseases thought to be induced by excessive cold. Sugar was classed among spices, such as cinnamon and caraway, which themselves had medicinal applications. The role of sugar as a preserving agent, especially for fruits, made it valuable to apothecaries who needed to store plant materials out of season. Sugar sweetened bitter drugs, and as a medicinal substance in its own right it could be nibbled during religious fasts such as Lent. In addition, the high price that sugar commanded (unimaginably high by modern standards) gave it mystique and enhanced its reputation as a medicine. Confections were also enjoyed as pleasurable foods with delicious flavors, vivid colors, and interesting textures.

These ideas, although at odds with many current perceptions about sugar and health, had worked their way deep into the consciousness of Europeans by the time of the great voyages of exploration, and until recently underlay the idea of sweetness as good. The special properties of sugar syrups when boiled, worked, and cooled gave us the ancestors of confections still eaten today. Some items appear originally to have been valued partly for the form they took, such as sugar candy formed in large crystals and sticks of pulled sugar. See PULLED SUGAR. Others were combined with various ingredients, for instance, caraway comfits, marshmallow, or licorice, or with almonds to make marzipan. See LICORICE; MARSHMALLOWS; and MARZIPAN. Candied ginger, candied fruit, and candied flowers exploited the preserving powers of sugar (and encompass the notion of storing, as conveyed by the idea of the *Konditor*). See CANDIED FLOWERS and CANDIED FRUIT.

Sugar could be mixed with gum Arabic or gum tragacanth to make a malleable paste similar to today's pastillage. See PASTILLAGE and TRAGACANTH. Ideal for conveying drugs, sugar could be cut into lozenges whose sizes were calculated to give accurately measured doses. Drugs could also be administered in a syrup, of which various types—electuaries, robbs, lohocks, and sherbets—derived from Arabic practice. Sugar-based mixtures could be used to convey aphrodisiacs or poisons. See APHRODISIACS. Syrupy mixtures also made cooling drinks and cordials, and the skills of the confectioner-apothecary often included the art of distilling alcoholic drinks flavored with fruit or herbs and sweetened.

Wheat flour also went into early confections. Prominent among these were wafers, which together with comfits and wine, were served at the end of meals, a habit that evolved into dessert. See WAFERS. Eggs whisked with sugar and mixed with flour and sometimes caraway seeds, and carefully baked at a low temperature until dried out, was known under various names, including Savoy biscuit, Naples biscuit, or diet bread, and may be connected to the origin of sponge cake. See SPONGE CAKE.

In the sixteenth century, the medicinal aspect of sugar work remained strong, and methods for working it were recorded by men of such subtle knowledge as Alexis of Piedmont and Nostradamus. See NOSTRADAMUS. In the parts of Europe that remained Catholic, some items became convent sweets, specialties of various religious establishments. See CONVENT SWEETS. So confections, in their journey westward through Europe and then across the Atlantic to the Americas, were freighted with far more than mere sweetness.

Confections to Impress

Confections were beautiful in their own right. In Italy, during the Renaissance, wealthy noblemen sometimes provided spectacular displays of intricate sugar sculptures known as *trionfi* to celebrate festivals or great events. Medieval feasts in England could also involve elaborate sugar work, presented as "sotleties" between courses to impress, amuse, and flatter the guests. See SUGAR SCULPTURE.

In sixteenth- and seventeenth-century England, making confections became a fashionable, creative pastime for aristocratic English women, alongside the more practical aspects of making up medicines. They perfumed and colored pastillage, then made it into striped or marbled lozenges to sweeten the breath, or shaped it as their fancy took them into gloves, shoes, keys, and numerous other ornamental items. Sugar syrup, boiled to a point at which it would candy, was molded into animal or fruit shapes, as was marchpane (marzipan), which was also made into large, decorated disks for celebrations such as the wedding feast. The women gathered fruit from their gardens and orchards and preserved it with sugar; made marmalade and fruit paste, which could be rolled into long strings and worked into complex knots; tried their hand at panning comfits; and distilled flower waters as well as more powerful alcoholic drinks. See FLOWER WATERS and FRUIT PASTES. They sometimes also made Savoy biscuits, other rich sweet cakes, wafers, macarons, and gingerbread.

These confections had to be shown off. They were often served in a special, small banqueting house, as part of a fashionable sugar banquet. See BANQUETING HOUSES. These collations of sugar work, sweet wines, and dairy dishes like syllabub, fool, and junket were highly popular. See FOOLS; JUNKET; and SYLLABUB. Books played a part in this fashion, especially during the seventeenth century, when several volumes of "secrets" including sugar work were published. These were often based on family manuscripts in which wealthy women recorded recipes for confections, or "banqueting stuffe," alongside recipes for cookery, medicine, perfumes, and cosmetics. Settlers took this habit to New England. Martha Washington's *Booke of Cookery* and *Booke of Sweetmeats,* from the family of Martha Dandridge Washington, is an example of such a compilation.

Both apothecaries and confectioners continued to trade on special skill and knowledge. Confections such as comfits and pulled sugar were tricky to make well and therefore best left to those with training. Books based on domestic manuscripts rarely give detail about either of these techniques. Comfit making required much attention to detail, as shown by information recorded by Sir Hugh Plat in *Delightes for Ladies* (1602). See PLAT, SIR HUGH. Artists, especially in the Netherlands, delighted in the complex textures of such confections and included them in many still-life paintings.

During the seventeenth century, published recipes began to show increasing professionalism. Sometimes they formed sections within larger works, as in *Cuisinier françois,* attributed to La Varenne (1651), or they appeared as separate small volumes. A notable example in English was *The Queen-like Closet* (1670), whose author, Hannah Woolley, claimed that she had raised her status from servant to free agent by practicing as a confectioner. Such books included recipes for preserved fruit, fruit pastes, marzipan, and increasingly elaborate pastry work.

The presentation of confections continued to evolve in the eighteenth century, especially under French influence. Ornamental desserts of different types of confections built up into tall pyramids on special saucers became fashionable at the French court, later replaced by intricate layouts including sugar sculptures, classical scenes, and gardens. *Le cannameliste français* by Joseph Gilliers (1751) showed idealized illustrations of elaborate table layouts from the mid-eighteenth century. See GILLIERS, JOSEPH.

Books conveyed knowledge and acted to some extent as advertisements for the skills and careers of confectioners. See CONFECTIONERY MANUALS. A notable example was Elizabeth Raffald, who worked in Manchester, and whose book *The Experienced English Housekeeper* (1769) details many recipes for confections, including ornamental jellies. But it was the shops that really brought in the customers. Bedecked with jars of sugar confections and fruit both fresh and preserved (confectioners were often fruiterers as well), their window displays were a source of amazement and wonder to all who passed by. In England, shopkeepers acted both as retailers and outside caterers, providing all kinds of food for parties, cakes for weddings and Twelfth Night, and ornamental desserts. London had several famous establishments, including one belonging to the Gunter family that became famous for a novel confection, ice cream, for which published recipes soon became available in books such as that by M. Emy. See EMY, M. and ICE CREAM.

Some books published in the late eighteenth and early nineteenth centuries were written by men who had been employed by Gunter's, notably William Jarrin. See JARRIN, WILLIAM ALEXIS. In the United States, sugar work was important in the cities of the East Coast; the earliest published work on the subject of pastry and sugar work appeared in Boston as *Seventy-Five Receipts for Pastry, Cakes and Sweetmeats* by Eliza Leslie (1827). Recipes for confections became increasingly detailed as knowledge such as the stages of sugar boiling lost its arcane and faintly magical-sounding overtones and became something controlled by weight, volume, and the use of thermometers.

Confections for Everyone

Industrialization, cheaper sugar supplies, changing social attitudes, and nonconformist religion all played a part in increasing the availability of confections in the nineteenth century. They were still loved for their flavors and textures. Sugar continued to be used as a preservative, and some of the old notions about its efficacy as medicine persisted. But confections of all sorts were also a source of profit, especially for individuals from sects like the Quakers, who sought to combine philanthropic work with making money in trades such as food production. In England, their drive laid the foundations for many chocolate confections.

Chocolate is the great contribution of the Americas to confectionery. Echoing the customs of the Aztecs, it was initially taken as a drink by Europeans. Sugar counteracted the bitterness of cacao, and like any other drink, it could be made up with substances thought to be good for health—wine, eggs, spices, and milk. Chocolate, like sugar, was an exotic, expensive novelty when it reached Europe sometime in the sixteenth century, and one that needed careful attention and special skills. A few chocolate confections were made from an early date (including, by the eighteenth century, various chocolate pastilles, creams, and chocolate puffs, like little chocolate-flavored meringues). However, it was nineteenth-century mechanization and industrialization that allowed enormous chocolate confectionery companies to develop on both sides of the Atlantic. Initially, they produced block chocolate for drinks, then as an ingredient for confectionery; eventually, they produced cocoa powder. See COCOA.

Some British chocolate manufacturers trace their origins to the craft confectioners of the eighteenth century, notably Fry's of Bristol (which merged with Cadbury in 1919) and Terry's of York. All are now part of Mondelēz International. The three original companies continued to produce a full range of sugar confections, as well as increasing volumes of block chocolate, and eventually devised ways of incorporating the two. Fondant, a soft, melting confection developed in the nineteenth century, provided the filling for both the earliest chocolate-coated candy bar and for a novelty in sweetmeats, luxurious chocolates presented in beautiful boxes. See CANDY BAR; CHOCOLATES, BOXED; and FONDANT. Other developments took place in Continental Europe, as Daniel Peter and Henri Nestlé worked on another novelty, milk chocolate. See PETER, DANIEL and NESTLÉ.

Milk and butter also went into a range of other confections that lent themselves to factory production. Toffee and butterscotch both became popular, made by numerous enterprises from local sweet makers to the newly emerging giants of the confectionery trade. Caramels were a North American innovation, made by Milton S. Hershey at his Lancaster Caramel Company before he went on to found his famous chocolate company. Toffee and caramels both became hugely popular in Britain and its current and former colonies. See BUTTERSCOTCH; CARAMELS; and TOFFEE.

The realm of sweetened flour-based confections also expanded during the nineteenth century. Cakes, cookies, British biscuits, and many sweet pastries developed numerous forms. Although the skills of the confectioner-sculptor were revived by Antonin Carême, desserts lost their emphasis on sugar confections. See CARÊME, MARIE-ANTOINE. Further opportunities for enjoying confections opened up with the popularization of exotic, expensive, and of course, fashionable drinks in the form of coffee and tea. The latter allowed the development of a whole new meal, afternoon tea, whose dainty rituals demanded the finest and most fragile cakes and pastries.

The original confections of the medieval apothecary existed alongside all these (as they still do today), produced by backstreet sugar boilers, craft confectioners, and the burgeoning new confectionery companies. They turned out vividly striped and brightly colored hard candy and sugar toys, cheap treats for children. Nineteenth-century innovation brought yet more novelties: fizzy sherbet powder, curiously elastic chewing gum, motto lozenges with little sayings written on them, and fortune cookies. See CHEWING GUM; FORTUNE COOKIE; and SHERBET POWDER. These developments continued into the twentieth century with products such as fruit-flavored gums like those made by the German company Haribo. See GUMMIES and HARIBO.

Confections had become part of consumer culture on both sides of the Atlantic. In both North America and Britain, they increasingly became products of large factories in the twentieth century. Although new shapes, textures, and colors of confection constantly appeared, many relied on techniques already known to medieval apothecaries or eighteenth-century confectioners. Innovation was more about new combinations, as in chocolate bars like the Mars bar, or in new ingredients that had technical functions, such as glucose, corn syrup, and modified starches. This approach contrasts with some parts of Europe, especially France, where many towns still have craft confectioners who make some local specialty, and Italy, where various biscotti and other pastries are highly regionalized. See BISCOTTI.

The names now used for retail premises—candy stores in the United States, sweetshops in Great Britain—reflect this move away from skilled artisan production in the back room of a shop to purely retail establishments. The journey of confections from health foods imbued with the magic of sugar, through the sparkling displays of eighteenth- and nineteenth-century craftsmen, to modern industry has brought them within the reach of everyone. This, in turn, has generated ambiguous feelings, as ideas about the negative effects of sugar on health and sugar addiction have increased. See ADDICTION. Yet the magic of confections is still alive, and brilliant displays of handcrafted sugar work, ingeniously decorated cakes, and boxes of truly delicious chocolates still amaze and delight.

See also BISCUITS, BRITISH; CAKE DECORATING; CANDY; CHILDREN'S CANDY; CORN SYRUP; DESSERT; GINGERBREAD; GLUCOSE; HARD CANDY; HERSHEY, MILTON S.; HONEY; LIQUER; LOZENGE; MACARONS; MARMALADE; MEASUREMENT; NOUGAT; PASTILLAGE; SUGARPLUMS; SWEET MEALS; TWELFTH NIGHT CAKE; and WEDDING.

David, Elizabeth. *Harvest of the Cold Months: The Social History of Ice and Ices*. London: Michael Joseph, 1994.

Hess, Karen. *Martha Washington's Booke of Cookery and Booke of Sweetmeats*. New York: Columbia University Press, 1995.

Işın, Mary. *Sherbet and Spice*. London: I.B. Tauris, 2013.

Mason, Laura. *Sugar-Plums and Sherbet*. Totnes, U.K.: Prospect, 2004.

Richardson, Tim. *Sweets: A History of Temptation*. London: Bantam, 2002.

Thick, Malcolm. *Sir Hugh Plat: The Search for Useful Knowledge*. Totnes, U.K.: Prospect, 2010. Not specifically about confections but contains an interesting section on sugar work.

Wilson, C. Anne. *Banquetting Stuffe*. Edinburgh: Edinburgh University Press, 1998.

Woloson, Wendy S. *Refined Tastes: Sugar, Confectionery and Consumers in Nineteenth-Century America*. Baltimore: John Hopkins University Press, 2002.

Laura Mason

confectionery equipment, like the tools used for making pastry, has changed very little over the last 200 years. Electricity has allowed for more powerful tools and equipment, and therefore great efficiency and perhaps better quality. The basic design of most hand tools, such as knives and spatulas, has not changed, but composite materials like plastics have made hand tools lighter and more durable. New synthetic coatings for bowls, pans, and pots, and higher-quality metals such as aluminum and stainless steel, have made these objects lighter and more efficient for conducting heat rapidly and evenly, which is essential when making candies and confections. Listed here are some of the specialized tools used for the confectioner's art.

Tools for Professional and Home Confectioners

An *acetate sheet* is used as a base to create designs and shapes in chocolate that can be transferred to desserts while keeping the chocolate shiny.

Caramel bars are 1-inch-square metal bars used to shape and hold caramel candy mixtures. They can be arranged into a wide variety of square and rectangular shapes. See CARAMELS.

A *chocolate transfer sheet* is printed with designs made of cocoa butter and dry food coloring that are transferred onto chocolate candies and truffles. See TRUFFLES.

A *comb* is used to create a decorative, textured line on candies and confections. Combs look like wide rulers with different-size ripped edges (teeth) on opposite sides; they are usually made out of sturdy plastic, rubber, or stainless steel. Some are triangular, with three different comb-edged widths.

Cutters and portion cutters include cookie cutters and handheld disc cutters with multiple wheel-shaped blades. A guitar cutter is made of stainless steel and cuts candies and confections into equal-size pieces in a variety of shapes, including rectangles, squares, triangles, and diamonds.

Dippers and forks are handheld tools used for dipping candies and truffles in tempered chocolate. They have a small handle with spiral, round, square, or fork-shaped ridge wires that allow excess chocolate to drip off before the confection is transferred to another surface to set up completely.

A *fondant funnel* dispenses equal portions of fillings for chocolates and marzipan and is used for making fondants. See CHOCOLATES, FILLED; FONDANT; and MARZIPAN.

A *flower nail* looks like a regular nail but has a larger flat head about 1.5 inches in diameter. It is used to make small designs that are transferred onto candies and confections.

A *marble slab* is useful for tempering chocolate by hand. Because the slab is porous, it cools the chocolate quickly.

In an *offset spatula*, a flexible blade is offset from the handle and stepped down, forming a "z" shape that makes this tool excellent for spreading mixtures in shallow pans and for moving candies and confections from one place to another without damaging their sides or top.

Pastry bags, sometime referred to as piping bags, are used for portioning out mixtures and for decorating. They are cone-shaped, with the narrow end open for fitting pastry tips, and are usually made of cloth lined with polyethylene. Disposable pastry bags are also available. *Pastry bag tips* fit in the narrow end of pastry bags. They can be bought individually or in sets that include multiple size openings and designs. A coupler is often included to secure the tips in the bag. In confectionery, pastry bags and tips are used for piping out truffles, filling truffle cups, and for molded candies.

Tools for Form and Design

A *blown sugar pump* is used to pump air into sugar to make delicate, three-dimensional designs, including clear bubbles. Pumps come in different styles but basically consist of a rubber bulb that is squeezed by hand, from which a flexible short tube protrudes; the tube ends in a short, rigid, copper or stainless-steel tube section. The pump slightly resembles a poultry baster.

Gum paste tools, sometimes called molding tools, are used for a variety of designing and sculpting work with gum paste (a mixture of egg whites, confectioner's sugar, and tylose powder) and marzipan. See TRAGACANTH. Usually purchased in a kit, they resemble handheld dental tools with a tool head on both ends and are normally made out of rigid plastic.

Molds come in a huge variety of shapes and sizes, including many seasonal, holiday, and special designs. Flexible plastic, silicone, and metal molds are used for solid filled and hollowed candies and confections including chocolate. Often several molds are contained on one sheet. Special molds for single objects are usually made of metal with two hinged sides. Molds called presses are used to shape gum paste, marzipan, rolled fondant, and modeling chocolate into leaf shapes and other designs.

Stamps, which create a design impression on candies and confections, are often custom-made. They come in a variety of materials, including wood, plastic, and metal.

A *stencil* is placed over or on a finished candy or confection to produce a design. A large variety of designs and sizes is available.

Specialized Equipment

A *chocolate tempering machine* melts and tempers chocolate to the correct temperature so that it will dry quickly and maintain its sheen when truffles and candies are dipped in it. A variety of sizes is available, ranging from a tabletop version that holds 1 pound to large, industrial machines that hold hundreds of pounds of chocolate.

A *pulled sugar light* is a special lamp that keeps a sugar mixture warm and pliable while it is being shaped (pulled). Although not necessary, a warming box that includes a light can also be used when doing pulled sugar work.

Thermometers that read from 100° to 400°F (38° to 204°C) are used to indicate the stages of cooked sugar that correspond to a temperature range, such as soft-ball, hard-ball, and so on. See STAGES OF SUGAR SYRUP. Electronic digital probe-type gauges as well as infrared laser-sight thermometers are also used.

See also CAKE DECORATING; COOKIE MOLDS AND STAMPS; PANS; and PASTRY TOOLS.

Bloom, Carole. *Truffles, Candies, and Confections: Techniques and Recipes for Candymaking*. Berkeley, Calif.: Ten Speed, 2004.

Bloom, Carole. *Intensely Chocolate: 100 Scrumptious Recipes for True Chocolate Lovers*. Hoboken, N.J.: Wiley, 2010.

Greweling, Peter P. *Chocolate and Confections: Formula, Theory, and Technique for the Artisan Confectioner*. Hoboken, N.J.: Wiley, 2012.

Carole Bloom

confectionery manuals are centered on the techniques used to manipulate sugar. They may also contain recipes for cakes and biscuits, ices, flavored drinks, alcoholic beverages, preserved fruit, medicines, cosmetics, and purely ornamental table decorations. These manuals are a subset of the comprehensive European cookbook. Their greatest utility lies in the preservation of foods for use in winter. They require specialized equipment and skills. More than most other culinary crafts, confectionery offers opportunities for ornamentation that range from the beautiful to the absurd.

The earliest published collections of confectionery recipes appeared in the small sixteenth-century European medical books and "books of secrets" published in Italy, France, England, and Germany. They contained medical and cosmetic receipts and in some cases instructions for preserving fruit, making pastilles, and concocting healing beverages. See FRUIT PRESERVES and MEDICINAL USES OF SUGAR. As Ken Albala explains in *Eating Right in the Renaissance* (2002), the conjunction of medical advice and confectionery was in accordance with the accepted doctrine of humors that had governed medical teachings since the first century C.E. Heat and cold, wetness and dryness, were attributes possessed by individuals and by the food and drink they consumed. When bodily humors needed to be tempered, that is, brought to a balanced center, the cold, dry melancholy person sought healing with warm, moist sugar. The sugared remedies were probably the least unpleasant ones available.

As early as 1555, *The Secrets of Master Alexis of Piedmont* described how to make plates with powdered sugar and gum tragacanth, which could be used to eat off of, and which could then be broken and themselves eaten. See TRAGACANTH. It would have been an attractive conceit in an age when fragile ceramic plates were beginning to replace wooden, metal, and bread trenchers. Marzipan confections were already present in the Middle Ages; in the sixteenth century, they were joined by fruit jams and pastes, sugar-coated seeds, and flavored pastilles. See COMFIT; LOZENGE; MARZIPAN; SUGAR; and SUGAR SCULPTURE.

The control of heat in sugar boiling was the core technique. See STAGES OF SUGAR SYRUP. Since the confectioner's options change with every few degrees of heat, it is not surprising that these stages had been named and described in French, German, and English. Other techniques in the confectionery books include freezing ices, making fresh cheeses, working with foams (egg whites and creams), and elaborately decorating cakes. See CAKE DECORATING and CHEESE, FRESH. In addition, jellies, custards, and salads are mentioned. See CUSTARD. Pierre de Lune's *Confiturier de la Cour* (1659) offered a recipe for a *Salade couronnée* that took up four pages and required carving a multitude of lemon-rind crowns. It served the same role as a *pièce montée*, dominating the table and causing wonder among the diners, as did the chocolate and ices in François Massialot's *Nouvelle instruction pour les confitures* (1692).

The typical seventeenth- or eighteenth-century manual contained recipes for a wide range of sweets, most of them sugar-based. These included nut-based sweets such as marzipan, Jordan almonds, and pralines, as well as boiled sugar candy, wafers, jellies, sweet biscuits, and other small baked goods, and, by the end of the seventeenth century, candied flowers, ices, and ice creams. Instructions might also be given for distillation and brewing. See CANDIED FLOWERS; HARD CANDY; ICE CREAM; PRALINE; and WAFERS.

Confectionery books addressed to women appeared in the seventeenth century. Hugh Plat's *Delights for Ladies* (1608) promised the reader "beauties,

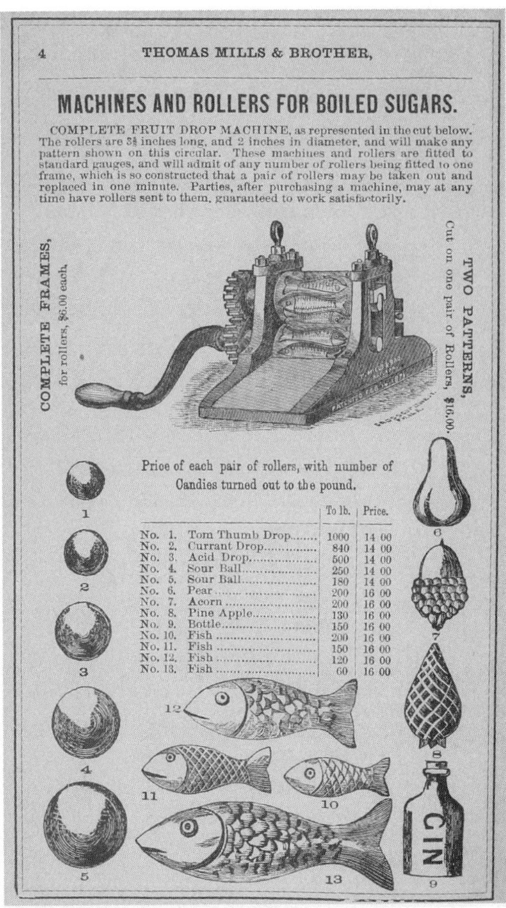

4 THOMAS MILLS & BROTHER,

MACHINES AND ROLLERS FOR BOILED SUGARS.

COMPLETE FRUIT DROP MACHINE, as represented in the cut below. The rollers are 3¾ inches long, and 2 inches in diameter, and will make any pattern shown on this circular. These machines and rollers are fitted to standard gauges, and will admit of any number of rollers being fitted to one frame, which is so constructed that a pair of rollers may be taken out and replaced in one minute. Parties, after purchasing a machine, may at any time have rollers sent to them, guaranteed to work satisfactorily.

COMPLETE FRAMES, for rollers, $6.00 each.

TWO PATTERNS, Cut on one pair of Rollers, $16.00.

Price of each pair of rollers, with number of Candies turned out to the pound.

		To lb.	Price.
No. 1.	Tom Thumb Drop	1000	14 00
No. 2.	Currant Drop	840	14 00
No. 3.	Acid Drop	500	14 00
No. 4.	Sour Ball	250	14 00
No. 5.	Sour Ball	180	14 00
No. 6.	Pear	200	16 00
No. 7.	Acorn	200	16 00
No. 8.	Pine Apple	130	16 00
No. 9.	Bottle	150	16 00
No. 10.	Fish	200	16 00
No. 11.	Fish	150	16 00
No. 12.	Fish	120	16 00
No. 13.	Fish	60	16 00

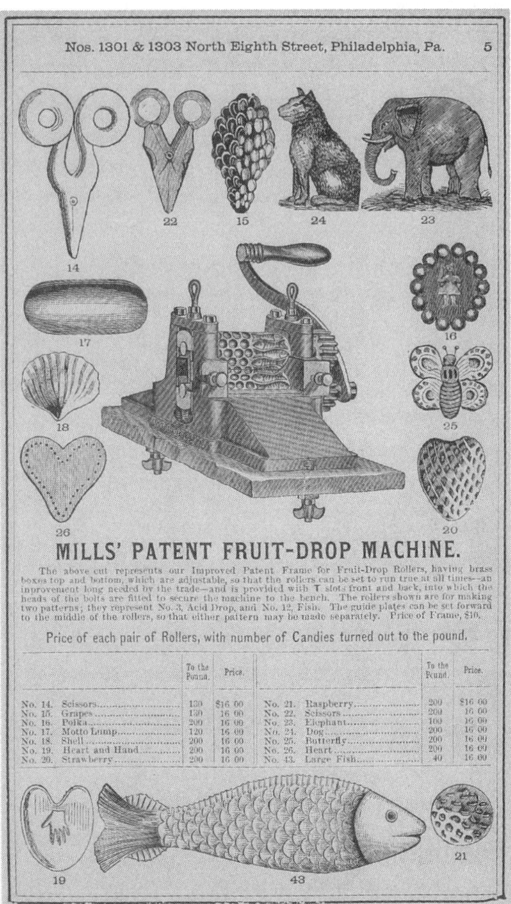

Nos. 1301 & 1303 North Eighth Street, Philadelphia, Pa. 5

MILLS' PATENT FRUIT-DROP MACHINE.

The above cut represents our Improved Patent Frame for Fruit-Drop Rollers, having brass boxes top and bottom, which are adjustable, so that the rollers can be set to run true at all times—an improvement long needed by the trade—and is provided with T slots front and back, into which the heads of the bolts are fitted to secure the machine to the bench. The rollers shown are for making two patterns; they represent No. 3, Acid Drop, and No. 12, Fish. The guide plates can be set forward to the middle of the rollers, so that either pattern may be made separately. Price of Frame, $10.

Price of each pair of Rollers, with number of Candies turned out to the pound.

		To the Pound.	Price.			To the Pound.	Price.
No. 14.	Scissors	130	$16 00	No. 21.	Raspberry	200	$16 00
No. 15.	Grapes	130	16 00	No. 22.	Scissors	200	16 00
No. 16.	Polka	200	16 00	No. 23.	Elephant	100	16 00
No. 17.	Motto Lump	120	16 00	No. 24.	Dog	200	16 00
No. 18.	Shell	200	16 00	No. 25.	Butterfly	200	16 00
No. 19.	Heart and Hand	200	16 00	No. 26.	Heart	200	16 00
No. 20.	Strawberry	200	16 00	No. 43.	Large Fish	40	16 00

The earliest confectionery recipes appeared in small sixteenth-century books containing instructions for medicinal and cosmetic preparations. By the late nineteenth century, confectionery manuals had become an important resource for professionals. Here, Thomas Mills & Brother show off the latest equipment in *United States Confectioners' Tool Works, Descriptive and Illustrated Catalogue of Goods,* 1886. WILLIAM L. CLEMENTS LIBRARY, UNIVERSITY OF MICHIGAN

banquets, perfumes and waters"; Hannah Wooley's *Ladies Directory* (1662) advertised preserving in jellies, candying fruits and flowers, cakes, comfits, and perfumes, as well as a suppositious cure for the plague. One of the handsomest confectionery books may be Maria Schellhammer's *Wohl-unterwiesenen Kochin zufallige Confect-Tafel* (Berlin, 1723) with its frontispiece illustrating the required equipment. Mary Eales (1718) was the first Englishwoman to publish a confectionery book, but it is to be hoped that none of her readers followed her advice to color pastilles with powdered cobalt blue glass.

Eighteenth-century France offered notable confectionery manuals: an expanded version of Massialot's *Nouvelle instruction pour les confitures* was followed by Menon's *Science du Maître d'hôtel confiseur* (1750). The most remarkable French books in this field were Emy's *Art de bien faire les glaces* (1768) with its charming rococo frontispiece of cupids making ice cream, and the superb *Cannemelist français* (1751) by Joseph Gilliers with engravings showing how to set up complicated geometrically perfect tables, as well as how to form pastillage flowers. Juan de la Mata's *Arte de repostería* (1755) illustrated that Spain, too, had a distinguished craft tradition. See EMY, M.; GILLIERS, JOSEPH; and PASTILLAGE.

The highly influential architectural fantasies in Marie-Antoine Carême's *Pâtissier pittoresque* (1815) ranged from the charming to the ungainly. Jules Gouffé divided his confectionery knowledge between his *Livre de conserves* (1869) and his *Livre de pâtisserie* (1873), which used chromolithography to show off *pièces montées*, pulled sugar work and petits fours to remarkable effect. See CARÊME, MARIE-ANTOINE.

Apart from *The Complete Confectioner* (1844), which acknowledged its debt to the English confectionery book by George Read, the American confectionery scene was quiet. Most contemporary candy-making books are addressed to the home cook, for hobbyists and people looking to make a little extra money. Candy manufacture became an industrial process, but pastilles (known in New England as NECCO Wafers) and cough drops (still made with boiled sugar) live on. See NECCO. Despite this competition, confectionery books continue to appear: books on candy making at home, especially for holidays, are popular; and professional confectioners share their secret techniques for new approaches with marzipan, chocolate, and, yes, boiled sugar.

See also JARRIN, WILLIAM ALEXIS; PUBLICATIONS, TRADE; and WEBER, JOHANNESE MARTIN ERICH.

Albala, Ken. *Eating Right in the Renaissance.* Berkeley: University of California Press, 2002.

Hyman, Philip, and Mary Hyman. "Les livres de cuisine imprimés en France du règne de Charles VIII à la fin de l'Ancien Régime." In *Livres en bouche: Cinq siècles d'art culinaire français du quatorzième au dix-huitième siècle*, edited by Sabine Coron, pp. 55–73. Paris: Bibliothèque nationale de France, 2001. A history of table service in France. Reprinted, Berkeley: University of California Press, 2007.

Notaker, Henry. *Printed Cookbooks in Europe 1470–1700: A Bibliography of Early Modern Culinary Literature.* New Castle, Del.: Oak Knoll, 2010.

Barbara Wheaton

confetti refers to both sugarcoated almonds presented to wedding guests in dainty tulle bags and the tiny bits of colored paper tossed into the air as the happy couple departs. Both trace their name back to the Latin *conficere*, meaning to "confect, compose, make." In England, as far back as the fourteenth century, the word "comfit" was used to describe nuts and seeds that were coated in sugar. See COMFIT. In French, the word is *comfit* or *confit*. Italians use *confetto* for the singular, *confetti* for the plural. Confection, confectionery, confectioner, comfit, and confetti—all are related.

The first sugarcoated nuts and seeds were made by apothecaries and used medicinally. They were the original sugarcoated pills. Depending on the seed, nut, or fruit in their center, comfits were believed to have various benefits. Some were eaten after a rich banquet to aid digestion. Those made with caraway or fennel seeds sweetened breath, hence Shakespeare's "kissing-comfits." Such comfits are still found in India, where they are known as sweet *saunf* or *valiary*.

At weddings, confetti were tossed over the heads of the bride and groom to ensure fertility. The tradition may have had its origins in ancient Rome, where wheat cakes were crumbled over the bride's head. Confetti were tossed at weddings in England, France, and other countries but were especially popular in Italy. In fact, the phrase *mangiare i confetti* is an idiom meaning "to attend a wedding," although the literal translation is simply "to eat confetti."

Confetti originally referred to the sugarcoated nuts and seeds tossed at weddings to ensure fertility. In 1894 the London stationery company J. & E. Bella commissioned the French Postimpressionist Henri de Toulouse-Lautrec to design this advertising poster, which depicts a happy young woman being showered with a new type of confetti, made of colorful paper.

Since they were expensive, comfits or confetti were status symbols and were served at christenings, birthdays, banquets, and other celebrations in addition to weddings. Desirable gifts, they were often presented in elegant silver or porcelain boxes, or in edible marzipan containers.

The skill and equipment needed to make confetti meant that most often professionals like apothecaries and, later, confectioners made them. But some household cooks produced them as well, judging by the recipe in Hannah Woolley's 1670 edition of *The Queen-Like Closet.* The equipment has changed dramatically over time and machines have replaced the hanging basin of the seventeenth century, but the basic process remains the same. The seeds or nuts are dried over heat, then sugar syrup is poured over them as they are swirled around to keep the syrup coating even and to keep the nuts separate. After each layer of syrup is applied and dried, another is added. The process is repeated until the desired coating is achieved.

Woolley's description made the difficulty clear:

> Move the Seeds in the hanging Bason so fast as you can or may, and with one Hand, cast on half a Ladle full at a time of the hot Sugar, and rub the Seeds with your other hand a pretty while, for that will make them take the Sugar the better; And dry them well after every Coat.

Later improvements obviated the need to put one's hands in the hot sugar syrup. But even in the nineteenth century when sugar was more affordable, the labor-intensive preparation meant that confetti remained expensive. Thus, some confectioners began to cut corners. To lessen expense and save time, they covered the almonds or seeds with flour before coating them with sugar syrup. That allowed them to build up the layers faster and use less sugar. It was a cheaper, quicker way to make edible confetti.

Another solution was to make ersatz comfits that were not intended to be eaten at all. They were created to be tossed. Made of plaster in the shape and size of the candied almonds, they were sold by the basketful and hurled at friends, lovers, and even strangers at celebrations. Tossing confetti was a way to flirt, to attract the attention of a prospective belle or beau.

When Johann Wolfgang von Goethe visited Rome in the late eighteenth century, he called the pre-Lenten carnival "a kind of small war, mostly playful." He described black coats spotted with white under a barrage of plaster confetti. By the time Charles Dickens visited in 1844–1845, the small war had escalated. Dickens said confetti turned carnival goers as "white as millers." To protect their clothes, they donned dusters; to shield their eyes, they wore wire masks.

At the end of the nineteenth century, a new type of confetti made its debut. In 1894 an advertising poster by Henri de Toulouse-Lautrec depicted a happy, smiling young woman being showered with colorful—and harmless—confetti made from paper. The poster was commissioned by J & E Bella, a London stationery company. Initial newspaper reports were nearly delirious about the new product. On 26 March 1894 *The New York Times* described a new carpet on the boulevards of Paris. "The confetti made a velvet soft to the feet, picturesque to the eye, and novel even to the most advanced taste," the newspaper reported.

Today, paper confetti explode from guns at carnivals, Wall Street parades, and weddings. Sugarcoated almond confetti are prized wedding favors. Happily, plaster confetti have disappeared.

Dickens, Charles. *Pictures from Italy.* Boston: Ticknor and Fields, 1867.

Mason, Laura. *Sugar-Plums and Sherbet: The Prehistory of Sweets.* Totnes, U.K.: Prospect, 2004.

Jeri Quinzio

convent sweets have been prepared in Roman Catholic female religious houses since the sixteenth century. The tradition began in Italy, Portugal, and Spain, where there had been ready exposure to Islamic confectionery and sugar. With the establishment of Portuguese and Spanish empires in the Americas and Asia, convent sweets spread around the globe and beyond the convent walls. Although the whimsical or sexual names of many of the sweets, such as tits, nun's farts, bacon of heaven, and little hams, suggest that they were frivolities, confectionery was a business, a metaphor for the spiritual life, a tool for diplomats and missionaries, and, like Baroque churches, an expression of the Catholic Counter-Reformation. Convent kitchens were also the first area where Western women made a mark on high cuisine.

Although convent sweets overlapped with the confectionery prepared by male guilds, the convent tradition achieved a particularly high standard that still persists. The most innovative and archetypal of these sweets, probably developed in Portugal in the late fifteenth and early sixteenth centuries, were made from beaten egg yolks and syrup. See EGG YOLK SWEETS; and PORTUGAL. *Ovos moles* (soft eggs), sometimes called *yemas* (yolks), are beaten egg yolks stirred in hot syrup to form a thick yellow mass, which is then used as a custard, as a pastry filler, or rolled into yolk-sized confections. Soft (like the yolks from which they were made), glowing, and golden, and thus redolent of divinity, sweetness, and grace, they remained edible for months. The process of making them was seen as analogous to the progress of raw, unrefined novices to full members of the spiritual community. Other versions of the technique yielded *huevos reales* (royal eggs), beaten egg yolks baked and then soaked in syrup, and *huevos hilados* (egg threads), beaten egg yolks trickled through a tiny orifice into hot syrup to form a tangled mass of threads.

A second category of sweets, those using fruits (in syrups, jams, jellies, and pastes, or candied and crystallized) and nuts (brittles, marzipans, and nougats), derived from Islamic practice. These confections, long known on the northern Mediterranean borderlands of Islam and Christianity, were familiar to the Moorish servants and slaves who worked in the convents, and were described in fourteenth- and fifteenth-century confectionery books. See CONFECTIONERY MANUALS; and ISLAM. Flour-based sweets, whose connection to the Islamic tradition is not entirely clear, make up a third category. Wafers, prepared for use in the Mass, were also eaten in secular contexts, sometimes with a sweet filling. See WAFERS. Flour-and-fat cookies (shortbread), light sponge cakes of eggs, flour, and sugar that appear to date from the fifteenth century, and pastries were also prepared. See SPONGE CAKE.

A final group of confections common in New World convents (though not in European ones) were made by boiling down milk, often with added sugar, to make syrup, variously known as *cajeta* or *dulce de leche*, and, with further reduction, fudge, frequently referred to as little ham (*jamoncillo*). See DULCE DE LECHE and FUDGE. It is tempting to speculate that the technique was introduced by Indians who made similar sweets and who, voluntarily or not, made the Pacific crossing from the Philippines to New Spain (Mexico) on the galleons that sailed annually from 1565 to 1815.

Across Europe, female religious orders paired with their male counterparts had been established from the Middle Ages on. Substantial convents housing as many as a hundred nuns, their servants, and lay helpers were built in cities, a reflection of and contribution to the level of culture and sophistication in these locales. The nuns, from elite families, were educated, forceful, and often without a religious calling. They sought diversions, ways to turn the products of the convent lands into income, and ways to honor their patrons. Elaborate confectionery was added to the singing, the embroidery, and the schooling of girls in the late sixteenth century, a time of reaction against the spread of Protestantism now known as the Counter-Reformation.

Simultaneously, Spain and Portugal were establishing empires in the Americas and Asia. See PORTUGAL'S INFLUENCE IN ASIA. Mexico (New Spain), which prior to 1585 had 4 convents, saw 7 more founded in the following 16 years, and by 1747 boasted 45. In Goa, the Portuguese trading post on the western coast of India, the Convent of Santa Monica was built in 1606. No order was more important in spreading the network of convents, and incidentally their sweets, than the Franciscan order of Saint Clare, created in the fourteenth century and now known in English as the Poor Clares. They set up convents in Madeira in 1496; Santo Domingo in 1551; Mexico City, La Paz, Osorno, and Tunia in the 1570s; Quito, Havana, Panama, and Chile in the 1590s; and in Puebla and Queretaro in 1606. In 1621 Sister Jeronima of the Assumption established one in Manila in the Philippines, having left Madrid 18 months earlier with two junior nuns, sailed for Veracruz, crossed New Spain, and then made the dangerous journey across the Pacific. In 1633 a sister convent was founded in Macao. By this time, it is estimated, there was a global network of 16,000 nuns.

Portuguese and Spanish nuns, in their home countries and in the New World, had access to the newly available fine sugar from plantations beyond the Mediterranean. See PLANTATIONS, SUGAR. They had fruits and nuts from convent orchards. Their egg yolks reportedly were leftovers—the whites had been used for starching clothes, for refining wine or sugar, and for applying gold and silver leaf to church altars.

Convent kitchens were large, set up for feeding the sisters and their staff, for preparing fine meals for visiting dignitaries, and for making sweets. Walls might be lined with tile; bench stoves and ovens were fired with charcoal or wood, depending on the temperature required. The kitchens were well equipped with balances, graters, skimmers, sieves, bowls, clay and metal pots and pans, spoons, knives, and molds. Servants and slaves grated sugar loaves, ground nuts, and stirred pots. The sisters monitored sugar temperatures by checking tactile and visual signs, and annotated instructions in fine manuscript cookbooks. See STAGES OF SUGAR SYRUP.

The resulting confections were offered as gifts to patrons, served at the festivities for the convents' patron saints, and sold to eager buyers. Convents and guilds together sold 400 pounds of confectionery in 1619 to the Mexico City government for the anniversary of the city's conquest on the Feast of San Hipólito. They helped prepare the confections that required 200 pounds of sugar and 100 dozen eggs when the viceroy visited Puebla in 1696.

Nuns rarely ventured beyond the convent walls, but their sweets were not restricted in the same way. Portuguese voyagers bound for Goa or Macao took as many as a hundred kegs of *ovos moles* to give as gifts on arrival (and as an appealing, digestible treat for the dangerous passage). Vasco da Gama, for example, presented sweets to the Zamorin of Calicut. Jesuit missionaries in Japan used confectionery as an enticement to conversion from 1543 until their expulsion in 1639. An unknown Japanese author penned *The Southern Barbarian Cookbook* sometime in the early seventeenth century. Although they are not identified with the Catholic faith, perhaps in view of the Jesuits' increasingly precarious situation, half of the book's 45 recipes are for the kinds of sweets associated with the convent tradition.

To this day, traces of convent sweets persist in Japanese cookery. See JAPAN. Egg threads are still made in Thailand and in Afghanistan, the latter perhaps a trace of the Portuguese envoy's visit to the court of Tamerlane. See THAILAND. In Spain, Portugal, and Latin America, the tradition is very much alive, updated in many cases with more recent sweet dishes such as cakes. Convent sweets of high quality, enjoyed by local constituencies and sought out by tourists, can still be bought at convent windows, from a chain of shops run by the Poor Clares in Spain, and from commercial operations preparing "traditional sweets." In the decades around 2000, commercial publishers in Argentina, Uruguay, Colombia, Mexico, Spain, Portugal, and doubtless other parts of the former Hispanic empires produced confectionery cookbooks. An Argentinian nun, Sister Bernarda, has a television show and includes a sweets cookbook in her line of publications; Sister Lucia Caram, also from Argentina, shares recipes on the Spanish cooking channel. While the reputation of convent confectionery remains high, it is unclear whether the dwindling number of nuns, who rarely have the support staff of the past, will be able to maintain the tradition.

See also BRITTLE; CANDIED FRUIT; CUSTARD; FRUIT PRESERVES; GUILDS; INDIA; LATIN AMERICA; MARZIPAN; MEXICO; NOUGAT; and NUTS.

Lavin-Maroto, Mónica. *Dulces hábitos: Golosinas del convento*. Recipes by Ana Luisa Benítz Muro. Mexico City: Editorial Clío, 2000.

Saramago, Alfredo, and Manuel Fialho. *Doçaria dos conventos de Portugal*. Lisbon: Assirio & Alvin, 1997.

Simeti, Mary Taylor, and Maria Grammatico. *Bitter Almonds: Recollections and Recipes from a Sicilian Girlhood*. New York: Bantam, 1994.

Rachel Laudan

cookie cutters are the modern descendants of ancient bread stamps and medieval cookie molds that were made of wood, stone, ceramics, wax, and other materials. These stamps and molds had incised motifs for imprinting bas-relief designs on top of the dough before baking. The figures included people, plants, animals, religious symbols, coats of arms, and scenes of daily life. Although these molds embossed the tops of the cookie dough, often with intricate designs, most of them did not also cut the dough into the shape of the cookie itself, which had to be done by hand with a knife or jagging iron, a small pastry wheel with a fluted edge for cutting a scalloped line through the dough. Bakers also pressed inverted metal, wooden, or glass drinking vessels onto the dough to cut out uniformly round shapes. See COOKIE MOLDS AND STAMPS.

By the late seventeenth century in England, bakers were using templates to guide the knife or wheeled cutter. By the early eighteenth century, English cooks were using shaped tin cutters for cutting cookie forms more quickly, whether from smooth, flat sheets of rolled-out dough or from dough that had been imprinted with a design from a mold. These included inverted metal cake pans as well as cutters made specifically for cookies. They were most likely crafted by tinsmiths who formed leftover strips of tin into simple shapes such as circles, squares, rectangles, and hearts. Eventually, these cookie cutters came to be less expensive substitutes for the intricately carved wooden molds used by professional bakers in Europe since the Middle Ages. Instead of embossed designs on top of the cookies, the simple shapes made by these cutters were decorated with icing, raisins, nuts, pieces of candied fruit, colored sugar, and even printed paper cutouts.

In the mid-nineteenth century, metal cookie cutters began to be mass-produced in Europe and North America for professional and home cooks alike. Popular shapes included men and women in traditional costumes, flowers, animals, Christmas trees, stars, and other holiday symbols. Some were also made in sets of graduated sizes, in a series of three, five, or more of the same shape that nested together for storage.

Since cookie cutters are designed to cut only the outline of a particular shape, the thin strips of pliable metal can be bent easily out of form, especially with repeated use. So some cookie cutters, especially those for use by professional bakers, have been made sturdier by attaching the cutter to a flat metal backing that has a C-shaped metal handle or a wooden or plastic knob on the back. This backing also makes it easier to press the cutter into the dough and lift it off without accidentally altering the shape of the cookie's outline. Since the late nineteenth century, multiple cutters, such as five interlocked stars or ten adjoined hearts, have also enabled bakers to cut several shapes at once, more quickly and without wasting as much dough. Another type of multiple cutter looks like a metal or wooden rolling pin covered with a series of adjoined metal cutters attached to the roller, which is pushed across the dough to cut a repeated series of adjacent shapes.

Cookie cutters today are made in a wide range of sizes and shapes, from traditional holiday symbols to contemporary comic-book characters and movie action-figures. A few are even fashioned to impress a design on top, such as the veins of a leaf or the spaces within a snowflake. Materials vary, too. For more than two centuries, tin has been the least expensive and most commonly used metal, but it rusts easily. Copper cutters are much sturdier and more attractive aesthetically but are costly and need to be polished periodically. Aluminum cutters with Bakelite handles were popular during the first half of the twentieth century, but they have been supplanted by stainless steel, especially for cutters used by professional bakers and industrial producers of cookies. Modern plastics are the least expensive materials, used for cookie cutters in the United States since the 1940s, but the cutting edge of a plastic cutter is less sharp than a metal one. However, plastic cutters are favored for use by children because these cutters come in many bright colors, are easy to clean, and do not have dangerously sharp edges.

The homey, often nostalgic, emotional appeal of cookie cutters has also been used as a marketing tool by makers of other products, who would attach a "free" cookie cutter to their package of cooking fats, cookie mixes, and recipe card sets. Some cutters, marked with a company's name or logo, are given away free in advertising promotions. Modern home cooks can purchase custom-made cookie cutters, too, shaped like their pet cat or dog, their house or boat, the logo of the college they attended, or their favorite sports team. In the history of cookie cutter production, these contemporary custom-made cutters have come full circle back to the original, handmade, individual cookie cutters of centuries past, before mass production began to dominate the cookie cutter industry.

See also ANTHROPOMORPHIC AND ZOOMORPHIC SWEETS; CHRISTMAS; GINGERBREAD; SPECULAAS; and SPRINGERLE.

Greaser, Arlene, and Paul H. Greaser. *Cookie Cutters and Molds: A Study of Cookie Cutters, Turk's Head Molds, Butter Molds, and Ice Cream Molds.* Allentown, Penn.: The Greasers, 1969.

Raffald, Elizabeth. *The Experienced English Housekeeper.* Lewes, U.K.: Southover, 1997. Reprint of 1769 edition.

Smith, Andrew, ed. *The Oxford Companion to American Food and Drink*, pp. 155–156. Oxford and New York: Oxford University Press, 2007.

Wetherill, Phyllis Steiss. *Cookie Cutters and Cookie Molds: Art in the Kitchen.* Exton, Penn.: Schiffer, 1985.

Sharon Hudgins

cookie jars are, simply put, storage containers for cookies or biscuits. However, they are more likely to be delightfully decorative than plain.

The term "cookie jar" or "cookie tin" reflects American usage; the English say "biscuit jar" or tin. That is because the Americans took the word *cookie* from the Dutch *koekjes*, the diminutive of *koek* or cake, whereas the English use the word "biscuit," derived from the Latin *panis bicoctus*, twice-cooked bread. Whether the containers hold twice-cooked biscotti, macarons, oatmeal cookies, or even commercial animal crackers, they are often as appealing as their contents. See BISCUITS, BRITISH.

In the seventeenth century a tightly lidded metal box was sufficient for biscuit storage. But in 1861, when the Licensed Grocer's Act allowed British groceries to be individually packaged and sold, specialized biscuit tins came into being. A few years later, offset lithography made it possible to print designs on the tins, and the creativity of the English tin maker burst forth. Reusable biscuit tins were made in the shape of castles, sets of books, grandfather clocks, and coronation coaches. They were decorated with colorful scenes of nature, tea parties, and holiday celebrations and, of course, prominently featured the brand name of the biscuit maker.

The process of press-molding glass was perfected in the United States in the early nineteenth century, and by the latter part of the century inexpensive glass cookie jars were being sold in both England and the United States. They were often made of pink or green glass and formed in the shape of a barrel, recalling the old general-store cracker barrel. By the late nineteenth century elegant biscuit tins, sans advertising, were also being made from lavishly decorated electroplated silver.

Round and barrel-shaped cookie jars made of stoneware became popular in the United States during the Depression of the 1930s. By the 1940s they were being created with great imagination. Rather than simple barrels, cookie jars were shaped to resemble overall-clad pigs, locomotives, rocking horses, smiling hippos, and teddy bears. Nursery rhyme characters like Little Miss Muffet, Humpty Dumpty, and Little Boy Blue were transmogrified into cookie jars.

During the 1950s TV and cartoon characters, including Davy Crockett, the Flintstones, Popeye, and Casper the Friendly Ghost, made their cookie-jar debuts. Disney characters, including Mickey and Minnie Mouse, Dumbo, and Goofy, likewise became cookie jars. Naturally, multiple versions of Santa Claus were also popular, as were corporate characters like Aunt Jemima, Mr. Peanut, and the Pillsbury Dough Boy. In the 1970s, fittingly enough, *Sesame Street*'s Cookie Monster became a cookie jar.

Even today, cookbooks and magazine features often headline cookie recipe sections with titles like "From the Cookie Jar," "From Grandma's Cookie Jar," or "A Cookie Jar Raider's Dream Come True." The accompanying illustration often portrays a homey kitchen scene with mom or grandma and children making cookies. However, today's cookie jars are as likely to contain cookies bought at a supermarket or baked with store-bought cookie dough as homemade-from-scratch cookies.

During the 1970s cookie jars became valued collectibles. Some collectors specialize in jars made by a particular manufacturer, others in themes like patriotism, sports, Disney characters, or TV shows. Some collect only from a particular time frame, especially the 1940s, which is thought of as the golden era of cookie jars.

Andy Warhol famously collected cookie jars from the 1930s and 1940s. After his death, the 25 April 1988 edition of the *New York Times* reported that his collection of 175 pottery cookie jars sold at auction for $247,830. The collection included pottery pigs, a chef's head, goats, Humpty Dumpty, and a panda. No doubt Warhol's celebrity inflated the price, which Sotheby's originally had estimated at about $7,000.

Today, illustrated guidebooks help collectors differentiate between reproductions and originals and offer price guidelines. Depending on their quality and desirability, the jars sell for as little as $30 to well over $1,000.

The term "cookie jar" can be heard in areas far from the kitchen. *Cookie jar accounting* describes a misleading practice in which a company understates its assets when doing well in order to overstate them when doing poorly. A thief is often said to have been caught with a "hand in the cookie jar." Cookie jars are associated with savings, much like a piggy bank, and advice columns recommend putting spare change in a "cookie jar fund." In fact, the second definition of "cookie jar" in the *Random House Dictionary of the English Language* is "a container used for storing money."

See also ANIMAL CRACKERS; AUNT JEMIMA; BISCOTTI; and MACARONS.

Moran, Mark F. *Warman's Cookie Jars: Identification & Price Guide*. Iola, Wis.: Krause, 2004.

Schweitzer, Sophia V. "The Art of the Biscuit Tin." *Smithsonian Magazine*, 4 April 2012. http://www.smithsonianmag.com/arts-culture/the-art-of-the-biscuit-tin.

Wilson, C. Anne. *Food and Drink in Britain: From the Stone Age to the 19th Century*. Chicago: Chicago Review Press, 1991.

Jeri Quinzio

cookie molds and stamps are used by cooks in many parts of the world to imprint designs—religious, secular, traditional, modern—on cookie dough, usually before it is baked. Sometimes the dough is baked in the mold or deep-fried on the mold. Descendants of the bread stamps used by ancient cultures, these baking utensils have a long history and encompass a wide variety of materials, forms, designs, and uses.

Historically, cookie molds have been made of wood, stone, ceramic (earthenware, stoneware, porcelain), metal, plaster, wax, and even thick pieces of leather. Some are now also made of glass, plastic, silicone, or resin. The mold has a concave design (a negative image, or reverse image) carved or otherwise shaped into it. With some types of molds, a piece of dough is first pressed into the mold, then the excess dough is cut away, and the dough is removed from the mold before being baked on a baking sheet or baking stone. Other types of molds are pressed, face down, onto a rolled-out sheet of dough, then removed from the dough, which is cut or trimmed into shapes before baking. These can be flat molds, known as boards, or rolling pins with designs incised in them. In all cases, a reverse imprint of the mold's design is embossed on the dough's surface. Examples of cookies molded in these ways include European springerle, speculaas, gingerbreads, and some shortbreads; Middle Eastern *ma'amoul*; Malaysian *kuih bangkit*; and Chinese and Japanese mooncakes.

Some metal, ceramic, and silicone molds function as baking pans. The dough or batter is baked in the mold, then turned out of the mold to cool, with the mold's shape imprinted on the cookie. French *madeleines*, Norwegian *sandbakelse*, some Scottish shortbreads, and some American holiday cookies are baked in molds that have single or multiple concave designs that are open at the top. Two-sided molds, usually made of iron, are used for making thin waffle- or wafer-like cookies imprinted on one or both sides. The dough or batter is enclosed and baked within the two sides of the mold. Examples include Norwegian *krumkake* and *goro*, Czech *oplatky*, Italian *pizzele*, and Indonesian *kue semprong*.

Rosette irons are a special type of cookie mold, resembling a branding iron, with a long handle perpendicular to a metal mold shaped like a flower, star, snowflake, Christmas tree, or other symbol. The metal part is first heated in hot oil, then dipped in batter, and quickly returned to the hot oil. After the bottom of the batter has been fried on the mold, the partially cooked batter is detached from the mold, turned over, and fried on the other side, producing a light, crisp cookie shaped like the mold. These kinds of fried, molded cookies, often garnished with sugar or honey, include northern European rosettes, Turkish *demir tatlısi*, Iranian *bamiyeh*, and Sri Lankan *kokis*.

Cookie molds and stamps allow bakers to turn out decorative cookies in shapes reflecting religious, secular, traditional, and modern motifs. Elaborately carved antique molds are now collectors' items.

Cookie stamps are usually made of carved wood or a ceramic material with a design molded into it; some are made from metal, glass, resin, or plastic. All have a handle on one side and a single design on the other. Most cookie stamps are round, although a few are square or made in other shapes. They are used for imprinting designs, one at a time, on a rolled-out sheet of dough that is then cut into individual shapes with a knife or cookie cutter. The stamp can also be firmly pressed onto a single small ball of dough, to flatten it out and form a roughly shaped round cookie with the design embossed on it.

European molded cookies are thought to be modern manifestations of sacrificial dough effigies made by pre-Christian people who practiced animal sacrifice to their gods. In those ceremonies, poor people who had no animals, or who could not afford to sacrifice one, substituted pieces of baked dough shaped like animals. Centuries later, in Europe, elaborately molded cookies became popular gifts, religious and secular celebration artifacts, decorations, teaching aids, and methods of spreading information visually, from biblical stories to political propaganda to the latest fashions. Intricately carved wooden molds were used to mass-produce honey-spice and egg-sugar cookies in thousands of different designs, from a few inches to 3 feet in size. Many museums in northern Europe now display collections of these historic hand-carved molds made between the sixteenth and nineteenth centuries.

Handmade cookie molds were popular baking tools in Europe, initially among the medieval bakers' guilds and later among home bakers, until simpler, mass-produced, less expensive metal cookie cutters began to replace them in the nineteenth century. Interest in making molded cookies at home was revived in Europe and the United States in the 1970s and 1980s, and artisans began making carved cookie molds with traditional designs, as well as ceramic molds with newer designs, to meet the demand. Some companies also began producing high-quality resin replicas of historic cookie molds from European museums and private collections. However, by the 1990s, less expensive, less well-made copies of traditional European cookie molds also arrived on the market, imported from China and Taiwan. Simple cookie stamps, handmade by artisans or mass-produced by baking-supply companies, have also gained popularity with home bakers in North America since the 1980s, because they are easier to use and less costly than more elaborate cookie molds.

See also COOKIE CUTTERS; GINGERBREAD; MADELEINE; MOONCAKE; SHORTBREAD; SPECULAAS; and SPRINGERLE.

Hardine, Anneliese. *The Edible Mass Medium: Traditional Cookie Molds of the Seventeenth, Eighteenth, and Nineteenth Centuries*. Cambridge, Mass.: Harvard University and Busch-Reisinger Museum, 1975. Catalog for the exhibition "Traditional European Cookie Molds," 6 November 1975–17 January 1976.

Hudgins, Sharon. "Edible Art: Springerle Cookies." *Gastronomica: The Journal of Food and Culture*, 4, no. 4 (2004): 66–71.

"Springerle and Speculaas Molds for Baking, Crafting, Decorating." http://www.houseonthehill.net/ (accessed 9 September 2013).

Watson, Anne L. *Baking with Cookie Molds: Secrets and Recipes for Making Amazing Handcrafted Cookies for Your Christmas, Holiday, Wedding, Party, Swap, Exchange, or Everyday Treat*. Friday Harbor, Wash.: Shepard, 2010.

Sharon Hudgins

cookies

See ROLLED COOKIES; BAR COOKIES; DROP COOKIES; and PRESSED COOKIES.

cooking irons for waffles, wafers, and rosettes are used to shape the batter or dough (sweet, savory, or unseasoned) that is cooked in or on them. They have, so to speak, a long, waffling trail through culinary history in terms of their form, purpose, and regional variations.

Waffle and wafer irons are similarly shaped and work the same way. Patterns (not necessarily identical) are impressed or incised in two facing metal plates of matching dimensions. The plates are joined at one side by a hinge or hinges. The irons are heated, then opened to fill with batter or dough and immediately closed for cooking. As the filling cooks or dough cooks (literally bakes) between the heated plates, it takes on the pattern of the plates, and often the form of the plates themselves. Some irons are large enough to make multiple wafers at a time; the size of each wafer is determined by the amount of batter or dough used with each portion.

These tools originally were called irons because they were made of cast iron and weighty. The handles were long for cooking over coals or fires on open hearths, often supported by a stand of some sort; or they were used on counters heated from beneath by hot coals. Wooden handles for insulation came later. See PASTRY TOOLS. As stoves evolved, so did the irons. For stovetop use, many irons have a cradle or frame for support so that the irons do not have to be held while cooking. A socket, in which the hinge rests, makes it possible to rotate the iron for even browning.

Wafer irons probably predate the waffle iron and were used in the Middle Ages (some references suggest even much earlier) to make plain wafers for religious Communion. Wafer irons produce thin, crisp wafers or cookies impressed with greatly varied designs incised in the plates from religious to geometric: scrolls, flowers, family crests, initials, and more. When wafers are warm, most are flexible enough to roll quickly into cones, tubes, tight cylinders, or drape over forms; they hold these shapes when cool. See WAFERS.

In the early twentieth century, waffle irons or bakers were electrified, and waffles enjoyed great popularity. The waffle maker could be used right on the dining table, and the waffles did not have to be turned. Further refinements for both waffle and wafer irons (which were also electrified) included lighter-weight grids of aluminum, nonstick finishes, heat controls, timers, and exteriors that appealed to the design fashion of the day. Today, these tools are often called bakers, since they are no longer made of iron or used over direct heat.

A standard waffle iron or baker is distinguished by deep indentations or grids. The depth of the grids and the shape of the overall unit vary: they can be round (sometimes in a series of hearts), rectangular, or square, and they are usually segmented so that the waffle can break apart easily. The indentations may be square, oval, or honeycomb in shape; some feature Mickey Mouse or religious saints. Scandinavian waffle irons make break-apart hearts, whereas Belgian waffle irons have much deeper impressions to yield thicker waffles.

Machines to make ice cream cones are also called waffle bakers, but the wafer they yield is thinner than a waffle, and they usually come with a cone form for shaping the warm cookie. See ICE CREAM CONES. Recipes vary to make the kind of waffle desired, from tender to crisp, sweet to savory, thick or thin.

Wafer irons are often named for the cookie they yield. In France, *oublies* and *galettes* are cookies with irons similarly named. Scandinavian cookbooks abound with recipes for *krumkake* from krumkake irons, as well as *strull* and *avlette*. Norway gets credit for *goro* baked in rectangular goro irons. Italian *pizzelle* cook in pizzelle irons (flat or wavy in shape), *cialde* in larger round cialde irons, and *ostie* in ostie irons. The Dutch make *stroopwafel* in the *stroopwafelijzer*. Although any wafer cookie batter or dough can, in principle, be baked in any of these specialized irons or bakers, many of the iron tools have slipped into the realm of antiquers as electric bakers have taken over their tasks.

The rosette iron (timbale iron or *waffelbackerei*) works differently. A patterned iron, attached to a metal rod with a heatproof handle, is heated in hot oil, dipped into a thin batter, and then returned to the oil to fry the batter crisp and golden. This pastry is eased off the iron to serve, often dusted with confectioner's or cinnamon sugar. The rosette is a common pattern for the iron, hence its name. Other forms include snowflakes, stars, interlocking rings, and butterflies. A solid iron (timbale iron) can be round, oval, rectangular, or square. It makes a crisp pastry to fill. Contemporary rosette irons usually screw off the rod, and some handles support two rods. Tools similar to the rosette iron are used for fried pastries in Asia.

See also BELGIUM; COOKIE MOLDS AND STAMPS; FRANCE; ITALY; SCANDINAVIA; and NETHERLANDS.

Fante's Kitchen Shop. http://www.fantes.com (accessed 20 November 2014).

Ojakangas, Beatrice. *Scandianavian Feasts*. New York: Stewart, Tabori, & Chang, 1992

Sonnenfield, Albert. *Food: A Culinary History from Antiquity to the Present*. Edited by Jean-Louis Flandrin and Massimo Montanari. New York: Penguin, 1999.

Jerry Anne Di Vecchio

Cool Whip is an artificial product intended to mimic whipped cream, composed mainly of water, hydrogenated vegetable oil, and high-fructose corn syrup. The flavor is bland and sweet, not really tasting much like a dairy product, with a texture somewhat denser than whipped cream. Cool Whip was invented sometime prior to 1966, when it was first introduced to the market, by Dr. William A. Mitchell, a food chemist in General Foods' Birds Eye division from 1941 to 1976. In that capacity he also formulated such other products and precursors as powdered egg whites, quick-setting Jell-O, Pop Rocks, and Tang. Within two years of its introduction, Cool Whip became the highest-grossing Birds Eye product. The whip has historically been marketed in 8-ounce plastic tubs in supermarket freezer cases, but aerosol versions are sometimes available. They are intended to compete directly with Reddi-wip, an aerosol whip made from dairy products by ConAgra. Cool Whip sold in the United States and Canada is manufactured in a factory in Avon, New York. It is now a flagship brand of Kraft Foods, which acquired the product through a series of mergers and divestments.

A commercial dating to the late 1960s advertised, "Cool Whip has all the good old-fashioned taste with lots less calories than whipped cream you have to make," implying that making fresh real cream was too much trouble. See CREAM. The product was shown being used on fresh fruit and strawberry shortcake. By 1992 a TV commercial featured the jingle "Cool Whip's the one, with the whip-creamy taste," and the product was shown in pudding parfaits and as a topping for waffles.

The nutritional panel on a package of Cool Whip lists the calories per cup as 381, of which 71 percent come from fat. Sixty-two percent of the fat, totaling 30.4 grams per cup, is saturated fat. From a shifting roster of fats, Cool Whip often uses hydrogenated palm kernel oil and hydrogenated coconut oil. Flavored Cool Whips and "free" Cool Whips are now part of the marketing strategy, including Original, Extra Creamy, French Vanilla, Chocolate, Strawberry, Cinnamon, Light, Reduced Fat, Free (fat-free), and Sugar-Free. Cinnamon and Strawberry have been only seasonally available at Christmas. Other chemicals in the recipe for Cool Whip include polysorbate 60, sodium caseinate, sorbitan monostearate, and xanthan and guar gums. Cool Whip was probably marketed by Birds Eye to compete with Kraft's Dream Whip Topping Mix, which had been introduced in 1957, nearly a decade earlier than Cool Whip.

In a product diversification strategy, Cool Whip rolled out a line of frozen frostings in 2012. The flavors were chocolate, vanilla, and cream cheese. According to Kraft Cool Whip Brand Manager Marjani Coffey, in an interview with *Marketing Daily*, "Consumers said that shelf-stable frostings were too sweet, too thick and too hard to apply without damaging the cakes or other baked goods in the process." The marketing tagline for the product, which is placed right next to Cool Whip in freezer cases, is "So good, you'll look for reasons to celebrate."

See also CORN SYRUP; ICING; and SHORTENING.

Cohen, Shoshanna. "Whipped Up: Cool Whip, for the Curious." *Culinate*, 2 February 2012. http://www.culinate.com/columns/spaghetti_on_the_wall/cool_whip.

Lukovitz, Karlene. "Cool Whip Frosting Breaks New Ground." *Marketing Daily*, 30 November 2012. http://www.mediapost.com/publications/marketing-daily/edition/2012/11/30/?print.

Robert Sietsema

cordials

See LIQUEUR.

corn syrup, or glucose syrup, is a clear, colorless sweetening liquid made from cornstarch. During the early nineteenth century, researchers in countries without easy access to cane sugar experimented with making sweeteners from other agricultural products, such as white or sweet potatoes. Beginning in 1836, American scientists tried to make sugar from cornstarch. They eventually succeeded, and by the end of the century, corn syrup was marketed under a variety of brand names. Corn syrup is not as sweet as cane sugar, but it is widely used in the commercial production of candy, preserved fruits, jellies, fruit drinks, and beer.

The Glucose Sugar Refining Corporation, formed in 1897, consolidated a portion of the corn syrup industry. In 1902 it merged with its largest competitor, the New York Glucose Corporation, to create the Corn Products Refining Corporation (CPRC). The company launched a major advertising campaign for its newly named premier product, Karo Syrup, which was promoted as a table syrup for pancakes and waffles and as an ingredient in recipes for homemade cakes, candies, beverages, sauces, and pies (such as pecan pie).

In 1957 Earl Marshal and Earl Kooi, scientists working for Corn Products, figured out how to make high-fructose corn syrup (HFCS) by refining corn starch into glucose and then adding enzymes to convert it into fructose (the predominant natural sugar found in fruit), which is about 2.3 times sweeter than glucose and 1.7 times sweeter than sucrose (common table sugar). It took another 10 years to perfect the formula, but at the time, HFCS was relatively expensive and cane sugar was cheap, so there was not much demand for it.

The 1973 U.S. Farm Bill created a system of price supports—direct payments to farmers based on target prices set by the government. Under this new system the government gave farmers "deficiency payments" to ensure that target prices were met. Corn growers, for instance, could grow all the corn they wanted, sell it at any price, and be assured of a profit through the government subsidy. Consequently, farmers planted more corn, which caused its market price to drop, making HFCS financially viable. In 1978 a new discovery made it possible to manufacture 90 percent fructose, which was much sweeter than cane sugar, and the HFCS industry took off. In 1980 Coca-Cola began to replace cane sugar with HFCS. By 1993 Americans were consuming 79 pounds of HFCS annually, and by 2004, 175 pounds per person—about 20 percent of that amount in soda. See SODA and SUGAR AND HEALTH.

Since the 1970s, HFCS used in processed foods and beverages has included both fructose and glucose, the proportions depending on its intended use. The HFCS used in baking is 50 percent fructose and 50 percent glucose. When used to sweeten soda, it is generally 55 percent fructose, although in some sodas fructose may be as high as 65 percent.

At the urging of sugar-beet growers in the United States, President Ronald Reagan, in May 1982, slashed the quotas placed on the importation of cane sugar, increasing its price to double what it cost in other countries. HFCS, therefore, became more attractive to food and beverage manufacturers. By 1984 Coca-Cola, Pepsi, and most other soda manufacturers had completely shifted to HFCS to sweeten their beverages. HFCS was also incorporated into a wide variety of other processed products, such as ketchup, cookies, pies, cakes, and candies.

Since 1973 the consumption of HFCS has soared 4,000 percent; it represents approximately 50 percent of the sweetener consumed in the United States. Americans down an average of 55 pounds of HFCS per year, and high-fructose corn syrup is also used in commercial foods and beverages produced in other countries. Although HFCS is chemically similar to table sugar (which has 50 percent fructose and 50 percent glucose), critics worry about its potentially deleterious health effects. A 2009 review of the literature on research into HFCS in the *Journal of Nutrition* concluded that HFCS may raise "insulin sensitivity, triglyceride and lipoprotein levels, and glycated protein levels" (Murphy, 2009). Another study, published in 2010 in *Cancer Research,* suggested an association between the consumption of fructose and pancreatic cancer. A study published in 2012 indicated that consuming HFCS may result in health consequences more serious than those arising from excessive amounts of natural sugar (Goran et al., 2012). To date, however, studies are insufficient to prove that HFCS is any less healthful than other types of sweeteners.

Due to the sweetener's poor image, however, several companies have removed HFCS from their products, or are at least considering such action. Many soft-drink companies, including PepsiCo, Dr Pepper, and the Coca-Cola Co., have reformulated their beverages, substituting sucrose for HFCS, and cane sugar soda is available in many countries.

See also FRUCTOSE; GLUCOSE; STARCH; SUGAR BEET; and SUGARCANE.

Bray, George A., Samara Joy Nielsen, and Barry M. Popkin. "Consumption of High-Fructose Corn Syrup in Beverages May Play a Role in the Epidemic of Obesity." *American Journal of Clinical Nutrition* 79 (April 2004): 537–543.

Goran, Michael I., Stanley J. Ulijaszek, and Emily E. Ventura. "High Fructose Corn Syrup and Diabetes Prevalence: A Global Perspective." *Journal of Global Health* 8, no. 1 (2013): 55–64.

Johnson, Richard J., with Timothy Gower and Elizabeth Gollub. *The Sugar Fix: The High-Fructose Fallout That Is Making You Fat and Sick.* New York: Pocket Books, 2009.

Kalamaras, Paula M., and Paul T. Kraly. *Sugar and Sweeteners: Trends and Developments in Foods and Beverages.* Norwalk, Conn.: Business Communications, 2003.

Murphy, Suzanne P. "The State of the Science on Dietary Sweeteners Containing Fructose: Summary and Issues to Be Resolved," *Journal of Nutrition* 139, no. 6 (June 2009): 1269S–1270S. http://jn.nutrition.org/content/139/6/1269S.full

Andrew F. Smith

cornstarch

See STARCH.

cosmetics, sugar in, falls into three broad categories: exfoliation, depilatory, and luster.

Exfoliation refers to the removal of dead skin cells, using abrasive particles suspended in oil or fat or stuck to the surface of a glove. The supposed benefits include a "younger, glowing appearance," although excessive exfoliation can lead to substantial skin damage. For those who nevertheless wish to abrade dead skin cells rather than wait for them to slough off naturally, sugar is a reasonable choice. Sharp-edged sugar crystals are suspended in olive oil or trapped in a bar of soap (either in commercial or domestic preparations). The crystals cut away the dry cells, but because they are soluble in water, they do not retain their edge long enough to cause serious damage to the skin.

The use of sugar in depilation makes a lot more sense. In the normal wax-based processes, hot wax can burn the skin; it can also adhere to the skin and cause damage when peeled off. Sugar depilation avoids this injury, since the depilatory material is used at or slightly above room temperature. The material, which can be made at home or purchased ready-made, is a paste prepared from eight parts sugar, one part water, and one part lemon juice (which helps to prevent the sugar from crystallizing as the mixture cools). The mixture is heated to around 248°F (120°C) and then left to cool, forming a thick paste or gel. To use it, the skin is first dusted with a light sprinkling of cornstarch or other powder so that the material will adhere only to the protruding hairs. The paste or gel is then applied. A strip of porous cloth is pressed onto the paste and then pulled off in the direction opposite to the hair growth, bringing hairs and paste along with it. The technique works well, although the removal process is purportedly still painful.

Finally, the presence of sugar in some cosmetics has been claimed to help produce surface luster; adding sugar to lipstick can make it appear more shiny. There may also be indirect effects, as in La Mer's Face and Body Gradual Tan, about which product innovator Loretta Miraglia has been quoted as saying, "The secret in this sauce is sugar. It creates a much redder color development—versus yellow—which is more natural and appealing." It is likely, in fact, that the dissolved sugar changes the refractive index of the water, which in turn affects the color balance of light scattered from the suspended droplets and particles (this trick has also been used by beverage manufacturers to enhance the color of drinks containing beta carotene). The sugar in and of itself is unlikely to produce such colors unless it is heated to unacceptably high temperatures, as in the final scene of the 1989 film *The Cook, The Thief, His Wife and Her Lover*, where a human body is coated with what appears to be a sugar glaze. But that, really, would be going too far in the use of sugar to promote beauty.

Shapiro, Bee. "Going Sunless but Glowing." *New York Times*, 26 June 2013. http://www.nytimes.com/2013/06/27/fashion/going-sunless-but-glowing.html?_r=0.

Toi, Ms. *Sugar Hair Removal: The Complete Book.* Kindle ed. Amazon, 2012.

Len Fisher

cotton candy, a confection made from melted sugar that has been flavored and finely spun into soft, pillowy threads, is a popular novelty dessert at festivals and fairs. Although production of the sweet was

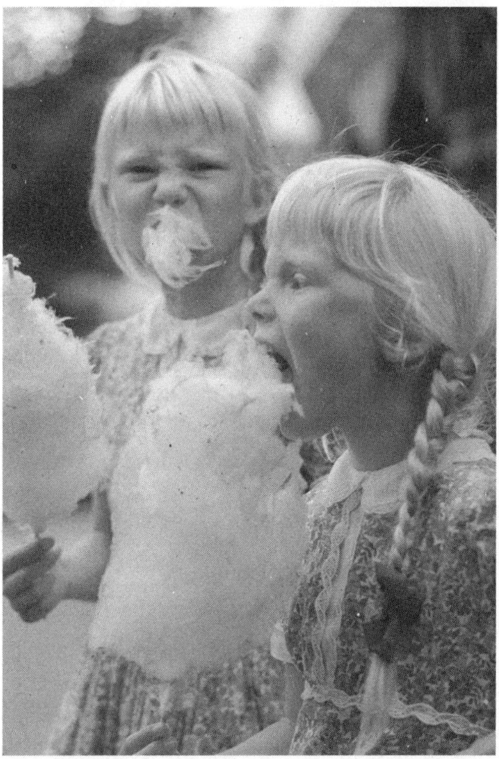

Cotton candy is made by melting flavored, dyed sugar until it turns liquid and then spinning it by machine into fine threads. Here, two girls in Copenhagen, Denmark, eat large, sticky swirls of cotton candy. GILBERT M. GROSVENOR / NATIONAL GEOGRAPHIC CREATIVE

not mechanized until 1897, versions of spun sugar threads are recorded as early as the sixteenth century.

A recipe for a "silver web" made from spun sugar, intended to adorn sweetmeats, appears in the 1769 edition of Elizabeth Raffald's *The Experienced English Housekeeper*. Recipes for a "gold web" and a dessert of spun sugar are also included. The late-nineteenth-century *Skuse's Complete Confectioner* suggests using spun sugar as a window dressing in shops. Charles Henry King's *Cakes, Cake Decorations and Desserts: A Manual for Housewives, Simple and Up-to-date* (1896) includes instructions for making large spun-sugar ornaments, as well as using the threads to decorate charlotte russes and tarts, and as handles for meringue baskets. See MERINGUE and TART.

Machine-spun sugar was invented in 1897 by Nashville, Tennessee, dentist William Morrison and confectioner John C. Wharton. They introduced their invention nationally at the 1904 World's Fair in St. Louis, calling the spun sugar it produced "fairy floss." Although at 25 cents per box, the cost of the dainty confection was half the admission to the fair itself, the floss was a wild success, and the duo sold 68,655 boxes.

In 1921 another dentist, Joseph Lascaux from New Orleans, engineered a similar machine, patenting the spun sugar it produced under the name "cotton candy" (a term that had first appeared in print only a year earlier). This name stuck in the United States, although spun sugar is still referred to as "fairy floss" in other parts of the world.

Gold Medal Products Co. debuted its model of a cotton-candy machine in 1949. It featured a spring base that made it more functional than earlier versions. Today, most cotton candy is still made using a Gold Medal machine, although subsequent models have been automated and streamlined. While much of the cotton candy produced in the United States is sold at festival and fairs, the newer machinery has made the candy more accessible, and it may now be found at shopping malls and stores. See FAIRS. Some high-end restaurants are now offering miniature versions of cotton candy for dessert, bringing what started out as carnival fare into the realm of haute cuisine.

To make the confection, sugar—often dyed and flavored—is melted until it becomes liquid. It is then spun in the machine, which forces the liquid through tiny holes that shape and cool the sugar. Once cooled, the sugar becomes a fine solid thread. These threads are collected and spun around a paper cone or stick to be served as a fluffy, giant mound. Although cotton candy is usually artificially flavored and colored in pink or blue hues, a regional variation is Vermont's maple cotton candy, flavored with pure maple sugar and boasting a natural off-white color. Because it is composed largely of air, a typical serving of cotton candy weighs only 1 ounce and contains about 105 calories.

Liberman, Sherri. *American Food by the Decades*. Westport, Conn.: Greenwood, 2011.

Mariani, John F. *The Encyclopedia of American Food and Drink*. New York: Lebhar-Friedman, 1999.

Toussaint-Samat, Maguelonne. *A History of Food*. New York: Wiley-Blackwell, 2008.

Emily Hilliard

court confectioners were an indispensable part of noble European households from the Renaissance right through the nineteenth century. Depending on the time and place, they created preserved fruit, candy, ice cream, and sugar sculptures, as well as numerous other sweet delights. Because they worked in private households, their raw materials were not subject to guild restrictions that defined what a confectioner was permitted to make. Since their role was expressly to turn expensive sugar into objects of conspicuous consumption, they were also not limited by the more mundane monetary considerations of artisans working for a broader market.

As the requirements of noble kitchens expanded in the Italian Renaissance, food preparation was increasingly divided into hot and cold, into kitchen and pantry (*cucina* and *credenza* in Italian). For both practical reasons (the ambient temperature of the work space was a factor, and the equipment differed) and as a matter of style, courses alternated between the two departments. Much like the musicians, painters, and other artisans in the pay of the nobleman, the role of the confectioner was to decorate the table and amuse the guests, often with impressively crafted sugar sculptures. See SUGAR SCULPTURE. Most of the Italian confectioners remain anonymous, but Luigi Fedele, who first worked at the court of Ferrara in the second half of the seventeenth century and later created sugar sculptures for Pope Innocent X, was so renowned that he had a madrigal composed in his honor.

The role of culinary display, if anything, only increased in France in the seventeenth and eighteenth centuries as courtiers tried to outdo each other at table. Here the confectioners had to keep an eye on the latest fashion. In *La science du maitre d'hotel confiseur* (The Techniques of the Steward-Confectioner, 1750) the prolific Menon explains, "The art of the *office* (pantry), the same as every other, has been improved through gradual changes; in so much as the earlier work is almost useless to today's pantry." Perhaps the best known of the eighteenth-century confectioners was Joseph Gilliers, the author of *Le Cannameliste français* (The French Sugar-Worker, 1751) who worked for a time as chief confectioner to the expatriate Polish king Stanisław Leszczyński. See GILLIERS, JOSEPH.

Elsewhere in Europe, noble courts first imitated Italy, and then France. Few, however, had the resources of Versailles. In Vienna, the Habsburg court depended on confectioners in town to supply many of its needs. The cost of purpose-made sugar sculptures gradually led to porcelain substitutes, most notably from Meissen. In Dresden, Munich, and Vienna, the court confectioner's job was increasingly to provide treats to display on ornate porcelain centerpieces rather than to make the centerpieces themselves.

As the style of service changed from the buffet-like *service à la française* to the sequential *service à la russe* subsequent to the French Revolution, the visual display requirements of confectionery became more modest. See DESSERT. Society changed too. At the beginning of his career, the great pastry chef Antonin Carême (1783–1833) created massive table ornaments, *pièces montées*, for the imperial court of Napoleon; at the end of his career, he created confections for the tables of the Rothschilds. See CARÊME, MARIE-ANTOINE.

See also EPERGNES and GUILDS.

Di Schino, June. "The Triumph of Sugar Sculpture in Italy 1500–1700." In *Look and Feel: Studies in Texture, Appearance and Incidental Characteristics of Food: Proceedings of the Oxford Symposium on Food and Cookery 1993*, edited by Harlan Walker, pp. 203–206. Totnes, U.K.: Prospect, 1994.

Haslinger, Ingrid. "Von Confecturn, Chocolade und Gefrornem Die Ehemaligen K. U. K. Hofzuckerbacker." In *Der süsse Luxus: Die Hofzuckerbäckerei und die ehemaligen K.U.K. Hofzuckerbäcker: Eine Ausstellung des Kulturkreises Looshaus*. Vienna: Kulturkreis Looshaus, 1996.

Michael Krondl

Cracker Jack, a confection made of popcorn, roasted peanuts, and molasses, was among the culinary wonders introduced at the 1893 World's Columbian Exposition in Chicago, alongside Pabst beer and Juicy Fruit gum. By 1896 Frederick and Louis Rueckheim, brothers and German immigrants who had started a local popcorn and candy business in 1872, had perfected the recipe and called it Cracker Jack—slang for "excellent" or "first-rate." They applied for a trademark on 17 February of that year, and it was issued 36 days later.

The brothers' marketing acumen was evident from the beginning, when the firm rolled out a national promotional campaign with the simple, alluring slogan, "The More You Eat, The More You Want." Cracker Jack was originally sold in large wooden tubs to retailers, but its wax-sealed package, which was developed in 1899, allowed consistent portion size and, more important, kept the contents crisp and fresh. That innovation, followed by moisture-proofing three years later, was suggested by Henry Eckstein, a friend and former general superintendent of the soap and lard manufacturer N. K. Fairbank Company. He did not actually invent the packaging, but paid a German scientist $500 to teach him how to make wax paper—and then improved on the process. The change (and subsequent advertising push) caused sales to skyrocket; the company was rechristened Rueckheim Brothers & Eckstein in 1903.

The new name coincided with expansion into a factory that covered an entire Chicago city block. By 1912 the company employed about 450 women and girls and 250 men and boys. See CHILD LABOR. That same year, redeemable coupons for adult clothing and goods such as watches and sewing machines, which

A vintage Cracker Jack box. This roasted peanut, popcorn, and molasses confection was first introduced in 1893 at the World's Columbian Exposition in Chicago.

had been given away with each box of Cracker Jack, were replaced by tiny trinkets and other prizes for children. With the success of this marketing ploy, the firm, which also made marshmallows and candies, became the Cracker Jack Company in 1922.

The "Sailor Jack" logo, introduced in Cracker Jack advertisements in 1916, was modeled after Frederick Rueckheim's grandson, Robert. In 1918 the logo was added to a red, white, and blue box, a symbol of an immigrant family's patriotism in a city that had become a hotbed of anti-German sentiment. Company ads exhorted consumers to save sugar and wheat and promoted Cracker Jack as "ideal wartime food," whether as breakfast cereal or an afternoon energizer. Men were advised to enlist in the Navy, just like Sailor Jack.

Cracker Jack was a moneymaker for concessionaires at theaters, parks, carnival midways, circuses, and, most famously, baseball parks. The earliest known connection between the game and the confection is an advertisement on an 1896 scorecard (in the digital collection of the National Baseball Hall of Fame & Museum) for a game played at Atlantic City, New Jersey, between the Atlantic City Base Ball Club and the Cuban Giants.

Cracker Jack was first sold at a Major League ballpark in 1907, and the two became inextricably linked in consumers' minds with the publication of the 1908 song "Take Me Out to the Ball Game." During a trip on the New York City elevated subway, vaudeville songwriter Jack Norworth (who authored "Shine On, Harvest Moon" among other popular standards) was inspired by the sight of a game advertised on the marquee at the Polo Grounds and penned the lyrics, which include "Buy me some peanuts and cracker jack / I don't care if I never get back." Tin Pan Alley composer Albert Von Tilzer wrote the jaunty melody. Neither man attended a Major League game until decades after the song was written. That the song is sung at every professional ballpark dates from the 1970s, when Chicago White Sox owner Bill Veeck encouraged broadcaster Harry Caray to serenade the fans during the seventh-inning stretch.

Early Cracker Jack baseball cards are greatly prized by collectors for their beauty and rarity. Printed in color, they feature players including Joe Jackson and Hall of Famers Ty Cobb, Honus Wagner, and Christy Mathewson, set against a red background. The 144 cards from the first series, printed in 1914, were available only inside boxes of Cracker Jack. They are scarcer than the cards of the following year, which could be ordered all at once, by mail; a very fine complete 1914 set commanded $502,775 at auction in 2010.

With the Rueckheims' savvy idea of placing a toy surprise inside each box of Cracker Jack, they parlayed a fun snack into a new form of entertainment—and created an American childhood ritual that gave great joy. Countless games, miniature books, spinning tops, rocking horses (as well as monkeys, bears, ducks, etc.), paper snap toys, acrobats on toothpicks, and optical illusion "Twirlies" remain treasured by collectors to this day. See CHILDREN'S CANDY.

The man who invented the little contrivances in their heyday, from 1938 to 1965, and had them manufactured in tin, paper, or plastic from his hand-carved wooden models, was C. Carey Cloud, a former cartoonist, illustrator, adman, and art director. In a 1979 "On the Road" interview with Charles Kuralt for *CBS Evening News*, he explained that he got started in the depths of the Depression when a friend said, "You're an artist, you can probably make a living designing Cracker Jack prizes." Cloud replied, "So I designed some little tin nodding-head animals. And took them out and got prices from die stampers and such...went to Cracker Jack, and they bought six million. And I thought, Where have I been all this time?" According to the inventor's best estimate, he created more than 700 million Cracker Jack toys, including the first all-plastic whistle.

The Cracker Jack Company remained in the Rueckheim family until 1964. It was sold to Borden, which, in turn, sold it in 1997 to the Frito-Lay division of food-and-beverage giant PepsiCo. In addition to increasing the peanuts in the "original" recipe (the peanut-to-popcorn ratio had become increasingly skewed in popcorn's favor), Frito-Lay rolled out Kettle Corn and Butter Toffee flavors in 2013. That year also brought Cracker Jack prizes with digital components, a Cracker Jack app that can be used to play "nostalgic" games (baseball, pinball) on smartphones and iPads; and a new brand called Cracker Jack'D with more intense flavors (some laced with caffeine), developed to appeal specifically to young male millennials.

See also UNITED STATES.

Chmelik, Samantha. "Frederick Rueckheim (1846–1937)." *Immigrant Entrepreneurship: German-American Business Biographies*. http://www.immigrantentrepreneurship.org/entry.php?rec=158.
Fussell, Betty. *The Story of Corn*. New York: Knopf, 1992.
Jaramillo, Alex. *Cracker Jack Prizes*. New York: Abbeville, 1989.
Martin, Dick. "The Man Who Gave Us Cracker Jack Toys." *Chronicle-Tribune Magazine*, 8 July 1973. http://www.c-carey-cloud.com/news-articles/man-who-gave-us-cracker-jack-toys.htm.
Smith, Andrew F. *Popped Culture: A Social History of Popcorn in America*. Washington, D.C., and London: Smithsonian Institution Press, 2001.
Strasberg, Andy, Bob Thompson, and Tim Wiles. *Baseball's Greatest Hit: The Story of "Take Me Out to the Ball Game."* New York: Hal Leonard, 2008.
Wilson, Mark R., Stephen R. Porter, and Janice L. Reiff. "Cracker Jack Co." In *Encyclopedia of Chicago*. Chicago: Chicago Historical Society, 2005. http://www.encyclopedia.chicagohistory.org/pages/2630.html.

Jane Lear

cream is the thick, fat-rich part of milk that rises to the top when fresh milk is left to stand. It can then be skimmed off for use as an enormously versatile substance in sweet dishes, where it provides a voluptuous contrast to crisp pastry, soft fruit, and jellied textures. There is no substitute for the distinctive flavor, smooth consistency, and pleasing mouthfeel of fresh cream—qualities it contributes to many desserts, especially silky custard-type dishes and ice creams. It is also frequently used in baking. Liquid or whipped cream is often served as an accompaniment to fruit or chocolate desserts.

Higher-fat cream, whipped until it holds its shape, is used for decorative piping; it also garnishes many desserts and features strongly in Central European cake and coffee traditions. Once whipped, cream can be folded into other mixtures; it lightens cheesecake fillings, makes mousses and fools airy, fills crisp pastries and brittle meringues, and serves as the basis for frothy syllabub. Combined with melted chocolate, cream makes a rich ganache mixture for layering in tortes. See TORTE.

The finest cream comes from cows that are humanely treated and carefully fed. Holstein cattle are the most common dairy breed worldwide because of their tremendous daily milk yield, but the Guernsey and Jersey breeds are considered the finest for the flavor, high butterfat content, and quality of their cream.

All cream, unless ultra-pasteurized, is highly perishable and should be stored in a closed container in the refrigerator, at the normal setting of 38° to 40°F (3° to 4°C). Regular cream lasts about ten days, but ultra-pasteurized can be kept for three to four weeks. Once opened, it should be handled like pasteurized cream.

Importance of Fat Content

The fat content determines the type of cream. Heavy cream has a butterfat content between 36 and 40 percent. High butterfat adds tenderness and moisture to baked goods. Many scones are called cream scones because they are made with cream. It is possible to substitute some other type of milk for the cream in these recipes and still have an acceptable result, but the scones will not be nearly as tender or moist as those made with heavy cream. Heavy cream is also used to make whipping cream. The fat is what helps stabilize cream after it is whipped, creating a more stable foam base that is easier to fold into a

This 1954 advertisement promoting the consumption of dairy products in Sweden uses the country's beloved summer berries to suggest that everything tastes "Twice as good with cream!"

mousse or curd. The fat also prevents the cream from freezing too hard when it is used in ice cream, leading to a creamier finished product.

Both the amount of fat in the cream and its temperature influence how well it will whip. Heavy whipping cream increases more in volume than light whipping cream, so a cream with a high fat content should be used for best results. For successful whipping, the cream, bowl, and beaters should be well chilled. Other ingredients, such as sugar or vanilla, should be added near the end of the whipping. Overwhipping can cause the cream to turn to butter. Lightly overwhipped cream can be corrected by gently folding in additional cold cream by hand.

There are three stages of whipped cream, each with a different use. The first, a light whip, is used as a topping for fruit dessert such as pies, crisp, or tarts. The cream should be whipped only until just thickened and semifluid like stirred yogurt. This more fluid state has a softer and lighter finish than a stiff cream. It can be lightly sweetened with sugar and flavored with pure vanilla extract or other complementary flavors. For folding into other ingredients, the cream should be whipped further to soft peaks. Stiff peaks are best for decorating and piping with a pastry bag, or for forming a quenelle of cream for plated desserts or for decorating a torte or tart.

Grades and Types of Cream

Several grades of cream are available in the United States. Some are available in other countries, but even in the English-speaking world they may be known by different names; for instance, heavy cream is called double cream in British English.

Half-and-half is a mixture of whole milk and cream that contains at least 10.5 percent but no more than 18 percent butterfat. It does not whip, but it can be used in many recipes instead of heavy cream for lower-fat cooking.

Light cream or coffee cream contains at least 18 percent but no more than 30 percent butterfat; it usually contains 20 percent butterfat. If it has 30 percent butterfat, it will whip, but the foam and structure will be weak.

Light whipping cream, the form most commonly available, contains at least 30 percent but no more than 36 percent butterfat. Cream must contain at least 30 percent butterfat in order to whip. Whipping cream will double in volume and is generally used as a topping.

Heavy or whipping cream must contain at least 36 percent butterfat. It can be readily whipped and will retain its whipped state longer than light whipping cream. Ultra-heavy cream or manufacturer's cream contains 36 to 40 percent butterfat. Avoid heavy creams that contain glycerides, which are added as emulsifiers, as is carrageenan for thickening and consistency.

Ultra-pasteurized cream has been briefly heated to temperatures up to 300°F (149°C) to kill microorganisms. It has a longer shelf life than regular cream but does not whip as well. It can contain additives and stabilizers, which impart a bitter flavor that must be masked by additional sugar and vanilla extract. See VANILLA.

Sour cream results from the addition of lactic acid bacteria to pasteurized cream with at least 18 percent butterfat to sour and thicken the cream. See SOUR CREAM.

Crème fraîche is heavy cream that has been slightly soured with bacterial cultures; it is neither as sour nor as thick as sour cream. It is a traditional product of Normandy in northern France.

Clotted cream is made by gently heating rich, unpasteurized milk until a semisolid layer of cream forms on the surface. After cooling, the thickened cream is removed. In the United Kingdom, clotted cream is strongly associated with the southwestern part of England, where it is eaten with scones and jam for a traditional cream tea. A similar product, called *kaymak*, is found in parts of Southwest Asia, where it is eaten with fruit preserves and sweet dishes, and used in pastries.

See also CAKE DECORATING and MILK.

Corriher, Shirley O. *Bake Wise*. New York: Scribner, 2008.

Dodge, Jim, with Elaine Ratner. *Baking with Jim Dodge*. New York: Simon & Schuster, 1991.

Mendelson, Anne. *Milk: The Surprising Story of Milk through the Ages*. New York: Knopf, 2009.

Jim Dodge

cream pie is a single-crust pie with a rich, sweet, custard-like filling, commonly thickened with flour or cornstarch and/or eggs, and in modern times also often having a whipped cream topping. Pies with a custard-type filling have been known since medieval times in Britain and Europe. *The Forme of Cury*, a cookery manuscript compiled around 1390 by the master cooks of King Richard II, contains a recipe for "daryols," which comprised "coffyns" (pie shells) filled with a mixture of cream, almond milk, sugar, and saffron and baked in an oven. See DARIOLE.

A huge range of flavorings and additional ingredients may be included in a cream pie, and recipes show much overlap with other sweet pies such as cheesecakes, sugar pies, and chiffon pies. See CHEESECAKE and CHIFFON PIE.

The first American recipe found to date that is called Cream Pie appears in *The Improved Housewife* (1844) by Mrs. A. L. Webster. It is filled with a thick egg custard "made very sweet," with raisins added and flavored with nutmeg, mace, and citron. A very simple recipe in *The Young Housekeeper's Friend* (1855) by Mrs. Cornelius instructs only to "boil and sweeten the cream, flavor it with grated lemon, and bake in a paste, about as long as pumpkin pie."

Several well-known regional variations have special status in the United States. Hoosier Sugar Cream Pie is the official state pie of Indiana, and Chess Pie is an intriguingly named popular treat in the southern states. The name and form of the latter most likely derived from the seventeenth-century English "cheesecakes" made without cheese, but having a similar texture and consistency. A strange but famous anomaly is Boston Cream Pie, which is not a pie at all, but a cake with a custard filling; it has been known since 1855. See BOSTON CREAM PIE.

See also PIE.

Smith, Andrew F., ed. *Oxford Encyclopedia of Food and Drink in America*. New York: Oxford University Press, 2013.
Willard, Pat. "Pie & Pastry." http://www.foodtimeline.org/foodpies.html.

Janet Clarkson

cream puff

See PASTRY, CHOUX.

crema catalana

See CRÈME BRÛLÉE.

crème anglaise

See CUSTARD.

crème brûlée

crème brûlée is a sweet egg-yolk custard made with cream. The cream, egg yolk, and sugar mixture is cooked, poured into individual ramekins, poached in a bain-marie (hot water bath), and then chilled. When the custard is firm, the top is covered with a layer of sugar that is browned by means of a salamander, broiler or butane torch (*brûlé* means "burnt" in French), forming a hard, caramelized crust on the surface.

The dessert is ubiquitous on restaurant menus today in the United States and in Europe, but its history is anything but straightforward. The English, French, and Catalonians all lay claim to the origin of the dessert. Many have attributed the creation of crème brûlée to the kitchens of Trinity College, Cambridge University in the nineteenth century, but this cannot be true. Although custards topped with caramelized sugar appeared in eighteenth-century English cookbooks, notably John Nott's *Cooks and Confectioners Dictionary* (1723), the origin of the recipe *in print* appears to be French. The British food writer Elizabeth David traced Nott's recipe for "Burnt Cream" to François Massialot's Crème Brûlée in *Cuisinier royal et bourgeois* (1691). The English translation of Massialot's book, *The Court and Country Cook* (1702), includes the crème brûlée recipe as "Burnt Cream." Unless a seventeenth-century precedent is found, Massialot seems to have been first in English as well as in French. This early recipe calls for milk, not cream, and the custard bakes in an oven, not a bain-marie. Massialot neglects to tell the cook to add sugar in the cooking stage, but refers to the sugar in the custard later in the recipe. If the omission was a mistake, it was never corrected.

Somewhat confusingly, Massialot has a similar recipe called Crême à l'Angloise in his *Nouvelle Instructions pour les Confitures* (1740 edition), which, like the modern crème brûlée, does call for the sugar to be cooked with the egg yolks. Elizabeth Raffald's recipe for "Burnt Cream" in *The Experienced English Housekeeper* (1769) is similar to Massialot's Crême à l'Angloise, except that she adds beaten egg whites to the custard mixture. The apparent name change for the same dessert prompted the editors of *Petits Propos Culinaires* to question whether French cooks got the idea to credit the English for the dish. However, Massialot's crème brûlée seems to disappear from French cookbooks only after the three-volume 1750 edition of *Le cuisinier royal*, not before; French cooks did not abandon the name crème brûlée. Although François Menon's *Soupers de la cour* (1755) contains a recipe titled Crème brûlée, it calls for cream, egg yolks, "a little sugar," and egg whites (producing a thinner custard), and when it is finished it resembles a warm crème caramel. After Menon, crème brûlée as a dessert name pops up in a few French cookbooks, but the recipes do not resemble either eighteenth-century version.

Crème brûlée is conspicuously absent from the major nineteenth- and early-twentieth-century French cookbooks, including Montagné's *Larousse Gastronomique* (1938). Nor is burnt cream common in nineteenth-century British cookbooks. Crème brûlée surfaces in Eleanor L. Jenkinson's *Ocklye Cookery Book* (1909), closely following Massialot's original recipe. *The Ocklye Cookery Book* is at least one source of the Trinity College origins story. Dione Lucas's *Cordon Bleu Cookbook* (1947) includes crème brûlée among the recipes she learned at the École du Cordon Bleu cooking school in Paris and later taught at the London École du Cordon Bleu, which she cofounded. However, the dessert was not particularly common, judging from prominent English-language cookbooks of the time. Crème brûlée reappears in a few English-language French cookbooks in the 1960s and 1970s, notably *Gourmet's Menu Cookbook* (1963) and Samuel and Narcissa Chamberlain's *Flavor of France* (2nd edition, 1969). Henri-Paul Pellaprat, codirector of the Paris École du Cordon Bleu and a prolific cookbook author, includes it in his *Everyday French Cooking for the American Home* (1978). Several twentieth-century southern cookbooks include the dessert, a few noting that it is a New Orleans specialty. By the time Patricia Wells published *Bistro Cooking* in 1989, she included a crème brûlée recipe, noting that it "seems to be one of the world's favorite desserts, at least in our time."

One plausible account of the late twentieth-century surge in the popularity of this dessert goes as follows: In 1975 Sirio Maccioni opened New York's Le Cirque restaurant and hired pastry chef Dieter Schorner. In his memoir, Maccioni recalls that "the most important dessert of the Schorner period was crème brûlée" (2004, p. 216). Maccioni takes credit "for reintroducing the dessert... and making it the most famous and by far the most popular dessert in restaurants from Paris to Peoria" (p. 216). The Catalonian dessert *crema catalana* is made the same way as today's crème brûlée. Maccioni claims it was *crema catalana*, which he tasted on a trip to Barcelona, that inspired him to return to New York and experiment with recipes. From there, he and Schorner created "Crème Brûlée Le Cirque."

See also CUSTARD.

Maccioni, Sirio, and Peter Elliot. *Sirio: The Story of My Life and Le Cirque.* Hoboken, N.J.: Wiley, 2004.

Petits Propos Culinaires 31 (1989): 61–63.

Kyri W. Claflin

crème caramel

See FLAN (PUDÍM).

crêpes

See PANCAKES.

crescent is the English term applied to baked goods whose form resembles a waxing moon. This use of the word first entered the language in the late nineteenth century as a loan translation of the French *croissant* and occurs alongside the French word, which was directly borrowed into English at roughly the same time. See CROISSANT. "Crescent" is also applied to the many similarly shaped baked goods of Central Europe that predate and presumably gave rise to the French croissant. Textual and linguistic evidence points to the origin of this family in the Bavarian dialect area of southern Germany and Austria, where *Kipfel* (sing. and pl.) and *Kipferl* (pl. *Kipferln*) are traditional crescent-shaped items; the former is attested in a text by the late thirteenth century. In Switzerland one finds the closely related *Gipfeli.* The names of these crescent-shaped items are derived from the word meaning "wagon stanchion"; such stanchions were typically curved and ended in a point (as can be seen in the heraldic use of the term *Kipfel*), thus resembling a horn.

The baked good itself expanded in two directions, with different approaches to naming. To the east and south of the South German/Austrian core area, especially in regions formerly linked politically to the Austro-Hungarian Empire, the name *Kipfel* was generally borrowed. Thus, we find Hungarian *kiflik,* Slovenian *kiflin,* Serbo-Croatian *kiflice,* and northern and northeastern Italian forms (*chiffel, chifeleti,* etc. in Friuli, Trieste, and Trentino; *chiffel* in Lombardy; *chifferi* in Liguria). It is even the name of a crescent-shaped pasta (*chifferi*). To the north and northeast of the core area, one finds instead native words that are derivatives—especially diminutives—of the word for "horn": in German *Hörnchen,* Czech *rohlíky/rohlíčky,* Slovak *rožky,* Polish *rogale* and *rogaliki;* the Yiddish name for crescents, *rugelach,* is borrowed from Polish. Interestingly, Serbo-Croatian includes, alongside the borrowed *kiflice,* the diminutive of "horn" in this application, *roščići.* The Italian word *cornetto/cornetti* (diminutive of "horn") may belong here too, though today it is essentially a regional name for the French-style croissant.

Central European crescents are typically made by cutting a triangular piece of dough that is then rolled and curved. Both sweet and savory varieties are widespread, and a range of dough types are employed: bread dough, short pastry dough, brioche dough, even potato dough. Sweet versions are often filled with nuts (especially walnuts), poppy seeds, fruit preserves, or sweetened cheese and can also be topped with powdered sugar and/or seeds or crushed nuts; savory versions are sometimes topped with salt, caraway, and the like, and used as sandwich rolls.

See also CHEESE, FRESH; FRUIT PRESERVES; NUTS; and POPPY SEED.

Fintor, Yolanda Nagy. *Hungarian Cookbook: Old World Recipes for New World Cooks.* New York: Hippocrene, 2001.
Metzger, Christine, ed. *Culinaria Germany.* Cologne: Könemann, 2006.

Anthony F. Buccini

Crisco

See SHORTENING.

crisp

See FRUIT DESSERTS, BAKED.

croissant, in its classic formulation, derives from a *pâte feuilletee* dough that also includes yeast and a larger portion of butter. Traditionally, it has a crescent shape (*croissant* being French for crescent), although with the popularization of industrially produced versions, the pure butter croissant has recently lost its curve. See CRESCENT.

Few foods have such potent emblematic power. Although produced internationally, croissants evoke France, bringing to mind visions of beret-wearing Frenchmen dipping their morning pastry into a steaming bowl of café au lait. Fewer foods still have histories as murky and steeped in erroneous culinary "fakelore." The most frequently repeated legend attributes the invention of the croissant to Viennese bakers, who during the 1683 siege of Vienna by the Ottoman Turks purportedly created a pastry inspired by the crescent of their enemy's flag. Alternatively, this same tale is recast during the Ottoman siege of Budapest of 1686.

The Vienna story has always held greater sway because it implicitly explains the origin of the word "viennoiserie," which the French use to refer to all croissant-related breakfast pastries. For this same reason, popular legend attributes the croissant's introduction in France to Marie Antoinette because she was Viennese. No evidence supports any of these tales, although crescent-shaped pastries had long existed across Europe, some dating back to the ancient world. The Austrian Kipferl can be documented to the thirteenth century, and the 1549 coronation banquet given to Catherine de' Medici by the Bishops of Paris included forty "gateaux en croissants." However, the croissant's *pâte feuilletée* dough dates only to the later seventeenth century.

The croissant appears to have been launched in Paris between 1837 and 1839 by the Viennese baker August Zang, whose Boulangerie Viennoise on the rue Richelieu also popularized the term "viennoiserie." Although the fashion for these pastries spread quickly, the first recognizable recipe for a croissant did not appear until the beginning of the twentieth century.

See also AUSTRIA-HUNGARY and VIENNA.

Chevallier, Jim. *August Zang and the French Croissant: How Viennoiserie Came to France.* 2d ed. North Hollywood, Calif.: Chez Jim, 2009.

Carolin C. Young

croquembouche (also croque-en-bouche) is a French dessert made by sticking together cream puffs with caramel. In the nineteenth century the pastry was formed using a cylindrical or other mold, though today it is more common to stack the puffs into a tall, pointed tower. Croquembouche literally means "crack (or crunch) in the mouth"—due to the consistency of the hardened caramel.

A pastry bearing this name became popular in the early nineteenth century, its invention being—like so many others—attributed to Antonin Carême. The great pastry chef does indeed give extensive instructions as well as several illustrations for very elaborate *pièces montées* called croquembouche in several of his cookbooks. See CARÊME, MARIE-ANTOINE.

In the nineteenth century the confections were not necessarily made with cream puffs. Alexandre Dumas, in his *Petit dictionnaire de cuisine* (1882), defines croquembouches as "pièces montées made with *croquignolles* [a crunchy cookie], *gimblettes* [jumbles, i.e., ring-shaped cookies], macarons, nougats and other crunchy pastries, which are combined with caramelized sugar and arranged on a base of puff pastry in the form of a large vessel [coupe]; this preparation is only used in the decoration of a ceremonial buffet table or as a buffet ornament for a grand ball." Glazed chestnuts and orange slices were also popular additions. The definition given by *Larousse Gastronomique* in the 1960s was not substantially different, even if the authors mention that the cream puff variant was the most common.

Today, the dessert is invariably made with cream puffs, though its ceremonial role persists. A croquembouche is commonly served at weddings, baptisms, and other occasions when an impressive presentation is required. Other than the tower form, confectioners advertise the pastry made in the form of churches, baby carriages, and even the hand of Fatima.

See also FRANCE and PASTRY, CHOUX.

Courchamps, compte de. *Néo-physiologie du goût, par ordre alphabétique; ou, Dictionnaire générale de la cuisine française, ancienne et moderne*. Paris: Bureau du Dictionnaire général de cuisine, 1839. http://catalog.hathitrust.org/api/volumes/oclc/40403364.html.

Montagné, Prosper. *Larousse Gastronomique: The Encyclopedia of Food, Wine & Cookery*. Edited by Charlotte Turgeon and Nina Froud. New York: Crown, 1961.

Michael Krondl

crostata

See GALETTE.

cupcakes are small, round, individual, iced snack cakes. Like muffins, they are sold with the fluted paper liners in which they are baked. The name "cupcake" was likely suggested by the cake called "cup cake," which emerged in the early nineteenth century as a quick and frugal alternative to pound cake, the best-loved company cake of the day. See POUND CAKE. In its original form, cup cake was a clever novelty in two different senses, both having to do with "cup." First, so it would be quick and easy to make, its ingredients were measured by the cup rather than weighed—then the usual practice when making cake—and, in most recipes, the measures followed some easily remembered formula, such as the favorite: 1 cup butter, 2 cups sugar, 3 cups flour, and 4 eggs. Second, to permit the cake to be made cheaply, with a minimum of butter and eggs, it was baked in individual molds, most often teacups or coffee cups, in which this rather dense, floury cake rose higher and lighter than if baked in a single large pan. The only alternative to cup baking would have been to leaven the cake with soda, but in the thinking of the day, soda was unacceptable in "nice" cakes meant for company, even quick, frugal cakes like cup cake. By the end of the nineteenth century, that thinking had changed, and cup cake, at least commonly, had acquired both soda and milk and had come to be baked in large pans, becoming the cake Americans still know today as the 1-2-3-4 yellow cake. See CAKE.

Some women, however, sometimes baked cup cake in individual molds simply because they liked the look of small cakes—and this is where the story of modern cupcakes begins. From the seventeenth century on, American women baked all sorts of fancy cakes in individual molds—not the teacups and coffee cups common for cup cake, but in individual tins made in a variety of clever shapes, including rounds, squares, oblongs, or hearts (which were particular favorites, especially for the popular "queen cakes"). When the modern individual cakes called "cup cakes" first emerged, at the end of the nineteenth century, they, too, were baked in such tins, as in Fannie Merritt Farmer's recipe in the original edition of *The Boston Cooking-School Cook Book*, published in 1896. Her recipe for Cup Cake (not yet Cupcake) does not hew to the measures of the classic 1-2-3-4 cup cake, which is to say, her "Cup Cake" is not actually cup cake. (Additionally, Farmer's recipe included an ingredient not traditionally found in cup cake recipes—mace—which connects her cup cake recipe back to the much earlier tradition of "spice cakes.") Farmer likely chose to title her recipe as she did because the cakes were baked individually, as cup cake once was and, in some quarters, continued to be. See FARMER, FANNIE. Within about 20 years, joined tins for the baking of cupcakes (as they were coming to be known) appeared on the market. (Joined muffin tins of a sort had debuted in the United States shortly after the Civil War.) See PANS.

Perhaps because of their small size, cupcakes began to be associated with children in the early decades of the twentieth century, whether they were made at home for birthday parties or purchased from a bakery. Ruth Wakefield's *Toll House Cook Book* (ca. 1936) includes a photo of cupcakes decorated with clown faces, and the many Betty Crocker cooking pamphlets from the 1940s aimed cupcakes at children. The 1967 edition of *Betty Crocker's Hostess Cookbook* offered the following advice: "Send leftover cookies or cupcakes home to your guests' children. You might even bake some extras with the children in mind." See BETTY CROCKER. A popular children's television show from the 1950s, *Howdy Doody,* featured a Hostess Cupcake ad, and Hostess created the character of Captain Cupcake in the 1970s to help advertise the tempting little snack cakes on television. (An anthropomorphic cupcake cop or sea captain, the cartoon character was sometimes seen with Hostess's first mascot, Twinkie the Kid.) Some elementary-school teachers even baked cupcakes for their students on special occasions. The growing embrace of muffin and cake mixes during the post–World War II period further spurred the cupcake's popularity, as did the burgeoning snack cake industry. The Taggart Baking Company of Indianapolis began making chocolate cupcakes in 1919. When the company was acquired by Continental Baking in 1925, the Hostess snack cake line was launched. Today, over 600 million Hostess cupcakes are sold annually across the United States. See HOSTESS.

The culture of the cupcake today has seen a shift away from cupcakes as a cheap snack food for kids to cupcakes as a trendy treat for adults. In fact, the global ascendancy of the cupcake appears to be tied to one adult cable-television series, *Sex and the City,* and one Greenwich Village bakery, Magnolia, which opened in 1996. In an episode from 2000, *Sex and the City*'s Carrie Bradshaw enjoyed a cupcake from Magnolia bakery. Since the airing of that segment, Bleecker Street, where the original bakery is located, has never been the same. Year-round, it is congested with tourists from all over the world. In a conciliatory gesture to the community, however, Magnolia stopped allowing buses to regularly disgorge hordes of visitors in search of the cupcake that Carrie Bradshaw ate.

It is hard to believe that the world's most famous cupcakes were, in fact, a complete accident. Seeking a use for the leftover cake batter from her signature coconut layer cakes, Alyssa Torry, Magnolia's original co-owner, began to bake cupcakes. Her customers loved them so much that she had no choice but to continue. Following the success of outposts in Chicago and Los Angeles, Magnolia opened its first non-U.S. store in Dubai in 2010. Cupcakeries hold particular appeal in countries where sweets are an important part of the culture, and where alcohol consumption is low or forbidden. Outside of the United States, besides offering a novelty, cupcake cafés tend to serve tea and coffee, avoiding the alcohol issue entirely. European capitals are now dotted with cupcake bakeries, and a similar trend is emerging in the Middle and Far East. Unlike ice cream, which appears to be equally popular among men and women, a higher percentage of cupcake customers tend to be women. The cakes' dainty, decorated nature may be the reason.

Like layer cakes, today's standard cupcakes are usually white, yellow, chocolate, or red velvet. The icing to cake ratio varies greatly, however. In some instances, the frosting is just a thin layer spread across the surface of the cupcake, but in others, icing is dexterously applied to a height of more than one inch. See ICING. Those who enjoy cupcakes frequently sample the icing before biting into the cake. The most popular icings are French buttercream and French meringue, but cream cheese and ganache frostings are gaining in popularity because they tend to be less sweet. Often a bakery will have a signature manner in which the frosting is applied, as well as signature colors, such as the pastel hues found at Magnolia Bakery.

While most cupcakes weigh in at approximately 3 ounces, some supersized cupcakes top the scales at six ounces and pack a whopping 900 calories per serving. Other bakeries opt for miniaturization and offer up one-bite, walnut-sized cupcakes containing fewer than 50 calories apiece. Mini cupcakes are not new. The culinary historian Meryle Evans fondly recalls the miniature cupcakes sold at Mrs. Holmes bakery in Asbury Park, New Jersey, before the outbreak of World War II.

The cupcake revolution may be an outgrowth of the 1970s food revolution that rejected the standardized, industrial version of bread and other baked goods. Many artisanal cupcake bakeries today use only high-quality, frequently locally sourced ingredients, and so, to a certain degree, the cupcake has come full circle, regaining its lost status as a fine cake. Cupcakeries can now be found in the chicest parts of cities both in the United States and abroad, and some brides and grooms are even rejecting traditional wedding cakes in favor of elaborately decorated cupcakes.

From Beverly Hills to Moscow, the humble cupcake has earned its place at the world's table due to its approachable, appealing nature.

See also BUTTERMILK; CAKE MIX; MERINGUE; and WEDDING CAKE.

Farmer, Fanny Merritt. *The Original Boston Cooking-School Cook Book, 1896*. New York: Weathervane, 1973.

Krondl, Michael. *Sweet Invention: A History of Dessert*. Chicago: Chicago Review Press, 2011.

Schmidt, Stephen. "Cakes." In *The Oxford Companion to American Food and Drink*, edited by Andrew F. Smith. New York: Oxford University Press, 2007.

Alexandra Leaf

custard is a mixture of whole milk, sugar, and eggs, generally flavored with vanilla and heated gently until thickened. Pale yellow to golden in color, it can be cooked in a saucepan, constantly stirred to make a sweet sauce that is sometimes known as custard sauce, boiled custard, or crème anglaise. See SAUCE. Alternatively, the raw mix can be poured into a dish or pastry crust to make a baked custard with a soft, set texture.

The name "custard" is also applied to a simpler, more convenient, and cheaper alternative made from packaged "custard powder" popular in the British Isles and Australia. These mixes contain no egg at all and are based on corn flour (cornstarch), flavorings, and colors, ready to mix with sugar and milk. Extremely popular in Britain, where they have come to be what most British people think of as custard, they are used mainly as sauces, substituting for egg-based custards. See UNITED KINGDOM.

The Science of Custards

Custard sauces that use egg as a thickener are notoriously tricky. Their texture relies on the coagulation of egg proteins as the mixture is heated. These proteins unfold to form a network that traps liquid, thereby yielding the velvety smoothness characteristic of custards. Beaten egg coagulates at about 156°F (69°C), although the presence of milk and sugar raises the coagulation temperature, so the mixture thickens at a temperature approaching 176°F (80°C). If heated beyond this point, the mixture will curdle and become spoiled. Heating the mixture in the top of a double boiler removes much of the risk from the process, and scalding the milk before adding it to the whisked mixture of sugar and eggs speeds up the process somewhat. Flour is sometimes added to stabilize the proteins, which allows the mixture to be heated to the boiling point (essential for cooking the flour).

Bird's Custard Powder is an eggless imitation custard powder developed in England in the 1840s by the pharmacist Alfred Bird, apparently because his wife, though fond of custard, was allergic to eggs. This advertisement appeared in the June 1901 issue of *The King* magazine. PRIVATE COLLECTION / BRIDGEMAN IMAGES

Baking the mixture is a gentler, less risky process, although precautions such as using a bain-marie are still advised for custards that do not involve pastry cases; these are usually removed from the oven while still soft in the middle. Caution is nevertheless needed, as they develop bubbles in the mix and lose their smooth texture if overcooked. The richness and texture of custards can be varied by increasing the number of eggs, using egg yolks only, or substituting cream for some or all of the milk. Such variations are seen most clearly in recipes that require baking.

Custard powder relies on starch as a thickener and must be cooked to the boiling point to gelatinize it; otherwise, the mix will not thicken and remains unpleasantly thin, grainy, and opaque. Mixes based on modified starches that gelatinize without heating are also available. When kept for any length of time, custard-powder custards are prone to weeping, or synerisis, as the starch stales. See GELATIN and STARCH.

Custard-Based Dishes

Egg-based custards are important both as sweet sauces and components in other dishes. For sauces, they are generally milk-based, or use small proportions of cream, and may be made with egg yolks rather than whole eggs. They can be added to fools and form an essential layer in trifle. See FOOLS and TRIFLE. The custard powder variety is often substituted; it also provides the base for banana custard, with slices of that fruit added. The notion of custard as a sauce runs deep in British food traditions, served alongside the numerous baked or steamed puddings traditional to dinner. Confusingly, the British would regard American packaged "pudding" mixes, which are also popular in parts of Europe and eastern Asia, as a form of custard.

The French name for a rich custard based on eggs, milk, and sugar is crème anglaise, presumably because of a perceived English fondness for this preparation. Used as a sauce for desserts based on fruit or cake, it has traveled the world as part of high-status restaurant cookery. Crème anglaise is also a component of the French dessert *île flottante* (floating island), for which the eggs are separated and the whites made into a poached meringue that floats as a praline- or caramel-decorated "island" on a custard made with the yolks. See MERINGUE. A rich custard with added flour to thicken and stabilize the mixture, used as a filling for pastries such as vanilla slices (Napoleons), is known in French cookery as crème patissière (pastry cream). Vanilla is by far the most popular flavor for all these custards, although almond, lemon, orange, coffee, chocolate, butterscotch, and alcoholic drinks such as rum may be added. Egg custard mixtures are also used as bases for ice creams and in cold dishes such as bavarois or "Bavarian cream," a molded, gelatin-set dessert. See DESSERTS, CHILLED and ICE CREAM.

Plain egg custard mixes can also be simply poured into a dish or a pie crust and baked until set. In British tradition, the latter are often made as individual "custards" using shortcrust pastry in small, deep, flowerpot-shaped molds. They can also be made as large custard tarts, known in North American cookery as custard pies, and cut into slices for serving. In this case the flavoring is usually a dusting of grated nutmeg over the top just before baking. Individual custard tarts, *pastéis de nata*, are a Portuguese specialty. See PORTUGAL. Made with egg yolks, butter, milk, and sugar syrup in puff pastry cases, they have a characteristic golden yellow surface speckled with dark spots. Cinnamon is a preferred spice for custards in Iberian traditions.

Baked custards have many variations. Cooked in individual caramel-lined molds, they form the crème caramel of French cookery and flan of Spanish-speaking countries. See FLAN (PUDÍM) and LATIN AMERICA. For crème brûlée, the custard, rich with cream and egg yolks, is baked alone and then finished with a caramelized layer of sugar to give contrast in both flavor and texture. See CRÈME BRÛLÉE.

The egg yolk and cream formula is the basis for many other sweet items and desserts. It is poured over apricots or other fruit and baked in tarts. Combined with chocolate and baked in ramekins, it becomes *petits pots au chocolat*; made with large amounts of lemon zest and juice, it becomes the filling for *tarte au citron*. Some other pie fillings, such as that for pumpkin pie, might be seen as special forms of custard, as might lemon curd (also known as lemon cheese), a popular preserve in British food traditions. See FRUIT PRESERVES. The curd is made with lemon zest and juice, eggs, sugar, and butter, yielding a translucent soft-set mixture that is used as a tart filling or spread. In Southeast Asia, coconut milk is used instead of cow's milk, as in the Thai *khanom krok*, little coconut custards, which, although sweet, are sometimes flavored with green onions or corn kernels.

History of Custards

The word "custard" derives from the French *crustade*, or pastry case, in which late medieval cooks baked egg and milk or cream-based mixtures with other ingredients, including sugar, spices, fruit, nuts, and meat (savory custards survive as quiche Lorraine). See PIE. A similar process occurred with the word "flan" in Spanish. "Dariole," another French word originally indicating an egg mixture in a case, came to mean a small custard tart in seventeenth-century English and now refers to the molds used to make them. See DARIOLE.

The seventeenth-century cookbook writer Robert May illustrated ornamental shapes made by cutting out pastry bases and adhering vertical walls to them to create elaborate little trough-like cases that were baked blind before being filled with custard. These treats were sometimes dredged with tiny comfits before serving and were eaten by spooning the mixture out of the (inedible) case.

By virtue of the egg, milk or cream, sweetener, and spice combination, other dishes in the early modern period can be thought of as types of custard. English cookery texts describe rich puddings made with eggs, cream, butter, sugar, almonds, pistachios, lemon, or other flavors that were originally boiled in skins and baked (they were later poured into pastry-lined dishes). Possets, ancestors of eggnog, also involved egg and cream mixtures that were thickened by allowing them to stand next to the fire. See EGG DRINKS. Custards could also be poured into dishes and steamed, or tied up in cloths and boiled. Little cold custards were served in porcelain cups as part of the dessert course. See DESSERT. Eighteenth-century cooks made numerous "creams" of eggs, cream, sugar and flower waters, spices, or nuts, all of which must have influenced the notion of custard, and which seem to have been extremely popular.

By the mid-nineteenth century, the word "custard" had come to mean more or less the same as it does today, and it was technology, not fashion, that led to a major change. Custard powder was developed in England in the 1840s by a pharmacist named Alfred Bird because, as the story goes, his wife, though fond of custard, was allergic to eggs. It is not clear which starch his original formula depended on, but cornstarch was first extracted in New Jersey in 1842. Initially used in laundries, a food grade of the starch soon followed, and custard powder quickly became popular in Britain and some British colonies, especially Australia. It never seems to have achieved widespread recognition in the United States, although pudding mixes, developed in the 1920s, are based on the same principle. Finally, custard pies, deliberately made with messy fillings, became important in early movies, though as ammunition, rather than food.

See also CREAM; EGGS; EXTRACTS AND FLAVORINGS; FLOWER WATERS; MILK; and VANILLA.

Davidson, Alan. *The Oxford Companion to Food*. Oxford: Oxford University Press, 1999.

Mason, Laura. "Custard and Pudding." In *Encyclopedia of Food and Culture*, Vol. 1, edited by Solomon H. Katz and William Woys Weaver. New York: Scribner, 2003.

May, Robert. *The Accomplisht Cook, or, The Art and Mystery of Cookery*. Totnes, U.K.: Prospect, 1994. Facsimile of the original 1685 edition, with a foreword, introduction, and glossary provided by Alan Davidson, Marcus Bell, and Tom Jaine.

McGee, Harold. *On Food and Cooking*. London: Scribner, 1984.

Laura Mason

dacquoise is a confection that looks like a cake but consists of two or three layers of hazelnut- or almond-flavored cooked meringue with a filling sandwiched between each layer. See MERINGUE. Buttercream is traditional, but fruit fillings and whipped cream are also commonly used. A dusting of confectioner's sugar may cover the top and sides of the dacquoise, or it may be spread with buttercream or left bare to show the beautiful layering of meringue circles and filling. A dacquoise can be made large, like a cake, or small, for individual desserts. Julia Child writes in *Mastering the Art of French Cooking* (1979, Vol. 2) that a great deal of disagreement exists in French cookbooks on what the layers should be filled with, and "since no one agrees on anything, you are quite safe in doing whatever you wish." This elegant dessert is found in pastry shops all over Paris, where it may be called a *Succès* or a *Progrès*. According to Child, the difference depends on whether ground almonds are used in the meringue or a mixture of almonds and hazelnuts. However, even this rule is not hard and fast. Older French cookbooks typically use one of these names instead of "dacquoise," regardless of the cake's composition. In his *Gastronomie pratique* (1928), Ali-Bab simply calls the confection a *gâteau meringué* (meringue cake) and recommends that it be filled with any sort of flavored cream, such as pistachio, chocolate, or mocha.

See also FRANCE and ICING.

Pellaprat, Henri. *La pâtisserie pratique*. Paris: Bibliothèque du journal "Le Cordon Bleu," 1928.

Time-Life Books, ed. *Cakes*. The Good Cook Techniques & Recipes Series. Alexandria, Va.: Time-Life Books, 1981.

Kyri W. Claflin

dairy

See BUTTER; BUTTERMILK; CHEESE, FRESH; CREAM; EVAPORATED MILK; MILK; SOUR CREAM; SWEETENED CONDENSED MILK; and YOGURT.

Dairy Queen, officially the American Dairy Queen Corporation, or DQ as it is known to its franchisers and fans, is one of the largest fast-food systems in the world today.

The company originated when John Fremont "Grandpa" McCullough and his son Alex operated the Homemade Ice Cream Company in Davenport, Iowa, in 1927. In the early 1930s, they moved their ice cream production into a former cheese factory in Green River, Illinois. The senior McCullough understood that ice cream served as a frozen solid at 5°F (−15°C) numbed the taste buds, and that it tasted more flavorful when soft. By experimenting, he discovered that fresh ice cream dispensed in a semi-frozen, custard-like state at about 23°F (−5°C) had the best flavor. The problem was that in the 1930s no equipment was available for dispensing semi-frozen ice cream that would also keep its shape. See ICE CREAM.

Despite these technical problems, McCullough continued to work on the development of a soft-serve frozen dairy product. In 1938 he was ready to test his idea on the public. The McCulloughs asked Sherb Noble, a good friend and customer, to run an "All You Can Eat for 10 cents" trial sale at his walk-in ice cream store in Kankakee, Illinois. The men made ice cream and scooped it into cups while it was still soft. Within two hours on 4 August 1938, 1,600 servings of this new dessert were served.

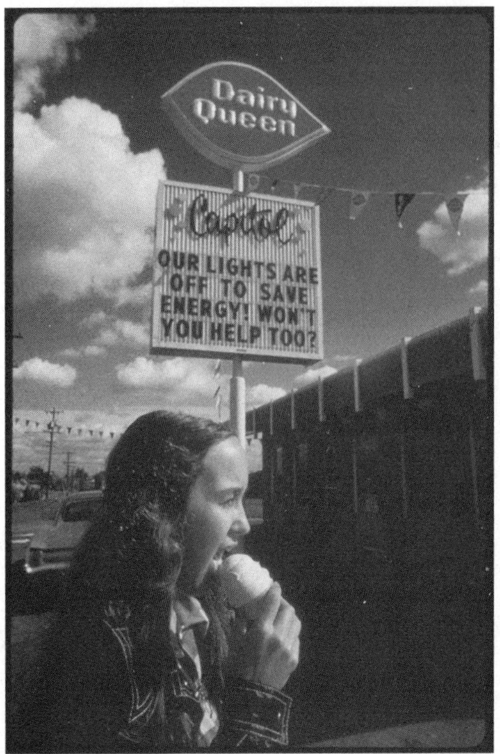

As a result of the 1973 oil crisis, the state of Oregon banned neon and commercial lighting displays. Some businesses, like this Dairy Queen in Portland, Oregon, used their unlit signs to convey energy-saving messages that could be seen during the day. PHOTOGRAPH BY DAVID FALCONER / U.S. NATIONAL ARCHIVES

Encouraged by the public's response, McCullough asked two manufacturers of dairy equipment to design and produce a machine that would dispense semi-frozen ice cream. Neither was interested. By chance, he read in the *Chicago Tribune* that Harry M. Oltz, who operated a hamburger stand in Hammond, Indiana, had patented a continuous freezer that would dispense soft ice cream. The men partnered in 1939, with the McCulloughs having exclusive use of the freezer west of the Mississippi River and Oltz having control to the river's east. Oltz moved to Miami, Florida, and established AR-TIK Systems, Inc. to promote soft-serve ice cream.

In 1940 Noble opened the first Dairy Queen store in Joliet, Illinois, under license from McCullough, who also created the Dairy Queen name. He grossed a whopping $4,000 in revenue that first season. In 2011 the Joliet City Council granted local landmark status to the nondescript whitewashed building on historic Route 66, where the first Dairy Queen cones were sold for 5 cents.

By the end of 1942, eight Dairy Queen businesses were in operation. Since manufacturing materials were devoted to the war effort, no new freezers could be built. During World War II, the McCulloughs kept busy developing their new franchise business and negotiating territories. Grandpa McCullough wrote many of these agreements on the back of napkins and paper sacks, an informal and haphazard procedure that would later cause untold problems for the company and the courts. Fast-food franchises were new at this time, although other entrepreneurs such as Howard Johnson had embraced the concept successfully in the 1930s.

In 1941 the McCulloughs opened another store in Moline, Illinois. It was this rectangular box store with its glass front, flat roof extended over the service window, and large sign featuring an ice cream cone with a curl that became the prototype for postwar expansion. "Curly" became the Dairy Queen soft-serve mascot; in the 1960s the ice cream cone sign was replaced with the more modernistic "red kiss."

Impressed by the long lines outside Dairy Queen shops, Harry Axene, a sales manager for a farm equipment company, approached Grandpa McCullough and negotiated a 50–50 partnership. In 1946 Axene called together all 17 Dairy Queen operators to form an organization to standardize operating procedures and to expand the company. By the end of 1948, 35 store owners came together to create the Dairy Queen National Trade Association. By 1950, 1,400 stores were serving a limited menu of sundaes and cones for immediate consumption, and pints and quarts to take home. Axene cut his ties with the company in 1949 and established the Tastee Freeze Company on the West Coast. In the 1960s, Dairy Queen purchased the franchise rights of Harry Oltz's AR-TIK Systems.

Dairy Queen opened its first store in Tokyo in 1972, and by 1976 there were 150 stores in Iceland, Guatemala, Trinidad, Panama, Hong Kong, and several other countries. The company also added new products. One major success was the Blizzard, a soft-serve concoction of ice cream blended with candy, cookies, and fruit. In the 1980s, the company purchased Golden Skillet, a fried-chicken chain; Karmelkorn Shoppes, Inc., a popcorn and candy franchise; and Orange Julius, a fruit-flavored blended drink and snack operation. See ORANGE JULIUS.

In 1997 Warren Buffett's Berkshire Hathaway Inc. of Omaha, Nebraska, purchased DQ for $585 million in stock and cash. The company now operates more than 6,000 restaurants in the United States, Canada, and 18 other countries.

See also BASKIN-ROBBINS; BEN & JERRY'S; ESKIMO PIE; and HÄAGEN-DAZS.

Derdak, Thomas, F. Uble, and P. R. Greenland. "International Dairy Queen, Inc." In *International Directory of Company Histories*, edited by Jay P. Pederson, Vol. 105, pp. 248–254. Farmington Hills, Mich.: Gale, 2010.

Jakle, John A., and Keith A. Sculle. *Fast Food: Roadside Restaurants in the Automobile Age*. Baltimore: Johns Hopkins University Press, 1999.

Joseph M. Carlin

dango are Japanese dumplings made from a dough formed into a ball and steamed. Although plain dango have been eaten in Japan since at least the eighth century, the customary practice of serving four dango as a sweet—on a skewer topped with sweetened soy sauce, azuki bean paste (*an*), or soybean flour (*kinako*)—developed in the early modern period (1600–1868) as an inexpensive treat sold by vendors. Dango can also be shaped into flat circles and boiled or grilled.

Dango are similar to mochi, but the latter are usually created from glutinous rice or other whole grains, whereas dango are traditionally made from nonglutinous rice flour, which gives them a chewy consistency like gnocchi. See MOCHI. As is characteristic of Japanese sweets, many seasonal varieties of dango exist. Moon Viewing (*tsukimi*) Dango are prepared in the autumn; Flower Viewing (*hanami*) Dango are snacks in cherry blossom season, giving rise to the saying "preferring dumplings to flowers," which indicates that the refreshments served at flower viewing parties often overshadow the beauty of the blossoms. Rice flour dango are preferred as confections, but savory dango made from wheat, buckwheat, and millet were staple foods before World War II. Farmers stuffed dango with vegetables flavored with miso and grilled plain dumplings for a quick meal. Dango can also be added to a clear or miso soup or to a sweet azuki bean soup called *shiruko*. See AZUKI BEANS. In some regions, dango were made from potatoes, nuts, or ground sesame.

See also JAPAN.

Nakayama Keiko. *Jiten wagashi no sekai*. Tokyo: Iwanami Shoten, 2006.

Eric C. Rath

Danish pastry

See LAMINATED DOUGHS.

dariole dates to medieval Europe and has never left the French dessert repertoire, although it is considered old-fashioned now. It is a small tart with a pastry shell and a flavored milk and egg custard filling. The flavorings include butter and sugar and a "perfume," such as rosewater, vanilla, cinnamon, or orange flower water. Some texts, such as *Le ménagier de Paris* (1393), give no recipe but simply list darioles on menus appropriate for weddings. Other texts, including *Le viandier* of Taillevent (published 1486) and early English manuscripts, have somewhat mangled instructions for making darioles. The Italian cook Martino (ca. 1465) offered a recipe for a single large custard tart called a *dariola*. The anonymous author of *Le pâtissier françois* (1655) includes a detailed dariole recipe that is for a single large tart made in a pastry-lined *tourtière*. By the eighteenth century, darioles were small custard tarts made in molds with fluted sides, and the word "dariole" now principally refers to this kind of mold. According to *Larousse gastronomique* (1938), dariole molds lined with puff pastry can be filled with frangipane, flavored with a liqueur, and sprinkled with powdered sugar after baking. See FRANGIPANE. In *Le livre de pâtisserie* (1873), Jules Gouffé flavors the custard with vanilla sugar, citron, orange, orange flower water, and crushed macaroons. Dariole does not appear in Julia Child's classic *Mastering the Art of French Cooking* (1961).

See also CREAM PIE; CUSTARD; and FLOWER WATERS.

Hieatt, Constance B., and Sharon Butler. *Curye on Inglysch*. Oxford: Oxford University Press and the Early English Text Society, 1985.

Redon, Odile, François Sabban, and Silvano Serventi. *The Medieval Kitchen*. Chicago: University of Chicago Press, 1995.

Kyri W. Claflin

dates are the fruit of the date palm (*Phoenix dactylifera*), a tree native to the deserts of North Africa and the Middle East. There are well over a thousand varieties of dates, ranging from dry and fibrous "camel dates" to moist and sweet medjools with their distinctive caramel-molasses flavor. They can be consumed in many stages, including the underripe *khalal* phase (crunchy and a bit astringent), the fully ripe *rutab* phase (moist and easy to spoil), and the *tamr* phase (wrinkled, less moist, and nonperishable) when most of the fruit are sold.

Date palms were probably first domesticated at least 5,000 years ago along the banks of the Tigris and Euphrates rivers. The trees favor intense heat and abundant below-ground water, making them a perfect cultivar for desert oases. Energy-filled and rich in nutrients, dates became culinary staples in desert cultures from northern India to Morocco. Appearing in many myths and religious accounts, date palms were often portrayed as the original "tree of life." Dates were a favorite food of Muhammad, who liked to eat them with cucumbers. Today, many Muslims break their Ramadan fast with a meal of dates. See ISLAM and RAMADAN. They are a common ingredient in many North African and Middle Eastern sweets, such as the date-filled cookie called *maʾamoul*. Date syrup, known as *rub* or *dibs* in Arabic, is used much like molasses as a sweetener. In Morocco, whole dates are frequently cooked in tajines with lamb or other meats.

Although the only large-scale date palm groves in Europe are found in the city of Elche in southeastern Spain, dates have been known for centuries in Western Europe. In medieval medicine, they were often eaten to "strengthen the womb" and to treat diarrhea and other stomach disorders. During the nineteenth century, dates became popular as sweet treats, either whole or as ingredients in dishes like date puddings. Today, sticky toffee pudding made with dates is a popular British dessert. See STICKY TOFFEE PUDDING.

Around 1765 a Spanish priest in Baja California planted the first date palms in the New World. Anxious to develop the arid regions of the America Southwest, the U.S. Department of Agriculture began importing date palms to southern Arizona and California in the late nineteenth century. From about 1910 on, the American date industry took root in California's Coachella Valley, about 20 miles southeast of Palm Springs, where summer temperatures can reach 120°F (49°C). The region's early date farmers concentrated on palms producing the *deglet noor* (in Arabic, the "date of light"), which is still the most common variety found in American supermarkets. Picked straight from the tree, deglet noors have a delicate, honey-like flavor. For commercial use, however, most deglet noors are usually dried for storage and then rehydrated with steam (which cuts the flavor) and pitted just before packing. The fruit soon became a popular ingredient for many baked goods, including date and walnut breads; various pies, puddings, and cakes; and even salads made with dates and other fruit. Many Coachella Valley date farms built roadside stands to sell their product to travelers. To cool off, visitors could also enjoy a date shake made from chopped dates, milk, and ice cream.

In 1927 a USDA botanist named Walter Swingle imported the first offshoots of the medjool date palm to the United States. Large, moist, and full-flavored, medjools were considered one of the premier date varieties. They were native to Morocco and Algeria, where a soil fungus had devastated the medjool orchards, but Swingle managed to find a few healthy offshoots in an isolated Moroccan oasis. In the 1940s the first medjool offshoots were released to commercial farmers in California and southwestern Arizona. When the trees finally bore fruit, medjools were recognized as the finest American-grown date. Beyond a small group of date fanciers, however, they never caught on with the broader American public. (In fact, the current American per capita consumption of dates is less than 6 ounces a year.) In recent decades, American medjools have found a market among immigrants from countries in the Middle East and North Africa, where dates are part of the culinary heritage and an important ingredient for holiday feasts. The Coachella Valley has for decades been the world's largest medjool-growing area. Based on plantings of young trees, it is projected that this region will soon be overtaken by the sprawling expanse of medjool date groves along the Colorado River near Yuma, Arizona.

Today, about 70 percent of the American date crop is deglet noors, mostly used by the baking industry. Medjools make up much of the rest; more than a third of this crop is shipped for export, mainly to Europe, Canada, and Australia. In cities with large immigrant communities, ethnic markets also sell imported medjools and various varieties from Israel, Saudi Arabia, and other Middle Eastern countries. A few Coachella Valley growers, like Oasis Date Gardens, also grow lesser-known dates such as the barhi, halawy, khadrawy, thoory, and zahidi varieties.

See also DRIED FRUIT; MIDDLE EAST; MOLASSES; NORTH AFRICA; and PALM SUGAR.

Hill, John. *A History of the Materia Medica*. London: T. Longman, C. Hitch and L. Lawes, 1751.

Hodel, Donald R., and Dennis V. Johnson. *Dates: Imported and American Varieties of Dates in the United States*. Oakland: University of California, Division of Agriculture and Natural Resources, 2007.

Popenoe, Paul. *Date Growing in the Old World and New*. Altadena, Calif.: West India Gardens, 1913.

Andrew Coe

Day of the Dead, celebrated by Christians on 1 November, draws on much older festivities that honor the deceased. When Pope Boniface IV first proposed a celebration in tribute to the Virgin Mary and All Saints in 610 C.E., the date chosen was 13 May to coincide with Lemuria, a Roman festival dedicated to ancestors. However, this celebration of all saints did not succeed; it was only some 200 years later that the holiday finally took hold. In 835 Louis the Pious, emperor of the Carolingian Empire, declared a celebration of the Christian saints in autumn, partly in an attempt to override the widespread pagan rituals practiced at that time of year. These festivities were likely related to the Celtic harvest festival of Samhain, when the souls of the dead were said to return to their homes. In the ninth century, under Pope Gregory IV, the Catholic Church finally mandated 1 November as All Saints Day. Next came the solemn mass initiated in 990 by Odily, abbot of Cluny, to commemorate all the dead in monasteries under his authority. This practice gradually spread throughout Europe, and 2 November was eventually established as All Souls Day in a further attempt to supplant the continuing pagan celebrations in honor of the dead.

In the northern hemisphere, Day of the Dead celebrations take place at a cold and dark time of year. Documents dating back to the early Middle Ages attest to the season's communal activities, including the late harvest. It is a time when people customarily sought to consolidate relationships through convivial rituals and liturgies before the winter set in.

In Mexico, at least two existing Aztec rituals, Miccailhuitontly, the Feast of the Young Dead, and Hueymiccailhuitl, the Feast of the Old Dead, facilitated the Catholic Church's integration of the pagan and Christian. The date 1 November is celebrated as Day of the Dead Children, while 2 November is the Day of the Adult Dead.

Because the influence of the Catholic Church has historically been very strong in Mexico, Italy, and Spain, Day of the Dead celebrations in these countries are emblematic of the holiday. Street markets, parades, and altars saturate the senses with fragrant, sweet smells from private and public kitchens. Cooks, momentarily akin to priests, officiate in culinary votive rituals that integrate the pagan with the Christian. In Europe, pristine altars covered in white linen display sweets like quince paste, roasted chestnuts, dried fig and almond bars, walnuts, and dates. Spain offers a variety of sweets in the shape of bones—realistic edible relics—some fried (like the *huesos de San Expedito*), others baked, such as the *huesos de Santo*, bones made of marzipan and sweet potato, egg yolk, or chocolate paste.

In Mexico in 1740, Friar Francisco de Ajofrín referred to the production and selling of *alfeñiques*, zoomorphic and anthropomorphic miniatures made of sugar. See ANTHROPOMORPHIC AND ZOOMORPHIC SWEETS. Sorrow and happiness merge in the virtual presence of the Great Dame—Death—as the dance of life is symbolically offered to the souls of the dead on baroque altars laden with sweets: decorated skulls made of sugar, *amaranto* (amaranth), and chocolate; *pan de muerto* (bread of the dead) made with flour, orange blossom water, pulque, and sugar, with its shape recalling a skull and crossbones; *calabaza en tacha*, made with pumpkin and *azucar de piloncillo* (unrefined cane sugar) syrup, and *taninole* (sweetened mashed pumpkin) beaten with milk. These votive sweets are accompanied by hot chocolate, pulque, mezcal, and tequila.

In the northern region of Lombardy, Italy, almond and cinnamon cakes called *pane dei morti* (bread of the dead) are baked for the holiday, along with *fave dei morti* (beans of the dead), sweetened bean-shaped cakes made of ground almonds. On the island of Sardinia, in Gilarza and Dorgali, they bake *tiliccas*, dough stuffed with grape paste, while in Palermo, Sicily, *pupi di zucchero* are offered up, mainly to children: sugar figures inspired by the puppets of the Opera dei Pupi. Nowadays, the *pupi* are often modeled after characters from popular culture, including Mickey Mouse and SpongeBob SquarePants. In Salemi, until the last century, *pane dei difunti,* bread braided in imitation of the crossed arms and hands of the deceased, was baked at home and distributed to the poor at the cemetery.

In Catalonia, Spain, small marzipan breads called *panellets* are popular. They are made from a paste of sweet potatoes, ground almonds, sugar, egg yolks, vanilla, and lemon peel. Chocolate, red currants, chopped hazelnuts, or pine nuts can be added before the cakes are baked in molds. In Madrid, the popular fried *buñuelos de viento,* stuffed with chestnut, pumpkin, or sweet potato paste, are reminders of the ethereal nature of life. They are eaten with hot chocolate along with marzipan *huesos de Santo.* In Extremadura to the west, Murcia in the east, and Andalucía in the south, *gachas de difuntos* are traditional, a sort of porridge made from the toasted flours of different grains cooked with milk or grape juice and flavored with cinnamon, aniseed, and ground cloves.

All these Day of the Dead offerings are examples of edible vanitas, intended to remind us who we are, where we come from, and where we will end up.

See also FESTIVALS; HALLOWEEN; ITALY; MEXICO; and SPAIN.

Armengaud, Christine. *Le diable sucré: Gâteaux, cannibalisme, mort et fécondité.* Paris: Editions de La Martinière, 2000.

González Turmo, Isabel. "Rituales alimenticios y ocasiones festivas (2)." *Demófilo: Revista de Cultura Tradicional de Andalucía* 9 (1992): 63–80.

Sike, Yvonne de. *Fêtes et croyances populaires en Europe: Au fil des saisons.* Paris: Bordas, 1994.

Soustelle, Jacques. *La vie quotidienne des Aztèques.* Paris: Hachette Littérature, 2008.

Alicia Rios

dental caries, the technical term for a cavity, describes the destructive outcome found in teeth following the bacterial-acidic attack on tooth structure. Those possessing a "sweet tooth"—a craving to eat sweet foods such as candy and pastries—are at greater risk of developing tooth decay because of its association with sugar consumption. The evidence that sugar plays a fundamental role in the development of dental caries is well documented and overwhelming. Sugar and other fermentable carbohydrates serve as a substrate for certain bacteria in dental plaque, and acid produced by this metabolic process induces the demineralization of enamel, making the tooth more vulnerable to decay.

Although the writings of Greeks, Egyptians, and Chinese document dental disease, the profession of dentistry emerged in the mid-nineteenth century as a discipline focused on treating diseases of teeth and associated supporting tissue. The understanding and treatment of dental caries first started with the tooth "worm theory," which posited that a tooth worm buried its way through tooth structure and caused a toothache by moving around. The pain subsided once the worm became tired and required rest. The exact image of this creature was not known, but folklore aided in the concept of how it might appear. The British believed that the tooth worm resembled an eel, whereas the Germans thought the maggot-like worm was red, blue, and gray in color. The treatment for "tooth worm" consisted of tooth extractions and traditional herbal remedies. The worm hypothesis evolved into more sophisticated theories on the acid production of oral microorganisms. Specific types of oral bacteria are able to produce many by-products from sugar consumption, including several types of acid. The acidic environment then promotes the breakdown of tooth structure and eventually cavities in teeth. The greater consumer demand for conservation of teeth eventually led to the development of dental restorations.

A steady annual rise in sugar consumption from 6.3 pounds per person per year in 1882 to its highest level of 107.7 pounds per person per year in 1999 shows that the U.S. appetite for sugar is remarkable. Over a five-day period, a person in 1882 consumed the same amount of sugar that is currently found in a 12-ounce can of soda, and today we consume the same amount of sugar in a mere seven hours. In 2011 a world population of 7 billion consumed roughly 165 tons of sugar. Developing countries, principally in Asia, are considered growing markets, while sugar consumption has leveled off in developed countries.

Even with the steady increase in sugar consumption over the past several decades, there has been a decrease in dental caries, which illustrates the multifactorial nature of dental caries. The development of tooth decay depends on the interaction of primary factors and is influenced by oral environmental and personal factors. The interaction of antibodies in the saliva or the roughness of the tooth surface will determine whether the bacteria survive, as well as their ability to attach to the tooth surface; the type of food ingested, such as "sticky" food that lingers in the mouth, will enhance the likelihood of decay; the bacterial composition and quantity of plaque will affect the outcome; and the frequency of tooth exposure to cariogenic (acidic) environments will also play a role. Arguably the most recognizable oral environmental factor exerting the greatest single influence on caries (in the United States) has been water fluoridation. The inclusion of certain dietary alcohols (polyols), such as xylitol in chewing gum, supports the remineralization of tooth enamel. See XYLITOL. Personal factors that correlate with dental caries include oral hygiene, education, income, dental insurance coverage, and oral health literacy.

Thanks to education from parents, dental hygienists, and dentists, we can indulge in sweets while still preventing dental decay by frequent brushing, flossing, using mouth rinses, and even chewing a sugar-free gum to increase salivary flow. See CHEWING GUM.

See also SUGAR AND HEALTH.

Black G. "A Plea for Greater Earnestness in the Study of Caries of the Enamel in Its Relation to the Practice of Dentistry." *Dental Brief* 15 (1910): 161–178.

Miller W. "Dental Caries." *American Journal of Dental Science* 17 (1883): 77–130.

Kevin A. Guze and Tom C. Pagonis

dessert, in the sense of a sweet, concluding course to a meal, is a French custom that developed slowly over several hundred years, reaching its current form only in the twentieth century. Even now, the practice of serving a final pastry or confectionery course is neither ubiquitous nor universal, even in France. Most cultures do not finish their meals on a sweet note, and even when they do, it is often no more than with a piece of fruit. In Renaissance Italy, sweet dishes were commonly interspersed with savory, as they were in Ottoman Turkey. Even the French make exceptions, occasionally starting a meal with melon or inserting a sorbet course between two savory dishes. Many cultures eat certain meals where sweets predominate. See SWEET MEALS. Nonetheless, with the growth of a globalized restaurant culture, the habit of finishing lunch or dinner with a sweet prepared dish is now familiar to everyone who can afford the bill.

Early Forms

The term "dessert" comes from the French verb *desservir*, meaning "to clear the table." It is mentioned as the penultimate course in two menus from the fourteenth-century *Ménagier de Paris*, in one case consisting of venison and frumenty (a sort of pudding), and in the other of a preserve (presumably made with honey), candied almonds, fritters, tarts, and dried fruit. The most common final course at elite medieval meals—referred to in France as *issue*—consisted of a sort of digestif of hippocras (spiced wine) and whole sweet spices, often candied. See COMFIT and HIPPOCRAS. It was only in seventeenth-century France that the final course in a multicourse meal came reliably to be called "dessert." But even then, it was not entirely devoted to sweet dishes any more than the preceding courses were consistently savory. In France, as in Italy and England, there were also meals made up almost entirely of sweets where the focus was on artistry mingled with ostentation, rather than on the food per se. In medieval and early renaissance England, a banquet of sweetmeats, sometimes termed simply "a banquet," might take the form of an entire meal devoted to sweets. This repast was occasionally served after a meal, which itself consisted of both sweet and savory dishes. The sweet banquet was sometimes served at a separate table, in a separate room, in a garden setting, or even in a separate "banketting house," where the tables would be set with displays well in advance. See BANQUETING HOUSES.

Until the seventeenth century, sweet and savory were not always distinct. In Christoforo di Messisbugo's sixteenth-century Italian banquet menus, meals typically began with an assortment of confectionery and concluded with more of the same. But just about every other dish in the intervening courses, whether a fish pie or stewed capon, had some sugar added to it, too.

The situation was not significantly different in France. Food historian Jean-Louis Flandrin has estimated that some 80 percent of still-extant French recipes for meat and fish dishes were sweetened in the fifteenth century. The number had dropped to around 50 percent a hundred years later, and in the seventeenth century, some 30 percent of these dishes were still being sweetened. Increasingly, though, the trend was to segregate sweet from savory. Just why this split occurred in France remains hazy, and the explanations are unsatisfactory. Flandrin implies that it signaled a return to earlier French habits, once Italian Renaissance fashions had waned (Italian food was notably sweeter than the French). Chauvinism may well have had something to do with the change; certainly, the first influential cookbook to be published following the period of Italian influence was self-consciously titled *Le cuisinier françois* (1651), the first cookbook ever to be characterized with a national identity. This nationalistic food consciousness and growing gap between sweet and savory also happen to parallel the demise of spiced food in France. Sugar was initially thought of as a spice; once it had been recategorized in people's minds as a confectionery and baking ingredient, it perhaps had no place in the new, mostly spice-free cuisine. This is not to say the change occurred overnight; *Le cuisinier françois* offered plenty of recipes for sweetened meat and fish dishes. Nevertheless, though sweet and savory were still served side by side, they were increasingly not blended on the same plate.

Service à la française

Affluent French seventeenth- and eighteenth-century menus most commonly consisted of three courses (*services*) made up of platters both large and small, each multidish course served more or less simultaneously buffet-style. This type of presentation was referred to as *service à la française* (even though it was commonplace all over Europe). Generally more and more sweet dishes were served as the meal progressed. In the first course they were rare, while the second course contained a scattering of side dishes called *entremets* (literally, "between the dishes"), which could be both savory and sweet. See ENTREMETS. In a menu from 1690, listed in François Massialot's *Le cuisinier roïal et bourgeois* (1691), members of the royal family and guests could choose among entremets of ham or pheasant pies but also blancmange, fritters (*beignets*), and apricot marmalade–filled tarts. See BLANCMANGE and FRITTERS. These sweet items were interspersed among 22 platters of roast beef, mutton, suckling pig, and "all sorts of poultry." Other menus suggest entremets of sweet omelets, fruit custards, crème brûlée, even a sugared artichoke custard. See CRÈME BRÛLÉE. It was only once this service had been fully cleared that the dessert course was served. The 1690 *Dictionnaire universel* defined dessert as "the last course placed on the table ... composed of fruits, pastry, confectionery, cheese, etc." This final course was the responsibility of the *office* or pantry, whereas the earlier dishes came from the kitchen. Accordingly, what characterized the dessert course was not so much that it was sweet, but that it was cold. It was also the most visually exciting part of the meal. Though some degree of spectacle distinguished every course, the final dessert service deployed the color, texture, and sculptural potential of confectionery with sometimes fantastic results. See SUGAR SCULPTURE. Broadly speaking, the confectioners followed the current style in the other applied arts. Thus, seventeenth-century dessert tables featured baroque pyramids of sparkling sweetmeats; eighteenth-century displays were replete with neoclassical statuary often set on a mirrored surface; the Romantic period saw *pièces montées* resembling crumbling classical ruins; and the Victorian period brought a ponderous historicism. With the arrival of *service à la russe*, these spectacular displays largely ceased to exist as table decoration was limited mainly to flowers and individual servings were brought to each diner in turn. In bourgeois homes, a fancy dessert might be displayed on the sideboard throughout dinner, but it was a shadow of its ancien régime ancestors.

According to Arthur Young (1792), an English writer visiting France on the eve of the Revolution, "dessert" was to be expected at even a modest meal. This practice apparently stood in marked contrast to the custom in England. "A regular dessert with us [the English] is expected," he explains in *Travels during the years 1787, 1788, and 1789*, "at a considerable table only, or at a moderate one, when a formal entertainment is given; in France it is as essential to the smallest dinner as to the largest; if it consists only of a bunch of dried grapes, or an apple, it will be as regularly served as the soup." Throughout his travels, Young described several of these desserts, which typically consisted of fruit, nuts, biscuits, and wine—more or less in line with the definition current in eighteenth-century England. Ephraim Chamber's *Cyclopaedia* (1741) defines dessert as "the last service brought on the table of people of quality; when the meats are all taken off. The dessert consists of fruits, pastry-works, confections, etc." Other English sources, however, limit dessert to a final course of fruit only.

The French system of serving meals in three or more courses concluding with one called dessert was emulated across Europe. Naturally, not everyone could afford the splendors of Versailles. Heinrich Klietsch's and Johann Hermann Siebell's *Bamberger Kochbuch* (1805), intended for both "noble and bourgeois tables," includes 78 suggested menus, mostly consisting of two courses. The first is exclusively savory, whereas the second may include anything from roast duck to capon pies to ice cream, sweet jelly, and cake. In addition to these menus, the authors include a selection of "dessert plates." Although not all are specified, those singled out include sorbet, ice cream, fruit, cookies, and "other confectionery." Given that these dessert plates are always listed as the last item of the second course, it is likely that they arrived at the table after the other items had been eaten, although no indication exists that the table had been cleared in the interim, as it was in France.

Service à la russe

French cuisine, the trendsetting style across ancien régime Europe, underwent its own revolution with the fall of the Bastille. With the decapitation of the old aristocracy, the grand, buffet-style courses made up of multiple dishes were supplanted by a form of sequential service adopted from a Russian model—hence the name *service à la russe*. The change was very gradual and not universally appreciated. The great chef Carême, for one, had little use for it. See CARÊME, MARIE-ANTOINE. In this new style, all the diners ate the same food, more or less, and the dishes arrived one after the other, much as they do today. The entremets, increasingly mostly sweet, shifted to the penultimate position, with dessert following. In other words, now two sweet courses concluded a meal. Flandrin points to the shift in language between menus in the eighteenth century, where "dessert" was the term for a course, to the late-nineteenth-century use of "desserts" (in the plural) to refer to the sweet foods themselves. By that point, the entremets often consisted of a sweet, creamy dish such as ice cream or bavarois, whereas dessert might include cakes, cookies, fruit, or petits fours. See DESSERTS, CHILLED; ICE CREAM; and SMALL CAKES. In France, a cheese course was sometimes slipped between the two.

By the 1950s, the entremets and dessert courses had elided into one, resulting in today's most common sequence of entrée, main course, salad, cheese, and dessert. The menus served at the Elysée Palace give some evidence that this shift toward the modern sequence occurred during World War II. Today, the distinction between entremets and dessert has mostly been lost. The most recent edition of the Académie française dictionary defines entremets as "a sweet preparation served after the cheese and which may take the place of dessert." At least when it comes to dessert, the West largely followed the French example.

Dessert in the United States

Initially, Americans aped the British model. They could, for example, look to Maria Eliza Rundell's widely reprinted *A New System of Domestic Cookery* (1807) for what was appropriate for a second course—mainly birds, game and shellfish, vegetables, fruit tarts, stewed apples, cheesecakes, and "all the finer sorts of Puddings, Mince Pies, &c." The book was apparently not intended for "people of quality," since it makes no mention of dessert. Robert Robert's *The House Servant's Directory* (1827) clearly aimed higher up the social scale. His dessert is served very much in the French manner: following two courses (served *à la française*) and a cheese course, the table is completely cleared before resetting for a sweet course of cake or possibly ice cream or blancmange. See BLANCMANGE and CAKE.

Hotels and restaurant menus in the latter half of the nineteenth century tended to break down sweet foods into two, not always easily understood, categories: pastry and dessert. The former included pies but also occasionally pudding; the second, fruit and nuts but also sometimes jellies, sponge cakes, ice cream, and charlotte russe. The distinction began to evaporate in the early twentieth century, even though fancy menus might well continue to include two sweet courses in the French style.

Today, a single dessert is the most common conclusion to a multicourse meal, though many fine dining restaurants make a habit of serving chocolates, petits fours, or some other sweet nothing after the official dessert has been cleared. See MIGNARDISE. As in France, dessert has also come to include any sweet food that might be served at the end of meal no matter when it is eaten, leading mothers to reprimand their children about not eating ice cream, cupcakes, pie, and other "desserts" before dinner.

See also CHARLOTTE; FRANCE; GELATIN DESSERTS; ITALY; PIE; PUDDING; and SPONGE CAKE.

Bibliothèque Municipal de Dijon. "Collection des menus." http://patrimoine.bm-dijon.fr/pleade/subset.html?name=sub-menus (accessed 1 April 2014).
Flandrin, Jean Louis. *Arranging the Meal: A History of Table Service in France.* Berkeley: University of California Press, 2007.
Krondl, Michael. *Sweet Invention: A History of Dessert.* Chicago: Chicago Review Press, 2011.
Messisbugo, Cristoforo di. *Banchetti compositioni di vivande, et apparecchio generale.* Ferrara: Giovanni de Buglhat et Antonio Hucher Compagni, 1549.
Rundell, Maria Eliza Ketelby. *A New System of Domestic Cookery.* Philadelphia: Benjamin C. Buzby, 1807.
"What's on the Menu?" http://menus.nypl.org (accessed 1 April 2014).
Young, Arthur. *Travels during the Years 1787, 1788 and 1789 Undertaken More Particularly with a View of Ascertaining the Cultivation, Wealth, Resources and National Prosperity of the Kingdom of France.* London: W. Richardson, 1792.

Michael Krondl

dessert design refers to the presentation of the course, generally consisting of sweet foods, that comes at the end of the meal.

Derived from the French verb *desservir*, dessert is what arrives after the table is "unserved" or cleared, and after our nutritional needs have been met; it is, in that sense, superfluous. See DESSERT. In his *Grand dictionnaire de cuisine* (1873), Alexandre Dumas wrote that there are three types of appetite: that which comes *from* hunger; hunger that comes *with* eating; and "that roused at the end of a meal when, after normal hunger has been satisfied by the main courses, and the guest is truly ready to rise without regret, a delicious dish holds him to the table with a final tempting of his sensuality." Dessert requires this third type of appetite; its aesthetic display and sensuous experience are of primary importance.

Dessert is as much about form as it is about taste. Confectionery and baking, from dough to caramel to marzipan, lend themselves readily to sculpture, for example. See SUGAR SCULPTURE. As a type of plastic art, dessert therefore is more likely to borrow from and contribute to the other art disciplines of its time, from architecture to fashion. Even the language of dessert making—molding, casting, dyeing, setting—and its associated tools have little in common with cooking. See CONFECTIONERY EQUIPMENT and PASTRY TOOLS. Desserts are shaped, constructed, and fabricated (and, now, mass-produced) with an eye toward form; taste is often secondary. They have long been prepared by professionals with specialized tools and equipment in facilities dedicated to sweets, explicitly separate from the kitchen. See PASTRY CHEF. Ultimately, dessert's place on and at the table is to amuse, not feed, and, historically, to communicate power or status, provide a locus for ritual and tradition, exchange cultural traits, even transcend the laws of gravity and physics. Desserts were made to awe, to show off, to delight. So what is dessert, after all? It is design: "the process of inventing things which display new physical order, organization, form, in response to function," as theorist Christopher Alexander explains on the first page of his landmark 1964 book *Notes on the Synthesis of Form.*

Luxury at a Large Scale

Sugar is the primary building material of dessert. Even before the idea of this separate and final course fully evolved, a tenth-century Arab recipe described marzipan shaped like fish and perfumed with camphor. See MARZIPAN and MIDDLE EAST. In early Renaissance Italy, Leonardo da Vinci wrote in *Notes on Cuisine* of the fate of his marzipan: "I have observed with pain that my Signor Ludovico and his court gobble up all the sculptures I give them, right to the last morsel, and now I am determined to find other means that do not taste as good, so that my works may survive." The ultimate luxury commodity, his chosen medium of sugar was preservable, malleable, and believed to have medicinal properties. See MEDICINAL USES OF SUGAR. And (unfortunately for Leonardo's sculpture), it was edible! Symbolically, technically, and gastronomically, sugar was the perfect material for public consumption—*panem et circenses* combined in one form.

From Lisbon to Antwerp, extravagant state, noble, or church banquets were followed by even more elaborate sugar collations. In a separate room, tables

This 1747 plate depicts the desserts of preserves, sugared almonds, fruit, and ices displayed on the head tables of a banquet given by Judas Thaddäus, Freiherr von Reischach, for the coronation of Holy Roman Emperor Francis I. Composed as architectural tableaux set in formal gardens, the desserts are allegories on historical events from the death of Emperor Charles VI to the election of Francis I. GETTY RESEARCH INSTITUTE abounded with large sugar-paste sculptures depicting important people, fantastic buildings, and mythological creatures, often gilded or silvered to underscore their richness. See BANQUETING HOUSES. Unlike the main meal, which was produced by the kitchen, the sugar work was created by individual artisans, sculptors, or apothecaries in their workshops. In 1574 sugar sculptures for a banquet given in honor of Henri III of France were the designs of Jacopo Sansovino, one of Venice's chief architects, whose loggetta still adorns the base of Campanile di San Marco. That a sugar sculpture might be on par with a building shows the primacy of sweets not as food, but as an expression of power and carrier of meaning, much like a church, a palazzo, or a fortress. See SYMBOLIC MEANINGS.

Innovation and Inspiration

The seventeenth and eighteenth centuries brought a number of innovations. The ascendance of the French court (and gardens) at Versailles brought with it a new style of dining in both preparation and presentation. Service *à la française* meant that the number of dishes for each course matched the number of diners and was served simultaneously, with dessert as a separate service. The kitchen was divided between the *cuisine*, where the meal was prepared, and the *office*, which was solely responsible for dessert, including ices. See ICE CREAM. Each household department produced complex menus, describing the courses and particular dishes. The office was also stocked with the latest innovations in design: sophisticated containers, molds, and freezing pots. Service *en pyramide* stacked multiple layers of preserved fruit, sugar pastes, and plant material on successively smaller tiers of silver or porcelain. Eventually, these dessert sculptures grew so extensive that they became entire miniature gardens, which remained on the table throughout the entire meal. And, finally, cookbooks with engraved plates of elaborate, expressly axial table plans rivaled design treatises on architecture, landscape, and fortification. Tables became landscapes unto themselves, in which the desserts represented statuary, plants, or buildings. The period's quest for verticality as a mark of (royal) triumph over a landscape was achieved far more easily with towers made of sugar on a dining table than with any building materials in a city or countryside.

Antonin Carême, known as the first celebrity chef (Talleyrand, Napoleon, and Tsar Alexander I were among his clients), and one of the last in a long line of culinary figures in French haute cuisine, was a celebrated creator of such tablescapes. See CARÊME, MARIE-ANTOINE. Working at a patisserie on rue Vivienne in Paris, he would walk across the street to the Bibliothèque Nationale, where he drew inspiration from the oversized illustrated catalogs depicting architectural wonders from Rome to Egypt. His resulting *pièces montées* (set pieces) included castles, pyramids, and temples inspired by ancient cultures and also borrowed from the neoclassical architecture that was being taught down the street at the École des Beaux Arts. For these confections made of spun sugar or *pâté morte* (dead pastry or decorative pastry without yeast), taste was irrelevant; the goal was appearance. In fact, although a few elements such as flowers or fruits may have been edible, the larger elements were often kept and stored for another occasion (bringing to mind the tradition of keeping slices of a wedding cake, or bride's cake, to celebrate anniversary years later). See WEDDING CAKE.

In 1803 Carême opened his own very successful patisserie, in which he displayed his *pièces montées* in the windows, bringing in tourists and locals alike. Previously available only to the elite, desserts now reached a larger public thanks to a drop in sugar prices resulting from increased production in the colonies. Newly affordable, sugar was used to sweeten chocolate, coffee, and tea and, inevitably, to create sweets to accompany them. As dining hours shifted to later in the day, these snacks filled a void in the long stretches between meals, and by the nineteenth century, teatime (the French *goûter*) was firmly established. See SWEET MEALS and TEA. From London to Madrid to Vienna, the political, social, and cultural life of the bourgeoisie centered around coffee, chocolate, and tea houses, whose delicate confections were supplied by patisseries. Porcelain plates, influenced by the rococo trompe l'oeil sugar sculptures of previous centuries, now displayed all manner of tarts and éclairs, whose size was more appropriate to this new meal. As the scale of desserts shrank, the influence of fashion and the decorative arts on their designs grew; color, texture, and pattern came to the fore. Since sugar was no longer a luxury (and therefore status symbol) in and of itself, desserts had to display artisanal quality and the latest fashion. Coupled with the emergence of nouvelle cuisine and service *à la russe* (courses served sequentially, allowing for food to be brought to the table fresh and hot), this new style of dessert brought with it a new appreciation for taste.

A Desire for Speed

Toward the turn of the twentieth century, dessert again began to change, and nowhere was this clearer than in the United States. The burgeoning (and busy) American middle class had few of the artisan bakeries available in continental Europe, and so the focus was on home cooking. Instead of relying on domestic help, Americans looked to science and technology. Into the void came kitchen machines like eggbeaters and chemical leaveners such as baking powder, all of which sped up the baking process. See CHEMICAL LEAVENERS and WHISKS AND BEATERS. Product manufacturers distributed cookbooks full of quick-bread recipes, encouraging the widespread adoption of such tools. Industrialization and mass production created a dessert culture that was more about speed than refinement, taste than presentation.

Today, after a century of mass-produced and machined biscuits and chocolates, dessert has lost its place at the table. Perhaps the clearest example is the recent food fad, the macaron. See MACARONS. The brand best known for macarons is the Parisian patisserie, Ladurée, which ran a fashionable nineteenth-century tea salon designed by the painter Jules Cheret, who took inspiration from the Paris Opera House. Ladurée's macarons are still made in France with the color palette of the original Cheret design, but they are flown in the tens of thousands each day to outlets worldwide and can be found in any major airport, usually just before the security gates. Even McDonald's recently introduced macarons in its McCafés. Once part of a tradition of confections to be savored in a social setting, today's macarons are a mass-produced item to be eaten alone, quickly—and usually on the go.

The Past in the Future

Interestingly, the most recent developments in dessert design harken back to the elaborate confections of Venice and Vienna when taste was secondary but the show was everything. Bompas & Parr, the British food designers (trained as architects) who repopularized jelly by treating it much like sugar sculptures of their day, use sweet as spectacle. For New Year's Eve in 2013 in London, in collaboration with food technology experts and pyrotechnicians, they created a multisensory firework display, in which revelers smelled and tasted fruity mists and edible banana confetti matched to the fireworks (all, of course, both halal and kosher). They must have been influenced by the description of a 1549 feast to welcome Philip II to the Netherlands, in which guests were led to an "enchanted hall" at midnight, where sugar collation descended from the ceiling, along with hail and perfumed rain made from sugar candy.

In the United States, the newest 3D printers can print chocolate, sugar, or candy, bringing the art of the confectioner and chocolatier to the home kitchen. The resulting elaborate creations can be made in a fraction of the time and with as little skill. One company, 3D Systems, is collaborating with Hershey's to offer 3D-printed food to consumers. See SUGAR, UNUSUAL USES OF. Whether a democratic experience like fireworks along the Thames, do-it-yourself (DIY) or mass customization, dessert is designed for and by everyone. But what of taste? Here, the dessert maker's dilemma parallels that of other design professionals in finding a balance of form and function.

See also CAFÉ; CAKE AND CONFECTIONERY STANDS; COMPETITIONS; CONFECTION; EPERGNES; GELATIN DESSERTS; LEAF, GOLD AND SILVER; PARIS; PLATED DESSERTS; SERVING PIECES; TROMPE L'OEIL; and VENICE.

Krondl, Michael. *Sweet Invention: A History of Dessert.* Chicago: Chicago Review Press, 2011.

Mintz, Sidney. *Sweetness and Power.* New York: Penguin, 1985.

Strong, Roy. *Feast: A History of Grand Eating.* London: Jonathan Cape, 2002.

Wheaton, Barbara. *Savoring the Past.* Philadelphia: University of Pennsylvania Press, 1983.

Denise Ramzy

desserts, chilled occupy the crucial middle ground between the frozen and the cool: chilling is an essential element in their creation and enjoyment. Most cold desserts are chilled in advance of serving, and gateaux or dessert cakes layered with whipped or enriched cream are often said to improve after a few hours—or even a rest overnight—in the fridge. Alchemical transformations achieved through setting and stabilizing in a truly cold rather than a merely cool place earn these chilled desserts a special category all their own.

Cold Chilled Desserts

These desserts are thoroughly chilled both to finish them—usually to ensure a set—and for service.

Bavarois

Also known as a Bavarian Cream or *crème Bavaroise,* this delicate egg-yolk custard, aerated with whipped cream and set with gelatin, is both a dessert in its own right and a key component of others. It can fill a cold charlotte or be molded with paper to stand proudly above the rim of the dish for a chilled "soufflé." See CHARLOTTE; CUSTARD; GELATIN; and SOUFFLÉ. Often scented with alcohol and flavored or decorated with fruits, nuts, or chocolate, the bavarois is chilled for four hours to preserve its fluffy lightness while ensuring a firm presentation. The great French chef Carême included bavarois recipes in his early-nineteenth-century cookbooks, though contemporary French sources tend to credit it as a Swiss invention, and the late-nineteenth-century chef Escoffier suggested that it should more properly be called a Muscovite. See CARÊME, MARIE-ANTOINE and DESSERTS, FROZEN.

Cassata

Sicilian cassata is composed of a set fruit cream (similar to *crème pâtissière*) sandwiched between savoy biscuit or sponge layers soaked in alcohol and enclosed in marzipan. It is chilled for approximately three hours before serving. See CASSATA.

Jelly

Often thought of as a children's dessert (in the form of Jell-O or packet jelly), a clear jewel-like jelly of fruit juice set with gelatin, agar agar, carrageen, guar or xanthan gums, or arrowroot, and sometimes flavored with wine or alcohol, can be a sophisticated dessert. Molded into beautiful shapes, it might be layered in different colors and flavors, made with milk for a creamy clouded effect, or have fruit suspended in it. See BLANCMANGE and MOLDS, JELLY AND ICE CREAM. It must be chilled in order to set fully and should be served very cold.

Refrigerator or Chocolate Biscuit Cake

Composed of a variable combination of broken-up cookies, butter, sugar, nuts, dried fruit, eggs, and chocolate, these cakes are not baked. Hard ingredients (butter and chocolate) are melted to facilitate mixing, and the result is formed into a log or loaf shape, hardened in the refrigerator, and served very cold in slices.

Partially Frozen Desserts

Some chilled desserts are more deeply chilled than others, or even partially frozen. Others are composed of a combination of frozen ingredients like ice cream or sherbet and nonfrozen ingredients like fruit, sauces, nuts, and other edible decorative elements, such as sprinkles or jimmies. See ICE CREAM; SAUCE; SHERBET; and SPRINKLES.

Parfait

A perfect balance of soft and firm, a harmony of whipped cream, egg yolks, sugar, and flavor (often alcohol), the classic French parfait has a smooth texture whose secret lies in technique. Instead of the usual custard found in ice cream, sugar syrup at 248°F (120°C) is beaten into egg yolks before mixing with the other ingredients and freezing for 3 to 4 hours. In the United States, the term "parfait" refers to a layered ice cream or frozen yogurt confection similar to a sundae.

Semifreddo

These "semi-frozen" ices, also known in Italy as *perfetti,* are soft and light in texture, somewhere between a mousse and an ice cream, one part custard and one part whipped cream. Although many recipes confuse semifreddo with parfait—and they are closely related as the alternate Italian name attests—they are technically different. For semifreddo, sugar syrup at 248°F (120°C) is added not to egg yolks, as for parfait, but to beaten egg white, as for Italian meringue. See MERINGUE. The result is an even lighter, softer texture. Many simpler recipes exist for domestic cooks that borrow the name, using less skilled techniques to achieve a similar texture. Some versions do not contain eggs at all, effectively being a semi-frozen uncooked cream. Others incorporate granular sugar into stiffly beaten egg white, as for French meringue. The majority comprise a light mixture of whole eggs and sugar whisked, zabaglione-like, over a double boiler and cooled before folding in whipped cream and perhaps incorporating other ingredients like fruit, honey, or chocolate. See ZABAGLIONE. Regardless of cooking technique, semifreddos are never churned in an ice cream machine and are usually frozen into molds, often in a loaf shape that is then sliced for serving. They do not freeze hard; sometimes they are only chilled in the fridge, not frozen. The end result must be cold enough to hold its form and be sliced, but still a bit soft.

Sundae

A sundae is an individual layered dessert of ice cream in one or more flavors, often served in a tall glass. See SUNDAE. It usually comprises a base layer of syrup or crushed fruit, followed by two scoops of ice cream finished with more fruit or syrup, a dry topping like crushed or chopped nuts, and a lavish flourish of whipped cream; it is always crowned with a maraschino cherry with its stem intact. Hot fudge sundaes have heated—usually fudge—sauce. Sundaes may be made more elaborate with layers of fruit instead of syrup, and with different combinations of sauces and decorations. They are often given evocative names, like the Dusty Road, a chocolate sundae sprinkled with malted milk powder; or the All-American Victory sundae in patriotic shades of red, white, and blue that was popular after World War II, composed of vanilla ice cream with a marshmallow topping and both maraschino cherries and fresh blueberries. The Knickerbocker Glory, an idea imported to the United Kingdom from the United States, is presented in a taller glass with chocolate syrup at the base, followed by three scoops of ice cream with alternate layers of various crushed fruits between them. The whole is topped with whipped cream and a maraschino or glacé cherry. An American parfait is similar, though it has no chocolate syrup and its three scoops of ice cream may be separated by either crushed fruit or fruit syrup. It also includes a layer of chopped nuts below the whipped cream. Health-conscious modern versions of the parfait are made with layers of yogurt and granola.

Peach Melba, constructed of vanilla ice cream topped with poached peaches and raspberry coulis, was created by the chef Auguste Escoffier for Dame Nellie Melba, to celebrate her 1892 Covent Garden performance in Wagner's *Lohengrin*. On its first outing, it was apparently presented on the back of an iced swan and topped with spun sugar. See ESCOFFIER, GEORGES AUGUSTE.

Poire Belle Hélène, invented by Escoffier in 1864 and named for the Offenbach opera, is a sophisticated relative of the sundae, composed of a poached pear, vanilla ice cream, and chocolate sauce decorated with crystallized violets.

Split

A split is a horizontally arranged variation on a sundae, classically including a banana, though variations including tropical fruits such as mango or pineapple are increasingly popular.

The classic banana split includes three scoops of ice cream in the center of a dish, bounded on both long sides with a banana sliced lengthways. Each scoop is topped with chocolate or fruit sauces, and the whole is decorated with whipped cream, chopped nuts, and cherries. Variations such as a banana-boat split may include sponge cake at the bottom of the dish.

See also BLANCMANGE; CHARLOTTE; CHEESECAKE; CHOCOLATE POTS AND CUPS; CREAM; CUSTARD; DESSERTS, FROZEN; FOOLS; MOUSSE; TART; and TRIFLE.

Black, Keda. *Sugar and Spice*. London: Hamlyn, 2008.

"More Perfect than a Parfait." http://www.itchefs-gvci.com/index.php?option=com_content&view=article&id=284&Itemid=628 (accessed 25 January 2014).

Tate & Lyle Refineries. *Sweet Success: The Tate & Lyle Cookbook*. London: Sackett and Marshall, 1977.

Jane Levi

desserts, flambéed, make dramatic use of flame to create spectacle for the diner. Whether deftly performed at a restaurant table with a spirit burner and polished copper pan, or rushed blazing from the family kitchen to a darkened dining room, a flambé can create a thrilling grand finale to a meal. Why stop at a few candles when you can set the whole dessert alight?

Technique

Flambéing is the technique of using alcohol to flame food. In dessert dishes it is usually employed as a final presentational step for a hot or warm dessert and therefore generally done in front of diners either at their own table or a side table. The dish is often briefly finished in butter and sugar (or sugar alone) to achieve some caramelization before the alcohol is added. For maximum effect, attractive cooking utensils—traditionally copper saucepans and chafing dishes—are used over a spirit burner or candle flame, depending on how much of the cooking has already been done in the kitchen. The method of flambéing varies according to how much sauce or juice is in the dish to be flamed. If little or no liquid is already present, the chosen spirit can simply be poured onto the dish and the pan either tilted to catch the flame or a match applied. If the dish is very juicy or has a sauce, then more spirit is usually required to obtain a good flame. It is heated separately in a ladle or small pan, set alight, and poured already flaming onto the dish. Once the flames have subsided, the dessert is served.

Alcohol

To obtain maximum flare, alcohol with a percentage volume of 40 or over is usually recommended for flambéing, selected according to the ingredients in the dish. Fruit liqueurs and strong alcohols like cognac, gin, vodka, bourbon, or whiskey are generally specified, using classic pairings like rum for bananas, kirsch for pineapple or cherries, curaçao for orange, brandy for coffee desserts, and so on. See LIQUEUR. There is disagreement on how much of the alcohol is actually reduced or "burned off" during the flaming process, and how much flavor the flambé imparts, but it seems safe to assume that part of the thrill of a flambéed dessert lies in its scent of almost-burned caramel and retained alcoholic content.

Dishes

Almost anything can be flambéed, and numerous recipes exist for grilled, baked, poached, and fried fruit desserts, from kebabs to cake and ice cream toppings, as well as layered, folded, or rolled pancakes with various stuffings and sauces sent aflame to the table. Savarins, vacherins, babas, meringues, bombes, and sweet omelets are all excellent subjects for the flambé treatment, generally given the epithet "Surprise" to indicate their fiery incarnation. A lick of flame gives a spectacular finishing touch to a Baked Alaska. See BAKED ALASKA. The truly classic dishes are those in which the flambé is a component part of the dish, the ones unimaginable—even unworthy of their name—without the flambé step.

Bananas Foster is a 1950s creation from New Orleans, a variation on a banana split made with baked bananas over vanilla ice cream with a dark brown sugar, cinnamon, and butter sauce, flambéed with rum.

Cherries Jubilee was created by Auguste Escoffier for Queen Victoria's diamond jubilee celebrations in 1897. Cherries are lightly poached in lemon syrup and served flambéed with cherry brandy or kirsch over vanilla ice cream.

Crêpes Suzette is the ultimate in table-side flambé, of disputed late-nineteenth-century origin and now somehow redolent of 1970s restaurants, mustachioed waiters, and polished copper pans. Thin pancakes are spread with sweet orange butter enriched with curaçao, briefly fried in foaming orange butter and deftly folded in three to make a round-ended triangle. Brandy, Cointreau, or Grand Marnier is added to the caramelized butter in the pan, ignited, and poured over the neatly stacked pancakes.

See also DESSERTS, CHILLED; ESCOFFIER, GEORGES AUGUSTE; NEW ORLEANS; and SUNDAE.

Capel, Barnard. *The Art of Flambé Cooking*. London: Iliffe, 1965.

Hansen, Christine E., Misha T. Kwasniewski, and Gavin L. Sacks. "Decoupling the Effects of Heating and Flaming on Chemical and Sensory Changes during Flambé Cooking." *International Journal of Gastronomy and Food Science* 1, no. 2 (2012): 90–95.

Nilson, Bee. *Fondue, Flambé and Side Table Cooking*. London: Pelham, 1972.

Jane Levi

desserts, frozen, are compositions with ice cream or frozen yogurt at their core, combined in various ways with other dessert ingredients such as sponge cake, biscuits, nuts, fruits, creams, and sauces. Distinct from desserts individually constructed on the spot from a combination of fresh and frozen ingredients, frozen desserts are built in advance from the components, frozen into a composed whole and presented in their entirety for serving. These creations may be as simple as an ice cream cake or pie, or as extraordinary as a molded and layered bombe in the shape of a ball, a fruit, or an architectural model.

With the right tools, any frozen matter can be sculpted and formed, and both ice and ices have long been carved and molded into specific shapes for elite tables. Elaborate molds were in use for high-status occasions as early as 1714, when a carved ice tree trunk set in chocolate foam soil and hung with 150 tiny fruit-shaped bombes was presented at a celebration given by the Austrian ambassador to Rome. By the early nineteenth century, fancy ices were commonly served in wealthy households, and as refrigeration technology developed in the later nineteenth century, ice cream in all its variations became accessible to a much wider range of people even as manufacturing innovations allowed for the mass production of inexpensive metal goods—molds among them. See ICE CREAM and MOLDS, JELLY AND ICE CREAM. The Victorian era saw an explosion in molded ice cream constructions, all the way up to the epic scale of Eppelsheimer's 39-inch-high, 17-liter ice cream Statue of Liberty of 1876. From the mid-twentieth century onward, frozen desserts that go beyond a straightforward tub of ice cream have also become an increasingly important category in industrial food production.

Molded Desserts

Desserts frozen in molds are perhaps the most spectacular of all frozen desserts. The molds themselves are often extraordinary and elaborate, and the internal engineering needed to ensure a stable result requires the layering of different styles of ice creams, sorbets, and other ingredients, which can lead to an interior as visually exciting as the exterior. Since a molded dessert needs to be soft enough to eat and cut while being firm enough to survive presentation and service, it is important to use a slow-melting ice on the outside, such as sorbet, and a softer one, like a parfait or spoom (a lighter, frothier sorbet), on the inside.

Bombe

Bomba in Italian, this is a molded ice cream dessert in a hemispheric shape, usually with one flat surface for stability on the plate when serving. Baked Alaska is a bombe that manages to be baked, frozen, and flambéed all at the same time. See BAKED ALASKA and DESSERTS, FLAMBÉED.

Crème à la Moscovite was a Victorian ice served partially, rather than fully, frozen. Related to the chilled dessert bavarois, the *Moscovite* was set with isinglass or gelatin, giving it a slightly jellied texture, and molded into a bombe or cylinder shape.

Nesselrode Pudding, a spectacular frozen dessert, is said to have been invented in 1814 by the great chef Carême for the Russian diplomat Count Karl von Nesselrode. See CARÊME, MARIE-ANTOINE. It is a rich cream custard enriched with sweet chestnut purée, currants, raisins, candied fruit, whipped cream, and maraschino liqueur. Molded in a bombe or a cylinder, it is served with a cold maraschino custard sauce.

Spumoni, an Italian ice molded in a hemisphere, is composed of two complementary layers, usually a custard-based ice cream on the outside and a semifreddo or parfait inside.

Tortoni or biscuit tortoni, a classic of New York City (although almost certainly descended from Menon's 1760 recipe for *biscuits de glace*), is a rich maraschino-flavored ice cream with biscuit crumbs mixed in and on top; the dessert is traditionally served in an individual paper case. It is unclear exactly how tortoni arrived in New York, but a recipe appeared as early as 1889 in *The Table*, a cookbook written by Alessandro Filippini, chef at the famous restaurant Delmonico's.

Frozen Versions of Other Desserts

Many commercial suppliers offer frozen variations of typical cakes and desserts, which can also be prepared at home.

Ice Cream Cake, Gateau, or Cheesecake

An ice cream cake or cheesecake is a layered construction starting with a base of sponge cake, brownie, or a crunchy crumb, sometimes topped with fudge sauce before adding the chosen ice cream or ice creams in layers, with or without more layers of cake, and with suitable decorations.

Arctic roll, a British commercial classic, is a log of vanilla ice cream surrounded with raspberry jam and light sponge cake—like a Swiss roll without the interior spiral effect.

Ice Cream Pie

Ice cream pies are made up of a deep, baked pie crust filled with freshly churned or softened commercial ice cream, and usually topped with whipped cream or custard and garnished with nuts, fruit, or other toppings. Eskimo Pie is, confusingly, not a pie, but the American name for a confection the British call a Choc Ice: a small block of ice cream, usually vanilla, encased in chocolate. See ESKIMO PIE.

Ice Cream Sandwich

The "bread" of the sandwich is usually made of triangular, circular, or rectangular wafers, which enclose a filling of ice cream. A fancier version, akin to a vacherin, may be made by using meringue instead of wafers. See MERINGUE and VACHERIN.

Layered Ice Creams

Simpler ice cream desserts are formed with layers of different ice creams, usually in a rectangular loaf-cake shape that is easily sliced. The Neopolitan is composed of two or more different flavored and colored ice creams, often vanilla, strawberry, and chocolate. Pückler is a German variation on the Neopolitan, including layers of crushed macarons soaked in liqueur along with the ice cream layers. Viennetta, a globally available Unilever product, is made of extruded rippled layers of ice cream alternated with sprayed layers of compound chocolate. It is available in various flavor combinations.

See also CHESTNUTS; CUSTARD; DESSERTS, CHILLED; and ITALIAN ICE.

Liddell, Caroline, and Robin Weir. *Ices: The Definitive Guide*. London: Grub Street, 1995.
"Nesselrode Pudding" and other frozen desserts at Historic Food, the website of food historian Ivan Day. http://www.historicfood.com/Nesselrode%20Pudding%20Recipe.htm (accessed 26 November 2014).
Stogo, Malcolm. *Ice Cream and Frozen Desserts: A Commercial Guide to Production and Marketing*. New York and Chichester, U.K.: Wiley, 1997.
Weir, Robin, and Caroline Weir. *Ice Creams, Sorbets and Gelati: The Definitive Guide*. London: Grub Street, 2010.

Jane Levi

dextrose

See GLUCOSE.

diabetes

See SUGAR AND HEALTH.

Diwali is India's most widely celebrated festival, an occasion that serves to remind humanity of the triumph of good over evil. On the night of the autumn new moon (between October and November), cities, towns, and villages in India sparkle with the glow of oil lamps, candles, and tiny string lights that decorate houses, walls, gardens, and public spaces. This array of lights is called *deepavali* in Sanskrit, and the modern Hindi term "Diwali" is derived from that. The festival is a most distinctive cultural and religious marker.

From the perspective of the agricultural calendar, Diwali is a postharvest celebration. It takes place after the main autumn crop has been harvested and there is cause to be thankful (except in years of disastrous droughts or floods) that the coming year's food supply is ensured. Preparing the land for the winter sowing is preceded by the enjoyment of autumn's bounty. Spiritually, however, Diwali is unique in being not only an affirmation of good over evil, but also an occasion celebrated by three religious communities: Hindus, Sikhs, and Jains. For Sikhs, Diwali is the anniversary of Guru Hargobind's liberation from imprisonment in 1619, whereas the Jains believe it to be the day when the great reformer Mahavira achieved nirvana.

For Hindus, Diwali is draped in a rich tapestry of myths that vary from region to region. See HINDUISM. In the north, it is a celebration of Rama's victory over Ravana. In the south, it honors Krishna's killing of the demon Narakasura. In the west, it marks the day when Vishnu banished the demon king Bali to the nether regions. In all these areas, Lakshmi, the goddess of wealth and prosperity, is worshipped during Diwali. For many business people, Diwali also marks the beginning of a new working year—a reflection of the occasion's agricultural roots. In the eastern states (Bengal, Orissa, and Assam), however, it is the goddess Kali who is worshipped on Diwali instead of Lakshmi, and the story of her conquest of evil takes precedence over other Indian myths.

Out of this diversity of faith and myth, one factor unites all who celebrate Diwali—the eating and exchanging of sweets. The sense of a new beginning, whether in the field, at home, or in a place of business, is accompanied by the hope of better things to come, and the natural culinary expression of that mood may be seen in the extraordinary variety of sweets prepared in different regions of the country.

In northern and western India, women labor for days in advance to produce items made with flour, semolina, rice flour, besan (chickpea flour), sugar, clarified butter, nuts, and milk evaporated to a fudge-like consistency. The resultant profusion of laddus, barfis, halvah, kachoris, puris, and other goodies are consumed by families at home and widely shared with friends, neighbors, and colleagues. See BARFI; HALVAH; and LADDU. The custom of visiting people and bringing brightly wrapped boxes of sweets is witnessed in every city and town. The professional confectioners are equally busy, churning out their specialties and creating displays that are appealing to both eye and tongue.

One of the most indulgent festive comestibles is *puran poli*, a flatbread stuffed with a sweetened mixture of chickpea flour and pigeon-pea flour, fragrant with cardamom, rosewater, and *kewra* (screwpine) flower water. See FLOWER WATERS and PANDANUS. The bread is fried in clarified butter and often dipped in warm, melted butter before eating. The *mawa kachori* is another seasonal stuffed treat, the filling made of solidified evaporated milk and chopped nuts. Another Diwali favorite is the *balushahi*, a richer, melting-in-the-mouth incarnation of a doughnut, emitting the aroma of clarified butter and gilded with festive silver foil. Among the laddus—round balls made with sweetened besan and aromatic spices—*motichoor laddu* is a particularly delectable version often served at Diwali. Tiny balls of besan dough are fried in clarified butter, dipped in syrup, and once cooled, formed into larger balls (sometimes with the addition of blanched almonds or pistachios) that are often decorated with edible silver foil.

In southern India, the same ingredients are used with a different culinary sensibility to create sweets for festive occasions like Diwali. Laddus, made with roasted besan, sugar, and prolific amounts of clarified butter, go by the name of *maladu, maavu laddu,* or *pottukadalai. Susiyam,* similar to *puran poli,* is made in the rounded shape of a laddu instead of a flatbread. The filling, consisting of cooked chickpeas (or Bengal gram), coconut, brown sugar, and toasted nuts, is stuffed inside a flour shell, shaped into a ball, and fried in coconut oil or clarified butter.

Milk plays the star role in items like rice pudding and a yogurt cheese called *shrikhand.* In eastern India, the traditional Bengali items such as sandesh, made with *chana* (or *channa*) or fresh curd cheese, also appear on the menu for Diwali. See SANDESH. Although Bengalis celebrate Kali Puja during Diwali, that presents no obstacle to their indulging in the lipid-rich laddus, barfis, and halvah that are so common in the northern and western parts of India.

See also FRIED DOUGH; INDIA; KOLKATA; and MITHAI.

Achaya, K. T. *Indian Food.* Delhi: Oxford University Press, 1998.

Banerji, Chitrita. *Eating India.* New York: Bloomsbury, 2007.

Krondl, Michael. *Sweet Invention: A History of Dessert.* Chicago: Chicago Review Press, 2011.

Chitrita Banerji

Dobos torte, pronounced *doboshe,* is Hungary's most iconic layer cake, a round cake consisting of six thin, buttery, sponge cake layers, five layers of chocolate buttercream, and a layer of hardened caramel covering the top. See CARAMELS and SPONGE CAKE. The top caramel layer is cut into individual slices (with a special Dobos torte knife) before it hardens, and those pieces are arranged on top of the cake. Dobos torte is served in nearly every *cukrászda* (patisserie) in the country.

Although Dobos torte is often mistranslated as "drum cake" (the Hungarian *dob* means "drum"), it is in fact named after its inventor, József Dobos (1847–1924), a baker, chef, prolific cookbook author, caterer, and culinary entrepreneur who came from a family of cooks going back generations. In 1878 Dobos opened a specialty gourmet shop in central Pest that sold an array of high-quality local foods and imported delicacies such as cheese, wine, caviar, and spices. The shop was known for its elaborate window displays and house-made products. Dobos's most important creation was his namesake cake.

The Dobos torte debuted in 1885 at the National General Exhibition in Budapest, where Dobos presided over an elegant pavilion staffed by more than 100 people. Queen Elisabeth and Emperor Franz Joseph were among the crowd who visited his pavilion. "Those present cheered the royal couple, who were served personally by Dobos himself, writes Tibor Éliás in his book *Dobos and 19th Century Confectionery in Hungary* (2010). "They of course also tasted the latest novelty, after which another royal cheer erupted—this time in honor of the creator of the cake" (p. 87). Afterwards, Dobos was made a purveyor to the Imperial and Royal Court.

The Dobos torte "was born as a result of continuous experimentation on the part of the ever creative Dobos," writes Éliás. The cake became a sensation not only in Budapest, but also throughout much of Europe, for several reasons. Unlike the other, more intricately decorated European cakes of the time, the Dobos torte, with its flat, shiny, unadorned caramel top, looked downright minimalist. The chocolate buttercream spread between the cake layers was also a new concept, and it became Dobos's signature (and secret) ingredient. Both the buttercream and hard caramel were innovations that gave the cake a significantly longer shelf life, with no need for refrigeration. Dobos brought his cakes with him during his frequent travels in Europe, and shipping the cakes throughout the continent became an important part of his business. He designed special wooden boxes to keep the cakes cool and perfectly intact during their journey. The Dobos torte was regularly served at social events throughout the Austro-Hungarian Empire.

During Dobos's time, his cake was much imitated by other patissiers in Budapest, but never successfully. Bakers did not figure out that cocoa butter was the secret ingredient in Dobos's smooth chocolate buttercream. Tired of all the bad imitations of his cake, Dobos donated his recipe to the Pastry and Honey-bread Makers' Guild in 1906 so that all pastry chefs would have access to the true recipe. Soon afterward, Dobos closed his shop. Despite his success, Dobos's life did not have a happy ending. He lost most of his fortune, which he had invested in war bonds, during World War I.

The Dobos torte is as popular as ever in Hungary today—and also in Austria and other countries that were part of the empire—but it is rarely prepared at home because it is so labor intensive. The Dobos torte (often written phonetically as Dobosh torte outside of Hungary) has also inspired cakes as far away as the United States. In New Orleans the Doberge cake is a layer cake usually filled with chocolate and lemon pudding and covered in buttercream or fondant. See FONDANT. In Hawaii the popular Dobash cake is a chocolate chiffon cake with a chocolate pudding or Chantilly cream filling. Though many Hungarian pastry shops prepare the Dobos in its classic form, modern bakeries also experiment and create versions that would have been unrecognizable to József Dobos. In Hungary, however, no matter how experimental a pastry chef gets with his or her Dobos torte, chocolate and caramel are always present. Even today, it feels like a little luxury to sit down with a slice of elegant Dobos torte.

See also AUSTRIA-HUNGARY; CAKE; LAYER CAKE; NEW ORLEANS; and TORTE.

Éliás, Tibor, and Katalin Csapó. *Dobos and 19th Century Confectionery in Hungary*. Budapest: Hungarian Museum of Trace and Tourism, 2010.

Carolyn Bánfalvi

Dolly Varden cake, a layer cake in the shape of a doll, inspires recollections of childhood whimsy. It has a long history within popular culture. Dolly Varden first appeared as a character in Charles Dickens's *Barnaby Rudge: A Tale of the Riots of Eighty* (1842). Described as a pretty, charming coquette, Dolly inspired fanciful portraits of her dressed in a cherry mantle and straw hat with red ribbons. All types of dedications to her followed, including flowered fabrics, parasols, paper dolls, dances, an amusing song, and even an iridescent trout. In the 1870s a fashion craze swept through London and New York, with *Harper's Bazaar* featuring "Dolly Varden Costumes"—flowered dresses with wide, bustled skirts.

Inspired by these colorful and multilayered dresses, admirers devised the Dolly Varden cake. In Australia, various recipes began to appear in the 1880s, and by around 1910 the recipe had become fairly standardized. It traditionally calls for a simple butter cake (butter, flour, sugar, a leavening agent, and eggs), sometimes flavored with lemon essence, split into two layers (or three, depending on the version of the recipe). This mixture is divided into two (or three parts) and one half is baked as is, with dried fruits and spices (raisins, cherries, currants, cloves, cinnamon, and nutmeg) mixed into the other. The cakes are stacked and joined together with a jam, icing, or a vanilla-flavored buttercream filling, creating a tiered result when the cake is cut and eaten. During the Depression years of the 1930s, when there was a scarcity of ingredients, many cookbooks contained an altered recipe for the cake that called for less fruit, spice, milk, and eggs, and with dripping (rendered animal fat) as a substitute for the butter.

As the recipe evolved to suit contemporary tastes and baking practices, modern ingredients like Maraschino cherries, cardamom, citron, walnuts, and coconut were added to the mix. In response to a craze for cake decorating among home cooks in the 1940s and 1950s, a new shape appeared in Australia and New Zealand alongside the tiered original—a rounded cake baked in a pudding tin. See CAKE DECORATING. The cake remained a novelty until the 1970s, when, possibly due to the popularity of the Barbie doll, a special Dolly Varden cake tin was manufactured and sold with decorative designs and instructions for crafting a dramatic cake. The deep tin formed Dolly's "dress," which encased an actual plastic doll placed in the center, usually a favorite of the child. The recipe showed how to use the doll, and instructed either removing the legs or carving out a hole at the center of the cake to accommodate its length.

Dolly Varden cake became irrevocably tied to birthday celebrations, though it was often relabeled. For instance, the Betty Crocker version of the cake is called "Fairy Tale Princess Cake," and cookbook recipes variously label it "Dolly Cake," "Princess Doll Cake," or "Barbie Cake." The cake continued to evolve to reflect popular trends and fashion fads, with most recipes from the 1980s onward recommending a cake mix as a quick alternative to allow more time for intricate decoration of the "dress."

While the original magic of Dolly Varden may have waned, the cake now serves as a springboard for the imagination, bringing delight to successive generations.

See also AUSTRALIA AND NEW ZEALAND; BETTY CROCKER; CAKE; and CAKE MIX.

Cedro, Carmel. "Dolly Varden: Sweet Inspiration." *Australasian Journal of Popular Culture* 2, no. 1 (2013): 37–46.

"Dolly Varden House Dress." *Harper's Bazaar.* New York Public Library Digital Gallery. http://digitalgallery.nypl.org/nypldigital/id?803737 (accessed 15 September 2014).

Humble, Nicola. *Cake: A Global History*. London: Reaktion, 2010.

Carmel Cedro

doughnuts are fried, doughy pastries leavened with yeast or chemical leaveners. They are found in myriad forms, shapes, and manifestations in almost every culture that has discovered the joys of fried food. In Alpine Tyrol, yeast-raised rounds are filled with preserves or cream; in New Orleans, sugar-dusted squares are a perfect partner for chicory-laced coffee. New Englanders have cider-scented dough circles and East Asians enjoy chewy *pon de rings*. See FRIED DOUGH and FRITTERS.

Perhaps the first reference to a doughnut-like pastry comes from Athenaeus, in the *Deipnosophists* (third century C.E.). *Enkrides* is "a small pastry deep-fried in olive oil and covered with honey afterward," he writes, a description that could easily apply to current Greek *loukomades*, though whether they were yeast-raised, as they are now, is anybody's guess. See ATHENAEUS. Doughnut predecessors also pop up in the medieval Muslim sources. *Zalabia* (the spelling varies) and *luqmat al-qadi* sometimes took the form of yeast-raised lumps of dough, as they do today. Morocco's doughnut-shaped *sfenj* have a clear ancestor in a recipe for *isfunj* found in an anonymous thirteenth-century Andalusian cookbook. See MIDDLE EAST; NORTH AFRICA; and ZALABIYA.

European Doughnuts

Most European countries have some version of a doughnut, which is typically associated with Carnival. See CARNIVAL. In Venice, *fritelle di carnevale* are fried dough balls enriched with dried fruit and spices. To make Lyons's sugar-dusted *bugne*, a yeast dough is tied in a knot. In Spain, *rosquillas de anis* are doughnut-shaped and flavored with anisette.

In Central Europe, Krapfen (one of many terms for a jelly doughnut) are documented as early as the thirteenth-century epic *Parzifal*. The fourteenth-century cookbook *Das Buch von guter speise* includes four recipes for fillings—all based on spiced apples—though none for the dough. A hundred years later, a Czech manuscript cookbook suggests a stuffing of figs, stewed pears, peaches, and sour cherries. Other sources recommend meat, fish, and vegetables. In Vienna, an ordinance from 1486 makes clear that the city was already supplied by professional doughnut bakers. By the late eighteenth century, jam-filled doughnuts were commonplace but, due to the cost of sugar, were expensive and accordingly not out of place at the fanciest occasions. According to contemporary press accounts, some 10 million Krapfen were served to the attendees of the Congress of Vienna during the 1815 carnival season alone. Today, jelly doughnuts are ubiquitous across Central Europe under an assortment of regional names and with a variety of fillings that may include jam, fruit butter, custard, chocolate, or liqueur-spiked cream. Israelis have adapted the carnival doughnut tradition for Hanukkah, serving jelly doughnuts (renamed *sufganyiot*) for the Festival of Lights. See HANUKKAH.

Early American Doughnuts

Parts of England, too, had a tradition of serving fritters for Shrove Tuesday, although most did not resemble anything we would call a doughnut. The one exception comes from Hertfordshire. William Ellis gives a recipe for these Hertfordshire Cakes, Nuts and Pincussions as early as 1750 in *The Country Housewife's Family Companion*, noting that they are made by shaping a yeast dough in the shape of walnuts. A little later in the century, a manuscript cookbook compiled by Baroness Elizabeth Dimsdale actually calls them "dow nuts." It is reasonable to assume that the New England settlers, many of whom traced their origin to precisely this part of England, brought the name and recipe with them, although as Puritans, they left behind any Carnival association.

In the New World, these fried dough balls were served year-round for breakfast, lunch, and dinner. Writers reminisce about eating the fried treats during the Revolutionary era; soldiers were feted with doughnuts before being sent to war. Even New England whalers, far from home, fried doughnuts in rendered whale blubber.

Noah Webster defined the doughnut as a "small roundish cake, made of flour, eggs and sugar, moistened with milk and boiled in lard" in his 1828 dictionary. The earliest American recipe for "Dough Nuts," inserted into an addendum to Susanna Carter's *Frugal Housewife* in 1802, does not specify the shape, but later recipes suggest that the "nuts" were made by rolling out the dough and cutting it into small squares or circles. The eventual torus shape seems to have been modeled on the jumble (a popular ring-shaped cookie) or possibly crullers, which were often twisted into a ring. In 1846 Mrs. Abell instructs the reader of her *Skillful Housewife's Book* to cut her "fried cakes" (basically cake doughnuts) as one would jumbles. Nonetheless, some 70 years later, a retired Maine captain named Hanson Gregory claimed that he had invented the holey doughnut in 1847. His was a delightfully improbable sailor's yarn, but it proved remarkably sticky for decades to come.

Ever in a hurry, Americans began to substitute chemical leaveners for yeast at least as early as 1829, when Lydia Maria Child included a recipe for pearlash-raised doughnuts in her best-selling *Frugal Housewife*. Later cookbooks would frequently include both so-called raised (yeast) and cake (chemically leaved) doughnuts, the relative merits of each being a point of contention even today. See CHEMICAL LEAVENERS.

Of course, New Englanders were not the only Americans to fry dough. During the nineteenth century, the ethnic fry-cake traditions of the Dutch, German, and French settlers began to hybridize with the Anglo-American practice. Mrs. Abell suggests adding raisins and currants to dough nuts to turn them into "New York Oley Koeks," her spelling of Dutch *oliekoeks*; some Pennsylvania Dutch families began using baking powder to make pre-Lenten *fastnachts* (similar to Krapfen); and in Louisiana, French and German traditions blended to create the beignet (not to be confused with the many varied *beignets* found across France). See PENNSYLVANIA DUTCH.

At the dawn of the twentieth century, doughnuts had become commonplace from Maine to Alaska; to many Americans, the homely pastries connoted a kind of wholesome domesticity. When the United States entered World War I in 1917, Salvation Army volunteers began to make the fried rings (alongside pies) as a way of boosting morale at the front. One Army lassie (as the young women were called) wrote, "Invariably the boys would begin to talk about home and mother while they were eating the doughnuts." Subsequent to the war, the Salvation Army used doughnuts to promote its cause, issuing posters that featured the lassies holding armfuls of "sinkers," condoning such Tin Pan Alley songs as "My Doughnut Girl," and even participating in the production of *Fires of Faith*, a mildly sensationalist Hollywood melodrama.

During World War II, the doughnut challenge was taken up by the Red Cross. Driven and operated by young women volunteers, retrofitted trucks were outfitted with gramophones, American cigarettes, magazines, and, most important, automatic doughnut frying machines. These "Clubmobiles" followed the advancing army through France, Italy, and right into Germany, often at enormous risk.

Once the European war was won, returning GIs were often held for weeks in huge tent cities. At one camp, near Reims, as reported by the *New York Times*, the soldiers downed a million cups of coffee and a half-million doughnuts each day. Once they returned home, a small number of veterans opened up doughnut shops of their own with the help of the GI bill.

Increasingly doughnuts, and doughnut shops, came to be associated with working-class Americans, not least a cartoon nuclear-plant worker named Homer Simpson. Before the advent of 24-hour fast-food chains, doughnut shops were one of the few places a factory worker or a cop on an early shift could grab some breakfast. William Rosenberg, the founder of Dunkin' Donuts, actively encouraged the police presence, figuring it would cut down on crime. Ever since, cops have been closely associated with doughnuts in the American imagination. The word "doughnut," due to its shape, has also picked up a host of secondary meanings, from a spare tire, to a maneuver made by an automobile, to a variety of sexual and sexual orientation slang that references the hole. See SEXUAL INNUENDO and SLANG.

Doughnut Chains

Following World War I and piggybacking on the sinker's new celebrity, several entrepreneurs made a stab at mechanizing the doughnut-making process. The most successful by far was Adolf Levitt, a Russian immigrant who founded the Doughnut Corporation of America. His doughnut-making gizmo, which made its debut in 1920, and accompanying proprietary mix eventually came to dominate the commercial bakery market. Levitt publicized October as doughnut month (doughnuts were a favorite Halloween treat) and sponsored the National Dunking Association. In 1940 the Association boasted 3 million members, including actor Zero Mostel, future television host Johnny Carson, and even choreographer Martha Graham. Levitt's Mayflower shops were the first national doughnut chain.

Following Levitt's lead, several doughnut businessmen succeeded in creating regional, and then national, doughnut chains. Shipley Do-Nuts originated in Houston, Texas, in 1936; Krispy Kreme was founded in Winston-Salem, North Carolina, in 1937; Winchell's in Temple City, California, in 1948; Dunkin' Donuts in Quincy, Massachusetts, in 1950; and Tim Hortons in Hamilton, Canada, in 1964. Several of these shops have expanded internationally, especially into the Middle East and East Asia. See CANADA; DUNKIN' DONUTS; and KRISPY KREME.

Starting in 1994, doughnuts began to get a gourmet makeover when, in Napa Valley, the celebrated chef Thomas Keller put a doughnut on the menu of the French Laundry. The same year, Mark Israel opened up a shop on New York City's Lower East Side using organic flour and glazing his yeasty rings with floral essence, passion fruit, and other outré flavors. Trendy restaurants followed suit, and by the first decade of the twenty-first century, fancy doughnut shops from coast to coast featured wacky flavors such as bacon maple, pumpkin spice latte, and Mexican mole, to say nothing of toppings ranging from Oreos to pulled pork and potato salad. In 2013 New York pastry chef Dominique Ansel made a splash with his trademarked but also widely copied "cronut," a fried ring of croissant dough filled with custard cream. Who could have guessed that people would stand in line for three hours for a fried lump of dough?

Abell, L. G. *The Skilful Housewife's Book, or, Complete Guide to Domestic Cookery, Taste, Comfort, and Economy: Embracing 659 Receipts Pertaining to Household Duties, Gardening, Flowers, Birds, Plants, etc.* New York: D. Newell, 1846.

Dimsdale, Elizabeth, and Heather Falvey. *The Receipt Book of Baroness Elizabeth Dimsdale, c. 1800.* Rickmansworth, U.K.: Hertfordshire Record Society, 2013.

Krondl, Michael. *The Donut: History, Recipes, and Lore from Boston to Berlin.* Chicago: Chicago Review Press, 2014.

Mann, Ludwig. "Krapfen." *Traditionelle Lebensmittel in Österreich.* 14 December 2009. http://www.bmlfuw.gv.at/land/lebensmittel/trad-lebensmittel/speisen/krapfen.html

Michael Krondl

dragées

See SPRINKLES.

dried fruit is a term that broadly covers any kind of fruit preserved by desiccation. In the context of baking derived from traditional British practice, however, the term is more specific, indicating dried vine fruit, sometimes mixed with small dice of candied peel. See CANDIED FRUIT. Dried fruit, in general, plays numerous roles in sweets, including direct use as snack food, as a component of confectionery items like energy bars, and as a dominant ingredient in rich fruitcake. See FRUITCAKE. Over a million tons of dried vine fruits are produced annually. Apricots, prunes, and figs are also dried and traded in substantial quantities; dates are the most important in global terms. See DATES.

Dried fruits are mentioned in ancient texts such as *Apicius*, the first comprehensive cookbook dating from the late Roman period. Their primary role was as a sweetener alongside honey and wine in a range of savory dishes. See HONEY. They became more significant in sweet dishes by the medieval period while still adding sweetness to savory foods. This role survives in Middle Eastern cuisines, for example, the use of dried apricots in *mishmishiya*, a lamb stew from Arabia and Iran. See MIDDLE EAST and PERSIA.

The traditional method of preparation is by sun drying, but this practice is being replaced by industrial processes to cope with demand, and also to produce a uniform product for mass marketing. Dried fruits store well, making them ideal for transport and trade. Their concentrated flavor and sugar content (sugars dominate their composition, ranging from 60 percent in apricots, prunes, and figs to nearly 80 percent in vine fruit) made dried fruits a sought-after commodity centuries ago when sugar was expensive, and they continue to be appreciated for their own textures and flavors, which are distinct from those of fresh fruit.

Vine Fruits

Vine fruits are derived from fresh grapes and have a long history in production, trade, and culinary use. In ideal conditions the fruit of *Vitis vinifera* will desiccate naturally on the vine and would have been gathered in prehistory before being developed and cultivated as a major trade item. Production and export are now dominated by Turkey and the United Sates, which account for half the world trade. The market demand for vine fruits has become very diverse, reflecting the globalization of baked goods and confectionery that often rely on them for their character.

Vine fruits are divided into three main groups. Raisins derive their name from the Roman word *racemus*, meaning a "bunch of fruit." They are generally the largest of the vine fruits and vary in color from brown to dark red. Sultanas were associated with the Ottoman Empire. They are generally pale yellow in color but can shade to green or gold. Currants are named after their medieval association with the Greek town of Corinth. The smallest of the fruits, they have a blue-black hue. Seedless vine fruit are now readily available, a great benefit for all bakers and makers of sweets, as stoning raisins was a sticky, much disliked kitchen chore. A single type of vine fruit, such as the currants used in traditional British Eccles cakes and Garibaldi biscuits, can give essential character to a particular baked good. More generally, a selection of vine fruits in baking provides immediate visual appeal but yields only modest flavor.

Other Dried Fruits

Other dried fruits include dried apricots prepared from the fruit of *Prunus armeniaca*, which can retain some of the character of the fresh fruit, particularly its color (especially when treated with sulfur dioxide). Three-quarters of the world's dried apricot crop is produced and exported by Turkey. A very different variety from the Hunza valley in Pakistan is dried on the trees and looks like a shriveled brown nut, but when cooked, it reveals an intense flavor. Dried apricots are a versatile ingredient that lends intense flavor and golden color to compotes, cheesecakes, cookies, cakes, and specialty breads, such as apricot *couronne*.

Prunes are the dried fruit of the plum tree *Prunus domestica*. The best-known variety is the *pruneau d'Agen* from France, with an aroma of almond. Although used in savory dishes such as tagines, prunes also have a role in baked goods, such as the *far Breton*, the signature dish of Brittany in which Armagnac-soaked prunes stud a thick batter cake.

Figs, principally the fruit of *Ficus carica* but occasionally of other species, are an important dried fruit crop in Turkey. Often called Smyrna figs, recalling their main port of export in Turkey (now called Izmir), they are made into *incir tatlisi*, a family of desserts made by rehydrating the dried fruit and stuffing them with walnuts and cream. Iran is also a major producer; their export fruits are of a smaller size. Figs were an important ingredient in medieval European food, for example, in the deep-fried fig pastries called *tourteletes in fryture*, described in the fourteenth-century *Forme of Cury* cookbook.

Apples are also dried to preserve the nutritional value of this highly perishable fruit. They find uses in confectionery and baking. Mulberries and sour cherries are dried on a modest scale from Turkey to Afghanistan for use as sweets and in compotes and baking.

Some more tropical soft-fleshed fruits are also dried. The smaller varieties of bananas are sun-dried whole to a soft, sticky consistency with a toffee-like flavor, very different from the hard banana chips now used in some baked goods. Sun-drying items such as mango slices is still carried out in a traditional manner in certain places, but tropical fruits like mangos and papayas are also processed into a form of candied fruit more acceptable to the tastes of the industrialized world.

See also APPALACHIAN STACK CAKE; FRUIT; FRUIT PASTES; FRUIT PRESERVES; and TURKEY.

Sun-Maid Growers of California. *Raisins & Dried Fruit: Serving the World Since 1912.* New York: DK Publishing, 2011. http://www.sunmaid.com/book (accessed 28 May 2014).

Phil Iddison

drop cookies are made by dropping cookie dough onto a baking pan from spoons or scoops, or by rolling dough into balls by hand and placing them on the pan. This method helps to produce uniform size and shape. Drop cookies are the most common type of cookie made because they are so easy to prepare. Flavors include chocolate chip, sugar, oatmeal raisin, and peanut butter. However, the variety of recipes is endless.

The most well-known drop cookie is the chocolate chip cookie, first developed in 1934 by Ruth Wakefield of the Toll House Inn in Whitman, Massachusetts. Mrs. Wakefield was an outstanding restaurateur and skillful chef. One day she cut a bar of chocolate into bit-size pieces and added them to one of her cookie recipes. The resulting cookies were so popular that they came to be served at the end of each meal at the inn. Soon the recipe was published in a Boston newspaper; it was called the Toll House Cookie. Mrs. Wakefield entered into an agreement with Nestlé that allowed it to print her recipe on their semi-sweet chocolate bars and then on bags of chocolate chips. See NESTLÉ. During World War II, GIs stationed overseas welcomed packages of Toll House Cookies from their families.

The most common flour used in drop cookies is all-purpose, a medium-protein content flour, which gives the cookies a good framework. Softer flours and starches, such as rice flour, cornstarch, oats, and cornmeal, are used to give different textures and flavors. Cake and pastry flours offer a finer texture and crumb.

A high percentage of solid fat forms the base of most drop cookies. It makes a somewhat soft dough that is easy to shape and that spreads nicely when properly baked. Butter is preferred for its maximum flavor and balanced taste. Liquid oils can be used in drop cookies, especially in vegan recipes. Usually, the fat is used at room temperature for even and quick aerating when beaten.

When all-purpose flour is used, the fat is creamed with the sugar only until smooth. When using softer flours and starches, all the ingredients are combined with the room-temperature fat and mixed until a smooth dough forms. Mexican wedding cookies are made using this method. With either method the dough should never be overmixed, as this could result in a tough dough or a weakened structure caused by overheating from the friction of mixing.

Cookie sheets should be lightly oiled or lined with parchment paper. The cookies should be spaced 2 or more inches apart to allow them room to spread; a crowded tray will not allow the heat to flow evenly. The cookie sheets should be positioned on the middle oven racks and rotated at least once from front to back for even baking and coloring. The cookies bake for 8 to 14 minutes at a temperature between 325°F and 375°F (163°C and 191°C).

Cookies should be cooled on the pan that is placed on a rack for even cooling. Placing them on a flat counter surface will trap the heat on the bottom, causing the bottoms to overcook; it could also create a vacuum that might generate steam and make the cookies soggy. Once completely cooled, the cookies may be stored in an airtight, covered container to preserve flavor and texture.

See also BUTTER; FLOUR; PRESSED COOKIES; and ROLLED COOKIES.

Amendola, Joseph. *Understanding Baking.* New York: Van Nostrand Reinhold, 1992.

Corriher, Shirley O. *Bake Wise.* New York: Scribner, 2008.

Jim Dodge

dulce de leche, literally "sweet of milk," is a caramel-flavored syrup made by boiling down milk with added sugar. It is found in various forms across Latin America: *cajeta* in Mexico (from the small wooden boxes in which it was traditionally sold), *manjar* ("delicacy") in Peru and Chile, *doce de leite* in Brazil, and *arequipe* in Colombia. If further boiled down, dulce de leche gives rise to fudgy confections (*jamoncillo* being one of the Mexican varieties). Although artisanal production continues, today homemade dulce de leche is more likely to result from simmering a can of condensed milk for several hours. Industrially produced versions are widely sold.

Dulce de leche may be eaten as is, spread on bread or crackers, or used as an ingredient in ice cream, tres leches cake, or as a filling in crepes. See TRES LECHES CAKE. In southern Latin America, it is sandwiched between cookies to make the very popular *alfajores*. Beginning in the 1990s, dulce de leche became popular in the United States and Europe in ice cream, tres leches cake, and banoffee pie (pastry or cookie crust filled with dulce de leche, cream, and banana, very popular in the United Kingdom since the 1970s).

The origins of milk sweets are unclear. Although today they occasionally crop up in Europe as *confiture du lait* (milk jam) in France or fudgy confections in Central Europe, they do not appear to have been part of the sweet repertoire of the Iberian empires. Dulce de leche, however, is found in the Philippines, and milk sweets are central to Hindu cuisine, raising the possibility that the technique was introduced to Latin America by passengers on the Spanish galleons that sailed between Mexico and the Philippines from 1565 to 1815.

See also LATIN AMERICA and MILK.

Presilla, Maricel. *Gran Cocina Latina: The Food of Latin America*, pp. 809–811, 834–835, 837–838. New York: Norton, 2012.

Rachel Laudan

dumplings, in a sweet context, usually refer to boiled or steamed balls of dough. In the Central European tradition, they may have a filling, and they can be served as a side dish or as a course in their own right. The *Appetit-Lexikon* (1894), a dictionary of gastronomy by Viennese authors R. Habs and L. Rosner, defines dumplings as a Sunday dish in the countryside, a side dish, or an addition to soups. Dumplings are typical of the South German and Alpine areas, various regions of the former Austro-Hungarian monarchy (Bohemia, Slovakia, Hungary), and parts of Eastern Europe, including Ukraine.

A bowl of mouth-watering dumplings is depicted on a wall painting in northern Italy that shows monks enjoying their meal around 1000 C.E. Dumplings were once the everyday fare of the poor, since the most basic ones called for only flour, water (or milk), eggs, and semolina. Bread cubes and, later on, potatoes were also used to make the dough. Dumplings were mostly topped with fried cubes of bacon when savory, or with hot cream or fruit sauce when sweet. See SAUCE. Dumplings with no meat filling became widespread Lenten fare, as most of the regions where they were prepared practiced Catholicism, under which roughly 150 fast days a year were observed until the beginning of the twentieth century.

Recipes for sweet dumplings began to appear in the seventeenth century, but they differed widely from what are now considered sweet dumplings. Perhaps the earliest recipe, from the early 1600s, appears in an anonymous manuscript in Prague's National Museum. Listed among a dozen recipes for savory dumplings is one for fruit dumplings made with plums that are mixed with diced white rolls and eggs, and then fried. Other early recipes include deep-fried almond dumplings to be served with sour-cherry soup; dumplings made from dried sour cherries, breadcrumbs, and eggs, also deep-fried and served with sour-cherry soup; and apple dumplings served with a soup made from wine, cinnamon, and sugar. In Bohemia, dumplings were made of farmer's cheese (*topfen*) dough or yeast dough, filled with plums or *powidl*, a very thick jam made of plums. These dumplings are still much appreciated there, as are semolina dumplings; both are served with melted butter and sugar. Less well known today are fried apple dumplings—apple cubes mixed with a dough made of flour, butter, eggs, and cinnamon—and plum dumplings based on noodle dough. It was only during the nineteenth century that a greater variety of sweet dumplings, many of which are still known today, began to appear in cookbooks. Yeast dough, potato dough, farmer's cheese dough, and choux pastry were and still are the most common types of dough used for dumplings.

Dampfnudeln (steamed noodles) are fist-sized dumplings made with flour, eggs, and yeast and cooked in a covered pan with a little milk and butter. Steamed *Hefeklösse* (yeast dumplings) are traditionally eaten with steamed prunes or dried apples and pears. *Zwetschgenknödel* (plum dumplings) belong to the large family of sweet, boiled, fruit-filled dumplings often made with potato dough in numerous variations; arguably the most famous are Austrian *Marillenknödel,* made with lush apricots and garnished with white breadcrumbs toasted with butter and sugar. The most popular sweet version of Ukrainian half-moon-shaped *varenyky* is filled with sour cherries and topped with sour cream.

A Viennese housewife in the second half of the nineteenth century would have served sweet dumplings for lunch, a tradition that endures today, especially on Fridays, although nowadays fruit-filled dumplings are most often eaten for dessert. New fillings have been added to the traditional repertoire, including chocolate, nougat, bilberries, and raspberries. One popular Viennese ice cream maker even offers *Eismarillenknödel* (ice cream apricot dumplings) consisting of apricot ice cream coated with vanilla ice cream and rolled in ground nuts. *Nockerl,* small oval dumplings made of a farmer's cheese dough, are frequently served with fruit purées for dessert—a smaller and lighter variation of traditional dumplings. Many cultures outside of Europe also steam or boil their sweets in the form of dumplings, among them South India's steamed *modaka* and Chinese *tang yuan.* See MODAKA.

Habs, Robert, and L. Rosner. *Appetit-Lexikon.* Vienna: C. Gerold's Sohn, 1894.

Zenker, F. G. *Anleitung zur feineren Kochkunst.* Vienna: Haas, 1824.

Zíbrt, Jan. *Staročeské umění kuchařské.* Prague: Dauphin, 2012.

Ingrid Haslinger

Dunkin' Donuts is an international restaurant chain specializing in doughnuts owned by Dunkin' Brands, which also owns Baskin-Robbins. As of 2014, the company had close to 11,000 stores in 31 countries and made over 70 varieties of doughnut. The first store—initially named Open Kettle—was opened by William Rosenberg (1916–2002) and his partner Harry Winokur in Quincy, Massachusetts, in 1950. It was renamed Dunkin' Donuts about a year and half later.

Rosenberg, the son of a struggling shopkeeper in Boston, worked his way up from a job as an ice cream truck driver during the Depression to owning, in partnership with Winokur, a mobile catering company in the aftermath of World War II. The New England–based business involved dispensing sandwiches, coffee, and a variety of sweet snacks, including doughnuts, from food trucks parked outside of factories. Noting the profit margin on coffee and doughnuts, as well as the success of Mayflower and comparable stores, and despite the objections of his business partner, Rosenberg decided to launch that first doughnut outlet in Quincy. At the time, doughnut shops typically limited their offerings to three or four flavors, but the fried dough entrepreneur experimented with dozens. Rosenberg writes in his autobiography that he was inspired to offer so many kinds by the proximity of the first Howard Johnson (also in Quincy), which sold some 28 flavors of ice cream. Unlike his competitors' stores, where patrons bought their pastries to go, Rosenberg included counters, stools, and a variety of beverages to encourage customers to linger. At many of the original outlets the bakers were visible through a window, hand-cutting the doughnuts and frying several batches a day to ensure freshness. See DOUGHNUTS.

With several of its own stores open, the brand began to franchise in 1955, choosing locations based on carefully researched metrics, including such factors as traffic patterns and demographics. One way the company's scouts determined family composition was to count the number of kids' bikes in the area. By 1960 the company had 100 stores, and by 1970 it began an ongoing expansion into Asia. The same year that saw the beginning of franchising also marked the forced departure of Winokur from the company. He went on to found Mister Donut, which was eventually reabsorbed into Dunkin' Donuts after both companies were bought by Allied Domecq in 1990. An independent offshoot of Mister Donut is still going strong in East Asia, with over 10,000 branches across the region.

As Dunkin' Donuts expanded, new products were added to the store's selection. In 1972 doughnut holes joined the menu; to appeal to children, they were named after the Munchkins in *The Wizard of Oz.* In time the menu expanded with muffins

(1978), bagels (1996), and a variety of sweetened beverages. In 2006 a consortium of private equity firms bought the company and made it independent again, reconstituting it, along with Baskin-Robbins, as Dunkin' Brands.

Today, Dunkin' Donuts American stores offer a variety of seasonal specialties such as the "blueberry cobbler" or the "Boston scream," an orange-frosted variation on the Boston cream doughnut. (This, the official doughnut of the Commonwealth of Massachusetts, is normally filled with vanilla custard and has a chocolate glaze.) Around the world, franchises have come up with such products as Korea's mochi doughnut made with glutinous rice; Indonesia's durian doughnut flavored with the Southeast Asian fruit with a notoriously overwhelming odor; the United Arab Emirates' date doughnut crowned with a chocolate-dipped date; and China's "seaweed floss" doughnut, topped with dry pork and seaweed.

See also BASKIN-ROBBINS and KRISPY KREME.

Aceto, Ali. "Global Donut Day: Spotlight on 12 Dunkin' Donut WonDDers Around the World." http://www.dunkindonuts.com/DDBlog/2013/06/global_donut_daysp.html#sthash.NQ7gx2vQ.dpbs (accessed 16 June 2014).

Krondl, Michael. *The Donut: History, Recipes, and Lore from Boston to Berlin.* Chicago: Chicago Review Press, 2014.

Rosenberg, William, and Brilliant Keener. *Time to Make Donuts.* New York: Lebhar-Friedman, 2001.

Michael Krondl

East Asia embraces long and broad historical continuities and connections in the confectionery cultures of China, Japan, and Korea that remain strong today. Sweets made from glutinous rice, for instance, are found in all these countries, as well as in Southeast Asia, notably Thailand and the Philippines. One can also trace the adoption of early versions of Western confectionery throughout Asia, as the example of Portuguese egg threads (*fios de ovos*) illustrates. See PORTUGAL'S INFLUENCE IN ASIA. This sweet, made by drizzling egg yolks into sugar syrup to form noodle-like strands, was originally a preserved food for Portuguese ships' captains and their officers embarking on voyages of discovery and trade. It was introduced to Japan in the sixteenth century, where it came to be known as egg noodles (*keiran sōmen*). See NANBANGASHI. Versions of this Portuguese recipe may be found in China, Thailand, and Cambodia.

Over the centuries Chinese confections spread to Japan and Korea, but China's historical influence on surrounding countries should be noted, especially in the dissemination of the ingredients for sweets, notably sugar, and the transference of the expertise to refine it. Sugarcane cultivation in south China dates to the third century B.C.E., and by the end of the 1800s sugar was China's third most important export item. Besides Chinese merchants, the Portuguese and Dutch (from the sixteenth and seventeenth centuries, respectively) also traded in Chinese sugar to Asian countries and Europe. Sugarcane arrived in Okinawa by 1600 from China, and the technology to refine sugar soon followed. The Dutch introduced sugar to Taiwan in 1624, and cultivation continued on the island after the Dutch were driven out in 1662 and Taiwan was incorporated into China's Qing empire in 1683. Japan sourced sugar from China beginning in the late 1500s, and Taiwan became the major supplier of Japan's sugar after its colonization of the island in 1895. China, India, and Thailand remain in the top five sugar-producing countries globally. Guangxi province is the largest sugar-producing region in China, followed by Yunnan. Xinjiang, Heilongjiang, and Inner Mongolia produce 90 percent of China's beet sugar.

Given that China is also one of the top five importers of sugar globally, it is not surprising that sugary confectionery is the largest sector of China's commercial confectionery market, in contrast to Japan and South Korea, where in 2012 chocolate amounted to about 41 percent and almost 60 percent of the total market, compared to just 6 percent in China. The Japanese favor chocolate bars and premium chocolates, but in South Korea most of the chocolate is destined for use in cakes and cookies. Overall, chocolate accounts for almost half of the Asia Pacific confectionery market, which includes Australia, China, Hong Kong, India, Indonesia, Japan, Malaysia, New Zealand, Philippines, Singapore, South Korea, Taiwan, Thailand, and Vietnam.

Mars Incorporated controls almost a quarter of the Chinese confectionery market, and the company also does significant business in South Korea, where it ranked among the top four sellers in 2012. See MARS. Offering Mars some domestic competition is China's Want Want Holdings, makers of popsicles, jellies, rice crackers, yogurt drinks, and other sweets. Ranked third in China is Lotte, a company founded in Tokyo but with its headquarters in Seoul. Lotte controls about 10 percent of China's market and also dominates among its competitors in Korea, notably the sweet makers Crown, Orion, and Haitai. Lotte, which produces biscuits, chocolates, chewing gum, candies, ice creams, and nutritional health supplements, is one of the top 10 confectionery companies globally in terms of market share. Japanese sweet makers Meiji and Morinaga are among the top 20 in the same rankings.

China has had a profound historical influence on the development of confectionery in East Asia, but in terms of the modern market for mass-produced sweets in the Asia Pacific, in 2012 Japan accounted for 37 percent of the region's confectionery market value, followed by China at 20 percent, India at about 5 percent, South Korea at 4.2 percent, and Taiwan at 3.2 percent. As China develops further economically, its market share will surely increase.

All the countries in East Asia have different local preferences in sweets; cereal bars, for instance, are becoming more popular in Japan but have yet to make significant inroads in South Korea and China. All three of these nations share a growing concern for healthy eating that might diminish sweet sales in the future, but that also offers niche markets for reduced-sugar confections in China and sugarless gum in Japan. Demand remains strong, nevertheless, especially for chocolate in Korea and Japan for holidays such as Christmas, Valentine's Day, and White Day, celebrated on 14 March when men are supposed to purchase sweets for female acquaintances. See VALENTINE'S DAY. Chocolate sales are also expected to rise in China as wealthier consumers seek premium sweets and become further acquainted with Western confectionery traditions.

See also CHINA; JAPAN; KOREA; SUGAR TRADE; and THAILAND.

"Confectionery in Asia-Pacific." MarketLine Industry Profile 0200–0710. October 2013.
"Confectionery in China." MarketLine Industry Profile 0099–0710. October 2013.
"Confectionery in South Korea." MarketLine Industry Profile 0117–0710. October 2013.
Mazumdar, Sucheta. *Sugar and Society in China: Peasants, Technology and the World Market*. Cambridge, Mass.: Harvard Asia Center Press, 1998.

Eric C. Rath

Easter is a spring festival, a time for celebration in the Christian calendar after a late winter fast, and one that contains echoes of older, pagan rituals. The holiday is celebrated with sweetmeats in exuberant variety, prepared throughout the Christian world at a season when the earth is still barren: nut cookies, buttery fruit breads, fruitcakes, marzipans, molded heaps of new butter and sweetened curds, chocolate eggs, and sugar-dusted butter lambs. Common to all these special foods is sweetness, and all are baked in a quantity meant for sharing. The sharing of foodstuffs, particularly when pleasurable, is a powerful weapon in the armory of all religions, a reality not lost on the pragmatic fathers of the early church, who adapted their celebration of resurrection to the old festival of procreation. Those who take their lead from the founding fathers of Rome—including Italians, Greeks, French, Spaniards, Portuguese, and Russians—named the festival for Pesach, the Jewish feast of thanksgiving at which sweetened unmilled grains are eaten. Those who took their lead from the Norsemen chose Eostre, Norse goddess of spring and rebirth, whose name has given the word "Easter" to English.

Alone among the feast days of the church, Easter's date is movable. Calculated according to the pre-Christian lunar calendar, it is further proof of a debt to the ancient rites of spring. Not all rituals associated with the old ways were welcomed by the new. Nuts and seeds could be considered acceptable symbols of resurrection, but not so the rowdy egg rituals—egg pacing, rolling, and cracking—associated with Eostre, which may or may not have been an invention of the Venerable Bede, anxious to distance his faith from pre-Christian rituals. Nevertheless, a memory of these activities survives in the chocolate eggs hidden for children by the Easter bunny, whose predecessor, the hare, Eostre's favorite (and still a creature associated with magic among the Celts), was charged with identical duties, though the beneficiaries were more likely to be young lovers in search of solitude.

Regional differences in climate and history influence the Easter menu, but the need for sweetness, the taste of ripeness and promise of harvest, is acknowledged by all. Eostre's sacred month is April, the planting month, the time when flocks and herds return to productivity, replenishing store cupboards, delivering fresh cream and newly laid eggs to restore health and hope at the darkest time in the farming year. All such foods were (and are, particularly in Eastern Europe but also in the more remote regions and islands of the Catholic Mediterranean) taken in a basket to the churchyard to be blessed; the same symbolic foodstuffs are eaten at funerals and by the graveside on Days of the Dead. See DAY OF THE DEAD and FUNERALS. Most curious of these preparations is the egg-cheese, a large round ball of hard-cooked custard drained overnight in cloth, prepared for the Easter basket by Ruthenes, a population of Ukrainians marooned in Slovakia who follow the ways of their forefathers. Cookbook author Catherine Cheremeteff Jones (2003) also recalls a meal of singular sweetness and richness shared with her Russian Orthodox family at Easter, when butter and cream were newly available in spring: "The centerpiece of the feast is *paskha*, molded and decorated sweetened curd-cheese enriched with additions of crystallized fruits, dried berries and nuts and traditionally eaten with *kulich*, a sweet, butter and egg-enriched bread baked in a tall round mold and traditionally taken to church to be blessed."

Sweet things, many of Arab origin, were traded from south to north. Exquisite miniature marzipan fruits exported from Sicily illuminate the Easter table in Holland. In Britain, historian Anne Wilson (1973) traces the origins of the Easter Simnel to festive biscuits made with fine flour, *simla*, milled by the Romans. The preparation vanished for a time to reappear—a form of resurrection—as rich fruitcake to be taken home at Easter. Baked on Mothering Sunday (Mid-Lent Sunday, a day on which the Lenten fast was relaxed) by young servant girls employed in Victorian households, this Easter message was layered and topped with marzipan. It is now somewhat confused by a decoration of fluffy toy chicks and sugar eggs with (or without) a rim of 13 little marzipan balls, one for each of those present at the Last Supper. See FRUITCAKE.

Evidence of similar confusion—a measure, perhaps, of reluctance to abandon the merry rites of spring for the somber rituals of the Christian Easter—was identified by artist Daniel Spoerri (1982) in the 1970s among the islanders of Greece. Whereas the Lenten fast was reported as strictly observed until midnight on Easter morning, thereafter the air was heady with the scent of Easter baking as every household set about the joyous task of exchanging sugared trays of sweet things—almond cakes flavored with rosewater, cinnamon-dusted butter biscuits, doughnuts drenched in honey—to be shared with all, whether neighbor or friend or passing stranger, a tradition surely as ancient as the rocks upon which the congregation built their church.

In bread-baking regions, traditional Easter cakes—yeasted doughs, sweetened and enriched—are sometimes baked in anthropomorphic shapes with unshelled eggs dropped in the belly or under the tail. See ANTHROPOMORPHIC AND ZOOMORPHIC SWEETS and BREADS, SWEET. In Germany, these breads can take the form of a fox or a hare, Eostre's favorite. In Italy, says cookery writer Ursula Ferrigno (1997), the most popular shape for sweet Easter breads is the dove, the symbol of peace, while in Spain and Portugal, sugar-dusted ring-breads come in the form of crowns or plaits with whole eggs tucked in the links. Although real eggs continue to play a central role in regions where the Easter traditions remain more or less unaltered, with the advent of moldable chocolate—a convenient material for sculpting and particularly popular with the sweet-toothed northern Europeans—eggs and baby animals as well as the Easter bunny, a reminder of Eostre's hare, began to appear in molded chocolate as Easter treats for children.

Sweetness shared not only confers a blessing on all who celebrate the risen Christ but also serves as a reminder of the need to restore fertility to nature, earth, and man.

See also BUTTER; CADBURY; CHOCOLATES, FILLED; CREAM; EGGS; HOLIDAY SWEETS; MARZIPAN; and MIDDLE EAST.

Ferrigno, Ursula. *Ursula's Italian Cakes and Desserts.* London: Metro, 1997.

Jones, Catherine Cheremeteff. *A Year of Russian Feasts.* London: Bantam, 2003.

Spoerri, Daniel. *Mythology & Meatballs.* Berkeley, Calif.: Aris, 1982.

Wilson, C. Anne. *Food and Drink in Britain.* London: Constable, 1973.

Elisabeth Luard

éclair

See PASTRY, CHOUX.

egg drinks go far back in time. Drinking raw eggs straight from the shell as a fortifier is undoubtedly as old as human beings themselves. With time, however, culinary refinement set in, and a whole family of egg drinks developed, in Europe consisting of many versions of hot and cold alcoholic drinks in the style of posset—hot, spiced milk curdled with wine or ale, with eggs later added. Caudle might be the earliest version, with the first recipe dating from early-fourteenth-century England. Thickened with bread as well as egg yolks, it is hardly a drink as such anymore but is very much a restorative, once favored for invalids and women in childbirth.

The most popular egg drink today is arguably eggnog. The name might be derived from egg and grog, the latter originating in the British Navy in 1740 as rum mixed with water. Once popular year-round as an individually prepared drink, eggnog in the English-speaking world today is mainly associated with the winter holidays and is often prepared in large quantities for a group. It typically consists of egg yolks, sugar, spirits (rum, brandy, vodka, or whiskey), milk, and cream, although some recipes add the dairy components immediately prior to consumption, after the sweetened base has aged. Aging for a minimum of three weeks and up to a year (though most often for the period between Thanksgiving and Christmas, when there is an abundance of eggs before winter) melds the flavors and yields a creamier consistency. Commercial versions (also nonalcoholic) tend to substitute the voluptuous richness of eggs with high-fructose corn syrup, carrageen, and guar gum. Despite ongoing health concerns regarding the consumption of raw eggs, scientific study has shown that using alcohol in the aging process kills salmonella, making aged eggnog potentially safer than a fresh version.

Many eggnog variations exist in the United States and elsewhere in the world. According to Myra Waldo's *Dictionary of International Food and Cooking Terms* (1967), residents of Wisconsin and Minnesota enjoy the Tom and Jerry, "a hot, frothy alcoholic drink made with beaten egg yolks, stiffly beaten egg whites, rum, sugar, boiling water, bourbon, and spices, served in mugs with a sprinkling of nutmeg." The origin of German *Eierlikör* or *advocaat* is said to lie with Dutch colonialists trying to imitate the creamy mixture of avocado ("advocaat") pulp, cane sugar, and rum they had been offered in Brazil, substituting egg yolk for the exotic fruit. German cookery books in the late nineteenth and early twentieth centuries offer many variants of egg drinks, among them the lighter *Eierwein*, egg wine (in its cold version, egg yolks mixed with sugar, nutmeg, and red or white wine), and the feistier *Hoppelpoppel* (a hot drink of cream boiled with vanilla, lemon zest, and sugar, thickened with egg yolks and given a kick with rum, arrak, or cognac). Today, *Eierlikör* is mainly consumed as a (delicious) topping for ice cream. In Puerto Rico, *coquito* calls for coconut milk and rum. Mexican *rompope* is flavored with cinnamon; Peru's *biblia* is made with the local Pisco, a spirit distilled from grapes.

A false friend is the New York soda-fountain drink called egg cream, which contains neither egg nor cream, but is made from soda water, sweet chocolate syrup, and milk. See SODA FOUNTAIN. Created in 1890 in a candy store with a soda fountain on New York's Lower East Side, it became the city's iconic drink. See NEW YORK CITY. Its name undoubtedly derives from the egg-white-like foam that develops on top of the soda when the carbonated water hits the chocolate syrup and milk. Along with soda fountains, the egg cream almost disappeared from New York in the 1960s, but it is experiencing something of a revival, and 15 March has been declared National Egg Cream Day in the United States. Finally, cocktails using raw egg merit a mention, such as Silver Gin Fizz (made with gin, lemon juice, sugar, carbonated water, and egg white) or Pink Lady (gin, grenadine, and egg white), which both use the egg white for texture, or Porto Flip, made from brandy and port and egg yolk for flavor and richness.

See also SYLLABUB.

Brown, John Hull. *Early American Beverages*. Rutland, Vt.: Charles E. Tuttle, 1966.

Coe, Andrew. "The Egg Cream Racket." *Gastronomica: The Journal of Food and Culture* 4, no. 3 (Summer 2004): 18–25.

Ursula Heinzelmann

egg yolk sweets, confections made from egg yolks and sugar, are synonymous with Portuguese cuisine. These rich concoctions, which many non-Portuguese find excessively sweet and cloying, are a hybrid between dessert and confectionery that originated in convent kitchens in medieval Iberia. See CONVENT SWEETS. Although egg sweets are also made in Spain, particularly in the Castilian region that shares much of its culinary heritage with Portugal, it is the Portuguese who elevated the egg sweet to iconic status, developing an extraordinarily extensive repertoire of recipes.

In Portugal during the Middle Ages, food was scarce, and eggs provided an important source of protein. Eggs (from hens, ducks, and other fowl) were readily available, relatively inexpensive, and, at a time when most Europeans spent more than half the days of the year in religious fasting, the devoutly Catholic Portuguese regarded eggs as permissible Lenten foods.

Eggs were also important in other ways. The whites were used in wine making, to clear the wine of lees. Traditional production methods required around eight eggs per barrel; the wine-making *quintas* (estates) sent the leftover yolks to convent nuns, a practice said to have been initiated by the pious king Philip III of Spain. (A belief still exists in Spanish folklore that a gift of eggs to the Clarissans will help guarantee good weather for a party.) A further surplus of yolks resulted from the inclusion of egg whites in the building material used for church walls and, according to popular myth, in the starch for nuns' habits. Finally, because egg whites were widely used in sugar refining (which the Portuguese had learned from the Moors), the nuns had ready access to an abundance of yolks. One effective method of preserving so many eggs was to cook the yolks with a large quantity of sugar. Many nuns found experimenting with confectionery a welcome distraction from the routine of contemplative life.

The most basic form of Portuguese egg confectionery is a sweet, thick sauce of cooked egg yolks and sugar called *ovos moles* (soft eggs) used as a custardlike filling for tarts and cakes, as a dessert sauce or topping, or as a filling for marzipan sweets. See PORTUGAL. *Fios de ovos*, sweet "threads" made by drizzling egg yolks through a sieve into boiling sugar syrup, is another basic preparation used in many different ways, either on its own or as a component of other desserts. Many variations of eggs and sugar exist, often with fanciful names such as "nun's bellies," "angel's cheeks," and "bacon from heaven."

In response to the overwhelming power of the Jesuit Order in Portugal and her colonies, the Jesuits and all other male religious orders, except Franciscans with duties in the colonies, were dissolved in the early nineteenth century, and the female orders were allowed to continue only until the natural death of the nuns. During this time, many recipes for sweets moved into the public realm to become part of the culinary repertoire of housewives and commercial manufacturers. Today, a resurgent interest in traditional Portuguese egg sweets has developed, particularly in the many regional variations that are once again being made in convents throughout the country.

Egg sweets and other convent desserts (*doces conventuais* in Portuguese), often adapted to make use of regional ingredients such as coconut milk and rice flour, are also found in all the former Portuguese colonies, as well as other places with a history of Portuguese influence. See PORTUGAL'S INFLUENCE IN ASIA.

See also FLAN (PUDÍM); PASTEL DE NATA; and THAILAND.

Goldstein, Joyce. *Savoring Spain and Portugal.* San Francisco: Weldon Owen, 2000.

Marques, Antonio Henrique R. de Oliveira. *Daily Life in Portugal in the Late Middle Ages.* Madison: University of Wisconsin Press, 1971.

Janet Boileau

eggs are one the most versatile ingredients in baking, used structurally for binding, texture, and aerating. Each egg has three parts: the shell, the white, and the yolk. The shell is thin and porous, usually white or brown, occasionally pale blue. The color of the eggshell is a result of the hen's breed and regional preferences. Inside, all eggs have similar nutritional content, cooking characteristics, and taste. The white or albumen, clear and thick, makes up about two-thirds of the center; it is mostly water with some protein. The other third is occupied by the yellow yolk or ovum, which contains the majority of the fat and protein. Both white and yolk coagulate at temperatures below the boiling point of water, characteristics much exploited to yield interesting textures.

Whole eggs are stirred and gently heated to thicken dishes like custards, creams, and ice creams (overheating causes curdling and failure of the dish). See CUSTARD and ICE CREAM. They are also beaten into mixtures for cakes such as fruitcake, and into batters to help leaven them. Beaten egg is brushed over many types of buns and pastries to give the finished item a gilded, soft shine.

The real power of the egg shows when it is used in separated form. The protein in egg whites can be whipped to form an airy cloud that leavens sponge cakes, soufflés, cookies, mousses, and marshmallows. Whipped egg white and sugar also makes frosting for cakes, toppings for tarts and pies, and gently baked, it becomes meringue. See ICING and MERINGUE. Care must be taken not to over-whip, as the mixture loses the ability to hold air.

Egg yolks contribute flavor and color to baked goods, but they are most essential in thickening semi-liquid sauces, mousses, custards, creams, and ice creams; in the correct proportions, they give silky textures. They can also be used instead of whole eggs for a richer and denser cake, cookie, or dough. Yolks are also much used in a special category of *yemas*, egg yolk sweets closely identified with Spain, Portugal, and areas influenced by them. See EGG YOLK SWEETS.

Most recipes call for large or extra-large eggs, which have the best ratio of egg white to yolk. For best results, the egg size specified in the recipe should be used. USDA grades refer to the quality of the egg both inside and out, the weight and other qualities influencing the egg's value. According to U.S. standards, graders hold eggs before bright lights called candling lights in order to gain a visual of the eggs' interiors. Random eggs are cracked open onto a flat surface so that the interior can be more easily inspected and compared to others from the same hen or group of hens. A fresh, good-quality egg will crack easily on the edge of a bowl with a nice clean break. The white should spread very little, form a beveled oval, and resemble thin, shiny Jell-O. See GELATIN DESSERTS. The yolk should be whole, upright, and round. If the egg white is as thin as water and spreads widely without a bevel, or if the yolk breaks or is flat and low, the egg is inferior and will perform poorly.

The finest eggs come from healthy hens that are raised humanely (as indicated by the Humanely Certified emblem on the carton). If farm-fresh eggs are not available, grocery-store eggs should be purchased refrigerated and in a carton to ensure that they stay fresh. The further from the sell-by date, the fresher they are.

Eggs should be stored refrigerated in their carton from 33° to 45°F (0.6° to 7°C)—the carton is designed to protect the eggs from picking up strong odors like garlic through their porous shell. They last up to one month when refrigerated but change slightly as they age. Eggs under a week old are preferred for baking. Cracked eggs will go bad within a day or two and are more prone to attracting bacteria. Discard any cracked eggs found in the carton.

Fresh eggs whip rapidly to their maximum potential and create stronger foam. They should be refrigerated until ready to use because they deteriorate rapidly at room temperature. Although eggs whip faster when warm, they do not whip to their maximum. If warm eggs are desired, they should not be allowed to stand at room temperature. Instead, the so-called Swiss method is used: place them in the top of a double boiler and whisk continuously until they reach warm or body temperature, about 98°F (37°C). Another traditional home method is to soak whole eggs in a bowl of warm water for 10 to 15 minutes; however, warming the eggs makes them more difficult to separate.

To freeze whole eggs, yolks, and egg whites, remove the desired part of the interior from the shell and place it in a tightly sealed container labeled with the date. Although frozen eggs can be stored for four to six months, the quality will be compromised. Thawed egg products should be stored in the refrigerator for no longer than three days, and frozen eggs cannot be refrozen once thawed.

When separating eggs, have two clean bowls side by side. Position the egg over the bowl intended for the whites. Crack the shell gently to form a clean break in the middle. Break it apart evenly into two halves, retaining the egg inside one of the halves. Then carefully pass the egg from one half to the other, back and forth, allowing the white to drop into the bowl below and keeping the yolk rotating between the two half shells. Use the edge of the shell to cut the white away from the yolk if needed. Place the now-separated yolk into the second bowl.

See also MARSHMALLOWS; MOUSSE; SOUFFLÉ; and SPONGE CAKE.

Hosking, Richard, ed. *Eggs in Cookery: Proceedings of the Oxford Symposium on Food and Cookery 2006*. Totnes, U.K.: Prospect, 2006.

McGee, Harold. *On Food and Cooking: The Science and Lore of the Kitchen*. New York: Scribner, 1984.

Jim Dodge

Emy, M., wrote the first book entirely dedicated to making ice cream, *L'art de bien faire les glaces* *d'office* (The Art of Making Ices for the Confectionery Kitchen), published in 1786 and written for professionals. Although the book is renowned, its author is a mystery. Presumed to be male (in mid-eighteenth-century France, a woman would not likely have been accepted as a professional confectioner and author), Emy is known only by his surname; his first name and dates of birth and death are nowhere recorded. His writing, however, reveals that he was a perfectionist—serious, opinionated, and passionate.

In his book, Emy explained how to make and freeze ices, ice creams, and mousses. He provided more than 100 recipes, some of them unique. Parmesan and Gruyère ice cream, anise mousse, and ice cream flavored with truffles (the fungi) were among his more exceptional ones.

Emy explored freezing techniques, equipment, health issues, and seasonality. Stressing the importance of using the finest ingredients, he explained how to judge them. He included instructions on molding ice creams into the fanciful shapes popular at the time, to resemble, for instance, asparagus and pineapple.

Emy was a pragmatist. Despite his emphasis on fresh ingredients, he suggested substituting jams when fresh fruits were unavailable. He tempered his instructions on making food colorings by warning that, because some people believed they were poisonous, such colorings had to be used judiciously. He disapproved of adding wine or spirits to ice cream but explained how to do so when an employer insisted on it. He could not resist adding that the results would not meet his standards.

Above all, he advised readers to follow his instructions precisely to achieve perfection. Whatever else he may have been, Emy was an unparalleled teacher.

See also CONFECTIONERY MANUALS; FRANCE; and ICE CREAM.

Emy, M. *L'Art de bien faire les glaces d'office*. Paris: Chez Le Clerc, 1768.

Jeri Quinzio

entremets are today disregarded bit players in the theater of upscale French and French-influenced menus. They appear at the end of the meal and are usually sweet. In the Middle Ages, though, entremets could be either a secondary dish at a meal in a prosperous household or, at royal or ducal courts, elaborate displays and dramatic or musical performances. The late-fourteenth-century *Ménagier de Paris* has many recipes for entremets, but few are sweetened. They feature meat, especially pork, fish, and eggs, as well as vegetables, but sugar is uncommon, and a meal typically ended simply with nuts and dried fruit with, perhaps, wafers. See DRIED FRUIT and WAFERS.

The fifteenth-century dukes of Burgundy went in for something quite different. At their most splendid banquets, the entremets came between the courses, not between the plates as a literal translation would suggest. They were not necessarily edible. A banquet of three courses (and many dishes) might have as its entremets a short dramatic performance, a display of the host's castles modeled in butter, or an imitation whale with musicians inside it. Lesser folk might bring entertainment to their tables with more or less suitable diversions that they, too, would call entremets. The guests at a wedding feast (although perhaps not the bride) could be entertained by a depiction of a woman in childbirth; the pious could be edified by a waxen head of John the Baptist on a platter. This robust tradition faded away by the end of the sixteenth century.

The term "entremets" remained but took on a different meaning in the seventeenth century with the coming of *service à la française*. This was still a two- or three-course meal. However, the emphasis was on laying out all the dishes for a course in a rigidly symmetrical fashion. La Varenne's *Cuisinier françois* (1650) and Pierre de Lune's *Nouveau cuisinier* (1659) include substantial numbers of entremets that are predominantly savory, as are most of the entremets in later menus, such as in the 1705 edition of Massialot's *Cuisinier roïal et bourgeois*. When sweet entremets do occur, they are most likely to be a form of custard or blancmange and appear on the table at the same time as their savory cousins. See BLANCMANGE and CUSTARD.

The more luxurious cookbooks included woodcuts or engravings showing the many ways that dishes could be arranged to meet the spatial and gastronomical needs of the time. This new system persisted on most upper-class European tables into the early years of the nineteenth century. A fine array of silver, ceramics, flowers, and *pièces montées* added to the spectacle. Complications proliferated. Thus, entremets made their way onto the patterned tabletop, slipping their way in between the more significant dishes. At times they were present with the hors d'oeuvres, the latter appearing in those days not as preliminary dishes but as minor dishes often placed around the outer edges of the formally arranged service—that is, outside the main works.

From the mid-seventeenth-century onward, a steady stream of French cookbooks appeared in English, often badly translated, bringing *service à la française*, hors d'oeuvres, and entremets with them. The English took to this new system with enthusiasm. Thus, John Nott tells his readers in his *Cook's and Confectioner's Dictionary* of 1723 that "Blanc-Mangers are us'd in Inter-messes, or for middle Dishes or Out-works." He goes on to say "then put it up in jelly glasses. These glasses you may set betwixt your plain jelly, or put it in a china bowl for the middle of the dish, or in cold plates for the second."

Over the course of the nineteenth century, entremets became an almost entirely sweet course of its own, sharing the bottom of the menus with "dessert" and "ices." There is only a slight remainder of the old mixture in the British "savoury." By 1938 *Larousse gastronomique* lists, under entremets, only sweets; the conversion had become complete.

See also DESSERT; ICE CREAM; and SUGAR SCULPTURE.

Flandrin, Jean Louis. "Ordre des mets, livres en bouche." In *Livres en bouche: Cinq siècles d'art culinaire français du quatorzième au dix-huitième siècle*. Paris: Bibliothèque nationale de France, 2001.

Ross, L. B. "Beyond Eating: Political and Personal Significance of the Entremets at the Banquets of the Burgundian Court." In *At the Table: Metaphorical and Material Cultures of Food in Medieval and Early Modern Europe*, edited by Timothy J. Tomasik and Juliann Vitullo, pp. 145–166. Turnhout, Belgium: Brepols, 2007.

Barbara Wheaton

epergnes are pyramidal dessert centerpieces of silver, gilt-bronze, ceramics, or glass featuring containers and baskets for the display and consumption of edible sweets, biscuits, fruits, and condiments. Many were designed with interchangeable elements and branches for candles and were displayed on raised mirrored platforms. A French-sounding moniker of unknown origin, the term "epergne" (sometimes epargne) was apparently coined in England in the early eighteenth century. In France, an epergne was called a *surtout de table*, *girandole garnie*, or *machine*; in Germany, it was a *Tafelaufsatz* or *Plat de Menage*, notwithstanding that these terms were not specific to dessert centerpieces and were applied to savory or figural centerpieces as well. Whereas "epergne" is not found in either Joseph Gilliers's *Le cannameliste français* (1751) or Henri Havard's *Dictionnaire de l'ameublement et de la décoration* (1894), both authors discuss and illustrate the *surtout*, which by the mid-seventeenth-century had supplanted the medieval standing salt on the princely table. Stefan Bursche, one of the earliest scholars to tackle the phenomenon of table decoration at European courts, also associates the *surtout* with the tradition of displaying pyramids of fruit at high-style baroque banquets in Italy and France. Both Julius Bernhard von Rohr, in his *Einleitung zur Ceremoniel Wissenschaft der Privat-Person* (1728), and François Massialot, author of *Cuisiner royal et bourgeois* (1705), described a *surtout* as a kind of *dormant* that remained in place for the entire meal, its containers refilled at intervals with savory foodstuffs and condiments and, finally, with dessert and its accompaniments.

English silver epergnes seem to survive in larger numbers than their French or German counterparts, though the latter are well documented by published engravings and in inventories. Eighteenth-century porcelain centerpieces range from the inventive Asian porcelain versions concocted by European silversmiths to the Meissen models introduced around 1740, which often survive in bits and pieces, the stand in one collection and the containers and cruets in others. Other European manufacturers produced porcelain centerpieces, following Meissen's lead. A Du Paquier porcelain version in the Hermitage features eight peasants with cups held aloft dancing around an elephant whose trunk was meant to dispense sweet dessert wine. The fragile glass epergnes regularly bestowed, according to archival evidence, by the Republic of Venice on special visitors and foreign princes are mostly lost.

Judging from the property in the Hofsilber- und Tafelkammer in Vienna and in the English royal pantry, epergnes and *surtouts* remained fashionable and necessary for court dining into the nineteenth century. Some are still employed at state occasions. The 1762 silver-gilt epergne by Thomas Heming in the Royal Collection was the most expensive item in the coronation service of George III. Even more

Epergnes are elaborate centerpieces for displaying sweets, biscuits, fruits, and condiments. Some have interchangeable elements, such as candleholders, for even more dramatic presentation. This striking epergne was made by the London silversmith William Cripps in 1753. IMAGE © STERLING AND FRANCINE CLARK ART INSTITUTE, WILLIAMSTOWN, MASSACHUSETTS. PHOTO BY MICHAEL AGEE

expensive was the epergne designed by William Kent for the prince of Wales in 1745, which was altered by Rundell, Bridge, and Rundell in 1829 by the addition of legs to raise its height. The gilt-bronze Milan centerpiece in the Hofburg in Vienna, a monumental classical revival ensemble made for the coronation of Emperor Ferdinand in 1838, stretches to 30 meters. A Gothic Revival epergne designed by William Burges for the marquess of Bute was manufactured by Barkentin & Krall in 1880–1881 and is in the Victoria and Albert Museum.

In the Victorian era, simpler epergnes emerged for the upper classes, made up of a central raised dish or urn flanked by smaller containers that might be attached or freestanding. In her *Book of Household Management* (1861), Mrs. Beeton called such stands "tazzas" and instructed: "With moderns the dessert is not so profuse nor does it hold the same relationship to the dinner that it held with the ancients.... The general mode of putting a dessert on table, now the elegant tazzas are fashionable, is, to place them down the middle of the table, a tall and short dish alternately; the fresh fruits being arranged on the tall dishes, and dried fruits, bon-bons, &c., on small round or oval glass plates. The garnishing needs especial attention, as the contrast of the brilliant-colored fruits with nicely-arranged foliage is very charming."

Eventually, epergnes became de rigueur for lesser tables, unleashing waves of affordable options in various media for every taste and budget. Apart from reproductions of eighteenth-century models and tazzas, elaborate new forms emerged, featuring a central vase or trumpet for flowers flanked by scrolling branches supporting smaller cups, flutes, or baskets. Google "epergne" to see the good, the bad, and the ugly of the Victorian and modern eras—many for sale, if only there were consumers for such by-now-anachronistic dining accessories. Apart from the occasional banquet of state, hotels, restaurants, and tea salons may be the only locations where epergnes are regularly employed today.

See also BONBONS; DESSERT; SERVING PIECES; and SUGAR SCULPTURE.

Barta-Fliedl, Ilsebill, Andreas Gugler, and Peter Parenzan. *Tafeln bei Hofe: Zur Geschichte der fürstlichen Tafelkultur*. Sammlungsband 4. Hamburg, Germany: Dölling & Galitz, 1998.

Brown, Peter, and Ivan Day. *Pleasures of the Table: Ritual and Display in the European Dining Room, 1600–1900*. York, U.K.: Fairfax House, 1997.

Bursche, Stefan. *Tafelzier des Barock*. Munich: Schneider, 1974.

Chilton, Meredith. *Fired by Passion: Vienna Baroque Porcelain of Claudius Innocentius Du Paquier*, pp. 848–911. Stuttgart: Arnoldsche, 2009.

Micio, Paul. "Early French Surtouts." *Silver Studies* 19 (2005): 79–97. Unpublished drawings and documents.

Maureen Cassidy-Geiger

Epiphany

See TWELFTH NIGHT CAKE.

Escoffier, Georges Auguste (1846–1935), a chef whose career spanned the splendors of the Second French Empire, the Edwardian era, and the early twentieth century, witnessed dramatic changes in French culinary fashion during his life. He ushered in many of those changes himself while serving as chef de cuisine and manager of the kitchens at the Paris Ritz and at the Savoy and Carlton in London, working with his friend and partner César Ritz.

Born near Nice, the young Escoffier learned to cook at his grandmother's side and later apprenticed at his uncle's restaurant in Nice. He went on to work at the Parisian restaurant Le Petit Moulin Rouge when it was at the height of its fame during the Second Empire. There, he proved his talent as chef to its powerful and wealthy patrons. By the late nineteenth-century's belle époque, the elaborate *pièces montées* of Marie-Antoine Carême were considered too old-fashioned for savory dishes, but Escoffier continued to conjure exquisite dessert *pièces montées*. His most well-known, *Pêche Melba*, named after the singer Nellie Melba, is still served today. Timothy Shaw (1994) describes Escoffier's original *Pêche Melba*—"its poached peaches rising up in a cone of gold from a silver dish... lay between the wings of a noble Lohengrin swan finely carved out of ice and lightly veiled in spun sugar" (p. 143)—as typical of his dessert creations. Another showpiece, *Belle de Nuit*, was a crescent moon ice carving perched on a larger block of ice that was lit from within by an electric bulb. The whole was draped with spun sugar and "surrounded by a profusion of ice cream and crystallized fruit" (p. 143).

In this 1926 photograph, the French chef and restaurateur Georges Auguste Escoffier is shown standing—rather Napoleonically—on a ship as it arrives in New York. Escoffier codified French cuisine in his masterwork, *Le guide culinaire* (1903), and his ideas about kitchen management, the use of fresh ingredients, and the proper demeanor of a chef continue to influence restaurant kitchens around the world. © BETTMANN / CORBIS

Considering that Escoffier created menus and dishes for the world's most famous people, including King Edward VII, the duc d'Orléans, and actress Sarah Bernhardt, it is only fitting that a spectacular sweets course would be the capstone of a magnificent meal. His cookbooks, however, reflect his practical nature. Escoffier's 1903 masterwork, *Le guide culinaire,* is a classic. In it, he writes that the book's dessert recipes are limited to the essential elements of pastry, confectionery, and ices that every trained cook must learn. The recipes are not intended for training a true professional pastry cook or confectioner; however, Escoffier believed that every chef should know how to prepare a complete meal (which always included dessert) should the need arise. His menus show that he often incorporated fruits into his desserts, perhaps reflecting his upbringing in the sun-drenched south of France.

See also CARÊME, MARIE-ANTOINE; FRUIT; PASTRY CHEF; and PLATED DESSERTS.

Escoffier, Auguste. *Memories of My Life*. Translated by Laurence Escoffier. New York: Van Nostrand Reinhold, 1997.
Shaw, Timothy. *The World of Escoffier*. New York: Vendome, 1994.

Kyri W. Claflin

Eskimo Pie, a slice of ice cream covered with chocolate, was conceived when an eight-year-old boy in an ice cream shop in Onawa, Iowa, wavered between spending his nickel on ice cream or chocolate candy. The shopkeeper decided to combine the two. The year was 1919, the shopkeeper was Christian K. Nelson, and the resulting confection became the Eskimo Pie.

Nelson made the product by dipping hard-frozen ice cream slices into heated chocolate. Rather than melt the ice cream, the process hardened the chocolate. Nelson called his invention the "Temptation I-Scream Bar" and sold it locally.

In 1921 he and Russell Stover became partners. Stover suggested the name Eskimo Pie. They received a patent for the process in 1922, but it was rescinded in 1929 because coating ice cream with chocolate was not a new idea. It was, however, a wildly popular one. As early as 1922, the partners sold a million Eskimo Pies a day.

Eskimo Pie's success rippled throughout the ice cream industry and inspired other chocolate-coated ice creams, including the Klondike Bar and the Good Humor Ice Cream Bar. See GOOD HUMOR MAN. The new products not only increased sales of cocoa and chocolate warmers; they also created a market for ice cream in winter.

Stover left the company in 1922 to concentrate on his candy business. Nelson struggled financially as a result of the patent litigation. In 1924 he sold the company to the manufacturer of its foil wrappers, now known as Reynolds Metals. He worked for the manufacturer until 1961, when he retired.

The company's frosty graphics feature snow globes, icebergs, igloos, and a cheery boy in a fur-trimmed parka. However, Eskimo Pie is now a controversial name among some Inuit. Today, Nestlé owns the Eskimo Pie brand.

See also ICE CREAM and NESTLÉ.

Funderburg, Anne Cooper. *Chocolate, Strawberry, and Vanilla.* Bowling Green, Ohio: Bowling Green State University Press, 1995.

Jeri Quinzio

Eton Mess is a British dessert made of broken meringue, fruit (traditionally strawberries), and whipped heavy (double) cream, mixed together into a sublime combination of textures and flavors. Some recipes include liqueur or a drizzle of chocolate.

Known as Eton Mess since the nineteenth century, the first mention of "Eton Mess aux Fraises" dates to a grand garden party in 1893 described by historian Arthur Beavan. It was attended by Queen Victoria on the eve of the marriage of Prince George, the Duke of York, and Princess May of Teck.

Similar desserts include Lancing Mess (made with bananas), served at Lancing College in Sussex, and Clare College Mush of Clare College, Cambridge University, which Sara Paston-Williams considers "the original recipe for this traditional pudding." However, the common belief is that Eton Mess was created at Eton College, a boys' school near Windsor, founded in 1440 by King Henry VI, where many important national figures have been educated. The dessert has many associations with the school: in the 1930s Eton Mess made of strawberries or bananas, with ice cream or cream, was sold at the school Sock Shop (a tuck shop or small grocery). Eton Mess is also served at the longstanding annual cricket match between Eton and Harrow, and at picnics for the school's 4 June celebrations marking the birthday of King George III, who maintained a close association with Eton.

In 1935 Eton Mess appeared on the menu at Royal Ascot, the famous horse-racing event near Eton; more recently, in 2013, a raspberry and lavender version was served there. Also in 2013, the world's largest Eton Mess was made in Soho Square in London. It contained 50 kilograms of fresh strawberries, raspberries, and blueberries and fed some 2,000 commuters.

Although the term "mess" may be associated with the messy appearance of the dish, it might also refer to an assortment of people who eat together. The word "mess" could also be used in the sense of a quantity of food, particularly a prepared dish of soft food or a mixture of ingredients cooked or eaten together, as in the term "a mess of greens" used throughout the American South.

See also CREAM; FRUIT; MERINGUE; and UNITED KINGDOM.

Paston-Williams, Sara. *Traditional Puddings.* Newton Abbot, U.K.: David & Charles, 1983.
Webb, Andrew. *Food Britannia.* London: Random House, 2011.

Helen Saberi

evaporated milk is milk from which the water has been partly removed. Because several canned products originally sold as "evaporated" and "condensed" milk are condensed through a process of evaporation, they have historically been surrounded by greatly confused terminology. Today, thick, syrupy, "sweetened condensed milk" is always made with added sugar, while the more fluid "evaporated milk" is produced by condensation/evaporation without added sweetening. In cookbooks published between about 1885 and 1940, however, it is often difficult to know which of the two is meant. See SWEETENED CONDENSED MILK.

Various forms of milk evaporated by long cooking have been used in India for centuries. But modern canned counterparts were technically far more difficult to manufacture than sweetened condensed milk. The latter, introduced in 1861, benefits from the preservative action of sugar. The Swiss-born pioneers of the unsweetened product, John B. Meÿenberg and Louis Latzer, began wrestling with the manufacturing process in 1884. Not until the early 1890s were problems of spoilage or unwanted clotting satisfactorily solved by the firm they had founded in Highland, Illinois, the Helvetia Milk Condensing Company (later Pet, Inc.). On the outbreak of the Spanish-American War, in 1898, Helvetia obtained a contract for supplying canned milk to the U.S. Army in Cuba and the Philippines. It was a major boost for both the company and the public image of unsweetened preserved milk. See SPANISH-AMERICAN WAR. In 1909, manufacturers solved the product's strong tendency to separate by homogenizing the milk, the first large-scale application of this process to any commercial form of milk.

Like sweetened condensed milk, the new product was far easier to store and transport without refrigeration than fresh milk. It had, and still has, a certain "cooked" flavor resulting from the caramelization of lactose. But if diluted with an equal amount of water, evaporated milk was more similar to fresh milk than the thicker, more syrupy sweetened condensed milk. If used undiluted, it was about as heavy as the "rich milk" or "top milk" (i.e., natural cream layer) that rose to the top of unhomogenized whole milk, and it soon became popular for some of the same uses as cream. Combining it with sugar in coffee, tea, or most desserts partly masked the caramelized note by allowing it to blend with other sources of sweetness.

The Evaporated Milk Association, founded in 1923, vigorously promoted the uses of evaporated milk in cooking, especially for desserts and sweets. In a series of recipe booklets the association gave methods for whipping chilled evaporated milk (with or without the aid of gelatin) to a simulacrum of whipped cream, or for using it in ice creams, frozen mousses, dessert sauces, puddings or pie fillings, pastry doughs, cakes, candies, and sweetened punches like eggnog. Recipes clearly inspired by the association's suggestions appear in many cookbooks of the 1930s and 1940s, including *The Joy of Cooking*, and in various compendia published by newspaper or magazine test kitchens. Evaporated milk is still favored by many cooks for making pralines, fudge, and caramels. See CARAMELS; FUDGE; and PRALINE.

The first successful versions of evaporated milk were at least as expensive as fresh milk or cream, but throughout the twentieth century the price dropped enough to turn the tables. By the 1950s and 1960s evaporated milk had been around long enough for many consumers to prefer it to uncanned milk on grounds of taste as well as economy. However, a period of campaigns against full-fat dairy products was then setting in. In response, during the late 1960s manufacturers introduced reduced-fat versions of evaporated milk. Today it is sold in whole-milk (3.25 percent milk fat), reduced-fat (2 percent milk fat), and nonfat versions. The consistency is often bolstered with carrageenan.

In the last several decades, U.S. sales of both sweetened and unsweetened canned milk have declined. Some of the slack has been picked up by immigrant groups, especially from the Latin American and Far Eastern tropics. Like sweetened condensed milk, unsweetened evaporated milk caught on in those regions without having to face any cultural prejudices in favor of dairy products genuinely or supposedly fresh from the farm; today it is prominently sold in U.S. neighborhood grocery stores catering to Latin American and Southeast Asian clienteles. In the eclectic culinary climates of both areas, it is sometimes combined with sweetened condensed milk.

Evaporated and sweetened condensed milk figure together in shortcut versions of *kulfi*, the rich Indian ice cream traditionally made with heavily reduced milk. In Hong Kong evaporated milk is now de rigueur in the filling for egg tarts (*dan tat* or *don tot*), a slightly anglicized offshoot of the *pastéis de Belém* brought by the Portuguese to nearby Macau.

Guangzhou- and Hong Kong–style dim sum parlors often include evaporated milk in jelled almond "curd" (*xingren doufu*), the steamed sponge cake called *ma la gao*, and sweet fillings for some of the flaky pastries generically known as *su bing*.

See also CHINA; CREAM; INDIA; MILK; PASTEL DE NATA; and ROMBAUER, IRMA STARKLOFF.

Mendelson, Anne. *Milk: The Surprising Story of Milk through the Ages*. New York: Knopf, 2008.
Selitzer, Ralph. *The Dairy Industry in America*. New York: Dairy & Ice Cream Field and Books for Industry, 1976.

Anne Mendelson

extracts and flavorings for preparing sweet confections and baked goods are essences drawn out from plant material that intensify and enhance the food and drink we consume.

Various means are employed to extract elements from the seeds, roots, stems, skins, juice, and blossoms of plants. These elements are then concentrated into essences, syrups, and oils, or into solids, which need to be pulverized. Many of these methods were used in the ancient world and are basically simple: simmering and boiling in liquid; pressing and squeezing; steeping, infusion, and maceration. Distillation is more sophisticated, as it requires boiling a liquid and then, by means of an enclosed vessel—a still—catching its vapor, which condenses into a purer form, or essence. The Greeks, Egyptians, Arabs, and Chinese understood this process as long as two millennia ago and used it much as we do today, to make alcohol, medicine, and perfume in addition to essences for flavoring.

Citrus

Lemon and orange, and to a lesser extent lime and grapefruit, are much used for flavoring. The zest of citrus fruit—the outer, colored part of the rind—contains its essential oil, which is highly aromatic, far more than the juice within. Pared or grated, zest brings liveliness to any concoction, whether savory or sweet (just be sure to avoid the bitter white pith). The cook can also rub a lump of sugar against the outside of a lemon or orange, for the sugar to absorb some of its oil. Another method, when making sweet bread, is to rub one's hands against the fruit and then immediately knead the dough to impart some of the oil's delicate fragrance.

The best commercial citrus oil is cold-pressed from the rind, which yields more intensity than extract or flavoring. Because of the large quantity of fruit needed, it is commensurately more expensive. The essential oil of the bergamot orange flavors Earl Grey tea.

Other Fruits

Fruit essences are made from the juice of certain fruits, especially strawberries, raspberries, and pomegranates, which are useful as flavorings for fruit compotes, pastries, and cocktails and lend an appealing pink tinge. The beautiful pomegranate, native to Persia, appears in ancient Greek, Hebrew, Egyptian, and Arab mythology and is still important to the cuisines of the Middle East and the Mediterranean. Fresh pomegranate juice can be concentrated and sweetened to make grenadine syrup to color and flavor cocktails.

Flowers

Orange flower water (orange blossom water) is distilled from the blossoms of the bitter orange. Used for compotes, puddings, pastries, and occasionally savory foods, orange flower water was the main flavoring in Europe before vanilla became available. It is still widely used in the Middle East.

Rosewater is more delicate than orange flower water. Both the water and essential oil are used in the Middle East, Balkans, and India for puddings, pastries, sorbets, and confectionery, including Turkish delight. See FLOWER WATERS.

The calyx or sepals of the hibiscus blossom are steeped like tea or sweetened into a deep red, sweet-and-sour syrup that is consumed in the Middle East and North Africa. With the rise of specialty cocktails, hibiscus syrup has become popular in the United States.

Nuts

The fruit of the almond tree has long been valuable in the cooking of Europe and the Middle East. The almond is also important for its oil, which comes primarily from the bitter almond (not cultivated in the United States). Almond extract or essence, used in desserts and baking, is processed and distilled from the residual crushed kernels of bitter almonds. Because the strongly flavored kernels contain toxic prussic acid, they must be heated before being eaten in any form. See NUTS.

Peaches, apricots, plums, and cherries are all cousins of the almond, so they have a natural affinity for one another. Noyau is a French extract made from the kernels of these fruits, which can be processed into a syrup or liqueur. Macarons are flavored with almond extract, but for *amaretti di Saronno* an extract of apricot kernels is used. See MACARONS.

Many sweet beverages are flavored with ground almonds, such as French *orgeat*, Latin American *horchata*, and British *ratafia*, all with traditions reaching far back in time. Hazelnut, walnut, and pistachio nuts are also processed into highly refined oil for baking.

Roots

Licorice ("sweet root") is the most popular root flavoring. Extract from the long taproot is sweetened with sugar and made into confections and candies with a distinctive black color. The licorice produced in the Netherlands and parts of Scandinavia is much stronger than American "lickerish," which is closer to candy. See LICORICE.

Sarsaparilla, from the root of the South American smilax plant, is a soft drink enjoyed in the American South. Root beer and birch beer are other soft drinks flavored with root extract.

Salep, a powder derived from the tubers of the Orchis genus of orchids, flavors milky drinks, custards, and ice creams. It is popular in the Middle East.

Seeds

Kola (cola) is made from the nut, or fleshy seed, of the kola tree. While initially bitter, the taste becomes sweet as it lingers on the palate. In its native West Africa, kola is chewed fresh, or else it is dried and crushed to make cola drinks. Kola contains a small amount of caffeine. American carbonated colas such as Coca-Cola and Pepsi-Cola belong to this family, however distantly. See SODA.

Stems

Mastic comes from the twigs of a shrub that, when cut, ooze a sticky resin. See MASTIC. The solidified resin is crushed and sweetened to make a flavoring and syrup. In the Balkans and Middle East, mastic is enjoyed in drinks, ice cream, chewing gum, and various candies like Turkish delight.

Leaves

The menthol in leaves of the mint family is highly aromatic. Peppermint is strongest, and its oil is extracted for use in candies and jellies, as well as toothpaste and pharmaceuticals. Spearmint more often flavors juleps, Middle Eastern tea, and fruit compotes. Corsican mint is the chief ingredient in crème de menthe liqueur.

Leaves of the rose geranium plant (*Pelargonium* or cranesbill) have a rose scent and were often used in the past to infuse desserts. Rose geranium can also be distilled into an essential oil.

The finest extracts and flavorings use natural products without synthetic additions or substitutes, and thus they are costly. Beware of products that seem surprisingly inexpensive. All flavorings should be used sparingly, especially oils and extracts, so as not to overseason food. The cook can always add more but cannot subtract.

See also LOKUM and MIDDLE EAST.

Arndt, Alice. *Seasoning Savvy: How to Cook with Herbs, Spices, and Other Flavorings.* New York: Haworth Herbal Press, 1999.
Davidson, Alan, ed. *The Oxford Companion to Food.* Oxford: Oxford University, 1999.
Stobart, Tom. *Extracts, Spices and Flavourings.* Harmondsworth, U.K.: Penguin, 1977.
Stobart, Tom. *The Cook's Encyclopedia: Ingredients and Processes.* New York: Harper & Row, 1981.

Elizabeth Gawthrop Riely

extreme candy describes overwhelmingly hot or sour candies marketed to consumers with an underlying dare: "This product may be too much for you to handle."

The Ferrara Candy Company is responsible for three classic early examples of extreme candies that are considered tame by today's standards. In the 1930s Ferrara introduced Red Hots (originally "Cinnamon Imperials"), small red cinnamon candies made by cold panning. See PANNING. The far spicier Atomic Fireballs followed in 1954—individually wrapped red jawbreakers that start out mild and quickly become hot and cinnamony thanks to cinnamaldehyde (the active ingredient in cinnamon) and capsaicin (a compound found in hot peppers). And in 1962 Ferrara introduced Lemonheads, hard lemon candies coated in sour sugar.

Children of the 1980s may remember DareDevils, jawbreakers that alternated rings of hot and cool flavors. Willy Wonka Brands (then owned by Chicago-based Breaker Confections) launched DareDevils in 1982 as a "Devilishly Hot" version of their popular Everlasting Gobstoppers. DareDevils have since been discontinued, but their insouciant name lives on in Dare Devils Extreme Sour Candy, sold both as individually wrapped hard candies and liquid sprays in flavors like "Death Drool." Made by the Foreign Candy Company, Dare Devils owe their extreme sourness to citric acid, malic acid, and sodium citrate.

Warheads, sour hard candies invented in Taiwan in 1975, were first distributed by the Foreign Candy Company in the United States in the early 1990s. See HARD CANDY. The challenge with Warheads is to get past the first intensely painful ten seconds; malic acid coats only the outside of the candies, leaving the more manageable ascorbic and citric acids behind for a mild finish. Children compete to see who can hold the most Warheads in their mouth for the longest time, and the still-popular Mega Warheads now carry the warning "Eating multiple pieces within a short time period may cause a temporary irritation to sensitive tongues and mouths." Label warnings notwithstanding, competitive consumption is part of the brand identity of many extreme candies. Toxic Waste Candy, similar to Warheads but with a sour liquid core to complement the sour exterior, has a challenge written onto each plastic waste-drum container: "How long can you keep one in your mouth?" A person who can manage 60 seconds is deemed a "Full Toxie Head!" But those who last under 30 seconds are labeled "Cry Baby!" or "Total Wuss!" Toxie Heads prove their mettle by posting YouTube videos of themselves keeping the candies in their mouths for the requisite minute or longer.

One issue with sour candies is that they are terrible for the teeth because enamel begins to break down at pH4, and most sour candies are at least a pH3. The problem is compounded with extremely sour candy; Warhead Sour Spray is a 1.6 on the pH scale, only about 0.6 less acidic than battery acid (though pH scales are logarithmic). See DENTAL CARIES.

In an attempt to make the world's hottest candy, several companies have turned to the hottest chile peppers. ThinkGeek, an online retailer, makes Ghost Pepper Super Hot Candy Balls from scorching-hot bhut jolokia, better known as ghost pepper, and Trinidad scorpion pepper. Vertigo Pepper Candy, a product of the appropriately named Bhut-pepper Company in Brooklyn, New York, contains five different chile peppers and measures 2 million Scoville heat units (SHUs), hundreds of times spicier than jalapeños. Although hot and sour tastes guarantee mouth burn, they do not necessarily translate into lucrative sales, for today's children seek ever more radical candy experiences. Thus, the most popular extreme candies are also interactive, with battery-powered delivery systems and all sorts of special effects.

See also CHILDREN'S CANDY and GAG CANDY.

Fabricant, Florence. "A Little Candy Makes the Heat More Bearable." *New York Times*, 15 September 2010.

Hartel, Richard W., and AnnaKate Hartel. "Sour Patch Candy." In *Candy Bites: The Science of Sweets*, 167–169. New York: Copernicus, 2014.

Max P. Sinsheimer

fairs are known today by many different names: show, fête, festival, market, and exhibition. An ancient tradition, a fair is a temporary gathering to display and trade products, goods, and animals. From a very early date, in order to attract crowds, fairs offered entertainment in the form of musicians, acrobats, jesters, and various contests. Delicacies and dainties, such as waffles and gingerbread, were for sale in great quantities at medieval fairs; professional vendors trolled the fairgrounds with portable ovens to sell their freshly baked goods to visitors.

The modern English word "fair" originates from the archaic word "fayre" and the Latin term *feria*, meaning "holy day." In medieval Europe, fairs developed as cyclical meeting places of local commerce and became, by the High Middle Ages, extremely important for long-distance and international trade. Fairs were habitually organized during the periods of saints' feasts, in the courts of churches and abbeys, or on village greens and plains near towns. Well-known examples of age-old English fairs are those held at Westminster on St. Peter's Day, at Smithfield on St. Bartholomew's, and at Durham on St. Cuthbert's Day.

A medieval fair normally began with three to eight days of preliminary work as goods were unpacked, exhibited, compared, and evaluated. The quantities for sale were revealed and prices were established, but this was a time for looking only. Next came the time for dealing, which lasted another three to eight days. The third and final stage of the fair consisted of settling and balancing accounts and arranging for credit. The layout of the fairs made comparing the quality of similar products quite easy. For instance, at the Lendit fairs, held in June on the plain between Paris and Saint-Denis, merchants from different towns (Louviers, Bernay, Lisieux, Vire, etc.) exhibited and sold their products in their own "streets."

Among the most important fairs in medieval Europe were the Champagne fairs, a series of six events, each lasting more than six weeks, and spaced throughout the year. Originally local agricultural and stock fairs, the Champagne fairs became important in reviving the European economy as they dominated commercial relations between the Mediterranean and Northern Europe. They served as a principal market not only for textiles, leather, and fur, but also for spices. For a long time, sugar and exotic spices (saffron, pepper, cinnamon, nutmeg, cloves, and ginger), essential for creating and flavoring cakes, biscuits, and other sweets, were very expensive and therefore available only to the wealthy classes. The best places for buying such sought-after ingredients were the fairs. The fairs were also important in the spread and exchange of cultural influences such as architectural and artistic ideas and innovations from different corners of Europe. Toward the end of the medieval period, developments in transport, especially in the sea transport of heavy goods, gradually made some fairs redundant. Better markets closer to the centers of production were available and growing. The majority of the Parisian fairs, for example, were now made needless by the permanent commercial market. While some fairs disappeared, others appeared, however, and even thrived because of their specialities—a good example are the fifteenth-century fairs at Lyons focusing on silks and spices. Frankfurt fairs remained the greatest European market for German products.

Edible souvenirs like gingerbreads and other sweet treats were sold and bought at fairs throughout

Europe. In England these souvenirs were commonly known under the collective name of "fairings." At Bartholomew Fair in Smithfield, fairings of gingerbread, made from a thick mixture of honey and breadcrumbs flavored with cinnamon and pepper and sometimes colored with saffron or sander (sandalwood), were sold from 1126 to 1800. See FOOD COLORINGS and GINGERBREAD. Ornamented by beautiful designs from wooden molds, the gingerbread fairings were decorated with box leaves nailed down with gilded cloves. See COOKIE MOLDS AND STAMPS. At Easter time in the northern counties of England, colored "paste eggs" were among the traditional fairings. Cornish fairings included a sweet and spicy ginger biscuit with sugar-coated almonds and caraway seeds, crystallized angelica, and macarons. See ANGELICA.

Toward the end of the medieval period, developments in transport gradually made some fairs redundant. However, fairs took on a new life on the North American continent, where they eventually became less about trade than celebrations of regional and ethnic production. The economic significance of fairs may have changed dramatically but they are still popular today. Countless fairs are organized periodically throughout the Western world, usually concurrently with anniversaries of important local historical events, or seasonal events such as harvest times, or holidays like Christmas, and often on dedicated, traditional fairgrounds. In the United States, county fairs exhibiting the equipment, animals, sports, and recreations associated with farming are an important part of cultural life in country towns. Their larger versions, the state fairs, often including only exhibits or competitors that have won in their categories at the various local county fairs, have been held annually since 1841. Home cooks vie for top ("blue ribbon") prizes for their pies and preserves, while fairgoers indulge in fair food both classic (cotton candy and funnel cakes) and newfangled (in Nashville, Tennessee, deep-fried Goo Goo Clusters, a milk-chocolate candy bar with caramel, marshmallow, and peanuts that is coated in batter before being fried). See COTTON CANDY and FRIED DOUGH.

Abu-Lughod, Janet L. *Before European Hegemony: The World System, A.D. 1250–1350.* New York: Oxford University Press, 1991.

Cavaciocchi, Simonetta, ed. *Fiere e mercati nella integrazione delle economie europee secc. XIII–XVIII.* Atti delle Settimane di Studi 32. Florence: Le Monnier, 2001.

Favier, Jean. *Gold & Spices: The Rise of Commerce in the Middle Ages.* Translated by Caroline Higgit. New York: Holmes & Meier, 1998.

Snodgrass, Mary Ellen. *Encyclopedia of Kitchen History.* New York: Fitzroy Dearborn, 2004.

Hannele Klemettilä

fantasy worlds made of sugar and sweets are part of the folklore of societies throughout the world. These "saccharotopias" typically combine surreal and unlimited amounts of candy and other edible delicacies with a life of leisure and carefree indulgence. They are special cases of the pastoral mode, with its sunlit paradise of natural fecundity (*locus amoenus*) and leisure (*otium*). Saccharotopias often include the "natural" foods of traditional pastoral—fruit, milk, and cheese—but they focus primarily on sweets.

The earliest saccharotopia is biblical. God speaks to Moses from the burning bush, promising to free the Israelites from slavery in Egypt and to bring them to "a land flowing with milk and honey" (Exodus 3.17: אֶל-אֶ רֶץ זָבַת חָלָב וּדְבָשׁ).

In modern times, the most famous sugar fantasy is the U.S. hobo ballad "Big Rock Candy Mountain." In the original version recorded by Harry McClintock in 1928, the world of the Big Rock Candy Mountain is a raunchy place with lakes of gin and whiskey, cigarette trees, and a hobo's whore, as well as lemonade springs and trees full of fruit, not to mention the rock candy crag. In 1949 the folksinger Burl Ives recorded an expurgated version that became a children's classic. Over time, other artists produced even blander lyrics: the gin disappears and whiskey turns to soda pop. Cigarette trees morph into peppermint. But the grittier Ives version is still the iconic image of America's leading saccharotopia, the sweetness of the candy nirvana powerfully contrasted with the portrait of the hobo life:

On a summer day
In the month of May
A burly bum came hiking
Down a shady lane
Through the sugar cane
He was looking for his liking
As he roamed along
He sang a song
Of the land of milk and honey
Where a bum can stay

For many a day
And he won't need any money

(Chorus)
Oh the buzzin' of the bees
In the cigarette trees
Near the soda water fountain
At the lemonade springs
Where the bluebird sings
On the big rock candy mountain.

Like all saccharotopias, though, this sugary Arcadia descends from a European archetype of unknown origin, the Land of Cockaigne. That legendary place of sweet-cramming debauchery and compulsive insobriety crops up in Italy (*Cuccagna*), as well as Germany (*Schlaraffenland* or slackerland), the Low Countries (*Koekange*), Spain (*Cucaña*), and in medieval England (Cockaigne). The name has even been connected, humorously, with modern London (Cockney). According to the *Oxford English Dictionary*, Cockaigne's etymology "remains obscure," but some authorities hypothesize that it derives from words for "cake," such as German *Kuchen* (the Brothers Grimm) or the Latin verb *coquere*, meaning "to cook." In English, it can be traced to the fourteenth century; in German, to thirteenth-century Latin drinking songs found at Benediktbeuern, the Bavarian monastery, lyrics that have retained their vitality as texts for Orff's *Carmina Burana* (*Ego sum abbas Cucaniensis / et meum consilium est cum bibulis*, which means "I'm the abbot of Cockaigne and I preside over a bunch of drunks").

Perhaps the fullest account of Cockaigne survives in one of the Harley manuscripts now in the British Library. Written down in Ireland around 1330, this naughty Middle English poem celebrates a place where naked nuns swim in rivers of milk, honey, and wine. A monastery has walls made of pies, with cakes for shingles and puddings for the pegs that fasten the posts and beams.

Cockaigne has inspired painters from Brueghel the Elder to Goya, who depicted a contemporary enactment of a Madrid folk ritual called *cucaña*, for which contestants shimmied up a very tall greased pole. Successful climbers were rewarded with an edible prize at the top. There are photographs of a similar *cuccagna* pole in Italy.

An entirely separate "Cockaigne" tradition arose in the Spanish Empire in the sixteenth century, in the Andean town that Pizarro called Jauja and established as the first capital of Peru in 1534. Before their defeat, the Incas had stored a vast amount of food in Jauja, which thereafter became famous throughout Spanish America as a proverbial paradise of easy

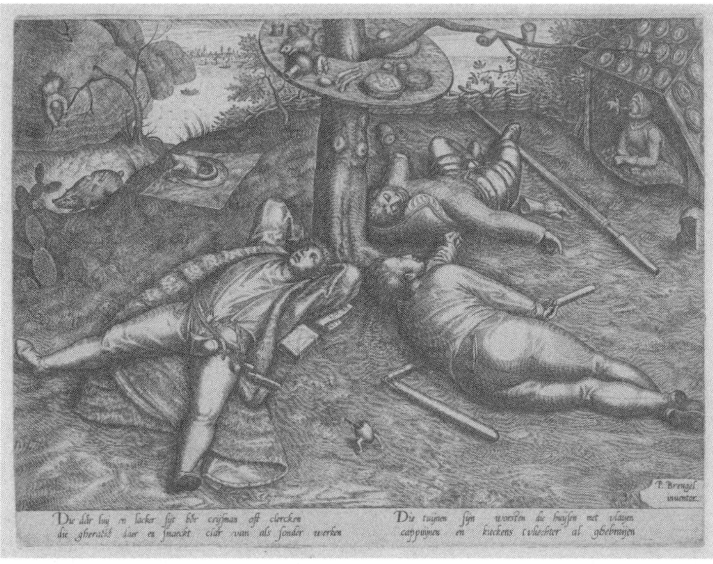

The legendary Land of Cockaigne, with its superabundant food and drink, has inspired artists for centuries. This engraving, attributed to the Netherlandish painter Pieter van der Heyden, was completed sometime after 1570.
THE METROPOLITAN MUSEUM OF ART, HARRIS BRISBANE DICK FUND, 1926

living. Even today in Mexico and its cultural hinterland across the U.S. border, the city of Jauja, *la ciudad de Jauja,* lives on in folklore as a mythic Shangri-La. The best evidence of this is a *corrido* of the same name. This popular Chicano song celebrates churches made of sugar, caramel friars, molasses acolytes, and side altars of honey. It can be heard on YouTube.

Pleij, Herman. *Dreaming of Cockaigne: Medieval Fantasies of the Perfect Life.* Translated by Diane Webb. New York: Columbia University Press, 2001.

Raymond Sokolov

Farmer, Fannie (1857–1915), was one of America's most esteemed cooking teachers and authors at the turn of the twentieth century. Renowned for her scientific approach to cooking and strict precision in measuring ingredients, she published her first book *The Boston Cooking-School Cook Book* in 1896. See MEASUREMENT. It was reprinted countless times. Farmer also took great pride in her courses in sickroom cookery. She wrote *Food and Cookery for the Sick and Convalescent* in 1904 and lectured at Harvard Medical School.

Farmer also had a whimsical side and a notable sweet tooth. Her works abound with cakes, cookies, pies, pastries, candies, ice creams, and puddings. *The Boston Cooking-School Cook Book* includes one of the first recipes for so-called brownies. They were not made with chocolate, but rather flavored with molasses, baked in individual shallow cake tins, and garnished with pecans. See BROWNIES. She made almond and cinnamon cookies shaped like horseshoes and studded with chocolate frosting nails. She sent her rolled wafer cookies to the table with ribbons around them and molded puddings into heart shapes for Valentine's Day. One of her Christmas desserts was a dish of ice cream covered with crushed macarons and topped with a crepe-paper-clad doll. In her December 1905 column for *The Woman's Home Companion* she wrote excitedly that she hoped it would "make many an eye twinkle at the Christmas dinner."

Farmer never met a marshmallow she did not like or could not mix into ice cream, frosting, or, especially, gelatin. Her salads were often as sweet as desserts. She gave the world the famous (or infamous) ginger ale salad. To make it, she added ginger ale to gelatin and then mixed in chopped cherries, celery, apples, and pineapple. See GELATIN and MARSHMALLOWS.

Remembered today for her stern insistence on level measurements, Farmer was also the woman who introduced ices and ice creams in the 1896 *Boston Cooking-School Cook Book* by writing, "How cooling, refreshing, and nourishing, when properly taken, and of what inestimable value in the sickroom!"

In this famous photograph, the Boston Cooking School principal Fannie Farmer (1857–1915) holds a measuring cup to a student, as if to reinforce her reputation as the "Mother of Level Measurements." © BETTMANN / CORBIS

See also CHRISTMAS; ICE CREAM; ICING; PUDDING; and VALENTINE'S DAY.

Shapiro, Laura. *Perfection Salad: Women and Cooking at the Turn of the Century*. New York: Modern Library, 2001.

Jeri Quinzio

fermentation is a process by which yeasts or bacteria produce alcohol, lactic acid, acetic acid, and other chemical byproducts as they metabolize sugars derived from varied sources. All sugars can be used as substrates for fermentation.

Alcohol Fermentation

By far the most widespread form of fermentation is the production of alcohol. Alcoholic beverages are produced by the action of yeasts (primarily *Saccharomyces cerevisiae* but also many others) on sugars found in honey, grapes, apples, and many other fruits, as well as cacti, tree saps, grains, starchy tubers, and milk. Indigenous people of most regions of the world developed distinctive alcoholic beverages made from available local carbohydrate sources. Simple carbohydrates ferment directly into alcohol. Yeasts are generally present on sugar-rich substrates, and fermentation will generally proceed spontaneously. For instance, raw honey diluted with water will inevitably begin to ferment, as will freshly pressed fruit juice.

In contrast, complex carbohydrates must first be broken down (by enzymatic processes) into simple sugars that will ferment into alcohol. Thus, it is always more technically difficult to produce beers and other grain- or starchy tuber-based beverages than wines and other alcoholic beverages made from fruits or other simple sugars. In the Western tradition of beer making, germination of grains, known as malting, produces such enzymes. This is the process used in making hopped barley beers and ales, as well as Egyptian *bouza*, African sorghum and millet beers, Central American corn beers, and many others. In the Asian tradition, the primary source of these enzymes is molds (primarily *Aspergillus* spp. but also *Rhizopus* spp.) grown on grains, such as Japanese *kōji*, Chinese *chu*, Korean *nuruk*, Indonesian *ragi*, Nepalese *marcha*, and others. The third source of such enzymes, generally regarded as the most ancient, is human saliva; chewed grain beverages, such as *chicha*, made from corn in the Andes Mountains of South America, continue to be produced in several different parts of the world.

Distillation is a process that concentrates alcohol (or other volatile substances). Only fermentation can create alcohol, and distillation can only concentrate alcohol that has already been fermented. Any type of fermented alcohol may be distilled. The process takes place in an apparatus known as a still. Distillation evaporates and then condenses the fermented alcohol, thanks to the different boiling temperatures of different substances. Alcohol boils at 173°F (78°C), whereas water boils at 212°F (100°C). So when fermented alcohol—a mixture of alcohol and water—is heated, the vapors contain proportionately more alcohol than the liquid, as does the resulting liquid when the vapors are cooled. With repeated runs through the still, a purer and purer product results.

Lactic Acid Fermentation

Another widespread form of fermentation is the metabolism of sugars into lactic acid by lactic acid bacteria. Many varied foods and beverages are products of this process: sauerkraut, kimchi, and other fermented pickles are lactic acid fermentations, in which plant sugars are metabolized into lactic acid by bacteria found on all plant life. Yogurt, kefir, and many cheeses also rely on lactic acid fermentation of milk sugar lactose. Yogurt and kefir are cultured by specific microbial communities that define the ferments, but lactic acid bacteria are present in all raw milk and will spontaneously *clabber* (sour) the milk if it is left unrefrigerated. Grains, too, will yield lactic acid after spontaneous fermentation.

Acetic Acid Fermentation

Another important metabolic product of the fermentation of sugars is acetic acid, more commonly known as vinegar. Acetic acid is not metabolized directly from sugars, but rather from alcohol. Thus, the fermentation of acetic acid from sugars is a two-stage process: first, the fermentation of sugars into alcohol; then a distinct microbial process in which the alcohol is converted into acetic acid. Vinegar can be made from any fermented alcohol or solution of fermentable sugars.

The bacteria that metabolize alcohol into acetic acid are known as *Acetobacter*. Acetobacter are aerobic organisms that can convert alcohol into acetic acid only in the presence of oxygen. This is why alcoholic beverages are typically fermented under conditions designed to exclude air, to avoid conversion of alcohol into acetic acid. But when acetic acid is the desired outcome, a vessel with a broad surface area is used to maximize contact with oxygen.

Mixed Fermentation

Many ferments involve some combination of alcoholic, lactic, and acetic fermentations. Until Louis Pasteur's 1860s research isolating yeast and other fermentation organisms, microorganisms always existed in communities, and many—arguably all—traditional ferments have involved more than a single type of fermentation. For instance, sourdough breads (and all bread until the isolation of yeast) are risen by a combination of yeasts and lactic acid bacteria. Similarly, in traditional fermented alcoholic beverages that rely on wild yeasts rather than isolated pure strains, the yeasts are always accompanied by lactic acid bacteria, and the products include not only alcohol but also lactic acid.

See also FRUIT; HONEY; MALT SYRUP; SAP; and YOGURT.

Katz, Sandor. *The Art of Fermentation: An In-Depth Exploration of Essential Concepts and Processes from Around the World.* White River Junction, Vt.: Chelsea Green, 2012.

Mollison, Bill. *The Permaculture Book of Ferment and Human Nutrition.* Tyalgum, Australia: Tagari, 1993.

Steinkraus, Keith, ed. *Handbook of Indigenous Fermented Foods.* 2d ed. New York: Marcel Dekker, 1996.

Sandor Ellix Katz

festivals, unlike quotidian rituals of blessing food or saying grace at the table to honor what we eat, highlight foods and dishes that reflect a community's religious, social, and cultural roots.

In Europe's traditionally Catholic countries, saints' days often have their own festivals, which are associated with particular sweets. In Sicily, to celebrate the 13 December holiday of Santa Lucia, a wheat and ricotta cream dish called *cuccìa* (related to the word for grain) is traditionally enjoyed. This practice has its roots in the seventeenth century, when residents of Palermo suffering from famine prayed to the Sicilian saint Santa Lucia, who hailed from Siracusa. When a boat carrying wheat arrived, the grain was quickly boiled instead of being ground into flour for pasta, and it was eaten with the local ricotta cheese. The ricotta cream version of *cuccìa* is specific to Sicily, where pasta and bread are banned on the holiday in commemoration of this historical event. In Sweden, St. Lucia Day is celebrated with saffron buns in assorted shapes (*Lussekatter*), whose golden hue brings light to the dark December days.

Christmas Eve in Provence is marked by the meatless *gros souper* (big supper), which is consumed before midnight mass. An important aspect of the meal is *les treize desserts de Noël*—the 13 desserts of Christmas, which symbolically represent Jesus and his 12 apostles. Thirteen desserts, including nougat, *mendiants* (dried fruit confections), and various fruits, are presented; tradition holds that each guest must taste at least one. See CHRISTMAS and NOUGAT.

In India, foods are ritually tied to the country's many festivals. The Hindu celebration of Diwali is very sweets oriented, with laddu made of chickpea flour, cardamom, sugar, and ghee one of the holiday's most typical offerings. See DIWALI and LADDU. *Jalebi* is a popular dessert made of a chickpea-flour batter fried until crisp and then drenched in a sugar syrup flavored with saffron and cardamom. Children enjoy candy toys during Diwali. Modaka, said to be the elephant-headed deity Ganesh's favorite treat, are small dumplings stuffed with jaggery (unrefined sugar) and coconut, either steamed or fried. Tradition calls for 21 modaka to be made as an offering during the Chaturthi festival in August. See MODAKA.

China's most popular sweet is the mooncake, which although tied to the Mid-Autumn Festival (sometimes called the Mooncake Festival), has many variations. The pastry is typically stuffed with lotus seed or red azuki bean paste; it sometimes contains a salted duck egg yolk, which symbolizes the full moon. The dessert is labor-intensive and almost always prepared commercially rather than at home. Mooncakes are also associated with festivals in Indonesia, Japan, Philippines, Thailand, and Vietnam, where for the New Year, *Tet Nguyen Dan* (or simply Tet) mooncakes are part of offerings made to the kitchen god Ong Tao. Families sometimes smear honey over the mouth of an image of Ong Tao to guarantee that he will say only pleasant or sweet things during the coming year. See MOONCAKE.

Fruit Festivals

Many festivals are based on seasonal fruits, especially strawberries, celebrations of which abound in North America and Europe. See FRUIT. Perhaps the most famous in the United States is held in Ponchatoula, Louisiana, which bills itself as the Strawberry Capital of the World. Bayou musicians perform at the city's three-day Strawberry Festival in mid-April, and there is a Strawberry Strut race, a parade and auction, and a college scholarship for each year's Strawberry Queen. Strawberries are consumed deep-fried, chocolate-dipped, blended in daiquiris, and by the dozens in a strawberry-eating contest. The festival is preceded by a Strawberry Ball at the end of March and followed by a Strawberry King and Queen Pageant and Grand Marshall Coronation at the end of May.

France's best-known salute to the strawberry takes place in Beaulieu-sur-Dordogne on the second Sunday of May. The highlight is a giant strawberry tart—as large as 26 feet across and containing as many as 1,700 pounds of strawberries—made by local bakers and served to all festival attendees.

Italy also has a variety of strawberry festivals. The *Sagra delle fragole* in Piedmont's hamlet of Fosseno features a *risotto alle fragole*. In Lazio, the town of Nemi celebrates *fragoline di bosco*, prized wild strawberries. During the festival, local girls in traditional dress walk through the crowds, handing out the small berries.

In Italy's Alto Adige (South Tyrol), apples are one of the leading crops. The three-day Bolzano Gourmet Festival, held in late May, showcases apples that have received the Protected Geographical Status certificate of Mela Alto Adige IGP/Südtiroler Apfel (Alto Adige and South Tyrol Apple). The event features educational programming and workshops in an apple orchard, as well as culinary demonstrations by top local chefs.

Confectionery Festivals

Europe's most popular chocolate festival is held in Perugia, Italy, in mid-October, where the city's famous Baci chocolates are prominently featured. Perugia's proximity to Spoleto and its world-renowned Spoleto Festival of culture may account for the Chocolate Festival's inclusion of exhibits, songs, and plays about chocolate.

Food fights are a feature of many culinary festivals in Spain. When the participants in *La Merengada* in Vilanova i la Geltrú—part of Carnival celebrations in late February or early March—run out of meringue pies to throw at each other, they substitute candies. A similar rite occurs in many Andalusian towns, including the regional capital, Seville, which holds the *Cabalgata de Reyes Magos* (Arrival of the Magi) festival on 23 December. Participants throw candies from floats, as they do during many Carnival festivals throughout the world. See CARNIVAL.

See also CHINA; CHINESE NEW YEAR; FRANCE; HOLIDAY SWEETS; INDIA; ITALY; SCANDINAVIA; SOUTHEAST ASIA; SPAIN; and UNITED STATES.

Field, Carol. *Celebrating Italy: The Tastes and Traditions of Italy as Revealed Through Its Feasts, Festivals, and Sumptuous Foods*. New York: Harper Perennial, 1997.

Fraioli, James, and Curti, Leonardo. *Food Festivals of Italy: Celebrated Recipes from 50 Food Fairs*. Layton, Utah: Gibbs Smith, 2008.

Doreen Schmid

Fig Newtons, trademarked by Nabisco, are popular bar cookies made of fig jam encased in cake-like pastry. They are surprisingly similar to the traditional fig rolls and *ma'amoul*, a sweet composed of shortbread pastry stuffed with figs, nuts, and other dried fruits, still popular today across the Middle East.

The technology that made Fig Newtons commercially viable in the United States has been subject to

Fig Newton cookies have been popular ever since their introduction in 1891, but in 2012 they were recast simply as "Newtons" to allow for an expanded line of fillings and to eliminate associations with what the manufacturer, Nabisco, feared was a "geriatric" fruit. PHOTOGRAPH BY EVAN AMOS

competing claims. One insists that Ohioan Charles Roser invented a machine around 1891 that allowed the cookies to be mass-produced by funneling the jam and the cookie dough separately but simultaneously. The other asserts that James Henry Mitchell of Philadelphia invented the cookie in 1891 when he came up with a duplex dough-sheeting machine and funnels.

Folklore maintains that the cookie was named after Sir Isaac Newton, but its more likely eponym is the Boston suburb of Newton. The Kennedy Biscuit Works of Cambridgeport, Massachusetts—the first company to produce Fig Newtons commercially, in 1891, soon after the machinery had been perfected—commonly named its products after nearby towns. Within a decade, following a massive nationwide merger of biscuit companies, Nabisco acquired the Biscuit Works. Today, the cookies are known simply as Newtons and encompass several varieties: crisp Fruit Thins, a whole-grain version, and fruit fillings other than fig. The 16th of January is National Fig Newton Day in the United States.

See also FRUIT PASTE and GASTRIS.

"Fig Newtons." http://www.foodtimeline.org/foodcookies.html#fignewtons (accessed 2 September 2013).

Judith Hausman

filo is the Greek name for the paper-thin pastry known as *yufka* in Turkish. It is made of durum wheat flour with a high gluten content, enabling it to be rolled or stretched very thin without tearing. The other ingredients are usually just water and salt, although some recipes may also include eggs or yogurt. Filo is rolled out in large circles using a long, thin rolling pin called an *oklava* in Turkish. Ottoman pastry chefs developed a faster method, first recorded in 1838, by which each walnut-sized ball of pastry is rolled to a saucer-sized circle, then piled up 10 at a time with starch sprinkled between each layer, and the whole pile rolled out simultaneously. See BAKLAVA.

When made at home for immediate consumption, filo sheets are used raw, but professionals half-cook them very briefly on a domed griddle, then dip them in water, and hang them up to dry, a process that enables the daily batch to be piled up without sticking together. Factory-rolled filo is thick and inflexible compared to the hand-rolled variety, and in Turkey it is used only as a last resort. In most urban neighborhoods, specialty shops exist where the paper-thin sheets are freshly rolled daily. In Greece there are no longer any artisans producing hand-rolled filo commercially, so consumers must rely on machine-rolled sheets.

In the past filo rolling was something that most country-bred Turkish boys learned to master, as we learn from a Turkish cookery book written in 1900 by an army officer named Maḥmūd Nedim for unmarried fellow officers. He writes that if his readers cannot roll out pastry themselves they should ask one of the soldiers, "most of whom know how to make yufka."

Flatbreads are of great antiquity in western Asia, but the very thin filo appears to be a Turkic innovation originating in Central Asia. Medieval Arab recipes often use the Turkish term *tutmaç* for this type of thin pastry. The eleventh-century Turkish-Arabic dictionary *Dīwān luġāt at-turk* written by Maḥmūd of Kashgar mentions *yufka* several times, including a dish made of filo folded and fried in butter and one variety of dough (*yalaci yuvga*) so fragile it crumbles at the touch. Since the Turks were a nomadic people, a type of bread that could be rolled out and cooked on a portable griddle in a matter of minutes was more practical than leavened bread, which needed time to rise and an oven for baking. In 1433 the French pilgrim Bertrandon de la Brocquière (1400–1459) encountered Turcoman nomads in the mountains of southern Turkey, who offered him fresh filo with yogurt, cheese, and grapes. The filo was made so quickly that Brocquière declared, "They make two of their cakes sooner than a waferman can make one wafer."

In addition to being eaten as bread with food, filo can be wrapped, folded, and layered with any number of savory or sweet fillings, and fried, baked, or cooked on a griddle. This versatility has given rise to a vast category of dishes throughout Central Asia, the Middle East, and the Balkans, from the simplest version described by Brocquière, who noted that the nomads "fold them up as grocers do their papers for spices, and eat them filled with the curdled milk [yogurt]," to baklava with 80 to 100 layers.

See also GREECE AND CYPRUS; MIDDLE EAST; and TURKEY.

Anderson, E. N., Paul D. Buell, and Charles Perry. *A Soup for the Qan*, pp. 3–4, 67, 315. London: Kegan Paul, 2000.

Işın, Mary. *Sherbet & Spice: The Complete Story of Turkish Sweets and Desserts*, pp. 181–183. London: I. B. Tauris, 2013a.

Işın, Priscilla Mary. "*Yufka*: Food for the Cook's Imagination." In *Wrapped & Stuffed Foods: Proceedings of the Oxford Symposium on Food and Cookery 2012*, edited by Mark McWilliams, pp. 222–228. Totnes, U.K.: Prospect, 2013b.

Kāshgari, Maḥmūd al-. *Compendium of the Turkic Dialects (Dīwān luġāt at-turk)*. 3 vols. Edited and translated by Robert Dankoff in collaboration with James Kelly. Cambridge, Mass.: Harvard University Printing Office, 1984.

Perry, Charles. "Filo." In *The Oxford Companion to Food*, edited by Alan Davidson. Oxford: Oxford University Press, 1999.

Priscilla Mary Işın

financier

See SMALL CAKES.

fios de ovos

See EGG YOLK SWEETS; PORTUGAL; and PORTUGAL'S INFLUENCE IN ASIA.

flan (pudím) is a word much in use when it comes to sweets, but as defined here, the words "flan" or "pudím" (pudding) are restricted to a dessert that is basically a firm custard made with considerable variation. As a custard dessert, flan is most often associated with Spain and the countries it colonized and traded with during the early era of sea exploration. The terms *pudím*, *pudim*, or *flan pudim* are also used in Portuguese-speaking countries. French versions of flan are called *crème renversée* and *crème caramel*; in Italy, it is known as *crema caramella*. In Brazil, *quindim*, *quindin*, and *pudim de leite* are versions of *flan pudim*. In Catalan, "flan" is spelled as *flam*. In parts of South America and the Caribbean, *quesillo* is interchanged with the word "flan." The Japanese call flan *purin*, an abbreviation of *pudingu*.

The signature of classic flan is caramel. Sugar, or sugar syrup, is caramelized and used to coat the cooking mold. See STAGES OF SUGAR SYRUP. The caramel hardens quickly. The custard mixture is added and the mold or molds are set in an insulating hot water bath (bain-marie) to cook in the oven or on top of the stove. The water moderates the temperature and keeps the edges of the custard from overcooking before the center is done. Steaming also works. Cooked flans must be removed from hot water or heat at once to avoid overcooking.

Flan may be served warm from the container in which it cooks, but typically flan is chilled to reach its maximum gentle, tender firmness—a solid state of varying density, depending on the ingredients used and their proportional relationship. As the flan cools, the caramel, which began to melt during the cooking process, continues to liquefy. When the flan is inverted from the mold, some of the caramel has sunk into the custard base, giving what is now the top its brown color. The liquid caramel helps the flan slip free and pools as a thin sauce around the dessert. Any caramel remaining in the mold usually has to be soaked free.

Custard, the essence of flan, has been recorded since Roman times, most astutely by Apicius in the first century. See CUSTARD. Flan custard is a combination of eggs that are beaten and blended with milk or cream (or with another liquid, purée, or even butter). For desserts, the custard is sweetened and usually flavored. The eggs create a sort of protein sponge that firms around the liquid to make it set or become semi-solid when cooked. If overcooked, the sponge tightens and breaks or curdles into liquid and rubbery lumps (a reaction called syneresis).

The number of eggs can vary, but one or two are needed at a minimum, or two to three egg yolks per cup of milk or liquid, plus sugar. Yolks make a thicker, more richly flavored custard, whereas whites deliver the most fragile and delicate one. Packaged flan or crème caramel mixes may not contain eggs, nor do the mixes require baking. Nonfat and lowfat milk with minimum eggs or whites make more delicate custards that firm at lower temperatures; richer cream and more yolks make custards with the smoothest and most unctuous impact. Recipes with a French heritage often call for extensively beating eggs and sugar, but beating just enough to blend thoroughly suffices. Straining is a superfluous effort. The amount of sugar influences how hot the custard must be to thicken, coagulate, or clot, and of course it influences the taste. The more sugar, the hotter the custard can get before breaking. Acid, such as lemon or fruit juice, causes custard to thicken at lower temperatures, but sugar counterbalances this.

Heating the milk before adding it to the eggs speeds cooking and also alters the milk proteins so that they form a thinner skin on the surface of the cold flan. Sweetened condensed milk, used particularly in Mexico, Central and South America, the Caribbean, and other hot-climate countries, dramatically raises the temperature to which flan can be heated, making it less prone to overcooking, and produces an even denser texture. See SWEETENED CONDENSED MILK. Cream cheese, another ingredient often used, adds more density, stability, and flavor to the flan. The best way to determine when flan is set, or done, is to shake the container gently: it is ready when the mixture jiggles just a little in the center. The old test of inserting a knife, to see if it comes out clean, works best when the custard is overcooked or on the verge of being so.

Flan welcomes flavors, especially vanilla. See VANILLA. The name often indicates the distinguishing ingredient: *flan de coco* (coconut), *flan de leche* (milk), *flan de queso* (cheese), *pudím de piña* (pineapple). Chocolate, coffee, and cinnamon flavors are popular. Pumpkin, guava, and apple purées—with or without milk—that are bound with eggs are classified as flans and may not include caramel. Some flans (puddings) are considered as such only in that they are unmolded; this type of flan may be based on fruit purée or juice firmed by gelatin.

See also FLAN (TART).

Andrews, Colman. *Catalan Cuisine: Europe's Last Great Culinary Secret*, pp. 51, 155, 249. New York: Antheneum, 1988.

Hale, William Harlan. *The Horizon Cookbook and Illustrated History of Eating and Drinking Through the Ages*, pp. 158, 706. New York: American Heritage, 1968.

McGee, Harold. *On Food and Cooking: The Science and Lore of the Kitchen*, pp. 54–56, 66–68, 71. New York: Scribner's, 1984.

Tousaint-Samat, Maguelonne. *History of Food*, pp. 356, 553, 554. Translated by Athea Bell. Cambridge, Mass.: Blackwell, 1992. Original French text, Paris: C. Bordas, 1987.

Jerry Anne Di Vecchio

flan (tart) is a simple open tart with a pastry crust filled with fruit, flavored creams, or any number of other ingredients. It is not to be confused with the custard-type dessert also known as flan (the word "flan" is derived from "flado," meaning a round, flat object). See FLAN (PUDÍM). Flans can be sweet or savory (a quiche is a flan). Dessert flans may be made with a sweet shortcrust (*pâte sucrée*), a shortcrust (*pâte brisée*), or even puff pastry. See PASTRY, PUFF. Special metal flan rings are bottomless so that the ring can be lifted straight up from the cooked tart before serving without disturbing its appearance. The flan can also be made in a tart pan with fluted sides and a removable flat metal disk on the bottom. After it is baked, the flan, supported from underneath by the metal disk, can be pushed up and out of the ring and placed on a serving plate. In both cases, the flan is perfectly formed and freestanding when served. For fruit flans, the fruit and the molded pastry can be cooked separately and then combined, or cut fruit can be arranged in the pastry shell before cooking.

In his *Livre de pâtisserie* (1873), Jules Gouffé gives a recipe for *Flans de Crème de Frangipane Meringuée*, in which the bottom of the pastry crust is covered with frangipane flavored with sugar, crushed macarons, and orange flower water. See FRANGIPANE. When the filled pastry has finished baking, meringue is piped over the top and the flan is put back into the oven until the meringue colors slightly. Gouffé then garnishes the dessert with preserved cherries.

Davidson, Alan, ed. "Flan." In *The Oxford Companion to Food*, p. 305. Oxford: Oxford University Press, 1999.

Montaigné, Prosper, ed. *Larousse gastronomique*. Paris: Librairie Larousse, 1938.

Kyri W. Claflin

floating island

See CUSTARD and MERINGUE.

Florentines are rich, round cookies made of caramelized toasted nuts and candied fruit, baked until golden brown, and then coated with dark chocolate. The contrasting textures and tastes make this pastry so special. Florentines are enormously popular worldwide but, like the savory dish "Eggs Florentine", they seem to have very little to do with the city of Florence. Unfortunately, disinformation often travels fast, and many sources erroneously claim that these delicious cookies originated in Florence. It is possible that the "Florentine" attribution arose from the Medici sisters' influential presence in France, since they originally hailed from Florence.

Florentine confectioners, especially Caffè Gilli, date the production of this sweet speciality only to the early twentieth century, when they were making *fiorentine*—small (3 centimeters), handmade chocolate pastilles (dark, milk, or white) topped with candied fruit, pistachios, or almonds. These ingredients are quite common to many Tuscan favorites, such as *cavallucci*, made with nuts, flour, spices, and honey, and panforte, made with candied fruit and nuts, so it is not surprising that they would show up in a new kind of cookie. However, these baked goods have little other resemblance to the Florentine cookie (neither has a chocolate topping, for instance).

In many English-speaking countries, such as Australia or South Africa, different versions of Florentines may be found that include ingredients like condensed milk, corn flakes, cranberries, and ginger. The well-known British chef Nigel Slater has offered recipes for Florentines with dried cranberries or poached pears in his food column in the *Observer*; he recommends hand chopping the candied peel and using only the finest dark chocolate.

Today, Florentines have finally come "home" to Italy. Numerous recipes can be found online, and articles about them are published in women's magazines. These recipes generally follow the classic version made with sugar, cream, butter, candied fruit, chopped and slivered almonds, and dark chocolate.

See also ITALY.

Ferrigno, Ursula. *La Dolce Vita: Sweet Things from the Italian Home Kitchen*. London: Mitchell Beazley, 2005.

Ottolenghi, Yotam, and Sami Tamimi. *Ottolenghi: The Cookbook*. Berkeley, Calif.: Ten Speed, 2013.

June di Schino

flour is the refined product that results from the milling of grain. Any type of grain can be milled into flours that range in consistency from coarse to fine, but for the purposes of baking, wheat flour is the most widely used. Whole-wheat flour is milled from the whole grain of wheat, also known as the wheat berry, which is composed of the bran, germ, and endosperm. The bran layer—the hard outer shell of the kernel—contains most of the fiber. The germ is the nutrient-rich embryo that, when cultivated, sprouts into a wheat plant. The endosperm is the largest part of the grain and is mostly starch. The flavor of whole-wheat flour is strong and distinctive. Refined white flours, by contrast, are made from only the endosperm. Since the sixteenth century white flour was sought out by the elite, in part because it was the most expensive, and fine pastry chefs favored white flour because it yielded the most delicate pastries and cakes. Only recently has whole-grain flour, long despised as peasant food, become something desirable, even trendy.

Processing

In the past, flour was stone ground, a slow milling process that causes less friction and heat, thereby preserving more of the nutrients in the wheat. With the invention of roller milling in Hungary in the mid-nineteenth century, and its spread throughout Europe and the United States in the late nineteenth century, stone-ground flour, especially in the United States, was relegated to a health-food fringe. Massive mills with high-temperature, high-speed steel rollers came to rule the industry. Although this high-speed process creates a much finer flour, it destroys many of the nutrients in the grain. Furthermore, while stone-ground flour is generally aged to improve its baking properties, industrial mills skip the expensive aging process. American mills generally bleach the flour with chemicals, including organic peroxides, nitrogen dioxide, chlorine, chlorine dioxide, and azodicarbonamide. (Japan stopped bleaching flour about 30 years ago, and the use of chlorine, bromates, and peroxides is not permitted in the European Union.) Bleaching has a negative effect on baking, as it toughens the dough, making it brittle, dry, and more difficult to work with.

Protein Content

Wheat flours are distinguished by how they are milled, the type of wheat, how it is grown, and the time of harvest. All of this affects the protein content, which in turn correlates to the amount of gluten in any given flour. Gluten helps create structure and determines texture in the final baked good. Flours with low protein contents produce crumbly tarts and tender, toothsome cakes, while higher protein results in hearty breads with a chewy crust. When the flour is moistened and then mixed or kneaded, the gluten is activated. The small air pockets that form are inflated by gases released by the leavening agent, which causes the dough to expand or rise. The more the dough is mixed or kneaded, the more the gluten develops. For this reason, batter cakes and cookie doughs are mixed only briefly, as overmixing causes the dough to toughen and dry out.

For light and airy cakes with delicate crumb, low-protein flour, either cake flour or pastry flour, is optimal. Most cookies use all-purpose flour with its moderate protein level to allow the dough to be rolled out. Pie doughs also require all-purpose flour so that they can be rolled out into large disks without breaking or crumbling. Shortbread or other butter-rich doughs that yield a fine, sandy crumb in cookies or tarts require lower-protein flours. Elastic doughs such as puff pastry need flour with more protein so that the dough will be firm enough to roll out and layer with butter. See CAKE; LAMINATED DOUGHS; PIE DOUGH; PASTRY, PUFF; ROLLED COOKIES; and SHORTBREAD.

White flour should be stored in a cool, dry area in an airtight container. Because it contains bran, whole-wheat flour easily turns rancid, and its flavor will dissipate. It should be stored in a cool, dry place for up to four months, or refrigerated or frozen for longer storage. The name given to the flour generally indicates how it is intended to be used.

Types of Wheat Flour

Bread flour is a strong flour, meaning that it has a high gluten content, usually around 13 to 16 percent protein. A handful of bread flour feels coarse and is slightly off-white in color. Bread flour is used for making crusty breads and rolls, pizza dough, and similar products.

All-purpose flour is formulated to have a medium gluten content of 10 to 12 percent, which makes it a good middle-of-the-road choice for a wide range of baking, from crusty breads to fine cakes and pastries. Even so, most professional bakers avoid all-purpose flour, preferring instead to use bread flour, cake flour, or pastry flour, depending on what they are baking.

Pastry flour contains about 8 to 10 percent protein. It can be used for biscuits, muffins, cookies, pie doughs, and softer yeast doughs. It is slightly more off-white in color than cake flour.

Cake flour, made from soft wheat, is slightly less strong than pastry flour, with a protein content of only 7.5 to 9 percent. Its texture is visibly finer than that of bread flour, and it is much whiter in color. Its fine, soft consistency makes it preferable for tender cakes and pastries.

Self-rising flour, all-purpose flour with measured amounts of baking powder and salt, is a commercial product created as a convenience for home cooks. It must be used very fresh, because when the flour is stored in the pantry, the baking powder quickly loses its effectiveness.

White whole-wheat flour is about 13 percent protein. It comes from a type of wheat that has no major genes for bran color. The bran of white wheat is not only lighter in color but also milder in flavor, making white whole wheat more appealing to those accustomed to the taste of refined flour. Its milder flavor also means that products made with white wheat require less added sweetener to attain the same level of perceived sweetness.

Whole-wheat pastry flour, or *graham flour,* is milled from low-protein soft wheat, with about 9 percent protein.

Regular whole-wheat flour, milled from hard red wheat, has a protein content of 14 percent. It is used in cookies, crusts, and creamed or batter cakes.

Gluten-free all-purpose flour was developed for those with gluten sensitivity. The flour can be used for cakes, cookies, breads, and breakfast items such as muffins, pancakes, and waffles. Unlike wheat flour, gluten-free flours are composed of a wide range of ingredients and vary greatly. The major difference is found in the first ingredient listed on the package label, which may be cornstarch, white and brown rice flours, or garbanzo bean flour. Each has a completely different flavor and effect on baked products, so manufacturer's instructions should be followed for each brand. The flours may also contain milk powder, tapioca flour, potato starch, xanthan gum, potato starch, tapioca flour, sorghum flour, and fava flour. Gluten-free baked goods do not keep well, so they are best eaten the same day they are baked.

Although it is generally safe to use pastry and cake flour interchangeably, it can be tricky to substitute flours with different protein contents. All-purpose flour can be used for most pastry doughs, but if a finer product is desired, its protein content can be reduced by removing two tablespoons from a cup of flour and replacing them with two tablespoons of sifted cornstarch. Conversely, the protein content of all-purpose flour can be increased by replacing two tablespoons of flour per cup with vital wheat gluten.

See also BREADS, SWEET; CHEMICAL LEAVENERS; MUFFINS; and PANCAKES.

Corriher, Shirley O. *BakeWise: The Hows and Whys of Successful Baking with Over 200 Magnificent Recipes.* New York: Scribner, 2008.

McGee, Harold. *On Food and Cooking: The Science and Lore of the Kitchen.* New York: Scribner, 1984.

Jim Dodge

flower waters, produced by steeping petals in water or by distillation, have been used since ancient times in medicine, perfumes, and cosmetics. The waters are also important in the kitchen as luxury flavorings, almost magically transforming food by imbuing a delicate fragrance, especially to sweet dishes. Rosewater and orange flower water are the best known, but other flowers can be used, such as screwpine, jasmine, rose geraniums, and ylang-ylang. Because their flavor can be intense, they should be used sparingly.

Rosewater

This flower water can be made from any sweet scented roses. The most famous is the ancient damask rose, but the cabbage rose, French rose, and musk rose are also used. Eglantine flower water from a wild rose, sometimes called sweet briar, is particularly popular in Tunisia. The ancient Egyptians, Greeks, and Romans extracted fragrance by steeping rose petals in water, oil, or alcohol. Although water distillation is still traditionally used in many Eastern countries, nowadays steam distillation is often the preferred method. Here, for instance, is how rosewater is made in Afghanistan today: The blooms are picked fresh in the cool, early hours of the morning. A large copper pot or cauldron is filled with water. The petals are added (the amount of water is usually about twice the weight of the petals), and the water is brought to a gentle boil. The pot is covered with a type of copper dome from which an attached pipe or tube leads to a glass bottle, into which the pipe neatly fits. Everything is sealed with dough to prevent the fragrant steam from escaping. The steam rises into the dome, and as it travels down the pipe, it is cooled by cold water, causing the steam to condense into droplets. The droplets travel along the pipe, and slowly the fragrant rosewater drips into the bottle. (Sometimes this rosewater is poured into another pot and slightly warmed again, then left to stand until a thin film of oil forms on the surface. The oil is skimmed off to make *atr* [attar], or oil of roses.) Orange flower water is traditionally made in much the same way.

The technique of distilling rosewater probably evolved in the third and fourth centuries C.E. in Mesopotamia. By the ninth century Persia was distilling rosewater on a large scale, and it was much used there and in neighboring regions. During the Golden Age of Islam in tenth-century Baghdad, famous for its lavish and sumptuous cuisine, rosewater was used extensively in sweet and savory dishes. See BAGHDAD.

The Ottoman Turks used rosewater to add fragrance to desserts, pastries (such as baklava), and sweetmeats (such as *lokum*), as well as to syrups and sherbets. The Turks introduced roses to Bulgaria, where the Valley of the Roses at Kazanluk is famous for its rosewater and rose petal jams. The use of rosewater spread to Europe via the Crusaders. In Elizabethan England, rosewater was used to flavor butter and sugar paste.

Colonial Americans, too, added rosewater to confectionery and desserts. Martha Washington's seventeenth-century *Booke of Sweetmeats* uses rosewater extensively in the recipes. Eliza Leslie (1857) pounded almonds for her almond pudding with "a few drops of rose-water to make them light and preserve their whiteness." Rosewater was added to syrups for use in beverages and also in savory dishes such as chicken pies and spinach. It was often purchased from the Shakers, a religious sect renowned for the purity of their products and who themselves fragranced their apple pie with it.

Rosewater today is used extensively throughout the Indian subcontinent, the Middle East, Central Asia, Turkey, and North Africa. It subtly perfumes biscuits, pastries, *jelabi*, firni, rice puddings such as kheer and *shola*, ice creams, *faluda*, and halvah, as well as drinks such as sherbets and sweet lassi, and sometimes savory rice dishes for festive occasions.

In the West adding a little rosewater to creams, sorbets, mousses, and jellies or sprinkling it over fruits, especially strawberries, transforms these dishes into something exotic.

Orange Flower Water

Sometimes called orange blossom water, orange flower water is distilled from the blossoms of bitter orange trees such as Seville orange and bergamot. It originated in the Middle East, where it is still produced, especially in Morocco and Lebanon. The water is used to add fragrance to syrups, pastries, sweets, and desserts. A teaspoon of orange flower water added to a coffee cup of boiling water, sometimes sweetened with sugar, is called "white coffee." A few drops added to sweetened cool water make a soothing infusion that is often given to children at bedtime. Moroccans frequently add orange flower water to tagines and sometimes sprinkle it over salads.

In the sixteenth century in the south of France, bitter oranges were widely cultivated to make orange flower water, initially for use in the perfume industry. By the seventeenth century in Europe, the water was flavoring almond cakes, rich seed cakes, biscuits, dessert creams, and custards. In Britain it was often used as an alternative to rosewater and added to desserts such as trifles and fools.

Orange flower water flavored *capillaire*, a fashionable nineteenth-century drink whose syrup was originally infused with maidenhair fern. It was also a key ingredient in orgeat, initially a beverage and later a syrup used to sweeten other beverages. American food writer Mary Randolph (1828) called orgeat "a necessary refreshment at all parties." Martha Washington's *Booke of Sweetmeats* uses orange flower water in a recipe for Hunny Combe Cakes.

Orange flower water is an ingredient in the famous New Orleans cocktail Ramos Gin Fizz and in the Mardi Gras orange cake. In France it flavors madeleines and is added to the *turrón* (nougat) of Spain. Further afield, it is added to little wedding cakes and to *pan de muerto* in Mexico.

Kewra Water

Sometimes known as *kewda*, kewra water is extracted from the flowers of the screwpine (*Pandanus odorifer*). See PANDANUS. It is similar to rosewater and is often used as an alternative or mixed with it.

India is a major producer of kewra, 90 percent of which grows in the state of Odisha. Its soft, sweet scent is prized for use in Indian and Sri Lankan cooking, mainly for desserts and sweets such as kheer, barfi, *jelabi*, rosogolla, and *ras malai*. Some Bengali sweets are dipped or soaked in kewra water to imbue a floral perfume. It is added to jams and conserves and sometimes sprinkled over elaborate rice dishes prepared for festive occasions. See INDIA.

Other Flower Waters

In Thailand flowers such as jasmine are picked at sunset when their fragrance is at its best and then steeped in cooled, previously boiled water overnight. This infused water is a traditional way of serving drinking water in Thailand, as well as an important ingredient in Thai desserts and sweets.

In Tunisia rose geranium flower water is popular in drinks, confections, pastries, and *mhalbiya*, a cake made with rice and nuts.

Ylang-ylang is added to ice cream in Madagascar, and in South East Asia it is used in sweets and soft drinks.

See also BAKLAVA; BARFI; EXTRACTS AND FLAVORINGS; LOKUM; MIDDLE EAST; ROSOGOLLA; and TURKEY.

Davidson, Alan. *The Oxford Companion to Food*. 3d ed. Edited by Tom Jaine. Oxford: Oxford University Press, 2014.
Ortiz, Elisabeth Lambert. *The Encyclopedia of Herbs, Spices, & Flavorings*. New York: Dorling Kindersley, 1992.
Saberi, Helen. "Rosewater, the Flavouring of Venus . . . and Asafoetida, Devil's Dung." In *Spicing Up the Palate: Proceedings of the Oxford Symposium on Food and Cookery, 1992*, edited by Harlan Walker, pp. 220–235. London: Prospect, 1993.
Thompson, David. *Thai Food*. Berkeley, Calif.: Ten Speed, 2002.

Helen Saberi

fondant (from the French for "melting") is an opaque, creamy white sugar-based mixture that can be used variously as a confection (usually flavored); as a filling for chocolates; or as a coating for cake or pastry. Once refined sugar became more widely available, confectioners began to experiment with its use in candies and icings, among which was fondant. See ICING. Changing the granular texture of sugar into a creamy substance is accomplished through a process of boiling the sugar with water and a small amount of glucose or corn syrup to 243°F (117°C) (the "soft-ball" stage) for a medium-firm texture. See CORN SYRUP and GLUCOSE.

For poured fondant, the hot syrup is poured onto a smooth surface such as marble and agitated after being first briefly cooled. Working the syrup in this way leads to an opaque and creamy mixture in which the particles of sugar are so small that they are imperceptible on the tongue. The fondant is then ready to be used, after being flavored as desired with mint, other flavorings, or small quantities of spirits or liqueurs.

Firm rolled fondant, also known as sugar paste, is often used to decorate wedding cakes. See WEDDING CAKE. It is made by combining confectioner's sugar, corn syrup, glycerine, and gelatin into a mixture firm enough to roll into thin sheets, which are then draped over the cake. This type of fondant is flexible enough to create decorative effects such as bows, flowers, and other ornamental flourishes. Buttercream icing usually coats the cake to act as an adhesive for the rolled fondant. See CAKE DECORATING.

See also GELATIN; STAGES OF SUGAR SYRUP; and SUGAR.

Edel, Matthew. "The Brazilian Sugar Cycle of the Seventeenth Century and the Rise of West Indian Competition." *Caribbean Studies* 9, no. 1 (1969): 14–44.

Greweling, Peter. *Chocolates and Confections*. Hoboken, N.J.: Wiley, 2007.

Robert Wemischner

food colorings have a long and somewhat problematic history. Written evidence for their use can be found as early as 1500 B.C.E. in Egypt and Europe. Color is such a strong gastronomical cue to flavor and freshness that there are strong incentives for its use not only as an embellishment but also as an adulterant. As a result, food colorings are highly regulated, and only a handful of compounds are approved for use. Colorings derived from natural sources that have a long history of use in food are generally regarded as innocuous, although naturally derived food colorings are not necessarily safe. For example, into the twentieth century, bluestone—copper sulfate—was used in pickle recipes to give the pickles a vivid green color. Unfortunately, like many natural mineral-based colorings, copper sulfate is toxic, albeit only mildly so.

The color of a substance depends on the interaction between the material and light. Light can either interact intimately with the molecules that make up a substance or can be physically scattered off of the structure of the material itself. Food colorings, whether naturally occurring or synthetic, contain a chromophore, a structural motif within a molecule that interacts with a specific wavelength of light in the visible spectrum. The molecule absorbs this light, so the remaining light reflected back to the eye no longer appears white. Chromophores that absorb green light, for example, reflect back red light.

Common chromophores found in food colorings range from the structurally simple azo and carotenoid motifs to complex ring structures and protein–pigment complexes. Most of these chromophores can be found in both naturally occurring colorants and synthetic colors. There are no natural sources of azo dyes known, and the protein–pigment complexes have not been synthesized. In addition to their chromophores, good colorings must be chemically stable, able to maintain their color while stored for long periods and during food preparation. This presents a challenge, as the structures, and therefore the colors, of many compounds are sensitive to changes in pH and temperature.

The synthetic azo dyes are also called coal tar dyes, not because they contain coal tar, but because they were first synthesized using chemicals distilled from the black, sticky residue that remained when coal was processed. Though they are no longer produced from coal tar distillates and can be synthesized from plant sources, the name has stuck. The azo colors approved for food in the United States or the European Union include Allura Red, Sunset Yellow, and azorubine.

Natural food-safe colorings are derived from a wide range of sources, including plants, insects, and bacteria. Natural colorings can be a single chemical compound, like beta-carotene, or a complex mix of pigments and uncolored compounds, as in caramel. Orange annatto powder is extracted from the seeds of the tropical achiote shrub; the color primarily results from bixin, which has a carotenoid chromophore. Paprika, turmeric, and saffron also contain a variety of carotenoid pigments. Salmon pink canthaxanthin (which gives flamingos their characteristic hue) and beta-carotene are also natural carotenoid colors. Although both these colorants can be extracted from natural sources, in practice canthaxanthin and beta-carotene are industrially synthesized.

Brown caramel color, produced by burning a mixture of sugars under controlled conditions, is a mixture of many different molecules with carbon skeletons. Natural sources of red colors include beet red—its color due to betanin, a molecule with an anthroquinone chromophore similar to that in D&C Green 5—and cochineal, a deep red powder made from crushed dried insects. Pure carminic acid, the anthroquinone pigment responsible for cochineal's red color, can be chemically extracted from the insects, or bacteria modified to produce it. Spirulina extract is an approved natural source for blue and green color. It is obtained from spiral-shaped bacteria that live symbiotically on tropical pond algae. The characteristic blue-green color of the dried extract derives from chlorophylls and phycocyanin protein–pigment complexes.

The playful nature of many confections encourages the use of color, and sugar is a particularly attractive base for a wide range of hues. See SUGAR SCULPTURE. The reflectance of the fine-grained solid produces a pure white, whereas large crystals can be clear as glass. Aqueous solutions of sugar are transparent and nearly colorless, and so will not distort or muddy colorings. Colors in food can also be created through purely physical processes. The opaque bright white of meringues is a result of light being scattered through a dispersion of two transparent materials—egg whites and air—with very different indices of refraction. Polar bears' fur is white for similar reasons.

See also ADULTERATION and VISION.

Mortensen, A. "Carotenoids and Other Pigments as Natural Colorants." *Pure and Applied Chemistry* 78, no. 8 (2006): 1477–1491.

Michelle M. Francl

fools have been a popular British dessert for many centuries. Nowadays they are usually a simple mixture of mashed or puréed fruit (raw or cooked, as appropriate), mixed with custard or whipped cream, although crème fraîche or yogurt are sometimes substituted. Fools are particularly suited to northern fruits such as gooseberries, raspberries, rhubarb, and damsons, but apples, blackberries, peaches, or more exotic fruits such as mango can also be used.

The name fool may be derived from the French *fouler*, meaning "to press" or "to crush." However, many early recipes in the sixteenth and seventeenth centuries contained no fruit and were merely a kind of custard made of cream, eggs, and sugar, often flavored with spices, rosewater, or orange flower water. See FLOWER WATERS. A likely explanation of the name is that fools, like trifles and whim-whams, are light and frivolous, mere trifles. In the early days, the words "fool" and "trifle" were frequently used interchangeably.

An early fool without fruit was Norfolk fool, popular in the seventeenth century. Custard was poured over a thinly sliced manchet (fine wheat bread) and decorated with sliced dates, sugar, and biskets (biscuits). Westminster fool also had bread as a base. The bread was soaked in sack (sweet wine) and covered with a rich, sweet custard flavored with rosewater, mace, and nutmeg.

Gooseberry fool, which became popular in Victorian times, was already known in the seventeenth century. Orange fool became a famous specialty of Boodle's Club in London, renowned for its cuisine. The club, founded in 1762, included famous members such as the dandy Beau Brummell and more recently David Niven and Ian Fleming. Boodle's fool has a base of sponge cake. Its creamy orange fool mixture, laced with orange liqueur, soaks into the cake to create a luscious, frothy dessert.

See also CREAM; CUSTARD; PUDDING; and TRIFLE.

Davidson, Alan. *The Oxford Companion to Food*. 3d ed. Edited by Tom Jaine. Oxford: Oxford University Press, 2014.

Helen Saberi

fortified wine differs from other sweet wines in that brandy (distilled grape spirit) is added to it, which yields a much higher alcoholic content. The additional alcohol is generally used to halt the fermentation abruptly before the yeast has converted all the grape sugar into alcohol (and various fermentation byproducts). Although the history of distillation goes back further, from about 1300 C.E., brandy was plentiful enough in Europe that small amounts were frequently added to various dry wines to make them more resistant to spoilage during transport. However, it was several centuries before someone added brandy directly to a fermenting wine for the first time, probably by accident, to produce a frankly sweet wine.

Madeira

The extra stability was particularly useful for the wine industry of the Portuguese island of Madeira off the northwestern coast of Africa, because Madeira's main markets were on the other side of the

Atlantic, in the Caribbean and North American colonies. Madeira's early wines, already documented in 1450, only 31 years after the island's discovery, resembled Malvasia Candida, a sweet straw wine from Crete. Over the late sixteenth and seventeenth centuries, wine production on Madeira grew dramatically. In the eighteenth century the increasing affluence, sophistication, and one-upmanship of American planters and merchants resulted in the importation of ever-finer Madeiras, leading to the development of the many styles we know today: dry Sercial, medium-dry Verdelho, sweet Bual (typically with 4 to 5 percent unfermented sweetness) and sweet Malmsey/Malvasia (typically with 5 to 10 percent unfermented sweetness), each named after the grape variety used. They are offered either as *colheita* (vintage) wines from a single year (declared on the label), or as blended multi-vintage wines of a minimum age (e.g., Reserve, which is aged 5 years; Special Reserve, aged 10 years). Bual has a rich, raisin flavor, while the lusher Malmsey offers a more pronounced interplay of acidity and sweetness. Vintage wines of both types can age for a century or more. Rainwater, mainly exported to North America, is a lighter style of slightly sweet Madeira made primarily from the Tinta Negra Mole grape.

Although Madeira's maritime climate, with a tropical influence and its terraced vineyards ascending to almost 2,750 feet above the Atlantic Ocean, creates special winegrowing conditions, the wines are more strongly marked by a unique aspect of the winemaking process. *Estufagem* imitates what wines shipped in barrels through the tropics would have undergone and gives Madeira wines their peculiar caramel-like flavor. It also hastens the oxidation that leads to the deep amber color with a distinctive green tinge at the rim of the glass. In the crudest form of this process (*cuba de calor*), the wine is directly heated to about 120°F (49°C) for three months, but today the majority of Madeiras exported are heated by the casks being placed in a sauna-like cellar (*armazém de calor*), and sometimes the finest wines are not heated artificially at all (*canteiro*). *Estufagem* was introduced during the eighteenth century, before the British influence on Madeira became stronger after the end of the Napoleonic Wars in 1814, which means that Madeira is actually a Portuguese-American wine, rather than a British one, as is often claimed.

Port

Fortification also appears to have come to the Douro Valley of Portugal during the first half of the eighteenth century. By 1800 the new sweet red port wines, typically with an alcohol content of 18 to 20 percent and 8 to10 percent grape sweetness, gradually replaced the region's previous style of more-or-less dry, full-bodied red in the main export market to England. Most of the region's wines then were like today's tawny ports—sweet, fortified port wines matured for between a few years and several decades in cellars located in the Oporto suburb of Villa Nova de Gaia, the home of the main port houses.

"Tawny" refers to the amber-brown color these red wines acquire through this aging process. The characteristic aromas are reminiscent of toffee, candied citrus peel, and roasted nuts. Today the finest ports of this kind are marketed either as single vintage *colheita* or as multi-vintage blends with declared minimum age (e.g., 10 Years Old, 20 Years Old). The older they are, the less grape tannin they contain and the more supple they taste, until, after about 30 years of aging, concentration through evaporation from the barrel increases the acidity content significantly. Unlike the single-variety wines of Madeira, port is always a blend of a handful or more indigenous grape varieties, most important Touriga Nacional and Tinta Roriz (known in Spain and many other countries as Tempranillo). Traditionally these grapes are fermented in shallow granite troughs called *lagares,* where they are foot-trodden to extract the maximum amount of color, tannin and aroma from the grape skins before grape spirit is added to arrest the fermentation. Today much of this treading is done mechanically.

Only during the early nineteenth century did the practice develop of bottling some ports after just a couple of years of cask maturation when they are still deep in color and full of fruit aromas and grape tannin. This is how vintage port tastes when released, as well as the lighter and less tannic late bottled vintage (LBV) port and the even simpler ruby port. All of these styles were at least indirectly the product of British influence on the region, dating back to the 1703 Methuen Treaty between Britain and Portugal. No other European wine has a more British image than Vintage port, which traditionalists in Britain did not consume before it had had 20 years of aging to soften the wines' often enormous tannins. Today, in England no less than in the important U.S. market, most vintage port is drunk much younger than that.

Sherry

Sweet sherry from the region around Jerez in Spain is a special case among sweet fortified wines, since the sweetness of a Cream sherry results from the blending of a fortified straw wine called PX (after the Pedro Ximénez grape from which it is exclusively made) with a fortified bone-dry Oloroso. The latter has been aged in a *solera,* a collection of casks to which younger wines are added so that they acquire character from the older wines it contains, yielding a wine with a consistent mature flavor. This blend yields a dark-amber to pale-brown wine with a rich, nutty, and dried fig or date character, with at least 15.5 percent alcohol and over 11.5 percent unfermented grape sweetness. Pure PX is mahogany brown with an enormously intense raisin aroma and flavor, and at least 21.2 percent grape sweetness. It is sometimes aged in cask for decades as a rare and unctuous specialty.

Other Fortified Wines

By the late nineteenth century, the wine industries of South Africa and Australia were producing modestly priced port- and sherry-style sweet wines on an industrial scale primarily to supply the British market. After World War II, when Britain's consumption of sherry declined significantly, they switched increasingly to dry table wine production. Only Rutherglen in Victoria, Australia, managed to build such a reputation for Tawny port (usually from the Shiraz, Mataro, and Grenache grapes) and similar sweet fortified wines from the Muscat grape that it defied this change in fashion. These wines can match the best Portuguese tawny ports, but they tend to be even lusher.

In recent years, with the resurgence of port's popularity, wines in this style have been produced in small quantities in an astonishing range of other wine-growing zones from California to Germany, and from all manner of grape varieties. None of these imitators can match Banyuls, though, the port-like fortified wine produced both as a vintage wine (resembling vintage port) and a blended non-vintage product (resembling tawny port) from the part of French Catalonia closest to the Spanish border. The greatest differences between these wines and port are their lower alcoholic content, typically about 16 percent, and the use mainly of Grenache grapes.

A footnote to the category of fortified wines includes wines made where there are no clear legal requirements, such as Commandaria from Cyprus. This straw wine made from the indigenous Mavro and Xynisteri grapes typically has full body comparable to a ruby port and a raisin character like PX.

See also FERMENTATION and SWEET WINE.

Hancock, David. *Oceans of Wine: Madeira and the Emergence of American Trade and Taste.* New Haven, Conn.: Yale University Press, 2009.

Mayson, Richard. *Port and the Douro.* Updated ed. Oxford: Infinite Ideas, 2012.

Stuart Pigott

fortune cookie is a folded, crescent-shaped wafer with a piece of paper tucked inside, most commonly distributed by Chinese restaurants in the United States. Over 3 billion are made each year.

Although the vanilla-flavored fortune cookie—with its distinctive shape and pithy sayings—has become an icon of Chinese culture in America, it most likely traces its roots to Japan, as the cookies are all but unknown in China. Similar crescent-shaped confectionery treats, known variously as *tsujiura senbei* ("fortune crackers") or *suzu senbei* ("bell crackers"), flavored with miso and sesame, are still sold by bakers in the former capital city of Kyoto. See KYOTO. The *senbei* are heated over fire with iron grills called *kata* and folded by hand, in contrast to the highly automated processes that produce American fortune cookies. Japanese immigrants brought the treat to California around the turn of the twentieth century. One of the earliest popular venues for the cookies was at the Japanese Tea Garden in San Francisco's Golden Gate Park.

By the end of World War II, fortune cookie production was largely taken over by Chinese immigrants, in part because of Japanese internment during the war. The cookies exploded in popularity in the postwar era, spreading eastward from California, to the point that they were used in a number of political campaigns in the 1960s and became an American staple by the 1980s. In addition to the original pithy and

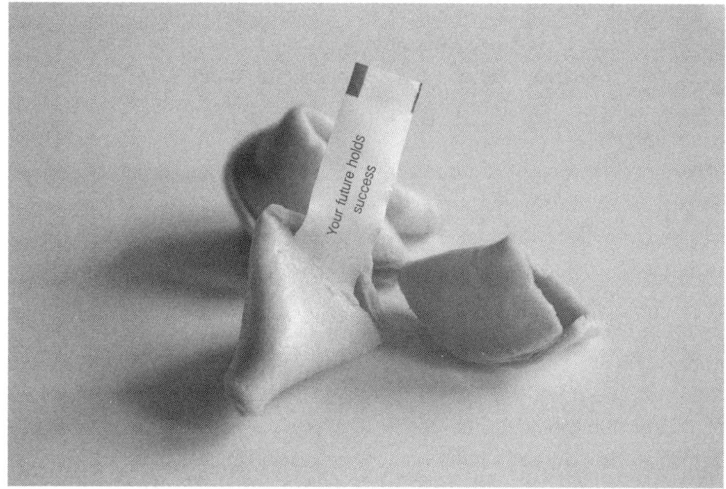

Although fortune cookies are universal at American Chinese restaurants, they are virtually unknown in China. These crisp, folded wafers were developed by Japanese immigrants to the United States at the turn of the twentieth century. © FLAZINGO PHOTOS, WWW.FLAZINGO.COM

prophetic sayings, fortune cookie slips sometimes include "lucky numbers," which many Americans now use to play the lotteries.

Today, there are fruit-flavored fortune cookies, giant fortune cookies, chocolate-dipped fortune cookies, dog fortune cookies, X-rated fortune cookie messages, and even Mexican fortune cookies shaped like tacos. Fortune cookies are also made in Brazil, Germany, Italy, and the United Kingdom.

Lee, Jennifer 8. *The Fortune Cookie Chronicles*. New York: Twelve, 2008.

Jennifer 8. Lee

Fourier, Charles (1772–1837), the utopian thinker often referred to as one of the earliest socialist theoreticians, is best known for the extraordinary level of detail in his elaborate—and often eccentric—vision of the future. Seventeen years old when the French Revolution erupted, his world turned upside down and his fortune lost, he retained a lasting hatred for what he disparagingly called "civilisation," including its sharp commercial practices (particularly those designed to manipulate commodity prices), toleration of poverty, and republicanism—especially its "Spartan" attitudes toward diet.

In Fourier's new society, called Harmony, everyone would live as they wished, recognizing their own tastes in work and in leisure and realizing these preferences in the company of like-minded people. In agrarian communities called phalanxes or phalansteries, one person of each gender and each temperament (a total of 1,620) would live together in beautiful buildings surrounded by fertile countryside, undertaking pleasurable work in short bursts, alternated with even more pleasurable leisure, all interspersed with up to nine delicious meals and snacks a day. No one would ever have to eat anything they did not like (such as turnips or cabbages, pet hates of Fourier's). Sex and food were to be recognized as the most important elements in this good life, taking their places together at the pinnacle of Harmonic religion. Fourier believed these were the essential human joys, especially food—and, in particular, sweet food—which, he pointed out, was the very first happiness of a child and the last one remaining to the elderly adult who had aged beyond the pleasures of the flesh.

The education of children would begin in the kitchen, and everyone would learn the science of "gastrosophy": a combination of learning to grow food, cook it, and match it to the temperament, health, and preferences of each individual. Sugar would play its part in international diplomacy. War would be replaced with giant worldwide gastronomic contests focused on the making of fine pastries, especially Fourier's favourite, the *mirliton*, a puff-pastry tartlet with an airy baked filling of beaten eggs and sugar enriched with crushed macarons and candied orange blossoms, pistachios, or other flavorings. As a result of beneficial climate change, crops—especially sweet fruits like Muscat melons and bergamot pears—would be plentiful and of a quality unimaginable in today's conditions. Most important, sugar would be cheaper than wheat. Thus, the bread of Harmony would be fruit compote: fruit cooked with a quarter of its weight in sugar, a food with multiple benefits demonstrating many of Fourier's core theories of economic efficiency and pleasure. First, fruit, and sugar would be cheap and plentiful, making this Harmonic bread an eighth of the price of "civilized" bread and equally accessible to rich and poor. Second, compote cuts down on wasted time and wasted food, as it can be made in advance and more quickly than bread, and it keeps better. Third, everyone prefers sweet food, especially women and children who, Fourier says, have a notoriously sweet tooth—rather like Fourier himself. Any concerns about the pernicious influence of too much sugar would be addressed by the ready supply of "balancing" acidic drinks such as lemonades and wines (and replaceable teeth). For sugar enthusiasts like Fourier, such a sweet life could be utopia indeed.

Barthes, Roland. *Sade, Fourier, Loyola*. Translated by Richard Miller. New York: Hill and Wang, 1976.

Bonnain-Moerdyck, Rolande. "Fourier Gastrosophe." In *Actualité de Fourier: Colloque d'Arc-et-senans*, edited by Henri Lefebvre, pp. 145–180. Paris: Éditions Anthropos, 1975.

Fourier, François Charles Marie. *Oeuvres complètes de Charles Fourier*. 12 vols. Edited by Simone Debout Oleszkiewicz. Paris: Éditions Anthropos, 1966–1968. See especially vols. 1, 4, 6, and 8.

Wilson, Bee. "Charles Fourier and the Phalansterian Banquet." In *The Meal: The Proceedings of the Oxford Symposium on Food & Cookery 2001*, edited by Harlan Walker, pp. 255–264. Totnes, U.K.: Prospect, 2002.

Jane Levi

France became one of the first countries to explore the possibilities of sugar when cheap supplies came flooding in from the Caribbean and South America at the start of the seventeenth century. French patissiers became the acknowledged masters of the art of cooking with sugar, taking over from the Italians. *Le pastissier françois*, published in Paris in 1653, was the first European cookbook devoted to pastry, clearly written by a pastry cook though the author is unknown. By midcentury a whole table at a banquet might be devoted to sweets, which also developed as a separate course to end the meal. The word "dessert" itself is derived from the French *desservir*, meaning to "clear the table of dishes" from the previous course. See DESSERT. It was in France that sugar specialties first emerged from the more day-to-day work of the patissier: *glaces* (sorbets and ice cream), *confiserie* (candies and petits fours), and *travail au sucre* (sugar sculpting), with a subspecialty in *chocolaterie* (chocolate work). *Boulangers* (bakers) had long plied their métier independently, baking in the *four banal* (communal oven) the wheaten loaves that were the staple food of the nation.

Following this lead over the centuries, a distinguished line of French pastry cooks developed. In 1751 *Le cannameliste français* appeared, a definitive guide to sugar work by Joseph Gilliers, head of the cold kitchen for Stanislaus, duke of Lorraine. See GILLIERS, JOSEPH. Early in the nineteenth century Marie-Antoine Carême created staggering architectural fantasies in sugar that he describes in *Le pâtissier pittoresque* (1815). See CARÊME, MARIE-ANTOINE and SUGAR SCULPTURE. That same year he cooked for the French Prince Talleyrand (a gourmet of renown) at the Congress of Vienna, as well as Tsar Alexander I when he visited France, before moving on to become chef to the British prince regent. Other important names include William Jarrin and Alphonse Gouffé, pastry chef to Queen Victoria. See JARRIN, WILLIAM ALEXIS. Today, French patisserie is global, led by pastry chefs such as the Lenôtre family, Pierre Hermé, and the Ladurée group, famous for their macarons. See HERMÉ, PIERRE; LENÔTRE, GASTON; and MACARONS.

Already in *Le pastissier françois*, the structure of classic French patisserie can be seen; here are the gâteaux and cakes, the genoises and biscuits, with the *crème pâtissière* (pastry cream) and *crème au beurre* (buttercream) to fill them. Pastries include choux and puff, immediately recognizable as the recipes we use today. Most obvious to any visitor to France are the classic French gâteaux, sometimes baked at home but most often bought in the patisserie for Sunday lunch or a birthday. Most popular is génoise, a simple sponge of whole eggs, sugar, and flour, sometimes butter too, cooked in a characteristic *moule à manqué* with sloping sides. See CAKE and SPONGE CAKE. Character is added to génoise with fillings of pastry or buttercream, with perhaps a

France has been known for the skill of its patissiers, or pastry chefs, since the seventeenth century. This etching by Abraham Bosse, titled *Pastry Shop*, depicts the activities that take place within, from rolling out dough to shaping and baking it. The verses explain that "This shop has delicacies / That charm in a thousand ways / Girls and little boys / Servants and wet nurses." METROPOLITAN MUSEUM OF ART, HARRIS BRISBANE DICK FUND, 1926.

sprinkling of rum or kirsch syrup on the cake itself. Favorite flavorings include coffee (*gâteau moka*), chocolate, orange (*gâteau Grand Marnier*), and berries such as raspberry and strawberry.

Biscuit is also a sponge, in which the eggs are separated and the whites whisked with some of the sugar so the finished cake is lighter and drier. The most famous is made in Savoy, perhaps because of its airy mountain location. Genoise or biscuit dough is spread on a lined baking sheet and lightly baked for a *gâteau roulé* (rolled cake). The filling should contrast with the sponge, with whipped cream and strawberries or red jam for a vanilla roll, or a pale filling for chocolate. Timelessly popular is *quatre quarts* (four quarters), the French name for pound cake, normally baked as a loaf to serve plain or with a thin lemon or orange icing. See POUND CAKE.

French artistic talent is further sparked by the versatile fluff of meringue. See MERINGUE. Plain meringues may be sandwiched with ice cream or coated in chocolate. For an architectural dessert, bars of baked meringue are mounted with more raw meringue and baked again to form *vacherins*, large or small baskets for filling with fruits and whipped cream. See VACHERIN. When ground almonds or toasted hazelnuts are folded into meringue and then baked in rounds, a whole series of meltingly rich gâteaux are created. *Gâteau succès* is sandwiched with praline cream, whereas *gâteau turquois* contains chocolate mousse. Most common are large or individual *gâteaux Dacquoises* (coming from the town of Dax) with various fillings, topped with a snowy dusting of confectioner's sugar. See DACQUOISE.

These cakes follow fashion, so that at the time of the French Restoration, the elegant table would be dominated by towering meter-high architectural temples and follies covered in fondant icing or pastillage in brilliant colors. See FONDANT and PASTILLAGE. By the turn of the nineteenth century and Escoffier, such grand gâteaux had diminished, but traces linger in *gâteau opéra*, a lavish layered confection of almond sponge cake, chocolate ganache, and coffee buttercream, topped with fondant icing that is still the challenge for advanced pastry students around the world. Gâteaux today are far simpler. "Cake," for example, is a sweet loaf flavored with combinations of coconut, hazelnuts, candied fruits, or chocolate. Chocolate mousse may be used to fill a chocolate cake, or a genoise sponge may be sandwiched simply with whipped cream and poached fruit. However, the building blocks remain the same—genoise, buttercream, pastry cream, and fondant icing are found all over the world and still convey a whiff of France.

Another family of French cakes and pastries has developed using puff pastry (*pâte feuilletée*), beloved for its buttery flavor and malleable, flaky layers that expand like magic into heart-shaped *palmiers* (shaped like a palm leaf, sometimes called "elephants' ears"), *papillons* (butterflies), or *langues de boeuf* (cows' tongues) glazed with sugar. See PASTRY, PUFF. Puff pastry will rise high to form *puits d'amour* (wells of love) filled with strawberry jam or red currant jelly. *Jalousies* (jealousies) can be large or small, made of bands of puff pastry filled with jam or apple purée and slashed so they resemble a window shutter (through which an illicit lover can be detected). Most famously, puff pastry is thinly rolled for *mille-feuille* (a thousand leaves), in the United States sometimes called a "Napoleon." Traditional *mille-feuille* is stacked with whipped cream, sometimes with pastry cream, often with berries, and topped with fondant or a caramel glaze; a modern deconstructionist version comes with filling and decoration scattered on the plate topped by shards of pastry pointing to the sky.

Choux pastry (*pâte à choux*) is another pillar of the French pastry repertoire. See PASTRY, CHOUX. Choux contains a high proportion of eggs and thus bakes to form crispy containers for fillings such as whipped cream, pastry cream, ice creams, and sorbet. Among the most famous of all French sweets are profiteroles, small balls of choux split and filled with vanilla ice cream and topped with hot chocolate sauce, and éclairs, bar-shaped pastries of choux with a piped filling of pastry cream—traditionally vanilla, coffee, or chocolate with contemporary variants running to mango, pomegranate, passion fruit, and more—topped with an icing of the same or a contrasting flavor. Choux pastry is the basis of timeless gâteaux such as *gâteau Paris-Brest*, a wheel overflowing with praline pastry cream and named for the Paris-Brest bicycle race that passed the door of the enterprising patissier who invented the cake. *Gâteau St. Honoré* is more elaborate, a wall of choux puffs stuck with caramel on a round of sweet pastry, encircling a mound of praline pastry cream lightened with whipped egg whites. The cream is named for *St. Honoré*, patron of pastry cooks and bakers.

In any French pastry shop window, small choux pastries play a part in the spread of *petits gâteaux* (little cakes). See SMALL CAKES. Mini-*gâteaux Paris-Brest* and *religieuses* (nuns) with robes created from éclairs catch the eye, as do *cygnes chantilly*, choux pastry swans with wings and a graceful neck, filled with a froth of whipped Chantilly cream. They may be flanked by *sablés* (butter cookies), the trendy ones flavored with herbs, and *lunettes* (spectacles) sandwiched with jam visible through two holes to resemble eyes. See SABLÉ. Almond-based cakes, called financiers as they are so rich, are baked in rectangular molds to resemble gold bars. Yet others are called *visitandines*, a reminder that such treats were for visitors, often a specialty of nuns. Nearby will be *biscuits à la cuillère* (ladyfingers) and madeleines, often flavored with honey. See MADELEINE. A recent American invasion of chocolate chip cookies and brownies has scarcely changed the scene.

France is the home of *petits fours*, a term that first appeared in *Pastissier françois* in 1653 and referred to the little ovens that had recently been invented, designed for baking miniature versions of almond cakes, puff pastries, and small cookies. These dry little cakes are often sold in bulk for nibbling at home, the nearest thing to cookies for the American cookie jar. In restaurants, a plate of petits fours covers a far wider range, including tiny sugar-glazed *fours* of almond paste; mini *quatre quarts* pound cakes; vanilla-tinged *palets de dames*, literally "ladies' palettes"; skinny, brown-edged *langues de chat* (cats' tongues); and baby madeleines. Recently, little macarons have appeared everywhere in a dozen flavors and colors, sandwiched with a further dozen fillings. Pastry chef Pierre Hermé created a rose macaron filled with rose cream, studded with lychees and raspberries, and topped with a red rose petal and called it Ispahan. There are now Ispahan croissants, gâteaux, ice cream, fruit jellies, jams, and even Ispahan yogurt.

Choice on the petits fours plate is widened by chocolate, whether as crisp, gold-flecked slivers or soft-centered truffles. See BONBONS; CHOCOLATE, LUXURY; and TRUFFLES. Almost unique to dinner-table offerings are fruits glacés, fresh fruits glazed with caramel, a treat that dissolves all too quickly in moist air. Cherries are favorites, with their protective skin and stems ready-made for dipping in the scalding sugar syrup; grapes are good, too. Strawberries can be glazed, but the caramel is fragile on the juicy fruit, making melted chocolate a better alternative. Candied fruits, whole fruits preserved and glazed in baths of sugar syrup, have been sidelined in recent times. See CANDIED FRUIT. However, at Christmas boxes of candied orange slices, greengage plums and apricots, rings of pineapple, and tiny white pears appear, glowing in neon colors. A stiff espresso is the best antidote to the sugar high the fruits deliver. Fruit jellies are an alternative, made from the pulp of tart fruits such as red and black currants, apples, or quince, cut in squares and arranged like a checkerboard. *Marrons glacés,* whole candied chestnuts, are an art in themselves. All come in *coffrets,* giant boxes designed for gifts. See CHESTNUTS.

The French love of sugar flourishes in festive sweets, particularly at Christmas. The season opens with *bûche de Noël,* a Christmas log created in rolled sponge and coffee or chocolate buttercream, coated in "bark" of more cream. See BÛCHE DE NOËL. Some logs have mushrooms of meringues sprouting from the sides, with branches and even an elf perched on top. Epiphany, the end of the feasting season on 6 January, is honored with a *galette des rois* (Kings' cake), of puff pastry enclosing a slim layer of almond paste. Hidden inside is the *fève,* once a simple dried kidney bean, but now a tiny china figurine of anything from a goose to a shepherdess to baby Jesus. Whoever wins the bean in his slice is king of the feast for the day. See TWELFTH NIGHT CAKE.

Christmas is the time for *pain d'épices* (spice bread), particularly in Burgundy and Alsace, where sheets of spice bread are fashioned into gingerbread houses complete with snowy gardens, tiled roofs, and Santa clinging to the chimney, all in sugar. Loaves of spice bread come with flavorings of candied orange or chocolate, and gingerbread men hang on the tree. See GINGERBREAD. French christenings, first communions, and sometimes just a birthday are marked with *dragées,* sugar-coated almonds in a rainbow of colors, pink or blue for the babies, with more sophisticated earth or pastel tones for grownups; each guest receives a little bag to take home. For a wedding, croquembouche is *de rigueur,* a spire of choux puffs filled with pastry cream and held in place with caramel glaze. The tower may be 3 feet or more high and calls for an expert hand, particularly with the festoons of white royal icing and dark chocolate cutouts that adorn the whole gâteau. See CROQUEMBOUCHE.

When do the French eat all these luscious cakes and pastries? The grander patisseries have a *salon de thé,* a space dedicated to cups of tea, coffee, and a pastry selected from the display in the main shop. See SALON DE THÉ. Ladies drop by for a morning pick-me-up or an afternoon of gossip with friends. A pastry is the reward for an obedient child on the way home from school. A tray of pastries, or more likely a whole gâteau, may be taken home to end Sunday lunch or dinner with friends. Sometimes a pastry is offered at the end of lunch or dinner in a restaurant, though dessert is the norm.

Many classic French desserts have a domestic touch, such as the custard sauce crème anglaise based on milk and eggs for serving with puddings or fruit compote. See CUSTARD. The childhood favorite *île flottante* is an island of poached or baked meringue floating in a sea of custard and topped with a trail of caramel; *oeufs à la neige* (snow eggs) are a smaller version. When set with gelatin, crème anglaise becomes a party dessert as *bavarois* (a creamy mold). See DESSERTS, CHILLED and GELATIN. Custard turns into crème caramel or flan when baked in a mold lined with caramel. See FLAN (PUDÍM). If the custard is made with cream instead of milk, left to set, and topped with caramelized sugar, it sets to a tantalizingly crisp *crème brûlée* (burned sugar). Credit for its invention is claimed by both Christchurch College in Oxford and Trinity College, Cambridge, though the first mention seems to have occurred in the French chef François Massialot's *Cuisinier roial et bourgeois* (1691). See CRÈME BRÛLÉE.

The favorite French family dessert must surely be chocolate mousse. The word for a frothy mixture, a mousse, is French, too. See MOUSSE. The froth is most often provided by eggs, egg whites, or whipped cream, all mild ingredients that need the punch of chocolate, praline, caramel, or an acidic fruit such as raspberry, apricot, orange, or lemon. The same flavorings are popular also in soufflés, or uplift may be supplied by alcohol such as Grand Marnier or the gold-flecked Danziger Goldwasser that inspires Soufflé Rothschild. See SOUFFLÉ. Soufflés may be hot, when they rise in the oven to the characteristic puffed shape, or molded as a cold or frozen soufflé with a collar that is discarded after the mixture has set. See DESSERTS, FROZEN. Even simpler is an omelette soufflée, in which the egg whites and egg yolks are divided, whisked with sugar, folded, and quickly fried in a bit of butter until puffy.

The most common dessert sauce is crème anglaise flavored with vanilla, coffee, or chocolate, or an herb such as mint or basil. See SAUCE. When eggs are left whole and whisked with sugar and sweet wine, *sauce sabayon* results, in France never served alone but poured over a slice of sponge cake or berries, then browned as a *gratin de fruits.* Sweet sauces of fruit almost always focus on berries, like Sauce Melba of puréed raspberries with a splash of kirsch, the renowned partner of poached peaches with vanilla ice cream. As far as fruit soups are concerned, the French seem to prefer their melon or berries left whole rather than liquid, but a few refreshing combinations such as chilled *soupe de cerises noires au vin rouge* (soup of black cherries in red wine) do appear sometimes. Equally unusual in France today are shimmering jellies molded with gelatin, isinglass, or carageen moss. Small portions sometimes appear on the tasting plates of modernist chefs, so perhaps the magnificent molded jellies shown in early photographs will one day return.

Puddings in France are rarely labeled as such. A bread pudding, for instance, would be called by its own name, such as *charlotte aux pommes* (apple purée baked in a mold lined with slices of buttered bread), or *pain perdu,* literally "lost bread" or French toast in the United States—slices of bread soaked in egg custard and fried until caramelized. See CHARLOTTE. Bread may be disguised as a *pouding soufflé* thickened with breadcrumbs, or a grander version flavored with raisins and candied fruit and baked in a little timbale as *pouding diplomate. Pouding de riz* is just that, rice pudding often enriched with cream. When cold, rice pudding may be set with gelatin, topped with poached fruits, and presented grandly as *Riz Condé,* named for a royal prince. Floppy, adaptable crêpes are the foundation of several French desserts, whether folded around poached fruit, rolled with a layer of chocolate sauce, or filled and baked with a fluffy soufflé mixture, or most famously spread with orange butter and flambéed with Grand Marnier as *Crêpes Suzette* (said to be the lady friend of the future King Edward VII).

For a fruit dessert in warm weather, seasonal fruits are macerated in a light sugar syrup, with a squeeze of lemon juice or a measure of white wine. Red wine is used to soak strawberries or sliced fresh peaches, particularly along the Loire where the dish is called *chicolle.* An eye-catching alternative is to caramelize sliced fresh fruits in butter and sugar, then flambé them with a generous dash of cognac. On a chilly autumn day, what could be wrong with a compote of poached apples or plums, or spiced pears in red wine? Winter oranges may be peeled, sliced, moistened with red wine, and sprinkled with crushed caramel. Just a few fruits—sliced apples or banana, rings of fresh pineapple, and small, firm strawberries—can be dipped in batter and deep-fried. And who could forget the French *beignets soufflés,* freshly fried fritters of choux pastry topped with sugar or melted jam and known universally as *pets de nonne* (nun's farts)?

Breaking new ground, many modern desserts cut down on the sugar in traditional recipes with variations such as mustard ice cream, or a purée of pears with parsley-root cream. The popularity of beetroot, an ingredient that is neither sweet nor savory, seems here to stay. Caramel sauce and chocolate candies are sparked with sea salt, while the chocolate itself is dark and intense rather than sweet. At the same time, sugar is straying into the rest of the meal, more as a condiment than a main ingredient. Several Paris restaurants offer savory-sweet courses (often as appetizers) such as a purple potato purée with raw and poached apples topped with a marjoram granité, both salty and sweet.

In any French patisserie, the in-house *tartes aux fruits* are a matter of pride. The simplest consist of a shell of sweet pie pastry filled with a single fruit, be it strawberries, raspberries, or peaches, and lightly glazed with red currant or apricot jam to pick up color and keep the fruit fresh. Often an underlayer of pastry cream adds richness and protects the pastry, particularly from a juicy fruit such as pear. Mixed fruit tarts always catch the eye with contrasting circles of red berries, red or green grapes, sliced oranges, banana, or kiwi. Many fruits are cooked in the pastry shell: pitted apricots or plums are arranged cut side upward, so the juice evaporates in the heat of the oven; thinly sliced pear halves may be set on a filling of almond paste or chopped chocolate, and baked to resemble the petals of a giant flower. Almost any fruit can be put to use in a tart—mango, quince, cherries, or lemon (often thickened to a curd with egg yolks and sugar). Apples are the most versatile filling of all, sliced, diced, or puréed.

In all these tarts, the fruits themselves are the decoration. A double-crust, covered tart is rare in France and is likely to be called a *tourte,* which is deeper and more substantial than a *tarte.* A *galette,* meaning a large, shallow round of pastry, can also be topped with fruit, as in the flaky *tarte aux pommes légère* (light apple tart) of puff pastry completely covered with thin slices of apple. See GALETTE and TART. Small *tartelettes aux fruits* follow the open-face lead of larger tarts, particularly with berries, presented perhaps as *barquettes* (shaped like a boat). Tartlettes may hold a lemon curd filling, or almond frangipane, or a mixture of walnuts and caramel in regions with walnut trees. See FRANGIPANE. In winter, *chaussons* (turnovers, literally "socks") are on display, particularly stuffed with apple or prune. A filling of fresh cheese in a dessert tart is a comparative rarity in France, found mainly in country districts where the milk is ultra-fresh.

French cooks are famous for living off the land, and nowhere is this clearer than in regional sweets. Brittany, for example is famous for its crêpes, particularly when made with buckwheat flour—buckwheat grows more easily than wheat in the thin Breton soil. For a quick snack, sweet crêpes may be simply sprinkled with sugar, spread with jam or melted chocolate, or moistened with rum or Grand Marnier. Far Breton is a batter pudding with prunes, cousin to the more famous *clafoutis Limousin* from central France, made with sour cherries (many a tooth has been broken on the pits). Other Breton desserts make the best of the excellent butter: *Gâteau Breton,* for instance, is the richest imaginable shortbread; *Breton sablés* (butter cookies) are scarcely less rich; whereas *kouign-aman* consists of croissant dough, rolled and folded with sugar to bake flat in succulent, flaky squares. Normandy, to the east of Brittany, is apple country, fertile ground for *tartes aux pommes* and the occasional apple dumpling (*douillon*).

Over to the north and east in Picardy and Champagne, the windswept land of sugar beets, sugar takes over in waffles and *tarte au sucre,* a yeast cake topped with butter and sugar, almost a sweet pizza. The region abounds in sugar candies with names such as the *bêtises* (mistakes) of Cambrai and the *abeilles* (honey bees) of Nancy. Bordering Germany, Lorraine is the ancestral home of madeleines and baba au rhum, while the cooks of Alsace are famous for their fruit tarts, just a little richer—topped with a cream and egg custard—and heavier—often using a yeast dough—than in the rest of France. See BABA AU RHUM. The Alsatian orchards running down the Rhine are the foundation of plum, raspberry, and pear liqueurs and white alcohols, as well as *fruits du vieux garçon* (bachelor's fruits) preserved in kirsch. The local jams and jellies are outstanding.

Three very different regions grow most of the nuts in France. See NUTS. The foothills of the Alps around Grenoble shelter groves of walnut trees for walnut cakes, tartlet fillings, and liqueurs. Further to the west across the Rhône rise the mountains of the Ardèche, home of almost all the edible chestnuts in France; less versatile than walnuts, most chestnuts end up candied or reduced to a sugared purée. The Rhône valley itself is lined with almond trees, the basis of so many classic gâteaux as well as nougat from Montélimar and *calissons,* almond-paste candies from Aix, the Provençal capital. See NOUGAT. There, in the Mediterranean sun, desserts yield to fresh fruits, starting with the melons of late spring and ending with the figs of fall. To fill gaps in supply during the cold months, almost every possible fruit is candied, a specialty of the hill town of Apt.

Running along the coast to the Pyrenees, fresh fruits also dominate, backed up by the occasional fruit tart, particularly flavored with lemon. In Languedoc, the local favorite *crème catalane* has a hint of Arab spice beneath a crisp caramel topping, in effect a crème brûlée. All across the south, deep-fried sweet pastries are common, from the twisted pastry *bugnes* of Arles to the *oreillettes* (little ears) of Toulouse, known as *merveilles* (wonders) in Bordeaux. Another Bordelais specialty, *cannelés,* chewy little cakes baked in fluted copper molds, are remarkably hard to concoct unless you know how (the batter must be cooked until it curdles and looks a horrible failure, redeemed by whisking in flour once the mess has cooled). See CANNELÉ.

Just occasionally in France do sweet oddities turn up, particularly in the countryside. One example is *Mont Blanc,* a sugary mountain of meringue, whipped cream, and chestnut purée, particularly popular in autumn. *Petits pâtés de Pézénas* from Languedoc, small pies shaped like mushrooms and filled with ground lamb and suet lavishly sweetened with sugar, hark back to medieval times. *Feuilleté Gascon* must be of Arab origin, a round galette of paper-thin dough layered with walnut or olive oil, a few slivers of apple or chopped walnut, and a sprinkling of Armagnac. Burgundian *tartouillats* are little cherry tartlets baked not in pastry but in a cabbage leaf. The famous *Tarte Tatin* is a curiosity in which apples are caramelized in butter and sugar in a deep pan, then baked with a pastry topping. When turned out, the mahogany-brown caramel gleams invitingly on the chunks of apple. Two sisters, the story goes, were left penniless by their father and turned to baking his favorite apple tart for travelers to the local railroad junction in Lamotte-Beuvron (Orléanais). See TARTE TATIN.

So many French sweets—mille-feuille, crêpes, crème caramel, chocolate mousse, *Tarte Tatin*—are now household names worldwide, a reflection of the ingenuity and manual dexterity of pastry cooks at home and in the professional kitchen. Long may such inspiration last!

See also CAKE DECORATING; CHRISTMAS; ESCOFFIER, GEORGES AUGUSTE; FRIED DOUGH; FRITTERS; FRUIT; HOLIDAY SWEETS; MIGNARDISE; PANCAKES; PARIS; SOUP; and ZABAGLIONE.

Carême, Antonin. *Le pâtissier pittoresque*. Paris: De l'Imprimerie de F. Didot, 1815.
Gilliers, Joseph. *Le cannameliste français*. Nancy: De l'Imprimerie d'Abel-Denis Cusson, 1751.
Hermé, Pierre. *PH 10: Pâtisserie de Pierre Hermé*. Paris: A. Viénot, 2005.
La Varenne, François Pierre de. *Le pastissier françois*. Paris: Chez Jean Gaillard, 1653.
Massialot, François. *Nouveau cuisinier royal et bourgeois*. Paris, 1691.

Anne Willan

frangipane refers to an almond-flavored pastry cream used to garnish cakes and to fill pastries and tarts of all kinds. An abundance of recipes demonstrates that any number of aromatics besides almonds can flavor the pastry cream (flour, butter, sugar, milk, whole eggs, egg yolks, and salt); Prosper Montagné's *Larousse gastronomique* (1938) does not even mention almonds. However, Ali-Bab's *Gastronomie pratique* (1928) distinguishes between basic pastry cream made with egg yolks and vanilla, and frangipane cream made with whole eggs, additional yolks, and crushed macarons. See MACARONS.

The name "frangipane" comes from the flowering tropical plant *Plumeria rubra* (also called Frangipani), an extract of which French glove makers had used to perfume their goods since the sixteenth century. According to Alexandre Dumas's *Grand dictionnaire de cuisine* (1873), this perfume was also used in pastry cream. In La Varenne's *Le cuisinier françois* (1651), *tourte de franchipanne* is a pistachio- and almond-flavored cream-filled tart. A second *tourte de franchipanne* for a fast day instructs the cook to "take the most beautiful flower that you can find" and soak it in egg whites. La Varenne calls for adding "flower water" to the mixture without further specifying which type to use, but presumably it is the same flower. See FLOWER WATERS. Since François Menon's *La cuisinière bourgeoise* (1760) recommends flavoring Crême à la Franchipane with orange flowers that have been grilled and chopped, the Frangipani flowers may have been used in the same fashion.

Since at least the nineteenth century, flavorings have included vanilla, crushed macarons, orange flower water, chopped pistachios (or mixtures of these ingredients), raspberries, and strawberries. Although Frangipani flowers are used today in salads and sweets on occasion, they do not seem to be trendy with professional bakers.

See also MARZIPAN.

Gouffé, Jules. *Le livre de pâtisserie*. Paris: Editions Henri Veyrier, 1998. Originally published 1873.

Kyri W. Claflin

fried dough as a term covers a large variety of globally distributed sweet foods produced by deep-frying dough in animal fat or vegetable oil. Because frying in fat is an expensive cooking technique, fried dough preparations were traditionally considered festive or celebratory foods. Although many are still associated with specific festivals or celebrations, others are now produced on a commercial basis for everyday consumption.

Made from a flour-based dough rather than a batter, fried dough can be distinguished from the more general term "fritter." See FRITTERS. In this regard it differs from such deep-fried sweets as *jalebi*, funnel cakes, and rosette fritters. Most recipes for fried dough call for flour (cereal or legume). However, in some cases the dough is made with limited amounts of flour, with the bulk provided by milk solids or vegetable pulp, as in Indian *gulab jamun* and Malaysian *kueh keria*, respectively. Although fried foods have ancient origins, and versions of fried dough are found throughout the world, several distinct categories can be identified on the basis of the dough preparation technique. Broadly speaking, these categories are unleavened dough, dough leavened by yeast or a chemical raising agent, and hot-water dough.

Unleavened Dough

The simplest type of fried dough is produced by frying unleavened dough. A Chinese example of this technique is *jian dui*, deep-fried sesame-seed-covered balls of glutinous rice flour that gain a hollow interior from the dough's expansion. A rather different form of unleavened fried dough is made by thinly rolling out a relatively stiff dough and cutting it into strips or other shapes. These strips can be folded, braided, or even formed into loose balls, as in the case of *Schneebälle* ("snowballs") from Rothenburg, Germany. Once fried, the dough can be sweetened by dusting with powdered sugar or dipping in honey or syrup. There are many regional names for this type of fried dough, including *pestiños* in Andalusia, *cenci* in Italy, *merveilles* in Southwest France, *origliettas* in Sardinia, and *boží milosti* in the Czech Republic. Modern recipes for fried dough strips can include chemical leavening agents. See CHEMICAL LEAVENERS. Though the addition of a leavening agent is not strictly required, it will produce a lighter product with an open texture, such as Latin American *sopaipillas* and Slovak *fánky*.

Leavened Dough

When unrolled leavened dough is fried, the action of yeast or of chemical leavening agents produces a product with a characteristically porous interior and a crisp or soft outer surface, depending on the specific recipe. Traditionally prepared for particular festivals or celebrations, fried leavened dough is also commonly sold commercially, the doughnut being the most prominent example. See DOUGHNUTS. One variation of fried leavened dough takes the form of large sheets or disks, variously called in North American "fried dough," "elephant ears," "beaver tails," or "flying saucers." These treats are frequently sold at festivals and fairs. Variations on this style of fried dough are served with either savory or sweet toppings, as in the case of Native American frybread and Hungarian *lángos*; or they can be eaten with sweet toppings exclusively, as is Bulgarian *mekitsa*. Many examples of smaller fried leavened dough products abound. In English-speaking countries they are often collectively described as "doughnuts," but this very large group of fried doughs includes *loukoumades* from Greece, South African *koeksister*, Mongolian *boortsog*, Japanese *sata andagi*, German *Krapfen*, *oliebollen* from the Netherlands, Indian *balushai*, and Lebanese *awwamaat*.

Hot-Water Dough

The final group of fried dough products is made from hot-water dough, produced by the addition of flour to a hot liquid, most often water and a fat. This type of fried dough is not as widely distributed as products made from leavened or unleavened dough. Nonetheless, recipes are described in the fifth-century collection of Apicius, indicating that this is an ancient method of making fried dough. Hot-water dough can be either a simple flour paste or enriched by the addition of eggs and butter to form a choux-type dough, as in the case of Italian *zeppole di San Giuseppe*, certain French *beignets*, and *pets de nonne*. Because these doughs are very wet, when they are fried, the outside of the dough forms a hard shell before the interior sets, resulting in a crisp-shelled, open-textured pastry that has given rise to such names as the Spanish *buñuelos de viento* ("wind doughnuts"). Fried hot-water dough products were common in European texts from the sixteenth to eighteenth centuries, when recipes often called for extruding the wet and sticky dough from a culinary syringe to produce long, thin "syringe fritters." Modern examples of syringed hot-water-dough fritters are Portuguese *farturas*, Spanish and Mexican *churros*, and Turkish *tulumba*.

See also FAIRS; FESTIVALS; HOLIDAY SWEETS; INDIA; and PASTRY, CHOUX.

Grocock, Christopher, and Sally Grainger. *Apicius*. Totnes, U.K.: Prospect, 2006.

Scully, Terrence. *The Opera of Bartolomeo Scappi (1570)*. Toronto: University of Toronto Press, 2008.

Adam Balic

Frisbie pie tins, made by the Frisbie Pie Company, were the inspiration for a popular American flying toy.

William Russell Frisbie launched his career by managing the Bridgeport branch of the Olds Baking Company of New Haven, Connecticut. In 1871 Frisbee purchased the shop and renamed it the Frisbie Pie Company. Frisbie assumed executive and marketing roles, his sister Susan baked, and his wife Marian Rose managed the plant. Although pies were the family specialty, Frisbie also sold a variety of standard baked goods. As time progressed, Frisbie's fame grew. Pie wagons supplied grocery stores, restaurants, and lunch rooms throughout southern New England. Advertisements published in the *Bridgeport Telegram* (Connecticut) proclaimed, "Frisbie's is the favorite pie with thousands." Pies of two sizes, but no specific flavors, were described as delicious, pure, juicy, and flaky crusted.

Frisbie's pies were sold in tin plates with his name imprinted in bold letters on the base. Customers paid a nickel deposit per plate, which was refunded upon return. College students were reportedly avid consumers of Frisbie's pies. They elevated the common pie tin to an athletic challenge in the 1920s and 1930s. Who threw the first Frisbie pie plate and when? History did not record the circumstances surrounding this event. Several universities and colleges claim the distinction, among them Yale (Connecticut), Middlebury (Vermont), and Harvard (Massachusetts).

The returnable pie tins manufactured by Bridgeport, Connecticut's Frisbie Pie Company inspired the flying discs called frisbees that have since become classic pieces of American sports equipment.

Walter Frederick Morrison, a West Coast inventor familiar with Frisbie's flying pie tins, began to experiment with plastic prototypes in the late 1940s. Morrison perfected the aerodynamics and capitalized on the then-current flying saucer fad. Morrison's Flyin' Saucer (1948) morphed into Wham-O's Pluto Platter (1951). Wham-O introduced the Frisbee novelty flying disc to the American public on 17 June 1957.

The Frisbee Pie Company disbanded in 1958. Table Talk Pies (Worcester, Massachusetts) purchased the rights to Frisbie's trademark but, as of 2013, no longer manufactures items with that name.

Stancil E. D., and M. D. Johnson. *Frisbee: A Practitioner's Manual and Definitive Treatise*. New York: Workman, 1975.

Lynne M. Olver

fritters, like the closely related fried dough and doughnuts, are a fried food preparation; the English word "fritter" derives from Old French *friture*, meaning "something fried." Although considerable overlap exists among these categories, in general, fritters are distinguished from other fried foods because they are made from batter rather than dough.

Globally, there are several common fritter-making techniques: using batter to encase fruit, molding fritters with a fritter iron, and pouring batter directly into hot oil. In Europe sliced apples encased in batter are common in historic texts and remain one of the most prevalent fruit fritters. Fresh stone fruits, dried prunes, pineapple, and banana are also popular fruit fritters. In Asia banana or plantain fritters are very widely distributed. They are made either by coating the banana in batter (called *kluay kaek* in Thailand, *pisang goreng* in Malaysia and Indonesia, and *pazham pori/ ethakka appam* in Kerala) or by mashing ripe banana to use as the basis of the fritter batter itself (*kolar pitha* in Bangladesh and *kolar bora* in Bengal).

Fritters made using metal molds or irons may be found in many cultures and are often referred to in historic European texts. See COOKING IRONS. Mold designs can be figurative or stylized. In the former case, they were once made in the form of coats of arms or animals and were used to garnish high-status dishes. Modern fritter irons are made in the shape of grids, stars, hearts, spirals, or flowers, and they often have evocative names. The fritters are known as *rosetbakkelser* (rosettes) in Norway, *struvor* in Sweden, and *dok jok* in Thailand. Turkey has *demir tatlisi* (iron pudding), Tunisia *chebbak el-janna* (windows of paradise), and Kerala *achappam*. Afghani fritters are called *kulcha-e-panjerei* (window biscuits); in Indonesia they are known as *kembang goyang* (swaying flowers).

The final class of fritter is made by pouring batter into hot oil. It can simply be dripped from the fingertips or from a spoon, or poured from a specialized utensil. In the tenth-century Baghdadi cookery book *Kitāb al-Ṭabīkh*, the batter for *zulābiyā mushabbaka* (latticed fritters) is poured through a hole in a coconut shell, whereas the sixteenth-century German recipe collection of Sabina Welserin calls for using a funnel to make *strauben*. See ZALABIYA. *Strauben* are still a specialty of southern Germany, Austria, and South Tyrol and are likely the source for funnel cake, a popular carnival food in North America. See FAIRS. By far the most widely distributed of the poured fritters are *jalebi* (as they are called in South Asia), a sweet food enjoyed in both Muslim and Hindu communities in the Indian subcontinent and throughout the Middle East as well as North and East Africa. They are a very popular sweet food during both secular and religious events, especially Ramadan and Diwali. See DIWALI and RAMADAN. The batter for these fritters is poured into hot oil in the form of spirals or roughly circular shapes. After frying, the *jalebi* are soaked in sugar syrup and then drained. This preparation gives them a crisp texture and a syrup-rich interior.

See also BAGHDAD; DOUGHNUTS; FRIED DOUGH; INDIA; MIDDLE EAST; NORTH AFRICA; PERSIA; and SOUTH ASIA.

Işın, Mary. *Sherbet and Spice: The Complete Story of Turkish Sweets and Desserts*. London and New York: I. B. Tauris, 2012.

Krondl, Michael. *The Donut: History, Recipes, and Lore from Boston to Berlin*. Chicago: Chicago Review Press, 2014.

Adam Balic

frosting

See ICING.

fructose, also called fruit sugar or levulose, is a monosaccharide. It is most commonly found in fruit (particularly apples, cantaloupes, pears, pomegranates, watermelon, and berries), but also occurs in animal tissues, tree saps (maple syrup), vegetables, and honey. Fructose is the sweetest sugar found in nature, about 1.7 times sweeter than glucose. See GLUCOSE.

When chemically combined with glucose, fructose forms sucrose, or common table sugar, a disaccharide that consists of 50 percent fructose and 50 percent glucose. See SUGAR. During metabolism, fructose is broken down and converted into glucose, which is used for energy or stored as fat. Unlike glucose, which is metabolized widely in the body, fructose is mainly metabolized in the liver.

For the past 40 years, commercial fructose has been produced by converting cornstarch into glucose, and then into fructose. The resulting product, called high-fructose corn syrup (HFCS), averages about 55 to 60 percent fructose, with the remainder being glucose. See CORN SYRUP. As HFCS is sweeter than table sugar, it is widely used in food manufacture, particularly in the soda industry but also in many commercial foods, including breads and other baked goods, candies, and fruit drinks.

Fructose has been part of the human diet for thousands of years, but recently the amount of fructose consumed has soared—as has the prevalence of obesity and metabolic syndrome (a group of risk factors that predict heart disease and Type 2 diabetes). Some researchers have proposed that the intake of excessive fructose as a free monosaccharide may have adverse health consequences, but to date, the evidence for deleterious effects is inconclusive.

See also HONEY; MAPLE SYRUP; SAP; STARCH; and SUGAR AND HEALTH.

Kalamaras, Paula M., and Paul T. Kraly. *Sugar and Sweeteners: Trends and Developments in Foods and Beverages*. Norwalk, Conn.: Business Communications, 2003.

Murphy, Suzanne P. "The State of the Science on Dietary Sweeteners Containing Fructose: Summary and Issues to Be Resolved." *Journal of Nutrition* 139 (June 2009): 1269S–1270S.

Andrew F. Smith

fruit has long been appreciated as a source of sweetness. Sweetness in fruit, a primary indicator of ripeness, guarantees digestibility in those wild-gathered foodstuffs on which our ancestors depended. "The Cree Indians of Canada," observed anthropologist Claude Levi-Strauss (1977), "believed that the Creator told humans that the first berries to be picked had to be boiled. Then the bowl had to be held first towards the sun, who was asked to ripen the berries, then towards the thunder who was asked for rain, and finally towards the earth, who was asked to bring forth her fruits."

When and under what circumstances fruit is eaten raw rather than cooked is a matter of latitude and climate. In temperate and tropical regions blessed with year-round sunshine, fruit is traditionally eaten raw at any time of day rather than as part of a meal, a casual attitude derived from easy availability. In northern lands, however, where the growing season is short and ripeness uncertain, fruit is traditionally eaten cooked and served as an integral part of a meal—usually, though not always, at the conclusion. Fruit soups sweetened with sugar are eaten at the beginning or the end of a meal in Scandinavia and Russia, while in Germany, fruit dumplings and strudels may be served after a soup as the main dish in a traditional family meal. See DUMPLINGS; SOUP; and STRUDEL.

From the limitations of climate, it seems, developed the northerner's habit of serving sugar-sweetened fruit-based desserts, including ices and sorbets, as a pleasurable conclusion to both formal and informal meals. This is not so in more temperate climes, although times are changing. Food writer Diana Farr Louis, reporting on the traditional foodways of Crete, noted the surprise of Westerners at the total absence of fruit-based desserts in the island's traditional menu: "For the Greeks and the Cretans, in particular, fruit is something that is eaten raw... but never, traditionally at any rate, encased in pastry or folded into a pudding" (2001).

Among northerners, sweetness in fruits is prized not only for pleasure but also as evidence of the triumph of man over nature, a costly business in Victorian Britain, when fashionable hostesses made reference to their husband's affluence by "showing an epergne"—an ornate serving dish with an array of tropical fruits ripened to perfection in artificially heated greenhouses—on the table as a prelude to dessert and the serving of the cheese course. See EPERGNES. This habit persists to this day in the offering of a small bunch of grapes on formally presented cheese boards.

Sweetness in fruit is most easily perceived through scent. See OLFACTION. Sight may deceive, but the nose never lies when choosing, say, a peach or a melon—explaining, perhaps, the attraction of seemingly rotten fragrances such as that of durian, a scent unpalatable to those who did not accept it in childhood, and—though rather less obviously—the smell of bletted fruits like medlars. The attraction of the semi-rotted is also present in fermented fruit juices. Although alcohol is undeniably the main attraction, wine connoisseurs instinctively reach for ripe-fruit metaphors—peach, black currant, blackberry, cherry, pear—to describe the complexity of fragrance and flavor.

The desire for additional sweetness in fruit in its role as pleasure-giver—as well as the need to add shelf-life—is satisfied by the ancient process of preserving or candying in honey or sugar-syrup, and in the preparation of fruit leathers and fruit pastes. See CANDIED FRUIT and FRUIT PASTES. Fruits were preserved in honey in ancient China, India, throughout the Middle East, ancient Egypt, and classical Greece. In Europe, on the rise of the Roman Empire, sweetness in the form of preserved fruits became a metaphor for civilization and the virtues of the rule of law, a concept as much philosophical as practical. Their equivalent today—fruit drinks and fruit purées sold fresh, canned, or frozen, particularly those marketed as without additional sweetening—rely on the ancestral memory of goodness associated with sweetness, and are commonly sold as health-giving whether or not this is true.

Fruit as pleasure-giver has long been explored in paintings, poetry, and myth. When Eve offered Adam a bite of that rosy-cheeked apple—or golden quince, as biblical scholars suggest—temptation lay in the sharing of sweetness as a metaphor for desire. Quince preserves remain the traditional symbol of happiness at Mediterranean weddings. In portraiture, a bowl of cherries conveys desirability and a ripe strawberry is a token of love; figs and pomegranates split open to show the seeds deliver their own libidinous message. If sweetness makes fruits desirable, there must also be sharpness: no rose without a thorn. The palate rejects blandness even when attracted by sweetness. *Naranjas de caña*, sugarcane oranges—the fruits of decorative orange trees planted in Spanish courtyards—are unpleasantly bland even though the taste is overwhelming sweet. The same was true of Europe's native wood

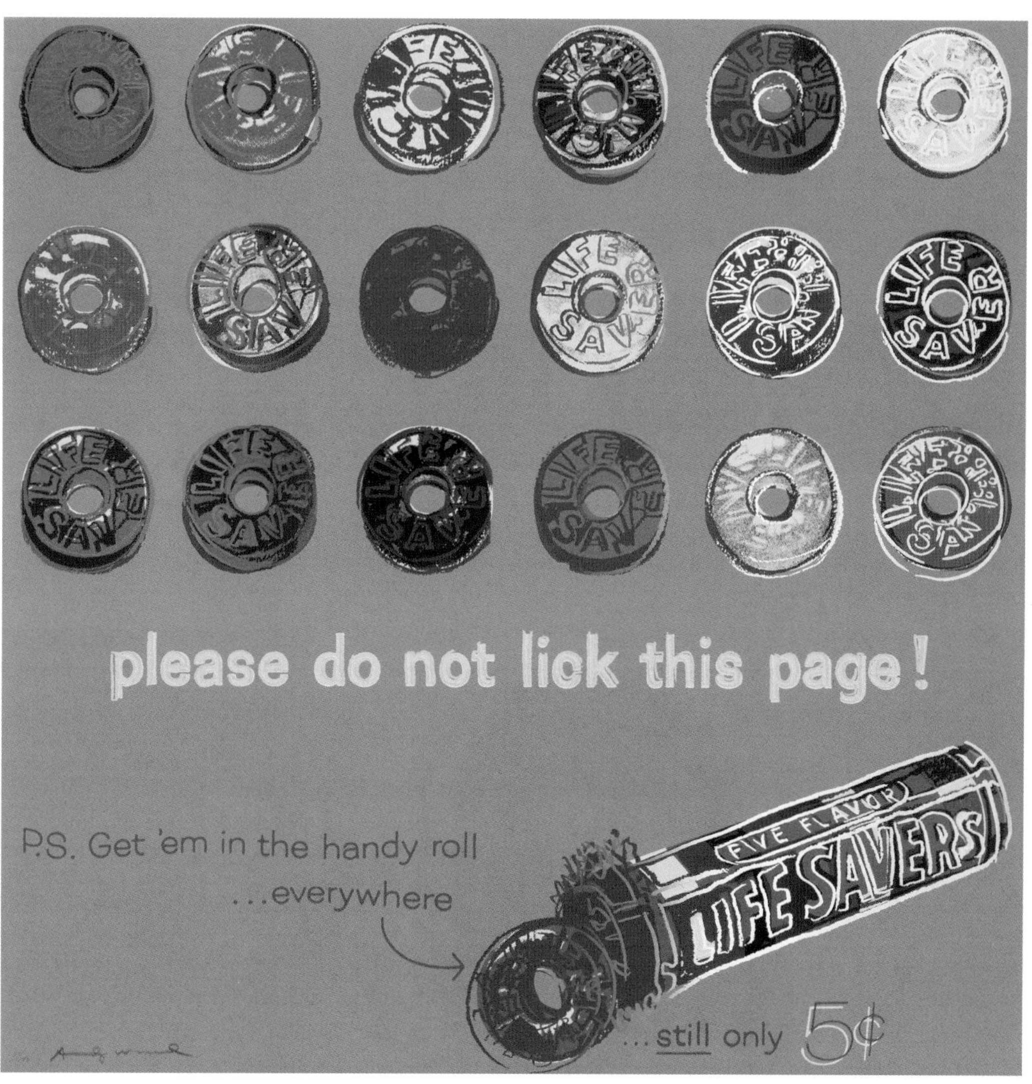
please do not lick this page!
P.S. Get 'em in the handy roll
...everywhere
FIVE FLAVOR
LIFE SAVERS
...still only 5¢

Andy Warhol, America's most famous pop artist, designed *Life Savers* in 1985 as part of his "Ads" series. This screen print celebrates the iconic hard candies called Life Savers that first appeared in a "Five-Flavor" roll in 1935; their flavors of pineapple, lime, orange, cherry, and lemon did not change for 70 years.

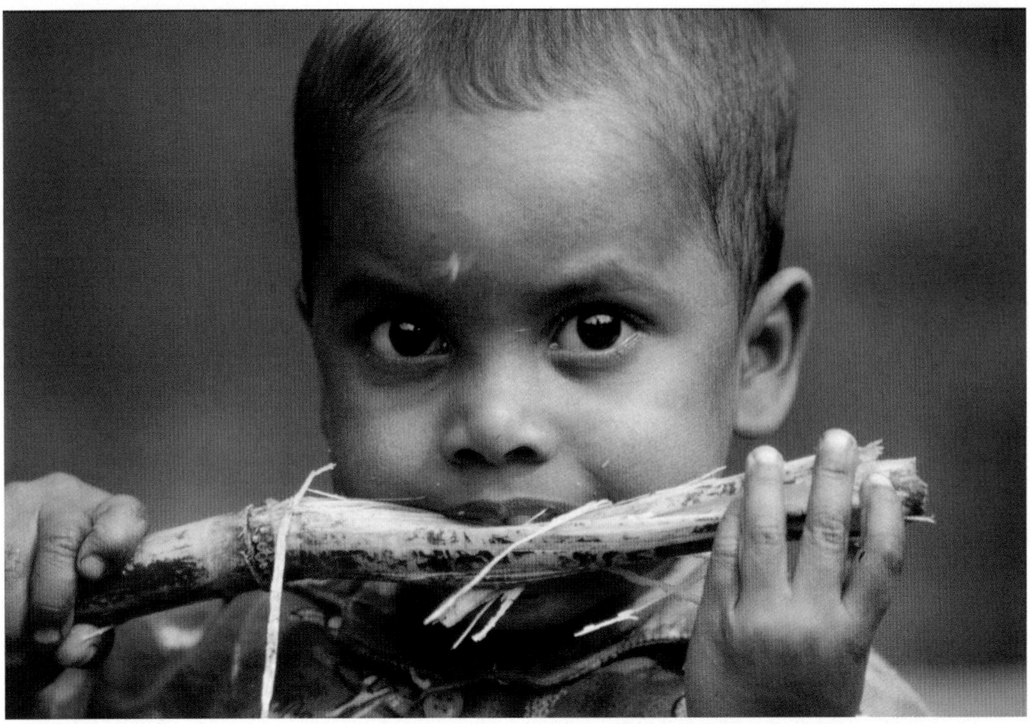

Sugarcane belongs to the genus *Saccharum*, which comprises tall, segmented grasses similar to bamboo but rich in sugar. *Saccharum officinarum*, the main cultivated sugarcane, has a reed-like stalk filled with sap. Here, a young boy chews a fibrous cane for a sweet treat. N. DURRELL MCKENNA, WELLCOME IMAGES

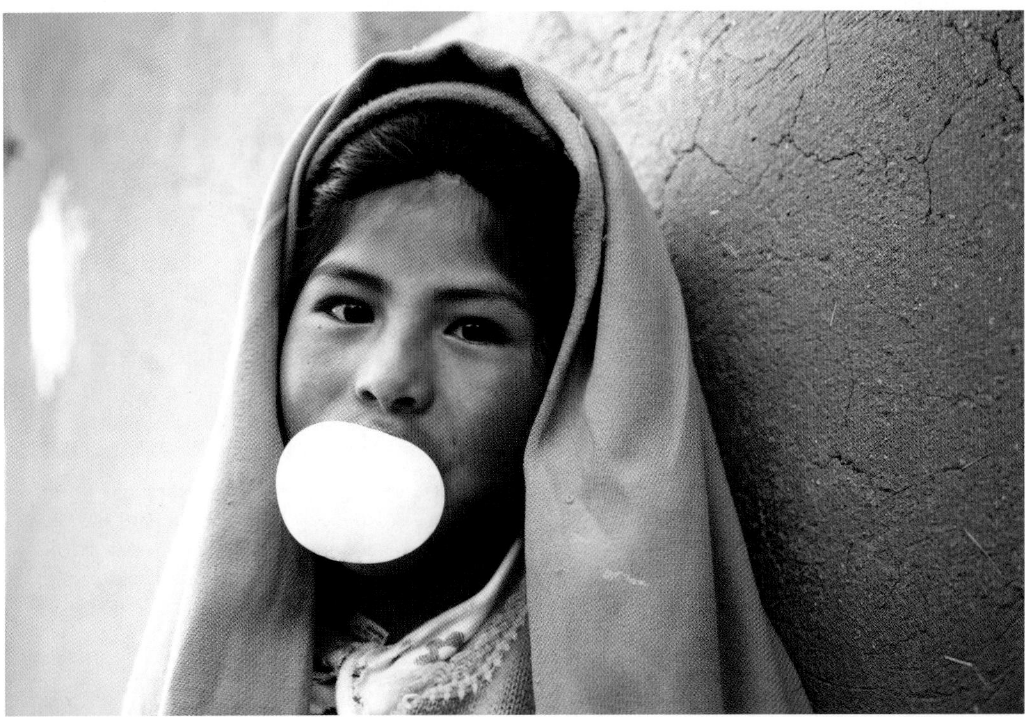

In 1928 Walter Diemer used latex to improve the elasticity of an earlier chewing gum formula. The result was Dubble Bubble, the first commercially successful bubble gum. Since then, the gum has spread worldwide, as evidenced by this young girl blowing a bubble in Potosí, Bolivia. PHOTO BY KIMBERLEY COOLE / GETTY, LONELY PLANET IMAGES COLLECTION

This portrait by the South African photographer Zwelethu Mthethwa (1960–) captures the proud grace of a sugarcane worker, who engages directly with the viewer, machete and cane stripper in hands silvered with dirt. © ZWELETHU MTHETHWA. COURTESY OF THE ARTIST AND JACK SHAINMAN GALLERY, NEW YORK

A dramatic pyramid of caramel-drizzled cream puffs, the French croquembouche makes frequent appearances at weddings and other ceremonial occasions. Its literal meaning of "crunch in the mouth" captures the caramel's crackle.

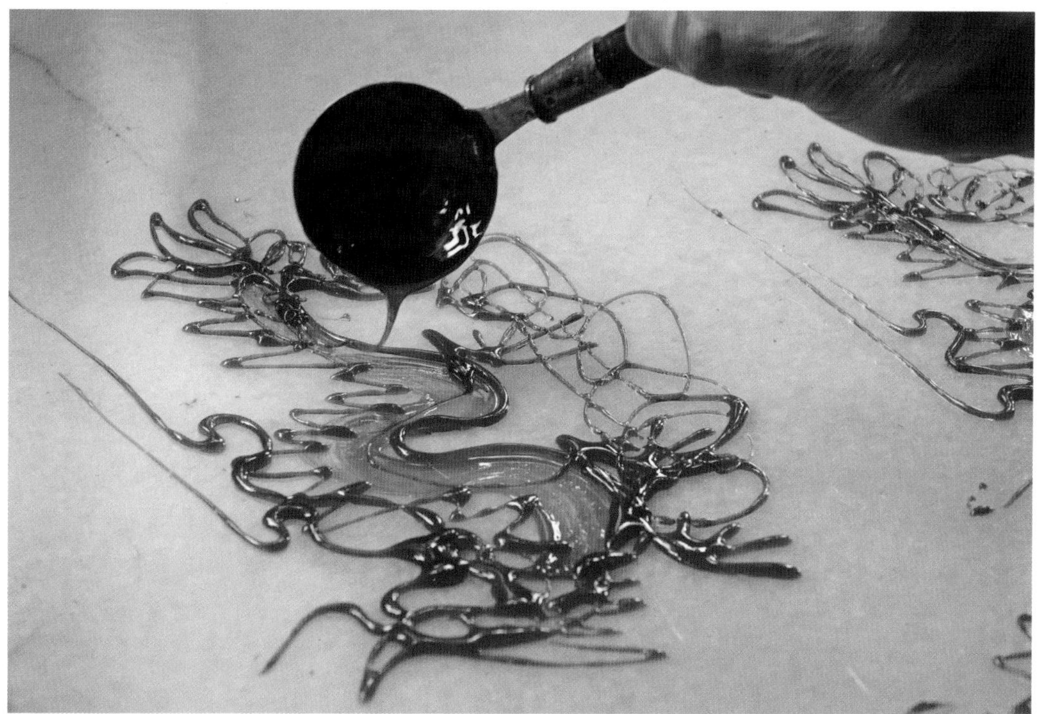

The Chinese folk art of sugar painting, creating fanciful forms out of caramelized rock sugar, is now recognized as part of China's cultural heritage. Regional practitioners can be found at temple fairs, at markets, and in parks. © HUPENG / DREAMSTIME.COM

Pastry chef Tracy Obolsky of the North End Grill in New York City transformed the Creamsicle ice cream treat of her childhood into a sophisticated pie made with a graham cracker crust, Bavarian cream, bitter marmalade, and orange gelée. Whipped cream and candied orange slices complete the dessert. PHOTO BY NIKO TRIANTAFILLOU / SERIOUS EATS

The American chocolate company Baker's was an early proponent of mass advertising. This ad plays on chocolate's Latin name, *Theobroma* (food of the gods), as cocoa is offered up to the Aztec king in a solid gold cup.

Child labor is an issue of global concern, especially in the chocolate industry, where young children are forced to work under often hazardous conditions. Despite lawsuits, the practice continues, particularly in the cacao-producing regions of West Africa.

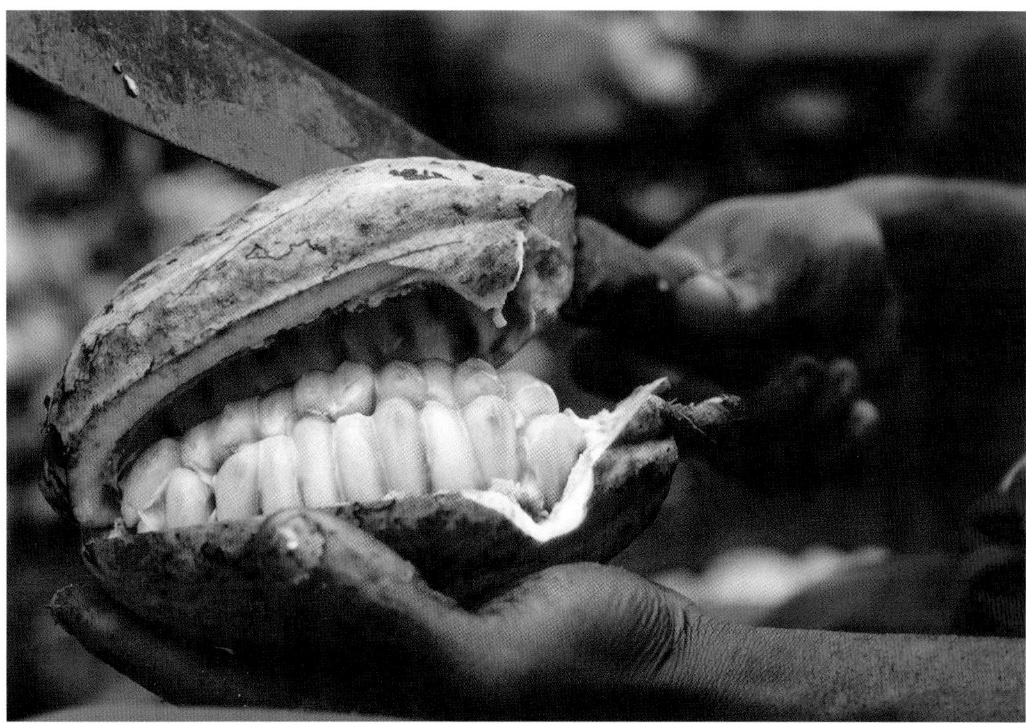

A farmer harvests the mature pods of the cacao tree (*Theobroma cacao*), the beans of which are used to produce chocolate. JAMES L. STANFIELD / NATIONAL GEOGRAPHIC CREATIVE

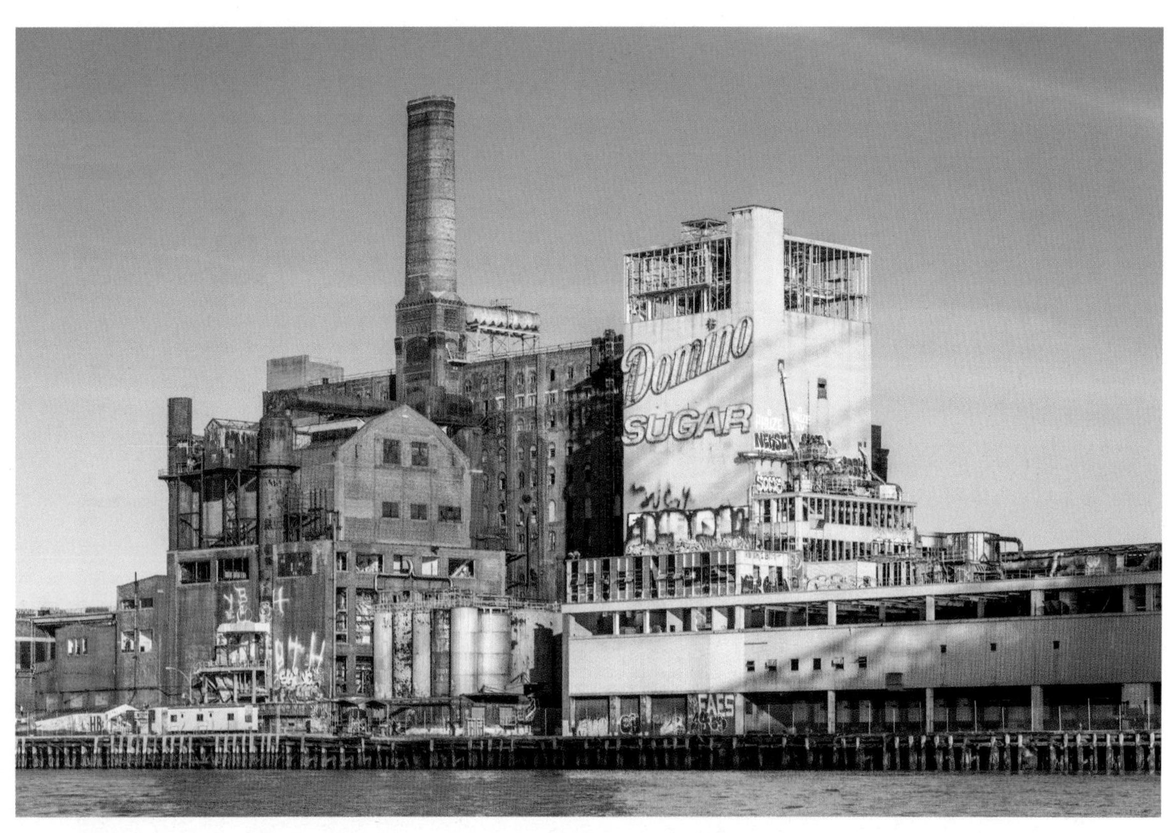

The Domino Sugar Factory in Brooklyn, New York, was built in 1856 and at one point processed over half the sugar used in the United States. It stopped operating in 2004. Paul Raphaelson sought to capture the factory's decay in a series of photographs titled *Sweet Ruin: The Brooklyn Domino Sugar Refinery* (2013–2014). © PAUL RAPHAELSON

In 2014 the American artist Kara Walker constructed a sphinx-like, 75-foot-long sculpture of white sugar and carved polystyrene in the abandoned Domino Sugar Refining Plant in Brooklyn, New York. *A Subtlety: The Marvelous Sugar Baby* comments on both New York City's plan to redevelop the factory as high-end condominiums and sugar's dark role in the slave trade. ARTWORK © KARA WALKER. PHOTO BY JASON WYCHE. COURTESY OF SIKKEMA JENKINS & CO., NEW YORK

This anonymous painting from around 1900 depicts a scene at Vienna's first coffeehouse, the Inn at the Blue Bottle, founded in 1683 by the Ukrainian Cossack Jerzy Franciszek Kulczycki, who had discovered coffeehouses while being held captive in Turkey.

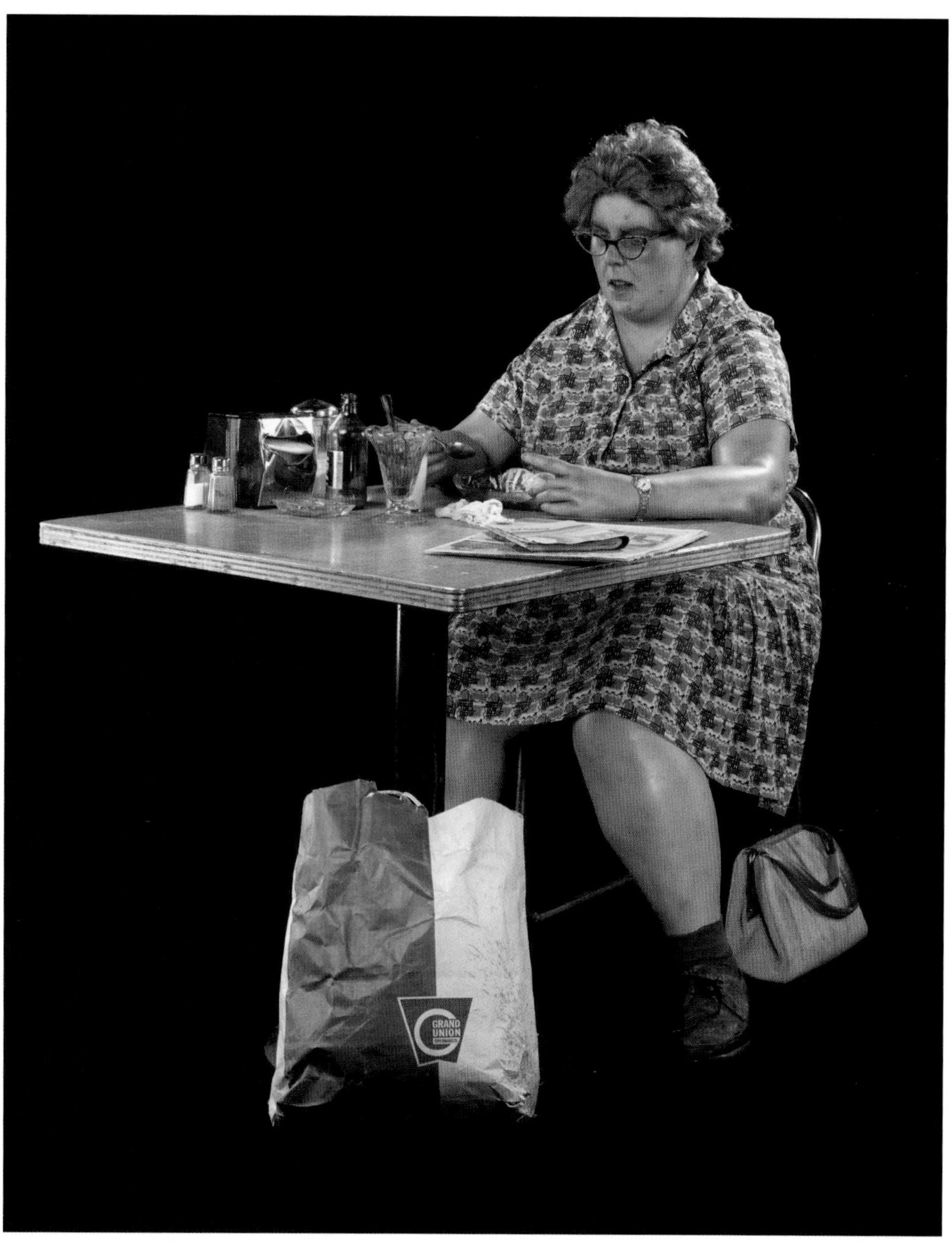

The American artist Duane Hanson was best known for his life-sized figural sculptures of middle-class men and women. *Woman Eating* (1971), a blunt representation of a woman eating ice cream, conveys isolation and the stigma of obesity. ART © ESTATE OF DUANE HANSON / LICENSED BY VAGA, NEW YORK, N.Y. / SMITHSONIAN AMERICAN ART MUSEUM, WASHINGTON, D.C. / ART RESOURCE, N.Y.

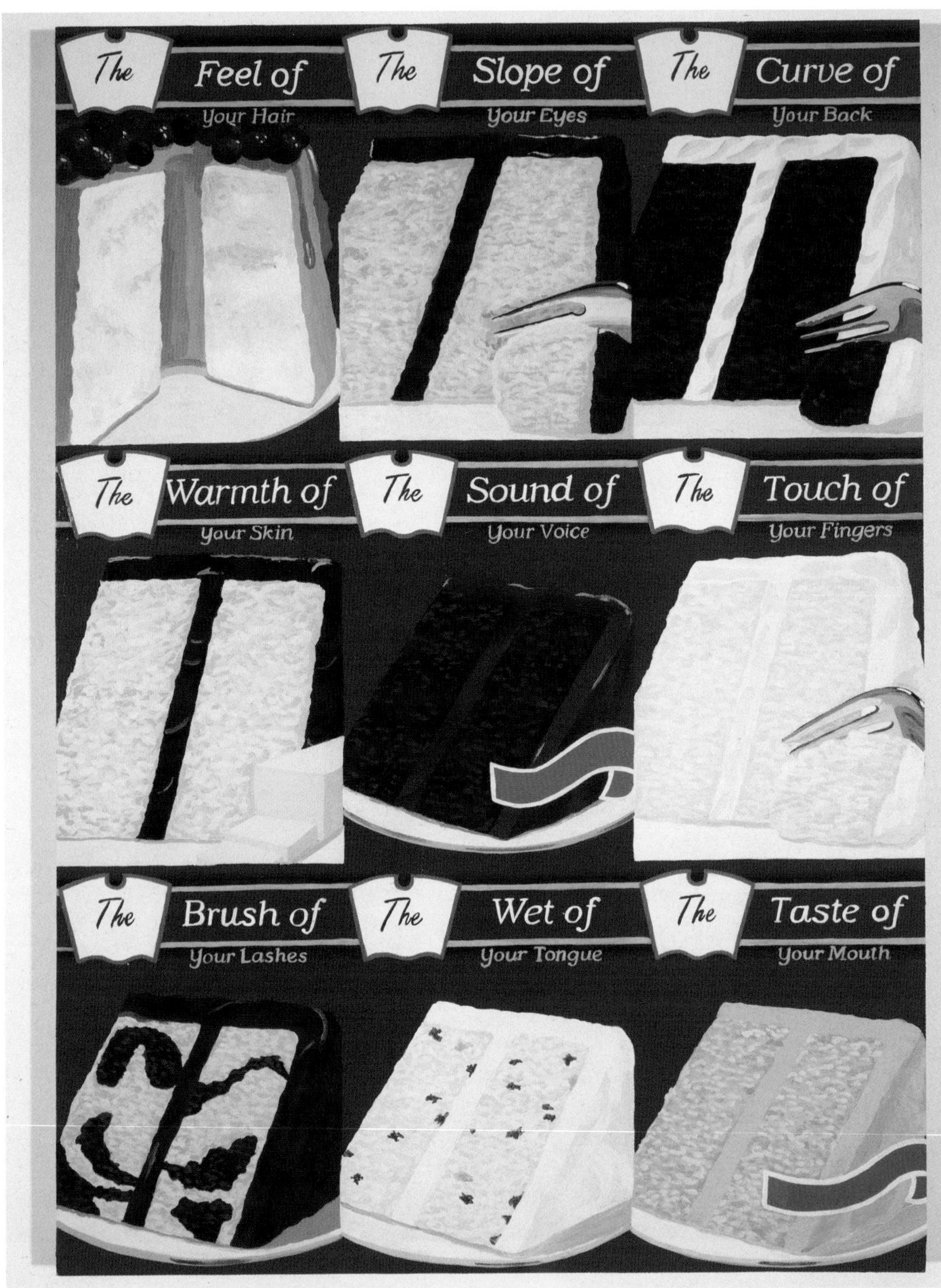

American artist Julia Jacquette borrows from old Duncan Hines cake mix boxes in this 1994 enamel on wood painting, recasting their wholesomeness as sensual dreams. The success of early cake mixes depended on convincing housewives that baking from a package was just as feminine and caring as making batter from scratch. COURTESY OF THE ARTIST

Although American artist Wayne Thiebaud never identified with Pop art, his paintings of commonplace items, especially his wonderful production-line pies, cakes, and cupcakes, likely influenced the movement. In *Boston Cremes* (1962), Thiebaud's lush strokes are the frosting on each slice. ART © WAYNE THIEBAUD / LICENSED BY VAGA, NEW YORK, N.Y. / CROCKER ART MUSEUM PURCHASE, 1964

The accoutrements of a well-set tea table—teapot, teacup and saucer, sugar cubes, and sugar spoon—are all visible in this 1730 American folk portrait of Susanna Truax, ascribed to the Gansevoort Limner (possibly Pieter Vanderlyn). Most likely all of these objects were imported. NATIONAL GALLERY OF ART, GIFT OF EDGAR WILLIAM AND BERNICE CHRYSLER GARBISCH

In his saccharine-sweet confectionery landscapes, many featuring cotton-candy clouds and nude women awaiting the viewer's pleasured gaze, American artist Will Cotton explores desire and the needs that fuel our consumer society. *Candy Curls* dates to 2006. COURTESY OF THE ARTIST AND MARY BOONE GALLERY, NEW YORK

In *Eyes Momma* (1987), Al Hansen, a member of the 1960s Fluxus art movement, played with the Hershey's candy bars he loved, using the wrappers and the name "Hershey" to create linguistic collages. COURTESY OF GRACIE MANSION GALLERY, NEW YORK strawberry, *Fragaria vesca,* considered of no interest to gardeners until the development of hybrids crossbred with big-berried, sharp-flavored New World varieties from Chile and North America. Victorian gardeners and plantsmen, experts in crossbreeding, nurtured new varieties of native species and experimented with seeds from elsewhere, resulting in the spread of fruit families into regions they would never otherwise have reached.

From these hothouse beginnings grew consumer expectations of fresh fruit on demand all year, leading to the development of methods of cropping and conserving freshness suitable for long-distance transportation. The results, as the Cree nation would certainly recognize, do not always deliver on expectations. Sourness can be softened by the heat of the fire, but sweetness is the gift of the sun.

See also DESSERT; DRIED FRUIT; FRUIT PRESERVES; ICE CREAM; and SHERBET.

Levi-Strauss, Claude. "The Roast and the Boiled." In *The Anthropologists' Cookbook,* rev. ed., edited by Jessica Kuper, pp. 246. New York and London: Routledge, 1997.

Louis, Diana Farr. *Feasting and Fasting in Crete.* Athens, Greece: Kedros, 2001.

Roach, F. A. *Cultivated Fruits of Britain.* New York: Blackwell, 1985.

Wilson, Constance Ann. *Food and Drink in Britain.* London: Constable, 1973.

Elisabeth Luard

fruit desserts, baked, refers to a grouping of desserts made of fruit baked with some version of a crust. Occasionally referred to as "spoon pies," the recipes are as much defined by their essential fruity nature as they are by their whimsical and often onomatopoeic names, which include "cobbler," "crisp," "crumble," "buckle," "betty," and "pandowdy." Their origins, along with their monikers, are universally murky. Some are closely associated with New England, indicating vague British derivations, but each has long passed into the collective American culinary lexicon.

With elements of folk tradition and unfussy informality, these desserts typically fall under the category of "country" or "rustic" recipes. Less exacting than pies or cakes and typically baked in pans and deep-set dishes, they double or triple easily to feed a crowd. Biscuit dough, breadcrumbs, free-form pie dough, or crunchy streusel largely comprise their toppings. See PIE DOUGH and STREUSEL. All of them benefit from a scoop of vanilla ice cream. When pulled from the oven as the fruit bubbles and the buttery pastry turns golden, these baked fruit desserts are winningly straightforward—that is, until it comes to strictly classifying them. Their plainness and universality invite myriad interpretations, which can vary from state to state or even town to town. Cooks can be vehement in insisting that their familial or regional version is the only correct rendering. And confusion frequently sets in when variations are subtle: What, for instance, exactly differentiates a crisp from a crumble?

The following definitions of individual desserts address their basic forms, with commentary on widespread variations if applicable:

- *Betty (or Brown Betty).* A New England favorite, in which fruit is layered with breadcrumbs (often mixed with butter), or sometimes cubes of bread, before baking. Apple is the fruit most commonly associated with a betty, though chopped rhubarb or thinly sliced bananas also work well.
- *Buckle.* More akin to a coffee cake, a batter is poured over or among fruit, often with the addition of a streusel topping. The finished dessert looks collapsed, or "buckled." Blueberry is the classic fruit for buckle; the berries stay handsomely suspended in the cake while maintaining their shape.
- *Cobbler.* No dessert in this group inspires as many broad interpretations. To many Americans, a cobbler is a deep-dish pie crowned with baking-powder biscuit dough (made with cream or buttermilk), which is often cut in circles or dropped by the spoonful atop fruit to give an appearance that is "cobbled together." Like pie, the versatile format works with almost any fruit that grows in North America, alone or in combination. Some cooks from the southern United States have variations that they defend vehemently: to them a cobbler is a rectangular pie, cooked in a pan with a bottom and top crust. And barbecue restaurants (and some home cooks) across the South and in Texas adhere to a cobble variation that resembles a buckle, with a milk-based batter poured over the fruit before baking.

- *Crisp and Crumble.* These deep-dish pies crowned with streusel, rather than dough, are practically interchangeable. Semantics come into play over differences in the streusel ingredients: some cooks and food writers insist that crisps include oats (in addition to or in place of flour) along with butter, sugar, spices, and sometimes chopped nuts, whereas crumbles call solely for flour. Others say it is the other way around. In any case, the term "crisp" is more common in the United States; the British use the name "crumble" more frequently. The French, too, have also enthusiastically adopted "le crumble."
- *Pandowdy.* A variant of the biscuit style of cobbler, except that the biscuit dough (often rolled out to form a solid covering over the fruit) is broken up during baking and pushed down into the fruit, allowing the juices to burble up and create a crisp, fruit-stained crust. The result is delicious but dowdy in appearance, hence the name.
- *Slump (or Grunt).* Solidly linked to New England, slumps and grunts resemble the biscuit approach to cobbler, except in this case the sweetened dough is often called a dumpling rather than a biscuit. These desserts are typically steamed atop the stove, though they may be finished in the oven for a few minutes to crisp their topping. The dumplings are said to grunt while steaming, and the final product certainly has a limp, or slumping, look.
- *Sonker.* The most obscure of the bunch is a soupy adaptation of cake-style cobbler particular to western North Carolina. Previously cooked fruit or sweet potato is baked with a flour–milk–sugar mixture the consistency of pancake batter.

Though they lack visual elegance, and popular recipes suggest vanilla extract and common spices like cinnamon and nutmeg as simple flavorings, imaginative cooks can elevate the aromas and tastes of these desserts to sophisticated heights. For example, in her book *Nancy Silverton's Pastries From the La Brea Bakery,* Silverton, one of the country's most accomplished pastry chefs, includes a chapter entitled "Cobblers, Crisps, and Crumbles." In it she advocates specific use of seasonal fruit (apples and pears in the fall, strawberries and rhubarb in the spring, stone fruit like peaches and apricots as well as berries in the summer) and in several recipes outlines a luxurious twist: she simmers a vanilla pod and its seeds in butter until the mixture browns and gives off a nutty, toasty perfume, and then she pours this over the prepared fruit of the dessert before adding the topping.

See also PIE.

Schreiber, Cory Schreiber, and Julie Richardson. *Rustic Fruit Desserts.* Berkeley, Calif.: Ten Speed, 2009.

Severson, Kim. "What You Call Your Pie Depends Upon Where You Live." *New York Times,* 1 July 2013. http://www.nytimes.com/2013/07/03/dining/in-search-of-the-sonker-a-sweet-denizen-of-surry-county-nc.html.

Silverton, Nancy. *Nancy Silverton's Pastries from the La Brea Bakery.* New York: Villard, 2000.

Bill Addison

fruit leather

See FRUIT PASTES.

fruit pastes are one of the oldest confections. Extended cooking of seasonal fruit with varying amounts of sugar produces thick, stiff, long-keeping preserves that have been used by most cultures over many centuries—as medicines, travel snacks, sweets, and desserts, and as accompaniments to both sweet and savory foods. Set with pectin and dried by long cooking, fruit pastes generally hold their shape outside a mold or package and are usually firm to the touch. The degree of firmness varies, and fruit pastes range from thick but spreadable butters and soft jellies that melt in the mouth to hard, chewy leathers, with a range of consistencies in between. Besides the length of cooking time and thus the degree of drying, the texture of fruit paste is dependent on the added sugar content: the higher the concentration of sugar, the less water the fruit jelly supports, resulting in a stiffer end result. Confectioners manipulate the sugar content of fruit pastes from little or none to equal parts, depending on the degree of tartness and stickiness required in the final product.

Long heating and additional evaporation bring out the deepest, richest hues of the fruit: berry colors intensify into the darkest pinks and reds; peaches and apricots produce a dark orange; green plums turn deep yellow, while purple plums become almost black; apples and pears move from light pink to a pale-pinky beige; and the ancient king of the long-cooked paste, the quince, produces an array of red-orange tones, from pale orangey-red at a fast open boil to the deep red of a long, close-covered simmer. It is no wonder that the varied, jewel-like glow and intense flavor of fruit pastes have long provided confectioners with the base for many of their most traditional fruit sweets.

Soft Pastes

Fruit Butter

Fruit butter is a thick but spreadable syrupy paste, usually made from sweet or sharp apples or pears. Made in tenth-century Arab kitchens from fruit pulp and honey vinegar, and in Victorian English kitchens using rum, today butters are best known in the Netherlands (*appelstroop*), Belgium (*sirop de Liège* for apple or *birnenhonig* for pear), Germany (*Apfelkraut*), Poland (*powidło*), and the United States (apple butter). The fruit is stewed with apple cider or vinegar for added sharpness and with spices such as cinnamon, nutmeg, allspice, and cloves. The strained fruit mixture is then cooked with sugar in a ratio of about 3 parts sugar to 1 part pulp until dark, thick, and creamy, and stored in jars. Usually a deep brownish black due to the long cooking and spices, it is eaten spread on bread or as an accompaniment to cooked meats, as well as being used as an ingredient in baking.

Fruit Jellies

The most yielding of the firmer fruit paste family, these jellies are nonetheless a quite different preparation from a light, fresh, gelatin-set dessert jelly. See GELATIN DESSERTS. Intensely fruity, jellied fruits or fruit jellies are soft yet firm sugar-covered sweets that keep for several months. In France, they are called *pâtes de fruit*; in Spain, *dulce de fruta*, often translated into English as Sephardi fruit paste. Pectin is a crucial element in the set of these jellies, so although they may be made in a multitude of fruit flavors (and therefore colors), they often contain apple purée as a thickener and to ensure the right texture and firmness. Two parts of puréed fruit or apple purée–thickened juice is cooked to 240°F (115°C) with one part sugar. Pectin is incorporated at a rate of up to three-quarters of a part, the mixture is returned to the boil, and lemon juice added to taste. The mixture is poured into prepared trays, sprinkled with granulated sugar, and left to set for a minimum of two hours before being turned to coat the other side with sugar. Once completely cooled, the jelly is cut into pieces—usually squares—and each one fully coated in granulated sugar. Fruit jellies keep for several months, at least. An alternative version may be set with agar instead of pectin. However, as a result of the protein content in agar, these jellies do not keep as long: weeks rather than months.

Medium to Firm Pastes

Fruit Cheese

Fruit cheese is a thick fruit paste, often set into a mold and presented as a shallow block for cutting, although it may also be set in a jar and either cut or spooned out. Commonly made with quince, apple, damson, gooseberry, or blackberry, fruit cheeses have a relatively high sugar content and an intense fruit flavor, and are usually eaten with hot or cold roasted meats, and sometimes with cheese. They are included in some of the earliest English recipe collections: in *Delightes for Ladies* (1609) Sir Hugh Plat gives a recipe for a version of plum or damson cheese that involves cooking the fruit to a pulp with rosewater or wine before finishing with sugar and molding. See PLAT, SIR HUGH. The basic method for preparing a standard fruit cheese is to chop the fruit and cook it to complete tenderness in a small amount of water, then push it through a sieve to make a smooth, thick pulp. This pulp is then combined with sugar in a ratio of 1 pint (600 milliliters) of pulp to 12–14 ounces (350–400 grams) of sugar. The mixture is gently heated and stirred until the sugar has dissolved, and then cooked, stirring frequently, for an extended period of up to an hour, until a channel is left in the paste when a spoon is drawn through it. Poured when hot into molds or shallow jars, fruit cheese sets firm when cool.

Quince Pastes

Quince pastes seem to have been known in most European cultures for many centuries, and quinces were stewed in honey for long keeping by the Romans in at least the fourth century C.E., and quite probably earlier. Medieval Arab confectioners developed the technique of stewing fruit pulp with refined sugar to make long-keeping pastes, and it is likely that the recipe arrived in Spain along with sugar in the twelfth century.

Cotignac is a version of *pâte de coings,* thick quince paste that originates in Orleans, France. It is molded in small, plain wooden boxes, or in large patterned molds that are sold as decorative blocks. This traditional delicacy was exported from France to England in the sixteenth century, where it was recorded with variable spellings, such as Sir Hugh Plat's "Quidini of Quinces."

Membrillo or *dulce de membrillo* is a very thick quince paste, perhaps the best known of this family of pastes, that takes its name from the Spanish word for quince. It is similar to fruit cheese and follows the same preparation method but generally contains more sugar—a 1 to 1 ratio of cooked fruit pulp to sugar—and requires even longer cooking. When the paste is done, the mixture not only holds a channel made with a spoon but also starts to come away from the sides of the pan. *Membrillo* is generally molded into rectangular blocks for slicing and is served with dairy cheeses, in particular Manchego, the Spanish ewe's milk cheese. It keeps extremely well in a cool, dark place, for at least a year. It can also be refrigerated for even longer keeping, though it may become sticky after some time in the refrigerator.

Quittenkäse or Quittenpästli is a centuries-old German or Swiss quince paste very similar to the southern European versions, though it can be even thicker than the Spanish *membrillo,* and is often made slightly tart with lemon juice or lemon zest. It is made all over Eastern Europe, from Croatia (*kotonjata*) to Hungary (*birsalmasajt*). The Hungarian version sometimes contains whole walnuts or almonds, or its outside is sprinkled with chopped nuts, and may be seasoned with cinnamon or cloves.

Very Firm Pastes

Fruit Leather

Fruit leathers are very solid fruit pastes that have been cooked as usual for a paste and then additionally dried out, either in a low oven or in the sun, for longer keeping. These drier pulps have also been recorded over the centuries, and *Delightes for Ladies* gives instructions for a medicinally tart dry cherry pulp, cooked with no additional sugar, and made even more sour with lemon juice or verjuice according to taste. Contemporary leathers usually have a little added sugar or honey—perhaps 2 tablespoons to 500 milliliters of fruit pulp. The pulp is cooked until very thick and then spread out in thin layers on trays and dried in a cool oven.

See also FRUIT; FRUIT PRESERVES; MARMALADE; MIDDLE EAST; PERSIA; and SPAIN.

Day, Ivan. "The Art of Confectionery." http://www.historicfood.com/The%20Art%20of%20Confectionery.pdf (accessed 20 January 2014).

Greweling, Peter P. *Chocolates and Confections: At Home with the Culinary Institute of America.* Hoboken, N.J.: Wiley, 2010.

Lal, Girdhari, G. S. Siddappa, and G. L. Tandon. *Preservation of Fruits and Vegetables.* New Delhi: Indian Council of Agricultural Research, 1960.

Mason, Laura. *Sugar-Plums and Sherbet: The Prehistory of Sweets.* Totnes, U.K.: Prospect, 2004.

Nasrallah, Nawal. *Annals of the Caliph's Kitchens: Ibn Sayyār al-Warrāq's Tenth-Century Baghdadi Cookbook.* Leiden, The Netherlands, and Boston: Brill, 2010.

Tate & Lyle Refineries Ltd. Home Economics Department. *Sweet Success: The Tate & Lyle Cookbook.* London: Sackett and Marshall, 1977.

Jane Levi

fruit preserves are an attempt to capture the magic of seasonal fruit and hold it in suspension for the months (or even years) to come. Sugar is the ingredient that offers the prospect of long keeping, and it is generally concentrated at around 60 percent in the jams, jellies, conserves, and syrup suspensions that make up the core members of this family. Shorter-keeping fruit preserves like compotes and curds may be less sweet. Almost all fruit preserves are cooked to a greater or lesser degree, both to kill microorganisms that might cause spoilage and to evaporate the right amount of water, depending on the texture and level of set desired. Uncooked fruit preserves keep for short periods of up to a week or depend on the presence of alcohol to preserve the fruit.

Preservation of whole and chopped fruits in honey is an ancient technique, recorded in Roman texts like Apicius. See ANCIENT WORLD. Citrus peels were salted for a day, then rinsed and conserved—as was done with dates or quinces—in boiled honey and spices; apples were stewed with honey and sometimes vinegar to make a thick sauce for immediate eating or keeping. Similar techniques are recorded in tenth-century Arabic texts as well as

Victorian-era food manufacturers often advertised their products alongside images of plump, happy toddlers to signify the new industrial age of safety and plenty, as in this advertising card for Thurbers' Fruit Preserves and Jellies, produced sometime between 1850 and 1900. LIBRARY OF CONGRESS

in the earliest English-language manuscripts. Preservation depends on boiling the fruit and the honey, and on keeping the product well sealed in cool, dark conditions. The introduction of refined sugar expanded the possibilities for preservation and the availability of these sweets to a wider group of people. Often used to medicinal ends, the technique of safely preserving fruits through successive boiling in sugar solutions was an important skill for the apothecary and the confectioner. It was a confectioner, Nicolas Appert, who in 1810 invented the first bottling process that safely preserved foods by boiling them in sealed glass jars, a technique later developed into industrial canning.

Chemistry of Jelled Fruit Preserves

All conserves are variations on a theme of cooked, set fruit preserves made with fruit and sugar. Although the specific techniques for making each one vary slightly, all depend on certain basic qualities of the core ingredients and how they interact under the application of heat. Every conserve relies on sugar for its preservation qualities and on pectin (or other jelling agents like carrageen or agar) for its jelling action; acid balance is required for both set and good flavor.

Fruit

Jams and jellies can be made from any fruit, alone or in combination. It should be dry, fresh, and ripe and, depending on size, used in whole pieces, chopped, or pulped. Since overripe fruit is lower in pectin and higher in acid, it is advisable to make jams and jellies from perfectly ripe or slightly underripe fruit, both to ensure a good set and to give better flavor.

Pectin

Pectin is the naturally occurring jelling agent contained in the skins, pith, cores, pips, and cell walls of fruits. The amount of pectin in fruits varies considerably, and before making jams or jellies, its level needs to be considered and the recipe adjusted accordingly. More pectin can be added to lower-pectin fruits, either by using jam-making sugar with pectin already added to it, or by adding apple juice.

Acid

Levels of acidity vary considerably among fruits. In making preserves, acid works to release pectin in addition to influencing the flavor of the final product. To release pectin, lemon juice should be added during the cooking process; as a flavor adjuster, it may be added once the setting point has been achieved.

Sugar

Sugar sweetens, preserves, helps the jelling action of pectin, and stops it from breaking down while the conserve is boiling. Since sugar also toughens fruit skins and slows down the initial release of pectin, it should be added only when the fruit is already softened, and should be fully dissolved before bringing the mixture to a boil. Coarser-grained sugar works best, since the larger crystals dissolve more quickly. The quantity of sugar to include is a matter of taste, but since it also affects the keeping qualities of the conserve, being aware of sugar's preservation effect is important. Traditional jam and jelly recipes usually suggest equal quantities of sugar and fruit, and if properly potted and sealed, these will keep in a cool dark place for at least a year. In some jams, sugar may be reduced to as little as one-fifth of the weight of fruit. However, as the sugar level reduces, so does the keeping quality, and at very low levels the jam will need to be used quickly (within a few weeks) and kept refrigerated to prevent spoiling.

Jam

Jam is a jellified preserve made with whole fruits and sugar. The fruit is boiled with sugar in solution until sufficient water has evaporated and a set has been achieved. As the mixture cools, the network of pectin molecules developed by the interplay between the sugar solution (measured by temperature and concentration) and acidity levels (measured by pH) ensures the formation of a firm yet soft jell, capable of supporting whole pieces of fruit. The fruit should be cooked but not overcooked, and the mixture should be sweet but not cloying. Overboiling and excessive reduction are to be avoided while ensuring that there is enough sugar and sufficient evaporation to allow long keeping. Some fruits, such as raspberries, apricots, or rhubarb, are macerated with sugar overnight to draw out the juice before cooking, but this preliminary step is not essential. The basic jam technique is to very slowly bring the softened fruit and sugar to a simmer in a nonreactive pan, stirring to make sure that all the sugar is dissolved as the fruit begins to cook. The mixture is brought to a rolling boil, where it is held until the setting point (approximately 220°F/104.5°C) is achieved. The set can be tested by dropping a spot of jam onto a cold plate, allowing it to cool, and gently pushing it with one's finger. If the surface wrinkles, the jam is done. Froth may be skimmed off as the jam cools, or a little oil or butter added to make it disperse. While still hot (185° to 195°F/85° to 90°C), the jam should be packed into sterilized jars, which should be filled to the top and well sealed. Because jam thickens as it cools, mixtures containing large pieces of fruit should be allowed to stand for about 10 minutes before packing to improve the distribution of fruit pieces. Alternatively, the jars may be filled, sealed, and processed in a boiling water bath.

Jelly

Whereas jams are prized for their fruitiness, jellies are judged on their clarity. The starting point is cooked fruit juice, produced by gently cooking the chosen fruit in the appropriate amount of water and then allowing it to drip through a fine mesh bag for up to 24 hours, resisting the temptation to squeeze the bag, as this will produce cloudy juice. The juice is cooked with sugar following a technique similar to that for jam, taking great care not to make it dark or syrupy through overboiling. As an alternative to the plate test, jelly can also be easily tested by dripping it from a wooden spoon: if it falls from the spoon in sheets, it is ready.

Compote

Stewed fruit compotes, often sweetened with additional sugar, are generally eaten as accompaniments to other foods, whether as a side dish to cooked meats or fish, spooned over breakfast cereals, or served with custard or cream as a simple dessert. Although they are not made for long keeping, the action of pectin and sugar seen in jams and jellies has the effect of preserving this fruit for several days. Compotes of fruit with honey were made for Roman tables, and similar dishes of sweetened stewed apples with almond milk and fig compote appear in *The Forme of Cury* (1390), the earliest English-language cookery manuscript.

Curd

Fruit curds are very thickly set egg and fruit custards that keep for an extended period of time in the refrigerator. See CUSTARD. Generally made with acidic fruits, particularly citrus, they are eaten on bread as a spreading preserve and used as fillings for tarts or in composite desserts such as lemon meringue pie (lemon curd) or key lime pie (lime curd). Egg yolks, sugar butter, and fruit juice are stirred constantly over a bain-marie or double boiler at gentle heat until a thick set is achieved, then used either immediately or packed into jars and sealed for later use.

Preserved Whole Fruits

There are many ways to preserve whole fruits, usually in syrups. The syrup may be made with sugar, honey, or a mixture of the two; flavored with spices or fragrant oils; or enhanced with alcohol. It might be a heavy, cooked syrup, or a simple one made through the action of the fruit leaching its juices slowly into sugar.

Bottled Fruit

Cooked bottled fruit. In his 1810 guide to preserving fruits, Nicolas Appert suggests simply cleaning fruit, adding it to a glass container, sealing the jar, and following the Appert process of boiling the jar until the fruit is cooked. Since the fruit is softened by cooking during this process, he suggests using slightly underripe but highly flavored fruits from the middle of the season; for some, such as strawberries, he recommends the addition of sugar to bring out their flavor and aroma.

Raw bottled fruit may be kept in sugar without cooking, though for a much shorter period than the cooked version. *Rysteribs*, shaken red currants, are a Danish technique for keeping fruit for a week or so to be eaten as a dessert or as an accompaniment to savory dishes. Cleaned currants are put into a jar with two-thirds their weight in sugar, kept in the fridge, and shaken periodically. In Sweden, *råröd lingonsylt* is a raw-stirred lingonberry jam that keeps the fresh flavor of the berries intact.

Fruit in Syrup

Fruits may be preserved in syrups of varying strength depending on how long you wish to keep them and how sweet you want the end result to be. They are generally blanched or cooked in syrup, then preserved in a sealed jar covered in syrup, often thickened. The blanching and cooking process may be repeated multiple times, for a more candied fruit, or just once, for a fresher presentation. In general, the longer the cooking and the thicker the syrup, the longer the keeping.

Mostarda di frutta. To make this traditional northern Italian preserve, blanched fruits, usually firm ones like quince, pear, or apple that will retain their shape during repeated heating, are simmered in an 80 percent sugar syrup for 10 minutes every 24 hours, for three to five days. The fruit is weighed down and left to soak in the syrup between simmerings. Just before bottling the fruit in its honey-like syrup, mustard oil is added. See MOSTARDA.

Spoon sweets. These Greek sweets are generally made in bite-sized pieces, of a size that will fit neatly into a teaspoon, and served with strong coffee as a snack. Fruits or green nuts like walnuts are simmered in very heavy sugar syrup (a ratio of 4 to 1 sugar to water), left to stand for 24 hours, and bottled in hot syrup. They keep for at least four months in a cool, dark place. See SPOON SWEET.

Fruit in Alcohol

There are several techniques for producing sweet, long-keeping fruit preserves in alcohol.

Cooked fruit. Fruits such as peaches, apricots, or pears are blanched, peeled, and briefly poached in sugar syrup. The fruit is placed in sterilized jars, to which equal quantities of thickened and cooled syrup and the chosen spirit (e.g., brandy, rum, bourbon) are added. The fruit should be kept for a month before eating and is preserved for a long time.

Raw fruit. German *Rumtopf*, French *confiture de vieux garçon*, and Anglo-American tutti-frutti are mixtures of soft summer fruits in rum, kirsch, or brandy. The fruit is gently mixed with up to 60 percent of its weight in sugar, placed in jars, and covered in the chosen alcohol. Left for a month before serving, the fruit must not be stirred until it leaves the jar. Other versions using stone fruits such as cherries depend on shaking to dissolve the sugar. The fruit is combined with 15 percent of its weight in sugar, covered with strong alcohol such as eau de vie, and shaken regularly. Such fruits may be eaten after 6 weeks and will keep for 12 months or so. See TUTTI FRUTTI.

Dried fruit can be soaked in grappa, eau de vie, or sweet wine to flavor and preserve it. No additional sugar is required. The fruit should be soaked for a month before eating and keeps well, improving in flavor for over a year.

See also CANDIED FRUIT; FRUIT; FRUIT PASTE; and MARMALADE.

Appert, Charles. *The Book for All Households; or, the Art of Preserving Animal and Vegetable Substances for Many Years.* Translated by K. G. Bitting. Chicago, 1920.

Henry, Diana. *Salt Sugar Smoke: How to Preserve Fruit, Vegetables, Meat and Fish.* London: Mitchell Beazley, 2012.

Mason, Laura. *Sweets and Sweet Shops.* Princes Risborough, U.K.: Shire, 1999.

Tate & Lyle Refineries Ltd. Home Economics Department. *Sweet Success: The Tate & Lyle Cookbook*. London: Sackett and Marshall, 1977.

Jane Levi

fruitcake is a mixture of butter, sugar, flour, and beaten egg, fragrant with spices and packed with dried fruit. Echoing medieval flavors, it is one of the glories of British baking and long considered a luxury food. According to Barbara Wheaton in *Savoring the Past*, the first "recognizable cakes" appear in La Varenne's 1651 *Le pâtissier francois*. In England, Robert May's 1685 recipe for "an extraordinary good Cake" is a yeast-leavened fruitcake, a style that lasted until the Victorian era. It was Ann Blencowe (1694) who pointed the way to today's cakes by using whisked eggs to aerate her yeast-free Brandy Cake.

Until the early nineteenth century, making a fruitcake, also known as a plum cake, was time-consuming: butter needed to be washed and rinsed in rosewater; the sugar was pounded and sieved; currants were sorted, washed, and dried; muscatel raisins were de-seeded and chopped; candied citrus peel was thinly sliced; almonds were blanched and slivered; and spices were freshly ground. Egg yolks had to be well beaten and the whites whisked with a wooden fork for hours until stiff. See WHISKS AND BEATERS. The cake mixture was spooned into a tin ring or a wooden "garth" resting on a metal sheet and lined with layers of paper to prevent scorching. Hours earlier the wood-fired bread oven had been heated with bundles of dry wood, then raked clear of ashes so that the temperature could be judged by sprinkling flour on the oven floor. See MEASUREMENT. The cake baked in the heat stored in the brickwork.

When the cast-iron cooking stove with its closed oven and more controllable temperature was introduced during the nineteenth century, cake making became easier, which in turn led to many more recipes. Mrs. Beeton (1861) includes 10 fruitcake recipes with beaten eggs and sometimes bicarbonate of soda to leaven the mixture. She also gives a recipe for an "economical" fruitcake. See BEETON, ISABELLA and CHEMICAL LEAVENERS.

Various ways have been devised to ensure that a cake made with less butter, sugar, or dried fruit than usual is still satisfying. A "boiled" fruitcake is made by first simmering dried fruit in milk or water before cooling and adding to the mixture, a method that helps to ensure a moist cake. Australian bakers sometimes add crushed pineapple to a fruitcake mixture to obtain a similar result. Particularly ingenious solutions were found during British wartime food rationing, such as a Christmas cake recipe advising that grated carrots could replace dried fruit, and gravy browning would improve the color of a fruitcake that lacked black treacle.

Regional and seasonal versions of fruitcake represent valued traditions. Simnel cakes, the light fruitcakes with a layer of marzipan baked into the center and associated with Mothering Sunday and Easter, were originally identified with certain towns in the north of England. See MARZIPAN. Scotland's Dundee cake, a light fruitcake with a crust of toasted almonds, is popular throughout Britain, whereas Scotch or black bun, a dark fruitcake enclosed in pastry and baked to celebrate Hogmanay, is rarely found south of the border. Bara brith is still baked today in Wales, and even in England. French bakers respect the origin of their fruitcakes and name them *le plum cake* and *le gâteau anglais*. Both are light mixtures in the style of a Genoa cake, or a guard's luncheon cake—a fruitcake served at the end of the midday meal in Victorian and Edwardian London, mainly in gentlemen's clubs. Although fruitcakes are normally baked in a round or square tin, some American fruitcakes are baked in a ring mold and encrusted with glazed candied fruits and nuts. See CANDIED FRUIT and DRIED FRUIT. Commercially prepared fruitcakes in this style, packaged in decorative tins, are available for sale online. During the Christmas season, thousands are shipped throughout the United States; a particular favorite comes from the Collin Street Bakery in Corsicana, Texas, whose family recipe, studded with pecans, is said to date from 1896.

The association of rich fruitcakes with the past has given them considerable cultural significance in Britain. During the seventeenth century, the cakes were iced with a poured sugar syrup, dried in the doorway of the oven. Opaque icing made with sugar and egg whites (later known as "royal icing") dates from early in the following century, with the next advance credited to Mrs. Raffald (*The Experienced English Housekeeper*, 1769), who introduced the custom of placing a layer of marzipan between the cake and the icing. See ICING. This style of iced fruitcake has become the epitome of celebration.

Fruitcakes intended for weddings, anniversaries, and Christmas are usually made well ahead to allow the flavor to mature; they are iced not long before the celebration. A Twelfth Night cake—the forerunner of the traditional Christmas cake—is a fruitcake made to celebrate the feast of Epiphany on 6 January, which should "eat well if twelve months old," as Dr. William Kitchiner wrote in *The Cook's Oracle* (1817). See TWELFTH NIGHT CAKE. Adding extra alcohol to a baked fruitcake with regular doses of brandy or sherry trickled into small holes in its base enhances both the cake's flavor and keeping quality.

The finest celebration fruitcake should be capable of being divided into numerous small portions suitable for serving to a large number of guests. Moreover, the cutting of a wedding cake is a significant moment during the celebration when the married couple both hold the knife to symbolize their new life together. See WEDDING CAKE. And by tradition the small cake at the summit of a tiered wedding cake is reserved for celebrating the christening of the firstborn.

See also BIRTH; CAKE; and WEDDING.

Beeton, Isabella. *The Book of Household Management*, pp. 854–856, 853–862. London: Ward Lock, 1861.
Henisch, Bridget Ann. *Cakes and Characters: An English Christmas Tradition*, pp. 203–213. London: Prospect, 1984.

Geraldene Holt

Fry's

See CADBURY.

fudge is a semisoft confection of American origin, also popular in Canada and the United Kingdom. From its first appearance in newspapers, magazines, cookbooks, and advertising pamphlets in the 1880s, fudge was promoted to the home cook and amateur candy maker as an innocent pleasure suitable for the domestic environment. Fudge was among the first candies to escape both the sexual overtones of luxury bonbons and the vulgar associations of penny candy. See BONBONS and PENNY CANDY. Early handmade fudge was cut into squares or diamonds, heightening the contrast to the sophistication of professional confectionery. Fudge's artlessness actually enhanced its appeal in genteel circles.

By the 1880s, due to improved processing methods, both the granulated sugar used to make fudge and the chocolate that was its preferred flavoring had become inexpensive. See CHOCOLATE, POST-COLUMBIAN and SUGAR REFINING. As sugar and chocolate became everyday staples, the world of confectionery goods that had once catered to wealthy male consumers was democratized and feminized. Fudge epitomized both trends. At the turn of the century, fudge-making and taffy-pulling parties for children became fashionable. Candy in this form was deemed a wholesome, even nutritious, treat. See CHILDREN'S CANDY and TAFFY.

An 1880s fudge-making fad among students at elite American women's colleges, especially Vassar, Wellesley, and Smith, fostered the use of the new creation. The young women made fudge in their dormitory rooms, often in tin boxes balanced on the chimneys of spirit lamps, and later in chafing dishes. (Occasionally, fire rather than fudge resulted.) One Vassar student is said to have made 30 pounds of chocolate fudge for an 1888 senior-class fundraiser. The Baker Chocolate Company of Dorchester, Massachusetts, manufactured unsweetened chocolate in tablet and powdered form that was featured in many fudge recipes. In turn, a Baker's advertising booklet "Choice Recipes" (published in 1902 in Dorchester, Massachusetts), by famed cooking teacher Maria Parloa and others, publicized college fudge. See BAKER'S.

Its identification with feminine and domestic leisure, its use as a homemade gift and an item for sale at school fairs and church bazaars, and its ritual integration into holiday celebrations made fudge instrumental in altering candy's rather extreme reputation as either a prestige good or a lower-class pleasure. Yet from the beginning, this homespun sweet was also important commercially. Fudge has been sold in candy shops and tourist spots since the late 1880s. Some fudge purveyors on Mackinac Island, Michigan, have been in business continuously since then.

Based on a supersaturated sugar solution devoid of nutritional value, fudge nevertheless received broad endorsement from an earlier generation of gastronomic trendsetters. Many cookbooks and women's magazines published after 1890, including the souvenir cookbook from the 1893 World Columbian Exposition compiled by socially prominent women, and the influential *Boston Cooking School Magazine*, contain fudge recipes. As recently as the 1980s, reputable nutritionists recommended fudge as an innocuous source of quick energy.

A crystalline candy, fudge is firmer than fondant yet softer than caramels, the sweets that are likely antecedents. See FONDANT and CARAMELS. Traditionally, fudge is made by gently boiling granulated sugar and milk to the soft-ball stage (234° to 240°F/ 112° to 115°C); adding butter; cooling the mixture somewhat (120°F/49°C); then beating until thick, creamy, and less glossy. See STAGES OF SUGAR SYRUP. Allowing the solution to cool before beating encourages the growth of small sugar crystals, essential to fudge's characteristic smooth consistency. To further encourage crystallization, marshmallow, corn syrup, invert sugar (a commercial fructose/glucose mixture), or fondant may be added. Fudge is poured while warm, then cooled completely before cutting into squares.

Along with chocolate, the earliest fudge flavorings included vanilla, butterscotch, maple sugar, and coconut. See BUTTERSCOTCH; COCONUT; MAPLE SUGARING; and VANILLA. The term "penuche" for brown-sugar fudge (early variants include *penucio, ponouchi,* and *penuci*) derives from the Mexican Spanish *panocha,* meaning coarse brown sugar. See SUGAR. Flavorings vary according to regional and national tastes, as well as current fashion. Rum-raisin and toffee are preferred in Britain, peanut butter in the United States. Louisiana pralines are essentially fudge-enrobed nut clusters. See PRALINE. Modern flavor innovations for fudge, such as cappuccino and salted caramel, abound. Nuts, especially peanuts, walnuts, and pecans, are often added to the mixture. See NUTS. Scottish tablet, a dense candy made of superfine sugar, condensed milk, butter, vanilla, and, optionally, whiskey and nuts, is sometimes identified as fudge. Fudge lends itself to embellishment, a fact reflected in lengthy product names, such as chocolate pecan brown sugar fudge. For many, fudge is now virtually synonymous with chocolate, and as an adjective, the term denotes the inclusion of chocolate in a dish, as in "fudge brownie" or "fudge sauce."

The origins of the word "fudge" (candy) are unknown, although the verbs "fudge" (meaning to fit together in a makeshift manner) and "fadge" (to cobble together) suggest intriguing possibilities, as does the meaning of "fudge" as nonsense. An 1883 article in the *New York Times,* "The Origin of Fudge," refers to one Captain Fudge, in the time of Charles II, who was so renowned for lying to his superiors that sailors would cry, "You fudge it" when they heard a lie. Indisputably, both the term "fudge" and the aroma of this sweetmeat were in the late Victorian air.

See also HARD CANDY.

Benning, Lee Edwards. *Oh, Fudge! A Celebration of America's Favorite Candy.* New York: Henry Holt, 1990.

Cooper, Gail. "Love, War, and Chocolate." In *His and Hers: Gender, Consumption, and Technology,* edited by Roger Horowitz and Arwen Mohun, pp. 67–94. Charlottesville: University Press of Virginia, 1998.

Woloson, Wendy A. *Refined Tastes: Sugar, Confectionery, and Consumers in Nineteenth-Century America.* Baltimore: Johns Hopkins University Press, 2002.

Keith Stavely and Kathleen Fitzgerald

funerals, or death rites, have historically been associated with foods that carry symbolic meaning. For the departed, sweet food and drink might be a necessary ingredient on the route to a successful afterlife, whether buried with them (as in the fruits found in ancient Egyptian burials, or the wine in Celtic graves of around 500 B.C.E.); left with the body by mourners as offerings (as in Ming and Song dynasty funerals in China); or ceremonially prepared and eaten in the presence of the dead person to ensure that his or her spirit departs in peace (as in ancient Greece). Throughout history funeral or wake food has operated as an important marker of the departed's status and respectability within the community, a convivial, generous gesture sent from beyond the grave. For the living, food may serve a specific ritual purpose, or it may simply be there to sustain emotionally and physically exhausted mourners who have stayed up all night at a wake or traveled a long distance to attend the funeral. In some rituals, sweet foods and drinks in particular play symbolic and practical roles, whether sustaining the living or appeasing the dead.

Tradition plays an important part in what is served at funerals, and even though the history that gives meaning to some habits may be forgotten, the foods themselves persist. The sweets and biscuits served in many European countries, particularly Italy, on All Soul's Day (the feast of commemoration of the dead) are often bean shaped, an echo of the black beans used in the ancient Roman ceremony of Lemuria, when ancestral ghosts were expiated. Currently, confections in the shape of bones and skulls often feature, as in the Mexican Day of the Dead celebrations, where sugar work reaches its peak in *calaveras*, perfect replicas of human skulls in white sugar, colorfully decorated and available in any desired size. See DAY OF THE DEAD. A more recent Mexican American tradition calls for *pan de muertos*, a rich coffee cake, ideally in the shape of a skull and decorated with meringues or pastry in the shape of tears or bones.

Many of the sweet funeral traditions of Anglo-Saxon culture appear to have roots in rural European communities, such as the traditional sweetened raisin pie still served by the Amish and Pennsylvania Dutch in the United States. See PENNSYLVANIA DUTCH. From at least the sixteenth century onward, it was most common in northern Europe for cakes, sweet spiced buns, or biscuits to be served with wine—either sweet wines like sherry or port or wines sweetened with sugar and mulled—or ale, either before departure to the funeral, as at the funeral for Samuel Pepys's brother in 1664, or afterwards. See FORTIFIED WINE and MULLED WINE. Similar cake-based refreshments were supplied to wake-keepers and funeral attendees in rural Ireland in the nineteenth and twentieth centuries. The Jamaican "nine nights" of wake and funerals feature cassava-based bammy, both to speed the spirit to the next world and to feed the mourners, while the corpse is sent to the grave with johnnycakes, a slightly sweetened cornbread, to ease the journey to the afterlife. In Hungary and Estonia, sweet cakes or pastries and wine or vodka are still served in the graveyard immediately after the funeral, in advance of the funerary feast.

Funeral biscuits were a particularly strong tradition in England, the Netherlands, Germany, and the United States—in some places until the late nineteenth century. Their exact composition varied according to location, but in England they were usually either a light sugared sponge biscuit, like a Savoy, Naples, or boudoir biscuit, or a shortbread, often with caraway seeds, and in the United States they were often sweetened with molasses. Decorated with hearts, the initials of the dead, and other suitable memorial symbols or wrapped in a commemorative paper, they were sometimes not eaten but kept as mementos for many years.

Although a lot of funeral feasts are savory, there are numerous examples of traditional funeral sweets and cakes around the world. In Iran, tea is served with dates and a sweet halvah of flour, sugar, and saffron at the final memorial service, and several Muslim countries follow the tradition of serving versions of halvah of ground nuts, flour, honey, and sesame or other flavorings. Orthodox Christian ceremony (including Greek, Romanian, Bulgarian, and Ukrainian) demands *kolyva*, a dish of boiled hulled wheat, to symbolize the resurrection, spiced and sweetened to symbolize the sweetness of heaven and God, and mixed with chopped walnuts, almonds, and other flavorings, such as sesame or parsley. See HALVAH and WHEAT BERRIES. The mixture is spread onto a tray and decorated with icing sugar and almonds, and served to everyone as they leave the funeral. In Tonga, the traditional sweet *topai* (or doughboy), boiled and served with sugar and coconut milk syrup, is commonly served at funerals, partly because it is so easy to prepare for large numbers of people. At Chinese funerals, mourners may be given a small piece of candy to consume before their return home, along with traditional red envelopes containing a coin, and perhaps more candy.

Funeral eating provides a means for the family and friends of the dead to mark their loved one's passing, cementing their continuing presence in the memory of a community of mourners, commemorating them with a meal or refreshment, and ensuring that the spirit is sent off in suitable style. As the *Tibetan Book of the Dead* has it, if you know how to die, you will know how to live (and vice versa)—so there is a lot to be said for doing it sweetly.

See also CHINA; ITALY; MEXICO; and UNITED KINGDOM.

Bendann, Effie. *Death Customs: An Analytical Study of Burial Rites.* London: Kegan Paul, Trench, Trubner & Co., 1930.

Brears, Peter, "Arvals, Wakes, and Month's Minds: Food for Funerals" in *Food and the Rites of Passage*, edited by Laura Mason, 87–114. Totnes, U.K.: Prospect, 2002.

Kremezi, Aglaia. "Kollyva, the Age-Old Greek Memorial Sweet." *Aglaia's Table* (blog). http://www.aglaiakremezi.

com/articles/general/kollyva-age-old-greek-memorial-sweet.html (accessed 18 September 2014).
Riley, Gillian. "Beans for the Dead." In *Proceedings of the Oxford Symposium on Food & Cookery, 1990: Feasting and Fasting,* edited by Harlan Walker, 173–174. London: Prospect, 1990.
Rogak, Lisa. *Death Warmed Over: Funeral Food, Rituals and Customs from Around the World.* Berkeley, Calif.: Ten Speed, 2004.
Thursby, Jacqueline S. *Funeral Festivals in America: Rituals for the Living.* Lexington: University Press of Kentucky, 2006.

Jane Levi

funnel cake

See FRIED DOUGH and FAIRS.

gag candy encompasses the candies with extreme flavors, funny names, unexpected ingredients, and surprising shapes that most children love. Some unusual candies, such as wax lips, were first manufactured in the nineteenth century. During the 1920s, the novelty candy trade offered chocolate-covered onions and cheese, and sweet pipes with tobacco made of little flakes of licorice.

A related genre was candy cigarettes made from chocolate or bubble gum (both wrapped in white paper), or from a chalky-tasting mixture of sugar and cornstarch. White with a pink tip, the latter looked something like real cigarettes. Some brands were made to exude a puff of powdery sugar if you blew into them, in imitation of smoke. Candy was packed into cellophane-wrapped, cigarette-sized packages emblazoned with real tobacco brands, such as Camel, Marlboro, and Chesterfield, but some companies used names that were merely evocative of the real thing, such as Lucky Star and Roundup, rather than actual brand names. In the 1960s, as concern about the health effects of cigarette smoking emerged, so did the fear that these candies might encourage children to smoke later in life. In response, some manufacturers altered their products. The word "cigarette" disappeared, and the products were renamed "candy sticks" or "stix." Efforts to ban the sale and manufacture of candy cigarettes failed in the United States, although other countries have banned them.

During the 1950s, large numbers of American children began celebrating Halloween by going door to door "trick or treating" for candy. See HALLOWEEN. Many gag candies were created to tap into the massive sales of candy around this holiday. Ferrara Pan Candy Company, a Chicago firm, already included Boston Baked Beans (candy-coated peanuts) and cinnamon-flavored Redhots in its product line; in 1954 it added the hotter-still jawbreaker-size Atomic Fireballs and in 1962 introduced very sour lemon drops. Just Born, makers of Peeps, created Hot Tamales, which look nothing like tamales but have a hot cinnamon flavor. See PEEPS. Special gag candies have been developed for other holidays as well. For Easter, there is a realistic-looking egg that bounces, and for a Christmas stocking stuffer, coal candy made from hard licorice is sold in a miniature coal scuttle with a tiny hammer for breaking it up.

Gag candies have also been associated with children's movies. Breaker Confections, a Chicago candy company, bought the rights to the Willy Wonka name from the 1971 musical film *Willy Wonka & the Chocolate Factory* and produced a series of candies, including "Everlasting Gobstoppers," mentioned in the movie. The company was eventually acquired by Nestlé, which began producing Wonka Bars in 1998. Sales were not strong, so Nestlé decided to discontinue the line. But in 2000, when director Tim Burton announced plans to remake the film, Nestlé jumped at the chance for product placement in the movie, providing hundreds of candy bars and thousands of props, and engaged in a massive promotional campaign for both the movie and the candy. The new movie was a tremendous success when it was released in 2005, as were the Nestlé candies featuring a cartoon likeness of Willy Wonka.

Certain gag candies cause unusual effects. Bloody Mouth Candy, for instance, is a hard candy that tints the eater's saliva blood red when chewed. Other candies produce black, blue, or green colors. Still other candies have shockingly unexpected flavors and

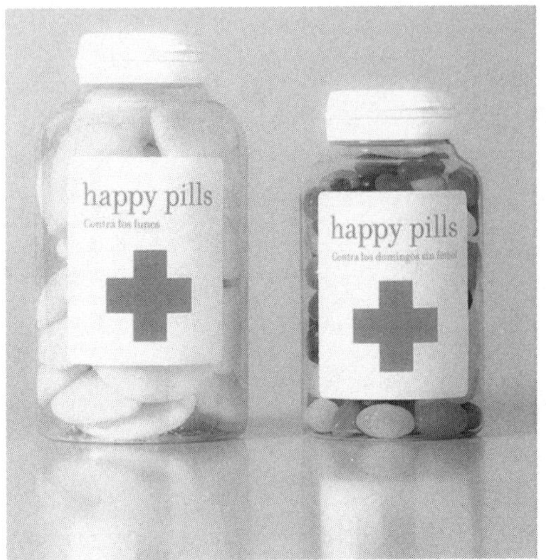

Vials and bottles filled with candy pills, often included in toy "Doctor" and "Nurse" kits, have been around for decades. This vial was designed by studio m for the candy store Happy Pills in Barcelona, Spain. © HAPPY PILLS

sensations, such as garlicky, mustardy, fishy, soapy, or salty flavors. Three unusual candies were hallmarks of the 1970s. General Foods released Pop Rocks in 1975, a hard candy with air pockets that contained carbonation, causing a crackling sensation when they melted in the mouth. Rumor had it that Pop Rocks exploded in the stomach, leading the company to discontinue the candy. Other unusual candies of the era included Zotz, a very tart hard candy that fizzed in the mouth, and orange and strawberry Space Dust, another crackling candy.

Vials and bottles filled with candy pills, often included in toy "doctor" and "nurse" kits, have been around for decades. As was the case with candy cigarettes, some authorities warned that children would confuse actual medication with candy, with potentially harmful or even lethal consequences. Nonetheless, candy pills remain on the market, updated with humorous labels such as "Madvil," "Damitol," and "Chill Pills."

In the 1980s manufacturers began to produce "gross-out" candy, such as Chocolate Snotty Noses, Dinosaur Dollops, White Chocolate Maggots, and Ear Wax Candy. Gelatin-based gummi candy lends itself to molding in all sorts of shapes and colors, and gummi worms are a perennial favorite. See GUMMIES and HARIBO. The realistic brown Gummy Earthworms have delighted children—and surprised fishermen. The NECCO candy company offers strongly flavored gummies in the shape of feet—Sour Stinky Feet and Hot Stinky Feet. See NECCO. Others have produced "erotic" sweets with anatomically explicit shapes.

All these candies pale before the myriad gross-out candies of the twenty-first century. In 2001 the Jelly Belly Candy Company released Bertie Bott's Every Flavour Beans in association with J. K. Rowling's Harry Potter books and movies. Flavors include Rotten Egg, Vomit, and Earthworm. The Danish candy company Dracco sells candy-pooping dogs, scorpion lollipops, and candy tongue tattoos. Fear Factor candy, based on the television series, includes crunchy worm larvae, slimy octopi, and frogs' legs served with a blood-red candy sauce. According to manufacturers, gross-out candy is one the fastest-growing segments of the candy market.

See also CANDY; CHILDREN'S CANDY; CHEWING GUM; EXTREME CANDY; and PENNY CANDY.

Richardson, Tim. *Sweets: A History of Candy*. New York: Bloomsbury, 2002.

Smith, Andrew F. *Junk Food and Fast Food: An Encyclopedia of What We Love to Eat*. Santa Barbara, Calif.: Greenwood, 2012.

Andrew F. Smith

galette is a flat, round cake made with pastry dough (short crust or puff pastry) and sometimes filled with rich frangipane. See FRANGIPANE. There are many kinds of galette, the most famous being the *galette des rois* (king cake) that dates at least to the Middle Ages. The *galette des rois* that is traditionally served on Epiphany contains a hidden bean or porcelain figure. The guest who gets the slice of cake with the bean is the "king" of the day or the feast. P. J. B. Le Grand d'Aussy writes in *Histoire de la vie privée des Français* (1782) that the *galette des rois* (also called a *gâteau à fève*, bean cake) was served on any joyous occasion, such as a baptism. He also writes that hot galettes were sold in the streets, and that "galette chaudes" was one of the famed street cries of Paris in the thirteenth century.

A galette can be a simple snack, as in the beloved children's story "Roule Galette," in which an old lady sweeps up bits of grain left in the granary to make a cake for her husband. In some areas of France, particularly in the South, a galette is made of brioche and flavored with lemon zest. In Normandy, galettes are made with puff pastry and are filled with fruit jam and crème fraîche. In France and French Canada, galette can also designate a cookie made from pastry dough covered in sugar and baked; in Brittany, the term designates a savory, filled buckwheat crêpe. In his nineteenth-century *Dictionnaire universel de cuisine pratique* (1894–1906), Joseph Favre laments that the galette is a heavy and indigestible cake, which suggests that the pastry chef's art of galette making has improved since Favre's time.

See also CHILDREN'S LITERATURE; FRANCE; PASTRY, PUFF; and TWELFTH NIGHT CAKE.

Gault, Henri, and Christian Millau. *Guide gourmand de la France*. Paris: Librairie Hachette, 1970.
Loomis, Susan Herrmann. *French Farmhouse Cookbook*. New York: Workman, 1996.

Kyri W. Claflin

gastris, an ancient Greek sweetmeat of the second century B.C.E. and a regional specialty of Crete, is important not just intrinsically but as a window into a lost world. Hardly any instructions for making sweets survive from classical Greece. The recipe is known because it happens to be quoted in the *Deipnosophists* of Athenaeus (book 14, 647d), a rich source for Greek and Roman food history written about 200 C.E.:

> Sweet almonds, hazelnuts, bitter almonds, poppy seeds: roast, watching them carefully, and pound well in a clean mortar. When well mixed, put into a small pan with boiled honey to moisten, adding plenty of pepper. It turns black because of the poppy. Flatten out into a square. Now pound some white sesame, moisten with boiled honey, and stretch two sheets of this, one below and the other above, so that the black is in the middle, and divide into shapes.

These instructions are one of the few remaining fragments of an ancient manual of bread and cake making by Chrysippus of Tyana in eastern Anatolia. He wrote in Greek at a time when eastern luxuries, captured in Roman wars, were all the rage in newly rich Italy. His audience may have consisted equally of educated Romans (Greek was the usual medium for scientific and technical texts) and their Greek-speaking cooks. This sweetmeat, its lost source, and its author are therefore evidence of an almost forgotten Mediterranean-wide gastronomic culture, as well as proof of a tradition of sweet specialties specific to certain Greek cities. All ingredients in gastris would have been locally sourced, with one exception: pepper, a rare, costly, and health-giving spice from southern India, which adds bite and exoticism. Thanks not least to Chrysippus himself, such local specialties would soon no longer remain local.

Dalby, Andrew. *Siren Feasts: A History of Food and Gastronomy in Greece*, pp. 162–165. London: Routledge, 1996.
Dalby, Andrew Dalby, and Sally Grainger. *The Classical Cookbook*, pp. 96–97. 2d ed. London: British Museum Press, 2012.
Olson, S. Douglas, ed. and trans. *Athenaeus: The Learned Banqueters*. Vol. 7. Cambridge, Mass.: Harvard University Press, 2011.

Andrew Dalby

gelatin, the transparent protein extract (collagen) that is crucial for holding liquids in suspension, gives shimmering architectural jellies, Bavarian creams, and similar preparations their drama. Water molecules bond with gelatin molecules to produce an elastic solid (colloidal sol). About 7 grams (1 tablespoon) of gelatin will bind a pint of liquid. Powdered, granular, or sheets of commercial gelatin first need to be hydrated in liquid three to four times their volume; they are then activated by heating (usually the soaking bath), or by adding a sheet to the hot liquid preparation. In the refrigerator, the gelatin solidifies by cooling slowly to a lower temperature. The gelatin network continues to tighten its water-holding capacity, but after aging over a few days, the bonds begin to break and liquid escapes (syneresis).

Cooks originally boiled calves' feet, skin, connective tissue, hartshorn shavings, or ivory dust to extract gelatin. Coastal cooks have used carrageenan and agar-agar made from red seaweeds such as Irish moss or dulse. In addition, isinglass, commercially extracted from the air bladders of some fish, also contains jelling compounds. (Cooked fruit purées, high in pectin, may also be molded.)

A molded gelatin dish is more easily released if the form is thinly coated with salad oil beforehand. When dipped in lukewarm water, the oil becomes fluid, but to break the 15 pounds of air pressure per square inch that holds the gelatin in the mold, the edges need to be loosened to allow air between the gelatin and container so that the gelatin will slide out.

See also GELATIN DESSERTS.

Charley, Helen. 1982. *Food Science.* New York: Wiley.
Vaclavik, Vickie, and Elizabeth W. Christian. 2007. *Essentials of Food Science.* New York: Springer.

Susan M. Rossi-Wilcox

gelatin desserts, also known as jellies, are made by a centuries-old practice that attests to the maker's exceptional skill. With today's ready-to-use commercial products, the triumph of molded gelatins sparkling on a candlelit mahogany dessert board to the admiration of dinner guests has been forgotten.

Gelatins can vary in flavor, shape, texture, color, and content. Thanks to its transparency and water-holding capacity as a setting agent, gelatin is one of the most versatile ingredients in a dessert maker's repertoire. The dazzling array of sweets that can be made from gelatin depends on several factors: the amount of liquid used, the flavoring components, and the treatment of the gelatin during the various phases of jelling: syrupy; slightly thickened; very thick; set, but not firm; firmly set.

When just ready to set, a fruit juice and gelatin mixture can be whipped into a light, opaque foam that is served after it has chilled and set. This type of gelatin foam is known as a whip, snow, or fluff. Fruit purée and chantilly (whipped cream) are often added to the foam to lend richness, and clear, colorful gelatin cubes or other ingredients may be folded in for embellishment. Sponges are similar to whips but incorporate beaten egg whites for more ethereal lightness. Both sponges and whips can be frozen to produce a semifreddo (the gelatin helps prevent the growth of large ice crystals). See DESSERTS, FROZEN. Whipped gelatin preparations may also be used as jelly-roll fillings and for unbaked fruit or cream pies. See PIE. For pies and tarts decorated with fruits, clear gelatin provides a shiny surface and helps keep the fruits and berries fresh. Although most fruits, including pineapple, can be treated this way, fresh pineapple must first be boiled for at least two minutes to denature the enzyme bromelain, which would otherwise liquefy the gelatin.

Classic French desserts, such as cold soufflés, Bavarian creams, and charlotte russes, all incorporate

After Jell-O was introduced in 1900, gelatin desserts quickly became mainstream in the United States, since housewives had only to stir the brightly colored fruit-flavored powder with water and chill it to set. This circa 1910 advertisement from the Genesee Pure Food Company was accompanied by recipes for each dessert. At the time, Jell-O came in seven flavors and cost 10 cents a package.

an egg-based custard (crème anglaise), whipped cream, fruit purée, and flavoring, usually a liqueur, which are stabilized with gelatin. See CHARLOTTE; DESSERTS, CHILLED; and SOUFFLÉ. These sweet jellies are beaten over ice until they begin to set; they are then poured into a distinctive mold and chilled before serving. A traditional Bavarian cream is molded in a ring form so that the accompanying sauce can fill the center, while a cold soufflé is served in ramekins or from a standard soufflé dish. A removable wax paper or tinfoil collar allows the mixture to set inches above the dish to resemble the rise of a hot soufflé. A charlotte russe is molded in a special tin that has been lined with a layer of sponge cake or ladyfingers. See SPONGE CAKE. The ingredients for these desserts can range from chocolate to any sweetened purée. For more predictable results, contemporary recipes for sweet mousses (mousselines) often suggest using gelatin in place of the tragacanth gum called for in older recipes. See MOUSSE and TRAGACANTH.

Eighteenth-century wooden molds were replaced by salt-glazed pottery and, later, by creamware manufactured by Spode, Wedgwood, and other firms. Fruits, such as carved melons or citrus rinds, have also served as molds to highlight the fruit used. When decorating a mold, a thin layer of the clear gelatin should first be poured into the form and allowed to congeal, to become the top layer of the unmolded jelly. Fruits, flowers, herbs, gold or silver leaf, and other edibles are held in place by this initial film, which is then covered with additional layers. Great care must be taken in the layering process. If too much gelatin mixture is added, lighter fruits such as peaches, strawberries, blueberries, mandarin oranges, and sliced bananas will float out of place. Each succeeding layer of gelatin should be syrupy and at nearly room temperature. If the gelatin is too warm, it will liquefy the layer below; if too stiff, air pockets will form and affect the transparency and surface smoothness. For large architectural jellies, individual layers can be molded in increasingly larger forms, including cake and pie pans, which will become distinctive features in the finished dessert. All gelatins must be carefully unmolded from the base upward. By temporarily placing skewers throughout an elaborated layered jelly, the piece can be re-refrigerated to ensure that all the layers bond.

When a lower ratio of liquid is used, gelatin produces a chewable gum. Firmly set jelly can be cut into shapes with cookie cutters or made into sweets. Turkish paste is a jelly made from cooked fruit or dried-fruit purée cut into squares and coated with powdered sugar or nuts. See LOKUM. Homemade marshmallows as well as the candy called pastels are made by incorporating whipped egg whites into syrupy gelatin and beating the mixture. See MARSHMALLOWS.

In the United States, gelatin desserts quickly became mainstream with the introduction of the commercial brand Jell-O in 1900 by the Genesee Pure Food Company. This brightly colored fruit-flavored powder was extremely easy to use; it had only to be stirred with water and chilled to set. By the mid-twentieth century Jell-O, and all sorts of desserts and salads based on it, had become a quintessential American food, living up to its early moniker as "America's Most Famous Dessert."

The popularity of gelatin desserts has not waned, but the desserts themselves have been reconfigured for a more sophisticated audience. Although ready-made gelatin mixes like Jell-O line grocers' shelves, fashionable restaurants nevertheless frequently include house-made gelatin-dependent desserts or elements in their elaborately constructed presentations.

See also GELATIN.

Child, Julia, Louisette Bertholle, and Simone Beck. *Mastering the Art of French Cooking*. New York: Knopf, 1961.

Escoffier, A. *The Escoffier Cook Book: A Guide to the Fine Art of Cookery*. New York: Crown, 1941.

Susan M. Rossi-Wilcox

gelt, chocolate "coins" (from the Yiddish געלט, for money or gold), are given to children as part of the current Jewish celebration of Hanukkah, the holiday commemorating the victory of the Maccabees over the Seleucid Greeks in 165 B.C.E. Special triumphal coins were struck after the victory, possibly serving as the inspiration for modern Hanukkah gelt. In any case, gelt started out as real coins given out, variously, as donations to the poor for ritual candles, as an incentive for children to study (as Maimonides taught), or as a bonus to teachers.

How chocolate gelt replaced real coins is a matter of colorful speculation, including the alleged prominence of Jews in eighteenth- and nineteenth-century chocolate manufacture. More concretely, in Belgium and the Netherlands, the feast of St. Nicholas (Sinterklaas or Santa Claus), which takes place on 6 December during the heart of the Hanukkah season (ranging from late November to late December), includes the offering of both chocolate and real coins (*Geld*) to begging students and children. It would be a mistake to draw too close a connection between this Christian tradition and Chanukah gelt—gelt is today a major part of Chanukah observance in Israel—but in America, where cultural assimilation has increasingly established Chanukah as a Jewish "Christmas," gelt can function as a comfortable alternative to Christmas presents. From modest beginnings by the U.S. chocolatiers Lofts and Barton's in the 1920s, the industry now offers the pious parent gold or silver foil-wrapped kosher-neutral (*pareve*), dairy (*milchik*), nut-free, and even Ghanaian fair-trade gelt.

See also HANUKKAH and JUDAISM.

Prinz, Deborah. "Christmas and Chanukah Chocolate Melt Together." *Petits Propos Culinaires* 89 (January 2010): 18–22.

Raymond Sokolov

gender in relation to sweets is a complex and multilayered subject, at least in Western societies. The English language adage "girls are made of sugar and spice and everything nice" encapsulates a widespread perception, reinforced by advertising and popular culture, that pairs women with sweetness and desserts. Countless Hollywood films present women gorging on ice cream and other sweets when abandoned by a lover or otherwise sad. This kind of response is rarely depicted with males, unless they are weak and overweight characters marked as "losers." In contemporary U.S. popular culture, whose global impact and marketing penetration are difficult to deny, women are presented as closely connected with and attracted to chocolate. In particular, bonbons and bite-sized delights reflect ideals of moderation while simultaneously expressing acceptable forms of eroticism and indulgence that can be enjoyed in solitary rapture. See BONBONS.

Rationalizations of these representations vary from scientific arguments that point to serotonin and dopamine levels in the premenstrual period and the significance of phenyl ethylamine and its endorphin-like effects on women's moods, to moral discourses that decry women's weakness and their inability to control themselves. Larger portions of chocolate are instead perceived as acceptable for male consumption—bars were provided to soldiers during World War II and many Europeans still remember American GIs distributing chocolate as they entered liberated territories. See MILITARY. In reaction, feminists have been keen to point out how these social customs and cultural notions are the result of oppressive power relationships, reinforced by pervasive advertisements that almost exclusively market ingredients and products for the domestic preparation of dessert and cake to women.

Other Times, Other Places

When it comes to sweets and gender, it is important not to generalize Western norms, ideas, and practices, since at other points in space and time the relationship is less marked, as in sub-Saharan Africa or Eastern Asia, or it is structured according to different notions. See SUB-SAHARAN AFRICA and EAST ASIA. For instance, in India, a country where desserts are pervasive and infinitely varied, on Bhai Phota (Brother's Day, also called Bhai Beej) sweets are presented to brothers and male members of the family. In the past, baby boys had their lips smeared with sweet substances before their first feeding, while fish was reserved for girls. Sweets are also strongly associated with weddings, regardless of the couple's religion.

In the Middle Ages, when sugar was still so rare in Europe that it was considered a spice, dessert production tended to fall into the domain of male specialists, especially for upper-class clients or for official occasions such as banquets and celebrations. Not only professional chefs and confectioners, but also pharmacists relied on technical skills honed by years of experience, and they were highly appreciated in the public sphere. In Italy, however, it was not unusual for women to produce pastries for sale, the same way they engaged in fresh pasta manufacture or cooked in family-owned eateries. As for consumption, sugar was not especially connected to gender. Rather, it was an expression of status and wealth due to its high cost. Yet dainty sweets were already associated with women—there is mention of *drageoirs* (elegant containers for sweets) being offered to the female guests at the wedding of Henry IV of England, while males were presented with plates of spices. As with any other edible substance, until the seventeenth century, the physiological qualities of sugar were framed in the medical and nutritional theories that considered the human body as regulated by four humors: blood, yellow bile, black bile (or melancholy), and phlegm, which also fell under the categories of hot, cold, moist, and dry. Although sugar was supposed to help warm the stomach during digestion, it was recommended that women avoid consuming it in excess because its moist nature would increase a woman's inherent moistness, turning her lazy and phlegmatic, while its hotness could make her more choleric and less feminine. See MEDICINAL USES OF SUGAR.

Romantic Sweets

From the eighteenth century on, upper-class women in France and England, as well as in other European countries, gathered in elegant cafés and consumed pastries with their beverages. They also patronized refined confectionery shops whose décor and service catered to the taste of the female clientele. As sugar became more available and its price fell, working-class women were able to add sugar or molasses to their tea, while upper-class women turned more to candies and dainty chocolate. See CHOCOLATE, LUXURY and CHOCOLATES, BOXED. Sweets came to symbolize men's romantic interest in women, a custom that continues today on Valentine's Day and, to a lesser extent, on Mother's Day. See VALENTINE'S DAY. Romantic messages were at times wrapped in paper that carried amorous messages, a peculiarity that is still found in Italian Baci chocolates. The connection between desserts and courtship was reflected also in the popularity of wedding cakes, larger and more spectacular than those used on other occasions, probably an echo of the stunning cakes consumed during noble banquets when sugar was still a luxury. See WEDDING CAKE.

Sex and Religion

Well into the nineteenth century, in Catholic areas of the Mediterranean like Sicily and Spain, nuns were renowned for their confectionery preparation, and in certain places this is still the case. See CONVENT SWEETS. It was not unusual for the daughters of noble families to be forcibly sent to a convent, where they learned to prepare delicious desserts that were then consumed by the upper classes. Nuns renounced the temptations of the flesh but toiled in the kitchen for others' delectation, reinforcing social and gender structures of power. The connection between nuns and sweetness was ironically consecrated by lay desserts such as *barrigas de freiras* (nun's bellies) in Portugal and *pets de nonnes* (nun's farts) in France.

These forms of irreverence connecting sweets and sex have ancient roots. The *minnuzzi ri Sant' Ajita* (Saint Agatha's little breasts) are little cassata cakes with a cherry on top that take their name from the martyr Saint Agatha, who had her breasts cut off. This specialty from Catania, Sicily, dates back to antiquity, when the followers of the goddess Isis—a symbol of motherhood—consumed sweet breast-shaped pastries to worship her. In Rome, the harvest goddess Demeter was associated with honey and flour sweets shaped like female genitalia, and the god Priapus—representing male potency—was honored with penis-shaped pastries. To this day, penis cake pans are available in novelty and sex stores, while erotic cakes shaped as sexual organs or representing sexual acts mark occasions like bachelor and bachelorette parties, where desserts are supposed to allude to upcoming postnuptial pleasures.

Advertising and Popular Culture

As candy and sweets became mass-produced and their consumption expanded during the Gilded Age, advertising and popular culture increasingly connected them to males—especially in the form of candy bars—as a sustaining source of energy and as a remedy against the temptations of alcoholism. See CANDY BAR. Simultaneously, bonbons—pure, graceful, and refined—were gradually presented as objects of female desire. As Western—and in particular American—products are making their way into other markets, these perceptions are being presented to populations that either did not traditionally consume great quantities of sweets or did not attribute any gender connotations to the consumption of sweets. The increased availability of snacks and desserts is thus shaping new needs and desires, influencing gendered notions attached to them.

Banks Nutter, Kathleen. "From Romance to PMS: Images of Women and Chocolate in Twentieth-Century America." In *Edible Ideologies: Food and Meaning*, edited by Kathleen Lebesco and Peter

Naccarato, pp. 199–222. Albany: State University of New York Press, 2008.
Dusselier, Jane. "Bonbons, Lemon Drops, and Oh Henry! Bars: Candy, Consumer Culture, and the Construction of Gender, 1895–1920." In *Kitchen Culture in America: Popular Representations of Food, Gender, and Race*, edited by Sherrie A. Innes, pp. 13–50. Philadelphia: University of Pennsylvania Press, 2001.
Krondl, Michael. *Sweet Invention: A History of Dessert*. Chicago: Chicago Review Press, 2011.
Richardson, Tim. *Sweets: A History of Candy*. New York and London: Bloomsbury, 2002.

Fabio Parasecoli

génoise

See SPONGE CAKE.

Germany is no exception to the general rule: for ancient Germans, as for others, sweetness was rare and highly coveted. Under Roman cultural influence from the first century B.C.E. until the fifth century C.E., apiculture became more sophisticated and honey more available, but the cultivated sweet fruits (cherries, plums, and apples) introduced by the Romans were regarded as a great luxury and reserved for those of high social standing. From the tenth century on, cane sugar from the Mediterranean was available, but for a long time it remained as expensive as exotic spices and was treated like medicine. See MEDICINAL USES OF SUGAR. At the end of the fourteenth century in Cologne, refined sugar was still more expensive than either ginger or pepper, with a pound of loaf sugar worth more than 16 liters of honey. Nevertheless, the quantity of sugar sold steadily rose throughout the fifteenth century, and by the 1450s sugar prices had fallen below those of ginger and pepper. But for far longer than elsewhere in Western Europe, honey was the Germans' sweetener of choice, often combined with sweet and tart fruit. See HONEY.

It was only in the mid-sixteenth century, after the founding of Germany's first sugar refinery in Augsburg in 1573, that sugar began to be indicated for culinary use, supplementing the honey in early gingerbread recipes. Sabine Welser, from a wealthy, patrician family, used sugar very liberally in her manuscript recipes for pies and tarts, and Marx Rumpolt, in his *Ein new Kochbuch* (1581), was the first to include a chapter devoted to *Zucker-Confect*, or sugar confections. Nowhere in his book is honey mentioned, perhaps, as he makes clear, because marzipan and *Zucker-Confect* are banquet foods reserved for the nobility. See MARZIPAN. On the rare, festive occasions when peasants could afford sugar, they tended to use it ostentatiously, sprinkling it over millet gruel, a festive dish served at weddings and christenings until well into the eighteenth century.

As elsewhere in Europe, sugar developed into an indispensable partner for coffee, tea, and hot chocolate. Following the example set by the French court, Germans not only sweetened the new, bitter-tasting beverages with sugar but also served sweet pastries or desserts alongside them, provided by *Conditoren* or *Zuckerbäcker*, literally "sugar bakers." In the seventeenth century Hamburg was the leading center in Germany for sugar refining and the sugar trade, due to the city's large number of Dutch refugees from the Thirty Years' War, who were already familiar with sugar from their Caribbean plantations. See PLANTATIONS, SUGAR; SUGAR REFINING; and SUGAR TRADE.

Scarcity

Sugar production altered dramatically in 1747, when Andreas Sigismund Marggraf and Franz Carl Achard successfully produced sugar from *mangelwurzel* (*Beta vulgaris*), known today as the sugar beet. See SUGAR BEET. In 1800 Germans consumed, on average, 1 kilo of sugar per year, about double what they had eaten a hundred years earlier. However, beet sugar really took off only in the 1840s, and between 1875 and World War I Germany became one of the world's great sugar exporters. Having become accustomed to ample and widely affordable provisions of sugar, Germans were forced to face scarcity due to wars and economic crises. See SUGAR RATIONING. During the British blockade in World War I, even seemingly abundant crops such as potatoes and sugar beets were quickly reduced to scarce commodities as people turned to them to compensate for the lack of fat and meat. In addition, the armament industry used fat and sugar to replace blocked imports of glycerine, which was necessary for the production of nitroglycerine explosives. The government also exported sugar, potatoes, and coal to neutral countries in exchange for raw materials to use in German factories. During World War II women developed their own methods of preparing starch from potatoes and syrup from sugar beets. Culinary ingenuity resulted in ersatz treats such as marzipan look-alikes made from grated potatoes or semolina mixed with a little sugar and artificial bitter-almond flavoring. See TROMPE L'OEIL. Postwar CARE parcels always contained sweet foods such as canned and dried fruits, honey, chocolate, and sugar, making sugar readily available once again. On the Berlin black market in 1947, 1 kilo of sugar could be had for 7 or 8 American cigarettes, while 1 kilo of various kinds of cooking fat cost 23 to 25.

In the 1950s there were still limits on food consumption for most people, but Sundays as well as holidays were once again marked by special meals, including sweets, whether stollen for Christmas or a chocolate pudding for Sunday dessert. See STOLLEN. Despite the overall constraints, concerns about overindulgence set in, and sugar (along with fat and overcooking) came to be regarded as the enemy of good health and slimness. Quark and milk, boiled fish, and boiled eggs were recommended, whereas tortes, chocolate, and whipped cream were blacklisted as sweet indulgences. See TORTE. By the 1980s dieting had become enormously popular, and so-called light products—diet foods with reduced sugar content or artificial sweeteners—proved a very successful new market for the food industry. In 1878 saccharine (first marketed in 1885) had been developed by a German chemist. This first artificial sweetener was readily embraced by the public (thereby alarming the beet-sugar industry), as rising affluence caused health problems such as obesity and diabetes, both of which were discussed as much in 1900 as they are today. In 1937 that original synthetic sweetener was joined by Cyclamat (sodium cyclamate); both stood in for sugar during the war. Today, agave nectar and concentrated fruit juices, mainly from apples, pears, and grapes, as well as all kinds of brown cane sugar and Stevia, are perceived as healthier and are used in place of white beet sugar in so-called health foods and organic products. See AGAVE NECTAR and STEVIA.

Characteristic German Sweets

In Germany, sweet foods are not limited to dessert. It is often said that the combination of spices, sweetness, fruit, and acidity still found in contemporary dishes such as sauerbraten is a German peculiarity, a medieval remnant proving the cuisine's backwardness. But this proclivity for sweet and sour can also be seen as a positive continuum. The French philosopher and politician Michel de Montaigne, traveling in the south of Germany at the end of the sixteenth century, commented favorably upon the meat served with cooked plums, pears, and apple slices, a custom that survives in the form of the poached pears and cranberries served with roast game to this day. In this context, it is interesting to note that with the pseudo-internationalization of food following World War II, Asian cuisine in Germany came to be associated with a number of sweet and sour recipes, typically involving canned pineapple.

Germany has a vast array of candies, many of which come from Haribo's wide selection of fruit gums (most notably Gummi Bears), licorice, chewy fruit candy, and marshmallows. See GUMMIES; HARIBO; LICORICE; and MARSHMALLOWS. In the late nineteenth century the first vending machines began to sell chocolate and other sweets, and later chewing gum and dextrose, often with cheap trinkets or collector's cards thrown in as additional temptations. *Brausepulver*, the German version of sherbet powder, merits special mention in no small part because it features in one of the most sweetly innocent sexual awakenings on film, when the protagonist in *The Tin Drum* (based on Günter Grass's novel) pours it into his girlfriend's belly button, spits into it, and licks up the foaming concoction. See SHERBET POWDER. *Brausepulver* has recently seen a nostalgic comeback. Chocolate remains a popular sweet, typically in the form of *Tafeln*, flat, square 100-gram bars. Germany is split between a recent foodie-driven rise in bitter dark chocolate with its higher cacao content and the much-loved milk chocolate, especially *Kinderschokolade* and the famous *Überraschungseier*, "surprise eggs."

The picture of sweet Germany would be greatly imbalanced without mentioning *Kaffee und Kuchen*, coffee and cake served in the afternoon in private homes or consumed in the country's numerous cafés or *Konditoreien*. See CAFÉ and KUCHEN. It is an informal way to mark a special event with a meal and can also serve as an excuse for (mostly female) friends to meet for a chat, referred to by the old-fashioned term *Kaffeekränzchen* or *Kaffeeklatsch* (coffee klatsch).

Until World War II home baking tended to be the norm, except for large sheet cakes, which in rural areas were brought to the local baker since they did not fit inside domestic ovens, and some households did not even have ovens. However, once the economy began to recover in the 1950s, housewives tended more often to buy prepared goods from the baker or *Konditor*, in particular, *Teilchen* or *Stückchen* (individual portions of cake) and small Danish pastries (*Plundergebäck*) filled with custard, almond paste, or fruit. For more festive occasions simple kuchen (mostly variations on pound cake) were, and still are, replaced by filled and garnished *Torten*, of which the most famous is arguably *Schwarzwälder Kirschtorte*. See BLACK FOREST CAKE. Equally popular for dessert is ice cream, which is served instead of cake in the summer, often in elaborate concoctions involving fruit, sauces, and whipped cream. In many regions, for a quick and simple Saturday lunch, a stew or hearty soup is followed by a sweet dessert. The Pfalz region is known for *Grumbeersupp un Quetschekuche*, potato soup traditionally eaten with a plum sheet cake made with a yeast dough. Once-popular cold fruit soups were formerly served for light summer lunches, a tradition that has nearly disappeared. See SOUP. Other old-fashioned sweet foods, such as baked or steamed yeast dumplings (*Rohr-* or *Dampfnudeln*), remain popular in the south. The dumplings, sometimes filled with fresh fruit or jam and served with vanilla sauce, take the place of cake. See DUMPLINGS. In the winter, baked apples are popular.

Before the days of Dr. Oetker's instant custard powder that need only be mixed with milk and brought to the boil, *Schokoladenpudding* was a favorite chocolate "pudding" made with eggs, like real custard. See OETKER. In many regions a kind of trifle, *Götterspeise* (literally, "the dish of the gods"), is made with custard, cream, jam, or fruit and sponge cake (dark pumpernickel bread is also used in the north). In the north of Germany, *Rote Grütze*, a mix of red fruit and berries thickened with various kinds of starch or gelatin, has been introduced from Scandinavia. See PUDDING and TRIFLE. Throughout Germany, fruit quark and farina pudding are popular, and *Kompott*, stewed fruit, is seeing a comeback.

As for holiday specialties, Easter brings lamb-shaped sponge cakes dusted with confectioner's sugar and bearing a small flag reminiscent of church processions, as well as chocolate bunnies and eggs with various fillings, wrapped in colorful foil. For Carnival a wealth of small pastries deep-fried in lard are made in numerous regional variations. See CARNIVAL; FRIED DOUGH; and HOLIDAY SWEETS. In the Rhineland, with its riotous parades, *Kamellen* (the local dialect for *Karamellen*, hard candies) are thrown into the crowd from the floats. Before Christmas children receive Advent calendars filled with chocolate or little gifts, and many towns feature an open-air *Weihnachtsmarkt* (Christmas market or fair), with many stalls offering *Glühwein* (mulled wine) and all kinds of *Lebkuchen*, as well as other candies and sweets. See FAIRS; GINGERBREAD; and MULLED WINE. On the evening of 5 December, children put out their polished shoes for *Nikolaus* (St. Nicholas), a cousin of America's Santa Claus, to fill them with goodies during the night. The treats traditionally consist of oranges, mandarin oranges, nuts, gingerbread, marzipan, and chocolates, but today small presents are often included. Throughout the entire Advent period, *Weihnachtsbäckerei* (Christmas baking) plays an important role. It is often an occasion for friends to gather, with children joining in. The most traditional German Christmas cake is stollen, but cakes with a poppy seed filling rolled up in a yeast dough are another Christmas tradition, with Silesian roots.

Heinzelmann, Ursula. *Beyond Bratwurst: A History of Food in Germany*. London: Reaktion, 2014.
Rumpolt, Marx. *Ein new Kochbuch*. Facsimile ed. Edited by Manfred Lemmer. Hildesheim, Germany, and New York: Olms, 1977. First published 1581.
Sheraton, Mimi. *The German Cookbook*. New York: Random House, 2014. First published 1965.

Ursula Heinzelmann

Ghirardelli, more than just chocolate, encompasses the story of immigration, the power of marketing, and the circle of urban renewal.

Italian-born Domingo Ghirardelli (1817–1894) founded Ghirardelli Chocolate Company in San Francisco in 1852. He had apprenticed at Romanengro's confectionery shop in Genoa before immigrating to Peru, where he opened his own shop, specializing in chocolate. While in Peru, Ghirardelli met fellow entrepreneur and land baron James Lick who, upon returning to the United States, sent word of the California Gold Rush to Ghirardelli.

Ghirardelli moved to California in 1849 and opened a general store in the town of Stockton, where he sold provisions, including chocolate, to successful miners who were looking for a taste of luxury. In the early 1850s he opened a second shop in San Francisco, which sold liquor, spices, coffee, and chocolate.

Three developments allowed the business to expand. The 1867 invention of the Broma process, which removes butterfat from cocoa solids without the use of alkalis, enabling the cocoa to mix easily with water or milk, allowed the chocolate to be shipped without turning rancid. Second, shipping possibilities expanded greatly with the completion of the transcontinental railroad in 1869. Finally, mass marketing and advertising during the Gilded Age—including a popular campaign about how to pronounce "Ghirardelli"—further drove demand for the chocolate confections. As a result, the business expanded to become the largest chocolate producer on the West Coast.

In 1893 the company acquired a textile mill on North Point Street in San Francisco. Over the decades, Ghirardelli built several additions to the structure, and the company remained in that location until 1964, when it relocated to San Leandro. The property was purchased by locals who wanted to save the building, which reopened in 1964 as a mixed retail space of shops and restaurants. A model for urban renewal in Boston and Baltimore, the complex, called Ghirardelli Square, was listed on the National Register of Historic Places in 1982.

The company itself underwent several changes. Golden Grain Macaroni acquired Ghirardelli in 1963, and as of 2013, it had become a subsidiary of chocolate makers Lindt and Sprüngli. Today, the company remains a bean-to-bar manufacturer, focused on premium quality, whose product line includes a range of bars, baking mixes and sauces, and cocoa powders.

See also CHOCOLATE, POST-COLUMBIAN; COCOA; and GUITTARD.

"About Ghirardelli." http://www.ghirardelli.com (accessed 10 March 2014).

Lawrence, Sidney. "The Ghirardelli Story." *California History* 81, no. 2 (2002): 90–115.

Pratt, Bland. "Ghirardelli Square—National Registry of Historic Places Inventory, Nomination Form." U.S. Department of the Interior, Heritage Conservation and Recreation Service, Washington, D.C., 1982. http://pdfhost.focus.nps.gov/docs/NRHP/Text/82002249.pdf.

Beth M. Forrest

Gilliers, Joseph (d. 1758) is best remembered as the author of *Le cannameliste français*, which was the most extensive manual for working with sugar written in the ancien régime. Published in 1751, the very year in which Diderot and d'Alembert brought forth the first volume of their famous *Encyclopédie*, the *Cannaméliste français* similarly features an alphabetized, dictionary-style format, reflective of the Enlightenment. Gilliers invented the word "cannameliste" from "canne" (sugar) to imply a person who works with sugar, so his book's title might be translated as "The French Sugar-Worker."

The book provides instructions for how to perform the wide-ranging functions of the *office*, the division of the kitchen in large, European households that created desserts in addition to preparing salads and liqueurs; supervising table settings and decoration; and caring for linens, silver, and the like. It includes advice about how to store fruits or transform them into jellies, as well as the best methods for making artificial flowers. The volume's extensive recipes for iced fruits, creams, and *fromages glacés* (which, confusingly, usually do not contain cheese) were among the first and most original in Europe. Gilliers also provided detailed instructions and diagrams for how to mold these iced confections into fanciful shapes imitating asparagus, boars' heads, fish, and other unexpected forms. See ICE CREAM.

Le cannemaliste français is most famous for its lavish, foldout engravings. Gilliers's designs for S-curved tables and intricate, three-dimensional *surtouts de table*, which sat in the center of the fanciest tables, exemplify the rococo style that flourished in mid-eighteenth-century France and betray a familiarity with the designs of the style's most renowned practitioner, Juste-Aurèle Meissonier (1695–1750).

Little is known about Gilliers's early life, except that he worked as a Chef d'Office for King Stanislaw Leszczyński (1677–1766), at the Château de Lunéville. The property belonged to the Duchy of Lorraine, which was given to Leszczyński in 1738 by his son-in-law, French king Louis XV (r. 1715–1774), as compensation for abdicating the Polish throne. It is presumed that Gilliers was a local boy from the region. He reported to M. François Richard, the Contrôleur des Offices who had worked for the deposed king since the time he had resided at the Château de Chambord (1725–1733). Gilliers was merely one of six assistants, who were further aided by two kitchen boys. Leszczyński also employed a full-time party planner, M. Dupuis, who held the title *Dessinateur des plaisirs*. All these workers, not to mention an extensive kitchen staff and other servants, reported to the Duke de Tenczin Ossolonski (1666–1756), the Grand Master of the Household, to whom Gilliers dedicated his book.

This large retinue sustained one of the most renowned pleasure palaces in Europe, which operated as something of a rival to the court of Versailles, especially after Madame de Pompadour (1721–1764) became the French king's mistress in 1745 and virtually ruled the realm, setting both policy and fashion. Leszczyński's daughter Marie (1703–1768) was the French king's wife, so, as a protective father, he naturally hoped to outshine the woman who had turned his son-in-law's head away from his beloved child.

The deposed ruler, who had failed so miserably at politics in Poland, excelled at hosting pleasurable, light-hearted entertainments and had a noted taste for the desserts and ices that featured at such events. He had, in fact, previously employed another famous Chef d'Office, Nicolas Stohrer, who joined Leszczyński's service during his 1719–1725 stay in Wissembourg. See STOHRER, NICOLAS. Stohrer left to join the queen's household when Marie married Louis XV in 1725, and then opened his own pastry shop on the rue Montorgueil in Paris. It is currently the oldest in the city.

If Gilliers's book disseminated the style of the extraordinary parties held at Lunéville as much as the recipes for appropriate sweets to serve at them, his designs seem downright conservative compared to engravings by architect Emmanuel Héré de Corny (1705–1763) of the wonders he had created at Lunéville, which included a grotto populated by 86 automatons in an idealized village as well as several whimsical garden pavilions used to stage the king's frequent banquets. A Turkish-inspired kiosk included a hydraulically powered table, which could rise up from the basement, and which was surmounted by an intricate porcelain *surtout* that depicted a pastoral landscape and sprayed jets of water.

Gilliers's masterwork records Lunéville's attenuated elegance, and its logical organization simultaneously reflects Leszczyński's court as a hub of Enlightenment thinking, where Voltaire (1694–1778), for example, was a frequent guest and where the former Polish king created and oversaw his own academy. However, the greatest importance of *Le cannameliste français* lies in its clearly written recipes, which, from ice cream to biscuits, helped popularize beyond this rarified universe many desserts that have become commonplace today.

See also DESSERT; DESSERT DESIGN; FRANCE; and SERVING PIECES.

Gilliers, Joseph. *Le Cannaméliste francais*. Nancy: Abel-Denis Cuisson, 1751.

Héré de Corny, Emmanuel. *Recueil des plans, élévations et coupes tant géometrale qu'en perspective des chateaux, jardins et dependences que le Roy de Pologne occupe en Lorraine [etc.]*. Paris, ca. 1750.

Muratori-Philip, Anne. *Le roi Stanislas*. Paris: Fayard, 2000.

Wheaton, Barbara Ketcham. *Savoring the Past: The French Kitchen and Table from 1300 to 1789*. New York: Touchstone, 1983.

Carolin C. Young

ginger

See SPICES.

gingerbread is a term that applies to a broad category of baked goods flavored with a combination of spices such as ginger, cinnamon, cloves, and nutmeg, and sweetened with honey, sugar, or molasses. Gingerbreads range from cakes to breads to cookies. Made from batters or doughs, and shaped in many forms, they can be soft or hard, thick or thin, glazed or unglazed, unadorned or decorated with icings, dried or candied fruits, nuts, marzipan, colored paper, or even gold leaf. Gingerbreads are closely associated with the Christmas season in several countries, but in many places they are also eaten year round. Although most gingerbreads are sweet, some are used as an ingredient in savory dishes, such as rich soups and sweet-sour sauces. Slices of gingerbread are often served as an accompaniment to fattened goose liver and duck liver.

Gingerbread History

Archeaological evidence shows that flat cakes made with honey and spices were baked by the ancient Egyptians, Greeks, and Romans. See ANCIENT WORLD. But the gingerbreads eaten today are descendants of those developed in northern Europe in the Middle Ages, when honey was the main sweetener available locally, and exotic, expensive spices

This lithograph of *The Gingerbread Seller* is from the series *The Cries of Paris* engraved by François Seraphin Delpech (1778–1825). Gingerbread, or *pain d'épices,* was often shaped in whimsical forms. MUSÉE DE LA VILLE DE PARIS, MUSÉE CARNAVALET, PARIS / BRIDGEMAN IMAGES

were increasingly being imported from faraway lands in the East to satisfy the medieval desire for highly spiced foods. See HONEY and SPICES. Honey-and-spice gingerbreads were first made in Christian cloisters and monasteries, before production shifted to professional bakers' guilds, and much later to home bakers. See GUILDS. A taste for gingerbread eventually spread throughout northern Europe, with certain cities becoming known for their own particular types of gingerbread: Ashbourne, Ormskirk, Grasmere, and Edinburgh in the British Isles; Paris, Strasbourg, Dijon, and Rheims in France; Dinant in Belgium; Nuremberg (Nürnberg), Aachen, Ulm, and Pulsnitz in Germany; Basel and St. Gallen in Switzerland: Toruń in Poland; Prague and Pardubice in the Czech lands; Pest in Hungary; Tula and Gorodets in Russia. Gingerbread recipes later spread around the world with Europeans who emigrated to North and South America, Australia, New Zealand, and parts of Africa.

Many early gingerbreads were made from a dough of rye flour and honey, flavored with spices that included cinnamon, cloves, nutmeg, anise, and ginger or pepper. Often the mixture was left in a moderately cool place for several months to ferment slowly like a sourdough, to develop the enzymes essential for the gingerbread's taste, texture, and preservation. After the remaining ingredients were added, the dough was shaped and baked. Over time, the variety of ingredients used in gingerbreads expanded to include wheat flour, eggs, butter, cane sugar, beet sugar, molasses, golden syrup, maple syrup, allspice, coriander, cardamom, saffron, almonds, hazelnuts, walnuts, currants, raisins, dates, grated lemon zest, candied orange peel and citron peel, rosewater, rum, brandy, milk, buttermilk, beer, licorice, crushed rock candy, crystallized ginger, and chemical leavenings. However, some baked goods called "gingerbreads" do not contain any ginger at all.

During the Middle Ages, the German city of Nuremberg—located at the crossroads of two major trade routes and surrounded by forests full of honeybees—became one of the most famous places for making gingerbreads in Central Europe. The

German term for these seductive sweets was *Lebkuchen* (or sometimes *Pfefferkuchen*, when their spiciness came from pepper instead of ginger). The stiff dough was pressed into highly detailed molds, usually made of carved wood, which imprinted intricate designs on top of the *Lebkuchen* before they were removed from the molds and baked in a hot oven. See COOKIE MOLDS AND STAMPS. The size and shape of the *Lebkuchen* were determined by the design of the molds, which ranged from a few inches to 3 feet tall and often depicted members of the nobility, religious figures, and coats of arms. Nuremberg *Lebkuchen* contained such costly ingredients, and was of such high quality, that it was sometimes used as payment for city taxes, and gilded *Lebkuchen* were given as special gifts to nobles, princes, and heads of state.

In the British Isles, gingerbread making dates from the fourteenth century, when the earliest gingerbreads were confection-like combinations of breadcrumbs, ground almonds, honey or sugar, and ginger. Originally eaten only by the upper classes, gingerbreads made with flour, treacle, and spices later became popular treats sold at markets and fairs. See FAIRS. Legend has it that Queen Elizabeth I enjoyed gilded gingerbread cookies baked in the shape of her suitors, courtiers, and guests, and that four centuries later Queen Victoria popularized gingerbreads as a British Christmas tradition. An old Halloween custom in northern England was for a maiden to eat a gingerbread cookie shaped like a man, to ensure she would soon find a husband. And witches were sometimes accused of baking and eating gingerbread effigies of their enemies. Gingerbreads shaped like pigs and men are still traditional for Bonfire Night (5 November) in Great Britain. See ANTHROPOMORPHIC AND ZOOMORPHIC SWEETS.

In Europe, as the demand for gingerbread increased and the prices of ingredients fell, faster production methods were developed. In the nineteenth century metal molds and cookie cutters, often mass-produced and less detailed in design, began to replace the elaborate handmade wooden molds of earlier times. Instead of intricately embossed designs on the dough, simpler decorations were added on top of the gingerbread cookies: nuts, candied fruit, sugar icings, and paper cutouts printed with seasonal or topical motifs. Shapes were simplified, too, eventually becoming the basic human, animal, and geometric forms common today. Artisanal bakers continued to leaven their dough with the natural yeasts present in it, but industrial bakers and home cooks began using baking soda, potassium carbonate, or ammonium carbonate to speed up the process. See CHEMICAL LEAVENERS.

Making gingerbread houses became a popular activity in Germany in the early 1800s. Ornately decorated heart-shaped *Lebkuchen* cookies also became a fad in Germany and Austria during the nineteenth century. Adorned with fancy designs and romantic sayings made from colored icing or printed paper cutouts, these large *Lebkuchen* hearts were often exchanged between sweethearts and given to wedding guests. They are still a popular souvenir at many Central European festivals and Christmas markets.

In some European countries, gingerbreads were a traditional food at many religious and secular events: Christmas, Easter, baptisms, birthdays, saints' days, a child's first day at school, conscription into military service, and departures on journeys. Elaborately decorated gingerbreads were often used as decorations, to be kept and displayed instead of eaten. An old custom still practiced in Central Europe and Scandinavia is to hang gingerbread cookies on evergreen boughs and Christmas trees in the house, and to display fancy gingerbread cookies in windows during the winter holiday season.

Gingerbread Varieties

In Germany today, *Lebkuchen* are produced in many sizes, shapes, flavors, colors, and textures: rounds, rectangles, squares, hearts, stars, pretzel forms, St. Nicholas (for the Christmas season), lucky pigs (for New Year), and rabbits (for Easter). See HOLIDAY SWEETS. The *Lebkuchen* dough ranges from "white" (light-colored) to different shades of brown. German *Lebkuchen* can be covered with white or chocolate icing; filled with marzipan or jam; or decorated on the top or bottom with whole or chopped almonds. Some versions are sweetened only (or primarily) with honey. *Oblaten Lebkuchen* are cookies whose dough is baked on top of a paper-thin edible wafer. Delicate, elegant *Elisen Lebkuchen* are a type of *Oblaten Lebkuchen* made with finely ground almonds, hazelnuts, or walnuts, and little or no flour.

Other types of gingerbread cookies—with a variety of different ingredients, shapes, colors, textures, and decorations—are known as *Printen*, *Honigkuchen*, and *Pfefferkuchen* in Germany; *Spekulatius* in the German Rhineland, *speculaas* in the Netherlands, and *speculoos* in Belgium; *Leckerli, Biberli,* and *Tirggel* in Switzerland; *pepperkaker* in Norway, *pepparkakor* in Sweden, *piperkakut* in Finland, and *pebernødder* and *brunekager* in Denmark; *piparkūkas* in Latvia and *piparkoogid* in Estonia; *pain d'épices* in France; *licitar* in Croatia; *mézeskalács* in Hungary; *perníky* in the Czech Republic and Slovakia; *turtă dulce* in Romania; *medinki* in Bulgaria and *medianyky* in Ukraine; *pierniki* and *pierniczki* in Poland and *prianiki* in Russia; ginger biscuits and ginger nuts in British Commonwealth countries; and gingersnaps in many English-speaking countries. Some towns and regions also have specific names for their own particular varieties of gingerbread cookies, including those made for local and regional holidays. Some of these cookies are elaborately decorated with white or colored icings, candies, paper cutouts, and even small mirrors, often with designs that have local cultural or religious significance.

The category of gingerbreads also includes many kinds of spice cakes. Leavened with soda, beaten eggs, baking powder, or sometimes yeast, they are made with the same spice combinations used in gingerbread cookies, usually have a somewhat dark color and dense texture, and are baked in many forms—flat, tall, round, square, rectangular, layers, and loaves. These include several kinds of British spice cakes, such as parkin made with oatmeal and treacle; Slavic honey cakes often made with rye flour and a smaller range of spices; and American gingerbread cakes, loaves, muffins, and cupcakes. Slices of gingerbread cakes are often garnished with lemon sauce, vanilla ice cream, or whipped cream.

Gingerbreads are popular in many parts of the world today because they are easy to make, use relatively inexpensive ingredients, are richly flavored, and can be baked in many forms. Gingerbread cookies, especially those cut in the shapes of gingerbread men and women, are particularly beloved by children. Amateur and professional bakers see gingerbread cookies as a blank canvas for their creativity in decorating with icing and other edible materials. The making of gingerbread houses at Christmas has spread from their origin in Germany to other countries around the globe, and gingerbread house contests have become popular community events in many places. Every year since 1991, the city of Bergen, Norway, has even sponsored the world's largest "gingerbread city" (*Pepperkakebyen*), a miniature city composed of more than 2,000 colorfully decorated and lighted gingerbread houses and other gingerbread buildings constructed by local children of all ages.

See also CHRISTMAS; EASTER; GERMANY; LEAF, GOLD AND SILVER; MOLASSES; NETHERLANDS; RUSSIA; SCANDINAVIA; and SPECULAAS.

Davidson, Alan. "Ginger Biscuits" and "Gingerbread." In *The Oxford Companion to Food*, edited by Alan Davidson, pp. 338–339. Oxford: Oxford University Press, 1999.

Franzke, Jürgen, ed. *Das Nürnberger Lebkuchenbuch.* Nuremberg, Germany: Verlag W. Tümmels, 2008.

Iaia, Sarah Kelly. *Festive Baking: Holiday Classics in the Swiss, German, and Austrian Traditions.* New York: Doubleday, 1988.

Klein, Udo. *Handbuch für de Weihnachtsbäckerei: Von Advent bis Silvester.* Cologne: Pfeifer & Langen, 1978.

Merinoff, Linda. *Gingerbread.* New York: Simon & Schuster, 1989.

Scharfenberg, Horst. *The Cuisines of Germany: Regional Specialties and Traditional Home Cooking.* New York: Poseidon, 1989.

Sharon Hudgins

glacéed fruit

See CANDIED FRUIT.

glaze

See ICING.

glucose (also called dextrose in the food industry) is a monosaccharide—the most basic form of carbohydrate—commonly obtained from plants, which manufacture it through the process of photosynthesis. Glucose is the main energy source for humans and most other organisms.

When consumed, glucose is absorbed by the intestines into the blood. In response to the rise in blood-glucose levels, the pancreas releases insulin, the central metabolic hormone. Cells that need glucose have specific insulin receptors on their surface, permitting glucose entry into the cells. When present in the blood, insulin directs some tissue cells to take up glucose, other cells to store glucose (in the form of glycogen) in liver and muscle cells, and still other cells to hold lipids (fats) in adipose tissue (body fat).

Insulin's absence signals cells to turn off the uptake of glucose, break down glycogen, release lipids from adipose tissue, and put glucose into the bloodstream. When oxidized in the body, in the process called cellular respiration, glucose provides energy for cells; carbon dioxide, and water are the waste products of that process.

Pure glucose has little flavor or color. Common table sugar (sucrose) is a disaccharide consisting of 50 percent fructose and 50 percent glucose. In the early nineteenth century, the starch from potatoes, sweet potatoes, and corn was converted into glucose syrup. By the beginning of the twentieth century, glucose was commonly used as a sweetener and sold as corn syrup, such as Karo syrup. See CORN SYRUP. A similar chemical process can convert glucose into fructose, a much sweeter monosaccharide.

See also FRUCTOSE and SUGAR AND HEALTH.

Hull, Peter. *Glucose Syrups: Technology and Applications.* Chichester, U.K., and Ames, Iowa: Wiley-Blackwell, 2010.

Salway, Jack. *Metabolism at a Glance.* 3d ed. Malden, Mass.: Blackwell, 2004.

Andrew F. Smith

Godiva is arguably the best known today of the large chocolate factories that emerged in Belgium in the late 1870s, arising mostly out of small, artisanal shops that served a fancy clientele. Mechanization and improvements in packaging and marketing led to the growing popularity of chocolate as its price declined. By the 1920s, chocolate had become a common treat that all social classes enjoyed. In the late 1940s, average per capita consumption was 1.1 kilos; by the 1970s, it had grown to 4.2 kilos per person, and it is close to 10 kilos today.

In the late 1920s, the Brussels area had some 90 chocolate manufacturers, including Joseph Draps, who, together with his family, produced pralines that were sold by local department stores. In 1945 the company opened its first shop in an upscale Brussels district and a second one in chic Knokke (on the Belgian coast), naming the products "Godiva," after the Anglo-Saxon legend of the woman who rode a horse naked to urge her husband to reduce taxes (her tactic was effective). Success came quickly and Draps opened more shops, including one in Paris in 1958, one on New York's Fifth Avenue in 1966, and one in Tokyo in 1972. The Campbell Soup Company became interested in this successful Belgian chocolatier and purchased the company in 1972. In 2007 Campbell sold Godiva to the Turkish Ülker Group. Today, Godiva has almost 10,000 points of sale all over the world and offers approximately 60 products, including the 72 percent Dark Chocolate Bar and Citron Meringue praline.

Godiva's success may be linked to the company's lowering of costs, finely tuned marketing, wealthy clientele, high-quality products (Belgian chocolate contains at least 35 percent cocoa butter, sometimes up to 85 percent), and continuous innovation in its product range. Godiva's history represents a genuine Belgian chocolate culture that has existed since the 1890s, when chocolate was first perceived as healthy, providing quick energy at a relatively low price, giving comfort in difficult psychological moments, and a genuine treat enjoyed on special occasions, such as the very popular children's holiday of Sint-Nicolaas (Saint Nicholas) on 6 December.

See also BELGIUM; CHOCOLATE, LUXURY; and CHOCOLATES, BOXED.

Scholliers, P. "De la boisson élitaire à la barre populaire: la production et la consommation du chocolat en Belgique aux 19e et 20e siècles." In *Chocolat: De la boisson élitaire au bâton populaire,* edited by Bruno Bernard et al., pp. 163–184. Brussels: CGER, 1996.

Special Issue: Bonbons, pralines, et squimaux, chocolats. Les Cahiers de la Fonderie 11 (December 1991).

Peter Scholliers

golden syrup is a pale gold, viscous treacle (molasses) with a light, intensely sweet flavor and a mild, slightly caramelized undernote. It is a by-product of cane-sugar refining that, like molasses, contains sugar that has failed to crystallize out of solution during the refining process; its distinctive color comes from the left-over impurities. See MOLASSES and SUGAR REFINING. An equivalent product is now produced from beet sugar by hydrolysis, in which sucrose is split into monosaccharides by the addition of acid.

More properly known in the United Kingdom under the trademark Lyle's Golden Syrup, it is a staple of the kitchen cupboard, packed in a distinctive green and gold tin bearing the biblical reference "out of the strong came forth sweetness" (Judges 14:14).

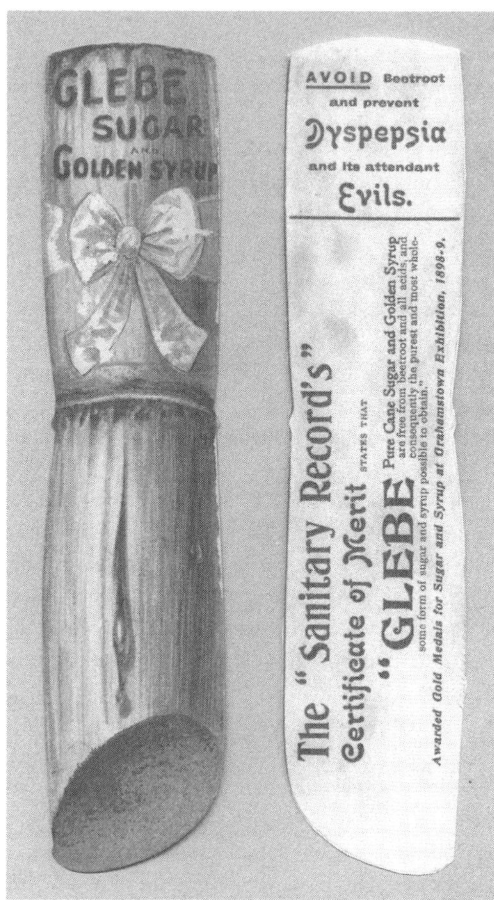

In 1865 John Kerr and Abram Lyle founded the Glebe Sugar Refinery in Greenock, Scotland. Most of their income soon came from Lyle's Golden Syrup, a light, mild molasses. This 1899 chromolithograph asserts the purity of their product. AMORET TANNER COLLECTION / THE ART ARCHIVE AT ART RESOURCE, N.Y.

Similar products, made from either cane or beet sugar, are produced in other countries, although they are uncommon in the United States, where corn syrup tends to take their place. See CORN SYRUP.

Pale golden syrup was first marketed commercially in the 1880s by Abram Lyle, who had a sugar refinery at Greenock, near Glasgow, in Scotland. Although other refiners also made similar products, Lyle's was of better quality and sold for a premium price; it became a financial savior for the company when sugar prices collapsed in 1883. Its distinctive packaging was devised in 1885.

Golden syrup provides an ingredient in confectionery; its sweetness and resistance to crystallization make it useful especially for toffee and caramels. See CARAMELS and TOFFEE. It lends sweetness to many desserts made in the United Kingdom and former British colonies, including treacle tart and steamed sponge or suet puddings. Golden syrup also goes into biscuits and sweet sauces and onto pancakes, porridge, and bread.

See also BISCUITS, BRITISH; SAUCE; SUGAR BEET; TATE & LYLE; and UNITED KINGDOM.

Blumenthal, Heston. *In Search of Perfection: Reinventing Kitchen Classics*. London: Bloomsbury, 2006.
Davidson, Alan. *The Oxford Companion to Food*. Oxford: Oxford University Press, 2006.
Munting, Roger. "Lyle, Abram (1820–1891)." In *Oxford Dictionary of National Biography*, 2005. http://www.oxforddnb.com/view/article/88654 (accessed 24 April 2014).

Laura Mason

The **Good Humor Man,** with his still popular Good Humor Bar, became the personification of one of the most successful of the countless ice cream novelties created in the early twentieth century. The confection was developed in 1920 when Harry Burt, a Youngstown, Ohio, candy maker, coated a slice of vanilla ice cream with chocolate. When Burt's daughter Ruth complained that eating it was too messy, his son Harry Jr. suggested putting a wooden lollipop stick in it. Burt did, and his children, like millions to come, were delighted.

Burt's genius was in marketing the product. He sold his "Good Humor Ice Cream Suckers" from a spotlessly clean white truck that announced its presence with bells from the family's bobsled. The Good Humor name originated in the ancient belief that the humors, or temperament, were related to diet, and Burt's belief that ice cream was a happy, healthy treat. See MEDICINAL USES OF SUGAR.

As the company expanded, Burt added more white trucks with bells. He hired and trained polite, personable men and provided them with pristine white uniforms. They represented the company so well that the Good Humor Man became a beloved figure in popular culture. He appeared in films, comics, radio programs, and children's books. The Good Humor Man was seen as friendly, reliable, and trustworthy, qualities also associated with the brand.

Company ownership changed several times until 1961, when the Unilever conglomerate acquired it.

The Good Humor ice cream bar debuted in 1920. As business expanded, its owner, Harry Burt, hired friendly salesmen to build the brand. Instantly recognizable in their white uniforms, Good Humor men quickly became beloved figures. This image is from *The Good Humor Man*, a 1950 film starring Jack Carson and Lola Albright.

Gradually, increased supermarket sales made the Good Humor Man less significant. Good Humor products, however, are still consumer favorites. The company, now Good Humor-Breyers, is one of the largest producers of branded ice cream products in the United States.

See also ICE CREAM.

Funderburg, Anne Cooper. *Chocolate, Strawberry, and Vanilla: A History of American Ice Cream*. Bowling Green, Ohio: Bowling Green State University Popular Press, 1995.

Jeri Quinzio

granita

See ITALY.

grape must is the unfermented juice of ripe grapes that comes off the wine press at the start of wine making. This juice is also used, boiled down to a third or a half of its original volume, to make *mostocotto*, sometimes called *sapa* or *saba*. The boiling process produces a rich, sweet syrup at little cost, used in the past as a substitute for honey or sugar. Some regional cuisines in Italy still use *mostocotto* in cookies and tarts. Versions of *mostaccioli* cookies from various regions include *mostocotto*, a practice that goes back to Roman times. In Emilia, the recipe for these spice cookies includes candied fruit; in Lazio, a seasoning of pepper; and in many areas, nuts or marzipan.

The condiment mustard gets its name from the grape must that was used as the base of a sweet and highly spiced confection made with fresh or candied fruits and seasoned with pungent mustard seeds, now best known as the industrial product *mostarda di frutta*, a speciality of Cremona. See MOSTARDA.

The genuine *aceto balsamico tradizionale di Modena* is made from the must of selected varieties of grapes boiled down to a third, sometimes with the addition of a mother vinegar, then matured and condensed by evaporation over the years in a succession of barrels of decreasing size. The barrels are made from different woods that impart their aromas to this highly complex substance—confusingly, not a vinegar, despite its name. The process of making wine vinegar is quite different; it uses uncooked grape must and a vinegar "mother" to obtain fermentation without the long and complex evaporation process that creates *balsamico*. Fraudulently flavored and sweetened vinegars called "balsamico" are not the real thing. A typical dessert of the Modena region is a plain vanilla ice with a dash of the genuine elixir poured over it.

Pekmez is the Turkish version of cooked grape must, made from grapes or carob pods; it adds a fruity flavor rather than the neutral sweetness of refined sugar and is used in both confectionery and savory dishes. See PEKMEZ.

The French definition of must, *moût*, is more complex and can include all the residues, skins, and pips of fruit. Known as the *marc*, this must can be distilled to produce fruit brandy, also called marc or grappa. The *moût* can be treated in various ways, by condensation or evaporation, with varying degrees of caramelization. It is often used to deglaze the pan in which meat or chicken has been cooked.

Verjuice or verjus—*agresto* in Italian—is the juice of sour or unripe grapes, used as a seasoning or cooking medium. It can be obtained by simply squeezing a handful of unripe grapes and straining the liquid into whatever you are cooking. Verjuice lends a fruity acidity without being as aggressive as wine or vinegar. Commercial varieties are often fermented or treated to last longer.

See also BISCOTTI; ITALY; SWEET AND SOUR; and TURKEY.

Benedetti, Benedetto, ed. *L'aceto balsamico*. Spilamberto, Italy: Consorteria dell'Aceto Balsamico, 1986.
Gotti, Marco Guarnaschelli. *Grande enciclopedia illustrata della gastronomia*. Milan: Garzanti, 2008.
Riley, Gillian. *Oxford Companion to Italian Food*. New York: Oxford University Press, 2007.

Gillian Riley

Greece and Cyprus, like other countries around the Mediterranean, have a tradition of sweets based on seasonal local ingredients. Since the dawn of civilization in Greece, ingenious cooks with limited means have found ways to create an amazing variety of frugal yet festive treats by complementing readily available fruits, vegetables, and nuts with flour, eggs, yogurt, and fresh cheese. Until sugar became affordable in the late nineteenth century, local honey or homemade grape molasses were used as sweeteners. See HONEY and PEKMEZ.

In Greece and Cyprus, sweets have never been served as the traditional conclusion to lunch or dinner. Fresh fruits are the usual ending for family meals, whereas sweets, simple or more elaborate, have traditionally been made for Easter, Christmas, and family feasts. Only children celebrate their birthdays in Greece; grown-ups feast on the day that the saint whose name they have been given is celebrated by the church. On that occasion, one or more special sweets are offered to the guests who visit the family to wish many happy returns to Constantine on 21 May, to Maria on 15 August, to Yiannis (John) on 7 January, and so on. In the late nineteenth and early twentieth centuries, the word *epidorpion* (dessert) was used in urban homes and restaurants that embraced the Western style, three-course meal. *Epidorpion*, a word from the Hellenistic vernacular, referred to the nuts, dried fruits, and honeyed flatbreads that accompanied the wine served after the meal in antiquity.

Because they were not made often, sweets are among the rare foods for which written recipes were kept. Even women who could barely write managed to record the ingredients for *melomakarona*—honey-doused Christmas cookies—or for the New Year's sweet bread in which a lucky coin is hidden; of course, they also kept notes on methods and the ratios of fruit to sugar for each of the numerous spoon sweets, the seasonal fruit preserves that are the cornerstone of traditional sweets throughout the Aegean.

Spoon Sweets

Even today, households keep a variety of spoon sweets in the pantry: *kydoni* (quince), *nerantzaki* (rolled Seville orange peels), and *vissyno* (sour cherry) are the most popular. Whatever each region produces is turned into *glyko koutaliou* (spoon sweet)—tiny whole tangerines, unripe pistachios or figs, heavily scented citrus blossoms, and the petals of pink roses. *Karydaki*, green, unripe walnuts from the mountainous regions, require a particularly lengthy process, whereas tiny eggplant is probably the most unlikely fruit of the garden to be simmered in syrup. Cooks boast of the color, texture, and taste of these preserves, which sometimes involve complicated procedures or use unusual ingredients. Calcium chloride was added to make crunchy fruit preserves long before Ferran Adrià and other "molecular chefs" deployed the chemical in their famous spherification technique. To welcome guests, a spoonful of these colorful syrupy morsels was traditionally offered on a tiny crystal plate presented on a tray with a glass of water. There was once an entire ritual governing which spoon sweets should be offered on each occasion. At weddings, for example, the preserves should be white—citrus blossoms and lemon or citron peel—while at various joyous family celebrations multicolored cherries, tangerines, and pistachios were served. On solemn days of mourning, people who visited the house would be offered dark preserves of tiny eggplant or whole unripe walnuts, with their slightly bitter flavor. In recent years, fruit preserves have come to be used as a topping for thick yogurt.

Fruit preserves with clear syrup, as we know them today, were once the privilege of the wealthy, as sugar was imported and expensive until the late nineteenth century. See FRUIT PRESERVES. Although from the fourteenth to sixteenth centuries sugarcane was cultivated and processed in Cyprus by the Venetians, and considerable quantities of sugar were exported to Venice, the sweet crystals were a precious commodity, hardly ever used by the locals. In the old days, fruits were preserved in honey and grape molasses (*petimezi*), the basic sweeteners of the region since antiquity. *Moustalevria*, a primitive pudding still popular today, is made by simmering grape must—freshly pressed grape juice—to concentrate its sweetness, with the addition of flour or cornstarch. See GRAPE MUST. *Soutzouki* (*soutzoukos* in Cyprus), a sausage-like sweet, is made by tying walnuts and other nuts on a string and dipping them several times in the thickened grape must, in a process similar to the one used in candle making. Interestingly enough, Cyprus is one of the few places where carob molasses, another primitive sweetener, is still used in some traditional sweets. Cypriot *pastelli* is a toffee-like sweet produced from cooked-down and dried carob molasses. The more common Greek *pastelli* is a totally different candy, made from honey mixed with toasted sesame seeds, with the occasional addition of almonds or walnuts.

Flour, Cheese, and Honey

Fried sweets vary by region and budget. By simply combining flour and water, with or without leavening, cooks with limited means always managed to create delicious treats like *tiganites*, frying spoonfuls of the mixture and serving the crunchy bites drizzled with honey and sprinkled with sesame or nuts. See FRIED DOUGH. For the pancake-like *laggites* of Thrace and the *laggopites* of Cyprus, the batter is cooked on a heated stone or griddle, much as was done in antiquity. With the addition of yeast, the mixture becomes *loukoumades* (fried dough puffs); when more flour is added, the dough can be shaped into little balls that are flattened before frying to make the Cypriot *pisia*. With more skill the dough is rolled into thin sheets of filo (*phyllo*), which can take myriad forms: *diples*, large or smaller pieces of thin dough, or *kserotigana*, the elaborate swirled filo ribbons of Crete, are fried in olive oil and again served drizzled with honey and nuts. Sheets of filo become the crust that encloses all kinds of seasonal ingredients: Cypriot *kolokotes* are small pies stuffed with grated squash or pumpkin, bulgur, and raisins. See FILO. A similar filling is used for the pan-size *kolokythopita*, or for cigar-like rolls that are baked all over the country as festive winter treats. *Kolokythopita* often hovers between sweet and savory with onions and aged cheese mixed with sugar, walnuts or almonds, cinnamon, and cloves.

In the spring, for the festive Easter sweets, *myzithra*—a ricotta-like fresh cheese produced since the dawn of civilization from sheep's and goat's milk during this season—is the main ingredient for many diverse small or larger pies. See CHEESE, FRESH and CHEESECAKE. Not surprisingly, flatbreads with fresh cheese and honey were the favorite treats of ancient Greeks and Romans; the Easter cheese pies of the Aegean and the similar ones of southern Italy seem to follow this ancient tradition. Fresh cheese mixed with honey and eggs, scented with cinnamon, lemon zest, or mastic, forms the stuffing for *melopita*, the traditional tart, or tartlets, in Santorini, Sifnos, and other islands of the Cyclades. See MASTIC. In Crete, filo crescents filled with sweetened fresh cheese are called *kalitsounia* and can be either baked or fried, much like the Cypriot *pourekia me anari*. The thick cream topping of sheep's milk is called *tsipa* in the Cypriot dialect. *Tsipopita*, one of the most unusual festive pies, is made by spreading the thick cream on filo, then rolling it tightly in a thin cylinder and coiling it to fit in a round pan. The next roll is coiled snuggly around the first and so on, until the pan is filled. After baking, *tsipopita* is doused in syrup and served cut into wedges.

Some of the most popular Greek sweets are the *glyka tapsiou* (sweets of the baking pan)—pies and all kinds of sweetened, cake-like breads typically enriched with almonds and walnuts. These baked goods are seldom served plain and are usually covered in syrup. *Karydopita* (walnut cake), *amygdalopita* (almond cake) and of course baklava, *galatoboureko* (sumptuous custard enclosed in filo), and *kadaifi*—little bundles of shredded filo stuffed with ground nuts—are some of the most common desserts in this category.

Baklava and other filo sweets are similar to those found in Turkey, as the technique of rolling paper-thin sheets was perfected in the kitchens of the sultan's palace in Istanbul. See BAKLAVA; ISTANBUL; and TURKEY. There are Lenten (vegan) versions of most traditional sweets, including baklava, which are baked using olive oil; in recent years, they have again become popular as people seek healthier-seeming desserts.

Along with fruit preserves, each home pantry always has one or two kinds of *koulourakia*, crunchy ring-shaped cookies baked with olive oil and scented with cinnamon, orange, aniseed, mastic, or ouzo. Cookies are baked in large quantities and kept in tins to serve with morning or afternoon coffee and to offer unexpected guests. The holiday season until the end of January was the time for baking the honey-drenched *melomakarona*, richly aromatic with spices that bring to mind the medieval *pain d' épices*; as well as the irresistible *kourambiedes*, buttery cookies with toasted almonds, dusted with confectioner's sugar. They were formerly a special Christmas treat, but now bakeries sell them every day. In Cyprus, similar buttery cookies are stuffed with pistachios and are traditionally offered at weddings. There, they are called *loukoumi*—not to be confused with Turkish Delight (lokum), also called *loukoumi* in Greece. See LOKUM. *Amygdalota*, flourless almond cookies fragrant with citrus-blossom water, are the festive treats of the islands, prepared with local almonds for weddings and christenings.

Foreign Influences

In the 1920s the first and most influential cookbook was published in Athens. It was written by Nicholas Tselementes, a chef who had worked in European and American hotels and who was determined to pull Greek cooks toward French cuisine and as far away as possible from their Eastern Mediterranean traditions. His book became the bible of the rising urban middle class, and "Tselementes" is still synonymous with "cookbook" in Greek. Half of the recipes—more than 250—are for desserts, but only about one fifth describe fruit preserves and a few traditional sweets. Tselementes's recipes for trifle, *tarte à l'orange*, and English Christmas pudding did not seem to inspire Athenians, but the rich layered cakes with whipped cream and chocolate became the envy of home cooks. They tried to reproduce them, copying the elaborate cakes the new posh patisseries were offering, undoubtedly following Tselementes's instructions. But one could not buy cream. Only evaporated milk was available at the grocery stores, and attempts to whip that milk with the newly invented hand-cranked egg beater proved impossible. Eventually, someone had the idea to use margarine for the creamy filling, and many cooks followed suit. Margarine was the common "butter" in Greece, since cow's milk butter was not traditionally produced, and the strongly flavored sheep's milk butter was used only occasionally in baking. Instant-coffee–flavored margarine was used for the "mocha" layered cake and cocoa powder for the chocolate. In the 1970s tins of Morfat, a new "whipped cream" for pastry, became an instant sensation. Produced from skim milk and vegetable oils, the white blob is fluffy and stable, and it is still used by many cooks who have no idea that they can make real whipped cream in the blender, in seconds.

In recent years, alongside the ubiquitous tiramisu and the brownies that home cooks prepare, mostly from prepackaged mixes, old-fashioned Eastern-influenced sweets have become popular again. Bakeries from Thessaloniki that specialize in sumptuous filo-wrapped treats have opened branches in Athens, and neighborhood bakeries all over the country sell versions of the traditional, syrup-drenched walnut and almond cakes, often topped with chocolate glaze.

See also ANCIENT WORLD.

Kremezi, Aglaia. *The Foods of Greece*. New York: Stewart Tabori and Chang, 1993.

Kremezi, Aglaia. "Nikolas Tselementes." In *Cooks and Other People*, edited by Harlan Walker, pp. 162–169. Proceedings of the Oxford Symposium on Food and Cookery, 1995. Totnes, U.K.: Prospect, 1996.

Kremezi, Aglaia. *The Foods of the Greek Islands*. Boston and New York: Houghton Mifflin, 2000.

Tselementes, Nik K. *Hodēgos mageirikēs* [Cooking Instructions]. 6th ed. Athens: Ekdosis pemptē epēuxmenē kai veltiōmenē, 1930. Originally published 1830 (Athens: Ekdosis V. Papachrysanthou).

Aglaia Kremezi

Gugelhupf (also written *Kugelhupf* and, in France, *kouglof*, *kougelhof*, or *kougelhopf*) is a light, mildly sweet cake traditionally leavened with yeast and baked in a distinctive sculptural mold made of glazed earthenware, but also of metal (tin or copper), and even bronze or cast iron. The cake is popular throughout a wide swath of Europe encompassing eastern France (Alsace in particular), South Germany, Switzerland, Poland, and regions formerly within the boundaries of the Austro-Hungarian Empire. It is also a traditional cake among the Pennsylvania Dutch, who refer to it as *Deitscher Kuche* (Dutch Cake). The old South German name consists of two words: *Gugel*, which derives from Latin *cucullus* (hood or bonnet), and *Hupf*, literally a hop or jump. Etymologists differ about the word's origin. The name of the cake may refer to a dance in which it was once a key feature. The Brothers Grimm wrote that the "hupf" may refer to the leap in dough volume caused by the yeast, though that is likely just a popular folk etymology.

In late medieval Austria, Gugelhupf served as the centerpiece for community events like weddings. True to the medieval meaning of Gugel (a festive headdress or decorative bonnet), this cake was ornamented with flowers, beech tree leaves, colored candles, and seasonal fruits in the form of a crown. Worn on the head of the bride, it entered the room with candles ablaze in order to launch the wedding feast into a lively dance that lasted as long as the candles remained burning. The association with a festive hat is further confirmed by the oldest known Gugelhupf recipe, preserved in the 1581 German-language cookbook of Hungarian-born Marx Rumpolt. In that recipe, Hat Cake, Rumpolt referred to the cake's hat shape and suggested that it be ornamented with flowers, herbs, and live chirping birds.

The origin of the hat design appears to be Byzantine, because a nobleman wearing a hat with a distinctive Gugelhupf shape while seated at a lavish banquet is depicted in a fourteenth-century fresco at Mount Athos in Greece. The precise evolutionary trail of this stylish hat and its westward movement into medieval Europe begs further research. What remains clear is that the cake molds derive from a similarity in shape or intentional imitation of these medieval hats. This should lend further weight to the argument that Gugelhupf was not originally a specific recipe (any more than it is today), but rather a term applied to certain types of festive cakes regardless of their ingredients or method of leavening. Over time, the basic design has assumed many forms, from elaborate geometrical patterns, to the more common "ribbed" shape vaguely resembling the spiraling twists of a turban, hence the alternative names "Turk's Turban" or "Turk's Head"—common descriptors for the molds made by nineteenth-century potters in the United States.

The refined cake that we know today displaced other much older and much more primitive yeast-raised cakes that had served as festive symbols for weddings, christenings, New Year's entertainments, in short, food associated with acts of commensality or with rites of passage as proposed by Austrian ethnographer Ernst Burgstaller. These old-style cakes were baked in earthenware pans, bowls, or even crocks. Thus, they lacked the eye-catching sculptural effect of the Gugelhupf.

In Austria's cities, these older, traditional poverty cakes disappeared during the early nineteenth century, because by then Viennese pastry cooks had expropriated the Gugelhupf, reinvented it, and integrated it into Biedermeier café culture. Thus, by the mid-1800s, it became a symbol of middle-class status, the Kaffeeklatsch circle, and genteel hospitality throughout the Austro-Hungarian Empire. That species of Gugelhupf, with its light, egg-rich crumb, its rosewater flavoring, chopped almonds, and elaborate shape lightly dusted with vanilla sugar, became codified in fashionable Viennese cookery by a number of Austro-Hungarian cookbook authors. Just the same, Austrian villagers did not forget their roots and thus transferred their older cake names to the Biedermeier form, to the extent that the Gugelhupf is still known locally in rural parts of that country under a variety of archaic medieval terms.

Still, mysterious legends about the origins of this cake persist. Perhaps foremost among them is the often repeated legend in French tourism literature that Marie Antoinette introduced the cake to France. Born in Vienna, she would certainly have known about Gugelhupf. If she made it fashionable at the French court, perhaps that alone provides us with legitimate seed for a culinary legend. But unfortunately for the myth mongers, several French museums own locally made Gugelhupf cake molds signed and dated from the 1600s, and many more cake molds in those collections are probably a century or so older.

Just as in Austria, the *kougelhopf* (as the cake is typically spelled there) maintains a dominant place in the food culture of Alsace. In fact, any Alsatian tourism bureau worth its annual budget will go out of its way to explain how important this cake is in local culture, even though the Alsatian origins are murky. Throughout Alsace, Gugelhupf is an accepted symbol of friendship, hospitality, mutual esteem, and so much a part of popular culture that the cake is served at all official receptions. And as in Austria, Alsatian Gugelhupf has displaced older and much more locally varied traditional cakes. It has condensed all the complicated culinary traditions of Alsatian and South German culture into the form of one symbolic coffee cake. Now marbled with chocolate or flavored with poppy seeds, it lingers on as ersatz "traditional fare" through the reinforcing promotions of tourist literature and regional cookbooks.

Today, Alsace is one of the few places where the traditional, yeast-leavened cake can easily be found. East of the Rhine, it is much more common to find recipes leavened with baking powder or, more laboriously, with beaten egg whites. The former is so ubiquitous that German baking powder typically features an image of Gugelhupf on the package. The cake has also mostly lost any ritual associations, instead being served for breakfast or as an afternoon snack, although in Poland, at least, Gugelhupf-like babas are still part of the Easter table, recalling the cake's celebratory past.

See also BABA AU RHUM; COFFEE CAKE; KUCHEN; PENNSYLVANIA DUTCH; VIENNA; and WEDDING CAKE.

Burgstaller, Ernst. *Österreichisches Festtagsgebäck.* Linz, Austria: Rudolf Trauner Verlag, 1983.
Doerflinger, Marguerite, and Georges Klein. *Toute la gastronomie alsacienne.* Vol. 2: *Plats sucrés.* Wettolsheim, France: Editions Mars et Mercure, 1979.
Rumpolt, Marx. *Ein new Kochbuch.* Frankfurt: Sigmund Feyerabend, 1581.
Währen, Max. "Die Märchenhaften Geheimnisse des Gugelhopfes und Ihre Enträtzelung." *Zürcher Backkunst* 1 (2004): 5–11.
Wiswe, Hans. *Kulturgeschichte der Kochkunst.* Munich: Heinz Moos Verlag, 1970.

William Woys Weaver

guilds and similar professional associations were present in Greek and Roman antiquity. However, with the fall of the Western Roman Empire, towns and cities shrank in size, and guilds waned with them. Because bakers' trades were indispensable to city-dwellers, they survived rather well through troubled centuries. The bakers were divided among proper bakers (*pistores*) and oven tenders (*fornarii*) who took care of communal ovens but also occasionally sold their own baked goods.

With Europe's improved economy and urbanization in the tenth and eleventh centuries, guilds reappeared, initially in the cities and small towns along the newly prosperous trade routes. In London, a guild of bakers obtained royal recognition by 1160. This guild may have served the royal household and possibly administered an early form of the Assize of Bread, a statute that regulated the price, weight, and quality of the bread sold in towns, villages, and hamlets from the thirteenth century on and was considered a crucial aspect of successful urban governance. The Assize of Bread was the first English law to regulate the production and sale of food.

As guilds specialized, they divided into new guilds. In Paris, Étienne Boileau, royal provost responsible for supervising trades, listed in his *Livre de métiers* (Book of the Trades, 1268) all the branches of the food trades (apart from the butchers, who had not filed their guild regulations). Each branch of the food trade had two or three different specialties, each with its own guild. The number of food professionals was higher in major cities. In the spring of 1288 Bonvesin da la Riva celebrated in his *De magnalibus urbis Mediolani* (On the Marvels of Milan) the many tradesmen who contributed to the city's renown; at the top of his list were 300 bakers, 440 butchers, 500 fishmongers, and more than 150 tavern keepers.

New Food Trades

New food-related trades and guilds emerged during the late Middle Ages. Their main purpose was to acquire exhaustive rights to prepare and sell certain types of foods that had not previously been regulated. The genesis of the cookie trade offers an illuminating example. Bakers throughout medieval Europe baked many varieties of bread, white and dark, eaten by different classes in society. During important religious holidays, bakers used some of their best wheat flour for cakes and pastries that could be sold only with the permission of the municipal authorities. Wealthy patrons, however, ordered their bakers to make such dainties all year round, and gradually the demand grew so great that authorities found it impossible to limit their production outside of holidays. Thus, the cookie trade was born. In Paris, cookie makers (*obloyers*) were granted privileges in 1270, and their status was confirmed by the king in 1397 and 1406.

The bakery trade continued to evolve. When the Paris pastry makers' guild was recognized in the fifteenth century, these professionals began to expand their selection of goods. In addition to meat pastries and tarts, they created sweetened products such as darioles, flans, and dauphins. See DARIOLE and FLAN (TART). In the meantime, candy makers had begun to split off from the grocers' guild (which had traditionally dominated the production of dragées, marzipan, and nougat) to form their own guilds in different parts of Europe, first in Spain, then in Sicily and northern Italy. See MARZIPAN and NOUGAT. Vendors of waffles and pastries became so important in late medieval Paris that they separated from the confectioners' guild (i.e., the professionals who produced comfits, all kinds of sweetmeats made from fruits, roots, or flowers preserved with sugar) and established their own guild. See CANDIED FLOWERS and COMFIT.

Craft Guilds

Craft guilds consisted of artisans and craftsmen in a particular branch of industry or commerce in a certain city or town. By joining together, these professionals were able to regulate competition among themselves and promote their own prosperity. They agreed on fundamental rules governing their trade, set quality standards, and policed their members' professional practices. Guild officials investigated complaints regarding bad workmanship and unfair competition and imposed fines on those who violated the guild's rules and standards.

Not all guilds were equal, and not all trades enjoyed the same social and economic status in their community: stronger and more prestigious guilds often subordinated others. Not only the wages but also the length of apprenticeship provide indicators of such differences. In Genoa, in 1230–1256, the annual income of a baker's assistant was among the lowest (10 soldi), as was that of cooks (3 lire, 12 soldi), while an apothecary's income (10 lire) was at the top end of the scale, and so was their social standing.

Among all professionals involved in the preparation of food, the confectioners were usually among the most highly regarded. Their skills were considered more advanced than those of ordinary cooks or bakers. A successful confectioner enjoyed a handsome income and a social standing clearly above that of most other food professionals. However, sugarworks like comfits were not the confectioner's exclusive domain. Because of their original medicinal uses, comfits were also produced by apothecaries, so the activities of these two highly regarded trades overlapped.

Apprenticeship System

Members of craft guilds were divided into masters, journeymen, and apprentices. The master was an established craftsman of recognized abilities—he possessed technical competence, wealth, and a respectable social position. He took on apprentices whom he trained in the elements of his trade, providing them with food, clothing, and shelter. In return, the apprentices worked for him without payment. The apprenticeship system secured the continuity of skills, tradition, and personnel on which the welfare of guilds depended.

The length of apprentice training varied between 2 and 12 years, depending on the craft: the longer the apprenticeship, the more prestigious the craft. Bakers' apprenticeships lasted four years, reflecting the trade's high standing. Even so, apprentices might serve the requisite number of years without acquiring proper skills, in which case the guild reserved the right to determine who was capable of practicing a craft. Among the many food trades, that of the cookie maker was considered very risky and laborious to learn in late medieval Paris. A professional cookie maker had to be able to make not less than 500 wafers (*oublies*) a day, in addition to 300 *supplications* and 200 *esterels* (two other kinds of wafers). See WAFERS.

New apprentices ranged in age from 8 to 17 years old. In many professions, the master was allowed to have only one apprentice in addition to his own son, but some professionals, such as dyers and goldsmiths, had the right to two. The number of butchers' and bakers' apprentices was not limited. Apprenticeship was only occasionally possible for girls.

After completing a fixed term of service, an apprentice became a journeyman, that is, a craftsman who could work for different masters and receive wages for his labor. Journeymen were not eligible to serve as guild officials, but most guilds allowed them to become members. If a journeyman wanted to better his position and obtain a master's title, he had to prove his skills by producing a masterpiece or by passing one or several tests. In Le Mans at the beginning of the sixteenth century, a candidate for master pastry maker had to demonstrate his competence and skills by using sugar loaves to make decent hippocras (sweetened and spiced wine). See HIPPOCRAS. The number of women working as day laborers (with journeymen status) in the urban trades is difficult to assess, but very seldom did they have the opportunity to become independent masters.

Merchant Guilds

Medieval merchant guilds were local associations, in a particular town or city, with privileges obtained from a local ruler granting the members exclusive rights to practice certain commercial activities. Merchant guilds became closely involved in regulating and protecting their members' commerce, not only locally but also at the level of long-distance trade. They controlled the distribution and sale of food, cloth, and other staple goods and hence obtained a monopoly over local commerce. They constrained foreign merchants and traders to pay fees if they wanted to participate in the local trade. Merchant guilds played a dominant role in the governance of many towns and cities.

Obviously, any craftsman could turn into a merchant by selling to the public. But the most prominent merchants conducted their business at a scale beyond the reach of ordinary guild masters. As for women, they did not usually have much to do with commercial food processing, but they were omnipresent in selling foodstuffs other than meat. Widowed women sometimes took over their late husband's business with the assistance of a male employee.

Decline of Guilds

From the twelfth to fifteenth centuries, guilds formed an important part of the economic and social fabric of Europe. Guilds contributed to the good government and economic prosperity of the towns and cities where they were located, setting and maintaining standards for the quality of goods and the probity of trading practices. In addition to their economic and educational functions, guilds served the social and religious needs of their members by building and maintaining guildhalls, churches, and chapels. Guilds performed charitable work not only among their own members but also within the community at large.

Guilds became long-lasting institutions because they offered efficient ways to promote the interests of professional groups while still competing against one another in a world that was constantly changing. The sixteenth century marked a turning point for most guilds. The growing pace of technological innovations and new opportunities for trade disrupted the control of craft guilds over particular industries. The merchant guilds, for their part, receded in importance when merchants became capitalistic entrepreneurs and formed companies. In Italy, Spain, and Germany, traditional merchant guilds survived into the early nineteenth century.

See also MEDICINAL USES OF SUGAR.

Desportes, Françoise. "Food Trades." In *Food: A Culinary History from Antiquity to the Present*, edited by Jean-Louis Flandrin and Massimo Montanari, pp. 275–286. New York: Columbia University Press, 2013.

Epstein, Steven A. *Wage Labor and Guilds in Medieval Europe*. Chapel Hill: University of North Carolina Press, 1991.

Epstein, S. R. "Craft Guilds, Apprenticeship, and Technological Change in Pre-industrial Europe." In *Guilds, Innovation and the European Economy, 1400–1800*, edited by S. R. Epstein and Maarten Prak, pp. 52–80. New York: Cambridge University Press, 2008.

Keene, Derek. "English Urban Guilds, c. 900–1300: The Purposes and Politics of Association." In *Guilds and Association in Europe 900–1900*, edited by Ian A. Gadd and Patrick Wallis, pp. 3–26. London: Centre for Metropolitan History, 2006.

Ogilvie, Sheilagh. *Institutions and European Trade. Merchant Guilds, 1000–1800*. Cambridge, U.K.: Cambridge University Press, 2011.

Hannele Klemettilä

Guittard is the oldest family-owned and operated chocolate company in the United States. Its continuity reflects the core value of sustainability the company has embraced since its founding. Guittard products are used by professionals and home bakers and also include ready-to-eat chocolate.

Etienne Guittard left his native France for California in the mid-nineteenth century to take part in the Gold Rush, intending to trade his family's French chocolate for mining tools. But he quickly realized the value of high-quality chocolate and decided to return to France to hone his craft. In 1868 he went back to San Francisco and opened Guittard Chocolate on Sansome Street. That same year, however, Guittard became part of a California Supreme Court case, when it was sued for trademark infringement. The company had misled consumers by calling its chocolate "Sweet German Chocolate," a name considered too similar to Baker's "German Sweet Chocolate." See BAKER'S.

In the twentieth century, Guittard overcame several challenges. The great 1906 San Francisco earthquake destroyed the factory, but the company recovered and relocated to Main Street. Next, the two world wars interrupted the global marketplace. Then the construction of the Embarcadero Freeway in 1958 forced the factory to move south of the city to Burlingame, California, while new automation within the chocolate industry challenged companies to balance economy with quality.

Today, the Guittard Company is involved with many organizations that promote sustainability by considering issues of the environment and producers along with the quality of the beans. Guittard purchases cacao beans certified by the Rainforest Alliance as fair trade. It is a member of the World Cocoa Foundation, which sponsors educational programs for youth in cacao-producing communities, and of the Cacao Livelihoods Program, which seeks to increase the economic viability of small-scale cacao farmers in West and Central Africa.

To improve the quality of chocolate and an understanding of terroir, Guittard established a line of single-varietal chocolates and became a founding member of the Heirloom Cacao Preservation Initiative, which seeks to identify and protect beans that produce chocolate of an exceptional quality and unique flavor. See CHOCOLATE, SINGLE ORIGIN. In 2007, company president Gary Guittard led the successful "Don't Mess with Our Chocolate" campaign that prevented the U.S. Food and Drug Administration from changing labeling laws to allow the use of the word "chocolate" by companies using cheaper substitutes. In this way Guittard circled back to the company's early years as a luxury purveyor, though from a very different perspective.

See also CHOCOLATE, LUXURY; CHOCOLATE, POST-COLUMBIAN; and COCOA.

Rosenblum, Mort. *Chocolate: A Bittersweet Saga of Dark and Light.* New York: North Point, 2006.

Beth M. Forrest

gulab jamun

See ZALABIYA.

gumball machines, with simple instructions like "Hold hand under opening. Insert coin. Crank knob," have made chewing gum readily available to the public on the go since 1888, when penny pieces began to be sold from a vending machine inside a New York City elevated rapid transit station. The hollow orbs of chewing gum covered in brightly colored candy shells known as gumballs were first sold from machines released by the Thomas Adams Gum Company in 1907. Traditional gumball machines, including the 1915 Digesto, and the Master Fantail manufactured in the 1920s and 1930s by Norris Manufacturing Company, consist of glass domes atop shiny chrome bases with coin slots, turning knobs, and chutes covered with metal flaps. Cheerful advertising decals attract customers, and discrete keyholes in the tops of the domes enable merchants to refill the machines. Founded in 1934, the Ford Gum and Machine Company sold tablet-shaped gum in rectangular dispensers that shared profits with service organizations such as the Lions Club

The first gumball machines to dispense candy-covered chewing gum came onto the market in 1907. They remain a favorite of children with a few coins to spare.

and Kiwanis International. Whether perceived in a positive or negative light, gum chewing has always been considered in relation to personal appearance, and the 1940s saw the advent of eye-level mirrors attached to gum-vending machines. In the early 1990s, OK Manufacturing of Salt Lake City, Utah, began distributing a 5-foot 8-inch attention-grabber called Gumball Falls. Holding up to 4,250 large gumballs, this machine releases a variety of flavored gumballs down dual spiraling tracks to the accompaniment of peppy music and flashing lights. In 2012 OK released a table-sized version that enables users to play pinball with a 1-inch gumball before it is dispensed.

See also CHEWING GUM.

Enes, Bill. *Silent Salesman Too: The Encyclopedia of Collecting Vending Machines*. Rev. ed. Lenexa, Kans.: B. and P. Enes, 1995.

Harley Spiller

gummies are relatively moist, chewy candies manufactured by immersing a sugar syrup in a gelling agent, pouring the mixture into a starch mold, and leaving it to solidify. Gummies are spiritual successors to the lozenges, pastilles, and other gum arabic- and gum tragacanth-based fruit gums that spread from the Middle East to Europe. See LOZENGE; PASTILLAGE; and TRAGACANTH. Modern gummies are a thoroughly industrial phenomenon, mass produced in factories, and with ingredient lists that typically include food dyes, artificial sweeteners, and gelatin. Gummies are easily molded and come in a bewildering array of shapes, from dinosaurs, sharks, frog legs, fried eggs, and phalluses to teeth, brains, aliens, hamburgers, and soda bottles.

Today's superabundant gummies have a common ancestor in the upright dancing gummi bear invented by Hans Riegel Sr., founder of the German confectionery company Haribo. See HARIBO. Introduced in 1922, Riegel's Dancing Bears (Tanzbären) were an immediate hit, helped along by their affordability: two Dancing Bears cost just a pfennig (one hundredth of a Deutschmark) during the hyperinflation years of post–World War I Germany.

Gummies were popular in Europe throughout most of the twentieth century, but they did not find a big American market until the 1980s. One early entrant was the Swedish manufacturer Malaco, which began exporting gummies to North America in 1957. Swedish Fish, which Malaco developed specifically for the North American market, are made with wine gum rather than gelatin, resulting in a firmer texture. Trolli, based in Fürth, Bavaria, first opened its factory in 1948, but it began targeting the American market only in 1975. Trolli's major innovation was to create double-layered gummies that combined gummi and foam textures; their fruit rings, such as apple rings and peach rings, remain popular, as does the "Trolli-Burger," a miniature gummi hamburger. In 1981 Trolli scored a big hit with brightly colored gummi worms, or crawlers, later developed in a sour variety.

Two companies both claim to have been the first to produce gummi bears in the United States, in 1981: the Herman Goelitz Candy Company (later the Jelly Belly Candy Company), based in Fairfield, California, and the Brock Candy Company, based in Chattanooga, Tennessee. Haribo, concerned by the growing competition, opened an American distribution center in Baltimore, Maryland, in 1982. Today, Haribo remains the largest gummi bear manufacturer in the world, producing 100 million gummi bears a day.

Jelly Babies, a popular British sweet, are somewhat like gummi bears, though with a harder outer shell dusted in starch and a jellied interior. They were invented in 1864 by an Austrian confectioner who gave them the rather horrifying name "Unclaimed Babies." In 1918, Bassett's, a British confectionery company in Sheffield, began producing a similar product, which they called "Peace Babies" to celebrate the end of World War I. Bassett's suspended production due to materials shortages during World War II, but relaunched them in 1953 as Jelly Babies. George Harrison reportedly loved them; at the height of Beatlemania fans would sometimes pelt them at the stage, much to the Beatles' irritation.

Not all gummies are anthropomorphic or zoomorphic. Gumdrops are cone-shaped gummies coated with sugar that have a soft, jelly-like texture. Spice drops are a variation on the gumdrop that feature flavors such as mint or cinnamon. DOTS, made by the Mason Division of Candy Corporation of America and now owned by Tootsie Roll Industries, claims to be America's "#1 selling gumdrop brand" since first being introduced in 1945. Jujubes and Jujyfruits, related wine-gum (starch-based) drops manufactured by the Heide Candy Company, first appeared in the 1920s with names that linked them to older gumdrops made from the fruit of the jujube tree. The link to jujubes is entirely nostalgic, as the modern candies contain no actual jujube fruit. In Canada jujubes, or jubes, are not a brand name but a broad group of related gummi candies.

Gummies hold a particular appeal for children, and youth-focused media companies have done well with gummi-based animations. In the mid-1980s and early 1990s Disney aired a television show called *Disney's Adventures of the Gummi Bears*, which featured anthropomorphic bears who could bounce away from hunters after drinking magic "Gummiberry juice." More recently, Gummibär, a singing and dancing animated gummi bear character created by the New Jersey-based entertainment company Gummybear International, surpassed one billion YouTube views.

Today, adults are more likely than ever to see the appeal of gummies. Gummi vitamins, developed to get fussy children to take their vitamins, proved so popular with adults that many adult vitamins and supplements now appear in gummi form. Less healthfully, alcohol-soaked gummies are popular party treats. The gummi fruit flavors mask the alcohol content, making them deceptively strong, and correspondingly dangerous for underage consumers.

Gummi manufacturers are tweaking their recipes and their advertising to appeal to changing consumer demands. Vegetarian gummies use pectin or starch in lieu of animal gelatin; organic gummies use organic cane sugar and organic fruit juices; and Kosher gummies use fish gelatin. Cavity-fighting gummi bears are being tested that incorporate xylitol, a sugar substitute. See XYLITOL. Sugar-free gummies are already available, though not always desirable. Haribo's sugar-free Gold-Bears use a hydrogenated syrup called lycasin that is not fully digestible by humans. The bags carry a safety warning stating that "some sugar-free candies may cause stomach discomfort and/or a laxative effect." Judging from Amazon reviewer comments, this warning may understate the case.

See also ANTHROPOMORPHIC AND ZOOMORPHIC SWEETS; GAG CANDY; and JELLY BEANS.

Deezen, Eddie. "When the Beatles Were Pelted with Jelly Beans," *Today I Found Out*, 11 August 2014. http://www.todayifoundout.com/index.php/2012/11/when-the-beatles-got-pelted-with-jelly-beans/ (accessed 15 September 2014).

Deis, Ronald C. "Candy Creations with Starch and Its Derivatives." *Food Product Design*, 1 September 1997. http://www.foodproductdesign.com/articles/1997/09/candy-creations-with-starch-and-its-derivatives.aspx (accessed 11 August 2014).

Khazan, Olga. "What's in Those Haribo Gummy Bears?" *The Atlantic*, 17 January 2014. http://www.theatlantic.com/health/archive/2014/01/whats-in-those-haribo-gummy-bears/283162/ (accessed 11 August 2014).

McGee, Harold. *On Food and Cooking: The Science and Lore of the Kitchen*. New York: Scribner, 2004.

Richardson, Tim. *Sweets: A History of Candy*. New York: MJF, 2002.

Romanowski, Perry. "How Products Are Made: Gummy Candy." http://www.madehow.com/Volume-3/Gummy-Candy.html#b (accessed 11 August 2014).

Max P. Sinsheimer

gummy bears

See GUMMIES and HARIBO.

Guriev kasha, a porridge of semolina layered with jam, honey, dried or preserved fruits, and candied nuts, carries the name of Count Dmitri Alexandrovich Guriev (1751–1825), minister of finance under Tsar Alexander I and a well-known gastronome. Legends abound about the origins of this extravagant dessert. Some sources say Guriev himself created the dish in the late eighteenth century. Others attribute it to a brilliant serf employed by a major in the Orenburg Dragoons, whose skill so impressed the count that he immediately bought the serf and installed him at his own estate.

A marriage between Russian comfort food and French haute cuisine, Guriev kasha appears in many variations, but the traditional recipe always includes golden skins formed by baking rich milk or cream in the oven. The skin that appears on the top of the milk is lifted off and used to separate the layers of semolina and its fillings. Then the porridge is sprinkled on top with sugar and browned under a salamander or broiler in the fashion of crème brûlée.

Guriev kasha appeared on the most fashionable menus of the nineteenth century, including the coronation menu for Tsar Alexander III. The dessert even figures in Russian history. In 1888, while traveling to St. Petersburg in his private train, Alexander III was about to partake of his beloved dessert when the train derailed at high speed, killing 23 people. His miraculous survival made Guriev kasha even more legendary.

Siutkina, Olga, and Pavel Siutkin. "Gur'evskaia kasha: Prav li Pokhlebkin?" [Guriev Kasha: Is Pokhlebkin Right?]. 5 July 2012. http://www.vkusitsvet.ru/tovarisch-est/istorii-ob-istorii/gurevskaya-kasha-prav-li-poxlebkin/ (accessed 7 August 2013).

Darra Goldstein

Häagen-Dazs belongs to the category of rich, dense, super-premium ice creams that have more butterfat and less overrun (air) than the average ice cream. Reuben and Rose Mattus created the upscale brand in their family-owned ice cream plant in the Bronx, New York. See ICE CREAM and BEN & JERRY'S.

In 1921 young Reuben immigrated to New York from Grodno, Belarus, with his widowed mother, Lea Mattus. Reuben tasted ice cream for the very first time on Ellis Island, where newcomers were treated to the luscious dessert because it reinforced the concept of America as the land of plenty. Initially, Lea earned money by cooking for single men in her neighborhood. Then she partnered with one of the bachelors to start a business making Italian ices in the Bronx. Lea took charge, and under her frugal management the business reaped large profits. She expanded her product line, adding ice cream novelties and bulk ice cream.

Reuben worked for his mother, learning every aspect of the business. In 1936 he married a gregarious, energetic young woman named Rose Vesel. Only months after their marriage, the newlyweds bought out Lea's partner. Reuben had fresh ideas for the business. He knew that the food industry was changing and that the Mattus company must change, too, but Lea vetoed his ideas.

After World War II, food conglomerates monopolized the space in supermarket freezers, squeezing small companies out of the marketplace. To prosper, the Mattuses needed a unique product that would fill a market niche overlooked by the big corporations. Reuben planned to survive by catering to a special segment of the market. He wanted to make an ultra-rich, top-quality ice cream that would attract consumers willing to pay extra for superior taste. Although Lea never put her stamp of approval on his plan, she gradually relinquished control.

In the late 1950s the Mattuses marketed a high-quality ice cream called Ciro's. Sales were very good, but Ciro's did not quite fulfill Reuben's vision. He continued to tweak his formulas until he created exactly the right flavors and texture. He wanted a sophisticated, cosmopolitan image for his new brand, so he put a map of Scandinavia on the container. He coined the name Häagen-Dazs because he wanted it to sound Danish.

Initially, the Mattuses sold only three flavors of their new brand: vanilla, chocolate, and coffee. They expected Häagen-Dazs to find a niche, but they were surprised by the nature of the market. Rose later described it as "an alternative market... steeped in the marijuana culture of the '60s." The brand's first fans "were a motley assortment of oddballs with long hair, fringe tastes, and decidedly eccentric business styles." Like cool evangelists, the hippies spread the word about the great new ice cream with the funny name.

In 1976 Rose and Reuben's daughter Doris Mattus Hurley opened the first Häagen-Dazs scoop shop, a successful venture that led to a chain of shops. In 1984 the Mattuses sold Häagen-Dazs to a food conglomerate, which later resold it. The brand expanded by adding new flavors and products, including ice cream bars, frozen yogurt, and sorbet. The company is now under the umbrella of General Mills.

Mattus, Rose Vesel, and Jeanette Friedman. *The Emperor of Ice Cream: The True Story of Häagen-Dazs*. New Milford, N.J.: The Wordsmithy, 2004.

"Rose Mattus, Co-founder of Häagen-Dazs Ice Cream Company, Dies at Ninety." *Canadian Press*, 30 November 2006.

Anne Cooper Funderburg

Halloween is a fall festival celebrated on 31 October, mainly in the British Isles and North America (although since the mid-1990s its celebration has become popular in parts of Continental Europe, Asia, and South Africa). The name Halloween derives from All Hallows' Eve, or the evening before All Saints Day, a Catholic celebration that was moved to 1 November (from its original date of 13 May) in the eighth century. The date was probably chosen to co-opt the pagan New Year's holiday of Samhain, celebrated by the ancient Irish Celtic tribes.

Because of its placement in the calendar, Halloween has always been associated with harvest and food. Apples were sacred to the Celts, and the red fruit has been part of Halloween throughout its history, serving as game (bobbing for apples), fortune-telling device (often involving paring an apple, with the form of the parings indicating a future spouse's initials), and food (most recently caramel apples, or apples on a stick covered with thick caramel sauce).

Halloween's association with sweets, however, may have begun because of another holiday that was added to the festival: in 998 C.E. All Souls' Day was designated as a day of memorial, celebrated on 2 November. The day was initially added to the celebration of All Saints' Day as a way for families to commemorate their own deceased members as they had the saints; by the sixteenth century "soul cakes" were distributed to beggars in exchange for prayers for the souls of loved ones in Purgatory. These small, flat, round cakes were usually made with milk, eggs, and spices, although sometimes fruit or seeds were added. "Souling" became the name for the act of going house-to-house begging for cakes, or offering a small musical performance in exchange for cakes.

In 1647 the British Parliament banned the celebration of all Catholic festivals, but Halloween was still enjoyed in Scotland and Ireland. The Irish have long celebrated Halloween with a traditional cake called "barm brack," made from dried fruit and strong black tea. See FRUITCAKE. This cake is often baked with small charms inside of it, giving it the name "fortune cake." Whoever receives a slice with, for example, a ring will be married soon, while a coin might indicate wealth, or a thimble, spinsterhood.

In the nineteenth century, as famine drove many of the Irish and Scots across the Atlantic to America, they brought their customs to the New World's large middle class, which had a fondness for parties and found Halloween, with its ghost stories and fortune-telling games, ideal for their children. By the 1870s American magazines were full of stories and articles about children's Halloween parties, with "pulling molasses candy" (also known as "pulling taffy") a typical activity (this candy, made largely from molasses, brown sugar, butter, and water, is pulled into long, thin strips as it hardens). See TAFFY. Pulling candy may have been especially popular at Halloween parties because of the way the strips occasionally curled to suggest arcane symbols and mysterious shapes. The fortune cake and apples remained characteristic Halloween party foods well into the twentieth century.

This Curtiss Candy Company advertisement appeared in *Woman's Day* magazine in 1956 with the tagline "Be Good to Your Goblins!" By the 1950s, homeowners preferred to give Halloween trick-or-treaters commercially wrapped treats rather than go to the trouble of making homemade doughnuts and taffy.

Around the turn of the twentieth century, commercially manufactured candy began to appear at Halloween. Sold for use at children's parties, the first store-bought Halloween candies were small sugar pellets sold in colorful containers (which are now highly collectible), but by the 1920s these had been replaced by candy corn, an inch-high, cone-shaped confection that combines white, orange, and yellow colors, roughly mimicking the appearance of corn kernels. First created by George Renninger at the Wunderle Candy Company in the 1880s, the candy combined mainly sugar, corn syrup, and wax, and, thanks to its autumnal colors, soon became a Halloween favorite. Produced now primarily by Brach's Confections, candy corn variants are made for other holidays (e.g., Indian Corn, which includes chocolate, is sold at Thanksgiving) and has spun off similar products, such as Brach's Mellowcreme Pumpkins, small orange and green pumpkin-shaped candies made from sugar, corn syrup, wax, and honey. Candy corn's distinctive shape and colors have led to reproductions in candle form and ceramics.

Trick or Treat

By the 1930s the American Halloween celebration had become largely the province of pre-adolescent boys whose mischievous pranks on the night had gradually become more and more destructive as they moved into urban areas, until many cities considered banning the festival altogether. However, homeowners soon discovered that it was more practical to buy off the pranksters with planned activities, which included parties, games, costuming, and foods. A famed 1939 article "A Victim of the Window-Soaping Brigade?" from *American Home* magazine suggests inviting the mischief-makers into the home for doughnuts and apple cider, and provides possibly the first national mention of the term "trick or treat." See DOUGHNUTS.

As a result of sugar rationing during World War II, the practice of trick or treat—in which costumed children go from house to house demanding treats in exchange for no tricks—did not become popular throughout the United States until the 1950s. See SUGAR RATIONING. Companies like Brach's, Hershey, and Nestlé started to target Halloween in both production and marketing, and homeowners agreed that it was far easier to hand out pre-made, individually wrapped treats than to cook their own mass quantities of doughnuts and taffy. See HERSHEY'S and NESTLÉ. The increasing boom in candy sales at Halloween led to an entire side industry of trick-or-treat bags and buckets—used by children to collect their voluminous Halloween sweets—often shaped and colored like jack-o'-lanterns.

Soon the popularity of candy corn was eclipsed by chocolate as the preferred Halloween treat. By the twenty-first century Halloween surpassed all other holidays—including Easter and Valentine's Day—in chocolate sales, with annual revenues in the billions. See VALENTINE'S DAY. Candy and cookie manufacturers now release products especially for Halloween each year. In 2012, for example, Oreo cookies made headlines with a special Halloween candy corn–flavored and colored version of the sandwich cookie in a "limited edition." See OREOS.

Halloween treats started to come under fire in the 1960s, as the urban myth of the razor blade in the apple spread. In 1974 a Texan named Ronald Clark O'Bryan earned the nickname "The Candyman" for poisoning his eight-year-old son Timothy with a cyanide-laced "Pixy Stix," a long straw usually filled with innocent dextrose and citric acid. O'Bryan's crime led to the notion of the anonymous poisoner of Halloween candy. Even though this myth had virtually no basis in fact, parents began to clamp down on trick or treat, while hospitals initiated programs to X-ray children's trick-or-treat bags. However, trick or treat proved to be too beloved a ritual to die, and it is now celebrated in areas of Europe and Japan as well.

Dia de los Muertos

In Mexico and Central America—where Catholic holidays combined with Aztec and Mayan traditions instead of Celtic—Halloween is seldom observed. Instead, Dia de los Muertos (Day of the Dead), a festival that combines commemoration of the dead with skull imagery, is celebrated on 2 November (although the festivities may begin on 31 October). The small sugar skull, made from a process known as *alfeñique* (in which items are molded from sugar paste), has become the primary symbol of Dia de los Muertos, although the skulls (which may be decorated with sequins and other inedible objects) are seldom consumed. *Pan de muerto*, or "bread of the dead," is a simple sweet bread (sometimes anise seed is added), which may be baked in the shape of bones or even a corpse, and is eaten as part of the festival, often at the graveside of a loved one. See DAY OF THE DEAD.

See also ANTHROPOMORPHIC AND ZOOMORPHIC SWEETS; BREADS, SWEET; and CHILDREN'S CANDY.

Good, Dan. "Candy Corn Oreos Hitting Store Shelves." *New York Post*, 10 September 2012.
Morton, Lisa. *The Halloween Encyclopedia*. 2d ed. Jefferson, N.C.: McFarland, 2011.
Morton, Lisa. *Trick or Treat: A History of Halloween*. London: Reaktion, 2012.

Lisa Morton

halvah means "sweetmeat" in Arabic, and diverse preparations throughout the eastern Mediterranean share this generic name. In Lebanon and Syria, in Israel and Jewish communities all over the world, and in Greece and the Balkans, halvah generally refers to a tahini-based sweet (also known as *halva, helva, halwa*, or *halawa*).

Halvah is first mentioned in the thirteenth-century Arabic *Kitāb al-Ṭabīkh* (The Book of Dishes), where *halwā yabisā* (dry sweetmeat) describes a sugar candy with almonds and sesame or poppy seeds, flavored with saffron and cinnamon. It appears to be similar to the sesame and honey candy called *pasteli* in Greek, a different type of confection. See GREECE AND CYPRUS. In his seventeenth-century *Seyahatname* (Book of Travels), Evliya Çelebi, the famous Ottoman chronicler of the eastern Mediterranean, mentions *tahin helvāsi* or *tahine*. He describes the street vendors of halvah in Istanbul, praises the quality of halvah in Bursa, and writes that Konya's most revered sweet was halvah. See TURKEY.

Sesame halvah is a combination of tahini paste and *natef*, an intriguing, sweet Arab dip made by boiling the root of soapwort (*Saponaria officinalis*) in water, then whipping the brown broth until it becomes white foam—an amazing transformation made possible by the presence of saponin in the root. The white foam is then mixed with thick sugar syrup, and tahini is added to make the halvah. The mixture is churned and beaten in a special machine, after which the resulting hard mass is transferred to a large bowl or trough in which strong young men knead it by hand. The somewhat irregular, fibrous texture of this coveted hand-kneaded halvah—still made in family workshops in Greece, Turkey, and the Middle East—distinguishes it from mechanically produced factory halvah with its compact, uniform texture.

It is unclear how and when halvah was adopted by the Polish Ashkenazi community and sold in Jewish dairy stores. Eastern European immigrants introduced halvah to the United States, and in 1907 Nathan Radutzky, a Jew from Kiev, became the first to produce halvah on New York's Lower East Side. His family continues to be the leading manufacturer of halvah in the United States. Now that modern chefs have rediscovered this ancient sweet, small producers have begun making organic, "gourmet" halvah spreads.

In Greece, tahini halvah is a very popular sweet, especially eaten during Lent. It is often called *halvas tou bakali* (the grocer's halvah) to distinguish it from homemade confections.

Flour, semolina, or cornstarch constitutes the main ingredient in a different kind of halvah that is popular in Iran, Turkey, Greece, and the Persian Gulf. To make this rich style of halvah, the starch is sautéed in butter and then moistened with sugar or honey syrup to make a soft, buttery sweet, one that can be traced back to medieval times. Al-Warrāq's tenth-century Baghdadi cookbook describes the cooking process and gives instructions for making date, apple, and carrot halvah—dishes later brought to India by the Mughals. See INDIA. Turabi Efendi's 1862 *Turkish Cookery Book* lists several of these so-called *helvāssi*. Some are made with wheat starch, whereas the recipe for *irimik helvāssi* calls for tiny pearls of sago, "small as gunpowder." Unlike *tahin helvāsi*, considered a poor person's sweet, these soft halvahs are often moistened with syrup mixed with milk and enriched with almonds, pine nuts, pistachios, and other nuts. This type of halvah is occasionally shaped with spoons, like quenelles, but more often it is transferred to molds, or spread on a pan, and left to set before being cut into squares or diamonds and served at room temperature. *Halvas simigdalenios* (semolina halvah) is the Greek version, for which semolina is toasted in olive oil instead of butter. There is also an old, frugal Greek version of olive oil halvah that uses chickpea flour instead of semolina.

See also MIDDLE EAST and NORTH AFRICA.

Krondl, Michael. *Sweet Invention: A History of Dessert*. Chicago: Chicago Review Press, 2011.
Saberi, Helen J., Helou Anissa, Esteban Pombo-Villar, Claudia Roden, and Alan Davidson. "A Spicy Mystery or With Soap on Our Hands and Foam at Our Mouths." In *The Wilder Shores of Gastronomy: 20 Years of the Best Food Writing from the Journal Petits Propos Culinaires*, edited by Alan Davidson and Helen J. Saberi, pp. 27–38. Berkeley, Calif.: Ten Speed, 2002.
Yerasimos, Marianna. *500 Years of Ottoman Cuisine*, pp. 239–241. Istanbul: Boyut, 2002.

Aglaia Kremezi

hamantaschen are triangular cookies filled with prunes, poppy seeds, jam, or even chocolate chips. These cookies are served at Purim, the holiday celebrating the Jewish people's deliverance from serious danger in the remote past. The word likely derives from the German *Mohntaschen,* poppy seed pastries, though some ascribe its origin to a combination of *Homen*—the Yiddish name for Haman, chief minister of the biblical Persian king Ahasuerus and enemy of the Jews (Esther 3:7)—and *tash* (pocket or bag) from the Middle High German *tasche.* Although in Israel these pocket pastries are called *oznei Haman* (Haman's ears), elsewhere the cookie's three corners are said to represent Abraham, Isaac, and Jacob—the three patriarchs whose merit saved the Jews. Hamantaschen have also been said to represent the wicked minister Haman's hat. In any case, eating these cookies symbolically commemorates Esther's cunning in saving the Jews from Haman's proposed annihilation in fifth-century B.C.E. Persia.

Sometimes made with yeast and sometimes from a short butter crust, hamantaschen are a relatively new addition to the global Jewish gastronomic scene, although similar filled pastries, like the *Mohntaschen,* were known in medieval Germany and Central Europe. One of the earliest American recipes for *Mohn Maultaschen* (poppy seed tartlets) may be found in *"Aunt Babette's" Cookbook: Foreign and Domestic Receipts for the Household,* published in Cincinnati in 1889 by the publishing company of Edward H. Bloch, a leader in the Reform Jewish movement. It calls for a filling of ground poppy seed, egg yolks, sugar, lemon peel, and crushed almonds both bitter and sweet, with raisins, citron, and rosewater as optional additions. Stiffly beaten egg whites are folded into this mixture, which is used to fill squares of puff pastry that are then shaped into triangles and baked in a hot oven.

Nineteenth-century cookbooks often give recipes for preferred Purim treats, such as the Purim Fritters (also called Queen Esther's Toast but known today as French Toast) in *Jennie June's American Cookery Book* (published by the American News Company in 1866), or Purim Puffs, basically a doughnut, in *The 20th Century Cookbook* (published in 1897 by C. F. Moritz and Adelle Kahn). At the beginning of the twentieth century in America, hamantaschen with a short dough became extremely popular, even among non-Jews. Traditional fillings included poppy seed or a thick purée of prunes or apricots called *lekvar,* a type of fruit butter. Today, Nutella, chocolate chips, lemon curd, and even Biscoff cookie spread are frequently used. See NUTELLA.

In the seasonal cycle of Jewish holidays, Purim's gastronomic position is quite important. Because it is the last festival before Passover, Purim is an occasion to use up all the previous year's flour. Hamantaschen, along with other sweets and fruit, are prepared and sent as gifts, called *shalach manot,* to neighbors, the poor, and the elderly. During the rest of the year, hamantaschen are often displayed with other pastries in Jewish bakery windows from Brooklyn to Paris.

See also JUDAISM; PASSOVER; and POPPY SEED.

Nathan, Joan. *Jewish Holiday Kitchen.* New York: Schocken, 2004.

Joan Nathan

hand pie

See TURNOVERS.

Hanukkah, also Hanukah, Chanukah, or Chanukkah, is the Festival of Lights celebrating the Maccabean victory over the Seleucids in 164 B.C.E. Arriving at the Temple to cleanse and rededicate it, the Maccabees found only enough sacred oil to light the menorah, the candelabrum, for one day. But a miracle occurred, and one day's supply lasted for eight. Therefore, for each of the eight nights of Hanukkah, an additional candle is inserted into the menorah, from right to left. The candles are lit by a *shammas* (or helper candle), from left to right, until on the final night an eight-candled menorah is aglow. After the candle ceremony, it is traditional to sing songs, play with a dreidel (spinning top), open presents, and eat latkes (fried potato pancakes) as well as other fried foods, including desserts fried in or made with oil. For example, Persian Jews eat *zelebi,* a snail-shaped, deep-fried sweet. See ZALABIYA. Jews in Latin America eat *buñuelos,* fried pastries introduced by Spanish settlers who likely learned to make them from Iberian Muslims.

Cheese-based dishes such as kugel and cheesecake are also eaten during Hanukkah to honor Judith's slaying of Holofernes, a general who attempted to demolish the town of Bethulia, Israel, in the sixth century B.C.E. Judith, a beautiful widow, gave Holofernes wine and cheese, and once the general became drunk, she cut off his head. Emboldened, the Israelites defeated Holofernes's terrified troops.

In Israel today, *sufganiyot* are the most popular Hanukkah treat. The word "sufganiyot" was a neologism for pastry, derived from the Talmudic *sofgan* or *sfogga*, meaning "spongy dough." *Sufganiyot* are basically raised jelly doughnuts rolled in sugar, a recipe brought by Jewish Central European settlers in the early part of the twentieth century. In Europe doughnuts (*Krapfen, pączki*) had long been fried for a variety of holidays by Germans, Poles, and others. According to Gil Marks (2010), the jelly doughnut's modern-day popularity dates from the 1920s when Histadrut, the Israeli labor federation, encouraged its compatriots to replace the homemade latkes (potato pancakes) popular among European immigrants with commercially produced *sufganiyot*. See DOUGHNUTS.

No matter the ethnic origin of the baker, every bakery in Israel makes *sufganiyot* for Hanukkah. Today, they are sometimes filled with foie gras, sometimes with dulce de leche—anything goes in the contemporary Israeli kitchen. See DULCE DE LECHE. In that spirit, rugelach—crescent or half-moon-shaped cookies made from cream-cheese-enriched dough and commonly filled with apricot preserves or chocolate—are now also popular at Hanukkah, even though they are not prepared with oil. See RUGELACH.

See also DOUGHNUTS; FRIED DOUGH; FRITTERS; GREECE AND CYPRUS; and PANCAKES.

Marks, Gil. *The Encyclopedia of Jewish Food*. Hoboken, N.J.: Wiley, 2010.

Nathan, Joan. *The Foods of Israel Today*. New York: Knopf, 2010.

Joan Nathan

hard candy is nearly as hard to define as it is to chew. In the United States, the term describes a wide variety of sweets, including drops, fruit lozenges, peppermints, lollipops, sour balls, candy sticks and canes, and rock candy. Familiar American brands like Life Savers, NECCO Wafers, Tootsie Pops, Boston Baked Beans, Red Hots, and Lemonheads use hard candy techniques—boiling sugar to the "crack" or "hard crack" stage—to create specialized tastes. See LIFE SAVERS; NECCO; and STAGES OF SUGAR SYRUP. The British-English notion of "boiled sweets" shares some similarities with North American "hard candy"; meanwhile, the Scots refer to "hard boilings," which include "soor plooms" (sourballs), "fizzy boilings" like sherbet lemons that explode as they dissolve in the mouth, and chalky, crumbly mints called "Berwick cockles" for their rounded shape ribbed with peppermint stripes. See SHERBET POWDER.

Temperature is of primary importance in making clear candies like fruit drops. When a syrup of sugar and water is cooked to the hard crack stage (once called the "caramel height") at the upper end of the temperature range for candy making, 275 to 338°F (135 to 170°C), the sugar syrup forms breakable threads. See CARAMELS. Cooking to a high temperature decreases the amount of water in syrup, and sugar syrup containing less than 2 percent water is optimal for hard candy, as it creates a clear, hard mass when cooled. Confectioners have also long known that crystals or "grain" can be produced when sugar is boiled, especially when it is stirred, a practice important for lower-temperature syrups, in which grain helps the mixture to harden on cooling. This process of crystallization, known as "graining," is desirable in certain confections, like fudge, but it is discouraged in clear hard candies made from high-temperature sugar syrups. See FUDGE.

The sucrose in sugar inverts to glucose and fructose when dissolved in water. See FRUCTOSE and GLUCOSE. Doctoring—adding inverting and flavoring agents—is a technique to control this inversion. To help prevent the formation of crystals, corn syrup, which does not crystallize, is often added to the sugar solution at a ratio of less than 3 parts corn syrup to 2 parts sugar. See CORN SYRUP. In pure, clear hard candy, tartaric acid or lemon may be added to enhance inversion and prevent graining or recrystallization. Acids prevent graining, while stirring induces graining. It is all about balance, which confectioners have perfected over centuries.

The boiled sugar syrup can be formed into shapes, poured into molds, pulled into rolls and cut, crystallized on a stick, or layered over a filling. Adding butter to the sugar syrup results in butterscotch; cooking at a slightly lower temperature with an even sugar and corn syrup ratio results in brittle; and adding flavorings results in mints or lemon drops. See BRITTLE and BUTTERSCOTCH. Hard candies must be wrapped or stored airtight in a dry place; otherwise, moisture will cause them to turn sticky or grainy, rather than retaining their smooth, glistening property.

Early accounts from China describe boiling barley and water to a hard consistency, then spinning it into sticks rolled in toasted sesame seeds. See BARLEY SUGAR. Persian exports of boiled sugar lumps were known in Europe by the twelfth century, and soon came to be flavored with violets, cinnamon, or rosewater and even gold leaf in *manus christi*. From the Persian *fanid* came the English penid or pennet, flavored with peppermint or oil of wintergreen for smokers or for medicinal uses. With the discovery of techniques like panning, sugar syrup could be poured in layers to form a smooth, hard coating. See PANNING. Sugar syrup made hard shells for spices, nuts, or shards of lemon or orange peel to sweeten medieval comfits, the precursor of hard candies such as cinnamon Tic Tacs. Candied flowers and larger comfits called dragées also used this sugar-coating process; however, comfits and their modern descendants are not technically hard candies, since the sugar syrup is taken only a few degrees above boiling. North Americans might consider the modern British Gobstopper, or jawbreaker, to be the ultimate layering of sugar to form a hard candy—it is a hard, round ball with varicolored layers that are revealed as the ball is sucked.

Rose acid, colored with cochineal, was a popular boiled sweet on the streets of London. The sparkling, glass-like appearance of hard candy prompted the desire for more vivid color than could be obtained from the bodies of insects, leading in the 1830s to the dangerous addition of synthetic pigments from lead- and mercury-derived reds to the then-novel coal-tar dyes. See FOOD COLORINGS.

Because of a belief in the medicinal properties of sugar and the precision with which sugar syrup must be treated, hard candy was once the province of apothecaries, but with mechanization in the mid-nineteenth century came the potential for mass production of boiled sweets, and penny candy became available to the masses, especially children. See CHILDREN'S CANDY and PENNY CANDY. By the early twentieth century, the perception of candy had come full circle from a valued and prescribed digestive to a craving that could lead to addiction. Thus, housewives were encouraged to make their own candy, not simply to avoid toxic dyes from coloring agents and the ink of the wrappers, but mainly to prevent moral dissolution from too much candy consumption.

See also CANDY; CANDIED FLOWERS; COMFIT; and MEDICINAL USES OF SUGAR.

Gott, Philip P. *All About Candy and Chocolate.* Chicago: National Confectioners' Association of the United States, 1958.

Mason, Laura. *Sugar-Plums and Sherbet.* Totnes, U.K.: Prospect, 1998.

Richardson, Tim. *Sweets.* New York: Bloomsbury, 2002.

Woloson, Wendy A. *Refined Tastes.* Baltimore: Johns Hopkins University Press, 2002.

Ardath Weaver

Haribo, a candy manufacturer, is an extremely well-known German brand whose signature product is Gummi Bears. The company's name is an acronym for Johann "Hans" Riegel Bonn. Riegel (1893–1945), a trained confectioner, started his own company from scratch in Bonn in 1920. He created the Gummi Bears in 1922, inspired by the costumed bears that were a featured attraction at fairs. In 1925 Riegel added licorice to his line of products, and the company's wheel-shaped licorice candies became extremely popular.

Like many of his contemporaries, Riegel recognized the importance of advertising early on, and in the mid-1930s he came up with the advertising slogan still used today: "Haribo macht Kinder froh" (Haribo makes children happy). Upon Riegel's death, his sons Hans (1923–2013) and Paul (1926–2009) took over, and Haribo thrived, with 1,000 employees in 1950. The company's dancing bears were renamed *Goldbären* (gold bears) in 1960 and trademarked in 1967; today, they are sold in 116 countries. The first TV ads appeared in 1962, and soon thereafter the phrase "und Erwachsene ebenso" (and grown-ups too) was added to the company's slogan to broaden its consumer base (in English-speaking countries, the slogan reads "Kids and Grown-Ups Love It So, the Happy World of Haribo").

Today, Haribo has expanded, with over 6,000 employees. In addition to its classic fruit gums and licorice and chewy candy varieties, the company releases a constant stream of new products to appeal to current tastes. Haribo has been the subject of controversies surrounding management succession, forced labor during World War II (which the company has denied), and the naming of some licorice products with the term *Neger* (Negro). In 1993 *Negergeld* (Negro money) was renamed *Lakritztaler*, licorice coins. See LICORICE.

See also ANTHROPOMORPHIC AND ZOOMORPHIC SWEETS; CANDY; and GUMMIES.

Grosse de Cosnac, Bettina. *Die Riegels: die Geschichte der Kultmarke HARIBO und ihrer Gründerfamilie.* Bergisch Gladbach, Germany: Bastei Lübbe, 2006.

Ursula Heinzelmann

Havemeyer, Henry Osborne (1847–1907), was to sugar what his contemporary John D. Rockefeller was to oil. Havemeyer masterminded the creation of the so-called Sugar Trust in 1887, after organizing the merger of a dozen and a half refineries in several cities. See SUGAR TRUST. Legal challenges began almost at once and continued past his death. Yet the American Sugar Refining Company—its official name—achieved a near-perfect monopoly, at one point controlling 98 percent of the country's sugar market. See AMERICAN SUGAR REFINING COMPANY.

Harry Havemeyer was born into a New York City family that had been in the sugar business for two generations. His paternal grandfather and a great uncle were German immigrants who apprenticed in London, then got jobs at a refinery in Lower Manhattan. In 1807 the brothers opened their own refinery, W. & F. C. Havemeyer, in a small building west of present-day SoHo. In 1856 Harry's father Frederick Christian Havemeyer Jr., with a cousin and a partner, took the business into the modern age by building a colossal, technologically advanced refinery in what is now the Williamsburg section of Brooklyn. Havemeyers & Elder employed several thousand workers and could produce 5 million pounds of sugar daily. It was Harry, though, who turned this enterprise into a sugar kingdom. In an often quoted letter, Harry's father wrote unambiguously to Harry's older brother, Theodore: "Get it down as a fact, that Harry is King of the sugar market."

Notorious for his abrasive personality, the stout, balding, white-mustached Harry became a favorite subject of caricaturists as he manipulated railroads to get preferential rates, granted rebates to wholesale grocers in exchange for selling only his sugar, and engaged in other questionable or illegal business practices designed to subdue competitors and discourage new entrants into the field.

Havemeyer's company primarily refined cane sugar, but he made substantial inroads into beet sugar refining as well. See SUGARCANE; SUGAR BEET; SUGAR REFINERIES; and SUGAR REFINING. Seeking to control his supply of raw materials, he invested in raw sugar sources, particularly in the plantations of the Caribbean. See PLANTATIONS, SUGAR. He also diversified horizontally, owning such things as cooperages for making sugar barrels.

Claus Spreckels, who refined Hawaiian sugar in California, was just one of many formidable rivals who eventually capitulated and joined the Sugar Trust. The Arbuckle Brothers were among the few who did not. These coffee roasters, as big in their realm as Harry was in his, patented a novel machine that packed coffee into paper bags. When they decided to use the machine for packing sugar, Harry retaliated by getting into coffee himself. Legendary price wars ensued, ending only after both companies had sustained enormous losses.

Harry married twice, each time to a member of the sugar-refining Elder family. After his divorce from Mary Louise Elder, her niece Louisine Waldron Elder became his wife. With Louise, Harry had three children and built a celebrated collection of European art, mostly Impressionist, which he pursued as aggressively as he had his sugar kingdom. (Many of his acquisitions hang in New York City's Metropolitan Museum.) A fellow robber baron of the period, Charles L. Freer, said of Harry's love of art: "No one can be more deeply touched by beauty than he, provided he is in a mood to enjoy it."

Havemeyer, Harry W. *Henry Osborne Havemeyer: The Most Independent Mind.* New York: H. W. Havemeyer, 2010.

Havemeyer, Louisine W. *Sixteen to Sixty: Memoirs of a Collector.* New York: Ursus, 1996.

Saltzman, Cynthia. *Old Masters, New World: America's Raid on Europe's Great Pictures, 1880–World War I.* New York: Viking, 2008.

Jeanne Schinto

Hermé, Pierre (1961–), has, since the late 1990s, been the most internationally renowned patissier of the grand French tradition and its greatest contemporary innovator. Jeffrey Steingarten dubbed him the "Picasso of Pastry" in *Vogue* magazine.

A fourth-generation pastry maker, Hermé left his native Alsace for Paris after the celebrated patissier Gaston Lenôtre (1920–2009) noticed him there before Hermé had even turned fourteen. Just five years later, Lenôtre entrusted a high-profile boutique to his wunderkind apprentice.

After military service and a stint at the Belgian chocolate firm Wittamer, Hermé returned to Paris, at the age of twenty-four, to take the helm at the pastry kitchens of Fauchon. There, he took inspiration from Paris's couturiers and began to debut his latest pastry creations in themed, seasonal collections—a practice that he has continued ever since. In 1994 Hermé released the first of his many books, *Secrets gourmands* (written in collaboration with Martine Gérardin), which won France's highest cookbook award and brought him national attention.

Three years later, Paris's oldest tearoom-cum-pastry-shop, Ladurée, featured Hermé in its new, marble-lined pastry palace on the Champs Élysées. Behind the scenes, he took charge of revamping the shop's classic macarons. See MACARONS. Within a year he was not only declared France's top pastry chef but was also the first in his profession to garner decoration as a Chevalier of Arts and Letters.

The Ladurée collaboration was short-lived, however. Accounts differ about whether it was the passionate artist and perfectionist or the bottom-line business types who initiated the break. But in 1998 Hermé launched the patisserie Pierre Hermé Paris in Tokyo. His debut in Japan was purportedly the result of contractual restraints imposed by Ladurée against his opening a rival business in France. However, the choice acknowledged and has subsequently fed the enormous Japanese appetite for traditional French pastry making.

After Hermé opened his first Parisian shop in 2001 on the rue Bonaparte and Ladurée opened one of its main outposts down the street in 2002, the macaron wars began. Parisians argued over which to buy, although, in essence, Pierre Hermé lay behind both versions. Traditionalists shop at Ladurée for classic flavors such as pistachio and rosewater, while the avant-garde go to Hermé for experimental tastes such as Szechuan pepper.

Hermé's innovations in French pastry making go far beyond the macaron's revival. His creative choice of ingredients includes using sugar as one would utilize salt. Conversely, he was the first to feature fleur de sel as one might showcase sugar. He makes liberal use of black pepper and other spices. He has also reinvented many classic recipes. For example, he makes *pâté feuilletée* by placing the butter outside of the flour mixture, although this dough is traditionally made the other way around.

His most famous signature dessert, the Isaphon, exemplifies his unique style of synthesizing classicism and innovation. It features a rose-flavored macaron, the size of an individual tart, which is filled with a litchi-infused rose cream and has a supporting rim of raspberries. A single rose petal, a raspberry, and a white-chocolate logo crown its top.

Hermé has retained an impeccable reputation for artistry, passion, and quality despite the global expansion of his brand.

Greenspan, Dorie. *Desserts by Pierre Hermé*. Boston: Little Brown, 1998.

Greenspan, Dorie. *Chocolate Desserts by Pierre Hermé*. Boston: Little Brown, 2001.

Carolin C. Young

Hershey, Milton S. (1857–1945), opened his own candy business after working as an apprentice in the shop of Joseph H. Royer, a confectioner in Lancaster, Pennsylvania. Hershey's first business, which sold taffy, nuts, and ice cream, opened in 1876 in Philadelphia. But it only lasted six years, owing in part to Milton's father's poor business acumen. After the shop failed, Milton followed his father out west to find his fortune mining silver in Denver, Colorado, an ill-conceived pursuit. But this adventure gave him his first break: in Denver he discovered a recipe for caramel that was superior to any he had ever tried. He brought that recipe back east and, after several more failed attempts, eventually succeeded with his Lancaster Caramel Company, which by 1890 made Milton Hershey wealthier than he had ever dreamed possible. The company grew to employ more than 1,500 workers in four factories, producing hundreds of varieties of caramels. But Milton Hershey wasn't satisfied. Business didn't excite him; invention did.

With their newfound wealth, Milton and his wife Kitty traveled the world, and in the course of their travels Milton tasted a new confection, milk chocolate, recently developed in Europe. At the 1893 Columbian Exposition in Chicago, Milton saw a tiny display of chocolate-making equipment from Dresden, Germany. The smell of roasting cacao beans caught his attention, and he announced immediately that chocolate would overtake caramels as the candy of choice. He bought the equipment right then and began experimenting. At first he made simple chocolate coatings for his caramels. Although European chocolate makers kept their methods of mixing milk and chocolate closely guarded, Milton eventually developed his own techniques for mellowing the chocolate—and reducing its cost—by adding milk.

Hershey believed that chocolate was as nutritious as meat, and he lauded its healthful properties. Convinced of chocolate's appeal, he sold the caramel business in 1900 and invested everything in a chocolate factory in the midst of cornfields in Dauphin County, Pennsylvania. He then set out to build a community—Hershey, Pennsylvania—that would be as wholesome as his chocolates. This was not the same kind of company town as DuPont's Wilmington, Delaware, or Deere & Co.'s Moline, Illinois. Milton Hershey told everyone, "I'm not out to make money. I have all that I need." He gave his workers insurance and retirement benefits, supported the local churches, and spared no expense on amenities for the community, including a theater, gymnasium, sports arena, public transportation, swimming pools, and a public school system.

Milton Hershey christened the town's main thoroughfares Chocolate and Cocoa Avenues. By 1911 the Chocolate Camelot that seemed as if it had sprouted overnight from the Pennsylvania farmland was the talk of the state. Milton Hershey was hailed as a visionary and his factory was humming, employing 1,200 workers and churning out $5 million worth of chocolate products annually, including iconic brands like Hershey's Milk Chocolate Bar (the Hershey Bar), Hershey's Milk Chocolate with Almonds Bar , Kisses, and Mr. Goodbar.

Without children of their own, Milton and Kitty established the Milton Hershey School for orphaned boys, and in 1918 Milton donated his entire interest in the company, worth $60 million, to the Hershey Trust for the benefit of the school. The trust, which still owns a controlling interest in the chocolate company, is now worth more than $8 billion, and the school has an enrollment of more than 1,800 disadvantaged boys and girls.

See also HERSHEY'S; KISSES; and REESE'S PIECES.

Brenner, Joël Glenn. *The Emperors of Chocolate: Inside the Secret World of Hershey and Mars.* New York: Random House, 1999.

Houts, Mary Davidoff, and Pamela Cassidy Whitenack. *Hershey.* Images of America. Cumberland, S.C.: Arcadia, 2000.

Joël Glenn Brenner

Hershey's, synonymous in the United States with chocolate, is the maker of a candy bar that has greatly influenced the American palate with its high sugar content and slightly sour off-notes, a taste truly distinctive from European chocolate. Introduced in 1900, the plain milk chocolate candy bar is the invention of Milton S. Hershey, a visionary who believed so strongly in the health and nutrient value of chocolate that he sold his successful caramel business for $1 million at the turn of the century to finance a massive new chocolate factory amidst the dairy farms of western Pennsylvania. See HERSHEY, MILTON S. Hershey taught himself the art of making milk chocolate—no easy task—and stumbled upon a method that allowed the lipase enzymes in the milk to break down the milk fat and produce "flavorful free fatty acids," according to Hershey chemists who later analyzed the process. In other words, the evaporated milk that went into his candy bar recipe was slightly soured. This flavor became the hallmark of the Hershey brand when the milk chocolate bar was introduced coast to coast in 1906. The first milk-chocolate candy available to most Americans, it became an instant hit.

Milton Hershey added almonds to the Hershey Bar in 1908. The nuts displaced some of the more expensive milk chocolate, making it easier to hold the price of the bar to a nickel. Hershey's automated, assembly-line factory, which cranked out bars by the millions, also provided a cost advantage, and he was often compared with Henry Ford, a man he greatly admired. Like Ford, Milton Hershey brought a luxury item to the masses. He introduced Kisses in 1907, Mr. Goodbar in 1925, Krackel in 1938, and with the purchase of the H. B. Reese factory just down the street in the early 1960s, Reese's Peanut Butter Cups were added to the Hershey line. See KISSES. The 1970s saw the addition of Rolo and Kit Kat, brands licensed from British candy maker Rowntree, and the introduction of a product very similar to M&M's, a peanut-butter-filled candy called Reese's Pieces that starred in the hit movie *E.T.* See M&M'S and REESE'S PIECES.

All these brands benefited greatly from Hershey's now ubiquitous practice of placing candy bars in gas stations, newsstands, diners, markets, and everywhere a salesman could imagine. Previously, candy sales had been limited to druggists and confectionery shops, but Hershey's aggressive approach paid off. By the 1920s the Hershey brand was cemented in the American psyche and the Hershey flavor ingrained in the memories of America's youth, though it has never received global acceptance. Outside the United States, a Hershey Bar is typically viewed as "cheap" chocolate because it contains so little cocoa butter. However, Hershey remains an iconic American brand and a favorite of millions.

See also CHOCOLATE, POST-COLUMBIAN.

Brenner, Joël Glenn. *The Emperors of Chocolate: Inside the Secret World of Hershey and Mars.* New York: Random House, 1999.
D'Antonio, Michael. *Hershey: Milton S. Hershey's Extraordinary Life of Wealth, Empire, and Utopian Dreams.* New York: Simon & Schuster, 2007.
Hershey Community Archives. Oral history collections, administered by the M. S. Hershey Trust.

Joël Glenn Brenner

Hinduism, one of the world's oldest religions, dates back more than 4,000 years. It is the faith of the majority of the people of India and also has adherents in other Asian countries, such as Nepal and Indonesia. From a relatively austere (though polytheistic) faith, as set out in the original texts of the four Vedas (approximately 1500 B.C.E.), Hinduism has evolved into a rich amalgamation of many local and regional beliefs and cultural practices. In folk idiom, the Hindu pantheon is often referred to as consisting of 33 million gods.

This protean vision is accompanied by a deeply intimate relationship between the individual and the divine, which is reflected in the attitudes and beliefs regarding food. The practice of animal sacrifice to placate the gods existed from ancient times, as can be seen in the texts of the Vedas and epics like the Ramayana (fourth to fifth century B.C.E.) and the Mahabharata (approximately fifth century B.C.E.). Over time, however, the rituals of worship, whether in the public domain of the temple or the private domain of the home, came to include the practice of offering a whole range of edible items, cooked and uncooked, to the gods. See TEMPLE SWEETS. The theory behind the practice was that offerings made with undiluted devotion and accompanied by the appropriate prayers and rituals were "accepted" by the deity, and this acceptance transformed ordinary food into something holy—prasad or sacred food. Subsequently, the human devotee could consume that prasad as a blessed gift from the god.

While sacrificing an animal like a goat or a buffalo is still occasionally carried out in certain areas, the vast range of food offered to the gods all over India is vegetarian. Some major temples, such as the Jagannatha Temple in Puri, Orissa, prepare daily meals consisting of rice and vegetable preparations cooked in a style that has remained unchanged for centuries. The food is offered to the temple deities five times daily by the priests and then distributed to the crowd of devotees. However, the most common items offered in worship, whether in the smaller temples, neighborhood shrines, or individual homes, are fresh fruits and sweets that can be homemade or store bought. In a tropical country like India, fruits are varied and available throughout the year and are immune from any taint of ritual impurity. Sometimes, the fruit can be transformed into a sweet. In Bengal, the birthday (in August/September) of the god Krishna, incarnated as a dairy farmer's son, is celebrated with sweets made from the pulp of the ripe *taal* (fruit of the toddy palm) combined with rice flour, grated coconut, and sugar. The mixture is deep-fried to produce crisp yet luscious fritters. The baby Krishna, often pictured holding a *naru* (a round ball of coconut and sweetened evaporated milk) in his hand, is referred to as Narugopal.

The systematic cultivation of sugarcane and the extraction of sugar from its juice began thousands of years ago in India, with references found in some of the Vedas and later in the Ramayana. That probably contributed to the predominance of sweet items in religious worship. Throughout the country, a whole parade of sweets made with flour, rice, coconut, semolina, milk, and dal, expressing the culinary genius of different regions, became the food of the gods. The humblest offering, available to the poorest of devotees, is the *batasha*, a small, round, meringue-like confection of whipped sugar, white or brown. *Batashas* have the advantage of lasting long even in tropical humidity and can serve as a small daily offering in home worship. They also lend themselves to large-scale distribution among the crowd present at a religious event.

Perhaps the most iconic sweet offering, found throughout India, is payasam or *payesh*—rice cooked in milk. See PAYASAM. Both ingredients have high symbolic value, rice as the life-sustaining staple and milk as the gift of the cow, an animal also considered sacred by Hindus. It should be noted that the payasam of India is not the same as the rice pudding of Western cuisine, since the latter usually contains eggs, which are nonvegetarian and, in ancient times, had strong associations of impurity. Other Western items, such as cookies, cakes, and pastries, which came to India in the wake of foreign colonization, are also excluded from the list of acceptable sweet offerings in Hindu worship because of the inclusion of eggs and their association with heathens.

Religious offerings have also been influenced by the Hindu philosophical tenet of three principal gunas (dominant traits)—sattva, rajas, and tamas—that characterize living creatures and earthly substances, including food. Each has distinctive attributes, and even gods are defined by the predominance of a specific attribute. For example, milk, evaporated milk (kheer or khoa), clarified butter, and rice, all of which are used to make sweets, are considered particularly suitable for the god Vishnu because he is associated with the sattva guna.

Achaya, K. T. *Indian Food*. Delhi: Oxford University Press, 1998.
O'Flaherty, Wendy Doniger. *Hindu Myths—A Sourcebook Translated from the Sanskrit*. London: Penguin, 1975.

Chitrita Banerji

Hines, Duncan (1880–1959), is the namesake of one of the most well-known boxed cake mixes in the United States since the mid-twentieth century. Often considered alongside Sara Lee and Betty Crocker, Duncan Hines, unlike these brands, was neither an invented character nor a pseudonym, but the first national restaurant critic in American history. See BETTY CROCKER and SARA LEE. An energetic, extroverted traveling salesman, Hines retired from business in 1936 to self-publish a best-selling restaurant guidebook, *Adventures in Good Eating*. Soon elevated to the status of "authority on American food," his persona became associated with notions of trust, honesty, and high standards in an era when middle-class diners traveling by automobile spurred the professionalization and expansion of the restaurant industry.

Due to his widespread, sterling reputation among consumers, Duncan Hines was often courted by food companies to sell their products. Despite his fear that endorsements would compromise his critical judgment, Hines eventually relented, forming Hines-Park Foods, Inc. in 1949 with a media executive, Roy Park. The Duncan Hines brand featured over 200 products, including canned produce, coffee, citrus juices, and salad dressings, as well as appliances, tableware, and even a credit-card service. At first, the best-selling item was Duncan Hines Ice Cream—no accident, for ice cream was Hines's favorite food, which he ate three times a day, including breakfast. The cake mixes were developed by Nebraska Consolidated Milling. They were distinguished by the requirement that cooks add fresh eggs to the mix rather than supplemental liquids, as was then the industry standard. Duncan Hines cookbooks of sweets recipes also sold well, a tradition that has endured into the twenty-first century.

The success of the ice creams and cakes mixes was immediate and took a large market share from established brands like Pillsbury. As a consequence, Hines-Park Foods drew attention from larger companies. Seeking to capitalize on the mid-century boom in food processing, Procter & Gamble purchased the brand in 1956 and whittled its portfolio down to the cake mixes. After Hines's death in 1959, his status as America's popular food expert was eclipsed by the next cohort of tastemakers, notably Julia Child. Duncan Hines the person, a critic, became just Duncan Hines the product, cake mixes.

Under Procter & Gamble's ownership, and then that of Aurora Foods and Pinnacle Foods, Hines baked goods have remained consistently popular. Although commercial fortunes can change at a whim, the future of Duncan Hines as an icon of American sweets appears to be strong. Dozens of cake flavors have been introduced, as well as mixes for brownies, muffins, and cookies, and frostings. With no face attached to the name Duncan Hines, the cake mixes have instead been associated with reliability, ease of use, and a sense of taste and texture that belies their industrial origin. The name has also taken on a non-culinary life of its own. By the twenty-first century "Duncan Hines" was such a part of many Americans' experiences with baked goods that dozens of hip-hop rappers' lyrics substitute his name for the word "cake," which in urban slang means "money."

See also CAKE MIX.

Hatchett, Louis. *Duncan Hines: The Man Behind the Cake Mix*. Macon, Ga.: Mercer University Press, 2001.

Hines, Duncan. *The Duncan Hines Dessert Book*. New York: Pocket Books, 1955.

Damon Talbott

hippocras, or hypocras, was a sweet, spiced medicinal wine familiar in late medieval and early modern Europe. To pharmacists, it was one of a class of "infusions" in which health-giving substances were combined with drinkable liquids: drinking hippocras was thus one of the more pleasant ways to improve one's health. The term was first recorded in the fourteenth century, and *vinum Hippocraticum* (as it soon became known in Latin to physicians and pharmacists) was still being prescribed in the late eighteenth century, but it is merely the best-known example of a class of medicinal wines that existed long before and still exist today.

Hippocras changed over time with the availability and reputation of individual spices. See SPICES. The precise recipe might vary in any case: hippocras was made to order, often from a doctor's prescription. Even the definition of "hippocras" was not fixed. In almost every source, the sweetener has to be sugar, more costly than honey (until the seventeenth century) and believed to be more health giving. The principal spice was usually cinnamon. Cloves and ginger were commonly included. Some sources say that the wine should be white—like the sugar—whereas others allow white or red as appropriate. Wines, like spices, varied in their medicinal effects. Hippocras was normally drunk cold; since the wine and nearly all the spices were (in terms of humoral theory) hot, adding further heat was not necessary or advisable.

Recipes are found in both cookery books and pharmaceutical manuals. This typical recipe dates from 1631:

> Take 10 lb. best red or white wine, 1½ oz. cinnamon, 2 scruples cloves, 4 scruples each cardamom and grains of paradise, 3 drams ginger. Crush the spices coarsely and steep in the wine for 3 or 4 hours. Add 1½ lb. whitest sugar. Pass through the sleeve several times, and it is ready.

From the fifteenth to eighteenth century, hippocras was consistently defined by the fact that it is strained through a woolen or cotton bag called a "hippocras bag" or "Hippocrates's sleeve." Steeping followed by filtering was the best way to produce a crystal-clear, fresh-tasting wine that had absorbed the full flavor of the required spices. It is uncertain whether the bag was named after the wine or the wine after the bag: it is also not quite certain that the name derives from that of the "father of medicine," the semi-legendary ancient Greek physician Hippocrates, although such is the usual view. Why the wine or the bag should be named after him is unknown. Despite widespread claims to the contrary, neither was invented by Hippocrates, who must have died about 1,700 years before the first recorded mention of either.

The procedure for making hippocras could be simplified by using a ready-made mix of ground spices. From the late-fourteenth-century household manual *Le mesnagier de Paris*, it seems that "spices for hippocras" were sold in this form by Parisian grocers.

Although the taste of good hippocras may resemble a sweet white vermouth, vermouth is not a hippocras by the usual definition, because its medicinal ingredients are herbs rather than spices. Ginger wine (though based on one spice rather than several) is a closer modern analog. The nearest ancient equivalent was the Roman *conditum*, a sweetened, flavored wine whose principal "active ingredients" were spices.

See also MEDICINAL USES OF SUGAR; MULLED WINE; and PUNCH.

Brereton, Georgina E., and Janet M. Ferrier, eds. and trans. *Le mesnagier de Paris*, p. 190. Oxford: Oxford University Press, 1981.

Uffenbachius, Petrus, ed. *Dispensatorium Galeno chymicum*, pp. 683–684. Hanau, Germany: Apud Dauid Aubri, 1631.

Andrew Dalby

holiday sweets are central to the observance of secular and commemorative occasions in societies throughout the world. Although all holidays are at heart commemorative, recalling some significant religious or historical event, they tend to become self-commemorative as well, accruing new traditions that are connected only indirectly or not at all to the essential nature of the original event. This process encourages the development of increasingly local traditions. Another, related process is that of grafting, by which a holiday belonging to a newly adopted religion incorporates elements of older traditions. The spread of Christianity famously involved such cultural absorption: the Christmas tree resulted from the association of Christmas with northern European pagan practices. See CHRISTMAS.

Inherent in holiday celebrations are opposing cultural tendencies of conservation and innovation. As commemorative events, holidays naturally encourage or even demand continuity of cultural practices through time, particularly in the realm of food. Long after certain dishes have disappeared from everyday life, they are prepared for special occasions, and thereby preserved. Furthermore, local ingredients and humble dishes maintain a central role in many holiday celebrations, especially those that are solemn in nature. Thus, sweetened wheat berries are frequently served at funerals and related commemorations of the dead (see the discussion of *kolyva* and *pastiera* below). See FUNERALS and WHEAT BERRIES.

At the same time, holidays are loci of innovation, into which the novel and exotic are naturally incorporated. This process involves not only unfamiliar ingredients but also dishes generally ascribed to differing socioeconomic realms, and in this way holiday foods serve to bind the various strata of society. Thus, on festive occasions, the middle class and poor tend as much as possible to surpass the limits of their usual diet and eat foods normally consumed only by the rich. For example, although in medieval Europe sugar and imported spices such as cinnamon, cloves, cardamom, nutmeg, and saffron were consumed with any frequency only by the rich, they gradually came to be featured in an ever-growing array of holiday dishes among the less well-to-do sectors of society.

Other key ingredients that marked sweet foods as celebratory were chocolate and highly refined wheat flour—as opposed to the less refined wheat flour and flours from other grains, such as rye, millet, barley, and oats, seldom found in holiday confections. See FLOUR. Yet other, more common ingredients like butter and other fats, milk and cheese, and some nuts, which in premodern times were expensive for the nonelite, further augmented the extravagance of celebration. The historical value of the European sweet Christmas breads made with dough from refined wheat flour enriched with eggs, milk, and butter and seasoned with sugar, spices, and candied fruit, derived not just from the effort required for their preparation but from the actual value of all the ingredients. Examples include Italian panettone and *pandolce*, German stollen, Dutch *kerststol*, and Norwegian *julekage*.

Other holiday dishes are rendered more specific to a given occasion through some aspect of their preparation, especially their shape (such as the Easter lamb cake or dove-shaped Italian *colomba pasquale*; the log-shaped French Christmas cake bûche de Noël; or the Hot Cross bun with its cross-shaped marking) or their color (red for Valentine's Day, red and green for Christmas, black and orange for Halloween, etc.). See EASTER; HALLOWEEN; and VALENTINE'S DAY.

An Archaic Family of Holiday Sweets

One old family of European dishes illustrates the role of symbolism in celebratory foods and highlights the development of *pastiera*, an elaborate and particularly rich dish that arose out of an older, very humble tradition.

In the Mediterranean world, preparations with whole grains developed symbolic religious significance in remote antiquity. In ancient Greece, they formed part of the ritual celebration of native divinities and were later grafted onto Christian observance, with the whole grains symbolizing the dual notion of death and resurrection. Various savory whole-grain dishes (generally combined with one or more legumes) persist to this day as celebratory foods in association with events of the Greek Orthodox calendar. The most notable is *kolyva*, a dish of boiled whole-wheat berries that, in numerous variations, is sweetened with honey or powdered sugar and fortified with crushed nuts, sesame seeds, and dried fruit. This dish is famously associated with funeral commemorations but is also consumed on various saints' days, All Souls' Day, and the first Saturday of Lent.

Within the Orthodox world, *kolyva* and its symbolic value were widely adopted beyond Greece for commemorative celebrations. The dish appears under the same name (in locally adapted forms) in the Balkans (Serbia, Bulgaria, Romania) and in the eastern Slavic lands (Ukraine, Belarus, Russia). A second but also ultimately Greek name for the dish, *kutia* (from the Greek *koukìa*, "kernels"), is also used in these Slavic lands as well as in Catholic Poland, where *kutia* is regionally featured in the traditional Christmas Eve meal. Interestingly, the dish also appears in various parts of southern Italy and Sicily—regions with deep historical connections to Greece—under the name *cuccìa* (from the Greek *koukìa*). In some places *cuccìa* is the name of savory wheat-berry preparations, but it is best known as a sweet concoction that includes nuts and candied fruits and nowadays also chocolate; the key ingredient is, however, fresh ricotta. In Sicily, sweet *cuccìa* with ricotta is eaten on Saint Lucy's Day (13 December), which formerly coincided roughly with the winter solstice in the old (Julian) calendar, with the traditional Greek symbolic value of death and resurrection clearly at play.

A particularly interesting development out of this tradition in southern Italy is the most famous of Neapolitan holiday sweets, *pastiera*, a pie with a *pasta frolla* (short pastry) crust filled with sweetened ricotta fortified with egg yolks and flavored with candied fruit and orange blossom water. See CANDIED FRUIT; CHEESE, FRESH; FLOWER WATERS; and PIE DOUGH. But what makes *pastiera* truly distinctive among ricotta-based pies is the de rigueur inclusion of cooked wheat berries; in this regard, the name for the dish in some Campanian dialects is telling: *pizza cu' gran*, or "pie with grain." *Pastiera* (attested as early as the seventeenth century) is made specifically for the Easter celebration. The ancient connection of a whole-grain sweet with death and resurrection clearly applies, but in this case it appears that the transfer from minor and more solemn occasions to the most important and joyous of Christian holidays occurred because of the complexity of the dish, both in terms of its preparation and expensive ingredients. The grain is necessarily still present, but here it becomes a complement to the enriched ricotta.

Other Noteworthy Families of Holiday Dishes

Fried Dough, Both Simple and Stuffed

Deep frying has always been a relatively expensive way to cook, but in the Mediterranean world, where olive oil and in some regions other vegetable oils were available, it has long been a feature of celebratory communal events, including holidays. Simple preparations of fried dough dressed with honey, syrup, or sugar are widely known from the Middle East to Spain, a culinary tradition that goes back as far as classical Greece and Rome; of similar antiquity are the analogs in Jewish and other Semitic cultures. Related preparations have also long been made for holidays across South and Southeast Asia. Indeed, this family of holiday sweets is one of the oldest and most widespread across the globe.

Beginning with some simple, nonfilled versions of fried dough (often quite soft and thus batter-like), the following examples can be noted:

- Indian jalebi has many regional variations. All are made from a yogurt-based batter that yields web-like forms when fried. Jalebi is often served in celebration of Indian nationhood. The Iranian analog, *zulbia*, and the compositionally identical but differently shaped *bamiyeh* ("okra"), are an important part of the celebration of Muslim holidays. In Arabic-speaking lands, *zulbia* also appear as a festive sweet with locally adapted versions of the name (*zalabiya, zlebia*). See ZALABIYA.
- North African *sfinj* are doughnuts, traditional in a Jewish context for regional Hanukkah celebrations; the Sicilian *sfingi* bear the same name and are featured in the celebration of the feast of Saint Joseph.
- Greek *loukoumadhes*, spherical and dressed with honey, are consumed throughout the year but are especially important at the feast of Saint Andrew.
- In southern and central Italy and southern Spain, relatively small bits of dough are fried and then piled together before being soaked with honey or syrup (in Italy, they are also decorated with colored sprinkles). In Campania, these confections, eaten during the Christmas season, are called *struffoli*; in Le Marche and the Abruzzo, essentially the same dish is called *cicerchiata* (named after the shape of vetch beans) and is part of Carnival celebrations. In Calabria and Sicily, the dish is likewise associated with Carnival, but the form of the individual bits of fried dough is elongated rather than spherical, as reflected in the name *pignolata* (cf. *pigna* "pine cone"). Closely related is the southern Spanish *piñonate*, which is, however, associated with Easter.
- Crisply fried strips of dough dressed with powdered sugar or honey are frequently part of Carnival celebrations. In Italy, they take on a wide variety of forms and names, of which *chiacchiere* is perhaps the best known. In Poland, one finds the very similar *chrusciki*; in Germany, *Scherben*.

- In the French-speaking world, beignets (with many regional names and variations) are part of the pre-Lenten celebrations of the Carnival period.
- Throughout Belgium, the feast day of the patron saint of each parish church, the *kermis* or *ducasse*, always involves the consumption of *smoutebollen* or *croustillons*, typically offered by food trucks specializing in deep-fried foods; these are balls of fried sweetened dough dusted with powdered sugar. The Flemish name, *smoutebollen*, derives from the fact that these confections were traditionally fried in *smout* (lard).

Holiday preparations in which the fried dough is stuffed with a sweet filling include Italian zeppole (for the feast of Saint Joseph or for Carnival), Polish *pączki* (for Carnival), German *Berliner* or *Pfannkuchen* (for New Year's Eve and Carnival), and Israeli *sufganiyot* (for Hanukkah).

Bread Puddings

Some old and ultimately elaborate holiday sweets developed out of the very humble European tradition of using stale bread as the basis for substantial everyday dishes, both savory and sweet (e.g., Danish *ølsuppe*, "beer soup"; German *Schwarzbrot* pudding, "black bread pudding"; and Silesian *Mohnpielen*, poppy seed dumplings). Of these, perhaps the most famous are the impressive English holiday puddings, such as plum pudding (Christmas) and figgy pudding (Christmas and Palm Sunday), which traditionally included breadcrumbs in their base. An elaborate sweet bread pudding strongly associated with the solemn occasion of Lent is the Mexican *capirotada*, an outlier of the Spanish family of (primarily savory) *migas* dishes. See PUDDING and SOUTHWEST (U.S.).

Highly Spiced Christmas Cookies

The high cost of oriental spices in Medieval Europe rendered them especially appropriate for use in festive sweets, and a great many cookie-like sweets from the late medieval tradition feature centrally in Christmas celebrations. A few notable examples:

- The German *Lebkuchen* family of biscuits stands out for its impressive combinations of flavorings including cloves, cinnamon, cardamom, coriander, nutmeg, mace, ginger, and anise. See GINGERBREAD.
- The Low Countries' speculaas use a similar array of spices and flavorings in biscuits of both simple form and complex molded shapes. See COOKIE MOLDS AND STAMPS and SPECULAAS.
- Southern Italian *mostaccioli* developed from Roman biscuits flavored with grape must (hence the name) to become highly spiced biscuits (with cinnamon, nutmeg, and clove) that contain chocolate in the dough and additionally receive a coating of melted chocolate. See BISCOTTI and GRAPE MUST.

See also CARNIVAL; CHINESE NEW YEAR; CHRISTIANITY; DAY OF THE DEAD; DIWALI; DOUGHNUTS; GREECE AND CYPRUS; HANUKKAH; INDIA; ISLAM; ITALY; JUDAISM; NETHERLANDS; PASSOVER; and RAMADAN.

Accademia Italiana della Cucina. *La Cucina: The Regional Cooking of Italy.* Translated by Jay Hyams. New York: Rizzoli, 2009.

Buccini, Anthony F. "Chi vuol godere la festa, digiuni la vigilia: On the Relationship between Fasting and Feasting." In *Celebration: Proceedings of the Oxford Symposium on Food and Cookery 2011*, edited by Mark McWilliams, pp. 66–75. Totnes, U.K.: Prospect, 2012.

Fletcher, Nichola. *Charlemagne's Tablecloth: A Piquant History of Feasting.* New York: St. Martin's, 2004.

Henisch, Bridget Ann. *Fast and Feast: Food in Medieval Society.* University Park: Pennsylvania State University Press, 1976.

Kochilas, Diane. *The Food and Wine of Greece.* New York: St. Martin's, 1990.

Montagné, Prosper. *The New Larousse Gastronomique.* Translated by Marion Hunter. New York: Crown, 1977.

Anthony F. Buccini

honey, composed mainly of fructose and glucose, is essentially nectar concentrated by honeybees to around 18 percent moisture. Besides tasting sweeter than table sugar, the fructose in honey is especially soluble in water, helping to make honey hygroscopic, or able to absorb moisture from the air. See FRUCTOSE. This quality means that honey is useful in baked goods as it keeps them from drying out. Honey also lends a lovely golden appearance and good flavor.

Honey was mankind's earliest and most potent form of sweetness and remained so in the Western world until the plantation system of sugar production developed in the seventeenth century and the price of

The first recorded beehives, shown on ancient Egyptian wall paintings, depict men removing honeycomb from cylindrical hives and packing it into jars. This French illustration, called "Bees," dates to 1900. It was intended for publication in Mexico. MUSÉE NATIONAL DE L'EDUCATION, ROUEN, FRANCE / ARCHIVES CHARMET / BRIDGEMAN IMAGES

sugar fell. See PLANTATIONS, SUGAR. Honey lost further ground as a sweetener when the process of extracting sugar from sugar beets was perfected in the early nineteenth century. See SUGAR BEETS.

Prehistoric honey hunters risked multiple stings to track down wild bee nests in rock crevices and tree hollows, as indigenous peoples still do today in places such as Nepal, the Amazon, and Africa. Bees and honey are depicted in rock art dating back at least 26,000 years. Wall paintings and records from ancient Egypt show how honey was first used in sweet food. Triangular cakes and containers of honey are shown in Rekhmire's tomb from around 1450 B.C.E. A Cairo museum has a honey cake from this era in the shape of a figure, like an early gingerbread man. See ANTHROPOMORPHIC AND ZOOMORPHIC SWEETS and GINGERBREAD.

Along with boiled-down grape must and dried fruits, honey was the main sweetener of food in ancient Greece and Rome. See ANCIENT WORLD; DRIED FRUIT; and GRAPE MUST. Particular honeys were famous. Archestratus, a Sicilian poet and gourmet who traveled around the ancient Greek world, recommends that the flat cakes of Athens be eaten with Attic honey from the herb-scented hills around Athens. Cheesecakes, breads, and sweets all used honey, and it is included in many of the recipes attributed to Apicius, compiled around the fourth century C.E., not only in dishes and sauces but also to preserve fruits and other fresh foods. See CHEESECAKE and FRUIT PRESERVES.

Honey predated cultivated sugarcane in India and was part of the ritualistic drink *soma* during the Rigvedic period of around 1700–1100 B.C.E. Although the culture of sweets in India is largely founded on sugar, a mixture of curds, ghee, and honey known as *madhuparka* was used by Aryans to welcome guests. Early medicinal works mention a sweet called *pupalika* that was a cake with honey at its center. See INDIA.

Medieval Persian and Arab cooks used honey alongside sugar in dishes such as halvah and baklava. It was such an important part of cooking in tenth-century Baghdad that one cookbook includes 10 different types. Honeyed foods were given to guests as part of the Arab tradition of hospitality. See BAGHDAD; BAKLAVA; HALVAH; and PERSIA.

The use of honey in pastries and other sweets spread westward with the Moors from the eighth century C.E., including the sweets made with nuts, honey, and egg white that are called *turrón* in Spain, *turrone* in Italy, and *nougat* in France. See NOUGAT. Sicilian food shows a layer of Arab influence today in sweet dishes such as *sfinci*, deep-fried balls of dough drenched in honey. See FRIED DOUGH.

Spiced honey gingerbreads, such as *Lebkuchen* and *Leckerli*, are a part of a long tradition in Central and Northern Europe. As they are today, these gingerbreads were elaborately decorated and molded into shapes such as the figures of saints, hearts, and pigs, or joined together into gingerbread houses. Stronger-tasting honeys from particular nectar sources, such as buckwheat honey, were favored for such recipes. *Lebkuchen* were first written about in Germany in 1320 when production was centered in monasteries, which often kept honeybees to produce wax for church candles; they were later made by bakers' guilds. See GUILDS. Nuremberg, as a center for Bavarian honey production as well as for the spice trade, was a prominent location for this activity.

In the seventeenth and nineteenth centuries, respectively, Europeans introduced honeybees (*Apis mellifera*) in North America and then Australia and New Zealand, where they thrived. In these regions, honey soon became a favorite ingredient in cooking as well as in baking, contributing flavor, shine, and sweetness to a wide variety of sweet and savory dishes. The *American Bee Journal* included honey recipes using honey beginning in 1876.

Symbolism

In Greek mythology, the infant Zeus was fed on honey, and in many cultures a ritual drop of honey was placed on the lips of infants, although today honey is not recommended for children under the age of one because of the risk of botulism. West Indians use a mixture of honey, oil, and spices called "Luck," and in Upper Burma a muslin cloth dipped in honey is given to the baby.

According to Jewish tradition, a child dips a piece of apple in honey on his or her first day of school to symbolize the sweetness of knowledge, and honey cake is served on the Jewish New Year to wish good fortune for the year ahead. See ROSH HASHANAH.

Honey has long been regarded as sacred. Offerings of honey cakes were made to the gods of ancient Egypt and Greece, and bees were seen as creatures that could fly between worlds. Honey is one of the five elixirs of immortality in Hinduism. See HINDUISM. The Old Testament describes the Promised Land as "flowing with milk and honey," and honey in general symbolizes sweet delight, as in the "Song of Solomon": "Your lips distil nectar, my bride; Honey and milk are under your tongue." See CHRISTIANITY. More recently, Sicilian newlyweds have been given a loving spoonful of honey to share at the bridal feast.

The changing symbolism of honey and bees reflects the preoccupations of each era. The ancient Romans admired how a honeybee would bravely die for its colony, while the Victorians saw bees as moral creatures that would sting the sinful. In the industrial age, honey came to be regarded as a symbol of nature, sometimes representing a lost rural idyll, as in W. B. Yeats' "bee-loud glade" in "The Lake Isle of Innisfree" (1890) or Rupert Brooke's wartime poem "The Old Vicarage, Grantchester" (1916): "Stands the Church clock at ten to three? / And is there honey still for tea?" Other artists and writers use honey to convey a more vital essence of life. German artist Joseph Beuys compared hive honey to blood (both substances are around the same temperature) and used it in his 1977 installation *Honey Pump at the Work Place*, for which he pumped honey in transparent pipes around a museum full of people from across the globe discussing how to change the world.

In the late nineteenth and twentieth centuries, architects have also been inspired by honey and beehives. The parabolic arches used by the Spanish architect Gaudi (1852–1926) are thought to have been inspired by the way honeycomb hangs in the wild. In 1921 Mies van der Rohe entered a submission called "Honeycomb" in a competition for a high-rise building in Berlin that was a prototype skyscraper; Frank Lloyd Wright used the hexagonals found in the honeycomb in his buildings from the 1920s onward.

In recent years, concern about mass honeybee deaths, including the phenomenon known as colony collapse disorder, has led to bees and honey being seen as an emblem of environmental vulnerability.

Honey and Health

Honey has been used for healing for at least 4,000 years. Many cultures in the ancient world used it in remedies for the skin, eyes, and ears, for wound treatment and gut health.

The first recorded prescription using honey is on a Sumerian clay tablet from around 2000 B.C.E. that recommends it be mixed with river dust, oil, and water; honey is also mentioned in Chinese literature from around this time. The ancient Egyptian Ebers papayrus (ca. 1550 B.C.E.) contains 147 prescriptions using honey, including formulas for ulcers and burns, and for skin conditions from scurvy, after circumcision, and to reduce inflammation.

The ancient Greek philosopher Democritus believed that moistening oneself inside with honey and outside with oil was a key to longevity, and followers of Pythagoras in the sixth century B.C.E. breakfasted on bread and honey for a disease-free life. The physician Hippocrates (ca. 450–377 B.C.E.) said that honey cleaned, softened, and healed ulcers and sores.

The Qurʾān states that God inspired bees to produce liquids of different colors that contain cures for man. Medieval Arab apothecaries used honey as well as sugar in preparations. Syrups could be sweetened with honey, and *lohoch* was a paste made of roots boiled up and mixed with honey and almond oil for throat and chest complaints. Honey continues to be used in pastilles and cough lozenges up to the present day.

Ayurvedic medicine specifies eight different kinds of honey to be used for healing, and doctors practicing this form of medicine still believe that the addition of honey makes a prescription work better, perhaps because the sugars it contains help burst the cell walls of the other bioactive ingredients so that they become more effective. The first book in English specifically about honey (and the only one until the twentieth century) was published in 1759 by a London apothecary, Sir John Hill, titled *The Virtues of Honey in Preventing Many of the Worst Disorders*.

While honey has continued to be used in folk and traditional medicines, especially in remote regions of Africa, Nepal, and Russia, it was largely dropped in the era of modern medicine and antibiotics. A 1976 editorial in *Archives of Modern Medicine* dismissed honey as "worthless but harmless." Piqued by this statement, Peter Molan, a biochemist in New Zealand, unearthed references in more than 100 published scientific papers that suggested honey was, in fact, actively beneficial. Since then, apitherapy, or the medicinal uses of hive products including honey, has grown apace.

Laboratory tests show the antimicrobial effect of specific honeys. Darker-colored honeys such as New Zealand manuka and Australian jarrah honeys are among those proved to be the most potent. Honey wound dressings have been licensed for use in Britain and the United States, as wound-care specialists say honey kills bacteria without damaging the surrounding tissues. All honeys are antimicrobial because their sugars kill bacteria and fungi, and also because honey is acidic. In addition, an active enzyme in honey can catalyze a reaction that produces hydrogen peroxide, which has a strong antimicrobial effect. Honeys, especially those from particular nectar sources such as buckwheat, have phytochemicals such as flavanoids that may further enhance their ability to heal.

Honey Production

The first recorded beehives, shown on ancient Egyptian wall paintings, depict men removing honeycomb from cylindrical hives and packing it into jars. The men are holding smoking bowls before the hives, a trick still used today to make the bees less likely to sting.

Bee-men in the forests of central Europe made ownership marks beside wild bee nests in trees and created detachable doors that enabled them to raid the colonies more easily. Log hives were hung in the trees or set on the ground; such hives eventually became a form of folk art, carved into figures such as bears or humans.

Woven wicker beehives were covered in cloom, a mixture of cow dung and lime. These wicker hives were replaced by the domed, woven straw hive called a skep, from the old Norse *skeppa* (grain basket). In rainy places, skeps could be placed in shelters or placed in niches built into a wall, known as bee boles. But the problem with such methods was that the bees were often killed when the honeycomb was removed. The loss of their bees upset the beekeepers; the many clerical beekeepers were especially troubled by the deaths they caused. It was a clergyman who eventually solved the problem. On 30 October 1851, the Reverend Lorenzo Langstroth conceived the idea of the "bee-space," a corridor around ⅜ of an inch wide that could be built between and around the honeycombs. This space was just enough for two bees to pass each other but not so big that they would start to build a comb to fill the gap. This invention allowed honey and brood comb to slide in and out of a moveable frame hive, enabling the beekeeper to remove the honey or inspect the bees without destroying the colony. Most commercial hives around the world now operate on this principle.

The other major advance for commercial honey production occurred in 1865 when Major Franz von Hruschka, an Austrian living near Venice, gave his son a piece of comb in a basket. As the boy swung the basket around his head, Hruschka noticed how the honey came out of the comb due to the centrifugal force, which became the prime method of honey extraction, replacing the earlier technique of squeezing honey from the comb.

Honey has been produced and exported for centuries. The major producers at present are China, India, Vietnam, Europe (particularly Germany, Hungary, and Bulgaria), Ukraine, the United States, Argentina, and Mexico. Honey is transported in large vats and blended by honey packers. Today, there is a greater emphasis on the organoleptic qualities of particular honeys, known as varietal or monofloral honeys, which are produced largely from specific nectar sources. Tupelo and sourwood honeys from the southern United States, avocado honey from Mexico and California, heather honey from the United Kingdom, wild thyme honey from Greece, chestnut honey from Spain and Italy, arbutus honey from Sardinia and Portugal, the butterscotch-like honeys of New Zealand such as rewarewa, the eucalyptus honeys of Australia, and leatherwood honey from Tasmania are just some of the kinds that are sought out by honey lovers. Honeydew honey, made from the sweet secretions of aphids feeding on tree sap, is another prized product, although its strong flavor is not to everyone's taste. See INSECTS.

Honey is graded according to various criteria, such as viscosity. In the United States, honey is described partly according to a range of colors on the Pfund scale, using the terms "water white," "extra white," "white," "extra light amber," "light amber," "amber," and "dark amber." Chefs and home cooks regard high-quality honey as a gourmet food to be drizzled on top of sweet dishes or onto a piece of cheese. The lower-grade honey used by the food industry is sometimes known as "baking honey." The most artisanal honey, sometimes called "raw," may be left as it is or barely heated, to no higher than the temperature of the hive, in order to retain more of its nutrients and flavor, and simply strained to remove bees' legs and wax. Commercial honey tends to be flash-heated and fine-filtered to keep it runny longer. Honey crystallizes at different rates according to its storage temperature and the composition of its sugars, with higher-fructose honeys such as acacia remaining liquid. Removing all particles and air bubbles from the honey slows down this crystallization process. Alternatively, a small amount of finely granulated honey can be stirred into honey to get a set or creamed texture of small, smooth crystals.

Some honey is diluted, "ultra-filtered," and then boiled to evaporate it back to a honey consistency. This process removes all the pollen and makes an anonymous substance that can no longer rightly be called honey. Fraudulent "funny honey" includes mixtures with inverted sugar and those that are not what they claim to be on the label, for instance, fake manuka honey. See ADULTERATION. Such products have traveled a long way from the natural beauty of honey as produced and stored by the industrious honeybee.

See also ISLAM; JUDAISM; MEDICINAL USES OF SUGAR; RUSSIA; and SYMBOLIC MEANINGS.

Crane, Eva. *The World History of Beekeeping and Honey Hunting.* London: Duckworth, 1999.
Kelly, Sarah. *Festive Baking in Austria, Germany and Switzerland.* London: Penguin, 1985.
Marchese, Marina, and Kim Flottam. *The Honey Connoisseur.* New York: Black Dog & Leventhal, 2013.
Munn, Pamela, and Richard Jones. *Honey and Healing.* Cardiff, U.K.: IBRA, 2000.
Ramírez, Juan. *The Beehive Metaphor.* London: Reaktion, 2000.
Ransome, Hilda. *The Sacred Bee in Ancient Times and Folklore.* London: Allen & Unwin, 1937.

Hattie Ellis

honeymoon today means a happy trip taken by a couple shortly after they are married. However, when the word "honeymoon" first appeared in the mid-sixteenth century, it had sardonic implications. The "honey" part of the compound, as one might expect, alluded to the sweetness of a new conjugal union. The "moon" part, however, was intended to undercut those sweet associations by implying that the joy of the couple was fleeting: it would soon wane, just as the full moon grows smaller with every passing night. This use of the word is clearly evident in a poem called "Cornucopiae" published by William Fennor in 1612. The "jovial time" of the poem's newlyweds is compared to a "honey-moon" that quickly turns from "clear" to "tenebrous":

> The jovial time of pastime and content,
> Which married persons do in kissing spend,
> Was scarce begun, when all their merriment
> By means of forked fortune made an end.
> And now their honey-moon, that late was clear,
> Did pale, obscure, and tenebrous appear;
> And thrusting forth her horns, did plain bewray,
> That some are cuckolds on their wedding day.

The sardonic associations that the word "honeymoon" possessed when it emerged more than 400 years ago persist in a contemporary idiom that first appeared in the 1870s—namely, "the honeymoon is over."

Fennor, William. *Cornu-copiae, Pasquils Night-Cap: or, Antidot for the Head-ache*. London: Thomas Thorp, 1612.

Simpson, J.A., and E. S. C. Weiner, eds. *Oxford English Dictionary*. 2d ed. 20 vols. Oxford: Oxford University Press, 1989.

Mark Morton

horchata, originally made in northern Africa from tiger nuts, is a refreshing drink perfect for hot climates. The small tubers of *Cyperus esculentus*, of the sedge family, were soaked, ground, and then sweetened to make *horchata de chufa*, a tiger nut drink still enjoyed in northern Africa and Spain today. Horchata made its way to Spain with the Muslim conquest prior to the year 1000; centuries later it spread from Valencia to the New World, where it took hold in Mexico.

Agua de horchata is a popular Mexican *agua fresca*, a fresh drink made with fruit, grains, pecans, almonds, and/or seeds, especially various types of melon seeds. Medium-grain white rice is the favored choice for Mexico's sweet horchata, which serves as the perfect antidote to too-spicy chiles. This type of horchata is made by soaking rice overnight in water until the water turns white and milky, then draining and puréeing the rice with a little fresh water to make a smooth paste. The rice paste is forced through a fine mesh sieve, adding more water as necessary. Horchata is most often flavored with *canela* (Mexican cinnamon, or true Ceylon cinnamon), cane sugar, and lime juice, which are added at the end of the process. The horchata may be thinned with cold water to the consistency of milk, although those who prefer a richer drink add whole milk, cream, or condensed milk. Horchata is more flavorful when made a day ahead, but the taste should be delicate, almost bland. The drink is served very cold over ice.

Horchata is the milky-white drink in the line-up of huge glass jars holding brightly colored fresh-fruit beverages that are found in traditional marketplaces throughout Mexico. Casilda's, the famous *aguas frescas* counter in Oaxaca's Juarez market, tops each glass of horchata with finely chopped cantaloupe, pecans, and a dollop of blood-red cactus fruit purée. When mixed, the drink turns a brilliant magenta.

See also MEXICO.

Muñoz Zurita, Ricardo. *Diccionario enciclopédico de gastronomía Mexicana*. Mexico City: Editorial Clío, Libros y Videos, 2000.

Nancy Zaslavsky

Hostess Brands, LLC is known for its line of sweet snack foods, including the iconic Hostess Cupcake, with its seven loop-de-loops of white icing, and Twinkies, the dessert cake with the reputation of being indestructible. Other popular snacks made by Hostess Brands include classic treats like Ding Dongs, Ho Hos, Donettes, Suzy O's, Sno Balls, Zingers Fruit Pies, and Baseballs.

Hostess Brands, LLC was formed in 2013 after almost a century of mergers and acquisitions and a decade of being in and out of Chapter 11 bankruptcies. What would become Hostess Brands took root in 1925 when the Continental Baking Company purchased the Taggart Baking Company of Indianapolis, the maker of Wonder Bread and a successful line of snack cakes. Continental would advertise these products under two trade names: "Wonder" for its bread products and "Hostess" for its cake products.

Although cupcakes have been part of America's culinary heritage since the nineteenth century, it was not until 1919 that the Taggart Baking Company introduced the first commercially produced cupcake. See CUPCAKES. These chocolate cupcakes, made from a devil's food cake recipe, were advertised under the Hostess name beginning in 1927, although they did not have the familiar vanilla crème filling with the seven distinctive white squiggles across the top until after World War II. In 1947 Hostess introduced the Sno Ball, a Hostess chocolate cupcake turned upside down and covered in marshmallow and coconut. In 1967 Hostess introduced a cream-filled cake called Ding Dong. Because it was similar to a snack cake called Ring Ding created by Drake's Cakes in 1958, Hostess had to call it Big Wheels on the East Coast. The problem was resolved in 1998 when Hostess purchased Drake's Cakes. Another popular Hostess cake is the Ho Ho, a chocolate cake with a pinwheel cream-filled design. This cake is similar to Drake's Yodels, created in 1963, and to Little Debbie's Swiss Rolls. See LITTLE DEBBIE.

Although cupcakes continue to be a Hostess staple, it was James A. Dewar's invention of Twinkies in 1930 that made the company's fortune and changed the snack-cake world forever. Dewar was the manager of the Continental Baking Company in Schiller Park, Illinois, which owned the Hostess trademark. He substituted a banana cream for the company's strawberry filling in Hostess's Little Shortbread Fingers and called the new product Twinkies, after a billboard advertisement for Twinkie-Toe Shoes. See TWINKIE.

In November 2012, Hostess Brands shut down production of their snack foods in the United States. Hostess products returned to the shelves in July 2013 after the company was purchased out of bankruptcy by the private equity firms Apollo Global Management and Metropoulos & Co. During this period of corporate uncertainty when Hostess products disappeared from store shelves, snack-food fans feared they might lose their favorite squiggle-topped cupcakes and cream-filled Twinkies forever. Their fear proved unfounded: Hostess's new managers targeted 160,000 stores to bring back these iconic brands onto the market, aggressively placing their snack foods in drug stores, vending machines, and dollar stores—in other words, anywhere you could buy a candy bar.

Hostess products have not only generated consumer loyalty but also a fan base that other consumer food product companies can only envy. In recent years Twinkies have made cameo appearances in films, television shows, and comic strips such as *Die Hard*, *Zombieland*, *The Simpsons*, "Wizard of Id," and *Family Guy*.

Beginning in the 1970s, Hostess actively focused its advertising on young people. The company printed baseball cards, featuring the Major League's biggest stars on its packaging, and advertised heavily in comic books with characters touting the benefits of Hostess snack foods. In one mini-episode in which Batman fails to stop a violent mummy with a ray gun, he cleverly subdues the mummy with a box of Hostess Twinkies, because mummies "can't resist that moist sponge cake and creamy filling!" This strange comic advertisement appeared in the April/May 1975 issue of DC Comics' *Beowulf*.

Twinkies are often made fun of or parodied. Dipping them into batter and deep-frying them may have started off as a joke, but deep-fried Twinkies are a staple at the Texas State Fair and other similar venues across the county. They were invented in 2001 by Christopher Sell, a native of Rugby, England, who operated a fish-and-chips restaurant in Brooklyn, New York. The shop was already selling deep-fried Mars Bars and Snickers, familiar treats in Scotland. One day Sell tossed a Twinkie into the boiling fat, and the rest is history.

See also SMALL CAKES.

"Hostess Cup Cakes: One of America's Most Popular Edible Icons." http://www.foodtimeline.org/foodcakes.html#hostess.

"Hostess Superhero Advertisements." http://www.comicvine.com/hostess-superhero-advertisements/4015-56171/.

Newman, Kara. "Deep-Fried Twinkies." In *Oxford Encyclopedia of Food and Drink in America*, 2d ed., Vol. 2, edited by Andrew F. Smith, p. 566. Oxford and New York: Oxford University Press, 2013.

Rourke, Elizabeth, Stephen Meyer, and David E. Salamie. "Hostee Brands, Inc." In *International Directory of Company Histories*, Vol. 133, edited by Jay P. Pederson. pp. 195–201. Farmington Hills, Mich.: Gale, 2012.

Smith, Andrew F. "Hostess Brands." In *Fast Food and Junk Food: An Encyclopedia of What We Love to Eat*, Vol. 1, p. 351. Santa Barbara, Calif.: Greenwood, 2011.

Joseph M. Carlin

Huguenot torte, neither French nor a torte, is a popular Charleston, South Carolina, baked apple and nut pudding with a meringue-like top. The recipe first appeared in the Junior League of Charleston's best-selling *Charleston Receipts* (continuously in print since 1950, with over 500,000 copies sold). Its author, Evelyn Anderson (identified in the book also as Mrs. Cornelius Huguenin), submitted the recipe for inclusion in the fundraiser cookbook in the late 1940s when she was making desserts for the Huguenot Tavern in the heart of the city's historic district. Remarried after the death of her first husband, she was contacted in the assisted-living facility where she lived in the late 1980s to discuss the recipe, which includes copious amounts of baking powder.

Mrs. Huguenin (now Florance) confirmed that she had adapted the recipe from one for Ozark Pudding that she had first sampled in the Mississippi River Delta, where pecans are indigenous. A twentieth-century conceit with no French antecedent—Charleston's large colonial population of Huguenots notwithstanding—the pudding calls for pecans or walnuts, neither of which are native to Charleston. Pecans were not generally planted in the Carolina low country surrounding Charleston until the twentieth century, when the rice plantations finally folded. And apples have never grown well there.

The gooey, extremely sweet dessert is still a favorite of Charleston's tearooms that open in the fellowship halls of the historic downtown churches during the city's famous house and garden tours in the fall and spring, as well as at the pervasive ladies' luncheons, garden clubs, and bridge games that still characterize the old southern port. Numerous deconstructed versions of Huguenot Torte appear on the menus of Charleston's popular restaurants, but the dessert is mostly confined to home cooks, who find its ease of preparation irresistible.

See also PUDDING and SOUTH (U.S.).

Taylor, John Martin. *Hoppin' John's Lowcountry Cooking: Recipes and Ruminations from Charleston & the Carolina Coastal Plain.* New York: Bantam, 1992.

John Martin Taylor

ice cream, the frozen mixture of sweetened and flavored cream or milk that is so universal today, was a precious indulgence when "One plate of Ice cream" was served at the table of King Charles II in 1671, according to Elias Ashmole's account in *The Institution, Laws and Ceremonies of the Most Noble Order of the Garter*, published a year later. At the time, kings, queens, and nobles might dine on ice cream. Commoners did not. Until the late eighteenth to early nineteenth century, the expense and difficulty of making ice cream limited it to upper-class tables.

Despite mythmakers' tales, neither Marco Polo nor Catherine de Médici introduced ice cream to European courts. Freezing is not described in Europe until the sixteenth century, and only then by scientists rather than cooks. Serving a plate of ice cream was not possible until the discovery of the endothermic effect, whereby a substance, such as cream, can be made to freeze by immersing or surrounding it with a mixture of ice and salt. Surrounding a cream mixture with ice alone chills but does not freeze it. Adding salt lowers the melting point of the ice and draws heat out of the cream, causing it to freeze. This mechanism, if not ice cream, was familiar as early as the thirteenth century, according to a contemporary description of the process by Arab medical historian Ibn Abu Usaybia.

Prior to the discovery of the technique of freezing, ice and snow were sought after and highly valued. Harvesting and then storing ice and snow for any length of time presented difficult challenges, but that simply added to the chilly substances' desirability. Ice was so highly regarded that a holiday was created for it in fourth-century Japan. On that day, the emperor gave chips of ice to palace guests. In ancient times, the Chinese, the Greeks, and the Romans all gathered and stored ice or snow. Icy sherbet drinks date back to medieval times in the Middle East. In the fifteenth century, the elites of Spain and Italy sent their servants to nearby mountains to gather snow. The servants wrapped the snow in straw and carried it back, on mules' backs or on their own. They stored whatever had not melted in pits or in simple icehouses built into the ground in cool, shaded areas. The ice and snow were used to chill drinks, decorate tables, and crown foods.

It seemed as if the world was waiting for ice cream to be created, despite the fact that from China to India to the Middle East and Europe, traditional medical and nutritional beliefs opposed iciness in the diet. Eating or drinking anything that was either exceptionally hot or cold was supposed to be avoided. Hippocrates had warned against "cold things, such as snow and ice," because they were "inimical to the chest." At various times and places, iced drinks were said to cause such ailments as colic, convulsions, paralysis, blindness, and even death. As late as the seventeenth century, the English diarist John Evelyn said he suffered "an *Angina* & sore Throat" because he had drunk wine with "Snow & Ice as the manner here is" when he was in Padua. Yet despite all the warnings and objections, ice and snow were prized and the discovery of the technique of freezing was acclaimed.

From Slush to Iced Cream

In the sixteenth century, the Italian scientist Giambattista della Porta experimented with freezing wine because, he wrote, "the chief thing desired at feasts" was wine as cold as ice. To freeze the wine, he immersed the bottle in a container of snow and saltpeter and turned the bottle until the contents froze. Since alcohol does not freeze solid, the result was a slushy drink that was soon the toast of noble Roman tables.

The freezing process made fanciful ice artistry possible. Cooks created marzipan boats and set them afloat on seas of ice. See MARZIPAN. They dipped fresh fruits in water, froze them, and displayed the shimmering fruits on dinner tables. Finally, they created sorbets and ice creams.

Cooks were already experienced in making flavorful drinks like the Middle Eastern sherbets. See SHERBET. Their repertoire also included an enormous variety of cream and custard dishes. See CREAM and CUSTARD. The next step was to turn these drinks into ices and the creams into ice creams.

In the latter half of the seventeenth century, ices began appearing in Italy, France, and Spain. Antonio Latini, chief steward for the Spanish prime minister in Naples, published some of the earliest recipes for ices, including one made with milk, in *Lo scalco all moderna* (1692). At the time, he also claimed that everyone in Naples knew how to make them. "Everyone" was, no doubt, an exaggeration. See LATINI, ANTONIO. But others in Naples and in France were beginning to publish recipes. Nicolas Audiger included detailed freezing instructions in his book *La maison réglée*, published the same year as Latini's first volume. Audiger did not have specific recipes for ices; he simply explained that to turn a drink like lemonade into an ice, one should double the sugar. Unlike Latini, however, he did give detailed instruction on how to freeze this doubly sweet lemonade. He said it should be put in a container, covered, and placed in a large tub filled with crushed ice and salt. After letting the container sit in the tub for a time, one should open it and stir the contents. The process should be repeated until the beverage turned into a sorbet. Though machine churning has replaced stirring by hand, the principle remains the same: moving the mixture as it freezes ensures that it will not simply harden into a block of flavored ice, but will be smooth and scoopable.

Audiger had just one recipe for ice cream. It was made with cream, sugar, and orange flower water, a delicate flavor that deserves a renaissance. See FLOWER WATERS. Other cooks published recipes for iced creams at the time, but their freezing instructions often failed to mention the all-important churning. The first ice cream recipe in an English cookbook appeared in *Mrs. Mary Eales's Receipts*, published in 1718. Titled "To Ice Cream," the recipe did not mention stirring.

Many early ice cream recipes seem tentative, as if the writer is not completely confident about the process. But in the eighteenth century, cooks became so comfortable with it that they experimented with flavors.

Confectioners' Creations

In France, in 1786, M. Emy wrote the first book entirely devoted to ices and ice creams and the most comprehensive one for generations. See EMY, M. His ice cream flavors ranged from cinnamon to saffron. His ices included pineapple, pomegranate, and rose. He also molded his ices and ice creams into decorative shapes.

Other confectioners began to do the same. Using molds of various shapes and sizes, they created realistic-looking peaches, strawberries, and pears to reflect the flavor of the ice or ice cream. They also molded ice cream into representations of hams, fish, and chickens that, happily, had nothing to do with the flavor of the ice cream.

They became so skilled at these trompe l'oeil ices that some eighteenth-century confectioners used them to trick guests. Dr. John Moore, an English resident of Naples, described a meal composed of ices in his 1792 book *A View of Society and Manners in Italy*. He wrote that when the king and queen of Naples paid a call on the nuns at a nearby convent, the royal party was presented with what looked like a cold luncheon consisting of meats, poultry, and vegetables. To their delight, the guests discovered the turkey was, in fact, a lemon ice, and all the other dishes were also ices in disguise. See TROMPE L'OEIL.

In the nineteenth century, British confectioners made ice cream in the shape of anarchists' bombs with flames made of spun sugar flaring from the top. The editors of *The Encyclopaedia of Practical Cookery* thought it "remarkable how much inclined some culinary professionals are to introduce the arts of warfare into their peaceful and uneventful occupations." The London-based Italian confectioner Giuliagmo Jarrin is credited with coining the term *bomba* to describe such ice creams. See JARRIN, WILLIAM ALEXIS.

America was slow to jump on the ice cream bandwagon. The cost and difficulty of obtaining ice along with the price of sugar meant that few could afford ice cream. Thomas Jefferson, for one, liked ice cream so much that he brought a recipe home from France and had his ice cream made at Monticello, where he maintained an icehouse. But few had the financial resources for their own ice house, and even professional confectioners could not get enough supplies to guarantee ice cream every day. Still, a certain Philip Lenzi advertised in a 1777 edition of the *New York Gazette* that he had ice cream to sell "almost every day."

Like ice and sugar, domestic ice cream recipes were hard to come by. Though imported and reprinted English cookbooks, such as the American edition of *The New Art of Cookery* (1792), included some recipes, Mary Randolph's *The Virginia House-Wife*, published in 1824, was the first native cookbook to offer recipes for ice cream and ices. Her many flavors included almond, chocolate, vanilla, and coconut. Most were flavors we enjoy today; the one oddity was her recipe for frozen oyster cream.

During the early nineteenth century, as ice cream became more affordable and available, Americans could buy it from confectioners, at cafés, and at pleasure gardens. These outdoor areas, long popular in England, were a cross between a garden and a café where patrons paid admission to stroll along tree-lined walkways, listen to musicians play, and enjoy delicacies like pound cake, lemonade, ices, and ice creams. Initially, the gardens were genteel havens for ladies and gentlemen, but eventually they became more democratic. Some served liquor and allowed dancing.

By the middle of the century, ice cream shops had opened in major cities. Some were tastefully decorated and catered to ladies by serving tea, sandwiches, and such drinks as sherry cobblers in addition to ice creams. Less elegant and expensive shops catered to working-class customers.

Egalitarian Ice Cream

In the era before mechanical refrigeration, ice had been as important an ingredient in ice cream making as cream, but supplying it was hardly big business. Like many others, Frederick Tudor's family harvested ice from a pond on their property near Boston, Massachusetts, and used it to make ice cream. Tudor saw the business possibilities in ice harvesting and decided to sell the ice in the West Indies. Despite a lack of interest from investors, he obtained the right to sell ice in Martinique in 1806, harvested enough to fill a ship, and set sail. The venture was a financial failure: much of the ice melted en route; moreover, Frederick's brothers, who had gone ahead to make arrangements, failed to provide an icehouse for storage once the shipment arrived. Nevertheless, Tudor persuaded a local restaurant owner to use the rapidly diminishing ice to make ice cream, and the local newspaper hailed his achievement.

In subsequent years Tudor and his associate Nathaniel Wyeth developed new harvesting, shipping, and storage techniques and ultimately shipped ice as far as India successfully (the Ice House in Chennai, India, still stands). Tudor became known as the "Ice King." His success inspired competitors, and by 1879 the natural ice industry was harvesting nearly 8 million tons of ice annually, employing thousands of men, and delivering ice to businesses and homes nearly everywhere. An icebox became a must-have kitchen appliance, and ice cream an affordable treat for ordinary families.

As the ice industry was developing, another innovation helped make ice cream a household item in the United States—an ice cream freezer that allowed the mixture to be stirred without the need to open the pot. In 1843 Nancy Johnson, a Philadelphian about whom little else is known, patented an ice cream freezer intended for home use. A crank on the outside of the tub was attached to a dasher, or paddle, inside the freezing pot. The person making the ice cream turned the crank, and the inner dasher churned the ice cream to a smooth, lush consistency. Others soon followed Johnson's lead and produced so-called patent freezers, which made it more cost-effective for professionals to make ice cream and much easier for home cooks to do the same. See ICE CREAM MAKERS.

By the late nineteenth century, ice cream making at home was widespread. Ice cream became as essential to birthday celebrations as cake. It went on picnics and raised funds for churches at ice cream socials. See ICE CREAM SOCIALS. Cookbooks abounded with recipes, and home cooks began emulating confectioners by molding their ice creams. Molds were sold in general stores and could be ordered from catalogs. Cookbook writers advised those who could not afford molds to improvise by using household items like baking powder cans. See MOLDS, JELLY AND ICE CREAM.

Expanding Opportunities

Commercial ice cream making expanded rapidly. In 1851 Jacob Fussell, a milk dealer from Maryland, was faced with an oversupply of cream. Rather than let it sour, he turned it into ice cream and sold it at a price that undercut the city's confectioners. Recognizing the potential of the ice cream business, he opened a factory and began production. Within a few years, he had become the first significant ice cream wholesaler in the country, selling to hotels, restaurants, and even churches. When his associate James M. Horton took over the business in 1874, he became the first to ship ice cream to foreign ports. Thereafter, ice cream was a favorite dessert aboard transatlantic steamships.

The United States had been late to ice cream making but, after the end of the Civil War, it led the world. European wholesalers bought American ice cream–making equipment, copied American products, and used American marketing techniques. Inexpensive ices and ice creams proliferated, and elite confectioners felt threatened by the competition. An 1883 edition of the *Confectioners' Journal* warned against the "fraudulent and depraved wares of the factories." It was no use. By then, street vendors were selling ice creams for pennies.

Italian immigrants in England and in the United States found work as ice cream peddlers in the late nineteenth century. Their ice cream was not of the same quality as that sold by confectioners, but it was welcomed by those who had never been able to afford any sort of ice cream. The peddlers sold ice cream in small glass containers called penny licks. They filled a glass with ice cream and the customer licked it out, without benefit of a spoon. When he finished, the peddler wiped the glass with a rag and filled it up for the next customer.

Somewhat more sanitary products were soon developed. Hokey-pokeys were slices cut from a brick of ice cream and wrapped in a piece of paper. Usually, the bricks were layered with three different flavors; each crosswise slice revealed all three, much to the delight of children. Ice cream sandwiches, first created by a street vendor on New York City's Bowery, soon became a favorite street food. Confectioners copied the idea, but served the sandwiches on small plates with ice cream forks. Forks were just one of the specialized implements created for ice cream. By the turn of the century, ice cream knives, spoons, dishes, bowls, serving pieces, and scoops all flourished. See SERVING PIECES.

The ice cream cone was originally eaten with a fork and served on the most elegant tables. See ICE CREAM CONES. Mrs. Agnes Marshall was an English cookbook author, teacher, and entrepreneur whose 1894 book *Fancy Ices* contained several recipes for prettily decorated ice cream cones. In one illustration, the ice cream cones are arranged in a pyramid atop a doily-covered platter. See MARSHALL, AGNES BERTHA.

In 1902 Antonio Valvona, an Italian living in England, received a U.S. patent for his "apparatus for baking biscuit-cups for ice-cream." He said they were to be "sold by the vendors of ice-cream in public thoroughfares." When ice cream cones were sold at the 1904 World's Fair in St. Louis, Missouri, they became an instant and widespread hit.

Initially, soda fountain proprietors resisted adding ice cream to their inventory because of the expense and difficulty of storage. It was inevitable, though, and before long ice cream sodas, sundaes, floats, banana splits, and other treats all became popular soda fountain offerings. The temperance movement and, later, Prohibition benefited the business greatly as soda fountains replaced saloons, and brewers became ice cream manufacturers. See SODA FOUNTAIN.

Street vendors' offerings expanded to include ice cream novelties such as Eskimo Pies, Good Humor bars, Popsicles (called Ice Lollies in England), and many others. See ESKIMO PIE; GOOD HUMOR MAN; and POPSICLE.

The Frozen Dessert Business

Ice cream–making equipment had improved over the years, and quantity production was possible by the early part of the twentieth century. By 1910 continuous-process freezers could produce up to 150 gallons of ice cream an hour. During World War I, ice cream making was banned in England. In the United States, sugar was restricted, so ice cream makers began replacing some of it with corn syrup and corn sugar. See CORN SYRUP. Some manufacturers used powdered milk and butter in place of the more expensive fresh cream. When the war ended, some substitutions continued.

In the 1920s mechanical refrigeration began to do away with the need for ice and salt, and before long with the natural ice industry. See REFRIGERATION. Refrigerated railroad cars sped national distribution. Technological advances including steam power, electric motors, homogenizers, and packing machines increased production capabilities. Scientific formulas designed to achieve specific butterfat content replaced old-fashioned recipes.

Howard Johnson opened his first soda fountain in 1925 in Quincy, Massachusetts, and soon became famous for the high quality of his ice cream, its 28 flavors, and the shops' highly visible bright orange roofs. One of the first to recognize the advantages of restaurant franchising, Johnson grew his business to include restaurants and hotels from Maine to Florida.

The Depression hit the ice cream industry hard, but portion control and other cost-cutting measures helped. So did offering customers a bargain. Five-cent cones and other nickel novelties were not very profitable, but they kept customers coming back. When the Depression ended, the ice cream business surged.

During World War II, England again prohibited ice cream making, as did Italy. But in the United States, ice cream was considered a morale builder and symbol of patriotism, thanks in large part to industry lobbying. In 1943 the U.S. Armed Forces became the world's largest ice cream manufacturer. The civilian business prospered as well, despite the rationing of some ingredients and difficulty of obtaining others. Before the war, quality ice cream had been made with a butterfat content of 14 percent. During the war, it dropped to 10 percent, and fewer flavors were produced to save on containers and transportation. Sherbet, or ice milk, was often served in lieu of ice cream. When the war ended, many manufacturers continued to make ice cream the same way.

After the war, munitions factories switched to turning out new cars and refrigerators with small freezing compartments. Homemakers began driving to the new supermarkets for their ice cream or going to drive-in soft-serve shops, instead of the local drugstore soda fountain. Prepackaged half-gallons of ice cream became the norm. Bigger was better, and quantity won over quality.

Before long, though, the tide turned, and companies such as Baskin-Robbins and Häagen-Dazs began to make richer, creamier ice cream. Young entrepreneurs like Ben Cohen and Jerry Greenfield, of Ben & Jerry's fame, opened scoop shops and sold rich creamy ice cream in an assortment of flavors. See BASKIN-ROBBINS; HÄAGEN-DAZS; and BEN & JERRY'S. In 1981 *TIME* Magazine pronounced ice cream "our guiltiest and most delicious sin."

In the twenty-first century, the frozen dessert business has become a vast multinational, multibillion-dollar enterprise dominated by international conglomerates Unilever and Nestlé. See NESTLÉ. Not every frozen dessert has a strict definition, but in general the market includes regular ice cream, which the United States Food and Drug Administration defines as containing not less than 10 percent milkfat; premium and super-premium ice creams, which can contain 18 percent; and French ice cream or frozen custard, which is made with at least 1.4 percent egg yolk solids. Although no hard-and-fast rule exists, sherbet is usually defined as a frozen, fruit-flavored dessert made with milk, whereas sorbet, often referred to as an ice, is made without milk. Gelato, or Italian ice cream, is generally lower in fat than most ice creams, and since it is served at a warmer temperature, its flavor may be more intense. Soft-serve is ice cream served as it is churned rather than being hard-frozen.

Today, in addition to finding ice cream at supermarkets, frozen dessert lovers can indulge at local scoop shops and new chain stores that are creating ice cream, gelato, frozen yogurt, and sophisticated soft-serve ice creams in all kinds of flavors. Although in every large-scale poll the most popular flavor continues to be vanilla, today's shops feature flavors ranging from Secret Breakfast, made with cornflakes and bourbon, to Honey Jalapěno Pickle. There has also been a resurgence of homemade ice cream, thanks to ice cream makers that work with the press of a button.

See also CREAM; ITALIAN ICE; MEDICINAL USES OF SUGAR; and SUNDAE.

David, Elizabeth. *Harvest of the Cold Months*. New York: Viking Penguin, 1995.

Day, Ivan. *Ice Cream*. Oxford: Shire, 2011.

Funderburg, Anne Cooper. *Chocolate, Strawberry, and Vanilla*. Bowling Green, Ohio: Bowling Green State University Press, 1995.

Quinzio, Jeri. *Of Sugar and Snow: A History of Ice Cream Making*. Berkeley: University of California Press, 2009.

Weir, Caroline, and Robin Weir. *Ice Creams, Sorbets & Gelati: The Definitive Guide*. London: Grub Street, 2010.

Jeri Quinzio

ice cream cones are edible cone-shaped pastries designed to hold ice creams or ices. Although their origins are controversial, the most plausible explanation is one of simple evolution. Ice cream manufacturers, faced with the challenge of creating a container, at the lowest possible cost, turned their skills as confectioners to adapting wafers to a new use.

In the seventeenth and eighteenth centuries, ice creams were rare and served only in aristocratic or wealthy households. They were eaten by the wealthy out of small porcelain, glass, silver, and pewter cups on a small plate, frequently with a small spoon.

The earliest reference to cones or cornets was by Antonio de Rossi, a Venetian confectioner in Rome, who produced, in 1724, a manuscript of recipes, including one for *cialdoni torcerli* or twisted wafers, which were shaped into conical containers, or cones.

The first pictorial evidence for ice cream cones is seen in an 1807 print by Debucourt showing a woman eating an ice in a cone in M. Garchi's casino café Frascati, in Paris.

Mrs. Agnes Marshall's *Fancy Ices* from 1894 offers two recipes for ice cream cones, the first known recipes published in English. Her Christina cornets were filled with vanilla ice cream mixed with finely diced, dried fruits. The cornets were piped with royal icing and dipped in chopped pistachio nuts. Her Margaret cornets were half-filled with ginger water ice, the other half with apple ice cream. Both were to be served "for a dinner sweet or dessert." See MARSHALL, AGNES BERTHA.

Numerous claims exist in the United States that the ice cream cone, or cornucopia, was invented at the 1904 World's Fair in St. Louis, Missouri. The fair popularized the cone, but it had already been in use in Europe many years before. Prior to the invention of the cone or cornet, the "penny lick" was the container in which ices were sold in Great Britain at the seaside and in the streets of towns and cities. Smaller sizes were sold for ½ d (halfpenny lick) and ¼ d (farthing lick). The "penny lick" was a small, low-quality, usually footed glass with a partially solid bowl and a small recess to hold the ice. The ice cream was "licked" out and the glass then returned to the vendor, who used it for the next buyer, frequently without washing it. These glasses were banned in England in the 1920s for spreading tuberculosis.

Waffle and sugar cones are variations on the simple cone, the waffle one being thicker and the sugar one containing more sugar, which gives it a firmer and more brittle texture. The Italian manufacturer Spica invented the Cornetto in Naples in 1959. The inside of this cone is coated with chocolate, sugar, and oil, making it possible to freeze the cone complete and filled, a technique that keeps it from becoming soggy. The Cornetto is one of the most successful ice cream products in the world. Spica is now owned by Unilever.

The ice cream cone is a convenient way to eat ice cream, but it is also one of the most ecologically sound pieces of packaging ever invented, since one consumes it.

See also ICE CREAM.

Weir, Robin. *Ice Creams, Sorbets and Gelati.* London: Grub Street, 2010.

Robin Weir

ice cream makers in the form of hand-cranked freezers were patented in the 1840s by a Philadelphia woman and a London confectioner. Their inventions revolutionized ice cream by creating a smooth, creamy texture that previous freezing methods did not produce. Other inventors improved upon their designs to create better ice cream makers for both household and commercial use.

In the ancient world, people used snow and ice to cool foods, but these natural refrigerants were in short supply during hot weather. Early scientists searched for a more reliable coolant, and someone discovered that putting saltpeter (potassium nitrate) in water produced a very cold liquid. By the mid-sixteenth century, Italians knew about this phenomenon and used it to make frozen concoctions called ices. See ITALIAN ICE. The French also learned the secret, and recipes for ices were published in Europe before 1700.

Until the 1840s, cooks used the pot freezer method to make ice cream. First, the cook removed ice from the icehouse or pit where large blocks of harvested natural ice were stored. He chipped the ice into small pieces and placed the chips, along with salt or saltpeter, into a wood tub. Then he poured his ice cream mixture into a tin or pewter pot and set it in the tub. He rotated the pot by hand and periodically used a long spoon to mix up the frozen particles inside the pot. His goal was to make a smooth

The American Machine Co. of Philadelphia manufactured the Gem Ice Cream Freezer in sizes ranging from two to fourteen quarts. This late-nineteenth-century advertising card shows how the cedar pail and stirrer move in opposite directions, causing "double action" that beats the ice cream mixture. BOSTON PUBLIC LIBRARY

frozen cream, but he generally produced a slushy concoction more icy than creamy.

In a variation on the pot freezer method, French cooks used a special pot or canister, called a *sorbetière*, which fit into a tall, cylindrical wood tub. The metal canister had a tight-fitting lid with a handle, which the cook grasped and turned to rotate the pot inside the tub. From time to time, the cook removed the lid and stirred the canister's ingredients with a spoon or spatula. Thomas Jefferson saw *sorbetières* when he lived in France (1784–1789) and acquired one for Monticello, his Virginia plantation.

In 1843 Nancy Johnson was issued a U.S. patent for a hand-cranked freezer, and Thomas Masters received a British patent for a design similar to hers. Johnson's device had four parts: a wood tub that held the salt and ice, a metal canister that held the ice cream mixture, a paddle or dasher that fit inside the canister, and a crank that attached to the dasher. The cook turned the crank, which rotated the dasher, churning the ice cream mixture inside the canister. The constant churning produced a frozen cream with a smooth, uniform texture.

Variations on Johnson's design were used for both home and commercial ice cream making in the nineteenth century. In the early 1900s, inventors patented special freezers for commercial ice cream manufacturing plants. These new freezers were designed for continuous, efficient production of large quantities of ice cream for the marketplace.

Electricity and mechanical refrigeration turned the hand-cranked ice cream freezer into an endangered species in the home. Families who could afford the latest labor-saving devices threw the old-fashioned freezer on the trash heap. New versions of the tub-and-canister freezer used an electric motor to turn the dasher, thereby eliminating the tedious, tiring hand-cranking. Another labor-saving option was making ice cream in the freezer compartment of a refrigerator. By the late twentieth century, cooks had a wide choice of efficient, easy-to-use ice cream freezers.

A compact, modern version of the hand-cranked freezer utilizes a double-walled bowl; the coolant is sealed between the walls, eliminating the messy, melting ice and salt. The cook puts the bowl in the freezer compartment of a refrigerator to freeze the coolant. Then the bowl is filled with the ice cream mixture and placed inside the housing. Like an old-fashioned freezer, this countertop version has a handle and a dasher. At intervals the cook turns the handle to stir the mixture and facilitate freezing.

Another option is the small electric ice cream maker that works in the freezer compartment of a refrigerator. The unit has paddles that turn slowly and automatically shut off while the ice cream is still soft. The ice cream ripens and hardens in the freezer. Some refrigerator manufacturers offer a built-in ice cream maker or a special electrical socket for one. Cordless, battery-operated ice cream makers have also been designed for use in the freezer compartment.

In the early twenty-first century, the most expensive ice cream maker is the self-contained freezer compressor unit. The cook prepares the ice cream mixture and presses a button to start the machine, the epitome of convenience and modernity. But the old-fashioned hand-cranked freezer is not totally extinct. At least one company still markets a hand-cranked freezer much like Nancy Johnson's, because many food lovers believe that hand-cranking makes the very best ice cream.

See also EMY, M.; ICE CREAM; MARSHALL, AGNES BERTHA; and REFRIGERATION.

Fallon, Peggy. *The Best Ice Cream Maker Cookbook Ever.* New York: HarperCollins, 1998.
Quinzio, Jeri. *Of Sugar and Snow: A History of Ice Cream Making.* Berkeley: University of California Press, 2009.

Anne Cooper Funderburg

ice cream socials became popular in late-nineteenth-century America as a result of the temperance movement, technology, and fundraising. Seeking sober alternatives to socializing, and employing ever-cheaper mechanical ice cream makers plus advances in commercial ice harvesting and storage, churches, synagogues, lodges, youth and other social clubs sponsored events based on selling ice cream to provide ongoing financial support for their organizations.

Offering usually a limited menu of flavors, and cake or pie to accompany the ice cream, the groups sold and served plates of ice cream to customers who, in summer, often sat at tables outdoors in imitation of popular commercial ice cream gardens, or in church fellowship or social halls converted for the event to ice cream parlors. The social might be timed to coincide with a community celebration or anniversary, with a holiday like the Fourth of July, or with a food festival such as those celebrating strawberries or blueberries. The social might also include music and games, with prizes for winners.

For centuries before the mid-1800s, ice cream had been an elite food, dependent on sufficient resources to buy or harvest and store ice for warmer seasons, plus household labor to make the treat. The invention of a geared, hand-cranked ice cream maker, patented in 1843 and thereafter manufactured for household consumption, put ice cream–making technology into middle-class domestic and social settings. See ICE CREAM MAKERS. Concomitantly, a trade in commercial ice harvesting ensured a year-round supply of natural ice, which was gradually replaced by the development of artificial refrigeration and ice production, particularly in the early twentieth century. See REFRIGERATION. These technologies, coupled with increased mid-nineteenth-century specialization in dairy farming near developing town and urban centers that assured regular supplies of milk and cream, plus ever-cheaper sugar, made ice cream popular among all strata of American society.

Recipes for ice cream abound in late-nineteenth- and early-twentieth-century cookbooks, and some, like Sarah Tyson Rorer's *Ice Creams, Water Ices, Frozen Puddings*, published in 1913, specifically addressed ice cream in all its forms. From time to time, large-quantity recipes for ice cream, pointing to production for socials, appear in community cookbooks published by charitable organizations to raise money. Occasionally, too, in manuscript cookbooks or handwritten recipe collections, ice cream recipes titled "for the church freezer," which call for larger quantities than a cook might make for family enjoyment, can be found.

Per-capita American ice cream consumption peaked during Prohibition in the 1920s. Ice cream socials were the epitome of good clean fun and continued well past the 1930s into the mid-twentieth century, especially among organizations dedicated to continued temperance, religious activity, or entertainment for youth. Groups, especially in rural areas, continued making their own ice cream, while those with access to commercially produced ice cream switched to buying it. Church and social groups still make ice cream for socials today, though ever more rarely.

See also ICE CREAM.

Quinzio, Jeri. *Of Sugar and Snow: A History of Ice Cream Making.* Berkeley: University of California Press, 2009.
Rorer, Sarah Tyson. *Mrs. Rorer's Ice Creams, Water Ices, Frozen Puddings.* Philadelphia: Arnold and Co., 1913.

Sandra L. Oliver

icebox cake, made from cookies or sweet crackers spread with whipped cream and chilled to form a solid, sliceable mass, descends from a 200-year-old family of desserts that includes trifles and charlottes. See CHARLOTTE and TRIFLE. Popularized by the proliferation of refrigerators (ice cooled in the later nineteenth century, then powered by gas or electricity in the early twentieth century), these desserts were promoted via cookbooks published by refrigerator makers, such as Alice Bradley's 1927 *Electric Refrigerator Menus and Recipes: Recipes prepared especially for the General Electric Refrigerator*. See REFRIGERATION. Magazines, newspapers, and cookbooks also provided recipes for icebox treats.

Early-twentieth-century versions of icebox cake often called for layers of ladyfingers or pieces of sponge or angel food cake dipped into custard prior to chilling in a form. See ANGEL FOOD CAKE and SPONGE CAKE. By the early 1930s, icebox cakes commonly used commercial cookies like vanilla wafers and chocolate wafers, layered with whipped cream.

Icebox cake precedents, such as the trifle in Hannah Glasse's 1805 *Art of Cookery*, call for macarons and cookie-like sweet cakes softened with sherry, topped with custard and jelly, and moistened further with syllabub, a wine-flavored whipped cream. See MACARONS and SYLLABUB. In the later 1800s, versions of charlotte russe sometimes called for gelatin-fortified whipped cream used with cake. See GELATIN. Maria Parloa's Charlotte Russe No. 2 recipe in her 1880 *New Cookbook and Marketing Guide* pointed the way to icebox cake with these instructions: "Have a quart mould lined with stale sponge cake. Fill it with whipped cream and set it in the ice chest for an hour or two."

See also CAKE.

Olver, Lynn. "Ice Box Cake (aka Refrigerator Cake)." http://www.foodtimeline.org/foodcakes.html#icebox (accessed 30 August 2013).

Sandra L. Oliver

icing is a sugar-based medium for enhancing and decorating many types of cake and other sweetmeats. Although a plain cake should still taste superb, it is often the icing on the cake that identifies it. Would we recognize an American carrot cake, the Dobos torta from Hungary, or a traditional British Christmas cake without their decorative layer of sugar?

Our love of sweetness may not be innate, but it is certainly ancient: honey brushed over an oven-hot cake was recommended in the fifth century by Apicius. Until smoothly ground icing sugar, or confectioner's sugar, was produced by commercial refineries in the nineteenth century, it was necessary to crush lump sugar in a mortar, then brush or shake the powdery grains through a fine-meshed cloth or sieve two or three times. See SUGAR and SUGAR REFINING.

Robert May's (1685) simple sugar glaze made by boiling sugar and water was poured over a newly baked fruitcake before drying in the oven. See FRUITCAKE. A layer of icing provides extra sweetness and also seals in the moisture and flavor of a cake. Ralph Ayres (1721), the cook at New College, Oxford, prepared the icing for a plum cake by beating sugar with egg whites for "half an hour or longer," thereby presaging present-day practice.

Ayres's icing was known as sugar icing until 1840, when Queen Victoria's wedding cake, weighing 300 pounds, was created. See WEDDING CAKE. To mark the occasion, the sugar plus egg white icing that covered the elaborately decorated and tiered confection was renamed "royal icing." Royal icing spread over marzipan on a rich fruitcake has become the accepted style for a celebration cake. The smooth, firm surface obtainable with royal icing is well suited to cake decoration involving piped emblems such as flowers, swags, and trellis patterns. See CAKE DECORATING.

Both Mrs. Raffald (1769) and Mrs. Beeton (1861) refer to the marzipan on a cake as almond icing, now also known as almond paste. See BEETON, ISABELLA and MARZIPAN. Blanched and ground almonds are mixed with icing sugar, egg whites, lemon juice, and brandy or rosewater to make a firm dough that is rolled out and placed on top of the cake. An English Simnel Cake has one layer of marzipan baked into the center and another resting on top of the cake. For a Battenberg Cake, the sections of colored sponge cake are held together by a sheet of marzipan enveloping the whole cake.

In the window of any French patisserie are examples of glacé icing with individual tarts, choux pastry éclairs, and sponge cakes gleaming with the smooth, satiny mixture. This soft icing is made by beating icing sugar with sufficient hot water until spreadable; it is usually flavored with vanilla extract, black coffee, chocolate, or citrus juice. Glacé icing is widely used by home bakers to give a professional finish to a cake.

In her chapter on pastes, icings, and glazes, Mrs. A. B. Marshall (1888), founder of a famous London cookery school, includes Vienna icing, made by blending icing sugar with butter, brandy, and maraschino. See MARSHALL, AGNES BERTHA. This icing is known today as buttercream or buttercream frosting, with milk or cream replacing the alcohol in Mrs. Marshall's recipe. Vienna icing "may be flavoured and coloured according to taste," says the author, and cupcake makers worldwide have risen to the challenge with a layer of various buttercreams, from lavender to pistachio, spread over the little paper-cased cakes. See CUPCAKES.

Not all icings require icing sugar. The different stages of boiled sugar syrup are deployed in making some frostings and icings, such as the billowing white meringue of American boiled icing. See MERINGUE and STAGES OF SUGAR SYRUP. Also described as seven-minute frosting, this icing is made by slowly adding a 238°F (115°C) sugar syrup to stiffly whisked egg whites while constantly beating until cool, usually for seven minutes.

Cooking a clear sugar syrup until it changes color to pale amber produces the glassy caramel icing of some Austrian and Hungarian cakes, such as Dobos torte. See DOBOS TORTE. The liquid caramel is either spread thinly over the top of the cake or poured onto oiled paper and allowed to cool before cutting to shape for decorating the cake.

Naturally brown cane sugars such as muscovado and demerara contribute an excellent butterscotch flavor to icing. Light, soft brown sugar is dissolved in heavy cream or butter over low heat, then brought to the boil and slightly cooled to produce an attractive fudge-like frosting. See SUGAR.

Fondant icing dates from the Victorian era and is more commonly prepared by professional bakers rather than home cooks. See FONDANT. A boiled syrup of sugar and glucose is cooled and kneaded on a cold surface until it becomes stiff and creamy. When required as icing, a piece of the sugar paste is softened with hot water until it reaches a pouring consistency.

The appeal of novelty cakes has led to the introduction of ready-prepared, colored sugar-paste icing that is rolled into sheets for draping over a cake before decorating. Small figures, animals, or other models for placing on the cake are made from the same mixture. The ease of using bought sugar-paste has spawned a thriving interest in cake decoration, and special decorating equipment, such as miniature pump-action sprays of food colors, have been developed for use with patterns and stencils—all intended to assist creativity. See CAKE DECORATION.

See also DOLLY VARDEN CAKE; PUBLICATIONS, TRADE; and SERVERS, SUGAR.

Ayres, Ralph. *Ralph Ayres' Cookery Book*, p. 13. Oxford: Bodleian, 2006.

Marshall, Agnes B. *Mrs A.B. Marshall's Cookery Book*, pp. 41–42. London: Simpkin, Marshall, Hamilton, Kent, 1888.

Geraldene Holt

Imperial Sugar Company, a major American sugar producer, was established in 1905 by Isaac H. Kempner (and other family members) and William T. Eldridge in what is today Sugar Land, Texas, a small community about 25 miles southwest of Houston.

Sugarcane had been grown in the area since the 1830s, when settlers found that the soil and climate, especially along the Brazos River, were conducive to its cultivation. See SUGARCANE and SUGARCANE AGRICULTURE. Samuel M. Williams and his brother grew sugarcane on their plantation on Oyster Creek, and in 1843 they produced enough to warrant construction of a small sugar mill on their property. This mill refined small quantities of sugar and also produced blackstrap molasses. See MOLASSES. Ed Cunningham subsequently acquired the Williams property and built a much larger refinery; in 1905 Isaac H. Kempner acquired the property in turn, naming his business the "Imperial" Sugar Company and expanding and diversifying its operations into areas unrelated to sugar refining. He even opened a bank. Kempner also built houses and stores for his workers in the company-owned town, which he named Sugar Land. The Imperial Sugar Company was incorporated in 1907, two years after its founding.

As sugar consumption increased in the United States during the first decade of the twentieth century, so did sugar production, and with the start of World War I in 1914 production increased further to supply European nations at war. When the United States entered the war in 1917 the demand for sugar outstripped supply, so the Imperial Sugar

Company imported raw sugar from the Caribbean in order to operate its refineries year-round.

The 1920s were years of change. The Imperial Sugar Company warded off efforts by Domino Sugar (then known as the American Sugar Refining Company) to control sugar production and distribution in the United States, and also held its own against the Texas Sugar Refining Company, which collapsed during the Depression. Imperial Sugar itself barely survived the Depression and did so only with a federal loan from the Reconstruction Finance Corporation. During the 1930s, the company innovated the packing of sugar in cotton bags, which were more convenient and sanitary than sugar scooped from barrels in stores. The company stopped growing sugarcane in Sugar Land in 1928 but continued to process raw sugar at its refinery in the city until 2003. See SUGAR REFINERIES.

After World War II the company expanded, producing more than 2 million pounds of sugar daily. The raw sugar came from the Dominican Republic, Brazil, Australia, and other countries. Imperial sold bulk sugar to candy manufacturers, bottlers, and other companies, and its products successfully competed against corn syrup and other cane sugar substitutes. See CORN SYRUP.

In 1988 the company merged with the Holly Sugar Corporation, a beet sugar refinery headquartered in Colorado Springs, and became the Imperial Holly Sugar Corporation. In 1996 it added the Spreckels Sugar Company of California and other companies, and Imperial Holly became one of the nation's largest refiners and distributors of sugar. Although Imperial Holly Corporation filed for bankruptcy in January 2001, the company survived; it closed its Sugar Land refinery in May 2003 but maintained refinery operations in California, Georgia, and Louisiana.

The current types of sugar marketed by Imperial Sugar are free-flowing sugar; granulated sugar; sugar shakers; light brown sugar; dark brown sugar; Stevia; and powdered sugar. See SUGAR. These products are sold under a variety of brand names, including Dixie Crystals, Imperial, Savannah Gold, NatureWise, and Holly, as well as private labels. The company also markets organic and fair-trade sweeteners and sweetener blends through partnerships, such as Natural Sweet Ventures, formed in 2010 with Pure Circle Limited to develop and commercialize Stevia sweetener blends; Louisiana Sugar Refining, formed in 2009 as a three-party joint venture with Sugar Growers and Refiners Inc. and Cargill Inc. to build and operate a cane sugar refinery in Gramercy, Louisiana; Comercializadora Santos Imperial together with Ingenios Santos, which markets sugar products in Mexico and the United States; and Wholesome Sweeteners, which sells organic, fair-trade, and other natural sweeteners such as agave syrup, honey, and Stevia. See AGAVE NECTAR and STEVIA. The Imperial Sugar Company also sells refined sugar, molasses, and other ingredients to industrial customers, principally food manufacturers, for use in candy, baked goods, frozen desserts, cereal, dairy products, canned goods, and beverages.

Imperial Sugar has changed hands many times, most recently in 2012, when it became a wholly owned subsidiary of Louis Dreyfus Commodities LLC, which combined its sugar holdings in Brazil and other places to create Ld Commodities Sugar Holdings, headquartered in Wilton, Connecticut.

See also AMERICAN SUGAR REFINING COMPANY; HAVEMEYER, HENRY OSBORNE; PLANTATIONS, SUGAR; SUGAR REFINING; and SUGAR TRADE.

Armstrong, Robert M. *Sugar Land and the Imperial Sugar Company*. Sugar Land, Tex.: R. M. Armstrong, 1991.

Black, Johnathan. *Sugarland, Texas: Including Its History, Sugar Land Ice and Sports Center, Teenstock Festival, Sugarland Mall, and More*. Earth Eyes Travel Guides, 2012.

Johnson, William R. *A Short History of the Sugar Industry in Texas*. Houston: Texas Gulf Coast Historical Association, 1961.

Andrew F. Smith

India is the second most populous country in the world after China and the seventh largest in area. No other country has such a diversity of climates and soils, races and languages, religions and sects, tribes, castes and classes, customs—and cuisines. Sometimes India is compared with Europe in its multitude of languages and ethnic groups—but imagine a Europe with eight religions (four of them born on Indian soil), each with its own dietary prohibitions and restrictions. This cultural diversity is reflected in the number and variety of sweets and sweet dishes.

Probably in no other part of the world are sweets (*mithai* in Hindi) so varied, so numerous, or so invested with meaning. See MITHAI. Sweets are an essential component of hospitality and celebration:

Indians send sweets to friends and family as gifts and consume them to celebrate passing an examination or getting a new job. They mark rites of passage, such as the birth of a child, pregnancy, marriage, even death. In the Hindu classification of foods by qualities, sugar, milk, and ghee, all ingredients in sweets, are considered *sattvic*—a Sanskrit term meaning "pure," "conducive to lucidity and calmness"—and can be eaten by everyone, even spiritual leaders and the most orthodox vegetarians. Sweets are also considered ritually pure and are offered to the gods and distributed to the devotees at Hindu temples. Sweets are sometimes eaten during fasts or used to break a fast.

Muslims also celebrate holidays and important religious occasions with sweets. For example, at the end of Ramadan, the fasting month, they prepare *khorma* (*khurma*), a thick pudding made of sautéed vermicelli, thickened milk, sugar, dates, and sometimes nuts, raisins, rosewater, and saffron for breakfast. See RAMADAN. India's Christians celebrate Christmas with delicious fruitcakes, while India's Parsi community (descendants of Persian Zoroastrians) enjoys dishes that reflect European, Iranian, and Indian influences, such as *mava malido*, an egg and semolina pudding, or *koomas*, a spiced baked cake.

Everyday Indian meals do not usually end with a dessert, except perhaps fruit or yogurt, sometimes sweetened. Instead, sweets and savory items are part of the late afternoon meal called tea or tiffin. Some sweets are made at home, but many are purchased from professional sweet makers, known as *halwai* or *moira* in Hindi. The process of making some sweets can be extremely lengthy and labor-intensive.

Unfortunately, the sweets served in Indian restaurants in the West—typically, kulfi, carrot halvah, ras malai, gulab jamun, and kheer—offer a limited introduction to the wonderful diversity and subtlety of Indian sweet dishes. A greater variety can be found in Indian sweetshops in large North American cities.

Historical Background

The earliest Indian sweet dishes were flavored with honey, dates, and fruits. The first sweet mentioned in the Sanskrit literature around 1000 B.C.E. is *apupa*, a round cake made of barley or rice flour baked in ghee and sweetened with honey. There are also references to *ksira*, milk and boiled rice, the ancestor of modern rice puddings.

Sugarcane grew in India from ancient times. Originally it was chewed, but during the first millennium B.C.E. Indians began to convert it to various products. The stems were crushed in a machine called a *yantra*, a large mortar and pestle turned by oxen that is still used in rural areas. The extracted juice, which contains up to 17 percent sucrose, was filtered and cooked slowly in a large metal pot fueled by the cane stalks. The thickened juice, called *phanita*, was similar to molasses and further concentrated and dried to make solid pieces of brown sugar, known as jaggery or gur. (The English word "sugar" comes from *sarkara*, the Sanskrit word for jaggery.) In the third century B.C.E., Indians discovered the technique of refining the juice into crystals, called *khand* (the origin of the English word "candy"). The Greek ambassador and writer Megasthenes (ca. 350–290 B.C.E.) was amazed by the sight of "tall reeds which are sweet both by nature and by concoction"—sugarcane, not known in Europe at the time—and "stones the colour of frankincense, sweeter than figs or honey." See SUGARCANE AGRICULTURE and SUGAR REFINING.

Later technological refinements, perhaps from Persia or Egypt, produced pure white loaves of sugar. The discovery that sugarcane could grow in the New World resulted in a decline in the Indian sugar industry, and by the nineteenth century sugar was imported from China and elsewhere. (Even today white sugar is called *chini* in Bengali and Hindi.) In 1912 the Sugarcane Research Institute developed hybrid sugarcanes using New World plants. Production increased dramatically, and today India is the world's second largest producer after Brazil. Indians are also the world's largest consumers of sugar, consuming 60 percent more than China's comparable population; middle-class Indians consume more sugar per capita than Americans.

Another source of sugar is the juice of palm trees, whose distinctive flavor makes it the preferred flavoring for certain sweets, especially in the winter. See PALM SUGAR.

In Ayurveda, the Indian system of medicine, dishes made from sugar were believed to have restorative powers and cooling properties. Even today, some sweet makers produce items containing ayurvedic herbs, such as *salan pak*, a Gujarati sweet made in the winter. It contains over 30 ingredients, including cloves, pepper, cinnamon, nutmeg, almonds, pistachios, Indian ginseng, and a whole host of ayurvedic herbs. *Salan pak* has a wonderfully complex, piquant flavor but can only be eaten in small amounts because of its powerful medicinal effects.

Ingredients

The word "sweet" encompasses a wide range of dishes, shown in the table below. After sugar, the most common ingredient is cow or buffalo milk. Milk has been an integral part of the Indian diet from ancient times. Cows have traditionally held a special place in Indian society, revered as the "eternal mother" for their usefulness as a source of labor and nourishment (excluding meat). Buffalo milk (from *bos bubalus*, a native species) has double the fat content of cow milk and is preferred by some sweet aficionados. See MILK.

An important component of sweets is khoa (*khoya*), a semi-solid or solid product made by slowly boiling milk until it thickens into a solid, constantly stirring to prevent caramelization. The ratio of milk solids to milk can range from 1:6 to 1:4. Before use it is often pulverized and sifted. *Chhana*, or curds, is made by bringing milk to a boil, then adding a souring agent, such as citric acid or old whey. This is done either while the milk is being heated, which makes a firmer product, or after it is removed from the stove. The curds are drained through a thin cloth and should be used immediately. Pressing the drained *chhana* under a weight to remove more moisture yields paneer, an ingredient often used in North Indian vegetarian dishes. Other common ingredients are chickpeas and lentils; rice, wheat, and other grains; fruits; vegetables; nuts (especially almonds, cashews, and pistachios); seeds (especially sesame seeds); and raisins. Clarified butter (ghee) is a preferred cooking medium. Popular flavorings include rose or kewra (screwpine) water, and spices, especially cardamom. See FLOWER WATERS; PANDANUS; and SPICES. Coloring agents include saffron, cochineal (red), and turmeric. Most sweets are subjected to some form of heat treatment that enables them to be preserved.

Some Categories of Indian Sweets

Category	*Examples*
Hard or semi-hard, dry	Halvah, barfi, laddu, peda, modaka, sandesh
In a liquid or syrup	Ras gulla, jalebi, ledikeni, gulab jamun, ras malai
Puddings	Payesh, payasam, pongal, kheer
Crepes	Pantua, malpoa
Yogurt	Shrikhand, misthi doi
European	Bibinca, fruit cake, biscuits
Crunchy	Chikki (peanut brittle), gur papdi

Varieties of Sweets

Some sweets are eaten everywhere in India, Pakistan, and Bangladesh; others are specialties of a region, city, even a single village. Some are variants of those found over an area extending from Turkey through the Middle East, and Central Asia to India, such as falooda, halvah, and jalebi. An entire encyclopedia could be devoted to Indian sweets; here, we have room only to list the main ones. Universally popular sweets include barfi, laddus, jalebi, halvah, and a rice pudding known variously as payesh, payasam, or kheer. See BARFI; LADDU; HALVAH; PAYASAM; and ZALABIYA.

A popular street food, jalebis (jalibis) resemble large pretzels. A thin batter of chickpea, urad dal, or white flour, sometimes mixed with a little yogurt, is extruded into hot oil to form large spirals that are soaked in warm sugar syrup for a few minutes. In northern India jalebis are enjoyed for breakfast, often with puris (puffed wheat bread) and halvah. A variation is *imarti*, which has a flower-like shape.

Unlike Middle Eastern halvah, usually made from sesame seeds, Indian halvah comes in two basic varieties: one made from semolina cooked with jaggery, clarified butter, and sometimes nuts and raisins, the other from vegetables (especially carrots and bottle squash), lentils, nuts, or sometimes khoa. Both versions require a lot of clarified butter and are moister and flakier than Middle Eastern halvah. Karachi halvah is a bright orange, somewhat rubbery, translucent halvah made from cornstarch, nuts, and ghee.

Kulfi, the Indian version of ice cream, is sweetened khoa frozen in cone-shaped molds. Unlike ice cream, the mixture is not churned, and the consistency is denser. Typical flavors include mango, pistachio, orange, rose, and saffron. Commercial kulfi may be frozen onto a stick for easy eating. It is often served with falooda, thin rice noodles scented with rosewater. *Sohan papdi* or *patisa* is a dry, very flaky dish made of chickpea flour, white flour, sugar, and a lot of ghee. It is often topped with *charmagaz*, a blend of almonds and pumpkin, cantaloupe, and watermelon seeds.

Rice pudding is a favorite throughout the subcontinent. Kheer, called *payesh* in Bengali, is made by slowly cooking rice and milk until the mixture thickens, then including sugar and flavoring it with kewra water. Almonds, raisins, and pistachios can be added. South Indians prepare a version called payasam. *Zarda* is a dish enjoyed by Muslims during religious festivals, such as Musharram and ʿId al-Fiṭr. Long-grain rice is cooked with sugar and aromatic spices, such as cardamom, cloves, and cinnamon, and sautéed in clarified butter. On special occasions, these and other sweet dishes are decorated with edible silver foil, called *vark*. See LEAF, GOLD AND SILVER.

Northern India

The main ingredient in Uttar Pradesh, Punjab, New Delhi, and other parts of northern India is khoa. It is a key ingredient in barfi and *pedha*, a round sweet flavored with chopped nuts and cardamom associated with the cities of Varanasi and Mathura. *Petha*, a famous dish of Agra, is a cross between fudge and preserves. Ash gourds are soaked in lime (calcium carbonate), boiled in alum powder and water, and then cooked again in sugar syrup. The result is a lovely, pale green, subtly flavored delicacy.

Rabri is thickened milk mixed with chopped nuts and the skin formed on the milk during cooking. *Firni* is a kind of custard made of rice flour or cornstarch cooked in milk with sugar, nuts, cardamom powder, and rosewater or kewra water. Gulab jamun are brown balls of khoa and flour that are fried and then soaked in sugar syrup.

Desserts do not play as large a role in the cuisine of the northernmost state of Kashmir as in other parts of India. The most popular include *akhor barfi* made from local walnuts; *firun/firni*, a custard made from ground rice, sugar, milk, saffron (which is native to Kashmir), and nuts and set in traditional earthenware pots; and *zarda*, a sweetened rice *pulao* prepared with nuts, saffron, and aromatic spices. The last two dishes are often served during ʿId al-Fiṭr and other Muslim celebrations.

Western India

In parts of western India, sweets are eaten during the meal itself, and often a pinch of sugar is added to vegetarian dishes. Laddus, especially *churma laddu*—deep-fried balls made from wheat flour and nuts—are popular. The Surat region of Gujarat is well known for the expertise of its sweet makers. A famous Surati sweet is *ghari*, a puri (circular wheat bread) with a sweet filling of khoa and nuts. It even has its own festival—Chandani Padva. Another famous Surati sweet is *halwason*—hard squares made from broken wheat, khoa, nutmeg, and nuts. *Mohanthal* is a kind of barfi made from chickpea flour, ghee, sugar, almonds, saffron, and pistachios. One of the most elaborate sweets is *sukhan feni*—very fine strands of sweet, flaky dough garnished with pistachios.

A traditional Maharashtrian sweet is *puran poli*, wheat pancakes filled with lentils and sugar, and served with hot milk or ghee. An emblematic (and very ancient) dish of Gujarat and Maharashtra is *shrikhand*—drained yogurt mixed with sugar, saffron, and cardamom and sometimes garnished with chopped nuts. Its unique sweet and sour taste makes it beloved by some and disliked by others.

The tiny state of Goa was part of the Portuguese empire for 400 years, and Portuguese influence is evident in the language and cuisine, especially the wide array of European-style cakes and pastries. See PORTUGAL'S INFLUENCE IN ASIA. *Bibinca* (*bebinca*) is a many-layered baked pudding made of egg yolks, sugar, flour, and coconut milk, and garnished with nuts. *Baath* is a cake made from semolina, eggs, ghee, coconuts, sugar, and caraway seeds.

Southern India

The most emblematic South Indian sweet dish is payasam, a pudding of rice and milk or coconut milk, sometimes with dal, fruit, raisins, and nuts. It often has a pinkish color because of the long cooking time that caramelizes the milk. In Kerala, the king of payasams served at festive occasions is *ada pradaman*, made from a special pressed rice, coconut milk, jaggery, coconut milk, coconut flakes, ghee, cardamom, cashews, and raisins.

In Tamil Nadu, a favorite sweet is *pal payasam*—small puris dipped in sweetened kheer and served hot or cold. The most important festival is Pongal, which is also the name of the dish served at this time: a mixture of boiled rice, dal, milk, jaggery, ghee, nuts, raisins, and coconut.

The city of Hyderabad, once home to the court of the Nizams, has a rich culinary and sweet culture influenced by Persian cuisine. *Double Ka meetha* (also known as *shahi tukra*) is a bread pudding (and probably an adaptation of English trifle) made from Western-style bread, khoa, saffron, and spices sautéed in ghee, soaked in milk, covered with sugar syrup, and baked. Vermicelli (*seviyan* in Hindi and Urdu) are very thin wheat noodles used in many dishes, including *reshmi zulfein,* made with lotus seeds and nuts, and *sevia ka muzaffar,* vermicelli with fried cardamom pods, thickened milk, and dried coconut. *Khubani ka meetha* is a very popular local dish made of cooked sweetened apricots topped with cream.

Eastern India

Bengalis—inhabitants of the Indian state of West Bengal and the Republic of Bangladesh—are famous for their love of *mishti,* or sweets, considered the apogee of the Indian sweet maker's art. Most commercial sweets are made from *chhana;* khoa is used mainly as a secondary ingredient. *Chhana*'s popularity in Bengal may have come from the Portuguese who lived in the region in the seventeenth century and specialized in the preparation of sweetmeats, breads, and cheese. The French traveler François Bernier wrote in 1659: "Bengal is celebrated for its sweetmeats, especially in places inhabited by the Portuguese, who are skilful in the art of preparing them and with whom they are an article of considerable trade."

The extensive use of *chhana* by professional sweet makers began in the mid-nineteenth century when B. C. Nag, N. C. Das, and other Calcutta sweetshop owners expanded their repertoire by inventing new varieties of sweets to serve an affluent and growing urban middle class. See KOLKATA. The most famous sweets are rosogolla, a light spongy white ball of *chhana* served in sugar syrup; *rajbhog,* a giant rosogolla; a dark-colored fried version called *ledikeni; cham cham,* small patties dipped in thickened milk and sprinkled with grated khoa; ras malai, khoa and sugar balls floating in cardamom-flavored cream; and *pantua,* sausage-shaped spheres fried to a golden brown and dropped in sugar syrup. See LEDIKENI and ROSOGOLLA. The apogee of the Bengali sweet makers' art is sandesh, small sweetmeats made from *chhana* and sugar, fried in clarified butter, and pressed into pretty molds shaped like flowers, fruit, or shells. See SANDESH.

Sweets generally made at home include *patishapta,* a semolina pancake filled with sugar, coconut, and khoa; *pithes,* coconut balls or disks coated in batter, deep-fried, and served in sugar syrup; and *malpoa,* patties made of yogurt, flour, and sugar, fried until golden brown, then dipped briefly in sugar syrup. *Misthi dol* or *lal doi,* yogurt sweetened with sugar, are standard ends to a Bengali meal.

See also COCONUT; DIWALI; HINDUISM; ISLAM; PERSIA; SOUTH ASIA; SUGAR; and SUGARCANE.

Achaya, K. T. *Indian Food: A Historical Companion.* New Delhi: Oxford University Press, 1994.

Bahadur, Om Lata. *The Book of Hindu Festivals and Ceremonies.* 2d ed. New Delhi: UBSPD, 1999.

Banerejee, Satarupa. *Book of Indian Sweets.* New Delhi: Rupa & Co., 1994.

Sen, Colleen Taylor. *Food Culture in India.* Westport, Conn.: Greenwood, 2004.

Sinha, Anil Kishore. *Anthropology of Sweetmeats.* New Delhi: Gyan, 2000.

Colleen Taylor Sen

insects, or at least traces of them, show up in just about every edible substance—even in something as innocent as candy. However, insects are sometimes intentionally made into candies in order to "gross out" the squeamish, or to demonstrate the eater's machismo. In the United States such candies have typically been little more than novelty items, such as the chocolate-covered ants introduced by Reese Finer Foods in the 1950s. Thanks to Groucho Marx, who quipped to Reese executive Morris H. Kushner that "I can't eat your chocolate-covered ants . . . the chocolate upsets my stomach," these treats became as much punch line as actual snack. Other consumers proved to have sturdier digestions. In 1956 the *New York Times* and the *Wall Street Journal* reported that Americans were developing a taste for exotic imported foods—and both chose chocolate-covered ants as the most newsworthy example.

Since then, the market for candy-encrusted bugs has proliferated. HOTLIX—a candy company in Grover Beach, California—is famous (or infamous) for its lines of creepy crawly confections. The company claims that its "owner found inspiration from the tequila with a worm." Whatever the origins, HOTLIX now produces and sells a wide range of products: Cricket Lick-It Suckers (blueberry, grape, orange, and strawberry lollipops, each with a crisply fried cricket inside); Ant Candy with Real Farm

Ants (disks of white and milk chocolate, studded with crunchy ants); and InsectNside Scorpion Brittle (a toffee-flavored slab of "amber" containing an actual scorpion). The company also offers a line of savory insect snacks. For a more grown-up taste, its Tequila Lollipops claim to feature real earthworms. A purist might demand *un gusano*, a maguey larva (*Hypopta agavis*) from the agave plant used to make mescal, but here the critter is more likely just another mealworm. Other insect confectioners produce such items as Butterfly Candy (a slab of strawberry-flavored hard candy enclosing a Bougainvillea blossom and a mealworm pupa), Milk Chocolate–Covered Crickets, and Watermelon Lollipops with mealworms inside.

Sometimes the insects are not *in* the sweets; they *make* the sweets. Bees, which convert nectar to honey, are the best-known example, but they are not the only ones. A group of insects called *Psillids* (including aphids and scale insects) collect sugar-rich sap from plants and turn it into honeydew. This honeydew can be collected by humans directly from leaves, or harvested by ants. The strong flavors of honeydews—*le miel de forêt, Honigtauhonig*, or *miele di bosco*—are distinctly different, varying according to the plant species from which the nectar is collected. It is used just as honey, either eaten directly, or as an ingredient in baking. Because some species of ants collect more honeydew than they need for immediate use, they have evolved a unique storage system. Honeypot ants (*Myrmecocystus* genus) feed the excess to certain specialized ants (called "repletes") that never leave their underground colonies. The repletes' gasters—the last section of their abdomens—swell to enormous size as they are filled with sweet syrup. These "sugar bags" are transparent, jewel-like spheres, between the size of a chickpea and a small grape. In semi-arid regions of Africa, Australia, and North and South America, people dig for these delicious repletes. Vic Cherikoff, who runs an Australian firm called Bush Tucker Party Ltd., prepares a special dessert named Honey Ant Dreaming. The recipe calls for filling small chocolate cups one-third full with sugar-bag honey, spooning on whipped cream, and then garnishing the top with a frozen honeypot replete.

Even if most Americans do not choose bugs as a special treat, they may still be eating them—and not just in the small, accidental amounts that government sanitary rules permit. "Confectioner's glaze," a more appealing name for shellac, gives some candies their appetizing shine. Less appetizing, however, is the fact that it is produced from a secretion made by female Lac Bugs (scale insects of the *Kerria* genus). These secretions are also used to make a red dye. More common is cochineal, a carmine coloring used in many candies, made from the dried bodies of another type of scale insect (*Dactylopius* genus). Cochineal was a very popular dye before aniline dyes, made from coal tar, were discovered in the nineteenth century. One might imagine that most people would prefer artificial food coloring from a nice clean laboratory to a natural one made from bugs that are farmed and scraped off of cactuses—but that is not the case. Cochineal is now more popular than ever. See FOOD COLORINGS.

In fact, bug confectionery seems to be experiencing a renaissance, at least according to a 2013 report by the U.N. Food and Agriculture Organization (van Huis et al.). "Fried insects embedded in chocolate or hard candy, and fried and seasoned larvae," the FAO writes, "can be found in the United States, while the world's most famous luxury stores, Harrods and Selfridges, sell fancy insect products in London." What would Groucho have to say?

See also GAG CANDY and HONEY.

Allen, Gary. "Insects." In *They Eat That? A Cultural Encyclopedia of Weird and Exotic Food from Around the World*, edited by Jonathan Deutsch and Natalya Murakhver, pp. 110–118. New York: ABC-Clio, 2012.

Condit, Jean. "Grasshoppers a la Mode: Strange Things Are Tickling Palates These Days. Coming Soon—Fried Bees, Chocolate-covered Ants." *New York Times*, 29 April 1956, p. 246.

De Foliart, Gene R., ed. *Food Insects Newsletter*. http://www.food-insects.com/a%20place%20to%20browse.htm (accessed 17 December 2014)

Hillery, Victor J. "Specialty Foods: Snails, Grasshoppers, Caviar, Ants Pop Up on More U.S. Menus." *Wall Street Journal*, 9 November 1956, p. 1.

Menzel, Peter, and Faith D'Aluisio. *Man Eating Bugs*, p. 29. Berkeley, Calif.: Ten Speed, 1998.

van Huis, Arnold, et al. "Edible Insects." FAO Forestry Paper 171, 2013. http://www.fao.org/docrep/018/i3253e/i3253e.pdf.

Gary Allen

Iran

See PERSIA.

Islam, the religion practiced by more than 1.5 billion followers of Prophet Muhammad around the world, reserves a special, even privileged, status for sweets. Dates and honey, in particular, remained primary even after sugarcane plantations and cane sugar refining spread throughout the Islamic world beginning in the seventh century.

Dates and honey have been valuable commodities since antiquity, not just as sweet foodstuffs but also for their medicinal properties. However, their high standing among Arabs was firmly established with the advent of Islam. The date palm was repeatedly mentioned in the holy Qurʾān as God's gift to His believers, and in the verses on the birth of Jesus, Mary was asked to shake the date palm in order to feed herself with the dates falling from the tree. The Prophet himself endorsed the date by saying that seven dates a day will keep poison and witchcraft away. His favorite was the Medina date variety *ʿajwa*, described as the food of heaven and used to help wean children. See DATES. Following the tradition of the Prophet, in some Muslim countries today, newborns are given a taste of dates or honey, in a ceremony called *taḥnīk*, and lactating mothers are fed a lot of dates. Modern medicine has shown that dates do indeed activate milk hormones and that they act as tonic for uterine muscles, which stimulate delivery contractions.

In the Qurʾān, Muslim believers are promised rivers of purified honey, and in another verse, honey itself is described as a healer for mankind. See HONEY. It is often praised as God's sweet medicine, unlike physicians' bitter medicines. From the early-fourteenth-century *Traditional Medicine of the Prophet*, known as *Ṭibb al-Nabī*, we know that the Prophet was partial to honey as food and repeatedly recommended it as medicine, especially for stomach and chest ailments. He is said to have enjoyed his first taste of the luxurious condensed pudding *faludhaj*, made of wheat starch, butter, and honey. Even after honey was often replaced in medieval times by cane sugar in making sweetmeats and pastries, it remained highly valued, especially in home cures like electuaries, pastes, and jams. Honey helped preserve the curative properties of the spices and herbs they contained and made them taste so palatable that many ended up being consumed for sheer pleasure.

Regardless of the type of sweetener used, since medieval times the eating of sweet foods has been generally approved of in the Islamic world. Following the ancient Galenic humoral theories of medicine embraced during medieval times, desserts and sweet drinks were usually offered at the end of the meal. Their hot and moist properties were believed to aid digestion, which was metaphorically described in terms of cooking. Also because of these properties, sweets were thought of as male sexual enhancers, a medicinal lore that still lingers today in some parts of the Muslim world. Today's groom, for instance, would be advised to eat at least 1 pound of dates on his wedding day.

The significance of sweets in Islamic religious and social rituals is manifested in the myriad varieties and abundant quantities consumed. Among these are the syrupy pastries enjoyed during the fasting month of Ramadan and the huge number of stuffed cookies like *kleicha* and *maʾmoul* baked especially for the two major feasts of ʿId al-Fiṭr (celebrating the end of Ramadan) and ʿId al-Aḍḥā (rejoicing over the performance of Hajj in Mecca). See RAMADAN. The Prophet's birthday, Mawlid al-Nabī, is a significantly sweet celebration, especially in Egypt, where decorated dolls of sugar and nuts are given to children. On other less joyous religious occasions, such as ʿĀshūrāʾ, the tenth day of the sacred month of Muḥarram, a sweet wheat porridge called harīsa is made and distributed, especially by Shiites mourning the death of Imam Ḥusayn, the Prophet's grandson. In Iran, this sad event is commemorated with the yellow rice pudding *zerde*, a dessert that in Turkey presides over occasions like wedding feasts.

The souls of dead Muslims have associations with sweets as well: after burial rites, date sweetmeats and starch-based puddings, cookies, and pastries are distributed to the poor. The same happens when the graves of family members are visited on religious feast days. Other Muslim rites of passage, such as circumcision and weddings, are closely associated with rich desserts like baklava. See BAKLAVA. Toffees and sugar-coated almonds are joyfully thrown by handfuls at the guests to the accompaniment of loud ululations. See CONFETTI. Immediately after a boy's circumcision, a piece of candy was traditionally popped into his mouth so that he would forget the pain.

A modern challenge caused by globalization and the rise of Muslim immigrants worldwide is halal dessert. Like halal meat for observant Muslims, desserts need to conform to Islamic law. No dessert *may contain alcohol; therefore, powdered pure vanilla* is substituted for vanilla extract, and gelatin must come from sources other than pigs, such as cows or fish, or any animal slaughtered ritually. Major stores have increasingly started to accommodate halal desserts. At the British department store Harrods, for instance, Belgian alcohol-free chocolate and sugar-coated dried fruits using halal gelatin are available for Muslims to purchase.

See also FRUIT PASTES; FRUIT PRESERVES; FUNERALS; MEDICINAL USES OF SUGAR; PALM SUGAR; and WEDDING.

Nasrallah, Nawal. *Dates: A Global History*. London: Reaktion, 2011.
Suyūṭī, Jalāl al-Dīn ʿAbd al-Raḥmān al-. *Traditional Medicine of the Prophet*. Translated by Cyril Elgood. Istanbul: Dar al-Fikr, 2007.

Nawal Nasrallah

isomalt is a polyol, or sugar alcohol. It is a colorless, odorless hydrogenated disaccharide that is used as a sugar substitute to replace sucrose, glucose, corn syrup, fructose, and the like in foods and drinks. Isomalt was discovered and developed in 1957 by scientists at the German company Südzuker AG, the largest sugar producer in Europe. The trademarked names for isomalt, Palatinose and Palatinit are derived from the Palatinate (Pfaltz) region of Germany, where isomalt was developed.

Isomalt has several advantages. It has properties similar to sucrose but half the calories, making it useful for lower-calorie foods. It has no aftertaste and a longer shelf-life than sucrose. Consuming isomalt does not substantially increase glucose levels in the bloodstream, so it is suitable for diabetics. Isomalt does not promote tooth decay, and products containing isomalt can be labeled "sugar free." See DENTAL CARIES. Although the excessive consumption of isomalt can cause diarrhea and gastric problems, it is approved for use as a food additive in most countries.

Isomalt is mainly used in baked goods—cereal, cereal bars, sponge cake, cookies, and biscuits—in hard candies, toffees, chocolates, and chewing gums, and in pharmaceuticals, such as throat lozenges and cough drops. It is also used for making decorative sugar sculptures, such as cast sugar (*sucre coulé*), as it does not crystallize as quickly as sucrose and can be heated without clouding. See SUGAR SCULPTURE.

See also CORN SYRUP; FRUCTOSE; and GLUCOSE.

Branen, A. Larry P., Michael Davidson, and Seppo Salminen, eds. *Food Additives*. 2d ed. New York: Marcel Dekker, 2001.
O'Donnell, Kay, and Malcolm Kearsley, eds. *Sweeteners and Sugar Alternatives in Food Technology*. Chichester, U.K., and Ames, Iowa: Wiley-Blackwell, 2012.

Andrew F. Smith

Istanbul is Turkey's largest city, known in antiquity as Byzantium and from the fourth century until the Turkish conquest in 1453 as Constantinople. The city was first settled around 6500 B.C.E., and it was through the surrounding region that agriculture spread from the Near East into Europe the following millenium. Istanbul owes its importance to a strategic location between Europe and Asia on a major shipping route through the Bosphorus Strait, which links the Black Sea to the Mediterranean. For nearly 2,000 years it was the capital of three successive empires: first the Roman (330–395 C.E.), then the Byzantine (395–1453 C.E.), and finally the Ottoman (1453–1922 C.E.), and so it has long been a cosmopolitan city inhabited by people of different faiths and diverse origins, as well as a center of international trade. Consequently, Istanbul has been the hub of three imperial cuisines that made use of both local and imported foodstuffs, ranging from caviar from the north coast of the Black Sea to spices from India.

In the early fourteenth century, during the Byzantine period, sugar of various types, as well as sugar candy and comfits "of every kind," arrived from Egypt, Damascus, Cyprus, and Rhodes and were traded in the city. After the Ottoman Turks conquered Istanbul in 1453, sugar was consumed in ever-greater quantities, and in the sixteenth century the Turkish scholar Mustafa Ali of Gallipoli likened the sugar of Egypt to "a sea flowing ultimately to Istanbul." The medieval Arab legacy of sweetmeats and sweet pastries was inherited and further developed by Turkish cuisine, a process that centered on the palace and Istanbul's elite ruling class. In this innovative cuisine, earlier Arab puddings such as *maʾmūniyya* (Turkish *memuniye*) made of chicken breast, rice, and almond milk were eventually transformed into deep-fried balls of rice helva sprinkled with sugar, nuts, and rosewater. Similarly, *kataif*, in its original Arab form a crumpet soaked in syrup, evolved into fine threads of cooked batter also known as *kataif*. Most of the innovations in Turkish confectionery emerged in Istanbul between the fifteenth and nineteenth centuries. Among these were boiled sweets known as *akide*, lokum (Turkish Delight), *kazandibi* (a type of caramelized milk pudding), *ekmek kadayıf* (syrup-soaked rusk eaten with clotted cream), and three confectionery items that evolved from sweetened medical preparations: *şerbet şekeri* (sherbet sugar), a soft toffee known as *macun*, and *çevirme*. See LOKUM and SPOON SWEET.

In the nineteenth century Europeans curious about "Oriental confectionery" looked to Istanbul. Perhaps the most prominent was Friedrich Unger, royal confectioner at the court of the first Greek king, Otto I (a Bavarian prince by birth). Unger left a detailed record of his research in *Conditorei des Orients* (1838), writing that in Istanbul he finally satisfied his "hunger for learning."

Under the Ottoman Empire's centralized administrative system, state functionaries like governors and judges were sent from Istanbul to towns and cities around the empire, where they introduced Istanbul dishes to the provinces. At the same time they carried local specialties back to Istanbul, so we find local sweet dishes like the *peynir lokması* (cheese doughnuts) of Lesbos adopted into mainstream Ottoman cuisine. In similar fashion, renowned palace dishes developed by inventive palace cooks spread to the tables of the upper classes, as demonstrated by "palace-style" confectionery recipes in cookery books, such as *saray etmeği* (palace-style bread pudding), *saray lokması* (palace-style doughnuts), and *süzme saray aşuresi* (palace-style strained aşure). *Aşçıbaşı*, a cookery book published in 1900 by Mahmud Nedim, an infantry lieutenant who was taught to cook as a child by his mother and wrote for bachelor colleagues who lacked his culinary skills, provides numerous examples of recipes collected in the places where he was posted, ranging from Erzurum in eastern Turkey to the island of Rhodes, in addition to mainstream dishes and two desserts of palace origin.

Istanbul's haute cuisine featured refined versions of commonly known confectionery and often included expensive ingredients such as musk, ambergris, and gold leaf. Despite the high price, consumption of musk rose to such a degree that in 1610 merchants were prohibited from selling musk on the open market until palace stocks had been replenished. In the Ottoman period sweetmeats flavored with fragrant flowers were popular, including violets, lilies, jonquils, and citrus blossom. Today, rose-flavored sweets and jam made with roses are still produced, although those made with other flowers are a rarity.

For connoisseurs only the finest ingredients were acceptable. One seventeenth-century Ottoman statesman insisted that his cooks use Syrian sugar candy rather than ordinary sugar for all the sweet dishes made in his kitchen. An improved version of *pelte* (a pudding of fruit juice thickened with starch) made by the religious scholar, poet, and gourmet Nevʾîzâde Atāī (1583–1635) not only used sugar candy but also required constant stirring for three hours. Such intensive labor was possible only at the palace and in wealthy households, which employed armies of kitchen hands as well as specialized cooks such as confectioners (*helvacı*) and baklava makers (*baklavacı*). Istanbul's guild system was the most extensive of any city in the empire, including several confectioners' guilds devoted to particular types of sweets and puddings. See GUILDS. In the seventeenth century there were 170 shops selling different types of helva, 70 selling *akide*, 70 selling other sweets, 20 selling *lokma* (doughnuts), 40 selling *sucuk* (strings of nuts coated with starch-thickened grape juice), and 15 selling *pelte*. The 50 *kadayıf* and 40 *güllaç* (starch wafers) shops did not sell finished desserts, but only semi-finished products (*kadayıf* threads, *kadayıf* pancakes and wafers) for completion at home. The same is true today, except that these products are now sold in supermarkets and groceries.

The most famous Turkish confectioner was Hacı Bekir, who was born in the province of Kastamonu around 1760 and apprenticed to a confectioner in Istanbul. In 1777 he opened his own shop, which still exists today. Hacı Bekir is believed to have perfected lokum and to have been the first person to export it in the mid-nineteenth century.

Istanbul was also renowned for the hundreds of itinerant vendors selling sweets and desserts in streets and parks, but modern health and safety laws mean that these hawkers have virtually disappeared. In the past the most common were sellers of *muhallebi* (milk pudding), various sugar sweets, ice cream, and sesame-seed helva.

The boiled sugar sweets known as *akide*, originally in lemon and musk flavors, were first made in Istanbul in the sixteenth century and became a symbol of loyalty to sultan and state. The soldiers of the

Janissary Corps presented them to the grand vizier, other dignitaries, and their own officers when they received their quarterly salaries. These newfangled sweets became so popular at weddings, the Şeker Bayram (a three-day festival marking the end of Ramazan), and other festivities that in the late sixteenth century black-market confectioners sprang up to meet the high demand.

Güllaç, a pudding associated primarily with Istanbul, is still made almost exclusively during Ramazan. Wafers are soaked in hot sweetened milk flavored with rosewater, then arranged in layers with ground nuts. It is mainly made at home, although especially during Ramazan it can be found in some Istanbul pudding shops.

Fruit preserves, in particular, those made from rose and quince, were nothing new, but from the fifteenth century onward these were joined by scores of new varieties. See FRUIT PRESERVES. Eighteen types were served at a royal circumcision banquet for two Turkish princes held in 1539, including watermelon, apple, cornelian cherry, eggplant, green walnut, pear, sour cherry, and carrot. The repertoire expanded steadily over the centuries to include green almond, mulberry, jujube, stonecrop, sage gall, persimmon, wild apricot, quince blossom, and judastree flower. Such preserves depended on the wide availability of sugar, which did not overwhelm the delicate flavor of fruits and flowers in the way honey and grape molasses did. See PEKMEZ. Offering fruit preserves to guests just before coffee became an established part of Ottoman hospitality rituals in the seventeenth century. Some preserves were brought to Istanbul from long distances: citron preserve from Egypt, quince jelly from Amasya, orange-flower jam from Chios, rose jam from Edirne, and ginger and mango jams from India. Topkapı Palace had a special kitchen for jam making known as the *reçelhane*.

Royal celebrations in Istanbul or Edirne often featured sculpted sugar models of gardens, castles, and animals that were paraded through the streets, then broken up and eaten by the crowd. Sugar mosques, castles, pavilions, and flowery meadows were made for the circumcision of Mehmed the Conqueror's sons Bâyezid and Muṣṭafā in 1457, and at another royal circumcision in 1582 hundreds of "wild animals and birds all of sugar" were carried in procession, including lions, tigers, elephants, camels, vultures, and peacocks, as well as backgammon and chess sets made of sugar. This custom gradually declined and finally died out in the early nineteenth century, around the time when French confectionery grew fashionable in Istanbul. In the 1840s Madame Meunier became one of the first foreigners to open a confectionery shop in the city.

Today, Istanbul is still famous for the diversity of its sweets and desserts, some specialties being particularly associated with the city, such as *ekmek kadayıfı* and *kazandibi*. Restaurants known as *muhallebici* serving a variety of milk puddings and a limited menu consisting of chicken soup and rice pilaf topped with chicken remain popular, although they have now expanded their menus to include *döner kebab* and sweet pastries. These restaurants can be traced back to the earlier *kaymak* (clotted cream) shops, where customers ate dishes of clotted cream sprinkled with sugar. See CREAM. The most celebrated of Istanbul's *muhallebici*s is the Pudding Shop in Sultanahmet Square, which became a meeting place for hippie travelers in the 1960s. It is still there, although serving a nontraditional range of food.

Sweets are often bought from famous confectionery shops such as Hacı Bekir or Cafer Erol and offered to guests in pretty lidded bowls (*şekerlik*) made of china or cut glass. Sweet pastries and milk puddings may be eaten at specialist shops renowned for particular varieties or purchased to take home. Sweets and pastries such as baklava are often taken to friends and family as gifts, and they are offered to guests as an accompaniment to tea or coffee, particularly during Ramazan and on other special occasions, as well as being served as dessert at ordinary meals. During the month of Muḥarram, many people make large amounts of *aşure* (sweetened whole-wheat pudding) to distribute to neighbors in small bowls.

See also FLOWER WATERS; MEDICINAL USES OF SUGAR; PUDDING; RAMADAN; TOFFEE; and TURKEY.

Işın, Mary. *Sherbet and Spice: The Complete Story of Turkish Sweets and Desserts*. London: I. B. Tauris, 2013.

Özdoğan, Mehmet. "Exploring Istanbul's Distant Past." In *Istanbul: Sultan of Lands and Seas*, edited by Filiz Özdem, translated by Mary Işın, pp. 9–25. Istanbul: YKY, 2009.

Pegolotti, Francesco Balducci. *La pratica della mercatura*. Edited by Allan Evans. Cambridge, Mass.: Mediaeval Academy of America, 1936.

Priscilla Mary Işın

Italian ice is a term that encompasses sorbetto, granita, and slush. Water ices rather than ice creams, they differ in texture but are all made with water, sugar or sugar syrup, and fruit or other flavorings, and are frozen to a nice cold slush rather than a hard block. A granita, usually of coffee or lemon, is a mixture of sugar syrup and a flavored liquid, with a lower ratio of sugar to liquid that causes it to freeze into shards or solid crystals after the freezing mass is broken up with a stout kitchen fork. Slush is also a water ice, frozen to a softer, slushier consistency. Sorbetto, or sorbet, is usually churned and frozen to a smoother, more compact texture. See SHERBET. In *More Classic Italian Cooking* (1978), Marcella Hazan writes that "an Italian ice is the most refreshing way to bring anything to a close—a rich and complex meal, a day in the sun, a happy evening with friends."

The prominent English writer Elizabeth David, in *Harvest of the Cold Months* (1995), her unsurpassed work on ice and ices, describes a seventeenth-century ice made with crushed melon seeds and flavored with orange flower water, which gives a vivid sense of what kind of ice can legitimately be called a sorbet. Vincenzo Corrado offers a fine selection of recipes for both sorbets and ices in his work *Il credenziere di buon gusto* (1778). A delicate jasmine sorbet and one flavored with cinnamon are outstanding, but some of his sorbets also include milk thickened with egg yolks.

Today's flavors are more pedestrian, ranging from the classic lemon to bubblegum. In the United States, the Italian ices called slush are served with a spoon-straw, a straw with a tiny spoon shape at one end, so that the slush can be eaten with the spoon to begin, then sipped as it melts. Originally peddled by immigrants from street carts, ices today are sold everywhere from street fairs to supermarkets.

See also FLOWER WATERS; ICE CREAM; and SHAVE ICE.

David, Elizabeth. *Harvest of the Cold Months*. New York: Viking Penguin, 1995.
Day, Ivan. *Ice Cream*. Oxford: Shire, 2011.
Quinzio, Jeri. *Of Sugar and Snow: A History of Ice Cream Making*. Berkeley: University of California Press, 2009.
Weir, Caroline, and Robin Weir. *Ice Creams, Sorbets & Gelati: The Definitive Guide*. London: Grub Street, 2010.

Jeri Quinzio

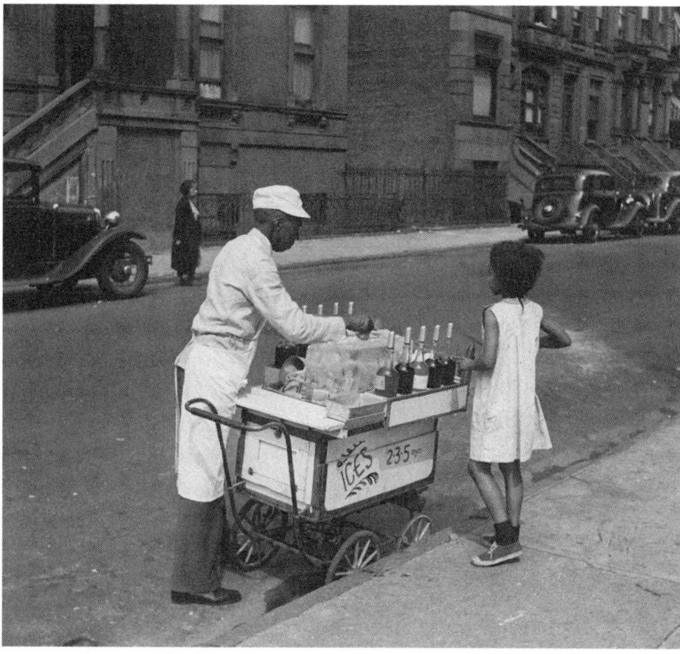

Water ices frozen to a hard slush are known in the United States as Italian ices, since they were originally sold by immigrant Italian street vendors. This 1940 photograph shows a vendor scraping ice from a block into a cup for a waiting customer, who will be able to choose among several flavored syrups. UNIVERSAL HISTORY ARCHIVE / UIG / BRIDGEMAN IMAGES

Italy comprises 20 regions, hundreds of provinces, and thousands of villages, nearly every one of which takes pride in its local specialty dessert. Some Italian desserts, like tiramisù and panna cotta, are known worldwide, but many more, like the peculiar but delicious *melanzana del cioccolato,* an eggplant-chocolate dish, are virtually unknown beyond the Amalfi coast. Like its cuisine in general, Italy's desserts feature local products, including the country's renowned citrus fruits, honey, and nuts.

In all of Italy, but especially in the south, dessert was a luxury, generally reserved for holidays and special occasions. By necessity, Italians have often added inexpensive local ingredients like chickpeas to stretch their supply of costly nuts. One example of this trick, still popular today, is *panzarotti con ceci,* dessert ravioli filled with jam-sweetened puréed chickpeas.

Cookies and Small Sweets

Many of the cookies and small sweets popular today in Italy date back to medieval and Renaissance times, like southern Italy's *mustazzoli,* originally made with reduced grape must but now more commonly made with just honey. See GRAPE MUST. In the Middle Ages, strong, "warm" spices like black pepper, nutmeg, and cinnamon were frequently used in sweets such as *pepatelli,* black pepper honey biscotti. See BISCOTTI. The Tuscan specialty of *panforte,* or "strong bread," is made with spices, candied and dried fruits, almonds, and honey. Coated with a thin, white, edible wafer and topped with confectioner's sugar, it is especially popular during the Christmas holidays; a similar Christmas sweet is *panpepato* (pepper bread), a specialty of Umbria. Also seasonally enjoyed are *cavallucci* (little horses), soft cookies made with honey, nuts, and anise. A Sienese sweet created in the Middle Ages, their name likely derives from the fact that they were offered to travelers who stabled their horses at local inns.

Savoiardi, ladyfingers first created in the early Renaissance and possibly popularized by the royal house of Savoy, are among Italy's most common cookies, and they serve as a key ingredient in hundreds of desserts, including charlottes, puddings, and tiramisù. See TIRAMISÙ. *Amaretti,* literally "little bitters," are small, round almond cookies made of sugar, almonds, and egg white. A speciality of northern Italy, their invention is attributed to Francesco Moriondo, a Savoiard pastry chef in the mid-seventeenth century. Amaretti can be either hard (*classici*) or soft (*morbidi*), and they can vary widely in size. Sicilian sesame lemon cookies appear under diverse names ranging from the elegant *biscotti Regina,* or "Queen's cookie," to the comical *strunzi di sciocca* (chicken shit) and *strunzi d'ancilu* (angel shit). *Baci di dama* (lady's kisses) are a specialty of Piedmont in northern Italy that consist of two small, round, hazelnut-almond shortbread cookies sandwiched together with a dark chocolate filling. *Pesche dolce* (sweet peaches) are among Italy's most unusual cookies, made of two half-round cookies held together with a creamy filling, then dipped in red-tinted liqueur and rolled in sugar. The cookies absorb the filling and liqueur to acquire the texture and fuzzy appearance of real peaches. There is even a faux peach pit in the center—a whole almond—the crowning touch to this culinary trompe l'oeil. See TROMPE L'OEIL.

Cannoli are a Sicilian specialty now famous around the world. These crunchy tubes of fried dough filled with sweetened ricotta were originally eaten only during *Carnevale* (Carnival), but today they are enjoyed year-round throughout Italy. See CANNOLI and CARNIVAL. In the past, when *Carnevale* was bawdier, the phallic shape of cannoli was exaggerated by making jumbo-sized ones called *cannolone.* Several other small sweets are traditionally served during Carnevale, including *bomboloni* (big bombs), fried hole-less doughnuts coated in granulated sugar and filled with custard or jam; *struffoli,* fried marble-sized balls of dough drenched in honey and sometimes sprinkled with colored sugar balls; and *zeppole,* fried dough puffs coated with granulated sugar. See DOUGHNUTS and FRIED DOUGH. *Cenci* are thin strips of dough fried coated with sugar, found throughout Italy under one cute name or another: *chiacchiere* (chatter), *zacarette* (shavings), *cenci* (rags), and *bugie* (lies).

Italy abounds with other festive regional sweets. In Sicily, marzipan plays an important role, particularly in the *frutta Martorana* molded to resemble fruits and vegetables, and named after the Monastery of Martorana, where the shaping technique is said to have originated. See MARZIPAN. *Pecorelle Pasquali* are marzipan Easter lambs, often filled with citron jam or pistachio cream. *Quaresimali* are Tuscan cookies that have been served for Lent since the Renaissance, when they were made with just water, flour, and caramelized sugar, which conferred a dark color symbolic of Christ's blood. *Ricciarelli* (curlies), originated in Siena in the Middle Ages and are associated with the Feast of the Annunciation on 25 March. Soft and oval-shaped, they are made with ground almonds, sugar, honey, and egg whites, and topped with confectioner's sugar or chocolate.

Cakes and Tarts

Cakes and tarts are not distinct categories in Italy, as they are in the United States; the word *torta* may refer to either. Few cakes are topped with icing but are instead moistened with liqueur syrups. Italian tarts are generally made with less filling and incorporate the crust into the filling for a cake-like texture. For this reason, most of Italy's tarts actually taste better the day after baking, once the filling has had a chance to be absorbed into the crust. Fillings include not only fruits and nuts but also vegetables, such as Tuscany's *torta co' bischeri agli spinaci*, with a ground-almond and spinach filling, and *scarpaccia*, with its sugar-sweetened zucchini filling. While fresh fruit does occasionally serve as a filling, jam and reduced fruit are more common.

Many Italian cakes are actually closer to sweet breads. *Bucellato* is a sweet, yeasted ring cake flavored with anise seeds and raisins; it is so ubiquitous in Tuscany, especially in the walled medieval city of Lucca, that people joke that "When Columbus arrived in America one of the first things he saw on shore was a man from Lucca selling an armful of *bucellato*!" *Colomba* is a dove-shaped sweet yeast cake traditionally filled with candied orange peel, topped with almonds and sprinkled with sugar. Numerous myths surround it. According to one story, on Easter Day in 1176 the city of Milan was on the verge of defeat in a battle against the invading Germans. When three doves suddenly appeared over the city, the battle shifted, and the invaders were vanquished. The Milanese celebrated by eating cakes in the form of the savior doves. *Pandoro*, a tall, star-shaped cake with a soft, brioche-like center, is often served in horizontal slices stacked to look like a Christmas tree; it comes boxed with a packet of confectioner's sugar to add a sprinkle of fallen snow. *Pandoro* may have originated with Renaissance Venetian bakers who dusted gold leaf onto cone-shaped cakes called *pan de oro* (bread of gold) for their wealthy customers. See VENICE. *Panettone*, a tall, dome-shaped yeast cake with the fruity aroma of raisins and candied oranges, is the quintessential Italian Christmas dessert. Although it probably originated in Milan in the fifteenth century, its familiar shape dates only to the 1920s. *Pinza*, an orange-scented yeast cake full of apples, dried fruit, and nuts, is served for the Feast of the Epiphany on 6 January, when, in small towns, friends and families exchange visits, tasting one another's *pinza* and voting on the year's best. Local lore has it that if a woman wants to be married within the year, she need only eat seven slices of *pinza* in seven different homes on 6 January. Eating the cake just after the New Year is supposed to bring anyone good luck, and some Italians will hold a linen-wrapped slice for months to preserve the promise of good fortune.

Crostata di visciole e ricotta is a Jewish-Roman specialty, a pie filled with sweetened ricotta and a layer of tart cherry jam. Also featuring fresh cheese is *cassata Siciliana*, a ricotta-filled sponge cake wrapped in marzipan, topped with a sugar glaze, and decorated with glistening candied fruit. See CASSATA. Recipes for *spongata*, a spongy pie filled with chopped walnuts and seasoned with spices and rum, can be found in fourteenth-century Italian cookbooks. Food historians believe it was either brought to Italy by the Jews or was based on an ancient Roman recipe for spiced bread. *Torta della Nonna* (Grandma's cake) is one of Italy's most popular desserts, a vanilla custard pie topped with pine nuts; *torta paradiso*, with its crunchy crust and lemony cake-like interior, is described by many Italians as *la torta dei ricordi* (the cake of memories), the sort of sweet their mothers had waiting for them on the kitchen table after school. *Torta degli Addobbi*, one of northern Italy's most beloved homemade desserts, shows up at virtually every potluck, birthday, and office party—a rich rice pudding flavored with almonds and oranges, baked, and then glazed with almond liqueur. The pudding, traditionally prepared for the Bolognese spring *Festa degli Addobbi*, is usually cooled before being cut into bite-sized diamond shapes that are served with toothpicks.

Chilled Desserts

Italy has many custards, made both with and without eggs. See CUSTARD. *Gelu di miluni*, watermelon custard, is a Sicilian specialty made with cornstarch and watermelon juice. It is served all summer, but notably on 15 July in Palermo, to honor the city's patron saint, Rosalia, and on Ferragosto, 15 August, Italy's ancient summer holiday celebration. The simplest of the many frozen and semi-frozen (*semi-freddo*) Italian desserts are *granita* and *sorbetto*, both essentially frozen water with flavorings. A fork is used to break the freezing mass of granita into crystalline shards, while sorbetto is generally churned to a smoother texture. Among the most popular granita flavors are lemon, coffee, almond, and pistachio. *Spumone* is the name for a category of semi-frozen and sweetened whipped cream desserts that can be made with all sorts of ingredients, including chocolate, fruit, and nuts. In the United States, "spumone" has come to mean molded ice cream in three layers—strawberry, vanilla, and pistachio—representing the colors of the Italian flag. See DESSERTS, CHILLED; DESSERTS, FROZEN; ICE CREAM; ITALIAN ICE; and SHERBET.

Pasta Desserts

During the Renaissance, pasta was a luxury food reserved for special occasions and often paired with other expensive items, such as sugar and cinnamon. In Italy today, many sweets are made with pasta, from Sicily's centuries-old *pistachio couscous* to modern creations such as chocolate-stuffed pasta shells and pasta chocolate truffles. All kinds of shapes are used in sweets recipes, including long pastas like spaghetti and tagliatelle. In Sicily, forkfuls of cooked spaghetti are fried and then topped with honey, orange zest, and crushed pistachios. In Emilia-Romagna, fresh raw tagliatelle are tossed with cocoa powder, crushed almonds, and sugar, and then baked in an open crust for a crunchy-chewy treat called *torta ricciolina* (curly pie).

Almost every region has its own sweet dessert ravioli, with variations in fillings, shapes, and cooking methods—ranging from boiled to baked to fried. *Caggiunitte* or *calzonetti*, an Abruzzo specialty, are fried ravioli filled with puréed chestnuts, chocolate, espresso, rum, and ground nuts. Marche's *ravioli dolci* or *cauciuni* are shaped like half-moons, filled with sweetened pecorino cheese, and baked. In Rome and the wider Lazio region, dessert ravioli are filled with ricotta that has been sweetened with either jam or sugar. Sicily's unique half-moon-shaped *'mpanatigghie* are filled with ground beef and chocolate before being baked. Some pasta desserts are mainly served during the Christmas holidays, including the Puglian *spaghetti latte di mandorle*, homemade spaghetti cooked in rich almond milk and topped with sugar and cinnamon; Lazio's *maccheroni Natalizi con le noci* (Christmas macaroni with walnuts); and *lasagne al forno*, lasagna layered with fresh sliced apples, dried figs, walnuts, raisins, and poppy seeds, popular in the Veneto region.

Chocolate

The Italians invented many chocolate desserts, among them chocolate custard and chocolate sorbet, and first mentioned in Antonio Latini's *Lo Scalco alla moderna* (1692). Italians were also the first to combine chocolate with coffee in both cakes and drinks. Italy remains home to some of the world's finest chocolate, manufactured by companies like Amedei, Domori, Ferrero, Majani, Novi, Perugina, and Venchi. According to the Italian food historian Clara Vada Padovani,

> The marriage of hazelnuts and chocolate was made in Turin, Italy, in the mid-1800s when the Napoleonic Wars blocked the transport of goods between America and Europe. *Oro bruno*, "brown gold," as they called cocoa powder, had become scarce, and Piedmont chocolate makers began to use hazelnuts, plentiful in the region, to extend their short supplies. The result was a creamy, flavorful delight that became an instant success. In 1867, this new chocolate treat was christened *Gianduia*, after a fictitious Turinese carnival character who loves good food and wine. It was formed into small candies, wrapped in paper, and given out at the Carnival in Turin.

Today in Italy, every *gianduiotto*—no matter the maker—comes wrapped in foil. In 2001 the Codex Alimentarius Commission of the World Trade Organization established gianduia as a fourth category of chocolate, after the milk, dark, and white varieties. Authentic *gianduiotti*, small gianduia chocolate candies, must weigh no more than 0.4 ounces, be shaped like an upside-down canoe, and possess the pronounced aroma of toasted hazelnuts. Baci (kisses), a trademark of Perugina, are round chocolate-hazelnut candies created in the 1920s, consisting of a hazelnut ganache center topped with a whole hazelnut and coated in dark chocolate. They come wrapped in silver and blue foil paper and include a waxed-paper message or poem. *Cremini* (little creams) are small squares with three layers of chocolate, usually dark, milk, and hazelnut. Mon Cheri, a liqueur-filled dark chocolate candy with a whole cherry in the center, was launched in 1956 by Ferrero. Rocher, also made by Ferrero, is a round candy filled with creamy chocolate, a crisp wafer, and a whole hazelnut, covered with milk chocolate and finely chopped hazelnuts.

See also BREADS, SWEET; CHOCOLATE, POST-COLUMBIAN; CHRISTMAS; NOUGAT; NUTELLA; ZABAGLIONE; and ZUPPA INGLESE.

Artusi, Pellegrino. *Science in the Kitchen and the Art of Eating Well.* Toronto: University of Toronto Press, 2003.
DePalma, Gina. *Dolce Italiano: Desserts from the Babbo Kitchen.* New York: Norton, 2007.
Grammatico, Maria, and Mary Taylor Simeti. *Bitter Almonds: Recollections and Recipes from a Sicilian Girlhood.* New York: William Morrow, 1994.
Granof, Victoria. *Sweet Sicily: The Story of an Island and Her Pastries.* New York: Regan, 2001.
Segan, Francine. *Dolci: Italy's Sweets.* New York: Stewart, Tabori & Chang, 2011.

Francine Segan

jaggery

See SUGARS, UNREFINED.

jalebi

See ZALABIYA.

jam

See FRUIT PRESERVES.

Japan is the largest confectionery market in Asia, famous for its traditional "Japanese sweets" (*wagashi*). It is also the largest consumer of chocolate in Asia. The perception that Japanese prefer confections that are less sweet than Western varieties is supported by the country's relatively low rate of sugar consumption.

Historical Overview

The history of Japanese confectionery begins with the "cookies" made in the prehistoric Jōmon period (10,000–400 B.C.E.). Walnuts, chestnuts, acorns, and horse chestnuts were important to the diet of the hunter-gatherer Jōmon people. Their "cookie" recipes entailed pounding nuts, kneading in meats, and grilling the confections on hot rocks near fire pits. The Jōmon cookie has disappeared, but the Japanese word for "sweets" (*kashi*), designating all types of confections today, literally means "nuts and fruits," which were the only "sweets" available to most of the population until the seventeenth century.

Fundamental ingredients for traditional Japanese confectionery, namely, rice, azuki beans, wheat, and millets, arrived from the continent in the Yayoi period (400 B.C.E.–300 C.E.). See AZUKI BEANS. Steaming proved the best way to prepare glutinous varieties of rice and millets, which could be formed into small cakes (mochi) either by hand or by mashing in a mortar with a pestle. See MOCHI. A more labor-intensive process involved pounding grains into flours and using the dough to make dumplings. See DANGO.

Production of flour foods advanced in the seventh through ninth centuries with the arrival of "Chinese sweets" (*tōgashi*) made from dough of rice and wheat flour formed into shapes and fried in vegetable oil. Documentation from the Heian period (794–1185) suggests that *tōgashi* had curious names and fanciful designs, such as Tied Rope, Fat Worm, Plum Branch, Taro Bud, and one sweet resembling a bellybutton. Some were flavored with cinnamon; others had stuffings of duck and vegetables. *Tōgashi* were occasionally sweetened with honey or with a decoction made from the sweet arrowroot vine (*amazura*). One *tōgashi* called *sakubei* may have been the first noodle made in Japan: it was eaten boiled and topped with vinegar, miso, or azuki. *Tōgashi* were served at courtly banquets with other dishes rather than as a separate course. They were also used as religious offerings to deities, and a few Shinto shrines continue to make the ancient confections that are otherwise unavailable today.

Another wave of continental foods arrived in the Kamakura period (1185–1333) when Buddhist monks introduced snacks (*tenshin*) into the monastic diet, such as steamed buns stuffed with vegetables

This mulberry-paper print by Utagawa Shunsho (1830–1854), from the late Edo period, depicts a rustic woman carrying a tray of rice cakes, with the rest of a meal wrapped in a decorative cloth. The tool on her back is used to cut mature rice stalks. GIFT OF JUSTINE LEWIS KEIDEL, 1991. THE WALTERS ART MUSEUM

(manjū) and *yōkan*, a vegetarian substitute for mutton made from mashed azuki beans, flour, kudzu starch, and flavorings. Popularized during the Muromachi period (1336–1573), manjū and *yōkan* became confectionery with the addition of sugar by the early modern period (1600–1868). See MANJŪ. The Portuguese, who arrived in 1543, imported sugar to Japan, as the Chinese and Dutch later did. The Portuguese also introduced cooking methods vital to the development of Japanese confectionery, including how to make candies and baked treats. See NANBANGASHI. However, the real surge in baking and Western-style confectionery occurred in the Meiji period (1868–1912). See JAPANESE BAKED GOODS.

By the late 1600s sweetened versions of rice cakes, dumplings, and manjū were becoming normative, and varieties of traditional confectionery reached their current form. See WAGASHI. Confectioners, who were purveyors to the imperial court in Kyoto or to the warrior government in Edo (Tokyo), cornered the market for imported sugar, using it for sweets that became the preferred refreshments for the tea ceremony. Catering to a more popular audience were sweet makers who employed domestic brown sugar and made rice crackers (*senbei*).

The shogun Tokugawa Yoshimune (1684–1751) recognized that imported sugar contributed to Japan's trade deficit, so he encouraged domestic cultivation, even planting sugarcane in Edo Castle as an example. By 1800 domestic sugar production was able to meet the country's demands. The island of Shikoku became famous for its high-quality refined sugar used in elite confectionery. See WASANBON. The Ryūkyū Islands (Okinawa) and Amami Ōshima produced brown sugar. Sugar was not used much in cooking until the Meiji period, when Japanese colonial policies led to the development of sugar plantations in Taiwan, and domestic consumption of sugar subsequently doubled in the last decade of the nineteenth century. By 1935, 90 percent of Japanese sugar came from Taiwan.

Confectioners became ubiquitous in Japan's early modern cities such as Kyoto and Edo. See KYOTO. One list dating to 1787 records in Edo more than 200 confectioners specializing in manjū, *senbei*, mochi, and dumplings. By 1811 the number of sweet makers in the city grew to more than 2,866 establishments. The development of the confectionery trade is also evidenced in the publication of confectionery cookbooks, of which about a half dozen examples survive dating back to the early eighteenth century. In 1841 sweet maker Funabashiya Orie popularized the treats sold in his shop in Edo with his recipe collection *Kashiwa Funabashi* (For Sweets, It's Funabashi).

The Modern Confectionery Industry

Chocolates arrived in Japan in 1878, and today chocolate products constitute the largest category of confectionery in terms of domestic sales, with annual per capita consumption reaching 1.67 kilograms. Dark chocolate has become popular in recent years, but the wide range of fillings and flavors—which include fruits and vegetables such as sundried tomatoes—distinguishes Japan's confectionery market, and foreign companies have taken notice. Nestlé markets Kit Kat candy bars in Japan in more than 80 varieties, including wasabi and soy sauce. Domestic confectioners have experimented with cookies that blend chocolate, pumpkin, and onion. The major chocolate companies in terms of sales are Lotte, Meiji Seika, and Ezaki Glico, which launched Pocky, its famous stick-shaped, chocolate-covered cookie in 1966.

Beyond chocolate, the second most popular sweets are sugar confectionery such as candies, mints, chews, and toffees. See TOFFEE. Morinaga, which pioneered selling domestically produced chocolate, dominates the sugar confectionery market with such products as its gummy Hi Chew, which debuted in 1975. Founder Morinaga Taichirō (1865–1937) worked for his uncle's ceramic retailing business and traveled to America in 1888 to expand his trade. When his business dealings soured, Morinaga found part-time work as a dishwasher and converted to Christianity. After briefly returning to Japan in hopes of missionary work, Morinaga opted to go back to America in 1892 to study Western confectionery. He worked in bakeries and with candy makers in San Francisco and Oakland, learning to make chocolates, gingerbread, nut cakes, angel food cakes, and candies. Morinaga returned to Japan in 1899 to open a small shop in Tokyo, where he initially tried to sell Western confections to other confectionery shops, but no one wanted to purchase his products until he began producing marshmallow confections, which were popular imports. His fame as a "Christian confectioner" spread among the Western diplomatic community and subsequently among Japanese government officials. Business flourished, and the company was incorporated in 1910, the same year Morinaga introduced chocolate bars to the Japanese market.

Ranking third in domestic sales is chewing gum, with sugarless gums the most popular by far. See CHEWING GUM. "Functional" gums that contain caffeine or claim to boost brainpower are also well liked among office workers and students. The leading manufacturer of chewing gum is Lotte, established in 1948 by Shin Kyuk-ho, a Japanese of Korean ancestry, who took the name for his company from Charlotte, the object of the protagonist's unrequited love in Goethe's novella *The Sorrows of Young Werther* (Lotte's company trademark is the "Sweetheart of Your Mouth"). Lotte sells the popular Crunky chocolate bar. The parent company, Lotte Holdings, includes Mary Chocolate, Ginza Cozy-Corner (a chain of cafés selling Western-style baked goods), and Krispy Kreme Doughnuts. Krispy Kreme arrived in Japan in 2006, bringing competition to Mister Donut, which has some 1,300 stores in Japan and has been headquartered in Osaka since 1983. See KRISPY KREME. Convenience stores, which are ubiquitous in Japan, have their own lines of sweets, such as Lawson's Our Café Sweets.

Sweets and Popular Culture

The introduction of a coin valued at 4 coppers in the late 1700s prompted vendors to switch from selling five dumplings on a stick to just four; some 200 years later, many changed to three dumplings in response to the popularity of the 1999 children's song "Three Dumpling Siblings" (*dango sankyōdai*). Two decades earlier, the kids' tune "Swim Mr. Grilled Sea Bream!" (*oyoge taiyakikun*), which describes how a small sea bream–shaped confection escapes to the ocean, had boosted that sweet's sales. Other sweets also have animated mascots. The hero Bean-paste Bread Man (Anpanman) debuted in 1973, showing what happens when a bun stuffed with sweetened azuki paste comes to life. Anpanman joins with other personifications of Western-style confections, including Meronpanna (Melon Bread, *meron pan*), to defeat the plans of Germ Man (*baikinman*) and his henchmen. Anpanman's cherubic persona appears on a variety of consumer goods, and there is a museum dedicated to him in Kōchi prefecture, where local trains display his face and play his theme song. Also heavily marketed is the chubby blue cat Doraemon, who first appeared in comic books in 1969 and subsequently became a television cartoon regular. Doraemon's namesake and favorite food is the Gong Cake (*dorayaki*), two pancakes sandwiching sweet azuki paste.

Responding to perceptions that men dislike sweets, Japanese confectioners tried in 2009 to market sweets with "masculine" names, such as Morinaga's Men's Ideal Pudding and a chocolate mousse-filled ice cream that Ezaki Glico's market research said men would crave for its fluffy texture. In 2010 Family Mart, Japan's third-largest convenience-store chain, sold My Sweets (*ore no suitsu*) for men, with blue rather than pink packaging. Puddings in the shape of breasts and buttocks have also debuted in attempts to appeal to other male sensibilities. On Valentine's Day, women purchase chocolate and other confections for male co-workers and friends; men are supposed to reciprocate on 14 March, "White Day."

Ehara Ayako, Ishikawa Naoko, and Higashiyotsuyanagi Shōko. *Nihon shokumotsushi*. Tokyo: Yoshikawa Kōbunkan, 2009.
Nakayama Keiko. *Jiten wagashi no sekai*. Tokyo: Iwanami Shoten, 2006.
Smil, Vaclav, and Kazuhiko Kobayashi. *Japan's Dietary Transition and Its Impacts*. Cambridge, Mass.: MIT Press, 2012.
Yoshida Kikujirō. *Seiyōgashi Nihon no ayumi*. Tokyo: Chōbunsha, 2012.

Eric C. Rath

Japanese baked goods merge Western influence with indigenous taste. The Portuguese introduced baking to Japan in the late 1500s, and the earliest Japanese baked goods are adaptations of Portuguese recipes, called in Japanese "Southern Barbarian Sweets." See NANBANGASHI. The Japanese word for bread, *pan*, reflects baking's Western origins. Recipes for baking bread and constructing ovens are found in a few early modern (1600–1868) culinary publications, but many Southern Barbarian Sweets, such as the golden Castilian Cake (*kasutera*), were adapted to be prepared without an oven by using a specially designed metal pan that could be set over a fire, with hot coals placed on top of the lid. Dutch merchants, who were the only Westerners allowed to live in Japan in the early modern period, maintained baking ovens in their enclave in Nagasaki. When the warrior government contemplated provisioning troops with bread, Egawa Tarōzaemon (1801–1855), a magistrate in charge of coastal defenses, summoned a Japanese cook who had served the Dutch to learn the craft of baking. In 1842 Egawa baked the first army-ration bread (*hyōrōpan*) and posthumously earned the title "Founding Father of Bread." The day Egawa baked his first loaf, 12 April, is dubbed Bread Day—a holiday known mostly to professional bakers today.

In 1858 the warrior government agreed to open up more ports to other Western governments, and within a few years Westerners established bakeries in these cities. By the time of the Meiji Restoration in 1868 that brought an end to the warrior government and ushered in a new regime eager to adapt Western reforms and culinary habits, Yokohama had four foreign-operated bakeries. Within a few years after the Restoration Japanese shopkeepers, many of whom had apprenticed to foreign bakers, opened their own stores. Prominent among them was Nakagawa Kahe'e (1817–1897), who sold baked goods and cookies (*bisuketto*) from the butcher's shop he opened in 1866.

Western-Style Sweets

The term "Western sweets" (*yōgashi*) was coined in the early 1870s to refer to recipes inspired by American and European confectionery. It was meant to distinguish foreign imports from native sweets (*wagashi*), but several Japanese sweet makers began creating European- and American-style pastries. Fūgetsudō, a confectionery company founded in the mid-1700s, sold bonbons and cookies in Tokyo beginning in 1874; in 1896 it offered éclairs and was the first confectioner in Japan to sell cream puffs (*shūkurīmu*), an adaptation of the French *choux à la crème*. Other entrepreneurs saw the opportunity to specialize in Western desserts. Fujii Rin'emon (1885–1968) opened his store Fujiya in Yokohama in 1910; it was the first bakery to sell British-style fruitcake at Christmas. In 1912 Fujii traveled to the United States and spent a year working in the food industry in Los Angeles. As of 1922, in addition to selling *shūkurīmu* and éclairs, Fujiya was the first bakeshop in Japan to offer "shortcakes" (*shōtokēki*)—layered sponge cakes with whipped cream. Fujiya's shortcakes decorated with strawberries became popular Christmas treats from the 1950s on. Bakery DONQ (pronounced *donku*) opened in 1905, introducing French bread and confectionery to Japanese consumers in Tokyo. Today, Fujiya and DONQ have outlets throughout Japan.

Confectioners frequently adapted Western sweets to native tastes. Kimura Yasube'e (1817–1889) opened his bakery Kimuraya in Tokyo in 1869; instead of using yeast as a starter for his baking, he added *kōji*, the mold-inoculated grain used in making sake. Yasube'e also experimented with using sweet azuki bean paste (*an*) as a filling, inventing Bean-paste Bread (*anpan*) in 1874. See AZUKI BEANS. *Anpan* quickly became well liked, and Kimuraya debuted a jam-stuffed bread (*jamupan*) in 1900. Equally as popular as *anpan* is Melon Bread (*meron pan*). The name suggests that this bun made of bread dough topped with cookie batter should also contain fruit, but it does not; the appearance of the bread most likely accounts for its name, since the surface looks like the skin of a golden muskmelon. The bun's yellow color from the cookie dough topping also justifies its alternate name, Sunrise Bread. Melon Bread is not to be confused with pastry containing chestnuts (*maron*, the Japanese cognate of the French *marron*), which are often used in confectionery in Japan.

Grilled Sweets

The Japanese word for baking (*yaku*) can also mean grilling, and many Japanese baked goods are actually grilled. A batter of flour, sugar, egg, and milk poured into heated metal molds around lumps of sweet azuki bean paste makes Grilled Dolls (*ningyōyaki*), bite-sized treats in the shape of puppets. Pouring the same mix into a mold shaped like a fish yields Grilled Sea Bream, a sweet invented by vendors in Tokyo in 1909, and one that remains a favorite sold at festivals. Gong Cake (*dorayaki*) consists of two round pancakes sandwiching a lump of sweet azuki paste. This sweet dates to the early modern period; eggs were added to the recipe in the late 1800s. In the area around Kyoto, Gong Cakes are called Mikasa, in reference to a famous poem about viewing the moon from Mount Mikasa in Nara City.

Baked goods, whether Southern Barbarian Sweets, Western-style pastries, or grilled confectionery, are widely available in Japan today. French and Danish pastries, cheesecake, chocolate cakes, and decorated cakes have been especially popular since the early 1970s.

See also JAPAN.

Miyazato Tatsushi. *Fujita gojūnen no ayumi*. Tokyo: Yumani Shobō, 2011.
Nakayama Keiko. *Jiten wagashi no sekai*. Tokyo: Iwanami Shoten, 2006.
Rath, Eric C. *Food and Fantasy in Early Modern Japan*. Berkeley: University of California Press, 2010.
Tojima Wako. *Meronpan no shinjitsu*. Tokyo: Kōdansha, 2007.
Yoshida Kikujirō. *Seiyōgashi Nihon no ayumi*. Tokyo: Chōbunsha, 2012.

Eric C. Rath

Jarrin, William Alexis (1785–1848), also called Guglielmo, was a confectioner and author of *The Italian Confectioner*, first published in 1820.

Born in the small town of Colorno, near Parma in northern Italy, Jarrin became a confectioner at a young age. The turbulent political background of the Napoleonic wars may have given him opportunities, and he was evidently ambitious. By 1807 he was working in Paris, where he made at least one elaborate sugar sculpture in honor of Napoleon Bonaparte. Jarrin claimed to have been attached to the emperor's household, and high-quality work in such an environment must have brought him into the same milieu as the famous chef and confectioner Carême. See CARÊME, MARIE-ANTOINE. In 1817 Jarrin moved to London, following in the footsteps of many skilled continental European craftsmen displaced by the political climate. The portrait frontispiece of the first edition of *The Italian Confectioner* states that Jarrin was "confectioner and ornament-maker" at Gunter's, a famous London confectioner. He subsequently opened his own shop on New Bond Street, in the heart of fashionable London.

William Alexis Jarrin was a worldly London confectioner whose book *The Italian Confectioner* was notable for its level of detail and accuracy. This portrait is from the third edition of the book, published in 1827.

The Italian Confectioner stands as the main monument to Jarrin's work and knowledge. Although the author's first language was French, he wrote in clear and expressive English. The book was reprinted in a number of editions over 40 years, often with revisions by the author, most of which were relatively small, although still useful. The 1844 edition, however, was significantly reorganized, with new material added to make it more useful as confectionery reached a wider market and mechanization began to make an impact.

The book takes its place in a wider tradition of European publishing on cookery and confectionery, but, at least in English, it remains unique in its level of detail and accuracy. In common with many confectionery texts of the eighteenth and early nineteenth centuries, *The Italian Confectioner* follows a relatively standard format, giving information about sugar boiling and recipes for specific candies, plus chapters on other important confections: syrups; fruit compotes, pastes, and preserves; comfits; creams; ices; biscuits; and distilling liqueurs and infusing ratafias.

Several chapters discuss making ornaments, including recipes for sugar-based pastes of the pastillage type, edible or otherwise. See PASTILLAGE. This information represented the culmination of centuries of practice and influenced the development of European porcelain, both in the form of decorative ornaments and in the tableware itself. Although Jarrin was not the only confectioner to discuss this material, he provides a depth of detail unrecorded elsewhere, capturing on paper techniques developed from the time of medieval *sotleties* and Italian *trionfi*. See SUGAR SCULPTURE. His rival Carême expressed ideas with more panache but was far less meticulous in detailing mixtures and processes. Jarrin's book is especially valuable to historians wishing to know more about the construction and presentation of ornamental desserts at the table, an important aspect of dining rituals.

Like Carême, Jarrin clearly regarded this branch of confectionery as an art closely related to sculpture, carefully explaining how to make molds from various materials, and how to gild, burnish, and varnish. A wooden confectionery mold signed by Jarrin, made by a skilled wood carver and displaying a then trendy Egyptian-influenced design, has recently come to light in a private collection. As a craftsman living by his skill, Jarrin took an interest in fashion and newsworthy events and made sure to flatter important patrons. Like many of his contemporaries he was also interested in innovation, and he improved and invented confectionery equipment.

In common with many tradesmen pursuing a fashionable clientele, Jarrin experienced financial problems and was declared bankrupt, first in 1828 and again in 1834. The 1828 files provide a wealth of information about his business. Valuations of shop fittings mention mirrors and fancy woodwork; molds made from copper, pewter, and tin; and the use of newly available "gas apparatus," evidently used for both lighting and fuel in the workshop. The accounts also allow a glimpse of an underresearched area of the confectioner's skill, that of outside catering for large parties and events at which he provided food of all types, not just sweetmeats.

Some details suggest a character that was touchy, concerned with providing a good appearance, and proud of his professional skills, but with little notion of financial control. In addition to bankruptcy, the more sombre side of Jarrin's life included friction with important clients when his ideas evidently did not coincide with theirs and family problems; his will mentions little beyond an estrangement between his wife and one of his daughters. Despite all these difficulties, Jarrin's book stands as a testament to a confectioner who was alert, inquisitive, and observant, full of enthusiasm for his craft, and possessed of an important vision.

See also CONFECTION; CONFECTIONERY EQUIPMENT; and CONFECTIONERY MANUALS.

Jarrin, William (Guglielmo) Alexis. *The Italian Confectioner.* London: printed for John Harding, 1820.

Mason, Laura. "William Alexis Jarrin: An Italian Confectioner in London." *Gastronomica* 1, no. 2 (2001): 50–64.

Mason, Laura. "William Alexis Jarrin and The Italian Confectioner." In *The English Cookery Book: Historical Essays*, edited by Eileen White, pp. 151–174. Totnes, U.K.: Prospect, 2004.

Laura Mason

jelly

See FRUIT PRESERVES.

jelly beans, a traditional "penny candy," became famous in the 1980s as U.S. President Ronald Reagan's favorite candy treat. Yet this all-American candy traces its origins to distant lands. In the mid-nineteenth century, immigrants from the Near East introduced Americans to lokum or Turkish Delight, a delicate candy flavored with rose and bergamot. See LOKUM. Local candy makers learned the secret of boiling sugar with cornstarch to produce the particular texture, a soft and slightly sticky gel that melted easily on the tongue. The candy syrup was poured into a pan, allowed to harden, and cut into squares dusted with fine sugar.

This simple candy evolved into the modern jelly bean with the rise of confectionery manufacture in the second half of the nineteenth century. Jelly beans are made in two stages. First, the soft center is poured and formed in cornstarch molds. Then these pieces are coated with sugar syrup in rotating heated pans to create the crunchy outer shell. See PANNING. The automation of the starch molding process in the "starch mogul," and the use of steam heat and power to automate the panning process, made it possible to manufacture jelly beans in quantity and to sell them cheaply. Although it is not known who originated the idea, references to jelly beans begin to appear in the popular press in the 1890s, and by 1905 the phrase "jelly bean" had been added to *Webster's American Dictionary*. Jelly beans quickly became a year-round penny favorite and—due to their egg-like shape—an Easter staple.

The inside of most jelly beans today is made with a cornstarch-based gel, which produces a firm, slightly sticky interior core. More tender jelly beans made with pectin are less common; they were popular some decades ago and are therefore considered "old-fashioned." The outer sugar shell of the jelly bean is typically infused with artificial flavors and colored with bright food dyes to create vibrant and appealing candies. Until recent decades, the center gel of jelly beans was not flavored.

The jelly bean was revolutionized in 1976 with the introduction of Jelly Belly, a new style of small, intensely flavored beans created with natural flavors. David Klein, a small candy entrepreneur, developed the name and the idea and teamed up with the Herman Goelitz Candy Company to manufacture the product. Klein's innovations included selling the beans in individual flavors and charging a premium price for what was once humble "penny candy." The Goelitz Company purchased the rights to Jelly Belly in 1980 and subsequently changed its name to the Jelly Belly Candy Company—a reflection of the huge success of the product.

See also PENNY CANDY.

"The Goelitz Family: Candy Corn & Jelly Belly." http://www.germanheritage.com/biographies/atol/goelitz.html.

Knoll, Corina. "Jelly Belly Creator Sour over Lost Legacy but Sees Sweet Future." *Los Angeles Times*, 22 June 2011.

Untermeyer, Louis. *A Century of Candy Making, 1847–1947: The Story of the Origin and Growth of New England Confectionery Company Which Parallels That of the Candy Industry in America*. New England Confectionery Co., 1947.

Samira Kawash

jimmies

See SPRINKLES.

Jordan almonds

See CONFETTI.

Judaism, the religious and cultural tradition that traces its lineage back to ancient Israel and the scriptural authority of the Hebrew Bible, has a long and varied engagement with sweets. The paradigmatic sweet of ancient Jewish tradition was honey (in Hebrew, *dvash*), which in the Bible refers both to the product of bees and to juices or pastes derived from dates, grapes, and figs. See FRUIT PASTES and HONEY. Honey is one of the two defining features of the promised land of Canaan ("a land flowing with milk and honey") throughout the story of the exodus and wandering of the Israelites (e.g., Exodus 3.8; Numbers 14.8). The mysterious natural process that produces honey resonates strongly with themes of revelation and preservation. Thus, the Bible describes manna, the magical food that sustained the Israelites in the wilderness for 40 years, as tasting like "wafers in honey" (Exodus 16.31). See MANNA. In subsequent rabbinic literature, *dvash* refers specifically to bees' honey, which highlights the remarkable status of the sweet substance in Jewish thought. According to the rabbinic interpretation of the biblical dietary code, honey is the only food product of a ritually unclean animal that is considered clean or kosher.

Honey is regularly associated with illumination. In the Bible, it is used as a metaphor both for the divine teaching or law (in Hebrew, *torah*) and for human wisdom (Psalms 19.8–11; 119.103; Proverbs 24.13–14). When Jonathan, son of King Saul, tasted wild honey in the woods, "his eyes lit up" (1 Samuel 14.27). The prophet Ezekiel recounts a vision in which he is commanded to eat a scroll inscribed with divine words, saying, "I ate it, and in my mouth it was as sweet as honey" (Ezekiel 3.3). This ingestion of words is echoed in a medieval European ritual of initiation for young students into the world of Torah study. On the first day of school (often coinciding with the festival of Shavu'ot, the traditional date of the revelation of the law on Mount Sinai), a slate with the letters of the Hebrew alphabet would be covered in honey, and the child would lick it off to ensure that the words of the Torah would remain sweet on his lips. He would then be presented with fruits, hard-boiled eggs (a symbol of renewal), and a honey cake inscribed with biblical verses or made in the shape of Hebrew letters. The Yiddish word for honey cake, *lekakh* (from the German *lecken*, "to lick"), provides a further association with learning through a pun on Hebrew *lekaḥ*, "instruction," as in Proverbs (4.2): "For I have given you good instruction (*lekaḥ*); do not forsake my teaching (*torah*)."

Rosh Hashanah and Passover

These connections to initiation and renewal also underlie the central role of honey in the meals for Rosh Hashanah, the Jewish New Year, which commemorates the creation of the world at the beginning of the harvest season. See ROSH HASHANAH. The consumption of sweets during the joyous celebration is already ordained in the Bible (Nehemiah 8.10), and honey cake is one of the most familiar desserts. Moreover, challah, the traditional bread of festive meals, is usually dipped in salt, but during Rosh Hashanah it is dipped in honey. The popular custom of dipping apples in honey, which originated in medieval northern Europe, connects the first fruits of autumn with the themes of sweetness and rebirth. Given the illuminating qualities of honey, this custom may also symbolize the opening of the eyes of the first humans in the Garden of Eden after they tasted the fruit of the tree of knowledge (Genesis 3.7). Ancient rabbinic sources speculated that the forbidden fruit was a fig, grape, or pomegranate, but the ubiquitous Christian identification with the apple may have influenced the medieval Jewish custom (though with a decidedly positive connotation), and apple desserts are common throughout the world during Rosh Hashanah, from European and Middle Eastern strudels, tarts, and compotes to apples cooked in honey and rosewater among Jewish communities in India.

The role of sweets during Rosh Hashanah is further highlighted by the banishment of bitter or sour foods from the festive meal, and in North African Jewish communities the tradition of avoiding all black foods even exists, since the color is associated with death and mourning. Other holidays, however, explore the interplay between sweetness and bitterness. Passover, the spring festival marking the liberation of the Israelites from bondage in Egypt, features a ritual meal called the seder (Hebrew for "order"), during which the exodus is retold and reenacted. See PASSOVER. The Bible identifies the meal's required components as roasted meat, unleavened bread (in Hebrew, *matzah*), and "bitter herbs" (Exodus 12.8). The bitter herb (in Hebrew, *maror*) broadly represents the hardships of slavery, but rabbinic sources debated which vegetables could be used, and many preferred lettuce, because it first tastes sweet and then becomes bitter, just as the Egyptians first treated the Israelites well and then "made their lives bitter" (Exodus 1.14).

A related symbolic Passover food is the sweet mixture of fruit and nuts called *ḥaroset*. The name derives from the Hebrew word for clay (*ḥeres*), which interprets the texture and color of the mixture as representations of the mortar used by the Israelites in their forced labor. Rabbinic sources specifically link the fruits in *ḥaroset* to Song of Songs (8.5): "Under the apple tree I awakened you; there your mother was in labor with you." According to rabbinic tradition, this refers to the enslaved Israelite women who, in order to circumvent Pharaoh's command that all male Israelite newborns be killed (Exodus 1.16), would give birth secretly in apple orchards. In Jewish mystical texts, the apple orchard is also a common symbol of divine presence. Thus, the bitter hardship of enslavement is tempered by the joyous knowledge of the divine role in the salvation of the children of Israel and their eventual liberation. This tempering is literally enacted during the Seder when a sandwich (in Hebrew, *korekh*) made of the bitter herbs and matzah, the bread of freedom, is dipped in the sweet *ḥaroset*.

Purim and Hanukkah

The sweetness of deliverance is also emphasized during Purim, which falls in late winter or early spring and commemorates the salvation of Jewish communities in the ancient Persian Empire from a plot to annihilate them. See PURIM. The biblical book of Esther recounts how the vizier Haman's evil plan was defeated by the Jewish queen and her wise cousin Mordecai. The appointed day of destruction was transformed into one of unbridled celebration: "a day of happiness and feasting, and a holiday, and [a day] of sending portions to one another" (Esther 9.19). The sending of portions to friends (in Hebrew, *mishloaḥ manot*) is restricted by rabbinic sources to foods that are ready to eat, and the most common items are pastries, candies, and fruits. Sweets are also central to the festive meal, both as symbols of deliverance and as good wishes for the future. Indeed, in many of the Muslim communities amid which Jewish people historically lived, the holiday was known as "the festival of sugar" (in Arabic, *eid al-sukar*).

The classic Purim sweets are figurative representations of Haman, which emphasize the dramatic reversal of fortune in the story. These range from Dutch and German gingerbread Haman figures to fried strips of dough called "Haman's ears" (in Hebrew, *'oznei haman*) around the Mediterranean. The most popular European and American treats are filled triangular pastries called *hamantaschen* (Yiddish for "Haman's pouches"), which likely derived their form and name from medieval German poppyseed pastries called *Mohntaschen*. See HAMANTASCHEN. The triangular shape has been variously interpreted in rabbinic sources as a representation of the pocket or purse from which Haman paid to secure the edict of destruction (Esther 3.9), his tricornered hat (likely an eighteenth-century anachronism), a variation on Haman's ears, or even the trio of patriarchs (Abraham, Isaac, and Jacob) before whose righteousness Haman lost his strength when he allegedly encountered them in a vision (which also offers a Hebrew pun on the name of the treat: *haman, tash kokho*, "Haman, his strength waned").

The themes of deliverance, preservation, and illumination are brought together in the celebration of Hanukkah, the winter festival of lights commemorating the rededication of the Temple in Jerusalem after the revolt of the Maccabees against their Greek oppressors. See HANUKKAH. According to rabbinic sources, the priests sought out unpolluted oil to light the sacred lamp in the Temple. They found only enough to last a single night, but the lamp miraculously burned for eight nights, providing enough time to prepare a new supply of pure oil. This miracle is commemorated by lighting candles for eight nights and eating foods fried in oil. In Spanish and Middle Eastern communities, these are typically pastries with sugar or honey coatings, such as *bimuelos*, dough fritters drizzled with honey. In northern European traditions, the chief representatives are latkes, potato pancakes often served with applesauce. The quintessential choice in Israel is the *sufganiyah*, which transforms *sufganin*, a spongy dough mentioned in ancient rabbinic sources, into a modern jelly doughnut. See DOUGHNUTS and FRIED DOUGH.

Another reconfiguration of older traditions is the widespread practice of distributing chocolate coins wrapped in foil, known as *gelt* (Yiddish for "money"). See GELT. A replacement for the real coins presented to children during Hanukkah in the nineteenth century, the custom grew out of an older practice of giving small amounts of money to religious teachers during the holiday, which may have been inspired by the etymological connection between the Hebrew words *ḥanukkah* (dedication) and *ḥinukh* (education). Once again, sweets are curiously entwined with the central Jewish themes of learning and preservation.

See also SYMBOLIC MEANINGS.

Cooper, John. *Eat and Be Satisfied: A Social History of Jewish Food*. Northvale, N.J.: Aronson, 1993.

Goodman, Philip. *The Hanukkah Anthology*. Philadelphia: Jewish Publication Society, 1976.

Marcus, Ivan. *Rituals of Childhood: Jewish Acculturation in Medieval Europe*. New Haven, Conn.: Yale University Press, 1996.

Marks, Gil. *Encyclopedia of Jewish Food*. Hoboken, N.J.: Wiley, 2010.

Nathan, Joan. *Joan Nathan's Jewish Holiday Cookbook*. New York: Schocken, 2004.

Segal, Eliezer. *Holidays, History, and Halakhah*. Northvale, N.J.: Aronson, 2000.

Edan Dekel

jujube

See GUMMIES.

junket is a dish of curdled milk with a soft-set texture and mild flavor, sweetened as a dessert. The milk is usually "turned" or "set" with rennet, although other agents can be used, including various plant juices, lemon juice, and buttermilk. In the United States it is made from packaged mixes that contain the rennet, sweeteners, and flavors such as strawberry or chocolate. In Britain, it is made with liquid rennet and sugar, and is sometimes flavored with vanilla or brandy or sprinkled with grated nutmeg or powdered cinnamon; clotted cream may be served on top. In Spain, a version traditionally made from ewe's milk is sold in small pots as *cuajada*; it is eaten with honey and walnuts. Icelandic *skyr* is also a junket-type product made with rennet combined with bacterial cultures similar to those used for yogurt.

An English recipe for junket from the seventeenth century made an appearance under the name of trifle, and rich versions of it could be made with cream; they may have been similar to the Italian cream cheese mascarpone, which is cream turned with rennet but then drained of whey. See TRIFLE. Popular in Britain well into the twentieth century, junket is now an unusual dish.

Originally, the name indicated soft, fresh cream cheese, and Elizabeth David considered that "junket" derived from the French word for rushes, the material used for making baskets to drain the curds. Junket also has an obsolete meaning as a sweet delicacy of any sort. Thus, the English phrase "going on a junket" came to mean a frivolous outing, especially one involving eating and drinking.

See also BUTTERMILK and MILK.

David, Elizabeth. *Spices, Salt and Aromatics in the English Kitchen.* Harmondsworth, U.K.: Penguin, 1970.

Laura Mason

King Cake

See TWELFTH NIGHT CAKE.

kisses, a century ago, referred to a broad range of sweets. In the United States a candy kiss was any soft, mouth-sized bite of candy. Europeans also used the word "kiss" for small sweet confections; Germans called meringue by the French word *baiser*, and many Americans used the English translation "French kiss." See MERINGUE. In northern Europe, variations on "kiss" have been used since the nineteenth century for small sweets, in particular, the "choco-kiss," a foamy marshmallow-like confection dipped in chocolate.

Today, Americans think of candy kisses as almost exclusively Hershey's Chocolate Kisses. Yet Hershey was a latecomer to the foil-wrapped kiss business. The most popular foil-wrapped chocolate morsel of the early twentieth century was Wilbur Buds, first sold in 1894. H.O. Wilbur and Sons secured the trademark to "Buds" in 1906, so when Hershey first started manufacturing its competing product in 1907, it settled for the more generic "Kisses."

Despite Wilbur's head start, Hershey had advantages in manufacture and distribution. Wilbur Buds boasted a distinctive petal design on the base of the cone that required each piece to be individually molded. In contrast, the Hershey's Kiss was flat on the bottom. When manufacture became fully automated in the 1910s, this advantage meant a machine could simply deposit the chocolate onto a moving conveyor belt. In 1921 new equipment automated the foil wrapping and also allowed for the inclusion of the paper "plume" (trademarked in 1924) that set Hershey's Kisses apart.

The Hershey Chocolate Company grew rapidly, and soon the distinctive Kiss overtook all competitors as the best-known chocolate morsel. But it was not until 2001 that Hershey overcame legal objections and successfully established a trademark on the word "Kiss" as it applied to candy.

The original milk-chocolate Kisses have been joined by variations, beginning with gold-wrapped Kisses with Almonds in 1990, white-coated Hugs in 1993, and dozens of limited-edition and holiday variations. Today, Hershey manufactures some 29 billion Kisses a year.

See also CANDY PACKAGING; HERSHEY, MILTON S.; and HERSHEY'S.

Kawash, Samira. "Kissing Cousins: The Hershey's Kiss and the Wilbur Bud." http://candyprofessor.com/2010/03/01/kissing-cousins-the-hershey's-kiss-and-the-wilbur-bud/.

Kawash, Samira. "Why a Kiss Is Just a Kiss." http://candyprofessor.com/2010/03/03/hersheys-why-a-kiss-is-just-a-kiss/.

McMahon, James D., Jr. *Built on Chocolate: The Story of the Hershey Chocolate Company.* Santa Monica, Calif.: General Publishing Group, 1998.

Samira Kawash

Kolkata (formerly Calcutta) is the chief city of the Indian state of West Bengal and the undisputed sweet capital of India, thanks to the Bengali people's passion for *mishti* (sweets). Job Charnock, an English trader who set up a trading post in the area at the end of the seventeenth century, is the putative founder of the city. Under the British East India Company, Calcutta became the administrative and

The sweets purveyor Girish Chandra Dey & Nakur Chandra Nandy still occupies the site where it opened in North Kolkata in 1845, and it retains its reputation for making excellent *sandesh*, a popular Bengali sweet prepared from *chhana* (fresh curd cheese) and sugar or palm-sugar jaggery. PHOTOGRAPH BY MICHAEL KRONDL © 2008

political capital of colonial India. During the nineteenth century, Calcutta reached its apogee as a center of culture, education, and the arts, a period that historians have come to call the Bengal Renaissance. After India gained independence in 1947, Calcutta became the capital of the state of West Bengal. In 2001 its name was officially changed to Kolkata, to reflect the Bengali pronunciation.

Bengali cuisine is noted throughout India for the sheer variety of its sweets, a phenomenon anchored in a long tradition. See INDIA and MITHAI. Medieval Bengali narrative poems, such as the *Chandimangalkabya*, are replete with descriptions of meals both epicurean and minimal, and most end with dessert, which could be as basic as a bowl of warm milk sweetened with cane sugar or *khejur gur* (sugar derived from the sap of the date palm tree). Items such as *pitha* (sweet dumplings), *payesh* (rice pudding), *naru* (round confections of sweetened coconut, sesame, or evaporated milk), kheer (condensed, sweetened milk), and *malpoa* (fritters made with flour and condensed milk, flavored with fennel and cardamom seeds, and soaked in syrup) feature recurrently. In modern times, the hallmark of Bengali hospitality is the offering of sweets to any visitor, even the unexpected one. Kolkata reflects this in the numbers of sweetshops that flourish in every neighborhood. Many of these have proprietary names, derived from the original confectioner who established the business.

Beginning in the mid-nineteenth century, the work of the professional sweet maker or *moira* who set up shop in Kolkata and nearby towns has dominated the world of Bengali confectionery. The demarcation between homemade and store-bought sweets coincided with the city's rapidly growing population and the widespread use of *chhana* (fresh curd cheese) as the primary ingredient. Manipulating this medium to create sweets of a remarkable range of textures is easier for professionals than for home cooks.

The two most famous Bengali sweets, sandesh and rosogolla, as well as a host of others like *pantua*, *rajbhog*, *chamcham*, and *danadar* are made with *chhana*. See ROSOGOLLA and SANDESH. Sandesh, whose texture can be soft (*narompak*) or firm (*karapak*), is often enhanced with flavors like mango, lime, rose petals, date palm sugar, and even chocolate. Its creation is attributed to the confectioner Paran Chandra Nag, who opened a sweetshop in 1826 in the Bowbazar area of Calcutta. His son Bhim Chandra Nag added variety and flair to his father's invention, and "Bhim Nag's sandesh" remained an emblem of excellence for many years. He is also credited with creating a special sweet called *ledikeni* in honor of the then Vicereine, Lady Canning. See LEDIKENI. Soon, there were plenty of other confectioners to cater to the Calcutta clientele. The shop named after Girish Chandra Ghosh and Nakur Chandra Nandy is one such example. It still occupies the North Calcutta site where it opened in 1845 and retains its reputation as an excellent sandesh maker.

The other Bengali favorite, rosogolla (a literal translation being "a ball in syrup"), is said to have been created and marketed in 1868 by Nobin Chandra Das, who started business in the Calcutta neighborhood of Baghbazar. His son, K. C. Das, expanded the family enterprise and applied available technology to streamline the production process and ensure the safety of his products. Not content with that, he also created a new sweet called *rosomalai*, which is a rosogolla floating in a sweet milky sauce scented with saffron. Today, the K.C. Das logo from Kolkata is seen on tinned sweets exported to other countries. See NOBIN CHANDRA DAS.

In the twentieth century, and especially after India's independence, Calcutta expanded southward, and the growth of the middle class resulted in a demand for high-quality sweetshops in the newer neighborhoods. A new generation of entrepreneurs created fabled stores like Balaram Mullick & Radharaman Mullick, Sen Mahasay, Jalajoga, Banchharam, Jugal's, and many others. Their confectioners, not content with simply reproducing traditional sweets or, in some cases, reviving items mentioned in early Bengali literature, experimented with new flavors and techniques to stir the increasingly globalized Bengali palate. The syrup for rosogolla, once made only with refined cane sugar, is now also created with date palm sugar, which is available in the winter. See PALM SUGAR. Fruits exotic and native, like mango, raspberry, kiwi, peaches, litchis, and watermelon, lend their fragrance and flavor to sandesh. Bengal is the only region in India where *mishti doi* or sweet yogurt is part of dessert, and a shop such as Jalajoga was famed for its version, made with rich milk and sporting a dense, pinkish-brown top layer of cream. The great Bengali writer Tagore honored it with the poetic moniker *payodhi*.

The changing population of Kolkata is reflected in the ownership of some sweetshops. Non-Bengalis, especially Marwari traders from Rajasthan, constitute a significant community, and some of them have ventured into the sweet-making business with enormous success. Probably the best known is Haldiram, originating in Rajasthan and selling both sweet and savory products all over India. Ganguram, established in Calcutta in 1885 by a confectioner from Uttar Pradesh, is noted for both its sweets and savory items that can be eaten as a small meal. Stores like these not only sell the usual Bengali sweets, they also produce items originating in northern India—rich halvas and sweets made with flour, sugar, *besan* (chickpea flour), evaporated milk, and clarified butter instead of the ubiquitous *chhana*. Kolkata has welcomed them with open arms, and Bengalis have joyfully expanded their dessert universe.

See also DATES and HALVAH.

Arndt, Alice, ed. *Culinary Biographies.* Houston, Tex.: Yes Press, 2006.
Dutta, Krishna. *Calcutta—A Cultural and Literary History.* Northampton, U.K.: Interlink, 2003.
Krondl, Michael. *Sweet Invention: A History of Dessert.* Chicago: Chicago Review Press, 2011.

Chitrita Banerji

kombucha is sugar-sweetened black tea fermented by a community of microorganisms into a tart, effervescent beverage, sometimes compared to sparkling apple cider. The fermented beverage kombucha is not to be confused with *konbucha*, a Japanese tea made from powdered *konbu* seaweed. Kombucha is typically produced by a symbiotic community of bacteria and yeast (SCOBY), generally referred to as a "mother," which takes the form of a rubbery disk that floats on the surface of the tea as it ferments. The community of organisms can also be transferred via the kombucha liquid itself, which can generate a new mother.

The kombucha SCOBY incorporates yeasts that metabolize sugar into alcohol, and acetobacter, which metabolizes alcohol into acetic acid in the presence of oxygen. Lactic acid and other bacteria may also be present depending on the SCOBY. Because of its oxygen requirement, kombucha is always made in an open vessel with a broad surface area exposed to air. The alcohol and acetic acid levels in mature kombucha can vary widely, depending on time and environmental conditions. Most kombucha is classified as a nonalcoholic beverage, containing less than 0.5 percent alcohol, though some are now being made and marketed as alcoholic beverages with higher alcohol content. Sugar and caffeine levels also vary in mature kombucha.

Although its precise origins are unknown (it was likely first used in the region of Manchuria), kombucha has long enjoyed acclaim in many varied locales around Asia and Central and Eastern Europe, and has been widely promoted as beneficial to health. Its use has been growing in the United States since at least the mid-1990s. Originally, kombucha was not commercially available; it spread exclusively through grassroots channels as enthusiasts grew more mothers and sought to share them. Today kombucha mothers and kits are widely available in the United States, and kombucha has become a big business, with hundreds of millions of dollars in sales and dozens of commercial manufacturers, ranging from small local enterprises to multinational corporations.

Katz, Sandor. *The Art of Fermentation: An In-Depth Exploration of Essential Concepts and Processes from Around the World*. White River Junction, Vt.: Chelsea Green, 2012.

Sandor Ellix Katz

Kool-Aid, an artificially flavored soft-drink powder, was invented in 1927 by American entrepreneur Edwin Perkins (1889–1961). Inspired by the success of the gelatin mix Jell-O and working in his mother's kitchen, Perkins invented a method to remove the liquid from Fruit Smack, a beverage concentrate he had developed a few years earlier. See GELATIN DESSERTS. The story of Kool-Aid reads as the prototypical rags-to-riches narrative of American ingenuity and hard work. Perkins initially manufactured and sold Kool-Aid in his hometown of Hastings, Nebraska, moving the company to Chicago once the product was established. The family-held firm was sold to General Foods in 1953, and Kool-Aid now belongs to the Kraft Foods Group, which acquired it in 1995.

Although Kool-Aid has been sold in various forms, including liquid concentrates and presweetened mixes, its most popular guise is a paper-and-foil sachet containing an unsweetened powder composed of citric acid, salt, ascorbic acid, artificial (and sometimes natural) fruit flavor, artificial color, and additives such as maltodextrin, corn starch, calcium phosphate, and BHA. The consumer makes the beverage at home by adding water and either granulated sugar or a sugar substitute to the unsweetened powder. Although Kool-Aid is best known for its conventional fruit flavors like cherry, grape, lemon-lime, orange, raspberry, and strawberry, it has appeared in a number of exotic flavors with whimsical names and lurid colors, such as Purplesaurus Rex, Sharkleberry Fin, and Solar Strawberry-Starfruit.

Kool-Aid's popularity comes from its vivid color and affordability. Perkins set the original price of the drink powder at 10 cents per package, and he reduced the cost to 5 cents during the Great Depression, keeping Kool-Aid well within financial reach of most American families. Sugar rationing during World War II limited both the production and sales of Kool-Aid, but the postwar era witnessed a boom that made Kool-Aid the generic name for any powdered soft drink in the United States. Kool-Aid's appeal to the pocketbook and the eye has maintained its fame, and the beverage powder now has a global reach. Kool-Aid is currently manufactured in both the United States and Mexico, and the quintessentially American beverage is sold worldwide in flavors geared to local tastes.

As an unsweetened flavor powder, Kool-Aid can be used to make many things other than the soft drink for which it is intended, and Kraft Foods's own website features recipes for popsicles, slushies, milk shakes, cakes, pie, and sorbet containing Kool-Aid powder. In addition, Kool-Aid's concentrated acids and coloring suggest a surprisingly wide range of other uses. Cooks have developed delicacies such as deep-fried Kool-Aid balls (brightly colored doughnut holes) and koolickles (Kool-Aid pickles), which transform a savory, green dill pickle into a sweet, crimson treat. Outside the kitchen, Kool-Aid can be used for its artificial coloring to make lip gloss, brightly colored modeling dough, and inexpensive watercolors for children, as well as to dye Easter eggs, fabric, and even hair. Kool-Aid's acidic composition lends itself to cleaning rust stains, removing chlorine from swimmers' hair, and preventing the buildup of limescale in water systems.

The widespread use of Kool-Aid as beverage, dye, and household chemical attests to its firm foothold in American culture. Roadside Kool-Aid stands, for example, have been just as popular as lemonade stands in the United States in certain regions and periods. Unsurprisingly, Nebraska has chosen Kool-Aid as its state drink, and since 2007, Perkins's hometown of Hastings has held an annual weekend festival called Kool-Aid Days, which boasts the world's largest Kool-Aid stand and sponsors a Kool-Aid drinking contest and the Miss Kool-Aid Pageant. More broadly, Kool-Aid has gained notoriety in popular culture from several disparate sources. Tom Wolfe's 1968 book *The Electric Kool-Aid Acid Test* documents the birth of the hippie movement by following countercultural figurehead Ken Kesey and his Merry Pranksters. The book's title refers to parties at which Kesey, the Merry Pranksters, and their guests drank LSD-spiked Kool-Aid to induce a group trip in search of intersubjectivity. American college students continue this tradition, albeit in a less hallucinogenic way, by partying with punch that combines Kool-Aid with vodka or grain alcohol. More sinisterly, the phrase "drinking the Kool-Aid," a metaphor for unquestioning groupthink, arose from the 1978 Jonestown Massacre in which some 900 followers of cult figure Jim Jones committed mass suicide in Guyana by drinking a toxic punch composed of Kool-Aid (or, as many contend, its less popular competitor Flavor Aid), cyanide, and prescription sedatives.

Kool-Aid is also famed for its marketing icon, the happy-go-lucky Kool-Aid Man. First introduced in 1954, the 7-foot-tall anthropomorphic pitcher of cherry Kool-Aid typically bursts through walls on hot summer days to the refrain of "Oh, yeah!" to offer refreshment in the form of Kool-Aid. The brand's mascot has undergone several transformations over the decades, including a digital makeover in 2013 that introduced a Facebook page, Twitter and Instagram accounts, and a smartphone app that lets users insert the Kool-Aid Man into their own photographs.

Adams County, Nebraska, Historical Society. "The Kool-Aid Story." http://www.adamshistory.org/index.php?option=com_content&task=view&id=32&Itemid=4 (accessed 22 November 2014).

Kraft Foods. "Kool-Aid." http://www.koolaid.com (accessed 22 November 2014).

Julie A. Cassiday

Korea is a peninsular country located in northeast Asia, bordering China and Russia to the north with Japan across the sea to the east. While at present the peninsula is divided into the two states of South and North Korea, historically the peninsula has been governed by a single polity since at least the early tenth century C.E. Sweets in premodern Korea (before the twentieth century) held an important function in both rituals and entertainment. The primary sweetener was honey—often referred to as *yak*, meaning "medicine." See HONEY. Fruit, glutinous rice, and azuki beans were also utilized for sweetness. See AZUKI BEANS. Some representative confections are *ttŏk* (rice cakes), *yakkwa* (fried honey cakes), *suksilgwa* (boiled candied fruits), and *yakpap* (medicinal rice). Presently, Koreans use the term *han'gwa* (Korean sweets) to refer to confections, with the exception of rice cakes.

Records of confections date back to the Three Kingdoms period (57 B.C.E.–668 C.E.), when an account was written concerning an ancestral rite held by King Suro (42–199) that included offerings of rice cakes and fruits. The subsequent Greater Silla (668–935) and Koryŏ (918–1392) periods saw two important developments that led to an increase in the number of confections and sweets. First, agriculture was greatly advanced, with more grains being produced, and second, Buddhist culture became prominent along with prohibitions against eating meat. Thus, more energy was put into specialized dishes, such as vegetarian fare, and confections. Buddhist practice also promoted the development of tea culture, and with that a class of confections known as *tasik* (foods for tea) became prominent. See BUDDHISM and TEA. The final premodern age was that of Chosŏn (1392–1910). This period was largely dominated by Confucianism, which emphasized the performance of various rites (especially marriage and ancestral rites) that required specific foods, including many sweets and confections. Sweets were generally consumed only during rites or on special days, although many exceptions existed. It was during this period that extensive records about sweets were kept, including recipe books that describe the types of sweets consumed and guidebooks that demonstrate precisely which sweets were offered in specific rites.

First among Korean sweets are rice cakes. They can be prepared in numerous ways and with many ingredients. Most commonly pounded glutinous rice is coated with azuki or roasted soybean powder; other varieties are made from steamed rice or glutinous rice wrapped around bite-sized pieces of fruits and nuts such as persimmons, apricots, chestnuts, or walnuts. A representative example is *songpyŏn*, glutinous rice cakes steamed on a bed of pine needles and stuffed with various ingredients such as sweetened chestnuts, honey, or sweet red azuki paste that yield different tastes and colors. Commonly made for the Harvest Moon Festival (the fifteenth day of the eighth lunar month, which falls in September or early October), these cakes were shared with neighbors as a means of extending goodwill and fostering communal harmony.

Yakkwa are part of a larger group of sweets known as *yumilgwa*, which are made from a mixture of kneaded grain flour, honey, and sesame oil that is pressed into various shapes and then fried in oil. The cooked cakes are sprinkled with various toppings such as pine nuts or sesame seeds. These fried treats were made in conjunction with auspicious occasions like marriages or sixtieth-birthday celebrations.

Suksilgwa are made by boiling fruits, nuts, or roots and then sweetening them with honey. There are two basic varieties of this treat. *Ran* refers to either fruits or roots that are boiled and then pounded until malleable before being covered in honey and sprinkled with coarsely ground pine nuts. Common examples include boiled chestnuts, jujubes, and ginger root. *Ch'o* are fruits boiled in honey-water and then sprinkled with either cinnamon powder or coarsely ground pine nuts, the most popular being boiled chestnuts and jujubes. Because they are so labor-intensive, *suksilgwa* were largely reserved for highly important occasions.

Yakpap also has a history dating to the Three Kingdom period: legend says that this sweet was offered to a crow that saved a king's life by informing him of an assassin lying in wait. To make *yakpap*, glutinous rice is steamed thoroughly; before the rice cools, jujubes, chestnuts, sesame oil, honey, and soy sauce are mixed in. *Yakpap* was a staple for the celebration of the first full moon of the lunar New Year, but like many of the treats just described, it was not necessarily consumed by the family alone, but rather shared with neighbors. Sharing confections was commonplace in premodern Korea and reveals the importance of harmonic relations within the village. Even in today's cosmopolitan Korea, an occasion such as moving into a new apartment is often marked by sharing *ttŏk* or another treat with one's new neighbors, a custom harkening back to premodern Korea when reciprocity and mutual assistance were prominent cultural traits.

The twentieth century has brought tremendous change to Korean cuisine in general and to sweets as well. During the Japanese colonial period (1910–1945), foodstuffs began to be commercially produced, and Western-style confections and candies were introduced. Following liberation and the Korean War (1950–1953), Western influence became even stronger thanks to the American presence in South Korea as well as to the foods—including both wheat flour and granulated sugar—that the United States provided as aid. In terms of sweets, the use of granulated sugar became common, and sweets began to mimic those in the West. One of the most well-known examples is the Choco Pie that was introduced in 1974 by the present-day Orion Confectionery Company. Interestingly, the Choco Pie is now said to be the most highly sought-after sweet in North Korea, perhaps demonstrating the dire situation of mass-produced sweets in the North. Traditional sweets remain popular and are frequently given as gifts and used in major life celebrations, such as marriages and birthdays.

See also CHESTNUTS.

Pettid, Michael J. *Korean Cuisine: An Illustrated History*. London: Reaktion, 2008.
Yi, Hyoji. *Han'guk ŭi ŭmsik munhwa* [The Food Culture of Korea]. Seoul: Sin'gwang ch'ulp'ansa, 2006.

Michael J. Pettid

Krispy Kreme is a chain of doughnut shops based in Winston-Salem, North Carolina. Despite their name, these southern pastries are neither crispy nor creamy, but rather are sweet, yeasty, and light. Although Krispy Kreme is maligned in some places for the high sugar and fat content of its doughnuts, in the company's home state of North Carolina, Krispy Kreme means more than just sweet indulgence; it is a cultural icon.

The company's signature neon HOT NOW sign flashes red when an Original Glazed doughnut slides out of the fryer and down a conveyor belt through a sugar-syrup bath, signaling that the doughnuts are ready for customers. Even just the phrase HOT NOW causes Krispy Kreme lovers to salivate. Yet the doughnuts need not be hot and fresh to be loved—a few seconds in the microwave returns them to their original, sublime state.

The Krispy Kreme Doughnut Company began in 1934 when nineteen-year-old Vernon Rudolph and his uncle left their general store in Kentucky to sell doughnuts in Nashville, Tennessee. A river barge cook is said to have created their recipe, likely related to New Orleans's yeast-raised beignets or German *Fastnachts*. In 1937 Rudolph opened his own Krispy Kreme shop in Winston-Salem and built it into a chain of family-owned stores, inventing an automated doughnut-making system. To ensure consistency, his proprietary recipe is still prepared only in the Winston-Salem mother plant; the dry mix is sent to more than 800 franchises in 23 countries around the world.

The basic recipe calls for a yeast-raised batter, which can include milk, butter, yogurt, eggs, vegetable shortening, and soy-based lecithin, as well as a plethora of chemical stabilizers. The Original Glazed doughnut, with 49 grams of sugar, weighs in at 190 calories, 100 from fat. However, many of the company's more than 50 varieties include ingredients that boost the calorie count of each doughnut to a whopping 300 or 400 apiece. See DOUGHNUTS.

Krispy Kreme doughnuts have become a cult treat. They are featured at the North Carolina State Fair as a sandwich base for hamburgers or sloppy joes—a concoction that obviates the kosher certification of the Winston-Salem plant. They also provide a new sweet and salty take on ham biscuits when used as a vehicle for country ham.

The company advertises its mission as "To Touch and Enhance Lives through the Joy That Is Krispy Kreme" and sells that experience as much as the pastry. Since 1955 Krispy Kreme has provided sales kits for group fundraisers, and its green dotted boxes with a dozen doughnuts brought in over $32 million last year for schools, churches, and civic groups. The annual Krispy Kreme Challenge licenses the trademark for a charity run benefiting the North Carolina Children's Hospital. Now in its tenth year, the race attracts more than 8,000 runners, who start at the North Carolina State University bell tower, run 2.5 miles to Raleigh's downtown Krispy Kreme store, consume one dozen Original Glazed doughnuts, and run the 2.5 miles back.

Krispy Kreme doughnuts are so beloved in North Carolina that they feature in bucket lists. After being diagnosed with amyotrophic lateral sclerosis, Chris Rosati of Durham, North Carolina, decided to fulfill his long-time dream of hijacking a Krispy Kreme truck to toss out free doughnuts. The company provided its 75th anniversary Krispy Kreme Cruiser and 1,000 doughnuts for a day; as Rosati distributed doughnuts from the bus, he said each box offered "12 chances to make somebody happy."

See also DUNKIN' DONUTS.

Carlitz, Ruth. "Hot Doughnuts Now: The Krispy Kreme Story." http://www.dukechronicle.com/articles/2003/10/22/hot-doughnuts-now-krispy-kreme-story (accessed 8 December 2013).

Krispy Kreme Doughnuts, Inc. "About Us." http://www.krispykreme.com/about-us/history (accessed 7 December 2013).

Mazzocchi, Jay. "Krispy Kreme Doughnut Corporation." In *Encyclopedia of North Carolina History*, edited by William S. Powell. Chapel Hill: University of North Carolina Press, 2006.

Ardath Weaver

kuchen is the German word for cake in general; within that term are many other designations for particular types of cakes. The menus of the German café-pastry shops known as *Konditoreien* traditionally offer small booklet menus listing *Kuchen* in subdivisions, depending on ingredients such as cheese, fruit, and cream. See CAFÉ. Some cakes, simply because they are round and especially if they were prepared without any flour or artificial leavening, are classified as *Torten*. See TORTE. In Bialystok, Poland, *Bialystoker kuchen* was the name for the poppy seed and onion bread roll we call a bialy, probably the result of that city's long commercial and political interaction with Germany, which added words to the local vocabulary.

In the United States, where so many classic baked treats have German origins, kuchen gradually has come to mean what we consider coffee cake or Danish (and which the Danes call *Wienerbrød*, Vienna bread). See COFFEE CAKE. These are most classically yeast-risen and moderately sweet cakes or buns accented with nuts, raisins, and aromatic spices such as cinnamon, nutmeg, and cloves. For some specialties, the yeast dough is folded with butter, as in puff pastry. See PASTRY, PUFF. Cinnamon rolls, crumb-topped flat twists known as bowties, braided pecan or almond rings, and what we call crumb cake (*Streuselkuchen* in German or, with apples, *Apfelstreusel*) are typical examples. See STREUSEL. For convenience and time-saving, these coffee cakes are often leavened with baking powder or baking soda instead of yeast. Depending on the quality of other ingredients and care in preparation, these quick kuchen-coffee cakes-Danish-Vienna breads can be very good, although they are generally disappointingly dry and bland, since they lack the winey aroma and lasting moisture that yeast imparts.

See also BREADS, SWEET; CAKE; GERMANY; and SCANDINAVIA.

Sheraton, Mimi. *The German Cookbook*. 50th anniv. ed. New York: Random House, 1965.

Mimi Sheraton

Kugelhupf

See GUGELHUPF.

kulfi

See INDIA.

Kyoto, Japan's capital from 794 to 1868, enjoys special distinction for its traditional Japanese confectionery (*wagashi*). See WAGASHI. Tea masters recognized the excellence of Kyoto confectionery in the early 1600s: the term "Kyoto Sweet" (*Kyōgashi*) first appeared in 1627 in the tea diary *Matsuya kaiki* (Matsuya Record of Gatherings). Within a decade, when many Portuguese-inspired recipes were included in lists of the city's "local products," Kyoto had become a center for "Southern Barbarian Sweets" (*nanbangashi*), rivaling Nagasaki. See NANBANGASHI and JAPANESE BAKED GOODS. By the end of the century, when the confectionery trade was fully established in Japan, Kyoto's sweet makers had opened branch shops in Edo (Tokyo).

Many of the nation's oldest confectioners are located or originated in Kyoto, including the venerable Kawabata Dōki, which has served the old capital for more than half a millennium. Kawabata Dōki, which began as a rice cake shop (*mochiya*), gained distinction after becoming a purveyor to the court in the late 1500s. Dōki produced *chimaki* (rice cakes or kudzu jelly wrapped in bamboo grass), and the shop became famous for its Flower Petal Cakes (*hanabira mochi*), which consist of a thin white rice cake folded over a small red cake next to a sliver of sweetened burdock root and white azuki bean paste (*an*) flavored with miso. *Hanabira mochi* are eaten at the New Year and are favored by tea masters for their celebrations (*hatsugama*) in the autumn. After the turn of the seventeenth century, sweet maker Toraya joined Kawabata Dōki in the ranks of court purveyors. Records show that Toraya supplied Southern Barbarian Sweets to the court as early as 1635. The same year Toraya was already producing its trademark *yōkan*, a sweet made from steamed azuki bean paste, sugar, flour, kudzu starch, and flavorings. See AZUKI BEANS. Novelist Ihara Saikaku (1642–1693) mentioned Toraya's *yōkan* along with Kawabata Dōki's *chimaki* in his hit publication *Nanshoku ōkagami* (The Great Mirror of Male Love), published in 1687. A branch store of Toraya opened in Edo by 1714; the main store moved to Tokyo in the Meiji period (1868–1912), although the confectioner still maintains two shops in Kyoto.

Kawabata Dōki, Toraya, and other confectioners serving the court, tea masters, and wealthy patrons crafted "superior confectionery" (*jōgashi*) using high-quality ingredients, particularly refined sugar, which was imported through Dutch and Chinese intermediaries in Nagasaki. In 1775 makers of *jōgashi* in Kyoto established a trade association (*nakama*). In return for making twice-yearly payments to the warrior government (from which the court purveyors Toraya and Kawabata Dōki were exempted), the association gained control of all the imported sugar brought into the city. By 1777 there were 284 Kyoto confectioners in the association, which sought to prevent nonmembers from producing or selling superior confectionery and prohibited its members from selling molds for sweets to outsiders. The association lasted until the Meiji government ended all such trade groups in 1868. However, Kyoto sweet makers understood the value of collectively promoting their trade, and they reorganized during the Meiji period to include 500 member stores. In 1900 they sent a delegation to the Paris Exposition.

Evidence of the technical skills of the city's confectioners is found in the cookbooks for sweets printed in Kyoto in the early modern period. Although there were hundreds of culinary texts dating from this time, many of which contain recipes for confectionery, the first entirely devoted to sweets was the anonymous *Kokon meibutsu gozen gashi hidenshō* (Secret Writings on Famous Japanese Confectionery New and Old), published in Kyoto in 1718 and followed by a sequel, *Kokon meibutsu gozen gashi zushiki* (Schema of Famous Japanese Confectionery New and Old), in 1761. Written for professionals, the texts describe how to make a variety of dry, moist, and Southern Barbarian Sweets. For their elite patrons, some confectioners created hand-painted pattern books to showcase the varieties of sweets they could produce. Kyoto sweets are distinctive for drawing on the long history, cultural milieu, and natural setting of the ancient capital, and the names of the sweets provide the main clue to these references. Kyoto confectioners sought out members of the aristocracy and tea masters to give their sweets artful designations. For example, Toraya claims that Emperor Kōkaku (1771–1840) gave the names "Belt of Jewels" and "Mountain Path in Spring" to two of its sweets and Emperor Ninkō (1800–1846) styled another confection "Garden of Autumn Leaves."

In addition to the elite tradition of sweets, many religious institutions in Kyoto have nearby sweet makers who created humbler confections that became nationally famous. Near the entrance to Imamiya Shrine are two confectioners specializing in Toasted Cakes (*aburi mochi*) made from soybean flour, grilled on a charcoal fire, and then glazed with sweet white miso. Shimogamo Shrine is said to be the birthplace of *Mitarashi Dango*, dumplings drizzled with soy sauce and syrup and served on a stick.

There are too many notable confectioners in Kyoto to list, but a few that are especially noteworthy include Chōgorō Mochihonbo, Kamesuehiro, Kameyamutsu, Matsuya Tokiwa, Suetomi, Shioyoshiken, Tsuruya Yoshinobu, and Tawaraya Yoshitomi (which operates a Kyoto confectionery museum, the Kyōgashi Shiryōkan), and Uemura Yoshitsugu.

See also JAPAN and PORTUGAL'S INFLUENCE IN ASIA.

Akai Tatsurō. *Kashi no bunkashi.* Kyoto: Kawara Shoten, 2005.

Aoki Naomi. *Zusetsu wagashi no konjaku.* Kyoto: Tankōsha, 2000.

Rath, Eric C. *Food and Fantasy in Early Modern Japan.* Berkeley: University of California Press, 2010.

Shashi Hensan Iinkai, ed. *Toraya no goseiki: Dentō to kakushin no keie.* 2 vols. Tokyo: Kabushiki Gaisha Toraya, 2003.

Eric C. Rath

laddu (also spelled *laddoo*), a round, sweet ball, is probably the most universally popular Indian sweet and one of the most ancient. It is given as an offering to deities at Hindu temples and served at many Hindu festivals and ceremonies.

The basic version (*besan laddu*) is made with chickpea (gram) flour, sugar, clarified butter, and cardamom powder. The flour is fried in the butter before adding the sugar and cardamom; when the mixture cools, it is formed into round balls around 1½ inches in diameter. They can be stored in an airtight container for up to a week.

Motichoor (meaning "crushed pearls") *laddu*, another very popular variety, are made from tiny balls of deep-fried chickpea batter soaked in sugar syrup. Regional variants include laddus made from wheat flour (Rajasthan), sesame seeds (Maharashtra), rice flour (Kerala), and beaten rice or rice flakes (Andhra Pradesh); sometimes grated coconut or coconut powder, roasted chickpeas, nuts, and raisins are added.

The most famous laddu is the one served at the Sri Venkateswara temple in Tirupati, Andhra Pradesh (the most visited temple in India and the world's second most visited holy place after the Vatican). Laddus are offered to Lord Venkateswara (an incarnation of Vishnu) and then distributed to the devotees. They are also sold in shops inside and outside the temple. These laddus are made from chickpea flour, sugar, clarified butter, cardamom, cashew nuts, and raisins. In 2008 they were granted Protected Geographical Indication status as a product with a specific provenance and composition. Another specialty of this temple is the *kalyana* (giant laddu), which is the size of a baseball.

See also HINDUISM and INDIA.

Achaya, K. T. *A Historical Dictionary of Indian Food.* New Delhi: Oxford University Press, 2002.

Banerjee, Satarupa. *Book of Indian Sweets.* New Delhi: Rupa & Co., 1994.

Colleen Taylor Sen

ladyfingers

See SMALL CAKES.

laminated doughs are made of layers of dough and fat, usually butter. *Pâte feuilletée*, or "puff pastry," is considered the king of laminated doughs. Croissant and Danish doughs belong to the same family, and all follow a similar construction. See CROISSANT and PASTRY, PUFF. No matter what form the laminated dough takes, its magical transformation in the oven depends on two elements: a flour-based dough and a fat. The pastry maker folds dough over the fat to enclose it, then rolls the dough out, and folds it over itself again and again, until it has dozens or even hundreds of very thin, alternating layers of dough and butter. As the pastry bakes, the steam from the fat releases and raises each individual layer of dough, creating a flaky mille-feuille (thousand leaves) effect. Proper puff pastry has many discernible layers of super-thin leaves of crisp, buttery dough.

The dough that folds over the butter, called *detrempe*, consists, at a minimum, of flour, water, and salt, although it usually contains some fat, too. This additional fat helps to prevent the principal fat being worked into the dough from bleeding into it as the dough is folded and rolled out.

The fat is traditionally butter. But animal fats, such as lard or duck fat, either used alone or in conjunction with butter, also have their place in these doughs. The hydrogenated vegetable fats used in mass production are second-rate, low-cost alternatives and are not recommended for reasons of quality and health.

Puff pastry dough typically contains around 75 percent butter relative to the weight of the flour, although some formulas, like those for inverted puff pastry and blitz puff doughs, use almost equal amounts of flour and butter. Croissant dough typically has a 3:10 butter-to-flour ratio of, which allows it to bake to a flaky texture on the outside and honeycombed within.

The pastry known as pithivier is an excellent example of a classic puff pastry product. The dough is rolled out to about ⅛ inch (2 centimeters) thick, cut into circles, layered with *crème d'amande*, topped with another layer of puff dough, scored in a pinwheel pattern, egg-washed, and baked. Pithiviers should rise 4 to 5 inches as they bake. For classic millefeuilles, the rolled-out puff dough is lined with parchment and baked with another pan on top of it, so the pastries turn out flaky without rising more than around half an inch. They are a perfect platform for topping with mousses and pastry creams. Palmiers are made from sheeted puff pastry dough that is layered with sugar, rolled up, and sliced into layered palm shapes that bake up crisp, sweet, and delicious.

Croissants are made from a leavened dough that rises thanks to the addition of commercial baker's yeast, a wild-yeast starter, or a combination of the two. Unlike puff pastry dough, croissant dough is sweetened, and it is hydrated with water and milk; whole eggs or egg yolks are also often added.

Croissant dough and American Danish dough are very similar, the primary difference being that croissant dough usually contains more butter and therefore bakes up flakier. A properly made croissant should shatter when bitten into and reveal a characteristically honeycombed crumb from the dough's fermentation and its gases that expand during baking. Croissants' taste should have a subtle acidity that balances the fat of the butter, without tasting at all sour.

See also BUTTER; FRANCE; PIE DOUGH; and SHORTENING.

Suas, Michel. *Advanced Bread and Pastry*. Farmington Hills, Mich.: Cengage Learning, 2008.

Ken Forkish

Latin America has essentially orderly, solid traditions of sweets that speak to the people's love of habit, not novelty. There is a soothing, reassuring stability in Latin American sweets that is also sensuous and magical.

For Latin Americans—who crave flavorful savory foods built in layers; who welcome the sting of hot peppers, the acid touch of citrus juices or vinegar, and the bite of raw onions in table condiments; and who seek vivid contrast between salty, sweet, bitter, acid, and the savory sensation of *umami*—dessert (*postre*) is meant to put a calming end to the sensory ride that is the Latin meal. Latin Americans are assertive in their savory cooking, and subtle, often minimalist, when making sweets and desserts.

The pre-Columbian peoples of Mesoamerica enjoyed honey-based treats and ambrosial tropical fruits, but the fundamental ingredient of the Latin American dessert tradition arrived in the New World with the Spanish after 1492 in the form of sugar and the sugarcane from which it is derived. See SUGAR and SUGARCANE. Muslims had introduced this perennial grass to the south of Spain in the eighth century, and tropical America proved an ideal environment for the South Asian native.

From Mexico to the southern tip of South America, Latin Americans are like a family that can trace its heirloom sweets back from generation to generation to a common source—the Spanish and Portuguese convents and monasteries that were founded in the early colonial period. See CONVENT SWEETS.

The cooks who developed and spread the Latin dessert-making tradition from Mexico and the Caribbean to the southern tip of Argentina worked their alchemy in the kitchens of the monasteries and convents that Spanish and Portuguese religious orders founded beginning in the sixteenth century. After the armies of conquest had subdued the native peoples, it fell to Franciscans, Dominicans, Jesuits, and others to propagate the Christian gospel and Iberian culture in the New World. The friars set about creating towns based on Iberian models and recreating the natural world they had known in Europe. They carried sugarcane and fruits such as peaches, apples, figs, grapes, plums, quinces, bananas, and oranges from one part of the Spanish colonial empire to the other.

The friars developed a reputation as gifted cooks who knew how to turn both Old and New World ingredients into tempting sweets, but it was the nuns who firmly planted Spanish sweet-making traditions

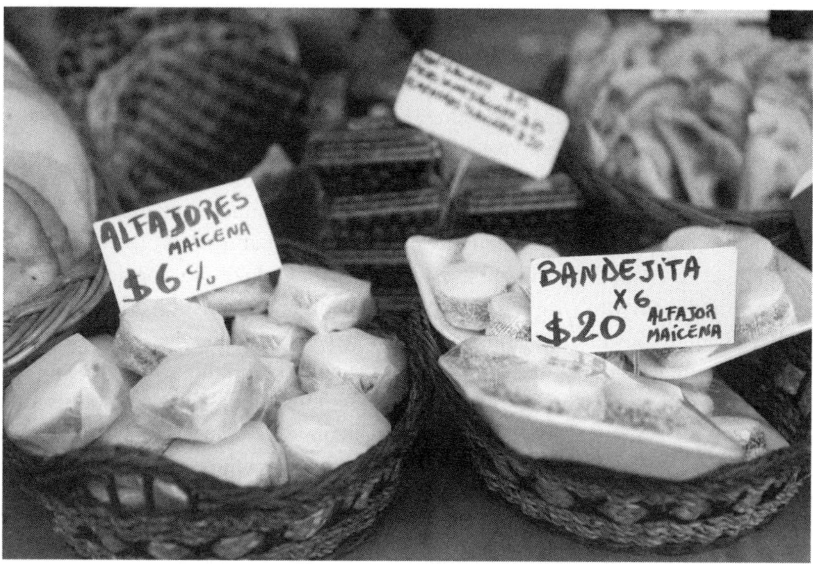

Alfajores, popular cookies often sandwiched together with dulce de leche, are offered for sale in Buenos Aires.
JILL SCHNEIDER / NATIONAL GEOGRAPHIC CREATIVE

in the New World. This was particularly true of nuns from Andalusia, which Christian rulers had wrested from Islamic control, and where convents were the repositories of Islamic recipes for sweets. See ISLAM.

The sisters were a peripatetic lot. Nuns of the Regina Angelorum monastery on Hispaniola (the island shared today by the Dominican Republic and Haiti) traveled to Cuba and Peru. The first nuns of the Santa Clara convent in Caracas, Venezuela, came from the Santa Clara convent in Santo Domingo, and the first nuns of the Carmelite convent of Trujillo, Peru, were from a sister convent in Quito. Such movement contributed to the dissemination of ideas and recipes.

The nuns' initial mission was to educate native girls who had been converted to Christianity by the friars. As more Spanish families settled in the colonies, some convents became boarding schools for upper-class young women, who brought with them retinues of servant girls. The nuns kept their charges virginal and prepared them to be good wives, teaching them cooking, dessert making, and other household skills. These lessons were at the same time imparted to their native, mestizo, and African servants.

Teaching monasteries benefited from monetary gifts from the parents of their aristocratic pupils, but nuns such as the Carmelites, who were cloistered and bound by vows of poverty, had to find other means of sustaining themselves. When times were hard and donations fell short, they produced special sweets to sell to the public. In a 1755 letter to his sister in Madrid, Guillermo Tortosa described the nuns of a convent in Puebla, Mexico, as "chubby, sweet white angels with heavenly hands." With those hands, he explained, they prepared delectable sweets for an important town festival. Their output, he wrote, included candied peaches, guava, pear, and quince, a caramelized goat's milk sauce called *cajeta,* egg sponge, and *mamón,* a type of genoise. Some of the sweets he described were traditional Spanish desserts, such as *tocino del cielo* ("heaven's bacon," an egg yolk custard), while others were Iberian desserts made with New World ingredients, such as the Brazilian egg and coconut custard *quindim.*

The story was repeated throughout New Spain. The nuns of La Concepción in Mexico City prepared sweet empanadas, the convent of La Encarnación in Lima was famous for its almond pastes, the Carmelites of Puebla were known for *dulce de cielo* (an egg-rich custard), and Puebla's Santa Clara convent was praised for a marzipan made with sweet potato (*camote*) paste mixed with unrefined sugar and molded into small sweet potato shapes. This heritage is echoed today in the names of Latin American desserts such as *suspiros de monja* (nun's sighs), *huevos espirituales* (spiritual eggs), and *suspiritos de Maria santísima* (little breaths of the most Holy Mary). Mexico and Peru, which were epicenters of viceroyal political power, had the greatest number of religious institutions, and therefore richer and more complex sweet cuisines than the Caribbean islands, where organized religion played a lesser role.

Not as rooted in convent traditions but reflecting a long-standing Spanish and Portuguese love affair with the combination of sweet and crunchy are the "fruits of the frying pan" (*frutas de sartén*), the fanciful name given in Spanish medieval cookbooks and later in colonial cookbooks to crisp, deep-fried pastries sprinkled with sugar or doused with syrup. See FRIED DOUGH. Another Islamic legacy in Latin America is fruit cooked in sugar syrup, either to sweeten the fruit for a silky dessert or to preserve it as an intensely concentrated confection, jam, paste, or candy. With an abundance of sugarcane and a cornucopia of tropical fruits, plantation kitchens produced prodigious amounts of guava marmalade, bitter orange shells in syrup, and many other stovetop desserts born of this mingling of traditions.

Perhaps the most beloved dessert tradition in Latin America—and yet another Iberian legacy—can be found in the many variations on the theme of sugar cooked with milk, egg yolks, or both, such as long-simmered rice puddings, the pan-Latin caramelized milk pudding or sauce called *dulce de leche*, and *natillas* that are like airy custards. See CUSTARD and DULCE DE LECHE.

Guavas or guava shells, native squashes, or cashew apples might take the place of peaches or quinces in fruit desserts and pastes. Pumpkin seeds, cashews, coconut, peanuts, and even starchy plantains came to fill the place of Spanish almonds and other nuts in the Latin interpretation of nougats, marzipan, and other candies. See MARZIPAN and NOUGAT. Allspice, vanilla, and cinnamon-scented *ishpingo* (*Ocotea quixos*) began gracing the same custards as traditional cloves and cinnamon. The "fruits of the frying pan" received novel additions such as pumpkin or corn, while yuca and sweet potatoes were used to make thick, sweet creams and puddings.

There are other important ethnic footnotes to this essentially transplanted Spanish and Portuguese story. Immigrants from many parts of the world brought their own favorite desserts to Latin America or found particular commercial niches there. For example, one can recognize a large, abiding African presence in the world of Latin sweets. In the massive kitchens of tropical plantations, or in any urban kitchen presided over by African matrons, a hybrid sweet cuisine came to be. But unlike the influence of Africans in other areas of cooking, it began as a matter of adopting the Spanish and Portuguese models. Later, emancipated slaves used the skills learned on plantations and in the homes of the rich to develop a unique repertoire of sweets.

Finally, to the mystification of cooks from other traditions, canned milk made an indelible mark on the map of Latin sweets. That fresh milk can be difficult to produce and store in the tropics was surely a factor, but what is at work is a cultural preference born a century ago, when U.S. companies began producing and exporting sweetened condensed milk and evaporated milk. Custardy sauces and flans made with these convenience products are a late but important chapter in the story of Latin America's centuries-old love affair with sweetness. See EVAPORATED MILK; FLAN (PUDÍM); and SWEETENED CONDENSED MILK.

See also BRAZIL; CANDIED FRUIT; EGG YOLK SWEETS; FRUIT; FRUIT PASTES; FRUIT PRESERVES; MARMALADE; MEXICO; PORTUGAL; SPAIN; and ZALABIYA.

Martínez Llopis, Manuel. *Historia de la Gastronomía Española*. Madrid: Editorial Nacional, 1981.

Presilla, Maricel E. *Gran Cocina Latina: The Food of Latin America*. New York: Norton, 2012.

Zolla, Carlos. *Elogio del Dulce: Ensayo sobre la dulcería mexicana*. Mexico City: Fondo de Cultura Económica, 1988.

Maricel E. Presilla

Latini, Antonio (1642–1692), was among the first to write about *sorbetto*. The author of *Lo Scalco alla moderna* (The modern steward), Latini rose from street urchin to knight in a life fit for a fairy tale. He was born in a small town in the Marche region of Italy in 1642. Orphaned at five, he seemed destined for poverty. But he found work as a servant and learned to read, write, cook, and manage a noble household. Eventually, he became steward to the Spanish prime minister in Naples, and in 1693, three years before his death, Latini was knighted.

Published in two volumes in 1692 and 1694, Latini's book was, as the title promised, modern for its time. He recorded some of the first recipes using tomatoes and chilies and wrote about cooking with fresh herbs rather than sweet spices. He described the *trionfi* (triumphs)—sparkling sugar sculptures, gleaming jellies, and shimmering ices—that dazzled the eye on regal banquet tables. See SUGAR SCULPTURE.

Although Latini asserted that everyone in Naples was born knowing how to make *sorbette,* he was among the first to write about them. The vocabulary of ices and ice cream evolved over time. Latini did not use the word *gelato,* and instead of today's masculine *sorbetto* (singular) and *sorbetti* (plural), he used the feminine *sorbetta, sorbette.* His flavors included lemon, sour cherry, and strawberry. He also made a cinnamon ice with pine nuts, and two different chocolate ices. His *Sorbetta di Latte,* milk sorbet, was flavored with candied citron or pumpkin. None of Latini's *sorbette* contained eggs or cream. His recipes lacked detail since, he said, he did not want to upset professional sorbet makers by revealing their secrets.

See also CONFECTIONERY MANUALS; ICE CREAM; and ITALY.

Latini, Antonio. *Lo scalco alla moderna.* 2 vols. Naples: Parrino & Mutii, 1692–1694. Reprint, Milan: Appunti di Gastronomia, 1993.

Jeri Quinzio

lauzinaj (*lawzinaj, lawzinaq, luzina*) is a pastry and confection whose main ingredient is almonds (in Arabic, *lauz*). "Supreme judge of all sweets," "stones of paradise," "food of kings"—such were the glowing epithets heaped on this quintessentially medieval dessert of the Arab-Muslim world. No wedding should be without it, and dreaming of it presaged jolly times. In addition to its seductive taste, lauzinaj was believed to have beneficial medicinal properties. It helped induce sleep, nourish the brain, and ripen cold humors in chest and lungs.

Medieval Arabic recipes describe making lauzinaj in two ways. *Lauzinaj mugharraq* (drenched lauzinaj) consisted of sheets of pastry as thin as the inner membrane of eggs, stuffed and rolled with ground almond or other nuts like pistachios or walnuts that had been mixed with an equal proportion of sugar and bound with rosewater, and sometimes luxuriously perfumed with musk, mastic, and ambergris. See AMBERGRIS and FLOWER WATERS. The rolled pastry was then cut into smaller pieces, arranged in a container, and drenched in fresh almond or walnut oil and rosewater syrup. These dainty almond rolls were precursors of baklava, a dessert closely associated with Ottoman cuisine. See BAKLAVA. Nowadays such rolls are more commonly called *asabi' il-'arous* (bride's fingers) in the Arab world.

Lauzinaj yabis (dry lauzinaj) was a confection reminiscent of marzipan. It was either made without cooking by blending equal amounts of finely crushed skinned almonds and sugar, bound and scented with rosewater, musk, and camphor; or else it was cooked by adding finely ground almonds to a boiling honey or sugar syrup, which was beaten and thickened to taffy consistency before being cooled and shaped. Whether raw or cooked, dry lauzinaj was artistically formed into animals and vegetables by means of special molds; rolled into cylinders and cut into fingers; or spread onto a greased surface and cut into triangles and squares.

The legacy of *lauzinaj yabis* proved to be far-reaching as it found its way to medieval Europe via Muslim Spain, the Crusaders, and Latin translations of books on dietetics and cookery, where it was recorded as *losenges* or *lesynges,* and by other spellings as early as the thirteenth century. Subsequently, while similar almond confections came to be called "marzipan" and "macarons" in Europe, the Arabic-derived name "lozenge" came to designate cough drops, regardless of shape or content. See LOZENGE; MACARONS; and MARZIPAN. The diamond shape so closely associated with lauzinaj further gave its name to the geometric form known as a lozenge. Evidence of this connection to shape can be found in the long tradition of the Iraqi diamond-shaped confection called *lauzīna,* whether it is made with almond, coconut, quince, or orange rind.

See also MIDDLE EAST and PERSIA.

Nasrallah, Nawal, trans. *Annals of the Caliphs' Kitchens: Ibn Sayyār al-Warrāq's Tenth-Century Baghdadi Cookbook.* Leiden, The Netherlands: Brill, 2007.

Rodinson, Maxime. "Venice, the Spice Trade and Eastern Influence on European Cooking." In *Medieval Arab Cookery,* translated by Paul James, pp. 199–215. Totnes, U.K.: Prospect, 2001.

Nawal Nasrallah

layer cake—the home cook's dessert showpiece—consists of two or more sponge or butter cake rounds with icing, jelly, or cream between the layers. After chemical leaveners, improved ovens, and tools became widely available around 1870, cooks began to create an astonishing array of layer cakes. See CHEMICAL LEAVENERS. Sponge, pound, and butter cakes were used to form the layers, with flavors as varied as rosewater, vanilla, chocolate, spice, fruit, and carrot. See POUND CAKE and SPONGE CAKE.

Recipes for mille-feuille, puff pastry with jelly or cream between the layers, were described in cookbooks in seventeenth-century France and eighteenth-century England, foreshadowing the layering of cakes. See PASTRY, PUFF. "Jelly cakes" first appeared in the 1830 edition of Eliza Leslie's *Seventy-five Receipts for Pastry, Cakes, and Sweetmeats.* The cake batter was initially baked on griddles like pancakes but later was spread in shallow jelly cake pans or made into thicker cakes that were baked and then cut horizontally after cooling. Jelly cakes became enormously popular; in 1891, 600 competitors entered the Illinois State Fair Jelly Cake competition. The winner caused a controversy by using Angel Food Cake for her layers. See ANGEL FOOD CAKE.

An icing of egg whites and sugar, often with coconut, replaced jelly between the multiple layers of white butter cake to form the White Mountain Cake popular in the 1860s. The filling for the Lady Baltimore Cake, named after a delectable cake described in the 1906 novel *Lady Baltimore,* included cooked figs, nuts, and dates, while the Lane Cake, created a few years earlier in Alabama, used bourbon, raisins, nuts, and coconut. Nuts and coconut adorn the more recent German Chocolate Cake that calls for Baker's German Sweet Chocolate. See BAKER'S. Boston Cream Pie, made with sponge cake filled with custard and topped with chocolate glaze, is now the official dessert of Massachusetts. See BOSTON CREAM PIE. Another official state dessert is Maryland's multilayered Smith Island Cake, consisting of yellow cake with rich chocolate fudge icing. Tall stacks of 10 or more thin cakes either iced or spread with jelly were once common for holidays and special occasions in the American South, although they are now rarely prepared at home. Such cakes include the dried apple–laden Tennessee Stack Cake and Kentucky Jam Cake. See APPALACHIAN STACK CAKE.

In nineteenth-century Europe, several decadent cakes and tortes, such as the Sachertorte and Dobos torte, were created by professional bakers. See DOBOS TORTE and SACHERTORTE. Mrs. Beeton's influential *Book of Household Management* introduced the British to the Victoria Sandwich, a two-layer cake with jelly, in 1861. This cake is still served at teas. Other well-known European cakes include the Opéra Gâteau, conceived in a Paris bakery in the 1930s and made of almond sponge cake with coffee and chocolate filling, and the Black Forest Cake, a rich concoction of thin chocolate cake layers, cherries, kirsch, and whipped cream. See BLACK FOREST CAKE. The Dutch-Indonesian cake *Spekkock* or *lapis legit* is made by baking very thin layers in succession to form a tall, multilayered spice cake.

Although layer cakes of a single color were often baked, two-layer cakes could combine silver (white) and gold (yellow), or light and dark (spice and chocolate). Three layers might have a contrasting color sandwiched between two matching cakes, while four layers could feature completely different colors, as in the Harlequin Cake. The stacking of colors could be quite striking. *Ice-cream and Cakes,* from 1883, offered a version of Neapolitan Cake with red, white, and green layers to replicate the 1848 flag of Italian unification. The Angel Cake still popular in the United Kingdom (not to be confused with American Angel Food Cake) has three layers—white, pink, and yellow—baked in square pans, cut into bars, and then topped with white icing. An 1877 version of Dolly Varden Cake called for four layers of chocolate, white, rose, and yellow, although later recipes generally alternated only light and dark layers. See DOLLY VARDEN CAKE.

Creative layer cake designs include the Checkerboard Cake, formed by three layers filled with alternating rings of light and dark batter. Britain's Battenberg Cake from the late Victorian era is a loaf composed of two upper and lower squares of pink and yellow cakes encased in almond marzipan. Cakes can be formed into elaborate three-dimensional shapes by using special pans or by carving the cake layers accordingly. Although tiered wedding cakes tower over bite-sized petits fours, both are technically layer cakes. See WEDDING CAKE.

American cookbooks for home cooks contained a variety of layer cakes. Some offered over 30 recipes; in 1907 May Elizabeth Southworth published *One Hundred & One Layer Cakes.* One of the earliest uses of the term "layer cake" was in a section header in an 1873 Ohio community cookbook, the *Presbyterian Cook Book.* Previously, recipes for layer cakes had appeared under specific names, such as Jelly Cake or Ribbon Cake. The proliferation of layer cakes caused a naming frenzy, which continues in contemporary cookbooks, although the popularity of this type of cake has diminished.

See also BEETON, ISABELLA; ICING; SOUTH (U.S.); and TORTE.

Krondl, Michael. *Sweet Invention: A History of Dessert.* Chicago: Chicago Review Press, 2011.
Southworth, May. *One Hundred & One Layer Cakes.* San Francisco: Paul Elder, 1907.

Patricia Bixler Reber

lead, sugar of, known to chemists as lead(II) acetate or Pb $(CH_3COO)_2$, gets its name not from its undeniable resemblance to rock candy but from its taste. It is sweet, roughly as sweet per teaspoon as sugar—and only slightly more lethal than strychnine.

In the nineteenth century, when mercury was used as a remedy for maladies as serious as syphilis and as commonplace as constipation, sugar of lead (*saccharum saturni*) was also part of the European pharmacopeia. Ironically, given that one symptom of acute lead poisoning is an upset stomach, the chemical was occasionally prescribed in low doses for intestinal maladies. Lead poisoning came to be called "colic of Poitou," due to the once widespread use of lead in that winemaking region.

Sugar of lead is chemically classified as a salt, an array of positive ions and negative ions, usually crystalline in appearance. The iconic example, table salt, comprises equal numbers of positive sodium ions and negative chloride ions in a cubic array. Perhaps surprisingly, not all salts taste salty. Though sodium chloride is the touchstone of salty tastes, there are literally millions of known salts, with tastes ranging from bitter to sweet.

Lead acetate—dipositive lead ions interspersed between negatively charged acetate ions—is a sweet salt. So is lead carbonate, as are salts of yttrium and beryllium. So many beryllium salts are notably sweet that the original name for the element was glucinium, from the Greek for "sweet." The obvious downside to all these noncaloric sweeteners is their toxicity. Ingesting as little as 3 teaspoons of sugar of lead would be quickly fatal to the average 70-kilogram Roman emperor.

The Romans were reputed to have used lead acetate as a sweetener. *Sapa,* and its more concentrated sister *defructum,* were syrupy sweeteners produced by boiling down must, a mildly fermented grape juice. See GRAPE MUST. Must contains acetic acid, a source of acetate ions, which will react with the metal vessels to produce metal acetates. Copper salts are bitter, imparting an undesirable taste to the *sapa,* but lead salts are sweet and so did not affect the taste of the sweet syrups. Pliny the Elder notes this in his *Natural History* with regard to the production of *sapa* and *defructum*: "Leaden vessels should be used for this purpose, and not copper ones...." Chemical analyses of *sapa* produced according to recipes dating from the classical Roman period, using kettles of similar metallic composition as those found at Pompeii and other sites, suggest that the lead content of *sapa* was 850 milligrams per liter, many thousand times higher than what is generally allowable in drinking water. Even diluted and used sparingly, sweetening with *sapa* posed a serious risk.

Interestingly, *sapa*'s sweetness does not result from sugar of lead. The sugar of lead in a liter of *sapa* is equivalent to roughly a pinch of sugar, imperceptible to most palates. However, the concentrated grape juice in *sapa* contains both the sugars glucose and fructose at concentrations that would mimic the sweetness of 1 cup of table sugar per liter, completely drowning out any sweetness attributable to the sugar of lead. Neither *sapa* nor *defructum* would be all that sweet to modern taste buds; simple syrup, which has similar culinary uses to *sapa,* contains about 4 cups of sugar per liter.

The practice of adding lead metal to fermenting alcoholic beverages such as wines and ciders, leading to the in situ formation of sugar of lead, did not end with the Romans but was commonplace in Europe until the modern era. Lead and lead salts are widely available, and they are as deadly to bacteria as they are to humans; vintners observed that filtering fermentation mixtures through lead sieves or dropping some lead shot into bottled wine noticeably reduced spoilage. A firm connection between ingesting low levels of lead in these beverages and lead poisoning was finally made in the early nineteenth century, in part because of the correlation between outbreaks of colic of Poitou and the arrival of wine shipments containing lead.

Grout, James. "Lead Poisoning and Rome." In *Encyclopedia Romana.* http://penelope.uchicago.edu/~grout/encyclopaedia_romana/wine/leadpoisoning.html (accessed 5 September 2012).
Tepper, Lloyd B. "Industrial Plumbism: Antiquity to Modern Times." *IA. The Journal of the Society for Industrial Archeology* 33 (2007): 53–66.

Michelle M. Francl

leaf, gold and silver, are produced the same way, by pounding a piece of the metal between vellum pads until it is no more than a few micrometers thick. As inert metals, both are harmless to the human body and, although indigestible, are consumed in such small quantities that they simply pass through the digestive system.

In the nineteenth century jellies were sometimes decorated with either silver or gold leaf, and Mrs. Beeton describes a Christmas jelly of red currant decorated with both gold and silver leaf to imitate flames. See BEETON, ISABELLA. In contemporary European and American sugar craft, both types of leaf are used. Sugared almonds, coated in silver and gold leaf, are often served at weddings. A cake to celebrate a silver wedding anniversary (25 years of marriage) may have edible silver leaf over the icing, although removable silver decorations are used more often. Fancy chocolates are occasionally decorated with a small amount of gold leaf, to suggest luxury, and gold dust is sometimes sprinkled on cocktails and champagne. In Great Britain, a specialist supplier called Wright's of Lymm sells gold and silver leaf for culinary use. Dust, petals, and flakes made of gold and silver sell in greater quantity than the leaf.

Gold and silver leaf are widely used to decorate confectionery in the Middle East and the Indian subcontinent, especially in Pakistan, Northern India, and Bangladesh. See SOUTH ASIA. Silver is used more widely than gold. In Arabic, gold and silver leaf are both known as *waraq*, which means "leaf" or "paper." Both types of leaf are called *vark* in Hindustani. The word might also derive from the Sanskrit word *varaka*, which means a "cloak" or "cloth," or something that covers something else. In traditional Ayurvedic medicine, silver is regarded as an antimicrobial astringent, and gold is regarded as an aphrodisiac. In the bazaar at Lucknow in Uttar Pradesh, gold and silver leaf are manufactured in the traditional way. It is claimed that both metals hold aphrodisiac properties, which possibly implies that their health benefits are secondary to the decorative qualities and air of opulence.

A wide variety of Indian sweets are decorated with silver. Gold leaf features in the extremely rich and luxurious cuisine of the Nawabs, notably in a sweet bread pudding called *shahi tukra*, but it is less frequently used than silver. Silver leaf is especially favored for barfi, a type of fudge made from condensed milk. See BARFI. It can also be used in savory dishes, especially korma—the fact that a korma is generally made with yogurt implies that in India silver is associated with creaminess.

Recently, some dispute over the vegetarian nature of *vark* has arisen, mainly because of its method of manufacture between vellum pads. Strict vegetarians do not eat *vark*. Purity is more of an issue, with many tested samples of *vark* found to contain traces of nickel, lead, copper, chromium, cadmium, or manganese.

See also INDIA and MITHAI.

Banerjee, Satarupa. *The Book of Indian Sweets*. New Delhi: Rupa, 2006.

Connoisseur Gold. http://ediblegold.co.uk.

Shipperbottom, Roy. "Gold and Silver Leaf." In *The Oxford Companion to Food*, 3d ed., edited by Tom Jaine. New York: Oxford University Press, 2014.

Joe Roberts

Lebkuchen

See GINGERBREAD.

ledikeni is made by forming a mixture of *chhana* (fresh curd cheese) and flour into ping-pong–sized balls and stuffing them with cardamom-scented *nakuldana* (sugar granules). The balls are then fried and subsequently soaked in sugar syrup to yield a slightly crisp exterior and soft, juicy interior; the melted sugar filling bursts in your mouth as you bite into this sweet.

The various legends of ledikeni's origin point to a confectioner's tribute to a colonial ruler. Ashoke Kumar Mukhopadhyay, a connoisseur of sweets, recounts (1999) that the sweet was prepared by the well-known confectioner Bhim Nag to commemorate the birthday of Countess Charlotte Canning, popularly referred to as Lady Canning, wife of the Indian Viceroy Charles Canning. Christened after the confectioner, Bhimnag is a famous sweet shop in North Kolkata owned and managed by Nag's family, whose roots can be traced to the Hooghly district. In another story, the shop is credited with the invention during Lady Canning's visit to Calcutta (Kolkata's earlier name) in 1856, before the Sepoy Mutiny. In a travelogue piece on sweetshops in Kolkata, Rimli Sengupta states that the sweet was created by Bhimnag to celebrate her visit. Though Lady Canning succumbed to malaria within five years of her arrival, her name has come to be associated with the popular sweet that continues to occupy a revered position in postcolonial Bengal.

Bhimnag, the shop known for the discovery of ledikeni, has a history of christening sweets in honor of its patrons; other popular ones include Nehru Sandesh, created in honor of Motilal Nehru's visit to Calcutta in 1927–1928; and Ashubhog, named after the shop's patron Sir Ashutosh Mukhopadhyay, an eminent Calcutta author. See SANDESH. However, Nandalal Bhattacharya (1999) points to a different tale of origin. According to this version, after the Sepoy Mutiny of 1857, confectioners in the Bengali city of Berhampore prepared a special sweet to honor Lady Canning, who was supposedly touring with her husband, the viceroy. The sweet was dubbed "Lady Canning," but the Bengali tongue transmuted it into ledikeni. In the decades following Lady Canning's untimely death, ledikeni became the sweet of choice at fashionable Bengali gatherings.

Although ledikeni is similar to *pantua* (another fried sweet), the molten sugar syrup of lightly flavored cardamom powder makes it distinctive. It is impossible to know whether or not Lady Canning ever tasted her eponymous confection, but the sweet continues to occupy a prominent place in the pastry cases of Bhimnag and other sweetshops throughout West Bengal.

See also INDIA and KOLKATA.

Bhattacharya, Nandalal. "Bengali Sweets: Chhana Based Sweets." *Loksanskriti Gabeshana* 2, no. 2 (1999): 199–207.

Mukhopadhyay, Ashoke Kumar. "Sweets of Kolkata." 11 May 1999. http://lokfolk.blogspot.in/2009/05/sweetsofkolkata-ashokekumarmukhopadhyay.html (accessed 10 April 2010).

Sengupta, Rimli. "Sugar Trail: A Homage to the Entrepreneurial Spirit of Kolkata's Historic Sweet Shops." *Outlook Traveller*, 1 December 2009. http://travel.outlookindia.com/printarticle.aspx?263212 (accessed 27 February 2013).

Ishita Dey

legislation, historical, covers the laws affecting the availability of sweets. Historically, the single most important law of this type has been the protective tariff on sugar. Tariffs and other trade protections have been enacted—and, notably, repealed—by virtually every major sugar-producing and sugar-consuming nation since at least the sixteenth century. Without tariff protection, large-scale plantation sugar production in the Caribbean and Pacific islands might never have developed, nor would the sugar-refining industries in Europe have had such phenomenal success. Ultimately, the steady increase in per capita sugar consumption in the modern period depended on trade policies that stimulated production and dramatically lowered the price of sweets. See PLANTATIONS, SUGAR.

Mercantilist policies in Great Britain, France, Spain, and Portugal restricted trade to their respective colonies before the eighteenth century. European colonial powers reserved for themselves the right to buy and refine the sugar from their own colonies, which could neither buy nor sell from foreigners, except at the cost of high trade duties paid to the colonizing country. Planters, importers, and refiners thus enjoyed a state-authorized monopoly, which encouraged them to invest in sugar plantations. Gradually, through the eighteenth and early nineteenth centuries, all European nations moved toward what they called "free trade." Free trade did not mean that there were no tariffs. Instead, it meant that international trade was allowed, and that the colonies could sell their goods more widely. As a result, larger quantities of sugar—most of it produced by slave labor—entered the world market at ever-cheaper prices. Sweetened tea, jam, candies, cakes, and cookies grew in popularity and became affordable for middle- and eventually even low-income consumers.

In the late nineteenth century, Germany and other European countries promoted their domestic sugar beet industries by paying subsidies to exporters. The resulting competition between beet and cane sugar brought down world sugar prices even more. High sugar tariffs in the United States encouraged farmers to grow sugar beets and also stimulated huge increases in cane sugar production in Hawaii, Puerto Rico, the Philippines, and Cuba, all of which paid low or no tariffs. Higher production in the United States and its dependencies brought lower prices, leading to a considerable expansion in the range and sophistication of sweetened foods.

Since the 1990s tariff protection has fallen out of favor worldwide, replaced by multilateral free trade agreements and import quotas. The United States restricts its sweetener market through marketing allotments and flexible tariffs tied to import quotas and domestic consumption. As a result of its multilateral trade obligations, the United States waives import tariffs on a significant amount of imported sugar. Mexico imposed antidumping tariffs on high-fructose corn syrup (HFCS) in the late 1990s in an attempt to protect its sugar industry against the U.S. corn industry. The United States filed complaints with international trade organizations, after which Mexico rescinded the tariffs but imposed a 20 percent consumption tax on HFCS-sweetened beverages. For several years Mexican Coca-Cola enjoyed a special following in the United States because it was cane sugar–sweetened and presumably had a more authentic flavor. The United States and Mexico resolved the dispute in 2006, and HFCS now enters the Mexican food supply while Mexico exports cane sugar to the United States. Some commentators note that U.S. corn subsidies have contributed to the overabundance of cheap, corn-sweetened beverages and foods in North American diets.

Legislation regarding sanitation and food purity has also shaped the history of sweets. Adulterants were formerly quite common in candy and sugar in Europe and the United States. See ADULTERATION. Artificial colors in candy were especially dangerous, since bright colors were achieved with lead, copper, and other hazardous elements. France passed the first general laws prohibiting food adulteration in 1802. By the 1830s it had enacted prohibitions on a range of chemicals, minerals, and other adulterants. In Britain and the United States, news reports of children poisoned by cheap candies galvanized public opinion. Great Britain implemented pure food laws in the 1860s, and the United States did so in the 1900s. England and the United States resisted stringent national laws because they seemed to impinge on free trade (in the British case) and independence from government interference in private affairs (in the American case). These laws, along with inspections intended to assure hygienic conditions in candy factories, were only sporadically enforced. In the twentieth century new methods of laboratory analysis have revealed the dangers of contamination and made it easier to test candies. In 1963 the Codex Alimentarius was created to coordinate food safety and hygiene standards for international trade. It has no regulatory capacity but issues guidelines and model national legislation. In the United States, the Food and Drug Administration regulates food safety and hygiene.

In light of public health concerns over rising rates of obesity, diabetes, and heart disease in the 2000s, some reformers have proposed consumption taxes on sweets as a way to shape consumer behavior. By imposing special taxes on high-calorie, low-nutrient foods such as soft drinks, they hope people will eat less of those foods. Hungary imposed such a tax in 2011. Denmark debated whether to do so, as did New York City. Policy analysts remain uncertain whether such measures improve health outcomes, or if they unnecessarily stigmatize poor people's food choices.

See also CORN SYRUP; FRUCTOSE; SUGAR AND HEALTH; and SUGAR TRADE.

Galloway, J. H. *The Sugar Cane Industry: An Historical Geography from Its Origins to 1914*. New York: Cambridge University Press, 2005.

Mathias, Peter, and Sidney Pollard. *The Industrial Economies: The Development of Economic and Social Policies*. The Cambridge Economic History of Europe 8. Cambridge, U.K.: Cambridge University Press, 1989.

Mintz, Sidney. *Sweetness and Power: The Place of Sugar in Modern History*. New York: Penguin, 1985.

Wilson, Bee. *Swindled: The Dark History of Food Fraud, from Poisoned Candy to Counterfeit Coffee*. Princeton, N.J.: Princeton University Press, 2008.

April Merleaux

Leibniz Keks, flat, crisp biscuits made from flour, butter (12 percent), sugar, and eggs, represent the very definition of sweet biscuits for generations of Germans, having been produced since 1891. Back then, the pioneering Hanover merchant Hermann Bahlsen (1859–1919) imported modern tunnel ovens from Glasgow, designed packaging as distinctive as the biscuits' advertising, and named them after the German philosopher Gottfried Wilhelm Leibniz, a native of Hanover. From the start the convenient little boxes of biscuits were aimed at hungry travelers in an age of urban growth and an expanding network of railways.

Five years earlier Jean Romain Lefèvre and Pauline Isabelle Utile in Nantes had come up with the Petit Beurre LU biscuit in exactly the same design—a flat rectangle with scalloped edges. English biscuits seem to have been the inspiration for both, and indeed Leibniz Keks were originally called Leibniz cakes. But Bahlsen soon switched to the phonetic German version of the word. This move might have been a nod to the Germanification trend of the era, which frowned upon foreign words. However, *keks* has become a false friend, since it stands for "cookies"

These crisp biscuits, named after the German philosopher Gottfried Wilhelm Leipniz, were originally packaged as convenient travelers' snacks. During World War I they became soldiers' rations, and today they are a popular everyday treat. RAINER ZENZ

or "biscuits" rather than cake—its official dictionary meaning since 1911 when it entered the definitive *Duden*. During World War I Bahlsen advertised the Leibniz Keks as soldiers' rations, even commissioning a postcard series from well-known artists to promote them.

Although still family-owned, Bahlsen has grown into an international conglomerate specializing in cookies and savory snacks like potato chips. In 2013 the large gilded bronze Leibniz Keks hanging outside the company's Hanover headquarters disappeared under mysterious circumstances (in ransom notes, the thief posed as the *Sesame Street* Cookie Monster); it reappeared just as mysteriously some months later.

Leibniz Keks are an essential ingredient for *Kalter Hund*, an icebox cake popularized in the late 1960s and early 1970s that has become fashionably retro today: Keks are layered in a rectangular cake pan with a rich mixture of cocoa, sugar, and coconut butter, then chilled and cut into slices to serve.

Heinzelmann, Ursula. *Beyond Bratwurst: A History of Food in Germany*. London: Reaktion, 2014.

Ursula Heinzelmann

lemonade, a refreshing beverage that has been enjoyed throughout the world for hundreds of years, consists simply of lemon juice, water, and sugar. Lemons and sugar—both originating in India and following the same route to the Mediterranean—are a natural pair. The addition of water creates a cooling drink in hot climates, such as India, where salt is often added. Lemonade can be served with ice, as is French *citron pressé*, or frozen into *granita*, Italian style. See ITALIAN ICE.

Lemonade is appreciated primarily as a pleasurable and refreshing beverage, but it has also long been valued for its healthful qualities. The earliest written recipes for lemonade, some flavored with fruits or herbs, appeared in Arabic, in a twelfth-century medical cookbook *On Lemon, Its Drinking and Use*. The author, Egyptian physician Ibn Jumayʾ, recommended the drink for stimulating the appetite, aiding digestion, curing inflammations of the throat, and even treating "the intoxicating effects of wine." Lemonade, he wrote, "quenches one's thirst and revives one's strength."

Health recommendations for lemonade, sometimes including such nourishing ingredients as barley, eggs, or sherry, appeared in "invalid cookery" sections of British cookbooks starting in the sixteenth century. Lemonade's most important contribution to health was certainly its strong dose of vitamin C, even before the human need for this vitamin was recognized. Scurvy killed more than 2 million sailors before the British Royal Navy in 1795 ordered that the sailor's daily rum-and-water grog should henceforth contain lemon juice, which effectively ended the 300-year plague of the disease. (Lime juice was used for a time in the mid-nineteenth century, but it was found to be less effective than lemon juice. This brief period when lime juice was used was what caused some to dub the British sailors as "Limeys.")

In northern Europe before the seventeenth century, the high cost of both lemons and sugar restricted lemonade consumption to a necessary expense for the sick or an extravagant pleasure for the rich. But after sugar prices collapsed in the early 1600s (due to the expansion of West Indies plantations), lemonade became much more affordable. *Limonadiers*, or lemonade men, dispensed the hugely popular beverage from metal tanks carried on their backs. French cookbooks of the mid-1600s offered scores of lemonade recipes, flavoring the drink with spices, flowers, and scents including ambergris, musk, cinnamon, rosewater, jasmine, and orange blossoms.

The practice of spiking lemonade with alcohol is nearly as old as the beverage itself, but the American temperance movement of the mid-1800s endorsed the innocent nonalcoholic version as a favored "temperance drink." First Lady Lucy Webb Hayes, who shunned alcohol in the White House of the 1870s, was dubbed "Lemonade Lucy," adding to the beverage's publicity. Even as the temperance movement faded, lemonade remained a refreshing and wholesome summer drink of choice in the United States, at picnics and carnivals, circuses and fairs. See FAIRS. Italian immigrants operated pushcarts or stands selling iced lemonade in the summer, in cities and at the seashore. Pink lemonade was associated with circuses, although the story of its origin, which attributed its invention in the 1870s to a circus vendor named Henry Allott after he accidentally dropped red cinnamon candies into a batch of lemonade, is likely apocryphal. Cookbooks of the period suggested flavoring lemonade with pink or red fruit such as watermelon, strawberries, or cherries, so pink lemonade was nothing new.

In the late 1800s many vendors used tartaric acid to imitate lemon flavor, merely floating lemon slices on the surface to resemble the genuine article. Sunkist Growers, a citrus marketing cooperative, introduced frozen lemonade in the 1950s, promoting it as "the coolingest cooler of them all." Bottled lemonades and powdered lemonade mixes, some containing citric acid and artificial colors, vary in quality. In Great Britain, "lemonade" or "fizzy lemonade" may refer to a commercially produced, carbonated, lemon-flavored drink quite different from the natural homemade beverage of lemons, sugar, and water.

Sonneman, Toby. *Lemon: A Global History.* London: Reaktion, 2012.
Tolkowsky, Samuel. *Hesperides: A History of the Culture and Use of Citrus Fruits.* London: J. Bale, Sons & Curnow, Ltd., 1938.

Toby Sonneman

Lenôtre, Gaston (1920–2009), rose from humble beginnings on a small farm in Normandy to become one of France's most successful patissiers, caterers, and retailers. As founder of the renowned Lenôtre cooking school in Plaisir, west of Paris, he trained hundreds of professional pastry chefs. At the time of his death, Lenôtre was head of a worldwide group of 60 boutique pastry shops in 12 countries, as well as proprietor of the Michelin three-star Paris restaurant Le Pré Catalan. Revenues from his empire totaled $162 million in 2008.

Lenôtre fits into a continuum of French master pastry chefs that began with Marie-Antoine Carême (1786–1833) and continues with Pierre Hermé (1961–), who, having served an apprenticeship with Lenôtre from the age of 14, has called Lenôtre the greatest influence on his career. See CARÊME, MARIE-ANTOINE and HERMÉ, PIERRE. While Lenôtre never renounced the butter, cream, and cheese that are at the heart of the cuisine of Normandy, he is best known for modernizing pastry making in the 1960s. He lightened the era's traditionally heavy sweets by substituting airy mousses, flourless creams, and tropical fruit purées for the dense flour- and sugar-laden cake layers and buttercreams of that era.

His creations presaged the advent of nouvelle cuisine in the early 1970s, which demanded a return to simple presentations and the freshest ingredients. Led by the French chefs Paul Bocuse, Roger Vergé, Jean and Pierre Troisgros, and others, the nouvelle cuisine movement grew out of the spirit of revolt spurred by the student riots that took place in Paris in 1968.

Lenôtre's aesthetic could be small and chic, or highly dramatic. His chocolates and individual pastries were models of precision, balancing flavors and textures, and exquisitely presented. For the 1984 marriage of Victoire Taittinger (of the Taittinger Champagne–producing family), he created a massive, multitiered cake decorated with bunches of spun-sugar grapes (for the bride) and rocket ships made from brown nougat and multifarious éclairs (for the groom). To celebrate Lenôtre's eightieth birthday in 2000, his apprentices constructed a dramatic 33-foot-high cake at the Trocadéro gardens.

See also FRANCE and PASTRY SCHOOLS.

Gault, Henri. "Nouvelle Cuisine." In *Cooks and Other People: Proceedings of the Oxford Symposium on Food and Cookery 1995*, edited by Harlan Walker, pp. 123–127. London: Prospect, 1996.
Levy, Paul. "Gaston Lenotre: Pastry Chef Who Brought Patisserie into the Modern Age." *The Independent*, 15 January 2009. http://www.independent.co.uk/news/obituaries/gaston-lenotre-pastry-chef-who-brought-patisserie-into-the-modern-age-1366591.html.

Elizabeth Field

licorice, or liquorice, refers both to the leguminous plant (*Glycyrrhiza glabra*), especially its root, and to confections made from it. Its Latin name, meaning "sweet root," was given by the first-century herbalist Dioscorides. Although many other spices and herbs are compared to licorice, including anise, star anise, fennel, and chervil, its flavor is quite distinct and usually much stronger. The fresh or dried roots can be chewed directly as a kind of breath freshener and tooth cleanser, a practice common in Jamaica and elsewhere. Normally, however, the roots are chopped and boiled in water; the resulting sweet, aromatic liquid is reduced and dried into a flat, hard sheet, which is either broken up or scored into small chips. This is true licorice in its purest form, without added sugar. Versions like this, or molded into sticks, lozenges, or drops, are still common in Southern Europe, the most highly regarded coming from Calabria and Spain. Throughout Italy one can find hard, pure licorice made by companies such as De Rosa, Amarelli, or the popular Tabu, which has other flavors added, including mint. Sen-Sen, once popular in the United States as a breath freshener, is similar, though it too contains other flavorings.

Licorice was long considered a medicinal plant, taken as a diuretic and expectorant and mixed into other medicines as a flavoring. As the original medicinal uses proliferated, they gradually encouraged popular consumption for pleasure. John French's *The Art of Distillation* (1651) provides a good example of how medicinal drugs become recreational. His recipe for Usque-bath or Irish aqua vitae is made with alcohol, sherry, raisins, dates, cinnamon, nutmeg, and "the best English licorish Sliced, and bruised." He explains that this preparation is commonly used in surfeits as a remedy for the stomach, but the pleasant flavor certainly commended it for any occasion.

During the twentieth century these medicinal associations were lost, and licorice is now mostly eaten as candy, although some modern medicinal uses still exist for substances derived from it. The active ingredient called glycyrrhiza has various negative side effects, so it is often removed from licorice-based medicines. In this form it is used to treat peptic ulcers as well as coughs and asthma. Some studies have shown that licorice also raises the blood pressure; others have connected licorice to lower testosterone levels in men. Licorice (*gan cao*) has played a major role in traditional Chinese medicine for a wide variety of ailments, especially those causing bodily inflammation.

Candy made from licorice usually includes sugar, cornstarch, gum arabic, or gelatin as a binder and to make it chewy. Ralph Thickness, in his *Treatise on Foreign Vegetables* (1749), provides several detailed recipes for licorice confections. Most include some form of starch, powdered sugar, and gum, as well as flavorings such as orange flower water. See FLOWER WATERS. His recipe for Liquorice Juice of Blois can still be followed today. Despite the name, it produces a solid candy:

> Take of Gum Arabick grossly pounded iv lb. Sugar iii lb. Liquorice, dried scraped and bruised ii lb. Infuse the Liquorice for twenty-four Hours in xxx lb. of water. Divide the strained Liqor into three Parts, in two of which dissolve the Gum Arabick over a slow fire, and pass it through a Hair-Sieve; then boil it with the remaining part of the Liquor to the consistence of a Plaister, adding the sugar toward the end, and stirring continually to make it white.

In the Netherlands, where licorice is highly popular, salt is traditionally added to "drop" or coin-shaped candies. Other shapes include Katjes Katzenpfötchen (little cat's paws). Germany's Haribo company produces colorful, unsalted Lakritzkonfekt. See HARIBO. In England the Pomfret or Pontefract Cake is a similar confection. Ammonium chloride is added to a version in Finland called *salmiakki*, which gives it a distinct alkaline flavor. These candies can also be used to flavor distilled spirits.

In the United States, licorice usually refers to a twisted stick of chewy candy, a long lace or whips, all of which are manufactured industrially. These might be black licorice, or strangely red, containing no actual licorice but artificially flavored to taste vaguely like strawberry. Twizzlers and Red Vines are the two best-known producers of this kind of licorice, though other companies have produced a wide range of flavors. Thus, licorice has become a generic candy type, as opposed to a particular flavor, in the United States.

There are also a wide range of confections flavored with licorice, such as small, candy-coated pellets; brightly colored pink, yellow, and blue layer-cake-like squares; soft black and white drops; and other curious shapes. These forms mixed together are known as "allsorts," the most renowned producer of which is Basset's in Sheffield, England.

Another iconic licorice-flavored confection are the small, candy-coated pellets known as Good and Plenty, which were once vigorously advertised on TV with the figure of Choo-Choo Charlie. This candy, like most licorice candies, has dropped dramatically in popularity in the United States. Once common candies such as crows, black jack, and plain black licorice whips are increasingly difficult to find.

See also CHILDREN'S CANDY; STARCH; and TRAGACANTH.

French, John. *The Art of Distillation*, p. 45. London: Richard Coates, 1651.
Thickness, Ralph. *Treatise of Foreign Vegetables*, p. 24. London: J. Clarke, 1749.

Ken Albala

Life Savers originated in 1912 when Clarence Crane, head of the Queen Victoria Chocolate Company, created a mint that would not melt like chocolate in the humid Cleveland, Ohio, summer. His Pep O Mint flavored candy with a center hole looked like a miniature life preserver. (Ironically, his son, the Romantic poet Hart Crane, leapt to his death without a life preserver in the Gulf of Mexico 20 years later.)

By then, the Life Saver formula had been sold to brothers Robert and Edward Noble of Greenwich, Connecticut, who packaged them in a foil tube. Candies with new flavors of Orange, Lemon, and Lime were crystalline rather than opaque. Other early flavors included WintOgreen, CinnOmon, ClOve, LicOrice, ChocOlate, MaltOmilk, CrystOmint, Anise, Butter Rum, Cola, and Root Beer. In 1935 the Five Flavor roll was introduced, containing Pineapple, Orange, Cherry, Lemon, and Lime candies.

During World War II, other candy companies donated sugar rations to the Life Savers Corporation, enabling the production of millions of candy boxes to pack into field ration kits as a reminder of home. "Life Saver Sweet Story" books, 10 rolls in a cardboard book-shaped box, became collectible Christmas treats. The candy rolled out in New York and Ontario, Canada, until a merger with Beech-Nut in 1956 moved production to Canajoharie, New York.

Kraft Foods bought the company in 2000 and production returned to Canada. The Wrigley Company purchased Life Savers in 2004, adding Pops, Gummies, Shapes, Hawaiian Fruits, and Fruit Tarts to the Life Savers brand. More than 40 flavors have been introduced in the candy's 100-plus-year history, among them Piña Colada, Tangerine, and Musk in Australia. The Life Savers Five Flavors, now Pineapple, Orange, Cherry, Raspberry, and Watermelon, are most often found in a bag or bulk pack of 20 rolls.

See also CANDY PACKAGING and HARD CANDY.

Ohio History Central. "Clarence A. Crane." http://www.ohiohistorycentral.org/w/Clarence_A._Crane (accessed 8 November 2013).
Wm. Wrigley Jr. Co. "Brands/Life Savers/History." http://www.wrigley.com/global/brands/life-savers.aspx (accessed 8 November 2013).

Ardath Weaver

Lindt, Rodolphe (1855–1909), improved the smoothness and melting quality of Swiss chocolate by devising a revolutionary method called "conching," whereby extra cocoa butter is kneaded into the chocolate mixture during the manufacturing process. The Lindt brand, over time, has attained almost iconic status: "Whenever I am driving from Switzerland to Austria...a few miles south of the city of Zurich [near the Lindt & Sprüngli factory in Kilchberg], I slow down, lower the car window...and inhale deeply and happily, because the air is always delightfully charged with the fragrance of chocolate." So wrote Joseph Wechsberg in the 19 October 1957 issue of *The New Yorker* magazine.

Rodolphe Lindt was born in Bern, Switzerland, into the family of a pharmacist politician. After training as an apothecary, he founded his own chocolate factory in Bern in 1879. At that time, chocolate was essentially just a mixture of cocoa solids and sugar, which tasted somewhat coarse and dry. To improve the texture, Lindt added extra cocoa butter to the mixture and invented a "conche" machine, with a long, heated stone trough, curved at each end and named for its resemblance to a conch shell. The machine was fitted with a roller to work the chocolate mass back and forth at a temperature of 131° to 185°F (55° to 85°C). Stone conches are still used today, in addition to modern rotary conches that knead the mass intensively. Conching may take from several hours to a week, depending on the quality desired. It improves the finished product's flavor and enables it to melt easily on the tongue.

In 1899 Lindt joined forces with Rudolf Sprüngli, who had built a chocolate manufacturing plant in Kilchberg, outside of Zurich. The facility is still used as one of the company's European production sites.

See also CHOCOLATE, LUXURY and SWITZERLAND.

Richardson, Tim. *Sweets*. New York and London: Bloomsbury, 2002.

Wechsberg, Joseph. "The Chocolate-Scented Air." *The New Yorker*, 19 October 1957, pp. 91–119.

Elizabeth Field

Linzer Torte, replete with spices and fruit, has for more than 300 years been the culinary representative of the provincial city of Linz on the Danube River in Upper Austria. Nineteenth-century travel books have two recurring themes in connection with Linz: *Schöne Linzerin*, beautiful Linz woman, and *Linzer Torte*. The beauty of the women of Linz was emphasized by their elegant traditional costume, including a precious golden bonnet. However, it is doubtful that they actually wore this costume for baking, as was depicted on the cover of one of the oldest Linz cookery books, published in 1846.

Linzer Torte is the oldest torte with a geographical designation. See TORTE. It developed over time from the multitude of exquisite almond cakes that were popular in Austria during the baroque period and eventually become well known throughout Europe, spreading along the trade routes that intersected Linz on the Danube in all directions. To this day, Linzer Torte is regarded as a traditional Christmas cake in Baden-Württemberg in southwest Germany. In Vienna, Linzer Torte was the most popular cake until the invention of Sachertorte. See SACHERTORTE. Emigrants took the popular cake to all continents. As early as 1855, Linzer Torte was well known in Milwaukee, thanks to the Austrian musician, painter, and poet Franz Hölzlhuber (1826–1898), who earned his living by baking Linzer Torte during a period of economic hardship. A century later other prominent émigrés, the von Trapp family of *Sound of Music* fame, spread Linzer Torte's reputation to Stowe, Vermont.

The earliest known recipes for Linzer Torte are found in the 1653 cookery manuscript of Countess Anna Margarita Sagramosa, now in the Stiftsbibliothek Admont in Styria, Austria. At that time Linzer Torte was served in the form of a *Schüsseltorte* (dished torte), which was essentially a sweet pie filled with stewed fruit. See PIE. The first printed recipe was published in 1718 in Augsburg as part of the famous *Neues Saltzburgisches Koch-Buch* by Conrad Hagger, who proposed the "good and sweet Lintzer-dough" for the torte. Today, the largest collection of historical Linzer Torte recipes may be found at the Upper Austrian provincial museum (Oberösterreichisches Landesmuseum) in Linz, but many Upper Austrian families guard their own traditional recipe, and each torte tastes a little different.

Owing to its expensive ingredients, Linzer Torte remained a status symbol well into the nineteenth century, especially when served to guests. Almonds and lemon zest, fresh butter, precious cane sugar, and the finest white flour were used for the dough, which was refined with prized spices like cinnamon, cloves, nutmeg, and cardamom. The earliest fillings consisted of desirable fruit such as quince and peach. Later, as spices were added in larger quantities and threatened to dominate the sweet quince aroma, tart red fruits were used instead, including red currants, cherries, and raspberries.

The torte's characteristic lattice decoration is mentioned from the start. Copperplates in Hagger's cookery book illustrate lattice toppings as impressive works of art, rolled or cut from the dough or applied by piping. However, not all early Linzer Tortes looked alike. Some were multilayered, filled with various fruits, and garnished with colored icing and candied fruit. See CANDIED FRUIT and ICING. Others featured an especially decorative spiral pattern. These variations in taste and appearance reflected the baroque sensibility.

Today, Linzer Tortes tend to be uniform in appearance. The classic Linzer Torte is now unthinkable without a lattice top, often decorated with slivered almonds. However, almonds have disappeared from the dough, replaced by hazelnuts, and occasionally walnuts. Combined with the spices, these nuts yield a darker dough; hence, the term "dark Linzer Torte" in contrast to the "light Linzer dough" made with almonds. In either case, the dough can be worked like a short crust or made using eggs and beaten until fluffy. See SHORTBREAD. Cinnamon, cloves, and red currant jam are generally used for the filling. The torte should be allowed to mature for a few days after baking for its fine taste to develop.

The light Linzer dough with almonds and lemon forms the base for a number of smaller pastries categorized as "Linzer Bäckerei" (baked goods), including *Linzer Augen* (eyes) and *Linzer Kipferl* (crescents), both filled with tart red currants. The simplest forms of *Linzer Bäckerei* are rolled cookies in the shapes of little stars, moons, rings, and so on. See ROLLED COOKIES. It is also possible to shape softer dough into *Linzer Stangerl* (little bars) and *Linzer Krapferl* (tartlets). All of these cookies, which are ubiquitous in Austrian pastry shops, may be filled with jam, coated with chocolate, and decorated with nuts and frosting. Linzer Torte's offsprings also include the popular *Linzer Schnitten* and *Linzer Weichseltorte*.

See also AUSTRIA-HUNGARY.

Faissner, Waltraud. *Linzerische Torten auf andere Art.* Erweiterte Neuauflage. Linz: Oberösterreichisches Landesmuseum, 2010.

Meixner, Maria E. *Das neue, große, geprüfte und bewährte Linzer Kochbuch. 13. Aufl.* Linz, 1846. http://www.alteskochbuch.at/kochbuchdrucke.html.

Schlager, Liselotte. *Linzer Torte.* Linz: Landesverlag, 1990.

Waltraud Faissner

liqueurs, including cordials and ratafias, represents a broad category of alcoholic beverages. Although they can be consumed neat or in cocktails, they are also called for in a range of cake and dessert recipes.

David A. Embury, in the 1958 third edition of his classic text *The Fine Art of Mixing Drinks,* devoted an entire chapter to the different types of liqueurs available and how to use them. Today, according to the Distilled Spirits Council of the United States, liqueurs outsell several other major spirits in America, including single-malt Scotch, bourbon, gin, tequila, and cognac. Liqueurs encompass alcohol produced from a wide range of ingredients and made all over the world.

The Alcohol and Tobacco Tax and Trade Bureau (TTB), which regulates the labeling and taxation of the spirits industry, uses the terms "liqueurs" and "cordials" interchangeably and makes no distinction between the two. The TTB's definition for the overall category centers on a few key points. A liqueur is a flavored spirit that must include at least 2.5 percent sugar by weight. The base can be any kind of spirit, and it can be mixed or redistilled with all sorts of fruits, flowers, plants, juices, or other natural flavorings and extracts made from infusions or macerations. The U.S. government has also set definitions for liqueur subcategories, such as sloe gin, sambuca, kümmel, triple sec, and ouzo.

According to the *Oxford English Dictionary* (*OED*), the first use of the word "liqueur," which comes from the French word *liquor,* occurred in 1742. Other sources suggest that it stems from the Latin word *liquefacere,* which means "to melt." The origins of "cordial" date back even further, to the late 1300s. The root of the word can be traced to the Latin word *cor,* which means "heart." Cordial originally referred to an invigorating drink that was comforting or exhilarating.

To confuse things even further, there are also ratafias to contend with. Jerry Thomas, a pioneering bartender in the 1800s, lists more than a dozen recipes for ratafias—flavored with everything from cherries to black currants to green-walnut shells to angelica seed—in the appendix of his seminal book *How to Mix Drinks, or The Bon Vivant's Companion* (1862). He starts off the section by stating that "every liqueur made by infusions is called ratafia; that is, when the spirit is made to imbibe thoroughly the aromatic flavor and color of the fruit steeped in it; when this has taken place the liquor is drawn off, and sugar added to it; it is then filtered and bottled." The earliest ratafias were made by crushing peach, cherry, apricot, or bitter almond kernels and infusing them in brandy or spirits for a few months; the kernels were then strained out and the alcohol sweetened. Later versions mixed juice pressed from fruits such as cherries, blackberries, and grapes with brandy and sugar and left the mixture to age—a safer process, as it eliminated any risk of cyanide poisoning from the kernels. The *OED*'s definition of "ratafia" is shorter but essentially the same as Jerry Thomas's, with the first reference dating back to 1670 from a print in the collection of the British Museum. And the dictionary adds another layer: "ratafia" also refers to a sweet French aperitif made from an aged mix of brandy and grape juice. It can also mean a cake or biscuit flavored with the liquor. Although the majority of people generally use the more general terms "liqueur" or "cordial," "ratafia" occasionally still shows up on menus and in cookbooks. The TTB, however, does not recognize it as a separate category.

Liqueurs can be divided into a few main categories. Many herbal liqueurs were originally created by alchemists or monks and were thought of as remedies for common ailments. They were used to sweeten bitter drugs such as quinine; however, today's products containing quinine are usually aperitif wines, not liqueurs. Spirits were originally used as the base since they could preserve the herbs, spices, and extracts—one reason why some believed that alcohol was the water of life. (The names "whiskey" and "eau-de-vie" originated as terms for the supposed "water of life.") The recipes for these elixirs were often secret and guarded carefully. To this day, only two people know the complete formula for green Chartreuse, which is made by French monks and calls for 130 different herbs and plants.

Other liqueurs are floral-flavored, like Crème de Violette, necessary for the delicious (and classic) gin-based Aviation cocktail. And a tremendous variety of fruit liqueurs exist—from best-selling triple sec and curaçao, both flavored with oranges, to cherry liqueurs like the Danish Cherry Heering, a key ingredient in the Singapore Sling. There is even Luxardo Maraschino Liqueur, which is distilled from Italian marasca sour cherries and aged in Finnish ash-wood vats.

Some brands use nuts, like the Italian hazelnut-flavored Frangelico that dates back to the 1700s. It is based on an elixir made by monks living in Piedmont. Cream versions are also an option, such as Baileys Irish Cream, one of the best-selling liqueurs in the world that calls for Irish whiskey. Coffee-and-rum-based varieties include Kahlúa and Tia Maria.

The category of liqueurs is certainly diverse, partially because many families traditionally produced their own liqueurs; a number of brands, like the Italian amaretto Disaronno, started out as personal recipes. Not that long ago liqueurs had a much larger mixological profile than they do today. In the 1950s, 1960s, and 1970s, liquor cabinets were filled with bottles of elixirs like Drambuie, a mix of Scotch, Scottish honey, spices, and herbs and the key ingredient in the classic Rusty Nail (one part Drambuie, one part Scotch). Harvey Wallbangers and Golden Cadillacs powered the 1970s nightlife scene, and both recipes require the sweet Italian liqueur Galliano, which is made from a secret recipe calling for 30 spices, herbs, and plant extracts. Galliano was also the secret ingredient in the Harvey Wallbanger cake, a Bundt cake as trendy in the 1970s as its namesake drink. But the granddaddy of all liqueur-centric drinks is the Pousse-Café, made by layering different liqueurs by their densities so that they do not mix. The finished product looks like an impressive—and colorful—slice of layer cake.

These concoctions were so popular that David A. Embury included this cautionary note in *The Fine Art of Mixing Drinks* (first published in 1948): "You probably would not try to eat a five-pound box of chocolates before dinner as an appetizer, and if you did try it you would probably get thoroughly sick. For precisely the same reason (only more so) you should not try to consume several cocktails whose principal ingredient is a conglomeration of heavy-bodied, high-proof, syrupy liqueurs."

His advice, on both ends, still holds up today.

Over the last few years, thanks to the rebirth of the cocktail and bartenders unearthing vintage recipes, interest in liqueurs has grown. But the learning curve is steep, since the current generation of bartenders and drinkers needs to be taught how to drink liqueurs and how to use them properly in cocktails. However, herbal liqueurs have certainly caught on. The bitter Italian Fernet-Branca has been embraced around the country by bartenders, who pour each other shots of the liqueur as a professional courtesy.

Importers both large and small are now flooding the U.S. market with products from across the globe, like the complex herbal Zwack Unicum from Hungary and the artichoke-based Cynar from Italy. And old favorites, such as the orange-and-cognac Grand Marnier and the citrus-and-brandy Tuaca, are making a play for new drinkers who might not have tasted their products before. These brands are sponsoring bartending contests and hiring celebrity ambassadors.

A number of new liqueurs have recently been created. The most popular (and easiest to find in the United States) is St-Germain, an elderflower-flavored liqueur produced in France and packaged in what looks like a jumbo belle époque perfume bottle. The concoction can be mixed with virtually any spirit and even dry white wine, which has made it ubiquitous in cocktail bars over the last few years. (It has done so well that rum giant Bacardi purchased the brand from its founder, Robert Cooper, in early 2013 for an undisclosed sum.) Another successful launch has been the French Domaine de Canton, a sweet ginger liqueur.

Even though many liqueurs hail from Europe, you need not travel far to find them. A number of craft distilleries across the United States, such as Clear Creek Distillery in Portland, Oregon, are making liqueurs from local ingredients; Clear Creek produces seven different bottlings, including cranberry, blackberry, loganberry, and cassis.

See also MEDICINAL USES OF SUGAR.

Embury, David A. "Liqueurs." In *The Fine Art of Mixing Drinks*, by David A. Embury, pp. 27, 177–188. New York: Doubleday, 1958.

Meehan, Jim. "Liqueurs." In *The PDT Cocktail Book*, by Jim Meehan, pp. 314–316. New York: Sterling Epicure, 2011.

Thomas, Jerry. *The Bartenders Guide: How to Mix Drinks*, pp. 228–233. New York: Dick & Fitzgerald, 1862.

Noah Rothbaum

literature, in its representation of sweets, presents a wide range of meanings, both positive and negative. Sweets appear in almost every form of imaginative writing from the Hindu Vedas onward. When sweets grace the table, they also grace the page. A society that develops a culture of sweets tends to both portray and examine that culture in its literature, both in the sense of celebrating the variety and frequency of sweet dishes, and in the depth of meaning that sweets carry in that literature. Sweets and sweetness are remarkably pliable, employed to illustrate notions of eroticism, aesthetics, innocence, immaturity, comfort, luxury, satire, disgust, and the uses of power, to name a few. Throughout history, the literature of sweetness has featured prominently in societies that brought confection to high levels of artistry, especially ancient India, where sugar refining was invented; the medieval Arab lands, which brought the art of sugar to new heights; late medieval and Renaissance Europe, which elaborated upon the mystical ramifications of sweetness; and the post-industrial Western world, in which sugar's declining expense brought it into every household.

Ancient and Classical Literature

The early history of sweets in literature is hardly distinguishable from the early history of sweets themselves, since much of our knowledge about ancient confectionery derives from imaginative writing. The first references to sweets appear in the Hindu Vedas (ca. 2000–800 B.C.E.). See HINDUISM. The Rig Veda describes the ancient Aryans as driving their chariots "while drinking honey, listening to the beautiful humming of the bees, with their chariots also humming like bees, drinking milk laced with honey." Cane sugar appears first in the Atharva Veda, used as a metaphor for love: the lover offers to enclose his beloved in a ring of sugarcane to both protect and entrap her. Specific sweets figure prominently in the Hindu epic Ramayana; for instance, Rama and the other princes of the narrative are conceived after their mothers eat magic portions of kheer, or rice pudding. Ganesh, the elephant god who was the legendary writer of the other major epic of the subcontinent, the Mahabharata, is associated with a gluttonous passion for *modaka*, a sweet dumpling still made during ceremonies to worship him. Numerous references to sweets occur throughout ancient Indian literature. See INDIA and MODAKA.

Although less prominent than in South Asia, sweets also feature in early East Asian literature. "Fried honey-cakes of rice flour and malt-sugar sweetmeats" appear in the third century B.C.E. Chinese poem "The Summons of the Soul" as an enticement for a lost soul to return to its body. More metaphorically, the "The Filial Piety Sutra" (ca. 589–906 C.E.), a key text of Mahayana Buddhism, describes the mother's "kindness of eating the bitter herself and saving the sweet for the child." See BUDDHISM; CHINA; EAST ASIA; and SOUTH ASIA. Honey-based sweets also figure somewhat in Ancient Greek and Roman literature (sugar was too rare for regular use) as luxurious comestibles. See ANCIENT WORLD and HONEY. In the climax of Aristophanes's allegorical play *Knights*, the demagogue Cleon withholds most of a *plakous* (a cake) from the Athenian people and loses their love. See PLACENTA. In Plato's *Republic*, Socrates approvingly notes the fact that the warriors of the *Iliad* abstain from sweets. Greco-Roman literature does make significant use of "sweet" (in Greek, *gluku*; in Latin, *dulcis* or *suavis*) as a rhetorical term, imbuing it with a range of aesthetic and emotional meanings. Sappho famously uses the term *glukupikron*, sweet-bitter, to describe the paradoxical intensity of erotic love, while Martial contrasts his "salty" satires with the sickly sweet poems of his rivals.

Medieval and Early Modern Literature

Medieval Arabic literature, which, like ancient Indian literature, was written in the shadow of sugarcane, is positively obsessed with sweets and sweetness. In one tradition collected in the *Ḥadīth*, even the prophet Muhammad sighs over *fālūdhaj*, a dish made of wheat, honey, and clarified butter, though the meaning of that sigh was roundly debated. See ISLAM; MIDDLE EAST; and PERSIA. Several stories in *1001 Nights* revolve around sweets, such as the battle between a husband and wife over a *kunafāh* (a fried pancake at that time) sweetened with cheap molasses instead of honey. Although satirists in every age use lowly food as a way of deflating noble abstractions and exposing pretensions, Arab satirists employ sweets with unusual abandon. The fifteenth-century satirical poet Ibn Sūdūn continually mentions bananas with honey and sugar syrup, about which he waxes, "My heart is madly in love since it misses you."

Following the lead of the Greeks and Romans, medieval European authors elevated sweetness to a term of indispensable poetic, religious, and social efficacy. "No word is used more often in the Middle Ages," writes Mary Carruthers, "to make a positive judgment about the effects of works of art" (2006, p. 999). Meanwhile, in Italian literature, the *dolce stil novo*, or "sweet new style," of Dante, Cavalcanti, and other poets heralded a new focus on courtly love and rhetorical artistry; it became one of the most influential literary movements in medieval Europe. Petrarch's *Rime Sparse* extended the power of sweetness by establishing it as a primary term for describing the complex experience of love, both earthly and divine.

Renaissance authors continued to concern themselves with the role of sweetness in aesthetic, erotic, and other kinds of social experience, but with new intensity, as cane sugar began to enter the consumer market in larger quantities and to take a major role in imperialist conquest. See SUGAR TRADE. When Frances Meres referred to his contemporary as the "honey-tongued" Shakespeare with his "sugared sonnets," he was drawing attention to the subtlety and erotic content of Shakespeare's poems. Shakespeare's plays also use sweetness in a variety of ways. "Sweet Valentine," calls Proteus in *The Two Gentlemen of Verona*, in a display of intense male friendship and (perhaps sexually charged) affection. "Sweets to the sweet," mourns *Hamlet*'s Gertrude as she scatters flowers over Ophelia's grave. In *Antony and Cleopatra*, Antony worries that all his former allies "do discandy, and melt their sweets / On blossoming Caesar" after Cleopatra's betrayal during the Battle of Actium. (The term "candy" entered English during the sixteenth century from Italian; "discandy" seems to be Shakespeare's invention.)

Starting in the seventeenth century, when chocolate and ever-cheaper sugar arrived in Europe, literature was more saturated with specific sweets, while the term "sweetness" grew so universal as to become essentially generic. Now available in large numbers to the middle and lower classes, sweets took on new meanings while retaining the older sense of luxury. In England, puddings, simple but rich, seem especially freighted in this regard, as evidenced by the Christmas pudding, "like a speckled cannon-ball," that caps the holiday meal in Charles Dickens's *A Christmas Carol*, and which Bob Cratchit regards "as the greatest success achieved by Mrs. Cratchit since their marriage." See PUDDING. But increasingly, sweets exhibit a dark side, evoking decay, mortality, and power, as in the quietly sadistic Guy de Maupassant story "The Cake," where being the cake cutter at a party is transformed from high honor to awful burden. The Industrial Revolution's increasing infatuation with and unease about rampant consumption (of not only sugar but also commodities more generally) no doubt play a significant role in this change of emphasis.

Modern and Contemporary Literature

The iconic sweet in modern literature is surely Marcel Proust's madeleine, the very crumbs of which call forth "the vast structure of recollection" that inspires his novel *In Search of Lost Time*. See MADELEINE. The association between sweets and memory runs strongly through twentieth-century literature, perhaps partly because of the increasing availability of sweets in childhood, which helped inspire sugary structures of recollection in adult writers. M. F. K. Fisher, another master of the connection between food and memory, opens her memoir *The Gastronomical Me* with a meditation on eating "the grayish-pink fuzz" from a kettle of strawberry jam, and evokes the childhood passion for sweets throughout her work.

Childhood experience, coupled with biological and cultural associations between sweetness and pleasure, frequently give sweets in modern literature the symbolic meaning of innocence (often lost) or of delight for its own sake. See SYMBOLIC MEANINGS. The joys and sadness of ice cream, for instance, surface in the work of such disparate poets as Osip Mandelstam ("Ice cream! Sun. Light airy cakes") and Wallace Stevens, whose "Emperor of Ice Cream" requests, "Let be be finale of seem." In Ludwig Bemelmans's story "Pêche Melba," a young girl in a convent school deploys the iconic sweetness of peach desserts as a form of resistance against her teachers' cruelty. For the child protagonist of William Gass's story "Sweets," cheap candy stands as "the center of all satisfaction." A scene in John Steinbeck's *Grapes of Wrath*—two impoverished boys are given a small and spectacular gift of penny candy—fuses innocent desire, the grinding suffering of poverty, and the potential of human generosity in a single red-striped sugar stick. See PENNY CANDY.

If sweets conjure innocence, they just as commonly evoke more adult experiences, such as sexual desire, guilt, disgust, and abuse of power. Writers frequently exploit this tension in sweetness between childhood pleasures and adult depredations. It is no accident that the eponymous protagonist of Terry Southern and Mason Hoffenberg's infamous 1958 pornographic novel is named Candy, or that, as in earlier literatures, sweetness is associated linguistically with (especially female) sexuality, as in phrases like "eye candy" for an attractive person, or "honey" and "sugar" as endearments for lovers. See SEXUAL INNUENDO and SLANG. Perceived links between sweetness and female appetite, coupled with contemporary rhetoric about the dietary perils of sweets, have also led to a strong association between sweetness and guilt, especially for female characters. See GENDER. Anita Desai's novel *Fasting, Feasting* features a bulimic teenage girl who binges guiltily and revoltingly on candy bars to a life-threatening degree—she comes to stand as a symbol in the novel for the errancy and feminization of modern American consumerism. Other works link femininity, sexuality, innocence, and sweetness through milder means, as in the magic realism of Laura Esquivel's *Like Water for Chocolate* or the celebration of the appetites in Joanne Harris's *Chocolat*.

Disgust, the dark side of pleasure, features prominently in modern depictions. In Thomas Pynchon's *Gravity's Rainbow*, Slothrop encounters a series of English hard candies, each redolent of revolting flavors like "mayonnaise and orange peels": biting into them is "like a journey to the center of some small, hostile planet." More disturbingly, authors often use sweetness to capture the intense disgust and horror of children forced too quickly into adulthood, as in Arundhati Roy's *The God of Small Things*, in which the "orangedrink lemondrink man," a sweets seller at a movie theater, molests the child Esthappen while promising sugary drinks and candy.

Roy's scene captures not only the ability of sweets to offend both one's senses and one's morality, but also the way in which sweets can be used as an instrument of oppression. Many modern portrayals of sweetness attest to its implication in structures of power and control. In Robert Graves's story "Treacle Pie," the nearly inedible pastry of the title forms the field on which a struggle of wills takes shape between the headmaster of a rigid boys' school and its new pupil. The eating of a magnificent rum jelly in Giuseppe Tomasi di Lampedusa's modern Italian classic *The Leopard* is described as if it were a great battle. One of the most influential uses of sweets to articulate power structures appears in Virginia Woolf's *A Room of One's Own*. Woolf contrasts two meals: one, at a men's college, ends with "a confection which rose all sugar from the waves," while the second, at a women's college, ends ignominiously in prunes and custard. "Now what food do we feed women as artists upon? I asked, remembering, I suppose, that dinner of prunes and custard." Women need not just rooms of their own, Woolf suggests, but also palatable, even beautiful food, if they are to create beauty.

Two areas of writing well attuned to the power and politics of sweets are African American and Caribbean literature, which, given the inextricable role that sugarcane has played in black slavery and West Indian colonialism, often view sweets as an instrument of white power and oppression. See COLONIALISM; RACE; and SLAVERY. Toni Morrison's novels frequently explore this issue; Morrison links confections with "capitalism, exploited labor, damaging white intrusion into black lives, and defilement," writes Dayle De Lancey (2000, p. 29). In *Tar Baby*, set partly on a Caribbean sugar island, one of the characters owns a candy company; *Song of Solomon* and *The Bluest Eye* also illustrate the devastating effects of sugar and sweets in black life. Caribbean novels, such as the opening section of Jean Rhys's *Wide Sargasso Sea*, often feature scenes on active or abandoned sugar plantations. See PLANTATIONS, SUGAR. Writers also reclaim tropes of sweetness for more positive uses, as in the Canadian writer Dionne Brand's *In Another Place, Not Here*, which opens by describing the love of two Caribbean women (one of them a sugarcane worker) as like "thiefing sugar."

See also CUSTARD; SITOPHILIA; SPIRITUALITY; and SUGARCANE.

Carruthers, Mary. "Sweetness." *Speculum* 81, no. 4 (October 2006): 999–1013.

Carson, Anne. *Eros the Bittersweet*. Champaign, Ill.: Dalkey Archive Press, 1986.

Deerr, Noel. *The History of Sugar*. London: Chapman & Hall, 1949.

DeLancey, Dayle B. "Sweetness, Madness, and Power: The Confection as Mental Contagion in Toni Morrison's

Tar Baby, Song of Solomon, and *The Bluest Eye.*" *In Process: A Journal of African American and African Diasporan Literature and Culture* no. 1 (2000): 25–47.
Gowers, Emily. *The Loaded Table: Representations of Food in Roman Literature.* Oxford and New York: Oxford University Press, 1993.
Krondl, Michael. *Sweet Invention: A History of Dessert.* Chicago: Chicago Review Press, 2011.
Masten, Jeffrey. "Toward a Queer Address: The Taste of Letters and Early Modern Male Friendship." *GLQ: A Journal of Lesbian and Gay Studies* 10, no. 3 (2004): 367–384.
Richardson, Tim. *Sweets: A History of Candy.* New York and London: Bloomsbury, 2002.
Tinsley, Omise'eke Natasha. *Thiefing Sugar: Eroticism between Women in Caribbean Literature.* Durham, N.C.: Duke University Press, 2010.
van Gelder, Geert Jan. *Of Dishes and Discourse: Classical Arabic Literary Representations of Food.* London and New York: Routledge, 2011.

David B. Goldstein

Little Debbie, one of the most popular snack brands in America, was named for the four-year-old granddaughter of the company's founders. In 1960, O. D. and Ruth McKee introduced a family pack of a dozen of their individually wrapped cookies, named the product line after Debbie, and used her image on the packaging. Ever since, the cheery girl in the straw hat has been a recognizable company symbol.

The McKees had gone into the bakery business in 1934, making cookies and snack cakes. In the 1940s they created the "Oatmeal Creme Pie," a soft oatmeal cookie sandwich with a creamy filling. It eventually became the first Little Debbie product, and remains one of the company's most popular items.

Marketing a low-price package of individually wrapped snacks was an innovative concept in 1960, and it proved highly successful. The company expanded and added products, which now include cupcakes, cookies, pastries, and muffins, as well as seasonal and holiday items such as heart-shaped brownies for Valentine's Day and summertime starfish cookies. Its brands include Drake's, Sunbelt, Heartland, and Fieldstone Bakery, in addition to Little Debbie.

The company prices its products competitively and builds considerable brand loyalty through community events and sponsorships. McKee products are sold throughout the United States, Canada, and Puerto Rico in grocery and convenience stores and in schools, hospitals, and on military bases. Privately held, the company commands a share of more than 50 percent of the snack cake market.

Debra McKee Fowler, the original Little Debbie, is now an executive vice president and a board member of McKee Foods Corporation.

See also HOSTESS; SARA LEE; and TWINKIE.

Feintzeig, Rachek. "Little Debbie, All Grown Up." Bankruptcy Beat, *Wall Street Journal*, 28 January 2013. http://blogs.wsj.com/bankruptcy/2013/01/28/little-debbie-all-grown-up/ (accessed 18 September 2014).
McKee Foods Corp. "McKee—A Family Bakery." http://www.mckeefoods.com/www/docs/1/About-McKee-Foods (accessed 18 September 2014).

Jeri Quinzio

Loft Candy Company was founded by the London-born William Loft (ca. 1828–1919) after he immigrated to New York in the 1850s. At first, he and his wife crafted handmade chocolates in their kitchen before opening a chocolate shop on Canal Street in 1860. Their son, George W. Loft (1865–1943), took over the business and expanded it, opening other retail stores beginning in the 1890s and building factories to supply them. Loft Candy Company became America's first retail candy-store chain, and by 1920 it was the largest retail candy company in America. During the 1920s Loft began promoting the brand by sponsoring radio programs. The Loft family lost control of the company in 1929, when the stock market crashed, and it was renamed Loft, Inc.

In 1930 Charles Guth (1876–1948) became president of Loft, Inc., and acquired other candy retailers, the Happiness Candy Stores and Mirror Stores in New Jersey. The combined operation owned 175 candy shops, soda fountains, and tearooms. See SODA FOUNTAIN. Guth was using Coca-Cola syrup in his soda fountains, but when that company turned down his request for a larger discount, he turned to the Pepsi-Cola Company—just before it went bankrupt for the second time. In 1931 Guth bought the firm and became president of both Pepsi-Cola and Loft. He put Loft chemists to work on reformulating Pepsi-Cola syrup and used his staff to restart the Pepsi-Cola Company. In 1933 Guth made a bold move: he started to sell 12-ounce bottles of Pepsi for the same price (5 cents) as Coke's 6-ounce bottle. Unsurprisingly, Pepsi sales took off. Within two years,

Pepsi had generated a $2 million profit and was the second-largest soft-drink company in America.

Guth left Loft in 1935 to work full time at Pepsi, where he was president and general manager. The executives of Loft, Inc., sued Guth in Delaware Supreme Court, claiming that he had used Loft employees, resources, and facilities to restart Pepsi, and that the successful Pepsi-Cola Company, in fact, belonged to Loft, Inc. In a landmark decision in 1939, the court decided that Guth had failed fiduciary responsibilities to Loft. Guth was removed from the presidency of Pepsi but continued to serve as general manager while the verdict was appealed; the Delaware Supreme Court upheld it in 1941. Guth was replaced as general manager of Pepsi and the two companies were combined. Loft candy stores were subsequently spun off from the Pepsi-Cola Corporation.

By 1941 Philadelphia businessman Albert M. Greenfield (1887–1967) had acquired control of Loft through his business, the City Stores Corporation. He expanded Loft's operations outside the New York area. By 1957 the company operated 300 stores on the eastern seaboard and the Midwest. It had more than 2,100 employees and sold more than 350 different products, including boxed chocolate assortments, gift baskets, and candy bars, the most famous being the Parlay bar. It also sold holiday treats, such as chocolate Easter bunnies and kosher chocolates wrapped in gold foil to simulate Hanukkah gelt (coins). See GELT.

Loft candy stores and the Barricini chocolate company (launched in 1931) were combined in 1970. By the mid-1970s there were 287 Barricini-Loft stores, which sold their own chocolates, imported chocolates, nuts, hard candy, and ice cream. During the next decade, the combined company faltered and cut the number of retail outlets. By 1985 it was down to just 40 stores in the New York area. The smaller company did not prosper, and by the 1990s all the shops had closed.

See also CANDY BAR and CHOCOLATES, BOXED.

Smith, Andrew F. *New York: A Food Biography*. Lanham, Md.: AltaMira, 2013.

Andrew F. Smith

lokum is the sweetmeat known as Turkish Delight in English. It is a thick, transparent jelly made of starch, sugar, water, and a wide variety of flavorings, such as fruits, nuts, mastic, and rosewater. When set, it is cut into cubes and sprinkled with a mixture of powdered sugar and starch. "Lokum" is a corruption of the original name *rahatü'l-hulkum* (ease to the throat), a figure of speech used to describe sweet, soft, and delicious foods as early as the tenth century, when the Arab writer Badi' al-Zamān al-Hamādhāni (969–1008) applied it to a type of marzipan. The expression was used during the Ottoman period for a pudding called *pelte* (from the Persian *pâlûda*, meaning "refined"), consisting of the starch-thickened juice of grapes or other fruits. Lokum developed in the eighteenth century as a very thick version of *pelte*. Although it has been suggested that lokum developed much earlier from ʿAbbāsid versions of *pelte* (*fâlûdhaj*) recorded in the tenth century, these recipes all contain oil or butter and produce not a sweet resembling lokum but a chewy toffee of the type also known as *sabuniyya*.

Lokum's other ancestor is a traditional sweetmeat known as *kesme* or *köfter*, consisting of boiled grape juice thickened with starch or flour, cut into lumps, and stored in jars for the winter. This product is still made in many Turkish provinces, such as Diyarbakır, Kahramanmaraş, and Kayseri. The substitution of sugar syrup for grape juice made it possible to develop a sweetmeat with a new range of sophisticated and expensive flavorings, such as musk and rose, which the distinctive taste of the grape juice would have overpowered. Other popular flavorings in the nineteenth century were clotted cream (*kaymak*), pistachios, almonds, pine nuts, violet, lemon, and bitter orange. At the Ottoman palace, pistachio- and musk-flavored lokum was preferred. "Double cooked" (*çifte kavrulmuş*) lokum, first recorded in 1924, is cooked for longer than normal, to a stiffer texture and darker color, and is cut into smaller cubes.

Foreign visitors to Istanbul in the early nineteenth century began to spread the fame of lokum, which became known in English as "lumps of delight" or "morsels of delight." The term "Turkish delight" was first recorded in the 1870s by the woman traveler E. C. C. Baillie, who wrote, "The sweetmeat known by that name in England is very different." European confectioners attempted to imitate the lokum using isinglass or gelatin, which produced a different texture. An example was Fry's Turkish Delight, still produced in England today. In the late nineteenth century the Frenchman Pretextat Lecomte investigated the manufacture of lokum in Istanbul and wrote that although the main ingredients are simply sugar and starch, the technique demands great skill: "It is in this that all the secret lies, and it should not be thought that this is a minor matter, which is why never, in Europe, has anyone succeeded in imitating *locoum*." To obtain the correct texture, the starch, sugar, and water mixture must be beaten without interruption in the same direction for two hours.

Another obstacle was the fact that the culinary use of starch was virtually unknown in most of Western Europe (although it had been used in the medieval period and makes a rare appearance in later cookery books). In eighteenth-century Europe starch was used not in cookery but to sprinkle on wigs, so the German name for starch remained *Haarpuder* (hair powder) long after wigs had fallen out of fashion. The only mention of starch in Mrs. Beeton's cookery book (1861) concerns starching linen, and the *Oxford English Dictionary* mentions no culinary uses for starch from the fifteenth to early twentieth centuries. In his Turkish–English dictionary (1890), Sir James Redhouse felt the need to specify that starch was "used for food" in his definition of the Turkish word for starch (*nişasta*). In Turkey, the Middle East, and Iran, on the other hand, starch had been an important culinary ingredient for more than a thousand years, and a large number of starch-based sweetmeats and puddings had evolved, including *güllaç*, *pelte*, *sucuk*, and *pestil* (fruit leather). See STARCH.

As lokum's fame grew in Europe, Istanbul confectioner Hacı Bekir began to export it in the mid-nineteenth century. A cartoon published in *Punch* magazine in 1861 bears the caption, "Latest Importation in Sweets, Rahat Lahkoum or Lumps of Delight," and in Charles Dickens's novel *The Mystery of Edwin Drood* (1870), Edwin Drood takes his fiancée Rosa to a "Lumps of Delight" shop.

Today, Turkish Delight is still popular and widely produced in Turkey. The most common varieties are rose, mastic, hazelnut, and pistachio, and although flavors like musk and violet are no longer available, newfangled flavors include banana, chocolate, and fig. Turkish Delight is usually cut into cubes or less often made into rolls filled with walnuts or clotted cream. Peak sales periods are the *bayrams* or religious holidays, when it is traditional to offer sweetmeats to guests. Istanbul is the principal producer, home to a number of traditional confectioners' shops such as Hacı Bekir and Cafer Erol, which produce their own lokum, and some large-scale manufacturers that sell wholesale and export. Other major centers of production are Safranbolu, Afyon, Konya, and Gaziantep.

See also EXTRACTS AND FLAVORINGS; FRUIT PASTES; GELATIN; ISLAM; MASTIC; NUTS; PEKMEZ; and TOFFEE.

Işın, Mary. *Sherbet and Spice: The Complete Story of Turkish Sweets and Desserts*, pp. 148–150, 154–55, 160–169. London: I. B. Tauris, 2013.

Nasrallah, Nawal, trans. *Annals of the Caliphs' Kitchens: Ibn Sayyār al-Warrāq's Tenth-Century Baghdadi Cookbook*, pp. 382–384, 387, 596. Leiden, The Netherlands, and Boston: Brill, 2007.

Perry, Charles, ed. *Medieval Arab Cookery*, pp. 84, 417, 456. Totnes, U.K.: Prospect, 2001.

Priscilla Mary Işın

lollipops have been a popular children's treat since the late nineteenth century. Today "lollipop" commonly refers to hard candy on a stick, but the word "lollipop" first appeared in British English in the early 1800s, well before the modern stick candy appeared sometime after 1890. In nineteenth-century Britain, any small children's candy could be called "lollipop," stick or not; at the same time, "lollipop" was frequently used metaphorically to refer to all manner of trifling amusements. In the United States, "sucker" was the preferred term for candy on a stick until the 1920s.

Some believe that the first lollipops were hard candy stuck on the end of a slate pencil, meant to keep school pupils' hands clean. As fanciful as this origin may be, the earliest documented manufacture of candy on a stick in North America occurred in 1895, when Canadian grocers Gilbert and James Ganong began pressing sharp wooden butcher sticks into warm blobs of hard candy to sell in their St. Stephens, New Brunswick, store. The term "all day sucker" to refer to candy on a stick came into popular usage in the late 1890s, suggesting that the grocers' idea spread quickly. Machines to automate inserting the stick in the candy first appeared in 1908.

The sucker offered obvious advantages over the traditional candy stick, and by the 1910s it was a staple children's candy. See CHILDREN'S CANDY. In contrast to the smaller morsels of traditional penny candy, suckers had substance, and sucker-eating could be stretched to fill an afternoon. See PENNY CANDY. After World War I, when rising sugar prices put pressure on the penny candy market, suckers (or lollipops) became even more popular.

Most of the best-known brands of today were created before World War II. Charms (now owned by Tootsie) is the oldest, going back to 1917. Dum

Dum pops were first sold in Ohio in 1924, and Tootsie Pop in 1931. Some parents and experts worried about the potential hazards of hard sticks in the mouths of tender youth. In the 1940s an inventor developed a flexible fiber loop suitable for toddlers, and so was born the safety lollipop, trademarked as Saf-T-Pop. These American classics are joined today by Chupa Chup, a Spanish lollipop first sold in 1958 and now the world's largest brand.

Carr, David. *Candymaking in Canada: The History and Business of Canada's Confectionery Industry*. Toronto: Dundurn, 2003.

Kimmerle, Beth. "Sweets Company of America." In *Candy: The Sweet History*. Portland, Ore.: Collectors Press, 2007.

"Lollipop History." http://www.spanglercandy.com/about-us/lollipop-history.

Samira Kawash

loukoumades

See ZALABIYA.

lozenge, in sweets and candy-making terminology, principally refers to the shape of a diamond or rhomboid cut from a thin layer and, by extension, to confections cut in this shape. Lozenges were usually cut from pastillage or similar types of paste made of sugar mixed with gum tragacanth. See PASTILLAGE and TRAGACANTH. The notion of the lozenge is closely linked to the original medicinal concept of confectionery, as something compounded to affect the health of the consumer. Sugar paste was an ideal vehicle for conveying powdered drugs. Apothecaries composed a mixture of sugar and soaked gum with drugs, flavors, and colors as required. This mass was thoroughly kneaded, then rolled out to a specific thickness, and divided accurately to give small, tablet-like sweets that contained measured doses of the active ingredient. See MEDICINAL USES OF SUGAR and PHARMACOLOGY. The shape was sometimes used with other mixtures, such as plain boiled sugar.

Making lozenges by hand was skilled work. E. Skuse, writing in *The Confectioner's Handbook* at the end of the nineteenth century, remarked that "the writer feels quite unequal to the task of making lozenge makers out of his readers; the process is simple enough, but it requires practice, and a good deal of it too, to mix and cut a sheet of lozenge paste as it should be." The problem, he explained, was that if the mixing process was overdone, it tended to discolor the paste, so that what was intended to be white dried to "a sort of greyish brown tint." Recipes included innocuous substances such as peppermint, rose (for sweetening the breath), ginger, or musk, and also more active ones—ipecacuanha (an emetic), paregoric (tincture of opium), or quinine. Lozenge making mechanized rapidly around the time Skuse wrote his book, remaining important until the advent of the modern pharmaceutical industry.

Early forms of the word "lozenge" appear in Old French and related languages used in the western Mediterranean. Dictionaries point toward a derivation from words used in that area to indicate slabs, for instance, in stone, such as tombstones. An alternative suggestion was made in the 1950s by Professor Maxime Rodinson, who suggested that the word derived from *lauzīnaj*, an Arabic term for an almond sweetmeat. See LAUZINAJ. Recent explorations of medieval Arabic cookery texts have not supported this theory, although diamond shapes are a favorite for baklava and some other Middle Eastern or Asian confections.

Whatever the derivation, for several centuries lozenges were hugely important as confections in Western European countries and then further afield. Over the years the word came to be more loosely used to refer to not only diamonds but also rounds, ovals, hearts, and other ornamental shapes in sugar paste. This type of sweet is now represented in the English-speaking world by various branded mint-flavored lozenges, cough lozenges, and the survivors of a late-nineteenth-century craze for conversation or motto lozenges.

Perhaps the most frivolous and potentially enjoyable form was the conversation lozenge, still made in the United Kingdom as Love Hearts, stamped with messages that range from the original nineteenth-century sentiments such as "Do you love me?" to those relating to more twenty-first-century concerns, including emailing and tweeting.

See also BAKLAVA.

Mason, Laura. *Sugar Plums and Sherbet: Four Centuries of British Confectionery*. Totnes, U.K.: Prospect, 1998.

Rodinson, Maxime, A. J. Arberry, and Charles Perry. *Medieval Arab Cookery*. Totnes, U.K.: Prospect, 2001.

Skuse, E. *The Confectioner's Handbook*. London, 1892.

Laura Mason

M&M's, with their shiny, colored candy coating protecting the chocolate inside, are the perfect embodiment of childhood. Each pellet-sized piece is like a special present just waiting to be opened and enjoyed. But the candy was never intended as a child's treat. Ironically, it was born out of war, made specifically for the soldiers of World War II who were stationed in tropical climates where chocolate bars would melt. The man who developed the M&M brand, Forrest E. Mars Sr., first saw confections like these on the battlefields of the Spanish Civil War in the mid-1930s. According to legend, Mars was traveling through Spain with a member of the Rowntree family, famous British confectioners whose business rivaled Mars's own. Both men were intrigued by the lentil-shaped chocolates the soldiers kept tucked away for a quick pick-me-up. Upon discovering the candy, they supposedly entered into a gentleman's agreement whereby Rowntree would take the idea back to the United Kingdom, introducing it as a product called Smarties, and Mars would bring the candy to the United States—where it became M&M's.

The truth of that tale is unknown. Forrest Mars had been kicked out of the family's American business, which had been producing Milky Way, Snickers, and Three Musketeers candy bars since the early 1920s; and he did depart from Britain before World War II, leaving his candy business, the third largest in the United Kingdom and best known for the Mars bar, in the hands of his top managers. See MARS. Because of his time abroad, when Forrest Mars returned to the United States in 1939, he knew better than most Americans that world tensions were high and that the country was likely headed toward war. If he planned to launch a new business, it was critical to secure a steady supply of chocolate, and that meant a visit to Hershey, Pennsylvania, home to the largest American chocolate manufacturer, the Hershey Chocolate Company. See HERSHEY'S. Mars's father, Frank Mars, was Hershey's biggest customer, using the firm's product to cover his company's popular candy bars. Several times a week, trainloads of chocolate left Hershey, Pennsylvania, bound for the Mars plant on Chicago's West Side. But on his return to the United States, Forrest Mars had to start from scratch. In a brilliant business move, he invited the eldest son of Hershey president William R. Murrie to partner in his new venture, asserting he would treat Bruce Murrie like family and even putting his name on the product, calling it M&M's for "Mars and Murrie."

Bruce Murrie was working on Wall Street at the time. At the urging of his father, he quit his job and joined in a limited partnership with Forrest Mars in the spring of 1940. Murrie put up 20 percent of the capital, and Mars contributed the rest. Murrie was named the company's executive vice president. He and Forrest Mars set up shop in Newark, New Jersey, with equipment imported from Italy that could candy-coat the chocolate. Manufacturing began almost immediately. With a steady supply of Hershey chocolate and 10 panning drums to apply the thin candy shell, the original M&M's were not stamped with a letter but did come in a variety of colors: brown, yellow, green, red, and occasionally violet. They were packaged in a cardboard tube that first hit store shelves in 1941. Sales were brisk from the beginning, and fearing encroachment from a competitor—like Rowntree's Smarties—Forrest

Mars patented the M&M's manufacturing process that spring.

His partnership with Murrie paid off handsomely. In 1942, when the government ordered severe rationing, M&M did not suffer; Murrie's father made certain the firm got all the supplies it needed. The War Department was initially M&M's biggest customer, and millions of M&M's went to bomber pilots stationed in North Africa and the Pacific Theater. See MILITARY. The Army also bought the candies for C-rations it distributed to soldiers in the Philippines, Guam, and other tropical climates. After the war the popularity of the brand followed the soldiers back home, although it took a few years for sales to regain their wartime peak. Forrest Mars blamed the dip on Bruce Murrie's poor sales efforts, and the two had a falling out in 1949. Eventually, Mars bought out Murrie's minority stake for $1 million.

In 1950 Forrest Mars began printing the letter *m* on the candy using black ink, yet another move designed to discourage copycats. Four years later, the peanut version of the candy was introduced, and the ink changed to the now familiar white. Oddly, the original peanut M&M's were all tan-colored; they were changed to match the hues of plain M&M's in 1960. With the peanut variety, Mars introduced its famous advertising slogan, "Melts in Your Mouth, Not in Your Hand," which lasted for decades. In recent years the company has become more creative with the brand, toying with its colors and candy fillings. Today, M&M's varieties include peanut butter, almond, raspberry, mint, and pretzel, in addition to the original plain and peanut. The company markets special color collections at holiday times and even sells special colors at its M&M World stores in iconic locations like Times Square and the Las Vegas strip. Consumers can also order specially printed M&M's online.

The candy has developed a cult-like following. A check of the Internet reveals all manner of myth and legend surrounding the taste of different flavors and the special powers attributed to the green M&M in particular. Musicians seem to have a penchant for M&M's, with many famous rock-and-roll bands requesting them backstage at rock concerts. Even the White House has specially packaged M&M's in red, white, and blue with the U.S. presidential seal. A multibillion-dollar brand, M&M's are sold around the world, and are just as popular in places like Japan and Israel as they are in the United States.

See also CANDY; CHILDREN'S CANDY; and PANNING.

Brenner, Joël Glenn. *The Emperors of Chocolate: Inside the Secret World of Hershey and Mars*. New York: Random House, 1999.

Broekel, Ray. *The Great American Candy Bar Book*. Boston: Houghton Mifflin, 1982.

Kimmerle, Beth. *Candy: The Sweet History*. Portland, Ore.: Collectors Press, 2003.

Joël Glenn Brenner

macarons (spelled with a single *o*) are colorful, filled cookies made from ground almonds, sugar, and egg whites that have become popular worldwide since the early 2000s. Any discussion of macarons must begin with the essential distinction between this French confection and the American macaroon, which refers most often to cookies made with sweetened coconut flakes. Macarons have a very simple ingredient list: almond flour, confectioner's sugar, sugar, and egg whites. Flavoring and coloring agents can be added to the shells, as long as they don't prevent the cookies from rising and obtaining their distinctive "foot," a narrow, delicate edge that indicates a macaron's overall quality. Macaron shells are thin and slightly crunchy, with a soft and moist interior. Achieving that perfect balance is where making macarons gets complicated, because the amount of air incorporated, the length of beating, and a temperamental oven can all affect the final result, which is why macarons are mainly made by professional pastry chefs, even though single-subject cookbooks on the topic for the home kitchen have recently proliferated.

Filled macarons were invented in the early twentieth century at the famed Parisian tea salon and pastry shop Ladurée. See SALON DE THÉ. Pierre Desfontaines, the second cousin of Louis Ernest Ladurée, had the idea of piping ganache on an almond-based shell and topping it with another shell. Although sweet macarons are standard, savory fillings, such as tomato jam or foie gras, are now also encountered, especially at restaurants where tasting menus offer a savory macaron as an amuse-bouche.

Macarons are believed to have appeared in Venetian monasteries in the eighth century, after the Arabs had brought almonds to Italy. Some sources state that in 791 a French abbey in Cormery began making ring-shaped almond cookies said to evoke a monk's belly button, though this version more likely emerged only in the nineteenth century. In any case, by the Middle Ages, almond-based foodstuffs were already popular throughout Europe. Legend has it that the macaron arrived in France with Catherine de Medici in 1533, when she married King Henry II, though like many similar food genealogies, this story is likely inaccurate. See MÉDICI, CATHERINE DE. In any case, a cookie made from almonds and sugar became popular in France, where various cities, such as Paris, Reims, Montmorillon, Saint-Jean-de-Luz, and Amiens developed their own distinct version. Nuns were often the driving force behind macarons, which they made for both nutritional and commercial purposes (baked goods, honey, and other food products were a source of revenue for most religious orders). See CONVENT SWEETS. Such was the case in Nancy, another French city famous for its macarons. In the late eighteenth century the nuns of Les Dames du Saint Sacrement's convent, who were forbidden to eat meat, began making macarons because they were nutritious. After the closing of the convent at the time of the French Revolution, two sisters began selling the macarons in order to make a living. They became legendary as "les Soeurs Macarons," to the point that a street now bears that name in Nancy. Nancy-style macarons are flatter than Parisian ones and don't have a smooth surface.

By the middle of the seventeenth century, recipes for macarons had begun appearing in French cookbooks. François Pierre de la Varenne's *Le Pâtissier François*, published in 1653, mentions macarons several times as elements of other recipes, seemingly to give those dishes body. The 1692 *Nouvelle instruction pour les confitures, les liqueurs, et les fruits* states that macarons are a combination of sweet almonds, sugar, and egg white, and offers instructions that include flavoring the batter with orange blossom water and icing them once baked, if desired. See FLOWER WATERS and ICING. From that point on, similar recipes for macarons appear regularly in cookbooks.

Nineteenth-century French confectionery cookbooks offer recipes for almond cookies that are made into a paste with egg whites and sugar (lemon zest is sometimes added), then combined with whipped egg whites, shaped into small mounds, and baked. Alexandre-Balthazar-Laurent Grimod de la Reynière's 1839 *Néo-physiologie du gout par ordre alphabétique, ou Dictionnaire générale de la cuisine française, ancient et moderne* lists no fewer than eight macaron recipes, including two for *macarons soufflés*, which could be closer to the light, meringue-based macarons we most often think of today. See MERINGUE.

If nineteenth-century books about Paris are to be believed, the city was teeming with macaron street vendors. Those vendors did not look like the elegant Ladurée, to be sure, but they testify to the lasting power of the combination of almonds, sugar, and egg whites. Today, cities large and small around the world have shops devoted to macarons, while pastry shops and supermarkets offer their own versions.

See also FRANCE.

Andrieu, Philippe. *Ladurée: The Sweet Recipes*. Paris: Hachette Livre, 2011.
Gordon, Kathryn, and Anne E. McBride. *Les Petits Macarons: Colorful French Confections to Make at Home*. Philadelphia: Running Press, 2010.
Hermé, Pierre. *Macarons*. London: Grub Street, 2011.

Anne E. McBride

madeleine is a small sponge cake in the shape of a shell that occupies a hallowed place in French patisserie. Madeleines have long been associated with the town of Commercy in Lorraine, whose bakers claim that the cake originated during the eighteenth century in the kitchens of the nearby chateau of Stanisław Leszczyński, father-in-law of Louis XV of France. The name of the cake is attributed to an elderly cook named Madeleine Paulmier (according to Bescherelle).

Nineteenth-century cookery books (those by Audot and Brisse, for instance) give recipes for madeleines as a modified pound cake or *quatre-quarts* mixture, a type of sponge cake with a sufficiently firm crumb to prevent its breaking apart when dipped into a cup of hot tea or a tisane. See POUND CAKE and SPONGE CAKE. A madeleine batter is made by beating together softened butter, fine white sugar, egg yolks, and wheat flour. The mixture is aerated with whisked egg whites and flavored with zest of lemon and orange flower water or brandy. Spoonfuls of the mixture are baked in special embossed madeleine tins that resemble small scallop shells. When baked and cooled, madeleine cakes are either left plain or dusted with confectioner's sugar. See SUGAR. Alternatively, a sugar glaze is brushed over the freshly baked cakes, which are replaced in the oven for a few minutes to dry.

Madeleine cakes are more attractive served upside down to display their distinctive shape, described by the writer Marcel Proust as "a little shell of a cake, so generously sensual beneath the piety of its stern pleating." Tasting a madeleine, dipped in linden tea, revived hidden memories that profoundly influenced Proust when writing his celebrated novel *A la recherche du temps perdu.*

The madeleine is considered so emblematic that it represented France in the European Union's Europe Day in 2006. The popularity of the cake remains undiminished, so in addition to the classic plain kind, many other versions are produced. Even Carême (1784–1833) listed half a dozen variations that include chopped pistachios, or currants, or candied peel. See CARÊME, MARIE-ANTOINE. Carême's *madeleines en surprise* are covered with a meringue mixture and replaced in the hot oven until lightly toasted. Today's madeleines may be filled with jam or fruit purée, or iced or frosted with chocolate. Yet all retain the characteristic indentations of the legendary little cake.

See also MERINGUE and SMALL CAKES.

Audot, L. E. *La cuisinière de la campagne et de la ville,* pp. 373–374. Paris: Audot, 1847.
Dumas, Alexandre. *Le grand dictionnaire de cuisine,* pp. 323–324. Paris: Veyrier, 1978.

Geraldene Holt

Maghreb

See NORTH AFRICA.

Maillard, Henri (1816–1900), was America's preeminent nineteenth-century confectioner. Celebrated in his adopted country for his Frenchness, he was sometimes considered too American in his native land. "Only a Yankee could have conceived the idea of creating an edible Venus de Milo," sniffed the French critic Eric Monod, echoing the sentiments of others in response to the 400-pound chocolate sculpture Maillard showed at the 1889 Paris Universal Exhibition.

This split identity characterized the career of Maillard, who immigrated to New York in 1848. At the 1876 Philadelphia Centennial, he included sugar models of such uniquely American figures as the Pilgrims and founding fathers, General Custer and Sitting Bull in one enormous exhibit, while flying the flags of both the United States and France above another. This latter exhibit demonstrated how cacao beans were turned into chocolate using French machinery available in the Machinery Hall's France section. Yet Maillard used "Henry," not "Henri," on the exhibit's signage and achieved great American success with the grand presidential party he catered at the White House on 5 February 1862. Hosted by First Lady Mary Todd Lincoln to unveil her renovation of the presidential mansion, the gala boasted as its centerpiece a Maillard-made confectionery steamship flying the Stars and Stripes, along with sugar models of Fort Sumter and the Goddess of Liberty.

Maillard's first chocolate factory-cum-shop and catering facility were in downtown Manhattan. By the 1870s the factory had moved up to West 25th Street, while the shop and a restaurant occupied part of the swank Fifth Avenue Hotel at 23rd Street. Photographs of the shop, circa 1900, show an Edwardian fantasy of mirrored walls, crystal chandeliers, mahogany display cases, and a cherub-painted ceiling. Surrounding the staff are tables of beautiful baskets and boxes of chocolates, as well as candy novelties like a life-size bust of a woman that could be mistaken for a customer. Chairs and tables along one wall reinforced Maillard's claim that his was "An Ideal Luncheon Restaurant for Ladies."

After Maillard's death, his son Henry Maillard Jr. moved the business slightly uptown, setting up first at Fifth Avenue and 35th Street in 1908, then at Madison Avenue and 47th Street in 1922. Hoping to expand beyond its reputation as a magnet for women, Maillard's added a men's-only restaurant with a separate entrance in the later location, which was visited by none other than James Beard. Maillard's also opened a branch in Chicago, on upscale Michigan Avenue.

Although Maillard's catering and restaurants attracted high society, its cocoa was marketed to a broader public. Free instruction in the art of preparing "Maillard's Chocolate for Breakfast, Lunch & Travelers" was given at Maillard's New York Chocolate School in the 1890s. The company's chocolate candies were popular well into the 1960s, long after the Depression had driven Maillard's other divisions into bankruptcy.

The Chicago restaurant was absorbed by the Fred Harvey chain, but Maillard's new owner ruined the New York locations, the last of which closed in 1942—a sad fate for the memory of the immigrant who had won World's Fair renown for his 200-pound chocolate vases and 3,000 kinds of filled chocolates.

See also CHOCOLATES, FILLED; CHOCOLATE, LUXURY; COCOA; and SUGAR SCULPTURE.

Blaugrund, Annette. *Paris 1889: American Artists at the Universal Exposition*, pp. 77–78. New York: Abrams, 1989.

McCabe, James D. *The Illustrated History of the Centennial Exhibition*. Philadelphia: National Publishing Co., 1876.

Francine Kirsch

malt syrup is an unrefined sweetener derived from germinated (sprouted) cereal grains, typically barley, in combination with other cooked grains. If malted barley alone is used, the resulting syrup may be called "barley malt extract," or just "malt extract," and the malt aroma will be more intense. Malt syrup is used in bread and other baked goods, jams, breakfast cereals, confectionery, and in brewing beer.

The first step in malting grains is to put them in a dark room and soak them in water. The germinating grains produce enzymes that convert starches into sugar to fuel growth. (Barley produces unusually active and abundant malt enzymes.) The maltster then halts enzymatic activity by quickly drying the sprouting seeds, which kills the seed embryo and preserves its nutrients. The malted grains are crushed, steeped in hot water, and mixed with cooked grains (unless it is a malt extract, in which case cooked grains are not added). Malt enzymes digest the starch present in the cooked grains, forming a slurry that is concentrated and evaporated by boiling off the water, or, in modern food-grade malt plants, by using a vacuum evaporator. The sticky dark brown syrup that is left is about half as sweet as table sugar, with a distinct flavor some have described as biscuity, honeyed, or, depending on the kilning technique, roasted, with chocolate and coffee-like flavors.

Unlike corn syrup, the predominant grain-derived sweetener used today, malt syrup has been around for several millennia. See CORN SYRUP. According to the food writer Harold McGee, malt syrup and honey were the primary sweeteners in China from around 1000 B.C.E. to 1000 C.E. Table sugar was too expensive for the peasantry, but malt syrup could be made from common household grains, such as rice, sorghum, and wheat. The classic sixth-century Chinese text *Qímín Yàoshù* (Essential Techniques for the Welfare of the People) includes chapters on how to prepare sprouted grains and how to extract malt sugar, or maltose. Malt syrup and maltose remain important ingredients in traditional Chinese confections such as Ding Ding Tong and Dragon's Beard Candy. See CHINA.

Malt syrup was not produced on a commercial scale in the United States until around 1920, when persistent sugar shortages led to greater interest in alternative sweeteners. See SUGAR RATIONING. Malt syrup was particularly attractive because it offered breweries devastated by Prohibition a potential new revenue stream. Instead of using malted barley as one of the four main ingredients in beer (along with hops, yeast, and water), some breweries simply canned malt syrup and sold it to consumers for use in cooking and baking. This "liquid malt extract" had good culinary uses, but it was also sold with a wink, since consumers could use the cans to illegally brew beer in their homes. Indeed, the LA Brewing Co. sold a malt extract that included a "Bohemian" hop flavoring, obviating the need for consumers to procure hops.

Malt extracts remain popular with home brewers today, but a greater volume of malt syrup worldwide goes into baking, confectionery, and even breakfast cereals. All malt products can be classified as diastatic (containing active enzymes) or nondiastatic (with enzymes inactivated by high processing temperatures). When diastatic malt products are used in baking, the enzymes can increase fermentation activity, helping to condition the dough. Care must be taken not to overuse diastatic malt or the finished product will come out "over-proofed," smelling of alcohol. Malt syrup also aids in the caramelization, or browning, of bread and pizza crusts, and dark malt extracts do the same in hearth breads. Of course, malt flavor is delicious in its own right, regardless of malt's functional attributes, and barley malt syrup is an essential ingredient in New York–style bagel recipes. In the United Kingdom, malt is the key ingredient in malt loaf, a sweet, dense, chewy loaf of bread. Light malt extracts lend many breakfast cereals sweetness and color. See BREAKFAST CEREAL.

Barley malt extract also appears on the ingredient lists of numerous popular confections and malt-based beverages. In the United Kingdom, Mars makes Maltesers, round milk chocolates with malt honeycomb centers; their United States counterpart, Whoppers, are malted milk balls produced by the Hershey Company. See HERSHEY'S and MARS. Both contain malted milk, a powdered blend of whole milk, malt extract, and wheat flour that was invented by William and James Horlick and trademarked under the "malted milk" name in 1887. Malted milk became a mainstay of soda fountains in the United States in the late nineteenth and early twentieth centuries, with soda jerks adding malted milk powder to milkshakes to form "malts." See MILKSHAKES and SODA FOUNTAIN. When light malt extract is incorporated into ice cream recipes, it helps control crystallization and imparts a rich toasted flavor.

As a sugar substitute, malt syrup has generally enjoyed a healthful reputation. In 1889 the Scotsman John Montgomerie filed an application for a U.S. patent on digestive biscuits, claiming his "malted bread" would make "nourishing food for people of weak digestion." Today, over 71 million packs of Digestives are sold every year in the United Kingdom. Ovaltine, a powdered malt mix invented in the late nineteenth century by a Swiss chemist, was a nutritional supplement believed to be especially good for infants, and by the early twentieth century it had become a popular children's drink in the United States and United Kingdom, often replacing hot chocolate. In the twentieth century, malt extracts often included cod liver oil to boost its value as a dietary supplement and to protect against rickets. Today, as fructose has fallen out of favor, malt syrup advocates may point to the absence of fructose in maltose. Maltose is a disaccharide, a combination of two glucose molecules, while sucrose (table sugar) is a combination of glucose and fructose. Malt syrup also contains some minerals and vitamins not present, or only minimally present, in other sweeteners. The recent rise of gluten-free dieting has made malt syrup a somewhat less desirable sweetener for many manufacturers. General Mills replaced malt syrup with molasses in their flagship Chex cereal and now advertises all but the Wheat Chex flavor as gluten-free.

Dillon, Sheila. "Malt." *BBC Radio 4 Food Programme.* Produced by Harry Parker. BBC, 28 February 2011.

Hansen, Bob. "Making Malt Extract." *Brew Your Own: The How-To Homebrew Beer Magazine*, May–June 2008. https://byo.com/stories/item/1101-making-malt-extract (accessed 11 August 2014).

McGee, Harold. *On Food and Cooking: The Science and Lore of the Kitchen.* New York: Scribner, 2004.

Miller, Ernest. "From Beer to Cookies: Malt Syrup Through the Years." *Food*, KCET Los Angeles, 24 April 2014. http://www.kcet.org/living/food/the-public-kitchen/from-beer-to-cookies-malt-syrup-through-the-years.html (accessed 11 August 2014).

"A New Sugar Substitute: Malt Syrup Is Indorsed by the Bureau of Chemistry." *New York Times*, 2 January 1920, 20.

Max P. Sinsheimer

manioc

See CASSAVA.

manjū, a traditional Japanese sweet, are steamed, stuffed buns made from wheat, rice, or buckwheat flour. Sweetened azuki paste (*an*) is the most common filling for manjū today, but the earliest manjū were vegetarian versions of meat buns. See AZUKI BEANS. According to one of many stories about their origin, Zen monks brought the recipe for manjū to Japan from China in the Kamakura era (1185–1333). The monks ate manjū stuffed with vegetables as snacks, sometimes in a broth. During the Muromachi period (1336–1573), peddlers dressed as monks sold savory manjū in medieval cities. By the late 1600s, "sugar manjū" stuffed with azuki paste became more prevalent than the savory type. The elite adopted manjū for use in the tea ceremony but commoners also enjoyed them, and the sweet remains one of the most popular of traditional confections in Japan, where there are many varieties. The flour to make Sake Manjū is kneaded with *amazake* (a rice beverage made from rice, water, and *kōji*—the mold *Aspergillus oryzae*), which imparts a tangy taste. Chestnut Manjū contain pieces of chestnut mixed with the sweetened azuki paste. Rikyū Manjū, alleged to be a favorite of tea master Sen no Rikyū (1522–1591), have brown sugar mixed into the flour. Tea Manjū are made with powdered green tea. Hot-spring resorts sell Hot Spring Manjū cooked by the steam of the hot spring. Savory versions of manjū survive as buns stuffed with meat (*nikuman*) or curry (*karēman*).

Nakayama Keiko. *Jiten wagashi no sekai*. Tokyo: Iwanami Shoten, 2006.

Eric C. Rath

manna is the magical biblical substance provided by God to sustain the Israelites as they wandered in the wilderness of Sinai for 40 years after the exodus from Egypt until they arrived in the land of Canaan. The name of the food itself evokes wonder and mystery. When the Israelites first saw it, they asked one another, "What is it?" (Hebrew, *mān hû'* [Exodus 16:15]), which yielded the name of the substance (in Hebrew, *mān*). The earliest Greek translators of the Hebrew Bible associated the sound of the word with Greek *manna* (meaning "morsel" or "crumb"), which became the standard term in English and other European languages.

The Israelites' question has confounded biblical readers since antiquity. The collection of disparate properties ascribed to manna cannot be reconciled perfectly with any known natural substance, a situation that underscores manna's inherent malleability as a symbol. It is first described as "bread from the heavens," which appeared daily with the morning dew as something "fine, flaky; as fine as frost on the ground," and which would melt when the sun grew hot (Exodus 16:4–21). It is said to look "like coriander seed" and its color is either "white" or "like the color of bdellium," a yellowish gum resin. Its taste was like "wafers in honey" or "the cream of oil" (Exodus 16:33; Numbers 11:7–8).

The Israelites were permitted to gather only enough manna each morning for a single day, since it would spoil rapidly and breed worms, except on the Sabbath, when the double portion collected the day before was miraculously preserved (Exodus 16:19–30). Manna could be boiled or baked, and in one detailed account the Israelites are said to "gather it and grind it between millstones or pound it in a mortar, and boil it in a pot and make it into cakes" (Exodus 16:23; Numbers 11:8). As is often the case with sweets, an all-manna diet eventually sickened the Israelites and drove them to violent complaint against God, who responded by forcing them to eat only quail meat until it came out of their noses (Numbers 11:4–20). Both the crime and the punishment highlight the principle that too much of a good thing can lead to dissatisfaction.

The manna stopped appearing as miraculously as it had begun once the Israelites reached their Promised Land. Its sustaining power was commemorated by the eternal preservation of one portion in a jar placed in front of the Ark of the Covenant (Exodus 16:34–35; see Hebrews 9:4), as well as by later references to its demonstration of God's nourishing spirit (Deuteronomy 8:3; Nehemiah 9:20; see John 6:31). Early postbiblical Jewish texts emphasized this aspect of manna by calling it "food of the angels" and a manifestation of God's "sweetness toward children" (*Wisdom of Solomon* 16:20–21), and further claimed that in the messianic kingdom God would feed the righteous with manna (*2 Baruch* 29:8).

Since antiquity attempts have been made to associate the biblical manna with natural phenomena in the Sinai Desert. Building on a tradition that goes back to the Hellenistic Jewish historian Josephus, many modern scholars have identified manna with a secretion produced by insects on the tamarisk tree (*Tamarix mannifera*), which shares several properties with honeydew produced by plant lice in the region. See INSECTS. Others have argued for a connection with a species of lichen (*Lecanora esculenta*) often spread by the wind in large quantities through the Central Asian steppes, although this species is not found in the Sinai region. Nevertheless, the symbolic demands of the biblical narrative prevent any perfect identification.

Ancient rabbinic tradition preferred to emphasize the wondrous nature of manna. It was thought to be one of 10 things produced at twilight on the sixth day of creation for the eventual preservation of humanity, alongside such items as Moses's rod, the rainbow, and the tablets of the law. It fell from the sky every day together with gemstones and pearls. It was used as perfume and cosmetics by the Israelite women. It was called the "food of the angels" because, like the angels, those who ate it did not have to relieve themselves since the manna was absorbed entirely into their bodies. Some sources claimed that manna could assume the taste of whatever food a person desired. Others argued that its taste differed according to the condition or age of the person eating it: to little children it tasted like milk, to youths like bread, to the elderly like honey, and to the sick like barley soaked in oil and honey.

Whether or not a scientific explanation can be offered, the various descriptions of manna associate it with another important symbolic food for the Israelites: honey. See HONEY. The country promised throughout their manna-eating journey is called a "land flowing with milk and honey" (e.g., Exodus 3:8), and manna shares both its sweetness and preservative qualities with honey. Likewise, the dual sustenance provided by manna and water in the desert suggests a parallel to the divine food and beverage of the ancient Greeks, ambrosia and nectar, which are also closely connected with honey.

See also CHRISTIANITY; JUDAISM; and SYMBOLIC MEANINGS.

Bodenheimer, Fritz S. "The Manna of Sinai." *Biblical Archaeologist* 10 (1947): 2–6.
Maiberger, Paul. *Das Manna: Eine literarische, etymologische und naturkundliche Untersuchung.* Wiesbaden, Germany: Harrassowitz, 1983.
Malina, Bruce J. *The Palestinian Manna Tradition.* Leiden, The Netherlands: Brill, 1968.

Edan Dekel

maple sugaring is the practice of making maple syrup from the sweet sap that flows from sugar maple trees in late winter–early spring. Owning a sugar bush—a stand of sugar maple trees—and a sugar house, and annually harvesting sap to make maple syrup, persists as a rural family tradition throughout New England, the Upper Midwest, and southeastern Canada. Only in these regions are there forests of trees full of running sweet sap, and this sap runs for only one or two months a year. Each spring, thousands of people go into the woods to tap the maple trees, harvest the sap, and move the sap into the many small sugar houses (or, in Canada, sugar shacks) that dot the region's heavily wooded landscape. Now a practice known to many, sugaring has long been a visible part of communities and landscapes in the northern forests of North America.

Sugaring is a communal practice. Maple trees grow interspersed with many other tree species (pine, birch, oak) in the forested landscape, and sugaring season draws many people into the woods to help with the harvest. There is only a small window of time when this can happen, which requires warm days and cool nights that permit the tree temperatures to hover between 40 and 45°F (4 to 7°C). People have to collect sap and boil it into syrup nonstop, day and night, an activity that leads to much conviviality: in Vermont, the tradition is boiling hot dogs in the evaporating sap for dinner; in Quebec, eggs are boiled in it for breakfast. In *How America Eats* (1960) food writer Clementine Paddleford described her foray into sugar making and tasting sap: "We drank sap fresh from the pail, a clear white

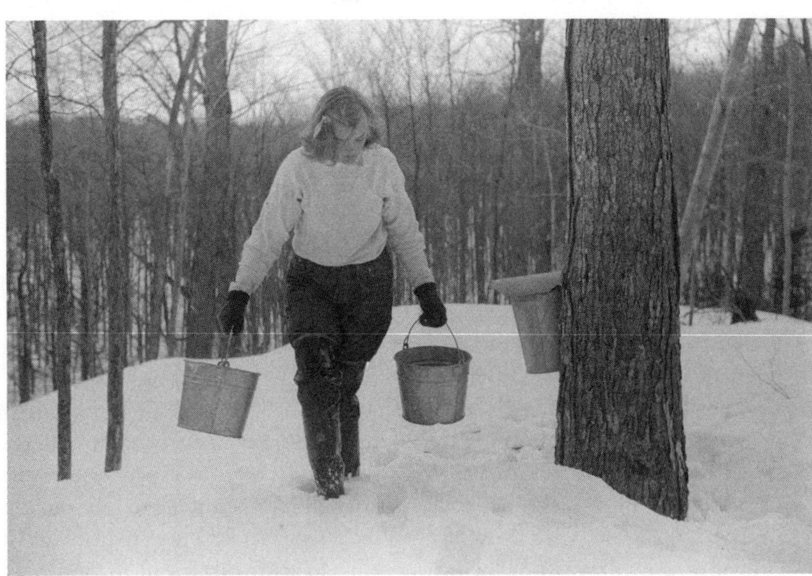

This 1940 photograph shows a young woman, Julia Fletcher, gathering sap from sugar maples on Frank H. Shurtleff's farm in North Bridgewater, Vermont. Sugaring remains a social event that draws people into the woods to help with the harvest. PHOTOGRAPH BY MARION POST WOLCOTT (1910–1990) / LIBRARY OF CONGRESS liquid, like sweetish rainwater. It tasted of sun, of the earth and the weather." Maple sugaring is a social *and* sensory experience.

Sugar Houses or Cabanes à Sucre

Sugar houses are the descendants of earlier open sheds that provided some protection for the large iron kettles used before the nineteenth-century invention of stainless-steel evaporators. Sugar houses vary in size and appearance but generally consist of one main room with a side room or two for wood, propane, and other materials needed to help the sap evaporate into syrup. Almost exclusively made of wood, sugar houses tend to have a steeply pitched roof to prevent pileups of snow, as well as a few windows to help let out the steam generated from the evaporator. Spending time in the sugar house with friends and family is commonplace, a rite of spring.

Unlike other functional buildings populating the region's still primarily agrarian and wild landscape, sugar houses are seen to be centers of both instrumental and social activity. Many, if not most, sugar makers sell their maple syrup. But when it is time to boil, the sugar house is transformed by the people who have come to talk, share food and drink, and help with the sugaring. The allure of maple sugaring may lie in being able to be with friends and family, warm in the middle of the snowbound landscape of late winter when sap is most often boiled. Sugaring stories often evoke an idealized view. As John Elder writes: "The sugarhouse was a beautiful sight when we arrived in the dusk. Steam was billowing out of the louvers we had so laboriously built, and a golden light from the Coleman lantern within was shining out of the open door ... illuminating both the steam and the smoke from our chimney" (2001, p. 92). It is in the sugar house that all the new season's maple syrup is first tasted and crucial decisions are made: the grade of each run, the possibilities for blending, the markets for selling, and the gifts to give to friends.

As a centuries-old tradition, sugaring involves many rituals. One is the annual sugar-on-snow party. These parties are held in small sugar houses but also at large maple festivals. There are many unconfirmed stories as to the origin of sugar-on-snow events, but what needs to happen *is* confirmed. Hot, thickened syrup is poured onto snow, creating a lacy pattern. By cooking the syrup to 234°F (112°C), it becomes thicker and develops a caramel flavor. When the syrup is poured onto the snow, the syrup hardens and contracts, creating a maple taffy of sorts. This taffy can either be eaten straight off the snow or twirled around a wooden stick. In some locales, the taffy is named "leather aprons" (in French Canadian, it is called *tire d'érable*). The resulting confection is served with a pickle and an unsweetened doughnut. See DOUGHNUTS and TAFFY. Sugar-on-snow is simultaneously hot and cold, sweet and sour, and making this dish remains part of the vibrant celebration of the North American sugaring tradition.

See also MAPLE SYRUP.

Elder, John. *Frog Run: Words and Wildness in the Vermont Woods.* Minneapolis: Milkweed Editions, 2001.

Lange, Michael. "Sweet Bedfellows: Continuity, Change and Terroir in Vermont Maple Syrup." *Digest: A Journal of Foodways and Culture* 1 (Fall 2012). http://digest.champlain.edu/vol1/article1_3.html.

Paddleford, Clementine. *How America Eats.* New York: Charles Scribner's Sons, 1960.

Amy B. Trubek

maple syrup is a sweetener made from intensive evaporation of the sap of maple trees. Most maple syrup is made by harvesting sap from the species *Acer saccharum*, the sugar maple. Sap can also be harvested from *Acer nigrum* (black maple), *Acer rubrum* (red maple), and *Acer saccharinum* (silver maple), but none have sap as sweet as the sugar maple. Sugar maple trees grow almost exclusively in the northeast region of Canada and the United States. Some stands may be found as far south as Georgia, but the larger tracts needed for sugaring are found primarily in the northern forest. Most of the commercially produced maple syrup comes from the Canadian provinces of New Brunswick, Ontario, and Quebec and the American states of Vermont, New Hampshire, New York, and Maine.

Sap is the lifeblood of any tree, bringing nourishment (water, sugar, nutrients) from the soil up to the branches, leaves, and fruit. See SAP. The uniqueness of the species *Acer saccharum* lies in its high percentage of sugar. Maple syrup is primarily sucrose, although some syrups, usually the darker ones, can also contain fructose and glucose. See FRUCTOSE and GLUCOSE. There are certain times of year when the sap flows the sweetest, generally as late winter turns to early spring. When the wood of the tree reaches the right temperature, between 40 and 45°F (4 to 7°C), the starches turn to sugars, and sweet sap begins to flow. The sap is harvested by "tapping" the trees. It takes 40 gallons of sap to make 1 gallon of syrup because what comes from the trees is primarily water. Making maple syrup is a major exercise in evaporation. See MAPLE SUGARING.

Maple sugaring long predates the establishment of strong national borders between the United States and Canada; fur trappers and traders were aware of and possibly trading syrup by the early 1700s. As early as 1672, a French Catholic missionary, during a journey on the northern side of Lake Huron, wrote of a baptism where "maple water" was used. In Vermont evidence exists that the Abenaki people taught the colonists how to gouge the sugar maple tree with an axe and then use bark buckets to collect the sap; settlers called maple syrup "Indian molasses." See NATIVE AMERICAN. By 1749 other settlers were writing about harvesting sap and boiling it down to maple syrup in large ironware kettles. In northern New England and southeastern Canada, most rural families owned lands with a "sugar bush," a stand of sugar maple trees. For most early settlers in the region, maple syrup was the only available sweetener, and more often than not the syrup was cooked down until it crystallized into maple sugar because it was easier to store. People would hack pieces from tubs or blocks of sugar to use either whole or heated back into liquid form.

Technologies of Production

The methods of procuring sap and making syrup used by the Native Americans and early settlers relied completely on natural conditions. Reed, bark, or wood spouts were used to draw off the sap into clay or bark vessels. The sap was boiled into syrup in large kettles, usually suspended by a metal rope hanging from a pole, over a constantly stoked wood fire. The pole was held up by two forked stakes. By the mid-1800s much of the process was brought indoors, initially in an open shed where the kettles were placed underneath the roof but still hung over an open fire. Later, enclosed structures and more efficient means of moving the sap from the trees to a holding tank and then to an evaporator were developed. By the late nineteenth century metal evaporators had been introduced. They were invented by David Ingalls in Dunham, Quebec, and soon updated and adopted by New England sugar makers. This technological innovation, along with others, allowed for the development of commercial maple syrup production. By the twentieth century the making of maple syrup had moved beyond the backyard woodlot.

Maple sugaring is an old-fashioned practice open to new technologies. One of the first was the invention of metal taps that could be inserted into trees to direct the flowing sap into metal buckets, which were then transferred into larger containers and transported by horse and wagon to the sugar house. Images of this process are still found on many jugs of maple syrup. Although taps are still central to the process of harvesting sap, today most maple sap is transported from the sugar bush by means of plastic tubing, with gravity or vacuum extractors pushing down the sap directly into the sugar house. There, machines perform reverse osmosis to remove much of the water from the sap. All this occurs before the sap is ever funneled into the flat metal evaporators that a century earlier had transformed the production of maple syrup and created new markets for this wild food.

Maple syrup is now an agricultural commodity, accounted for and supervised by state and provincial agencies and trade associations. Canada and the United States are the only two maple syrup–producing countries in the world. In 2009 worldwide production of maple syrup was estimated at 13,320,000 gallons, with Canada accounting for 82 percent of that production. Quebec is by far the largest maple syrup producer in Canada, and in the world, with 75 percent of all maple syrup worldwide coming from this province. The central and eastern part of the province is responsible for most of this maple syrup. In the United States, Vermont is consistently the leading producer of maple syrup (40 percent of total production in 2013), followed by Maine and New York. Other states making maple syrup include New Hampshire, Pennsylvania, Michigan, Wisconsin, Ohio, Connecticut, and Massachusetts. In 2013 U.S. domestic production of maple syrup was 3.2 million gallons.

Quebec now sells maple syrup solely under the auspices of the Quebec Federation of Maple Syrup Producers. About 85 percent of production is sold to packers or bulk buyers and exporters who redistribute bulk or prepackaged maple products. These products can be sold to food stores, supermarkets, and gift shops in both domestic and international markets. Producers can sell maple products of only 5 liters or less directly to the consumer. In the United States, by contrast, maple syrup remains primarily a small-scale enterprise for individual sugar makers. In Vermont, it is estimated that over 3,000 people actively tap trees to make and sell maple syrup, with some tapping 100 trees and others tapping thousands. Making maple syrup has become a new growth area in Vermont agriculture. In 2000, 1 million taps were installed; by 2012 there were over 3 million.

Grading and Tasting Syrup

Anyone who wants to sell syrup, whether from the farmstead, to the general store or to major blender/packers, must adhere to state or provincial regulations. The primary regulations seek to ensure that all maple syrup sold is pure (not adulterated) and consistent according to grade. See ADULTERATION. In the United States, grade was usually defined as a combination of appearance by color and density. There have been different names for these grades, but until recently the four grades were Fancy, Medium Amber, Dark Amber, and Grade B. Sitting in a sugar shack, watching the sap evaporate into syrup in the large stainless-steel evaporator, the sugar maker *looks* for the moment when the density and color are uniform. Density is determined when a small bit of syrup is poured into a hydrometer and measured; the goal is 66 percent or 67 percent Brix (a scale indicating sugar content). See BRIX. All grades of maple syrup have the same density. As of 2014, all maple syrup produced in the United States and Canada began to use a unified grading system that relies on taste as well as appearance. All maple syrups for consumption are now called Grade A. The four different categories are Golden, Delicate Taste; Amber, Rich Taste; Dark, Robust Taste; and Very Dark, Strong Taste.

The sweet yet earthy complexity of maple syrup means that this wild food is still in demand even though new technologies have created simple and inexpensive sweeteners. In the United States, maple sugar candy remains a popular treat found in shops all over New England. The syrup is cooked at high heat long enough to reach a crystalline stage; it is then poured into molds, often in the shape of a sugar maple leaf, where it cools into a fudge-like candy. Maple butter is made by heating the syrup to the soft-ball stage at 235°F (113°C) and then chilling it quickly and stirring until it reaches a creamy consistency. See STAGES OF SUGAR SYRUP. "Sugar-on-snow" is an old-fashioned treat for the sugaring season. Thickly boiled sap is poured in lacy patterns onto snow, where it immediately hardens into a taffy-like confection. Pouring maple syrup over pancakes and waffles for breakfast is a national American tradition, even if many Americans use Aunt Jemima or other "faux" syrups instead of the real thing. See AUNT JEMIMA. In Quebec, several desserts made with maple syrup are central to the region's culinary repertoire, especially *pouding de chomeur* (poor man's pudding). This simple dish involves pressing biscuit dough into individual cups or a baking dish, pouring a mixture of maple syrup and cream over the dough, and then baking it in the oven. *Tarte au sirop d'érable* (maple syrup pie) is like a sugary pecan pie without the nuts.

Maple syrup is a long-lived sweetener with a bright future. Consumers of all types increasingly desire maple syrup, as other sweeteners, such as high-fructose corn syrup and cane sugar seem fraught with problems. See CORN SYRUP. Maple syrup is a flavorful natural product. More demand exists for maple syrup in the United States now than since before World War II, and sugar makers cannot keep up with it. In addition, the syrup is regularly shipped to countries around the globe, including Japan, Thailand, and Australia. Maple syrup is thus not an artifact of a rural agrarian past, but a vital part of everyday life.

See also CANADA and MOLASSES.

National Agricultural Statistics Service. "Maple Syrup Production." http://www.nass.usda.gov/Statistics_by_State/New_England_includes/Publications/0605mpl.pdf.

Nearing, Helen. *The Maple Syrup Book*. White River Junction, Vt.: Chelsea Green, 2000.

Trubek, Amy. "Sweetness and Taste: Mapping Maple Syrup in Vermont." In *At Table: Dialogues on Food and Architecture*, edited by Samantha Martin-McAuliffe. New York: Berg, forthcoming.

Amy B. Trubek

marmalade generally refers to a chunky, sweet-sharp, semi-liquid jelly laced with chopped Seville (bitter) orange peels. Although the word "marmalade" may be applied to other fruits or vegetables suspended in jelly, according to a 2001 law, products labeled as marmalade in the European Union must be made with citrus fruit only. A mainstay of British breakfasts, marmalade is typically eaten on buttered toast. It has been extolled by writers and poets from T. S. Eliot to Ian Fleming (James Bond enjoyed Frank Cooper's marmalade at breakfast every day).

The Portuguese *marmelada,* from which the English "marmalade" derives, comes from *marmelo,* or quince. The origins of today's preserve date back over 2,000 years to a solid cooked quince and honey paste similar to contemporary *membrillo,* the Spanish quince paste. See FRUIT PASTES. Used as a preserve and reputed remedy for stomach disorders in ancient Greece and Rome, quince marmalade was eagerly taken up by the Spanish and Portuguese during medieval times after they learned about it from the Moors, who had settled the Iberian Peninsula in the eighth century. In the late Middle Ages, marmalades began to be sweetened by sugar rather than honey, a transition that continued into the sixteenth century.

The first shipments of *marmelada,* packed in wooden boxes, arrived in London in 1495. Expensive and imbued with purported medical and aphrodisiac powers, it was a popular food among noble families, who served it after feasts as a digestive sweetmeat. Around this time, northern Europeans also prepared cooked quince and sugar preserves called alternately *chardequince, condoignac, cotignac,* or *quiddony.*

The Scots pioneered marmalade's switchover from quince to bitter orange in the eighteenth century. The preserve's texture was now thinner, and it was served as a breakfast and teatime spread rather than as an after-dinner digestive. By the late nineteenth century, orange marmalade was being mass-produced by venerable British firms, including Frank Cooper and Keiller's.

As the British Empire expanded, orange marmalade traveled to British colonies around the globe. It was never embraced as a spread as enthusiastically in the United States as in Britain but was used more often as a flavoring for baked goods. Because Seville oranges are available for only a few weeks in January and February, contemporary home cooks view marmalade making as a seasonal ritual.

See also FRUIT and FRUIT PRESERVES.

Field, Elizabeth. *Marmalade Sweet & Savory Spreads for a Sophisticated Taste.* Philadelphia: Running Press, 2012.

Wilson, C. Anne. *The Book of Marmalade.* Philadelphia: University of Pennsylvania Press, 1999.

Elizabeth Field

Mars, Inc. is the largest candy company in the United States, boasting such venerable brands as M&M's, Milky Way, Three Musketeers, Snickers, Skittles, Starburst Fruit Chews, and Twix. With its purchase in 2008 of the chewing gum giant Wm. Wrigley Jr. Co., it added brands like Life Savers, Altoids, Doublemint, and Orbit to this iconic lineup, becoming a confectionery behemoth with global sales estimated at more than $30 billion. It is one of the largest privately held firms in the United States, being wholly owned by the Mars family of northern Virginia. The company operates a pet food division and owns Uncle Ben's Rice and other food brands, but the majority of its sales derives from candy brands that are household names worldwide.

Mars's beginnings are twofold, stretching back to the turn of the twentieth century when Frank C. Mars watched his mother cooking. Frank was a sickly child, struck by polio, and spent practically all of his youth indoors. He soon found he had a knack for making confections. At age nineteen, he struck out on his own, selling his candies door-to-door to small shopkeepers in and around Minneapolis-St. Paul. In 1902, the same year he opened his firm, he married Ethel G. Kissack; their only son Forrest was born two years later. But the business was not successful, and in 1910 Ethel filed for divorce, sending Forrest to live with her parents in Canada. Soon afterward, Frank remarried (another Ethel, coincidentally) and moved west to Seattle, where he tried his hand at a new business, but it, too, failed. Returning to Minneapolis-St. Paul, with no available credit, he and Ethel set up shop in a modest room above a kitchen, and Frank began making small batches of candy that Ethel took to sell on the trolley cars each morning. The biggest seller was a butter-cream concoction that eventually made its way into Woolworth and a dozen or so smaller retailers. By 1923 Frank Mars had finally found success. But what happened next is where the story gets sticky. To hear Frank Mars's son Forrest tell it, Forrest is the one who gave Frank the idea that turned the business into a million-dollar enterprise.

Father and son had not seen each other since the divorce, but they happened to meet when Forrest was working one summer as a traveling salesman while attending college at Yale. During lunch at a five-and-dime, while they were drinking malteds, Forrest claims he came up with the idea to put the flavor of a malted milk shake in a candy that could be sold nationwide, not just locally. Based on that advice, Frank Mars invented the Milky Way in 1924, a combination of caramel and fluffy nougat surrounded by a solid coating of chocolate. The Milky Way was strikingly different from competing bars. First, the chocolate covering kept it fresh, so it could be sold coast to coast. Second, because malt-flavored nougat—made of egg whites and corn syrup—was the bar's main ingredient, the Milky Way appeared larger but tasted just as chocolaty and cost less to produce. The Milky Way brought in sales of nearly $800,000 its first year on the market.

Seeing Eye to Eye

When Forrest Mars graduated from college and joined his father's business, he expected to be rewarded handsomely for his contribution. But the two men did not see eye to eye. Forrest wanted to expand the business rapidly, into Canada and beyond. However, Frank Mars had failed many times before striking it rich with the Milky Way, and he did not share his son's enthusiasm. After Forrest threatened and insulted him, Frank decided he had no choice but to buy his son out of the business, giving him $50,000 if he would disappear and never contact his father again.

Undaunted, Forrest Mars set out for Europe to seek his fortune. He traveled to Switzerland first to learn the fine art of making chocolate and then settled in England. In the small industrial town of Slough outside London, he set up shop in a tiny factory with some second-hand equipment and began making a version of his father's Milky Way bars, which he egotistically dubbed the Mars bar. Unable to afford to manufacture his own chocolate, he purchased his chocolate covering from Cadbury and sweetened the bar slightly to appeal to British taste. See CADBURY. He traveled to London to sell the bars to shopkeepers himself and soon acquired a loyal following. By the end of 1933, the Mars bar's popularity had grown to the point where Forrest could enlarge the factory and automate it, and soon sales expanded into other European countries. The success of the Mars bar abroad soon rivaled the success of its American cousin and became the foundation for an empire that quickly eclipsed Frank Mars's U.S. firm.

Brand Confusion

Forrest nevertheless was not satisfied until he regained control of his father's Chicago-based business in 1960, finally reuniting his firm with its American counterpart. In the meantime, Forrest had founded M&M's in the United States, which went on to lead the American candy conglomerate, now renamed Mars, Inc., with headquarters just outside of Washington, D.C.—a fact that surprises many Europeans who have always considered Mars a British-based company. Mars, Inc.'s two-pronged beginning has also resulted in continued confusion over the Mars and Milky Way brands. In the United States the company sells a Mars bar, but it is not the same as the British Mars bar, which is really an anglicized version of the Milky Way. Instead, the American Mars bar has caramel, nougat, and whole almonds buried inside, and it is covered in a thick milk chocolate coating.

The firm's global beginnings have given it an unprecedented advantage in the modern age, for Mars, Inc. was a global powerhouse long before the idea of global brands became necessary in the age of the internet. The firm operates on six continents and in more than 180 countries. The Mars family has always understood that the world is, in fact, a very interconnected place, and their business reflects that global pursuit. From the beginning, Forrest Mars said he wanted to build a global empire, and that is exactly what he did. He died in 1999 at the age of 95.

See also CANDY BAR; CHEWING GUM; LIFE SAVERS; and M&M'S.

Brenner, Joël Glenn. *The Emperors of Chocolate: Inside the Secret World of Hershey and Mars*. New York: Random House, 1999.

Joël Glenn Brenner

Marshall, Agnes Bertha (1855–1905), was among the foremost Victorian cookbook writers. Born in Walthamstow, Essex, she was one of the daughters of John Smith, a clerk, and his wife Susan. Her father died when she was young, and her mother remarried. Sadly, little is currently known of her education or where she learned to cook. The only clue to where she trained may be found in an

Agnes Marshall (1855–1905) was one of the foremost Victorian cooks and an extraordinary businesswoman who founded a cookery school, wrote cookbooks, sold hand-cranked ice cream machines and ice cream molds, and started a weekly magazine called *The Table*. This print is of unknown origin.

1886 interview of her husband in the *Pall Mall Gazette*: "I should tell you that Mrs. Marshall has made a thorough study of cookery since she was a child, and has practiced in Paris and Vienna with celebrated chefs."

Following her marriage to Alfred William Marshall at St. George's Church, Hanover Square, in 1878, the path of Agnes Marshall's career becomes clearer. If she were alive today, Mrs. Marshall would be judged a formidable force in business; for a Victorian woman, she was truly extraordinary. In 1883, following her purchase of property on Mortimer Street in London (a very unusual transaction, since women had earned the legal right to purchase property, particularly with their own money, only in 1870), Mrs. Marshall opened a cookery school. She started with no pupils on the first day, but a year later she was demonstrating to classes of up to 40 people, five or six days a week.

In 1885 *The Book of Ices* was published, followed by *Mrs. A. B. Marshall's Book of Cookery* in 1888, *Mrs. A. B. Marshall's Larger Cookery Book of Extra Recipes* in 1890, and, finally, *Fancy Ices* in 1894. See ICE CREAM.

Prompt to respond to commercial opportunities, Mrs. Marshall offered a range of hand-cranked ice cream machines, which even today prove to be faster and more reliable when pitted against modern electric machines. See ICE CREAM MAKERS. Once the ice cream was made, Mrs. Marshall was there to offer a huge range of splendid molds in which to form the ice cream, and ice caves to freeze it solid. See MOLDS, JELLY AND ICE CREAM. *Fancy Ices* took her ices to a more elaborate and embellished level, and this book includes the earliest reference in English to putting ice cream in a cone. See ICE CREAM CONES.

In 1886, no doubt using the facilities of the cookery school, Mrs. Marshall launched a weekly magazine called *The Table*, and in 1888 she was the first person to suggest, in the magazine, using liquefied gas for ice cream making at the table. In 1892 she undertook an extensive lecturing tour of major cities in England, taking the stage with a team of helpers to cook an entire meal in front of audiences of up to 600 people.

The staggering scale of Mrs. Marshall's achievements is arguably unequalled. She was a unique one-woman industry, and her recipes were always concise, accurate, detailed, and successful. She deserves much more credit than she has been given by history.

Weir, Robin. "Marshall, Agnes Bertha (1855–1905)." In *Oxford Dictionary of National Biography*, edited by H. C. G. Matthew and Brian Harrison. Oxford: Oxford University Press, 2004.

Weir, Robin, et al. *Mrs. Marshall. The Greatest Victorian Ice Cream Maker*. West Yorkshire, U.K.: Smith Settle, 1998.

Robin Weir

Marshmallow Fluff is an iconic brand of marshmallow cream manufactured by the Durkee-Mower company of Lynn, Massachusetts, since 1920. See MARSHMALLOWS. The sticky sweet spread is a staple comfort food in New England, where it is best known as an essential layer of the fluffernutter—a Marshmallow Fluff and peanut butter sandwich.

The sugary spread known as Marshmallow Fluff is so beloved in its home state that legislation is pending to make the fluffernutter—a combination of Marshmallow Fluff and peanut butter—the official state sandwich of Massachusetts. © DURKEE MOWER INC.

Fluff is also a versatile baking ingredient. It can substitute for marshmallows as a topping on hot cocoa or sweet potatoes, or serve as a sweet adhesive in whoopee pies, frostings, fudge, Rice Krispies treats, meringues, salads, candies, fillings, chiffon pies, sorbets, shakes, and cheesecakes. Diluted, it becomes a dessert sauce.

Durkee-Mower whips Fluff's four ingredients—dried egg whites, corn syrup, sugar syrup, and vanillin—batch by batch to ensure consistency. The surface of Fluff is smooth like a melted marshmallow, but once breached, reveals a light, stiff porous interior that turns glassy smooth again upon standing. The confection spreads and sticks, but does not drip. It expands and contracts with temperature, requires no refrigeration, and apparently holds up in zero gravity. Sunita Williams, an astronaut and Massachusetts native, squirreled away her own jar of Fluff onboard the International Space Station. For New Englanders like Williams, Marshmallow Fluff is the stuff of home. Generations of northeasterners will argue that Fluff is quintessential to their childhood, be it the wholesome 1950s or the far-out 1970s.

Marshmallow Fluff was invented in 1917 by Archibald Query, a French-Canadian immigrant and candy maker living in Somerville. Query sold the recipe to returning World War I veterans H. Allen Durkee and Fred L. Mower, who founded Durkee-Mower and began selling the concoction door to door. By the 1920s Fluff was being advertised in Boston newspapers. In 1930 the company debuted the "Flufferettes," a female vocal trio who sang dreamy odes to Fluff on the Yankee Radio Network. In 1961 Durkee-Mower developed the "Fluffernutter" trademark. Around this time, Fluff packaging adopted its signature look—a blue-and-white label sketched in classic "Dick, Jane, and Spot" style and a ruby-red lid. The iconic jar has remained unchanged since, inspiring powerful Pavlovian responses among the long-initiated.

Apart from strawberry and raspberry varieties, released in 1953 and 1994, respectively, Marshmallow Fluff has remained its simple self. The Lynn factory, built in 1950, remains Fluff's sole locus of production and uses the same basic methods and machinery from that era. The company has not changed its jar design since 1947 and rarely advertises. Although Fluff can be found in 28 states and 10 countries, the vast majority is sold in upstate New York and New England. In these regions' grocery stores, Fluff can be found in its familiar place alongside the peanut butter, no mere third wheel to jelly.

Marshmallow Fluff is not the only commercially available brand of marshmallow cream. Kraft has marketed Jet-Puffed Marshmallow Crème since 1961, and Limpert Brothers, Inc., of Vineland, New Jersey, has sold a more syrupy marshmallow cream as an ice cream topping since 1913. Paradoxically, Limpert Brothers also markets its product under the name Marshmallow Fluff. In one of the stranger deals in American business, Limpert Brothers and Durkee-Mower agreed to share trademark rights in 1939, provided that Limpert Brothers sold wholesale and Durkee-Mower sold for individual use only, except in New England. The two Fluffs are, in a sense, nonoverlapping magisteria.

In 2006 Marshmallow Fluff's retro reputation found itself in the crosshairs of the twenty-first-century fight against childhood obesity. Massachusetts State Senator Jarrett Barrios proposed limiting servings of Marshmallow Fluff in public school lunches to one per week. Indignant, Massachusetts State Representative Kathi-Anne Reinstein counterclaimed that the fluffernutter ought to be crowned as the state sandwich.

Barrios, who was not raised in Massachusetts, did not anticipate the public outcry he encountered. He quickly rescinded his proposal and promised to support Reinstein's instead. His spokesman assured the Associated Press that Barrios loved Fluff as much as the next legislator.

That same year, the annual "What the Fluff" festival debuted in Archibald Query's hometown of Somerville. Billed as an "ironic tribute," the recurring festival has featured Fluff cook-offs, Fluff-inspired games, Fluff-sculpted hair-dos, Fluff science experiments, and impersonations of Query and the Fluff-erettes. The outpouring of love has proven anything but ironic—the festival draws several thousand people every year.

Durkee-Mower, Inc. "Marshmallow Fluff Homepage." http://www.marshmallowfluff.com.
Liesener, Katie. "Marshmallow Fluff." *Gastronomica: The Journal of Food and Culture* 9, no. 2 (Spring 2009): 51–56.
Union Square Main Streets. "Fluff Festival." https://unionsquaremain.org/fluff-festival.

Katie Liesener

marshmallows are light, spongy confections made of sugar or corn syrup, water, and a gelling agent that have been whipped and set to capture an airy density. The modern marshmallow is also typically coated in cornstarch, sugar, or chocolate, as naked marshmallow is pertinaciously sticky to the touch.

The marshmallow takes its name from the marsh mallow (*Althaea officinalis*), a wetland weed native to Europe. A spitting image of its cousin the hollyhock, the marsh mallow sports a tall, sturdy stalk and pale pink flowers. Mucilage (similar to sap) is found throughout the plant's body but especially in its thick, fibrous root. Physicians of the ancient world recommended extracting the mucilage by boiling the root and consuming it with milk, honey, or wine to cure a variety of ailments. The Greek naturalist Theophrastus noted that meats cooked with marsh mallow cleaved together—a dramatic exhibition of the plant's supposed flesh-healing powers! In fact, he was witnessing the stickiness that would make the mucilage the first gelling agent of the marshmallow.

Over the centuries, marshmallow mucilage proved most effective as an antidote to cough and sore throat. (Modern medical studies have verified that marshmallow root does indeed soothe inflammation in mucous membranes.) In the nineteenth century European physicians prescribed boiling down the mucilage with sugar to create a palatable cough syrup. In

This advertising card, produced by The Campfire Co. sometime around the turn of the twentieth century, encouraged consumers to use marshmallows in their dessert recipes. For centuries confectioners had made marshmallows in individual batches, but by the early twentieth century, automation meant that these treats could be mass produced. BOSTON PUBLIC LIBRARY

France, the mucilage was whipped with sugar and egg whites to create lozenges. See LOZENGE and MEDICINAL USES OF SUGAR. By century's end, French confectioners had dropped the medicinal mucilage for more readily available gelatin. The French also traditionally used rosewater to flavor their marshmallows, which emerged a delicate pink. Although marshmallows may have lost their eponymous ingredient, in France today they can still be found blushing a similar hue as the mallow's blossoms.

In the nineteenth century marshmallows immigrated to the United States, where their next major innovation awaited. At the time, confectioners made marshmallows by whipping the necessary ingredients and letting the foam set in individual cornstarch molds. By the early twentieth century, however, marshmallows could be produced in large batches. In 1954 Alex Doumakes, of the American marshmallow company Doumak, invented an extrusion process by which marshmallows were forced through a chute and cut to their desired size. The innovation reduced the time required to make a marshmallow from 24 hours to 1 hour.

Today, marshmallows are mass-produced and sold throughout the Americas, Europe, and Asia. Although they can be eaten plain, they are often gussied up in various candy iterations. Peeps and Circus Peanuts, for example, cast marshmallows into whimsical shapes. See PEEPS. In Japanese Tenkei candies, marshmallows are filled with jam or cream. Mallomars and MoonPies pair chocolate-coated marshmallows with graham cracker. See MOONPIES. Chocolate-covered marshmallows are popular the world over, but the French are especially attached to their chocolate-coated marshmallow bears, an iconic childhood treat.

Marshmallows are also a versatile ingredient, lending their fluffy sweetness to fruit salads, cookies, Rice Krispie treats, and rocky road ice cream. In 1917 Angelus Marshmallows (once made by Cracker Jack) commissioned a recipe booklet to popularize novel uses of marshmallows. Thanks to the booklet, they became a favorite topping for hot cocoa and for sweet potatoes, especially at Thanksgiving.

These seasonal uses hint at another fateful property of the marshmallow: thermoreversibility. That is to say, marshmallows can revert to their original viscous state when heated. Quick to note the gooey lusciousness of a toasted marshmallow, the Imperial Candy Company launched the Campfire Marshmallows brand in 1917, explicitly promoting the candy as a camping staple. Before long, campers were sandwiching toasted marshmallows between graham cracker and chocolate, and the s'more was born. See S'MORES.

The most recent development in marshmallows has been toward batch-made boutique brands. Countering the homogeneity of mass-produced marshmallows, independent confectioners experiment with different densities, flavors (by adding fruit syrups, herbs, or spices), and textures (by coating with cookie crumbs, bacon bits, or the like). A British company has fully realized the marshmallow as a blank canvas by custom-printing marshmallows with clients' personal photographs. Marshmallows can also be modified by replacing the usual gelatin with fish gelatin (for kosher marshmallows) or agar (for vegan ones).

Culinary developments may aim to sophisticate the humble marshmallow, but the confection's lasting cultural impact seems tied to childhood. Some American cities celebrate Easter with "marshmallow drops," events in which helicopters rain marshmallows on earthbound children. Popular toy blow-guns made of PVC pipe shoot miniature marshmallows as ammunition. In the movie *Ghostbusters* (1984), marshmallows are forever personified by the Stay Puft Marshmallow Man, a cartoonish villain of bloated, springy step. In the world of psychology, Stanford researcher Walter Mischel's famed "marshmallow test" of 1970 presented children with a feat of forbearance—eat one marshmallow now or wait 15 minutes to be rewarded with two—and immortalized the marshmallow as the supreme symbol of temptation.

See also ANCIENT WORLD; CHILDREN'S CANDY; GELATIN; JAPAN; and MARSHMALLOW FLUFF.

"History of Campfire Marshmallows." *Campfire Marshmallows*. http://www.campfiremarshmallows.com/about/history-of-campfire-marshmallows/ (accessed 26 January 2014).

Phillips, Roger, and Martyn Rix. *The Botanical Garden*. Vol. 2: *Perennials and Annuals*. Buffalo, N.Y.: Firefly, 2002.

Porcelli, Lesley. "How Sweet It Is: The Perfect Sweet Potato Casserole." *Saveur*, 26 October 2011.

Rivenburg, Roy. "A Puff Piece." *Los Angeles Times*, 3 March 1995.

Tobyn, Graeme, Alison Denham, and Margaret Whiteleg. *The Western Herbal Tradition: 2000 Years of Medicinal Plant Knowledge*. New York: Churchill Livingstone/Elsevier, 2010.

Katie Liesener

marzipan is a firm paste of finely ground nuts, almost always almonds, and sugar, sometimes bound with either whole eggs or egg whites. It may be scented with rosewater or orange flower water, but the main flavor and aroma come from the nuts. As a result of its fine flavor and versatile texture, marzipan has many uses in confectionery, baking, and dessert making, working equally well in baked and unbaked goods. It can be modeled or molded into shapes, used as a covering for celebratory cakes, rolled thinly as a layer in pastries, or baked into biscuits and petits fours. It has been a prime component in fancy baking and decorative sugar craft over many centuries, and remains an important celebratory confection, particularly for a wide range of festival and holiday sweetmeats. See HOLIDAY SWEETS.

Mixtures of honey and nuts, which have been known for thousands of years, are the precursors of many sweet nut confections, marzipan among them. However, it is the cultivation and refinement of sugar in sixth-century C.E. Persia that we have to thank for the development of the fine, long-keeping sugar–nut paste we know as marzipan today. See SUGAR and SUGAR REFINING. In English, we use the German name *marzipan*, and that nation is still renowned for its very fine product. Debate persists over the origin of the word, but it seems to have come initially to southern France and Italy from the Persian and Armenian *marzuban*, applied to jewel boxes and both the wooden box and marzipan it contained, only later evolving to focus on the contents. The French (*massepain*), Spanish (*mazapán*), and Italian (*marzapane*) words may also refer to either the month of March or to pastries and bread, hinting at a connection with a time of year or simply to confectionery in general. In England, the earliest marzipan cakes were similarly called "marchpane," and these flamboyantly iced, gilded, and decorated sweetmeats certainly sound like festive jewels for the dessert table.

How to Make Marzipan

There are several techniques for making marzipan, depending on the desired consistency. Whereas homemade marzipan is generally raw, confectioner's marzipan is gently cooked to 356–392°F (180–200°C) to both sterilize and manage the moisture content, which according to European Union rules should be no higher than 8.5 percent. Great care must be taken to ensure that the nuts are not overworked to the extent that they become oily. Bitter almonds may be added in small proportions to enhance the almond flavor, which may be more or less desirable depending on the intended use of the marzipan.

Homemade Marzipan

Most domestic recipes call for 2 parts ground blanched almonds and 1 or 1½ parts fine confectioner's sugar. These ingredients are kneaded together with either egg white or egg yolk, the latter often specified in recipes for celebratory cakes, where the whites are used for the icing.

Raw Marzipan

This is the basic professional-grade marzipan, consisting of 2 parts almonds to 1 part sugar. The almonds are blanched and skinned, and left to soak in cold water until use. The nuts are ground with the sugar in fine granite rollers, using water to reduce oiling. The mass is then gently cooked in a double-walled pan, to sterilize it and reduce the water content, until almost dry to the touch.

French Marzipan

To make a whiter French marzipan, the almonds are ground before sugar syrup or glucose is added. See GLUCOSE. The mixture is cooked to a smooth paste, which is then turned out onto a slab and spread thinly to cool quickly.

Macaron Paste

For this version, blanched almonds and sugar are milled along with egg white. More egg white is added depending on the final desired consistency, in a proportion of up to one-tenth of the weight of the nuts. See MACARON.

Variations

Although true marzipan is made with almonds in a 2 to 1 proportion of nuts to sugar, a number of variations exist:

Almond icing. Sometimes used as an alternative description for marzipan, almond icing is a much sweeter, less nutty confection. It contains up to 75 percent sugar and only 23 to 25 percent almonds.

Almond paste. Also used as an alternative name for marzipan, almond paste is a different and cheaper product to manufacture, with a higher sugar content. Generally made from equal quantities of nuts and sugar, it is sometimes used as a substitute for marzipan in pastry fillings or mass-produced chocolates.

Frangipane. Not strictly speaking a marzipan, frangipane is used as a lighter marzipan-like filling, made with equal parts almond, butter, sugar, and eggs. See FRANGIPANE.

Hazelnut marzipan. Hazelnuts are used as an alternative to almonds, ground together in a proportion from 1½ to 2 parts nuts to sugar. Almonds may be mixed in according to taste.

Mazapán de pili. In the Philippines, a version of marzipan is made with local pili nuts.

Mazpon. This is a Goan variation on marzipan made with local cashew nuts.

Persipan. Blanched apricot or peach kernels, with a flavor between sweet and bitter almonds, are used to create persipan, commonly made in Germany and elsewhere as a high-quality but cheaper substitute for marzipan.

Pistachio marzipan. This vivid green marzipan is made with pistachio nuts, ground together in a proportion of 1½ to 2 parts nuts to sugar. Almonds may be mixed in according to taste and cost.

Uses of Marzipan

Marzipan is a crucial ingredient in numerous cakes and breads, from German stollen to Danish *Kransekage*, as well as being a filling for pastries. See STOLLEN. It is also formed into quite specific sweets and cakes, many of which are traditional for special occasions or festive times of year.

Modeling and Molding

Marzipan's firm yet pliable texture allows it to be formed into intricate models of every imaginable shape and size. Colorful marzipan fruits and animals for Christmas and for Easter eggs and lambs are produced all over Europe. Many of the forms are traditional, such as German breads (*Marzipanbrot*) and potatoes (*Marzipankartoffeln*) for Christmas, or Martorana fruits, also known as *pasta* or *frutta reale,* made for All Saint's Day in Sicily. Forms may be modeled by hand, and either painted, sprayed, or rolled in edible dyes or powders to enhance a realistic finish. Others are shaped in metal or plastic molds. Wooden molding boards are used for making evenly sized and shaped pieces—round, oval, or pear-shaped—for enrobing in chocolate. All kinds of marzipan sweets may be finished using special tools such as cutters, nippers for edge crimping, and decorative rollers for making uniform patterns on marzipan sheets. See CONFECTIONERY EQUIPMENT.

Cakes

A thick layer of marzipan between the fruitcake and icing is a critical element in many large celebratory cakes, such as British Christmas or wedding cakes. See FRUITCAKE and WEDDING CAKE. Simnel cake, for Easter, includes a layer of marzipan in its center, and a baked and glazed top layer of marzipan decorated with 11 marzipan balls to represent the 12 disciples minus Judas.

Confections

There are numerous special small marzipan cakes or sweets made in Germany that come from two distinctive schools, those of Lübeck and Königsberg (today's Russian Kaliningrad). See NIEDEREGGER. The latter traditionally tastes a little less sweet and comes in the form of petits fours cut with special crimped cutters. The result can resemble a vol-au-vent and be partially filled with boiled apricot jam or liqueur fondant, topped with a firmer fondant and decorated. See FONDANT. The overall characteristic, though, is to let the pieces set for 24 hours before browning them in a hot oven.

See also CAKE DECORATING; FLOWER WATERS; GERMANY; and NUTS.

Mason, Laura. *Sugar-Plums and Sherbet: The Prehistory of Sweets.* Totnes, U.K.: Prospect, 2004.

Rodinson, Maxime, A. J. Arberry, and Charles Perry. *Medieval Arab Cookery.* Totnes, U.K.: Prospect, 2001.

Storer, E. *The Complete Book of Marzipan.* London: Maclaren and Sons, 1969.

Unger, Friedrich, and Priscilla Mary Işın. *A King's Confectioner in the Orient.* London: Kegan Paul, 2003.

Jane Levi

mastic is the crystallized sap of the mastic tree (*Pistachia lentiscus* var. Chia), a kind of wild pistachio shrub or small tree. *Lentiscus* (or *Schinus*) shrubs grow wild all over the eastern Mediterranean shores, but only on the southern part of the island of Chios do the plants produce mastic. Pink peppercorns (*Schinus molle*) and sumac (*Rhus coriaria*) are two other flavorings from plants of the same family that grow in different parts of the world. The word "mastic" derives from the ancient Greek verb *mastichao* (to gnash the teeth); "masticate" has the same origin.

Mastic crystals were the most glamorous of the various ancient resins, certainly more so than gum arabic or tragacanth. See TRAGACANTH. Chios mastic (*masticha*) has a subtle, fruity flavor and a distinct sweet aroma that other natural gums lack. These characteristics made it a precious commodity beginning in Roman times. Its crystals were used as chewing gum and breath freshener, as well as medicine. See CHEWING GUM. Recent studies have proven that mastic oil, extracted from the crystals, does indeed possess antibacterial properties that may be beneficial against stomach ulcers.

Since early Byzantine times, mastic crystals have been used as flavoring for *mastichato*, a most sought-after aperitif mentioned by Alexander Trallianus (ca. 525–ca. 605 C.E.). This drink, along with mastic crystals, used to be Chios's main export. A similar smooth, mastic-flavored drink is still produced on Chios and is frequently referred to as the "ladies' ouzo."

Today, ground mastic is used to flavor breads and cookies in Greece and throughout the Middle East and North Africa. It should be added sparingly, as large quantities yield a bitter and turpentine-like taste. Lokum (Turkish Delight) is flavored with mastic, as is *dondurma*—the famous Turkish eggless ice cream. See LOKUM. The enviable, strand-like texture of *dondurma* is sometimes mistakenly attributed to mastic; however, it is *salep*, the powerful ancient thickener extracted from the starchy bulb of the orchid *Orchis mascula*, that gives the frozen dessert its texture. A similar mastic-scented ice cream is called *kaimaki* in Greece. *Ypovrichio* (submarine) refers to a spoonful of sugar paste scented with mastic, served submerged in a glass of cold water—hence the name. The anointing oil used by the Greek Orthodox Church includes mastic along with other aromatics.

Mastic production has remained unchanged for centuries. The whole family tends and carefully prunes the trees in winter. In summer, skilled workers make slits on the trunk and lower branches to collect the mastic "tears" throughout the fall. Picking over and sorting the crystals is a long and tedious process. The medieval *mastichochoria*, the mastic-producing villages of southern Chios, were built by Genoese rulers between the thirteenth and fourteenth centuries. Unlike other villages of the island, they are constructed around central towers, with tall external walls that offered protection from pirates and thieves who coveted the valuable produce. During the more than four centuries of Ottoman rule that followed, mastic production was directly overseen by the sultan.

In recent years, after a period of steady decline, mastic sales have surged worldwide, thanks to research and promotion. In 1997 Chios mastic was named a European Union Protected Designation of Origin (PDO) product. It is now sold as not only a flavoring but also the key ingredient in various health products and cosmetics.

See also GREECE AND CYPRUS; ICE CREAM; MIDDLE EAST; and NORTH AFRICA.

Braudel, Fernand. *The Mediterranean and the Mediterranean World in the Age of Philip II.* New York: HarperCollins, 1992.
Chios Mastiha Growers Association. http://www.gummastic.gr/index.php?contentid=72&langflag=_en.
Kremezi, Aglaia. *The Foods of the Greek Islands.* Boston and New York: Houghton Mifflin, 2000.

Aglaia Kremezi

mead, made from honey, water, and yeast, may be mankind's earliest crafted alcoholic drink. Honey mixed with water ferments by means of yeasts, both in the air and within the honey itself, which feed on its sugars. See HONEY. This process would occur naturally if rain chanced to fall into a bowl of honeycomb. Early observers likely took note of the resulting drink's intoxicating powers and were spurred on to make more.

Many different styles of mead evolved and are still made today. The drink can be dry or sweet, with an alcohol content generally ranging from around 8 to more than 16 percent. Mead can be sparkling, distilled, or spiced. When flavored with herbs and spices, mead is called metheglin, a drink considered to have healthful properties. Cornwall and Wales were known for their mead, and the Celtic words *meddyg* (healing) and *llyn* (liquor) provide the etymological root for this drink. Fruit meads, made with honey and fruit juice, are called melomel and have many variations. Pyment is made with grape juice, cyser from apples, black mead from black currants, red mead from red currants, morat from mulberries, and myritis from bilberries.

The ancient Greeks and Romans made many kinds of honeyed drinks. Pliny's recipe for mead in the first century C.E. was to mix honey and rainwater in a proportion of 1 to 3 and to keep it in the sun for 40 days. A spiced combination of mead and wine called mulsum cheered the chilly Roman troops occupying northern Europe and is thought to be the origin of mulled wine. See MULLED WINE.

While wine took over in southern countries, honey drinks remained prominent in the north, both as mead and as honey beers. In 300 B.C.E. Pytheas, a Greek mariner, sailed north of Britain for six days and reached a land of barbarians who "from grain and honey made a fermented drink." Pliny commented on how the people of the British Isles consumed great quantities of the honey brew. In Wales, freemen could pay dues to the king in the form of mead, and a free township had to supply "the worth of a vat of mead to the King, which ought to be capacious enough for the King and his adult companion to bathe in it."

Like honey, mead is much linked to love and virility. The term "honeymoon" is thought to come from the month-long celebrations of nuptials when mead was drunk. See HONEYMOON. In the Indian Rigveda, Vishnu created a mead-spring from one of his footprints, and all who drank from it became highly fertile. Chaucer writes in "The Miller's Tale" of the carpenter's beautiful wife having breath honeyed by meeth (mead) and braggot, a honeyed ale: "Her mouth was swete as braggot or the meeth."

The drink is also associated with both fighting and the camaraderie among fighters. A Scottish saying claims that mead drinkers have the strength of meat eaters. The epic poem *Beowulf*, set in Denmark around 700 C.E., includes warriors taking "joy in their mead," and Shield Sheafson, scourge of many tribes, is described as a "wrecker of mead-benches." In Teutonic mythology, warriors getting to Valhalla quaffed sparkling mead offered by divine maidens. Wooden bowls called mazers, some elaborately ornamented with silver, were used for the communal drinking of mead.

Sir Kenelm Digby (1603–1665) collected recipes, including 108 for mead and other honey drinks, which were published posthumously in *The Closet of the Eminently Learned Sir Kenelme Digbie Kt. Opened*. The book reveals the wide culture of this tradition and includes a recipe for Elizabeth I's metheglin, flavored with thyme, rosemary, and bay leaves.

By this stage, however, mead was on the wane in Europe. Imported drinks such as wine were growing in popularity, and the dissolution of the monasteries by Henry Vlll in the mid-sixteenth century had eliminated an important source of honey, since monks kept bees to produce wax for pure and sweet altar candles.

Mead remained the preferred drink in Russia until the early eighteenth century. It is still popular in Ethiopia and Eritrea, where it is called *tej*. Elsewhere, honey drinks continue to be made as a country craft. Brother Adam (1898–1996), the Devon-based beekeeping monk who traveled the world in an effort to breed the best bees, would offer guests his famous heather-honey mead, sometimes cooled first in a stream near his apiary on Dartmoor. He recommended that mead be kept in oak casks for at least seven years to mature. Contemporary mead makers agree that the drink improves with age.

Some mead is made commercially, although too often the drink's name has been tarnished by the mixing of poor-quality wine with poor-quality honey. But good mead is undergoing a revival. Its sweet form goes well with desserts, cheese, nuts, and pâtés, as a bottle of Sauternes would. Connoisseurs praise distilled mead for its floral, honeyed bouquet and rounded finish. Mead is still part of country fairs and honey shows, and meads of many styles from all over the world compete in the Mazer Cup International, held annually in Boulder, Colorado.

See also HIPPOCRAS and SWEET WINE.

Crane, Eva. *The World History of Beekeeping and Honey Hunting*. London: Duckworth, 1999.

Furness, Clara. *Honey Wines and Beers*. Mytholmroyd, U.K.: Northern Bee, 1987.

Gayre, G. R. *Wassail! In Mazers of Mead*. London: Phillimore & Co, 1948.

Heaney, Seamus. *Beowulf*. London: Faber and Faber, 1999.

Hattie Ellis

measurement is essential to cooking. We measure time and temperature, amounts and ingredients, with greater or lesser precision, according to

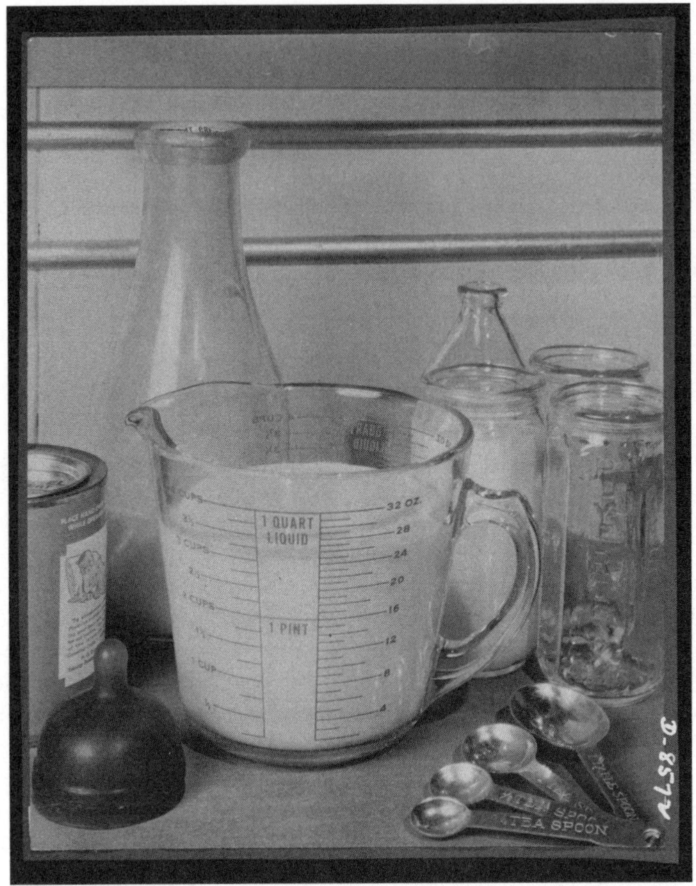

The manufacture and sale of standardized tools, advocated in the United States by Fannie Farmer, occurred in fits and starts. This 1943 photograph promotes a new type of glass measuring cup with easy-to-read markings, useful for preparing infant formula or for following recipes precisely. LIBRARY OF CONGRESS

need and the tools (personal experience, measuring cups and spoons, scales, thermometers) available to us. Baking especially demands measurements that are close and standardized, in part because certain chemical reactions require precision, and in part to ensure replicability. Nevertheless, what, why, and how we measure are determined more by culture, history, economics, philosophy, and law (France established the metric system by law in 1790, Britain in 1824, and the United States settled on the uniform standards in 1836) than by science. This is particularly true of the late nineteenth century in North American culinary history, a period characterized by far-reaching changes in dietary practice and culinary science precipitated by industrialization, urbanization, gender, class, and social stratification, as well as by equally significant improvements in the technologies of measurement.

The move to standardization, especially in the United States, is often attributed to the Boston Cooking School, and two of its directors, Mary J. Lincoln and Fannie Farmer. See FARMER, FANNIE. Farmer's canonical *Boston Cooking-School Cook Book* was among the first to insist on accurate measurements, and it is widely said to be the first to utilize level measurements as standard practice. Farmer's insistence on level measurements was important for another reason. *The Boston Cooking-School Cook Book* assisted the move away from scale (weight) measurements, which persisted in the United States well into the nineteenth century, to volume (cups and spoons).

Before Farmer and the rise of home economics and scientific cookery, recipes utilized a variety of methods of measurements. Common units of measurement included "alum the size of a cherry," "knobs" of butter, or "butter the size of a walnut." Historians have demonstrated that widespread disagreement existed about how to measure butter, sugar, flour, and other kitchen staples. Even references to seemingly standard measures, such as a "cup" of flour or a "teaspoon" of sugar, could mask substantial variations, since terms like cup and spoon did not reference a uniform amount or standardized implement or tool. The manufacturing and retail of standardized tools occurred over several years, and in fits and starts—first to appear in the 1880s were measuring cups, followed by measuring spoons.

The move to standardization occurred in an era in American culinary history preoccupied with the development of a progressive and scientific approach to domestic work in general, and to cooking in particular. Farmer referenced this change, writing that she hoped *The Boston Cooking-School Cook Book* "may awaken an interest through its condensed scientific knowledge which will lead to deeper thought and broader study of what to eat." These changes in domestic life mirrored changing understandings about the role of women in the household and in society. Standardization was also facilitated by urbanization and an increasing degree of culinary cosmopolitism in urban social life.

Efforts to standardize culinary measurements continue to influence kitchen work. Recipe developers and cooks must choose between the U.S. Customary System (the inch-pound system) and the International System of Units (the metric system). Perhaps more significantly, there are differences in how we measure liquids and dry ingredients, and especially between measurements based on weight and volume. Most home cooks use uniform measuring cups and spoons, but even these standardized tools allow for significant variation—a cup of any ingredient (flour is especially troublesome) may vary in amount depending on several factors, including how densely the food is packed. See FLOUR. Culinary professionals, and especially pastry chefs, rely extensively on weight measurements and scales when the need for precision is critical to taste, presentation, and replicability. Other metrics include "ratio cooking," which uses weight rather than volume measurements and "parts," or ratios of critical ingredients to one another. Bread bakers, in particular, base successful formulas on such ratios.

Oven temperatures are notoriously inexact. Before the advent of calibrated thermometers, cooks might gauge an oven as slow, moderate, or fast by one of several mechanisms, including the "hand test," or by sprinkling flour on the oven floor and timing how long it took to turn golden or dark brown. (A similar test used instead a strip of white paper.) The need for precision in pastry and confectionery kitchens has similarly prompted the development of increasingly sophisticated tools of measurement. There are specialized thermometers, for example, for dough (to determine the thermal death point, or the temperature at which yeast dies), as well for candy, chocolate (important for tempering), and especially sugar. There are several different thermometers for measuring the stages of boiled sugar, including Baumé hydrometers, which measure the concentration of sugar in a liquid in degrees, and Brix hydrometers, which measure sugar in liquids by decimals. See BRIX.

Although standard measurements are essential in baking and confectionery, there may also be a soft tyranny in the drive for precision, hinted at by the nearly simultaneous appearance of standardized measurements and the rise of socially ambitious cookery in the late nineteenth century. In the process, other social values and manners often associated with the middle class, including an aversion to excess, may have helped to undermine our sense of cooking and eating as gustatory pleasures. Hence, one of the casualties of scientific standardization may be taste, not only in its gustatory sense, but also in the aesthetic sense of taste as a skilled practice. Another unintended side effect of greater standardization may be a loss of culinary skill and creativity of the home cook. Uniformity in measurement practices should therefore be counted as sometimes an aid and sometimes an impediment to good cooking.

See also CONFECTIONERY EQUIPMENT; PASTRY TOOLS; SACCHARIMETER; STAGES OF SUGAR SYRUP; and PASTRY TOOLS.

Carlin, Joseph M. "Weights and Measures in Nineteenth-Century America." *Journal of Gastronomy* 3 (1987): 67.

Duran, Nancy, and Joe Jaros. "American Measurement: Refining Cups and Spoons for Scientific Cooking in the Late 19th–Early 20th Century." *Journal of Agricultural & Food Information* 11 (2010): 19–22.

Shapiro, Laura. *Perfection Salad: Women and Cooking at the Turn of the Century*. New York: Modern Library, 2001.

Sokolov, Raymond. "Measure for Measure." In *The Cooking Pot: Proceedings of the Oxford Symposium on Food and Cookery, 1988*, edited by Tom Jaine, pp. 148–152. Totnes, U.K.: Prospect, 1989.

John E. Finn

Médici, Catherine de (1519–1589), the sometime queen, queen mother, and regent of France, never had it easy. In her own day, she was vilified for exerting too great an influence on the affairs of France, and excoriated for surrounding herself with Italians. Writers over the last two centuries have attributed to her the introduction to France of everything from artichokes to ice cream, some even claiming that she brought the very idea of haute cuisine to her adopted homeland. More recently, food historians have dismissed anything of the sort, relegating the poor queen to little more than a footnote in the history of French cuisine. The truth is undoubtedly more nuanced.

Caterina de'Medici, as the Italians knew her, came from the great Florentine merchant family, the only daughter of Lorenzo de'Medici and Madeleine de la Tour d'Auvergne, a French duchess. In 1533, at the age of 14, the orphaned Caterina was betrothed to Henry d'Orleans, the second son of Francis I. After a ceremonious wedding in Marseilles, attended by her uncle, Pope Clement VII, and Francis I of France, the Italian teen largely disappeared from view. Commentators have rightly pointed out it is unlikely that the 14-year-old had much influence on the French court when she first arrived, culinary or otherwise, or that she was accompanied by a large entourage of Italian cooks as she left Marseilles. There is certainly no documentation of ice cream in France or Italy in her lifetime. See ICE CREAM. She seems to have lived in relative obscurity until the death of her royal father-in-law, after which her husband ascended the throne in 1547 as Henri II.

It was only then that the 28-year-old Catherine stepped into the limelight, first as queen and then queen regent after the untimely death of her husband in 1559. In the years that followed, she would become the most powerful woman in the history of royal France. She spent enormous fortunes patronizing the arts and architecture (in Paris, the Tuileries gardens are all that remain of her once grand palace). She became renowned for staging great public festivals where mock jousts, musical entertainments, ballet, and even fireworks competed for attention. The Italian influence was unmistakable in both the music and the staging of the banquets. Was this entirely Catherine's doing? Undoubtedly not. Italians set the fashion across Europe in the sixteenth century. Certainly, Francis I had been a great Italophile and had introduced many southern innovations to his court. In France, Italians were instrumental in setting up the manufacture of satin, stockings, cotton, ribbons, silk faience, glass, mirrors, and other luxury goods. In later years Italian artisans set up cafés and lemonade stands. See LEMONADE. That said, it would be hard to believe that Catherine's Medici lifestyle and powerful coterie of Italian hangers-on did not have significant influence on culinary fashion during her decades of dominance.

But was her involvement in pastry more personal? Her library contained at least one copy of Bartolomeo Scappi's influential *Opera*, first published in Venice in 1570, with its recipes for fried cream puffs and biscotti (there called *mostaccioli alla Milanese*). See BISCOTTI. According to the early-nineteenth-century Irish writer Sydney Morgan, Francis I had actually put Catherine in charge of the royal household, including the *office* where confectionery was made: "les patisseurs de la Dauphine shed a glory on the whole order, by the ingenuity they displayed in their architectural and allegorical structures." See SUGAR SCULPTURE. Whatever the truth of this assertion, it is clear that the prevailing fashion in confectionery changed during Catherine's years in power.

It is worth comparing a banquet celebrating Catherine's coronation in 1549 to a later feast given in honor of Anne of Austria, the Medici queen's new daughter-in-law in 1571. The earlier occasion had a decidedly medieval sensibility, with vast piles of game birds, hare, and rabbit. There were plenty of old-fashioned French pastries like cream tarts (*darioles de cresme*), date tarts, marzipan, choux pastry rings, crescent-shaped cakes, stirrup-shaped cakes (*estris*), various wafers, little flaky pastries, and "tartres de Millan" (a sort of shortbread moistened with curds). See DARIOLE; MARZIPAN; PASTRY, CHOUX; and WAFERS. The confectionery supplied by Pierre Siguier, apothecary and spicer, was also decidedly medieval. He provided "spices, dragées, hippocras, wax and other drugs furnished for the feast." See HIPPOCRAS. Fast forward some 20 years and the occasion might as well have taken place in Venice or Ferrara. The evening began with dinner, which was followed by dancing and finished off with a meal of sweetmeats (here called a *collation*, the French take on the Italian *collazione*). See DESSERT and SWEET MEALS. The display included preserves, both dry and liquid, sugared nuts, fruit pastes, marzipans, biscuits, and "every kind of fruit in the world." See FRUIT PASTES; FRUIT PRESERVES; and SUCKETS. There were even the sort of sugar sculptures for which Italian artisans were famous. Among these were Minerva and other classical figures, as well as trompe l'oeil meat and fish made of tragacanth paste. See TRAGACANTH and TROMPE L'OEIL.

Italian confectionery was no doubt the most advanced in the sixteenth century, in part because Venice and other Italian towns led Europe in sugar refining, and in part because of the peculiar nature of Italian Renaissance courts, which sought to outdo their neighbors through the magnificence of their patronage of the arts, including confectionery. See VENICE. This was a magnificence that both Francis I but most especially his Medici daughter-in-law would seek to emulate—if not exceed.

See also FRANCE and ITALY.

Danjou, Félix. "Festin donné à al royne Catherine au logis episcopal de l'évesché de Paris, le dix-neuvieme jour de jouing 1549." In *Archives curieuses de l'histoire de France*, series I, Vol. 3, p. 418. Paris: Beauvais, 1838.

Heller, Henry. *Anti-Italianism in Sixteenth-Century France*, p. 189. Toronto: University of Toronto Press, 2003.

Morgan, Sydney. *The Book Without a Name*, p. 10. Paris: Baudry's European Library, 1841.

Wheaton, Barbara Ketcham. *Savoring the Past: The French Kitchen and Table from 1300 to 1789*, p. 52. Philadelphia: University of Pennsylvania Press, 1983.

Michael Krondl

medicinal uses of sugar may seem counterintuitive in modern Western society, where sugar is considered a substance at worst inimical to health and at best a guilty pleasure carrying empty calories. However, in most past civilizations sugar was not merely the spoonful that helped the medicine go down, it *was* the medicine. This medicinal usage is rooted in ancient dietetic theory.

Sugar is a giant grass, *Saccharum officinarum*, native to the highlands of New Guinea, but there are also species found in India. Indians were the first to cultivate and process sugar, and the Sanskrit word *sarkara* is the origin of the Arabic *sukkar*, our "sugar," as well as the word in most other languages. See SUGAR. The Latin epithet *officinalis* that is sometimes used in place of *officinarum* for the plant's botanical name denotes that the substance belongs in the medicine cabinet. In the Ayurvedic system of ancient India, sugarcane juice is used to increase *kapha*—the dosha or bodily humor that regulates fluids in the body and lubrication. By this logic the juice serves as an expectorant in coughs, as an aphrodisiac that increases the libido, and as a diuretic to detoxify the kidneys. See APHRODISIACS. The ancient *Charaka Samhita* offers one of the earliest references to sugar's medicinal value: "The juice of the sugarcane, if the stalk is chewed with the aid of the teeth, increases the semen, is cool, purges the intestines, is oily, promotes nutrition and corpulency and excites the phlegm."

Sugar was brought to China from India along with Buddhism, and there it was considered nourishing for the spleen, strengthening for *qi* (vital energy), and having a cleansing property. It was also thought to generate bodily fluids, an idea that may have been borrowed from Ayurveda.

The ancient Greeks did not know sugar, although it was briefly encountered in the expeditions of Alexander the Great into South Asia. The Romans, too, were only familiar with sugar as an exotic medicine. Pliny the Elder mentions it in his *Natural History* as a medicine, as does the botanist Dioscorides, who wrote that "there is a kind of concreted honey, called *saccharon*, found in reeds in India and Arabia Felix, like in consistence to salt, and brittle to be broken between the teeth, as salt is. It is good for the belly and the stomach being dissolved in water and so drank, helping the pained bladder and the reins [kidneys]." The great physician Galen also mentions sugar briefly, saying that it is less sweet than honey but has the same medicinal properties.

Sugar was much more familiar to medieval Persian and Arab physicians. Avicenna in his *Canon of Medicine* not only uses sugar in many compounds but also mentions sugar-coated pills: "In the case of pills, some doctors give them a coating of honey, or boiled honey, or boiled sugar... Various expedients may be adopted to meet various temperaments or personal proclivities, thus enabling the patients to swallow the drug without being aware of it being a 'medicine.'" See PHARMACOLOGY.

After the year 1000, when trade connections to the East gradually proliferated, sugar became more familiar in Europe but still retained much of its medicinal association, inherited largely from traditions in the Muslim world. As a sweet substance, sugar, according to humoral physiology, was considered a heating and moistening aliment, one that is especially nourishing. In fact, for anyone but the choleric in whose bodies sugar might burn up, it was believed to be an ideal food.

By the late Middle Ages the culinary and medicinal use of sugar reached an unprecedented level, and the cane began to be grown in Sicily and islands such as Madeira and the Canaries. See SUGARCANE. The historian and first librarian of the Vatican Library, Bartolomeo Sacchi, better known as Platina, wrote that sugar is nourishing and good for the stomach, and that there is no dish not improved by sugar. This approbation became so widespread that Europeans became virtually addicted to sugar, especially after it was grown in the Caribbean and used to sweeten new caffeinated drinks like coffee, tea, and chocolate.

It was this very success and ubiquity that gradually stripped sugar of most of its supposed therapeutic value in Western medicine. Not only did new chemical and mechanical theories of physiology replace the humoral system, but also empirical evidence steadily mounted that sugar does little else than provide calories. Nonetheless, it continued to be used by habit in medicine. In the eighteenth century, for example, the French physician Louis Lemery prescribed it for colds and chest disorders and for cutting through viscous phlegm, much as sugar is still used today. Its use in formulating syrups and electuaries, as well as in making pills palatable, has remained standard right down to the present. Sugar is still a major ingredient used by the pharmaceutical industry, and when the price of sugar goes up, so does the price of drugs.

See also ANCIENT WORLD; COMFIT; PANNING; and SUGAR AND HEALTH.

Anderson, E. N. *Food in China*, p. 240. New Haven, Conn.: Yale University Press, 1988.

Avicenna. *Canon of Medicine*. Translated by O. Cameron Gruner, p. 485. New York: AMS, 1973.

Forbes, Robert James. *Studies in Ancient Technologies*. Vol. 6, p. 102. Leiden, The Netherlands: Brill, 1966.

Lemery, Louis. *Traite des Aliments*, p. 207. Paris: Pierre Witte, 1705.

Platina. *De honesta voluptate*, p. 156. Tempe, Ariz.: Medieval and Renaissance Texts and Studies, 1998.

Ken Albala

Mehlspeise, literally "flour food dish" in German, is today roughly translated as "dessert" or "pastry," but in earlier times the meaning was quite different. Until the late nineteenth century, in Catholic Austria, Bavaria, and the adjoining regions, Mehlspeise referred to a wide variety of flour-based foods, from strudels and vegetable tarts to dumplings and noodles.

J. G. Krünitz's *Oekonomische Encyclopädie* (Economic Encyclopedia, 1802) defined Mehlspeise as "any dish prepared from flour, so that [the word] can therefore also be understood to include dumplings, pancakes, noodles, etc. In particular, only certain soft-textured (pap-like) foods are considered Mehlspeisen, which are baked in a mold or bowl and contain mainly flour but also rice, sago, noodles, etc. with various fruits and other nourishing or flavor-enhancing additions." As the *Encyclopädie* implies, these dishes were predominantly sweet, but not always; a strudel might be filled with crayfish or apples, while pasta could be sprinkled with sugar or baked with Parmesan cheese. What characterized them was that they were all meatless and thus permitted on the many fast days prescribed by the Catholic calendar. Many regional cookbooks include a Mehlspeise category in the fast-day recipe section.

As elsewhere in Europe, meatless days were hardly abstemious for those who could afford fine food, and in Central Europe starchy side dishes were often served along elaborate fish preparations. However, as social status decreased, these flour-based foods became an ever more central component of the meal. Bavaria and the territories of the Hapsburg Empire were almost entirely landlocked, and although fresh fish were caught in the rivers and raised extensively in reservoirs, they were never as abundant or available as in countries with long seacoasts. In the nineteenth century some Czech peasants found fish to be such a rarity that they served fish-shaped loaves instead of the traditional carp for Christmas dinner.

If Central European Renaissance cookbooks are any guide, even the literate elite ate a great number of grain-based foods. The culinary guides have extensive sections devoted to porridge (*Muß*) of every description (predominantly meat-free, though not always). Many of these gruels were sweetened with fruit or honey (or grated honey-sweetened gingerbread) by poorer folk, and with sugar by the elite. The sixteenth-century citizens of Jindřichův Hradec in southern Bohemia made a specialty porridge with blueberries, flour, and gingerbread called *žahúr*, leading them to be called by the local nickname *žahúři*. Fitting more neatly into the *Encyclopädie's* definition, myriad varieties of fruit dumplings, sometimes fried rather than boiled, as is the case today, were another Renaissance favorite. See DUMPLINGS. Early versions often incorporated dried or fresh fruit into the dough, whereas today, fruit-filled dumplings such as the Wachau's *Marillenknödel* enclose whole fresh apricots in dough. Pancakes, sweetened with fruit butter, honey, and later sugar, were also commonly eaten as meatless, flour-based main courses. In much the way Italians of a certain class might make a meal out of pasta, Central Europeans often turned noodles into supper, but rather than dressing them with a savory sauce, they frequently topped them with cottage cheese, poppy seeds, and grated gingerbread or another sweetener.

Central European cookbooks devoted extensive sections to Mehlspeisen. Maria A. Neudecker lists some six dozen recipes explicitly categorized as Mehlspeisen in her 1806 *Die Baierische Köchin in Böhmen* (The Bavarian Cook in Bohemia). There are five strudels filled with ingredients from crayfish to chocolate, a wide assortment of dumplings, waffles, and baked puddings. Other recipes, such as one for *Kugelhopf* or various kinds of *kolatschen*, are closer to the more contemporary sense of Mehlspeisen as a hearty flour-based dessert. A hundred years later, the category has become even more blurred. The 1903 version of Katharina Prato's bestselling *Die süddeutsche Küche* (South German Cookery) still includes recipes for crayfish strudel (both with sugar and without) and macaroni with ham and cheese, but she also offers recipes for plum dumplings, *Kaiserschmarrn* (a partially shredded pancake), and polenta topped with butter, cinnamon, and sugar. The great majority of these dishes would still have been considered main courses, though not all.

As the hold of Catholic food observances faded in the twentieth century, so did the habit of eating flour-based foods as a main course, though not entirely. It is not considered odd to make a filling meal of dumplings or pancakes even if there is little Lenten association. When it comes to the term "Mehlspeise" itself, contemporary Germans barely use the word. It is still widely used in Austria, and to some degree in neighboring Bavaria, though the meaning no longer includes savory dishes as it once did. Today, the word is used broadly for just about any cooked sweet. This usage extends to the plural Mehlspeisen, in Austria sometimes used in place of "dessert" for the final sweet course of a meal.

Krondl, Michael. *Sweet Invention: A History of Dessert.* Chicago: Chicago Review Press, 2011.

Krünitz, J. G. *Oekonomische Encyclopädie.* Vol. 87. Berlin: Joachim Pauli, 1802.

Zíbrt, Čeněk. *Staročeské umění kuchařské.* Prague: Dauphin, 2012.

Michael Krondl

meringue is a billowy blend of whipped egg whites and sugar, with the addition of an acid, such as cream of tartar or lemon juice. When incorporated with an invisible ingredient, air, this foam multiplies eight times from its original unbeaten state, producing one of the most vital cornerstones of the confectionery kitchen, used in a myriad of pastries and desserts.

As far back as the seventeenth century, beaten egg whites and sugar were molded into small open baskets called "paper coffins." The renowned nineteenth-century French chef Marie-Antoine Carême was likely the first to use a pastry bag to pipe meringue, rather than shaping it with a spoon. Piped meringue made possible the creation of elaborate vacherins (large meringue shells) and other showpiece confections, such as Baked Alaska, a dramatic layer of meringue spread over an ice cream center and browned in the oven, one version of which is said to have been created for Delmonico's New York restaurant to commemorate the Alaska Purchase. See BAKED ALASKA; CARÊME, MARIE-ANTOINE; and VACHERIN. The early twentieth century gave us the pavlova, a heavenly meringue cake that is topped with fruit and whipped cream from Australia and New Zealand, which was devised in honor of ballerina Anna Pavlova. See PAVLOVA.

History

Legends claim that the airy mixture of meringue was named after the Swiss village of Meiringen, or even after the French Merovingian kings, but these etymologies are false, and uncertainty surrounds the origins of meringue and its name. We do know that meringue developed from the egg-white mixtures whisked with bundles of cleaned twigs that appeared in European cookery texts in the sixteenth and seventeenth centuries, generally with the addition of cream of tartar. See WHISKS AND BEATERS. When sugar began to replace cream of tartar in the seventeenth century, the mixture became even lighter and was referred to as "sugar puff." By the eighteenth century recipes close to those known today for modern meringue were already well known.

Written recipes for egg whites whipped with sugar appear in early English cookbooks, although they were not yet called "meringue." For instance, Lady Elinor Fettiplace's receipt book (1604) includes a brief recipe called White Bisket Bread, which calls for 1½ pounds of sugar, a handful of fine white flour, and the whites of 12 beaten eggs—proportions surprisingly similar to those used for meringue today. The first documented recipe actually titled "meringue" was published in François Massialot's *Le cuisinier roïal et bourgeois* (1691).

The Science of Meringue

When a recipe specifies using only two or three ingredients, such as egg whites, sugar, and an acid, achieving perfection can be a challenge, as is the case with meringue. So it is helpful to understand the chemistry of egg foams. See EGGS. Egg whites are composed of proteins and water. When beaten and combined with air, the albumen, or thick white of the egg, separates into gaseous foam, a stable mass of tiny bubbles coated with a thin layer of water. When air and acid are incorporated into the whites, or when the mixture is exposed to heat with the help of steam, the bonds of the whites unfold, denaturing the proteins and making it possible for them to join and solidify. As meringue cooks, another protein, called the ovalbumin, goes to work and changes the fluid foam into one that is solid, thus preventing collapse of the structure.

Beating whites to the correct consistency can be a baker's nemesis. It is essential to begin with a clean bowl and whip, whisk, or beaters that have been wiped lightly, usually with an acid such as white vinegar, to remove any trace of fat. Eggs that are closer to their expiration date make the best candidates for meringues; because the whites are thinner, they beat up faster, quickly attracting air cells. Very fresh eggs have thicker whites and should be stirred or blended together with a whisk or fork before whipping, to achieve even viscosity. The whites must be completely free of egg yolk; cold eggs are easier to separate. Using a copper bowl to whip egg whites produces a more stable foam and greater volume. Some pastry chefs advise against using salt when beating egg whites because they believe it leaches water from the whites and increases beating time. Because whipped egg whites are fragile, tender handling is always required. Overbeating or overheating can ruin a meringue.

Methods for Making Meringue

Three methods exist for incorporating sugar into the egg foam: French, Swiss, and Italian. The least stable of the meringues but most popular and easiest to make is the common or French meringue. Here, sugar is whipped into room-temperature egg whites, at about 70°F (21°C), without the use of heat. To make Swiss meringue, the whites and sugar are first whipped with a balloon whisk in a bowl set over a hot-water bath (bain-marie) and warmed to 110° to 120°F (40° to 50°C) to dissolve the sugar; the mixture is then beaten until cool on medium-high speed in a stand mixer. Italian meringue, the strongest of the three, starts with egg whites at room temperature. After whipping the whites to soft peaks, a hot sugar syrup is added and the mixture is beaten until cool. All three meringues should contain cream of tartar or lemon juice for stability and added volume, and should be whipped until thick, smooth, and glossy.

Sugar is the invaluable ingredient that captures air, creates volume and texture, and provides the gift of sweetness to meringues. Extracting cane juice from the sugarcane plant began in Southeast Asia thousands of years ago. India deserves credit for transforming cane juice into granules more than 2,000 years ago. A fine grained sugar is favored for making meringues because it is quick to dissolve and has the ability to entrap air well. See SUGAR and SUGAR REFINING. If unavailable, it can be made by finely grinding granulated sugar in a food processor. Confectioner's sugar, also called powdered or 10X, is a blend of granulated sugar and 3 percent cornstarch. Its powdery texture is achieved by milling granulated sugar 10 times (hence the name 10X). The presence of cornstarch in meringue is believed to aid in absorbing moisture.

Cream of tartar is an acidic ingredient extracted from wine residue that forms on the inside of wine vats. Its primary usage in meringue preparations is to stabilize beaten egg whites and increase volume.

There are two types of meringue, *soft* and *hard*. Achieving one or the other depends solely on the amount of sugar incorporated—soft requires less, whereas hard requires more. Generally, the ratio of sugar per egg white is 2 to 4 tablespoons, but the exact quantity used within this ratio is guided by the specifications of the recipe.

Soft meringues not only use less sugar, they require less beating time and shorter baking in a moderate oven at 325° to 350°F (163° to 177°C). Popular recipes made with soft meringues include pie toppings, sponge, chiffon and angel food cakes, soufflés, mousses, chewy cookies, buttercreams, and other frostings.

Hard meringues use the maximum amount of sugar and require more beating time and longer baking. These confections are slowly baked in a low oven at 200° to 225°F (93° to 107°C). They should remain light in color, with no sign of browning (unless made with ground nuts, cocoa, or espresso powder). To maintain the white color and optimum crispness, hard meringues are often dried in an unlit oven for several hours or overnight to remove all moisture. This procedure applies to vacherins, meringue nests, crisp cookies (such as kisses), and ornamental decorations like meringue mushrooms.

Baking is not recommended during humid weather because of the negative effect it has on all baked meringues. Soft meringue made on days with high humidity can result in a gummy texture, while hard meringues lose their crispness. Sugar and egg whites attract moisture, which often causes "weeping," brown beads of melted sugar that form on the surface.

Tricky as working with meringue may be, once the baker gets a feel for the process, the rewards are great and enable the baker to produce a delightfully diverse array of baked goods.

See also FRANCE.

McGee, Harold. *On Food and Cooking: The Science and Lore of the Kitchen*. New York: Charles Scribner's Sons, 1984.

"Meringue Musings & History." 10 September 2012. http://www.epicureanpiranha.com/2012/meringue-musings-and-history/.

Muster, Douglas. "The Origins and History of Meringue." http://www.inmamaskitchen.com/FOOD_IS_ART/meringue2.html.

Toussaint-Samat, Maguelonne. *History of Food*. Translated by Anthea Bell. Cambridge, Mass.: Blackwell, 1992.

Carole Walter

Mexico to this day show traces of three distinct traditions in its sweets. Pre-Hispanic sweets included fruits, saps, and honey, although chocolate, now so much part of the Western sweet kitchen, was then prepared as a cold, bitter, spiced drink. In the colonial period, the largely Islamic-derived sweet kitchen of late medieval Spain was further developed and adapted to the products of the New World. Starting in the mid-nineteenth century, immigrants introduced other sweet traditions and new technologies that allowed for the flourishing of new kinds of sweets.

The Aztecs, the Mayas, and the many other peoples living in what is now Mexico enjoyed a variety of fruits. See FRUIT. In the tropical lowlands, they picked, for example, pineapple, cherimoya (*Annona cherimola*) and guayabana (soursop, *Annona muricata*), and creamy orange mamey (*Pouteria sapota*). On the high, arid central plateau, they gathered little golden apple-shaped tejocote (*Crataegus Mexicana* in the hawthorn family) and tiny black garambullos that outlined the branches of the old man cactus (*Myrtillocactus geometrizans*), as well as vivid pink and yellow pitahayas (Hylocereus family) and pink and green *tunas* and *xoconostle* from the nopal or paddle cactus (Opuntia family). To make a long-keeping sweet paste, they macerated and dehydrated the *tunas*. See FRUIT PASTE. They extracted the sweetness from mesquite pods by boiling and evaporation; they sucked the juices of maize and relished young cobs for their sweetness. They made syrup (*aguamiel*) from the sap of agaves and collected honey from the combs of native bees (*Melipona beechiae*), the papery nests of wasps (*Brachygastra mellifica*) and ants. See AGAVE NECTAR; HONEY; and SAP. Scholars believe the Indians showed a preference for a sweet/hot flavor profile that is still much appreciated.

In 1521 the Spanish conquered Mexico City. They quickly introduced new plants and animals, such as the European honeybee, cattle, sheep, goats, wheat, citrus, and above all sugarcane. Within a few years of the Conquest, Hernán Cortés established a sugar plantation near Cuernavaca, a hundred miles to the south of Mexico City. Other plantations and refineries soon followed. See PLANTATIONS, SUGAR and SUGAR REFINERIES. The Spanish sweet tradition was expanded to include American fruits and nuts, particularly pecans and peanuts. Chocolate was used to make a hot, sweet, spiced drink, though rarely in baking or confectionery.

Just as important, the Spanish brought with them the ovens, stoves, and implements of European kitchens and bakeries, as well as cookbooks and know-how about baking and confectionery. They also continued traditional European ways of organizing male kitchen workers into guilds of bakers, who turned out sweet breads (pan dulce) as well as regular bread; cake makers; and biscuit makers, who prepared "fruits of the oven" (*frutas de horno*), essentially cookies of different combinations of wheat flour, sugar, eggs, milk, and water. Confectioners created what are now known as traditional sweets (*dulces tradicionales*). Included were wafers (*obleas*), fruit- and nut-based confections deriving from the Islamic tradition, egg yolk and sugar confections developed in Portugal and Spain, and boiled-down milk confections. See EGG YOLK SWEETS; ISLAM; and WAFERS.

The sweet goods prepared by male guilds overlapped with those made by women in haciendas, town houses, and, above all, convents. See CONVENT SWEETS. A tradition of manuscript cookbooks flourished, a high proportion of the recipes being for sweets. The sophisticated, diverse sweet tradition of the colonial period was underwritten by the wealth that flowed from the colony's fabulously rich silver mines.

The culmination of the colonial tradition can be appreciated in the 800 or so sweet recipes in the first published Mexican cookbook, *El cocinero mexicano*, which appeared in 1831, immediately after independence from Spain. Cake and pastry making (*pasteleria*) is the subject of the first of six sections. Represented are puff pastry (*hojaldre*); choux pastry (*masa real*, "royal" dough); pastries for empanadas and raised pies; cookie doughs (*regalo de horno*, gift of the oven); buñuelos, which merit 30 recipes; and *bizcochos* (which usually contain flour, sugar, eggs, and sometimes lard, occasionally a leavening agent). See FRIED DOUGH; PASTRY, CHOUX and PASTRY, PUFF.

Desserts and confectionery (*reposteria*) make up the remaining five sections. Tortas, puddings, and bread- and *bizcocho*-based sweets include both sweet and savory "cakes"; Anglo-style "pudines," among them Indian (hasty) and plum pudding; and a series of variants on bread pudding (golden soup, *sopa dorada*) and French toast (*torrejas*). See PUDDING. The eclectic section that follows begins with egg sweets (the convent-developed egg-based confectionery), gelatins, and creams (identified as French). See DESSERTS, CHILLED and GELATIN DESSERTS. It continues with *antes*, elaborate composed dishes served at the start of the meal, often sponge cake covered with a fruit paste and topped with spices, dried fruits, and syrups. *Postres*, the dishes served after the meal, cross the sweet/savory divide. Medieval/Islamic blancmange (*manjar blanco*), a purée of chicken, rice, and almonds, for which 10 recipes are given, is joined by dishes such as pork meatballs in syrup with raisins, almonds, and pine nuts; a paste of ground chickpeas or dried broad beans with sugar and milk; and a variety of flans (*leche cuajada*). See BLANCMANGE and FLAN (PUDÍM).

Then come dry preserves, mainly candies, marzipan and nougat (*turrón*), crystallized fruits, compotes (poached fruits), and conserves (jams and marmalades), fruit pastes or cheeses (*cajetas*, little boxes from the containers in which they were stored), and syrups. See FRUIT PRESERVES; MARZIPAN; and NOUGAT. A couple of sections on sorbets, ices (*helados*) made with cream and eggs, fruit waters, and liqueurs round out the extensive range of sweets. See ICE CREAM and SHERBET.

Since galleons sailed annually between New Spain and the Philippines (with links to Panama and Lima, Peru), the sweets described in *El cocinero mexicano* reached Asia and reunited with those in other Spanish colonies. And since this cookbook was the model for other foundational cookbooks published elsewhere in Latin America, Mexican sweets continued to have influence beyond the country's boundaries.

The third stage in the evolution of Mexican sweets began after independence and is still progressing today. Cake shops, coffee shops, and tearooms in the European tradition, and soda fountains in the American, provided new places where respectable women were welcome and could consume sweets on a regular basis outside the home. See CAFÉ and SODA FOUNTAIN. The cake shops El Globo (1884) and Pasteleria Ideal (1927) still exist, while the restaurant, confectionery, and bakeries of Sanborns, founded by Walther and Frank Sanborn in 1903 (acquired by Walgreens in 1946 and since 1985 in the hands of Grupo Carso), remain draws for the middle class in the centers of every major Mexican town.

New immigrants from the Spanish Basque country at the beginning of the twentieth century took over the baking industry, at least in Mexico City. They were probably responsible for the popular sweet breads for Day of the Dead (*pan de muerto*) and Three Kings Day (*pan de tres reyes*). See DAY OF THE DEAD and TWELFTH NIGHT CAKE. On a daily basis, bakery shelves are stacked with an enormous variety of small, mildly sweet breads (pan dulce), the most popular being *conchas* (shells) eaten for breakfast or with chocolate before retiring to bed. See BREADS, SWEET. Chinese immigrants introduced salted, aniseed-flavored dried fruits (*see mui*), which were Mexicanized as bright pink tamarind and mango *chamoy* sold alongside the *dulces tradicionales*. Japanese immigrants were almost certainly responsible for the popularity of shaved ice with syrup (*raspados*), and Lebanese for widely available Middle Eastern pastries. See SHAVE ICE.

Refrigeration meant a proliferation of cold sweets. Starting in the early twentieth century, ice cream makers (*neveros*) appeared in town squares, twirling metal buckets of fruit, cheese, and nut mixtures in wooden tubs of ice. In the 1950s those of Tocumbo, a remote town in the central state of Michoacán, began selling fruit pops (*paletas michoacana*); now their townsfolk have outlets all over Mexico. In the 1960s and 1970s custard ice cream makers set up business, followed by international chains such as Baskin-Robbins. See BASKIN-ROBBINS.

Condensed milk transformed home desserts. See SWEETENED CONDENSED MILK. Nestlé's La Lechera condensed milk cans and cookbooks offered tantalizing, easy recipes. Their recipe for *flan magico*, flan prepared in a pressure cooker, became to all intents and purposes the national dessert. The chief challenger was gelatin, opaque with condensed milk or transparent with fruit juice. See GELATIN DESSERTS. In the late twentieth century gelatins became yet more glorious with colored-syrup flower shapes embedded by syringe. Then came *pastel de tres leches*. See TRES LECHES CAKE. Most recently, *chocoflan*, a flan recipe mixed with a packaged chocolate cake recipe that separates into two layers, has become the rage.

By contrast, home baking of cakes, cookies, and pies remains unusual, even though ovens have been commonplace in well-to-do homes for a century and are creeping into the kitchens of even the poorest. Instead, women turn to supermarkets and small entrepreneurs for cookies, pies, and cakes, which are still reserved for birthdays and other celebrations. The prestige line of cookies, many of them wafers, is Mac Ma, with its own line of stores. Then comes Marinela, part of the Bimbo baking empire, founded in 1945 by Catalan immigrant Lorenzo Servitije and associates. Among its offerings are cookies such as Mexican wedding cookies (*polvorones*), Lors (an Oreo type of cookie), Principe ("Prince," a chocolate cream sandwich), and individually wrapped pies (pecan, pineapple) and snack cakes. In 1956, following its purchase of extrusion machinery for cakes, Bimbo began producing snack cakes, the most popular being the Gansito, a chocolate-covered sponge with a white creamy center containing strawberry jam.

Mass-market confectionery is dominated by Mars, Nestlé, Frito-Lay, Kraft, Ferrero, and Hershey's, which turn to firms such as Grupo Piasa for high-quality sugar from modern mills. See HERSHEY'S; MARS; and NESTLÉ. Medium-size Mexican companies such as La Lorena and Dulces Vero, and a host of tiny ones, turn out hard candies, tamarind candies, and chamoy-flavored sauce for use on fruit. Nestlé is the biggest seller of drinking chocolate, still the major use of chocolate.

Modern Mexican sweets are consumed across the Americas thanks to over 34 million Mexicans in the United States, as well as Bimbo's presence in Latin America and the United States.

See also CHOCOLATE, PRE-COLUMBIAN; PORTUGAL; and SPAIN.

Barros, Cristina, ed. *El cocinero mexicano*. Colección Recetarios antiquos. Mexico City: CONACULTA, Culturas Populares, 2000. Reprint of the 1831 edition.
Curiel, José Luis. *La dulcería Mexicana: Historia, ciencia y tecnologia*. Mexico City: Limusa, 2007.
Maza, Josué de la, ed. *Dulces momentos con la lechera*. Mexico City: Nestlé, 1998.
Zolla, Carlos. *Elogio del dulce: Ensayo sobre la dulcería Mexicana*. Mexico City: Fondo de Cultura Económica, 1988.

Rachel Laudan

The **Middle East**—Egypt and the Fertile Crescent countries, with Arabia as a late-joining partner—is where agriculture began around 11,000 years ago with the domestication of that versatile grain, wheat, which has figured ever since in so many sweets and pastries. It is also where literature began 4,500 years ago, but early scribes gave regrettably little thought to our curiosity about what they ate.

For instance, *šʿ-t*, one of the scores of ancient Egyptian words that can be translated as "bread," might have been sweetened with dates or date juice, or maybe not. The Babylonians made something called *qullupu* for the monthly Eshshēshu festival, and from context we can be sure it was made with honey, linseed oil, or dried fruits, but was it a sweetened bread, a fried pastry, or a rich pudding? The Hittites were a little more forthcoming about their baked goods, but they often represented the names with Sumerian logograms such as NIN.DA$_4$, rather than spelling them out in Hittite, so we do not know what they actually called them, which might have cast some light on what they were like. Fortunately, what seems to be a translation of NIN.LÁL into the related Luvian language, *malitiwallas kuisa*, gives a little clue, because it means "honey bread (shaped like a) fang."

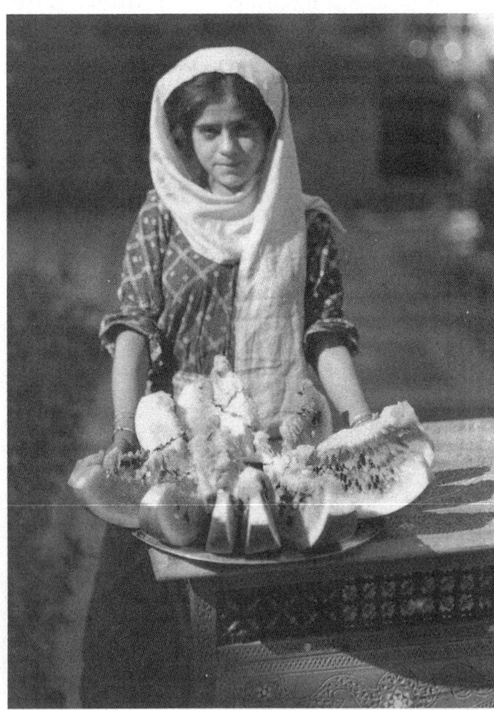

A young woman displays watermelon for sale at a railway station in Syria. JULES GERVAIS COURTELLEMONT / NATIONAL GEOGRAPHIC CREATIVE

Yes, a fang. The sweets that were recorded in ancient times were made for religious occasions and often had symbolic shapes, especially in Egypt. See SYMBOLIC MEANINGS. At the same time, ordinary people were probably making humbler sweets for everyday use that perhaps resembled some that are current in present-day Oman, such as a sort of pudding made by boiling date juice with flour and a little butter until thick.

In the sixth century, we suddenly know a good deal about everyday foods in one particular area, western Arabia. Muslims had a pious interest in the life of Muhammad, and religious scholars felt an obligation to learn everything about the Arabic language in which the Qurʾān was written, so over the next two centuries a colossal amount of data was collected on early medieval Arabia. See ISLAM.

From what the scholars recorded, it is clear that meat was a highly regarded food for special occasions, but the everyday cuisine was overwhelmingly based on dates, barley, and dairy products. The dates meant that many dishes were more or less sweet, but this fairly wholesome diet suffered grievously from monotony. See DATES. The eleventh-century Moorish linguist Ibn Sīda compiled a glossary of Arabian food names that suggests a desperate desire to wring variety out of this severely limited pantry.

For instance, he lists separate words for dried dates steeped in milk (*siqʿal*), pounded dates thrown in buttermilk (*raḍḍ*), milk poured over dates (*majīʿ*), pitted dates mixed with milk (*waṭīʾa*), cottage cheese pounded with dates (*ʿabītha*), toasted barley mixed with dates (*bakīla*), dates kneaded with toasted barley (*ʿujjāl*), and so forth. Of this repertoire, the only Arabian sweets that the seventh-century Muslim conquests spread to other countries were *hais*, which was originally dates mixed with butter and cottage cheese—later medieval recipes would substitute cake crumbs, nuts, and sesame oil for the last two ingredients—and *ʿaṣīda*, a simple peasant porridge optionally sweetened with dates. In its turn, *ʿaṣīda* was later rendered more grand by using flour instead of barley grits and adding nuts, sugar, and other upscale ingredients.

Tenth-Century Haute Cuisine

On conquering Persia, the Arabs discovered the splendor and luxury of its imperial court and speedily jettisoned their ancestral dishes in favor of Persian cuisine. See BAGHDAD and PERSIA. The caliphs of Baghdad organized cooking contests among their boon companions, just as Persian emperors had, and gentlemen of their court kept collections of favorite recipes, just as Persian noblemen had. In the tenth century, a book titled *Kitāb al-Ṭabīkh* (The Book of Dishes) was compiled from these court recipe collections, so we know a very great deal about what the aristocrats of Baghdad ate during its golden age, the eighth through tenth centuries.

Most of the sweets in this book have Persian names: various delicate puddings called *fālūdhaj*, fancifully shaped fritters (*zulābiyā*) dipped in honey, and, above all, marzipan (*lauzīnaj*) in a pastry wrapper so delicate that one poet compared it to grasshoppers' wings. See MARZIPAN and ZALABIYA. It was immersed in sugar syrup and sesame oil until it was eaten. According to a famous anecdote, when a rough Turkish warrior named Toghril Beg conquered the city in 1055, Baghdadis presented him with some *lauzīnaj* in the hope that he would appreciate their precious, sophisticated civilization. Unfortunately, he is said to have responded, "These are good noodles, but they need garlic."

The most esteemed meat dish, *jūdhāb*, was itself partly a sweet. As meat roasted in a tandoor oven, a tray of pudding (the *jūdhāb* proper) was inserted under it so that the pudding could be enriched with the running fat and meat juices. The diner received a serving of roast meat on top of a portion of this *jūdhāb*, which could be a bread or rice pudding, a cornstarch-thickened pudding flavored with fruits such as apricots or mulberries, or even a tray of fried bananas or crepes folded around a ground nut filling. So, it was basically sugar, starch, meat, and fat—scarcely what your doctor would prescribe, and your doctor would probably not be surprised that it was very popular.

As they represented courtly tastes, the recipes emphasized expensive ingredients. *Khabīṣ*, a sort of fruit- or nut-flavored pudding adopted from the Aramaic-speaking Christian population of the Fertile Crescent, was usually thickened with flour or crumbled biscotti (*kaʿk*), but in this book one luxurious recipe substitutes ground almonds. *Muhallabiyya* was basically rice pudding, but two recipes in *Kitāb al-Ṭabīkh* were custards flavored with nuts. (Medieval Arab rice puddings were often enriched with shredded chicken breast, so many a *muhallabiyya* resembled the medieval European *blancmanger* and the modern Turkish *tavuk göğsü*.) See BLANCMANGE.

A newly recorded pastry, which would become very important in later centuries, was *qaṭāʾif*, a sort of eggless crepe made by kneading a stiff dough and then gradually working in enough water to make it slack. Relatively slack, that is—*qaṭāʾif* could be rolled out for frying or baking, but the batter would be thin enough for dipping food for frying. See FRIED DOUGH. In *Kitāb al-Ṭabīkh*, the crepes were usually fried and sweetened a bit like modern pancakes, but the most distinctive treatment was to fry them on one side only, leaving the upper sides tacky; top them with sweetened, ground nuts; fold them over and seal; and then deep-fry the resulting packets.

Egypt had made two contributions to the sweets repertoire. One was *kaʿk* (from Coptic *kʾaakʾe*), a sort of ring-shaped biscuit that has survived to the present. The other was an extra-thin flatbread, *kunāfa* (Coptic *kenephiten*), which served as a wrapper in sweets.

After learning of pulled taffy (*fānīdh*) from Iran, Baghdad cooks had started exploring the higher densities of sugar syrup. In *Kitāb al-Ṭabīkh*, a sort of nougat called *nāṭif* was made by beating thick hot syrup with egg whites. It could also be made with boiled honey, but from this point on sugar quickly replaced honey in confectionery. See NOUGAT and TAFFY.

The Thirteenth Century

Three substantial cookbooks date from thirteenth-century Egypt, Syria, and Iraq and share a common repertoire of dishes. To take one example, *Kitāb Waṣf al-Aṭʿima al-Muʿtāda* (The Description of Familiar Foods) includes most of the tenth-century sweets, although *zalabiya* is now made by dribbling leavened batter into boiling oil, in the manner of Pennsylvania Dutch funnel cakes. See PENNSYLVANIA DUTCH. The cuisine is less extravagant than that of the Baghdad of the caliphs, and various new dishes have been invented, such as *qāhiriyya*, a ring of pistachio paste dipped in batter, deep-fried, and drenched in syrup. A number of new desserts have been created based on stuffing or layering *qaṭāʾif*.

Some of the sweets resemble more recent Arab favorites. *Luqam al-qāḍī*, little deep-fried pellets of dough dressed with sugar syrup, have scarcely changed since the thirteenth century. A cannoli-like pastry called "Zainab's fingers" (*aṣābiʿ Zainab*) resembles modern Arab pastries with similar names, except that the tube that is stuffed with nuts was made of noodle paste and cooked by frying, while the modern versions use filo dough and are baked. See FILO. A pastry not given a name in the books was what is now called *kunāfa* in the Arab world—thin strings of batter dribbled on a heated tray to make something that looks like semi-cooked vermicelli. This would be kneaded with butter and baked, making the pastry known as *kadayıf* in Turkish, *kadaifi* in Greek, and—somewhat confusingly since it is nothing of the kind—"Shredded Wheat pastry" to many Americans.

Experimentation with sugar syrup was ongoing. A sort of cookie called *aqrāṣ mukallala* was glazed by dipping it into very thick syrup, and a new variety of *lauzīnaj* was virtually the same as modern nougatine (sugar cooked without water to the hard crack stage, then stirred with almond paste). Hard candies (*aqrāṣlīmūn*) had been invented and were colored red, yellow, or green, like lemon drops or Life Savers. See HARD CANDY; LIFE SAVERS; and STAGES OF SUGAR SYRUP.

The Moors transmitted the Middle East's knowledge of sweets to Europe during their occupation of Spain (717–1492) and Sicily (827–1224), starting with the culture of the sugarcane. See SUGARCANE. *Lauzīnaj* spread under a new name, *makhshabān*, giving European words for this product, such as Spanish *mazapán* and English marzipan. Along with the knowledge of syrup the Moors passed on the technique of candying. A third-century Damascus cookbook titled *Kitāb al-Wuṣla ilā al-ḥabīb* gives a recipe for candying gourd, which is essentially identical to the Spanish *dulce de calabaza*. An anonymous thirteenth-century Moorish cookbook gives a recipe for puff pastry under an Arabic name (*muwarraqa*) and a Spanish one (*folyatil*), both meaning "leafy," which suggests that puff pastry might have been a joint invention of the Moors and the Spanish. See PASTRY, PUFF.

The Turkish Period

Already in the thirteenth century, Arab cuisine had started to show the influence of the Turks who had been moving into the region from Central Asia, first as mercenary soldiers, then as rulers. Along with Turkish breads and pastas, a few sweets appeared in the Arab cookbooks. One was *qarni yārūq* (split belly), which was made by kneading flour and water as if for noodles but with the addition of some melted butter. This rich paste was rolled out thin, cut into strips, and fried crisp. Dressed with syrup and pistachios, it was like a slightly crumbly, deconstructed baklava. See BAKLAVA.

Another was *qāwūt*, a sweetened mixture of grain and nuts fried in butter that was originally served to women in childbed. It paralleled a traditional Middle Eastern food, not recorded in the medieval books but clearly of great antiquity: boiled whole grain sweetened and served on religious occasions. See WHEAT BERRIES. Grain symbolizes rebirth, so Christians made this dish for Easter and the feast of the martyr St. Barbara. Shiite Muslims made it on ʿĀshūrāʾ, the tenth day of the month of Muharram, which is the anniversary of the martyrdom of the caliph ʿAli, so Muslims know this dish as *ʿāshūrāʾ*.

By the end of the sixteenth century, the Ottoman Turks had conquered the entire Arab world east of Morocco, except for the remoter parts of Arabia. Originally, the Ottomans' idea of haute cuisine was derived from books written in thirteenth-century Baghdad, but as the capital of a large and wealthy empire, Istanbul quickly developed its own style, the cuisine of elaborate kebabs, eggplant stews, stuffed vegetables, and baklava-type pastries that now dominates the eastern Mediterranean. See TURKEY.

Today

Even centuries ago, Middle Eastern pastries and confections tended to avoid the sweet–sour combination, which was considered appropriate only for meat dishes. As a result, the sole fruit regularly used in sweet preparations has been the very sugary date. Mixed dried fruits, however, are cooked together as fruit compote, *khoshāf*.

Some of the medieval pastries have survived to the present: *zulābiyā* (also called *mushabbak*, meaning "lattice"), *qaṭāʾif*; *aṣābiʿ Zainab* (or related names meaning "lady's fingers," such as *ṣawābiʿ al-sitt*), and *luqam al-qāḍī*. Puddings are still popular: *muhallabiyya* (usually thickened with cornstarch), *rizz bi-ḥalīb* (rice pudding, which has medieval antecedents), and *mughlī* (a nut-enriched cross between a pudding and a custard). See PUDDING. At one point in the late Middle Ages, a crumbly butter cookie evolved under the name *ghurayba* (literally, "the little extraordinary thing"). Borrowed in Turkish, it was pronounced *kurabiye*, the name by which it has become known in the West through its Greek spelling, *kourambies* (pl. *kourambiedes*).

If you look into a bakery in most of this area, you will be struck by the predominance of Turkish baklava-type pastries. The Turkish influence is strongest in Damascus, which was a local center of administration under the Ottoman government. Damascus still has a significant Turkish population and is known for making the best baklava-type pastries in the Arab world. Other widespread Turkish sweets are *qamar al-din*, the famous "apricot leather," and *sujuq*, a confection made by dipping a string of walnut meats into a boiling mixture of grape syrup and cornstarch, as if dipping a candle. The name means "sausage" in Turkish, and the product does end up looking like a rather lumpy sausage.

Particularly characteristic of northern Syria is *ḥalāwat jibn*, a versatile sweet that is a little difficult to classify. It is made by toasting flour with butter and stirring it with syrup—making a sweet roux, in effect. When the mixture thickens, the cook kneads it with crumbled mild cheese to make something with a texture oddly reminiscent of a washcloth. It can be eaten by itself or rolled around a stuffing such as nuts.

The most famous Egyptian sweet is *om ʿAli* (mother of Ali), a sort of bread pudding made by baking torn-up pieces of bread or filo dough with milk and nuts. It is suspected that this dish is actually adapted from the English bread pudding, which was introduced at a hospital in Upper Egypt during the early twentieth century by a nurse named O'Malley.

Iraq shows recent Iranian influence, for instance, *rangīna*, a confection of dates and toasted flour, and *nūni panjara*, fritters cooked with a special iron like the Italian *rosette*. Iraq has indigenous specialties of its own, such as deep-fried cardamom-flavored cakes called *ṣalūq*. The Persian Gulf cooks much like Iraq, except that there is far less Turkish influence.

The southern and eastern Arabian Peninsula cooks rather differently. Most sweets in Oman are pudding like, thickened to one degree or another with starch, agar agar, or other products. In ascending order of firmness, they are *sakhana*, *khabīṣa*, and *ḥalwā*. Some have unusual flavorings, such as fava beans or even garlic, and concentrated milk figures in many *ḥalwās*, possibly reflecting Indian influence. See HALVAH and INDIA. Oman is closer to Bombay than to Baghdad and has adopted at least one Indian dessert, the Indian vermicelli, *siwāya*, cooked with sugar and nuts.

Yemen, at the southern tip of the Arabian Peninsula, is one of the world's poorest countries. Its traditional sweets are usually flavored with honey, which is considered medicinal and also blessed, because it is mentioned in the Qurʾān. Despite the country's poverty, surprisingly expensive honey boutiques are located in Sanaa. A typical sweet is *fatūt*, crumbled bread that can actually be mixed with anything but very often is flavored with honey or bananas. The specialty of Sanaa is *bint al-ṣaḥn*—layers of leavened dough, stacked up, baked, and served with butter and honey. In Sanaa, this dish is usually served at the beginning of the meal.

See also HONEY and NORTH AFRICA.

Abdennour, Samia. *Egyptian Cooking and Other Middle Eastern Recipes*. Cairo: American University, 2011.

Hamad, Sarah al-. *Cardamom and Lime: Recipes from the Arabian Gulf*. Northampton, Mass.: Interlink, 2011.

Helou, Anissa. *Lebanese Cuisine*. New York: St. Martin's, 1998.

Ibn Sīda. *Al-Mukhaṣṣaṣ*. Vol. 3, Book XI, pp. 57–64. Beirut: al-Maktab al-Tījārī lil-ṭibāʿa wal-Tawzīʿ wal-Nashr, 1965.

Nasrallah, Nawal. *Annals of the Caliphs' Kitchens: Ibn Sayyār al-Warrāq's Tenth-Century Baghdadi Cookbook*, pp. 374–432. Leiden, The Netherlands, and Boston: Brill, 2005.

Perry, Charles, trans. "*Kitāb Waṣf al-Aṭʿima al-Muʿtāda* [The Description of Familiar Foods]." In *Medieval Arab Cookery*, edited by Maxime Rodinson and A. J. Arberry, pp. 373–450. Totnes, U.K.: Prospect, 2000.

Roden, Claudia. *The New Book of Middle Eastern Food*. New York: Knopf, 2000.

Charles Perry

The **Midwest (U.S.)** is the area of the United States encompassing Illinois, Indiana, Iowa, Kansas, Michigan, Minnesota, Missouri, Nebraska, North Dakota, Ohio, South Dakota, and Wisconsin. Long before this official definition, however, Midwesterners themselves were characterizing their region and its food. In 1842, for example, Mrs. Philomelia Ann Maria Antoinette Hardin published the wonderfully titled *Every Body's Cook and Receipt Book: But More Particularly Designed for Buckeyes, Hoosiers, Wolverines, Corncrackers, Suckers, and All Epicures Who Wish to Live with the Present Times*, giving the Midwest its first truly regional cookbook. Hardin's book, purportedly the first printed west of the Alleghenies, wasn't a collection of recipes that she culled from cooks in the East Coast or England. She speaks to the stomachs around her, with recipes for "Hoosier Pickles" and "Buckeye Rusk." Here is her recipe for "Wolverine Pudding":

> A quarter of a pound of buiscets [*sic*] grated, a quarter of a pound of currents cleanly washed and picked, a quarter of a pound of suet shred small, half a large spoonful of pounded sugar, and some grated nutmeg; mince it all well together, then take the yelks [*sic*] of three eggs, and make it all into balls as big as turkey's eggs; fry them in fresh butter of a fine light brown.

This was a dessert to get a Wolverine through a Michigan winter, and if readers lived in Ohio, Indiana, Kentucky, or Illinois, they could find recipes to satisfy their sweet tooth, printed alongside "Valuable Rules" for making medicine, raising honey bees, or cultivating fruit trees. Hardin's book firmly roots its advice and recipes in the region now called the Midwest. See PUDDING.

The term itself, as it refers to the stretch of the United States east of the Ohio River and west of the Missouri, did not come into American usage until the 1890s, and Hardin's title hints at the difficulty of describing this region's character. Buckeyes, Hoosiers, and Wolverines still embrace those nicknames, but people from Kentucky or Illinois are not likely to see themselves as Corncrackers or Suckers. Midwestern sweets are marked by this clash in the region between continuity and change. From the Native Americans' precolonial use of *sinzibuckwud*—the Algonquin word for "tree sap" that literally means "drawn from wood"—to the maple candy that Pa gives his daughters in Laura Ingalls Wilder's popular *Little House on the Prairie* series ("It was better even than their Christmas candy"), to the 568,000 gallons of maple syrup produced by Ohio, Michigan, and Wisconsin in 2013, Midwestern sweets have been created and consumed in response to the needs and desires of the people who live there; people who have constantly inherited, invented, and adapted their food from the land around them; and the people, sometimes very different from themselves, who live alongside them. See MAPLE SUGARING; MAPLE SYRUP; and NATIVE AMERICAN.

The Great Plains states of Kansas, Iowa, the Dakotas, and Nebraska have given Americans one vision of the Midwest: a heartland of small towns and agrarian values, where endless acres of cereal crops, such as corn and wheat, unfurl among silos and farmhouses, as a classic dessert like sugar cream pie cools on the sill. Also known as Hoosier pie, farm pie, Indiana cream pie, and finger pie, because you stir it with your finger, this simple mix of flour, butter, salt, vanilla, and cream originated with the Amish and perhaps Quaker communities who settled in Indiana in the early nineteenth century. See PIE. Over 600 miles away, in the Dakotas, recipes brought in the same period by Danish, Swedish, and Norwegian immigrants give a sense of the communities who would come to represent Middle America: the *krumkake* is a waffle cookie with Scandinavian origins that traditionally shows up for Christmas celebrations, alongside the *sandbakelse*, a sugar cookie baked in a fluted tin, and the rosette, an ornate, wafer-sized, deep-fried pastry. Powdered sugar might dust any of them. With their ties to the old country and ongoing presence at today's tables, these desserts testify to America's belief in the Midwest as a place of family and tradition, where sweets offer one of life's simple pleasures.

This vision differs from the Midwest of the Great Lakes states, in which Rust Belt industrialization, widespread immigration, and urban values, with Chicago's mighty skyline beckoning, define the region. Here, tradition and innovation work together. Immigrant sweets such as the Italian *cassata* cake found in Cleveland bakeries or the Polish *pączki* in Detroit, filled with cream or jam and reminiscent of a jelly doughnut, give the Midwest its signature character, but so do desserts like the brownie, said to have been invented by a chef at the Palmer House Hotel in 1893 during the Columbia Exposition. See CASSATA and DOUGHNUTS. Apparently, one Mrs. Bertha Palmer asked the chef to make a "ladies dessert"—not so messy as a piece of pie, not so big as a slice of cake—that she could include in the lunch boxes for women working at the fair. Voilà, the brownie. See BROWNIE. The Twinkie and the Cracker Jack also came from Chicago. See CRACKER JACK and TWINKIE. In this vision, Midwestern sweets are as diverse as its cities' inhabitants and inventors, with Indian *gulab jamun* (fried balls soaked in sugar syrup) and sweet potato pie brought north during the Great Migration as symbolic of Midwestern sweets as the famed cherry pies of Michigan's Lower Peninsula or its Mackinac fudge.

These competing visions of the Midwest as city and country fail to capture the rich complexity of the region, where small-town and big-city ideals constantly mix. A city such as St. Louis preserves its German heritage with a fruitcake called stollen, and a town of 27,000, as Mansfield, Ohio, was in the 1920s, can give birth to a mass-market product such as the Klondike bar. See STOLLEN. In fact, the Midwest is where the national food industry began and is currently housed. General Mills, Hostess Brands, the Kellogg Company, Kraft Foods, Nabisco, Quaker Oats, and Sara Lee all started in the Midwest. See HOSTESS and SARA LEE. Wherever people are eating a mass-produced dessert, whether it is wrapped in plastic or pulled from the freezer, they are eating Midwestern fare, a regional vision of food that has reached around the globe.

Fertig, Judith M. *Prairie Home Cooking: 400 Recipes that Celebrate the Bountiful Harvests, Creative Cooks, and Comforting Foods of the American Heartland*. Boston: Harvard Common Press, 1999.

Lewis, Jenny. *Midwest Sweet Baking History: Delectable Classics around Lake Michigan*. Charleston, S.C.: History Press, 2011.

Wolff, Peggy, ed. *Fried Walleye and Cherry Pie: Midwestern Writers on Food*. Lincoln: University of Nebraska Press, 2013.

Eric LeMay

mignardise, also called "friandise," is a general category that includes many kinds of little sweets—small cakes, cookies, macarons, chocolates, candied fruits, and pralines—served most often at the end of a meal with coffee and liqueur. The word comes from the French *mignard*, meaning "delicate" or "pretty," which in turn derives from the medieval word *mignon*, meaning "small." Mignardise can be synonymous with the petit four (literally, "small oven"), which appears to be a creation of the nineteenth century. The famous French chef Marie-Antonin Carême claimed that the name referred to the baking of these small cakes in a slow oven whose heat dissipated after the large desserts had finished baking. See CARÊME, MARIE-ANTOINE. In his *Physiologie du goût* (1826), Jean Anthelme Brillat-Savarin refers to the "multitude of delicate pastries which make up the fairly new art of baking little cakes." M. LeBlanc, author of Roret's *Nouveau manuel complet du pâtissier* (1829), refers to the confection of petits fours as a branch of patisserie in which particular commercial bakers specialized. He advises professional bakers to have two ovens, including a smaller oven devoted to baking petits fours and all sorts of small cakes, to save on cooking fuel. By the time LeBlanc was writing, there were already at least 50 different types of ovens that the professional baker could purchase.

See SMALL CAKES.

Brillat-Savarin, J. A. *The Physiology of Taste*. Translated by M. F. K. Fisher. Washington, D.C.: Counterpoint, 1999. Originally published in 1826.

Montagné, Prosper, ed. *Larousse gastronomique*. Paris: Larousse, 1938.

Kyri W. Claflin

military sweets are often overlooked, with studies of food and the military generally focusing on the nutritional content of rations. After all, as the popular saying goes, "An army travels on its stomach." However, since the creation of the U.S. Armed Forces, sweets have sustained our servicemen and women emotionally and physically. Sweets have also served as a goodwill ambassador of sorts, distributed to foreign populations by American troops for generations.

The Revolutionary War–era Continental Congress first established an official field-feeding program for the military in 1775, attempting to standardize rations and their preparation. The basic "garrison ration" allocated per soldier per week typically included beef, pork, or salt fish; bread or flour; milk or either cider or spruce beer plus a small stipend; and peas or beans. Slight variations on this garrison ration remained the standard for servicemen under all conditions, whether they were in camp, in the field, or in combat, from the Revolution through World War I.

By World War I, the military had created a slightly broader range of rations, designed for use under varying conditions of warfare. There existed, for example, reserve rations, trench rations, and

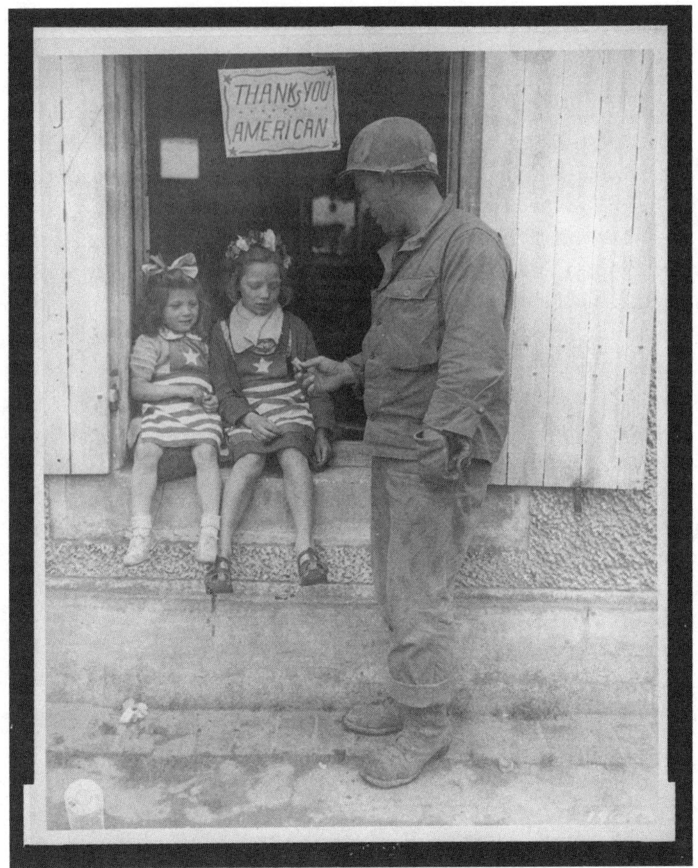

Sergeant Walter P. Goworek, from Jersey City, New Jersey, treats two girls dressed up for a 1944 Fourth of July celebration in La Mine, France, to some G.I. candy. The sign in the background indicates the French feeling of gratitude toward their American liberators. SIGNAL CORPS PHOTO / LIBRARY OF CONGRESS

emergency rations. Some of these rations included chocolate bars, which dispensed energy and morale, the Quartermaster Corps declared.

Following the war, the government attempted to improve rations based on soldiers' complaints. It was suggested that all rations could be improved by adding chocolate, among other items, to the basic pattern of canned meat, tinned bread, and beverage (previously, only some rations contained chocolate). By 1922 an Army specification for rations mandated that each include 3 ounces of corned beef or chocolate—an interesting equivalency.

During World War II, a multitude of new rations appeared for use in varying climates and conditions of warfare. There were, for example, rations specific to ground troops, aviation crews, for use in tropical climates, for high-altitude climates, for desert climates, for use in lifeboats, for use immediately prior to combat, for distribution by the Red Cross to prisoners of war, and so on. Most of these rations contained sweets, and a popular slogan of the period declared, "Candy is a fighting food." Sweets in these rations included candy-coated peanuts or raisins, hard candies, caramels, chewing gum, fudge disks, cookies, candy bars, pudding, chocolate drops, pan-coated cream centers, fondant creams, gumdrops, and jelly and licorice drops. See CANDY BAR; CARAMELS; CHEWING GUM; FONDANT; HARD CANDY; and LICORICE. Some of these sweets were commercial products, like Tootsie Rolls and M&M's. Others were items specifically designed for military use, like the notoriously unappealing D-bar.

Field Ration D, also known as the D-bar, was a chocolate ration bar produced by Hershey's for the military. The D-bar was meant to be consumed in emergency situations when no other food source was available; thus, the military's requirements were as follows: that it weigh 4 ounces (112 grams), be high in food energy value, withstand high temperatures, and taste "a little better than a boiled potato," so that soldiers would not be tempted to snack on it for fun.

Soldiers almost unanimously hated the bars. In 1943 the Army asked Hershey's to produce a more traditional chocolate bar with improved taste, one that would still survive the extreme heat of the Pacific Theater. The resultant Hershey's Tropical Bar (often erroneously called the D-ration throughout the war, despite its new formula) better mimicked a normal chocolate bar in its shape and flavor than the original D-ration, which it gradually replaced by 1945. Still, nearly all U.S. servicemen and women found the Tropical Bar tough and unappealing. Nonetheless, an estimated 3 billion D-rations and Tropical Bars were distributed to soldiers throughout the world between 1940 and 1945.

Military rations have evolved nearly continuously since World War II, but once sweets found their way into government-issue rations, they never left. Today, the official ration of the U.S. Armed Forces is known as the Meal, Ready to Eat (MRE). These MREs offer a variety of sweets, including a broad spectrum of cookies, cakes, and candies, some of which are iconic, commercially produced treats such as Skittles, Reese's Pieces, and M&M's. See HERSHEY'S; M&M'S; and REESE'S PIECES.

Although the military did not officially include sweets (outside of the occasional sugar for coffee, or perhaps syrup or molasses) in its earliest rations, the writings of soldiers from all conflicts dating back to the Revolution mention the consumption of, and comfort provided by, sweets obtained privately. Other evidence of the consumption of individually acquired sweets abounds; records show that, for example, during World War I, the American Red Cross distributed some 5.5 million chocolate bars to doughboys stateside, and that during World War II the Wakefields of cookie fame reportedly sent their Toll House chocolate chip cookies to servicemen and women all over the world.

Any analysis of sweets and the military must also note that America's servicemen and women have, over the years, earned a reputation for sharing their sweets. During the World Wars, they often distributed sweets to the civilians they encountered, including survivors of the concentration camps of World War II. This concept of using sweets to spread goodwill continued into the Cold War period and beyond. During the Berlin airlift in 1948, for example, American plane crews dropped an estimated 23 tons of chocolate, chewing gum, and other candies over various locations in the city. The tradition of handing out sweets continues to this day. Sadly, there can be unintended negative consequences to these goodwill gestures, as in the case of starved concentration camp survivors who became ill after eating calorie-dense chocolate shared by troops, or children who have been injured because of their proximity to soldiers from whom they sought candy.

Whether created specifically for the military or commercially produced, included in standard, government-issue rations, or obtained via alternate routes like post exchanges or care packages, sweets have provided servicemen and women with energy and morale for generations. Sweets have also become a calling card of the American military, used to generate goodwill around the globe. While today's servicemen and women still consume and share old standards like the ever-hardy M&M's, there are now healthier alternatives like the HooAh Bar. Reminiscent of the D-ration of yesteryear, this nutrition bar comes in the timelessly appealing flavors of chocolate and mocha. Although current dietary trends may warn of the dangers of too much sugar or other empty calories, sweets in the U.S. military are sure to endure.

Brown, W. C. "The U.S. Army Emergency Ration." *Infantry Journal* 16, no. 7 (1920): 656–660.

Koehler, Franz A. *Special Rations for the Armed Forces, 1946–1953.* Washington, D.C.: Office of the Quartermaster General, 1958.

U.S. Army Natick Soldier Engineering Center. "A Historical Look at Rations." Last modified 20 May 2010. http://nsrdec.natick.army.mil/media/fact/food/Historical_Rations.pdf.

U.S. Army Quartermaster Foundation. "U.S. Army Quartermaster Corps History." Last modified 2 September 2008. http://www.qmfound.com/history.html.

Melissa Ziobro

milk in the strictly biological sense is both the first and the most chemically complex food encountered by any mammal in a lifetime of eating. Cow's milk, like that of less familiar dairy animals including goats, sheep, and water buffaloes, has literally innumerable components that take on still more complexities in handling and cooking. For this reason, it can play enormously diverse roles in making all kinds of sweets.

Simple gravity easily splits unhomogenized cow's milk into two parts. A lactose-rich water-based solution (whey) holding suspended particles of a major milk protein called casein sinks to the bottom as "skim milk" in any container. A top layer containing the much less dense milk-fat globules along with a small amount of the basic solution rises to the top as "cream." See CREAM. Both parts can be manipulated into other forms through means including the action of lactic acid bacteria and/or some enzymes, possibly combined with heat. See BUTTERMILK; CHEESE, FRESH; SOUR CREAM; and YOGURT. Agitating cream (or whole milk, or yogurt) under the right conditions produces butter along with a whey-like solution, true buttermilk. Various Old World peoples had mastered these and other transformations in ancient (in fact, prehistoric) times. Bacterially cultured products flourished from the Balkans eastward; concentrates of boiled-down milk were beloved in India; and simple unripened cheeses were familiar from northeastern to northwestern Europe.

By contrast, milk and cream not modified by fermentation, curdling, or churning did not achieve huge culinary importance in Western Europe and North America until well into the Industrial Revolution. Only with nineteenth-century advances in transportation, refrigeration, and sterile packaging could "sweet" milk and cream safely reach a large, mostly urban market. Almost at once, the technology also arrived for manufacturing sweetened condensed and evaporated milk as well as producing butter on an expanded commercial scale. See BUTTER; EVAPORATED MILK; and SWEETENED CONDENSED MILK.

The dietary importance of fermented milk products declined in Western Europe and North America throughout the nineteenth century, while "sweet" milk and various derivatives became safe, cheap, and universally available. Their expanded role rested on the same pursuit of manufacturing innovation that was simultaneously bringing Western consumers refined white flour and sugar—those other prerequisites for making many sweetened items that swiftly multiplied on the tables of all but the poorest classes between the end of the Civil War and the start of World War I.

Of the specialties that either originated or gained popularity at this time, sweetened beverages included cocoa and hot chocolate, milk punches, eggnogs, and milkshakes. See COCOA; EGG DRINKS; and MILKSHAKE. Chemically leavened cakes using milk or cream as the principal liquid and butter as shortening enjoyed a tremendous vogue, along with custard-based desserts and starch-bound milk puddings. Milk was also the usual liquid used in fudge, caramels, penuche, and many other candies, along with a host of frostings and dessert sauces. Ice cream became far easier to prepare at home, thanks to the invention of hand-cranked freezers; new whisking or beating devices enabled cream to be whipped in a few minutes. In the Old World, butter-based pastries like puff paste were largely products of the same era, as were buttercream frostings or fillings.

After the start of the twentieth century, some products of the older preindustrial milk technologies enjoyed a certain resurgence. Their rediscovery has been encouraged in the last few generations by increased immigration to the United States from such regions of the Old World as the Balkans, the Middle East, parts of the former Soviet Union, and the Indian subcontinent. For instance, the fudge-like milk sweet called khoa and sweetened versions of yogurt-based lassi are to be found wherever people from India have settled. See INDIA. In another vigorous trend, immigration from Latin America has created an audience for dulce de leche and canned-milk flans. See DULCE DE LECHE and FLAN (PUDÍM).

Simultaneously, "sweet" fluid milk is being explored as never before, as a way to differentiate products aimed at a growing bevy of specialized clienteles. Though campaigns against dietary fat and cholesterol are now on the wane, they continue to generate sales of milk classified by butterfat content, from "fat-free" up through 0.5, 1, and 2 percent to so-called whole milk. (At a standardized 3.25 percent, this last is actually well below the average fat content of cow's milk not subjected to the centrifuging, partial recombining, and homogenizing processes universally used in today's dairy industry.) Other niche versions of milk have been developed in response to the problem of lactose intolerance. Various dietary agendas have inspired manufacturers to create white, pourable plant-based mixtures sold as "almond milk," "rice milk," "soy milk," and so forth, though they are completely unrelated to milk. For purposes of dessert making, great caution should be used in substituting reduced-fat, reduced-lactose, or plant-based products for whole milk (or cream, which has its own family of imitations) in recipes.

See also CARAMELS; FUDGE; ICE CREAM; ICING; LATIN AMERICA; PUDDING; REFRIGERATION; SAUCE; AND WHISKS AND BEATERS.

Du Puis, E. Melanie. *Nature's Perfect Food: How Milk Became America's Drink.* New York: New York University Press, 2002.

Kindstedt, Paul S. *Cheese and Culture: A History of Cheese and Its Place in Western Civilization.* White River Junction, Vt.: Chelsea Green, 2012.

Mendelson, Anne. *Milk: The Surprising Story of Milk through the Ages.* New York: Knopf, 2008.

Selitzer, Ralph. *The Dairy Industry in America.* New York: Dairy & Ice Cream Field/Books for Industry, 1976.

Valenze, Deborah. *Milk: A Local and Cultural History.* New Haven, Conn.: Yale University Press, 2011.

Anne Mendelson

milkshakes and malteds are cold, thick, creamy beverages made by combining milk, ice cream, iced milk, sorbet, or yogurt in a blender or mixer. To enhance the flavor, the mixologist has a vast range of options, including chocolate, coffee, malted milk, vanilla extract, honey, fruit syrups, juices, spices, and liqueurs. In different regions of the United States, the milkshake is variously called a frappe, a frosted, a thick shake, a cabinet, or a velvet.

The milkshake's exact origins are unknown, but evidence indicates that it began as a soda fountain drink in the 1880s or earlier. See SODA FOUNTAIN. The ingredients and flavors resembled those of such traditional treats as English syllabubs and eggnogs. See EGG DRINKS and SYLLABUB. James Tufts, a soda fountain manufacturer, patented the Lightning Shaker for mixing milkshakes in 1884. The shaker, which was bolted to a counter, held one or two glass canisters with metal tops. The mixologist poured the milkshake ingredients into a canister and turned a crank to blend them. An 1890 dictionary defined milkshake as "an iced drink made of sweetened and flavored milk, carbonated water, and sometimes raw egg, mixed by being violently shaken by a machine specially invented for the purpose."

The Tufts trade catalog stated that the milkshake "has sprung into great popularity in the South in a surprisingly short time. Wherever it has been properly introduced, it has immediately become extremely popular." The catalog included a recipe that called for milk, shaved ice, and flavored syrup (preferably chocolate or vanilla), with the option of adding port wine. Other early recipes recommended whiskey to give the drink a little extra punch. To make a richer, thicker drink, upscale soda fountains used heavy cream or ice cream along with milk in their shakes.

Malted milk originated as a nutritional supplement and found a second market as a flavoring for malted milk shakes. Brothers William and James Horlick emigrated from Britain to Chicago, where they formed the Horlick Food Company to make a dietary supplement for infants and invalids. They knew that malt sugars aid digestion, but moist malt ferments easily. In order to make a nonalcoholic digestive aid, they had to prevent fermentation. They employed a vacuum process to dry wheat and barley malt, which they pulverized and packaged as a powder. In 1875 they received a patent for their new product, and two years later they opened a factory in Racine, Wisconsin. See MALT SYRUP.

Horlick's powder tasted best when mixed with milk, but the milk supply was not always safe in the days before refrigeration and government regulation. See MILK. To ensure the purity of their product, the Horlicks bought dairy farms, raised their own cows, and made powdered milk. They mixed the dry milk with the other ingredients in their product, and the consumer added water to convert it into a liquid. Horlick's malted milk sold briskly, so other companies, including Carnation and Borden's, began to market similar mixtures. An unknown mixologist came up with the idea of adding malted milk powder to milkshakes. The result was a hearty, filling drink that became very popular, especially with men.

Horlick's success inspired another Racine entrepreneur to invent an electric drink mixer to blend malted milk powder with liquids. Frederick Osius, the ingenious powerhouse who ran Hamilton Beach Manufacturing, created the Cyclone Drink Mixer in 1910. The Horlicks refused to bankroll the start-up costs for production, so Osius journeyed to New York to find investors. When he ran short on cash, he persuaded the owner of the Caswell-Massey store on Broadway to lend him money, with a Cyclone mixer as collateral. The novel blender created a sensation at the Caswell-Massey soda fountain, and malted sales soared. When the sales manager for a milk company saw the Cyclone, he immediately grasped its potential. He bought blenders from Osius and gave them to his customers, who ordered large quantities of malted milk. In 1922 Osius sold Hamilton Beach and moved to Miami, where he continued to develop new mixers.

In 1936 Earl Price invented the Multimixer, an automated milkshake machine that made up to five shakes simultaneously. Countless soda fountains, restaurants, and roadside stands used the Multimixer because it was a sturdy, reliable machine that produced tasty shakes. Although the Multimixer was efficient, fast-food outlets wanted something even quicker and simpler. Premade machine-mix milkshakes, containing artificial flavorings and chemicals instead of fresh ingredients, became a favorite shortcut in the fast-food industry.

"Horlick's Achievement." *The Pharmaceutical Era*, 24 August 1905, p. 189.
"Malted Milk: The New National Drink." *The Soda Fountain*, March 1928, pp. 41, 76.
Stone, Fanny S. *Racine, Belle City of the Lakes, and Racine County, Wisconsin*. Vol. 2. Chicago: S. J. Clarke, 1916.
Tufts, James W. *Arctic Soda-Water Apparatus: Book of Directions*. Boston: Tufts, 1890.

Anne Cooper Funderburg

Milky Way

See MARS.

mince pies, small pies filled with a sweet mixture known as mincemeat, are essential to the British Christmas. They are double crusted, round, and baked in patty pans or little foil molds. Plain or sweet short crust, or puff pastry, is used, according to taste. See PIE DOUGH. The top crust is now often cut in a star shape, just one more innovation in the long history of these pies. The mincemeat filling, homemade or purchased, consists of minced or chopped dried fruit (currants, raisins, sultanas); candied peel; apple; beef suet (or sometimes butter or vegetable fat); sugar; sweet spices such as cinnamon and cloves; and brandy to taste. The "meat" element of the name is explained by the former addition of meat to these ingredients.

Made at home or by craft or industrial bakers, mince pies are consumed in vast quantities from early December onward; eaten as snacks or offered as hospitality; accompanied by tea, coffee, sherry, or mulled wine. Although mince pies are known in the rest of the English-speaking world, enthusiasm for them is variable outside of the British Isles. They are sometimes made as large pies in the United states.

Myths have accrued to mince pies for centuries—for instance, that the spices represented the gifts of the Magi, and that Elizabethan shapes echoed the crib the infant Jesus lay in. There is little historic evidence to support this lore, and examination of early recipes shows that, under various names—minc'd pies, shred pies, secrets pies—these pies once took their place among pies of many types. In early modern European cookery, pie fillings combined meat or fish, dried fruit, spices, and sugar (in relatively small amounts in early recipes). Robert May (*The Accomplisht Cook*, 1685) gives recipes typical of the time, always including meat of some description (or fish or eggs for meatless days). He includes recipes for pies in the French and Italian fashions, and his book illustrates numerous different forms, including small, round pies that are tall in relation to their diameter, and more ornate shapes. See PIE.

Eighteenth-century mince pies took elaborate forms, such as crescents, fleurs-de-lis, and trefoils, shaped in molds with straight sides and turned out before baking. They were arranged in kaleidoscopic patterns on plates for the table. By the nineteenth century the shape had settled down to the small circular ones still made, sometimes with short-crust bases and puff pastry tops. The filling ingredient that changed most over the years was the meat. Tongue, mutton, beef, and tripe (as well as fish such as herring, salmon, or salt cod) are mentioned in earlier recipes. In the nineteenth century, beef was the usual choice, but it had vanished from recipes by the start of the twentieth century. A sweet lamb pie including currants survived until the twentieth century in the Lake District.

The combination of a dried fruit filling and an outer pastry layer, made by wrapping the pastry around the filling rather than using a mold, occurs in other British contexts. See FRUITCAKE. These baked goods tend to be regional and include Eccles cakes and Chorley cakes (both originating in Lancashire), and Banbury cakes (Oxfordshire). Black bun, made in Scotland, is a large pastry cake with a dense filling of currants, traditional to Hogmanay (New Year). Curiously, an Italian regional speciality known as *spongata* (illustrated in a board game dated 1691, and given in a recipe by the confectioner

William Jarrin in 1820) is similar in general plan to "cakes" of this type; it is a large pastry-wrapped confection of dried fruit. Still made in the Parma area and also traditional for Christmas, to British palates, *spongata* is inevitably reminiscent of mince pies. See JARRIN, WILLIAM ALEXIS.

Mason, Laura, and Catherine Brown. *The Taste of Britain*. London: Harper, 2006.

May, Robert. *The Accomplisht Cook*. Totnes, U.K.: Prospect, 2000. A facsimile of the original 1685 edition, with a foreword, introduction, and glossary supplied by Alan Davidson, Marcus Bell, and Tom Jaine.

Laura Mason

miracle berry is a bright red berry from the *Synsepalum dulcificum* shrub native to West Africa, which has traditionally been used to make sour soups and palm wine more palatable. Although the berry has very little flavor of its own, it has a miraculous effect on taste buds. For up to two hours after eating a miracle berry, the taster experiences acidic and sour foods as deliciously sweet. The secret behind this taste transformation is miraculin, a protein that binds to sweet receptors on the tongue. When the mouth environment becomes acidic, the miraculin molecule changes its shape and activates those sweet receptors. Miraculin is sensitive to heat, so cooking the berry eliminates the effect. After eating a miracle berry, anything tart can be gobbled up like candy, though bitter flavors are not affected. Lemons, limes, and grapefruits are popular foods at "flavor tripping" parties, where people gather to share the odd taste experience of miracle berries.

Although the berries can be eaten fresh, they are highly perishable, so they are more commonly available as freeze-dried tablets. Miracle berries have not been approved by the FDA for use in the United States as a food additive, but they have found commercial success in Japan, where dieters and diabetics alike can enjoy low-calorie food with all the sweetness of a sugary dessert.

See also SUB-SAHARAN AFRICA.

Yong, Ed. "How the Miracle Fruit Changes Sour into Sweet." *Not Exactly Rocket Science*. 26 September 2011. http://blogs.discovermagazine.com/notrocketscience.

Anna P. Goldstein

mithai, meaning a "sweet," derives from the Sanskrit *mishta* (sweet) and is a word universally understood in India, despite the country's huge variety of languages and dialects. It is the most joyful word in the Indian culinary universe, not only connoting items with a sweet taste, but also evoking a sense of social communion, festivity, sharing, and celebration. Although items eaten during religious celebrations are often called mithai, the term has no religious overtones. For Hindus and Muslims, the two main religious communities of India, as well as for others, mithai constitutes an integral part of gustatory pleasure. See INDIA.

Primarily, *mithai* is a Hindi/Urdu word, an umbrella term incorporating a huge variety of confections made in northern and western India. The eastern Indian sweets made with *chhana* or fresh curd cheese are usually not referred to as mithai by the local population, although people from other parts of India might choose to do so. The common ingredients of what is called mithai are flour; sugar; legumes (mostly chickpeas); nuts like cashews, almonds, and pistachios; clarified butter; and kheer/khoa (thickened, evaporated milk). They are often perfumed with cinnamon, cardamom, saffron, rosewater, and kewra (screwpine) water. The aroma of good mithai is rich and toasty, and lingers in the air and on the palate.

The ubiquitous laddus (ball shaped sweets) and barfis (rectangular sweets) of northern India are what mostly come to mind as mithai. See BARFI and LADDU. However, an extraordinary variety of textures and shapes is to be explored in the world of mithai. The jalebi (derived from the Arabic *zalabiya*), for instance, is made with a batter that is any combination of chickpea flour, rice flour, wheat flour, and urad dal flour. The batter is piped into hot oil to achieve a convoluted shape and then dropped into syrup. The jalebi is crisp on the outside and juicy inside. A similar product is the *imarti* or *amriti* made with urad dal flour colored with saffron, but its texture is softer and denser than that of the jalebi.

Mithai also includes a wide range of halvahs (halwas). See HALVAH. These are made with flour, semolina, several kinds of legumes, vermicelli, and among Muslims, even eggs. Halvahs are cooked in clarified butter and often enriched with khoa and perfumed with sweet, aromatic spices. A particularly rich product is called *sohan halwa*, made with a combination of milk, sugar, cornstarch, and copious quantities of clarified butter. The product is supposed to have originated in ancient Persia, from where it reached India. At one point, Multan in Pakistan became famous for its *sohan halwa*. The notable thing about this confection is its hard and brittle texture, unlike the fudge-like texture of most halvahs. The large amount of clarified butter used to make *sohan halwa* results in an extraordinarily emollient mouth feel, despite the crisp texture. In some families, *sohan halwa* is made with wheat starch, obtained by repeatedly washing the wheat flour in water until the gluten is isolated. Mostly, however, *sohan halwa* is made by professionals, and certain sweetshops in both India and Pakistan are famous for this product.

See also HINDUISM; ISLAM; KOLKATA; NUTS; and ZALABIYA.

Achaya, K. T. *Indian Food*. Delhi: Oxford University Press, 1998.

Chitrita Banerji

mochi, in Japanese, refers to rice cakes and other dumpling-shaped foods made from sticky substances. Mochi are similar to dango, except that mochi are traditionally made with pounded whole grain and dango are from flour. See DANGO. Rice cake mochi are made from polished glutinous rice, which becomes naturally sticky when steamed. Traditionally, the steamed rice is pounded in a large mortar with a pestle to form the cakes, a labor-intensive process, which, coupled with the fact that polished rice was expensive, made rice cakes a luxury food. Rice cakes can be formed into many shapes and are integral to ceremonies and seasonal observances. Depending on the region of Japan, round or square rice cakes are used in the savory New Year's soup called *ozōni*. Also synonymous with the New Year are the rotund and thick mirror cakes (*kagami mochi*) created as offerings to deities and as symbols of prosperity. Rice flour has replaced pounded grain in most versions of mochi confectionery, of which there are countless varieties. Rice flour cakes stuffed with sweetened azuki bean paste (*an*) are wrapped with pickled cherry leaves to make Cherry Leaf Cake, a favorite during cherry blossom season. See AZUKI BEANS. Mochi can also be stuffed with strawberries, or covered with azuki paste or sesame seeds. Mochi ice cream is an invention of Los Angeles's Japan Town. Before World War II, rice cakes were reserved for special occasions, but other varieties of savory mochi were eaten daily. The latter were made from wheat or millet, nuts, sweet potatoes, taro, or bracken (*warabi*), created with or without a filling, and grilled or added to soups and porridges.

Rath, Eric C. "The Magic of Japanese Rice Cakes." In *Routledge History of Food*, edited by Carol Helstosky, pp. 3–18. New York: Routledge, 2014.

Eric C. Rath

modaka, an ancient sweet that may date back to around 200 B.C.E., is a stuffed dumpling especially popular in western and southern India. The dough is made of rice or wheat flour shaped into little packages that are filled with grated coconut; jaggery (unrefined sugar); nuts (often cashews); sometimes khoa (milk solids, made by boiling down milk); and cardamom powder. Modern versions incorporate ingredients such as chocolate, mango, almonds, paneer, tomatoes, chopped nuts, and dates. They can be steamed and served with ghee (clarified butter) or deep-fried.

Modakas are the favorite food of the Hindu deity Ganesh, the elephant-headed god who is often depicted holding a modaka in one of his four hands. His nickname is *modakapriya*, meaning "one who loves modakas." During the festival Ganesh Chaturthi, a major event in western India, a *puja* (ceremony) honoring Ganesh always ends with offering the image of the deity 21 modakas. After the ceremony, modakas are distributed to the devotees.

Ganesh is said to have once cursed the moon for making fun of him for eating so many sweets, which is why the moon waxes and wanes, regularly losing its beauty and sometimes vanishing altogether. The modaka itself has been compared to the moon, its segments representing the moon's phases. A related sweet is the *karanji*, a crescent-shaped modaka.

See also HINDUISM and INDIA.

Achaya, K. T. *A Historical Dictionary of Indian Food*. New Delhi: Oxford University Press, 2002.
Bahadur, Om Lata. *The Book of Hindu Festivals and Ceremonies*. 2d ed. New Delhi: UBSPD, 1999.

Colleen Taylor Sen

molasses (known as treacle in England) is a thick, syrupy liquid that ranges from dark brown to almost black in color. It is a byproduct of sugar production and can be prepared from cane, sugar beets, or grapes. See SUGAR REFINING. The English word comes from the Portuguese *melaço,* which in turn is derived from the Latin *mellacium,* meaning "must" from honey (*mel*).

There are several varieties of molasses, beginning with the lighter type prepared from the first boiling of the cane, which is known in the southern United States as cane syrup or light molasses. See CANE SYRUP. The second boiling of the sugarcane juice produces dark molasses, and the third yields bitter blackstrap molasses. If the first or second molasses has been bleached with sulfur, it is known as sulfured molasses and has a distinctive taste. Recently, this type of molasses has become less popular because of concerns about the use of sulfur in its production.

Historically important in the United States, molasses was the primary sweetener in the country up until World War I, when it was replaced by refined sugar. In the colonial and Revolutionary War period, molasses played an even greater role in the diet. It was widely consumed by the poor, who often subsisted on molasses accompanied by bread as their sole staple. In the late 1700s many Massachusetts fishermen and their families ate as much as 30 gallons of it annually. In the American South, molasses constituted a significant portion of the slave diet, along with cornmeal and smoked pork. But its most prominent colonial use was in the production of molasses beer and rum, a major beverage of the era. See RUM. The conversion of molasses into rum for use as a trade good for the purchase of slaves is a hallmark of one leg of the triangular transatlantic slave trade. See SLAVERY.

The syrup's early dietary importance is evidenced by the 1733 Act for the Securing and Encouraging the Trade of His Majesty's Sugar Colonies in America. The so-called Molasses Act taxed molasses imported from anywhere other than the British sugar islands. Raw sugar and molasses were shipped for refining into sugar either to Europe or to the colonies that would become the United States. Regulating the source of molasses was an attempt to keep the colonists economically tethered to England and a way of maintaining economic and political control over the cane-growing colonies as well. The Act was largely ignored. In 1763, out of 15,000 hogsheads of molasses brought into Massachusetts, 14,500 were smuggled in. The tariffs were reduced somewhat in the Molasses Act of 1764, but the reductions were too little, too late. Along with the better-known tax on tea, the Molasses Acts are considered to be a cause of the American Revolution.

Molasses remained a staple of the diet of the middle and lower classes in the American North and the South until well into the twentieth century. It was sold from barrels by grocers and in general stores, and used in classic American recipes such as gingerbread, Indian pudding, anadama bread, shoofly pie, gingersnaps, Boston brown bread, and Boston baked beans. By the end of the nineteenth century, molasses began to be canned, and trade brands developed, such as Grandma's and Br'er Rabbit. In the early twentieth century Noah Taussig brought together a consortium of molasses producers under the name American Molasses Company and worked with the Food and Drug Administration during World War I to promote the consumption of molasses in order to save sugar.

Today, molasses is considered by many to be a health food. It has approximately the same amount of calories as sugar, but it contains glucose and fructose and only about half of the sucrose of sugar. See FRUCTOSE and GLUCOSE. It is high in magnesium and manganese and a good source of vitamin B_6 and potassium. For these reasons, while molasses can still be readily found in many grocery stores, it is also available in health food stores, especially blackstrap molasses, which is reputed to have increased health benefits. Molasses, however, was not healthy for the ocean in September 2013, when a leak from a pipeline in Hawaii owned by Matson, the state's largest cargo shipper, leaked some 233,000 gallons into Honolulu Harbor from one of the last remaining sugar export routes from Hawaii to the mainland. The leak caused the death of 26,000 fish and other marine animals and put molasses in the news once again, ironically exposing an unhealthy aspect of what is widely regarded as a health food.

See also BOSTON MOLASSES DISASTER; COLONIALISM; LEGISLATION, HISTORICAL; PEKMEZ; SUGAR BEET; SUGAR TRADE; and SUGARCANE.

Brower, Robert W. "Molasses." In *The Oxford Encyclopedia of Food and Drink in America,* 2d ed., edited by Andrew F. Smith, Vol. 2, pp. 601–603. New York: Oxford University Press, 2012.

Taussig, Charles William. *Some Notes on Sugar and Molasses: Being the Story of an American Industry.* New York, 1940.

Warner, Deborah Jean. *Sweet Stuff: An American History of Sweetener from Sugar to Sucralose.* Washington, D.C.: Smithsonian Institution Scholarly Press in cooperation with Rowman & Littlefield, 2011.

Jessica B. Harris

molds, jelly and ice cream, shape jellies (gelled juices) and ice creams for dramatic presentation. Early European and American molds were produced largely from pewter, a metal that transmits heat fairly slowly and allows for a brief immersion in warm water or for standing at room temperature, a process that melts a very thin layer of the jelly or ice cream and permits it to be unmolded without losing its shape or the decorative pattern from the mold. Other materials used in the manufacture of molds have included red-ware, yellow-ware, ironstone, copper, stamped tin, and steel. Today, molds are often made of flexible silicone.

Ice cream and jelly (the historical term for gelled juices) were originally luxury dishes, served primarily to the elite who could afford the ice houses necessary for chilling during the warm months. Because these desserts lent themselves to dramatic presentation, molds were made in a great variety of sizes and fanciful shapes. There were patriotic themes (George Washington, his hatchet, or Lincoln); gender themes (dolls and flowers for girls; vehicles or drums for boys); and holiday themes (Christmas trees or St. Valentine's Day hearts). Small molds in the form of hearts, spades, clubs, and diamonds; cylinders and cubes; and assorted fruits and vegetables chilled single-portion servings. Larger sizes (e.g., a 1-pint pumpkin mold and a 1-quart clover mold) could handle a crowd. Represented among the larger molds were special ones for bombes—ice cream desserts consisting of two or more layers of variously flavored ice creams frozen in a large, round, bullet- or melon-shaped mold. See DESSERTS, FROZEN. One imaginative example is the "watermelon bombe," molded in a deep bowl, which contains three layers—green for the outer rind, white for the inner rind, and red for the pulp, with a sprinkling of chocolate chips for the pits. To achieve the distinct layers, the green-tinted ice cream is spread against the outside of the mold and frozen. When it is firm, a thin layer of white ice cream is added, and the mold is returned to the freezer. The red interior with chocolate chips is frozen last.

The Mello-Roll, a tubular form served in a waffle cone shaped to hold it horizontally, was invented in 1912. Its inventor, C. W. Vogt, patented the mold in 1913 and later sold it to Borden. Mello-Rolls came in vanilla, chocolate, strawberry, chocolate ripple, and chocolate fudge ripple flavors and were sold in local candy stores in New York and Canada.

This plate from *Mrs. Seely's Cook Book* (1902) shows decorative jelly and pudding molds, which were very fashionable at the turn of the twentieth century. Lida Seely's New York employment agency provided domestic servants to the wealthy. Her cookbook covers French and English cooking, as well as the duties of various household staff.

Molds for shaping jelly were generally less complicated, though for special presentations a hollow circle was used to create a ring of molded jelly whose center could be filled with a pyramid of fruits. In the twentieth century molds may simply have been any container on hand—often plastic—that could tolerate both heat and cold; often the jelly (usually made from commercial Jell-O, which had been introduced in 1897) was simply spooned out rather than being unmolded. See JELL-O. Layered Jell-O molds were *de rigueur* for American housewives in the 1950s. To achieve a dramatic effect, a package of Jell-O was dissolved in the prescribed amount of boiling water (or a mixture of boiling water and fruit juice) and poured into the bottom of a large (preferably tube) pan. It was then placed in the refrigerator for a few hours until completely set. Meanwhile, a second flavor of Jell-O was dissolved in water or juice and cooled until chilled but not yet set; it was added when the first layer had hardened, and the mold was once more refrigerated. A third flavor of Jell-O was dissolved in water and cooled, then added in turn once the second layer was firm. The mold was sometimes enriched with sliced fruits in colors and flavors appropriate to each layer. Unmolding this large concoction required expertise; the practiced cook learned to briefly almost submerge the chilled mold in a large bowl of warm water to facilitate the unmolding process. The amount of liquid used to dissolve the Jell-O was often reduced by a few tablespoons to make the Jell-O firmer and less likely to spread uncontrollably when unmolded.

Molded jellies have once again become chic, thanks in part to the fantastic creations of Sam Bompas and Harry Parr, whose London company Bompas & Parr creates entire cities and landscapes of shimmering molded jelly. Bompas & Parr offers a wide range of molds, including bespoke forms for individualized creations.

See also DESSERTS, CHILLED; GELATIN; GELATIN DESSERTS; and MARSHALL, AGNES BERTHA.

Bompas, Sam, and Harry Parr. *Jelly with Bompas & Parr: A Glorious History with Spectacular Recipes*. London: Pavilion, 2010.

Kander, Mrs. Simon. *The Settlement Cookbook*. Milwaukee, Wis.: Settlement Cook Book Co., 1901.

Marshall, Agnes B. *The Book of Ices*. London: Marshall's School of Cookery, 1885.

Randolph, Mary. *The Virginia Housewife*. Washington, D.C.: Davis and Force, 1824.

Alice Ross

mooncake (*yuebing*) is the traditional Asian pastry eaten during the Mid-Autumn Festival, one of the most prominent annual holidays celebrated on the fifteenth day of the eighth lunar month, which usually falls in September or early October. Typical mooncakes are round or rectangular; most consist of a thin, tender pastry skin surrounding a sweet, dense filling, often with a center of salted duck egg yolk. This pastry is especially beloved by the Chinese for its rich flavor and the role it may have played in Chinese history. According to one folktale, about 700 years ago, during the Yuan dynasty, China was ruled by the Mongols who had invaded from the north. To secretly plot the Mongols' overthrow, the Chinese shared their planned strategy in paper messages that were hidden in the fillings of mooncakes. The Chinese won the battle, and to this day mooncakes are credited with the victory. Mooncakes are given to friends, relatives, and business associates, and as a sign of respect to one's boss. They are usually served with tea.

Mooncake varieties are numerous, and the filling and outside pastry vary with the region and country. In southern China, the cakes are typically round or rectangular, and the filling is usually made from red azuki bean paste, lotus seed paste, sweet black bean, or mung bean paste; it may have a salty duck egg yolk in the center, as a symbol of the full moon. A more

Tender pastry encloses a sweet, dense filling in mooncakes, the favored sweet during the Chinese Mid-Autumn Festival. A salty duck egg yolk is sometimes hidden in the center to symbolize the full moon. LYBIL BER

opulent variety, called "five kernel," is filled with five types of nuts, dried fruits, and seeds, coarsely chopped and held together with a maltose syrup.

Traditional mooncakes have an imprint on the top displaying the Chinese characters for longevity or the rabbit of longevity, who is said to live on the moon holding a mortar and pestle. Some mooncakes have a bakery name pressed on the top, or they may indicate the type of filling inside.

Over time the crusts and fillings of mooncakes have changed, although the traditional varieties are still widely available and considered the most desirable. Taro paste, pineapple, even durian-filled mooncakes have become popular fillings among overseas Chinese. Contemporary mooncake fillings may consist of yogurt, jelly, chocolate, and fat-free ice cream.

See also AZUKI BEANS; CHINA; and ICE CREAM.

Simonds, Nina, Leslie Swartz, and the Children's Museum of Boston. *Moonbeams, Dumplings, and Dragon Boats.* Boston: Harcourt, 2002.

Stepanchuk, Carol. *Red Eggs and Dragon Boats: Celebrating Chinese Festival.* Berkeley, Calif.: Pacific View, 1994.

Nina Simonds

MoonPies were first baked by the Chattanooga Baking Company in 1917. Originally designed for coal miners who could not take a work break for a meal, the MoonPie was solid, filling, and circular, fitting snugly inside a worker's clothes or carried easily in the hand. Earl Mitchell Sr., a bakery salesman, came up with the idea of layering graham crackers with marshmallow; he later added more graham crackers and coated the entire pie in chocolate. The four main flavors of MoonPies produced today are chocolate, vanilla, strawberry, and banana.

In the 1930s, MoonPies sold for a nickel apiece, and southern workers fortified themselves with the snack. They soon became an iconic southern treat; paired with the regional RC Cola, they were immortalized in Big Bill Lister's honky-tonk song "Gimme an RC Cola and a MoonPie." Since 2008, revelers in Mobile, Alabama, have brought in the New Year with a six-hundred-pound electronic MoonPie that is raised high into the sky as midnight strikes. In addition, MoonPie eating contests and festivals take place throughout the South.

When southern workers migrated north after World War II, they brought MoonPies along. By 1960 the pies were being produced in the Northeast, where they were called Scooter Pies, after the baseball great Phil "Scooter" Rizzuto of the New York Yankees. The Little Debbie Marshmallow Pie, produced by McKee Foods, is a similar snack. See LITTLE DEBBIE. In 1964 the Chattanooga Baking Company introduced the Double-Decker, a double-stacked MoonPie with three cookies and two layers of marshmallows.

During a rebranding effort in 1998, MoonPies adopted the tag line "the only one on the planet," and they are still marketed as being "outta this world!" Also in 1998 the Mini MoonPie was introduced as a response to mothers who wanted a smaller size that would not spoil their children's dinner. Chattanooga Baking Company often partners with other companies in Tennessee, such as Mayfield, which debuted "moon pie" as its newest flavor of ice cream in 2003: it contains vanilla ice cream, "French silk ribbon" chocolate, and chocolate-covered graham pieces. A million MoonPies leave Chattanooga each day to be distributed across the United States.

See also SMALL CAKES and SOUTH (U.S.).

Dickson, Ron. *The Great Moonpie Handbook.* Gretna, La.: Pelican, 2010.

Rebecca Tolley-Stokes

Morocco

See NORTH AFRICA.

mostarda is a typical Italian condiment made from slightly unripe fruit such as apples, pears, peaches, cherries, figs, melon, pumpkin, and citrus peel that have been preserved in syrup, often with a decisive piquant taste from ground mustard seed. Although the word *mostarda* sounds similar to the French *moutarde* or English *mustard,* the word derives from the Latin *mustum ardens* (fiery grape must), fresh grape juice boiled down to a thick syrup with the spicy addition of mustard seed. Whereas the French and English forms of mustard refer to both the plant and the finished product, in Italy mostarda only refers to the fruit-based condiment, while *senape* means "mustard."

Like those of most Italian specialties, the characteristics of mostarda vary from region to region, town to town, and even family to family. The fruit can be of a single kind or assorted; it can be whole, sliced, or sieved; and the syrup can be made of sugar or reduced grape must. See GRAPE MUST. The amount and quality of mustard seed vary considerably, too, from absent to explosive; it can be added in either powdered form or as an essential oil.

Mustard was already appreciated by the Greeks and Romans, who marinated *brassica* leaves in vinegar. The ancient Romans learned many methods of food preservation while trading in the Orient, and certainly in India, where chutney is prepared with fruit and mustard seed, ingredients important to mostarda. Lucius Junius Columella, writing in *De re rustica* (first century C.E.), makes the earliest distinction between mostarda and mustard. He uses mostarda, which he calls *mustaceum*, for preserving meats, in contrast to mustard, or *sinapsis*, which accompanies boiled foods. In ancient times, this latter condiment was mixed with finely chopped almonds and fennel.

A Latin recipe from the important fourteenth-century manuscript *Liber de coquina* is probably the first to indicate how to reduce must to prepare mostarda: "Sic para mustum pro mustarda conficienda: accipe mustum novum, fac eum bullire quod quarta pars solum remaneat vel tertia... Et valet pro carnibus porcinis vel tincis salsatis" (This is how to prepare the must to make mostarda: take fresh must, and boil it down to a third... This is ideal for pork, marinated tench or other dishes).

Mostarda can be found in many regions of Northern Italy. In Piedmont it is known as *cugnà*, a mixture of spiced fruits always served with *bollito misto*, mixed boiled meats. The *mustarda* from Asti is made of quince, walnuts, and dried fruit, preserved in wine must without mustard seed. In Lombardy the fruit is generally preserved in sugar syrup. Mantua has a long history of mostarda produced by *speziali* (pharmacists and spice dealers). It was kept in decorative ceramic jars; Isabella d'Este, marchesa of Mantua, was particularly fond of this luxury. The painter Andrea Mantegna was known to cultivate quinces for his mostarda, and at the wedding banquet of Vincenzo Gonzaga, duke of Mantua, to Margherita Farnese, *mostarda amabile per savore* (sweet mostarda as an accompanying sauce) was served. The particular flavor of Mantuan mostarda derives from the use of a special local apple *campanina*. To this day, delicatessen shop windows in Mantua display large wooden barrels of this appetizing mostarda, which can often be bought directly from the producer.

However, Italy's most famous mostarda is *la mostarda di Cremona*, with its glistening whole fruits. The English tourist Edith Templeton (1954) described it as "a jewel of a dish, much too beautiful to be eaten, with cherries like antique coral, green figs like emeralds." The very first reference to this mostarda can be found in a curious letter from 1397, now in the civic archives of Voghera, that describes a Christmas feast recommending mostarda for capons and wild game. In the French text *Ouverture de cuisine par maistre Lancelot de Casteau* (1604), the first recipe "pour faire moustarde de Cremone" appears, which is very similar to the present-day version.

Italian artists seem to have been especially fond of Cremona mostarda. The composer Giuseppe Garibaldi was a devotee, and Giuseppe Verdi was considered a "mostarda ambassador." The poet Opprandino Arrivabene wrote: "There is nothing more wonderful in Cremona than the mostarda and the torrone." An 1860 publication on Cremona cites the mostarda factories recognized for their excellent quality and exportation. Although the continual exposure to heat and strong vapors were deleterious to workers' health, conditions today have radically improved.

Mostarda is also made in Emilia-Romagna, and the town of Carpi is well known for its version, which has a quite different consistency resembling a thick jam with no added spices. In *La scienza in cucina e l'arte di mangiare bene* (1891), Pellegrino Artusi gives a recipe for Tuscan mostarda made with apples and pears flavored with powdered white mustard. Mostarda can also be found in southern Calabria and Sicily, where the fruit is cooked and preserved in wine must with no mustard.

The taste for mostarda used to be rather limited in Italy, as it united contrasting sweet and spicy flavors. Today, with the influence of Indian, Chinese, and Thai cuisines, attitudes have changed, and assorted cheeses with mostarda or honey are a very popular *aperitivo*.

See also FRUIT.

Bertinelli Spotti, Carla, and Ambrogio Saronni. *La mostarda di Cremona*. Cremona, Italy: Cremonabooks, 2001.

Ridolfi, Franco. *Mostarda di frutta*. Milan, 1996.
Templeton, Edith. *The Surprise of Cremona*, pp. 42–44. London: Eyre & Spottiswoode, 1954.

June di Schino

mousse designates a wide variety of desserts. The category can be essentially defined as chilled airy confections made from one of four bases: whipped cream; beaten egg whites; gelatin (in combination with one of the first two); or sugar syrup meringue (also called Italian meringue) combined with whipped cream. Mousses lend themselves to an endless choice of flavorings. In the eighteenth century, a mousse was served in a large silver goblet made especially for this dessert, presumably to retain the icy chill that was a marker of a dessert intended for elite tables. For his *Mousse à la crème*, François Menon begins by whipping the cream and advises that if the cream does not froth up (*mousser*) properly, the cook must add beaten egg whites. If done by hand (for Menon, with a bundle of twigs, but later with a whisk), beating the eggs whites properly requires effort. Electric beaters now supply the elbow grease for many cooks. In both cases, the rapid whipping motion enables the cook "to harvest the air" and turn the egg whites into a frothy, stiff structure (McGee, 2004). For his *Mousse de chocolat*, Menon incorporates melted chocolate into fresh egg yolks, which he then adds to the cream and froths up the mixture as in his first recipe.

These techniques, published in 1750, are not far from how we still make mousse today. One way to create a chocolate mousse is to melt the chocolate over low heat or in a bain-marie to avoid burning the chocolate. When it is melted, beat in the egg yolks one at a time. Other flavorings, such as orange liqueur, can be added at this point. The melted mixture should cool slightly. Whip the egg whites to stiff peaks and gently fold them into the chocolate base, making sure not to leave streaks of egg whites suspended in the mousse. Pour the mousse into any serving dish, including eighteenth-century silver goblets if you have them, and chill until the mousse is firm. Mousse can be made and served in a charlotte mold, a glass bowl, or a single large or individual small porcelain dishes. In France, a small porcelain dish of chocolate mousse is sometimes called a *pot de crème*, but that dessert is more accurately custard. The difference is that for custard, the eggs are not whipped but thickened by the slow addition of scalded milk or cream (and flavorings) and poured into ramekins that are then poached in a water bath in a slow oven.

Chilled and frozen soufflés are not true soufflés at all, but mousse that is poured into a soufflé mold lined above the rim with paper or tin foil and then frozen. The trick to getting the extra volume needed for a chilled soufflé is to beat the egg whites to very stiff peaks before folding them into the base. Sometimes gelatin is added to help stabilize the mixture. When the paper is carefully removed before serving, the soufflé gives the impression, the illusion actually, that it has risen above the dish like a real soufflé does when it bakes. See SOUFFLÉ.

See also CUSTARD; GELATIN; MERINGUE; PASTRY TOOLS; and WHISKS AND BEATERS.

Child, Julia. *Mastering the Art of French Cooking*. New York: Knopf, 1979.
Gourmet's Best Desserts. New York: Random House, 1987.
McGee, Harold. *On Food and Cooking*. Rev. ed. New York: Scribner, 2004.
Menon, François. *La science du maître d'hôtel, confiseur*. Paris: Chez Paulus-du-Mesnil, 1750.

Kyri W. Claflin

mud pie, also called Mississippi Mud Pie, is a style of twentieth-century American rich chocolate desserts variously composed of pudding (custard), cake, biscuits, ice cream, whipped cream, marshmallows, and liqueur presented in a cookie crust. Hot fudge or chocolate syrup completes the presentation. The dessert's name playfully recalls the color and consistency of the warm, gooey, mud pies of childhood.

The concept of mud pie descends from European culinary traditions of combining creamy custards with cake or biscuits. Elizabethan-era trifle, nineteenth-century Viennese chocolate tortes, 1900s fudgy brownies, 1920s black bottom pie, 1950s ice cream novelties, and 1960s southern-style Glorified Brownies paved the culinary trail.

According to the earliest print reference for mud pie in the United States, it was made, but not invented, by the wife of a rising-star chef based in Long Beach, California, circa 1965. Early 1970s newspapers include mud pie recipes in readers' exchange columns and in lists of local fair contest winners, suggesting that the recipe was circulating among home bakers at that time. In the mid-1970s the Chart House restaurant chain added mud pie to its dessert menu, elevating the confection's popularity to the national level. Upscale restaurants, corporate kitchens, and home cooks embraced the mud. Although it is true that some mud pie recipes come from Mississippi, no evidence exists to suggest they originated there. Dirt Dessert is a simpler version assembled with packaged commercial products.

de Groot, Roy Andreis. "Hot Fudge Poured over a Rich Mud Pie for a Special Treat: Dessert Topped with Hot Fudge." *Chicago Tribune*, 25 April 1982, p. SA4.
Dosti, Rose. "Culinary SOS: A Sweetheart of a Fudge Cake." *Los Angeles Times*, 24 March 1976, p. G9.
Flanary, Mildred K. "Chef of the Week: Gill, a Gourmand, on the Go." *Independent-Press Telegram*, 1 August 1965, p. W12.

Lynne M. Olver

muffins are defined in various ways, depending on period, place, and the people describing them. To further complicate matters, muffin-type foods themselves are known by different names. Eighteenth-century teacakes, colonial American gems, Civil War cornmeal cupcakes, and nineteenth-century corn sticks all fall into the muffin family. Crumpets, scones, biscuits, and buns are close relations.

The English word "muffin" derives from the Low German *Muffe* (pl. *Muffen*), meaning "little cake." Old French *moflet* or *mouflet* denotes a kind of soft bread.

There are two kinds of muffins: (1) English muffins, made with yeast, descend from ancient Celtic griddle cakes. Plain and chewy, they are gently pulled apart and served at breakfast or tea with jellies, preserves, honey, or butter. (2) American muffins are chemically leavened, enriched, semi-sweet quick breads baked in individual portions. Although American muffins can be split, warmed, toasted, and spread with dairy products or fruit preserves, they are generally consumed "as is" at room temperature for breakfast, brunch, or light snacks.

American muffin flavors generally mirror popular quick breads. Instead of being baked in loaf pans, the batter is spooned into hoops, patty pans, gem pans, or muffin tins. Traditional flavors include corn (hominy, mush, Indian), blueberry, apple, milk (buttermilk, cream), rice, oatmeal, banana, and zucchini. "Healthy" muffins contain bran and graham. Savvy consumers examine fat and carbohydrate content to determine the "healthiness" of the product.

American-style mini-muffins were trendy in the 1930s. Oversized gourmet muffins were promoted in the 1980s. Muffin tops (muffin crowns) were introduced in the 1990s. Contemporary palates embrace savory muffins (macaroni & cheese), supersweet presentations (raspberry chocolate chunk), and experimental flavor combinations (chocolate carrot).

David, Elizabeth. *English Bread & Yeast Cookery*. New York: Penguin, 1980.
Weinstein, Bruce, and Mark Scarbrough. *The Ultimate Muffin Book*. New York: William Morrow, 2004.

Lynne M. Olver

mulled wine, a hot blended drink made of wine, sugar, fruit, and spices, has been known since at least Roman times. Popular throughout Europe, most versions are made with dry red wine or rich fortified wines, such as port, or a mixture of the two. Sometimes spirits or liqueur is added.

The wine is sweetened with sugar (best first dissolved into a syrup) or honey (traditional in southeastern Europe), and seasoned with a variety of spices (whole rather than powdered), such as cinnamon, nutmeg, cloves, mace, ginger, allspice, star anise, vanilla, cardamom, peppercorns, juniper berries, and fennel seeds. For maximum flavor the spices are best left to infuse overnight or are cooked in the sugar syrup and strained before serving. Other additions can include lemon or orange juice and peel, the inclusion of clove-studded oranges being typical of a similar drink called *bishop*. Chopped apple, raisins, and almonds can also be added and served with the wine. Depending on the combination of ingredients, the wine may be sweet, spicy, or fruity. Mulled wine with cinnamon and egg yolks was considered a hot and healthy drink until the early nineteenth century. See EGG DRINKS.

The drink's various names refer to the wine being heated, boiled, or burnt. The word "mulled" for heated wine first appeared in the early seventeenth century but is of unknown origin. Contemporary mulled wine is not boiled, as the high heat burns off the alcohol and removes the wine's character.

German *Glühwein* and Scandinavian *glögg* are popular at Christmas and the New Year. Both names mean "glowing-hot wine," and they are often made with raisins, almonds, and cardamom and served with spiced biscuits. In the United States, National Mulled Wine Day is unofficially celebrated on 3 March, though it is unclear who proclaimed this date. Likely, it is a (misguided) marketing ploy by wine or spice producers, as the date is late in the season for the enjoyment of hot wine.

As wine and fruit juice are corrosive, pottery or silver vessels were traditionally used for mulled wine, or a red-hot poker was plunged directly into the liquid to heat it. Modern recipes recommend the use of noncorrosive stainless-steel or enamel pots.

See also FORTIFIED WINE; GINGERBREAD; HIPPOCRAS; and SPICES.

Spencer, Edward. *The Flowing Bowl.* London: Grant Richards, 1903.

Elizabeth Gabay

munchies, a term used to describe any general feeling of hunger, is most often associated with the intense hunger experienced after the use of marijuana. Consequently, those experiencing the munchies are often not particular about how they assuage their cravings. Anything from gourmet cuisine to cold, five-day-old pizza can be effective. However, sweets are often considered to provide the quickest and most satisfying relief. After all, the brain associates the sweet with coveted energy for the body, and there is convincing evidence that marijuana use intensifies the enjoyment of sweet things.

A noted scientific study conducted by Japan's Kyushu University in conjunction with the Monell Center in Philadelphia has found that cannabinoids, the active ingredient in marijuana, act directly on taste receptors on the tongue to enhance sweet taste. In other words, marijuana makes sweets taste even sweeter. Mice given cannabinoids consistently experienced enhanced sweet taste responses, while there was no effect whatsoever on responses to salty, savory, or bitter taste stimuli.

Numerous websites for marijuana aficionados present lists of favorite foods for satisfying the munchies; sweets consistently account for half or more, with salty and savory foods comprising the remainder. Most frequently mentioned sweets include candy, ice cream, cookies, pastries, and soft drinks.

Stromberg, Joseph. "A Scientific Explanation of How Marijuana Causes the Munchies." Smithsonian.com, 9 February 2014. http://www.smithsonianmag.com/science-nature/scientific-explanation-how-marijuana-causes-munchies-180949660/

Yoshida, R., et al. "Endocannabinoids Selectively Enhance Sweet Taste." *Proceedings of the National Academy of Sciences USA* 107, no. 2 (December 2009): 935–939.

Roy C. Towlen

Nanaimo bar is a type of unbaked cookie that is assembled in a pan, chilled, and then cut into rectangles. The bar is made up of three layers: a cocoa, coconut, and graham cracker crumb base; a layer of custard buttercream; and a topping of chocolate.

The Nanaimo bar is perhaps best described as a product of industry. It is an amalgam of several processed foods, containing as it does white sugar, confectioner's sugar, cocoa, vanilla custard powder, chocolate baking squares, graham cracker crumbs, and dried coconut. Such innovations certainly reduce preparation time. They also hint at the bar's provenance: the recipe most likely came together when such ingredients were increasingly available, affordable, and popular. The Nanaimo bar made one of its first published appearances in 1953, in pseudonymous *Edith Adams' Fourteenth Prize Cookbook*, part of a series of readers' prize-winning recipes published by the newspaper *Vancouver Sun*.

The city of Nanaimo on Vancouver Island, British Columbia, has played a substantial role in ensuring the longevity and widespread popularity of its eponymous dessert. From a mayor-initiated competition to determine the ultimate Nanaimo bar recipe (1986), to the current "Nanaimo Bar Trail Map" featuring local eateries that make, sell, and deconstruct the bar, the now iconic treat has become a product of the tourism industry. As a home-baked dessert, the Nanaimo bar also enjoys a long-standing presence at church lunches, afternoon teas, fundraisers, potlucks, family reunions, and wedding or baby showers. However, this catering to family and community appetites generally remains outside official discourse.

See also BAR COOKIES.

Adams, Edith. *Edith Adams' Fourteenth Prize Cookbook.* Vancouver, B.C.: Edith Adams' Cottage Homemakers' Service, *Vancouver Sun*, 1953.

"Nanaimo Bars." http://www.nanaimo.ca/EN/main/visitors/NanaimoBars.html (accessed 31 August 2013).

Newman, Lenore Lauri. "Notes from the Nanaimo Bar Trail." *Canadian Food Studies / La revue canadienne des études sur l'alimentation* 1, no. 1 (2014): 10–19.

Alexia Moyer

nanbangashi, literally "southern barbarian sweets," refers in Japan to confections introduced by the "southern barbarians," that is, Westerners, chiefly the Portuguese during the mid-sixteenth to early seventeenth centuries. Portuguese merchants and missionaries helped to popularize the consumption of eggs and sugar, and these are focal ingredients for nanbangashi, which include baked goods and candies. Before the Portuguese arrived in 1543, sugar was known in the ancient period in Japan as a medicine; commoners consumed eggs, but the elite avoided them, at least for formal banquets. Jesuit missionaries presented sweets to Japanese warlords and potential converts, while Iberian merchants developed a market for the sugar they brought from China by teaching the Japanese how to work with the sweetener and how to bake. Anti-Christian edicts barred the Portuguese from Japan in 1639, but nanbangashi only grew in popularity. The names of the most popular nanbangashi indicate their Iberian origins and include cookies (*bōro*); the golden Castilian sponge cake (*kasutera*) made rich with copious amount of eggs; small bumpy candy called *konpeitō* that come in various colors and are an adaptation of the Portuguese anise candy *confeito*; and hard-crack "caramels" (*karumeira*). See CARAMELS; COMFIT; and SPONGE CAKE.

See also JAPAN and PORTUGAL'S INFLUENCE IN ASIA.

Rath, Eric C. *Food and Fantasy in Early Modern Japan.* Berkeley: University of California Press, 2010.

Eric C. Rath

Napoleon

See PASTRY, PUFF.

Native American sweets included sweet-tasting roots, berries, fruits, saps, and syrups. For the Natives of North America, all of nature was their supermarket, and they had an encyclopedic knowledge of plants and animals. Many plants, whether gathered or cultivated, had multiple uses. Certain tribal groups were stationary, whereas others remained on the move, collecting and hunting as they migrated. Each territory had its own specific plants and animals, and different tribal groups used the same plant in a variety of ways. In addition, Native Americans sometimes "tended" wild plants to ensure their ongoing harvest. This entry provides a brief overview of some of the plant foods used for their sweet qualities by Native Americans.

Maple Sugar

Although many trees such as birch (*Betula* spp.), ash (*Fraxinus* spp.), hickory (*Carya* spp.), and box elder (*Acer negundo*) have sap that can be made into sweet syrup, or evaporated for sugar, maples (*Acer* spp.) have rich and very high-volume sap. See MAPLE SYRUP and SAP. Chippewa, Iroquois, Potawatomi, Dakota, and other tribes living in maple-growing regions made "Indian sugar" and maple syrup from "sugar trees" or maples, with the sugar maple (*Acer saccharin*) the most prolific in yield. Maple sugar was described in treaties as a tribal right and a significant part of the diet. If correctly tapped, the trees were not damaged and were used annually for years.

In March or April depending on the latitude, during the Sugar Moon, the "juice" or sap was at the peak of sweetness. Hollowed trees were filled with hot rocks and the collected sap was boiled and evaporated to create maple sugar. In later years, iron kettles were used for boiling the sap. Sap was sometimes allowed to sour to create "vinegar." Thimble berries, a type of blackberry (*Rebus Canadensis*), were mixed with maple sap and water to create a beverage used by the Iroquois in longhouse ceremonies. On occasion the sap was fermented and used to create beverages like beer. Maple sugar was a stable commodity more easily transported, stored, and traded than maple syrup. The sugar cakes made were used to season food, frequently instead of salt, in all forms of cookery; they were also mixed with other foods and added to hot or cold drinks, depending on the time of year. Birch bark molds weighing 100 pounds apiece were a trade commodity, and maple sugar was sometimes used as currency. Small, formed maple sugar cakes were made into shapes like flowers or bear paws and decorated with porcupine quills as special gifts, or they were offered for sale. Potawatomi children made candy by cooling maple sap in the snow. Large quantities of maple sugar meant food for the winter months, a necessity for survival for many tribal groups.

Corn, Maize, Indian Corn

Some archaeologists have recently speculated that corn was developed as an important domesticated plant not for the food value of the ears, but primarily as a source of sugar. By removing the ears from the stalk when they are young or "green," the ears will have absorbed some of the sugar but the stalk will still hold most of the sugar. An early explorer writes from Roanoke in 1585 that "we have found here maize...whose ear yieldeth corn for bread... and the cane maketh very good and perfect sugar." In caves throughout the Southwest and Utah, archaeologists have found discarded quids of yucca (*Yucca* spp.), mesquite beans (*Prosopis* spp.), maize husks (*Zea mays*), bulrush plants (*Scirpus* spp.), agave (*Agave* spp.), and prickly pear (*Opuntia* spp.). Chewing quids of these sweet plants would have been like indulging in a candy bar, with the quids discarded, for future archaeologists to find, when they were no longer sweet.

In a process called "sweet corning," the ears were picked when sweet and cooked; the kernels were dried and later reconstituted by placing them in hot water. When these kernels were ground and combined with water, they made a sweet drink. Soft and sweet corn, called "papoon," was a food favored by many children of the northeastern tribal groups. The Corn Planting Moon in May was followed in August by the Green Corn Moon. In the Southwest, the Hopi would make corn balls from finely ground sweet corn by mixing the corn with water and potash, and cooking it by dropping the balls in boiling water, or baking them in corn husks. The Cheyenne used a similar process for corn balls that figured in their eagle-catching ceremony. Numerous tribes throughout much of the United States grew various types of corn, including sweet corn. The Iroquois evaporated cornstalk syrup to make a corn sugar. The Pawnee dried cornsilk and mixed it with ground corn as a sweetener. The Hopi would use baked and dried corn kernels to sweeten dishes during the winter. Masticated corn was also used to sweeten foods. Dried and roasted kernels were mixed with cornstalk syrup to create a candy that sometimes included seeds and nuts.

After maple sugar collection, usually in March, the Mohawk would prepare for corn cultivation. Green corn was ripened in water for several months and then eaten as candy. The Iroquois preserved green or young corn by parching it over a fire and then removing the kernels from the cob. This allowed the corn kernels to be stored and reconstituted later with water. Once ground, this meal was mixed with maple sugar and would be taken on hunting or other trips. It could be mixed with water and eaten either cold or hot. Mohawk corncakes sometimes included vegetables or fruit, such as squash or berries, and could be made into betrothal or funeral cakes. The cornstalk was used as a storage container for maple sugar and other items, with corncobs as stoppers (cobs at the time were much smaller than our modern ones).

Stevia

Stevia rebaudiana Bertoni is known for its sweet taste. Native to the New World, over 80 species of Stevia exist. The plant's range was restricted to temperate parts of the United States, Central America, and South America. It was mainly used for medicinal purposes, and many of its varieties actually have a bitter taste. See STEVIA.

Honey

Honeybees arrived in North America in the seventeenth century, traveling by sea with European immigrants, and beekeeping quickly spread in the American colonies. Some bees escaped and established feral populations, whereas others remained domesticated and cared for by the colonists. The arrival of honeybees in a new area was said to signal to the Native Americans that the colonists were not far behind. See HONEY.

Juniper

With *Junipernus* spp. quite abundant in certain areas with a diverse range, juniper berries are quite sweet and were eaten by the Utes and other tribes. The Apache roasted the fruit; other tribes dried the fruit, crushed and stored it, or used it as a spice. Gum from the juniper was also chewed as a special treat. The Navaho ground the fruit to eat in corn mush and also to make into candy.

Mesquite

Honey mesquite (*Prosopis glandulosa*) and other varieties of mesquite (*Prosopis* spp.) similarly have a wide range throughout the South and Southwest and were heavily used by many Native peoples. When the beans are ground and mixed with water and dried in the sun, the mixture creates a very sweet cake. Pods are also mashed and boiled, and the gum is eaten as a candy. Sometimes this gum is mixed with saguaro syrup to create a conserve. The pods are eaten raw like candy or ground and mixed with water to make a drink, which Gary Paul Nabhan (1985) has described as "sweet, like carob or chocolate pudding in flavor and texture."

Saguaro

Saguaro (*Carnegia gigantea*) fruit is much appreciated by the Apache, Pima, and Papago. It is eaten raw or dried in the sun; the fruit is cooked into a type of butter, while the juice is made into a jam, as is the pulp; the dried fruit is shaped into blocks as a way of preserving it for future use. Strained, boiled pulp is thickened into a light brown syrup used as a sweetener.

Agave

The leaves and hearts of the American century plant (*Agave* spp. and *Agave americana*) are cooked on hot stones for several days, then eaten or pounded into flat cakes that have a sweet taste. They are very fibrous and can be carried while traveling, although the fiber is not swallowed. The heart of the plant and fruit heads are also cooked, dried, and eaten as candy. The Apache take the thick, juicy base of the leaves and center to make a "head" that is baked slowly in a pit oven of heated stones covered with dirt until it turns very sweet.

Fan Palm, California Fan Palm

The fruit of the fan palm (*Washingtonia filifera*), which is very sweet, is eaten raw or sun-dried; the juice is mixed with water for a beverage.

Prickly Pear

The *tuna* or fruit of the prickly pear cactus (*Opuntia* spp.) is used by the Apache, who boil it down into a stiff jam they call "tuna cheese" or *queso de tuna*. The tuna is also pit-roasted, dried, and made into jelly.

Berries and Fruit

Native American grapes (*Vitis vinifera, Vitis* spp.)—Muscadine and other varieties—had broad geographic distribution and were eaten fresh, dried, crushed, and preserved. They were used to make all sorts of cakes and preserves by a wide range of tribal groups, including the Mendocino, Cherokee, Iroquois, Lakota, and Pawnee. Seasonal berries and fruits included blueberries (also called huckleberries or hurtle berries) (*Vaccinium* spp.), raspberries (*Rubus* spp.), blackberries (*Rubus* spp.), and *Fragaria Virginia* and other varieties of strawberries (*Fragaria* spp.), as well as various fruits of the *Prunus* spp. family, including plums, cherries, and peaches. (The last of these was introduced by the Spanish but quickly spread by Native Americans.) All were highly prized as fresh fruits by varied tribal groups, but as a result of their perishable and seasonal nature, they were frequently sun-dried for future use, or made into preserves and concentrated syrups. Dried fruit was reconstituted with water and made into cakes with cornmeal, or cooked into a sauce. The dried cakes were used as travel food by the Iroquois. The Navajo considered strawberries a delicacy.

Hickory

Hickory (*Carya* spp.) nuts were pounded by the Creek and placed in boiling water, then strained to yield a thick "milk," described by John Bartram in the eighteenth century as being as sweet and as rich as fresh cream. This milk was used with cornmeal to make cakes and as an ingredient in cooking. The nuts were also eaten plain or roasted and used as seasoning.

Pinyon and Various Pines

Pinyon (*Pinus* spp.) are found throughout the Great Plains and parts of the Southwest. The nuts are a special delicacy, and the sap is used for candy and can be chewed like gum.

Camas

The explorers Lewis and Clark wrote that "among these last [roots] is one which is round and much like an onion in appearance and sweet to the taste; it is called Quamash and is eaten either in its natural state, or boiled into a kind of soup or made into a cake called 'pasheco.' After our long abstinence, this was a sumptuous treat." The root of camas (*Camassia quamash*), tasting a little like a pumpkin, was used from the Rocky Mountains west and throughout California.

Sweet Root

The peeled roots of sweet root (*Cymopterus newberryi*) have a pleasant taste and are eaten by the Hopi and Navajo.

Sweet Potato

The Cherokee and Seminole used the tubers of the sweet potato plant (*Ipomoea batatas*) for food, including roasting in ashes and mixing with cornmeal to form a kind of bread.

See also AGAVE NECTAR.

Coe, S. D. *America's First Cuisines.* Austin: University of Texas Press, 1994.

Gasser, R. A. "Regional Signatures of Hohokam Plant Use." *Kiva: Hohokam Ethnobiology* 56, no. 3 (1991): 207–226.

Larsen, E. A. "Pehr Kalm's Description of Maize, How It Is Planted and Cultivated in North America, Together with the Many Uses of This Crop Plant." *Agricultural History* 9, no. 2 (April 1935): 98–117.

Moerman, D. E. *Native American Food Plants: An Ethnobotanical Dictionary.* Portland, Ore.: Timber Press, 2010.

Nabhan, G. P. *Gathering the Desert.* Tucson: University of Arizona Press, 1985.

Smalley, J. A. "Sweet Beginnings: Stalk Sugar and the Domestication of Maize." *Current Anthropology* 44, no. 5 (December 2003): 675–703.

Daphne Derven

NECCO is the oldest candy company in the United States and has been satisfying America's sweet tooth since before the Civil War. Oliver B. Chase, a druggist from England, is credited with inventing the first candy-making machine in the United States in 1847. See CHASE, OLIVER. He used the device for stamping out sugar wafers called "lozenges." See LOZENGE. Based on the immediate success of these flavored candy lozenges, Oliver and his brother Silas Edwin founded Chase and Co. in South Boston that same year. Today, the wafers are believed to be the oldest American product continuously manufactured and sold in its original form. In 1901 Chase and Co. combined with two other candy companies to form the New England Confectionery Company (NECCO). NECCO's world headquarters is located in Revere, Massachusetts.

Chase's flavored lozenges were surprisingly popular, probably because they were cheap and durable. These sweet lozenges were carried by Union soldiers, who called them "Hub Wafers," "Hub" being the nineteenth-century nickname for Boston where they were made. By 1899 the U.S. government was including candy in soldiers' rations in the hope of increasing caloric intake and improving their endurance and health. See MILITARY. The U.S. War Department shipped 50 tons of candy to Spanish-American War battlefields and requisitioned the company's entire output of hardy NECCO Wafers for soldiers during World War II. See SPANISH-AMERICAN WAR.

Throughout most of the company's history, these candy wafers ensured its financial success. The treats were a favorite during economic hard times because a roll of wafers cost just a few cents and could be doled out to children, one at a time, for days. They have served other purposes, too: the rugged wafers have been used as rifle-range targets, poker chips, and checkers. Admiral Richard Byrd took two tons of NECCO Wafers on his polar expedition in the 1930s; decades later, kitchen doyenne Martha Stewart used them to make roofs for gingerbread houses.

Other successful NECCO products include Canada Mints, Mary Jane peanut-butter chews, and Sky Bars, the first multicenter candy bar, which was promoted with a sky-writing campaign in 1938 to capitalize on America's aviation craze. The company also makes Squirrel Nut Zippers, Peach Blossoms, Candy Buttons, and Haviland Mints. NECCO candies that did not stand the test of time included Hoarhound Ovals, Jujube Monoplanes, Whangbees, and Climax Mint Patties.

"Conversation hearts," a Valentine's Day staple, were invented by Silas Chase in the 1860s. See VALENTINE'S DAY. The concept dates back to the late 1800s, when printed sayings on colored paper were placed in "Cockles," small crisp candies in the shape of a scalloped shell. In 1866 another Chase brother, Daniel, invented a process that allowed the sayings to be printed directly on the candy. The heart-shaped conversation candies later called Sweethearts got their start in 1902. These familiar candy hearts have cute little sayings such as "Be Mine," "All Mine," "Crazy 4U," and "Cutie Pie." Today, they are also available in Spanish. In 2004 the U.S. Postal Service issued a 37-cent stamp with the image of two overlapping Sweethearts candies saying, "I ♥ YOU." Sweethearts became an American icon, even though they disappeared from the market for nearly 20 years. These crunchy, chalky, pastel candies, smaller and thicker than a NECCO Wafer, were hugely successful when first introduced and remained so for the next 50 years. But in an incredible miscalculation, NECCO discontinued the conversation hearts in the 1950s, only to reintroduce them in the 1970s when the company came under new management. NECCO turns out 8 billion (13 million pounds) of the sweet treats every year for Valentine's Day. If you are of a certain age, the colorful hearts were probably as much a part of your childhood as they are for kids today. Although many of the 100-plus ways of saying "I love you" featured on the hearts have changed, especially since the early 1990s, the candy's formula and the way the hearts are produced remain virtually the same.

NECCO was a highly successful business for over a hundred years, but by the 1960s it had stagnated by relying on existing products and failing to innovate, modernize, or update its antiquated production facilities. NECCO was still using a leather conveyor-belt system and wooden troughs instead of stainless steel, and some said the company's aging production facility looked like a candy-making museum. Furthermore, NECCO did no consumer marketing whatsoever. The company was losing money and approaching bankruptcy. In 1963 UIS Co., a New York holding company, purchased NECCO and installed a management team to turn things around. On 28 December 2007 American Capital Strategies Ltd. announced that it had invested in the company. American Capital partnered with Clear Creek Capital LLC and Domenic M. Antonellis, president and CEO of NECCO, in the investment.

NECCO now fully operates in the present. The company recently launched a website for custom candy. At MyNECCO.com, customers can personalize their own NECCO Wafers or Sweethearts in consumer-sized quantities and create one-of-a-kind candies for any occasion. These special candies are promoted as perfect favors for weddings, baby showers, graduations, birthday parties, and business outings.

See also CANDY and CHILDREN'S CANDY.

Brokel, Ray. *The Great American Candy Bar Book*. pp. 75–77. New York and Boston: Houghton Mifflin, 1982.
Dusselier, Jane. "Bonbons, Lemon Drops, and Oh Henry! Bars: Candy, Consumer Culture, and the Construction of Gender, 1895–1920." In *Kitchen Culture in America*, edited by Sherrie A. Inness, pp. 13–49. Philadelphia: University of Pennsylvania Press, 2001.
Foglino, Annette. "The History of Sweetheart Candies." *Smithsonian Magazine*, 8 February 2011.
Morave, Natalie. "The History of Candy Making in Cambridge: NECCO." 2001. http://www.cambridge-history.org/discover/candy/necco.html.
Mote, Dave. "New England Confectionery Co. NECCO." In *International Directory of Company Histories*, edited by Tina Grant, Vol. 15, pp. 323–325. Detroit: St. James, 1996.

Joseph M. Carlin

Nestlé, with more than 300,000 employees, production sites in over 80 countries, and an annual turnover of around $100 billion, is the world's largest food producer, with headquarters on Lake Geneva in Vevey, Switzerland. The company's origins were certainly on the sweet side, when Frankfurt-born pharmacist Henri Nestlé (1814–1890), in Switzerland in 1867, came up with Farine Lactée, a milk powder for infants that could be mixed with water as a replacement for breast milk. Grown-up sweets came into the picture when Nestlé merged with the Swiss chocolate makers' trio of François Louis Cailler, Daniel Peter, and Charles Amédée Kohler in 1929. See PETER, DANIEL. The three had long experimented with combining milk and chocolate and relied on Nestlé's condensed milk for their production (the first milk chocolate had actually been marketed in 1845 by Jordan & Timaeus in Dresden, Saxony, 30 years earlier than in Switzerland). Nestlé's initially small company prospered long after his death, expanding rapidly after 1898 by taking over European (and later worldwide) rivals. The most important addition to the Nestlé portfolio was the industrial production and marketing of instant coffee in 1938 under the Nescafé brand, which created a perfectly complementary product mix of coffee, milk, and chocolate. Since then, the company has also branched out into condiments (Maggi), pet food (Purina Alpo), bottled water (Vittel and Pellegrino), and cosmetics (L'Oréal).

The official company slogan is "Good Food, Good Life," but ultimately that means good food according to Nestlé. The giant conglomerate has not only shown a strong interest in emerging and new markets (entering them with "popularly positioned products" adapted to each individual market), it is also working relentlessly to add as much value to raw products as possible, in order to achieve independence from floating market prices and create maximum shareholder value (in the financial world, Nestlé shares tend to be seen as not cheap but virtually risk-free). The very opposite of the kind of direct producer–consumer exchanges that occur at farmers markets, Nestlé's business model is to sell products for much more than the value of their original raw ingredients, whether coffee (Nescafé and Nespresso, as well as many more local brands), wheat (cereals, pasta, and frozen pizza), or milk (a wide array of milk powders, condensed milk, and infant formulas, as well as ice cream and yogurt). Although the threat of rising cacao prices is repeatedly mentioned in financial reports, few of the vast selection of sweet snacks under the Nestlé umbrella actually contain very much cacao, including KitKat (produced in the United States by Hershey's), Lion, Munchies Milky Bar, Perugina Baci, Quality Street, Smarties, Wonka Bars, or Nesquik instant chocolate. See COCOA.

In fact, Nestlé is as torn in its identity as in the contrast between its high-end products such as Cailler chocolate and the affordable caramel-filled Rolo. On the one hand, the company has been positioning itself as above all concerned with health and well-being, selling diet products and initiating nutrition institutes and councils. On the other, it is making its money with sugar- and fat-laden foods such as sweets, ice cream, and pizza. This split identity may be one of the reasons the company has repeatedly faced controversy. In addition to criticism surrounding nutrition-based health issues, including the undeclared use of GMO products, Nestlé has been accused of price fixing, raising infant mortality in third-world countries through the promotion of its baby formula, commercializing natural water supplies in the form of bottled water, tolerating deforestation, and turning a blind eye to child labor.

Schwarz, Friedhelm. *Nestlé: The Secrets of Food, Trust and Globalization*. Toronto: Key Porter, 2006.

Ursula Heinzelmann

The **Netherlands,** situated along the North Sea opposite Great Britain, have always been strong in trade. Sugar was imported in medieval times, mainly from Italy and Portugal. Products made with sugar, such as *suikerbrood* (cinnamon bread, literally "sugar loaf"), were well liked but expensive; they were consumed especially during public holidays. Because of their expertise, Dutch confectioners were invited in 1514 to work at the court of Maximilian I, emperor of the Holy Roman Empire, and in 1522 at the court of Ferdinand I, archduke of Austria. See COURT CONFECTIONERS.

The Dutch established trading relations with overseas countries in the seventeenth century. In Surinam and the islands of the Caribbean, in particular, they developed their own sugar plantations. See PLANTATIONS, SUGAR. Raw sugar was refined in Amsterdam. Around 1660, Amsterdam boasted more than 50 refineries, about as many as in the rest of Europe. Cane sugar became an important export product. Although the price of sugar went down in the domestic market, it remained a luxury item. Sugar and imported spices resulted in new kinds of pastry, such as gingerbread: *peperkoek*, literally "pepper cake," and *kruidkoek*, "spice cake," the predecessors of the typically Dutch honey cake (*ontbijtkoek*). See GINGERBREAD.

Public Holidays and Feast Days

The Dutch added luster to public celebrations by baking all manner of delicacies, and they took this custom with them when they fanned out to other continents in the seventeenth century. On New Year's Eve, Dutch immigrants in the United States baked *koekjes*, *wafels*, and *krulkoeken*. The Americans adopted these delicacies as *cookies*, *waffles*, and *crullers*. Elsewhere, Dutch names for various types of pastry were taken over as well. For example, the name *krakeling* (cracknels) stuck in France and Indonesia, and *wafel* (waffle) in Germany, Scandinavia, and Russia.

The most popular Dutch feast day, celebrated since the seventeenth century, is the feast of St. Nicholas (*Sinterklaas*). This holiday was brought to the United States by the Dutch, where *Sinterklaas* developed into Santa Claus. Dutch children were (and are) given sweets like marzipan (*marsepein*), fondant (*borstplaat*), gingerbread men (*speculaaspoppen*), and spiced biscuits (*speculaasjes*). See GINGERBREAD; MARZIPAN; and SPECULAAS. St. Nicholas distributes spice nuts (*pepernoten*), ginger nuts (*kruidnoten*), gingerbread (*taaitaai*), meringues (*schuimpjes*), and confectionery (*suikergoed*). In the nineteenth century, the custom of consuming pastry and chocolate shaped in the form of letters—*amandelletters, banketletters, boterletters,* and *chocoladeletters*—was introduced for St. Nicholas Day.

Cookies of All Sorts

Over the course of the eighteenth century, the price of sugar dropped still further, which made sweets more affordable for increasing numbers of people. It became customary to fill pastry with almond paste, called *banket*. A fashion arose for serving coffee and tea, sweetened with sugar and accompanied by cookies or pastry, at home. In the nineteenth century a switch from cane sugar to industrially produced, cheaper beet sugar took place, resulting in an increase in sweets consumption and the production of all kinds of new products, each of which had its own name. See SUGAR BEET. From 1900 on, specialized factories were set up to manufacture a wide assortment of cookies, including *bastognekoeken, bitterkoekjes, eierkoeken, gevulde koeken, janhagel, jodenkoeken, lange vingers, makronen, mariakaakjes, pindarotsjes,* and *roze koeken*—each made with distinct ingredients and methods.

Seeing in the New Year traditionally entails preparing deep-fried doughnut balls (*oliebollen*), apple turnovers (*appelflappen*), and apple fritters (*appelbeignets*). Christmas festivities include eating almond pastry rolls (*banketstaven*), Christmas loaves (*kerstbroden, kerststollen*), Christmas cookies (*kerstkransjes*), and turban-shaped cakes called *tulbanden*. See CHRISTMAS.

Confectionery

During the Middle Ages, children were given sugar balls on special occasions, but specialized types of sweets date only to the end of the eighteenth century. The best known are bull's eyes (*babbelaars* or *toverballen*), marshmallows (*spekjes*), dolly-mixture (*tumtum*), and acid drops (*zuurballen* or *zuurtjes*). Fairground attractions include cinnamon sticks (*kaneelstokken*), nougat (*noga*), cotton candy (*suikerspinnen*), and sticks of rock sugar (*zuurstokken*). See FAIRS. A typical Dutch custom, known since the late eighteenth century, is to offer people rusks with aniseed comfits (*beschuit met muisjes*) on the birth of a child: blue ones for a boy and pink for a girl. See COMFIT.

Thanks to Dutch innovations in the eighteenth and nineteenth centuries, chocolate became available in the form of tablets, slabs, and bars. In the late eighteenth century, Caspar Flick's Amsterdam chocolate factory began manufacturing chocolates that are still called *flikjes*. In 1828 the Dutchman Casparus van Houten Sr. took out a patent for an inexpensive way to separate the fat from cocoa beans, which boosted the production of chocolate products. See COCOA and VAN HOUTEN, COENRAAD JOHANNES. In 1907 the Dutch firm of Kwatta produced the first wrapped chocolate bar, which was intended for the army. The best-known names of chocolate bars were *Kwatta* and *Koetjesreep*, literally "cow-bar," a kind of imitation chocolate bar with a cow on the wrapper. These Dutch products have now been replaced by international brands like Mars, Snickers, and M&M's. But Dutch youngsters still relish a bread topping called *hagelslag*, chocolate sprinkles, which dates back to the beginning of the twentieth century. See SPRINKLES.

A typical Dutch product is licorice (*drop*), a delicacy in the Netherlands since the eighteenth century. The Netherlands is currently the largest licorice-producing nation in the European Union. There is a wide selection of sweet and salty types, and a corresponding variety of names, mostly based on the taste, such as *anijsdrop* and *laurierdrop* (anisette and bay-leaf flavored), or on the form, such as *muntdrop* and *veterdrop* (coin or shoestring-shaped). See LICORICE.

Desserts

In the beginning of the nineteenth century, people began to mark the end of a meal by eating a simple sweet dessert, which was given the Dutch name of *toetje* ([little] afters). Of the many possible offerings, a typical selection might include *lammetjespap* or *zoetepap* (meal pap), *griesmeelpudding* (semolina pudding), *havermoutpap* (oatmeal porridge), *karnemelkspap* (buttermilk mush), *rijstepap* (rice pudding), and *watergruwel* (gruel). In the 1960s and 1970s, all segments of the population got into the habit of ending dinner with a ready-made dairy dessert. The Dutch Dairy Board strongly promoted a variety of dairy products like *vla* (custard), pudding, and yogurt in various flavors, sold in cartons that could be kept fresh in the fridge. Since then a multitude of varieties of this typically Dutch dessert have been produced, with continually changing names.

See also COLONIALISM; CONFECTION; CUSTARD; DOUGHNUTS; FRIED DOUGH; HOLIDAY SWEETS; NOUGAT; PUDDING; and SUGAR REFINERIES.

Burema, Lambertus. *De voeding in Nederland van de Middeleeuwen tot de twintigste eeuw.* Assen, The Netherlands: Van Gorcum, 1953.

Jobse-van Putten, Jozien. *Eenvoudig maar voedzaam: Cultuurgeschiedenis van de dagelijkse maaltijd in Nederland.* Amsterdam: SUN, 1995.

Van der Sijs, Nicoline. *Chronologisch woordenboek van het Nederlands: De ouderdom en herkomst van onze woorden en betekenissen.* Amsterdam: Veen, 2001.

Van der Sijs, Nicoline. *Cookies, Coleslaw, and Stoops: The Influence of Dutch on the North American Languages.* Amsterdam: Amsterdam University Press, 2009.

Van Otterloo, Anneke H. *Eten en eetlust in Nederland (1840–1990): Een historisch-sociologische studie.* Amsterdam: Bert Bakker, 1990.

Nicoline van der Sijs; translated by Frits Beukema

neuroscience, the study of the human nervous system, offers a number of intriguing insights into the perception of sweetness. Sweetness is one of the most important sensory signals for our brain to detect, typically signaling calories, which are essential for energy and growth. While sweetness can be detected (or sensed) only by a certain class of taste buds in the oral cavity (concentrated primarily on the tongue), the neuroscience evidence demonstrates just how important the integration of cues from every one of our senses is to the perception of how sweet something tastes (to us) and also how much we happen to like the experience. See SWEETNESS PREFERENCE.

Taste buds sensitive to sweetness can be found all over the tongue but tend to be concentrated around the tip. The taste buds transmit information to the brain about the chemical properties of the soluble (or sapid) compounds in the mouth. The latest evidence demonstrates the existence of a taste map in the brain (specifically in the insula), with sweet tastes activating one area, sour tastes another, and so on.

Difficulty of Directly Tasting Sweetness

The various receptors found in the oral cavity can interact and mutually suppress one another. This phenomenon, known as sensory suppression, makes it difficult for the brain to assess just how sweet a food really is (based on nothing more than what happens to be signaled by the various gustatory receptors). What is more, the temperature at which a food or drink is tasted can also play havoc with our ability to ascertain the sweetness of that which we are consuming. Just think about how cloyingly sweet most colas taste when served warm. The actual sweetness obviously has not changed—what has changed, and dramatically, is our perception of the taste. However, even if we were able to accurately ascertain the sweetness of a foodstuff, we certainly cannot stick everything we come across into our mouths in order to decide whether or not it tastes sweet.

Multisensory Perception of Sweetness

Given the difficulty of assessing sweetness directly (or any other taste property, for that matter), our brains have evolved to utilize information from the other senses, such as olfaction and vision, in order to try and infer, or predict, whether a particular foodstuff is likely to be sweet or not, long before it ever reaches our mouth. Put simply, the challenge for the brain is to integrate the gustatory cues from the tongue with olfactory information from the nose, as well as any oral-somatosensory, visual, and even auditory cues that may be available. See OLFACTION; SOUND; and VISION. Sometimes our brain combines signals from the senses in ways that are surprising. So, for example, the brain frequently shows evidence of sensory (often visual) dominance. What this means in practice is that if one changes the color (or visual appearance) of a food, it could well change the perceived taste or flavor of that food. Evidence also suggests that the brain sometimes combines sensory cues in ways that are nonlinear (either super-additively or sub-additively). Such observations, worked out in the cognitive neuroscience laboratory, have created great excitement in the food and flavor industries, as they seem to offer the promise of delivering flavors more cheaply (and, who knows, perhaps more healthily) by getting the combination of food-related sensory cues just right.

In nature, a natural correlation exists between the ripening of fruits and their transition from green and sour to the redder, riper, and hence sweeter end of the spectrum. Perhaps as a result of our brain's picking up on this correlation, coloring a food or beverage red has been shown to be a particularly good cue to sweetness (e.g., in a beverage). See FOOD COLORINGS. Indeed, the very development of trichromatic color vision in our hairy ancestors may have developed in order to enable them to more effectively pick out the ripe red fruits out among the dark green canopy. Whatever the cause, nowadays, as the expression goes, we eat with our eyes. As such, our brain uses visual cues in order to determine, or predict, what a food will taste like. This is something that appears to occur relatively automatically, and within a matter of milliseconds. Hence, one of the ways in which the sweetness of a food or beverage can be changed is simply by changing its color. Our brain uses the color to make a prediction, and as long as our experience matches it when we put whatever it is in our mouth, we will likely see "assimilation"—that is, we will experience what we expected. It is only when the experience (e.g., of sweetness) is drastically different from what we expected that one may see a "disconfirmation of expectation," which, on occasion, can lead to a rebound effect whereby we rate the food as tasting less sweet than we otherwise would.

People in the West describe certain smells such as vanilla, strawberry, and caramel as sweet, yet anyone who has ever tried biting into a pod knows that vanilla actually tastes very bitter. So why then do most of us describe such smells as sweet? Is this anything more than merely a metaphorical use of language? The evidence suggests that it is. Indeed, a fascinating body of research by Dick Stevenson and his colleagues in Australia has demonstrated that foods really do taste sweeter when a sweet-smelling aroma is added. This factor might be part of the reason why vanilla ice cream is so successful, as at very low temperatures the taste buds do not work so well, as noted above. It appears that our brains learn the associations between particular (especially novel) aromas and particular taste qualities within a few exposures to their paired presentation in food and drink. Learning has even been shown to take place in the absence of any awareness of the contingency.

Such exposure-dependent learning helps to explain why it is that aromas like benzaldehyde (the cherry-almond smell associated with Bakewell tart) will likely smell sweet to a Westerner, whereas consumers from Japan, where such desserts are uncommon, may instead associate (and hence integrate) the smell of benzaldehyde with monosodium glutamate (MSG) because those ingredients co-occur more frequently in the foods of the region, such as, for example, in pickled condiments. These multisensory interactions between taste and smell in food can sometimes be super-additive.

Neuroscientists distinguish between sensory-discriminative and hedonic responses to foods. On the one hand, we can estimate how sweet a particular dessert is—this is a sensory-discriminative judgment. On the other, we may find that level of sweetness very pleasant, or we might judge it excessively sweet—this is a hedonic response. By putting people into a brain scanner, and seeing where the pattern of blood flow changes ("which part of the brain lights up," as it were), neuroscientists have been able to establish that different parts of the brain are responsible for coding these different responses to taste and flavor. The insula, often referred to as the primary taste cortex, appears to code the sweetness of a food (that is a sensory-discriminative attribute), whereas the orbitofrontal cortex (OFC), a roughly walnut-sized structure located between the eyes and back a bit, codes for the reward (or hedonic) value of a food. So, for example, if a hungry participant is fed a sweet dessert, something that she really likes, then activity will likely initially be seen in both of these brain structures. However, if the participant continues to eat until sated, then the activity in the OFC will drop off, while the activity in the insula will remain relatively unchanged. The OFC not only codes for the reward value of food; it is also a key integration site where gustatory, olfactory, visual, and oral-somatosensory textural cues, and presumably even auditory cues, are integrated. Intriguing neuroimaging research has shown that the activity in the OFC increases when we experience a congruent combination of taste and smell (sweetness combined with the smell of strawberry, say) and declines when we are exposed to an incongruent combination of inputs (sweetness with the smell of chicken broth, say). Such brain responses can be thought of in terms of the notion of super-additivity and sub-additivity.

Intriguingly, our response to sweetness changes over the course of development. Young children appear to like sweetness more than adults, presumably a sensible strategy for a growing organism. Even as adults, though, the population seems to segment into sweet likers and sweet dislikers. Such differences reflect more than simply a difference in sensitivity to sweetness. Future neuroimaging research may be able to help scientists determine whether such differences, both developmental and individual, are reflected in the response of the OFC, or in some other brain region.

One bizarre neurological condition that highlights the importance of the insula to our perception of, and response to, food comes from those rare patients suffering from Gourmand's syndrome. Following brain damage, such individuals suddenly develop a profound and enduring interest in everything food-related. Brain scans have revealed that these rare patients have normally suffered damage to the right anterior part of the brain. Such neurological damage can shift a person from "eating to live" to "living to eat."

Prescott, J. *Taste Matters: Why We Like the Foods We Do.* London: Reaktion, 2012.

Small, D. M. "Flavor Is in the Brain." *Physiology and Behavior* 107 (2012): 540–552.

Spence, C., and B. Piqueras-Fiszman. *The Perfect Meal: The Multisensory Science of Food and Dining.* Oxford: Wiley-Blackwell, 2014.

Trivedi, B. "Hardwired for Taste: Research into Human Taste Receptors Extends beyond the Tongue to Some Unexpected Places." *Nature* 486 (2012): S7.

Charles Spence

New England (U.S.) is a region known for such classic early American desserts as pumpkin pie, Indian pudding, and Indian meal pound cake, all of which evolved from English recipes adapted to the native ingredients corn and pumpkins. Another group of sweets, including apple and mincemeat pies, apple dumplings, hard and soft gingerbreads, and Election cake, relied on the apples and wheat that settlers had brought with them, along with familiar recipes from their English homeland.

Some of these desserts migrated westward as New Englanders settled elsewhere in the country. Others nearly vanished, overtaken by new styles in sweet cookery, particularly cakes, cookies, and cold desserts in the nineteenth century, a process speeded by the adoption of chemical leavens, inexpensive fine wheat flour and white sugar, and ingredients like baking chocolate. See BAKER'S; CHEMICAL LEAVENERS; and SUGAR. In the twentieth century, commercial products and recipes from test kitchens broadened dessert offerings, while blurring the distinction between national dessert trends and traditional regional ones.

Pies and Pudding

Apple, mincemeat, and pumpkin pies have graced New England's Thanksgiving dinner and other significant dinners for nearly three centuries, in addition to being a popular choice for daily fare. See PIE. In her diary, midwife Martha Ballard of Augusta, Maine, recorded making these three pies nearly year-round in the early 1800s, rarely mentioning any others. Puritan settlers did not observe Christmas, with which mincemeat was strongly associated in England. Unwilling to give up mincemeat, however, they repurposed the pie for Thanksgiving celebrations, which made seasonal sense—as a kind of butchering-season preserve, mincemeat recipes call for meat, suet, apples, raisins, spices, and cider. Cooks baked apple pie from fresh apples from autumn through winter, as long as they stored well, and from dried apples when the fresh ran out. Colonial cooks discovered that sliced pumpkin cooked up much the way apples did, but the custard-based pumpkin pie we know today was developed from English milk puddings. See PUDDING.

The New England version of the milk and cornmeal pudding called Indian pudding is sweetened with molasses. (Southern versions usually use sugar.) The several sorts of Indian pudding varied in consistency from firm enough to be boiled in a pudding bag to baked puddings with eggs and even flour added. Indian pudding is still made occasionally at home today, and it is sometimes served in restaurants.

Apple dumplings—pastry-wrapped apples—were boiled individually in cloths in early New England. They were replaced by baked versions in the later 1800s. Other nineteenth-century apple desserts, including homely pandowdys and apple roly-poly puddings using pastry or biscuit-like dough (sometimes boiled in a cloth, sometimes baked), gave way in the 1900s to nationally popular crisps with streusel toppings. See FRUIT DESSERTS, BAKED.

Molasses Cakes and Gingerbreads

Molasses, derived from cane sugar and imported from the West Indies as a sweetener, predominated in the eighteenth and nineteenth centuries for common baking in most New England households. See MOLASSES. White or brown cane sugars accrued to the gentry and, up until the later 1800s and early 1900s, were reserved for special occasions and for preserves, except in economically depressed regions and households. Apple cider reduced to thick syrup, called cider molasses, served well as a substitute.

Several varieties of gingerbread, including hard sugar and soft molasses gingerbreads, commonly appear in American cookbooks, and they were popular in New England as well, where molasses was most commonly used. Subcategories of gingerbreads evolved nationally into varieties of soft molasses and ginger cookies. In New England, versions of soft molasses cookies using drippings or bacon fat were made on fishing boats at sea and in lumber camps. See DROP COOKIES and GINGERBREAD.

Molasses-sweetened cakes and doughnuts, common in the past all over New England, persisted in more isolated parts of the region, particularly in Maine, where they can still be found, though rarely. See DOUGHNUTS. Molasses blueberry cake, still made there, is an example, though the sugar-sweetened one is more common.

Maple sugar desserts are another New England specialty. Nearly always, in the earliest days of maple sap harvesting and boiling, the goal was to produce maple sugar as a substitute for cane sugar, or to produce maple molasses. Baked goods, confections, puddings, and pies made with maple sugar and syrup carried the distinctive maple flavor. In more recent times, maple syrup, most strongly associated with Vermont, is used in desserts for its own sake. See MAPLE SUGARING and MAPLE SYRUP.

Election Cake, a yeast-leavened cake made in the tradition of English festival cakes and rich bread, was traditionally associated with annual election and militia training days during the late 1700s and into the early 1800s. In-town households expecting to offer hospitality to rural visitors coming for the day made the cakes with enriched yeast dough containing eggs, butter, sugar, and currants or raisins; they were also sometimes iced. See CELEBRATION CAKES.

Brownies and chocolate chip cookies are now ubiquitous American desserts, but they appeared first in New England. In the 1896 *Boston Cooking School Cook Book*, Fannie Merritt Farmer included a brown-sugar version she called "Brownies"; today they are called "blondies." She published the chocolate-flavored brownie recipe in 1906. See BROWNIES and FARMER, FANNIE. Ruth Wakefield, in Whitman, Massachusetts, is generally credited with mixing broken chocolate bars into brown-sugar dough to create Toll House Cookies, named for a restaurant she and her husband operated.

Travelers and locals continue to enjoy many of New England's traditional desserts. For example, chefs offer Indian pudding on dessert menus, and it is conveniently canned for home consumption. Pies are de rigueur at church and lodge bean suppers, and local eateries known for serving them have parking lots full of cars.

Child, Lydia Maria. *The American Frugal Housewife*. 12th ed. Boston: Carter, Hendee, and Co., 1833. Reprint, Worthington, Ohio: Worthington Historical Society, 1965.

Cornelius, Mary Hooker. *The Young Housekeeper's Friend: Or, a Guide to Domestic Economy and Comfort*. Boston: Tappan, Whittemore, & Mason, 1850.

Farmer, Fannie Merritt. *The Original Boston Cooking-School Cook Book, 1896*. New York: Crown, 1973. Facsimilie reprint of the first edition of the *Boston Cooking-School Cook Book*.

Parloa, Maria. *The Appledore Cookbook, Containing Practical Receipts for Plain and Rich Cookery*. Boston: Andrew F. Graves, 1880.

Simmons, Amelia. *American Cookery: Or, the Art of Dressing Viands, Fish, Poultry and Vegetables*. New York: Dover, 1984. Facsimile of the 1796 version, with introduction by Mary Tolford Wilson.

Sandra L. Oliver

New Orleans, the Queen City of the South and the largest city in the state of Louisiana, abounds with sugar-laden dishes, served from breakfast through dessert, many with centuries of tradition attached. As the oldest and most historic sugarcane-producing U.S. state Louisiana, not surprisingly, is known for its tremendous affection for sweets. Jesuit priests planted the first sugarcane there in 1751, and by late 1795, Etienne de Bore had perfected the process of crystalizing brown sugar from cane. See SUGAR and SUGAR REFINING.

Even New Orleans's governmental rule played a part in the prevalence of sweets. Until the Louisiana Purchase in 1803, the Code Noir governed societal norms among the white, free black, and slave population. Under the code, slaves were allowed to purchase their freedom and, additionally, all slaves were allowed one free day each week. On the slave's day off (frequently Sunday), many became street vendors, peddling tempting sweet treats such as tac-tac (popcorn balls bound with cane sugar) and earning money that eventually bought freedom for many of the enslaved and their families. See RACE and SLAVERY. Sugared native pecans served in paper cones, flat ginger cakes called stage planks, and *la colle*—a cake made with molasses and roasted peanuts and pecans—were also popular street foods.

Praline vendors abounded, as did calas ladies. See PRALINE. Their special street call "Calas, calas! Belle calas tout chaud!" rang through the streets of the French Quarter, the Vieux Carré. Calas are ancient rice cakes that originated in the rice-growing regions of West Africa, namely Ghana, and were popularized in New Orleans by the enslaved from that area. Like the more famous beignet sold from stands in the French Market, calas were often consumed for breakfast. Rice was also an integral ingredient in *riz au lait*, a type of rice pudding made with leftover rice and milk and served warm for break-

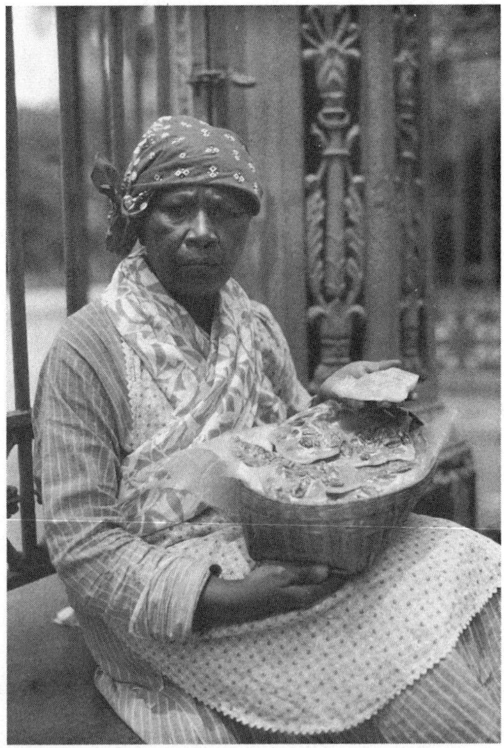

A vendor sells pralines in New Orleans's historic French Quarter in 1929. NGS IMAGE COLLECTION / THE ART ARCHIVE AT ART RESOURCE, N.Y.

fast. It was called rice blancmange when chilled for dessert. See BLANCMANGE and PUDDING.

By the early 1900s, horse- and mule-drawn carts traveled New Orleans's suburbs selling waffles and other sweets. Sam Cortese, a son of Sicilian immigrants, began selling Roman Taffy Chewing Candy from a cart in 1910. Today, Cortese's grandson Ronald Kottemann continues the family tradition using the original, mule-drawn cart.

Sicilians also popularized a shaved ice treat flavored with brightly colored, flavored sugar syrups sold from handcarts in the streets. In 1939 a New Orleans machinist, Ernest Hansen, invented an electric ice shaver that transformed blocks of ice into a fluffy, fine, snow-like ice that became known as the Sno Bliz or, more commonly, the SnoBall. See SHAVE ICE.

Flour was available from the city's earliest days, and the thrifty Creoles never wasted any. New Orleans French bread (known from the twentieth century as "poor boy bread") is a unique, light, airy loaf with a shattering crust that becomes stale within 24 hours. Slices of stale French bread soaked in egg and sugared milk, laced with brandy or vanilla, were called *pain perdu* or "lost bread" and served with cane syrup for breakfast. See CANE SYRUP.

Another favorite use for stale French bread is a custard-like bread pudding incorporating local ingredients like pecans, topped with liqueur-laced sauces, and served either cold or warm. Canned fruit cocktail became a popular addition in the early twentieth century, and later, white chocolate became another. Commander's Palace restaurant is renowned for its soufflé-style bread pudding.

Creole cream cheese, a soft cheese much like a *fromage blanc*, was made by clabbering fresh milk. It was most frequently eaten sweetened with sugar for breakfast but was also served frozen for dessert once ice became available in the early 1800s. See CHEESE, FRESH.

Although claimed across the southern United States as a classic dessert, pecan pie is also a Louisiana favorite. Native pecans are an important ingredient in a cookie called "cocoons." The pointed oval, sugared shortbread cookies were named for their resemblance to the silky threads that envelop the local moth's larvae in autumn.

By the late 1800s, strawberries and citrus were widely cultivated in south Louisiana. Springtime strawberries are preserved, incorporated into cakes, and frozen into Sicilian-style ice. See ITALIAN ICE. The citrus crop inspired sweets such as candied citrus peel and marmalade. See CANDIED FRUIT and FRUIT PRESERVES. Ambrosia, made with local satsuma oranges, imported coconut and sugar, and served in glistening crystal bowls, was a fixture of Christmas and other winter holiday celebrations. See AMBROSIA.

New Orleans became the nation's top banana port in the early 1900s. In 1951 Owen Brennan, founder of Brennan's Restaurant, asked his chef Paul Blange to create a flaming dessert utilizing the tropical fruit, and Bananas Foster was invented. See DESSERTS, FLAMBÉED.

The king cake tradition, which originated in Catholic France, is a Mardi Gras staple. The brioche dough ring, sprinkled with sugar in Carnival colors of purple, green, and gold, contained a hidden favor, originally a bean. Over time the favor became a tiny porcelain doll and then a plastic baby doll. The recipient of the hidden favor was named king or queen for the day, and was usually tasked with purchasing the next king cake. See BREADS, SWEET; CARNIVAL; and TWELFTH NIGHT CAKE.

Founded in 1855, the Elmer's Candy Company still supplies New Orleanians with Heavenly Hash and Gold Brick chocolate Easter eggs. "Turtles," small chocolate patties containing chopped pecans and sporting whole pecans to imitate a turtle's legs and head, are another popular twentieth-century candy.

In 1933 Beulah Ledner created the Doberge cake, inspired by the Austro-Hungarian Dobos torta. See DOBOS TORTE. Thin sponge cake layers are filled with custards flavored with chocolate, lemon, or caramel and finished with buttercream and poured fondant icing. See FONDANT. Ledner sold her recipe and her business to Gambino's Bakery, which continues to make the popular cakes today.

The story of New Orleans's sweets would not be complete without the mention of sodas and cocktails. Local pharmacist I. L. Lyons created a bright red sugar syrup flavored with almond and vanilla that he named "Nectar." When combined with soda water and ice cream, topped with whipped cream and a cherry, it became the iconic Nectar Soda sold at pharmacy soda fountains throughout the twentieth century. See SODA FOUNTAIN. Sweet cocktails like the Ramos Gin Fizz, Brandy Milk Punch, the Grasshopper, and the Hurricane were all invented in New Orleans, where they are still enjoyed.

See also SOUTH (U.S.).

Bienvenu, Marcelle. *The Picayune's Creole Cook Book*. Sesquicentennial ed. New Orleans: Times-Picayune, 1987.

Tucker, Susan. *New Orleans Cuisine: Fourteen Signature Dishes and Their Histories*, pp. 179–191. Jackson: University Press of Mississippi, 2009.

Poppy Tooker

New York City's unique position, for most of its history, as America's leading seaport, financial center, and immigrant mecca has made it an anomaly in all culinary departments, sweets included.

The Dutch, who founded New Amsterdam in the seventeenth century, bequeathed a distinctive repertoire of sweet baked goods. Washington Irving, in "The Legend of Sleepy Hollow," praised "the doughty doughnut, the tender *oly-koeck*, and the crisp and crumbling cruller." He might have added to this list pancakes and waffles, the small puffed pancakes known as *poffertjes*, and the little flat cakes known as *koekjes*, or, in English, "cookies."

The *oly-koeck* was a small ball of sweet raised dough fried in hot oil or lard, hence the name, which means "oil cake." A kind of proto-doughnut, it could be plain, with a dusting of sugar, or packed with nuts, raisins, or currants, and apple, and spiced with cinnamon, cloves, and ginger. See DOUGHNUTS.

The cruller, from the Dutch *krullen* (to curl), was sweet dough pulled into an oblong twist or formed into a ring. It became one of New York's iconic street foods, sold by wandering peddlers and at market food stalls like the one described by Walt Whitman in 1842 in one of his early journalistic pieces for the *New York Aurora*.

An influx of émigrés displaced by the French Revolution introduced New Yorkers to the pleasures of French pastry and confectionery, as well as to the ices and ice creams that Italians had popularized

Arnold Eagle, a Hungarian-American photographer and cinematographer, took this photograph of a New York City candy store in 1935 as part of the Federal Art Project. THE MUSEUM OF THE CITY OF NEW YORK / ART RESOURCE, N.Y.

in Paris. Auguste Louis de Singeron, one of many stranded noblemen, opened a patisserie in lower Manhattan that offered inventive treats like New Year's cakes decorated with arrow-pierced hearts and frolicking cupids, and a marzipan replica of the Tuileries Palace. See ICE CREAM; ITALIAN ICE; and MARZIPAN.

In pocket-sized gardens like the one created by the Frenchman John Contoit in present-day Tribeca in the early nineteenth century, patrons could enjoy lemonade, pound cake, and ice cream in three flavors: vanilla, strawberry, and lemon. See LEMONADE and POUND CAKE. Ferdinand Palmo, an Italian, operated a dazzling Broadway emporium, the Café des Mille Colonnes, where the Italian ices were judged "not inferior to those of Tortoni in Paris."

The early gardens and ice cream cafés evolved into palatial "saloons" like Taylor's and Thompson's. Located on Broadway, in present-day Tribeca, these glorified ice cream parlors were among the city's finest restaurants.

On the sidewalks and in the city's bustling markets, pie was king. See PIE. Throughout the nineteenth century New Yorkers consumed almost unimaginable quantities, 22 million pies in 1895, in sizes ranging from tiny "buttons" to giant holiday pies. The city's largest pie bakery turned out 20,000 pies a day: apple, peach, custard, rhubarb, plum, lemon, and coconut, with mince and cranberry sold during the Christmas season.

Surging immigration brought millions of new foreigners to the city in the late nineteenth and early twentieth centuries, providing New Yorkers with an exotic palette of sweet delicacies from the four corners of the earth. In the teeming Syrian quarter near the Washington Market, where the World Trade Center once stood, the curious could try exotic sweets like baklava, halvah, and kanafi. See BAKLAVA and HALVAH.

Jewish immigration from Eastern Europe and Russia profoundly changed the city's palate, adding foods both savory and sweet that became, and in some cases remain, synonymous with New York. These include New York–style cheesecake, charlotte russe, egg creams, and Nesselrode pie. Most had their heyday between 1920 and 1960, then declined along with the traditional delicatessen.

Cheesecake, in one form or another, had been traditional all over Europe for centuries, but with the invention of cream cheese in the late nineteenth century, it took on a new smoothness, lightness, and richness, resting on a thin sponge crust or, later, a crust made from graham crackers. See CHEESECAKE. It was the dessert par excellence at celebrity-packed delicatessen restaurants like Reuben's, the Turf, and Lindy's, where it attained star status. "It stands half a foot tall, it measures one foot across," Clementine Paddleford wrote of the Lindy's cheesecake. "Its top is shiny as satin and baked to the gold of the frost-tinged oak" (1949, p. 61). Today, Junior's in Brooklyn owes much of its reputation to its cheesecake, a denser, less sweet version of the classic New York style.

Charlotte russe was a popularized version of the French molded dessert known as *charlotte à la Parisienne* or *charlotte à la russe*. See CHARLOTTE. Priced at a nickel or less and sold in the cool months, a classic charlotte russe consisted of four ladyfingers encircling a small mountain of whipped cream topped with a maraschino cherry. It was served in a frilled paper cup with a false bottom to push the ingredients upward for eating.

Nesselrode pie recast Nesselrode pudding, another French classic, in pie form. See PUDDING. It was popularized by Hortense Spier, whose wholesale bakery on the Upper West Side supplied the pie to restaurants all over the city in the 1940s and 1950s. Her dessert, omitting the traditional candied or puréed chestnuts, was a rum-accented Bavarian cream with candied fruits poured into a pie shell.

The deceptively named egg cream contained neither eggs nor cream. It was a refreshing, bubbly combination of seltzer, chocolate syrup (more often than not, Fox's U-Bet), and milk.

Industrially produced soft drinks, candies, and sweets crowded out the old favorites, which linger only in the memory, like the Brooklyn Dodgers. The sole modern-day equivalent is the black and white cookie, a large shortbread-like disc whose two hemispheres are covered by chocolate and vanilla fondant icing. The cookie, nearly ubiquitous in New York bakeries, attracted national attention in 1998 when the comedian Jerry Seinfeld, in an episode of *Seinfeld*, praised it as a symbol of racial harmony. Holding it aloft, he exclaimed: "Look to the cookie!" See BLACK AND WHITE COOKIES.

See also NETHERLANDS.

Berg, Jennifer. "From the Big Bagel to the Big Roti? The Evolution of New York's Jewish Food Icons." In *Gastropolis: Food and New York City*, edited by Annie Hauck-Lawson and Jonathan Deutsch, pp. 252–273. New York: Columbia University Press, 2008.

Dayton, Abram C. *Last Days of Knickerbocker Life in New York*. New York: Putnam's, 1897.
Markfield, Wallace. "The Egg Cream Mystique." *New York* (Sunday magazine of *New York Herald Tribune*), 8 November 1964, pp. 12–13.
Paddleford, Clementine. *How America Eats: Best Recipes of 1949*. New York: United Newspapers Magazine Corp., 1949.
Rose, Peter G. *The Sensible Cook: Dutch Foodways in the Old and New World*. Syracuse, N.Y.: Syracuse University Press, 1989.

William Grimes

New Zealand

See AUSTRALIA AND NEW ZEALAND.

Niederegger, a family-run business in the port city of Lübeck on the Baltic Sea, is the most important marzipan producer in contemporary Germany. See MARZIPAN. During medieval times, Lübeck belonged to the Hanseatic League and was among the richest cities of the Holy Roman Empire. Marzipan was first mentioned there in a guild decree of 1530 that granted exclusive production rights to apothecaries, as sugar was still a very rare ingredient, considered of medicinal value, similar to many spices. When both sugar and almonds became more commonly available and affordable, marzipan moved from the province of the apothecaries to that of confectioners.

In 1806 Johann Georg Niederegger (1777–1856), a young pastry chef from Ulm, took over Konditorei Maret in Lübeck (founded in 1786); in 1822 he opened his own establishment on Breite Strasse. Over the years Konditorei Niederegger branched out into marzipan production. Up to this day sumptuous gâteaux and chocolates are produced and consumed in an elegant café opposite the town hall. Today, over 500 people work for the seventh generation of Niedereggers, who refuse to reveal the secret ingredients beyond almonds and sugar that go into their marzipan, although some people suspect it is rosewater, which many ancient Arab recipes mention.

Niederegger marzipan is shaped, colored, and coated into over 300 different figures ranging from traditional loaves, eggs, Easter bunnies, and pink pigs (a symbol of good luck on New Year's Eve) to all kinds of fruit and vegetables (a traditional Christmas gift) and even tools and cars. Niederegger also offers marzipan-flavored tea, coffee, and cocoa, as well as marzipan liqueur and other products.

See also GERMANY and MEDICINAL USES OF SUGAR.

Wiehmann, Otto, and Antjekathrin Grassmann. "Niederegger, Johann Georg." In *Neue Deutsche Biographie (NDB)*, Vol. 19, pp. 222–223. Berlin: Duncker & Humblot, 1999. http://daten.digitale-sammlungen.de/0001/bsb00016337/images/index.html?seite=236 (accessed 1 November 2013).

Ursula Heinzelmann

Nobin Chandra Das (ca. 1846–1925) is the founder of a Kolkata sweetshop best known for its rosogolla (or rossogolla), a milk-based, syrup-soaked dumpling that is one of India's most popular sweets. See ROSOGOLLA. According to family records, Nobin Das was descended from a line of sugar dealers who had fallen on hard times, which led the young man to take up the profession of *moira* (confectioner), a noticeable step down the social ladder. By 1864 he had set up shop in the Baghbazar district of Kolkata, then the wealthy capital of the British Raj. See KOLKATA. Legend has it that Nobin Das created rosogolla by a process of trial and error, eventually coming up with a method of boiling balls of fresh curd cheese in sugar syrup until they swelled with the sweet liquid. The inhabitants of Baghbazar, who used to like making up rhyming verses, honored him with a suitable ditty: "Baghbazarer Nobin Das / rosogollar Columbus" (Nobin Das of Baghbazar / the Columbus of rosogolla). Whether Nobin Das did, or did not, invent the sweet is highly contentious in parts of India. It is plausible that Nobin Chandra Das did no more than refine and popularize an already extant sweet. The moist sweetmeat was apparently discovered by Kolkata society when Raibahadur Bagwandas Bagla, a wealthy businessman, stopped by the store to get a drink of water for his son. The son tasted the rosogolla, and word of the spongy delight spread like wildfire.

The Das family business expanded when Nobin's son Krishna Chandra Das opened up his own shop in 1930 and expanded the franchise to other stores in Kolkata. He also added canned rosogolla to the repertoire. The original N. C. Das shop closed in 1965 following the promulgation of the short-lived West Bengal Channa Sweets Control Order, which placed restrictions on fresh curd cheese–based sweets, the Communist government's theory being that this action would free up more milk supplies for everyday use. K. C. Das just barely survived the year-long prohibition. Today, K. C. Das has over 20 stores in Kolkata and Bangalore and distributes its canned rosogolla worldwide.

See also INDIA and MITHAI.

K. C. Das. *Sweetening Lives for 75 Years.* ca. 2006.
Krondl, Michael. *Sweet Invention: A History of Dessert.* Chicago: Chicago Review Press, 2011.

Michael Krondl

nonpareils

See SPRINKLES.

North Africa, which stretches along the Mediterranean coast from Egypt to Morocco, boasts a population with a prodigious sweet tooth. Consequently, the range of North African sweets is impressive. The Ottomans ruled over most of North Africa, although not Morocco, which explains why Moroccan sweets exhibit an older, Persian influence rather than a Turkish one. In fact, much of Middle Eastern and North African cooking can be traced back to Persian cuisine, mainly because Baghdad's ʿAbbāsid caliphs favored Persian cooks, and as they expanded their empire, they took them along. See BAGHDAD and PERSIA. Once the invaders settled, they taught the local cooks, leaving a strong Persian culinary legacy that can be detected even now, centuries later.

Although certain sweets are shared in various versions among the different countries (Egypt, Sudan, South Sudan, Libya, Tunisia, Algeria, Morocco, and Western Sahara), others are specific to a single country. One sweet that has crossed from the Middle East to North Africa and is shared with slight variations throughout is *ghrayba,* a shortbread made with flour and butter that can be made using plain flour or ground almonds or a mixture of the two.

Zlabia (also *zalabia* or *zulābiyā*) is another sweet common throughout the region. See ZALABIYA. This fritter is made in a variety of forms. One common method is to pipe a yeast-leavened batter through a thin nozzle into hot oil to form intricate rosettes, which are fried until golden and then dipped in sugar syrup or hot honey. Rice pudding is also a common dessert, as is a smooth, milky pudding called *muhallabiyya* (also spelled *muhallabia*). Orange blossom water is the main flavoring for these puddings, as it is for sugar syrup or honey in most of North Africa, except for Tunisia, where geranium water is favored. Unlike in the Middle East, rosewater is rarely used. See FLOWER WATERS.

In Morocco, couscous can also be served as a sweet by steaming and mixing it with confectioner's sugar and ground toasted almonds. In Egypt, where it is sold on the street, raisins instead of nuts are added to the couscous.

Egypt

Egypt, separated from the rest of North Africa by a huge tract of Libyan desert, belongs more to the Middle East rather than to North Africa, both culturally and in its cuisine. See MIDDLE EAST. Most Egyptian sweets (as well as savory dishes) are closer to those of its neighbors to the East. Still, Egyptians have their own distinctive sweets, the most famous being *om ʿAli* (mother of ʿAli), a bread pudding made with very thin flatbread (*reqaq*) layered with mixed nuts and moistened with sugar-sweetened milk before baking. There are several stories behind the name, none of which can be verified. One dates the sweet to the first wife of the thirteenth-century ruler Sultan ʿIzz al-Dīn Aybak, whose son was named ʿAli. The sultan's second wife also bore him a son. When the sultan died unexpectedly, it was assumed that the throne would pass on to the first-born ʿAli, but the second wife wanted power to go to her son. To prevent this, Umm ʿAli had the second wife killed, and then prepared the dessert to celebrate the first son's ascension to the throne. Whether the sweet is really named after her cannot be verified, but what is certain is that *om ʿAli* is one of Egypt's most iconic desserts, with a lovely, flaky texture when properly prepared.

Bassbussa is another typical Egyptian sweet, a sponge cake made with semolina and garnished with almonds, then soaked in sugar syrup. *Bassbussa* is found with slight variations in other Middle Eastern and North African countries that came under Ottoman rule (called *nammura* in Lebanon, *hʾrisseh* in Syria, and *revani* in Turkey).

Maghreb

Kaʾb el-ghzal (gazelle's horn) is the Moroccan sweet par excellence, made by wrapping the thinnest pastry dough around sweet almond paste flavored with

A proud sweets seller exhibits his dried fruits and confections in Morocco's famous Marrakech souk. © RAOUL D.

orange blossom water and mastic (the dough is also made with orange blossom water). The filled dough is then shaped into a thin, raised crescent similar to a horn; hence its name. It is served at all celebrations and also offered with mint tea to visitors in between meals. *Ka'b el-ghzal* is also found in Algeria and Tunisia; however, in the latter country, *ka'b el-ghzal* describes a shortbread cookie made with chickpea or sorghum flour, whereas in Algeria, the pastry is similar to the Moroccan one. The Moroccan version is the finest and most delicate.

North Africa does not have a tradition of specialist sweet makers comparable to that of the Arab world, where sweet making is the preserve of specialists. By contrast, North African home cooks know how to make the whole range of sweets and take pride in making their own pastries. They will only buy commercial sweets from pastry shops that employ women who were formerly home cooks like themselves. Each of these professional women has her own specialty; some make only *warqa*, the Moroccan analog to filo (known as *malsuqa* in Tunisia), made by dabbing a very wet dough onto a hot plate (*tobsil*) until the plate is covered with a very thin round sheet of pastry. See FILO. *Warqa* is used in both savory and sweet preparations. Home cooks will sometimes hire these expert women pastry chefs to prepare sweets in large quantities when they are hosting a *diffa* (reception) for either a wedding or other celebration. Of course, as North Africa becomes more and more modern, increasing numbers of men are doing the same job.

Warqa is also used on its own to make *bstila au lait* (literally, "milk pastilla," though it is actually made with custard). Sheets of *warqa* are fried and layered with custard, which is sprinkled with crushed toasted almonds and cinnamon. The flavoring of the custard varies but traditionally it is orange blossom water and ground mastic.

M'hanncha is a variation on *ka'b el-ghzal*, in which instead of using pastry dough to wrap around the almond paste, cooks use *warqa*. In Morocco, the sweet is served sprinkled with powdered sugar and cinnamon; in Algeria, it is sometimes soaked in sugar syrup or honey.

Another typical Moroccan sweet is *ch'bakkiyya*, which during Ramadan is served with *harira*, a thick soup that is the first thing people eat to break their fast. Known as *griouch* in Algeria and in some parts of Morocco, *ch'bakkiyya* is made by plaiting thin strips of dough, which sometimes have a little ground sesame mixed in with the flour, to form small, intricate pastries that are fried and then dipped in hot honey or sugar syrup. North Africans traditionally used heated honey to sweeten their pastries, but today they more often use sugar syrup because it is cheaper. Sometimes the syrup is flavored with orange blossom water (Morocco and Algeria) or geranium water (Tunisia).

If *ka'b el-ghzal* is the Moroccan sweet par excellence, the Tunisian one is *maqrud*, stamped cookies filled with dates or crushed almonds that are fried, then dipped in honey or sugar syrup.

Health and Religion

In the West, people do not associate sweets with healthy eating, but in North Africa, some sweets are considered health-giving. One is the Moroccan *amlou*, a thick dip or spread made by finely crushing unpeeled toasted almonds with honey and argan oil to produce a luxurious almond "butter" to spread on crackers or bread or simply to scoop with a spoon. *Sellou* is another "medicinal" sweet given to women after childbirth to restore their health. It is a slightly different kind of nut butter made by grinding toasted or fried almonds and toasted sesame seeds and mixing them with toasted flour, cinnamon, anise, and mastic before moistening the mass with clarified butter. The clarified butter makes *sellou* last much longer than if it were made with regular butter. Some people make the mixture firm, whereas others make it loose.

The Tunisians have their own equivalent of *sellou*, called *zrir*, which can be made in several different ways—with ground sesame seeds, butter, and sugar syrup, or with added ground hazelnuts, pistachios, or walnuts. The Algerian version is called *bsissa* and is made with toasted chickpeas and wheat that are ground, then mixed with clarified butter and honey and served on the seventh day after the birth of a child.

A good time to sample sweets in North Africa is during Ramadan, when no food or drink is allowed to pass believers' lips from sunrise to sunset. See RAMADAN. However, at dusk, the feasting starts. Typically, people ease back into eating and drinking with a few dates and a drink of water or juice. They then go to pray, and only after that do they sit down to a full meal, which always ends with sweets—at other times of year, fruit is the usual dessert. Because people stay up most of the night, receiving guests or visiting family and friends, sweets are an essential part of life during Ramadan, both as an offering to guests and as a present when one visits others, or even as a gift sent to loved ones. Sweets are also everywhere to be seen on the street, piled high in pastry shops and sold from street stalls that are set up temporarily during Ramadan.

See also BLANCMANGE; CUSTARD; FRIED DOUGH; ISLAM; and MASTIC.

Aït Mohamed, Salima. *La cuisine egyptienne*. Marseilles, France: Autres Temps, 1997.
Bennani-Smires, Latifa. *La cuisine marocaine*. Paris: J. P. Taillandier, 1971.
Boubezari, Karimène. *Ma cuisine algérienne*. Aix-en-Provence, France: Edisud, 2000.
Guinaudeau-Franc, Zette. *Les secrets des cuisines en terre marocaine*. Paris: J. P. Taillandier, 1981.
Kouki, Mohamed. *Cuisine et pâtisserie tunisiennes*. Tunis, Tunisia: Maison Tunisienne de l'Edition, 1977.

Anissa Helou

Nostradamus (1503–1566), born Michel de Nostradame in Saint-Rémy de Provence, was an itinerant apothecary, astrologer, and healer. As an apothecary, he perfected his skills in confectionery and jam making. From the Middle Ages to the nineteenth century in France, sugar was sold by the apothecaries' guilds, because it was considered medicinal, warming, and an effective laxative. See GUILDS and MEDICINAL USES OF SUGAR. As sugar refining became more widespread across Europe, sugar came into greater use as a flavoring for food; a preservative of fruits, flowers, and some vegetables; and as ornament in confectionery.

Nostradamus produced a number of compilations of "useful secrets" covering jams, cosmetics, and electuaries, which were intended for high-born "ladies" of the elite, who would not have cooked, but who would have been concerned with beauty treatments, preserving fruit, and home remedies. His *Traité des fardemens et des confitures* (Treatise on Make-up and Jams) appeared in 1552; *Bâtiment des recettes* (Building of Recipes) and *Excellent et moult utile opuscule* (Excellent and Very Useful Little Work) were published in 1555. In these works, Nostradamus demonstrated his knowledge of both sugar and honey, explaining the processes of sugar refining and clarifying, and insisting on using the best ingredients. As he wrote in *Opuscule*, "From good wares good products are made, and from ugly or bad, bad work." His recipes ran the gamut from preserved lemon and orange peels to quince jelly, marzipan, toothpaste, hair dye, remedies for plague, and love potions. Although Nostradamus remains best known today for his *Prophesies*—predictions written in rhyme—his contributions to the art of preserving and confectionery should not be overlooked.

See also CANDIED FLOWERS; CANDIED FRUIT; SUGAR; and CONFECTIONERY MANUALS.

Wheaton, Barbara Ketcham. *Savoring the Past: The French Kitchen and Table from 1300 to 1789.* Philadelphia: University of Pennsylvania Press, 1983.

Elizabeth Field

nougat is an elegant, crisp yet chewy aerated confection of honey, sugar, and egg whites containing nuts and sometimes dried fruits. It has a long history and several variations, identified with different names according to type and country of origin. Versions of nougat were probably known in ancient Greece and Rome, although the skills of early Arab confectioners seem to have refined the recipe into the pale, light versions predominant in Europe since the mid-sixteenth century. A tenth-century Persian text contains perhaps the most poetic celebration of its beauty, flavor and mouthfeel, describing nougat as looking as solid and luminous as silver, stuffed with exquisite nuts and flower-like dried fruits, and tasting as soft and sweet as lips.

Whether making the original Persian *natif*, Turkish *gaz*, French *nougat*, Spanish *turrón*, or Italian *torrone*, the basic technique is the same. Honey and sugar syrup are boiled to the cracking point, added to just-beaten egg whites, and hot, lightly roasted nuts, either whole or chopped, are mixed in. Once beaten together, the mass is poured into flat trays, generally lined with a layer of edible wafer paper, where it is spread or rolled to a thickness of 1 to 2.5 cm, topped with another layer of wafer paper, lightly pressed, cooled, and cut into rectangular bars or smaller rectangular pieces. Contemporary commercial nougat may have its texture manipulated to be shorter and less chewy with the addition of fat, milk powder, or confectioner's sugar during the final beating.

Nougat can be made with any nut or mixture of nuts. Almonds are traditional, especially in regions with substantial almond production; they are often combined with pistachios, although there are also versions using hazelnuts, walnuts, or seeds. In some cases, dried fruits may be included, and variations on this theme are becoming more and more common in European and American sweetshops, as are chocolate-coated bars of nougat. See DRIED FRUIT. Smaller pieces of nougat enrobed in chocolate have long been included in preselected boxes of bite-sized chocolate sweets, and many common chocolate bars include nougat, whether in the form of chips, as in Toblerone, or with a filling based on a whipped chocolate nougat, like Milky Way or Mars Bars. See CHOCOLATES, BOXED and MARS. German nougat is an exception, being eggless, smooth, and chocolaty, and much more closely related to gianduja or praline. See PRALINE.

Origins and Names

Although it is frequently suggested that the Romans had a nougat-related honey and nut confection called *cupedia*, the Latin word is, in fact, a general term for dainty, desirable delicacies, both sweet and savory. The Sicilian alternative name for torrone, *cupeta*, refers to this Latin root. The confection we know today owes more to its Arabic origins, and it is assumed that the Moors brought the necessary skills and ingredients (such as almond trees) with them to Spain in the eighth century, and that nougat entered France from Turkey via the port of Marseilles in the mid-sixteenth century. In neither case did the early Persian names of *helva* or *natif* travel with the confection; neither did the Arab confectioners' tendency to perfume the nougat with spices or flower waters. See FLOWER WATERS. The Italian and Spanish names refer to the roasted nuts (from the Latin *torrere*, "to toast"), whereas the French name evokes a nut cake (from the Latin *nux*, meaning "walnut," and French *gâteau*, meaning "cake"). In other parts of Europe, such as Austria and Hungary, nougat's name, translated as "Turkish honey," refers to its mid-sixteenth-century arrival from Turkey.

Types of Nougat

Regardless of regional origin, there are three main categories of nougat, most readily distinguished by color.

White Nougat

White nougat with almonds is probably the most commonly recognized nougat, well known as *nougat de Montélimar* in France, *torrone di Cremona* or *di Benevento* (with hazelnuts) in Italy, or *turrón di Ali-*

cante in Spain. It is made by heating sugar syrup or glucose with honey at 285° to 300°F (140° to 149°C), depending on how hard or chewy the confectioner wants the final result to be: the lower the temperature, the chewier the nougat (French-style nougat tends to be slightly chewier, whereas the Spanish versions aim for a crisper, crunchier texture). This hot, sweet mixture is then beaten into stiffly beaten egg whites until well incorporated and thick. Lightly roasted, skinned nuts (and fruit if desired) are added before finishing with edible paper as described above.

Brown Nougat

Light-brown nougats range from a slightly golden off-white to a more caramel hue and acquire most of their color from a second cooking of a white nougat mixture, which begins to caramelize the sugars, as in *turrón di Agramut* from Lleida in Catalonia. The darker caramel shades often result from the use of ground roasted nuts in the mixture, or from grinding up the result of the first cooking before the second caramelization, as in the Spanish *Jijona turrón*, which (unusually) has no paper on its outside.

Black Nougat

The closest in form to the Roman honey-nut confections *itria*—balls wrapped in paper—and flat-rolled *gastris* honey-nut sweets, this eggless, darkest of all nougats is known as *nougatine* in France and *mandorlato* in Italy. See GASTRIS. It was made for sale in sweetshops in England in the early nineteenth century under the name "almond hardbake." This type of nougat is very dark brown in color and has a slightly more brittle texture than other nougats. Cooked only once like white nougat, the sugar is caramelized rather than made into a syrup, and warmed honey is usually added in a higher proportion than in other recipes. This sweet mixture is heated to a somewhat higher temperature—up to 310°F (155°C)—and no egg white is used. Toasted nuts are added as usual. It is generally sandwiched between two pieces of edible paper and presented in a style similar to white nougat.

Seasonality

In southern Europe nougat is often thought of as a confection for celebrations like Christmas, and it is one of the 13 traditional desserts included in the French Provençal Christmas meal. See CHRISTMAS. Nougat is also enjoyed at Easter and other holidays in Spain and Italy. Some smaller makers (such as Confiserie Foque in Signes, France) follow this seasonality in their production cycle, producing nougat only between the middle of September and the end of December. It is possible that this seasonality partly originates in the timing of the almond harvest, which usually begins at the end of August. Thus, the freshest almonds could be used while the new honey was being collected and the hens were still laying, before the darkest days of winter set in. Today's commercial production is now more likely to include corn syrup than sugar and fragrant honey, but in the fine nougat made by regional specialists, one can still taste the light, honeyed confection chewed with enjoyment for millennia.

See also ANCIENT WORLD; HONEY; NUTS; and STAGES OF SUGAR SYRUP.

Durand, Jean. *Le nougat de Montélimar: Legende, histoire, portraits.* Pont-Saint-Esprit, France: La Mirandole, 1993.

Işın, Mary. *Sherbet & Spice: The Complete Story of Turkish Sweets and Desserts*, pp. 126–136. London: I. B. Tauris, 2013.

Mason, Laura. *Sweets and Sweet Shops.* Princes Risborough, U.K.: Shire, 1999.

Nasrallah, Nawal. *Annals of the Caliph's Kitchens: Ibn Sayyār al-Warrāq's Tenth-Century Baghdadi Cookbook.* Leiden, The Netherlands, and Boston: Brill, 2010.

"Spanish Turrón (Nougat): Sweet Arab Heritage in Spain." http://www.foodswinesfromspain.com/spanishfoodwine/global/products-recipes/products/4446282.html (accessed 24 January 2014).

Jane Levi

Nutella is the brand name of the popular chocolate-hazelnut spread made by Italian confectionery company Ferrero and distributed to 75 countries worldwide. See ITALY. Though hazelnuts and chocolate are now thought of as a classic combination, Italians have historically paired the two not necessarily for taste, but for reasons of economy. In 1806, during the Napoleonic Wars, Napoleon issued the Continental Blockade, an embargo on British trade, which caused the price of chocolate to become extremely expensive. In response, chocolatiers in Turin, Italy, began adding chopped hazelnuts, plentiful in the region, to chocolate to stretch the supply.

In the 1940s, as a result of World War II, chocolate once again became expensive in Italy, so pastry maker and Ferrero company founder Pietro Ferrero turned to the hazelnut and chocolate pairing, dubbing his version *pasta gianduja* after the classic Piedmontese carnival character Gianduja. When his product first appeared on the Italian market in 1946, a kilo of chocolate cost six times more than the same amount of *pasta gianduja*. Ferrero's product was originally formed into loaves and wrapped in foil, but he eventually developed a more spreadable version, packaged it in a jar, and named it *supercrema gianduja*. In 1964 Pietro Ferrero's son Michele Ferrero renamed the product Nutella, with the intention of distributing it across Europe.

After almost 20 years of successful sales in Europe, Nutella was first imported to the United States in 1983. Today, the kosher spread made from sugar, palm oil, ground hazelnuts, cocoa solids, and skim milk is sold throughout the world. It is a popular breakfast item and has been incorporated into numerous recipes, including those for brownies, pies, and cake icing.

Bourin, Jeanne. *The Book of Chocolate*, p. 139. New York: Flammarion, 2005.
"The History of Nutella." http://www.nutellausa.com/history.htm (accessed 15 October 2013).

Emily Hilliard

Spice Islands nutmegs were so prized that elaborate implements were devised to grate them efficiently and without waste. Ranging from tinned iron to carved wood and silver, most grinders featured a lidded compartment where the nutmeg could be stored. PHOTOGRAPH BY MICHAEL FINLAY

nutmeg and nutmeg graters have enhanced many a dessert and beverage. The fruit of the nutmeg tree, *Myristica fragrans*, is unique in providing two distinct and wonderfully aromatic spices: nutmeg, the seed of the tree; and mace, the dried aril, a reddish lacy covering of the seed's shell. The main source of nutmeg is the Banda Islands in the Moluccas, the Indonesian Spice Islands. See SPICES.

Nutmeg has been used, in finely grated form, as a prized flavoring in culinary recipes since medieval times, and it was believed to have medicinal properties. In Elizabethan England, physicians, claiming nutmeg as the only curative for the plague, charged huge prices for what had until that time been seen as no more than a cure for the common cold and flatulence. Nutmeg was, and still is, used widely in desserts, fruitcakes, flummeries, possets, and the like, as well as in savory dishes such as spiced meats and Scottish haggis.

Although any fine kitchen grater can be used to powder the nutmeg, a wide variety of graters made specifically for this purpose can be found. Almost all involve a simple nail-pierced tinned-iron grating surface and a hinged lidded cavity where the nutmeg may be stored. Such graters are made in many designs and materials, ranging from the precious—silver (and occasionally even gold), Bilston enamels, and silver-mounted shells—to the simple, including coquilla nuts and the more prosaic japanned tinned iron. Variety exists because a principal use of nutmeg during the eighteenth century was as an additive to the highly popular concocted drinks of the era, such as rum punch. See PUNCH.

Although nutmeg was generally grated into the punch during its making, in order that he could add further spice to his taste, the gentleman-about-town would carry a pocket grater in an attractive design.

See also CUSTARD.

Milton, Giles. *Nathaniel's Nutmeg: How One Man's Courage Changed the Course of History.* London: Hodder & Stoughton, 1999.

Michael Finlay

nuts are tree fruits enclosed in hard shells (with the exception of peanuts, which are actually legumes). Part of the human diet since prehistory, their shells are frequently found on archaeological sites. They can be gathered, stored, and transported with ease and combine concentrated nutrition with excellent flavor. These properties have assured their preeminence in many food cultures, and their perceived high value gives them a prominent role in sweets.

In terms of world production, coconut and peanut dominate. See COCONUT. Walnuts, chestnuts, almonds, hazels, and pistachios are also important, and all have a role to play in sweets. Although the production of cashew nuts is significant, they are primarily used in savory dishes and are only just beginning to penetrate into the domain of sweet goods as a substitute for more expensive nuts. The major exception is India, where cashews traditionally appear in a great number of sweets, including barfi and halvah. See BARFI and HALVAH. Pecans, Brazil nuts, macadamia nuts, and pine nuts complete the list of nuts that have local or minor use in sweets, for instance, the Brazil nuts used to decorate luxury fruitcake. See FRUITCAKE.

The principal culinary nuts have a fat content ranging from 50 to 75 percent. Predominantly unsaturated, fat from nuts gives high calorific values, except for chestnuts, which are lower in fat and calories. See CHESTNUTS. Nuts are significant sources of carbohydrates and fiber, and they contain appreciable quantities of various vitamins, trace elements, antioxidants, and phytochemicals. In sweets they contribute significantly to the energy density but are also highly nutritious, balancing the "empty calories" of sugar.

Production of tree nuts requires investment in land and money and is long term. Commercial storage and transport are straightforward, and world trade continues to expand steadily, with new countries investing in production. The United States has become the dominant almond producer, while China has recently risen in the league of walnut producers.

Walnuts, the fruit of *Juglans regia*, and their close relative, the pecan from *Carya illinoinensis*, have similar characteristics and roles in European and American food, respectively. They are incorporated into breads, cakes, brownies, pies, and candies such as the Walnut Whip. They contribute crunch and flavor and have the added advantage of an intriguing shape, which lends them to decorative roles.

Almonds, from *Prunus amygdalus*, have two forms: bitter and sweet. The former are the original wild form, containing a bitter glycoside that creates prussic acid on crushing; while poisonous in large quantities, bitter almonds add a desirable dimension of flavor to baked goods. Sweet almonds have been selectively bred for a milder taste. They are used extensively in sweet foods, whether as whole kernels, nibs, flakes, or ground. Ground almonds have found key uses in marzipan and flourless tortes. See MARZIPAN and TORTE. Combined with eggs and sugar, they yield luxurious gluten-free cakes with a dense but melting texture. Toasted and crushed almonds form the basis of praline, and frangipane, a mix of butter, sugar, egg, and ground almond, is used in dishes such as England's famous Bakewell pudding. See FRANGIPANE and PRALINE. Almonds are especially important as centers for panned sweets, such as sugared almonds or confetti. See CONFETTI and PANNING.

Hazelnuts are one of our oldest foods, found at a Mesolithic site in Scotland dating back 10,000 years; they are now processed into the chocolate spread Nutella on an industrial scale. See NUTELLA. Roasted whole hazelnuts appear in many confections, including the chocolate-enrobed Baci. See BONBON and PERUGINA. They are also crushed or ground for use in cakes, cookies, and meringues. Unlike other nut trees, the hazel, *Corylus avellana*, produces nuts relatively young, as a bush rather than as a full-grown tree.

Chestnuts, the fruit of *Castanea sativa*, are native to Europe and Asia Minor, and related species are spread across Asia to Korea. They are farinaceous in consistency, with low fat and protein content. Most of the nut production is used in savory dishes, but marrons glacés have a niche position in the international world of sweets, and chestnut flour is used locally in breads and pancakes.

Pistachio, the vivid green fruit of *Pistacia vera*, is a latecomer to Western cuisines. Many people first encountered it in the green component of the tricolor ice cream popularized by Italian culture. See ICE CREAM. Apart from this and minor use in cake decorating, the pistachio was confined to Middle Eastern food until the later part of the twentieth century. However, its use has spread rapidly, and the United States has almost matched the production of the nut's culinary heartland, Iran and Turkey. The kernels are ground and used in *fistikli ezmesi*, the Turkish equivalent of marzipan, which is a speciality of Gaziantep; they are also used in baklava, as are walnuts. See BAKLAVA.

Nuts with minor regional importance include macadamias, originating in Australia, and pine nuts, which decorate cakes and sweets around the Mediterranean. Another minor nut with regional prominence is *mahlab*, the kernel of the *Prunus mahaleb* cherry, which has a flavor similar to bitter almond. The crushed kernels are used in Cypriot *flaounes*, a complex Easter bread with sweet and savory ingredients, and Turkish *paskalya çorek*, where, together with mastic, it yields the taste and aroma characteristic of this sweet bread. See MASTIC. The kernels of apricot stones find a similar use in amaretti.

Peanuts are a swiftly grown annual crop, *Arachis hypogaea*, whose physical development as it fruits is quite extraordinary. The fertilized flower stem extends and buries itself into the soil to allow the nut pod to develop. World production is in the tens of millions of tons, a small proportion of which finds its way into sweets. Peanut butter, ubiquitous on the supermarket shelf, has diverse uses in baking. Peanut candies such as Reese's Peanut Butter Cups and Snickers are famous brands. See REESE'S PIECES. The nut is also now established as a cheap substitute for more expensive tree nuts in a range of brittles, nougat, and bakery goods. See BRITTLE and NOUGAT.

See also BREADS, SWEET.

Albala, Ken. *Nuts: A Global History*. London: Reaktion, 2014.

Rosegarten, Frederic, Jr. *The Book of Edible Nuts*. Mineola, N.Y.: Dover, 2004.

Phil Iddison

Oetker is the best-known German food brand, according to public opinion surveys. The company started with baking powder before turning to the manufacture of custard powder, the product with which it is most closely associated. However, Dr. August Oetker KG has grown into a conglomerate that transcends foodstuff production to rank among Germany's largest internationally operating family-owned and family-run companies.

It all began in Bielefeld in 1891, when pharmacist August Oetker (1862–1918), a baker's son, hit upon the idea of selling "Backin" baking powder in small, standardized envelopes, each for 500 grams of flour. Oetker branded the baking powder with a distinctive logo—a silhouette of a woman's head—and his own name, the title of "doctor" signaling quality. From the start Oetker ran an intense and hugely successful advertising campaign. Backin was patented in 1903, and 50 million envelopes were sold in 1906. From 1908 on, the company's very modern marketing campaign was managed by a special department at the Oetker factory. In 1911 Oetker published *Schulkochbuch,* a cookbook for school kitchens, and a baking cookbook appeared in 1930. The company also introduced cooking demonstrations and public tastings, and later pioneered advertising on TV.

However, the postwar economic recovery meant that in the mid-1950s less baking was done at home, and more products were purchased at bakeries. The amount of flour sold diminished by half, whereas the expenditure on prepared baked goods doubled. But housewives still had to demonstrate their skills, and *Obsttorte,* a prebaked sponge or short pastry base covered with fresh, tinned, or poached fruit and a glaze, became a favorite homemade dessert. It was easy and quick to make and considered tasty and healthy. Oetker compensated for losses in Backin sales by launching a similarly packaged powdered jelly glaze in 1950, which became an instant hit.

Today, Oetker sells a wide range of cake and pudding mixes, and the company's holdings have diversified into other areas, such as shipping, hotels, banking, sparkling wine production, soft drinks, and breweries, with frozen pizza now the top seller under the Oetker brand. Recently, the family's political and economic ties to the Nazi regime were revealed.

See also GERMANY.

Ritter, Johannes. "Bielefelder Familienunternehmen: Oetkers braune Vergangenheit." *Frankfurter Allgemeine.* http://www.faz.net/aktuell/wirtschaft/unternehmen/bielefelder-familienunternehmen-oetkers-braune-vergangenheit-12622536.html (accessed 18 October 2013).

Ursula Heinzelmann

olfaction, the sense of smell, contributes noticeably to perceptions of sweetness. Sweet is generally considered to be one of the five principal qualities of the sense of taste—or *gustation*—along with sour, salty, bitter, and umami (umami refers to the savory taste, associated with glutamates, whether naturally occurring or synthetic). Sweet taste sensations arise primarily from the activation of specialized receptors on cells located in taste buds on the tongue. Yet people also perceive sweet notes in certain odors: in the fragrances of flowers and perfumes, and, significantly, in the aromas of foods. Many food aromas seem distinctly sweet—consider, for instance, the sweet scent of a ripe banana. So how does olfaction contribute to the sweet flavors of foods and beverages?

When we chew a morsel of food or sip a beverage, the resulting perception of flavor arises in part from the activation of gustatory receptors in the tongue and oral cavity, but more substantially from the activation of olfactory receptors in the nose (and from the activation, in the oral cavity, of somatosensory receptors, which convey information about texture, pungency, and temperature). When we take food in the mouth, airborne molecules reach olfactory receptors in the nose by an indirect route, traveling *retronasally*, through the back of the mouth. (When we sniff, the odor-producing molecules reach the olfactory receptors directly, traveling *orthonasally*, through the nostrils.) The critical role that olfaction plays in the perception of flavor becomes apparent when the sense of smell is taken away or blunted—for instance, when a head cold or allergy blocks our nasal passages, preventing the airborne molecules from reaching olfactory receptors and thereby dampening flavors. In a related vein, the tendency for elderly people to report that, over the years, foods "lose" their flavor largely reflects the substantial decline with age in olfactory sensitivity.

The role of olfaction can be easily demonstrated by filling a small cup with an assortment of different fruit-flavored jelly beans. See JELLY BEANS. Shut your eyes to avoid color cues and, with one hand, pinch your nose closed. Then, with eyes still shut and nose still pinched, pick out one jelly bean, put it in your mouth, and bite into it. As long as your nose remains closed, the jelly bean will have little flavor beyond sourness or sweetness, which comes from gustation, or pungency, which comes from somatosensation. Lacking direct olfactory information or indirect color cues about the flavor, it is difficult to identify the fruit by gustation alone. Unpinching your nose, however, releases a torrent of flavor, making it much easier to identify the fruit—as berry or peach, grape or banana. Further, with nasal passages open, the jelly bean, now full-flavored, may appear notably sweeter.

Odors that are themselves described as sweet can augment or enhance sweet tastes, even though the odors produce no sweetness through the gustatory sense. Adding a few drops of sweet-smelling vanilla to morning coffee, for example, makes the coffee taste sweeter, even though pure vanilla evokes no gustatory sweetness. This can be confirmed by pinching the nostrils to block olfaction while sipping the coffee and then comparing sweetness, now from gustation alone, with and without the added vanilla. See VANILLA. Robert Frank and Jennifer Byram showed that adding strawberry odor enhanced the sweetness of a sugary food but adding peanut butter odor did not. On the other hand, adding strawberry odor did not enhance the saltiness of a salty food. Odors enhance taste qualities when the qualities of the odors and tastes are similar. This is not surprising. But what makes odor qualities and taste qualities similar? Why, for example, are certain odors, such as vanilla, perceived as sweet?

Sweet tastes are first and foremost associated with the presence of sugars in foods, and hence with calories—and an adequate intake of calories is critical to health and well-being. Consequently, sweet tastes presumably evolved to be intrinsically pleasurable and rewarding. Although sugars can weakly stimulate the olfactory sense, the rich flavors of milk, fruits, and other foods arise mostly from the large number of odorous molecules that are specific to each food and that give each food its characteristic flavor. To the extent that some of the odorous molecules are associated with the presence of sugars in foods, olfactory receptors that respond to these molecules may have evolved an intrinsic capacity to produce pleasant, rewarding, sweet sensations.

An alternative explanation, however, does exist. When people experience particular odors in close conjunction with particular tastes, the odors may take on the associated taste qualities. In support of this hypothesis, Richard Stevenson, Robert Boakes, and John Prescott showed that after pairing a previously tasteless odor with a sweet taste, the odor itself appeared sweet. In a similar vein, using behavioral training and testing methods, Shree Gautam and Justus Verhagen showed that in rats, as in humans, odors became sweet only after the odors were paired with sugar. And using methods of neuroimaging, Dana Small and her colleagues observed, in regions of the human brain associated with flavor perception (insula, orbitofrontal cortex, and anterior cingulate cortex), especially significant neural responses to mixtures of perceptually similar olfactory and gustatory stimuli, such as vanilla and sugar.

A final observation: experiencing vanilla together with sugar makes vanilla taste sweet like sugar, but it does not make sugar taste like vanilla. In general, taste donates while olfaction receives. This asymmetry doubtless evolved from the natural capacity of sugars, and other sweet-tasting substances, to be pleasurable and rewarding, and of the biological advantage to having a flavor system that can effectively learn which odors are consistently associated with these sweet stimuli. Analogous processes likely mediate the association of other odors with bitter tastes, which often characterize the presence of poisonous substances. The inverse is not true, as there is no equivalent biological basis for taste qualities to signal odors. The brain appears to be so configured that it readily allows one-way transfers of qualities, such as sweetness, from taste to odor.

See also AROMA; SWEETNESS PREFERENCE; and VISION.

Frank, Robert A., and Jennifer Byram. "Taste-Smell Interactions Are Tastant and Odorant Dependent." *Chemical Senses* 35 (2010): 767–776.

Gautam, Shree Hari, and Justus V. Verhagen. "Evidence That the Sweetness of Odors Depends on Experience in Rats." *Chemical Senses* 13 (1988): 445–455.

Rozin, Paul. " 'Taste-Smell Confusions' and the Duality of the Olfactory Sense." *Perception & Psychophysics* 31 (1982): 397–401.

Small, Dana M., and John Prescott. "Odor/Taste Integration and the Perception of Flavor." *Experimental Brain Research* 166 (2005): 345–357.

Small, Dana M., Joel Voss, Y. Erica Mak, Katharine B. Simmons, Todd Parrish, and Darren Gitelman. "Experience-Dependent Neural Integration of Taste and Smell in the Human Brain." *Journal of Neurophysiology* 92 (2004): 1892–1903.

Stevenson, Richard J., Robert A. Boakes, and John Prescott. "Changes in Odor Sweetness Resulting from Implicit Learning of a Simultaneous Odor-Sweetness Association: An Example of Learned Synesthesia." *Learning and Motivation* 29 (1998): 113–132.

Lawrence E. Marks

Orange Julius is a frozen drink made from orange juice, crushed ice, sugar, and a "secret ingredient" that may contain powdered milk or egg whites and vanilla flavoring. The drink was originally sold from Orange Julius stands that became an iconic part of the Southern California landscape and eventually spread nationwide.

The brand was founded in 1926 when real estate broker Willard Hamlin secured a corner storefront in downtown Los Angeles for Julius Fried's orange juice stand. This was the height of the soda fountain boom, with consumers developing a passion for novelty drinks. See SODA FOUNTAIN. Hamlin decided to invent his own concoction, the Orange Julius, which quickly became the stand's hottest seller. Hamlin quit real estate and opened counters selling nothing but Orange Julius everywhere from Los Angeles to New York's Times Square. For an energy boost, customers could have a raw egg cracked into the drink before blending. The brand's mascot was a red devil who appeared over the tagline: "A Devilish Good Drink."

The Great Depression curtailed the business, but after World War II Hamlin rode the franchise boom to open stores (many in an eye-catching modernist style) across Southern California's spreading suburbs and particularly in the new retail malls. He also expanded the offerings to include hot dogs and hamburgers and new Julius flavors like pineapple and strawberry. In 1967 Hamlin sold Orange Julius to International Industries, a franchise specialist that began a national and international expansion of the brand. The company was bought and sold several times before International Dairy Queen purchased the company in 1987. Today, Dairy Queen stores sell eight flavors of "Julius Originals" drinks, including the original orange flavor. Hamlin's formula remains a closely guarded secret, leading fans to experiment with many different ingredients, including vanilla pudding mix, raw egg whites, and whole milk, to re-create the drink at home.

See also DAIRY QUEEN.

Wilbur, Todd. *Top Secret Recipes: Creating Kitchen Clones of America's Favorite Brand-Name Foods*, p. 95. New York: Plume, 1993.

Andrew Coe

Oreos, the world's top-selling cookie, manufactured by the Nabisco Company, are a sandwich biscuit consisting of two crisp chocolate rounds with a vanilla cream filling.

Until the twentieth century, cookies in America were generally homemade or bought at local bakeries; mass-produced cookies like Oreos became popular around the turn of the century due to the relatively inexpensive cost of sugar, the development of new manufacturing technologies, and the rise in popularity of such treats. The National Biscuit Company (Nabisco) introduced the Oreo Biscuit in 1912, the same year they released the Lorna Doone, a square shortbread cookie. Oreos were first sold to grocer S. C. Thuesen in Hoboken, New Jersey, and were launched nationally one month later. What is now referred to as "milk's favorite cookie" was not the first of its kind, however. Nabisco had previously offered a similar product dubbed "Bouquet," and the Sunshine Biscuit Company had launched its chocolate sandwich cookie, the Hydrox, in 1908.

The name Oreo was invented by Nabisco, but its origins remain unclear—not even Nabisco cites a definitive story. Some food historians speculate that the name derives from the French word for gold (*or*), and in fact the cookie's name was printed in gold lettering on the original package. Others, less convincingly, suggest that the name comes from the Greek *oros*, meaning "mountain," whose root is "*ore-*"—the claim being that these flat cookies were originally shaped into mounds. Although the "Oreo" part of the name has remained the same, the tagline has evolved. In 1921 the Oreo Biscuit became the Oreo Sandwich. Then, in 1948, it was changed to Oreo Crème Sandwich; in 1974 it morphed again into Oreo Chocolate Sandwich, which it remains today.

The Oreo has also undergone evolution in its design. The size of the cookie has fluctuated, with today's version being slightly smaller than the original, although larger than intermediate renderings. And although the chocolate rounds have always been docked and embossed (cut and stamped), the original bore a wreath of petals said to have been designed by Nabisco employee William Turnier. In 1924 a pair of turtledoves was added to the wreath. The look of today's Oreo—a series of four-leaf clovers surrounding the word "OREO" set within the Nabisco logo, all surrounded by a dotted line and a ridged outer edge—was created in 1952.

Little is known about the ingredients in the original Oreo recipe. In recent years the type of fat used in both the cookies and the cream has been altered. In the mid-1990s the lard used in the filling was replaced by partially hydrogenated vegetable oil; however, due to rising health concerns about trans fats, the recipe was again changed in 2005 to a blend of canola and palm oils. Oreos received kosher certification in 1998, and modern Oreos are egg- and dairy-free, making them suitable for vegetarians and vegans.

Today, there are over 40 flavors and varieties of Oreo cookies—ranging from Double Stuff, introduced in 1975 and offering additional cream filling; Minis; Golden Oreos, vanilla rather than chocolate cookies; and the Triple Double, three cookies sandwiched with cream between each layer. Variations in filling exist, including peanut butter, mint, and chocolate, as do extravagant limited edition versions such as Birthday Cake; Ice Cream Rainbow Shure, Bert!; and Banana Split Crème. Organic Oreos, made with organic flour and sugar, were added to the brand's line in 2007. Although most variations did not appear until well into the latter half of the twentieth century, a lemon cream-filled Oreo was introduced in 1920; it was discontinued four years later. A similar flavor reemerged as a limited edition variety in 2013, this time with a vanilla wafer instead of a chocolate one. Nabisco, now owned by Kraft, also offers other Oreo-brand products, including piecrust "Cakesters"—a soft, cake-like version of the cookie—fudge-covered cookies, and ice cream cones.

Oreos have become an icon of American culture, so much so that popular "personality tests" have been devised according to how the subject prefers to eat the cookie—whether biting down on the whole sandwich at once or taking it apart to scrape off the creamy filling with the teeth. "Oreo" is also used perjoratively to refer to African Americans who reflect too many attributes of the dominant white culture. Although Nabisco's superior marketing and distribution contributed to the Oreo's early success and helped it to outsell the Hydrox cookie (which was discontinued in 2003, with a brief return for its 100th anniversary in 2008), the brand's ability to remain classic while evolving with changing consumer taste and desire is largely responsible for its standing as the best-selling cookie in the world. As of 2011, over 491 billion Oreos had been sold worldwide. The Oreo is now available in over 100 countries and has inspired and been incorporated into a number of popular recipes, including cookies-and-cream ice cream, brownies, milkshakes, cheesecakes, and pies.

Elliot, Stuart. "The Oreo Turns 100 with a Nod to the Past." *New York Times*, 27 February 2012. http://www.nytimes.com/2012/02/28/business/media/the-oreo-turns-100-with-a-nod-to-the-past-advertising.html?_r=0 (accessed 20 October 2013).

Mariani, John F. *The Encyclopedia of American Food and Drink*, p. 225. New York: Lebhar-Friedman, 1999.

Smith, Andrew. *The Oxford Encyclopedia of Food and Drink in America*. 2d ed. New York: Oxford University Press, 2013.

Emily Hilliard

The **Pacific Northwest (U.S.)** includes the entire northwest corner of the United States and Canada. The region is prized by cooks for its superior tree fruits, nuts, and berries. The lush valleys of British Columbia, Washington, and Oregon form a large, fertile growing region that is sandwiched between the Coastal range on the west and the rugged Cascade and Rocky Mountain ranges on the east, stretching over 400 miles north to south. The area's dry and sunny days and cool nights are optimal for flavor and color development and mean fewer disease problems. Crops grow slowly and develop rich, complex flavor profiles.

Wild fruits and nuts grow in abundance throughout the region and were a food source for Native Americans. Many fruits were dried and used to supplement their meals during the long winter months when food was scarce. See NATIVE AMERICAN. By 1830, early settlers could plant their own crops from seeds purchased at Hudson Bay Company outposts. Eighteen years later, the first commercial crops were planted in Oregon's Willamette Valley after Henderson Luelling and his brother, Seth, transported 700 grafted fruit trees, bushes, and berries planted in the beds of their wagons over the Oregon Trail. "Bing," the main variety of cherry produced in the United States, was named in 1860 after nurseryman Seth's Chinese foreman, Ah Bing, who grafted the tree on which they grew. Today, in the summer, fresh Bing cherries are often made into a compote with local raspberries, blackberries, and blueberries and served over chiffon or pound cake, or barely cooked with a small amount of sugar and a splash of local eau-de-vie for a sauce for ice cream.

Another popular ice cream topper is local strawberries. The industry was born when farmers started growing strawberries as a crop while they waited for their newly planted fruit trees to reach maturity. The berries thrived, and in 1870 Asa Lovejoy opened the first cannery and began shipping berries across the country to the East Coast. In 1920, Oregon and Washington were the first to develop the preservation of fruit by freezing strawberries in barrels, which were then shipped by rail to East Coast preserve factories. Today, although the much-anticipated strawberry crop is small, it is still considered a regional treasure, and the sun-ripened berries are cherished by locals for their excellent flavor and juicy flesh that is a brilliant red inside and out. During the season, most dessert tables will feature them in some form—strawberry shortcake, strawberry pie, or fresh strawberry sauce over homemade ice cream. With strawberries' exceptionally short season, these simple old-fashioned desserts have remained favorites because they showcase the berries and bring out the best of their luscious flavor. See PIE; SAUCE; and SHORTCAKE.

Almost all of the nation's commercial blackberries and black raspberries, and a high percentage of the red raspberry and blueberries, are grown here. Many blackberry cultivars, like the highly regarded "Marion" (commonly called marionberry), tayberry, and loganberry, are prized by local cooks for their excellent flavor. Fresh raspberries are available locally during summer and into fall, as well as high-bush blueberries, which grow in the same regions.

With the abundance of fresh berries available locally in the Pacific Northwest, desserts served during

June and July always feature fresh berries in one form or another. The best blackberry pie is made with the flavorful wild Pacific trailing blackberry, but more often it is made with commercially grown berries like Marions, a regional favorite. The fine flavor of Marions is so intense that this simple old-fashioned dessert needs only sugar, a splash of lemon juice, a thickener, and pastry to make an exceptional sweet ending.

Cobblers and crisps made with berries, fruits, and nuts, or a mixture of them depending on what is in season, are also widely popular. Cobblers are most commonly made by tossing the fruit with sugar and a thickener, topping with a short pastry, and baking until the crust is a rich golden brown. However, they are also served with a cooked fruit filling with tender biscuits baked on top. See FRUIT DESSERTS, BAKED.

The most traditional Pacific Northwest desserts—pies, cobblers, crisps, and cakes—are made with the beloved native wild huckleberry. Twelve species grow in the Pacific Northwest and one of them—the sweet purple berries of *Vaccinium membraceum*—was a significant industry a hundred years ago. From mid-August to mid-September, large huckleberry camps were set up near ancient huckleberry fields, where families picked and often canned huckleberries on the spot. Professional pickers sold their berries to a distributor, who hauled the berries to urban markets for resale and processing.

Native Americans have gathered huckleberries in the Gifford Pinchot National Forest near Mount St. Helens for thousands of years. The berries, picked and dried on tule (rush) mats in front of a smoldering log, were eaten with dried game and fish throughout the harsh winters. During the Depression, as more and more unemployed workers left the cities for the mountains in hopes of making enough money picking huckleberries to feed their families, a conflict arose with the Native Americans whose ancient berry picking fields had been invaded. They took their grievance to the U.S. Forest Service, and the issue was resolved with the Handshake Agreement of 1932 that reserved a portion of the Indian Heaven Huckleberry Fields solely for Native American use during the season. The treaty is still being honored today, and huckleberry pie is still as popular today as it was a hundred years ago. It is the quintessential Pacific Northwest dessert.

Besides the wide variety of wild and commercially grown berries, there is also a thriving tree fruit industry, including apples, pears, cherries, apricots, plums, and peaches.

From mid- to late summer and into fall, when tree fruit are perfectly ripe and harvested, local dessert choices expand exponentially. Sweet cherries, peaches, nectarines, pears, and apples are transformed into mouth-watering desserts that tend to be rustic rather than fussy, with the fruit occupying center stage. Apple crisp is popular, baked with blackberries, huckleberries, or chopped hazelnuts, while pears are often poached in spiced red wine or used as a main ingredient in cakes. It is also not unusual to find tree fruit served as a last course with locally produced cheese and nuts, following the French tradition. Local apples, cherries, and plums, as well as several berries, are made regionally into eau-de-vie, which is often served with sweets for dessert.

Almost all of the country's hazelnuts are grown from the very southern end of Oregon's Willamette Valley into southern Washington. The orchards are distinguished by the deep emerald green canopy that protects the nuts when, in late September or early October, they drop to the ground when ripe. These premier nuts are best known for their large size and superior flavor, making them a favorite of chefs. Chopped hazelnuts are widely used paired with chocolate or fall fruits—hazelnut chocolate mousse, pear and hazelnut tart, and hazelnut apple crisp can often be found on regional menus. Ground hazelnut flour is a favorite of pastry chefs when they want a rich, nutty pastry or a gluten-free substitute for wheat flour.

Ice cream is still as popular a dessert now as it was a hundred years ago. In the past few years, there has been an increase in small, independent ice cream producers who use local ingredients in ice creams, such as Honey Balsamic Strawberry with Black Pepper Ice Cream or Melon Ice Cream with shards of razor-thin prosciutto. See ICE CREAM.

Sweet endings in the Pacific Northwest appear to have new beginnings.

See also DRIED FRUIT; FRUIT; FRUIT PRESERVES; NUTS; and UNITED STATES.

Agricultural Marketing and Resource Center. "Commodities and Products: Fruits." http://agmrc.org/commodities__products/fruits/ (accessed 16 April 2014).

Germplasm Resources Information Network. "History of Fruit Growing in the Pacific Northwest." http://www.ars-grin.gov/cor/cool/luelling.html (accessed 16 April 2014).

Hibler, Janie. *The Berry Bible*. Las Vegas, N.V.: AmazonEncore, 2010.

Janie Hibler

palm sugar is one of the world's oldest sweeteners, distinguished from cane sugar in Singhalese chronicles dating from the first century B.C.E. It is produced and consumed across a swath of Asia stretching from the Philippines to India and Sri Lanka. For anyone accustomed to thinking of sugar as either white or brown and just plain sweet, palm sugar is surprising in its complexity, ranging in color from pale yellow to almost black and with a flavor that, in addition to sweet, can be salty, sour, bitter, smoky, or any combination thereof. See SUGAR.

Palm sugar is produced by boiling sap collected from the cut inflorescence of many palm varieties, including palmyra (*Borassus flabellifer*), coconut (*Cocos nucifera*), kithul or fishtale (*Caryota urens*), date (*Phoenix dactylifera*), silver date (*Phoenix sylvestrus*), aren (*Arenga pinnata*), and nipa (*Nypa fruticans*) palms. Prior to cutting, the inflorescence is softened by beating with a stick or mallet to initiate the flow of sap. The sap is captured in tubes suspended beneath the cut inflorescence and collected twice a day; tappers often add a fermentation prohibitor such as lime, calcium carbonate, or tannic bark. Some tappers and sugar makers (often one and the same individual) include a ritual as part of the sap collection process. On northern Sumatra, ethnic Batak, most of whom are Christian, request permission from God before collecting sap. On Bali, it is believed that if the tapper speaks with or is spoken to by anyone while transferring collected sap to the pan where it is to be boiled, the sugar will become spoiled.

Once collected, the sap is reduced by evaporation, boiled and stirred for several hours in large, uncovered cauldrons. During boiling, some makers add ingredients to alter the color of their sugar; for example, Batak add the spongy reddish fiber that lines the inside of mangosteen peels to make their product darker. Once the sap has been sufficiently reduced, usually to a viscosity somewhere between the soft- and hard-ball candy stage, it is poured into molds made from coconut halves, bamboo tubes, strips of rattan joined to form a circle, and other materials, and left to cool and solidify. See STAGES OF SUGAR SYRUP. In southern Thailand, the sugar is whipped with large whisks until it is stiff, then formed without the use of molds into lumps or swirl-topped mounds and left to dry. In Sarawak and Sabah states on Malaysian Borneo and on Sri Lanka, the sugar is taken from the fire when still liquid, allowed to cool, and then poured into jars, tubs, or bags.

In local languages palm sugar might be named for its color (*gula merah* or "red sugar" in Indonesia), its traditional provenance (*gula jawa* in Indonesia, *gula Melaka* in Malaysia), the variety of palm from which it is made (*gula nipa* and *gula aren* in Indonesia, *gula apong* or "floating sugar" on Malaysian Borneo, in reference to the nipa palm, which grows in water), or the sugar-making process (*pakaskas* in the Philippines from *kaskasin*, which refers to the process of "scraping" the sugar from the boiling sap). Palm sugar is *duong thot not* in Vietnamese and *scor thnout* in Khmer. In India, it is called gur or, confusingly, date sugar (whether or not it is made from date palms) or jaggery, a word that also refers to dark brown cane sugar.

No matter which palm it is made from, palm sugar has a lower glycemic index and is less sweet than cane sugar. The palm sap that becomes sugar has also long been used to make intoxicating toddy and distilled arak, as well as vinegar. Palm sugar is an ingredient in a staggering variety of sweet and savory foods, from Thai *somtam* (green papaya salad) to innumerable Indian sweets.

See also INDIA; MAPLE SUGARING; PHILIPPINES; SOUTH ASIA; SOUTHEAST ASIA; STICKY RICE SWEETS; SUGAR AND HEALTH; and THAILAND.

Grimwood, Brian E. *Coconut Palm Products: Their Processing in Developing Countries*. Rome: Food and Agriculture Organization of the United Nations, 1975.
Moody, Sophy. *The Palm Tree*. London: T. Nelson and Sons, 1864.

Robyn Eckhardt

pan di spagna

See SPONGE CAKE.

pancakes are thin, flat cakes made by pouring or ladling a liquid batter onto a hot greased surface, and baking them there until done. The simplicity of the required ingredients and equipment means that pancakes are one of the most ancient foods created by humans. Pancakes called *tagenites* made from wheat flour and soured milk and served warm with honey are mentioned in Greek writings from the fifth century B.C.E., but it is generally accepted that some form of pancakes has been made since prehistoric times.

Pancakes Large and Small

Two key features distinguish pancakes from other starch-based staples. The first is that liquid batter (at times very thick) is used, in contrast to the firm dough required for shaping bread. The second is that gluten is not required for successful formation—indeed, gluten is not generally desirable, as pancakes are intended to be soft, not stiff—which means that a much greater range of grains can be used.

Flour or meal made from true cereal grasses, such as wheat, oats, barley, rye, maize, and rice, collectively form the base of most pancakes eaten around the world. The grain-like seeds of plants that are not technically grasses, such as buckwheat (related to rhubarb) and amaranth (related to pigweed), and starches derived from many other seeds and plants, such as pulses (peas, beans, lentils), potato, cassava (tapioca flour), and chestnuts, may also be used. This enormous flexibility in the basic ingredient has led to pancakes being a truly global food—one that has crossed the East–West culinary divide in a way that bread has not.

The basic pancake batter may be varied in an almost infinite number of ways. It may be plain and simple, rich and sweet, or spicy and savory. Additional ingredients such as berries, nuts, or chocolate chips may be included in the batter, or the cooked pancake may be folded or rolled around a filling (sweet or savory), or served with a sauce alongside. The batter may even be colored, either artificially or with such natural ingredients as beet juice, spinach juice, or turmeric.

In terms of thickness, pancakes fall into two broad groups. The thin, unleavened form is exemplified by the classic French crêpe and embraces many European specialties (most of which are sweet dishes), such as the *palatschinken* of Central and Eastern Europe, Poland's *naleśniki*, and Spanish *frixuelos*. The thicker, fluffier, leavened type is that of the American hotcake, Australian pikelet, Scottish drop scone, and Russian blini (yeast-raised, classically made from buckwheat, and often savory). Many other national specialties fall somewhere between these styles, for example Austrian *Kaiserschmarrn* (characteristically shredded before serving), German *Pfannkuchen* (the word can mean both pancake and doughnut), Czech *livance*, and Danish *æbleskiver* (plump, round balls that traditionally contain an apple filling).

The diameter of the pancake depends on personal and national preference, and is limited only by the diameter of the cooking pan or surface. The pikelet of Australasia is a few bites in size, and several are cooked at the same time in the pan, whereas Ethiopian *injera* may be several feet across, with a single pancake ample enough to satisfy several people. In some countries special pans have been devised with indentations for cooking multiple pancakes at once, such as Denmark's *æbleskiver* and Sweden's *plättar*.

Pancakes may also serve as the base for other dishes, especially cakes. *Gâteau mille crêpes* (thousand crêpe cake) consists of a large stack of thin crêpes sandwiched together with a sweet filling, which is then cut into slices like a cake. Hungary's *rakott palacsinta* is not dissimilar. In Russia, blini are layered with farmer's cheese and dried fruit, or sometimes simply jam, to make a tall *blinchatyi pirog*.

Cooking Pancakes

Although the word "pancake" is attested in English since the beginning of the fifteenth century, the exact characteristics covered by this name are far from certain. Recipes for simple, everyday dishes were not written down in times past, as they would have been part of every cook's and housewife's repertoire. Recipes that do appear in pre-nineteenth-century cookery texts are frequently unclear, and many dishes referred to as "pancakes" appear to more closely resemble what we would now define as fritters (fried in deep fat), waffles (cooked between two heated plates), or omelets (a predominantly egg mixture). See FRITTERS. There is also recipe confusion and overlap with hoecakes, johnnycakes, griddle cakes, flapjacks, slapjacks, and other similar articles. In some instances even today, "pancakes" turn out to be flatbreads, made from stiff dough that has been kneaded and rolled or pressed out.

The first written recipe in English for something unequivocally a pancake in form and method of cooking appears in the *Good Huswife's Handmaide for the Kitchin*, published in 1588:

> Take new thicke Creame a pinte, foure or fiue yolks of Egs, a good handfull of flower, and two or three

> spoonfuls of ale, strain them altogether into a faire platter, and season it with a good handfull of Sugar, a spooneful of Synamon, and a litle Ginger: then take a frying pan, and put in a litle peece of Butter, as big as your thombe, and when it is molten browne, cast it out of your pan, and with a ladle put to the further side of your pan some of your stuffe, and hold your pan aslope, so that your stuffe may run abroad ouer all the pan, as thin as may be: then set it to the fyre, and let the fyre be verie soft, and when the one side is baked, then turne the other, and bake them as dry as ye can without burning.

Leavening is not essential to pancake batter, but it does yield a lighter, fluffier result. Pancakes can be raised with eggs, yeast (including that in ale or beer), baking powder, or baking soda. See CHEMICAL LEAVENERS; EGGS; and YEAST. Snow can also be used (see below), and stiffly beaten egg whites folded into the batter make an especially fine and light pancake. Leavening may also be achieved by allowing natural fermentation of the batter, which adds a characteristic sour taste to the pancake, as in traditional Russian blini made with buckwheat flour; bubbly-surfaced Ethiopian *injera* made from teff flour and water left to stand for several days; and the very similar Somalian *lahoh*, made from sorghum flour and water.

In its simplest form, a pancake can be made from flour and water only, but it would not be a delicious pancake. The choice of liquid used in the batter makes its own significant contribution to the style and flavor of the pancake. Milk in any of its myriad forms may be used, depending on preference and availability: skimmed milk serves the purposes of economy, and cream makes for a rich taste and texture. See CREAM and MILK. Especially notable is buttermilk, which is acidic, and hence assists the leavening action of baking soda, if it is used. See BUTTERMILK. Nondairy "milks" may also be used, as they characteristically are in Asia. Good examples include tiny rice flour and coconut milk pancakes called *kanom krok* in Thailand, and *serabi* in Indonesia. Virtually any liquid can be used, of course, and in the past, ale and wine were popular and common. The ale could also serve as the source of the yeast, which helped lighten the mixture.

For something so essentially simple, specific instructions nonetheless exist for making certain types of pancakes. Most often the pancake is turned to cook first on one side, then the other, but some thin pancakes, such as Moroccan *beghrir*, call for cooking one side only. When turning pancakes, the question frequently arises as to whether the pancake should be turned with a spatula or tossed. Although there is much sentiment and hype about tossing pancakes, tossing is not necessary, and it is fraught with risk to the pancake and to kitchen surfaces. However, tossing is a good party trick, and it is required at the traditional pancake-tossing races at Shrovetide.

In the Christian calendar, Shrove Tuesday is most closely associated with pancakes because it was traditionally the day to use up all eggs and milk before the long period of abstinence known as Lent. The most famous event of this day is a pancake race. Pancake racing is said to have begun in the distant past, when a woman making pancakes heard the church bell and, not wanting to waste her efforts, ran quickly to church, tossing her pancake as she went. Since 1950 the towns of Olney, England, and Liberal, Kansas, have held an International Pancake Race.

Pancakes lend themselves to serving in a wide range of situations. Their inherent simplicity means that they are most commonly associated with informal events such as family breakfasts, and they are favorites for campfire cooking. Glamorous versions are suitable for fine dinner parties and other entertainments. A prime example is the famous dessert Crêpes Suzette, whose origins are controversial. The chef Henri Charpentier claimed to have invented the dish in 1895 when he rescued a dessert from disaster in the royal kitchen of Edward, Prince of Wales (the future Edward VII). Charpentier renamed the dessert in honor of the prince's female companion and served it to great acclaim—or so the story goes. Although called by different names, recipes for essentially the same dish appeared in the cookbook published in 1896 by Oscar Tschirky, maître d'hôtel of the Waldorf-Astoria Hotel in New York, and in the English edition of Auguste Escoffier's *Guide culinaire*, published in 1903. Interestingly, neither recipe calls for a final stage of flambéeing, which is today considered intrinsic to the dish.

Pancakes in America

In America, the skill of pancake making certainly arrived with the earliest European settlers, and the national repertoire has been greatly expanded since then by migrant populations from around the world. The first authentic American cookery book, Amelia Simmons's *American Cookery*, was published in 1796.

It contains a pancake recipe that shows adaptation to local ingredients. Although the recipe specifies frying, it does not indicate how much fat to use, so the "Federal Pan Cake" may have been more like a fritter.

> Take one quart of boulted rye flour, one quart of boulted Indian meal, mix it well, and stir it with a little salt into three pints milk, to the proper consistence of pancakes; fry in lard, and serve up warm.

An English cookbook widely reprinted in the young republic, *A New System of Domestic Cookery* by Maria Eliza Ketelby Rundell (1807), gives instructions for snow pancakes:

> Is an excellent substitute for eggs, either in puddings or pancakes. Two large spoonfuls will supply the place of one egg, and the article it is used in will be equally good. This is an [*sic*] useful piece of information, especially as snow often falls at the season when eggs are dearest. Fresh small beer, or bottled malt liquors, likewise serve instead of eggs. The snow may be taken up from any clean spot before it is wanted, and will not lose its virtue, though the sooner it is used the better.

The quintessential modern American pancake is leavened with baking powder and served with maple syrup. See MAPLE SYRUP. It is a staple at breakfasts in family kitchens and in diners across the country. In some regions it is known as a hotcake. The phrase "hot cakes" appears to be an American invention, and first appeared in 1683 in a letter from William Penn, governor of Pennsylvania, to the "Committee of the Free Society of Traders of that province residing in London." The "hot cakes" to which he refers, however, are clearly not pancakes in the accepted sense of the word today. Penn is writing of the food of the Native Americans when he says "with hot cakes of new Corn, both Wheat and Beans, which they make up in square form, in the leaves of the Stem, and bake them in the Ashes." See NATIVE AMERICAN. Similar confusion exists with other references to hot cakes or hotcakes over the next few centuries—it is impossible to know for certain if they were fritter-like or flatbread-like.

The phrase "selling (or "going off like") hotcakes" also first appeared in an American publication, in 1839. In *The Adventures of Harry Franco*, a novel about the great financial panic of 1837, Charles Briggs writes: "'You had better buy 'em, Colonel,' said Mr. Lummucks, 'they will sell like hot cakes.'"

The modern concept of a hotcake as a pancake could not have appeared before the development and widespread use of chemical leaveners, which did not occur until the late eighteenth century. But once commercial baking powder became available in the mid-nineteenth century, powder-risen pancakes rapidly became an American favorite. An English reporter described his experience of an American breakfast in an article titled "Hotel Life in New York," in the 27 December 1860 issue of the *London Times*. He notes that "breakfast may be obtained from half-past 6 till 11, and on a scale of which even our neighbours north of the Tweed [i.e., in Scotland] have no conception." The intrepid reporter tackles steak, potatoes, and fried oysters, after which the waiter prevails upon him to try something more:

> ... a little broiled fowl, or an omelet? Well, you will have some hot cakes? Hot cakes are an American institution (every custom, I should remark, is termed an "institution" in America).
>
> These hot cakes resemble crumpets, and are generally served in a pyramidal form, a large cake forming the base, and the small one the apex of the pile. A little butter is placed between each cake, and syrup (refined molasses) poured over the whole.

See also CHESTNUTS and TAPIOCA.

Albala, Ken. *Pancake: A Global History*. London: Reaktion, 2008.
Davidson, Alan. "Pancakes." In *The Oxford Companion to Food*, pp. 571–572. New York: Oxford University Press, 1999.
Montagné, Prosper. *Larousse gastronomique*. Edited by Charlotte Turgeon and Nina Froud. London and New York: Hamlyn, 1961.
"Pancakes & Crepes." http://www.foodtimeline.org/foodfaq2.html#pancakes.
Smith, Andrew, ed. *Oxford Encyclopedia of Food and Drink in America*. 2d ed. New York: Oxford University Press, 2012.
Toussaint-Samat, Maguelonne. *History of Food*. Translated by Anthea Bell. Malden, Mass.: Blackwell, 2000.

Janet Clarkson

pandanus, though largely unknown to cooks and chefs in the West, is an important flavoring and coloring ingredient in the sweets repertoire of South and Southeast Asia, from India to the Philippines.

Pandanus is a genus of flowering trees and shrubs that includes over 600 species of tropical and subtropical plants native to Asia. *Pandanus amarillifolius* (formerly *Pandanus odoratissimus*), usually called "pandan" or "screwpine" in English, is the species that provides cooks with pandan leaves (*bai toei* in Thai, *daun pandan* in Malay, *pandan* in Tagalog, *sleuk toey* in Khmer, *la dura* in Vietnamese, *rampe* in Sinhala, and *su mwei ywe* in Burmese). The leaves give a delicate scent and flavor reminiscent of basmati rice, with hints of rosewater and vanilla. They also lend an attractive light green tint.

The male flowers of several species of pandanus are the source of "screwpine essence," an aromatic, pale orange liquid used in South Asian cooking to flavor sweets and drinks. See EXTRACTS AND FLAVORINGS.

Pandan leaves look a little like narrow gladiolus or daylily leaves: bright green, long, flat, and pointed. They are available fresh in Asia, Hawaii, and Australia, and occasionally in colder-climate regions. In North America and Europe, however, cooks more commonly have access only to frozen pandan, which also works well. To use pandanus, tie several leaves in a knot and then simmer in water, milk, or coconut milk until they have released their aroma and green color; the knot enables them to be lifted out easily when the dish has cooked.

In Malaysia, Indonesia, and India, pandan leaves are most often cooked with rice to add a light green tint and impart an aromatic flowery flavor; they also perfume coconut-milk-based desserts in Southeast Asia. These days in Asia, a number of factory-made ingredients, such as tapioca balls, fine rice noodles, and rice-flour-based sweetmeats are dyed green with vegetable dyes to evoke pandan.

See also INDIA; PHILIPPINES; SOUTH ASIA; and SOUTHEAST ASIA.

Bremness, Lesley. *Herbs*. London: Dorling Kindersley, 1994.
Norman, Jill. *The Complete Book of Spices*. London: Dorling Kindersley, 1990.

Naomi Duguid

pandowdy

See FRUIT DESSERTS, BAKED.

panning is the process for making sugared almonds, comfits, dragées, jelly beans, M&M's, and numerous other items in which nuts, spices, and pieces of candied fruit, fruit paste, sugar paste, or chocolate are coated with sugar shells. See COMFIT; FRUIT PASTES; and JELLY BEANS. The principles behind it have been known since at least the early medieval period in the Middle East.

Confectioners differentiate between hard panning—using sugar syrup in a slow process to make smooth, hard-centered items—and soft panning, which uses sugar and glucose syrup in a rapid process to make irregularly shaped candies with a soft bite. Chocolate can also be used as a coating in panning, as in chocolate-covered raisins.

Simple in principle, the panning process is, in fact, complex. For hard panning, first ingredients for the centers are prepared by shaping and drying with gentle heat in a warm room; nuts also require sealing with gum arabic and flour. These steps are important, as even tiny amounts of moisture or oil can discolor the surface of finished items.

Next, the centers are placed in large pans that are mounted at an angle. These revolve, tumbling the contents, and successive "charges" of syrup of relatively low concentration are added, a process known as "wetting." Air, supplied to the pans through nozzles, dries each charge in a thin layer before a subsequent one is added. This, too, is important, as inadequately dried sugar gives the finished sweets a grayish cast. Air temperature varies according to the type of center: for instance, cold air is recommended for sugared almonds, warm air (104°F [40°C]) for nonpareils. Other ingredients such as perfume or color can be added to the syrup and dustings of starch help to build up the coats and absorb syrup. This "engrossing" is repeated until the coating achieves the desired thickness. A final panning with beeswax, carnauba, or paraffin wax yields a polished surface. The small silver balls used for cake decoration are made by panning with silver dust or leaf in the final stages of production. See LEAF, GOLD AND SILVER.

Panning is a skilled process in which subtleties of speed and temperature (for both pans and airflow) and concentration of the syrup are crucial. It is also time consuming: engrossing is slow and can be intermittent; soft panned items need periods of drying on trays both during the process and afterward.

Illustrations in early confectionery books show panning done by hand. They imply that confectioners vigorously shook the sweets in shallow, bowl-like balancing pans suspended over burning coals, thereby exaggerating a process that actually requires gentle heat and thorough stirring. Careful attention to syrup concentration produces different surface textures, and drying between coats is essential for good results. The technique of adding subsequent coats explains one of the great mysteries of British childhoods: how the enormous sweets known as gobstoppers can change color as they are sucked.

Lees, R., and B. Jackson. *Sugar Confectionery and Chocolate Manufacture.* Aylesbury, U.K.: Leonard Hill, 1973.
Richardson, Tim. *Sweets: A History of Temptation.* London: Bantam, 2002.

Laura Mason

pans come in a vast assortment of shapes, sizes, and materials. The correct pan is as essential to many cakes as the batter itself. For example, French cake pans have sloping sides that make possible an even coating of melted fondant icing for classic gâteaux. English cake pans with straight sides are deeper than American ones so as to accommodate heavier fruit-laden batters; shallow American pans are designed for stacked layer cakes that are tall with straight sides. Even tart pans are different: a French tart pan is made of metal with a decorative, fluted edge and a removable base for easy unmolding, whereas an American pie plate has sloping sides for ease of serving the pie directly from it. The oval, deep English pie dish is unknown in either country.

Today's most favored baking pans are made of heavy-gauge aluminum or Pyrex (tempered glass); others are available with a nonstick finish, or are made from cast iron or silicone. Because Pyrex transmits heat very efficiently, glass pans require a cooler oven temperature, so bakers are advised to set their ovens 25°F (–4°C) lower than when using other pans. Cast iron transmits heat inefficiently, so some recipes suggest preheating these pans before filling them with cake batter or dough. Silicone pans are appreciated for their flexibility and nonstick property, which eliminates the need for greasing, a necessary step for most baked goods to ensure their release from the pan. Paper cake pans are also on the market, although they are mainly for professional bakers.

Round pans are suited for baking single- or multilayered cakes, and elongated loaf pans accommodate quick breads. Standard rectangular pans range in size from 5 × 8 inches to 18 × 24 inches and are useful for bar cookies and brownies. See BAR COOKIES and BROWNIES. Muffin and cupcake pans are made of individual cups joined together in a rectangular form. Historically, muffin tins were made from individual cups soldered together into three or four rows. Today, they come in many different patterns, ranging from miniature to large, shallow indentations for baking crusty muffin tops. Some pans have sculpted patterns in the bottom; when inverted for serving, the cakes display a decorative top. See CUPCAKES and MUFFINS.

Cookie sheets, jellyroll pans, and sheet-cake pans are generally interchangeable. The most important

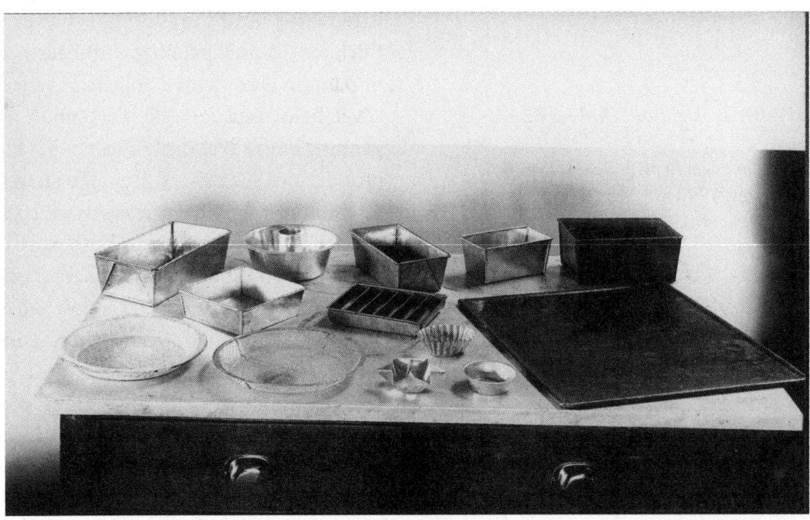

This photograph of various pans, plates, sheets, and molds for baking appeared in a 1912 Cornell University Household Economics and Management bulletin on "Choice and Care of Utensils." CORNELL UNIVERSITY LIBRARY

feature is a low lip edge, as a deep pan would present problems in removing drop, rolled, or pressed cookies. See DROP COOKIES; PRESSED COOKIES; and ROLLED COOKIES. Many bakers favor cookie sheets with only a small, curved lip on one narrow side that enables the baker to pick up the sheet; it is very easy to lift or slide cookies from the three lipless sides. Shallow, 1-inch deep rectangular jellyroll pans are usually 10 × 15 inches. Like cookie sheets, they are frequently lined with parchment paper so that the baked goods will not stick.

Pie pans, also called "tins" or "plates," are generally made of Pyrex, aluminum, coated steel, or stoneware. Standard pans are 1½ inches deep; "deep dish" pans, at 2 to 2½ inches in depth, can accommodate more filling. Pie pans are available in sizes ranging from 6 inches to 12 inches in diameter, the most popular being 9 and 10 inch. Some (particularly those made of Pyrex or stoneware) have fluted edges to facilitate making a decorative finish to the crust. See PIE. Tiny tartlet molds, including fluted and unfluted barquette tins, are used for miniature confections; various sizes of round, shallow pans, usually with fluted sides, are specifically designed for quiches and tarts.

Round torte or spring-form pans, with removable bottoms, are usually manufactured from sheet aluminum. See TORTE. This fairly flexible material permits the opening and closing of the pan's overlapping sides, which are secured by the use of spring clasps. These pans, ranging from 5 to 14 inches in diameter, can be 3 to 7 inches deep for home baking; commercial pans may be deeper still. After the torte is baked and cooled, the sides are released, opened, and removed. Sometimes the torte is easier to slice and serve from the pan bottom itself, particularly when it is large or fragile, but the baked layer may also be removed to a cake plate for slicing and serving.

Special-purpose baking pans include aluminum angel food cake pans and Turks' head or turban molds with a removable bottom and spiral patterning on the sides; both types have a central tube that allows the heat to penetrate the batter more efficiently and ensure that the cake will cook evenly. Similar pans, without a removable bottom and generally made from cast iron, aluminum, or silicone, are called Bundt pans, after the coffee cake–style Bundt cake that unmolds with a decorative pattern. See ANGEL FOOD CAKE and GUGELHUPF.

See also BREADS, SWEET; CAKE; FRISBIE PIE TINS; and LAYER CAKE.

Franklin, Linda Campbell. *300 Years of Kitchen Collectibles*. 5th ed. Iola, Wis.: K. P. Krause, 2003.

Alice Ross

Paris, the capital of France, is one of the world's great gastronomic centers. Its proximity to the famed butter of Normandy and to high-quality French flour gave the city a natural advantage in pastry making that continues to the current day. However, its fame owes at least as much to the systemized culinary techniques that its best practitioners spread internationally.

From Antiquity to Renaissance

Paris's fertile surroundings allowed for the successful cultivation of many fruits from an early date. The Roman emperor Julian's fourth-century description of the native Parisii tribe records that they were even growing figs by covering the trees to protect them from the harsh winter. *Mesnagier de Paris* (ca. 1393) provides advice to a Parisian housewife on how to cultivate violets, mint, raspberries, currants, seedless grapes, cherries, and plums. Pears were so ubiquitous that the French word *poire* could be used as a synonym for dessert. Apples were nearly as prevalent and remain a staple.

By the *Mesnagier*'s era, the city had become a thriving international metropolis with a wholesale market to match. Contact with the East during the Crusades brought exotic sugar and spices in increasing quantities. Other products came from regions across the kingdom and beyond.

Having survived Roman occupation, Viking invasions, and years of relative obscurity, Paris had become the capital of West Francia with the accession of Hugh Capet to the throne in 987. But from the twelfth century the city's expansion accelerated phenomenally. Its population exploded from an estimated 3,000 residents in 1100 to around 200,000 by 1300. A central, wholesale market at Les Halles was established by 1137 and quickly expanded, especially after the construction of permanent buildings in the 1180s. By the *Mesnagier*'s era, one could buy waffles, sugar in myriad forms, dragées, and other sweets from an impressive list of expert vendors. The core of the city began to take on recognizable form with a highly legislated food market at its physical and metaphorical epicenter.

The almond- and butter-rich *gâteau du roi*, which is still made throughout northern France for Epiphany, hearkens back to this era. This tradition remains so popular in Paris that many patissiers set up outdoor stands exclusively to sell this cake during the season. See TWELFTH NIGHT CAKE.

By the sixteenth century the city excelled at elaborate sugar sculptures and pastries for lavish entertainments, such as the multisensory *magnificences* organized by Catherine de Médici for the Polish ambassadors in 1573. See MÉDICI, CATHERINE DE and SUGAR SCULPTURE. These effete celebrations differed little from analogously regal events held elsewhere in Northern Europe. However, they are remarkable because they occurred not quite a year after one of the city's bloodiest episodes, the crown-endorsed St. Bartholomew's Day Massacre, which left thousands of Protestants dead. This was but one battle in nine gruesome Wars of Religion that rippled through France from 1562 until 1594. Nevertheless, in the midst of this tumult, the Venetian ambassador to France raved about the astounding array of food products available in Paris and lavished praise on its patissiers and caterers.

Ancien Régime

Paris and its cuisine grew increasingly sophisticated through the seventeenth century. Paradoxically, however, the city did not develop a distinctive gastronomic style until the court definitively left it.

Louis XIV moved the court into full-time residence at Versailles in 1682. Paris then became the center of French counterculture. The city's first extant café, Le Procope, opened just four years later to serve the newly imported beverage coffee to a clientele featuring freethinkers. The institution of the café has epitomized Paris ever since. See CAFÉ.

The Procope's Italian-born founder gained as much renown for his ices as for his coffee. Although glacés had been served privately to elite Parisians a century earlier, they henceforth became a favored treat for public consumption at fashionable venues in the Palais Royal and on the Boulevard des Italiens, such as Tortoni's.

The first book devoted solely to ices was written and published in Paris by M. Emy in 1768. This volume features ice creams with an egg-custard base, which are not dissimilar to those now produced by Paris's famed glacier Berthillon (founded 1954). See EMY, M. and ICE CREAM.

A craze for thick, slightly bitter hot chocolate, which continues to be popular, matched that for glacés. Both emerged from the application of Enlightenment logic to colonial products. More broadly, they contributed to Paris's emergence in the eighteenth century as Europe's preeminent source of luxury goods from fashion to furnishings.

Pastry techniques made the most significant and resonant advances. Parisian manuals such as Augustin Roux's *Dictionnaire domestique portatif* (1762–1764) demonstrate that even before Paris spawned the world's first restaurant, it had developed and refined the pastry techniques that continue to underpin the French tradition.

Many of the most renowned practitioners had foreign origins. Nicolas Stohrer, who in 1730 founded Paris's oldest extant patisserie, is presumed to be from the area of Wissembourg where he apprenticed. He is credited for bringing the *baba* to Paris. See STOHRER, NICOLAS. Other new forms of biscuits, macarons, gâteaux, madeleines, and brioches that became similarly associated with the city also originated elsewhere. Paris was the hub where ideas were exchanged even as techniques codified.

Although Marie Antoinette never said, "Let them eat cake," on the eve of the French Revolution of 1789, this apocryphal phrase succinctly conveys the fact that while many struggled to afford bread, wealthy Parisians of the ancien régime were spoiled in their choice of fine pastries.

Post-Revolution to Belle Époque

In the post-Revolutionary era, the production and marketing of sweets (as was the case for many luxury trades) carried on strangely unaffected and simultaneously transformed. The newly rich enjoyed spending publicly with "see and be seen" bravura. This resulted in more glamorously appointed patisseries, cafés, and shops as well as inventiveness fueled by the need to captivate a fickle audience. Alexandre-Balthazar-Laurent Grimod de la Reynière (1858–1837) documented this phenomenon in the world's first food journal, which debuted in Paris in 1803.

Marie-Antoine (Antonin) Carême (1784–1833) was that generation's most celebrated patissier and chef. See CARÊME, MARIE-ANTOINE. Although he worked privately, he created dazzling, architectonic *pièces montées* for public balls. More important, he "doubled" (by his own estimation) the range of French pastries and techniques and disseminated them through books that garnered international attention. Although his work incorporated ideas taken from stints in London and Vienna, he extolled his native Paris as the globe's gastronomic capital.

Carême's *Pâtissier royal parisien* appeared the same year as Napoléon Bonaparte's ultimate defeat. Although French military dominance ended in 1815, Paris's reputation as preeminent in European gastronomy ascended ever higher. Carême's protégés Jules Gouffé (1807–1877) and Auguste Escoffier (1846–1935) continued this trend into the twentieth century. See ESCOFFIER, GEORGES AUGUSTE.

The city itself also grew exponentially, doubling its population from 700,000 in 1815 to a whopping 1.7 million in 1861 and an all-time high of 2.9 million on the eve of World War I. New immigrants, such as Viennese-born August Zang, who in Paris in the late 1830s produced the first recognizably flaky croissant, added their traditions to the mix. See CROISSANT. However, regional and national differences got smoothed into a system no less regimented than the military.

These developments continued largely unchecked until World War I, with the exception of the infamous Siege of Paris of 1870 and the ensuing chaos of the Paris Commune. Nevertheless, Ladurée bears witness to the rapidity with which many businesses oddly thrived upon these traumatic events. A fire during the 1871 Commune burned down the original bakery of 1862. This allowed for the construction of a luxurious tearoom designed to appeal to women, whose purchasing power had already been realized by newfangled department stores such as Le Bon Marché (founded in 1852).

As steamboats, railways, and eventually automobiles brought increasing numbers of visitors to the City of Lights, its spectacle crescendoed to a feverish pitch. Glittering events and personalities often received a commemorative dessert. Many remain classics today. Escoffier invented the Poire Belle Hélène in 1864 for Offenbach's operetta *La belle Hélène*; and even the Paris-Brest bicycle race that started in 1910 received its own pastry in the shape of a wheel.

World War I to the Present

World War I took an especially hard toll on Paris, which was closer to the battle lines than any other major city. Sugar and coal were the first goods to be rationed; fancy pastries were entirely banned. As a supply hub, the city became adept at prefabricating food in large quantities. Prospere Montagné (1865–1945) learned to organize approximately 16,000 bread rations per sitting that could be reheated on the battlefield. His techniques soon found their way into civilian production after the war, alongside a vogue for American jazz, cocktails, and refrigerators.

Nevertheless, a conservative backlash fought to preserve traditional craftsmanship from architecture to gastronomy. Created under this impulse in 1929, the Meilleurs Ouvriers de France (best workers of France, known as MOFs), which includes categories for chocolatiers and patissiers, guard classical techniques through rigorous and extensive training.

When Paris capitulated to the Nazis in June 1940, huge swaths of the population simply fled. The city was already in rough shape economically. Yet, in spite of rationing, pastries and other luxury goods remained available to collaborators as well as to black-market purchasers.

However, German occupation cost Paris its hitherto unassailable self-assurance, which negatively affected its food. By the 1970s American-style supermarkets sold packaged sweets and rubbery croissants throughout the city, and even many specialty patissiers increasingly cut corners.

At the top of the market, Paris gradually reestablished itself as a world-class capital for luxury goods, including sweets. Parisian chocolate, exemplified by the masterful sculptures of Patrick Roger, is as stunning as it is intense. Parisian sophisticates ignited the recent worldwide craze for macarons as devotees of rivals Ladurée and Pierre Hermé sparked heated debates on the subject. See HERMÉ, PIERRE. Competitions to determine the capital's best examples of classics such as croissants, éclairs, and the Paris-Brest have recently mushroomed. Raised public awareness has been met with a proliferation of high-end patisseries. That the world's first dessert-only restaurant, Dessance (serving three-course meals of sweets), opened in Paris in early 2014 bears witness to the city's ongoing ability to innovate even as it upholds classical standards.

See also BABA AU RHUM; FRANCE; MACARONS; MADELEINE; PASTRY, CHOUX; and PASTRY, PUFF.

Brereton, Georgina E., and Janet M. Ferrier, eds. *Le Mesnagier de Paris*. Paris: Librairie Française, 1994.

Carême, Antonin. *Le pâtissier royal parisien*. 2 vols. Paris: Dépôt des moulins, 1854.

Escoffier, Auguste. *Memories of My Life*. New York: Van Nostrand Reinhold, 1997.
Grimod de la Reynière, Alexandre Balthazar Laurent. *Almanach des gourmands*. Paris: Mauradan, 1803.
Jones, Colin. *Paris: The Biography of the City*. London: Penguin, 2005.
Roux, Augustin. *Dictionnaire domestique portatif*. 3 vols. Paris: Vincent, 1762–1764.

Carolin C. Young

Passover, the eight-day festival of freedom celebrating the Exodus from Egypt, is probably the foremost Jewish holiday today. It is also one of the world's oldest continually observed festivals. No products made from regular flour and no leavened food (more precisely, no fermented foods) can be eaten at Passover. This practice is based on a passage from Exodus 12:15, "For seven days you are to eat bread made without yeast. On the first day remove the yeast from your houses, for whoever eats anything with yeast in it from the first day through the seventh must be cut off from Israel." *Pesach* in Hebrew means "passing by" or "passing over"; the holiday was called Passover because God passed over the Jewish houses while slaying the firstborn of Egypt. During most Jewish ceremonial meals throughout the year, two loaves of the sweet, enriched bread known as challah are served, but on Passover three matzahs are placed on the table instead. Matzah, the unleavened and quickly baked bread prepared for Passover, reminds contemporary celebrants that the Jews fleeing Egypt had no time to leaven their bread or to bake it properly.

Today, the eight-day festival maintains its family character, beginning with the traditional Seder meal at home. The central object of every table is the Seder plate arranged with symbolic foods, including *haroset*, a sweet fruit and nut blend symbolizing the mortar that Jews used to build the ancient Egyptian pyramids or buildings (it is not clear that it was the pyramids). While the Ashkenazic mixture typically contains apples and walnuts, the Middle Eastern and Sephardic versions often include dates, but other ingredients vary according to the country and sometimes even the city of origin. Besides these symbolic foods, Passover recipes themselves have evolved over the years, reflecting the foods of the countries to which Jews immigrated. To compensate for the absence of flour demanded by the biblical rule, Jews throughout the world have created all kinds of baked goods, such as soaked matzah and, later, matzah cake meal made from carefully watched flour, meaning that it has not touched any other flour or been near anything fermented during the year, ensuring that it is acceptable for Passover.

Some Passover favorites include flourless tortes using egg whites beaten until stiff, ground nuts, sugar, and egg yolks; sponge cakes containing matzah meal or potato flour; macaroons made from almonds or coconuts; *Schaumtorte*, a large meringue filled with strawberries; and *chremslach* or *krimsel*, fritters made from dried fruit, nuts, and spices, and sometimes stuffed with apples or jam. Beet or carrot *eingemachts* (preserves) were traditionally popular in Lithuania and Russia. Jews from Morocco make preserved fruits to eat as a sweet at Passover, such as candied eggplant and candied oranges. Jews from Salonika ate candied almonds. In the United States today, Americans enjoy fruit-flavored jelly slices or jelly rings coated with chocolate. Increasingly popular desserts are made from matzah coated with chocolate or a toffee-like, buttery, crunchy topping. And in Israeli homes, one can find every imaginable Passover sweet known to mankind.

See also JUDAISM.

Nathan, Joan. *Joan Nathan's Jewish Holiday Cookbook*. New York: Schocken, 2004.

Joan Nathan

pastel de nata (pl. *pasteís de nata*), perhaps the most ubiquitous of all Portuguese sweets, is an egg custard tart. The pastel de nata can be found in every pastry shop in continental Portugal as well as on Madeira and the Azores Islands, where the tarts are commonly referred to as *queijadas de nata*.

The pastel de nata originated sometime prior to the seventeenth century in the Santa Maria de Belém quarter of Lisbon. Pastry production provided religious orders with supplemental income, and the monks of the Monastery of the Hieronymites first created these tarts to help offset monastery expenses. The tarts were made from yolks left over from eggs whose whites were used to starch clothing and purify wines. See EGG YOLK SWEETS. Following the Liberal Revolution of 1820, Portuguese religious orders were closed; as a means of survival, the Hieronymite monks contracted with a nearby bakery to produce and sell their tarts. These particular pastries became known as Pasteís de Belém, and the monks' original recipe was patented and registered. These tarts continue to be made and sold at the Antiga Confeitaria de Belém, Lda., their recipe still a closely guarded secret.

Though regional variations exist, the pastel de nata is commonly made of puff pastry, egg yolks, sugar, and flour. See PASTRY, PUFF. Some recipes also call for lemon peel, cream, vanilla, and milk. Whatever the combination of ingredients, a pastel de nata hot from the oven—often sprinkled with cinnamon and powdered sugar—is a divine tribute to Hieronymite ingenuity.

See also PORTUGAL.

Duarte, Frederico, Pedro Ferreira, and Rita João, eds. *Fabrico Próprio: O design da pastelaria semi-industrial portuguesa*. Portugal: Pedrita and Frederico Duarte, 2008.

Ortins, Ana Patuleia. *Portuguese Homestyle Cooking*. Northampton, Mass.: Interlink, 2013.

Pasteís de Belem. "History: The Taste of Tradition." http://www.pasteisdebelem.pt/en.html (accessed 2 September 2013).

Vieira, Edite. *The Taste of Portugal: A Voyage of Gastronomic Discovery Combined with Recipes, History and Folklore*. London: Grubstreet, 2013.

Frances Baca

pastila is an ethereal fruit confection that is one of Russia's oldest sweets, likely dating back to the fourteenth century. It originated as a way to preserve the apple harvest by cooking tart, pectin-rich apples until soft, then sieving them into a purée dried slowly in the oven. (The name derives from the Latin *pastillus*, meaning a "small loaf.") Two Russian towns lay claim to pastila: Kolomna, near Moscow, where the confection was probably first produced, and Belyov, near Tula, where the recipe was perfected. The secret to excellent pastila is the addition of air through copious beating and through egg whites, which turn the dense apple paste into a light, airy mass. After whipping the apple purée until light, egg whites beaten stiff with a little sugar are folded in (the original sweetener was honey). This mixture is spread in a thin layer on a baking sheet to dry for several hours at low heat in the oven. The Belyov version calls for reserving a little of the beaten apple mixture to spread between layers of the baked pastila. The stacked confection is then returned to the oven to dry a little more, resulting in a surprisingly moist confection that is sweet yet tart, less gelatinous than marshmallow, and softer than meringue. Although apples are traditional, pastila can also be made from berries and even hops, a version touted in the nineteenth century as a hangover cure.

During the Soviet era, the art of making pastila was largely lost, but now it is experiencing a revival. A museum devoted to pastila opened in Kolomna in 2009, and in Belyov a campaign is under way to restore the gravesite of Amvrosy Prokhorov, the nineteenth-century merchant whose layered pastila gained renown throughout Russia and Europe.

See also RUSSIA and GURIEV KASHA.

Stepanova, Ekaterina. "Muzei Rossii: Muzei kolomenskoj pastily." Natsional'nyi Fond Sviatogo Trifona, 4 July 2012. http://www.stfond.ru/articles.htm?id=9579&print=true (accessed 8 August 2013).

Darra Goldstein

pastillage is a malleable sweet dough made of powdered sugar, water, binding agents such as gum tragacanth or gelatin, and acid (vinegar or cream of tartar) that is used in making edible decorations.

In recipes and illustrations dating back to the seventeenth century, pastillage is presented as part of the confectioner's arsenal to impress the British and French nobility. Only the very rich could afford the expense of processed and pulverized white sugar and the artisanal expertise of dedicated pastry chefs.

The dough can be tinted with food colors, but historically it has remained a pristine white. After kneading, the dough is rolled thin and cut into shapes with a sharp knife following a paper template or with cutters. It can also be pressed into cavity molds and released. The pieces are laid flat to dry, or draped along curved objects until they hold their shape. The dough starts to crust immediately and fully hardens within 24 hours. Once dry, any rough edges are often sanded, and separate pieces are attached to one another using royal icing or sugar cooked to 320°F (160°C). See ICING and STAGES OF SUGAR SYRUP. In contemporary show work, an airbrush is often used to lend color and texture to the completed piece. The final results are sturdy and can be used as candy dishes, ornamental supports in wedding cakes, and architectural structures. See WEDDING CAKE. Today, pastillage is mostly used in competition work as a *pièce montée* for buffets.

Pastillage is not delicate enough for forming realistic sugar flowers or sculpted figurines, which are typically made of derivatives called sugar paste (in the United Kingdom and South America) or gum paste (in the United States). Nor is it used for icing cakes, for which a more emollient version exists by the names of sugar paste (United Kingdom, South Africa, and Australia) or rolled fondant (United States). See FONDANT.

See also CAKE DECORATING; CARÊME, MARIE-ANTOINE; COMPETITIONS; and TRAGACANTH.

"Royal Sugar Sculpture: 600 Years of Splendor." Bowes Museum, Barnard Castle, 2002. http://www.historicfood.com/Royal-sugar-Sculpture.htm.

Ron Ben-Israel

pastry, choux, or cream puff pastry, when baked or fried yields a crisp exterior surrounding a characteristic hollow center, ready to be filled. Made from a paste of butter, water (or milk), flour, and eggs, this workhorse in both the savory and sweet sides of the kitchen relies for its leavening on eggs and the steam created by the water in the dough. Notable for being twice cooked, once on the stovetop and then baked or fried, versions of this dough have been around at least since Roman times. Choux pastry was widely used in the Renaissance; Bartolomeo Scappi includes a recipe for it in his 1570 *Opera,* using the dough to make fritters. See FRITTERS. In pre-Revolutionary France this pastry dough was known as *pâte royale;* Republican France renamed it *pâte à choux,* since it was mainly used to make "petits choux" or cream puffs, which were seen to resemble *choux* (cabbages).

Whatever it is called, this dough is versatile. On the savory side, it is mixed with cheese to make *gougère* and with mashed potatoes to make *pommes dauphines,* which are fried. The dough is also widely used to create sweet fritters, whether Spanish *churros* or *buñuelos de viento,* Neapolitan *zeppole di San Giuseppe,* French *croustillons* (also known as *pets de nonne*), or America's "French" crullers. See FRIED DOUGH. In the French pastry repertoire, baked versions of the dough result in cream puffs, éclairs, miniature swan-shaped pastries, Gâteau St. Honoré, and Paris-Brest, among other configurations. For these particular sweets, the dough is variously shaped, baked, and finally filled.

McGee, Harold. *On Food and Cooking.* New York: Scribner, 1984.

Robert Wemischner

pastry, puff, is a dough made by layering a flour–water paste with butter, resulting in very thin layers that "puff" up when baked into delicate layers or leaves; both the French *pâte feuilletée* and Italian *pasta sfogliata* derive from the word "leaf." Bakers have figured out two ways to do this. In a technique documented in medieval Arab sources, dough smeared with liquid fat is shaped into a cylinder and then rolled thin. This technique was certainly used in medieval and early modern Spain and is still used to make Neapolitan *sfogliatelle.* The origin of the French technique, in which the flour–water paste is repeatedly folded around solid butter, rolled out, and refolded, is much more controversial. According to one story, a French pastry cook's apprentice named Claudius Gele invented puff pastry in 1645, inspired by the diet of flour, butter, and water that his sick father was ordered to follow. An even more improbable tale ascribes that same discovery to the baroque French painter Claude Lorrain. Whether this technique was invented independently in France or developed out of the Arabic approach is difficult to verify. There is mention of a *gâteau feuillé* as early as 1311, although what this pastry actually was is pure conjecture.

Whatever its origins, the idea of layering or laminating fat, most commonly butter, into a dough of flour and water certainly gained favor in Europe, from Spain to France to Italy and beyond, and has become a staple of the pastry kitchen throughout the region. Puff pastry is considered the consummate example of the pastry maker's art, requiring precision, patience, and time. See LAMINATED DOUGHS.

Ever since La Varenne's *Pastissier françois* (1653) included the first printed recipe for *pâte feuilletée,*

Risolles aux poires—pear jam enclosed in light envelopes of puff pastry—are a specialty of France's Savoie and Haute-Savoie regions. PHOTOGRAPH BY MARC LE PRINCE the basic method for making the dough has remained largely the same. In general, the weight of flour and fat is equal. The flour is mixed with water and often a small amount of fat into a smooth, elastic dough called the *détrempe* (from the French word *tremper*, meaning "to dip or soak," alluding to the process of using one's fingers or hand to combine the dough and water). This dough is set aside to rest under refrigeration so that it will be easy to roll during its multiple layering, known as the lamination process. Then the laminating fat is worked until it is malleable but not greasy and shaped into a thin sheet, sized to fit within the détrempe when it is rolled out.

The process of rolling out the dough to enclose the butter, known as *beurrage*, may be done in one of four ways. In the first method, the dough is rolled into a symmetrical four-petaled clover shape with the center left a bit thicker than the four "petals." The butter is then placed into the center of this "flower" and the petals are folded over the center to enclose it. The second method involves rolling the détrempe into a rectangle three times as long as it is wide. The dough is visually divided into thirds, with the butter placed on the middle third. The unbuttered dough to the left and right of the buttered third is then folded over the butter to enclose it. In the third method, the dough is rolled out to a rectangle, and one half of it is covered with the butter layer. The unbuttered half is then folded over the buttered half, and the seams are sealed. The final method, called *pâte feuilletée renversée* (or *inversée*; reverse or inverse puff pastry), is the opposite of the three previous methods. It calls for placing the butter packet on the outside of the dough to enclose it.

No matter which method is used, the dough is then rolled out with long strokes, using even pressure to ensure that the butter and dough are flattened to equal thicknesses. This rolling and folding process is known in French as the *tourage*. The resulting rectangle is then folded in one of two ways. A simple fold has three dough layers enclosing two layers of butter; the process of rolling and folding is repeated a total of six times. The four-layered book fold also encloses two layers of butter, but the rolling and folding are repeated only four times. In both cases, the dough is chilled well between each "turn" to allow the butter to solidify and the gluten in the dough to relax.

"Rough" or "quick" puff paste, arguably a variant of flaky pie pastry, involves a simpler process in which butter, cold but still malleable, is cut into large pieces and mixed directly with the flour, ice water, and a bit of salt. The resulting dough is then patted into a rectangle on a floured surface with firm, steady strokes of the rolling pin before being rolled out, folded, and chilled. This process is repeated three times, with the dough refrigerated after each rolling. The finished dough yields less distinct individuation of layers and only a moderate amount of inflation during baking.

Puff pastry has many uses, both savory and sweet. It can be rolled around a filling, as in Beef Wellington or salmon coulibiac, or form the base for numerous tarts and tartlets. Perhaps the best-known use of puff pastry is in the classic mille-feuille (thousand-layered pastry) or Napoleon, for which the dough is rolled into rectangles and, after baking, cut and layered with pastry cream; the top layer is traditionally coated with fondant. See FONDANT. The pastry shell known as vol-au-vent, containing savory and often creamy fillings, is another common use for the dough. Puff pastry also forms the basis for smaller pastries such as *chaussons* (turnovers usually filled with cooked fruit), *sacristains* (rectangular strips of dough encrusted with sugar and almonds), *allumettes* ("matchsticks"—thin strips of dough often coated with fondant), and palmiers (palm-leaf shaped cookies, sugar-coated and caramelized).

When properly made, puff pastry is light and airy, boasting impossibly thin, fragile, melt-in-the mouth layers, a miracle of pastry engineering based on a mere handful of ingredients.

See also FRANCE; PASTRY, CHOUX; and PIE DOUGH.

Bertinet, Richard. *Pastry*. San Francisco: Chronicle, 2013.
Gisslen, Wayne. *Professional Baking*. 6th ed. Hoboken, N.J.: Wiley, 2013.
Perry, Charles. "Puff Paste Is Spanish." *Petits Propos Culinaires* 17 (June 1984): 57–62.
Pfeiffer, Jacquy. *The Art of French Pastry*. New York: Knopf, 2013.

Robert Wemischner

A **pastry chef** is the person responsible for designing the dessert menu in a restaurant, hotel, or pastry shop. The pastry chef typically works in consultation with the chef in charge of the savory side of the kitchen to ensure harmony in the meal from start to finish. Depending on the size of the establishment, pastry chefs might work on their own or with a team, which can vary in size from one other

In this engraving from around 1690, called "Costume for a Pastry Cook," a pastry chef is fantastically outfitted in the tools and creations of his trade. It was published by Gerard Valck, a Dutchman better known for his cartographic publications. PRIVATE COLLECTION / THE STAPLETON COLLECTION / BRIDGEMAN IMAGES

person to dozens of employees in a hotel. When a restaurant cannot afford to employ a full-time pastry chef, one might be asked to consult and create a dessert menu that a more junior cook will execute, or the chef-owner might take on that responsibility. Because not all customers order desserts, whether for dietary or financial reasons, the pastry kitchen is often an area of the restaurant where budgets are trimmed.

Many restaurants, including high-volume operations, do not employ pastry chefs but instead rely on manufactured desserts. Some of these might be custom-made for a specific restaurant, or the establishment can choose from a large selection of standard offerings. Some independent restaurants have neither the need nor the budget for a pastry chef; these also tend to rely on consulting pastry chefs, who create a dessert menu that can be executed by an existing employee. The consultants might come in several times a year to give the menu seasonal tweaks or make other adjustments. Fine-dining restaurants, especially those with a prix fixe tasting menu that includes desserts, are more likely to have a named pastry chef whose reputation serves to attract diners.

Restaurant pastry chefs rarely create large-scale desserts, other than the occasional wedding or birthday cake and, depending on trends, full pies or cakes from which slices are served to diners. They focus instead on plated desserts, which are created and served in individual portions. See PLATED DESSERTS. These desserts typically comprise multiple components, such as a cake, tart, or similar item with a smooth filling or topping like custard or pastry cream; an ice cream, sorbet, or other frozen or iced element; and a textural component like meringue, caramel shards, or crumbly freeze-dried fruit bits. In hotels, pastry chefs can handle large banquets, parties, and conferences and thus often create showpieces for display, along with a large variety of desserts that can be kept at room temperature on a buffet table for a couple of hours and serve hundreds of people, something that is harder to achieve with frozen or plated desserts. Verrines—layered desserts served in glasses or cups—are popular in high-production settings. See VERRINE.

Pastry chefs in pastry shops handle a different type of high-output production, focusing often on items such as macarons, éclairs, and other individually sized pastries, along with cakes and tarts one might purchase for a dinner party, and viennoiseries such as kouign-amann and croissants. In order to stand out in an increasingly competitive marketplace, many pastry chefs develop specialties that can attract media and consumer attention.

The first celebrity pastry chef is also one of the most celebrated figures of modern cookery. Marie-Antoine Carême was born in Paris in 1783 and died in 1833 after authoring such books as *Le Pâtissier royal parisien, Le Pâtissier pittoresque,* and *L'art de la cuisine française au 19-ème siècle.* See CARÊME, MARIE-ANTOINE. Sculptural showpieces, a Carême trademark, are still a skill pastry chefs must master in competitions (even if restaurant pastry chefs, other than those in hotels, rarely find time to compete). See COMPETITIONS and SUGAR SCULPTURE. Today, some modernist pastry techniques have evolved from classic French ones. In particular, Albert Adrià of elBulli in Spain developed a large range of new practices, such as making spherified purées and edible landscapes. Other technologies, including the use of liquid nitrogen, have allowed for ice cream made à la minute or containing more alcohol than is possible with a normal freezer. See SUGAR IN EXPERIMENTAL CUISINE. Pastry chefs have taken more liberties with their menus to reflect seasonality and their own flavor preferences, resulting in a greater diversity of desserts. However, despite these innovations, typical French techniques and dessert components, from doughs to pastry creams to cakes, remain the foundation of dessert menus and training curricula around the world.

Because pastry chefs often toil in a windowless basement, particularly in large cities, once they reach a certain level of fame working for someone else, their careers generally become less linear than those of savory chefs. For a time some opened dessert-centric restaurants, but that trend seems to have peaked in the mid-2000s. Pastry chefs who can capitalize on visibility from their work in high-profile restaurants can move into product development, consulting, or the creation of more traditional pastry or ice cream shops. They can also often parlay their fame into cookbook contracts and television appearances.

As pastry chefs have gained more attention from media and consumers throughout the United States, they have been asking for more official recognition in the form of awards, like those bestowed by the James Beard Foundation or *Food & Wine* magazine. As of 2014, however, the James Beard Foundation still only granted one award in this area, for best pastry chef in the country.

See also CROISSANT; DESSERT; DESSERTS, CHILLED; DESSERTS, FROZEN; ICE CREAM MAKERS; MACARONS; and PASTRY, PUFF.

Montagne, Prosper. *Larousse Gastronomique.* Rev. ed. New York: Clarkson Potter, 2001.

Poulain, Jean-Pierre, and Edmond Neirinek. *Histoire de la cuisine et des cuisiniers.* Paris: Éditions LT Jacques Lanore, 2004.

Anne E. McBride

pastry schools in the United States assumed their current form during the second half of the twentieth century as the result of a unique confluence of governmental and cultural factors. Today, bakers and pastry chefs commonly learn their craft through on-the-job training, apprenticeships, and culinary schools. Although certificates and degrees are not required to work in the industry, a formal culinary education has become the preferred method for jump-starting or advancing a culinary career.

Early cooking schools catered primarily to upper-class women who studied for social and domestic prowess, as opposed to job preparation. In England,

Edward Kidder operated one of the first cooking schools to include mostly baked goods during the early to mid-1700s. By the late 1700s, Elizabeth Goodfellow in Philadelphia had established a similar program in her city bakeshop for well-heeled ladies. Eliza Leslie, the heralded author of books on cookery and etiquette in the 1800s, was one of Goodfellow's more accomplished pupils. In the larger American port cities, cooking schools were not uncommon by the nineteenth century. Already in the mid-1800s, French chef Pierre Blot had established the New York Cooking Academy, which offered separate classes for upper-class women, domestic servants, and professional cooks. In London in the late 1800s, Agnes Marshall, the acclaimed nineteenth-century English ice cream maker and culinary writer, frequently lectured on cookery and frozen desserts. See MARSHALL, AGNES BERTHA.

By the end of the nineteenth century, the United States had established land-grant colleges that provided an educational outlet for women in the form of home economics. While men learned agricultural and mechanical skills at these colleges, many women chose domestic science as a route for professional and educational fulfillment. The Boston Cooking School (of Fannie Farmer fame), New York Cooking School, and Philadelphia Cooking School continued the popularity of home economics and afforded women a new avenue for success in a growing profession. See FARMER, FANNIE.

Baking and pastry instruction in an academic setting for career preparation is a modern phenomenon. Luxury hotels had already developed training centers for their staff, including cooks and bakers, in the early twentieth century. The Smith-Hughes Act of 1917 provided U.S. federal funds for vocational training, and by 1927 the Frank Wiggins Trade School in Los Angeles offered what is considered the first professional culinary training program, derived from its home economics program. In Chicago, the School for Professional Cookery (Washburne School), another early culinary program, began in 1938. Before World War II, only eight American culinary vocational programs existed. After the war, the newly passed GI Bill included provisions for assisting veterans with tuition costs, thereby adding additional federal funding to higher education. In 1947 the Culinary Institute of America (CIA) opened the first culinary program in a higher education setting. It was customary for these early cooking programs to include the basics of baking and pastry as a component of the culinary curriculum. The CIA was among the first colleges to pioneer standalone 15- and 30-week baking programs in the early 1970s.

In Europe, bakers traditionally comprised a separate guild from pastry makers. See GUILDS. Cooks belonged to another occupation entirely. In American higher education, baking and pastry arts merged into a single academic field as cooking schools proliferated and specialized in the 1980s and 1990s. The first certificate and degree programs in baking and pastry were offered by the CIA in the late 1980s, soon followed by Johnson & Wales University, California Culinary Academy, and the French Pastry School in Chicago (Washburne). The venerable Le Cordon Bleu in Paris, in operation since 1895, eventually added a separate bakery (*boulangerie*) diploma in 1998.

In 1976 the American Culinary Federation (ACF) established a formal culinary apprenticeship program, followed four years later by a baking and pastry apprenticeship. The status of chefs skyrocketed during this time, in no small part thanks to cooking shows and channels like the Food Network. Culinary and baking and pastry programs became firmly entrenched in the higher education landscape as hundreds of public and private programs began appearing in the 1980s. In 1986 the ACF established the Educational Foundation Accrediting Commission (ACFEFAC) to programmatically accredit culinary schools based on industry standards. By 1989 the ACFEFAC added separate standards to evaluate baking and pastry programs. Finally, in 1990, the U.S. Department of Education designated culinary and baking and pastry programs with their own Classification of Instructional Programs codes, used to track and report fields of study within the U.S. higher education system.

According to the National Center for Education Statistics, by the early twenty-first century, there were more than 400 higher education culinary programs in the United States, down from a high of 700 a decade earlier. Only 189 colleges and institutes, however, offer a baking and pastry certificate or degree, and the ACFEFAC accredits 80 of those programs. There are, of course, innumerable specialized professional development courses for bakers, pastry cooks, and chefs, as well as similar offerings for the hobbyist. Common courses include artisan breads, European pastries, chocolate work, confections, showpieces, wedding cakes, sugar artistry, and plated desserts. The baking and cupcake craze, bolstered by popular culture and reality TV competitions, has only increased esteem for the baking and pastry arts.

See also PASTRY CHEF.

Diamond, Becky L. *Mrs. Goodfellow: The Story of America's First Cooking School.* Yardley, Pa.: Westholme, 2012.

Shapiro, Laura. *Perfection Salad: Women and Cooking at the Turn of the Century.* New York: Farrar, Straus and Giroux, 1986.

Weir, Robin. "Marshall, Agnes Bertha (1855–1905)." In *Oxford Dictionary of National Biography.* New York: Oxford University Press, 2004.

Glenn R. Mack

pastry tools, the varied implements from spoons to ovens used in making sweets, have remained essentially the same through the years. But in many cases, technology has improved their precision. Today's well-calibrated ovens are a vast improvement over wood-fired ones that required a cook to be a keen judge of heat since they lacked any temperature control. In the past, cooks might put a piece of paper in the oven and judge the temperature by the time it took for the paper to turn brown. They timed baked goods by saying a prayer or a series of prayers. They would, no doubt, be impressed by the accuracy of today's tools and their nearly infinite variety.

Today, thermometers are accurate, reliable, and highly specialized. Oven thermometers include the cable thermometer, which can be read without opening the oven door. Point-and-shoot infrared thermometers capture the invisible infrared energy naturally emitted from all objects. When aimed and activated, the thermometer instantly scans the surface temperature of an object from up to 2 feet away. This tool is useful for taking oven temperature as well as the temperature of different areas in the refrigerator or room. Instant-read thermometers are invaluable for determining temperatures of sugar syrups and baked goods. See STAGES OF SUGAR SYRUP. They are so universal that chef's jackets are usually designed with a pocket on the sleeve to hold one. Many pastry chefs still rely on their noses and sense of timing to judge when items are done; however, electronic timers are helpful when many things are baking at the same time.

Although spoons are one of the most basic baking tools, the symbol that best represents the pastry chef is the whisk. See WHISKS AND BEATERS. Once made from a handful of twigs, wire whisks now come in an assortment of shapes and sizes and are useful for both stirring and beating mixtures. An enormous balloon whisk, 14½ inches in circumference, is more effective than a spatula for folding one mixture into another. Some pastry chefs make their own whisks for spun sugar by cutting the loops of a whisk to form a metal whisk "broom."

Mechanical stand mixers are used for heavy-duty mixing in both commercial and home kitchens. Attachments include flat-paddle beaters for general mixing and whisk beaters that whip as much air as possible into a mixture. The latter are perfect for beating egg whites or batter for sponge-type cakes. Many cooks rely on hand-held electric mixers for small tasks.

Once found only in professional kitchens, food processors are now common in home kitchens. They are indispensable for grinding nuts and chocolate, grinding sugar to a superfine consistency, making pie crust, and purééing fruit. Blenders, too, have traveled from the professional to the home baker. The hand-held immersion blender is an excellent tool for smoothly emulsifying ganache, cream sauces, and quantities too small for a stand mixer.

Scales are essential in a baker's kitchen. Most bakers prefer the metric system, which makes it easier to scale recipes or formulae up or down.

Most new inventions build on already existing products. The microwave oven, invented in 1947, is a significant exception. It is unequaled for concentrating liquids without introducing caramelization and provides the fastest method for melting chocolate. See CARAMELS.

Basics

An assortment of mixing bowls is essential for any baker. They may be made of stainless steel, earthenware, glass, or even bamboo. Glass bowls are microwavable, nonreactive, and do not retain odors. Double boilers, also known as bain-maries, may be a specialized set of two pans with the smaller one fitting over the larger, or simply a bowl set over a saucepan. They are valued for even and gentle heating in making sauces and curds and for melting chocolate.

Baking pans include round, square, rectangular, spring-form, tube, loaf, sheet, and muffin pans made

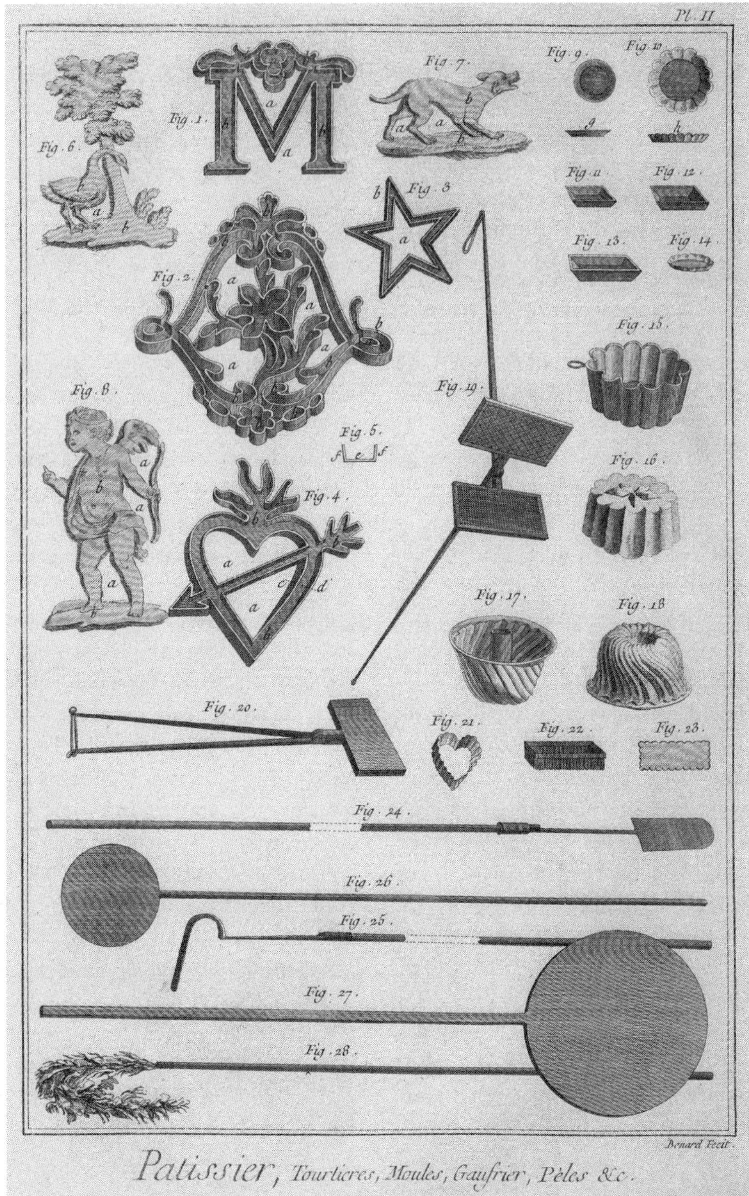

This plate from Diderot and d'Alembert's *Encyclopédie*, published between 1751 and 1772, illustrates the article "Pâtissier." Pastry tools are grouped into sections: tin molds, almond paste or biscuit cakes in the shape of figures and animals, tart dishes, a mold and a cake in the form of a Turk's cap, waffle irons, a heart-shaped tin dough-cutter, and utensils for the oven. GETTY RESEARCH LIBRARY

from a variety of materials. Rimless baking sheets or the backs of sheet pans are used for baking cookies. Pie pans, tart pans with removable bottoms, round pizza pans, flan rings, and sheet pans are all among the baker's supplies. Heavy-gauge aluminum pans with a dull finish are ideal. Dark or glass pans require baking at 25°F (−6°C) lower than the suggested temperature. Silicone is a poor conductor of heat and is therefore most effective for small pans used for cupcakes or *financiers*. See CUPCAKES and SMALL CAKES. Silicone has excellent release if cooled completely before unmolding.

Cookie bakers have a nearly infinite variety of plain and fancy cookie cutters to choose from. They also use ice cream scoops of varying sizes to dispense portion-controlled cookie dough. See COOKIE CUTTERS; COOKIE MOLDS AND STAMPS; and MOLDS, JELLY AND ICE CREAM.

Spatulas are another basic tool available in various materials and sizes. Silicone spatulas are resistant to high heat, which makes them invaluable for stirring sugar syrups, caramel, curds, and cream sauces. Their flexibility also makes them effective mixing-bowl scrapers.

A small metal spatula, straight or offset, with a narrow 4-inch blade, is one of the most often used implements in a pastry kitchen. It is perfect for leveling measuring spoons, dislodging crust from the sides of pans, frosting the sides of cakes, and making swirls in frosting. A long, narrow metal spatula is used for smoothing the tops of cakes or dislodging the bottom of a tart. A broad, inflexible grill spatula or pancake turner is convenient for lifting frosted cake layers and tarts.

Every baker has at least one rolling pin. The two most commonly used types are 20-inch-long solid silicone or wooden pins and small rolling pins, which are very useful for smaller pieces of fondant and tartlet dough. See FONDANT. When rubbed with flour, a knitted cotton rolling-pin sleeve works wonderfully to prevent sticking. (Pastry chefs use rolls of knitted cotton sleeving, available at surgical supply stores, which can be cut to exact size.)

Stainless-steel fine-mesh strainers, or sieves, are valuable for a wide range of activities from sifting flour to straining berries for purées, preserves, lemon curd, and cream sauces. The chinois is a conical sieve that is used with a pestle to help push the contents through the mesh.

Bench scrapers are the pastry chef's third hand. Metal bench scrapers are excellent for cleaning counters without scratching them. They are effective for gathering up dough, keeping the edges of dough even, and cutting dough. Because they are flexible, plastic bench scrapers are ideal for scraping a bowl or scooping up fillings. Wire racks are a necessity for cooling baked goods.

Specialized Equipment

Today's bakers, both amateur and professional, can choose from a vast array of utensils. Disposable pastry bags and plastic squeeze bottles are used for piping and decorating cakes and cookies, and for piping caramel, chocolate glaze, and purées when plating desserts. An advantage of the plastic squeeze bottle is that the contents can be kept warm by placing the bottle in a hot-water bath.

Reusable liners are useful because absolutely nothing sticks to them, making them ideal for caramel, meringues, and ladyfingers. See CARAMELS and MERINGUE. Sometimes called super-parchment or reusable parchment, they also make cleanup easy. Food service-quality Silpat, a combination of silicone and fiberglass, is not quite as nonstick as Teflon-type liners. However, it is more durable and is safe for temperatures up to 480°F (250°C), whereas the Teflon-type liner is rated as safe only up to 425°F (220°C). Parchment is ideal for lining the bottoms of cake pans. It enables the cake to release perfectly when unmolding and, if left uncoated, helps to remove the bottom crust easily for sponge cakes that will be brushed with syrup.

The Microplane grater is the most effective tool to remove the maximum amount of citrus zest quickly and easily without the bitter pith. Old-fashioned cone-shaped ridged reamers, often made of wood, efficiently extract juice from citrus fruit. Silicone brushes are best for brushing syrup onto cakes and glazes onto pastry. They are easier to clean than other brushes and are practically indestructible.

Propane torches do more than brown the top of crème brûlée. They are also used to heat the sides of a stand-mixer bowl, to warm the sides of cake pans and flan rings for perfect unmolding, and to caramelize meringue or powdered sugar on top of pies and tarts.

Baking professional-looking cakes is easier with such helpers as cake strips. Ideally made from silicone, they wrap around pans to promote evenly baked layer cakes. For large cake pans, strips can be made from aluminum foil folded around wet paper toweling.

Long-bladed serrated knives work best to cut layer cakes in half horizontally, a process called torting. See TORTE. A sturdy, heavyweight turntable is needed when frosting and decorating large tiered cakes.

Cake decorating tips and tubes help cooks make fanciful decorations on cakes. Larger tubes, referred to as pastry tubes, are used to pipe festoons of whipped cream, pastry cream, meringue, and batters such as ladyfingers and cream puffs. Cardboard rounds are invaluable for supporting cake layers. Slim gold or silver foil cake rounds, rather than corrugated rounds, are preferred, as they require less decorative piping to hide the sides.

Other helpful baking aids include silicone mats that help keep dough from sticking; large, soft silk brushes for whisking excess flour from dough without marring it; and wheels used to cut pastry and pizza.

Flour dredgers are canisters with small holes in the top. They are used to sprinkle the counter and pastry dough evenly with flour, though many pastry chefs use their hands. Hands, after all, have always been an essential baker's tool.

Krasner, Deborah. *Kitchens for Cooks: Planning Your Perfect Kitchen.* New York: Studio, 1996.

Wolf, Burt. *The New Cooks' Catalogue.* New York: Knopf, 2000.

Rose Levy Beranbaum

pavlova, a large meringue cake smothered with thick whipped cream and decorated with fresh fruits such as strawberries, kiwi, or passion fruit, exemplifies the practice of naming fashionable foods after celebrities. Meringue cakes were already circulating in North America (e.g., Foam Torte and Kiss Cake) and were known in Britain, Australia, and New Zealand when the Russian ballerina Anna Pavlova first toured Australia and New Zealand in 1926. Press reports emphasized the lightness of her dancing and the beauty of her costumes, and three food items reflecting these qualities were named "pavlova." First was a multicolored, layered jelly (appearing in the Davis Gelatine Company's recipe book in Australia in 1926 and in New Zealand in 1927). Next came small, crisp, coffee- and walnut-flavored meringues, devised by Rose Rutherford in Dunedin, New Zealand, around 1928. The third appeared in 1929, when "Festival," a contributor to a New Zealand rural magazine, named her meringue cake recipe Pavlova Cake. The ballerina's popularity helped cement the new name, and by 1935 several different pavlova recipes were known. No single foundation recipe existed from which all later versions derived. A similar process of renaming existing recipes occurred in Australia, though possibly later, since no printed recipe for pavlova has been found there that predates 1937.

By the 1950s both Australians and New Zealanders considered the pavlova their own. In 1973 a Perth chef, Bert Sachse, claimed that he had invented the recipe in 1935. Similar stories of origin were recorded from Sydney and Wellington, but none can be substantiated. Such claims led to the so-called pavlova wars, a rivalry underpinned by the creationist belief that recipes are invented. On the contrary, detailed chronological examination of recipes for meringue cakes and pavlovas demonstrates an *evolutionary* process.

Pavlovas were at first baked in two layers, later as single cakes; thickness, rather than the addition of cornstarch, predisposed them to soft centers. As with other forms of meringue, beaten egg whites and sugar are the foundation, with vinegar (or another acid) used to stabilize the foam. Cornstarch, vanilla, boiling water, and baking powder are optional extras. Although ingredients have shown only minor variations since the 1930s, mixing methods have changed significantly. Electric mixers allowed all-in-one mixing, reducing the level of skill needed. Cooks developed recipes for pavlovas to be cooked in electric frying pans and in microwave ovens. An uncooked variant was developed in New Zealand, and a rolled pavlova emerged in Australia.

From the 1950s, as afternoon teas declined, the pavlova was transformed into a special occasion dessert, invariably with the essential cream and fruit embellishment. Now internationally known, the pavlova has spread throughout the world, along with the debate over its origins.

See also MERINGUE.

Leach, Helen. *The Pavlova Story: A Slice of New Zealand's Culinary History.* Dunedin, New Zealand: Otago University Press, 2008.

Helen M. Leach

payasam is a sweet dish prepared from rice, pulses, semolina, or other starchy ingredients simmered in milk to produce puddings of varying thicknesses. It is an integral part of South Indian meals, especially feasts to mark auspicious occasions. Payasam is also used as an offering in temples and Hindu rituals, as well as being integral to traditional *thali* meals in restaurants that specialize in South Indian vegetarian meals.

In Andhra Pradesh, Tamil Nadu, and Kerala, this dish is called *payasam*; in Karnataka, *payesa*; *payesh* in Bengal; *sangom kher* in Manipur; and *kheer* or *firni* in North India. Each version of the dish uses a local variety of rice or some other regional grain. In Manipur, *sangom kher* is cooked with purple or black rice. In Bengal, payesh is prepared from a variety of short-grain rice called *atap chal* (sundried rice).

Classic versions of payasam are prepared from rice bran (*aval*) or dehydrated rice granules (*ada*). In addition, payasam is made from *semiya* (vermicelli), *sago* (semolina), and pulses, particularly moong lentils (*cheru payar*). *Kooto payasam* from mixed lentils and *nei payasam* from broken wheat are also common.

This age-old dish has been a subject of experimentation in recent times, with cooks adding fruits such as jackfruit, mango, and pineapple and vegetables like beets, carrots, red pumpkin, and bottle gourd to give the pudding a new twist. A report in the *Hindu* (6 August 2012) noted that Kerala Tourism's annual payasam festival to mark the harvest festival of Onam in Thiruvananthapuram in 2012 included both old and new payasam recipes. These recent innovations may be nothing new, however; evidence of vegetable- and fruit-based payesh recipes dates back to at least 1900. Bipradas Mukhopadhyay lists recipes of payesh prepared from potato, bottle gourd, raw mango, orange, seeds of jackfruit, sweet potato, and other foodstuffs in his book on desserts *Mistanna Pak* (1906).

In the southern state of Kerala, payasam is usually served at the end of a *sadya*, an elaborate vegetarian meal served on special occasions. It is also offered in temples across South India. At the Sabarimala Ayyappa Temple, *aravana payasam*, prepared from jaggery, ghee, and a special variety of rice called *unakkalari* (red-colored raw rice), is so popular that Ayyappa devotees can order the *prasadam* online through the courier company DTDC. Payasam and its counterparts payesh and kheer are also prepared at home for special occasions. One pan-Indian practice is a bowl of payasam/payesh/kheer cooked to celebrate a birthday or any good news. In Bengal, payesh is the first morsel of solid food given to a child during *annaprasan*, the rice-feeding ceremony. For the ceremony, the pudding is prepared from rice, milk, and sugar, although date palm jaggery (*nalen gur*) often replaces sugar during the winter months. This typically homemade dish has attracted the attention of the giant food corporations, so ready-to-make MTR Vermicelli Payasam Mix, Bambino Vermicelli Payasam Kheer Mix, and GITS Basmati Rice Kheer Mix can now be bought in any Indian supermarket.

See also INDIA.

Achaya, K. T. "Pāyasa(m), pāyesh." In *A Historical Dictionary of Indian Food*, 2d ed., p. 180. New Delhi: Oxford University Press, 2002.

Mukhopadhyay, B. *Mistanna Pak*. 2d ed. Vols. 1 and 2. Kolkata: Bengal Medical Library, 1906.

Ishita Dey

Peeps, extruded marshmallow confections marketed to coincide with American holidays, have excited a cult following for reasons likely relating to their garish colors, sweet flavorlessness, and aggressively cute and childish shapes. See MARSHMALLOWS.

Peeps are made by Just Born, a company founded in 1932 by a Russian immigrant named Sam Born, who had arrived as a candy maker in 1910 and opened a Brooklyn candy-making and retail store in 1923. In 1953 the company, by then based in Bethlehem, Pennsylvania, acquired the Rodda Candy Company, which made a line of hand-piped marshmallows in the shape of yellow chicks, marketed at Easter to fill baskets. Sam Born's son, Bob, a physicist and engineer, encouraged the mechanization of the process, and eventually the product line expanded to different shapes for different holidays, including pumpkins at Halloween, reindeer and snowmen at Christmas, hearts at Valentine's Day. Today the company claims to be "the world's largest manufacturer of novelty marshmallow treats" and to produce enough Peeps in one year to circle the globe twice.

The Peeps' mute, fixed expressions, flexibility, and curious properties—they can be cut with scissors, stacked and used as craft materials, and inflated in microwave ovens, leading to filmed "jousting contests" people post in online forums—have made Peeps a subject of fascination that has little to do with actually eating them. Scientists have tried to dissolve them in acetone and sulfuric acid. Bloggers leave them out for months and years to look for mold or signs of spoilage (in vain; the marshmallow hardens). The candies made the switch to ironic pop culture commentary in a way that other stolid mass-produced brands did not.

Some people actually enjoy eating them. The fine coating of sugar provides a pleasing contrast to the interior, which is drier and firmer than most marshmallows. Even when Millennial irony and artisan interest have shifted focus, Peeps are likely to march on, as imperturbable as they are indestructible.

Magner, Mike. "The Peep: A Marshmallow Confection That Has Ascended to Easter Heaven." *National Journal Daily*, 28 March 2013.

Ohlin, Martin, and Mark Masyga. *Peeps: A Candy-Coated Tale*. New York: Harry N. Abrams, 2006.

Corby Kummer

pekmez (*petimezi* in Greek; *vincotto, sapa,* or *saba* in Italian; *dibs el inab, debess ennab,* or *debs el enab* in Arabic) is an ancient, traditional ingredient of the Mediterranean pantry. The Romans called this grape molasses *defructum*. It is made from freshly extracted grape juice that is simmered to condense to roughly one-third or one-fourth of its original volume. This lengthy process makes the dark and syrupy molasses expensive and rare, and the small quantities produced every fall disappear fast.

Until the nineteenth century, when sugar became affordable, this concentrated grape syrup was an essential sweetener throughout the Mediterranean, along with honey. It keeps practically forever, and its flavor is not just sweet but much more complex, with slightly bitter undertones due to the caramelization that occurs during the lengthy cooking.

In ancient Greece and Rome, as well as Persia and other Eastern Mediterranean countries, many types of fruit preserves were made with grape molasses; even today, quince and pears are traditionally cooked in grape molasses in parts of Greece and Turkey. See FRUIT PRESERVES. In the mountain villages of Italy's Romagna, the dark, densely flavored *savôr* is a jam of fall fruits made with the syrupy molasses from the local sangiovese grapes. *Savôr* traditionally accompanies the pungent *formaggio di fossa,* the sheep's or cow's milk cheese of the same region that ripens in special underground pits.

Italian recipes with names beginning with *mosto* or *must* indicate foods that were traditionally made with grape molasses—the poor people's sweetener of old. When sugar became affordable, it replaced the dark syrup in most recipes. Thus, the formerly *mosto*-sweetened *mustaccioli* (or *mostaccioli*), festive cookies of Napoli and other parts of Italy, are now sweetened with sugar, honey, and spices; they get their molasses-like color from cocoa powder. In Greece, however, bakeries still sell *moustokouloura,* ring-shaped cookies sweetened with grape molasses. They are brown and not particularly attractive, but their deep flavor is ample compensation for their homely appearance.

Tahin-pekmez—grape molasses mixed with sesame paste, 2 parts tahini to 1 part grape molasses—is a hearty traditional Turkish breakfast with ancient roots, also popular in Lebanon and other countries of the Middle East. Pekmez lokum (*moustoloukouma* in Greek) is a luscious, sugarless Turkish Delight made with grape molasses and walnuts or other nuts. See LOKUM. Homemade pasta is drizzled with *petimezi* on the island of Lemnos, and on neighboring Samos grape molasses sweetens *loukoumades,* traditional fried dough puffs. See FRIED DOUGH.

Small amounts of *petimezi* are used to sweeten some old Greek vinegar sauces, like the traditional *savore* of Tinos island, a pungent garlic, herb, and vinegar marinade-like sauce, similar to Spanish *escabeche,* in which fried or grilled fish was preserved in the old days.

Grape molasses dribbled over snow is said to have been the first-ever frozen dessert. Today, the syrupy pekmez is drizzled over yogurt, ice cream, or porridge to add a complex layer of sweetness. As an additional benefit, grape molasses is a naturally healthy alternative to sugar, rich in iron, potassium, and other antioxidants. No wonder chefs and bartenders throughout the world have begun experimenting with this precious old-fashioned ingredient.

See also ANCIENT WORLD; GREECE AND CYPRUS; HOLIDAY SWEETS; MIDDLE EAST; and TURKEY.

Halici, Nevin. "*Pekmez* in the Anatolian Kitchen." In *Taste: Proceedings of the 1987 Oxford Symposium on Food and Cookery,* edited by Tom Jaine, pp. 100–102. London: Prospect, 1988.

Işın, Mary. *Sherbet and Spice: The Complete Story of Turkish Sweets and Desserts*. London: I. B. Tauris, 2013.

Karababa, E., and N. D. Isikli. "*Pekmez*: A Traditional Concentrated Fruit Product." *Food Reviews International* 21, no. 4 (2005): 357–366.

Aglaia Kremezi

pennets

See HARD CANDY.

The **Pennsylvania Dutch** culture of "sweets," which includes both confectionery (*Zuckerwerk*) and pastry (*Backwerk*), represents one of the richest regional cuisines in the United States. Referred to as "Dutch" by the colonial English, a medieval term for anyone from the Rhine Valley, this group created a hybrid food culture that evolved out of three basic eighteenth-century immigrant components:

the Palatine, or *Pelzer Drittel* (which also includes German-speaking Alsatians); the Swabian, or *Schwowe Drittel* (largely derived from the German state now called Baden-Württemberg); and the *Schweizer Drittel*, or "Swiss Third," represented by the Swiss Reformed, Mennonites, and Amish. Added to this hybrid mixture are influences from larger British-American cultural patterns. The Amish, who compose about 5 percent of the total Pennsylvania Dutch population, have since the 1930s been a tourist icon for the whole culture, yet the Amish have in fact had very little influence on the overall development of sweets among the Pennsylvania Dutch.

While each group may claim culinary professionals who became leaders in the area of "sweets," it was the Swabian component that produced the most long-lasting contributions. The nonurban Plain Sects (like the Amish) devoted themselves to farming, while the Swabians became the pretzel bakers, the hotel owners and country innkeepers, and the fancy food entrepreneurs. This culinary dichotomy between town and country existed well into the 1960s, with the country Dutch eating one way and the urban Dutch eating another. Thus the discussion of sweets ultimately devolves into a barometer of class and economic status, especially since sugar was at one time a costly social dividing line.

In that respect, Pennsylvania Dutch culture was always separated when it came to sweets. Sweet foods were consumed only during holidays or festive occasions like weddings, or even more so during funeral banquets. Furthermore, confectionery was not the same as pastry, a fact well reflected in the professional confectionery books from the period. The foremost regional county towns offered a welcoming environment for emigrant confectioners and pastry bakers to set up shop and then meld their talents with local expectations, and from this process many new foods and dishes emerged. One example is George Girardey, who authored a number of cooking manuals in the 1840s. He received confectionery training in Philadelphia, and then moved to Hamilton, Ohio, where he became well known in that Pennsylvania Dutch community as the Philadelphia ice cream man.

Newspaper advertisements in the eighteenth and nineteenth centuries reveal not only a large array of imported shop goods, including even Nuremberg gingerbreads and marzipan, but also the elaborately carved molds used by central European bakers for such festive foods as paste sugar ornaments, clear toy (barley sugar) candies, springerle cookies, and even bread and pie crusts made specifically for the Pennsylvania market. See BARLEY SUGAR; COOKIE MOLDS AND STAMPS; GINGERBREAD; MARZIPAN; and SPRINGERLE. During the period of industrialization following the Civil War, several enterprising Pennsylvania Dutch confectioners reinvented themselves as "manufacturing confectioners," a term applied to firms that both sold confectionery and made the tools and utensils required by the trade. See CONFECTIONERY EQUIPMENT. For this reason, southeastern Pennsylvania became one of the primary centers of candy manufacturing in the nineteenth century, with Reading the uncontested candy capital of the Dutch Country, a reputation that lives on in Luden's Cough Drops. However, one of the most internationally famous names is Milton S. Hershey (1857–1945), a chocolate manufacturer of Mennonite ancestry who first opened his shop in Philadelphia in the 1890s, then later established a chocolate empire near Harrisburg, Pennsylvania. See HERSHEY, MILTONS and HERSHEY'S.

Candy (*Zuckerwerk*)

While the economic environment of rich Pennsylvania county towns like Reading, Lancaster, and York could support professional confectioners and a wide array of sweet goods, the targeted market was the urban middle and upper class; the situation was quite different in rural households and in general home cookery. It was common for rural Pennsylvania Dutch to buy confectionery from shops only for seasonal occasions like Christmas—marzipan and clear toy candies are prime examples—otherwise confectionery in the home was more or less based on molasses, since it was cheap when in season during cold weather. See MOLASSES.

The most popular candies still made at home are *Moschi*, a hard molasses candy containing nuts (peanut brittle is considered a type of *Moschi*), *Meerschaum* (sea foam candy), and "bellyguts," pulled molasses taffy braided to resemble the intestines of a pig. Another regional specialty is *Quitteschpeck* (quince paste), pureed quince cooked thick with sugar and cooled to form a thin sheet, which is then sliced into a variety of shapes and dipped in sugar. See FRUIT PASTES. A similar paste candy is made with pears, persimmons, and sugar, or with equal parts of cooked pureed chinquapins (wild chestnuts) and sugar. This type of homemade candy, which appeals to children, was once commonly sold in nineteenth-century cake and mead shops, often small stores run by impoverished widows who also sold a variety of cakes and cookies to support themselves. Women and children socialized in the cake and mead shops, since strong alcoholic beverages were not served.

With the advent of the home economics movement in the 1890s and a proliferation of fundraising cookbooks for churches and other community organizations, home candy making moved into higher gear. All sorts of recipes were developed to raise money for special causes, and the fall of the price of sugar brought these confections within reach of even the poorest working families. Opera Fudge became popular during this period and is still one of the trademark confections of Wertz Candies, an old-fashioned candy shop in Lebanon, Pennsylvania. See FUDGE. One of the most popular late-nineteenth-century candies still made today is known locally as "flitch candy" or "candy flitch"—mashed potatoes mixed with confectioner's sugar—in short, potato fondant. See FONDANT. It became the poor man's substitute for marzipan, to the extent that some home cooks even flavored it with almond extract.

On the northern edge of the Pennsylvania Dutch country, where rich farmlands meet the coal mining region, candy coal, or "black diamonds" (colored black and flavored with anise or licorice), became a popular local item and one of the iconic products of the former Mootz Candies of Pottsville (now Michael Mootz Candies of Wilkes-Barre). Teaberry candies are also characteristic of the northern Dutch counties, especially the area northwest of Reading and Harrisburg. The most common teaberry candy is a form of pink granulated sugar shaped like tiny pebbles and used to decorate cakes and cookies. This candy is also ground to a powder and added to cake batter to make teaberry-flavored cakes. Where teaberry candies are scarce or unavailable, country cooks take pink NECCO wintergreen lozenges, soak them overnight in milk, and use this pink milk to both flavor and color their cakes and cookies. See NECCO. Teaberry candy or the NECCO lozenges are also used to flavor teaberry ice cream, one of the most popular brands being Leiby's, produced in Tamaqua, Pennsylvania.

Finally, in the southwestern corner of the Dutch Country, especially in Bedford and Somerset Counties, where maple sugaring is a major local industry, various candies and confections based on maple sugar are gaining popularity. See MAPLE SYRUP and MAPLE SUGARING. Due to the encouragement of the Pennsylvania Association for Sustainable Agriculture, there is now an active campaign to employ local maple sugar in Pennsylvania Dutch recipes as part of an effort to enhance regional tourism.

Cakes and Pastries (*Backwerk*)

Out of the more than 1,600 distinctive dishes documented in the Pennsylvania Dutch region of the United States, a good portion consists of cakes and various types of pastries. Many of these are not found in cookbooks or in restaurants, but rather remain within the sphere of home cookery. The oldest and most traditional term for cake in Pennsylvania Dutch is *Siessbrod* ("sweet bread"), which implies that the basic dough is the same as bread, but then other ingredients (like eggs, butter, sugar or honey) are added to give it a festive character. See BREADS, SWEET.

The most universal *Siessbrod* is called *Deitscher Kuche* (Dutch Cake), the culture's equivalent of South German *Gugelhupf.* See GUGELHUPF. Dutch Cake baked in elaborate molds was made for Christmas and New Year's, and there are about 30 basic variations, depending on local custom and religious affiliation. Another yeast-raised cake is known as *Datsch* or *Datschkuche*, which was essentially a poverty dish baked down-hearth in ashes, without expensive sugar, dried fruits, saffron, or other ingredients associated with festive dishes. Heavy and dense, it served either as bread or dumpling eaten with stewed fruit or sweet gravy. Today, *Datsch* is generally baked in a *Schales* pan, a broad, shallow earthenware or metal baking dish 11 to 14 inches in diameter and about 1 inch deep.

Hutzelbrod also belongs in the *Siessbrod* category, since it consists of sweetened sourdough formed into a long "log" filled with dried fruit and nuts. The surface of the roll is ornamented with fancy strips and cutouts of dough, all of which is then glazed with honey and milk. Since these breads were usually large (sometimes four feet long), they were normally made by professional bakers who had ovens large enough to accommodate them. Like the giant gingerbreads made by Pennsylvania Dutch bakers for window displays during the holidays, *Hutzelbrod* was essentially a Christmas food. See CHRISTMAS.

Historically, the Pennsylvania Dutch could be divided along economic lines into "cake families" or "pie families," with cakes signifying a more urban and well-to-do social status. Moravian Sugar Cake (made for the Moravian Love Feast), Schwenkfelder Wedding Cake (a saffron flavored *Siessbrod),* and Weaverland Wedding Bread (a sweet flower-shaped saffron bread made among the Old Order Mennonites) are exceptions, in that they were made communally for specific religious functions. Other cakes, such as Apeas (from *pain d'épice*), were prepared at home as coffee cakes, as were hundreds of different sorts of crumb cakes, fruit-covered yeast cakes, and crossover desserts like Shoofly Cake, which began as Centennial Cake, a molasses crumb cake baked in a cake tin; it later migrated to a pie shell for more convenient eating at farmhouse tables, and it is now known as shoo-fly pie. See COFFEE CAKE; KUCHEN; and PIE.

A full inventory of Pennsylvania Dutch pastries is impossible here, especially since many of the more unusual dishes would require extensive explanation. But a few of the most popular pies are Lemon Sponge Pie, Montgomery Pie, Funny Cake, Apple Schnitz Pie, Fish Pie (a lemon filling with cookie dough crust), Strip Pie (fruit tarts with cookie dough crust and strips across the top), and various cheese pies, such as Beer Cheese Pie, with a pretzel crust. Some pies are highly localized, such as the Maple Cream Pie of Somerset and Bedford Counties.

Also highly localized are many of the cookie recipes—sugar cookies in particular. Some can be traced to specific places of invention: snickerdoodles (from *Schnecknudle*) were created in Reading, Pennsylvania; Christmas Antler Cookies come from Pottsville; Frackville Pretzels (doughnuts shaped like pretzels) originated farther north; Lebanon Rusks (yeast-raised potato dough flavored with rosewater) are from Lebanon; and Teaberry Butterfly Cookies come from the Mahantongo Valley. Universal among the Dutch are traditional Christmas gingerbreads and honey cakes (*Lebkuche*). Most recently, whoopie cakes (or whoopie pies) have entered the culture via the Big Valley Amish of Mifflin County, who introduced them from the Midwest in the late 1960s. See WHOOPIE PIE.

See also PHILADELPHIA.

Fasolt, Nancy. *Clear Toy Candy: All About the Traditional Holiday Treat with Steps for Making Your Own Candy.* Mechanicsburg, Pa.: Stackpole, 2010.

Healy, Dorothy W., ed. *Typical Pennsylvania Recipes.* Allentown, Pa.: Allentown-Bethlehem Gas Company, 1950.

Hutchinson, Ruth. *The Pennsylvania Dutch Cook Book.* New York: Harper & Brothers, 1948.

Rohn, Mrs. Mahlon. *Lancaster County Tested Cook Book.* Lancaster, Pa.: Privately published, 1912.

Shoemaker, Alfred L. *Christmas in Pennsylvania.* 50th anniv. ed. Edited by Don Yoder. Mechanicsburg, Pa.: Stackpole, 2009.

Weaver, William Woys. *Pennsylvania Dutch Country Cooking.* New York: Abbeville, 1993.

William Woys Weaver

penny candy remains common in the contemporary lexicon, even though few candies can now be bought for a penny. The term "penny candy" broadly refers to cheap, bulk, sugar-based candies usually associated with children. Over the nearly two centuries of the term's existence, relatively little has changed in its meaning.

In the United States, the origins of penny candy can be dated to 1847, when small boiled sugar sweets were pulled, crimped, colored, striped, twisted, and cut to fit the mouths of eager children. The 1847 invention of the hand-cranked lozenge candy machine by Oliver Chase in Boston made rapid mass production of boiled sugar candies possible for candy makers both large and small. Some of the dies for early candy machines resembled pennies, providing another explanation for the origin of the phrase, as the penny candies actually mimicked money in sugar form. Other dies resembled fruits, nuts, figures, animals, ships, and other objects that doubled as sugary toys for children to play with and suck on. In 1851 the first revolving steam panning cookers were imported to Philadelphia, revolutionizing the laborious process of sugar panning jujubes, gumdrops, and dragées. See PANNING. All manner of these candy-coated treats, previously unattainable by the masses, were now available in bulk at confectionery shops, usually sold by the scoop or piece and starting at a penny each. The proliferation of penny goods, as they came to be known in the nineteenth century, allowed children of various means to spend their own coins at the candy counter, while adults and the upper classes consumed fancier boxed chocolates and bonbons. See BONBONS; CHOCOLATES, BOXED; and CHOCOLATE, LUXURY. The strong distinction between the confectionery preferences of children and adults remains, despite the waning tradition of the old-fashioned candy store today.

See also CHILDREN'S CANDY.

Untermeyer, Louis. *A Century of Candymaking, 1847–1947: The Story of the Origin and Growth of New England Confectionery Company Which Parallels That of the Candy Industry in America*. Boston: Barta, 1947.

Woloson, Wendy. *Refined Tastes: Sugar, Confectionery and Consumers in Nineteenth-Century America*. Baltimore: Johns Hopkins University Press, 2002.

Ryan Berley

Persia, to use its traditional name, is the civilization that dominates the Iranian Plateau, that rugged highland that separates India from the Middle East and borders on the steppes of Central Asia. There has been culinary cross-fertilization in all directions throughout this area, but mostly it has been a matter of Persia influencing its neighbors. One reason is that Persia often dominated them politically; another is simply that, despite its huge extent and dispersed population centers, Persia has spent much of the last 2,500 years politically unified, with a wealthy royal court that could support a haute cuisine.

During the Sassanid Empire (224–651), cuisine was a sharp marker of social rank. In a short sixth-century tale that has been translated as "King Ḫusrav and His Boy" ("boy" in the sense of page or servant), the king examines a young man who wants to join his retinue by quizzing him on what is finest in 13 categories. It reads suspiciously like a handbook of gourmet trends for the social climber. Three of the categories are sweets, more or less. The main one is *rōn-khwartīg* (side dishes). Unvala, the English translator of this tale, interpreted *rōn-khwartīg* as "pastries," but several of these dishes were still being made in Baghdad three centuries later, and they were all either puddings or sweetmeats. There were marzipan-like pastes of almonds (*lōzēnag*) or walnuts (*gōzēnag*), a "coarse" or perhaps "greasy" sweet (*shaftēnag*), a snow-white sweet (*vafrēnag*), several items with illegible names, and *charb-afrōshag*, or "fat *afrōshag*." Later, in the thirteenth century, an Arab scribe wrote down a recipe for *afrūshiyya*, which was made by boiling honey with cornstarch and sesame oil.

The very finest *rōn-khwartīg*, the social climber needed to know, was *pālūdag*, a word that literally means "refined." In the later Arab cookbooks this word would refer to a pudding thickened with cornstarch, and presumably it meant the same to the Sassanids. In the sixth-century tale, *pālūdag* was flavored with apple and quince juices.

One of the two remaining categories of sweet in the tale is *hambuk*, roughly translatable as "preserved fruits." See FRUIT PRESERVES. They were probably preserved in sugar—the best, declares the young man confidently, were ginger root and a bland Indian fruit called *myrobalan*. The last category is nuts, or more precisely seeds, because it includes hemp seed and even lentils dressed with olive oil. See NUTS. The finest nut, says the young man, is hempseed fried in the fat of wild goat. Since wild animals have little fat, this looks a lot like conspicuous consumption, as does the *rōn-khwartīg* that was made with the fat of the proverbially lean gazelle. (In later centuries, the tale of Ḫusrav and the young man was later translated into Arabic, and this last sweet appears in that telling as a pudding made of milk, rice flour, and gazelle fat.)

Nuts such as coconut, acorns, and chestnuts were all eaten with sugar, and there was an "excellent sweet" consisting of dates stuffed with walnuts. See DATES. This usage shows an enduring Persian taste: centuries later, when we finally read of Persian pastries, they usually have a filling of sugar and nuts.

The Sassanids had already made contributions to sugar technology by developing a technique of refining sugar that involved boiling the crude syrup with milk in order to remove impurities. See SUGAR REFINING. The resulting refined sugar was proverbially white, and also rock-hard. Its name, *tabarzad* (struck with a hatchet), refers to the fact that sugar had to be hacked from a sugar loaf before it could be pounded to usable granules. See SUGAR. The Sassanids also invented pulled taffy (*pānīdh*).

After Muslim armies conquered Persia in 651, the Arabs speedily abandoned their traditional foods for the cuisine of the glittering Persian court. Several of the ancient Persian sweets survived in the cuisine of the Baghdad court during the eighth through tenth centuries: *lauzīnaj, jauzīnaj,* and *fālūdhaj*. See BAGHDAD and LAUZINAJ. Other sweets with Persian names were recorded in Arab cookbooks of the tenth and thirteenth centuries, and some may date from the Sassanid period as well. These include *khushkanānaj*, the probable ancestor of all Middle Eastern cookies, made by kneading dough with sesame oil and stuffing it with sugar and almonds before baking. Another cookie, *kulaijā*, was similar but was shaped in a mold.

Zulābiyā, the most influential Persian sweet of all time, has generally been described as something like the Pennsylvania Dutch funnel cake—a fritter made by dribbling batter into boiling oil, either in a lattice pattern or a free-form shape. See ZALABIYA. However, in the tenth-century book *Kitāb al-Ṭabīkh*, *zulābiyā* is described as leavened dough formed into decorative shapes before frying. In thirteenth-century Arab cookbooks we usually find the funnel cake recipe, but sometimes *zulābiyā* is made by frying a nut filling dipped in batter.

There are not many direct Persian culinary sources for the later Middle Ages, although the poet Abū Ishāq-e Hallāj (d. 1427), familiarly known as Bushaq, gives some glimpses. His nearly untranslatable poems are parodies of famous Sufi mystical poems, with all references to the Divine Beloved replaced by the names of foods. (Humorous though the effect is, Bushaq was a Sufi himself.) For instance, he mentions *yakh dar behesht*, a cornstarch-thickened sweetmeat flavored with rosewater that is still made; the name means "ice in heaven."

The earliest Persian cookbooks, both written by royal chefs, date to the sixteenth century. They include some old favorites such as *pālūda* and *zulābiyā*, as well as an interesting pastry called *qutāb*, which was in effect a large, deep-fried, semicircular samosa. The later of the two books, *Maddet ol-Hayât*, happens to include the earliest recipes for baklava. See BAKLAVA. They scarcely resemble what we know as baklava today, consisting of thin flatbreads stacked up in a pan with a sweet filling between every two layers, drenched with syrup and butter, and cooked in a pan. They would have been soggy rather than crisp, and the filling in this case was not nuts but lentils. (Lentils were included among the nuts in the story of King Ḫusrav and his page.)

Today, Persian sweets are generally eaten alone, not as part of a meal, which may explain why a relatively narrow range of sweets is made at home. They include the rice pudding *shir berenj*, which may have been adopted from India in ancient times, and two other puddings, *sholeh zard*—a softer rice pudding of Mongolian ancestry flavored with saffron—and *ferni*, a baked pudding made from rice flour. There are shortbreads that include rice (*nan-e berenji*) or chickpeas (*nan-e nokhodchi*). The very descriptively named *gusht-e fil* (elephant's ear) consists of deep-fried thin sheets of dough.

A wider variety is made by professional confectioners. *Sohān*, a specialty of the ancient city of Qom, is a sort of cross between a very buttery brittle and a somewhat crumbly fudge. Like many Persian sweets, it is flavored with saffron, rosewater, and nuts. A somewhat different version, *sohān-e asali*, is made from boiled-down honey. *Sohān-e asali* is traditional at Nouruz, the Persian New Year, which falls on the spring equinox. Sweets are prominently featured at Eid al-Fitr, the feast marking the end of the Ramadan fast, the particular favorite being *zulābiyā* (these days often spelled and pronounced *zoluūbiyā or zolbiyā*).

Many Iranian cities have their own specialties. In Isfahan, it is *gaz*, a nougat flavored with manna, the sugary substance found on tamarisk trees that have been attacked by a certain scale insect. See MANNA and NOUGAT. The sweets capital is Yazd, an ancient oasis located between the two great Iranian deserts. It is famous for *baghlāvā* (baklava) and a number of sweet nut-paste confections called *louz*—diamond-shaped confections of ground nuts, perhaps descended from the ancient *lōzēnag*. Yazdi *ghotāb* is a spherical nut-stuffed pastry, deep-fried and then glazed. There are a number of cookie-like pastries, such as the rice-based *ke'k-e yazdi*. The most elaborate specialty is *pashmak* (wool), which looks like cotton candy but is made by a technique similar to Chinese pulled noodles. Soft hot candy is stretched and folded repeatedly until it turns into a mass of threads.

This mountainous country has an ancient tradition of harvesting ice in winter and storing it in underground ice houses called *yakhchāls* to chill fruits and puddings. When the technique of producing subfreezing temperatures by adding salt was introduced from Europe in the nineteenth century, Persians began making ice cream (*bastani*), by preference flavored with saffron, cardamom, and pistachio. See ICE CREAM.

Ice has also been pressed into service for that most ancient of Iranian sweets, *pālūdag*. Now usually pronounced *fāludeh*, it is still sweetened with cornstarch but is no longer a "trembling" pudding, as Bushaq called it. A cornstarch pudding is cooked until quite firm and then sliced into vermicelli-like threads, which reside at the bottom of a glass of fruit juice or rosewater-flavored syrup, typically with ice for summer.

See also CHESTNUTS; FLOWER WATERS; FRIED DOUGH; MARZIPAN; PUDDING; SPICES; and TOFFEE.

Batmanglij, Najmieh. *Food of Life: Ancient Persian and Modern Iranian Cooking and Ceremonies*. 4th ed. Washington, D.C.: Mage, 2011.

Nasrallah, Nawal. *Annals of the Caliphs' Kitchens: Ibn Sayyār al-Warrāq's Tenth-Century Baghdadi Cookbook*. Leiden, The Netherlands: Brill, 2005. See pp. 374–432.

Unvala, J. M., trans. *Ḫusrau i kavâtân u rêtak ê, The Pahlavi Text "King Ḫusrav and His Boy."* Paris: Geithner, 1921.

Charles Perry

Perugina is an Italian chocolatier and confectionery based in Perugia (Umbria), Italy, whose most famous product is a hazelnut-filled chocolate called Baci. The company was founded in 1907, but since 1988 it has belonged to the Swiss-based multinational food and beverage company Nestlé. See NESTLÉ.

The name "Perugina" (feminine form of the adjective "Perugian") is shorthand for the company's original full name: *Società Perugina per la Fabbricazione dei Confetti* (Perugian Company for the Manufacture of Confections). This company was founded by four partners, including Francesco Buitoni, son of the founder of the Buitoni food company. In the 1920s, the Buitoni family extended its control over Perugina, with the Buitoni and Perugina companies remaining in close association until their sale in 1988 (principally to Nestlé). Both Buitoni and Perugina expanded internationally in the 1930s, first to France, and then to the United States, with further expansion after World War II.

Perugina produces a wide range of confections, including chocolate drink mixes, ice cream bars and cones, seasonal baked goods (panettone, colomba), and caramels ("Rossana"), but chocolates remain the core of the business. Of these, the Baci ("kisses") are the most popular. They are made of dark chocolate (now also of white chocolate) in which hazelnut bits and a whole hazelnut are embedded. The packaging of individual Baci is particularly distinctive and attractive: each is wrapped in blue and silver foil, beneath which is a slip of paper with a proverb or aphorism about love or friendship written on it, translated into five languages.

See also CHOCOLATE, LUXURY and ITALY.

Perugina. "La Storia." http://www.perugina.it/storia (accessed 15 December 2013).

Anthony F. Buccini

Peter, Daniel (1836–1919), created milk chocolate in 1875, an innovation that laid the groundwork for the worldwide success of the Swiss chocolate industry. A butcher's son who worked as a candle maker in Vevey, Switzerland, Peter married Fanny Cailler, the eldest daughter of François-Louis Cailler, founder of one of the first chocolate factories in Switzerland, in 1863. As the candle-making trade foundered, due to the introduction of kerosene in Switzerland, he subsequently opened his own small chocolate factory.

Daniel Peter, the inventor of milk chocolate, called his product "Gala Peter," combining his name and the Greek word for "milk." This poster from around 1900 uses a depiction of two Berber men and a camel in the desert to suggest the keeping power of Peter's chocolate. Made from Nestlé's dried milk powder, Gala Peter did not spoil. KHARBINE-TAPABOR / THE ART ARCHIVE AT ART RESOURCE, N.Y.

Other confectioners had tried to add milk to chocolate to create a smoother, sweeter blend than dark chocolate, but they had failed, because adding milk resulted in a too-liquid mix that turned rancid easily. In the early 1860s, Peter came across a new children's food that was being made from thickened milk and flour by his neighbor in Vevey, the chemist Henri Nestlé. See NESTLÉ. He came up with the idea of mixing Nestlé's dried milk product with chocolate powder and sugar, thereby overcoming the problems associated with using fresh milk. In 1875 his milk chocolate for drinking appeared, followed by chocolate for eating in the 1880s.

The addition of powdered milk enabled manufacturers to cut down on the proportion of expensive cocoa in their products, and also provided Peter with a new product with which to compete with more established chocolatiers, including Cailler, Philippe Suchard, and Charles-Amédée Kohler.

See also CHOCOLATE, POST-COLUMBIAN.

Freedman, Paul, ed. *Food: The History of Taste.* Berkeley: University of California Press, 2007.

Elizabeth Field

petit four

See SMALL CAKES.

PEZ are small candies that were invented in Vienna, Austria, in 1927, when Eduard Haas III created a breath mint made of pressed sugar and peppermint oil, which he advertised as "the mint of the noble society." Haas coined the name PEZ by combining the first, third, and eleventh letters of the German word for peppermint, *Pfefferminze*. PEZ candies were initially marketed as a product for adults, so it is not surprising that the first dispensers, which came on the market in 1949, strongly resembled cigarette lighters. In the 1950s the company continued to use scantily clad pinup girls to promote its products, but once PEZ broke into the American market in 1953, the company recognized the potential in targeting children. The PEZ girls were given a more respectable look, and the dispensers (which still resembled cigarette lighters to some extent) got character heads that pivoted back to dispense the candy. The first models sporting Mickey Mouse and Donald Duck heads appeared in 1962. Today, new dispensers hit the market every two months. PEZ is currently sold in some 80 countries around the world, with three- to eight-year-olds being the main consumer target group.

This young target group has inspired new flavors. Orange, lemon, cherry, strawberry, and raspberry have emerged as classics. Cola was introduced in the late 1990s. Passing fads produced such flavors as pineapple, watermelon, and green apple. Peppermint, the original flavor, is available once again after a long production break.

The candy's hallmark shape has not changed since 1927. They resemble small rectangular bricks, with rounded corners that facilitate removal from the molds after pressing. Another obvious feature is the elongated depression in the middle that makes them more chewable, because the typical PEZ lover always pops a handful into his or her mouth at once and immediately bites into them.

See also CANDY and CHILDREN'S CANDY.

PEZ. "History: From 1927 until Today..." http://www.pez.at/en/Company/History (accessed 3 October 2014).

Martin Hablesreiter and Sonja Stummerer

pharmacology, the study of drugs and their effects, deals with how medicine is made and how it is delivered; in short, how to sugarcoat the bitter pill. The clichés may be hard to swallow, but the metaphors are grounded in reality: sugar is commonly used in making and administering drugs, both licit and illicit.

There is more to sugarcoating than meets the eye, or even the tongue: sealing, subcoating, smoothing, coloring, and polishing are involved in the process. Perhaps people would be less inclined to take their meds if the color were irregular, so manufacturers strive to prevent mottling. Sugarcoating was proposed by a pharmacist from Chambéry named M. Calloud in 1854; the idea was to envelop medicinal substances to disguise their unpleasant taste. His recipe, perhaps inspired by a French formula for happiness (*vivre d'amour et d'eau fraîche*), consisted of flax seed, white sugar, and spring water. Later, many layers of syrups with increasing concentrations of dye were applied, a process that could take days.

A breakthrough came in 1973 with a patent for "dry edible non-toxic color lakes" of submicron-particle

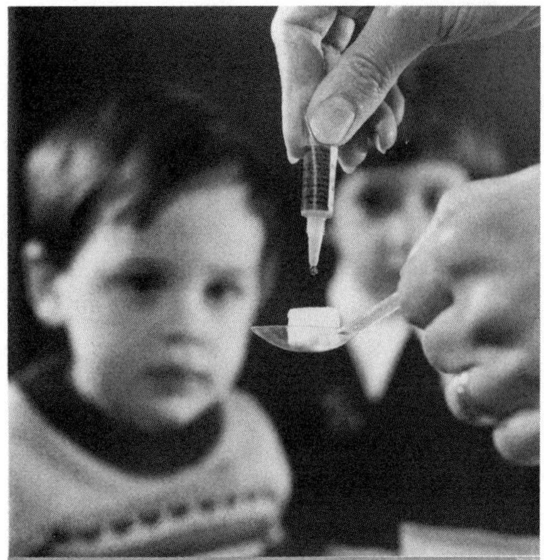

The polio vaccine is dripped onto a sugar cube for an awaiting patient, circa 1980. For well over a hundred years, sugar has helped medicine go down. WELLCOME LIBRARY, LONDON

size. Much as "color lakes" may suggest pills on a summer afternoon diving into a lake (rather like the old M&M's commercial), here "lake" refers to an insoluble dye (the kind used for food coloring). The pigment is manufactured by precipitating the dye with a binder, often aluminum oxide (Al_2O_3). Combining an aluminum lake and an opacifier dispersed in a syrup solution made it possible to reduce the number of applications of coating. Now color-matched concentrates can be added to the coating solution. Alternatively, a film-forming polymer in aqueous solution is applied to the surface of the tablet, a procedure called film coating.

Sugar is an excipient, a substance that contributes to the physical composition of the drug or aids in delivery of the active ingredient. Excipients are generally regarded as inert (having no physiological effect) and therefore safe. Occasionally, though, a difference in reaction to a generic drug versus a brand-name drug is attributable to an excipient. And excipients, even naturally occurring sugars, sometimes have adverse effects: fructose, for those who are susceptible, may cause hypoglycemia; lactose can cause diarrhea and vomiting; sucrose, of course, is infamous for its role in causing dental caries. See DENTAL CARIES.

Excipients bind ingredients together; they help the pill, once ingested, to disintegrate; and they add volume, ensuring that the pill is easy to handle and swallow and that the active ingredient is at the right concentration. Excipients also serve to protect the active ingredient from moisture and light, and, of course, to sweeten.

Sweeteners, found in most pills and syrups as well as in medicated cough drops, include sucrose, fructose, dextrose (glucose), and lactose, as well as synthetic sweeteners such as aspartame and saccharin. See ARTIFICIAL SWEETENERS; FRUCTOSE; and GLUCOSE. Sweeteners constitute as much as half the percentage by weight of typical oral medications taken by children; the percentage is even higher for some antibiotics, cough syrups, and cold medicines. Nonsugar sweeteners sweeter than sucrose (e.g., aspartame) are useful to manufacturers because less is needed, and the bulk of the pill can therefore be kept small. Nonsugar sweeteners may be recommended to patients, to avoid dental caries and reduce the risk of diabetes, when medication must be taken chronically.

In drug manufacture, sucrose is frequently combined with other ingredients to obtain a particular effect. Compressible sugar (direct compacting sugar) consists of sucrose plus a small amount of starch, maltodextrin, or invert sugar, as well as a lubricant. Compressible sugar is the filler in chewable tablets; it may also bind or sweeten. Confectioner's sugar, sucrose (at least 95 percent) mixed with finely ground cornstarch, is also used to sweeten. See SUGAR. Its virtues are rapid dissolution and fine particle size, which contributes to pill uniformity. Sugar spheres, spherical granules 200 to 2,000 microns in diameter, form the basis of many time-release capsules, known formally as multiparticulate sustained release formulations. The spheres are coated first with the drug, then with a polymer. When the pill is ingested, a bit of the drug escapes through the mesh of the polymer, and as the polymer erodes, the active ingredient continues to be released little by little.

Some pills contain sugar (plus other excipients) without the active ingredient; these are placebos, notably used in clinical drug trials as controls. "Placebo" originally meant something that would please the patient; but in pleasing the patient, the physician was often prescribing in the dark, without having first established that the medicine did any good. Thus placebos came to be associated with medical quackery. Today, sugar pills are more commonly associated with the "placebo effect," a sensation of relieved symptoms in the absence of an active drug.

Sugars in the form of complex carbohydrates attached to protein or fat molecules (glycoproteins and glycolipids, respectively) are ubiquitous in living cells. Such sugary molecules are the focus of glycobiology, a term coined in 1988 by the Oxford University biochemist Raymond Dwek. This field explores making drugs out of sugars, or sugar-containing molecules: heparin, a common anticoagulant, is one such drug. A sugar-based vaccine against *Haemophilus influenzae* type b (Hib) has nearly eliminated the meningitis, occasionally deadly, this organism causes. The sugars fucose and mannose have been used to treat rare disorders in which normal protein glycosylation (the addition of sugar to protein) is impaired. Sugars may also figure in therapies for diseases whose underlying cause is dysregulation of the inflammatory response, such as rheumatoid arthritis and Crohn's disease. Nanoparticles coated with sugar molecules may one day serve as cancer drugs that can target tumor cells.

Sugar in the form of sugar cubes has been used as a vehicle to administer drugs. Following the lethal poliomyelitis epidemics of the early 1950s, the Salk vaccine, consisting of virus particles inactivated by formaldehyde, was administered by injection. Batches of vaccine in which not all the virus had been inactivated caused a terrible outbreak of polio in 1955, and the vaccine was badly discredited. By passaging virus through cultured cells, a process called attenuation, Albert Sabin knocked out the capacity of the virus to cause disease, though it still elicited an immune response. The Sabin vaccine was not injected but, rather, dripped onto sugar cubes and, between 1964 and 1979, deliciously administered to millions of children. This vaccine additionally promoted "contact immunity," as vaccinated children spread the vaccine strains to unvaccinated children. But the vaccine strains proved unstable, occasionally causing paralysis. Eventually, the Salk vaccine was reinstated, a development that has decidedly lessened the pleasure of vaccination.

Sugar cubes for drug delivery achieved notoriety when, in the 1960s, lysergic acid diethylamide (LSD), championed by the indefatigable Timothy Leary, ushered in the psychedelic era. Sugar cubes soaked in LSD, it was claimed, would vaccinate users against the terminal boredom of the unenhanced mind. LSD, a hallucinogen, binds to serotonin receptors on the surface of certain neurons, causing the neurons to slow down and stop firing, but the exact mechanism by which it causes hallucinations remains unknown.

Another way to sweeten mind-altering drugs is to swirl them into brownie batter. See BROWNIES. The original recipe, found in *The Alice B. Toklas Cookbook* (1954), is likely to yield a fruitcake- or figgy pudding–like affair, having as ingredients black pepper, nutmeg, cinnamon, coriander, dates, figs, almonds, peanuts, butter, sugar—and, of course, *Cannabis sativa* (marijuana). The cookbook recommends that it "be eaten with care. Two pieces are quite sufficient." Today's college students (not for nothing is it called higher education) are likely, instead, to follow a traditional chocolate brownie recipe, although the most popular method of taking marijuana remains inhalation. (Sweetened marijuana is not uniquely the gift of Western culture, however, as *bhang*, a concoction of cannabis leaves, milk, sugar, and spices, is drunk in India.)

The latest version of an edible mind-altering drug is Molly-on-a-lolly. Molly, another name for Ecstasy (3,4-methyl-dioxymethamphetamine), can be obtained in powder form and sprinkled on a lollipop, which both improves its taste and alleviates the less-than-delightful side effect of jaw clenching.

Sugar has thus played on the imagination of physicians, chemists, biologists, and hippies—all of whom, in one way or another, have sweetened those substances they believed do us good.

See also MEDICINAL USES OF SUGAR; SUGAR AND HEALTH; and SUGAR CUBES.

Alper, Joseph. "Searching for Medicine's Sweet Spot." *Science* 291, no. 5512 (23 March 2001): 2338–2343.

Kumar, A., A. T. Aitas, A. G. Hunter, and D. C. Beaman. "Sweeteners, Dyes, and Other Excipients in Vitamin and Mineral Preparations." *Clinical Pediatrics* 35, no. 9 (September 1996): 443–450.

Lesney, Mark S. "More Than Just the Sugar in the Pill," *Today's Chemist at Work*, January 2001, 30–36. http://pubs.acs.org/subscribe/archive/tcaw/10/i01/html/01lesney.html (accessed 20 September 2014).

Offit, Paul A. *The Cutter Incident: How America's First Polio Vaccine Led to the Growing Vaccine Crisis.* New Haven, Conn.: Yale University Press, 2005.

Rowe, Raymond C., Paul J. Sheskey, and Sian C. Owen. *Handbook of Pharmaceutical Excipients.* 5th ed. London: Pharmaceutical Press, 2006. See pp. 744–747 and 750–753.

Shapiro, Arthur K., and Elaine Shapiro. *The Powerful Placebo: From Ancient Priest to Modern Physician.* Baltimore: Johns Hopkins University Press, 1997. See pp. 28–42.

Swarbrick, James, and James Boylan, eds. *The Encyclopedia of Pharmaceutical Technology*. 5th ed. New York: Marcel Dekker, 2002. See pp. 525–526.

Karen Pepper

Philadelphia has a long history of confectionery that is unique both in terms of the highly specialized profession that evolved there and the pervasive influence the Philadelphia trade had on American confectionery in general. From the very earliest establishment of the city, confectioners held a special place in the community of food purveyors who derived their economic success from the mercantile nature of Philadelphia's colonial trade networks. The Caribbean provided a ready source of sugar and exotic fruits. Shipping connections with Spain, Portugal, and the Mediterranean ensured a steady flow of luxury products such as fresh oranges, lemons, almonds, and syrups, while the city itself provided a niche market among the wealthy merchant class, whose lavish entertainments created a demand for European-style caterers and confectioners.

The earliest Philadelphia confectioners of record were generally of British origin, many of them women (especially Quakers), or immigrant German confectioners trained according to prevailing French notions of taste and presentation. Newspaper advertisements from the mid-eighteenth century onward listed the many enticing products of the city's confection shops, including ices, puddings, sorbets, fruit tarts, and a vast array of candies, and they point to a noted preference for *pièces montées*, ornamental table constructions made of paste sugar. See SUGAR SCULPTURE. The popularity of sugar-work decorations for Philadelphia banquet tables continued well into the nineteenth century. Furthermore, it is evident from newspaper notices that these figures were displayed in shop windows and available for rent, along with fancy furniture and table settings. Thus even urbanites of relatively modest means could contract with the shops to create lavish dinners and decor, if only for one evening.

The French Revolution and the slave rebellion in Haiti, both of which sent thousands of French-speaking refugees to Philadelphia in search of safety and a new life, also helped to establish the city as a preeminent center of American confectionery. Many well-known French cooks and confectioners took up residence in the city and quickly earned local reputations for ice creams, caramels, flavorings, chocolates, and fine pastries. It was also during the 1790s that *fromage glacé* (molded ice cream) became an integral part of city entertainments. See ICE CREAM. Molded raspberry ice creams with a center core of mocha-chocolate were given pride of place at debutante balls into the 1950s. One of the best-known French confectioneries from the nineteenth century was the firm of Henrion & Chauveau, whose chocolate caramels were unrivaled in the United States. See CARAMEL and CHOCOLATE, LUXURY.

The city's large and affluent Quaker community also took a keen interest in confectionery, since this was considered a reputable line of work, and from a business standpoint it was an extension of the many complex and interlocking relationships among Quaker merchants, Quaker banking, and the large community of Quaker farmers in the surrounding counties. Those farmers provided the city with excellent farm produce, including the high-grade cream for which Philadelphia ice cream became famous. See CREAM. Elizabeth Goodfellow (1768–1851), a confectioner who moved in and out of Quakerism through a succession of widowhoods and marriages, established one of the most influential cooking schools in the United States prior to the Civil War, though she is perhaps best remembered today for introducing lemon meringue pie into American cookery. However, the most famous American Quaker confectioner is doubtless Stephen Whitman, who in 1842 established a chocolate company that survives to this day as a division of Russell Stover Candies. The Whitman's Sampler, introduced in 1912, has become an American culinary icon. See CHOCOLATES, BOXED and CHOCOLATES, FILLED. Another Quaker firm, Croft, Wilbur & Company (founded in 1865), survives as the Wilbur Chocolate Company, now located in Lititz, Pennsylvania.

The fame of Philadelphia ice cream is largely attributed to the British-born confectioners George and Eleanor Parkinson, who established their ice cream empire in the 1820s. The grand banquet held in Philadelphia for the Marquis de Lafayette in 1824 provided the Parkinsons with an opportunity to introduce vanilla ice cream in which flecks of the vanilla beans could be observed. This proof of purity and integrity of ingredients became a permanent feature of Philadelphia-style vanilla ice cream. Their son, James Wood Parkinson (1818–1895), also became a noted confectioner, whose restaurant in a refurbished mansion was considered one of the high altars of American cuisine prior to the Civil War. Parkinson continued his fame and influence as an editor for the *Confectioners' Journal* (1874–1956), a trade publication begun in Philadelphia and now a lasting historical record of American confectionery during its early years of industrialization. See CONFECTIONERY MANUALS and PUBLICATIONS, TRADE.

Many of the leaders in mechanized confectionery were located in Philadelphia, among them the Thomas Mills Manufacturing Company (1863–1967), famous for its candy-making tools. See CONFECTIONERY EQUIPMENT. Among the manufacturing confectioners (firms that made both confections and tools) the names of Valentine Clad and George Endriss remain well known to collectors of fine molds, cookie prints, and copper utensils. See COOKIE MOLDS AND STAMPS. Candy factories abounded in nineteenth-century Philadelphia due to the ease of shipping products on the Pennsylvania Railroad. Many candies from that period still survive, including candy corn for Halloween, developed in the 1880s by the Wunderle Candy Company; Good & Plenty licorice candies, introduced in 1893 by the Quaker City Confectionery Company; and Goldberg's Peanut Chews from the 1920s—not to mention bubblegum, a creation of the Frank H. Fleer Company, which began selling the gum in 1928. See CHEWING GUM and HALLOWEEN.

Philadelphia's position as America's candy capital has declined since the 1940s, but the tradition lives on in Shane Confectionery (opened in 1863), the oldest surviving sweet shop in the United States, and still operating from the same store (now restored) in Philadelphia's Old City. See SWEET SHOPS. Furthermore, the Retail Confectioner's Association of Philadelphia has kept Philadelphia at the forefront of American confectionery by sponsoring its annual Philadelphia National Candy Gift and Gourmet Show, the uncontested trial ground for all that is new and innovative in the world of American sweets.

Confectioner's Journal (Philadelphia), 1874–1956.
Diamond, Becky. *Mrs. Goodfellow: The Story of America's First Cooking School.* Yardley, Pa.: Westholme, 2012.
Huling, Charles C. *Notes on American Confectionery.* Philadelphia: Author, 1891.
Huling, Charles C. *Revised American Candy Maker.* Philadelphia: Author, 1908.
Parkinson, Eleanor, ed. *The Complete Confectioner.* Philadelphia: Lea and Blanchard, 1844. Reissued in 1849 by her son, James Wood Parkinson.
Rorer, Sarah Tyson. *Mrs. Rorer's Home Candy Making.* Philadelphia: Arnold and Co., 1889.
Wilbur Chocolate Company. *Cooks' Tours through Wilburland.* Philadelphia: Wilbur Chocolate Co., 1912.

William Woys Weaver

The **Philippines** is an archipelago of 7,107 islands located east of the Southeast Asian mainland. More than 300 species of edible fruits and nuts are found in the country. It is customary in all three major regions—Luzon, Visayas, and Mindanao—to end a meal with a selection of locally available fruits in season. Among the most popular fruits are mango, *atis* (sugar apple), *lanzones*, bananas, and citrus fruits like *dalandan* (native orange) and *suha* (pomelo)—fruits that are meant to be enjoyed in their naturally ripened state. The tradition of dessert as the last course of a meal is more Western than Asian. In the Philippines, the native way of eating is viewed not as a progression of courses but as a display of both savory and sweet dishes that allows the diner to visually plan how to allocate "stomach space" to the meal at hand. It was only after 350 years of Spanish colonial rule, and 50 more of American that the Western notion of *postre* (the Spanish term for after-dinner sweets) and the serving of American cakes and pies for dessert finally made their way into the Filipino mindset.

Native Sweets

Despite four centuries of daily exposure to Western culinary habits and preferences, Filipinos stay true to preserving what was theirs. Native sweets have endured, but they are primarily eaten for breakfast or *merienda* (snacks in between meals). The majority of these sweets are referred to as *kakanin*, from the Tagalog word *kanin*, which means "cooked rice." Although *kakanin* are mostly rice based, using both regular and glutinous varieties, other sources of starch include roots, tubers (cassava or *ube* [purple yam]), grains like corn and millet, *saba* (cooking banana) and vegetables like *kalabasa*, a type of squash.

Although *kakanin* employ only three basic ingredients—starch, sugar, and liquid—the permutations of cooking and variations in regional styles produce an infinite number of sweet concoctions of different textures, levels of sweetness, stickiness, and artistry of presentation. Sometimes flavoring agents such as pandan (screwpine), anise, or sesame seeds are used, but the main flavors come mostly from the varietal choices of rice, root crops, and the wrapping leaves or bamboo containers that impart their own unique flavors and aroma to the *kakanin*. These sweets are usually served with grated *panocha* (solid blocks of *muscovado*), red or white sugar, and grated coconut. See SUGAR.

The use of glutinous rice, which produces "sticky cakes," originated in Laos, Thailand, and Cambodia and eventually spread to East Asian countries. Evolutionary and anthropological studies have shown that local peoples from this "glutinous rice zone" preferred this quality in their rice and therefore selected glutinous varieties for replanting and use for future generations.

According to the methods used for cooking them, there are four major categories of commonly available rice-based *kakanin*:

1. ***Suman*** consists of boiled whole-grain glutinous rice wrapped in either banana leaves or a coconut frond. In Bicol and Samar, more exotic leaves such as *hagikhik* (ti leaves) are used. Most common are *suman sa ligia*, made from rice treated with lye (which leaches the color from the banana leaf and turns the rice green) and served with *latik* (coconut caramel); and *suman sa ibos*, glutinous rice, coconut milk, and salt cooked in a tube-shaped coconut frond.
2. ***Puto*** is steamed, leavened *galapong* (soaked and ground nonglutinous rice) of different sizes and shapes, usually prepared in round molds or square pans. Most *puto* makers use natural leavening agents such as *lavadura* (a rice-based starter) or baking powder. The *galapong* can also be flavored with purple yam, pandan, or brown sugar and topped with grated cheese just before steaming. Christmas is usually celebrated by eating *puto bumbong*, made with ground *pirurutong* (a violet variety of glutinous rice), steamed in a bamboo tube, and topped with grated *panocha* and coconut. Several regions are known for their *puto*: *Putong Polo* (Bulacan), *Calasiao* (Pangasinan), *Binan* (Laguna), *Manapla* (Negros Occidental), and *cassava puto* (Sorsogon, Bicol).
3. ***Bibingka*** is a baked confection made of ground regular rice batter (*galapong*) or grated cassava mixed with eggs, coconut or evaporated milk, and sugar. The mixture is covered with a flat metal tray on which hot coals are placed in order to caramelize the top as the sweet bakes over a slow fire in a makeshift clay or concrete oven. In Luzon, *bibingka* is topped with *kesong puti* (carabao white cheese) and salted duck egg and served with grated coconut. In the Visayas, the sweets are called *bingka* and are leavened by *tuba* or coconut toddy (fermented coconut sap) and baking powder. They are usually served simply dusted with sugar.
4. ***Kalamay*** is a thick mixture of ground glutinous rice, brown or red sugar, and water or coconut milk cooked in an uncovered vat called a *kawa* or *taliasi* that rests on a pit filled with wood fire. When thick and almost solid, the mixture is formed into patties or served in coconut husks. There are many superstitions connected to making native sweets; those surrounding *kalamay* are among the best known. In Sariaya, Quezon, *kalamay* making is a traditional part of wedding rituals. A huge pit for making the sweets is dug before the wedding and lit with firewood. After the wedding, the pit must be covered immediately to prevent further use; otherwise the unfortunate bride will turn into an annoying gossip and loudmouth. In San Pablo, Laguna, one local *kakanin* maker watches out for drunks, because a drunken man getting close to her *kalamay* will render the sweet a lumpy failure, and "when you have one drunk around, he will attract more of them."

Many other types of native sweets are not rice-based. The most common are *guinataan* or root crops; sago and jackfruit simmered in coconut milk and sugar; and iced desserts such as *halo halo* ("mix mix"), *mongo con hielo* (mung beans) and *mais con hielo* (creamed corn). Traditionally served in tall parfait glasses, iced desserts have layers of beans, corn, palm seeds, agar agar, *macapuno* (also known as "coconut sport" or "mutant coconut"), and fresh fruits such as jackfruit, melons, or mangoes—all topped with shaved ice and evaporated or condensed milk. Special versions are topped with *pinipig* (pounded immature rice), ice cream, and flan.

Foreign Influences

The Spanish left a legacy of sweets, most of which are egg-yolk-based desserts, biscuits, and cookies. See SPAIN. From the 1600s to the late 1800s, egg whites were used as a binding agent in building the walls of churches and cathedrals. Local women were taught by the nuns to make egg-yolk-based classics such as flans, *yemas* (egg yolks and sugar pastry balls dipped in sugar or hard caramel), and *tocino del cielo* (a very rich flan made of egg yolks, sugar, and butter steamed in small molds in a bain-marie or water bath). See CONVENT SWEETS; EGG YOLK SWEETS; and FLAN (PUDÍM). Many bakeries were established near churches; the most famous is the 140-year-old Panaderia de Molo in Iloilo, Visayas, which still produces egg-yolk-based biscuits such as *galletas, biscocho, barquillos, hojaldres, broas,* and *rosquetes.*

American influence is expressed in the profusion of chiffon cakes, pies, and tarts adapted to local tastes by the use of native ingredients, which gave rise to such delicacies as *ube* cake, mango tart, and *buko* (young coconut) pie. See CHIFFON CAKE and PIE. Local bakeries and restaurants are quick to bring to Manila and other cities trendy baked goods or sweets from the United States, including cronuts, s'mores, cupcakes, the New York-based Momofuku Milk Bar crack pie, and Nutella soup. See CUPCAKES and S'MORES.

Recently, European baked goods such as French macarons have been featured in local food magazines and appeared on social media sites like Instagram and Facebook, and cooking classes on these delicate confections sell out quickly. See MACARONS. The media recently reported on the Philippine obsession with Trader Joe's Speculoos Cookie Butter, a peanut butter alternative made from ground Dutch and Belgian shortbread cookies and vegetable oil. See SPECULAAS. In early 2014, Eric Kayser, a Paris-based artisan baker, opened a branch of his Eric Kayser Artisan Boulanger at the Power Plant Mall in Makati; people line up not only for croissants (plain, almond, and chocolate) but also for his praline, pistachio, and lemon cream pastries and his brioche with white chocolate chips.

Because the Filipino appetite for sweets is all embracing, the home table accommodates both domestic and imported goods. However, native sweets remain the preferred comfort food, and Filipinos living both in the islands and abroad continue to crave *puto, suman,* and *bibingka.*

See also EAST ASIA.

Besa, Amy, and Romy Dorotan. *Memories of Philippine Kitchens: Stories and Recipes from Far and Near.* New York: Stewart, Tabori and Chang, 2006.

Davidson, Alan. *The Oxford Companion to Food.* Oxford: Oxford University Press, 1999.

Olsen, K. M., and M. D. Purugganan. "Molecular Evidence on the Origin and Evolution of Glutinous Rice." *Genetics* 162, no. 2 (2002): 941–950.

Amy Besa

pica is the scientific term for the craving and subsequent consumption of nonfood items. It is not an acronym, or an abbreviation, or a famous physician's last name. *Pica pica* is, in fact, the genus and species of the common magpie. Because of their attraction to shiny objects, magpies were thought to be birds with an indiscriminate appetite. (As it turns out, they don't swallow these items; they build their nests with them.) By analogy, the human condition of desiring nonfood items was given the name "pica" in the sixth century by a Byzantine physician, Aetius of Amida.

Although pica may seem to be a mere curiosity, it is actually ubiquitous. There are written descriptions dating back to the fourth century B.C.E., and archaeological evidence suggests that it may be millions of years old. Physicians, explorers, slavers, missionaries, and anthropologists have described its occurrence in almost every country. It is found with greatest frequency among pregnant women and young children, especially those living in the tropics; in some countries it is a hallmark of pregnancy.

Pica Substances

While there are many craved nonfood items, particular terms are used for the most common types of cravings. These terms combine the Greek names of specific items, such as *geo* (earth), *amylon* (starch), and *pagos* (hard objects, in this case ice), with *phagein* (to eat), thus yielding geophagy, amylophagy, and pagophagy. However, not just any type of earth (or starch or ice) will do. Just as we now know that the magpie's appetite is not indiscriminate—those nonfood items in their beaks are housing materials, not lunch—pica cravings are also very specific.

Take geophagy, for example. It is manifested differently throughout the world: Mexican women prefer adobe, women in the American South are partial to plastic baggies of white clay sold in convenience stores, and Zanzibari women excavate and bake their own clays. But around the world, texture and smell are the most important qualities of geophagic earth (and most of the other nonfoods craved). The smoothest soils (i.e., those high in clay content) are the most sought after, from the Arctic to the Amazon, and everywhere in between. The smell of earth, especially after it is dampened, is the other important criterion for soil selection.

Earth as a Delicacy

Although the lengths that people go to remove dirt from their clothes, bodies, and homes make it hard to believe, "good dirt" is an absolute delicacy the world over. For geophagists, finding earth that has the "right" smell and texture brings immense pleasure, in the same way a warm Krispy Kreme doughnut might for others. Indeed, some of the terminology used for geophagic earths is similar to that for sweets. For example, in Haiti, geophagic earth is known as *bonbons terres,* and pregnant women there relish it like candy. Along the Swahili coast, geophagic earth is described as *tamu,* meaning both "sweet" and "delicious," even though there is nothing sugary per se about the earths. Sometimes the connection is even more literal: in a Georgia hospital, a birthday cake was spotted that was made out of baked red clay, topped with butter and salt. Earth is not the only nonfood snack that is relished; hunks of raw starch (amylophagy) were once typically stocked in the snack aisle of grocery stores in the South, right next to the cookies and candy.

Strength of Cravings

To say that geophagists "eat earth" does not convey the often imperative nature of their drive. In fact, the desire for pica substances is so overwhelming that the strength of these cravings has been equated with those for tobacco, alcohol, and drugs for hundreds of years. Today, in online discussion groups about pica, people regularly use terms and phrases such as "addiction," "getting clean," and "staying off the stuff." See ADDICTION.

Compelled by these cravings, people go to extreme lengths to eat the earth that their hearts desire. They may be secretive about the whereabouts of their clay pit, walk many miles to the site with "good dirt," tussle with the cattle who are also eating "their" clay, and hide their behavior from family members.

Given this strong desire, it should be no surprise that people have a very hard time ceasing their pica behavior. Nineteenth-century descriptions of the punishment meted out to slaves who engaged in pica make it clear that even terrible physical punishment, including whippings and iron masks, was no deterrent. These days, threats from family members, admonishment from physicians, and promises to God are often of no avail.

Explanations for the Behavior

Although pica has been dismissed as pathological and aberrant for many centuries, evidence currently available suggests that pica may actually be adaptive. Experimental data indicate that the binding capacity of at least some pica substances makes them capable of shielding us from damage that would otherwise be inflicted by harmful chemicals and pathogens. The clay content may also have soothing anti-diarrheal or anti-nausea effects, similar to Kaopectate. (Indeed, Kaopectate takes its name from one species of clay, kaolin.) Furthermore, the demographic profile of those who engage in pica most frequently—pregnant women and young children living in the tropics—is also consistent with this hypothesis, since they are most biologically vulnerable.

See also SWEETNESS PREFERENCE.

Young, Sera L. "Pica in Pregnancy: New Ideas about an Old Condition." *Annual Review of Nutrition* 30 (2010): 403–422.

Young, Sera L. *Craving Earth: Understanding Pica; The Urge to Eat Clay, Starch, Ice, and Chalk.* New York: Columbia University Press, 2011.

Young, Sera L., Paul W. Sherman, Julius B. Lucks, and Gretel H. Pelto. "Why On Earth? Evaluating Hypotheses about the Physiological Functions of Human Geophagy." *Quarterly Review of Biology* 86, no. 2 (2011): 97–120.

Sera Lewise Young

pie, at its most elemental, consists of some food completely or partially enclosed in dough and baked. This simple concept has given rise to an almost infinite number of variations, including some of the most popular and iconic dishes in the Western world.

In the English language, the words for various categories of pie are first attested in the medieval period—specifically, "pie" appears in 1303, "pasty" in 1296, "flan" (as "flawn") in about 1300, and "tart" in about 1400. See FLAN (TART) and TART. The actual physical pie, however, undoubtedly predates

The American photographer Berenice Abbott was hired by the Works Progress Administration to chronicle the buildings and neighborhoods of New York. This 1936 photograph, part of her *Changing New York* project, shows an automat at 977 Eighth Avenue, where a slice of pie was delivered at the push of a button. THE MUSEUM OF THE CITY OF NEW YORK / ART RESOURCE, N.Y.

the written record by millennia. Wrapping food in dough before cooking is a very ancient and widespread practice (it is most likely that cooking on hot rocks or boiling preceded oven-baking the dish, as less fuel was needed) and probably developed simultaneously in several areas where cereal grain was the staple food. We know that the ancient Greeks and Romans enjoyed food wrapped in dough, although existing records do not contain sufficient details of ingredients or methods to be certain of the type of pastry used or the style of these "pies."

The pie as we know it today came into being in medieval Europe, where the raw materials were in abundance: forests for wood (baking requires a lot of fuel), wheat for the best pastry, and hard fats such as lard and butter (oil does not make superb pastry.) See BUTTER; FLOUR; and PIE DOUGH. An open fire is fine for boiling liquid food in pots, or for roasting large pieces of meat on spits, but it is problematic for small pieces of food, soft foods such as fruit, or dishes requiring gentle cooking, such as custards. See CUSTARD. To solve this problem, cooks turned to professional bakers' ovens, and since metal baking pans were rare, they created thick, hand-raised pastry shells called "coffins" to hold the contents. See PANS. This method of cooking is reflected in the name *bakemete* ("meat" in the generic sense of any food), used to indicate a pie of small, soft, or mixed ingredients. A fifteenth-century Bake Mete recipe (Harleian MS. 279) turns out to be a tart of pears and "gobbets of marrow" in saffron-flavored custard cooked in "fair little coffins."

The hard pastry coffins also facilitated preservation of the dish. By today's standards, pies in this pre-refrigeration era were kept for a frighteningly long time. William Salmon's *The Family Dictionary: or, houshold companion*, published in 1695, contains a recipe for a Boar Pie, which advises that, if sealed with butter, "it will, if it be not set in a very moist place, keep a whole Year." The third advantage of the hard pastry coffin was that it functioned as its own container, which, along with its storage potential, enabled pies to be sent long distances as gifts, or to be used as provisions for sea voyages.

It is commonly said that the tough, thick pastry of these coffins was "not meant to be eaten," but in an era when every grain of cereal was hard-won, and absolutely nothing was wasted, this is difficult to believe. It is likely that the well-to-do themselves did not eat 2-inch-thick hard pie-shells made solely from rye flour and water—but these crusts were surely given to those lower down in the pecking order. There is also evidence from medieval cookery books that pastry was crumbled and used to thicken liquid dishes, and that the coffins were occasionally refilled.

Gervase Markham, in his *English House-wife* (1615), was adamant that "our English Hus-wife must be skilfull in pastery, and know...what paste is fit for every meate, and how to handle and compound such pastes," and he gives general advice on a number of different types of pastry, some of which are clearly meant to be eaten. The first known explicit instructions for "short" edible pastry appear in *A Propre New Booke of Cokery* (1545), but from hints in much earlier recipe manuscripts it is apparent that pastry meant to be enjoyed as an intrinsic part of the dish was already in existence well before this date.

> To make short paest for tarte.
>
> Take fyne floure and a cursey of fayre water and a dyshe of swete butter and a lyttel saffron, and the yolckes of two egges and make it thynne and tender as ye maye.

Cookery texts from Continental Europe show a large range of types of pastry and fillings. *Le ménagier de Paris* (1393) includes "pies of turtle-doves and larks," "pies of cow and talemouse" (a cheese and egg tart), and "sugared meat tarts." Lancelot de Casteau's *Ouverture de cuisine* (Liège, 1604) gives instructions for "paste of fine flour with eggs & butter and a little water," which is clearly intended to be eaten. The first comprehensive French text devoted to the art of the pastry cook (credited to Pierre François de la Varenne), *Le pâtissier françois* (Paris, 1653), contains instructions for several types of pastry, from robust "coffin" dough made with rye flour and hot water to thin, multilayered puff pastry made with butter. See PASTRY, PUFF.

Unfortunately for the cook and the historian, there is no consistent correlation between the style and the usage of the words "pie," "tart," and "flan," even within national boundaries. In France, a flan remains a fruit- or custard-filled tart, whereas elsewhere the Spanish caramel custard is the more common meaning. See FLAN (PUDÍM). In the north of England, the word "tart" is commonly applied to the double-crust version, which is called a "pie" in the south of the country. Similarly, the unqualified word "pie" in Australia indicates a double-crust meat pie, but in the United States it just as regularly evokes a sweet, single (bottom) crust dish. To confuse the issue further, several iconic American pies are not pies at all: Boston cream pie is indisputably a cake, and whoopie pie is a type of soft cookie. See BOSTON CREAM PIE and WHOOPIE PIE.

American Pies

When the first English settlers moved to North America, they took with them, as migrants inevitably do, their own recipes and style of cooking. Just as inevitably, they found the conditions quite different from their homeland, and they had to adapt their cooking to the locally available ingredients. Their English wheat did not thrive in New England, and the settlers were quickly forced to adopt maize as their staple food. The small amount of wheat that was available in the early decades of the colonies was more economically diverted to use in pies rather than bread. This situation surely sowed the seeds of the excellent reputation of New England's pies, and of its citizens' love of pies at breakfast.

Conversely, the apple seedlings that these early folk brought to their new home thrived, and New England apple orchards proved prolific. Americans did not invent apple pie, but there is no doubt that the roots of the nation's love for it were laid down within the first decades of the seventeenth century.

Unlike many New World foods, the pumpkin was quickly adopted by Europeans familiar with other members of the gourd family, and recipes for "*pompion*" pie appear in seventeenth-century European cookery books. Amelia Simmons, the author of the first genuinely American cookbook, *American Cookery* (1796), gives two recipes for pie made with *pompkin*,

Hostess Twinkies are so famously supercharged with sugar that they were successfully used as the "Twinkie Defense" in the murder trial of San Francisco city supervisor Dan White. Apparently, these ultra-sweet snack cakes are popular with superheroes and mummies as well.

Colorful Indonesian *kue*, traditional bite-sized desserts, are often presented on a platter called *jajan pasar* (market treats) and given as gifts during Javanese holidays. PHOTO BY GUNAWAN KARTAPRANATA

Paeksŏlgi, a type of Korean steamed rice cake (*ttŏk*), represents purity and is traditionally served on a child's first birthday. The unusual yellow variety shown here is covered with powdered pumpkin. NATIONAL MUSEUM OF KOREA, SEOUL

This young man in Murshidabad, India, is expert at preparing *khejur gur*, syrup processed from the sap of the date palm. © GAUTAM PAUL 2009

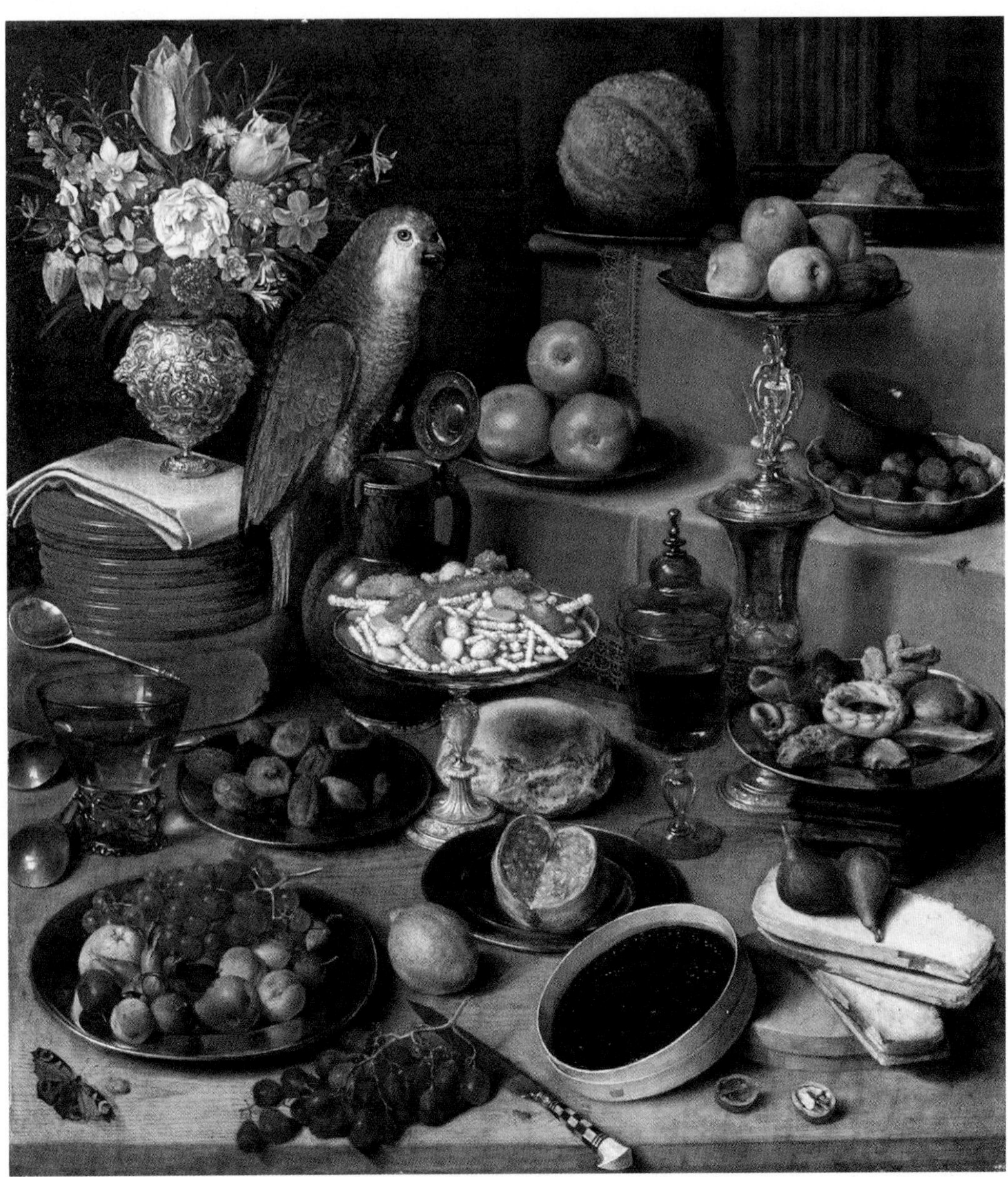

The table in German artist Georg Flegel's *Large Food Display* (ca. 1630) is resplendent with fruit, nuts, pastries, and, at the center, sweetmeats and ragged comfits in a silver compote. It conveys wealth and cultivation while also recognizing symbols of Christian faith.

Wealthy eighteenth-century patrons commissioned elegant porcelain ice cream buckets to keep their ice cream cold at the table. This bucket, made by the Sèvres Royal Manufactory in 1771, held the ice cream in a liner surrounded by ice mixed with salt. Porcelain was favored because it didn't corrode from the salt. THE NELSON-ATKINS MUSEUM OF ART

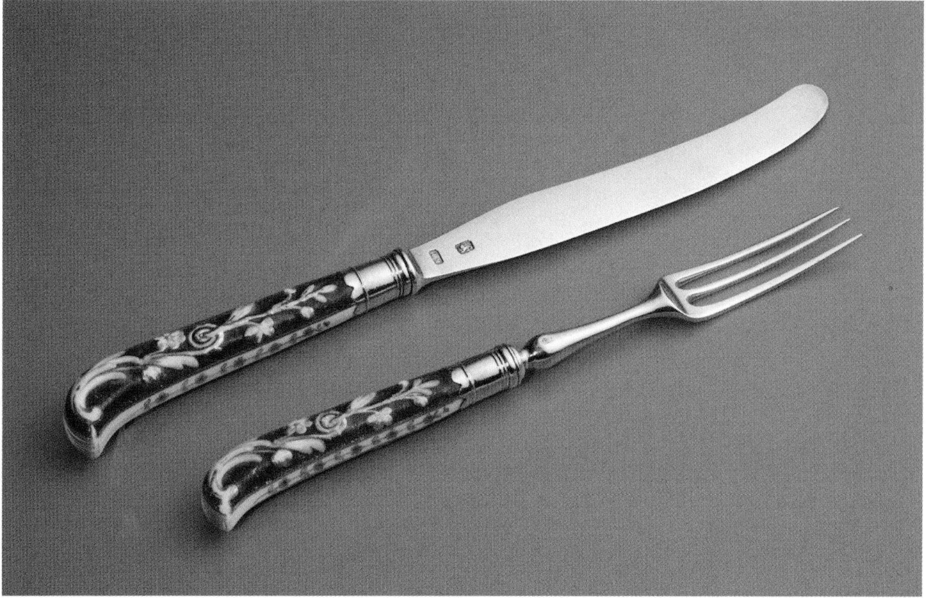

This silver gilt and porcelain dessert fork and knife come from a set of six, made in London around 1772, most likely by the silversmith Richard Parr. The knife shows the scimitar-shaped blade that was prevalent before being superseded by the straight blade. Both the blade and the tines of the fork are gilded to avoid oxidation on contact with acidic fruit. IMAGE © STERLING AND FRANCINE CLARK ART INSTITUTE, WILLIAMSTOWN, MASSACHUSETTS. PHOTO BY MICHAEL AGEE

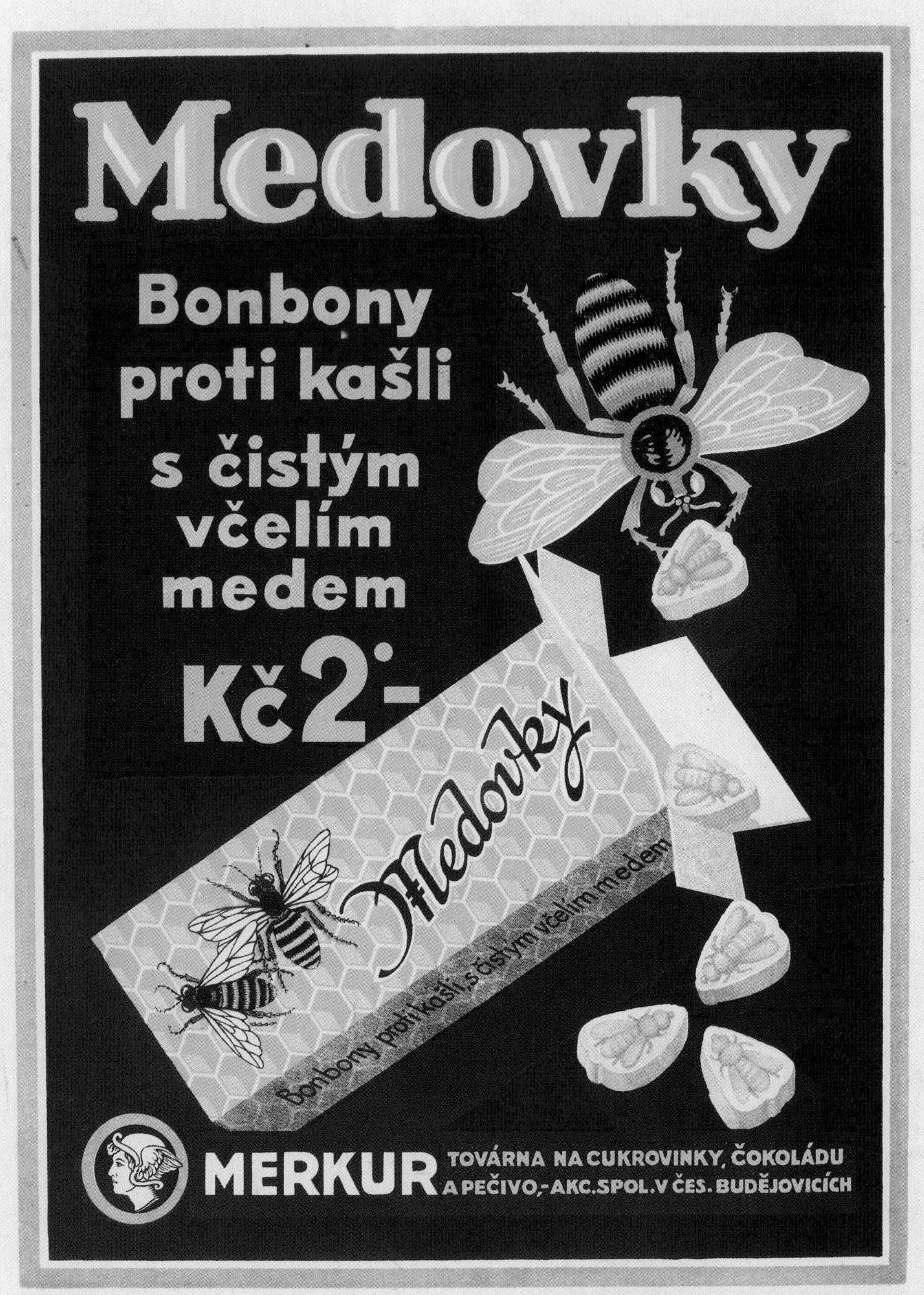

This Czech poster from around 1900 advertises flavored lozenges made with "pure bee honey." Lozenges are closely linked to the original concept of confectionery as medicine, for which materials are compounded to heal those who are sick. WELLCOME LIBRARY, LONDON

66
Une Confisseuse. Eine Zückerbacherin od. Candiferin.
1. Sucre fin de Canari. 1. Canarien Zückher. 2. Sucreries en piramide. 2. ein Aufsatz
mit allerley Candierten Sachen. 3. fruits confits. 3. eingemachtes Obst. 4. toutes sortes de
Sucreries et confitures. 4. allerley köstl: gebach ū: candiertes Zückerwerckh. 5 plusieurs cho-
ses confites. 5. allerley kleine überzogne Sachen. 6. forme de noix empoivree. 6. Pfeffer-
Nüsse 7. boulettes d'Ambre. 7. Bisam Küglen. 8. Cannelats. 8 Zimmet Mandel 9.
Pain d'Anis. 9. Anis Brod. 10. un cornet. 10. eine Gstattel oder düte
Cum Priv. Maj.
I. F. Schmit sculps.
M. Engelbrecht excud. A.V.

The French language maintains a clear distinction between sugar workers (*confiseurs*) and pastry cooks (*pâtissiers*), for whom sugar is but one ingredient among many. In this color engraving by Martin Engelbrecht from around 1735, a confectioner is festooned with bonbons and other sugary treats. BIBLIOTHEQUE DES ARTS DECORATIFS, PARIS / ARCHIVES CHARMET / BRIDGEMAN IMAGES

Frangipani (*Plumeria rubra*) is a deciduous shrub whose fragrant flowers come in shades of pink, yellow, and white. It is the namesake for frangipane, an almond-flavored pastry cream, which was originally perfumed with the blossoms' essence. PHOTO BY MINGHONG

The wonder of this berry from the West African shrub *Synsepalum dulcificum* is its miraculous ability to render sour tastes sweet. So it's no surprise that the berry's active ingredient, which binds to sweet receptors on the tongue, is called miraculin. PHOTO BY HAMALE LYMAN

Mary Curtis Ratcliff's series of decorated cakes, called *Mixed Messages*, plays on the tension between the sweet and the repressed. *Homage to Barbara Bush* (1996) pays tribute to former First Lady Barbara Bush by suggesting her shock of white hair and pearls. © MARY CURTIS RATCLIFF

Joseph Marr's sugar sculptures have an aesthetic borrowed from antiquity, but his techniques are decidedly modern. He uses a three-dimensional scanner to print a mold of his model and then fills the mold with sugar syrup and leaves it to harden. *Cherry Laura,* with its reference to sugar as a form of bondage, is from the 2011 series *Desire is a Trap*.

The hyperrealist Italian artist Roberto Bernardi turns everyday objects into compositions of luminous beauty. His 2012 oil painting *Le Due Luci* (The Two Lights) conveys lollipops' essential deliciousness and delight. COURTESY OF THE ARTIST

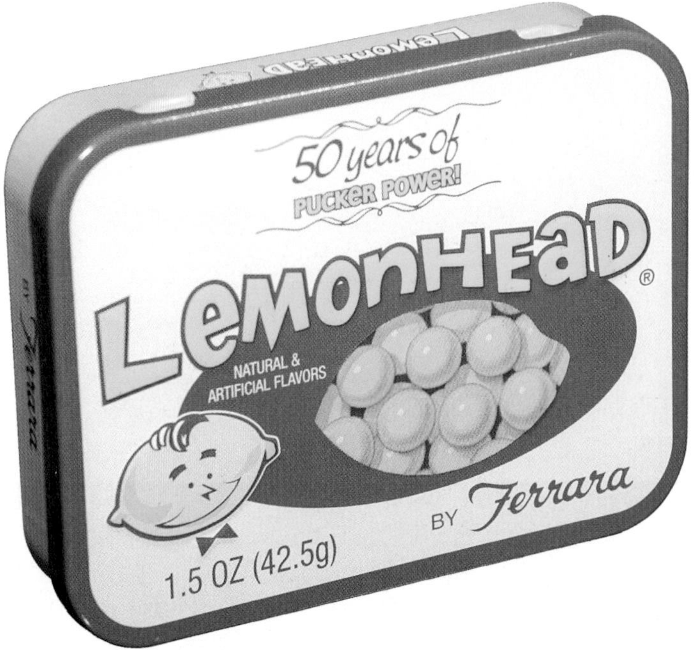

The Ferrara Candy Company was one of the first to experiment with hot and sour candies, developing the popular Red Hots in the early 1930s. Lemonheads, hard lemon candies coated in sour sugar, were introduced in 1962. This retro candy tin commemorated the 50th anniversary of the Lemonhead brand. © FERRARA CANDY COMPANY

A beloved confection of fresh milk curd and sugar syrup, rosogolla is most closely associated with the West Bengal sweets-making tradition. K. C. Das, a rosogolla maker's son, pioneered the technique of canning the sweet so that Indian expats throughout the world could enjoy it. © K. C. DAS GRANDSON PVT. LTD.

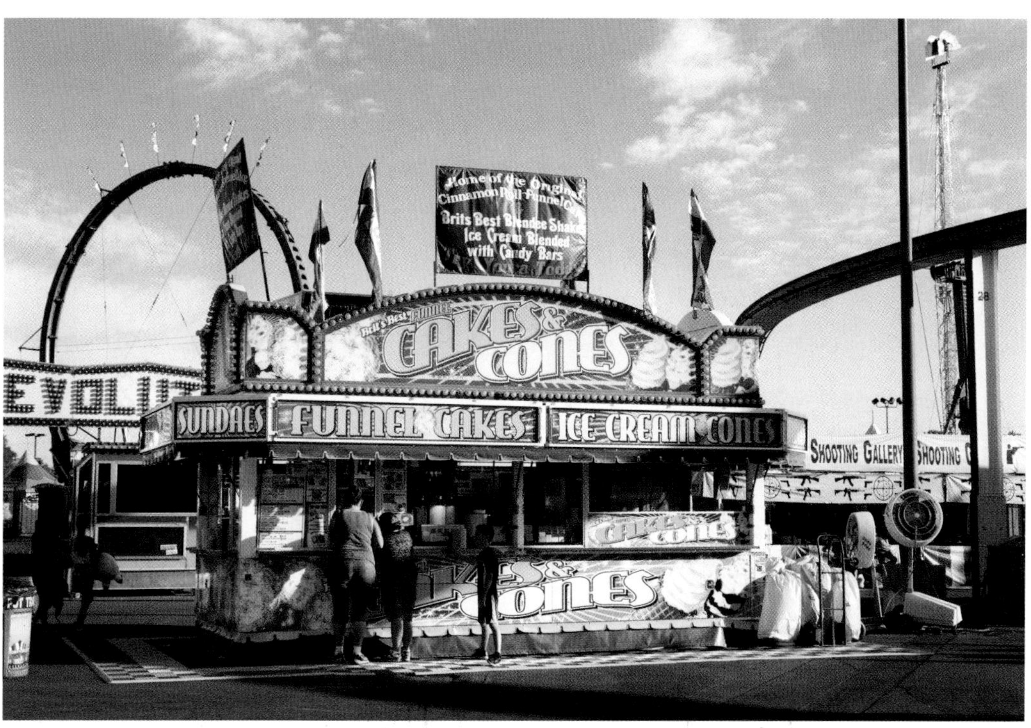

A funnel cake and ice cream cone vendor at the 2012 California State Fair in Sacramento, California. Ice cream cones were popularized in the United States at the 1904 St. Louis World's Fair. LIBRARY OF CONGRESS

The abolitionist movement in England identified sugar as the root cause of slavery and the symbol of its evils. This 1792 etching by the British caricaturist James Gillray satirizes one of his favorite targets, King George III. Abolitionists had urged a sugar boycott in 1791; here George and his wife, Charlotte, propose giving up sugar in their tea, to their daughters' dismay. © THE TRUSTEES OF THE BRITISH MUSEUM

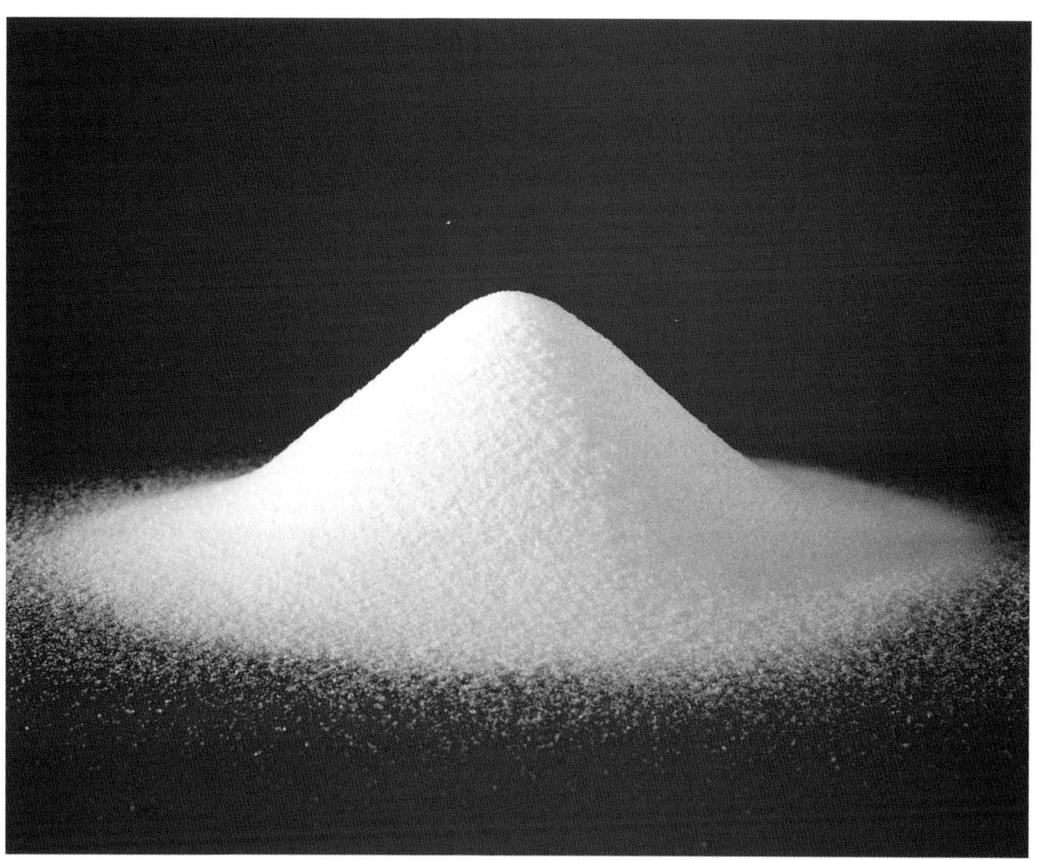

Shimon Attie's series *White Nights, Sugar Dreams* (2000) explores the relation between sugar and blood, both of which are necessary to life. But imbalance—as happens with diabetes—can be dangerous. Attie's beautiful C-prints meditate on his own illness and that of others, provoking fascination and fear.

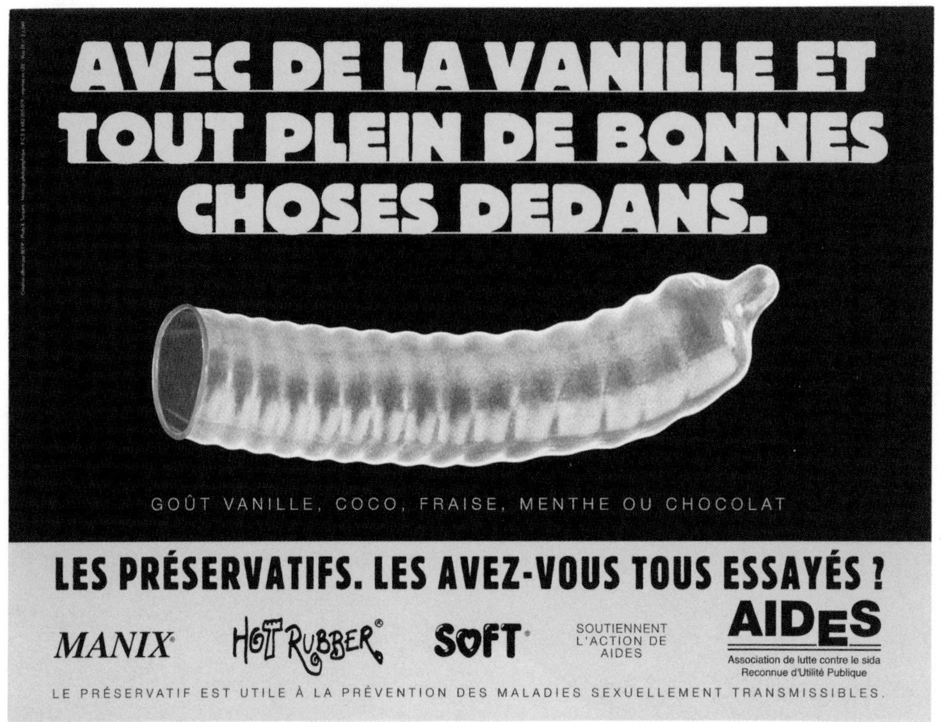

This condom advertisement by the Association de Lutte Contre le SIDA (Association for the Fight against AIDS) carries the message "With vanilla and lots of good things inside... vanilla, coconut, raspberry, mint or chocolate flavor. Condoms—have you tried them?" Color lithograph by R. Turqueti [199?]. WELLCOME LIBRARY, LONDON

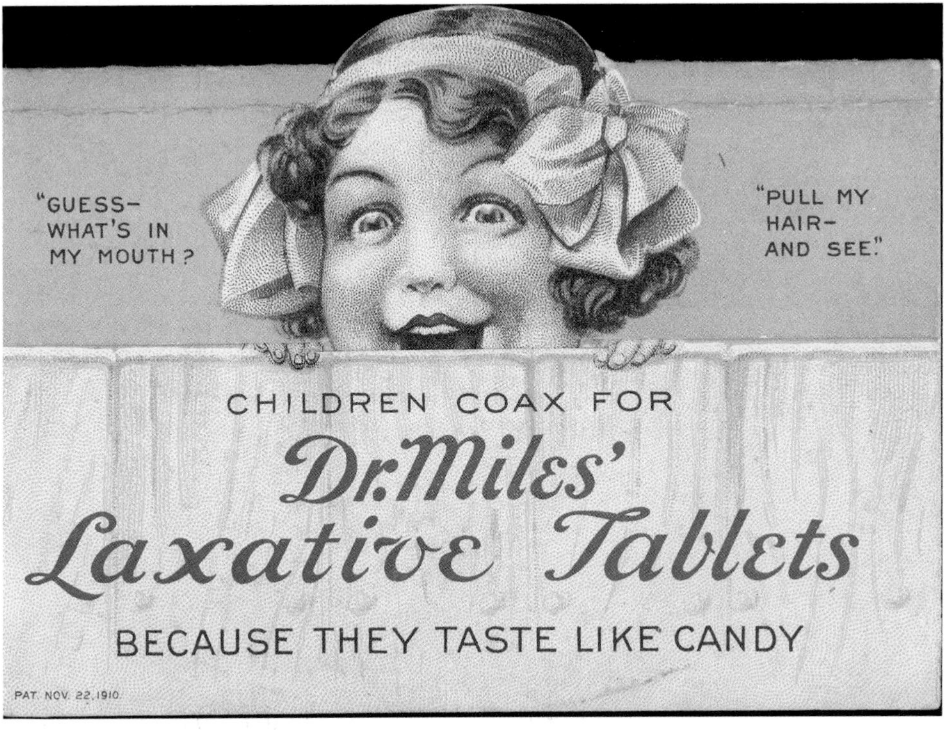

Pharmaceutical companies have long sought to sweeten bitter pills. Medicines were, and still are, marketed in candy flavors to appeal to children and grownups alike.

the second being sweetened with molasses. See MOLASSES. A similar situation existed in regard to the sweet potato (often called "Spanish potato"), which made for an easy adaptation of European pies made with root vegetables and tubers.

A huge repertoire of pies (particularly sweet pies) has developed in the United States since those early days. In addition to apple, pumpkin, and sweet potato, several others justify particular mention. Shoo-fly pie is a Pennsylvania Dutch specialty reminiscent of English treacle tart, but made instead with molasses. Its name supposedly comes from it being as attractive to flies as to humans. See PENNSYLVANIA DUTCH. Pecans are indigenous to North America and are similar in appearance to European walnuts, so it is perhaps surprising that recipes for pecan pie do not appear until the late nineteenth century. See NUTS. Key lime pie owes its origins to the invention of condensed milk in the United States in 1856—an invention that must have been a godsend to cooks in pre-refrigeration days in the dairy-poor (but lime-rich) Florida Keys, who adapted the cream pie concept to the new product. Lemon meringue pie is another example of a dish evolving from an earlier concept. Lemon-flavored cream and custard puddings and pies existed in medieval times, and meringue was perfected (probably in France) in the seventeenth century. See MERINGUE. The same process applies to the Southern favorite, chess pie, which has similar features to seventeenth-century "cheesecakes without cheese." See CHEESECAKE. Chilled chiffon or refrigerator pies seem to be particularly popular in the United States, and grasshopper pie—a mint and chocolate concoction with a cookie crust—is a relatively recent addition to the scene, appearing in the 1950s.

The modern pie comprises a vast number of styles, including open-face pies, which lack a top crust; double-crust pies, with a top crust; lattice-topped pies, with dough strips woven across the top; and deep-dish pies, lacking a bottom crust but always with some type of upper crust. Pies made with a dough casing can also be "raised" or freestanding (without a pie plate) or shaped as portable pockets, baked or fried, and eaten out of hand, in which case they are regionally known as "hand pies." Pies with a bottom crumb crust are most often used for unbaked fillings such as puddings, chiffon, Bavarian cream, or ice cream. See DESSERTS, CHILLED and DESSERTS, FROZEN. Pies with a crumb (streusel) topping may have a crumb or pastry bottom crust with either a sweet or savory filling; these are related to crumb-topped fruit crisps and shoo-fly pie, while cobblers, slumps, grunts, and spoon-pies are in the same family but are usually topped with biscuit dough or dumplings. See FRUIT DESSERTS, BAKED and STREUSEL.

The love of pies has been incorporated into the American national identity. The phrase "as American as apple pie," first cited in the 1920s, is now in common usage, and American soldiers fought for "Mom and apple pie" during World War II. It is also indisputable that pies play important roles in the nation's cultural events and celebrations. There are regional preferences and specialties, of course, but the whole nation appears to go pie-crazy at Thanksgiving. Clementine Paddleford, in her book *How America Eats* (1960), wrote:

> Tell me where your grandmother came from and I can tell you how many kinds of pie you serve for Thanksgiving. In the Midwest two is the usual, mince and pumpkin.... Down East it's a threesome, cranberry, mince and pumpkin, a sliver of each, and sometimes, harking back to the old days around Boston, four kinds of pie were traditional for this feast occasion—mince, cranberry, pumpkin and a kind called Marlborough, a glorification of everyday apple.

Many states have nominated a pie as an "official" state food, including Delaware (peach pie), Florida (Key lime pie), Indiana (sugar cream pie), Maine (blueberry pie), Oklahoma (pecan pie), and Louisiana, which alone has chosen a savory pie—the Natchitoches meat pie. See STATE DESSERTS. With such a volume of popular and governmental support, it seems likely that America's love affair with the pie is set to continue indefinitely.

Clarkson, Janet. *Pie: A Global History*. London: Reaktion, 2009.

Hess, John H. and Karen. *The Taste of America*. Grossman, 1977.

Hieatt, Constance B., Brenda Hosington, and Sharon Butler. *Pleyn Delit: Medieval Cookery for Modern Cooks*. Toronto: University of Toronto Press, 1996.

Simmons, Amelia. *American Cookery*. 1796. Facsimile ed. Bedford, Mass.: Applewood, 1996.

Smith, Andrew, ed. *Oxford Encyclopedia of Food and Drink in America*. 2d ed. New York: Oxford University Press, 2012.

Willan, Anne, with Mark Cherniavsky and Kyri Claflin. *The Cookbook Library*. Berkeley: University of California Press, 2012.

Janet Clarkson and Susan G. Purdy

pie dough, a simple blend of flour, fat, flavoring, and liquid, is magically transformed by heat into a crust with deliciously varied qualities: buttery, tender, and flaky (for fresh fruit pies); tender and crisp (for open-face tarts); tender but sturdy (for soft custard pies); or tender and crisp but moisture-proof (for hand-held juicy pies or turnovers). The type of fat in the dough is a determining factor. Many American bakers today prefer to use a blend of fats, namely butter plus a small amount of shortening, which bakes into a rich, buttery crust that is tender, "short," and also exceptionally flaky—the latter a characteristic uniquely important to American bakers.

Flakiness is created when ice-cold fat is lightly mixed with the flour and salt, then pinched into large flakes; when this dough is baked in a sufficiently hot oven, steam quickly forms, separating the starch layers and pushing up the air pockets left by melted fat so that the heat can set the starch into flakes. By contrast, the classic French dough *pâte brisée,* made with virtually the same ingredients (little or no sugar but always containing all-butter), has a higher fat-to-flour ratio and is mixed differently: butter is worked into the dough slightly more, by a technique called *fraisage,* by which bits of dough are pushed together with the heel of the hand on the countertop. *Pâte brisée* has a buttery flavor and toothsome texture but is somewhat less obviously flaky.

American pie dough descended from the British model and originally used lard and suet as fats, but over the past nearly 200 years, tastes and recipes have changed. In 1911, Crisco, a solid all-vegetable shortening, was introduced to the American market. After World War II, because it was heavily advertised, cheap, easy to store, and produced tender results, Crisco quickly became American bakers' favorite fat. It was not until 1961, when Julia Child and colleagues asserted in *Mastering the Art of French Cooking* that butter plus a small amount of shortening yields the best result, that bakers turned once again to a blend of butter and other fat. This trend prevails today, although some home bakers now rely on a shortcut, using store-bought crusts they shape and fill themselves.

Wheat flour, the pie baker's most important ingredient, contains gluten, an essential element that gives dough its structure. This stretchy, elastic substance develops when two of wheat's several proteins are mixed with water: glutenin gives dough strength, while gliadin provides elasticity. Pie dough needs some gluten to bind it together, but not too much, or it will become tough. Different types of flour, with different gluten levels, absorb differing amounts of water, and all of these factors affect the resulting crust. For all-purpose pie crusts, most home bakers get excellent results using all-purpose unbleached flour, generally milled from a blend of hard and soft wheat containing roughly 10 to 13 percent gluten. For very tender baked goods, one can also use a low-gluten (8 to 9 percent protein) pastry flour, milled from soft wheat and able to hold a lot of fat without toughening, or a blend of pastry flour and all-purpose flour. See FLOUR.

Fat, depending on the type used, and the way it is mixed into flour, affects pie dough's texture, tenderness, richness, and taste. Fat coats the elastic strands of gluten in wheat flour, making them slippery, separated, and softened; some fats coat gluten more completely than others. The more the fat is worked, or rubbed, into the flour in the dough, the more moisture-proof, tender, and less flaky the dough will be.

Unsalted U.S. Grade A or AA butter gives dough the most delicious, rich flavor. Because salt levels vary with the brand, it is best to use unsalted butter in all baking. Butter, about 81 percent fat, contains proteins, dry milk solids, and water. It must be kept very cold during handling; if it warms up, it can release water that may develop gluten in the flour. See BUTTER.

The flakiest crusts are made with 100 percent fats such as lard (rendered from pork fat, which must be fresh to avoid an off flavor) or vegetable shortening. See SHORTENING.

Flakiness occurs when very cold solid fat is pinched with flour, or "smeared" into it with the heel of the hand, to make "leaves" of fat between layers of flour starch. The larger and colder the leaves of fat, the larger the flakes in the crust. When this dough is placed in a sufficiently hot oven (425°F [218.3°C] for the first 15 minutes of baking), liquid in the dough quickly turns into steam, which immediately causes the gluten strands and starch between the fat layers to puff up, set, and create flakes before the fat melts. Shortening has a higher melting point than butter, so it doesn't melt as fast, allowing steam to push up even more flakes before it succumbs to the heat.

Liquid is needed in pie dough to moisten and activate some (but not too much) gluten in the flour, giving dough structure. Cold liquid, such as ice water, is preferred, because cold inhibits gluten development, helping dough's tenderness, as does the addition of an acidic ingredient such as vinegar, lemon juice, buttermilk, sour cream, or yogurt. See BUTTERMILK; SOUR CREAM; and YOGURT. Acid literally cuts the gluten strands in flour, making them "shorter" (as in "short," tender dough) so they do not become elastic or tough. Also, an acidic dough will set up faster in the heat of the oven.

Many bakers like to add an egg yolk to pie dough along with liquids, because it contains natural lecithin that helps make dough pliable for easy handling; the yolk also adds richness, color, and a little flavor. A whole egg (with the binding/drying action of its white) is added only to make a crust stronger and sturdier—good qualities for moist fillings. See EGGS.

Vodka occasionally appears as a liquid ingredient in pie dough, replacing a portion of the water in specially formulated recipes. It is considered a novel tenderizing agent because, although it is a liquid and can moisten flour, it contains 40 percent ethanol (alcohol). Since this is not water, it will neither bind with or nor develop gluten. Alcohol vaporizes during baking and leaves no trace flavors.

Flavoring such as salt adds flavor to dough while enhancing the strength of the gluten; tender pie dough uses small amounts of salt. A little salt also makes sweets taste a little sweeter. Sugar, in small amounts, gives flavor and, because it caramelizes, enhances the color of a baked crust; however, since sugar weakens the elasticity of gluten, excessive amounts of sugar can transform a pliable, easy-to-handle pie dough into a sandy, crumbly texture that is very difficult to roll out. See SALT and SUGAR.

Corriher, Shirley. *BakeWise: The Hows and Whys of Successful Baking, with Over 200 Magnificent Recipes.* New York: Scribner, 2008.
Hamel, P. J., ed. *The King Arthur Flour Baker's Companion.* Woodstock, Vt.: Countryman, 2003.
McGee, Harold. *On Food and Cooking: The Science and Lore of the Kitchen.* New York: Scribner, 1984.
Purdy, Susan G. *As Easy as Pie.* New York: Atheneum, 1984.
Sultan, William J. *Practical Baking.* 4th ed. New York: Van Nostrand Rheinhold. 1986.

Susan G. Purdy

pièces montées

See SUGAR SCULPTURE.

piloncillo

See SUGARS, UNREFINED.

piñatas, candy-filled papier mâché ephemeral art, are a staple in Mexican fiestas ranging from the traditional Christmas *posadas* (the nine days preceding Christmas) to birthday parties. Piñatas come in all shapes and sizes and are used in celebrations of all kinds, including secular and religious holidays, bridal showers, and political rallies. These colorful containers have now made their way into mainstream culture, appearing at children's birthday parties throughout the United States.

From its likely origins in China and subsequent travels through Italy and Spain and finally to Mexico and the United States, the piñata tradition has remained basically the same: a candy-filled container that is broken by a blindfolded player. Marco Polo, on his twelfth-century visit to China, is said to have encountered the custom of breaking a figure of an animal as part of the New Year's celebration. The tradition eventually spread to Italy and Spain, where it was laden with new meaning: as part of Lenten festivities, the piñata came to symbolize the battle between good and evil. Breaking it open with a decorated stick, participants were rewarded with candies for having vanquished evil and temptation. In Spain, *el baile de la piñata,* celebrated on the first Sunday of Lent, continued the tradition as blindfolded participants struck a clay pot filled with candy until it broke.

The Spanish brought this tradition to the Americas and used it to proselytize the indigenous populations. Serendipitously, the Aztecs already had a somewhat similar celebration, during which a treasure-filled clay pot was struck and the offerings spilled to honor their god Huitzilopochtli; the Mayans also played a game in which blindfolded players struck a clay pot hanging from a string. Thus, the Spanish found an easy corollary and aligned the game with three theological teachings of the Catholic Church: faith, hope, and charity. The pot covered with colorful *papel de china* (tissue paper) represented evil or the Devil, who is often attractively disguised to attract gullible sinners. The shape of the traditional piñata with its seven-pointed star, one for each of the seven deadly sins, had symbolic value; the candies, fruit, and toys represented earthly pleasures.

Thus, the game symbolized blind faith (the blindfolded player) conquering evil. Second, the colorfully decorated pot is a symbol of hope as it hangs overhead—in the heavens. It is only by breaking the pot with virtue (the colorfully decorated stick) that the hope for a reward for good acts can be realized. Finally, as the vessel that holds all good is broken, everyone enjoys the blessings, the reward for leading a good life.

Today, the religious symbolism of the piñata has been all but lost, although breaking a piñata remains one of the essential elements at the *posadas*, during which parishioners go from house to house asking for lodging, as the holy family did on Christmas Eve; each of the *posada*'s nine nights concludes with the breaking of a piñata. The original clay pot has given way to a papier mâché construction that uses reed cane and paper to construct elaborate and colorful shapes that range from Disney characters to political figures. At Easter, popularly known as *el día de la coneja* (the day of the rabbit), a piñata in the shape of a giant Easter egg or a rabbit is broken by Mexican and Latino families at outdoor picnics throughout greater Mexico, including the American Southwest.

Invariably, the piñata is filled with candy, most often individually wrapped hard candies. While in the more traditional Christmas celebration, the piñata is filled with *colación*, a sugarcoated anise seed hard candy, at Easter it is filled with traditional Easter candies, such as *tamarindo*, jelly beans, peeps, and marshmallow eggs.

See also FESTIVALS and MEXICO.

Cantú, Norma E. "Piñatas and Paper Arts." In *The Oxford Encyclopedia of Latinos and Latinas in the United States*, edited by Suzanne Oboler and Deena Gonzalez, Vol. 2, pp. 382–384. New York: Oxford University Press, 2005.

Devlin, Wendy. "History of the Piñata." http://www.mexconnect.com/articles/459-history-of-the-pi%C3%B1ata (accessed 2 May 2014).

Norma E. Cantú

Pitts, ZaSu (1894–1963), enjoyed a long career as an actress that began during the silent-screen era and lasted almost 50 years, through talking pictures, vaudeville, Broadway, radio, and television. In her early twenties she was sent to Hollywood by her widowed mother to earn a few dollars at the film studios, and by 1917 was cast in her first film, *The Little Princess*, opposite Mary Pickford. Her transition to the talkies was seamless. Pitts was cast in many comic roles, which made the most of her big, woeful eyes and nervous, fluttering hands.

Pitts delighted in preparing candies for her friends and colleagues on the set, and she brought this joy to the writing of a cookbook that was published late in the year of her death. *Candy Hits* is organized along the lines of Pitts's career path, beginning with four basic candy recipes in "Silent-Screen Days," and continuing to more complicated procedures in "Talking-Picture Days." The recipes are enhanced by Pitts's humorous stories, including how she learned to dip chocolates—she advises cooks to pray before beginning that adventure. The "Stage-Tour Collection" includes recipes Pitts collected while touring, while "Television Days" contains mostly fruit and nut desserts the actress prepared for dinner parties. Pirate's Treasure, made with fresh coconuts, was one of her favorites, as were Texas Tycoons, crispy, brittle treats made with pecans, butter, and sugar. The final section, "Candies for Holidays," includes seasonal

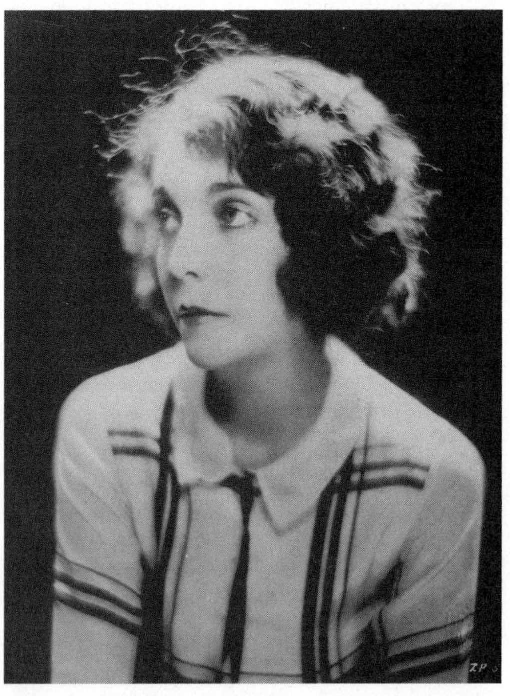

The silent-screen star ZaSu Pitts used to bring homemade candy to Hollywood parties. At the end of her life she penned *Candy Hits*, a charming cookbook of her favorite recipes.

treats, such as lollipops, fondant Easter eggs, and candy apples.

Pitts, ZaSu. *Candy Hits: The Famous Star's Own Candy Recipes.* Compiled by Edi Horton. New York: Duell, Sloan and Pierce, 1963.

Katie Guthorn

placenta is an ancient Roman cake of goat's cheese and honey layered between a dried semolina pastry (called *tracta,* which some consider to be an early form of pasta) and an outer wheat pastry shell with a central knob of dough. The top and edges were scored, and the cake was said to resemble the seed pod of the mallow flower. This Roman dish was descended from the Greek *plakous,* which is normally understood to mean a flat cake, although some scholars believe it was named from the fact that it was "full of individual flat sheets." The name survives in many European languages, particularly the Rumanian *platchynta,* which resembles the ancient cake, and the Hungarian *palacsinta,* which now refers to crepes. See ANCIENT WORLD and PANCAKES.

The Greek dramatist Antiphanes described the ancient pastry this way: "The streams of the tawny bee, mixed with the clotted river of the bleating she goat, placed upon a flat receptacle of the virgin daughter of Zeus, delighting in 10,000 delicate veils—or shall I simply say *plakous.*" In Greek and Roman culture, *plakous* was both a delicate dinner dessert and a sacrificial cake. It was offered at the sanctuary of Demeter and Kore in Corinth before the second century B.C.E., and ceramic votive offerings of these cakes were also found at the site. A detailed Latin recipe is preserved in Cato the Elder's agricultural manual *De Agricultura*; the fact of its presence in the collection, along with a number of other similar cakes, is assumed to reflect the need to make regular offerings to the gods in the course of maintaining a successful farm.

At some point in the Middle Ages, the word *placenta* came to be used for the human afterbirth, which has a coincidental resemblance to the ancient cake. Throughout history the human afterbirth has been cooked and consumed by new mothers; it is said to resemble liver in texture. Currently, the placenta may be dried and rendered into pill form so that new mothers may benefit from the recognized reduction in the incidence of postpartum depression in those who consume the organ. Votive offerings in the form of cakes formed to resemble the organ were also traditionally made by new mothers in many primitive cultures, a perhaps not coincidental link to the original ancient sacrificial cake.

Athenaeus. *The Deipnosophists,* 449c. Edited by S. D. Olson. Loeb Classical Library 235. Cambridge, Mass.: Harvard University Press, 2008.

Brumfield, Allaire. "Cakes in the Liknon: Votives from the Sanctuary of Demeter and Kore on Acrocorinth." *Hesperia: The Journal of the American School of Classical Studies in Athens* 66, no. 1 (1997): 147–172.

Cato the Elder. *De Agricultura,* ch. 76. Rev. ed. Translated by W. D. Hooper; revised by H. Boyd Ash. Loeb Classical Library 283. Cambridge, Mass.: Harvard University Press, 1935.

Grandjouan, Clairève. "Appendix 1: The Food of the Heroes." In *Hellenistic Relief Molds from the Athenian Agora,* pp 57–68. Hesperia Supplements 23. Princeton, N.J.: American School of Classical Studies at Athens, 1989.

Lincoln Placenta Encapsulation. http://www.lincolnplacenta.com.

Sally Grainger

plantations, sugar, are large-scale enterprises that grow and process sugar for distant markets. Historically, the term "plantation" was sometimes used for products such as fish and iron, but the typical plantation produced tropical plants such as rubber, oil palm, cotton, coffee, and, above all, sugarcane, for the European market. Because sugarcane requires not only abundant water but higher temperatures than those found in the temperate zones, from the fourteenth century on, Europe turned to overseas plantations to acquire its sugar. See SUGARCANE. It looked first to the Mediterranean, then to the Atlantic islands, then to tropical colonies in the Americas and the Caribbean, and finally to European- or American-controlled tropical lands worldwide. The height of sugarcane plantation culture was in the Caribbean around 1800. From the late nineteenth century on, cane plantations faced fierce competition from the temperate sugar beet. See SUGAR BEET. It should be noted that India, China, and Southeast Asia did not adopt the system of sugar plantations.

Since plantations were so isolated, they were at once intensely local and part of far-flung global networks. Politically, they were controlled by Europe or by former European colonies, particularly the Portuguese, the Spanish, the English, the Dutch, the French, and the Americans. Their capital came from

In his series *Sugar Children*, the Brazilian artist Vik Muniz focuses on the children of plantation workers on the island of Saint Kitts. To create these works, Muniz took a Polaroid of his subjects, then used that image to draw each child using sugar as a medium. He photographed the drawing to get the finished result. *Valentina, the Fastest* dates to 1996. ART © VIK MUNIZ / LICENSED BY VAGA, NEW YORK, N.Y.

Europe, their labor from the non-European world—first from Africa, then from Asia. They were large-scale enterprises, employing from 50 to 200 people in the eighteenth century, and even more later on. Because as much productive land as possible was turned over to sugar, provisions for the owners and managers, and to some extent for the enslaved as well, were imported. Legally, the plantation owners and managers took discipline into their own hands, with cases rarely being referred to European courts.

By the fourteenth century, Europeans had learned from Islam how to grow, crush, reduce, and refine sugar, establishing plantations in Crete, Cyprus, and Sicily in the eastern Mediterranean. Enslaved war captives from different parts of the Mediterranean and the Black Sea provided the labor.

In the fifteenth and sixteenth centuries, as the Spanish and Portuguese empires expanded, they established plantations in the Atlantic islands, New Spain, and Brazil. Sugar was shipped from Madeira from 1455, and from the Canaries from the 1480s. One of Cortés's first actions after the Spanish conquest was to establish sugar mills south of Mexico City in the late 1520s, and by the 1540s sugar mills dotted the northern coast of Brazil. Enslaved Africans were imported to provide labor. See SLAVERY.

Growing the cane was the work of field laborers, who planted the crop (it had to be replanted every two years), weeded it, harvested it, and with the help of ox carts hauled it to the mill. In the most modern of the mills, the vertical three-roller mill—perhaps brought to Spanish America by voyagers on the galleons that sailed annually between Acapulco in what is now Mexico and Manila in the Spanish-owned Philippines—replaced rotating stone and platform presses. Three vertical iron-plated rollers, moved by overhead gears, were powered by a water mill, windmill, or oxen. A slave fed the cane through the first and middle roller; another fed it back between the middle and third roller. The cane juice dribbled out to a collecting pan below. The bagasse (crushed cane) was thrown away.

The juice moved through a pipe to a boiling house lower down the hill, which at some point became equipped with a sequence of six copper boiling pans. Slaves moved the juice from pan to pan as it became successively thicker and boiled at a higher temperature. To get rid of the impurities, they added blood, lime juice, or lye. When the sugar began to granulize, they took it from the last boiling pan, strained it, and put it in clay jars to cure into brown sugar in the purging house. If a finer, whiter sugar was required, they packed damp clay on top of the jar. Water trickled through the sugar, removing the impurities and leaving white "clayed" sugar behind. See SUGAR REFINING.

The Portuguese and Spanish exported much of the sugar in addition to consuming it locally. Profits were sufficiently large that in New Spain (Mexico), for example, the owners of the sugar mill of San Juan de Atotonilco set aside the income from 6 percent of its sugar loaves for the construction of the convent of Santa Rosa in Puebla. The lower-quality molasses that was a byproduct of this process was either sold locally as a cheap sweetener or was distilled into cane liquor (rum, aguardiente) in the plantation distillery. See MOLASSES and RUM.

Between the 1630s and the 1650s, the Dutch came to control the northern part of Brazil and its sugar plantations. When they lost hegemony over the area, cosmopolitan Dutch merchant families introduced skilled workers and knowhow to the Caribbean. Royalist refugees from the English Civil War of 1642–1651 began planting and processing sugar on the island of Barbados. By the mid-seventeenth century, the island was given over to sugar monoculture, shipping some 5,000 tons in 1650 and five times that in 1700. From the 1740s, the French colony of Saint Domingue (Haiti) and the English colony of Jamaica became the largest sugar producers in the region, though plantations were found throughout the Caribbean islands.

From the fifteenth to the mid-nineteenth century, the main labor force consisted of enslaved men and women from sub-Saharan Africa. Disease, heavy labor, and often inadequate diets meant that the population was not self-sustaining but had to be constantly supplemented by a fresh supply of slaves. All in all, some 11 million Africans were forcibly moved to the New World, overwhelmingly the largest group of migrants, and making this the largest population movement in the preindustrial world. Women as well as men worked in the fields and as domestic servants. They were also expected to grow much of their own food in small plots of land allotted for this purpose. Those who escaped the harsh conditions on the plantations, the Maroons, had no hope of returning to their own lands but had to find secure refuges in the New World.

In the nineteenth century, the Caribbean sugar plantations began a long decline. In 1804, Haiti became an independent republic following a successful slave revolution. One European and American nation after another banned the slave trade and abolished slavery. The plantation economy shifted once again to tropical regions controlled by Europe or the United States, notably Hawaii, Queensland, Zanzibar, Natal, Fiji, and the Indian Ocean islands. Within the United States, sugar was grown in Texas and Louisiana. Slave labor was replaced by indentured labor, primarily Asian, but also with workers from the Caribbean and the Atlantic islands.

Toward the end of the century, beet sugar, which grew in temperate climates, challenged cane sugar. The cane industry, exemplified by the Hawaii Sugar Planters Association, responded by setting up research stations to investigate all aspects of breeding, growing, crushing, and refining sugar. New varieties of cane were introduced as a result of this work. See SUGARCANE AGRICULTURE. Steam, and later electric, power replaced animal, wind, and water power in the mills. Techniques developed for beet sugar, such as a partial vacuum to speed up evaporation, were also adopted by the cane sugar industry. By the late twentieth century, sugar plantations were fully mechanized, as huge machines prepared the ground and harvested the cane, trucks moved it to refineries, and the refineries themselves were automated. See SUGAR REFINERIES.

Historians have produced a number of theories about the role of sugar plantations in world history. In 1944, Eric Williams, an economic historian and later prime minister of Trinidad and Tobago, argued in *Capitalism and Slavery* that black slavery generated the capital that financed the Industrial Revolution. After decades of research and debate, historians have concluded that this cannot have been the case, since the combined profits of the slave trade and Caribbean plantations made up no more than 5 percent of Britain's national income. In 1985, Sidney Mintz, in *Sweetness and Power*, argued that sugar played a key role in the growth of capitalism and imperialism as it was transformed from a luxury to a necessity, acquiring new uses and meanings and becoming "one of the people's opiates," at least in the British Isles.

The legacy of the sugar plantations is seen in the crumbling great houses that have been turned into tourist attractions, such as the country houses and merchant mansions in England and New England built with the proceeds from sugar and filled with furniture made from mahogany trees cleared for cane fields, or in the Tate Gallery in London, funded by the Tate family, partners in Tate & Lyle, the major British sugar refiners. See TATE & LYLE. Most of all, though, this legacy is seen in Africans in Brazil and the Caribbean; Indians in Fiji and Guyana; Chinese, Japanese, Koreans, and Filipinos in Hawaii; Indians in Mauritius; and all the other millions of people moved around the world to supply the European demand for sweetness.

See also SUGAR.

Barrett, Ward. *The Sugar Hacienda of the Marqueses del Valle.* Minneapolis: University of Minnesota Press, 1970.

Curtin, Philip D. *The Rise and Fall of the Plantation Complex: Essays in Atlantic History.* Cambridge, U.K.: Cambridge University Press, 1990.

Daniels, John, and Christian Daniels. "The Origin of the Sugarcane Roller Mill." *Technology and Culture* 29, no. 3 (1988): 493–535.

Mintz, Sidney. *Sweetness and Power: The Place of Sugar in Modern History.* New York: Viking, 1985.
Schwartz, Stuart B. *Tropical Babylons: Sugar and the Making of the Atlantic World, 1450–1680.* Chapel Hill: University of North Carolina Press, 2003.
Williams, Eric Eustace. *Capitalism and Slavery.* Chapel Hill: University of North Carolina Press, 1944.

Rachel Laudan

Plat, Sir Hugh (1552–1608), was an Elizabethan and Jacobean gentleman who lived in London and wrote on many scientific and culinary topics. Almost half of his book for women, *Delightes for Ladies,* published in 1600, is devoted to candying and preserving. The origins of most of the recipes are traceable in his surviving manuscripts. Not all are Plat's own recipes; a third are from a manuscript he acquired, probably dating from the 1550s, including an extended passage that covers the whole process of comfit making, long regarded by historians as written by Plat. See COMFIT. Plat's fascination with technology is reflected in many of his recipes. He revels in the complexity of sugar-plate making, describing how to mold sugar, and marzipan, into intricate shapes. See MARZIPAN and SUGAR SCULPTURES. He also liked "conceits," created by shaping marzipan to resemble cooked rabbits and birds: "a [sugar] banquet may bee presented in the forme of a supper." Living flowers might be candied in a garden "so you may bid your friends after dinner to a growing banquet."

Plat consulted professionals at work, including his school friend the apothecary "Mr Parsons" and "Mr Webber one of her ma[jes]ties privie Kichin." He was keen to outdo them; by following Plat's recipe for syrup of violets "you gaine one quarter of sirup, more than diverse Apothecaries doe." From personal knowledge of London tradesmen Plat gives money-saving advice: "the garble [broken pieces] of almonds will make a cheap paste" of marzipan; musk sugar is worth the trouble it takes to make because "it is sold for two shillings the pound"; and, because confectioners only use the peel, "you may buy the inward pulp of Civill Oranges . . . of the comfit-makers for a small matter" to make orange juice. Plat's book was part of a general upsurge of writing on fruit and flower preservation at the time, and its 23 editions are indicative of its popularity.

See also CANDIED FLOWERS; CANDIED FRUIT; and FLOWER WATERS.

Thick, Malcolm. *Sir Hugh Plat: The Search for Useful Knowledge in Early Modern London.* Totnes, U.K.: Prospect, 2010.

Malcolm Thick

plated desserts refer to sweet offerings, usually served at the end of a meal but also as snacks, that are individually composed on a plate, in a bowl, or using another serving vessel. They are generally for the enjoyment of a single diner, although they can be shared.

Presentation has long been an important aspect of desserts, particularly in public settings such as restaurants and hotels. The nature of desserts—intended to be celebratory and indulgent rather than nourishing—is no doubt one reason for that. The fact that desserts tend to be made in advance and served cold or at room temperature, allowing for time to shape, mold, and decorate them, might be a factor, too. Complex dessert decorations go back centuries, particularly for cakes. In his 1846 British cookbook *The Modern Cook,* Charles Elmé Francatelli, chef to Queen Victoria, advised decorating wedding cakes with "blossoms or sprigs—or, even wreaths of orange-flowers," and he garnished genoise cakes with pistachios, currants, meringue pearls and leaves, and stripes or dots of "any kind of bright preserves." See CAKE DECORATING.

Elaborate decoration of plated desserts in the West is more recent and probably stems from the innovations—beginning in the 1960s and continuing into the 1980s—of the nouvelle cuisine chefs in Lyon and Roanne, France, such as Paul Bocuse and the brothers Pierre and Jean Troisgros, who took over their parents' Roanne restaurant at the Hôtel des Platanes in 1954. The Troisgros's restaurant had a trolley that rolled onto the dining room floor, and guests were offered "Le Grand Dessert," a selection of cakes, pastries, poached fruits, ice creams, and sauces that were plated at tableside according to each diner's preference. French chefs influenced by this nouvelle cuisine style, including Daniel Boulud and Jean-Georges Vongerichten, brought the ideas and aesthetic to the United States in the 1980s. However, they plated desserts according to their or their pastry chefs' taste, rather than according to the whim of their guests.

The same basic French elements remained at the heart of plated desserts for the next decade, with a

Presentation has long been an important element of the dessert course, particularly in public settings such as restaurants and hotels. This image is from a decidedly nonpublic setting, a White House State Dinner on the occasion of French president François Hollande's visit on 11 February 2014. The White House pastry chef Bill Yosses crafted a bittersweet chocolate malted ganache from Hawaiian chocolate. BILL YOSSES

reliance on fruit coulis, vanilla sauce (crème anglaise), apricot glaze, and candied fruit—particularly the maraschino cherry. See CANDIED FRUIT and SAUCE. Mint sprigs and whipped cream were also common elements. Jacques Pépin, in his 1988 book *The Art of Cooking*, garnished most of the desserts simply with those elements—an orange tart in the book is plated only with mint and candied orange peel.

A typical example of a plated restaurant dessert in the 1980s was the Big Boy chain's Hot Fudge Ice Cream Cake, which comprised two rectangles of rich chocolate cake sandwiching a rectangle of vanilla ice cream. A squirt and a half of fudge was placed on each corner, and a dollop of whipped cream was piped onto the center with a star tip. The cake was topped with a maraschino cherry.

Cooks at home and in restaurants were already getting more playful, however. In a summer fruit feature in 1979, *Bon Appétit* magazine advocated serving blackberries layered with whipped cream in an oversized wine glass, and presented strawberries and blueberries in a large, shallow Martini glass drizzled with liqueur-spiked vanilla sauce. A dozen years later the style had not changed much, although the flavorings became more elaborate. In 1991, in a similar summer feature, *Bon Appétit* presented sliced peaches and whole raspberries in a goblet of sweetened wine flavored with orange zest and cinnamon. But new elements of luxury were being added: gold leaf adorns chocolate cake on a hotel buffet in a 1991 issue of *Bon Appétit*. More elaborate plate decorations were also coming to the fore, as readers were taught to shape leaves out of chocolate and to garnish cheesecake with white chocolate shavings.

The 1980s and 1990s were also the heyday of fruit coulis dotted with crème anglaise, or vice versa, created by running a toothpick or skewer through them so that the sauces would streak slightly. See SAUCE. Symmetry was generally expected in plated desserts in the 1980s, but a new aesthetic emerged in the 1990s as squeeze bottles came into play. Multiple sauces often crisscrossed or dotted dessert plates.

Meanwhile, at higher-end restaurants, the architectural artistry (often called "tall food") spearheaded by Alfred Portale at New York City's Gotham Bar and Grill was within a few years being copied elsewhere in the city, in restaurants such as Aureole, which opened in late 1988. Tom Vacarro, the dean of baking and pastry arts at the Culinary Institute of America, recalls that the introduction into pastry kitchens in the late 1980s and early 1990s of new flexible molds that could be shaped according to pastry chefs' whims allowed them to create stackable items. So, for example, a devil's food mousse cake could be topped with a chocolate disk, and a blueberry-infused panna cotta could be unmolded on top of that. Such desserts were often accompanied by even taller decorations made of chocolate or spun sugar. When guests saw these new, eye-catching presentations being brought to neighboring tables, they were often convinced to place a dessert order themselves.

By the mid-1990s, desserts garnished with other desserts were not uncommon. An example is the key lime pie at the Greenhouse Grille in Sanibel, Florida, featured in *Nation's Restaurant News* in 1995, which was garnished with a miniature key lime ice cream cone filled with key lime sorbet. More elaborate serving vessels came into play, too, such as a hand made out of ice that was used to serve sorbet at the Mansion Kempinski Bangkok in 1995.

By the turn of the twenty-first century, as food's role in American popular culture became more pronounced, dessert presentations were subject to many shifting fads and styles. Deconstructed desserts, in which all of the elements are presented in unconventional ways, continue to move in and out of fashion. One example is the deconstructed s'mores at Recette in New York City, made by streaking marshmallow sauce on a plate and quickly torching it with a blowtorch. A streak of ganache is placed beside the sauce, and it is topped with a scoop of graham cracker ice cream, cocoa nibs, and a house-made graham cracker. See S'MORES.

Miniature desserts have also come into fashion. They were introduced to chain restaurants by Cliff Pleau, the corporate chef of Seasons 52, a restaurant founded in 2003 specifically for aging baby boomers. Charged with only offering menu items with 450 or fewer calories, Pleau devised "mini indulgences," small layered parfaits served in cylindrical dishes resembling shot glasses. They were so popular that they soon spread to other chains, and independent restaurants picked up on them when they discovered that customers who were hesitant to commit to large desserts were willing to order one or more smaller ones.

As the twenty-first century approached its second decade, the naturalist aesthetic that began to pervade savory cooking also found its way onto dessert plates. Pastry chefs began crumbling chocolate cookies to resemble soil—something that had been happening on kids' menus for awhile (atop chocolate pudding studded with gummy worms). At Town House in Chilhowie, Virginia, in 2009, chef John Shields made a dessert called "purple mountains," a yogurt sorbet that he shaped to look like rocks using a super-cold "anti-griddle." Shields coated the sorbet with powdered macaroons mixed with powdered anise. Next to the mountains he served smaller "hills" made of buttercream flavored with anise and pastis. The mountains were nestled in a dark mocha curd and surrounded by black sesame oil.

Throughout their decades of evolution, plated desserts have remained a reflection of their time, in their own way reminding diners where they are and leaving them with a final memory of the meal they just enjoyed.

See also DESSERT; DESSERTS, CHILLED; and DESSERTS, FROZEN.

Francatelli, Charles Elmé. *The Modern Cook: A Practical Guide to the Culinary Art in All Its Branches.* New York: Kegan Paul, 2005.

Pépin, Jacques. *Jacques Pépin's The Art of Cooking.* New York: Knopf, 1992.

Wemischner, Robert. *The Dessert Architect.* Clifton Park, N.Y.: Cengage Learning, 2009.

Bret Thorn

The **politics of sugar** reflect the fact that every industry has a political dimension, and the larger the industry, the more complex and dynamic its politics. Thus only some of the most interesting examples of sugar politics can be discussed here.

Because sugar remained a rare luxury for centuries after its introduction into Europe in the twelfth century, its politics reflected its modest economic status until trade accelerated in the mid-seventeenth century. By then, England, France, Holland, and Denmark had joined Portugal and Spain in establishing sugarcane operations in the Caribbean and along the Atlantic coast of South America, notably in Brazil. See SUGARCANE and SUGARCANE AGRICULTURE. By the eighteenth century, sugar had already seduced the middle class. The proliferating working class of the nineteenth-century Industrial Revolution demanded it for factory tea breaks and family suppers known as high tea, transforming sugar into an essential food. The soaring sugar trade dominated Britain's economy, and the politics of sugar dominated the national economic agenda. To supply sugar in huge quantities at affordable prices, the industry relied on enslaved Africans and their descendants to work the sugarcane plantations. See PLANTATIONS, SUGAR and SLAVERY.

Slavery and Sugar

The triangular commerce between Europe, the New World, and Africa generated an all-pervasive slave-sugar industrial complex that included slave traders; carters, dock workers, and harbor officials; shipbuilders and shipyard workers; seamen, captains, and ship's bursars; freight forwarders, insurance agents, and customs agents; refiners, packagers, and bakers; grocers and confectioners; and brokers and commercial agents known as factors—all demanding (and sometimes receiving) assistance in the form of subsidies and economic protection or monopolies. See SUGAR TRADE.

This powerful and profitable industry operated within Britain's mercantilist economic system, which dominated from the sixteenth to the late eighteenth century and favored the metropolis and its shipping interests, refineries, and associated trades at the expense of subservient colonies. Sugarcane had to be refined in Britain and, to prevent defiant colonials from establishing their own refineries, the metropolis imposed onerous duties on refined sugar. See LEGISLATION, HISTORICAL and SUGAR REFINERIES.

Rise of the West India Interest

Within these mercantilist parameters, the powerful West India Interest sugar lobby worked hard to obtain favorable terms and conditions. The leading planters, often absentees who preferred the metropolis to their colonial sugar estates, established England's most formidable lobby and threw themselves into politics. In the days of rotten boroughs, they bought parliamentary seats, and by the mid-eighteenth century they held the balance of power in the House of Commons. They could save governments from non-confidence votes, a service for which governments later repaid them.

The West Indians parlayed their political support into peerages and infiltrated the House of Lords. The absentee planter Lord Hawkesbury, later Earl of Liverpool, was president of the Privy Council for Trade and a fervent advocate for the West India Interest, including the slave trade. Other West Indians held municipal offices: William Beckford, the fabulously wealthy heir to vast Jamaican sugarcane estates, was twice lord mayor of London.

The West India Interest set new standards for political pressure tactics. They were organized, focused, and capitalized. They intermarried and allied themselves with influential landed and mercantile interests. See SUGAR BARONS.

Rum Deals and Snow for Sugar

The West India Interest lobby persuaded lawmakers to institute the extremely profitable naval rum ration—half a pint of molasses-derived grog per seaman. See RUM. After the Seven Years' War (1756–1763), in a deal nicknamed Snow for Sugar, the lobby convinced the English government to return the prolific sugar island of Guadeloupe to France and to retain the giant fur-trading colony of Canada. Guadeloupian sugar would have benefited consumers, but it would also have competed mercilessly with the eroding West Indian sugar operations.

In the early nineteenth century, after the collapse of Haiti's sugar commerce triggered a soaring European demand for British sugar, consumers demanded the right to buy cheaper, free-labor East Indian sugar. The West India Interest fought back, and by appealing to their past service as agents of civilization who also brought Christianity to native and African heathens, and dismissing the consumers' right to less expensive sugar, the Sugar Interest bested their East Indian economic rivals, whose sugar was cheaper and free labor. In 1799 the Interest also won the right to found the West India Dock Company and was awarded a 21-year monopoly to load and unload all West Indian produce at the docks on the Isle of Dogs in East London, then the world's largest.

In their competition for capital investments and loans, the stakes for the West Indians were high. Sugar was a risky business because planters were in perpetual need of legislative support to avert catastrophes such as dramatic drops in the price of sugar, sharp increases on sugar duties, foreign competition, and publicity about the brutality of sugar slavery. By the turn of the nineteenth century, the sugar lobby was losing many of these political battles. Economic theories favoring liberalization and free trade were challenging the protectionist policies that meant preferential duties for West Indian sugar. In addition, lobbyists for the growing abolitionist movement that targeted sugar slavery were implacable opponents.

Abolitionists

The abolitionist movement was as diverse as the slave-sugar complex. It included slaves, free or freed blacks, English workers, Quakers, reformists, free traders, and others who hated slavery and identified sugar as its root cause and the symbol of its evils.

As the movement set out to work through legally sanctioned means by lobbying parliament from the late eighteenth century to 1807, when the slave trade was abolished, its members were split on whether to demand an end to the institution of slavery itself, or only an end to the slave trade that fed the institution. Most blacks and a great number of women supported immediate emancipation, but, for the sake of solidarity, they acquiesced in their leaders' more cautious, "gradualist" positions.

The abolitionists quickly learned effective lobbying. Their leaders involved themselves in the political stratagems and alliances that move the parliamentary process along, and participated in the official inquiries and studies that precede new laws. Fact-finding was a crucial tactic. Between 1787 and 1790 the abolitionist Thomas Clarkson visited and described slave ships, and his official evidence on the "monstrous inequity" of the slave trade ran to over one thousand pages. In the House of Commons, William Wilberforce displayed a wooden model of the *Brookes,* a Liverpool slave ship, with 482 recumbent Africans jammed into its hold as he urged members to vote against the slave trade. Abolitionists also distributed *Brookes* prints, the first mass-distributed political poster.

In 1787, outside Parliament, they formed the Society for the Abolition of the Slave Trade, which spawned a network of local abolitionist associations: more than 200 in 1814, and more than 800 by the mid-1820s. This network petitioned Parliament, preached the tenets of abolitionism, raised money to publish and distribute tracts and other literature, and contributed pro-abolition letters and articles to newspapers and magazines.

The slave-sugar lobby fought back, but Lord Grenville's new Whig government, which included the abolitionist foreign secretary Charles Fox, was in tune with the popular will. In 1807, on its 16th appearance, the Abolition of the Slave Trade Act passed 115 to 15 in the House of Commons and 41 to 20 in the House of Lords, and became law on 25 March 1807.

The slave trade was now illegal. Abolitionists hoped that planters, deprived of new supplies, would be forced to improve their slaves' working and living conditions, and that, as the slaves died off, so would the institution of slavery. To stamp out slave smuggling, abolitionists also lobbied for a clerical tool to detect smuggled African imports. But the Slave Registration Bill, passed against ferocious West Indian opposition because it required slaveholders to register each slave, failed to sound slavery's death knell.

The abolitionists regrouped and, in 1823 they founded the male Anti-Slavery Society. Though they could neither vote nor petition Parliament, abolitionist women formed Ladies' Anti-Slavery associations, writing and distributing abolitionist literature, fundraising, collecting signatures on petitions that abolitionist men presented to Parliament, and boycotting slave-grown sugar. These associations also embraced immediate abolition and threatened to stop donating to the Anti-Slavery Society unless it dropped its gradualist stance. In 1830, in response, the Anti-Slavery Society opted for the immediate abolition of slavery.

In 1833, when the Slavery Abolition Act finally passed, its full title trumpeted the compromises politicians had crafted to ensure its passage: "An Act for the Abolition of Slavery Throughout the British Colonies; for promising the industry of the manumitted Slaves; and for compensating the Persons hitherto entitled to the Services of such Slaves." Slaves, however, got not one cent.

The West India Interest, masters of sugar politics, lost their battle to retain slavery but won huge concessions. They warned that emancipation would devastate the sugar industry, and if slave owners were not compensated they would stop issuing credit, honoring bills of exchange, and shipping out essential supplies. In consequence, the colonial economies would be destroyed and the government would fall.

The Whigs, cornered, agreed to compensation, but with the caveat that the applicants must make their claims in England, which would force them to satisfy their creditors as soon as they were paid. The act also forced the slaves into a transitional "apprenticeship," a slave-like arrangement devised to help planters develop a wage-labor system.

After slavery was abolished, the politics of British sugar focused on lowering its price and supporting the powerful sugar refineries. In 1846, sugar duties were repealed, and foreign slave-grown sugar was admitted into the domestic market. Soon Cuba, with more than three million slaves, was exporting half its sugar to Britain; it had become the Caribbean's most spectacularly successful sugar producer.

Post-bellum Sugar World

After the Civil War ended American slavery in 1863, the politics of sugar in the former slave state of Louisiana changed drastically. Most plantations lay in ruins, planters were heavily indebted, and uncooperative bankers refused to lend them money. Desperate and nearly bankrupt, they could muster little political leverage against the lobbying power of the sugar refiners, who wanted cheap sugar from any source, notably domestic beet and foreign cane sugar. More gallingly, planters were even forced to pay and make other concessions to their former slaves, now busily establishing themselves as free political beings. Ironically, these freedmen made the sugar plantations where they had lived and worked together the locus for recruiting, proselytizing, and organizing their mutual aid societies, political clubs, and militias.

The planters resisted ferociously. They withheld wages, resurrected patrols to keep the freedmen on the plantations, and fired those who registered to vote or left the cane fields to attend political meetings. They formed secret societies pledged to restoring white supremacy. In 1877 they also founded the Louisiana Sugar Planters' Association and created a sugar lobby to influence federal tariff policymakers and to share research information.

Reconstruction ended in 1877 when the Republican Party withdrew federal troops from the South in return for the electoral votes to send Rutherford Hayes to the White House, despite his having lost the popular vote. Whites again held the whip hand, and black sugar workers were disempowered and disregarded. Violence, intimidation, and killing became the order of the day, and the politics of sugar were now played by powerful industry lobbies.

American Sugar Barons Take Over Hawaii

The Civil War that devastated Louisiana's sugar industry fueled Hawaii's, which skyrocketed as it strove to satisfy the voracious appetites of the sugar-deprived North and gold-enriched California. Many of the new planters were Americans who, in 1875, over the bitter opposition of Louisiana and other southern states, succeeded in winning duty-free status for bringing Hawaiian sugar into the United States.

The politics of sugar in late-nineteenth-century Hawaii were so brutal that President Bill Clinton apologized for them in the late twentieth century. In 1887 the Hawaiian League, a quasi-secret, American-dominated cabal of sugar planters, forced Hawaii's king to accept the "bayonet constitution," which transferred most of his power to a cabinet they dominated, granted voting rights to non-Asian foreigners, and imposed heavy property qualifications that eliminated most native Hawaiians. Four years later, Queen Lili'uokalani, King Kalakaua's sister and successor, attempted to abolish the "bayonet constitution" and to limit American political power in Hawaii. The sugar plantocracy, outraged, arranged for U.S. Marines to overthrow Lili'uokalani, who was forced to abdicate. President Grover Cleveland later called Lili'uokalani's ouster "an act of war" perpetrated on behalf of the Hawaiian sugar interests. But the American sugar barons wanted even more: free access to the huge American market, and they lobbied hard until the United States annexed Hawaii, which in 1900 became an American territory.

Forced Labor in the Sugar Beet Fields

The politics of North American sugar also dealt with the challenge of recruitment for the arduous, relentless, and low-paid work of harvesting sugar beets. The Depression produced enough desperate people to man the fields. But World War II lured so many away to the military and better jobs that the sugar industry appealed for help. The American and Canadian governments responded by drafting workers from the ranks of conscientious objectors, German prisoners of war, and Japanese Americans and Japanese Canadians. They classified the latter as "aliens" and shipped them to remote detention camps and, in 1942, to beet-sugar farms in the U.S. states of Oregon, Utah, Idaho, and Montana, and the Canadian provinces of Alberta and Manitoba. Then they promoted beet sugar as a "patriotic" commodity.

Cuba's 10-Million-Ton Sugar Harvest

After Haiti's sugar industry collapsed following the 1804 Revolution, Cuba's industry soared to become the Caribbean's largest, with the United States its most important customer. Cuban sugar brokers, resenting Spain's corrupt and inefficient administration, sought closer connections and even annexation to the United States. Meanwhile, Americans bought Cuban sugar estates and worked and intermarried with Cubans. By the time of the Spanish-American War in 1898, American interests controlled Cuba's sugar industry; after the war the United States granted Cuban sugar preferred status in the American market. See SPANISH-AMERICAN WAR.

Soon after seizing power in 1959, Fidel Castro began wholesale nationalization of sugar holdings; in his revolutionary Cuba, politics focused on sugar as an economic lifesaver. Following the Soviet model, confiscated plantations became state farms, and workers were guaranteed permanent employment. When they drifted off to easier, equally secure jobs, Castro ordered soldiers into the cane fields. Despite low productivity, Castro staked Cuba's economic health on sugar, specifically a projected 10-million-ton sugar harvest in 1970. The yield came close—8.5 million tons, 90 percent better than in 1969, the Year of the Decisive Effort—and for two decades thereafter, with sweetheart agreements with the Soviet Union that kept sugar prices high, Cuba's leaders made sugar the economic motor of its revolution.

When the Soviet Union collapsed, Cuba's sugar-based economy, which was 85 percent dependent on Soviet markets, collapsed along with it. Production and prices plummeted. The old politics of sugar had become obsolete.

Black Sugar

In the Dominican Republic, the politics of sugar always include the issue of the Haitian cane workers who are essential to the industry. To ensure a steady supply of labor, the Dominican government used to bribe Haiti's usually dictatorial presidents to provide *braceros*. These arrangements ended in 1986, after the dictator Jean-Claude "Baby Doc" Duvalier was expelled from Haiti. Today, Haitians and their descendants still cut Dominican cane, but almost all are defined as "illegals" who can be deported at will.

Unrefined Politics of Sugar

The art of lobbying is one of sugar's enduring legacies, and both beet and cane interests benefit from the supposed "right" of citizens to enjoy abundant amounts of sugar at cheap prices.

Within the sugar industry, refiners have replaced producers as power brokers, and many dominate production as well. In the United States, the sugar lobby spends millions of dollars annually to persuade lawmakers to preserve legislative protection for cane- and beet-sugar producers, millers, and refiners by levying a prohibitive tariff that cripples foreign sugar trying to compete in the U.S. market. See SUGAR LOBBIES. Big Sugar has also devised ways to bypass U.S. anti-trust laws, primarily by marketing through cooperatives. Sugar growers have won exemptions from some labor regulations, such as the obligation to pay overtime wages.

The politics of sugar extend into pressuring nongovernmental organizations (NGOs) such as the World Health Organization and policymakers for government food guidelines to defy known health guidelines about restricting sugar consumption. The stakes are high. These guidelines influence food labeling, government dietary education, and even school lunch programs. Worldwide, millions of people depend for meals on NGOs that base their menus on World Health Organization guidelines. As type 2 diabetes and obesity ravage much of the world's population, sugar lobbies shamelessly work to keep the sweet stuff flowing.

See also SUGAR AND HEALTH; SUGAR RIOTS; and SUGAR TRUST.

Abbott, Elizabeth. *Sugar: A Bittersweet History*. London: Duckworth, 2009.
Butler, Kathleen Mary. *The Economics of Emancipation: Jamaica and Barbados, 1823–1843*. Chapel Hill: University of North Carolina Press, 1995.
Midgley, Clare. *Women against Slavery: The British Campaigns, 1780–1870*. London: Routledge, 1992.
Mintz, Sidney W. *Sweetness and Power: The Place of Sugar in Modern History*. New York: Penguin, 1985.
Pares, Richard. *A West-India Fortune*. London: Longmans, Green, 1950.
Ragatz, Lowell. *The Fall of the Planter Class in the British Caribbean, 1763–1833: A Study in Social and Economic History*. New York: Octagon, 1963.
Rodrigue, John C. *Reconstruction in the Cane Fields: From Slavery to Free Labor in Louisiana's Sugar Parishes, 1862–1880*. Baton Rouge: Louisiana State University Press, 2001.
Sussman, Charlotte. *Consuming Anxieties: Consumer Protest, Gender, and British Slavery, 1713–1833*. Stanford, Calif.: Stanford University Press, 2000.
Williams, Eric Eustace. *Capitalism and Slavery*. London: Andre Deutsch, 1964.
Woloson, Wendy. *Refined Tastes: Sugar, Confectionery, and Consumers in Nineteenth-Century America*. Baltimore: Johns Hopkins University Press, 2002.

Elizabeth Abbott

Pop Rocks

See CHILDREN'S CANDY.

Pop-Tarts, toaster-ready breakfast pastries with a sweet filling, have appealed to American consumers for almost five decades, thanks to their convenience, high sugar content, long shelf life, and low cost. In 1964, Post Foods introduced a pastry called Country Squares that could be heated in a toaster, but the company was slow to market it, and sales were stagnant. The Kellogg Company saw an opportunity and launched Pop-Tarts in 1967. The product soon took off, and by the 1990s sales in Kellogg's toaster-pastry category had tripled. Pop-Tarts became the nation's fastest-growing breakfast product, with 29 flavors in both frosted and unfrosted varieties. However, consumer complaints in 2006 forced Kellogg's to eliminate the phrase "made with real fruit" from the packaging.

Children are the greatest consumers of Pop-Tarts. Kellogg's targets them by offering flavors like Knock Knock Jokes Wild Berry, Barbie Sparkleberry, American Idol Blue Raspberry, NASCAR Brown Sugar Cinnamon, and Pictionary in its Printed Fun line. Pop-Tarts reflect popular culture with their brand licensing of blockbuster animated and family films like *Shrek the Third*, which lures children into selecting products associated with favorite characters. Critics complain that such licensing provokes unhealthy food choices based on market forces.

Walmart's intricate inventory tracking system has revealed that Strawberry Pop-Tarts are the most commonly purchased food item for survival before and after natural disasters. When people prepare for hurricanes, they stock up on Pop-Tarts because the food can be eaten without heating, is appropriate for any meal, and has a long shelf life.

Hamilton, Jon. "Big-Box Stores' Hurricane Prep Starts Early." NPR, 26 August 2011. http://www.npr.org/2011/08/26/139941596/big-box-stores-hurricane-prep-starts-early (accessed 6 October 2014).
Linn, Susan and Courtney L. Novosat. "Calories for Sale: Food Marketing to Children in the Twenty-First Century." *Annals of the American Academy of Political and Social Science* 615, no. 1 (2008): 133–155.

Rebecca Tolley-Stokes

popping sugar is no longer just a candy in the form of Pop Rocks; it is also an ingredient with which chefs, particularly those with modernist inclinations, are experimenting to add unexpected texture and sensation to their food. The company Molecule-R, which sells popping sugar, describes the chemical process by which carbon dioxide is added to melted, cooled sugars (sucrose, lactose, and glucose; some manufacturers use corn syrup as well). As the mixture hardens, the carbon dioxide becomes trapped in the sugar, releasing with a pop when it encounters moisture, as in one's mouth. Most pastry chefs purchase unflavored versions of popping sugar from companies like Molecule-R and WillPowder and add their own flavorings. Popping sugar's surprising effect on unsuspecting diners makes it popular with pastry chefs who like to experiment with physical and molecular gastronomy.

Like many modernist products, popping sugar first emerged in food manufacturing. William A. Mitchell, a food chemist for General Foods, was trying to create an instant carbonated soda but failed to make a satisfactory one. He shelved his formula, which was rediscovered by another chemist 20 years later and developed into the candy Pop Rocks, which were introduced in 1975. Within a few years rumors began to spread that the candy, when mixed with Coca-Cola, would make the stomach explode, and the product's popularity plummeted. Pop Rocks briefly disappeared from the market in the mid-1980s, but today they are once again being sold and appreciated worldwide. Chefs who use unflavored popping sugar appeal to their customers' nostalgia for childhood.

See also CHILDREN'S CANDY; COOL WHIP; and SHERBET POWDER.

Rudolph, Marv. *Pop Rocks: The Inside Story of America's Revolutionary Candy*. Sharon, Mass.: Specialty Publishers, 2006.

Anne E. McBride

poppy seed comes from the opium poppy flower, *Papaver somniferum,* whose unripe pods are incised to collect the latex known as opium, an alkaloid drug that contains a mixture of morphine, heroin, and codeine. The seeds are incapsulated in the poppy pod and harvested only when the plant is fully ripe and the opium latex flow has stopped; if the pod is not incised, the latex can still be removed when the pod is almost completely dried. At this point the seeds are devoid of opiates and are mature enough to yield a satisfactory amount of poppy seed oil, which is one of the major reasons for the plant's cultivation.

The poppy plant is believed to have first been domesticated in Mesopotamia, with almost all sources acknowledging that the earliest mention of the opium poppy is in Sumerian texts dating as far back as 4000 B.C.E. Poppy's sedative powers were apparently recognized early—the Sumerians called it *hul gil, hul* meaning "joy" and *gil* meaning "plant." Various sources mention that the poppy's cultivation in Asia Minor dates back to the Hittite period around 2000 B.C.E. The Hittite fertility goddess Kubaba is always depicted with a poppy pod in her hand, and her legacy continues into the later Greek and Roman periods, when poppy continued to serve an iconic role. The poppy is referred to in Homer's *Iliad* and *Odyssey* (850 B.C.E.). Representations of the Greek and Roman gods of sleep, Hypnos and Somnus, show them wearing or carrying poppies. Poppy in classic Greek culture has its roots in the Minoan Poppy Goddess of the Bronze Age. Depictions of the poppy plant continued to turn up in Anatolian cultures: Seljukid period tiles and tombstones often feature depictions of the poppy, and Ottoman kilims and carpets have stylized poppy pod motifs.

Poppy seed comes in three colors—dark (blue), medium (light brown), and light (creamy white)—which are similar in flavor but preferred for different purposes. The food writer Harold McGee notes that the bluish tint of the dark variety is actually an optical illusion caused by miniscule calcium oxalate crystals covering the brown seed. The light brown variety is often reserved for oil pressing in Turkey. The bluish–dark gray variety is most commonly used for baking purposes, often ground into a paste to bring out its nutty taste. In Turkey the poppy-paste rolls *haşhaşlı çörek, haşhaşlı açma, katmer,* and *nokul* can be sweet or savory, in either case usually combined with ground walnuts.

The use of poppy seed in sweets is most widespread in German, Austrian, and Hungarian baking traditions: *Blechkuchen* (sheet cake) with poppyseeds, *Mohnstollen* (poppy stollen), *Mohnstriezel* (rolled poppy seed cake), *Mohnstrudel/Mákosrétes* (poppy seed strudel), *Mohnkuchen/Mákos pite* (poppy seed cake), *Mohnkuchen mit Streuseln* (poppy seed streusel cake), *Mohntorte* (poppy seed torte), and *Kindli* (poppy seed cookies) being the most common. The Purim sweet *Hamentashen,* often filled with a ground, sweetened poppy-seed paste, has numerous variations in all European countries with Ashkenazic Jewish populations. See JUDAISM.

The rolled poppy seed cakes made in eastern Europe and the Balkans are regarded almost as national desserts. The Slovenian national specialty *Premorska* or *Prekmurska gibanica* (Prekmurian layer cake) and the Croatian *Međimurska gibanica* (Medjimurian layer cake) are cakes layered with poppy seeds, walnuts, apples, raisins, and curd cheese. *Potica,* another Slovenian speciality, is of such importance that it has even been depicted on postage stamps. The filling can consist of nuts, raisins, and sometimes apples, but a poppy seed filling is essential for the Christmas table. Although most of these rolled cakes are shaped in the form of logs to reveal a spiral design when sliced, they are sometimes baked in special tube cake pans or manipulated into a horseshoe shape.

Germknödel and *Mohntaschen* or *mákos metélt* are sweet dumplings with ground poppy seeds, sugar, and melted butter, served as desserts in Austro-Hungarian cookery. See AUSTRIA-HUNGARY. Pancakes, crepes, flatbreads, or flat griddle cakes made of egg-based batter, yeast dough, or a plain flour and water dough can be served spread or filled with poppy paste; such preparations include the Austrian *Mohnpalatschinken,* Hungarian *mákos palacsinta,* and Slovenian *gıbíce.*

Poppy-seed-based sweets symbolize abundance and fertility, and thus are very popular for festive occasions like Easter or weddings, but most of all for Christmas or New Year's Eve, when the tiny seeds augur a plentiful harvest in the new year. Flat noodles with poppy seeds, melted butter, and sugar; rolled poppy seed cakes; and a poppy seed bread pudding are special treats. *Mohnpielen,* a bread pudding soaked in milk and doused with rum, once prepared only for Christmas Eve in the eastern German region of Silesia, is today found throughout Germany; Hungary's *mákos guba mézzel* is very similar. *Kut'ia* is a traditional Russian Christmas porridge of wheat berries with honey and poppy seeds; during Lent the wheat berries are cooked in poppy seed "milk"—water in which ground poppy seeds have steeped. See WHEAT BERRIES. In Lithuania and eastern Slovakia, small biscuits are dunked in cold poppy seed milk for the traditional Christmas Eve meal, *kūčios.*

See also HOLIDAY SWEETS.

Bogataj, Janez. "Taste Slovenia." Ljubljana, Slovenia: Rokus Gifts, 2007.
Gergely, Anikó. *Culinaria Hungary.* Cologne: Könemann, 1999.
Kaneva-Johnson, Maria. *The Melting Pot: Balkan Food and Cookery.* Totnes, U.K.: Prospect, 1999.
Tan, Aylin Öney. "The Poppy: Potent yet Frail." In *Food and Morality: Proceedings of the Oxford Symposium on Food and Cookery 2007,* edited by Susan R. Friedland, pp. 279–281. Totnes, U.K.: Prospect, 2008.

Aylin Öney Tan

Popsicle is a brand name for the frozen novelty known elsewhere as the ice lolly, freezer pop, or ice block. It has generic status in the United States. In a legend disclaimed by the inventor himself, the original Popsicle is said to have appeared in 1905 when eleven-year-old Frank Epperson left a glass containing water, powdered soda mix, and a stick outside overnight, only to discover it frozen the next morning. Epperson began selling Popsicles to the public in 1923, but he quickly sold his rights to the new product and its production process. By 1925 the Joe Lowe Company of New York was marketing the patented Popsicle throughout the United States. This novelty—composed of water, sugar, corn syrup, stabilizers, and artificial flavor and color, and frozen on a birch-wood stick—gained instant popularity due to its low price, bright colors, and convenience. Popsicles have typically figured among the frozen treats sold from ice-cream carts and trucks, and the Eighth Air Force of the United States declared Popsicles a symbol of American life during World War II.

The Popsicle brand subsequently expanded to include novelties like the Creamsicle, Fudgsicle, and yogurt-based Yosicle. The brand was bought in 1989 by Unilever's Good Humor division. A host of new flavors, many associated with candies, such as Jolly Ranchers or Sour Patch Kids, or with animated characters, such as Hello Kitty or SpongeBob SquarePants, have appeared since, but cherry remains the most popular flavor among the over two billion Popsicles sold annually. Although Unilever fiercely defends its Popsicle trademark, competitors offering low-calorie, fresh-fruit, and artisanal flavors now sell frozen pops that run the gamut from chocolate-avocado to mango-chili.

See also CHILDREN'S CANDY; GOOD HUMOR MAN; and ICE CREAM.

Castella, Krystina. *Pops! Icy Treats for Everyone.* Philadelphia: Quirk Books, 2008.
Unilever United States. "The Popsicle Story." http://www.popsicle.com/article/detail/107646/the-popsicle-story-popsicle-ice-pops (accessed 22 November 2014).

Julie A. Cassiday

Portugal, with its rich variety of confections, is a nation of dessert lovers. Sweets abound: on holiday tables, in corner cafés, and as ever-present daily delights. Portuguese desserts can be generally characterized as exceptionally sweet, with a heavy emphasis on sugar and egg yolk combinations. These egg-based creations and a wide assortment of other sweet treats are consumed not only after meals, but also in the morning with a strong cup of Portuguese espresso, or in the afternoon as a midday indulgence. As so simply stated in *Fabrico Próprio,* a compendium of Portuguese confectionery: "We, the Portuguese, cannot live without cakes."

The history of Portuguese sweets began with the Moors, who occupied the southern Algarve region from the eighth to thirteenth centuries. They planted vast groves of almond trees, and almond desserts—often combined with figs and honey—are still commonly found throughout Portugal. Prince Henry the Navigator established sugarcane plantations in Portugal's Atlantic colonies in the fifteenth century, and by 1500 Madeira had become the largest producer of sugar in the western hemisphere, soon to be dwarfed by cane cultivation in the Portuguese colony of Brazil. See BRAZIL and PLANTATIONS, SUGAR. Egg whites were widely used to refine sugar, and the increase in Portuguese wine exportation to England in the seventeenth century resulted in a further bounty of leftover yolks (egg whites were used to clarify some wines). The abundance of yolks and sugar led to a proliferation of new desserts. Religious orders of the seventeenth and eighteenth centuries capitalized most successfully on these ingredients, creating a vast array of *doces conventuais* (convent sweets) that were offered to visiting dignitaries and sold to supplement clerical income. Several classic Portuguese desserts—pastel de nata, *barriga de freira, toucinho do céu,* to name just a few—originated in convents and monasteries, and are still eaten today. See CONVENT SWEETS.

In addition to fanciful convent sweets, pastries enjoy a notable role in Portuguese dessert culture. Cafés and *pastelarias* (pastry shops) stock a variety of popular baked goods—*palmieres, queques,* and *bolos de arroz* among them—and their delicious flavors and modest prices ensure a steady stream of regular customers. These cakes, cookies, and pastries are so widely available and expertly produced that they are very rarely made at home.

From elaborate egg-based sweets to simple pastries, the Portuguese enjoy a wide assortment of tempting and unique desserts. The following is a small selection of the most familiar and distinctively Portuguese sweets.

Cakes and Cookies

Bolo de Mel

The richly spiced *bolo de mel* (honey cake) originated on the island of Madeira in the mid-fifteenth century, during the expansion of sugar plantations on the island. Originally made with molasses but now often prepared with honey, this dense cake also features almonds, walnuts, candied peels, candied fruits, prunes, or a hint of Madeira. It is usually made in large batches and will keep up to a year without losing flavor. Traditionally considered a Christmas treat, *bolo de mel* is now eaten year-round.

Bolo Rei

Introduced to Portugal via France in the nineteenth century, *bolo rei* (king cake) is the ubiquitous Portuguese Christmas cake. Traditionally round with a hole in the middle (resembling a crown), the brioche-like cake is packed with raisins, nuts, and crystalized fruits. *Bolo rei* customarily contains a small metal charm—an owl, a key, a heart—and a dried broad bean; the one who finds the charm is cheered, and the one who finds the bean buys next year's cake. See TWELFTH NIGHT CAKE. However, most modern versions of *bolo rei* have since eliminated both the charm and bean, in the interest of food safety.

Pão de Ló

Pão de ló (sponge cake) is a simple and much-loved Portuguese dessert commonly consisting of flour, eggs, sugar, salt, and lemon or orange peel. The best-known recipes are from the northern provinces, with regional differences in the proportion of eggs, flour, sugar, and cooking times. *Pão de ló* is served plain and, in addition to being enjoyed fresh, is also used day-old as the basis for puddings and other desserts. The Portuguese introduced an early form of *pão de ló* to Japan during the sixteenth century, and it is still enjoyed by the Japanese and referred to as *castela, kasutera,* or *pan.* A half-baked version of *pão de ló* known as *alfeizerão* is eaten like pudding. See JAPANESE BAKED GOODS.

Suspiros

One of the few egg-white-based desserts in the Portuguese repertoire, *suspiros* (literally, "sighs") are crisp meringue cookies flavored with lemon. *Suspiros com ovos moles* is a variation from the southern Algarve province, where a sweetened egg yolk filling is spread between two cookies.

Toucinho do Céu

Among the many *doces conventuais, toucinho do céu* (bacon from heaven) is a rich and moist cake that was created by nuns in the northern Trás-os-Montes province. It is composed of flour, sugar, butter, eggs, egg yolks, ground almonds, and cinnamon. The original convent recipe was heavier, quite possibly including lard instead of butter, though the name may simply be metaphorical, to reflect the richness of the dessert.

Custards and Puddings

Arroz Doce

Found on every typical Portuguese dessert table is the beloved *arroz doce* (rice pudding), whose origins lie in the northern Minho region. This creamy pudding is made much like risotto, using short-grain rice cooked with milk. Sugar, egg yolks, salt, and lemon peel are also combined in the mixture. The finished dessert is sprinkled with ground cinnamon, often laid in intricate, lace-like patterns. A variation on this dessert is *aletria*, where the rice is substituted with angel hair or vermicelli pasta.

Farófias

The origin of *farófias* is not clear, though the similarity to—and possible derivation from—the English "Floating Island" dessert is notable. *Farófias* is one of the few Portuguese desserts to feature egg whites, rather than the customary yolks. The egg whites are beaten to soft peaks and poached in milk, then spooned over a lemon-flavored custard, and lightly dusted with cinnamon. See MERINGUE.

Leite-Creme

Though egg custard puddings are produced throughout Europe, the Portuguese version known as *leite-creme* originated in the northern Beira province. Rather than being baked in an oven, *leite-creme* is made on the stovetop and uses milk rather than cream. Common *leite-creme* ingredients are flour, sugar, vanilla, egg yolks (fewer or more depending on the richness of the desired result), and the characteristically Portuguese additions of lemon, cinnamon, or port wine.

Pastel de Nata

Perhaps the most well-known of all Portuguese pastries, the pastel de nata is commonly made of puff pastry, egg yolks, sugar, and flour. Some recipes also call for lemon peel, cream, vanilla, and milk. See PASTEL DE NATA and PASTRY, PUFF.

Pudim Flan

Though said to have originated in Spain and France, pudim flan (crème caramel) is widely enjoyed by the Portuguese; in the Azores it is also known as *pudim veludo* (velvet pudding) or *pudim de leite* (milk pudding). The Portuguese version is sometimes thickened with egg yolks rather than whole eggs, and it may not always be served with the customary caramel sauce. Milk, eggs, and sugar are the common base of pudim flan, with varying additions of vanilla, port wine or brandy, and lemon or orange peel. See FLAN (PUDÍM).

Egg Confections

Barriga de Freira

One of many *doces conventuais, barriga de freira* (nun's belly) was first produced in the seventeenth century by nuns in the western Beira Litoral province. The origin of the name is unknown, though the variety of cleverly named *doces conventuais* attests to the humor and inventiveness of medieval clerics. Egg yolks form the base of this dessert; they are combined with crumbled bread, sugar, butter, lemon peel, nuts, and sometimes dried fruit or port wine. This mixture is often spooned into rice paper casings whose bulging half-moon shapes do indeed resemble a plump belly.

Fios de Ovos

Made from sugar, egg yolks, and water, *fios de ovos* (egg threads) is served as a garnish on cakes and puddings, as a filling for cakes, or simply by itself in small, sweet mounds. The strands are made with a special funnel by means of which egg yolks pass through tiny, narrow openings and drop carefully—without touching—into boiling sugar syrup. *Fios de ovos* is also found in Japan and Thailand, most likely brought there by Portuguese explorers during the sixteenth century. See PORTUGAL'S INFLUENCE IN ASIA.

Ovos Moles

Considered one of the best-loved and most distinctive of Portuguese desserts, *ovos moles* (soft eggs) was created by the nuns of Aveiro, in the northern Beira Litoral province. Originally consisting of only egg yolks, sugar, and water, a modern variation substitutes rice flour for some of the yolks. Soft and spreadable, *ovos moles* is an extremely adaptable dessert: it can be glazed between layers of pastry, drizzled over fruit or puddings, or squirted into fanciful maritime-themed rice paper casings and popped directly into one's mouth. In Aveiro, *ovos moles* is also sold in small wooden barrels (some only big enough to fit a spoon) that are colorfully decorated with nautical scenes.

Papo de Anjo

Papo de anjo (angel's double chin) is a *doce conventual* that originated in Mirandela, in the northern Trás-os-Montes province, sometime in the fourteenth or fifteenth century. Though regional variants exist, the original Mirandela recipe features egg yolks, sugar, fruit preserves, and cinnamon. The egg yolks are baked, next boiled in sugar syrup that is lightly flavored with orange or lemon peel, and then served as moist, spongy cakes.

Fried Delights

Fatias Douradas

Fatias douradas or fried bread (also called *rabanadas*) seems to have spread across Portugal from the northern Minho region. This dessert is customarily served at Christmas Eve, and in the Azores it is enjoyed as a Carnival specialty. Similar to French toast, this treat consists of bread bathed in milk and egg, fried, and dipped in syrup or honey, or sprinkled with cinnamon and sugar.

Filhós

Traditionally made on Christmas Eve or during Carnival, *filhós* (also known as *bêilhoses* in the Alentejo region) are crisp, delicate fritters made in a variety of styles, often from pumpkin or squash mixed with flour, eggs, and brandy, and sprinkled with cinnamon and sugar. *Malasadas*, the Azorean version of *filhós*, are made without pumpkin or squash; they resemble raised, sugared doughnuts, and are another treat whose popularity has spread through Portuguese immigrant communities worldwide.

Sonhos

Another staple on Portuguese Christmas Eve tables, *sonhos* (literally, "dreams") are light, fried doughnuts found throughout Portugal. Made from sweetened choux pastry dough, they are drizzled with orange- and brandy-flavored syrup and rolled in cinnamon and sugar.

See also EGG YOLK SWEETS and FORTIFIED WINE.

Anderson, Jean. *The Food of Portugal.* New York: William Morrow, 1986.

Duarte, Frederico, Pedro Ferreira, and Rita João, eds. *Fabrico Próprio: O design da pastelaria semi-industrial portuguesa.* Portugal: Pedrita and Frederico Duarte, 2008.

Vieira, Edite. *The Taste of Portugal: A Voyage of Gastronomic Discovery Combined with Recipes, History and Folklore.* London: Grubstreet, 2013.

Frances Baca

Portugal's influence in Asia resulted from the Atlantic kingdom's expansion into the Indian Ocean in the closing years of the fifteenth century. Subsequently, the Portuguese established colonies in Goa, Malacca (now Melaka), and Macao, from where traders and missionaries fanned out through the region. While their success in bringing Christianity to this part of Asia was somewhat limited, the Portuguese had a profound influence on the region's cuisines, introducing novel foods from Europe and the New World, as well as Iberian cooking techniques. Their legacy is particularly evident in the case of sweets.

Cakes, cookies, pastries, desserts, candies, and sweet preserves with probable Portuguese origins are found all over Asia, wherever the Portuguese settled or traded. Unlike other European colonial powers, which discouraged interracial liaisons, the Portuguese actively encouraged settlers to marry local women and to populate the empire with Catholic subjects. The frequency of miscegenation meant that Iberian culinary influences penetrated local cultures with unusual rapidity.

The development of Portuguese sweet making in Asia was also fostered by the entry of Iberian nuns into the region in the early seventeenth century. Like their counterparts in Portugal, the nuns at the Santa Monica convent in Goa were renowned for their baking and confectionery skills. See CONVENT SWEETS. Young Christian women from throughout Portuguese Asia were sent to Santa Monica (Asia's largest convent) for an education, which included the domestic arts. Returning home, these women passed on their skills within their local communities.

The Portuguese were experts at candying, jam making and sweet preserves, desserts, cakes, and confectionery. Some of the less perishable kinds of sweets were carried on ships as indulgences for the crew and extra nourishment for the sick. In foreign lands, sugar, marzipans, and sweet preserves were presented to local dignitaries as tokens of respect and offered as trade goods. See FRUIT PRESERVES and MARZIPAN. Portuguese marmalade, in particular, was appreciated for its fine quality. See MARMALADE. In 1638 the German traveler Johan Albrecht de Mandelslo enthused over the "tarts, Florentines, egg sweets, perfumed marzipans, fruit syrups and conserves" served in the dining hall of the Jesuit College in Goa.

The Portuguese grew sugarcane in the fertile region around their settlement in Bengal and introduced superior refining methods. See SUGAR REFINING and SUGARCANE AGRICULTURE. In Goa, *bebinca,* a rich layered cake made with coconut milk, rice flour, and sugar; *dodol,* a palm sugar fudge; preserves such as *mangada* (from mangoes) and *figada* (from bananas); and various confections made with cashews and almonds are legacies of the Portuguese presence, which endured until India annexed Goa in 1961. See PALM SUGAR.

In Japan, European foodways were promulgated by the Japanese wives and servants of Portuguese traders living in Nagasaki, giving rise to a new culinary classification, *nanban ryori.* This "Southern Barbarian cuisine" included sugary confections and cakes, known collectively as *nanbangashi,* several kinds of which are still being produced in Japan by artisanal bakers and confectioners. See JAPAN; JAPANESE BAKED GOODS; and NANBANGASHI. Among these, *kasutera* (castella), a sponge cake traditionally made in Nagasaki and related to the Portuguese *pão de ló,* is one of the most popular. Spiky boiled sugar candies called *konfeito* (from the Portuguese word for comfits), presented as a gift to feudal lord Oda Nobunaga by the missionary Luis Frois soon after the Portuguese arrival in Japan, are still painstakingly made by hand. See COMFIT. *Keiran somen,* a specialty of Fukuoka, are sweet egg noodles in the tradition of Portuguese *fios de ovos.* They are still made by a few *wagashi* specialists, using the traditional Portuguese method of drizzling egg yolks into boiling sugar syrup. See EGG YOLKS SWEETS and WAGASHI.

The peanut, a Portuguese import from South America by way of Africa, gave rise to the peanut brittle and peanut candies that are now hugely popular in China. See BRITTLE and CHINA. Although Macao has now reverted to Chinese rule, Portuguese-style *pastelaria* (cake shops) remain a fixture, some aficionados claiming that the *pastel de nata* from Macao is even better than the Portuguese original. In Hong Kong, *pastel de nata* gave rise to the dim sum dessert known as egg tart. See PASTEL DE NATA.

In Thailand, Marie Guimar, the part-Portuguese wife of an influential member of the Siamese court, is credited with teaching the Thais to make many of the "temple sweets" that are served during religious festivals and on special occasions. In the vicinity of the original Portuguese settlement in what is now Thonburi, a baked cookie with likely Portuguese origins called *kanom farang kuti jin* is still being made. Other Thai sweets attributed to the Portuguese include *foy thong, thong yip, thong yot,* and *mo kaeng.* See THAILAND.

Over time, recipes for Portuguese desserts and baked goods were modified by replacing wheat flour with rice flour and removing dairy products such as milk and cream. Sweet bean paste, cashews (introduced from Brazil by the Portuguese), rice flour, coconut, and other locally available ingredients replaced Iberian commodities such as quince paste, ground almonds, and rich egg custards. Methods were also adapted to suit local kitchen technologies. Cakes that were traditionally baked in an oven might be steamed, or browned in a contraption fashioned to mimic the top-down heat of a salamander.

Because cakes and sweets were so closely associated with Catholic ceremonial events, they were much in demand in devoutly Catholic Luso-Asian societies. Many confections and baked goods are still closely associated with religious occasions, such as Easter, Christmas, baptisms, and saint's days. Some take elaborate shapes or are formed to represent religious objects, such as the bones of a saint or the crown of Jesus. Two pastries still made throughout the Lusophone world, *coscurão* (sheets) and *fartes* (pillows), represent the bed linen of the Holy Infant. Macanese cooks refer to *aluwa,* their version of Indian *halwah,* as his mattress. See HALVAH.

In Malaysia and Indonesia, cakes called *putugal* and *bolo/boru* (Portuguese for "round"), *dodol*-like fudges, mango pudding, and *kaya,* a sweet spread made with coconut milk, sugar, and eggs, are thought to be Portuguese in origin, as are thin wafer cookies called "love letters" and sweet fritters called *sonhos* (dreams). In Sri Lanka, *bolo fiado,* a layer cake, and cookies called *fuguetes* attest to the Portuguese presence there. Versions of Sri Lanka's signature Love Cake, made from semolina with spices, cashews, and in some variations a candied squash preserve similar to Portugal's *doce de chila*, are made in Eurasian households throughout the region.

See also BEAN PASTE SWEETS; COCONUT; CUSTARD; NUTS; and PORTUGAL.

Commissariat, M. S. *Mandelslo's Travels in Western India (1638–1639)*. New Delhi: Asian Educational Services, 1995.

Krondl, Michael. *Sweet Invention: A History of Dessert*. Chicago: Chicago Review Press, 2011.

Menezes, Maria Teresa. *The Essential Goa Cookbook*. London: Penguin, 2000.

Sen, Colleen T. "The Portuguese Influence on Bengali Cuisine." In *Food on the Move: Proceedings of the Oxford Symposium on Food and Cookery 1996*, edited by Harlan Walker, pp. 288–298. Totnes, U.K.: Prospect, 1997.

Tetsuya, Etchu. "European Influence on the 'Culture of Food' in Nagasaki." Translated by Fumiko F. Earns. *Crossroads: A Journal of Nagasaki History and Culture* 1 (1993): 107. http://www.uwosh.edu/faculty_staff/earns/etchu.html (accessed on 4 October 2014).

Yu, Su-Mei. "Thai Egg-Based Sweets: The Legend of Thao Thong Keap-Ma." *Gastronomica: The Journal of food and Culture* 3, no. 3 (2003): 54–59.

Janet Boileau

pound cake is a British invention from around the end of the 1600s or early 1700s—the actual date is uncertain—whose name derives from its proportion of ingredients: one pound each of flour, sugar, butter, and eggs. The cakes were large, dense, and buttery, and they kept extremely well at room temperature, an important factor at a time when all baking was accomplished in brick ovens, and when cakes were baked only occasionally. It was advantageous to have a cake on the sideboard for the family to nibble on or to serve in case company dropped in.

Pound cakes depend upon the creaming method to make them rise. Beating the butter with the sugar creates a multitude of tiny air bubbles that expand in the oven's heat to raise the cake during baking. The eggs, in addition to acting as leavening agents, add moisture in the form of fat and water and contribute to the cake's tenderness. Some cookbook authors of the nineteenth century firmly believed in adding the yolks and whites separately to a pound cake batter, claiming that the beaten whites bumped up the level of aeration. No chemical leavening is used in a true pound cake.

Before the invention of the electric mixer, pound cakes were labor intensive, requiring at least one hour of whipping the batter with a hickory rod or wooden spoon. See PASTRY TOOLS and WHISKS AND BEATERS. Housewives used imagination to vary the flavorings of their pound cakes, adding caraway seeds, cinnamon, nutmeg, aniseed, rosewater, orange or lemon essence, or even dried fruits. Mace became the spice of choice in the southern United States. See DRIED FRUIT; EXTRACTS AND FLAVORINGS; FLOWER WATERS; and SPICES.

Versions of pound cake appear throughout Europe. For example, the French *quatre quarts* maintains the 1:1:1:1 ratio of the four major ingredients, while in the German *Eischwerkuchen* (*Ei* = egg, *schwer* = heavy), each ingredient weighs as much as the eggs.

Patent, Greg. "Please Don't Call It Pound Cake." *Gastronomica: The Journal of Food and Culture* 9, no. 3 (2009): 59–62.

Greg Patent

praline, in its simplest form a confection of nuts and sugar, is a representative dish of the Francophone Atlantic world. It is a French recipe ascribed to César, duc de Choiseul, comte du Plessis-Praslin, an early seventeenth-century marshal and diplomat. In a widely circulated though unverifiable story, du Plessis-Praslin inspired his cook, possibly one Clément Lassagne, to name the sweet invention in his honor. Originally made of caramelized and sugarcoated whole almonds, pralines were a treat reserved for the elite. Only in the late 1600s, following the praline's invention, did sugar shift from a rarity and luxury to a common and necessary ingredient consumed nearly the world over. Various iterations of the praline have since diffused across former French colonies, echoing similar, though unrelated, international sweet treats; these include the global assortment of nougats, brittles, and marzipans, all of which fuse nuts (tree nuts, peanuts, or nut-like drupes like almonds and pistachios) with sugar or honey.

In France, *pralin* now refers to roasted almonds, or sometimes hazelnuts, that have been coated in boiled sugar and crushed to form a crumbled or pasty topping or filler for candies, cakes, pastries, and ice creams. When mixed with chocolate, *pralin* becomes *praliné*, a petit bonbon made famous in Belgium. See BONBONS. It was in Brussels in 1912 that the chocolatier Jean Neuhaus II invented the creamy fondant-filled chocolate shell that Belgians call their praline. The Neuhaus brand still sells the quintessential Belgium chocolate praline today.

The praline has also reached iconic status in New Orleans, Louisiana, where the abundant pecan tree yields the nut that gives the candy a distinctly local flavor. See NEW ORLEANS. The Deep South praline folds toasted whole or chopped pecans into sugar, butter, and milk or cream; sometimes vanilla, molasses, or caramel is added. Boiled, then constantly stirred over medium-low heat, the creamy mixture thickens to a fudge-like consistency. The resulting batter is spoon-dropped onto a butter-greased baking sheet or parchment paper and allowed to cool. Rich and caramel brown in color, round or oval, the southern praline is most often eaten in hand like a cookie.

Though a slew of legends have traced the existence of the New Orleans praline to as early as the 1720s—some tales give credit to the newly arrived Ursuline nuns for introducing the confection—these stories are almost certainly a bit of local mythmaking. Sugar and milk were rare commodities in eighteenth-century Louisiana; France, followed by Spain, rarely if ever sent sugar to their young colonial outpost, while the local sugar industry did not develop until the 1790s. Instead, the earliest mentions in the historical record to a New Orleans praline culture occur in the late nineteenth century. Newspaper articles from this era trace this praline's beginnings to the earlier antebellum period, when it became fashionable for affluent white homes to include a platter of pecan pralines with lunch or dinner.

Following the American Civil War, and the subsequent federal emancipation of all enslaved persons, African American women in New Orleans became intrinsically and intimately tied to the praline. Known in the regional French vernacular as *marchands des pralines* (praline merchants) or *pralinières*, these women made their pralines at home but sold them in the city's streets. Alongside the traditional pecan praline, they sometimes sold a cochineal-dyed variety called "pink poodles" and a coconut-flavored version named "white mice." Several of these *pralinières* became locally famous; etchings of them appeared in cookbooks, travelers recorded their street-vendor songs, and newspaper accounts documented their lives. Selling their wares from baskets, these praline ladies often chose creative nicknames and divided up the city into territories: Praline Zizi occupied a corner of the French Quarter's Jackson Square, Gateaux Bon Marché ("Inexpensive Cake Lady") plied her praline trade for over 30 years in the downriver Marigny district, and one Mary Louise cornered the market on Tulane University's campus. Most always dressed in a tignon headscarf and apron, the *pralinières'* romanticized and archaic Old South era uniform should be considered a shrewd marketing device that provided economic freedom and independence for these women.

The praline has since become deeply tied to New Orleans's culinary culture. Everything from ice cream to bacon is pralined, or praline-coated, in caramelized sugar and pecans. Confectionery shops dedicated to the praline and geared toward tourists dot the modern French Quarter. And *pralinières*, including a few men, still sell the confection from baskets in just about every corner of the city.

See also BELGIUM; FRANCE; and NUTS.

Nunez, Chanda M. "'Just Like Ole' Mammy Used to Make': Reinterpreting New Orleans African-American Praline Vendors as Entrepreneurs." MA diss., University of New Orleans, 2011. http://scholarworks.uno.edu/cgi/viewcontent.cgi?article=1127&context=td (accessed 4 October 2014).

Rien Fertel

preserves

See FRUIT PRESERVES.

pressed cookies are made by forcing a smooth cookie dough through a cookie press or pastry bag fitted with a disk or nozzle that forms each cookie into a uniform shape on a baking sheet. The cookies are embossed with the same, usually symmetrical, design on top. Also known as spritz cookies, from the German word *spritzen* (to squirt), these cookies probably originated in Germany, where they have long been a traditional sweet at Christmas time. Now popular throughout northern Europe, they are also eaten in other parts of the world where European immigrants have settled.

A cookie press is a specialized baking utensil made of metal or plastic, consisting of a tube with a plunger at one end and a selection of removable disks, or templates, that can be fitted on the other end. These disks have designs cut into them that shape the dough as it is squeezed through the tube by the plunger and extruded onto a baking sheet. Most cookie presses are operated by hand, although some used by professional bakers are electric. A pastry bag, usually fitted with a large star or ribbon nozzle, can also be used for making pressed cookies. These utensils make it easy to produce large batches of identical cookies in a short time.

The dough consists of butter or vegetable shortening, flour, sugar, eggs, a small amount of baking powder, and flavorings such as spices, cocoa powder, extracts (vanilla, almond, rum), and grated lemon or orange zest. The dough can also be tinted with food colorings. Savory spritz cookie doughs contain less sugar and are flavored with fresh or dried herbs, paprika, chili powders, ground pepper, grated cheeses, and other seasonings.

Shapes include squares, rectangles, circles, pinwheels, rosettes, spring flowers, Halloween pumpkins, stars, wreaths, snowflakes, and Christmas trees. The cookies can also be decorated with colored sugar granules, chocolate sprinkles, chopped nuts, candied cherries, chocolate chips, nonpareils, colored dragées, confectioner's sugar glaze, melted chocolate, or icing piped onto them with a cake decorator.

Dainty little spritz cookies are often served with afternoon tea or coffee, with after-dinner coffee, and with mulled wine during the winter holidays. Since these cookies are so quick and easy to make in large quantities, they are also popular for cookie exchanges and are sometimes even used as decorations for other kinds of baked goods.

See also DROP COOKIES and COOKIE MOLDS AND STAMPS.

Handbuch für die Weihnachtsbäckerei: Von Advent bis Silvester. Cologne: Pfeifer & Langen, 1977.

Iaia, Sarah Kelly. *Festive Baking: Holiday Classics in the Swiss, German, and Austrian Traditions*. New York: Doubleday, 1988.

Sharon Hudgins

Priapus was a rustic Greek god. He is not one of the Twelve Olympians and is never mentioned in the Homeric epics, but like other Greek deities, he found his way into Roman religion and Latin literature. Humans looked to him for the protection of orchard fruit and the guarantee of male sexual potency, both themes embodied in his typical representation, a wooden statue whose exaggerated erect phallus was an explicit warning that fruit thieves of either sex would be raped.

Intruders having been scared off, Priapus's second typical form was a statuette of a smiling, homely figure whose apron, visibly supported by his phallus, offers a lapful of ripe fruit to the householder and his guests. Such Priapi in bronze and terracotta have been found by archaeologists at Pompeii and elsewhere. Two literary sources confirm that edible Priapi in the same style were made for display at banquets. One is a verse couplet from a series written by Martial, around 100 C.E., to accompany surprise gifts: "*Pastry Priapus*: If you want to be replete you can eat our Priapus: you can even nibble his loins and you'll still be clean."

The second source is a scene in "Trimalchio's Feast," the best-known episode of the first-century *Satyricon* by Petronius. A *pompa* or set-piece display of fruits, cakes, and sweets is presented before the desserts, with a pastry figure of Priapus as its centerpiece. Just like the bronze figurines, he wears "an apron, supported in the usual way, loaded with grapes and fruits of every kind." The diners' greedy fingers soon discover that these are not real fruits but fruit-shaped sweetmeats overfilled with sticky saffron sauce. Allowing for fictional exaggeration, this scene makes clear Priapus's role as patron of the fruits and sweets at a banquet, and it confirms the skills that Roman confectioners employed to change sweets into fruits, and gods into pastry.

Courtney, Edward. *A Companion to Petronius*. Oxford: Oxford University Press, 2001.

Petronius. *Satyrica*. Translated by R. Bracht Branham and Daniel Kinney. London: Dent, 1996.

Schmeling, Gareth L. "Trimalchio's Menu and Wine List." *Classical Philology* 65. no. 4 (1970): 248–251.

Andrew Dalby

profiterole

See PASTRY, CHOUX.

proverbs abound in all cultures, and those involving food are among the most common. Given their desirability, sweet foods are featured more often than not. The reason is that the realm of proverbs is the familiar: their purpose, after all, is to render abstract conventional wisdom into concrete and memorable forms by invoking everyday objects and situations. Few things are as familiar to a community as its food culture; hence the kitchen, dining room, and taste buds are frequently mined in the creation of proverbs. For example, in the sixteenth century, the sage counsel that mere words cannot bind people became the proverb "Promises are like pie crusts—made to be broken." In the early eighteenth century, the truism that people have hidden agendas inspired the saying "He woos for cake and pudding." In the late eighteenth century, the notion that things are defined by their opposites prompted the maxim "Every white has its black and every sweet has its sour."

Proverbs continue to be a feature of contemporary speech: parents still chide their children for having unreasonable expectations by saying, "You can't have your cake and eat it too." However, proverbs have lost the authoritative status that they enjoyed centuries ago. The ancient esteem for proverbs is attested by the very existence of the Old Testament's Book of Proverbs, which includes maxims such as "Eat thou not the bread of him that hath an evil eye, neither desire thou his dainty meats" (Proverbs 23:6). Aristotle, too, is said to have written a now-lost work on proverbs. During the Middle Ages, hundreds of proverbs emerged, such as the twelfth century's "Dearly bought is honey licked from a thorn." Many more proverbs were resurrected in the sixteenth century, when the Dutch humanist Erasmus published a collection of 3,000 proverbs derived from ancient Greek and Roman sources, including "Hunger makes beans taste like sugar" and "Everyone thinks his own fart smells sweet."

The veneration of proverbs began to wane in the eighteenth century, when they came to be seen as evidence of vulgarity rather than sophistication. In 1741, Lord Chesterfield belittled "common proverbs" because they were

> proofs of having kept bad and low company. For example, if, instead of saying that tastes are different... you should let off a proverb, and say "that what is one man's meat is another man's poison"... everybody would be persuaded that you had never kept company with anybody above footmen and housemaids.

It is probably not a coincidence that the status of proverbs began to decline as the scientific method began to emerge, for folk sayings couldn't compete with hard empirical evidence. The wisdom of "an apple a day keeps the doctor away" diminished once scientists discovered that the caffeic acid that naturally occurs in apples is a carcinogen.

The culinary and gastronomic conventions of a culture are, of course, reflected in the food proverbs that the culture produces. The ancient Romans, for example, used to say "from eggs to apples"—meaning "from beginning to end"—because it was their custom to begin a meal with an appetizer of eggs and end it with a dessert of apples. In China, proverbs that mention rice proliferate, such as "You can't eat the rice cake in a picture." Halvah, a soft dessert made from honey and sesame seeds, appears in many proverbs from the Middle East, including "When things don't go right, even halvah will break your tooth" and "Your mouth won't get sweet just by saying 'halvah.'"

In England, where honey was the primary sweetener up until the sixteenth century, that nectar-based bee product is found in dozens of proverbs, including "Honey catches more flies than vinegar"; "Where bees are, there is honey"; "He who shares honey with a bear, has the least part of it"; "He that in his purse lacks money, has in his mouth much need of honey" (meaning that if you lack resources you need to use sweet words); "Lick honey with your little finger" (meaning that even with desirable things you should exercise moderation); and "He licks honey through a cleft stick" (meaning that he is making things difficult for himself).

Cake, too, makes frequent appearance in the proverbs of England, such as "Life is not all cakes and ale"; "Bread today is better than cake tomorrow"; "Eaten cake is soon forgotten"; "A cake eaten in peace is better than two in trouble"; "A bad custom is like a good cake—better broken than kept"; "If wishes were butter-cakes, beggars might bite"; and "My cake is dough" (meaning "my plans have failed"). Other sweet items appear less often in the proverbs of England. Notable exceptions are "He spits out secrets like hot custard" and "Jam tomorrow and jam yesterday, but never jam today."

In the United States, where everything is as "American as apple pie," it is not surprising that apples are a staple of proverbial phrases, as in "Eat an apple going to bed, make the doctor beg his bread"; "Adam ate the apple, and our teeth still ache"; "An apple never falls far from the tree"; "If you don't like my apples, don't shake my tree"; "One bad apple spoils the barrel"; and "There's little choice in a barrel of rotten apples."

Over the centuries, some proverbs have ceased to be current, and their meaning might now seem obscure. For example, nowadays one rarely hears the English proverb "The devil makes his Christmas pies of lawyers' tongues and clerks' fingers," meaning that the lies of lawyers and the prevarications of their clerks are encouraged by corrupt officials. Also obsolete is "Every cake has his fellow," meaning that every person has a match or soul mate. Some forgotten proverbs only make sense when their historical context is restored: the sixteenth-century adage "Pie-lids make people wise" seems nonsensical until we remember that back then the lid—or crust—of a pie was not always intended to be eaten but rather functioned to protect the inside from insects and vermin. Only when this "pie-lid" was removed would someone become "wise" as to the contents of the pie.

On the other hand, some proverbs do continue to be used even after they cease to make literal sense. The proverbial phrase "to bet dollars to doughnuts" is still familiar, even though inflation has diminished the impact of the wager's original disparity. Likewise, the saying "the proof is in the pudding" remains popular today even though it doesn't, upon scrutiny, actually make much sense. We have to go back to the early seventeenth century to find its original, meaningful form: "The proof of the pudding is in its taste." Other food proverbs have also changed over time. "To eat humble pie," for example, was originally "To eat umble pie," the umble being deer offal that was sometimes cooked into a poor-man's pastry. Although the words "humble" and "umble" are unrelated, their coincidental resemblance prompted people to unwittingly replace the less familiar latter word with the more common former one.

Other changes to proverbs reflect a desire to enhance the sayings. The early sixteenth-century proverb "Many things fall between the cup and the mouth" evolved by the mid-nineteenth century into the now familiar "There's many a slip 'twixt cup and lip" because rhyme and rhythm make it easier to remember. Literary techniques are also at work in other proverbs, including parallelism (as in "The nearer the bone, the sweeter the flesh" and "A black plum is as sweet as a white"), alliteration (as in "The more crust, the less crumb" and "No sweet without sweat"), and antithesis (as in "Sweet meat must have sour sauce" and "A honey tongue, a heart of gall"). Humor, too, is not alien to proverbs, as in these two maxims from sixteenth-century England: "A turd is as good for a sow as a pancake" and "You were a sweet nut if you were well cracked."

Baz, Petros D. *A Dictionary of Proverbs, with a Collection of Maxims, Phrases, Passages, Poems, and Anecdotes from Ancient and Modern Literature.* New York: Philosophical Library, 1963.

Mieder, Wolfgang. *A Dictionary of American Proverbs.* New York: Oxford University Press, 1992.

Tilley, Morris Palmer. *A Dictionary of the Proverbs in England in the Sixteenth and Seventeenth Centuries.* Ann Arbor: University of Michigan Press, 1950.

Wilson, Frank Percy. *The Oxford Dictionary of English Proverbs.* Oxford: Clarendon, 1970.

Mark Morton

psychoanalysis is concerned with the associations and displacements that occur around a given concept. So, if a patient discusses sweets, the analyst will not be as much focused on what sweets actually are—how they affect physiology, taste buds, or the brain—as she would be with what sweets represent for the patient. While empirical studies on sweets and their physiological effects might be of some interest to the analyst, she would above all ask questions about the emotional and mental associations of sweets for the individual. The most telling of these associations often occur in the realm of the unconscious; a patient for whom sweets are a central issue would need to explore well beyond the surface of concrete data to reach the significance of sweets in his or her life. This type of inquiry foregrounds dreams, indirect links, repeated patterns of anxiety, and childhood memories.

There are as many directions in which sweets can be interpreted in psychoanalysis as there are people. The father of modern psychoanalysis, Sigmund Freud (1856–1939), made an association among sweets, eroticism, and the oral phase of sexual development, wherein the love-object is thought of as "sweet" and "appetizing," creating the desire to "devour . . . with love." Freud states also that "in dreams sweet things and sweetmeats stand regularly for caresses and sexual gratification." An excessive focus on sweets can also be the "the very first sign of [a] patient's neurotic illnesses," as is the case with a patient who for a period in his childhood "would not eat anything but sweets." Karl Abraham (1877–1925) found that "neurotic men with a strongly suppressed libido" have a compulsive desire for sweet things, especially if the connection is made via "sucking at sweets very slowly." The association is not limited to men: one female patient of Abraham's substituted chocolate for masturbation, thus regressing to the oral stage of sexuality. As can be seen from these brief examples, sweets are associated with displaced and repressed sexual desire, activating guilt and pleasure at once. They also bring back strong suggestions of infancy and childhood.

Beyond the fundamental connection to sexual desire, the psychoanalytical interpretation of sweets is vast and cannot be summarized under one rubric. There are related avenues to consider, such as the role of sweets in eating disorders, cravings, and depression. Psychoanalysis remains cognizant of these, but unlike, say, cognitive behavior therapy or social work, it does not focus on giving the patient a specific remedy. Thus, for example, rather than telling a patient who is fixated on sweets what to do to eliminate the fixation, the analyst works alongside the patient to find ways to illuminate what sweets mean for the patient, and how they have come to be used to address an anxiety that is not immediately apparent. This process takes a long time and might remain open-ended. But it can, in its own right, shed light on the unconscious and the hidden links between sweets and the patient's concerns and behavior.

Abraham, Karl. *Selected Papers of Karl Abraham, M.D.* Translated by Douglas Bryan and Alex Strachey. London: Hogarth, 1927.

Ellman, Stephen J. *Freud's Technique Papers: A Contemporary Perspective.* London: Karnac, 2002.

Freud, Sigmund. *Three Case Histories.* Translated by Philip Reiff. New York: Collier, 1963.

Leyla Rouhi

publications, trade, which arose in late-nineteenth-century Europe and the United States, were a vital source of information for both commercial bakers and pastry chefs in the burgeoning restaurant and hotel business. Trade journal publishers also produced high-quality professional pastry manuals.

For most of the 1800s, the confectionery shown in books remained well beyond the skill level and customer base of most bakers—their authors wrote and cooked mainly for wealthy patrons. Only at the century's end, with printing techniques greatly improving and transportation and industry making baking products widely available and affordable, did trade publications geared for middle-class tastes, celebrations, and pocketbooks arise.

Because the authors of these books and articles were businessmen as well as practitioners of the trade, their advice was often as much financial as it was aesthetic, concentrating on "cheap cakes for quick sale" or promising "to guide the sincere baker into the most profitable channels of expression." Trade publishers commonly set up shop in an industrial city: Chicago rather than New York; Manchester or Glasgow in addition to London; Milan rather than Rome; Nordhausen and Dresden in recently unified Germany.

To emphasize their credentials to prospective readers, authors often listed the medals and prizes they had won at trade exhibitions and competitions. Trade publishers enhanced the importance of these events by commissioning books like the 1903 *Confectionery Critiques,* containing one judge's opinions on a recent London exhibition ("every intending competitor should read," advertised the book's publisher). Even in deprived, post–World War II England, the major baking trade publisher released *Exhibition Goods* in 1951. Although the typical baker could only dream of showing at an exhibition, the coverage provided by these publications afforded inspiration and access to the most up-to-date trends in pastry making, which could be copied on a less ambitious level.

Hoping to attract top confectioners who could explain their craft, publishers often hired the owners of the numerous baking schools that were springing up, men like St. Louis–based British émigré Joseph Lambeth and Chicago-based German émigré John Zenker, whose pastry work was renowned throughout the country. Sometimes their articles were collected into a book. In Zenker's case, the Bakers' Helper publishing company turned his columns for *Bakers' Helper* magazine from 1948 to 1950 into *Artistic Cake Decorating from A to Z.* Other school owners—like New York's E. M. Berling, Manchester's Ernest Schulbe, and Dresden's Erich Weber—self-published, as did supply and product companies like Fred Bauer and the Calumet Baking Company, both headquartered in Chicago. Where the publisher was also a supplier, catalog pages often blended in seamlessly. Trade books might also carry outside advertising: Maclaren's 1903 *Book of Cakes* included full-page ads for everything from icing colors to "butter flavor" flour to Egso (a "natural egg yellow"), and even advertisements for other publishers' books.

In the United States, in particular, trade publishers often catered to immigrant men. Herman Hueg, acknowledging the nation's large number of German-born bakers, produced bilingual publications: his 1892 book-cum-catalog, *Ornamental Confectionery and The Art of Baking in All Its Branches,* had sold 90,000 copies by its 1905 tenth edition. But literacy could be a problem even for native English speakers. In 1925 the aptly named confectioner W. C. Baker celebrated that "every baker today is at least able to read," but five years later E. M. Berling remained cautious, explaining that his manual was "presented . . . in language easy to understand and excluding all high-class expressions." The editors of John Zenker's book addressed another potential shortcoming when they claimed that cake decorating "can be mastered by people who are not artistically inclined."

By the late 1800s, the United States already had three trade journals: *Confectioners' Journal, Confectioner and Baker,* and *Bakers' Helper. Bakers' Helper* remained America's top title for decades, issuing many manuals along with its twice-monthly magazine. In England, *The Practical Confectioner* and *The Bakery and Confectioner's Journal* vied with two Maclaren publications, *Confectionery & Baking Trade* and *The British Baker,* the second of which became dominant. Like its British and American counterparts, Italy's *Giornale dei pasticcieri et confettieri* (Journal of Pastry and Confectionery) published manuals in addition to a magazine.

The interwar years of the twentieth century were trade publishing's zenith, when color printing and photo reproduction combined to produce both magnificent books and informative journals, as well as supply catalogs as deluxe as the books: United Yeast Company's large-format catalog, with full-page color plates, came with an embossed metallic cardboard cover. Despite the nation's ethnic diversity, trade publishers in the United States embraced an all-American stance during this and the post–World War II era, unlike their European counterparts, who offered manuals in many languages (such as Germany's Erich Weber and Heinrich Killinger) as well as translations of German, Swedish, Swiss, and Danish publications (such as Britain's Maclaren). See WEBER, JOHANNES MARTIN ERICH.

The line between the professional and amateur began to blur in the late 1940s when Chicago supplier Dewey McKinley Wilton discovered that his pricey professional cake decorating courses, meant for veterans on the GI Bill, were attracting hordes of housewives. By 1960, his firm's first "amateur" manual was in its fifteenth edition, and by the mid-1970s, Wilton's books were as vivid and their creations as intricate as the 1920s professional manuals had been.

By the late twentieth century, books for amateurs were frequently more eye catching and certainly more affordable than any professional manuals. While trade journals like *Pastry & Baking* in the United States, the *British Baker,* and Canada's *Bakers Journal* were keeping professionals, especially those working for large hotels or chain restaurants, abreast of the latest business and technological news, a growing breed of mass-circulation magazines for enthusiastic amateurs and semiprofessionals offered more in the way of creative inspiration, sometimes from renowned pastry chefs themselves. By the first decades of the twenty-first century, glossies like *American Cake Decorating* and Britain's *Cakes & Sugarcraft* and *Cake Craft & Decoration* had been joined by a host of "one-off" cake decorating magazines and the web-only *Cake Central.*

See also BAKER'S; FOOD COLORINGS; and CONFECTIONERY MANUALS.

Baker, W. C., *Mastercraft in Cakes and Decorating.* Chicago: Bakers' Helper, 1925.

Hueg, Herman. *The Art of Baking and Ornamental Confectionery in All Its Branches.* Long Island City, N.Y.: Author, 1905.

Lewis, T. Percy, and A. G. Bromley. *The Book of Cakes.* London: Maclaren & Sons, 1903.

Francine Kirsch

pudding, originally a term derived from the French *boudin* (itself from the Latin *botellus,* "sausage") and reserved for a sausage-like item (as in "blood pudding"), is now most frequently a dessert, although its nature varies widely by region. In North America, "pudding" is a custard-like concoction. In the United Kingdom, it can refer to the sweet course that ends a meal; to any food considered suitable for this course; or, more specifically, to suet pastry or sponge-cake-type mixtures (whether steamed, boiled, or baked), batter mixtures, or baked milk and cereal mixtures. Other cultural variations include the North American "hasty pudding" or cornmeal mush, the Indian rice-and-milk-based sweet kheer, and the blood-and-chocolate pudding called sanguinaccio from Puglia. See SANGUINACCIO. A related word, *pudim*, occurs in Portuguese; and *budino* is an Italian custard-like dessert. The British usage of the term "pudding" is so inclusive as to be almost universal, and every culture that eats bread has some version of bread pudding. However, as Alan Davidson notes in *The Oxford Companion to Food*, "To focus attention on the British usage [of the term] is legitimate, since pudding may be claimed as a British invention, and is certainly a characteristic dish of British cuisine" (2006, p. 638). See UNITED KINGDOM.

In the late nineteenth century British pudding gained a reputation as plain, even boringly so, lacking the nuance, artifice, and drama of other desserts. Victorian examples such as "Cold Shape" were stubbornly, drably antipoetic. Nonetheless, pudding inspires fierce devotion in a nation that has always harbored an achingly sweet tooth. British puddings exist under several broad categories, including milk or "nursery" puddings, made with a starch such as rice, tapioca, or sago; suet puddings; batter puddings; and sponge puddings (often either boiled or steamed). Many of these are served with a sauce, often custard. See CUSTARD. Despite having some ingredients and techniques in common with savory puddings (such as steak and kidney in a suet crust), pudding arguably has no single defining characteristic; indeed, nailing down a definition is almost impossible. One recurrent theme is substantiality—unsurprising, given Britain's notoriously chilly and damp climate. Less obvious are the perceptions of gender appropriateness that the substance of a pudding gave rise to. The lighter "puddings"—creams, fools, flummeries, junkets, syllabubs, and possets—were seen as feminine, whereas heavy suet puddings were "manly." See FOOLS; GENDER; JUNKET; and SYLLABUB.

History

A remarkably direct line can be traced from the spiced, savory sausages of classical antiquity to the rich, sugary desserts of today. After the departure of the Romans from England, boiled suet sausages became a staple of the Anglo-Saxon diet. Medieval palates favored the blending of savory, sweet, and spicy flavors, and puddings at this time were likely to include both meat and sugar. The antecedent of the famous Christmas plum pudding was a "plum pottage" containing meat and dried fruits. Such combinations originated in the extensive Arabic influence on medieval European cooking.

Sugar became a primary cooking ingredient rather than a seasoning in the early modern period, as New World slave plantations began exporting it to Europe. See PLANTATIONS, SUGAR and SUGAR TRADE. Although sweet items were still served alongside meats and vegetables, and many dishes retained both sweet and savory flavors, overtly sweet puddings began to evolve into a class of their own, particularly among those who could afford to use greater quantities of sugar. The Elizabethans developed the "pudding pie" (a pudding baked in a dish and covered with a pastry lid) to eliminate the use of animal guts, but perhaps the single greatest innovation in pudding's history is the pudding cloth, which food historian C. Anne Wilson called "a vital factor in the expansion of pudding-eating" (1984, p. 285). A pudding cloth is mentioned in a 1617 recipe for Cambridge Pudding, and in the 1670s Hannah Woolley gave two recipes for almond pudding: one in guts, and one to be boiled in a "napkin." As puddings proliferated, regional specialities, such as "Devonshire whitepot" using the famous Devon cream, began to appear. In 1747 Hannah Glasse offered two recipes for haggis, oats and offal cooked in a sheep's stomach. One, "To Make [A Haggis] Sweet with Fruit," offers an example of what distinguished a sweet from a savory pudding, namely, currants, raisins, and half a pint of "sack" or sweet, fortified wine. By this time the meat had begun to disappear from mince pies and Christmas "plum" puddings; recipes suggested filling boiled suet pudding with either meat or fruit, rather than both. The eighteenth century saw the advent of batter puddings such as Yorkshire pudding, baked and served with a roasted joint (but sometimes eaten as a sweet—a practice that survives in Yorkshire). It also saw a proliferation of puddings based on almonds, carrots, lemons, oranges, or other fruits, baked in pastry crusts.

In the Victorian era, the mass production of the pudding tin allowed even housewives with no servants and little cooking expertise to make complex puddings, while the overall distinction between sweet and savory puddings continued. However, as potatoes became more widely accepted by the middle classes, they began to replace suet puddings as meat's starchy companion. Along with the growth of the British Empire, a characteristically Victorian nationalistic mythology grew up around the British pudding and the country's particular skill in making it. As one commenter from *The Saturday Review* wrote in 1860 of the de facto national dish eaten by British colonialists at sweaty Christmas dinners in India: "We, too, may see in our... determination to eat plum pudding at Agra and Lahore, a sign that we are determined to have our own way wherever we go, and that we are a very vital and self-sufficing people." The sense of nation and past that now attaches so strongly to pudding was thus already developing; in Thomas Hardy's *The Mayor of Casterbridge* (1886), the old-style frumenty serves as a symbol of vanishing rural customs.

Decline and Revival

Sweet puddings continued to proliferate, though many were simply minor modifications within the larger theme of suet, sugar, and dried fruit. This (perceived) monotony was one of the factors contributing to the decline of the traditional English pudding in the twentieth century. Other reasons include the dieting craze induced by the fashion for boyish figures of the 1920s; wartime food rationing that made key ingredients scarce; a new breed of housewives with little time for the long steaming and boiling required; cheaper meat, and central heating, both of which reduced the need for filling, carbohydrate-rich puddings.

Across the Atlantic, at the close of the Great War, came the first powdered pudding mixes: the My-T-Fine brand debuted in 1918. Following World War II, in 1949, the *New York Times* raved about "Amazo" cornstarch-based instant pudding. Amid a cultural backlash against the Victorians and an increasing emphasis on lighter foods, scientists experimented with artificial ingredients. These mixes, often eaten alone as a snack, remain popular in Continental Europe and Southeast Asia (as in Indonesian *puding coklat*), as well as in North America.

Renewed interest in traditional puddings came from food writers in the 1970s and 1980s, notably Jane Grigson. Lamenting the downfall of the pudding in her landmark *English Food* (1974), she provided a carefully curated selection of recipes, part of a nascent consciousness of British culinary heritage. The publication of a *Book of Traditional Puddings* by the National Trust (1983) and the 1985 establishment of a "Pudding Club" dedicated to their preservation suggested both the hold the pudding retained on the British cultural imagination, and the widespread concern at its apparent disappearance. By 2000 the American food magazine *Gourmet* could state that "British chefs have rediscovered the 'pud,' that odd collection of boiled, steamed and baked desserts with funny names." Contemporary British chefs like Nigella Lawson, Jamie Oliver, and Heston Blumenthal have all published their own versions of traditional pudding recipes.

The resurgence of the pudding raises some questions about the nature of its appeal. After all, even pudding's defenders admit its shortcomings; as food historian Jeri Quinzio diplomatically puts it, "Warm, milky rice pudding... [occupies] a special place that has much to do with nostalgia and little to do with flavour" (2012, p. 90). The answer lies partly in the fact that pudding embodies the complex relationship between sweetness and sentimentality. Ironically, however, the traditional suet or steamed pudding is now primarily produced either commercially or by professional chefs, and is frequently deployed by the latter as a marker of their authenticity, homeliness, Britishness, or class affiliation. Members of Britain's Pudding Club are "bound by our enthusiasm for something wonderful and unchanging... something childish and yet enduring" (2012, p. 7). This powerful sense of the past appears to be pudding's greatest advantage and also disadvantage. Puddings fell out of favor, in part, because they seemed anachronistic, yet precisely because they are antiquated enough to be viewed romantically—as a nostalgic relic of a disappearing way of life—they are regaining popularity. Pudding is thus doubly nostalgic: it belongs not only to a departed sociocultural moment, but also to one's own (even if partially imagined) childhood.

See also BLANCMANGE; CHRISTMAS; CUSTARD; ETON MESS; FLAN (PUDÍM); PAYASAM; SPONGE CAKE; STICKY TOFFEE PUDDING; and TRIFLE.

Davidson, Alan. "Pudding." In *The Oxford Companion to Food*, 2d ed., pp. 638–639. New York: Oxford University Press, 2006.

Paston-Williams, Sara. *The National Trust Book of Traditional Puddings*. Newton Abbot, U.K.: David & Charles, 1983.

Pudding Club, The. *Great British Puddings*. London: Ebury, 2012.

Quinzio, Jeri. *Pudding: A Global History*. London: Reaktion, 2012.
Turner, Keith, and Jean Turner. *The Pudding Club Book: 100 Luscious Recipes from the World Famous Pudding Club*. London: Headline, 1997.
Wilson, C. Anne. *Food and Drink in Britain: From the Stone Age to Recent Times*. Harmondsworth, U.K.: Penguin, 1984.

Abigail Dennis

pulled sugar is used in many traditional, eye-catching candies, including North American candy canes, British seaside rock and humbugs, French *berlingots*, and Swedish *polkagrisar*.

To make pulled sugar, sugar syrup is boiled with glucose (to prevent graining or recrystallization) to the hard crack stage (302°F [150°C]), then allowed to cool slightly before being literally worked by pulling the mass, stretching it into a rope, folding it and pulling again—a process repeated until the sugar becomes satiny and opaque. A skilled confectioner can do this by hand with astonishing speed and apparent ease, although machines are now mostly used for this hot and potentially dangerous task. Often the sugar is divided into parts, some of which are colored or left clear to make contrasting stripes or patterns on the mass before it is drawn out to its final length.

The Scottish Edinburgh rock and Turkish *peynir şekeri* also use the same technique, but the syrup is boiled to a lower temperature and the final confection is allowed to grain, yielding a powdery, melting texture.

Although the origins of this technique are unknown, they must be ancient. A clue to the introduction of pulled-sugar confections to the European world lies in the word "pennet," an old English name for pulled-sugar sweets apparently similar to Edinburgh rock. This word ultimately derives from the Arabic *al-fanid* and is related to the archaic Spanish *alphenique* and Portuguese *alfenim*, both denoting pulled sugar. The association of a precise skill with a word originating in an area responsible for both growing sugar and transmitting the skills for working with it suggests that the two moved west together during or shortly after the Muslim conquest of the western Mediterranean, and also pinpoints the magical ability of sugar to transmit far more than mere calories.

Mason, Laura. *Sugar-Plums and Sherbet: The Prehistory of Sweets*. Totnes, U.K.: Prospect, 2004.

Laura Mason

punch, which generally refers to a blended drink of sweetened alcohol flavored with fruit and spices, has its origins in Persia and India. Nonalcoholic, iced sherbets made with sugar, lemon juice, and water and flavored with flower waters had been discovered by Europeans. One apocryphal story has Saladin serving sherbets to King Richard during the Crusades. See FLOWER WATERS and SHERBET. In India, among non-Muslims, alcohol was added to make a delicately perfumed drink called *pale-puntz*, "consisting of Acquaevitae, Rose-water, juice of citrons and sugar," as described in *Mandelslo's Travels in Western India*, 1638–1639. These Indian "punches" were made with arrack (distilled palm wine) and cane sugar or jaggery, a sticky, dark brown palm sugar refined with lime juice. See PALM SUGAR. A popular theory concerning the name suggests that "punch" is a corruption of the Hindi *panch*, meaning "five," referring to the five elements of strong (alcohol), weak (water or fruit juice), sour (citrus juice), sweet (sugar), and spice, all essential to the making of punch.

In reality, punch was, and is, made in any number of variations: three (alcohol, sugar, and fruit; or alcohol, sugar, and milk or eggs); four (alcohol, sugar, citrus, and water); and five or more ingredients. The spice used is typically nutmeg. See NUTMEG. Nonalcoholic punches eliminate the alcohol. From the beginning, punch has been described as being made and served in a bowl, and drunk together with friends and at celebrations.

The earliest references to punch outside of India are from the American colonies in the 1630s. In England, although the earliest references appear only in the late seventeenth century, following the Restoration, they suggest that punch was known earlier. British sailors were likely familiar with a simple, rough beverage, whereas merchants from the East India Company introduced a posher version.

Based as it is on spirits (initially, arrack and brandy, then rum from the eighteenth century on), with the addition of citrus juice and various forms of sugar as the sweetener, punch was different from the traditional European blended drinks made with wine, beer, cider, and milk, spiced, enriched, and sweetened with honey. See SYLLABUB. Molasses was used in the vinegar-based drink switchel popular with farmers in colonial America, while Central American *ponche navideño* calls for *piloncillo* (dark brown sugar). See SUGAR.

A good balance of acidity and sweetness was an important element of eighteenth-century punch. Proportions varied, depending on the sourness or sweetness of the fruit and the type of alcohol used, but a Caribbean rhyme suggests that a perfect balance was found in "one of sour, two of sweet, three of strong and four of weak." This proportion appears to be the usual one in the West Indies, Europe, and America during the eighteenth century. Punch often accompanied fried fish, cheese, and turtle soup—the fattiness of these foods being cut by the punch's acidity. It is unclear whether serving punch with savory foods meant that early versions of the drink were less sweet, but the literature reveals frequent mention of the sharp acidity of lemons leading to extreme stomach cramps.

The eighteenth-century punch-making process began with a "sherbet" of sugar dissolved in citrus juice. Over time tastes appear to have changed, and the sugar–acid balance became less important, with the result that punch became sweeter. A simple sugar syrup, often readymade, became increasingly common, and a greater range of fruits was used. Recipes moved from advising the cook to "sweeten to taste" to listing specific quantities of ingredients, regardless of a given fruit's acidity.

Although growing concern in the late eighteenth century over slavery had a passing effect on the use of "slave sugar" and rum, punch became increasingly popular in Continental Europe and America in the early nineteenth century. See SLAVERY and SUGAR TRADE. A fashion for flaming punch developed, thanks in part to the caramel flavor created by the flame. In Germany, the popular *Feuerzangenbowle* (fire-tong punch), in which a lighted rum-soaked sugar cone was allowed to drip into the punch, was later captured in Helmut Weiss's film *Die Feuerzangenbowle* (1944). In France, flaming brandy or rum was added to the punch. In *Manuel complet de la maitresse de maison et de la parfaite ménagère* (3d ed. Paris, 1834), Elisabeth Celnart suggests a November tea party with a large bowl of flaming punch surrounded by a variety of little sweets and cakes. In Britain, heated drinks such as mulled wine merged with punch, and steaming bowls of punch became a traditional Christmas drink. See MULLED WINE.

Pineapple-flavored rum had been popular since the eighteenth century. Some early American punches used peach brandy. Flavored liqueurs and eaux-de-vie, especially orange and cherry, became popular in the nineteenth century, providing extra alcohol, fruit, and sweetness, often enhanced by the addition of pieces of fruit. Fruit punches, with less emphasis on the sweet–acidic balance, have continued to evolve. Contemporary examples include Spanish sangria, Mexican *ponche navideño* with acidic *tejocote* (*Crataegus pubescens stipulacea*) and tamarind, stewed until soft; Guatemalan *ponche navideño* with various dried fruits, pineapple, papaya, mango and peaches, mamey (*Mammea Americana*), and coconut; and Austro-Hungarian *Krampampuli* with raisins, crystallized ginger, and dates.

The development of the ice trade, of refrigeration and ice production, encouraged the making of iced punches. Inspired by Persian sherbet and an infatuation with the Orient, iced Punch à la Romaine, made with fruit juice, whisked egg whites, and alcohol, was often served in ornate glasses as a palate cleanser between courses at grand dinners.

Several punch-flavored cakes exist. Swedish *punsch*, by law made with arrack, is particularly sweet, and is used to flavor small cakes called *Punschrullar*, made of biscuits and cacao covered in green marzipan and dipped in chocolate. Rum, oranges, and lemons are used in Germany, Austria, and Hungary to flavor *Punschtorte*. In Finland, Runeberg's Torte is a small pastry seasoned with bitter almonds, Swedish *punsch*, and raspberry jam. It is traditionally served with a glass of punch from early January into February, to commemorate the birthday of the poet Johan Ludvig Runeberg, who was said to have enjoyed the confection with *punsch* for breakfast. An American trifle is sometimes called a Punch-Bowl Cake because it is made and served in a punch bowl. Eliza Acton, in *Modern Cookery for Private Families* (1845), gives a recipe for Punch Sauce made with brandy, rum, white wine, oranges, and lemons for serving with "custard, plain bread and plum-puddings."

Punch bowls, often large enough to serve a crowd and grand enough to be displayed, were produced in all materials and many styles. Ornate bowls on a pedestal were used for more formal events; some American glass bowls have detachable pedestals, so bowl and pedestal could be inverted to form a cake stand. See CAKE AND CONFECTIONERY STANDS. Special ladles, with long handles and bowls of silver (sometimes crafted of coin), were also devised for serving punch.

Alongside the twenty-first-century revival of cocktails have come a number of attempts to revive punch as well, but they have proved less successful for a number of reasons. A cocktail serves one person, whereas a bowl of punch needs a crowd. Cocktails thrive on a careful balance of new and unusual combinations, sometimes exotic and bizarre. Good punch, often drunk in greater volume, requires delicacy, less sweetness, and fresh fruit to succeed.

See also COLONIALISM; HIPPOCRAS; POLITICS OF SUGAR; and RUM.

Künster, Silke von. *Bowlen und Punsche*. Niedernhausen, Germany: Falken, 2000.

Lina (pseudonym). *Die Köchinn, wie sie sein soll und muss: Perfect kochen zu lernen*. Munich: A. Weber, 1836.

Spencer, Edward. *The Flowing Bowl*. London: Grant Richards, 1903.

Terrington, William. *Cooling Cups and Dainty Drinks*. London: George Routledge and Sons, 1869.

Thomas, Jerry. *How to Mix Drinks, or the Bon-Vivant's Companion*. New York: Dick and Fitzgerald, 1862.

Wondrich, Dave. *Punch: The Delights (and Dangers) of the Flowing Bowl*. New York: Perigree Trade, 2010.

Elizabeth Gabay

qaṭā'if (often pronounced *'aṭāyif* in modern Arabic) is a crepe of considerable antiquity—the name may come from an Aramaic verb meaning "to make dough." Today the *qaṭā'if* might be made like a Western crepe, but the traditional technique is to knead a stiff, leavened dough and then work in enough water so that it can either be rolled out thin or used as a batter or a dough.

The oldest *qaṭā'if,* typically fried and then rolled around a filling of nuts, appear in a tenth-century cookbook from the court of the Abbasid caliphs. A sweet called *khushkanānaj min qaṭā'if maqlī* (a cookie made from stuffed crepes) was made by frying a crepe just long enough to stiffen one side, with the upper side remaining tacky, so that it could be folded around a nut filling, sealed shut, and deep-fried. This sweet may have been a recent invention, because in North Africa it was called "Abbasid *qaṭā'if.*" It is still made in Arab countries; the Turks call it *dolma kadayıf.*

Later cookbooks added new recipes, such as a stack of crepes (*abū lāsh*) and *jamāliyya,* a deep-fried pastry made by sealing two crepes together around a filling. There was already confusion between *qaṭā'if* and thin baked or griddled flatbreads. In an unrecorded process, a pastry wrapper in the form of vermicelli-like threads evolved around the thirteenth century, the Arabs calling it by an old flatbread name, *kunāfa,* and the Persians, Turks, and Greeks by forms of *qaṭā'if* (respectively *ghatāyef, kadayif,* and *kadaïfi*).

Today, both the half-cooked crepes and the vermicelli-like product are usually bought from pastry shops and stuffed at home. The usual filling for both is sweetened ground nuts, but clotted cream and white cheese are also used. When the filling is cheese, the Turks refer to the vermicelli-like version as *künefe,* a form of the Arabic name *kunāfa.*

See also MIDDLE EAST; NUTS; PANCAKE; PERSIA; and TURKEY.

Helou, Anissa. *Lebanese Cuisine.* New York: St. Martin's, 1998.

Rayess, George. *Rayess' Art of Lebanese Cooking.* Beirut: Librairie du Liban, 1966.

Charles Perry

race is connected to sweets in many and various ways. Central to any discussion of the relation between the two is power and the ways in which it informs our historical and contemporary understanding of sweetness. In many cultures, sweets have had a history as commodities of racism, or as objects used to distribute racist imagery, messages, and logic. Several racial or ethnic groups have been linked with negative connotations involving certain sweets (Haribo black licorice, for example). Focused on here is the African American experience in the United States, and the associated stereotypes, racist depictions, and health issues related to this experience.

Production

Two commodities—sugar and slaves—were significant to the growth of transatlantic commerce, and the production of sugar is directly tied to the enslavement and exploitation of Arawaks, Africans, and African Americans whose labor helped the Atlantic economy to burgeon. From the sugar plantations of the Caribbean to those of the American South, enslaved peoples worked the sugarcane fields and plantations and were essential to the Triangle trade. See PLANTATIONS, SUGAR and SUGAR TRADE. Across the ocean, for a long while, Pacific Islanders were the source of cheap labor in the sugarcane fields of Australia. Whether in the East or the West, the campaign for sugar functioned to enhance the lives of some while degrading the lives of many others. Due to sugar's status as a luxury item, it sold for high prices, making investment in its production and trade profitable, especially for European merchants. For the enslaved in the United States and the Caribbean, sugar production was especially arduous work, with seasonal rotations and long hours for those who worked in labor gangs. The paltry rations given sugarcane workers further reduced their life expectancy. See SLAVERY.

As agents of reproduction, women were especially affected by the back-breaking toil of sugarcane production. In addition to working long hours, women generally had the responsibility for feeding their families. It is not well known that the antebellum food-service industry provided some opportunities for black women to participate in the early American economy. While free black men primarily dominated the catering industry, some enslaved, but mostly freed, African American women, like the higglers of the British Caribbean and *quitandeiras* of Brazil, sold foods and beverages as hucksters and hawkers. Success from these modest ventures was often measured by the ability to secure one's freedom or augment family earnings. By capitalizing on menial occupations, these early entrepreneurs profited from the sugar and molasses that figured in the sweetening of many beverages and ice cream, cakes, pastries, fritters, pralines, calas (rice cakes), and other baked goods. See NEW ORLEANS and PRALINE. Even after the Civil War, African American women are said to have passed on the art of making fudge, taffy, pecan caramels, and all sorts of brittles to their children.

Stereotypes and Racist Depictions

While African Americans continued to experience some economic advancement in the food industry, Reconstruction ushered in new, racist ideologies that were expressed in popular and material culture.

Carrie Mae Weems's series *Ain't Jokin* (1987–1988) explores racist stereotypes by pairing mundane but culturally loaded objects with acerbic commentary. *Black Man Holding Watermelon* asks why African Americans are so closely associated with the fruit; those familiar with that stereotype might ask, What is wrong with this picture? © CARRIE MAE WEEMS. COURTESY OF THE ARTIST AND JACK SHAINMAN GALLERY, NEW YORK

From the 1880s to the 1930s, black people were portrayed in almost universally derogatory ways as very dark, nappy-headed, bulging-eyed, childlike, and overly deferential. And they were almost always depicted as happy, with an uncontrollable appetite for watermelons.

From minstrel shows to sheet music, postcards to photographs and films, African Americans were caricatured as stealing, eating, and even becoming watermelons. The meanings of this association are many, but the imagery was mainly intended to depict African Americans as simple-minded, content to laze around and happily eat watermelon. The early twentieth century, for example, witnessed white functions and events where blacks provided the entertainment by engaging in watermelon-eating contests. A 1937 cover of *Life* magazine helped to perpetuate these stereotypes by depicting a wagon full of watermelons with an African American man, his back bared, sitting on the edge of a cart looking out toward a dirt road, with farmland on either side. Another image accompanying the story was captioned "The watermelon starts its journey to market in an ordinary wheelbarrow pushed by a grinning Negro."

In her installation *Ain't Jokin,* the visual artist Carrie Mae Weems (b. 1953) emphasizes the cultural potency of race and mundane objects of material culture like sweets. One of the images, *Black Man Holding Watermelon,* forces viewers to ask why African Americans are associated with the fruit; those familiar with the stereotype might ask, what is wrong with this picture? Using watermelon and other sweets, artists such as Weems highlight how such foods remain culturally explosive. In 2008 this stereotype boldly emerged when, during and immediately after the successful presidential bid of Barack Obama, images began circulating that showed watermelons on the White House lawn, one bearing the caption "No Easter egg hunt this year"—evidence not only of the pervasiveness of this particular sweet, but also of the enduring legacy of racial associations that it continues to invoke.

More recently, controversy erupted on the Internet when the opinion columnist Theodore Johnson pointed out that the familiar jingle "Turkey in the Straw" blaring from many ice cream trucks could be associated with the "coon songs" of the past. Though the actual song has a long history that predates its arrival in America, lyrics that originated in blackface minstrelsy were sometimes added to the melody. The words of one song in particular—"Nigger Love a Watermelon Ha! Ha! Ha!," written by Harry C. Browne in 1916—make reference to watermelon as the "colored man's ice cream." Johnson notes that the impact of racism is enduring, especially when it is hidden in "the nooks and crannies of wholesome Americana."

Health Disparities

The relation between African Americans and watermelon is not wholly unfounded, although it is greatly exaggerated. Watermelon is, in general, a familiar fruit in Southern foodways. However, African American dietary habits, choices, and cooking methods, though largely Southern in derivation, have evolved from a long history of slavery, oppression, and segregation, resulting in decidedly different health outcomes today. See SOUTH (U.S.).

Though health disparities exist among all racial and ethnic groups across socioeconomic strata, it has been argued widely that there is a higher prevalence of obesity and weight-related diseases—cardiovascular problems and diabetes, for example—among African Americans. According to some studies, the reasons for these disproportions are not well understood. Others maintain that rather than the foods themselves, it is the long-held cultural beliefs, behaviors, and attitudes informing cooking methods—including the excessive use of sweeteners and fats—that have contributed to these health concerns. See SUGAR AND HEALTH. At least one study suggests that among today's African American youth and children, when compared to European Americans, there is an elevated preference for sweet tastes that begins in childhood. The same study found that, beyond young adulthood, African Americans may derive comfort and sustained pleasure from the repeated intake of sweet tastes in order to alleviate stresses stemming from racial inequalities.

Ironically, in 2014, the African American visual artist Kara Walker paid homage to the "unpaid and overworked Artisans who have refined our Sweet tastes from the cane fields to the Kitchens of the New World" by creating a sphinx-like, 75-foot sculpture of white sugar and carved polystyrene. The figure, titled *A Subtlety: The Marvelous Sugar Baby*, bears a likeness to countless caricatures of African American women—heavyset, thick-lipped, wide-nosed, and kerchief wearing. In this sculpture, Walker not only encapsulates vestiges of entrepreneurship, stereotyping, and health, but like Carrie Mae Weems, she draws attention to the destabilizing tensions of representation, race, and power that most likely will forever link African Americans to white sugar sweetness. See ART.

James, Delores C. S. "Factors Influencing Food Choices, Dietary Intake, and Nutrition-Related Attitudes among African Americans: Application of a Culturally Sensitive Model. *Ethnicity and Health* 9, no. 4 (November 2004): 349–367.

Johnson, Theodore R., III. "Talking about Race and Ice Cream Leaves a Sour Taste for Some." *NPR Code Switch: Frontiers of Race, Culture, and Ethnicity*. National Public Radio, 21 May 2014. http://www.npr.org/blogs/codeswitch/2014/05/21/314246332/talking-about-race-and-ice-cream-leaves-a-sour-taste-for-some (accessed 22 May 2014).

Mintz, Sydney. *Sweetness and Power: The Place of Sugar in Modern History*. New York: Penguin, 1995.

Schiffman, Susan S., Brevick G. Graham, Elizabeth A. Sattely-Miller, and Measha Peterson-Dancy, "Elevated and Sustained Desire for Sweet Taste in African-Americans: A Potential Factor in the Development of Obesity." *Nutrition* 16, no. 10 (2000): 886–893.

Walker, Juliet E. K. *The History of Black Business in America: Capitalism, Race, Entrepreneurship*. 2d ed. Chapel Hill: University of North Carolina Press, 2009.

Psyche Williams-Forson and LaDonna Redmond

Ramadan is the holiest month in the Muslim lunar calendar, during which the consumption of sweets reaches dizzying heights. After abstaining from food and drink from sunrise to sunset, fasters gratify their deprived appetites with a varied meal known as *iftar*, followed by some ultra-sweet desserts. Such indulgences might have been largely encouraged by a widely circulated, albeit questionable, oral tradition of the Prophet Muhammad that describes true believers as lovers of sweets. Another tradition says that true believers love dates. See DATES and ISLAM. Indeed, Muslims worldwide traditionally break their daylong fast with a few dates, following the Prophet's example, along with some water or yogurt. It should be noted that modern medicine has given its nod of approval to this sweet ritual: while the body rapidly gets the nourishment it needs, the dairy slows down elevated sugar levels.

The sugary Ramadan lavishness may historically be traced back to medieval times, when sugarcane cultivation became widespread in the Middle East with the rapid expansion of the ruling Muslim empires. See SUGARCANE and SUGARCANE AGRICULTURE. We have ample evidence of the dizzying arrays of confections, including sculpted ones, made in the kitchens of the elite and at the specialized sweets-markets. But in relation to Ramadan accounts of customs and practices, the Egyptian Fatimid era from the tenth to the twelfth centuries offers the most detail, as related in Nasir Khusraw's *Safarnama* and al-Maqrizi's *Khuṭaṭ*.

For the Fatimids, dessert was a celebratory food, and they took great pains to impress with it. In the royal kitchens, hundreds of dessert chefs were employed and immense quantities of ingredients were used to prepare the enormous platters distributed to high and low, rich and poor, in celebration of Ramadan. They were loaded with stuffed cookies like *khushkananaj* and *basandūd*; shelled nuts, raisins, and dates; and the ring-shaped hard sugar-candy *sukkar Sulaymānī*. Also included were the sweet digestives *juwarishnat*, *natif* (nougat), and *fanīdh* (pulled taffy). See NOUGAT and TAFFY. Cooks began preparations for these gift trays 10 weeks ahead of time. During the Ramadan *iftar* meal, colored hard candies (*halwa yabisa*) outlined the table, and bowls of condensed puddings were abundantly arranged across it. See HARD CANDY. Servers would begin arranging the banquet table at midnight. A citrus tree, complete with branches, leaves, and fruit, all made of sugar, served as a fabulous centerpiece. Underneath were arranged almost one thousand sugar statuettes. To celebrate the end of Ramadan, two huge sculpted sugar palaces were placed at both ends of the dining table. See SUGAR SCULPTURE.

Sweet celebrations continued to be important in Ramadan during the time of the Ottomans. Puddings, thick starch-based halva, syrupy pastries, jams and electuaries, toffees, nougats, and many other desserts comparable to those served in Egypt appeared on the table, along with a host of other sweets either adapted or invented. Baklava loomed large. See BAKLAVA. The most famous Ramadan tradition goes back to the end of the sixteenth century, when the Baklava Procession was first held annually on the fifteenth day of the month. Hundreds of trays of baklava for the janissaries were baked in the palace kitchens. Tied in cloths to keep the sticky pastries clean of dust, these trays were carried to the barracks in pomp.

Today, Muslims typically first wash down the *iftar* meal with fruits or light milk *muhallabiyya* puddings thickened with cornstarch or rice flour. The Iranian variation called *zerde* is tinted yellow with saffron, while the Indian *kheer* uses vermicelli noodles for a starch. See INDIA and PERSIA. Dried fruit compote (*khoshaf*) is popular in Egypt and Turkey. Its Indonesian counterpart *kolek/kolak* is made with coconut milk, palm sugar, pandan leaves, and fresh and dried fruits. It is not unusual for sweets to be consumed even within the course of the meal itself. In Morocco, for instance, the spicy *harira* soup is eaten together with *shabbakiyya*, flower-shaped cookies fried and drenched in honey.

After some rest, people go out to socialize and enjoy desserts with tea or coffee, or they patronize all-night dessert shops where popular Ramadan confections are offered. These are mostly sticky, rich, fried treats, often filled with nuts or sweet cheese or clotted cream and drenched in syrup. *Qatayif* (Arabian pancakes), *kunafa* (vermicelli-like pastry), and baklava are ubiquitous in the Middle East. See QAṬĀ'IF. Even more widespread is the latticed *zalabiya*, called *mushabbak* in the Levant, *zulbia* in Iran, and *jalebi* on the Indian subcontinent and in Afghanistan. See ZALABIYA. Semolina is found in such Ramadan favorites as the moist semolina cakes variously known as *basbousa* in Egypt, *nammora* in Lebanon, *hareesa* in Syria, and *qalb el-louz* in Algeria; in Afghanistan and on the Indian subcontinent, semolina is cooked into a dense pudding called *suji halwa*. See HALVAH. A Ramadan sweet indigenous to Southeast Asia and southern China is *kuih* (and other linguistic variants), made in many different ways, the most common of which is the Indonesian layered multicolored steamed cake *kue lapis*. It consists of steamed thin layers of batter made with flours of tapioca, rice, and mung beans, mixed with sugar syrup, coconut milk, and pandan leaves. All these sweets are available year round, but they are most frequently consumed during Ramadan.

In Iraq and other Gulf countries, the children receive their own share of Ramadan sweet delights by going door to door singing and asking for sweets. This practice, called *Qarqīʿān* or *Majīna*, takes place in the middle days of Ramadan and is believed to date back to the birth of the Prophet's grandson Hasan ibn Ali on the fifteenth of this month. The children of Medina, the story goes, gathered around the prophet's house singing *Qarrat al-ʿain* (Congratulations), and the Prophet rewarded them with sweets, dates and raisins.

See also CHINA; DESSERT; DRIED FRUIT; FRIED DOUGH; MIDDLE EAST; SOUTH ASIA; SOUTHEAST ASIA; and TURKEY.

Işın, Mary. *Sherbet and Spice: The Complete Story of Turkish Sweets and Desserts*. London: I. B. Tauris, 2013.

Sharif, Dima. "Ramadan Special 2013: A Focus on Ramadan Culture and the Spirit of Ramadan." *Dima Sharif: Bringing Food to Life* (blog), 8 July 2013. http://www.dimasharif.com/2013/07/ramadan-special-2013-focus-on-ramadan.html (accessed 22 October 2014).

Nawal Nasrallah

Reese's Pieces, Hershey's popular candy shells filled with a peanut butter mixture, would never have become famous without the help of competitor M&M's.

The fact that M&M's had been America's best-selling candy since its introduction in the early 1940s infuriated Hershey executives, especially because

Milton Hershey's right-hand man William Murrie had helped Forrest E. Mars Sr. launch the M&M brand. Hershey's had supplied M&M's with chocolate and helped the business throughout World War II when rationing made supplies scarce. Murrie's son Bruce went into business with Forrest Mars, representing the second M on M&M's, but Forrest forced Bruce out when he had no further use for his Hershey connections. See HERSHEY'S; MARS; and M&M'S.

In 1954 Hershey's went head-to-head against M&M's with its own product, called Hershey-ets. But Hershey-ets proved difficult to sell because it was nearly impossible to describe them without invoking the competition's name—the products were simply too similar. Hershey abandoned Hershey-ets in the 1970s. But the leftover Hershey-ets candy-making equipment gave marketers an idea. Instead of making a product exactly like M&M's, Hershey's could make a candy more like its best-selling Reese's Peanut Butter Cup. However, creating a peanut-butter center that did not leak peanut oil was not easy. Hershey's turned the job over to an outside food-science firm that developed a special paste dubbed "penuche"—a blend of peanuts and sugar that contained very little peanut oil, so the filling would not spoil or soften the candy coating over time.

To avoid comparison with M&M's, Hershey executives decided that the new product would not contain chocolate. The candies were brown and orange, reflecting the Reese's brand, and the name Reese's Pieces was born. The candies were introduced nationally in 1980, and Hershey had high hopes for the brand. But after a promising start, sales began to fall, putting Hershey's multimillion-dollar investment in jeopardy.

In October 1981 Universal Pictures approached Mars, Inc. about using its M&M's product in an upcoming movie about an alien stranded on Earth who befriends a little boy. The boy would use the M&M's to lure the tiny alien out of his backyard and into his home. But the executives at Mars refused, fearing that any association with an alien creature could send the wrong message about its product. So Universal turned to Hershey's. They offered Reese's Pieces a shot at the movie, telling Hershey executives the movie would boost candy sales and, in return, the candy could promote the movie. Hershey executives signed an agreement pledging $1 million worth of candy promotions for *E.T.* in exchange for the opportunity. A step beyond traditional product placement whereby a consumer product appears in a show or film, this was one of the first cases of "brand integration," in which a brand features prominently in the actual plot.

When *E.T.* opened, it immediately began breaking box office records around the world, and sales of Reese's Pieces skyrocketed. The Reese's Pieces brand has remained popular with consumers ever since, although sales dipped again shortly after the movie hype died down. Nevertheless, the idea of candy-coated pieces remains a Hershey staple, and today the company sells many Pieces varieties, including Almond Joy, Peppermint Patties, Hershey's Special Dark, and Hershey's Milk Chocolate with Almonds. No doubt if Mars had accepted the Universal offer, none of these candies would exist today.

See also HERSHEY, MILTON S.

Brenner, Joël Glenn. *The Emperors of Chocolate: Inside the Secret World of Hershey and Mars*. New York: Random House, 1999.
D'Antonio, Michael. *Hershey: Milton S. Hershey's Extraordinary Life of Wealth, Empire, and Utopian Dreams*. New York: Simon & Schuster, 2007.
Hershey Community Archives. Oral history collections, administered by the M. S. Hershey Trust.

Joël Glenn Brenner

refrigeration is the chilling of a food or a liquid from the ambient temperature to a lower one by removing heat through convection or conduction. Refrigeration enables liquids and foods to last longer because the microorganisms naturally occurring in them (bacteria, yeasts, and molds) multiply most readily in a temperature range of 77°F (25°C) to 86°F (30°C). Reducing the ambient temperature in and around the food by refrigeration significantly slows down the ability of the microorganisms to multiply, thereby reducing the likelihood that the food will spoil.

The earliest form of refrigeration was achieved simply by surrounding the food or liquid with ice or snow in order to reduce the temperature. Consuming chilled food was a novelty, and the sensation was greatly enjoyed. Affluent families farmed ice from rivers and lakes on their estates to store in specially constructed icehouses designed to keep the ice from melting for as long as possible. They were usually sited under trees or on the shady side of a building, often partially or completely below ground. The ice, insulated with wood and straw, could be kept year round for making ice creams and other chilled desserts. See DESSERTS, CHILLED; DESSERTS, FROZEN; and ICE CREAM. In harsher climates, cold temperatures were easier to maintain; Russian noblemen, for instance, had vast, naturally cooled cellars that were perfect for aging mead. See MEAD and RUSSIA.

Freezing preserves liquids and foods for months, and in some cases for years. Freezing cools a chilled food or liquid to below its freezing point, where it solidifies. This point varies according to water content. The higher the water content of a food, the more solid it will be at the freezing point of water. Freezing a liquid requires more science than mere refrigeration. The addition of various salts (e.g., sodium chloride, or table salt) to ice reduces the temperature of the ice. It is possible to reduce the temperature of ice to about 6°F (−21°C) by adding salt, a practice historically used in the production of sorbets and ices. See ITALIAN ICE and SHERBET. Today, rock salt is added to ice to more effectively freeze the custard when making ice cream in hand-cranked machines. A temperature of −3°F (−16°C) can easily be achieved at home by this method. See ICE CREAM MAKERS.

When and where this endothermic effect of salt on ice was discovered is unknown. The historian Joseph Needham, in his monumental work *Science and Civilisation in China*, considers it unlikely that the freezing effect of salt solutions was a European discovery; he believes that it reached Europe from the East via the Arabs and Moors during their time in Spain (711–1492 C.E.). The first European record of the endothermic effect dates to 1530, when the Italian physician Marco Antonio Zimara of Padua wrote in his *Problemata* about the use of niter (sodium nitrate) for chilling liquids.

Commercial Ice Trade

By the nineteenth century, supplying ice for chilled and frozen confectionery, as well as for keeping perishable food from spoiling, had become big business. Wealthy people in major Western cities had iceboxes (early refrigerators), into which the local iceman delivered, on a regular basis, big blocks of ice. This business was labor and transport intensive and depended on the weather for the production of ice. In 1842 the entrepreneur Frederic Tudor began shipping ice from the United States to England, and in 1850 Carlo Gatti shipped ice from Norway to London. Other companies shipped ice from the United States to South America and even to India (Chennai's famous icehouse stored ice shipped from the States by Frederic Tudor; it is now the Swami Vivekananda House). However, with the advent of mechanical refrigeration, this industry died out.

Mechanical Refrigeration

The first known method of mechanical refrigeration was demonstrated in 1756 by William Cullen, a surgeon and chemist at Edinburgh University. In 1842 John Gorrie designed a system to refrigerate water to produce ice, but it was a commercial failure. Six years later, Alexander Twining initiated commercial refrigeration in the United States, and by 1856 mechanical refrigeration had developed into an industry.

Though refrigerated railroad cars using a mixture of salt and ice were introduced in the United States in the 1840s, it was not until the 1860s that mechanical refrigeration came into use on the railroads. In the mid-twentieth century, refrigerated trucks became commonplace on the roads. Mechanical refrigeration meant that meat and perishable foods could be shipped, frozen, to Europe and North America from Australia, New Zealand, or Argentina, and still arrive frozen and in good condition. Professional confectioners were early adopters of this method, especially the Sara Lee Company in the United States, which revolutionized the process in the 1950s. See SARA LEE. The new equipment enabled bakeries to broaden their offerings with a wider selection of ice creams and cakes iced with buttercream.

Domestic mechanical refrigerators first appeared around 1914–1915. They came with small freezer boxes inside that were usually suitable only for making ice cubes for drinks. The larger refrigerator compartment, however, enabled the owner to keep milk and cold drinks, as well as milk-based desserts, blancmanges, trifles, puddings, jelled desserts, and, soon enough, icebox cakes. See BLANCMANGE; GELATIN DESSERTS; ICEBOX CAKE; PUDDING; and TRIFLE.

Freeze-Drying

Freeze-drying, developed during World War II, consists of freezing a substance in a vacuum in order to remove any water or ice. Used extensively for pharmaceutical products, it was adopted in the latter part of the twentieth century for culinary use, to make freeze-dried ice cream that could be stored unrefrigerated and then rehydrated to be eaten by astronauts, among others.

Freezing with Liquid Nitrogen

Freezing by means of cryogenic liquids was first mentioned in 1894 by James Dewar at a lecture at the Royal Institution in London. Astonishingly, the Victorian cook Mrs. Marshall mentioned this method in her magazine, *The Table,* on 24 August 1901, suggesting that it would soon be possible for guests to make their own ice cream at the table. See MARSHALL, AGNES BERTHA. Although the process had been familiar to food technologists for decades, it was not until 1999, when Heston Blumenthal used it to great effect in his restaurant The Fat Duck, that the technique came to the notice of the public. Blumenthal continues to experiment today, with liquid-nitrogen–chilled ice creams made of chicken puree and curry, or of frozen reindeer milk and bacon.

David, Elizabeth. *Harvest of the Cold Months: The Social History of Ice and Ices.* London: M. Joseph, 1994.
Needham, Joseph. *Science and Civilisation in China.* Cambridge, U.K.: Cambridge University Press, 1976.

Robin Weir

religion

See BUDDHISM; CHRISTIANITY; HINDUISM; ISLAM; and JUDAISM.

Rigó Jancsi, the Hungarian cake named for a Gypsy violinist, is literally the stuff of legend. Dazzling stories surround it, but few details of its creation are known. What is certain, however, is that this luscious torta (cake) was the result of an affair that began in 1896 Paris. Rigó and an American millionairess from Detroit, Clara Ward—by marriage the (Belgian) Princess Caraman-Chimay—met in Café Paillard, one of the grand restaurants of the boulevards. Some say on that occasion, with music the food of love, the Gypsy virtuoso played his violin to irresistible effect. Others characterize the princess as an adventuress ready to bolt. Whether one or the other is the case, or both, the two ran off together, divorced their respective spouses, and, in time, married.

Clara Ward was an American millionairess who became a princess after marrying a Belgian prince, but she left him for a Hungarian Gypsy violinist named Rigó Jancsi. Their love affair inspired a rich chocolate sponge cake that still bears the violinist's name. In this 1905 photograph, Clara Ward poses provocatively above her lover.

To the European aristocracy into which Clara's husband, the Prince Caraman-Chimay, was born, the scandal was profoundly shocking. To the populace, especially that of Hungary, where Johnny Rigo was the hometown boy, he and his princess were almost folk heroes. Eventually, someone—no one knows who or exactly when—created a voluptuous cake (layers of chocolate sponge filled with chocolate cream, and glazed with chocolate) inspired by the flamboyant pair. In one version of the story, it was a pastry chef; in another, it was the Gypsy who asked for a cake that would be "dark and ruggedly handsome like Rigó Jancsi himself, sweet as their love, and delicate as his wife."

Whatever the origins of this now-classic cake—and despite the existence of numerous photographs and postcards of the couple, and even a lithograph of the two by Toulouse-Lautrec—more than a century after its creation, this edible symbol of love and lust remains the chief remembrance of Rigó Jancsi and his exploits. Still a favorite, not only in the countries of the old Austro-Hungarian Empire, but elsewhere in Europe, the United States, and Australia, it lives on as a testament to consuming passion.

Katona, Csaba. "'Európa legérdekesebb hercegnője'—egy normaszegő nő a 19–20. század fordulóján" ["The Most Interesting Princess of Europe"—A Woman against the Rules at the Turn of the 19th and 20th Centuries]. *Turul* 86, no. 3 (2013): 100–107.

Cara De Silva

rock is a traditional confection of British seaside resorts made from pulled sugar. Made in long sticks, flavored with mint or fruit essences, it has a brightly colored, often red, exterior. The white inner core mysteriously encloses letters spelling the name of the resort, or sometimes has a complex pattern—a flower, a fruit, a face—running its length.

Making rock is simple in principle. Sugar is boiled to the hard crack stage 302°F (150°C) then divided and colored, usually adding red to a small proportion and leaving the rest plain. See STAGES OF SUGAR BOILING. The uncolored batch is pulled until it is white, and some of it is shaped into a short, thick cone and kept warm. The colored batch is divided into strips, and the design is built up with some of the pulled colored sugar. For instance, a letter *O* is formed by wrapping a cylinder of white sugar in an outer coat of red. These lengths containing patterns are assembled around the cone, the whole is wrapped in pulled sugar, and a colored coat is added to the exterior. A machine spins the cone of rock into long, slender cylinders that are gently rolled until cool to keep their cylindrical form. Then they are cut into short lengths, revealing the pattern across the ends, and wrapped in cellophane along with a picture of the resort in which they are sold.

Rock has been sold as a souvenir in the United Kingdom since the late nineteenth century. The notion of putting lettering in sugar sticks was mentioned by Sir Henry Mayhew in *London Labour and the London Poor* in 1864, but pulling striped sugar into lengths (as seen in candy canes) is an older idea. See CANDY CANES. The association of pulled sugar with the seaside is mysterious but may originally relate to the concept of sugar as an ingredient that counteracted cold in the Galenic system of humors. See MEDICINAL USES OF SUGAR. Although rock with complex patterns in the middle seems to have developed in an English context, Italian illustrations from the nineteenth century show vendors pulling sugar as a novelty sold on the beach in Naples.

See also BOARDWALKS and HARD CANDY.

Mason, Laura. *Sugar-Plums and Sherbet: The Prehistory of Sweets*. Totnes, U.K.: Prospect, 2004

Laura Mason

rolled cookies are prepared from a dense dough that is rolled flat and cut into a variety of shapes. They are most popular during celebrations and holidays, when they are colorfully decorated, iced, or covered with confectioner's sugar, glazes, fondant, colored sugars, or small candies. See FONDANT and HOLIDAY SWEETS. Sugar cookies are common, since they are a good canvas for added flavors. Ingredients such as chocolate, mint, cinnamon, nutmeg, ginger, or nuts may be added to the cookie dough; gingerbread cookies are especially popular. See GINGERBREAD and NUTS.

The dough typically contains flour, butter, sugar, eggs, and baking powder. All-purpose, or medium-protein flour, is used because it creates an elastic dough that can be rolled into a thin layer while holding its shape. Great care should be taken when mixing the dough. There are two basic ways to make dough for rolled cookies. The first, known as the creamed method, calls for creaming room-temperature fat with sugar. Then eggs or liquids, and finally the dry ingredients, are added and mixed only until the dough forms. For the one-stage method, all the ingredients are added to the bowl and mixed at slow speed for a few minutes until they are evenly incorporated. With either method, the dough should never be overmixed because that toughens it.

After the dough is made it should be covered and refrigerated for about 30 minutes before rolling, which allows the protein to relax and form a firmer mass that is easier to roll. Keeping the counter lightly dusted with flour when rolling allows the dough to glide rather than stretch. Stretching overactivates the gluten in the dough and causes the cookies to shrink and become oddly shaped.

Rolled cookies are usually baked at 300° to 325°F (148° to 163°C). These low temperatures allow the oven heat to slowly penetrate the cookies for even baking and browning. The cookies should cool on the pan, placed on a rack. Once cool, they may be decorated, and then stored in a covered airtight container.

See also BUTTER; DROP COOKIES; EGGS; FLOUR; ICING; and PRESSED COOKIES.

Amendola, Joseph. *Understanding Baking: The Art and Science of Baking.* 2d ed. New York: Van Nostrand Reinhold, 1992.

Corriher, Shirley O. *BakeWise: The Hows and Whys of Successful Baking with Over 200 Magnificent Recipes.* New York: Scribner, 2008.

Jim Dodge

Rombauer, Irma Starkloff (1877–1962), and her daughter, Marion Rombauer Becker (1903–1976), were authors of the *Joy of Cooking*, one of the most important twentieth-century American cookbooks. First published by Rombauer at her own expense in 1931, it grew to become both a beloved national institution and (under Becker) a prodigious one-of-a-kind kitchen encyclopedia.

From the outset, the St. Louis–born mother and daughter's Midwestern German roots strongly influenced the selection of material, particularly regarding sweets. Both women loved a wide range of American cakes, pies, confections, and other desserts, from brownies to persimmon pudding. But they remained especially devoted to the pastry and dessert traditions of the German-speaking community in which they had grown up. Through *Joy* they introduced many American cooks to—among other things—German Christmas cookies (*Lebkuchen*, *Springerle*, "Cinnamon Stars"), Linzer Torte, almond torte, hand-stretched strudel, and sweetened yeast-raised cakes like *Kugelhupf* and *Dresdner stollen*.

The authors always remained vigilantly up to date on new developments in cakes, pastries, candies, and ice creams. In 1936, long before rival kitchen bibles like *The Boston Cooking-School Cook Book* had mentioned electric mixers, Rombauer was giving directions for mixer-method cakes. When Becker took over the work (from 1962 to 1975), she added great amounts of useful technical information on the properties of different flours, sugars, fats, and kinds of baking pans. She deleted a considerable amount of older material derived from manufacturers' proprietary formulas. Seeking to expand the work's international focus, she also introduced many new recipes, including genoise, chocolate mousse, baklava, and Turkish delight.

For all of *Joy's* credentials as a distinguished teaching tool and reference work, the quality that its admirers most treasured during Rombauer's and Becker's lifetimes was an engaging conversational verve that moved one early user, the popular illustrator James Montgomery Flagg, to describe it as "the first cookbook that could be called human."

See also BROWNIES; FARMER, FANNIE; GUGELHUPF; PANS; SPRINGERLE; and STOLLEN.

Mendelson, Anne. *Stand Facing the Stove: The Story of the Women Who Gave America the "Joy of Cooking."* New York: Henry Holt, 1996.

Anne Mendelson

Rosh Hashanah is the Jewish New Year. The anniversary of the Creation, it is a time for self-examination and repentance. Ancient people had no organized New Year, but rather calculated the year from the new moon nearest to the beginning of the barley harvest in spring (at Passover) or to the ingathering of the fruits (Sukkot) in autumn. Rosh Hashanah, which is celebrated in early autumn, was eventually adopted as the beginning of the festal year, and today it is one of the great solemn days in Judaism. See JUDAISM.

The Rosh Hashanah table is laden with delicacies representing optimism for a sweet future. Dishes abound with honey, raisins, carrots, and apples—all sweet seasonal reminders of hope for the coming year. At the commencement of the Rosh Hashanah meal, Jews around the world say a blessing over an apple, symbol of the Divine Presence, dipped into honey to augur a sweet year. Some Jews also eat a date or a pomegranate. *Lekakh*, Yiddish for honey cake, is the traditional eastern European cake served on the first night of Rosh Hashanah; it is also eaten as a sweet throughout the year. Today, honey cake, once a simple honey-infused cake, has taken on a more gourmet aspect with the addition of chocolate, ginger, apples, or apricots. In North African Jewish communities, dainty finger pastries oozing with honey syrup, shaped like rolled cigarettes, are served. In the Ottoman Empire, baklava with a sugar or honey syrup were served. See BAKLAVA. Zelebi, snail-like rolls of dough dipped in honey, are served in Persian and Iraqi communities. Although apple desserts abound at Rosh Hashanah because of the apple's symbolism, the South German and Alsatian tradition of serving an Italian plum tart called *Zwetschgenkuchen* has become increasingly popular.

Nathan, Joan. *Joan Nathan's Jewish Holiday Cookbook.* New York: Schocken, 2004.

Joan Nathan

rosogolla, often spelled rasgulla, is a popular Indian ball-shaped sweet prepared from *chhana* (fresh milk curd) soaked in sugar syrup. These moist treats are a common sight at sweet shops across the subcontinent. In India, rosogolla is primarily associated with West Bengal, where it is just one, if perhaps the best known, of numberless *chhana*-based sweets. *Chhana* from cow's milk is considered best for rosogolla. To make *chhana,* acid—most traditionally the whey from a previous batch—is added to hot milk to coagulate it. Once the curds are drained, artisans take extreme care to squeeze out any excess water. The mixture is traditionally kneaded by hand on a wooden board, although kneading machines are now common. The *chhana* is rolled between the palms to form small balls, which are then cooked in sugar syrup. Though the ingredients are simple, the technique demands considerable skill. In *Mistanna Pak,* a two-volume compendium of sweets published in 1906, Bipradas Mukhopadhyay cautioned readers to be attentive while boiling the *chhana* balls. After adding the balls to the bubbling sugar syrup, cold water must be sprinkled over them to prevent them from crumbling—a common defect.

More recently, sweet makers have been experimenting with flavors like chocolate, orange, and others to give rosogolla a new twist. One such interesting innovation is the now-famous baked rosogolla available in Kolkata at Balaram Mullick. Those on a diet can enjoy low-calorie rosogolla.

There are various claims and counterclaims regarding the origin of the sweet, and the argument is often as heated as it is esoteric. Some believe that rosogolla was first prepared by the sweet makers of Odisha, while others insist that it was invented in Bengal. The most common view is that Nobin Chandra Das invented the sweet in Kolkata (Calcutta) in 1868; there is even a plaque commemorating the spot. See KOLKATA and NOBIN CHANDRA DAS. Sweet makers are called *moira* in Bengali, as are the caste members (part of the Nabasankha group) associated with confectionery and sugar production. The story goes that Nobin Moira came from a family of sugar traders that had fallen on hard times. After at least one false start, in 1866 he opened a sweet shop in the Bagbazaar district of North Kolkata. Two kinds of sweets were popular among the patrons: *sandesh* and sweets made of dal (lentil) or other flour. See SANDESH. As related in a booklet called *Sweetening Lives for 75 Years,* published by K. C. Das, the patrons were bored and demanded something different, so Nobin came up with "Sponge Rosogolla." The sweet gained popularity following a visit by the wealthy businessman Bhagwan Das Bagla to Nobin's shop. Nobin offered Bhagwan Das Bagla's thirsty son rosogolla along with some water, and the sweet's fame soon spread far and wide.

Though Calcutta's Nobin Moira is popularly called the Columbus of rosogolla, the food historian Pranab Ray, in his work *Banglar Khabar* (1987), points out that by 1866, Braja Moira had already introduced rosogolla in his shop near Calcutta High Court. Yet another tale claims that Haradhan Moira invented rosogolla in Phulia, some 50 miles to the north of Kolkata. Haradhan Moira used to prepare sweets for the local zamindar, a feudal lord who could collect taxes from the villagers. One day a little girl from his household visited the sweetshop, and she was crying. To comfort her, Haradhon Moira dropped a ball of *chhana* into some piping hot sugar syrup, and rosogolla was born. Claims to the origin of rosogolla do not stop here. Gopal Moira from Burdwan district created a sweet similar to rosogolla, called *gopalgolla. Mistikatha,* a newsletter published by the West Bengal Sweetmeat Traders Association, points out that many other artisans prepared similar sweets carrying a variety of names, including *jatingolla, bhabanigolla,* and *rasugolla.*

While debates regarding rosogolla's origins continue, it is important to note that Nobin Moira's enterprising son Krishna Chandra Das and grandson Sharadacharan Das were instrumental in putting rosogolla on the global map, thanks to their innovative technique for making canned rosogolla. In 1930 Krishna Chandra Das opened his own shop with his younger son Sharadacharan Das. When Sharadacharan Das took over the business after his father's death, he incorporated the shop as a company, and in 1946 he rechristened it K. C. Das (P) Limited. He was instrumental in designing the steam-based cooking technology used in the K. C. Das factories in Kolkata and Bangalore. Yet even if canned rosogolla is available anywhere, and anytime, the best rosogolla remains a piping hot one straight from the kitchen, cooked late in the evening in a local Bengali sweet shop. Even better is rosogolla soaked in sugar syrup prepared from *nalen gur* (date palm jaggery), a treat available only from October to December. See PALM SUGAR.

See also INDIA and MITHAI.

Banerji, Chitrita. "How the Bengalis Discovered *Chhana* and Its Delightful Offspring." In *Milk: Beyond the Dairy: Proceedings of the Oxford Symposium on Food and Cookery 1999*, edited by Harlan Walker, pp. 48–59. Totnes, U.K.: Prospect, 2000.

Haldar, J. *Bengal Sweets*. Calcutta: Chuckervertty, Chatterjee & Co., 1921.

Ray, Pranab. *Banglar Khabar*. Calcutta: Sahityolok, 1987.

Ishita Dey

rugelach are crescent or half-moon-shaped cookies usually made with a cream-cheese dough. Although popular for Hanukkah and Shavuot (the holiday celebrating the giving of the Torah), they are also eaten throughout the year. The name likely derives from the Yiddish or Slavic *rog*, meaning "horn," with the addition of *lakh*, the diminutive plural. Originating in Eastern Europe, and related to *Schnecken* (sweet buns), *Kipfel* (bread crescents), and *Kupferlin* (almond crescents), rugelach are now probably the most popular American Jewish cookies.

Rugelach dough was originally made with yeast, butter, and sour cream, but in the United States, thanks to the popularity of Philadelphia brand cream cheese, it evolved into the short cream-cheese pastry most often encountered today. According to Gil Marks in *The Encyclopedia of Jewish Food*, the first known recipe for rugelach with a cream-cheese dough appeared in *The Perfect Hostess*, written in 1950 by Mildred O. Knopf, sister-in-law of the publisher Alfred A. Knopf. Mrs. Knopf explained that the recipe came from Nela Rubinstein, wife of the famous pianist Arthur Rubinstein. But it was Mrs. Knopf's friend Maida Heatter who put rugelach on the culinary map in 1977, when she published her grandmother's recipe in *Maida Heatter's Book of Great Cookies*. This recipe remains the most sought after of all Mrs. Heatter's recipes and is the prototype for the rugelach most often found today in upscale American bakeries and discount stores like Costco. Like doughnuts and bagels, rugelach now come in a multitude of flavors, even jalapeño, although the most popular are chocolate and apricot. For those who obey the Jewish dietary laws, pareve versions of rugelach using soy-based Coffee Rich creamer and margarine instead of cream cheese are also available.

See also HANUKKAH and JUDAISM.

Marks, Gil. *The Encyclopedia of Jewish Food*. Hoboken, N.J.: Wiley, 2010.

Nathan, Joan. *Jewish Cooking in America*. New York: Knopf, 1994.

Joan Nathan

rum, sometimes spelled *rhum*, is the generic term for alcohol distilled from fermented sugarcane, either in the form of cane juice or cane-based molasses. Once Europeans began cultivating sugar in their colonies in the 1400s, it was inevitable that rum would be invented. Sugar had previously been imported to Europe from the Arab world, where distilling was used primarily to refine medicines and perfume, since drinking alcohol is prohibited to Muslims. In Western Europe, where there were no such restrictions, distilling was a common skill, and there was a brisk trade in brandy and other liquors known under the collective name of *aqua vitae*, or "strong waters." It was common knowledge that most sweet liquids could be fermented and distilled, so it is surprising that the Europeans did not make rum for over a hundred years after sugarcane first became available to them.

It is very difficult to pinpoint the first instance of alcohol distilled from sugarcane. The cocktail historian David Wondrich cites the Indian historian Ziauddin Barani, who wrote in 1357 that a sultan of Delhi, who died in 1316, had prohibited the distillation of wine from granulated sugar. That lone reference aside, the next appearance of rum is in the mid-sixteenth century, when plantation workers in the Portuguese colony of Brazil ran sugarcane juice through a still to make low-quality rum. The first mention of this drink is in a report by Governor Tome da Souza of Bahia, who wrote in 1552 that the slaves were more passive and willing to work if allowed to drink *cachazo*. That term, which is colloquial Portuguese for a low-grade alcohol typically used for pickling, signals the quality of the resulting beverage. The first detailed description of the Brazilian rum called cachaça, from George Margrave's *Historia Naturalis Brasiliae* of 1648, calls it "a beverage fit only for slaves and donkeys," revealing that the drink had not been improved in almost a hundred years.

In the Portuguese, Spanish, and French colonies in the New World, rum remained a crudely distilled beverage for centuries. In those countries, powerful aristocrats held monopolies on distilling brandy, and they wanted no competition from other spirits that might reduce the value or volume of their exports. In 1647 the Portuguese government ordered that only slaves were to drink cachaça; since slaves had no bargaining power, there was no incentive to make a better product. For hundreds of years cachaça was made in crude stills and stored in clay jars that imparted an earthy flavor; it was not until the late nineteenth century that any concerted attempt was made to improve it.

The situation in the British colonies was different, as the mother country had no valuable trade in distilled alcohols and no incentive to suppress new drinks. The first mention of rum in English is in a letter from the colony of Barbados in 1651, which states, "The chief fuddling they make in this island is *Rumbullion* alias *Kill-Divil*, and this is made of sugar canes distilled, a hot hellish, and terrible liquor."

As there was no suppression of the trade, local sugar planters started experimenting and quickly realized the commercial potential of fermenting molasses, a byproduct of sugar refining. See MOLASSES and SUGAR REFINING. There was little demand for molasses in the 1500s, since the sticky liquid was much more difficult to transport than crystalline sugar and had a heavy and less desirable flavor. Some molasses was used as a sweetener by slaves and the poor who lived near plantations; the rest was usually dumped into rivers. As molasses was a product with a longer shelf life than sugarcane juice, and one that had previously been thrown away, the economic advantages of using it were obvious. As it happened, the caramelized flavor of molasses made more desirable rum, with a smoky sweetness to balance the harsh spirit.

Demand for the new drink grew, but the islands were not the best place to make rum in volume, as there was a limited amount of timber to feed the fires of the distilleries. A solution beckoned—ship the molasses to fellow British colonists in New England, where there were unlimited forests and a supply of skilled labor, in exchange for codfish, meat, grain, and other foodstuffs that were expensive or unavailable in the Caribbean. By 1657 a thriving rum trade had developed between the southern and northern colonies, causing the General Court of Massachusetts to declare overproduction a problem. A market was quickly found, as rum became one of the components of the Triangle trade that brought molasses from the Caribbean to be made into rum and exchanged for slaves to work the sugar plantations. See PLANTATIONS, SUGAR and SLAVERY.

Rum became an integral part of trade inside the colonies, which had a chronic shortage of English hard currency. Wages were paid and land sold for prices denominated in gallons of rum, and it became the primary trade good with the native tribes. Rum also became part of the colonial American medicine chest, recommended to purify stale water, ward off diseases of "foul air," and banish chills in winter. It was drunk recreationally in many ways—mixed with warm molasses to make a beverage called blackstrap; with berries and vinegar in drinks called shrubs; with hot cider for wassail; and with cream, eggs, and beer to make flips. See EGG DRINKS.

It was in colonial America that rum was first used in cooking, notably in cakes involving rum raisins, apple tansy pastries, and rum and berry sauces. One questionable item is the rum cake in which fruit is candied and mixed with the batter before baking, followed by the cake being soaked in rum and aged before consumption. Though this is allegedly an American variant on a British steamed pudding said to be popular since the seventeenth century, the oldest surviving recipe is from the 1840s. There are also claims that this item originated in Bermuda or Jamaica, but in all cases contemporary documentation is lacking.

A more authentic eighteenth-century rum dessert—though one that is remarkable to modern diners—is the omelette filled or topped with rum-apricot sauce and sprinkled with powdered sugar. This recipe was popularized by Thomas Jefferson's cook James Hemings after he left Jefferson's service, and was one of many items made with fruit sauces cooked with rum. The most common dessert in colonial America was probably Indian pudding with hard sauce—a steamed pudding made with cornmeal, milk, and molasses topped with a glaze of rum, butter, and sugar. See PUDDING.

It is difficult to determine accurately when rum was first used in cooking, because many recipes merely specified a "hard sauce" that could be made with rum, whiskey, or brandy, depending on what was available. The rums and whiskeys of the 1700s were all similar in that they were harsh and unaged when typically consumed. (Although it was known at least as early as 1737 that aging improved rum, this step was left to purchasers; for makers to barrel-age and mellow spirits before selling them was not common practice until the 1830s.) It is difficult to accurately recreate early recipes involving rum because it is almost impossible to find rum as bad as the best that could be had in that era.

Once rum was improved by aging, Europeans began drinking it in punches and investigating how it might be further used in cooking. See PUNCH. Rum production in all colonies of the British Empire was spurred when the navy adopted rum as the tipple of choice; it replaced a brandy ration for which the principal supply came from France. The army followed, and the switch kept British government commerce inside British colonies. Rum was made in 1793 in Australia and in India in 1805.

The first European culinary hit involving rum was the *baba au rhum*, based on a traditional Polish yeast cake and invented by exiles in Paris in 1835. See BABA AU RHUM. A variant on this dessert, with lemon juice and rum in equal amounts, is a specialty of Naples. Rum balls were invented around 1850, probably in Germany, where they are called *Rumkugeln*. The basic recipe of rum, coconut, and chocolate spread to England, where the confection became a Christmas specialty, and around Europe, where many regional variations developed. In the twentieth century, desserts based on rum and coconut became popular worldwide, and in Mexico, coconut rum sauce was added to the traditional *tres leches* cake for a regional hit. See TRES LECHES CAKE. Elsewhere in Latin America, rum-cinnamon sauces laced with star anise were first recorded as cake glazes in Colombia in the early twentieth century, along with a cake called *pastel borracho*, made with rum, prunes, and crème anglaise. See CUSTARD.

The late twentieth century saw a proliferation of rum brands and styles, along with greatly increased sophistication among consumers, and the use of rum in sweets has expanded correspondingly. Brands now on the market range from those with vodka-like clarity to heavily aged styles with the depth and smokiness of Scotch whisky, giving rum drinkers unparalleled choice, and cooks a wide palette of flavors to work with.

See also SUGARCANE and SUGAR TRADE.

Curtis, Wayne. *And a Bottle of Rum: A History of the New World in Ten Cocktails*. New York: Crown, 2006.
Foss, Richard. *Rum: A Global History*. London: Reaktion, 2012.
Smith, Frederick H. *Caribbean Rum: A Social and Economic History*. Gainesville: University Press of Florida, 2005.
Williams, Ian. *Rum: A Social and Sociable History*. New York: Nation Books, 2005.

Richard Foss

Russia was famed in medieval times for its wild hives, so abundant that travelers tell tales of honey dripping right from the trees. See HONEY. Although sugar eventually supplanted honey for preserving and baking, the Russians remain devoted to honey's taste and nutritive powers.

The *Domostroi*, a sixteenth-century book of household management, describes several different types of mead, all fermented from wild honey: boiled, white (made from light, clear honey), honey (with a greater proportion of honey to water), ordinary, boyars' (the honeycomb was left in for the initial fermentation), spiced, and berry. See MEAD. Berry meads offered the further advantage of preserving large quantities of perishable summer fruits. Another old honey-based drink is *sbiten'*, for which honey is heated with water and spices, and sometimes fortified with vodka or brandy.

As sugar gradually entered elite kitchens in the second half of the seventeenth century, the Russians clearly distinguished between preserves made with honey and those made with sugar. Most prized of all were the honey's "tears"—the pure liquid that drips naturally from the comb. The Russians made other sweeteners by boiling down fruits such as grapes and watermelon into syrup known generally as *patoka* (a word later used to describe molasses, a byproduct of sugar refining). See PEKMEZ and MOLASSES. *Patoka* was used to preserve nuts, ginger root, fruits, and even vegetables like carrots, turnips, and radishes, by cooking the foodstuff gently in the syrup until glistening. Sugar-rich vegetables like beets, pumpkin, and carrots were turned into *paryonki*, chewy treats made by baking the thinly sliced vegetables at low heat until their sugars caramelized, then air-drying them.

The Russians relished fresh apples, cherries, pears, plums, melons, and berries in season, eating them fresh, baking them (especially apples), and using them to sweeten porridge. The seventeenth-century German scholar Adam Olearius described an exquisite Russian apple with flesh so translucent that when held up to the sun, the seeds could be seen right through the skin (this was probably the Yellow Transparent apple). Fruit not eaten fresh was put up for preserves or used to flavor a wide range of cordials and liqueurs.

Once they gained access to sugar, wealthy households also frosted and glacéed fruit. Grapes, gooseberries, lingonberries, cranberries, and currants were dipped in beaten egg white, then rolled in fine sugar and dried slightly in a warm oven. Apricots, peaches, pears, cherries, and sweetmeats such as plums stuffed with nuts were cooked lightly in syrup, then dusted with crystalline sugar to create jewel-like confections known as "dry Kiev jam" (analogous to the "dry" suckets of Elizabethan kitchens, distinct from the "wet" confections preserved in syrup). See CANDIED FRUIT. Catherine the Great took such a liking to these candied fruits that in 1777 she issued an edict requiring that hundreds of pounds be supplied to the court. Fruit juice was boiled into *ledentsy*, clear, hard fruit drops. In the homes of the wealthy, all of these sweet foods, known collectively as *zayedki*, were served at the end of the meal, in a special course.

Dried fruits and nuts, including raisins, apricots, cherries, dates, prunes, almonds, walnuts, and hazelnuts, were also enjoyed as *zayedki*. See DRIED FRUIT. Local stone fruits were dried in the great Russian masonry stove. More exotic fruits were initially brought by caravan from China and Central Asia, but as Russia's territorial ambitions expanded, so did access to produce. Beginning in the seventeenth century, territory stretching east to Siberia and Central Asia, south to the Caucasus, and west to the Baltic states came under the empire's control; in the twentieth century the Soviet Union covered one-sixth of the world's landmass, giving Russians access to all sorts of Eastern fruits and confections, including figs, sultanas, halvah, and lokum. See HALVAH and LOKUM.

Traditional Sweets

In addition to a wide range of preserves and beverages, Russians prepared other types of sweets, although it must be stressed that for the most part these treats were reserved for the well-to-do, as the serfs, and later the peasants, subsisted on meager grain-based diets; only on feast days and major holidays like Easter were they able to indulge. *Pastila* is among the most distinctive: puréed, sweetened apples are whipped with egg whites and dried slowly in the oven to form a light confection. See PASTILA. An old term for fruit leather is *levashniki*. Fruit, usually berries, was cooked with *patoka* and puréed, then spread into a thin layer and dried. See FRUIT PASTES.

Excellent cakes were baked in the masonry stove as the temperature fell after bread baking. The most widespread, and still popular today, are *pryaniki*, firm gingerbread shaped into decorative forms, either by hand or in wooden molds. See GINGERBREAD. Originally made with rye flour, honey, and berry juice, Russian gingerbread dates back to pre-Christian times; spices were added in the Middle Ages. Variations include *medovik* and *kovrizhka*, both of which call for a higher proportion of honey that yields a more pronounced honey flavor.

Holidays featured special foods. From pagan times, even before Russia adopted Christianity in 988 C.E., *bliny* (or *blini*, yeasted pancakes made with a variety of flours) were baked to mark the return of the sun in late winter; they are also a symbolic funeral food. Though not intrinsically sweet, *bliny* in the nineteenth century were also encountered in a Europeanized, crêpe-like form spread with jam or honey (chocolate is often used today). Another ancient holiday dish is *kut'ya*, wheat berries cooked with honey, poppy seeds, and nuts and served with dried fruit compote at Christmas. In some families, a spoonful of the honey-soaked grain was tossed up to the ceiling. If it stuck, the next season would bring a bountiful harvest. See WHEAT BERRIES. At Easter, *paskha* (a rich, sweet cheesecake) and *kulich* (a tall, yeasted, enriched loaf) celebrate the end of the 40-day Lenten fast. See EASTER and BREADS, SWEET.

Russia Meets the West

Although sugar had been known in Russia as early as the thirteenth century, traditional sweets were, until centuries later, made with honey or another liquid sweetener. Demand for sugar rose only in the mid-seventeenth century, when the use of tea became more widespread. Imported at great cost, chiefly through the far northern port of Arkhangelsk, sugar remained a luxury available only to the wealthy. Russia's first domestic sugar refinery opened in Saint Petersburg in 1719, at Tsar Peter the Great's prompting. By the end of the eighteenth century, Russia had 20 sugar factories, and the first factory for refining sugar beets was built in 1802. By 1900, Russia was one of the world's great sugar producers. Nevertheless, devout Russians were reluctant to accept sugar in any form, since it was commonly refined with blood and therefore forbidden for fast days, which number nearly 200 in the ecclesiastic year.

Thanks to Peter the Great's westernizing reforms, the eighteenth century witnessed profound changes in all aspects of Russian life, including cuisine. If, when Peter took the throne, the affluent were still enjoying *zayedki* at the end of the meal, by the mid-eighteenth century they were eating *desert* (dessert), a cognate pointing to high society's growing infatuation with all things French. See DESSERT. The nobility began to employ foreign chefs, who accelerated the introduction of new dishes and methods of preparation. By the mid-nineteenth century the Russian elite regularly consumed desserts from the classical European repertoire, such as *macédoine de fruits*, Viennese torte, and chestnut croquembouche. See CROQUEMBOUCHE. Other creations, like Guriev kasha, were a hybrid of Russian and French practices. See GURIEV KASHA.

Churned ice cream arrived from the West at the end of the eighteenth century. See ICE CREAM. However, Russians had long enjoyed their own frozen dairy treat in the form of *molochnaya stroganina*, made by freezing fresh, rich milk and shaving long, thin strips off the mass with a sharp knife (this process is used today to make an appetizer of frozen fish). *Stroganina* was a seasonal treat made possible by the winter cold. Even today Russians eat ice cream outdoors year round.

The Soviet Period

In the aftermath of the 1917 Revolution, food became an ideological tool. Candy was particularly useful, since it was now produced for the masses, often for educational purposes. "New Weight" candies introduced the metric system in a pleasing way. Wrappers for "Red Army" candies, with Russian Civil War images and catchy rhymes, were designed by the great poet Vladimir Mayakovsky. The consumption of candy, once considered nonessential, became a cultural imperative.

Chocolate, however, remained a symbol of bourgeois decadence, providing fodder for Alexander Tarasov-Rodionov's classic early Soviet novel *Chocolate* (1922), which chronicles the downfall of a functionary through the twin temptations of chocolate and lust. But with Stalin's mid-1930s campaign to make life "better" and "more cheerful," chocolate was promoted, along with champagne, as proof that the Soviet Union could provide its proletariat with luxury goods. Nine chocolate factories were built under the Five-Year Plans, and vast amounts of cacao beans were imported for domestic production.

Although Soviet champagne and chocolates never achieved high quality, ice cream undeniably contributed to the betterment of Soviet life. In 1936, Anastas Mikoyan, the minister of foreign trade, toured the United States, where he became enthralled with American ice cream–making technology. See ICE CREAM MAKERS. Seeing an opportunity to overtake America in ice cream production, he immediately imported the necessary equipment, and the first Soviet ice cream factory opened in 1937. Mikoyan decreed that every Soviet citizen should eat no less than five kilos of ice cream a year.

Despite the Soviet Union's chronic food shortages, hard candies—distinguished by colorful, charming wrappers—were never in short supply. Other Soviet-era treats included a marshmallow-like confection called bird's milk, and sweet soy sticks made by the Red Front candy factory. See BIRD'S MILK. Nevertheless, Russians continued to be avid makers of jams and preserves at home, for winter sustenance. When President Mikhail Gorbachev introduced sugar rationing in 1988 to stem the production of moonshine, consumers began hoarding sugar, one of the few reliably available products. Sugar virtually disappeared from the stores, at which point Muscovites were assured three kilos apiece during the jam-making season as a goodwill gesture.

Post-Soviet Russia

After the Soviet Union collapsed in 1991, the market was flooded with brightly packaged foreign brands, and Western fast-food chains appeared. Snickers candy bars were sold at kiosks alongside the suddenly old-fashioned-looking hard candies. McDonald's brought milkshakes to Moscow in 1991 (although the Russians had enjoyed their own version for decades), and Dunkin' Donuts arrived in 2010, displacing the city's iconic outdoor doughnut stands. See DUNKIN' DONUTS. But the past was not forgotten. When, in 2000, the Brooklyn-born chef Isaac Correa opened a popular fusion restaurant in Moscow, he called it The Hive. The restaurant's signature was gorgeous honey presented in sake cups with tea. Harking back to a profligate past was the restaurateur Arkady Novikov's dessert of "wild" strawberry soup, made from berries grown throughout the winter in greenhouses.

Russians today are attempting to resurrect many treasures of Russian cuisine that had disappeared during the 70-odd years of Soviet rule. Young entrepreneurs are bringing renewed attention to such beloved sweets as *pastila,* preserved fruits, and of course, special honeys.

Goldstein, Darra. *A Taste of Russia.* 3d ed. Montpelier, Vt.: Russian Life Books, 2012.

Gronow, Jukka. *Caviar with Champagne: Common Luxury and the Ideals of the Good Life in Stalin's Russia.* Oxford: Berg, 2003.

Smith, R. E. F., and David Christian. *Bread and Salt: A Social and Economic History of Food and Drink in Russia.* Cambridge, U.K.: Cambridge University Press, 1984.

Darra Goldstein

sablé is a French butter cookie in the shortbread family that may have originated in Normandy. The cookie or biscuit is usually sweet and may be sandwiched in pairs with a filling. Normandy lies on the northwest coast of France, where the Atlantic provides a mild, even climate with ample rainfall, leading to a long tradition of dairy farming. High-quality butter is a key ingredient of the sablé, along with flour, egg yolks, and sugar. A little salt and vanilla, or perhaps lemon, almond, or chocolate, are the only other flavorings. For a savory sablé, grainy Parmesan or similar hard cheese is grated and mixed into the dough.

The name "sablé" derives from the French word for sand, *sable,* referring to the cookie's tender, crumbly texture; it likely derives from pastry that used to be known as *pâte sablée.* Describing this pastry in *La Bonne cuisine française* (ca. 1890), Émile Dumont notes, "Pâte sablée is called this because as one eats, it breaks into little particles like grains of sand." To produce the desirable texture, cooks and pastry chefs have various techniques for achieving that graininess, such as using large-crystal "sand" sugar, adding the sugar or flour in two separate stages, using part confectioner's sugar and part granulated sugar, chilling the dough before cutting it, and so forth.

Besides giving the sablé a rich flavor, a high butter content with minimal handling inhibits the formation of gluten strands in the flour, which would make the dough tough or elastic. The butterfat shortens the dough by breaking up the gluten, hence the terms "shortbread" and "shortening." "Simple as this dough is to prepare," writes Madame E. Saint-Ange in *La Bonne Cuisine* (1927), "it nonetheless has one essential requirement: that it be worked rapidly with a rather cool hand. If the work takes a long time, the dough loses its sandy character; and there is quite a lot of butter, so if your hand is warm it will melt as you work and mix badly with the flour."

See also SHORTBREAD.

Saint-Ange, Evelyn. *La Bonne Cuisine de Madame E. Saint-Ange: The Original Companion for French Home Cooking.* Translated by Paul Aratow. Berkeley, Calif.: Ten Speed, 2005.

Elizabeth Gawthrop Riely

saccharimeter is a scientific instrument used for sugar analysis that evolved from the simpler polariscope used by the French savant Jean-Baptiste Biot (1774–1862). From his experiments in light reflection in the second decade of the nineteenth century, Biot found that when he passed polarized light through some substances, the plane of polarization would rotate. He also found that cane sugar and beet sugar act the same in this regard, while other substances do not. Thus, a polariscope would enable him to distinguish sucrose from other sugars (such as glucose) that rotate the plane of polarization in the opposite direction. When Biot found that the strength of the sugar solution determines the extent of optical rotation, he realized that a polarimeter (a polariscope that measures this rotation) could be used to determine the quality of sugar for commercial or tax purposes. In the 1840s a French optical instrument maker named Jean-Baptiste François Soleil designed a polarimeter specifically for sugar analysis and termed it a saccharimeter. As subsequent improvements made saccharimeters more reliable and user

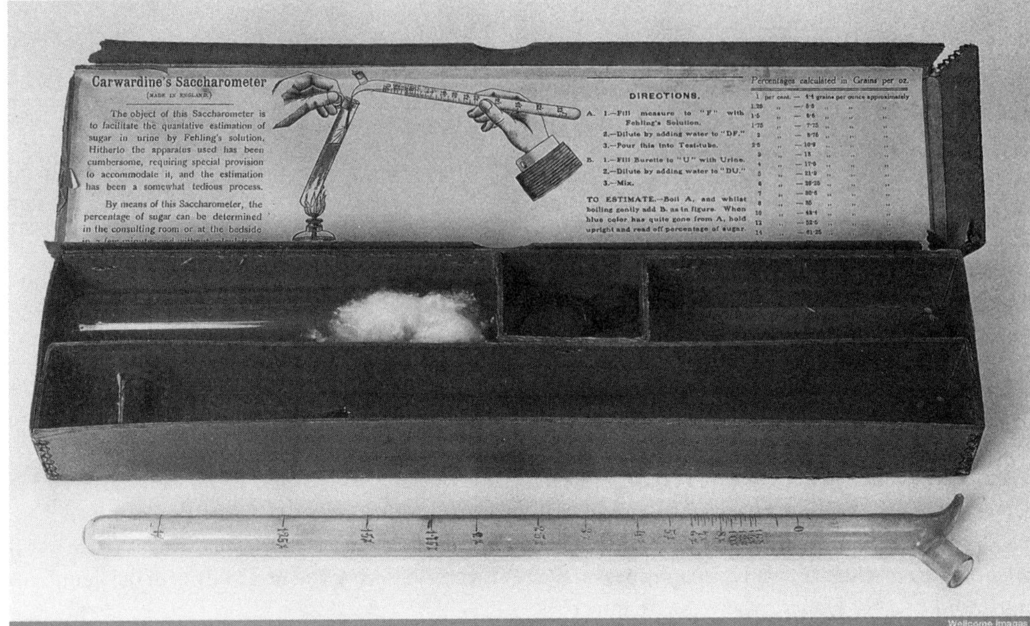

The Carwardine Saccharometer was invented around 1894 by Thomas Carwardine, a physician at Middlesex Hospital in London. Saccharometers and saccharimeters both test for the presence of sugar in urine, an indicator of diabetes, but saccharometers measure the specific gravity of a solution, while the more modern saccharimeter measures its light polarization. WELLCOME LIBRARY, LONDON

friendly, these optical instruments came into widespread use in countries around the world.

Saccharimeters are still used today for sugar analysis. They are also used to determine the sugar content of wines and other vegetable products. And they are used by doctors who diagnose diabetes by determining the sugar content of urine.

See also GLUCOSE and SUGAR.

Warner, Deborah Jean. "How Sweet It Is: Sugar, Science, and the State." *Annals of Science* 64, no. 2 (2007): 147–170.

Deborah Jean Warner

saccharine

See ARTIFICIAL SWEETENERS.

Sachertorte, Vienna's famous chocolate cake, is easily that city's most storied confection. The cake is almost the personification of the sweet—and perhaps somewhat staid—elegance that still hovers over the old Habsburg metropolis. As described by the authors of the comprehensive *Appetit-Lexicon* (1894), the pastry is "a superior sort of chocolate cake, distinguished from her rivals primarily by the chocolate gown she wears over her blouse of apricot jam." Poetic hyperbole aside, the definition of what can legally be called a Sachertorte in Austria is very specific. The *Österreichisches Lebensmittelbuch* (the Austrian food codex) devotes six pages to a precise definition of cakes and related confectionery, starting with the celebrated Sacher. To summarize, the cake itself needs to be a chocolate sponge (minimum 15 percent chocolate solids); nuts can be added, as long as the name reflects the addition. The cake must then be covered with apricot preserves, and finally with a fudgy glaze containing chocolate and sugar. Forgeries that contain such verboten additions as buttercream, ganache, or raspberry jam may be perfectly delicious, but they are not a Sacher.

The original is named after Franz Sacher, a caterer who worked in Vienna and nearby Bratislava (then Pressburg) in the middle years of the nineteenth century. According to a story recounted by his son Eduard, the elder Sacher began his career as an apprentice in the kitchens of Prince Metternich, then the most powerful politician in the Habsburg Empire. One day in 1832 the 15-year-old Franz was apparently asked to make dinner for the great statesman and three of his friends. It was supposedly for this intimate fete that the culinary prodigy whipped up that first Sachertorte. The story is a good one, and it has been repeated so often that it has the ring of truth (not least by Eduard Sacher, who used it to good effect to promote his five-star hotel). The trouble is that Franz Sacher himself told a different tale. In a 1906 interview for the *Neues Wiener Tagblatt*, the 90-year old recalled first making the cake in the 1840s when he ran a restaurant and catering business in Bratislava. There is a certain logic to this. The cake is custom built to hold up to the stresses of catering. It need not be refrigerated, and the apricot glaze keeps it from drying out—the main reasons that the Hotel Sacher has been able to maintain a flourishing mail order business in the confection ever since the 1900s. Since there are no documents confirming either story, the question arises of which to trust: the memory of the nonagenarian inventor or the promotional efforts of his hotelier son?

If there is controversy regarding the cake's birth date or place, it is nothing compared to the legal storm unleashed in the twentieth century when new owners took over the Hotel Sacher and decided to assert their ownership of the Sacher trademark. In the 1920s, like Vienna itself, the hotel and family had fallen on hard times. This circumstance led to the sale of the hotel to one set of owners and the recipe to another. As of 24 July 1934, Demel's, Vienna's most famous pastry shop, put the "Eduard Sacher-Torte" on its menu. Meanwhile, at the hotel, the "Original Sacher-Torte" took pride of place. Hans Gürtler, one of the hotel investors and a lawyer, took Demel's to court and eventually won the trademark dispute in 1938—even as the Nazis were marching into town. But that wasn't the end of it. The suit resurfaced after the war and eventually made its way to the Austrian Supreme Court. At each stage of the appeals process, culinary experts and famous chefs stood on the witness stand, testifying about the dueling recipes. The point of contention was whether Franz Sacher's original cake had one layer (Demel's recipe) or two (the hotel's). The judges, however, were more interested in the intellectual property aspect of the case rather than the fine details of baking. They ruled that while the original cake indeed had a single layer (the hotel's cake was apparently split in the 1920s), the Hotel Sacher retained the right to call its bilevel confection "the original." As a result, we have the Original "Sacher-Torte" and all the other Sachertortes. It is easy enough to taste the hotel's version, as their kitchens make over 360,000 of them a year and ship them worldwide. The Original Sacher-Torte needs no more refrigeration than it did when Franz Sacher ran his catering business over 150 years ago.

See also AUSTRIA-HUNGARY; LAYER CAKE; and VIENNA.

"Codexkapitel/B 34/Konditorwaren Abschnitt Konditorwaren traditioneller Art und Herstellungsweise mit entsprechender Bezeichnung." In *Österreichisches Lebensmittelbuch*, 4th ed. http://www.lebensmittelbuch.at/konditorwaren/.

"Der Alte Sacher." *Neues Wiener Tagblatt*, 20 December 1906, pp. 8–9.

Michael Krondl

salon de thé is a French food-service establishment that focuses on serving tea and coffee accompanied primarily by pastries and other sweet foods. Many exist as part of a pastry shop, though it is now not uncommon for cafés and restaurants to offer this same sort of service and describe themselves as a "restaurant, café, bar, salon de thé." The salon de thé retains a heavily gendered and class association as a respectable gathering spot where bourgeois women would congregate in the afternoon, and its design reflects a certain propriety. As opposed to the French café, which is often on a street corner or a square, open to the street, and with tables oriented so that the clientele and passersby can stare each other in the face, the typical salon de thé would be located on the second floor, removed from the potentially prurient gaze of the pedestrian, yet often hung with mirrors so that the women patrons could gaze at and assess one another.

The term is a literal translation of "tearoom" and is an adaptation of the British original. According to the author of *Les consommations de Paris* (1875), the habit of eating meals in pastry shops was also a trans-Channel import. The first actual tearoom in Paris was opened in the 1880s by the brothers Neal, who ran a stationery and book store, the Papeterie de la Concorde, on the Rue de Rivoli. Initially, their salon de thé was no more than a couple of tables

A *salon de thé,* or tearoom, was a fashionable British import to France. This lithograph of *The Tea Shop* by Francis Donkin Bedford appeared in *The Book of Shops* (1899). © THE ESTATE OF FRANCIS DONKIN BEDFORD. PRIVATE COLLECTION / THE STAPLETON COLLECTION / BRIDGEMAN IMAGES

behind the counter, and its menu was limited to tea and cookies (biscuits); eventually, the brothers set up a proper tearoom upstairs. By 1900 five o'clock tea was all the rage, taken at pastry shops but also at the tearooms of swank hotels like the Ritz. Just how much actual tea anyone drank is questionable. Parisian women were more likely to prefer coffee or (hot) chocolate. However, neither the beverage nor the generally sweet food that accompanied it were the point for the French woman of leisure, as novelist Jeanne Philomène Laperche (writing under the pseudonym Pierre de Coulevain) noted in 1903: "The tea-room... makes a pleasant halting-place between her shopping and her trying-on [of clothes]. It answers two purposes—her wish to be sociable and at the same time exclusive." In the early part of the twentieth century, the salons spread across France and eventually lost most of their English associations; drinking tea remained a largely bourgeois affectation.

Today, the traditional salon de thé has a decidedly old-fashioned, stuffy quality, perceived as a gathering place for women of a certain age or, in the case of marquee tearooms such as Ladurée, as a tourist trap. For a younger crowd, a more contemporary, informal version (still called a salon de thé) has taken its place. The purpose remains the same, even if rooibos and brownies have replaced lapsang souchong and a *religieuse,* the mirrors now sport frames from Morocco, and the socializing takes the form of tweets and Facebook updates.

See also CAFÉ; FRANCE; and TEA.

Abbot, Mary. *A Woman's Paris; A Handbook of Every-Day Living in the French Capital.* Boston: Small, Maynard & Co., 1900.

Husson, Armand. *Les consommations de Paris.* Paris: Hachette et cie, 1875.

Krondl, Michael. *Sweet Invention: A History of Dessert.* Chicago: Chicago Review Press, 2011.

Michael Krondl

salt, technically known as sodium chloride (NaCl), is one of the most important compounds in the human body. The *International Journal of Food Science & Technology* summarizes salt as a flavor enhancer due to its effect on different biochemical mechanisms. Salt regulates fluids in the body, assists in proper function of the adrenal glands, stabilizes heartbeats, balances sugar levels, aids in muscle contraction and expansion, and helps with communication within the nervous system. In the perception of taste, its role is essential. Without salt, the tongue would detect only the basic flavors of food.

Salt is essential to kitchen methodology, too. Ice cream owes its very existence to the discovery that when salt is mixed with ice, the melting point of the ice is lowered. That allows a mixture—such as that of cream, sugar, flavoring, and a bit of salt—to freeze and become ice cream. Today, most ice cream makers have self-contained freezers that require neither ice nor salt, but the original salt and ice mixture gave birth to the ice creams and ices that the world now enjoys. See ICE CREAM.

There are numerous types of salts. Kosher salt, which originates from the sea or from the earth, is the most widely used in American professional kitchens because it has a larger grain that is easily picked up with three fingers to season dishes; it also disperses quickly and has a mild flavor. Another widely used salt is sea salt. Sea salt can come in crystalline or flaked form. It brings a punch of flavor to food and can also add a slightly briny note. Some specialty salts include black sea salt, pink Himalayan salt, volcanic red salt, seaweed salt, smoked Alaskan sea salt, Japanese sea salt, and cherry-smoked salt.

In bread baking, adding a 1.5 to 2 percent ratio of salt to flour, by weight, can enhance the flavor and texture of all breads. Furthermore, the addition of salt to items such as pretzels and buns after baking adds an entirely new dimension to baked goods. Whole-wheat flour benefits from salt because salt removes water from the wheat and brings the aroma and taste of the flour to the fore. The addition of salt to bleached flour can bring balance to an otherwise alkaline-tasting product. Salt should be used in bread baking to enhance the natural flavor of the ingredients; too much of it will destroy both flavor and enzymatic reactions in the dough.

Gluten development is further assisted by the addition of salt. When the gluten structures start to tighten, the dough holds on to carbon dioxide that has been released by yeast during fermentation. Salt will also control the yeast and prevent too much fermentation, which can lead to over-proofed dough. Starches in the flour are converted to simple sugars that feed the yeast. Salt's regulatory effects on the yeast allow some of these sugars to remain, causing the dough to form a beautiful golden crust when baked.

Salt also balances sweet, and it enhances nuances of flavor in ingredients such as chocolate and caramel. A small amount of salt added to chocolate can bring out fruit flavors as well as other tangy and spicy notes that would otherwise go unnoticed. While caramel can be overly sweet, the slightest hint of salt will bring out its hidden smoky and buttery flavors. See CARAMELS. In cakes, the presence of salt adds more depth. When egg whites are whipped and then folded into a batter, a small amount of salt helps the egg whites to hold their structure and add volume to the cake batter, which in turn produces a greater yield and a fluffier cake. See CAKE; EGGS; and MERINGUE.

Salt also plays a key role in leavening dough. Cookies, for instance, owe their light texture to chemical leavening with the assistance of an acid salt. See CHEMICAL LEAVENERS. When an acid salt, such as baking soda (sodium bicarbonate, or $NaHCO_3$), is added to dough, it releases carbon dioxide, just as yeast does in bread baking, the only difference being that the carbon dioxide is released at a specific temperature during the baking process, instead of before baking.

Dessert lovers especially prize the flavor and complexity of fleur de sel (flower of salt), once traditionally defined as the finest hand-harvested sea salt. In Guérande, Brittany, the chore was entrusted to women because men were considered too rough for such a delicate operation. *Fleur de sel de Guérande* is still hand-harvested, but some fleur de sel is now gathered mechanically. Today flurries of fleur de sel, whether artisanal or industrial, are sprinkled onto or into all manner of sweets—chocolates, caramels, ice creams, cakes, brownies, and cookies.

An appreciation of salt is paramount for the development of a chef's career. Great chefs understand the true complexity of salt, even though most people perceive it as a simple ingredient.

Kurlansky, Mark. *Salt: A World History*. New York: Walker, 2002.

Moss, Michael. *Salt, Sugar, Fat: How the Food Giants Hooked Us*. New York: Random House, 2013.

Mindy Segal

sandesh is the Bengali word for "message," as well as a popular sweet prepared from *chhana* (fresh curd cheese) and sugar or palm sugar jaggery cooked together to varying consistencies, depending on the desired result, which can be meltingly tender or dense and chewy. Sandesh is often pressed into decorative wooden molds and is sometimes filled or flavored with essences both native and exotic. Its preparation requires synergy between a *ununer karigar* (an artisan skilled at cooking the mixture), his skill with a *tadu* (a long ladle with a wooden blade used to prepare the sweetened mixture), and a *patar karigar*, an artisan who sits near a wooden board (*pata*) and magically rolls out sweets with his fingers.

In an occupation that seems to breed invention, regional sweet makers have developed numerous local specialties. For instance, in Chandannagore (part of the former French colony of Hooghly), in the early nineteenth century, Lalit Mohan Modak, grandson of Surjya Kumar Modak, created a wooden mold shaped like a palm kernel (*talsansh* in Bengali). A denser *chhana* was added to molded sweets with a rosewater-scented filling to meet the request of a local strongman who wanted to surprise his son-in-law on the occasion of Jamaishasthi, the feast honoring sons-in law. Popularly known as *Jalbhara talsansh sandesh*, this nineteenth-century creation from Surjya Modak's humble establishment still draws many sweets lovers to the two shops run by his descendants.

Over time, sandesh flavored with kiwi, strawberry, mango, vanilla, and chocolate have been introduced. Low-calorie sandesh and diabetic sandesh prepared from *chhana* and sucralose are popular among weight watchers. While sandesh is just one of many sweets made and sold in most business establishments, Kolkata's renowned Girish Chandra Dey & Nakur Chandra Nandy prides itself for specializing in selling "only sandesh" throughout the year.

See also INDIA; KOLKATA; MITHAI; and PALM SUGAR.

Haldar, J. *Bengal Sweets.* Calcutta: Chuckervertty, Chatterjee & Co., 1921.

Taylor Sen, Colleen. "*Sandesh*: An Emblem of Bengaliness." In *Milk: Beyond the Dairy: Proceedings of the Oxford Symposium on Food and Cooking 1999*, edited by Harlan Walker, 300–308. Totnes, U.K.: Prospect, 2000.

Ishita Dey

sanguinaccio is a kind of lightly sweetened sausage or pudding made in various ways throughout Italy with coagulated pig's blood. When prepared in the form of a sausage, it is usually boiled for eating. Sanguinaccio is especially popular in northern Italy, Lombardy, and the Veneto in particular. In Val d'Aosta it is known as *boudin*, from the French, while in Tuscany it is known as *biroldo*. There are many dialect versions as well. Typical ingredients, depending on the region, are grape must, pine nuts, walnuts, chocolate, sugar, candied citrus, and milk. In Naples the pudding might be served with ladyfingers. Although sweet, sanguinaccio is not served as an after-dinner dessert; it stands on its own or is perhaps used as a dressing for pasta, as in the *lasagnette al sugo di sanguinaccio* (*laganèdda cu sangìcchja*) typical of the Gargano region in Apulia, where it is prepared during the pig slaughter. The pig's blood is seasoned with lard, sugar, cocoa, cinnamon, tangerine zest, milk, and salt before being tossed with the pasta.

Gotti, Marco Guarnaschelli. *Grande enciclopedia illustrata della gastonomia*. Milan: Reader's Digest, 2000.

Clifford A. Wright

sap is a fluid that moves in either the xylem or phloem vascular system of a plant. Xylem sap is a watery solution of minerals taken up from the soil by the roots. It moves in xylem cells (vessel elements, tracheids) that form long rows of cylindrical pipes. The flow is driven by evaporation from the leaves, and a large tree can easily take up more than 100 liters of water a day in this way. Plants go through the trouble of extracting water from the soil with one primary goal: producing sugar. Most of the water is lost while obtaining carbon dioxide from the atmosphere and in photosynthesis, a process that converts light energy into chemical energy and stores it in the bonds of sugar molecules. Plants use phloem sap to distribute the energetic sugars throughout the organism, where they are used in growth and metabolism, and for producing sweet fruits such as apples. The liquid flows in sieve element cells, which form a channel network running throughout the plant. Phloem sap contributes to many natural sweeteners, such as flower nectar and palm sugar. See PALM SUGAR.

Sap contains a diversity of sugars, including glucose, fructose, sucrose, sorbitol, mannitol, raffinose, and stachyose. See FRUCTOSE; GLUCOSE; and SORBITOL. Most plants, however, transport sucrose, commonly known as table sugar. See SUGAR. Although the sugar concentration varies among species, phloem sap typically contains 20 percent sugar, twice as much as Coca-Cola (10 percent). There are two good reasons why phloem sap contains so much sugar. First, it is difficult for animals and insects to feed directly on the phloem, because their guts cannot process the very high sugar content. Second, while sweet sap has the greatest transport potential, viscosity impedes flow, and 20 percent is the most effective concentration for long-distance transport. Although plants have generally evolved toward this optimum, a number of unusually sweet plants exist. This group consists primarily of crop plants such as corn (41 percent) and potato (50 percent), the sugar junkies of the natural world.

Both xylem and phloem sap can be tapped for use in sweeteners, but owing to the plant's natural defenses, it is usually only possible to extract miniscule amounts of sap. A notable exception is found in the production of palm sugar, where phloem sap readily flows from cuts made to the inflorescence, or the flowers. A well-known sweetener that originates directly from xylem sap is syrup made from sap tapped from trees in the early spring, when cool nighttime temperatures are followed by days with rapid warming. See MAPLE SYRUP. Maple and birch xylem sap tapped under these conditions contain a few percent sugar; the sap is subsequently boiled down to produce syrup.

See also NATIVE AMERICAN.

Jensen, Kaare H., Jessica A. Savage, and N. Michelle Holbrook. "Optimal Concentration for Sugar Transport in Plants." *Journal of the Royal Society Interface* 10, no. 83 (2013): 20130055. http://rsif.royalsocietypublishing.org/content/10/83/20130055.full.pdf (accessed 7 October 2014).

Kaare H. Jensen

Sara Lee, one of the best-known producers of refrigerated and frozen baked goods in the United States, became famous for such products as pound cakes, coffee cakes, and New York–style cheesecake. See CHEESECAKE; COFFEE CAKE; and POUND CAKE. The company's memorable and long-running slogan, "Everybody doesn't like something, but nobody doesn't like Sara Lee," was written by Mitch Leigh, composer of the musical *Man of La Mancha*. Operating around the globe and now encompassing far more than baked goods and breads, Sara Lee's major brand-name products include Ball Park Franks, Chef Pierre pies, Hillshire Farm meats, State Fair foods, and Jimmy Dean foods.

The original company began in 1935 when 32-year-old Charles Lubin and his brother-in-law, Arthur Gordon, bought a small Chicago-area chain of neighborhood bakeries called Community Bake Shops. The company prospered. When Lubin took over sole ownership in 1949, he named his first product, a cream-cheese-based cheesecake, after his then eight-year-old daughter and changed the name of the business to Kitchens of Sara Lee. In 1951 Lubin introduced the soon-to-be famous All Butter Pound Cake, followed by the All-Butter Pecan Coffee Cake. Both were enormously popular.

Most baking companies attract customers by keeping prices low. Lubin's marketing strategy was to focus on quality first, even though some of his products sold for twice the price of the competition. He demanded fresh milk, pure butter, and real eggs in his baked goods. His cheesecake contained almost a pound of quality cream cheese. The excellence of the ingredients was touted in the company's advertising. One ad campaign carried the tagline, "Sara Lee Cakes, they're all better because they're all butter." Until the early 1950s, however, because of their perishability, Sara Lee Kitchens had to limit the delivery of fresh-baked cakes to a 300-mile radius of Chicago.

By 1953 Lubin had perfected a line of frozen bakery products that retained the quality he demanded while offering mass-distribution capabilities. The following year, working with the housewares manufacturer Ekco, the company developed an aluminum foil pan in which products could be baked, quickly frozen, shipped, and sold. Sara Lee frozen products would be in all 48 states by 1955. Over 200 frozen Sara Lee products are sold nationwide today, including Cream Cheese Cake, Butter Pecan Coffee Cake, All Butter Chocolate Cake, Banana Cake, Apple'n Spice Cake, and Chocolate Brownies.

Lubin's aluminum baking pan was a major revolution in the food industry and helped usher in the era of convenience foods. In 1954 Swanson used Lubin's innovation to introduce TV dinners, and within a year Sara Lee began selling its cheesecake nationally. At this time the dessert was still closely associated with Germans, Jewish Americans, and New York City, but thanks to the company's wide reach, cheesecake soon lost its ethnic and regional associations.

In 1956 Sara Lee was acquired by Consolidated Foods Corporation, headed by Nathan Cummings, a successful Canadian-born importer of general merchandise whose first venture had been to purchase a small biscuit and candy business, which he later sold for a profit. In 1939, at the age of 43, Cummings had borrowed $5.2 million to buy C. D. Kenny Company, a Baltimore wholesale distributor of sugar, coffee, and tea. He built his new company through acquisitions, a strategy he followed until retiring from active management in 1968. Because Sara Lee was one of Consolidated's best-known brand names, in 1985 the company adopted Sara Lee as its corporate name, and the Kitchens of Sara Lee was renamed Sara Lee Bakery.

On 4 July 2012, Sara Lee Corporation was split into two companies. The North American operations were renamed Hillshire Brands (makers of Jimmy Dean, Ball Park, and State Fair brands), while the international coffee and tea businesses became D. E Master Blenders 1753. The Sara Lee name continues to be used on bakery products and certain deli products distributed by Hillshire Brands.

Gabaccia, Donna R. *We Are What We Eat: Ethnic Food and the Making of Americans.* Cambridge, Mass.: Harvard University Press, 2000.

Salamie, David E. "Sara Lee Corporation." In *International Directory of Company Histories*, Vol. 99, edited by Jay P. Pederson, pp. 390–398. Detroit: Gale Cengage, 2009.

"Sara Lee Corp." *Advertising Age*, 15 September 2003.

Joseph M. Carlin

sartorial sweets—clothes made with sugar—are surprisingly ubiquitous. Sugar weaves its way into fabrics both synthetic and natural, and clothing made of sweets offers a provocative aesthetic.

Several familiar fabrics are manufactured from molecules of sugar that nature has already stitched together. Cotton and linen consist largely of cellulose, a polymer in which glucose molecules are connected to each other, much like a line of dancers linking arms. Cotton fibers are unbranched, spiraling chains of cellulose, the strength of the fiber being directly proportionate to the length of the chain.

Linen is constituted of a cellulosic polymer derived from the bast fibers of flax plants. More brittle than cotton (think of all those wrinkles), linen consists mainly of glucose and xylose; other sugars are present in small amounts. See GLUCOSE.

Seersucker, a lightweight cotton that requires no ironing, is favored for summer suits and tropical climates. The weave is such that the cotton puckers into characteristic squares or rectangles. The puffed shapes, reminiscent, perhaps, of plump rice grains, give seersucker its name, which in Hindustani means "rice pudding and sugar" (*kheer aur shakkar*), an appellation that originated with the Persian *shiroshakar*, or "milk and sugar."

The Japanese company Sugar Cane & Co. produces a sturdy denim from sugarcane. And a vegan version of leather is made by cultivating bacteria in sweetened green tea until a sheet forms, which can then be cut and fashioned.

Rayon, sometimes called "artificial silk," is a cellulose-based synthetic. Adipic acid, one of the main components of nylon, another synthetic, is produced from sugars extracted from fruit peels. A new manufacturing process for obtaining adipic acid, less costly and more efficient than the original one, may help nylon once again step out in style.

Sweet Crinoline

Starch, a sugar polymer, lends stiffness and shape to fabric, expanding the ways in which it can be fashioned into clothing. See STARCH. The stiffness of starch should not, however, distract from the more playful—and seductive—ways in which sugar is incorporated into apparel.

Cellulose can be digested only by bovine, ovine, or caprine diners. Insofar as it refers to a straw boater, the expression "I'll eat my hat" thus cannot be applied literally. Nevertheless, a variety of edible "hats," mostly cakes shaped and frosted accordingly, have made it possible to swallow one's words.

The jacket of Herb Albert's Tijuana Brass mid-1960s record album, *Whipped Cream & Other Delights*, featured a woman lusciously clothed in whipped cream, licking some off her finger. A fabric called whipped cream came into style at about the same time: the "textured whipped cream mod dress" was made of white fabric with a wavy pattern that looked slightly quilted—and very *à la mode.*

Hearts Worn on Sleeves, and Melting

More recently, the Ukrainian pastry chef Valentyn Shtefano created for his bride a dress consisting of

1,500 cream puffs; one can only wonder how the wedding feast ended. Shown in Munich in 2010 was a German chocolate bubble dress, so called, apparently, because of the shape of its skirt. More chocolate fashions are displayed at the annual Salons du Chocolat held in Paris, Tokyo, and New York. The gowns, inspired by chocolate, certainly look delicious, though it is not clear whether they are actually edible. Those preferring greater exposure might order, perhaps as a Valentine's Day special, a chocolate thong.

Designed for a younger crowd are candy necklaces, consisting of small, disk-shaped NECCO-like candies with holes in the middle, strung on a string. If long enough, the necklaces can be worn and eaten simultaneously. See NECCO.

As this brief glimpse into the sweeter side of the textile and fashion industries indicates, sugars continue to be reconfigured into fabrics and sweets concocted into ready-to-wear marvels.

See also SUGAR, UNUSUAL USES OF.

Akin, Danny E. "Linen Most Useful: Perspectives on Structure, Chemistry, and Enzymes for Retting Flax." *ISRN Biotechnology* 2013 (2013), Article 186534. http://dx.doi.org/10.5402/2013/186534 (accessed 1 June 2014).

Collop, Chelsey, and Meilssa Deffenbaugh. "Cotton Classroom." Colombia, Mo.: Project Cotton, Department of Textile and Apparel Management, University of Missouri, 2008. http://cotton.missouri.edu/Classroom-Chemical%20Composition.html (accessed 29 May 2014).

Colman, David. "Summer Cool of a Different Stripe." Thursday Styles, *New York Times*, 20 April 2006.

"Local Scientists Make Nylon Out of Sugar." *Today Online*, 31 March 2014. http://www.todayonline.com/daily-focus/science/local-scientists-make-nylon-out-sugar (accessed 9 May 2013).

Karen Pepper

sauce often completes a dessert. Whether served on a plate, in a bowl, or in a glass, dessert gains a punctuation mark from a hot or cold sauce served on, under, or beside it to amplify a principal flavor or provide contrast. There are seven main categories of dessert sauces:

1. *Fruit-based*, in the form of a coulis made from sweetened or unsweetened fruit puree. Coulis is sometimes thickened with starch or other thickeners such as agar or fruit pectin. Liqueur can be added to augment the flavor. See STARCH.
2. *Custard-based*, such as crème anglaise, often considered the queen of dessert sauces. Crème anglaise is a pourable stirred custard made from egg yolks, sugar, milk, and often cream, which may be flavored in many different ways, either during cooking or before serving. See CUSTARD. Whole vanilla beans are a common and traditional flavoring element, but whole, fragrant spices such as cinnamon, cloves, and star anise, and herbs such as thyme, tarragon, and rosemary, are often used to infuse the sauce with a complex flavor and then removed once the desired intensity of flavor has been achieved. See VANILLA. Crushed coffee beans and whole tea leaves are other flavor enhancers.
3. *Sabayon* (zabaglione or zabaione, believed to date from the sixteenth century), an emulsified sauce made from a mixture of eggs, sugar, and a sweet wine (traditionally Marsala), dry wine, Champagne, or spirits, including *eau de vie*. See ZABAGLIONE. The mixture is heated over a bain-marie (a simmering water bath upon which a nonreactive bowl is placed) and whipped until thick and foamy. It is served warm or cold.
4. *Caramel-based*, with or without the addition of a dairy enrichment such as cream or butter. See STAGES OF SUGAR SYRUP.
5. *Chocolate-based*, using cream or milk, or both, and sometimes butter, depending on the desired thickness, and varied according to the viscosity of the chocolate when melted; white, milk, or dark chocolate may be used as the basis of the sauce.
6. *Flavoring-based*, such as coffee, tea, wine, and liqueur, with alcohol enhancements and various sweeteners other than refined sugar, including maple syrup and agave syrup. See MAPLE SYRUP and TEA.
7. *Semi-solid sauces*, such as hard sauce, a mixture of butter, sugar, and usually rum or brandy. Such thick sauces resemble an icing that melts when ladled over a warm dessert. See ICING. They originated in England and have been used in the United States since the late nineteenth century as an accompaniment to steamed and bread puddings.

No matter which sauce is used, the idea of providing contrast in flavor, and often in texture, is paramount. For example, a sweet dessert is well complemented by a tart or even acidic sauce, as in a white chocolate mousse served with a tart citrus sauce, either lemon- or lime-based. On the other hand, an only slightly sweet rhubarb tart could be accompanied by a vanilla crème anglaise to achieve an overall mellow sweetness in the dessert. From the point of view of texture and mouthfeel, silky smooth sauces of all kinds provide contrast to a wide range of desserts, from crunchy praline-based ice cream to flaky stacks of puff pastry layered with pastry cream and fresh fruit.

Dessert sauces can also offer temperature contrast. Perhaps the best illustration of this concept is the classic American hot fudge sundae, in which hot and cold coexist in a single spoonful. See ICE CREAM. In a slightly different way, the beloved American dessert apple pie à la mode reveals how temperature variations can elevate the simple to the sublime; as the ice cream melts, it turns into a cool sauce beside the warm pie. See À LA MODE.

Davidson, Alan. *The Oxford Companion to Food.* New York: Oxford University Press, 1999.
Peterson, James. *Sauces: Classical and Contemporary Sauce Making.* 2d ed. New York: Wiley, 1998.
Roux, Michel. *Sauces.* New York: Rizzoli, 2010.

Robert Wemischner

Scandinavia historically refers to Norway, Sweden, and Denmark, countries in which sweets are very popular and well integrated into the culture, even though the concept of a formal dessert course is relatively modern.

Before sugar reached northern Europe, Scandinavians relied on honey and fruit extracts for sweeteners. In the Middle Ages, spice cakes made of rye, oats, and honey were enjoyed, as were sweets that could be baked over an open fire with special cast-iron equipment. Sugar changed all that. Like much of Europe, Scandinavia has a dark chapter in its history: in 1672, Denmark established a colony on St. Thomas in the Caribbean, and thus took part in the sugar trade based on slave labor. See SLAVERY and SUGAR TRADE. As new methods of baking reached the north from France and Austria, sugar became a sought-after commodity. Scandinavian bakers traveled to Vienna, bringing back new ideas that led to the creation of different kinds of baked goods, in which the bourgeoisie was eager to indulge. What Americans know as "Danish pastry" is one such result; its Danish name of *wienerbrød* (Viennese bread) reveals its origins. See VIENNA.

Bakeries were situated primarily in cities and towns, while home baking took place in rural areas, mainly on large farms and estates that had sufficient staff, easy access to dairy, and money to buy sugar. In this way country houses and bakeries throughout Scandinavia were responsible for developing a wide range of cakes and desserts named after famous people. Napoleon cake is a classic *mille-feuille* made with red currant jelly; Sarah Bernhard consists of a macaron topped with chocolate ganache and coated in dark chocolate; and *Prinsesstårta* is a beloved Swedish cream-filled layer cake draped with a sheet of pale green marzipan. See MARZIPAN.

In the late 1800s, inviting people for a "cake table" was a popular rural pastime in Sweden. Fifteen to twenty different cakes would be served with coffee, cold milk, and sugar. This tradition soon extended to funerals. People were invited home for cakes and coffee after the church ceremony, or they gathered at the local community center, which was used for gatherings and celebrations. On a more daily basis, coffee breaks, known familiarly as *fika* in Swedish, have been part of life throughout Scandinavia for the last 200 years. They are an informal way for women to meet and share a cup of coffee, some cake, and the latest gossip. Today, they have largely been replaced by the coffee break at work.

In the early 1800s, in the larger cities, cafés called *konditori* began to open, and some, such as La Glace in Copenhagen and Sundbergs Konditori in Stockholm, still exist to this day. See CAFÉ. *Konditorier* in Copenhagen were particularly famous for their celebrity patrons, including Hans Christian Andersen and the philosopher Søren Kierkegaard. Throughout Scandinavia these pastry shops offered a public space where people could meet and be seen in society.

Spices

Thanks to trade with the Hanseatic League, spices have been present in Scandinavia since the fifteenth century. They were used mostly in *mjød*, or mead, a fermented honey drink. See MEAD. When spices became more affordable around 1700, they began to be used more commonly. In Scandinavia, cinnamon, cardamom, and vanilla have been especially popular in baking for the last 200 years.

Vanilla is a basic ingredient in many cake recipes and is also found in candy and caramels. See CARAMELS. Cinnamon is used in many ways. Arguably most famous is the cinnamon bun, of which commercial and home versions exist, along with regional variations. The *kanelsnegle* is a Danish pastry for which cold butter is rolled into dough that is coiled around a sweet cinnamon filling. The most widespread cinnamon buns, called *kanelbullar*, are made with yeast dough, with melted butter added. They are offered by almost every baker throughout Scandinavia. Similar to *kanelbullar* are *kardemummabullar*, which use ground cardamom instead of cinnamon. Cardamom is used throughout Scandinavia to enhance the flavor of almost all variations of *blødt brød*—the soft, sweet, yeasted wheat bread that forms the basis of many buns and cakes.

The most popular Danish Christmas cookies are *peperkaker, pebernødder, brunkager*, and *ingefærkager*—and their counterparts in Norway and Sweden—all of which are very thin, crisp cookies aromatic with spices like ginger, cinnamon, and cloves. The original recipes for these gingerbread cookies date back to the 1200s and 1300s. For best results the dough should rest for several weeks before being rolled out, to enhance the flavor of the spices. A cookie cutter cuts the *peperkaker* into various decorative shapes, while *pebernødder* are formed into small round balls. No master recipe exists; instead, there are many regional variations, and bakers prize their generations-old family recipes.

Seasonality

In Scandinavia everything is seasonal, even sweets, with different cakes served in winter and summer. Although this tradition historically had to do with a scarcity of ingredients, it continues today. Winter means that nuts, dried fruit, and spices are used for flavoring, whereas summer offers an abundance of berries: strawberries, raspberries, gooseberries, red and black currants, and rose hips. In particular, layer cake, variously known as *lagkage, blødkage*, and *tårta*, and traditional for birthday parties throughout Scandinavia, is made very differently depending on the season. In the summer a sponge cake is cut into three layers, each of which is spread with cold custard and fresh berries. In the winter, jam or plain whipped cream replaces the berries. See CUSTARD; LAYER CAKE; and SPONGE CAKE. The cake is usually decorated with marzipan, chocolate, or confectioner's sugar. Layer cakes can be simple or elaborate, baked at home or bought from the local bakery. After World War II, new products like prebaked cake layers and instant custard powder came onto the Scandinavian market. With a jar of jam and whipped cream from a spray can, one could make a layer cake in 30 minutes, not an uncommon practice even today.

In Denmark the first apples of September are baked into the traditional apple cake—thick apple sauce layered with sweet roasted bread crumbs and whipped cream, and served cold. Because Norway and Sweden have much shorter growing seasons, summer is fleeting, making the first berries of the season cause for celebration. They are added to cakes, luscious puddings and pies, and pressed for juice and made into preserves. See FRUIT PRESERVES. Especially prized in northern Scandinavia are tart lingonberries and golden cloudberries. Elderberries and aromatic elderflowers are also made into refreshing summertime drinks and desserts throughout the region.

Other Baked Goods

Scandinavia has a wide variety of baked goods that are often served together on the afternoon or early evening cake table, a tradition celebrated especially by the older generation, for whom "seven sorts" of cakes were standard. More recently it has become fashionable among young people to invite friends for an old-fashioned cake table in a kind of retro gathering.

The selection of baked goods includes pastry, dry cakes, cream cakes, coffee cake, and, of course, the famous butter cookies. Danish pastry is eaten all over Scandinavia. Danish bakers added *remonce*, a sweet paste of sugar, butter, and nuts or marzipan, to the *wienerbrød* dough, and sometimes spices like cardamom or poppy seeds. Seasonal fruits or berries provide an alternative filling. Danish pastry is often eaten in the morning, like a croissant; when served in the afternoon with coffee, it is made larger and called *wienerbrødsstang*, meaning a "long piece" of pastry. *Borgermesterkrans*, or "mayor's wreath," is another *wienerbrød* variation.

Cream cakes became very popular in the late 1800s because of the strong tradition of dairy products in Scandinavia. The technologies of the Industrial Revolution allowed for cream and other dairy products to be kept cool in refrigerators, so that cakes could last throughout the day, which gave the bakers an opportunity to be creative. They came up with a range of cream cakes made with puff pastry, short crust, choux pastry, and yeast dough. See PASTRY, CHOUX; PIE DOUGH; and PUFF PASTRY. Each type of cake has a distinctive name, such as the medallion, two round pieces of short-crust pastry filled with cream and a little fruit compote and decorated with chocolate or icing. See ICING. A favorite type of small cream cake is the *semla,* a cardamom-scented yeast bun bursting with a mixture of marzipan and cream and topped with whipped cream and a dusting of powdered sugar, traditionally served at Shrovetide, the period of indulgence before Lent. Cream cakes are eaten for an afternoon coffee break, after dinner, or for a special occasion, although they can also be enjoyed simply on a rainy day or for some *hygge,* a Danish word that describes a special kind of comfort. These cakes are often purchased at a bakery. They must be eaten the same day due to their fresh ingredients.

Dry cakes have a longer shelf life, since they don't contain any fresh dairy products. A typical dry cake is the so-called Napoleon's hat, which consists of short-crust pastry and marzipan dipped in chocolate and formed into a shape resembling Napoleon's hat. *Linse* is a type of short-crust pastry with a custard filling. *Mazarin* also has a short crust but is an open tart filled with marzipan, sugar, and butter. One variation includes fresh lingonberries, which in Sweden are often glazed with icing. Another famous dry cake is *kransekage,* made with marzipan, sugar, almonds, and egg whites. *Kransekage* became very popular among the aristocracy in the 1700s, when almonds were quite expensive, as a way to show off their wealth.

The horn of plenty—*overflødighedshorn,* or cornucopia—was created in the 1700s as a reference to Greek mythology. The horn was built out of rings of the *kransekage,* with small marzipan cakes inside. The idea is to fill the horn so full that the little cakes will spill over in abundance. It is made for special celebrations, weddings, christenings, and confirmations.

Pound cake, called *sandkage* in Danish, is every housewife's savior. It is very popular for home baking and always appears on the cake table. The cake stores well and is therefore handy for unexpected guests, for whom the tradition is always to offer coffee and cake.

Småkager are butter cookies, an everyday treat with coffee. Fifty years ago, all housewives kept a store of *småkager* for unannounced visits. Once private homes were equipped with their own ovens, baking these cookies was easy to do, and they lasted for weeks in an airtight container.

Fried Pastries

The Scandinavian dessert repertoire includes a variety of fried goods, many of which date back to the days before ovens were common. Using cast-iron molds, they could be prepared over an open fire. Today these traditional cookies and cakes are rarely made at home, usually only at Christmas. *Klejner* or *fattigman* are crisp, twisted strips of dough often flavored with lemon zest and fried in hot oil. They vary from region to region: in Norway they are made with yeast and frequently decorated with icing after cooling; in Denmark they have no yeast and are served plain. *Æbleskiver,* with their pancake-like batter, are a Danish Christmas tradition. Traditionally, these plump pancakes are baked with either a slice of apple or prune sauce inside, though that practice is no longer common. They are fried in a little shortening or butter in a special cast-iron pan with round indentations. Sadly, very few Danes make *æbleskiver* by hand anymore, generally choosing to buy them frozen and reheat them in the oven. *Æbleskiver* are served with raspberry jam and powdered sugar; a glass of *gløgg* or mulled wine is the classic accompaniment. See MULLED WINE.

At Christmas, Norwegians serve *krumkake,* a thin, crisp waffle pressed in an ornately decorated two-sided iron that leaves its impression on the finished waffle. See WAFERS. While still warm, the *krumkaker* are rolled into cones; they are typically served with cloudberry jam. *Rosette* or *struvor* belong to an old tradition in Scandinavia. Like *krumkaker,* they are made with a special iron, often floral in shape, which is dipped into a liquid batter and then into hot oil. Today, rosettes are most often prepared in Scandinavian communities in the United States.

Candy and Licorice

Today, the Scandinavian sweet tooth is visible in worldwide brands of candy and candy stores. Modern Scandinavian candy stores are like supermarkets, where customers help themselves to a variety of candy and pay by weight. These shops have replaced the older style of shops where candy was bought and paid for individually. See PENNY CANDY. Such old-fashioned candy shops, called *slikbutikker*, existed in virtually all Scandinavian cities and towns. They are often described in children's literature, as in Astrid Lindgren's *Pippi Longstocking*. See CHILDREN'S LITERATURE.

The Scandinavian love of licorice is a big part of the region's candy tradition. See LICORICE. Licorice was first used as a cough medicine purchased at the pharmacy. As a nonmedicinal treat, licorice root became very popular in the early 1800s, and Scandinavian candy factories have been producing a range of hard, soft, sweet, and salty licorice for the last 200 years. There are now hundreds of corporate and artisanal brands to choose from.

Bolsjer are small, decorative pieces of hard candy made of pure sugar and fruit concentrates, or of other essential flavors. See HARD CANDY. A few small artisanal producers still exist, such as Sømods Bolcher in central Copenhagen.

Over the past 50 years, many new, foreign products have been introduced to Scandinavia. However, when it comes to sweets, tradition remains strong. Although a significant number of small bakeries have closed over the last 20 years or so, a new generation of artisan bakers is making sure that the high-quality handmade products Scandinavian bakers are known for do not disappear. New trends are reinvigorating old traditions, such as the combining of chocolate and licorice in inventive cream cakes, or the use of fresh fruit instead of commercially prepared jam. Danish *flødeboller*—chocolate-coated marshmallows, sometimes with a layer of marzipan—have experienced a renaissance as chocolatiers experiment with new flavors like passion fruit, colorings like beet juice, and spices like cardamom.

Finland

Among the Nordic countries, Finland is often seen as an outlier, partly because Finns don't speak the mutually intelligible languages of the Danes, Norwegians, and Swedes. The country's culinary traditions differ, too, having been influenced by Russia rather than by the French haute cuisine embraced by the royal kingdoms of Denmark, Norway, and Sweden. Finnish culinary practices tend to be less elaborate than those of its neighbors. With nearly 40 different types of edible berries, Finland often features fruit in desserts, along with an enticing array of dairy products. In the summer, berries are baked into *mustikkapiirakka*, Finland's iconic blueberry pie, or pressed and whipped into light-as-air *vispipuuro*, a lingonberry and semolina pudding. The oven-baked Åland pancake, a specialty of the Baltic islands between Finland and Sweden, is based on semolina or rice pudding inflected with cardamom and served with stewed prunes and whipped cream. On the mainland, Tiger Cake, a chocolate-marbled pound cake, appears on the coffee table that is as much a tradition in Finland as elsewhere.

Like other Scandinavians, Finns love salty licorice, especially the extremely strong *salmiakki*. They also share a love of crisp, deep-fried battercakes in the form of *tippaleivät*, which are traditionally served for May Day along with *sima*, a lightly carbonated lemon mead. The Russian influence can be seen in the use of sour cream in coffee cakes, and in the fresh cheese used for cheesecakes. See CHEESECAKE and COFFEE CAKE. Cardamom is a favored spice that shows up not only in sweet desserts, but also in enriched breads like *pulla*. See BREADS, SWEET. All manner of fruit soups—from blueberry in summer to mixed dried fruit in winter—remain popular in Finland. See SOUP.

Boll-Johansen, Hans. *Ved bordet: Madkultur i nord og syd.* Copenhagen: Gyldendal, 2003.

Ellison, J. Audrey, ed. and trans. *The Great Scandinavian Cookbook: An Encyclopedia of Domestic Cookery.* New York: Crown, 1967.

Favish, Melody, trans. *Swedish Cakes and Cookies.* New York: Skyhorse, 2008.

Gold, Carol. *Danish Cookbooks: Domesticity and National Identity, 1616–1901.* Seattle: University of Washington Press; Copenhagen: Museum Tusculanum Press, 2007.

Karg, Sabine, Regula Steinhauser-Zimmermann, Irmgard Bauer, et al. *En kulinarisk rejse gennem tiderne: En kogebog med opskrifter fra stenalder til middelalder.* Brøndby Strand, Denmark: Communicating Culture; Zug, Switzerland: Museum für Urgeschichte(n), 2011.

Tanttu, Anna-Maija. *Northern Flavours: Food from Finland.* Helsinki: Otava, 2007.

Trine Hahnemann

semifreddo

See DESSERTS, CHILLED.

servers, ice cream, constitute an entire category of serving utensils. Despite the fact that food chilled by ice existed in ancient Rome, and that forms of ices and ice cream became fashionable in elite European circles in the seventeenth century, the development of utensils specific to its serving is primarily an American story. See ICE CREAM. European serving methods in the pre-mechanized eighteenth and early nineteenth centuries included elegant porcelain serving pails with matching or glass cups that would have needed little more than a serving spoon or even a tablespoon to serve the ice cream. A simple, small teaspoon could have scooped the ice cream out of a cup. Spoon-like implements with straight edges—ice cream spades—exist from the eighteenth century.

In the mid-nineteenth century, ice cream and its servers came to newly rich middle-class diners as part of an ever-expanding market for specialized flatware in the United States. The crank-driven home ice cream maker, the increased long-distance transport of large masses of ice by railway, and the lowering of sugar prices all came together in the mid-nineteenth century to broaden the volume of ice cream being served. To these developments was added the discovery of the Comstock Lode of silver in Nevada in 1859. From this easy supply of silver flowed a river of fancy new implements that complemented changing culinary tastes. Ice cream was among the foods that inspired creative and specific serving implements. It was thought to be best served with a spade or a "slice." However, some serving sets included a pierced, pointed serving spoon that could lift a block of ice cream from the ice and let any melted water run off. The spoon could be paired with a knife that could also be used for cutting ice cream or cake. The frozen-solid hardness of ice cream and sorbets inspired the market for often gilded and engraved, specially designed, sharp-edged forks and spoons, ice cream spades, slices, saws, and hatchets.

These ice cream spades, saws, and hatchets appeared in endless possible patterns thanks to new technologies like the steam-driven, double-sided die-stamp that enabled more efficient production of sometimes elaborate motifs on both sides of the utensils' handles. The wide range of patterns, as well as the variety of solutions for serving large quantities of ice cream, appealed to American consumerism. Yet, despite the number of patterns available for servers, and individual flatware to match, the ice-cream server often did not match the service pattern. Instead, it was a key example of the American fascination for developing function-specific utensils. Thus, an ice cream hatchet's handle might try to replicate, in silver, an actual hatchet.

Serving ice cream, preferably with dramatic implements, played a leading role in the conspicuous consumption of those who could afford luxurious trappings. This service was accompanied by the display of specialized implements, especially forks, with which to eat the ice cream and sorbets. Even though ice cream was enjoying similar levels of democratization in Europe, these implements were more successful in the United States, thanks to skillful marketing that played on social insecurities, which implied that to be socially acceptable, one needed food-specific designs. The idea of eating ice cream and sorbet with an individual fork appeared as early as the 1840s, when Americans were still sensitive about not being savvy about fork usage.

The masculinity of the forms of some ice cream servers suggests that the owners of such pieces were not embarrassed to consider themselves products of American prosperity, rather than of the refined European aristocracy associated with ice cream in previous centuries. The hatchet and spade forms may also suggest that the serving of ice cream was exclusively the province of the butler or male server, rather than of a maid, given the force that was likely needed to cut the ice cream. A large amount of frozen ice cream might have been set in tower-like displays, some on stands with polar décor. The ice cream was then cut with a silver spade, hatchet, saw, or serving knife on the dining room sideboard to avoid melting in transit; a spade was used to portion the ice cream for each plate, from which it was eaten with a special fork, small spade, or shovel, all with a knife edge for cutting.

By the end of the nineteenth century, as refrigeration and the cost of ice cream fell, ice cream became a mass-market product. Nonetheless, elegant menus still showed a fascination with palate-cleansing ices served between courses, presented in glass containers from the pantry so that no fancy servers were needed. More significantly, the broader market meant that the ice cream servers were often relegated to the kitchen, and so less costly materials were used.

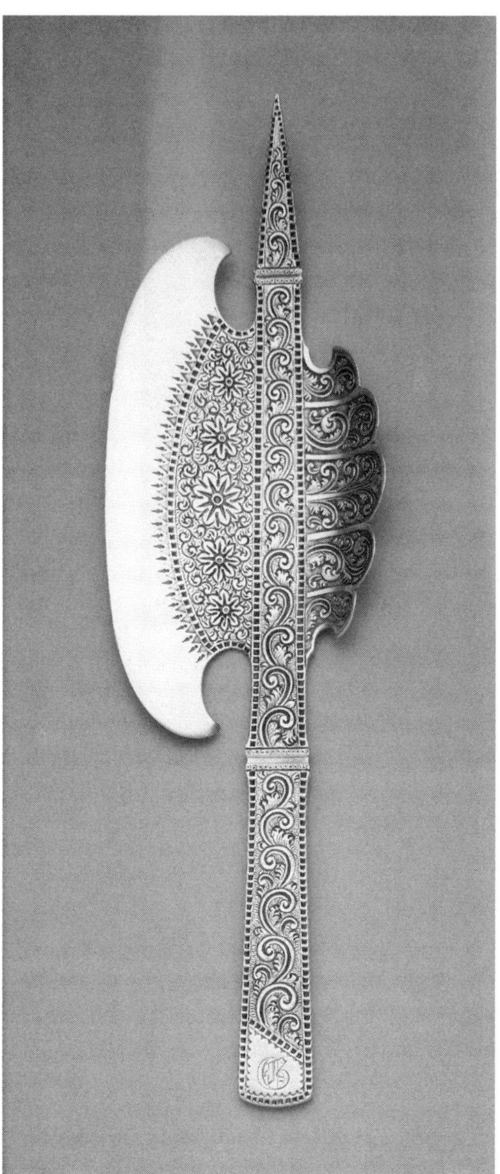

An engraved silver ice cream hatchet made by the Gorham Manufacturing Company, circa 1880. The growing popularity of ice cream in mid-nineteenth-century America, along with the proliferation of specialized tableware during the Gilded Age, inspired elegant serving pieces designed to cut through the treat's frozen mass. DALLAS MUSEUM OF ART, GIFT OF DR. AND MRS. DALE BENNETT / BRIDGEMAN

As ice cream became standard with birthday cake, some twentieth-century ice cream servers doubled as cake servers, using a sharp or serrated edge for both. With mass-market appeal, stainless steel came to the fore between the world wars, and even silver servers often featured stainless-steel blades for strength. More casual presentations of the late twentieth and early twenty-first centuries have introduced brightly colored handles and circular metal scoops with a metal band that rotates to push the ice cream out into attractive balls for cones or bowls. Other innovations, such as cold-resistant silicone handles or metals that can be warmed to extract hard-frozen ice cream or sorbet from commercial containers, have replaced the spade or hatchet-like servers. Today, ice cream, no longer a luxury item, arrives in individual servings, including the cone, or with a spoon with which to eat it.

See also REFRIGERATION; SERVERS, SUGAR; and SERVING PIECES.

Coffin, Sarah D., et al. *Feeding Desire: Design and the Tools of the Table, 1500–2005*. New York: Assouline, 2006.

Sarah D. Coffin

servers, sugar, are necessary tools for the table, since sugar is used to adorn desserts and sweeten beverages. Over the years, as the forms of sugar have changed, so have the implements designed to serve it. An early place to store sugar on the table or sideboard was the sugar box, which was succeeded by the sugar bowl, and then the sugar caddy, primarily used to hold sugar for beverages. Sugar was retrieved from these boxes and bowls by means of nips or snips, scissors or tongs. Other early tools included casters or sugar sifter spoons used to shake sugar over fruit or other confections. In more recent years, sugar has been provided inelegantly at the table in simple paper packets or tubes, especially in restaurants.

Within the limited categories of sugar servers, there are many varieties in design. The greatest impact on the development of these objects occurred after the sixteenth century in Europe, when the introduction of tea, coffee, and chocolate led to a craze for these items among the elite. Although none of these beverages were generally imbibed with sugar in their native lands, Europeans perceived them as bitter. Before long, objects specifically designed around sugar added to the status of the beverage service and complemented the beautiful vessels made to hold them. During the late seventeenth and eighteenth centuries, as tea, coffee, and chocolate pots and sugar bowls came into prominence, so too did

These silver sugar casters, made in Paris between 1730 and 1740, depict slaves carrying sugarcane, a reminder of sugar's bitter origins. © RMN-GRAND PALAIS / ART RESOURCE, N.Y.

various forms of nips, snips, tongs, and scissors. See CHOCOLATE POTS AND CUPS.

Sugar boxes date back to the sixteenth century as storage containers appropriate for either the table or sideboard, for use with dessert or with the wine, which was sometimes sweetened. The significance ascribed to sugar can be seen in the generally high artistic levels of these objects, in their fine materials (often silver), and in their engravings and ornamentation.

Sugar caddies evolved as part of the tea equipage. Tea caddies were usually provided in pairs, for different types of teas, and sometimes included a third, larger box for sugar. This combination, usually made of silver but housed in a wooden box with mounts, evolved in the eighteenth century. Toward the end of that century, the tea set, which could include coffee and chocolate pots and hot-water urns, generally also included a matching sugar bowl, in which case the sugar caddy or box was replaced in a tea caddy set by a mixing bowl for the tea.

Sugar bowls appeared predominantly on the tea table, with coffee and chocolate at breakfast, or at the end of a meal. As sugar and tea became more affordable, the bowls grew in size. Early sugar bowls were often round in shape, their forms and decoration frequently reflecting those of the teapot. However, the first sugar bowls were not considered part of a set, and hence did not need to match. To keep the sugar clean and fresh, the bowls had covers that were lifted for retrieving the sugar with tongs or scissors; these implements never stayed in the sugar bowl, as is often common practice today. Silver and the prized porcelain imported from Asia, or of eighteenth-century European manufacture, were considered worthy materials for serving valuable sugar.

Sugar nips, nippers, or snips refer to the sharp-edged implements used to cut sugar into pieces small enough for serving. Sugar arrived from the refinery in loaves, cones, or coarse chunks that had to be separated and broken down further. See SUGAR REFINING. Scissor-like objects, generally known as sugar nips, with sharp, sometimes ridged fingers, were used to cut the lump sugar into small portions. The sugar could then be ground in a mortar, cut into even smaller pieces, or grated before being placed in a caster for sprinkling over food; the action of shaking created an even finer granulation. Cone and loaf sugar continued to be used throughout the nineteenth century in the United States, especially in rural areas, although once commercially granulated sugar became affordable, the cones were relegated to the kitchen.

Sugar tongs and scissors were designed for picking up lumps of sugar to put into a tea, coffee, or chocolate cup; the names reflect the different forms. Early sugar tongs often included two hinged or connected arms that could be pinched to grab a small lump of sugar. Some had sharp edges at the terminals to facilitate further crumbling. Sugar scissors, as the name suggests, were fashioned in the form of an X, with open, circular finger holes by which to grip and close the ends of the scissors around a lump of sugar. The scissor form became popular in the second quarter of the eighteenth century and remained so into the twentieth century, especially after Henry Tate introduced the sugar cube in London in the 1870s. See SUGAR CUBES and TATE & LYLE. However, in the latter part of the eighteenth century, a simple, flat, elongated U shape became fashionable; it was easy to craft from a single sheet of silver and could be bright-cut or engraved with delicate decoration. With the increased consumption of tea, and the ever-increasing sizes of teapots and their accompanying sugar bowls, these tongs were easily made longer to accommodate the new bowl sizes. Tongs and scissors were not generally part of the tea set, but the U-form tongs sometimes did share engraved designs and initials, even armorials, with the sugar bowl.

Casters are usually found in the form of small towers, most frequently with baluster or octagonal sections and removable pierced domed caps. Initially they held sugar that had been grated from cones or chunks; as sugar became more refined, they later held granules and confectioner's sugar. See SUGAR. When casters first appeared in England in the late sixteenth or early seventeenth century, they were considered appropriate gifts for noblemen, on the order of objects like pomanders for spices and perfumes. Some early standing table centerpieces featuring "salts" for another prized commodity included some sort of pierced component, possibly for sprinkling sugar or spices. The development of the three-caster box or set, with one larger sugar caster and two smaller ones for pepper and dried mustard, did not appear until the era of the English dessert banquet in the late seventeenth century. See BANQUETING HOUSES.

Sugar sifter spoons function in much the same way as casters, holding grated lump, granulated, or confectioner's sugar that can be sprinkled by shaking the spoon from side to side. Their sharp-edged pierced decorations allow sugar to sprinkle through the piercings. While the exact date of their origin is unclear, the earliest sifter spoons, with fairly deep bowls and long handles, seem to have appeared in the latter part of the eighteenth century. Their popularity in the nineteenth century and later is probably due to the advent of mechanized sugar refining and the patenting of a powdered sugar machine in 1851, which meant that sugar could be sprinkled in a more highly refined state from the spoons.

See also SERVING PIECES.

Glanville, Philippa, and Hilary Young, eds. *Elegant Eating: Four Hundred Years of Dining in Style.* London: V & A Publications, 2002.

Trager, James. *The Food Chronology: A Food Lover's Compendium of Events and Anecdotes, from Prehistory to the Present.* New York: Henry Holt, 1997. See p. 246, citing Boston candy maker Oliver Chase's patent.

Sarah D. Coffin

serving pieces are the objects and tools devised for presenting sweets. Historically, they were treasured—stored separately and not in daily use. Examples include the Limoges enamel valued at the sixteenth-century Valois court, or the Venetian bowls in Henry VIII's Whitehall Glasshouse. Some pieces were exotic, such as the gilded and lacquered "wicker China" at Salisbury House, London, in 1612. In Renaissance Italy, tin-glazed *istoriato* dishes painted with classical myths were popular. Dutch and English customers had tin-glazed plates painted with moralizing or mocking rhymes, successors to the earlier trenchers, which were disks of thin beech wood. Painted and gilded with a motto or a biblical text, these delicate mats had a plain side for candied fruit. See CANDIED FRUIT.

Imported Chinese porcelain arrived in Italy beginning in the late fifteenth century, and from the mid-sixteenth century it rapidly became the desired material for serving fruit across northern Europe. The silver-mounted Imari porcelain service of Charles of Lorraine (now in Vienna's Imperial Silver Chamber) shows how colorful ceramic services imported from China and Japan retained their appeal well into the eighteenth century.

In the early seventeenth century, fruit, a prestigious delicacy, was set out on broad "scalloped" dishes, as listed in Charles I's inventories in the 1630s; beginning in the 1660s, this style was superseded by standing dishes on trumpet feet. For evening parties at courts, sugared fruit was piled up in decorative silver trays. Apart from the decorative pastry lids on pies and tarts, height was the desired effect.

Service en pyramide created height by stacking graded salvers called *porcellanes*, a term used from the mid-sixteenth century, even though the salvers were not always made of porcelain. At the 1668 peace celebrations at Versailles, dessert was served in *seize porcelains en pyramide*.

New delicacies such as flavored creams required new serving wares. Between 1637 and 1639, Viscountess Dorchester's dessert closet contained a sugar box, "cream bowls of china garnished with silver, China dishes, glasses and bottles . . . 5 drawers full of Chinay dishes and glass plates, a dozen tortus shell dishes." Robert May, in *The Accomplisht Cook* (1678 edition), recommended "little round Jelly glasses," to be stacked up on salvers. Before the early eighteenth century, flat ceramic plates and dishes were hard to fire in kilns. Metal or lead glass offered an alternative: "The broader your cream dish, the more beautiful your cream will look," as Rebecca Price advised in 1681. She also recommended a silver server (salver) for "Jelly Lemons" and a salver for "Spoonefulls of Spanish Cream." In 1702 the French chef Massialot recommended "China" for wet sweetmeats in his *Nouvelle instruction pour les confitures*.

Porcelain offered shiny color and ornament for ladles, bowls, and dishes for cream and compotes, as well as for plates painted with flowers and dessert tureens shaped like fruit. At Chelsea in 1755, a "compleat service for the dessert" featured large cabbage leaves, vine leaves, and small sunflower leaves. By the 1770s, European porcelain factories were making special ice-filled ceramic bucket-shaped containers, with a central saucer, for serving ice cream. See ICE CREAM. The Meissen, St. Cloud, Chantilly, and Sèvres factories all supplied porcelain handles for dessert flatware. At Williamsburg, Virginia, in 1770, Governor Botetourt had a case of flatware "with China handles," plus gilt-handled dessert sets, standard since the late seventeenth century. Diners often carried small folding pocketknives for fruit.

A new implement, a silver trowel devised for dexterous lifting of delicate pastries and cakes, was adopted from Oslo to London by 1720. Porcelain and creamware trowels soon followed. For serving ice cream, two-handled glass or porcelain cups, presented on small salvers, became standard, as depicted in M. Emy's *L'Art de bien faire les glaces d'office* (1768). See EMY, M. Silversmiths created spades with curved sides to slice the ice cream. See SERVERS, ICE CREAM. Gilding remained the preferred finish for both serving implements and dessert wares. In the 1760s the botanically knowledgeable second Duchess of Portland ordered a complete service, including black-currant and strawberry leaf dishes for fruit tarts, candelabra formed as plant stems with insects and butterflies, and serving spoons and forks with leaf-encrusted handles and bowls. These themed dessert services suited the eighteenth-century concept of summer dining al fresco in garden houses and grottoes, or on a boating lake, as at Wanstead House.

At all social levels, setting out a dessert was a valuable skill. Banquets (desserts) at sixteenth-century European courts are known about mostly from descriptions by heralds and stewards, images of royal marriages, feasts of knightly orders (the Garter, St. Esprit), and feasts held for imperial elections. In the late seventeenth and early eighteenth centuries, professional table deckers created striking effects with silver, glass, and porcelain. For evening assemblies from the 1740s, epergnes in all these materials, with small hanging baskets for sweetmeats and sugared fruit, were popular. See EPERGNES. For large feasts, serving wares were rented from goldsmiths, glass sellers, and confectioners. In the 1760s, Domenico Negri depicted on his trade cards the fanciful dessert centerpieces on Chinese, marine, and classical themes available to rent from his premises at the Sign of the Pineapple in London's Hanover Square.

Exceptional creations attracted comment in the press: the royal goldsmith Hugh Le Sage made for the Prince of Nassau "a very curious piece of wrought plate (for a desert) of exquisite workmanship" (*Daily Advertiser*, April 1731). For the Duke of Richmond, a 1730s list of "Things to be gott in Paris" included a confectioner and "a compleatt sett of desert dishes with looking glasses." Mirror centerpieces, fashionable from the early eighteenth century, were dressed with clusters of porcelain figures and sugar flowers, which were replaced in the early nineteenth century by gilded stands for fruit or fresh flowers.

French and English handbooks of instructions, such as Hannah Woolley's *Queenlike Closet or Rich Cabinet . . . of Rare Receipts (for) . . . Ingenious Persons of the Female Sex* (1670) or *The Whole Duty of a Woman* (1737), stress the importance of symmetry in the layout but rarely specify the dishes. In Manchester the confectioner Elizabeth Raffald recommended a "Deep China Dish" as the centerpiece for a dessert. Classes for women in pastry making and dessert planning were held in London in the 1720s and later.

Wealthy owners of costly porcelain dessert services often showed them in glazed display cases near the dining room, as at Apsley House, London, and Alnwick Castle. Exceptional eighteenth-century Sèvres services can be seen at Waddesdon Manor, the Rothschild Collection (Paris), and Woburn Abbey. Other European porcelain services made for imperial and princely households are in St. Petersburg, Vienna, and Munich. Beginning in the 1760s, creamware, aimed at middle-class consumers, offered a cheaper decorative substitute for porcelain. The best known are Queens Ware services from Wedgwood's factory, often decorated with transfer printing; Leeds potters produced a variety called pearlware. Baskets with pierced borders were popular at all social levels. These English wares were widely exported.

Once the concept of the restaurant was invented in Paris in the 1760s, this new setting increasingly offered an agreeable environment alongside confectioners' shops for respectable women to eat in public, and restaurants gradually transformed the preparation of sweets. More-complex and fashionable delicacies such as ice cream, puff pastry, and meringues became treats to be prepared by professionals and consumed away from home. See MERINGUE and PASTRY, PUFF. Serving wares for commercial eating places were elaborate, adopting conventions such as special tiered stands for cakes, and tall glasses for iced confections. See CAKE AND CONFECTIONERY STANDS.

Beginning in the early nineteenth century, the variety of serving implements for desserts multiplied, driven by new dining practices, industrial innovation, and the constant invention of novelties. In the 1840s, Elkingtons, an entrepreneurial Birmingham firm, and Christofle in Paris almost simultaneously invented techniques for electroplating flatware. Shiny but much less expensive than sterling silver, and more durable than the earlier silver substitute known as Sheffield plate, this new material was fashioned into a huge range of slices, scoops, knives, and spoons.

American manufacturers were inventive in devising tools for particular delicacies. This "jewelry of silver," a term used in *Scribner's Monthly* 1874 article "The Silver Age," ranged from oyster forks to "knife-edge ice cream spoons," sawback cake knives, and servers for asparagus, celery, berries, pastries, and salad.

Machine-made pressed glass offered a decorative and colorful alternative to cut glass, which continued to be admired throughout the nineteenth century. Mid-nineteenth-century housewives appreciated colorful porcelain dishes and plates that reproduced rococo design of the 1740s and 1750s, including shell-shaped baskets and comports for fruit. As illustrated in Mrs Beeton's *Book of Household Management* (in many editions from 1861), dessert tables were still laid in a symmetrical arrangement, echoing the location of the earlier savory dishes, with the addition of trowels, grape scissors, and decorative serving spoons, as well as small knives, spoons, and forks with gilded or mother-of-pearl handles. See BEETON, ISABELLA.

Today, informality in eating, driven by a lack of time to prepare foods as much as by changing attitudes to diet, means that desserts are rarely elaborately presented at home. However, a birthday or other celebration still merits a special effort, such as bringing out a treasured old dish or bowl and small forks. Restaurants and caterers for large dinners compete to present their confections with style, although the wares and tools are usually simple, practical expressions of contemporary design.

See also BANQUETING HOUSES; FRUIT; and SUGAR SCULPTURE.

Belden, Louise Conway. *The Festive Tradition: Table Decoration and Desserts in America, 1650–1900.* New York: Norton, 1983.

Bursche, Stefan. *Tafelzier des Barock.* Munich: Editions Schneider, 1974.

Glanville, Philippa, and Hilary Young, eds. *Elegant Eating: Four Hundred Years of Dining in Style.* London: V & A Publications, 2002.

Lehmann, Gilly. *The British Housewife: Cookery Books, Cooking & Society in Eighteenth-Century Britain.* Totnes, U.K.: Prospect, 2003.

Philippa Glanville

sexual innuendo has coupled sweetness with love and sexuality since ancient times. In the Old Testament's Song of Solomon, the female speaker equates her lover with sweet apples:

> As the apple tree among the trees of the wood, so is my beloved among the sons. I sat down under his shadow with great delight, and his fruit was sweet to my taste. (2:3)

In his fourth-century work *The Fall of Troy*, Quintus Smyrnaeus alludes to "love's deep sweet well-springs."

In the late thirteenth century "sweetheart" arose in English as a term of endearment, followed shortly after by "sweeting." In the late sixteenth century "sweetikins" appeared: "She is such a honey sweetikins," wrote Thomas Nashe in a pamphlet from 1596. "Sweetling" and "sweetie" appeared in the mid-seventeenth century, while "sweetie-pie," "sugar pie," and "sugar" emerged as terms of endearment around 1930. In 1969 The Archies released their hit song "Sugar, Sugar," in which a "candy girl" is advised to "pour a little sugar" onto her boyfriend.

Not surprisingly, "honey" has also long been used as a term of endearment. In a fourteenth-century manuscript called "William and the Werewolf," the hero tells his beloved, "Mi hony, mi hert, al hol thou me makest" (My honey, my heart, you make me completely whole). In a sixteenth-century bawdy poem by the Scottish poet William Dunbar, a woman calls her lover "my swete hurle bawsy, / my huny gukkis" (my sweet calf, my honey cakes). In the late nineteenth century "honey bunny" appeared, though a precursor might be found in a 1719 poem by Thomas D'Urfrey in which a lover proclaims, "My Juggy, my Puggy, my Honey, my Bunny."

Sweet foods have also been used in sexual contexts to represent various parts of the human body. Slang words for the buttocks, for example, have included "hot cross buns" and "pound cake." In addition, baked goods have been used as metonyms for female breasts, as with "cupcakes," "apple dumplings," and "love muffins," but more often they are imagined as sweet globular fruits: apples, oranges, cantaloupes, mangoes, and especially peaches and melons. Sweet foods have also inspired several slang names for the penis, including "custard chucker," "ladies' lollipop," and "sweet meat." Slang names for the vagina have included "honey pot," which was first used in a narrative published in 1673 called *Unlucky Citizen*: "Desiring by all means to gain his will on the Wench, and to have a lick at her Honey-pot." "Jelly roll" was a popular slang name for the vagina in the 1920s, as was "fur pie" from the 1930s onward. The 1999 film *American Pie*, in which a teenager copulates with a warm apple pie, appears to have prompted the recent use of "apple pie" as a slang synonym for "vagina."

The lyrics of many popular songs construe sexuality in terms of sweet foods. The term "jelly roll," as mentioned earlier, was used as a slang name for the vagina and appeared in numerous jazz and blues songs of the 1920s, such as "I Ain't Gonna Give Nobody None o' My Jelly Roll," "Nobody in Town Can Bake a Jelly Roll Like Mine," and "The New Jelly-Roll Blues." The latter song, as recorded by Peg Leg Howell in 1926, includes these suggestive lyrics:

> Jelly roll, jelly roll, ain't so hard to find.
> Ain't a baker shop in town bake 'em brown like mine
> I got a sweet jelly, a lovin' sweet jelly roll,
> If you taste my jelly, it'll satisfy your worried soul.

Sexual innuendo also characterizes the lyrics of Bessie Smith's jazz classic "I Need a Little Sugar in My Bowl," which she recorded in 1931: "I need a little sugar in my bowl, / I need a little hot dog, between my rolls." Smith's song "Kitchen Man" from 1929 is equally suggestive:

> When I eat his doughnuts
> All I leave is the hole
> Any time he wants to
> Why, he can use my sugar bowl.

Songs that made risqué use of sweet foods persisted throughout the twentieth century. Roosevelt Sykes, in 1961, sang, "I'm the sweet root man, try this potato of mine." In the 1970s The Guess Who sang about a woman withholding sex from a man in their song "No Sugar Tonight." Steve Miller admired a woman's breasts when he crooned, "I really like your peaches, want to shake your tree," and the Rolling Stones equated "brown sugar" with young black women: "Brown sugar how come you taste so good? / Brown sugar just like a young girl should." In some song lyrics, sweet foods were employed as stand-ins for an erect penis: Tom Waits, in "Ice Cream Man," sings, "I got a cherry popsicle right on time / A big stick, mamma, that'll blow your mind," while 50 Cent in "Candy Shop" says, "I'll take you to the candy shop, / I'll let you lick the lollypop." Contemporary pop stars continue to honor the tradition of sweet and bawdy lyrics. In her 2013 album *Blow*, Beyoncé croons, "Can you lick my Skittles, it's the sweetest in the middle, / Pink is the flavor, solve the riddle."

See also GENDER and SLANG.

Morton, Mark. *Dirty Words: The Story of Sex Talk.* London: Atlantic, 2005.
Thorne, Tony. *Dictionary of Contemporary Slang.* New York: Pantheon, 1991.

Mark Morton

sfogliatelle

See PASTRY, PUFF.

shape, perhaps against expectation, influences the way we perceive sweetness, leading to the question of whether sweetness itself has a shape. While the question might seem like a nonsensical one, a growing body of empirical evidence now documents the fact that the majority of Western consumers will match sweet-tasting foods with rounded (rather than angular) shapes. Why such an association should exist is not altogether clear. It may have something to do with the fact that both sweetness and roundness are treated as positive sensory attributes. By contrast, most Westerners match bitterness, sourness, and carbonation with more angular shapes, the link in these cases perhaps being that all three cues are associated with stimuli that are potentially dangerous or bad for us, and hence generally best avoided.

Shape Symbolism in Action

Foods are typically rated as tasting sweeter when they are served in a round format rather than a more angular one. Such an observation may help to explain why consumers complained following the introduction of the new, rounder Cadbury Dairy Milk chocolate bar in 2013, saying that the confection tasted sweeter following its change in shape. Mondelēz International, the company that currently makes the product, asserts that the recipe hasn't changed. In the future, food companies may be able to use the crossmodal correspondence between roundness and sweetness to enhance the design of their product offerings.

Furthermore, once it is realized that taste attributes can be communicated by means of shape cues, a rich world of "synesthetic marketing" opens up. It can be argued that the labels, logos, and packaging of sweet products should be rounder (to set up the right expectation in the mind of the consumer), while products that are bitter or carbonated should be angular.

Desserts are rated as tasting significantly sweeter if served from a round plate than from an angular one, while food served from a white plate is perceived as tasting sweeter than food served from a black plate. Presenting a dessert on a round white plate may thus allow the chef to reduce the sugar content while not compromising on taste. No wonder, then, that many restaurateurs are now starting to sit up and take note of the emerging research on shape symbolism and taste.

Cross-Cultural Differences in the Shape of Sweetness

Intriguingly, recent cross-cultural research has highlighted the fact that not everyone experiences the same cross-modal associations when it comes to the shape of taste. The semi-nomadic Himba tribe of Namibia, for instance, actually shows the opposite pattern of results from Westerners, associating sweetness (as in milk chocolate) with angularity. Further research is needed in order to determine why this should be so.

See also VISION; SOUND; and SWEETNESS PREFERENCE.

Bremner, Andrew, Serge Caparos, Jules Davidoff, Jan de Fockert, Karina J. Linnell, and Charles Spence. "'Bouba' and 'Kiki' in Namibia? A Remote Culture Make Similar Shape-Sound Matches, but Different Shape-Taste Matches to Westerners." *Cognition* 126, no. 2 (2013): 165–172.

Spence, Charles. "Unravelling the Mystery of the Rounder, Sweeter Chocolate Bar." *Flavour* 2 (2013): 28. http://www.flavourjournal.com/content/2/1/28 (accessed 7 October 2014).

Spence, Charles, and Betina Piqueras-Fiszman. *The Perfect Meal: The Multisensory Science of Food and Dining*. Chichester, U.K.: Wiley-Blackwell, 2014.

Charles Spence

shave ice is the term used in Hawaii for thinly shaved ice doused in fluorescent, tropical-fruit-flavored syrups and served in a paper cone. The dropped "d" is typical of the Hawaii Creole English (commonly known as pidgin) that is widely spoken in the islands. Shave ice is one of a large family of shaved ice treats around the world that are enjoyed for the delicate consistency of their ice flakes, which hold the syrup in suspension. Snow cones or snow balls, more commonly sold in the mainland United States, are made of crushed ice.

The history of shave ice and snow cones is yet to be written, though certain preliminary observations are possible. Although there were probably hand-shaved predecessors (still found in Mexico, for example), to make either type on a commercial scale requires large-scale ice harvesting or artificial refrigeration, a machine for shaving or crushing, sugar, and artificial flavors and colors. This suggests an origin sometime in the early twentieth century. The distribution of shave ice maps fairly closely onto early-twentieth-century Japanese emigration routes to Hawaii and the Americas, and to the slightly later expansion of the Japanese empire across East and Southeast Asia (though how shave ice ended up in the Caribbean is obscure). This trajectory, along with the widespread occurrence of Japanese-made machinery, indicates an origin in Japan, possibly Okinawa, the main sugar-growing area in that country. Snow cones appear to have been an American innovation, though the crushed ice balls of India may be an independent invention.

Shave ice lends itself to more exuberant variants, such as sweetened azuki beans in the bottom of the cup and ice cream on the top in Hawaii, or condensed milk or Calpis (fermented goat's milk) in Japan. Filipino *halo halo* is a riot of textures and flavors, including sweetened beans, jackfruit, gelatinous young coconut, and fresh fruits, all covered with syrup or condensed milk.

See also AZUKI BEANS; ICE CREAM; and SWEETENED CONDENSED MILK.

Laudan, Rachel. *The Food of Paradise: Exploring Hawaii's Culinary Heritage.* Honolulu: University of Hawaii Press, 1996.

Rachel Laudan

sherbet refers to both a sweet chilled drink and a lush frozen dessert. Although it resists strict definition, sherbet is a delight to drink or eat. The name derives from the medieval Arabic *sharāb*, meaning a drink or a dose of water, medicine, or other liquid; this word was adopted into Urdu as *sharbat* and into Turkish as *şerbet.* By the late Middle Ages *sharāb* had become a notorious euphemism for an alcoholic beverage; the alternate form *sharbāt* (along with *sharbat* and *şerbet*) came to mean a sweet, nonalcoholic, fruit-based beverage, not necessarily chilled. The essential thing about a *şerbet* is sweetness, which is considered auspicious in Turkey and the Middle East. In Turkish, "To sense someone's pulse and serve sherbet" means to use tact. In Egypt, the phrase "sherbet flows in her veins" means that a woman is sweet, delightful company; it does not mean that she is cold-blooded.

Traditional sherbet beverages are sweetened with sugar or honey, and are made with a variety of fruits, flowers, and herbs, including lemon, pomegranate, quince, strawberry, cherry, orange, rose, orange blossom, tamarind, mulberry, and violet. They are both everyday drinks and festive ones, served at weddings, births, and circumcision ceremonies. In Turkey, a bride-to-be is said to have drunk *şerbet* when she agrees to marry, and *şerbet* is prepared to mark the betrothal. Iranians drink *sharbat* as part of the festivities at Nowruz, the New Year holiday celebrated on the first day of spring. On such occasions, sherbets are traditionally presented in elegant glass cups covered with rounds of embroidered silk and placed on decorated trays. On more ordinary days, street vendors throughout the Middle East sell sherbets from large flasks and announce their presence with tinkling bells, much like ice cream peddlers in the West.

Sherbet makers also mixed dried fruits and flowers with sugar to make sherbet powders, a kind of instant sherbet that could be easily transported, then mixed with water and chilled for a refreshing beverage. The powders were sold throughout the region and even imported to England during the seventeenth century. In their modern form, sherbet powders are a child's treat. Twenty-first-century English children eat sweet fizzy sherbet powders by dipping lollipops into the powder and licking it off. Sherbet Fountains, paper tubes of sherbet powder with licorice straws, are also popular with young children. See SHERBET POWDER.

Sherbet in Europe

The word *sharāb* entered European languages in the late medieval period, resulting in words like *sciroppo* and *syrup* via Latin. The first Western mention of sherbet appeared only in the sixteenth century, when it was recorded in Italian as something that Turks drank. Italians adopted the word as *sorbetto*, rather than *scerbetto*, due to a folk etymology connecting it with *sorbire*, "to sip." From *sorbetto* came the French *sorbet* (1553), Spanish *sorbete*, and Portuguese *sorvete.* English might be the only Western language that adopted the word "sherbet" directly from Turkish.

In the early seventeenth century the English writer and traveler to the Middle East George Sandys described "sundry sherbets... some made of sugar and lemons, some of violets, and the like." Nineteenth-century novelist James Morier described the flavor of Persian sherbets as "so mixed that the sour and the sweet were as equally balanced as the blessings and miseries of life."

Sherbet remained a drink until seventeenth-century Europeans discovered the endothermic effect whereby ice, when combined with salt, lowers the temperature of a substance enough to freeze it. Early freezing pots for making ices and ice creams were called *sorbetières*, sometimes spelled *sarbetières* or *sabotieres*. In Italy, the word *sorbetto* was used for both frozen ices and frozen ice creams well into the eighteenth century, when *gelato* became the term for ice cream.

In most countries, sorbetto or sorbet came to mean a frozen water ice made from a basic sugar syrup to which fruit juices, additional water, herbs, flavorings, wine, or spirits are added. Beaten egg whites, fresh or pasteurized, are often used to lighten sorbets. Today, commercial sorbets may also include stabilizers, emulsifiers, and other products to create a smoother, longer-lasting product.

In the United States, the word "sherbet" eventually came to be used for frozen mixtures that contained milk rather than cream, but the term was a fluid one. In her 1913 book *Ice Creams, Water Ices, Frozen Puddings*, the American Sarah Tyson Rorer wrote that a water ice should have the appearance of "hard, wet snow. It must not be frothy and light." She defined sherbet or sorbet as being composed of the same mixture as water ice, but it had to be stirred constantly and have meringue mixed in. Her sherbets did not contain milk. See ITALIAN ICE and MERINGUE.

Soda fountain manuals from the early twentieth century include sherbet recipes that call for such ingredients as gelatin, cream of tartar, beaten egg whites, cream, or milk. But generally in the United States, sherbet is an ice milk. During World War II restaurants and soda fountains promoted sherbet since it was made with milk rather than cream, which was in short supply. Half-and-half sundaes were made with a scoop of sherbet and a scoop of ice cream. See SUNDAE. Today, frozen sherbets are sold in many flavors, including pomegranate, lemon, grape, raspberry, lime, and peach, though the flavors are not yet as numerous as those used in Middle Eastern beverage sherbets.

Midmeal Sorbets

In Victorian England, elaborate multicourse meals began with a hot soup course. Then, after three more courses, the second half of the meal often began with a cooling sorbet or punch much like the Middle Eastern sherbet drinks. See PUNCH. The preeminent English cookbook author Agnes Marshall wrote that these sorbets should be of a "light, semi-frozen nature.... They are generally prepared by first making an ordinary lemon-water ice, and adding to this some spirit, liqueur, or syrup for flavouring, and fruit for garnish, and are named accordingly rum sorbet, cherry sorbet, and so on." She said they should be served in glasses or fancy cups. Mrs. Marshall used the terms "sorbet" and "water ice," but not "sherbet." See MARSHALL, AGNES BERTHA.

The midmeal sorbets were generally made with enough liquor to prevent their freezing solid, so that they would be slushy. Roman Punch, ubiquitous on nineteenth- and twentieth-century menus in England and the United States, was one of the most popular. Recipes vary. One of Mrs. Marshall's was basically a lemon water ice with Jamaica rum added; another was a lemon water ice with beaten egg whites, brandy, and champagne. Her recipe for American Sorbet was similar to the others but flavored with Catawba wine (an American red wine) or champagne. Its unique quality was that it was served in ice glasses, made by freezing water in tin molds shaped like cups. Mrs. Marshall included an ad for the molds at the back of the 1894 edition of her book *Fancy Ices*. See MOLDS, JELLY AND ICE CREAM. Some twenty-first-century menus have revived the midmeal sorbet, but the practice has not regained its former popularity.

Today, the U.S. Food and Drug Administration (FDA) defines sherbet as a frozen dessert with a milk-fat content of not less than 1 percent, or more than 2 percent. It defines water ices as similar to sherbets, except that no milk or milk-derived ingredients may be used. No definition is provided for sorbet. Generally, in the United States and Europe, sorbet does not contain dairy products and is usually hard-frozen rather than resembling the slushy mixtures of yesteryear. In the Middle East and Middle Eastern restaurants everywhere, sherbet is still the sweet chilled drink that so impressed sixteenth-century European travelers.

See also CHILDREN'S CANDY; CREAM; ICE CREAM; MIDDLE EAST; and SODA FOUNTAIN.

Davidson, Alan, ed. *The Oxford Companion to Food.* Oxford: Oxford University Press, 1999.

Rossant, Juliette. "The World's First Soft Drink." *Saudi Aramco World,* September–October 2005.

Weir, Caroline, and Robin Weir. *Ice Creams, Sorbets & Gelati.* London: Grub Street, 2010.

Robin Weir and Jeri Quinzio

sherbet powder is a mixture of sugar, tartaric acid powder, bicarbonate of soda, and lemon flavoring. It combines sweetness, sharp acidity, and a sensation of fizz, and was described by Tim Richardson, in *Sweets: A History of Temptation* (2002), as "one of the most nutritionally unjustifiable and gastronomically obscure foodstuffs available to man (or child)."

This inexpensive confection is essentially a U.K. specialty beloved of children between six and ten. As "Rainbow Crystals," arranged in colored stripes in the jar, it decorates the sweetshop shelves, waiting to be weighed out and tipped into flimsy paper bags; a cheap lollipop (a boiled sweet on a stick) is added to make a "sherbet dab." Sherbet Fountains are paper tubes filled with the powder, each one sealed around a hollow tube of licorice that serves as a drinking straw for imbibing the contents. "Flying saucers" are fragile discs of wafer, domed in the middle and pressed together in twos to enclose the powder; and sherbet lemons are lemon-flavored boiled sweets filled with the powder. Sherbet also flavors tablet-like confections of powdered sugar stamped out under high pressure. Of these, Love Hearts, descendants of Victorian motto lozenges, are the most distinctive.

Sherbet powder dates to the mid-nineteenth century, when it was discovered that bicarbonate of soda and tartaric acid, developed by the chemical industry, produced a powder that effervesced when combined with water. The idea rapidly evolved into a dry mix for making fizzy lemonade, a cheap version of the popular iced lemon sherbet drink.

Other countries are less enthusiastic about sherbet powder, although the French Coco Boer, a concoction of powdered licorice and bicarbonate of soda sold in tiny tins, follows the notion of a powder to make a drink that combines novelty and appeal to youngsters.

See also LEMONADE; LICORICE; and LOLLIPOPS.

Mason, Laura. *Sugar-Plums and Sherbet: The Prehistory of Sweets.* Totnes, U.K.: Prospect, 2004.

Laura Mason

shortbread, a flat, fragile, crumbly pastry, has been defined by the term "short" since medieval times. "Shortness" was created by using lots of butter or lard, rubbed into flour and baked, to make a flaky or crumbly texture. See SHORTENING. Sweetness came from sugar, caraway comfits, sugared almonds, or candied peel. See COMFIT. In the late 1500s, some recipes were described in English as "short-cakes." More palatable than a hard, salty, twice-baked biscuit, they were a popular treat in the centuries that followed, and they flourished in many different forms.

Shortbread belongs to an extended family of baked goods. Among those found in Europe are French *galettes.* See GALETTE. Flat, round shortcakes in a pebble *(galet)* shape, they are perfumed with cinnamon, rum, or bergamot. Greek *kourabiethes* contain some egg and are flavored with almonds, ouzo, and vanilla. Once baked, they are thickly coated with confectioner's sugar. Small, round English shortcakes include Derbyshire wakes cakes, with currants, caraway, and lemon; Goosnargh cakes from Lancashire, flavored with coriander or caraway; and Shrewsbury cakes, which include spices and rosewater. See SMALL CAKES.

It is in Scotland's culinary history, however, that a recipe titled *Short Bread* appears in the nation's first published cookery book, *Mrs McLintock's Receipts for Cookery and Pastry Work* (Glasgow, 1736). Her buttery, caraway-flavored dough has a "mutchkin of barm" (the yeasty foam created by fermentation), which may explain its "bread" tag. A *Scottish Shortbread* recipe, in Mistress Margaret (Meg) Dods's *The Cook and Housewife's Manual* (Edinburgh, 1826), has the proportions 3:2:1 of flour, butter, and sweetening, which remains the norm. Dods also calls it—possibly for the benefit of English readers—a "Short Cake." The recipe yields a 1-inch (2 cm) thick cake, made oval, square, or round in shape and either plain or with additions of candied peel and almonds. Besides the highest quality ingredients—especially good-flavored butter—careful blending and "firing" (baking) are considered essential for the finest results. Dods advises adding more almonds and butter if the cake is to be sent as a "holiday present to England."

Being raised to the status of a special food gift certainly increased this shortbread's fame. But it would not have flourished without the talents of skilled Scots bakers. During the period of the Auld Alliance with France (1295–1560), when there was much interchange between the two countries, French pastry cooks worked in Edinburgh. According to archive records from the 1500s, Scots bakers who made sweet cakes became known as "Caik-baxteris." Like French pâtissiers, they were distinct from the bread bakers, and it can be expected that they practiced their art to high levels of perfection.

Evidence of Scottish shortbread's reputation appears in advertisements in English newspapers. The *Hereford Journal* in 1825 describes it as "Scots shortbread, an Exquisite Cake." In 1837 a London baker's advertisement in the *Morning Post* states that his shortbread "is made in the same way, and in as high perfection, as it can be had in Scotland."

During the 1800s, shortbread's Scottish credentials were also noted by leading English cookery book authors, including Eliza Acton (1845) and Mrs. Isabella Beeton (1861), which added to its national, and global, commercial success. Popular not only as a year-round gift, "shortie," as it is affectionately known in Scotland, is also an essential treat at festive times such as Hogmanay (New Year), when it is joined by black bun and drams of Scotch whisky.

While the 3:2:1 proportions have remained more or less constant, not all shortbread is made with white flour. On Orkney, where a tasty Neolithic barley known as "bere" is still grown and milled, bakers add a little of this flour to their shortbread. Others add rolled oats to provide more flavor and texture. Some use rice flour, or fine semolina, to make the shortbread grittier; or some cornstarch to make it more meltingly smooth.

Flavors, shapes, and textures always evolve. While new innovations with chocolate and caramel in "millionaire" shortbread make their mark, old traditions live on. Oldest perhaps is the thick round of shortbread shaped like a Yule bannock, with its edges pinched to symbolize the sun's rays. Harking back to ancient folklore is the belief that this shape gave the cake magical powers at the darkest time of the year. Shortbreads shaped in a round, thistle-decorated, or plain wooden mold still have their edges shaped in the form of the sun's rays.

"Petticoat tail" shortbread, cut in wedges, is yet another variation. One theory of its origins suggests that it emulates the bell-shaped petticoats worn in the 1800s. Whether true or not, this type was considered appropriate for a "ladies'" tea table. Men preferred to get their teeth into shortbread baked into thick fingers.

According to a member of the Scottish Association of Master Bakers, a tax ruling in the late 1900s threatened to classify shortbread as a "common biscuit." Not so, argued the bakers: it has a long and distinguished history as "a specialty item of flour confectionery." The evidence they presented proved their case, and the historic distinction between shortbread and biscuit was preserved. See BISCUITS, BRITISH.

See also BUTTER; SABLÉ; SHORTCAKE; and SHORTENING.

Mason, Laura and Catherine Brown. *The Taste of Britain.* London: Harper, 2006.

McNeill, F. Marian. *The Scots Kitchen: Its Traditions and Lore, with Old-Time Recipes.* Glasgow: Blackie, 1929. Reprint edition, edited and introduced by Catherine Brown, Edinburgh: Birlinn, 2010.

Catherine Brown

shortcake is a cake made "short"—in its old English sense meaning "easily crumbled"—by the incorporation of fat such as butter, lard, or cream into the dough. The *Good Huswifes Handmaide for the Kitchin* (London, 1594) contains a recipe "To make short Cakes," in which the finest flour is worked with cream or butter, sugar, sweet spices, and egg yolks, so that "your paste wil be very short, therefore yee must make your Cakes very little."

There are regional differences in the use of the words "shortcake" and "shortbread" and in the differentiation, if any, between the two. In Britain (especially in Scotland) shortbread is the more common term and specifically refers to a sweet, buttery pastry with a crisp, cookie-like texture. See SHORTBREAD. In the United States, shortcake usually indicates a cake made with a rich, soft, scone- or biscuit-like texture, which is then split and filled with fruit.

The most famous and popular version in the United States is undoubtedly the strawberry shortcake. A short piece in the *New-York Farmer and American Gardener's Magazine* in 1835 suggests that the cake was not at that time widely known: "In several parts of New-England... a short-cake is made, and while hot is cut open, and strawberries sweetened with sugar are put in. This cake is said to be delicious." By 1867 strawberry shortcake was considered sufficiently iconic to be served along with other "popular Yankee dishes" at the American restaurants at the great International Exposition in Paris.

Strawberry shortcake remains one of America's most popular desserts, with recipes for it (and other shortcake variations) still appearing regularly in books, magazines, and websites throughout the country.

See also CAKE; SHORTENING; and UNITED STATES.

Ross, Alice. "July and Strawberry Shortcake." *Journal of Antiques & Collectibles,* 20 July 2000. http://www.journalofantiques.com/hearthjul.htm (accessed 8 October 2014).

Smith, Andrew F. *Oxford Encyclopedia of Food and Drink in America.* 2d ed. New York: Oxford University Press, 2012.

Janet Clarkson

shortening is fat used for cooking. Although the term is broad enough to encompass all sorts of fats (including liquid oils), as commonly understood, shortenings tend to be solid or semisolid at room temperature, since only these fats will make a dough "short," meaning friable, or easily crumbled. They may be derived from animal, vegetable, or compound substances. Shortening can be used as an ingredient (in butter cake or lard pie crusts, for instance) or as a cooking medium (for deep-fried doughnuts or fritters). The modern usage dates to the nineteenth century and is generally a North American term.

The purpose of shortening in sweets depends upon the recipe. In cakes, it renders the texture soft and tender. It also adds volume to the batter. In cookies and sweet biscuits, shortening provides a chewy feel or crisp bite, depending upon the proportion. Pastry cut with shortening results in a flaky yet sturdy product capable of supporting fillings. See PIE DOUGH. Because shortening adds moisture in the form of fat (rather than water) to baked products, it contributes to the natural shelf life of the product. Shortening is also sometimes employed in confectionery, most notably in butterscotch and buttercream frostings.

With the exception of butter, shortenings are generally valued for being flavorless. Leaf lard, the highest-grade animal shortening, contributes almost none of its own taste to the product. Commercial products have long promoted this neutral quality. With the exception of butter, most shortenings can be stored in airtight containers at room temperature.

Lard

Lard is rendered pig fat. Humans have used hogs for food and cooking since prehistoric times. The fat from the pig was employed from these very early days as a cooking medium and ingredient. Uses and recipes evolved according to the needs and tastes of various cultures. How was lard discovered? Like most early foods, probably by accident. Presumably, when early cooks finished cooking hog pieces, they noticed the thick fat (lard) that had congealed after cooling.

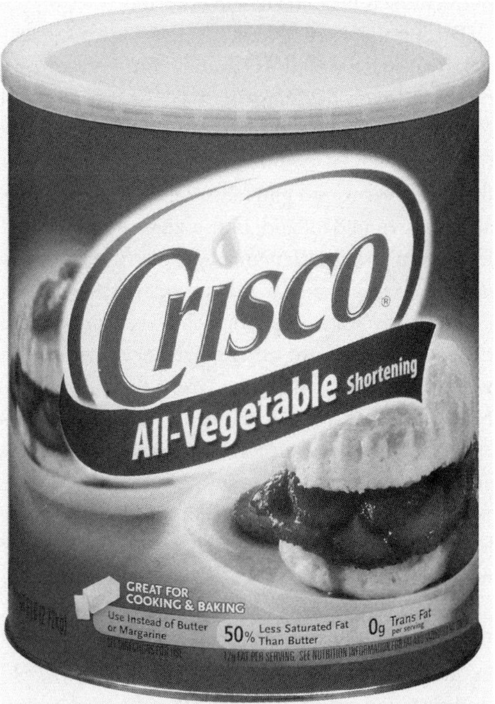

Although solid shortenings get a bad rap these days for their saturated fat, they're invaluable in baking for the tender, flaky goods they produce. © THE J. M. SMUCKER COMPANY

Leaf lard, considered the finest grade of lard, surrounds the kidneys of the hog. Commercial leaf lard surfaced in the 1880s. Like other shortenings, leaf lard was used for frying and baking. Its "flavorless" quality made it especially appealing because, like the vegetable shortening Crisco (its competitor in later years), lard barely changed the flavor of the finished dish.

Margarine

Also known as "artificial butter," "red butter," "moonshine butter," "city butter," "margarine butter," "oleomargarine," "oilymargarine," and "butterine," this shortening compound was introduced by Hippolyte Mège-Mouriès, a French chemist, in response to Napoleon III's call for a butter substitute suitable for field soldiers. Mège's 1867 process was patented in England in 1869 and in the United States in 1973. At about the same time, a similar process was patented by Henry E. Bradley of Binghamton, New York (U.S. Patent #110-626, 3 January 1871).

American margarine production was firmly established by 1873. Founding investors of the Oleo-Margarine Manufacturing Company in New York City claimed that the new "butter" was genuine—only the means of producing it were artificial. Production costs were significantly cheaper than for traditional dairy butter, so return on investment was guaranteed. Period newspapers confirm that "city made" butter was used in fashionable hotels, restaurants, and steamship companies.

The American dairy trade objected strongly to competition from margarine. Industry leaders launched powerful campaigns stating that this adulterated product was manufactured under filthy conditions with inferior ingredients. They also argued, quite rightly, that unscrupulous venders were cheating consumers by passing off yellow-dyed margarine as butter. The U.S. Internal Revenue Service responded by requiring special retail licenses and taxes on both white and dyed margarine.

American consumers readily embraced this cheaper butter substitute. Recipes required no adaption or calculations when using margarine instead of butter. The chief complaint centered on color. Annatto, a red dye used for coloring margarine and cheese, was readily available for consumers who desired a yellow product resembling traditional butter. During World War II, margarine was promoted by home economists as a better choice than butter. By then, the product had improved greatly in terms of flavor and nutritional value. In the 1950s, popular cookbooks and baking mixes began substituting the generic term "shortening" for "butter," leaving the ingredient decision to the consumer.

Margarine sales soared again in the 1970s, when health professionals educated consumers about the dangers of saturated fats and cholesterol. Margarine was actively promoted as a healthier choice than butter. New products proliferated in various textures (solid, whipped, and liquid) and types of packaging (sticks and tubs). In the 1980s, margarine-butter blends and diet (reduced-calorie) margarine were introduced. Twenty-first-century consumers still generally choose margarine over butter.

Vegetable Shortenings

Cottolene (N. K. Fairbank & Co., 1892), Crisco (Procter & Gamble, 1911), Primex (Procter & Gamble, 1926), Parfay (Swift & Company, 1930), Spry (Lever Brothers, 1932), Swiftning (Swift & Company, 1947), and Golden Fluffo (Procter & Gamble, 1955) were vegetable-based products marketed to American consumers as "digestible" and "pure." Originally sold in tins, these semisoft shortenings were promoted for frying as well as baking. Vegetable shortenings were embraced in particular by the Jewish community, because according to kosher laws they were considered "pareve"—suitable for use at meals containing meat. Corporate kitchens produced booklets touting better flavor, crispier crusts, and richer results. Hydrogenation made the product shelf-stable. Historic descriptions concerning health and cleanliness in the realm of food production help twenty-first-century readers understand why "modern" homemakers favored commercial products over "natural" ingredients.

Cottolene is generally recognized as the first hydrogenated vegetable shortening available to American consumers. It was introduced in 1892 by the N. K. Fairbank & Co. of Chicago, and Produce Exchange of New York. While primarily marketed as a cooking medium, Cottolene could have been used as a baking ingredient.

Crisco was the first vegetable shortening to attain national popularity. Actively promoted by Procter & Gamble, Crisco's slogan was "It's Digestible." Famous home economists worked in the company kitchens and wrote dozens of cookbooks encouraging modern cooks to try this new product. In 1937 Crisco introduced "Super-Creamed" Crisco, a fluffier product for even greater digestibility. Sales results and consistent product evolution attest to the staying power of this iconic American foodstuff, although in response to recent health concerns, Crisco reformulated its product in 2012 to eliminate all trans fats. Some of the fat it contains is still hydrogenated, however.

See also BUTTER.

"Crisco." In *Encyclopedia of Consumer Brands*, Vol. 1: *Consumable Products*, edited by Janice Jorgensen, pp. 139–142. Detroit: St. James, 1994.

Knightly, W. H. "Shortening Systems: Fats, Oils, and Surface-Active Agents—Present and Future, *Cereal Chemistry* 58, no. 3 (1981): 171–174. http://www.aaccnet.org/publications/cc/backissues/1981/Documents/chem58_171.pdf (accessed 8 October 2014).

Ross, Alice. "Cottolene, and the Mysterious Disappearance of Lard." *Journal of Antiques & Collectibles*, February 2002. http://www.journalofantiques.com/Feb02/hearthfeb.htm (accessed 27 February 2014).

Wiest, Edward. *The Butter Industry in the United States: An Economic Study of Butter and Oleomargarine*. New York: Columbia University Press, 1916.

Lynne M. Olver

sitophilia describes sexual arousal involving food. It is arguably the most socially acceptable type of paraphilia. Within studies that address paraphilia more broadly, sitophilia has yet to receive sustained scholarly attention due to the lack of clarity as to whether it represents a deviant or a normal sex practice. In all probability, the word "sitophilia" was imported into the sexual sphere in the late twentieth century from biology, which labels a genus of weevils that threaten food stores as *Sitophilus* and several species of food-loving fungi as sitophilia. An expansion of the sensuality inherent in food preparation and consumption into the realm of the erotic, sitophilia realizes the alleged aphrodisiac properties of foods such as oysters or chocolate by making them into a sexual fetish. See APHRODISIACS.

Whether viewed as a result of the reciprocity of bodily appetites, a conflation of the cardinal sins of gluttony and lust, a disavowal of the mother's absent phallus, a fixation on food as a transitional object, or the product of classical conditioning, sitophilia frequently involves sweets such as candy, whipped cream, honey, ice cream, syrup, and cake. Specific sitophilic practices are remarkably diverse and can include everything from eating or drinking a fetishized food from a partner's body to using food items as surrogate genitalia. For example, the invention of edible underwear in 1975 has resulted in sex toys such as the trademarked Candypants, as well as candy G-strings and crotchless gummy panties, while those excited by wet and messy fetishism, known as sploshing, enjoy bodies liberally doused with viscous substances like whipped cream, custard, pudding, chocolate sauce, or cake batter.

The relative acceptability of sitophilia involving sweets is nowhere more evident than in sexual nicknames that include the words "sugar," "honey," and "sweet," or in Hershey's Kisses, a foil-wrapped candy that locates amatory and gustatory pleasures in the mouth. See KISSES; SEXUAL INNUENDO; and SLANG. Numerous bakeries, confectioners, and chocolatiers similarly link sugar to the erotic by adopting suggestive names (Chocolate Fetish, Cake Fetish, or Sweet Fetish), marketing overtly sexual products (chocolates shaped like breasts or lollipops representing a penis), and developing salacious flavors (e.g., Orgasmic Organic Ice Cream's Chocolate Climax, Strawberry Seduction, and Kinky Karamel). The mass media has in effect made sweet-focused sitophilia into the neophyte's fetish by advising men and women alike to include food play with fruits, chocolate, flavored syrups, whipped cream, and the like in their repertoire of healthy and normal sex practices.

Popular culture plays an important role in promoting sugary sitophilia. For instance, the cover of Herb Alpert and the Tijuana Brass's 1965 album *Whipped Cream & Other Delights* features a photograph by Peter Whorf that has titillated many a splosher: an apparently nude woman sits in the middle of a mound of whipped cream with one dollop on her head and another on a finger poised at her parted lips. Similarly, Ken Russell's 1975 rock opera *Tommy* includes a sexually charged food orgy in which Ann-Margret portrays a psychotic break by throwing a champagne bottle into a television set, surrendering to the fountain of bubbles, baked beans, and melted chocolate spewing from the broken screen, and then writhing through the ensuing mess while passionately embracing an oversized sausage-shaped pillow. The 1986 film *9½ Weeks* presents a tamer sitophilic seduction when Mickey Rourke feeds Kim Basinger, among other foods, maraschino cherries, strawberries, Vicks Cough Syrup, red gelatin, and honey, before they have sex on the kitchen floor. Sitophilia moves onto the kitchen counter in the 1999 movie *American Pie*, in which high-school senior Jim (played by Jason Biggs) has sex with a warm apple pie. Evidently, almost everyone finds frisson in sugar and spice and everything nice.

See also ANTHROPOMORPHIC AND ZOOMORPHIC SWEETS.

Laws, D. Richard, and William T. O'Donohue, eds. *Sexual Deviance: Theory, Assessment, and Treatment.* 2d ed. New York: Guilford, 2008.
Love, Brenda. "Sitophilia." In *The Encyclopedia of Unusual Sexual Practices*, pp. 264–265. Fort Lee, N.J.: Barricade, 1992.
Money, John *The Lovemap Guidebook: A Definitive Statement.* New York: Continuum, 1999.

Julie A. Cassiday

slang—mocking, sneering, casting a jaundiced eye on the world's proprieties—is by its nature sour. It finds approval hard, congratulation challenging, and affection almost impossible. Yet even if slang's oldest meaning of "sugar" is money, and the second oldest a euphemism for the most common term for defecation, slang, for all its skepticism, cannot resist the tempting possibilities of "sweet." It has no word for "love," but someone can "be sweet on" someone else, and the trope "good enough to eat" characterizes a wide range of human love-objects. But slang has its limits. The presence of sweetness—whether the term itself; semantic equivalents such as "honey" or "sugar"; specifics such as "cake," "toffee," "candy," or "lollipop"; or a variety of brand names such as M&M's (drugs in pill form)—is regularly turned on its head in a wide range of negative definitions. In slang's upside-down, inside-out, tweaked, and twisted world, even sweet can turn sour.

Let us begin, then, with "sweet" itself.

Judged by slang's mainly concrete lexis, the word "sweet" manages quite a few abstractions. There is the ironic sweet: a "sweet mess," "take your own sweet time"; there is the approving sweet, applicable to people, objects, actions, and events. There is sweet in human terms, which can mean gullible, but also dexterous and expert; in criminal terms, it can mean devoid of suspicion, as well as simple and lucrative (when describing a crime as safe). To "be sweet" is to be amenable; this usually occurs as "keep/have someone sweet"—to keep someone well disposed toward oneself, especially by complaisance or bribery. Given the traditional equation of little girls with "sugar and spice," it can also imply effeminacy when used of a male, thus yielding compounds such as "sweet kid," "sweet girl," or "sweetmeat"—prison terminology for a younger prisoner who joins up with an older man. (Sweet, when referring to real females is, of course, standard.) As noted earlier, to be "sweet on" is to be in love with or infatuated by, though it can also mean nagging, pestering and insistent, and, free of relationships, simply satisfied or happy. Australia's "she's sweet" or "she'll be sweet" means everything is satisfactory, as does "she's be apples" or "she'll be apples." That which is easy or pleasurable can be "sweet as a nut," "sweet as honey," or "sweet as a lolly."

Sweet can act as an intensifier: "sweet (bleeding) Jesus!", "sweet Christ!", and others. It can refer to the beloved, the "sweet papa" or "sweet mama" (though the inference is of financial transaction and the primary synonym remains "sugar daddy"); thus it can also modify the world of commercial sex, giving the "sweet mack" or "Sweet Willie," a (relatively) gentle pander. The pimp is also a "sweetman," although the word can cover a less compromised lover—what makes him sweet are the gifts he brings, and perhaps his "sweet-mouth" (his verbal skills).

In standard usage, to "sweeten" is to adulterate with sugar; its slang definitions include to bribe, to flatter, or to mollify (typically a con man's anxious victim). The trickster is the "sweetener," a term that can also mean a bribe; a word of encouragement, or a threat of force; the lips; and, slang's male viewpoint aforethought, the penis. Sometimes sweet can be taken literally, as in the short-order jargon's "blonde and sweet" (coffee with cream and sugar). "Sweetness and light," meaning whiskey, suggests a positive image of the liquor's effects (not exactly what Matthew Arnold was thinking of in *Culture and Anarchy*).

What works for sweet also works for sugar, typically in its use for a range of wealthy lovers—"sugar daddy," "sugar papa," "sugar-pops," "sugar mama," or "sugar mummy"—although this latter should not be confused with the "yummy mummy," a British confection suggesting that sexiness need not terminate with maternity, and which in turn is synonymized by pornography's blunt acronym, the MILF. "Yummy" can also be used of a nubile teenager and is kin to "yum-yum," used around 1880 for sex, and for a female who might permit it.

"Sugar" picks up on the monetary associations of "sweeten," to mean a bonus or a bribe, and the verb form means to bribe or to present a fake image. A "sugar-bag" accepts such gifts, though the second-rate materials used for such containers have led to the meaning "second-rate" for the word's adjectival form. Inferiority also accompanies the compound "tea-and-sugar," usually joined to a bandit or burglar, both petty thieves. It is also—though here the link is only assonant—a euphemism for "shit" (either as excrement or used as an exclamation), though, like shit, sugar can also mean money. The terms "big sugar" and "heavy sugar" refer to substantial sums of money, while a "heavy sugar daddy" or "heavy sugar papa" is a woman's generous or exploitable older lover. Men turn the tables with "sugar basin," the vagina, into which they deposit "sugar," or semen. The "sugar-bush" is the pubic hair, and the "sugar-stick," inevitably, the penis. The nineteenth-century exclamation "sugar, cock your legs and cry" signifies triumph or delight among members of the underworld and is accompanied by standing on one leg, cocking up the other, and shouting "Sugar!" Perhaps it equates with modernity's approving "sweet!"

Like sugar, the term "candy" is far more common in the United States than elsewhere. The word can mean something admirable or desirable. It can refer to money or someone seen as "sweet," with or without sexual overtones. And, like sugar, candy can codify the names of a variety of drugs, usually narcotic. An underlying image of "softness" that parallels "sweet" can suggest effeminacy, even homosexuality, and a "candy-ass" is a weakling, though in the 1920s and 1930s, "candy-leg" suggested a wealthy and attractive young man—an early form of "chick magnet." Candy's best known combination is "arm candy," a pretty girl adorning the sugar daddy's arm, but it also provides the synonymous "eye candy" and "brain candy," meaning superficially attractive but intellectually undemanding.

Terms of Endearment

Sugar and sweet are both enlisted as terms of endearment, but they are not alone. The equation of the loved one and the toothsome treat—one who is "good enough to eat"—is venerable. "Thy lips, O my spouse, drop as the honeycomb: honey and milk are under thy tongue," declares the Song of Solomon around 200 B.C.E., and the pattern has continued. "Honey," with its combinations "honeychild," "honey-chops," "honey-dip," "honey-baby," "honey-pot," and "honey-bun," arrived in the early twentieth century, as did "crumpet." The equation seems unquenchable, and endearments include "honey-bunch," "honey-bunny," "honeybugs," "honey-cunt," and "honeypie." As with sugar, there are less appetizing senses, notably the ironic: a "honey of a mess" is problematical. "Honey" can denote various bodily fluids, whether sexual or excretory—the best known of the latter is "honey cart," used in various forms of public transport to describe a container for what an earlier world, equally euphemistic, termed "gold." The rival images combine in the eighteenth century's "all honey or all turd with them," said of those whose relationship fluctuates violently between amity and enmity.

"Sweetie," "sweetie-pops," "sweetycakes," "sweetie-pie," "sweet pea," and "sweet potato pie" are other modern terms of endearment. "Cake" has been popular in the United States for a century, while "lollipop" has been common since 1850.

"Tart" is perhaps the most interesting. Now seen as a pejorative (other than in Australia and Liverpool, where it remains neutral), the word began life positively. The *Slang Dictionary* of 1859 explained: "Tart, a term of approval applied by the London lower orders to a young woman for whom some affection is felt. The expression is not generally employed by the young men, unless the female is in 'her best,' with a colored gown, red or blue shawl, and plenty of ribbons in her bonnet—in fact, made pretty all over, like the jam tarts in the swell bakers' shops." (Beware, however, of compound tarts: rhyming slang is pervasive, and the "raspberry," "strawberry," "cherry," and "treacle" varieties all mean breaking wind.)

Moving on to the physically attractive, one definitely finds more of the same. A pretty girl can be "jam," "crumb," "cupcake," "raspberry," and "peach" (and the intensified "peacherino"). "Cheesecake," a pin-up, appeared around 1930 (its male counterpart, "beefcake," is slightly younger).

Other expressions of affection or approval include "dishy," "tasty," "fruity," "scrumptious," "flavor," "slice," and "yummy." Endearments have included a "banana," a "basket of oranges" (a reference apparently to glittering nuggets of gold as well as fruit), one who is the "jammiest of the jam" or the "real raspberry jam," a "bun," "butter," a "cutesie-pie," a "dixie cup," a "creamie," a "pancake," a "pastry," and even a "penn'orth o' treacle."

Sometimes sweet turns sickly and endearment turns to abuse. Such terms include "pieface," "muffin," "fruitcake," "jellybean," "jellyhead," and "social doughnut hole"—in other words, a human "nothing."

Parts of the Body

The vocabulary of food has been enthusiastically colonized for parts of the human body. But sweetness—perhaps inevitably, given its adoption by the world of affection—tends to one area: the sexual. While there are exceptions—"biscuit" (the head), "cakehole" (the mouth), "jelly snatchers" (the hands), and the rhyming "tarts" (gooseberry, jam, raspberry, or strawberry) for heart—the primary links remain lubricious. If the beloved is "good enough to eat," then slang's appetite also encompasses her or his constituent parts.

The female breasts include the sixteenth-century "apples," eighteenth-century "dumplings," and such modernisms as "cupcakes," "chestnuts," "grapes," "jujubes," "mangoes," "pippins," "melons," and "grapefruit." The penis, traditionally seen as a weapon, can also be sweet—the "banana," "candy cane," "cinnamon stick," "gobstopper," "lollipop," "tit-bit," and "yum-yum." Terms for the vagina include "bit of jam," "brownie," "cherry pie," "date," "orange," "doughnut," "fig," "jelly roll," "muffin," and "pancake." See SEXUAL INNUENDO.

Slang's sweet shop is capacious, and its cookie jar is deep. We can but nibble. "Cake" is both "sweet" and "soft," both literally and metaphorically. The latter image has recruited it to mean a fool, a weakling, a fop, or a dandy; and a simple task is a "piece of cake." The former attribute gives us an attractive woman, a prostitute, and the female genitals. Then there is shape: cakes are stereotypically round. This gives us the buttocks and breasts; it can also refer to a disk of crack cocaine. The "cake-eater" (elsewhere "cookie-pusher") was an effete young man who attended smart tea parties and charmed old ladies; the inference was "gay," though it might also have been "rich."

Above all the cake is "taken": "take the cake" means to surpass, to outdo (context determines a positive or negative inference). Nor is this exemplary cake alone: an individual or a circumstance may take the "bakehouse," the "baker's shop" or "bakery," the "beer," the "candied peel," the "duff," the "flour," the "gingerbread," the "pastry," the "peach," or the "scone." Assonantly, the cake, "crumb," or "currant" may also be "captured" or "copped."

Similarly, one may "take the biscuit," even the "pickled biscuit," but while U.K. biscuits are seen as sweet, American ones are not. For Americans, the word is "cookie," and cookies, far from being taken, are in various synonyms—"chuck," "flip," "heave," "shoot," "throw," "toss," "woof"—lost (in other words, cookies are "vomit"). Cookies are more productive than cake and can mean a person ("sharp cookie," or "smart cookie"); like other objects of sweetness, they offer images of desirability and "softness." Then there is "Oreo," that cookie which, being black on the outside and white within, has been adopted as a pejorative in the fraught world of race. See OREOS.

So many sweets. No room for "licorice stick" (the clarinet), "taffy" (nonsense), or "treacle" (flattery), or for the sugared delights of "kugels," "jellybeans," "flummery," and "twinkies." It's enough to "give you diabetes," or at least a "toothache," but for slang even these are not a problem: both phrases just mean "you're sweet."

See also GENDER; PHARMACOLOGY; SPORTS NICKNAMES; TWINKIE; and SYMBOLIC MEANINGS.

Green, Jonathon. *Green's Dictionary of Slang*. London: Chambers, 2010.

Jonathon Green

slavery refers to the brutal system of production in which people are forced to labor for overseers who reap large profits from their work.

As the European craving for sugar exploded in the mid-seventeenth century, planters devised ways to provide huge quantities at affordable prices. Labor was an essential element in the production process, and because sugarcane is a demanding and labor-intensive crop, the acquisition of slaves seemed an obvious solution. See SUGARCANE.

From 1630 to 1660, England, France, Holland, and Denmark established large-scale sugarcane operations in the New World, following the example of Portugal and Spain. Labor remained the most urgent issue. The indigenous peoples who had been forced into slavery were dying out, killed by overwork, malnutrition, brutality, despair, and European diseases. European indentured workers and prisoners fared little better. Frustrated sugar planters turned to Africa, kick-starting an international slave trade that transported millions of Africans into slavery, of whom 6 million were eventually sold as sugar slaves.

This drawing from William Clark's pictorial work *Ten Views in the Island of Antigua* (London, 1823) depicts slaves digging holes and planting sugarcane. © THE BRITISH LIBRARY BOARD

On the Middle Passage, the route between Africa and the New World, Africans were crammed into filthy, unventilated holds and given inadequate food and water. The men were shackled; the women and children, in separate quarters, were not. Traumatized and grief-stricken, the Africans mounted revolts that began off the West African coast and persisted throughout the Middle Passage, which lasted from five weeks to three months. An estimated 15 percent died from disease, suicide, and brutality.

On their arrival in the New World, the slaves were sold, renamed, branded, issued identical cheap garments, and shackled. Then came a sad march to their new master's sugar plantation, where resident Creole slaves were instructed to orient them, a process known as "seasoning." Two out of seven Africans died of disease and despair at this stage, and suicide was common.

Sugar Plantations

The plantations, which ranged from hundreds to thousands of acres, featured cane fields known as "cane pieces," pastureland and woodland for fuel, and self-contained villages. These villages included the infrastructure of sugar production: a mill, boiling and curing houses, often a rum distillery, and sheds and barns for the bagasse, or cane leavings, and for supplies, equipment, and livestock. There were homes for the overseer, chemist, and other white employees. The planter's "great house" loomed over the slave quarters, built either as barracks or as rows of thatched-roof shacks. Many plantations contained gardens or "provision grounds" for their slaves to grow their own food, instead of providing food for them. See PLANTATIONS, SUGAR.

Plantations operated like factories, with vast assembly lines of work gangs performing specialized tasks with rigid scheduling. Each gang—Great Gang, Second Gang, and sometimes a Third Gang—was selected for strength, ability, and blackness, and each had a slave driver. Except in the early days of the slave trade, when more African males were imported, females predominated in the fields. The elderly, the disabled, adolescents, and all slave children from four or five years of age on were pressed into the Hogmeat Gang, which scavenged food for the animals, weeded gardens, and did odd chores, under its usually female slave driver. Male slaves also worked as boilermen, coopers, mechanics, wheelwrights, carpenters, blacksmiths, masons, carters, loaders, mule handlers, stock keepers, cooks, grass cutters, rat catchers, fishermen, and watchmen.

To control their hostile labor force, planters hired white overseers, usually bachelors, who used whips and corporal punishment. Slave drivers also stalked the fields, flogging recalcitrant, slow, ailing, or weak slaves. They were "official tyrants" whom planters and overseers consulted and indulged as long as they were ruthless. What deeply complicated the slaves' personal relationships was that these drivers were fellow slaves, mostly powerful males whose privileged positions depended on their continued willingness to monitor and punish the field slaves, even their own wives, sisters, daughters, and mothers. The exception was the Hogmeat Gang driver, who was usually a slave woman.

Sugarcane Crop

In July or August, slave gangs prepared the cane pieces for planting by slashing and burning grass, shrubs, and old cane. The work was dangerous, as slaves contended with swinging machetes, smoke, snakes, and armies of rats that inhabited the fields. (One plantation caught 3,000 rats in just six months.)

Next came cane holing, the backbreaking job of digging precisely measured holes and building ridges around them from scooped-out soil. Then pairs of slaves inserted three cane tops into each hole and packed it with manure, seaweed, or sludge before covering it with earth. As the planted cane grew, the slaves reinforced the ridges, weeded the thousands of rows between the cane holes, removed dry stalks, and pruned. Many plantations staggered their planting schedules so that slaves finished the dreaded job of cane holing in one field only to repeat it in another. See SUGARCANE AGRICULTURE.

When the cane matured, the gangs harvested it. Since the sugar content of cut cane decreases as it dries out, the gangs had to haul it to the mill for immediate processing. There it was crushed between giant rollers, a dangerous operation that cost many exhausted slaves their hands or arms and made amputees a common sight.

Once milled from the cane, the sap was piped along to be boiled and clarified, and slaves risked being scalded. In the final stages, the syrup was cooled and cured and readied for shipment. Some plantations distilled rum. See RUM. The cutting-milling-boiling-distilling cycle lasted for five months. To urge their slaves to persevere in their superhuman efforts, planters offered them hot cane juice or tots of rum laced with sugar.

Planters also kept oxen and mules to power the mills and assigned field slaves the additional chore of picking grass for animal fodder before they could tend their own gardens and cook their meals. Nonetheless, determined slaves, usually women, assiduously worked their provision grounds, raising crops that improved their family's nutrition and could be sold or exchanged for goods otherwise unavailable.

Female slaves, most barred from the skilled trades that males alone could aspire to in the sugar hierarchy, coped with pregnancy, childbirth, and raising children, whom most planters considered a drain on plantation coffers. Mothers were denied enough time for nursing and child care and were made to entrust their infants to slaves too old to do any other work. Except in Cuba, where planters allowed mothers time to breastfeed two or three times a day, babies were fed bread, flour, and sugar mashed into pap. Everywhere, the mortality rate of enslaved children was high.

A separate contingent of often lighter-skinned slaves, many the progeny of their master, overseer, or white visitors, served as housekeepers, cooks, laundresses, cleaners, and babysitters. They lived in the great house and had little to do with the slave quarters. Their work was less onerous than field work, but they were always on call, and women were sexual targets. Housekeepers, often their masters' mistresses, were in danger from jealous white wives who supervised and hated them and their mixed-race children.

The literal and figurative shadows of the great house darkened all slave life, even in the quarters. Slave housing reflected how whites valued some slaves over others, and rewarded skilled boilers, carpenters, and others with larger and better homes. Slave family life was complex. After the abolition of the slave trade in the nineteenth century shut down the African source of new slaves, some planters forced their slaves to marry so that their offspring could create a new supply. Other unions were illicit, as slaves from different plantations sometimes defied orders and met surreptitiously. Slaves feared committing themselves to unions easily shattered if one spouse was sold away. When unions failed, the slaves separated and lived alone or tried again. Blood relations were strong, and shipmates from the Middle Passage always treated each other as kin. But slaves did not yearn for children they could not protect from abuse or save from the misery of slavery.

Racialism as Ideology

Sugar slavery's most insidious creation was the racialism that was the sugar world's organizing principle, and also its justification for enslaving Africans. This racist ideology borrowed from Christianity and pseudo-science, and referenced complex racial distinctions based on bloodlines. See RACE. Surrounded and outnumbered by the slaves they oppressed, whites needed social arrangements and power structures that would keep them safe from their victims.

Yet this carefully enunciated racism coexisted with its polarity of legal freedom. Manumission was possible, and sometimes light-skinned and beloved slaves were freed, as were those too old and decrepit to work, whose "freedom" saved the planters money but actually meant homelessness, starvation, and death for its luckless recipients.

As racial slavery evolved in the seventeenth and eighteenth centuries onward, legal texts known in the British colonies as Slave Codes and in other colonies as Black Codes, premised on slaves being troublesome property, prescribed slavery's operation. Varying little from colony to colony, they acknowledged interracial hatred, anticipated revolt, and prescribed brutal and mutilating punishments, including cutting off genitals and slow incineration.

Black Codes criminalized almost every slave misdeed, defined running away as the theft of the slave owner's property, and dealt harshly with marronage (joining fugitive slave settlements). Despite the horrendous punishments prescribed, sugar slaves engaged in chronic resistance, including sabotage, suicide, marronage, and armed uprisings. They malingered, broke their hoes, burned cane fields, mutilated livestock, stopped work, sang satirical songs, and stole whatever they could, with sugarcane heading the list. They plotted uprisings that, in Haiti, burst into full revolution, overthrew slavery, and created the world's first black republic.

After the phony freedom of apprenticeship—a transitional and mostly unsuccessful arrangement devised to help planters in the British colonies develop a wage-labor system—ended abruptly in 1838, slavery was abolished in the British West Indies, and over the next 50 years it was abolished in the rest of the sugarcane world, including Cuba and Brazil. Slavery ended, but its impact on slave descendants lingers to this day.

See also SUGAR BARONS and SUGAR REFINING.

Follett, Richard J. *The Sugar Masters: Planters and Slaves in Louisiana's Cane World, 1820–1860.* Baton Rouge: Louisiana State University Press, 2005.

Forster, Elborg, and Robert Forster, eds. *Sugar and Slavery, Family and Race: The Letters and Diary of Pierre Dessalles, Planter in Martinique, 1808–1856.* Baltimore: Johns Hopkins University Press, 1996.

Goveia, Elsa V. *Slave Society in the British Leeward Islands at the End of the Eighteenth Century*. New Haven, Conn.: Yale University Press, 1965.

Hall, Douglas. *In Miserable Slavery: Thomas Thistlewood in Jamaica, 1750–86.* Kingston, Jamaica: University of the West Indies Press, 1999.

Moitt, Bernard. *Women and Slavery in the French Antilles, 1635–1848.* Bloomington: Indiana University Press, 2001.

Tomlich, Dale W. *Slavery in the Circuit of Sugar: Martinique and the World Economy, 1830–1848.* Baltimore: Johns Hopkins University Press, 1990.

Elizabeth Abbott

slump

See FRUIT DESSERTS, BAKED.

small cakes are baked in individual small molds meant for single servings. We can be certain that small cakes came early to America, for Pilgrim father Edward Winslow brought a set of 12 banqueting trenchers to Plymouth Colony. The kind of banquet for which these trenchers were purposed was actually a little meal of sweets, which included the small Italian biscuits often called "prince bisket." In modern terms, these were firm sponge cakes baked in home-sewn individual paper cases or round or rectangular metal or ceramic molds. Toward the end of the seventeenth century, prince bisket was joined on banqueting tables by new small cakes called Portugal cakes, which were an English invention. Portugal cakes were composed of roughly equal weights of flour, butter, sugar, and eggs, plus (in most recipes) a handful of the small raisins called currants, all of which were beaten together with the hand until the batter was aerated so that the cakes would rise light in the oven. Portugal cakes were baked in small tartlet molds called pattypans, about 24 of which were needed for one batch of cakes in 1-pound proportions.

The banquet faded around 1700, but American women continued to bake both of its small cakes long thereafter. Sponge biskets, often called Naples biscuits in America after 1800, remained favorite accompaniments to ice creams until around 1850, when they were subsumed by the modern French ladyfingers. Portugal cakes, increasingly known as queen cakes after 1770 and often baked in heart-shaped pans, were still considered fashionable for tea parties into Fannie Farmer's day. See FARMER, FANNIE.

Over the course of the eighteenth century, Portugal cakes gave rise to a large family of "rich cakes" that were likewise composed of equal weights flour, butter, sugar, and eggs and leavened by air beaten into the batter. One of these cakes, pound cake, became extraordinarily popular in America, as did two other rich cakes that American women invented out of pound cake during the 1830s: the almond-flavored, brilliant white lady cake, and the citrusy, deep-yellow golden cake. See CAKE and POUND CAKE. Although typically made up as large cakes, these cakes were also sometimes baked individually—"in small tins, such as are used for queen-cake, or Naples biscuit," wrote antebellum cookbook author Eliza Leslie. The decision to bake these cakes individually was sometimes tied to presentation: small cakes looked pretty when jumbled in a cake basket or stacked in a high pyramid on a party table. But women sometimes chose to bake rich cakes individually out of practicality. Said Leslie, "It may be recommended to novices in the art of baking, to do every thing in little tins or in very shallow pans; there being then less risk than with a large thick cake." In the 1830s, when women baked cakes in a Dutch oven or brick oven, whose heat was uncertain, and when, more crucially, fine rich cakes were never chemically leavened, and were therefore dense and resistant to baking through, small rich cakes were far less apt to emerge from the oven disappointingly clammy and streaked than large, thick ones.

This simple fact of cake chemistry brings us to the small cake that became the mother of all modern American butter cakes, as well as eventually giving rise to today's most familiar American small cake. In the 1820s, seeking a cake that was cheaper than pound cake yet nice enough to serve to company, American women invented so-called cup cake. See CUPCAKES. This cake was made with only about half as much expensive butter and egg in ratio to flour as true pound cake, and yet it rose palatably light without soda (the use of which would have made it decidedly *not* "nice"), precisely because it was baked in teacups. By the late 1830s some women had already modified this cake by adding milk and soda, making a plainer cake, but a larger, lighter, more convenient one that could be baked in a single pan. Thus, yellow cake, the first modern American butter cake, was born. The cupcake, as we now understand it, would have to wait another half century for its debut.

Small Cakes in the Gilded Age

Toward the end of the nineteenth century, French cooking became fashionable among the American middle classes. Besides bringing many new dishes into the American repertory, the French cooking vogue ushered in new meal styles, as well as new styles of serving and presenting foods. Among the new serving notions was the doily-covered silver or china platter holding a tempting assortment of individual pastries, cookies, and small cakes. Such platters were set out for the final dessert course at dinners à la russe, at ladies' luncheons and teas, and at parties. It was primarily to fill such platters that, between roughly 1885 and 1915, American women created a new generation of small cakes.

These cakes can be divided into two groups. One group comprised individual cakes of familiar American types: modern butter cakes, pound-type cakes, and modified molasses gingerbreads. See GINGERBREAD. Fannie Farmer outlined five such cakes in the original 1896 edition of *The Boston Cooking-School Cook Book*, including a plain modern butter cake (or "yellow cake") called Cup Cake and a molasses-pecan cake called Brownies. In most of these recipes, including her Cup Cake, Farmer called simply for baking the small cakes in "shallow tins" or "individual tins," but in her recipe for Brownies she wrote, more specifically, "small, shallow fancy cake tins." A photograph in a 1904 issue of *The Boston Cooking-School Magazine* shows us exactly what the tins for molasses brownies—and, presumably, for the other small cakes of the day—looked like. Variously shaped as rounds, ovals, rectangles, and triangles, with fluted walls and narrow bottoms, the tins appear to be virtually the same as the individual tartlet or cake molds imported today from Europe by American cookware shops. Farmer, in effect, Frenchified the old American small-cake tradition, thereby producing suitable articles for the slot labeled "fancy cakes" inscribed in countless period dinner, tea, and party menus.

The other group of new small cakes comprised petits fours, which American women of the Gilded Age understood to be dainty cake sandwiches cut in rectangles or other shapes, filled with whipped cream or jam, dipped in fondant, and topped with a nutmeat or candied flower petal. See CANDIED FLOWERS and FONDANT. The French made such cakes with the enriched sponge cake called génoise, for which American women usually substituted either pound cake or a new butter cake/sponge cake cross invented specifically for this purpose.

Petits fours are still with us, as are various more recently arrived French small cakes, including madeleines, financiers, canelés, and the multifarious dainties presented as *mignardises* in ambitious restaurants. See MIGNARDISE. Also sometimes seen in the United States are fancy small cakes from other parts of Europe, such as the Viennese *Indianerkrapfen* and the Italian *sospiri*. But the small cake that won the day in America was, of course, the cupcake, or so it came to be spelled in the early twentieth century, when the fancy tins gave way to the convenient connected cupcake pan, and cupcakes tumbled from tea and party tables into children's lunchboxes.

See also BANQUETING HOUSES; BROWNIES; CHEMICAL LEAVENERS; DESSERT; and SPONGE CAKE.

Belden, Louise Conway. *The Festive Tradition: Table Decoration and Desserts in America, 1650–1900.* New York: Norton, 1983.

Driver, Christopher, ed. *John Evelyn, Cook: The Manuscript Receipt Book of John Evelyn.* Totnes, U.K.: Prospect, 1997.

Farmer, Fannie Merritt. *The Boston Cooking-School Cook Book.* Boston: Little, Brown, 1896. Facsimile, New York: Weathervane, 1973.

Farmer, Fannie Merritt. *The Boston Cooking-School Cook Book.* Boston: Little, Brown, 1914.

Hill, Janet M. "Seasonal Recipes." *The Boston Cooking-School Magazine* 8, no. 10 (May 1904): 505.

Leslie, Eliza. *Directions for Cookery in Its Various Branches.* 31st ed. Philadelphia: Carey & Hart, 1848. Facsimile, with introduction by Louis Szathmáry, New York: Arno, 1973.

Stephen Schmidt

s'mores first appeared as a published recipe in *Tramping and Trailing with the Girl Scouts* (1927), where they were called "Some Mores." This now iconic combination of marshmallows, Hershey's milk chocolate, and graham crackers was suggested as a campfire dessert: marshmallows are roasted on a stick over an open campfire, then sandwiched between two graham crackers along with squares of milk chocolate to make a sweet, gooey treat. It is unclear whether the Girl Scouts actually invented s'mores or whether they were known before the recipe was published. The combination of a smooth chocolate covering, sticky-soft inside, and crisp base was certainly familiar to American consumers: the popular Mallomar cookie had been introduced in 1913, followed by MoonPies in 1917; both consisted of chocolate-covered marshmallow on a crisp cookie layer. See MOONPIES. However, the fire-singed marshmallow of s'mores distinguished and intensified their sweetness, making them a summertime favorite, especially for children, for whom they remain lovingly associated with camp and campfire songs.

The ingredients for s'mores are much older than the confections themselves. Modern marshmallow confections were first made in France around 1850, when candy makers used the root of the swamp mallow plant to bind egg whites, corn syrup, and water to create handmade confections. See MARSHMALLOWS. In the late nineteenth century, a recipe of corn syrup, cornstarch, sugar, and gelatin made the mass production of marshmallows in cornstarch molds possible, and they became popular sold in tins. In 1948 a new extrusion process and a "jet-puffed" method that infused the marshmallow with air sped up production even more. By 1955 there were over 30 commercial manufacturers of marshmallows in the United States; at present only three remain. Graham crackers, created in the 1820s by health and nutrition reformer Reverend Sylvester Graham, were popularized by the Nabisco Company at the turn of the twentieth century, and Milton Hershey introduced the first mass-produced chocolate bar in the United States in 1900. See HERSHEY'S.

Today, contemporary pastry chefs create refined and dramatic versions of the s'more by layering house-made marshmallows with Graham crackers and top-quality chocolate. "S'more" has also become a special flavor for brownies, cupcakes, and ice cream. So beloved are these treats that 10 August is celebrated as National S'Mores Day in the United States.

Tramping and Trailing with the Girl Scouts, pp. 68–69. New York: Girl Scouts of America, 1927.

Judith Hausman

soda is a generic term for carbonated beverages dispensed from fountains or sold in bottles or cans. Depending on the region, these are also known as soft drinks, soda pop, fizzy drinks, or tonic, or called by brand names such as those of the three leaders: Coke, Pepsi, or Dr Pepper. All sodas are carbonated, sweetened, and flavored, features that distinguish them from noncarbonated energy and sports drinks, juice drinks, and flavored waters.

Carbonated water and sweeteners are the most important ingredients. Sodas are sweetened with sugars (regular soda) or artificial chemicals (diet soda). The other ingredients—sodium, caffeine, organic acids, coloring agents, and flavor additives—are present in amounts too small to have much effect on nutrition or health. A typical 12-ounce cola, for example, contains only 30 milligrams of sodium and 35 milligrams of caffeine, low in comparison to other sources. The flavor additives are deeply guarded trade secrets, but include fruit and herbal extracts. The acids and flavors help to counteract the otherwise overwhelming sweetness of these drinks.

Regular Sodas

A 12-ounce regular soda typically contains 40 grams of sugars—the equivalent of *ten* teaspoons. Sodas are, in effect, systems for rapid delivery of large amounts of sugars into the blood stream. The sugars are glucose and fructose, derived from high-fructose corn syrup (HFCS) or, occasionally, cane and beet sugar (sucrose). See CORN SYRUP; FRUCTOSE; and GLUCOSE. Until 1984, American sodas were largely sweetened with cane or beet sugar. But these are more expensive than HFCS because of quotas, tariffs, and corn subsidies. When taste tests proved that consumers could not tell the difference between sodas made with sucrose or HFCS, companies switched to the cheaper alternative. In some cane-growing countries, such as Mexico, sodas are still sweetened with sucrose but increasingly diluted with the less-expensive HFCS. Because some European countries grow sugar beets, and former colony trading partners grow sugarcane, the European Union continues to favor sucrose.

Sugars account for all of the 150 calories in a 12-ounce drink. As the size of drinks increases, the sugars increase, and so do the calories. A vending machine's 20-ounce bottle provides about 250 calories from its 16 teaspoons of sugars. A movie theater's 64-ounce "Double-Gulp" could, in theory, contain as much as 54 teaspoons of sugars and 800 calories, but it is typically poured over ice. The more ice, the less sugar and, therefore, calories.

Less sugar is desirable because the sugars are almost entirely responsible for the health effects of sodas. Sugary drinks contribute to poor diets, weight gain, and obesity-related conditions such as type 2 diabetes, heart disease, and stroke. Sugars provide no nutrients; their calories are "empty." Worse, the sugars come in liquid form and constitute "liquid candy." Preliminary research in animals suggests that consuming sugars as liquids rather than in solid foods bypasses regulatory systems that control appetite and food intake. Studies of human eating behavior support this idea: sodas encourage people to consume more calories from other foods. Sugar alone does not have this effect; people eating jelly beans compensate for candy calories. Neither do liquids necessarily; soups help people lose weight. These observations explain current dietary advice to "drink few or no regular sodas" as a means to reduce intake of sugar and its nutritionally empty calories. See SUGAR AND HEALTH.

Sodas would not be a health concern if people did not drink so many of them. But in America, sodas together with energy and sports drinks are the fourth leading contributor to adult calorie intake, and the third for children. These drinks account for 36 percent of added sugars in American diets, and sodas alone provide twice as much sugar as is recommended for daily diets. Dietary surveys find half the population to maintain that they consume no sodas at all, meaning that the other half must drink much more. Five percent of the population admits to drinking at least 48 ounces a day. Men drink nearly twice as much soda as women, especially when they are single. The highest intakes are reported by boys ages 12 to 19, and people who are from the South, black, Hispanic, or of low income. Even children ages 2 to 5 drink an average of 6 ounces a day. Soda use declines with education, income, and age, which makes it an indicator of low social status and low income—characteristics most associated with high rates of obesity and related health conditions. The one hopeful sign is that soda consumption in the United States has been declining since the late 1990s, as health-conscious Americans increasingly turn to less sugary sports drinks, teas, diet drinks, and bottled water.

The industry reports that American companies produced 30 gallons of regular carbonated sodas per capita in 2012, down from 41 gallons in 1998. Because inventory is tightly controlled, the industry says that virtually all the soda it produces is purchased. If we assume that all purchased soda is consumed, these figures translate to a per capita intake of 320 12-ounce servings per year, down from 437 per capita in 1998. The difference between slightly less and slightly more than one serving a day may not appear serious, but the industry views the decline as a crisis.

To expand sales, soda companies have moved their marketing overseas. On a worldwide basis, the industry produced 194 billion liters of regular sodas in 2012. For the 7 billion people in the world, this works out to 78 12-ounce servings per capita per year. The range of consumption is large, from less than ten a year in some countries in Asia and Africa, to more than one a day in Mexico and Argentina. Soda companies view high-population countries such as China, India, and Indonesia as prime markets for expansion. Public health experts predict that an increase in obesity prevalence is sure to follow.

Diet Sodas

Diet sodas contain no or little sugar and provide no calories. Instead, they are artificially sweetened with aspartame, acesulfame K, sucralose, Stevia, or other nonnutritive chemicals. See ARTIFICIAL SWEETENERS and STEVIA. Even though there is little evidence to support the idea that diet drinks help with weight loss or maintenance, they account for 30 percent of soda sales in America. Their most frequent drinkers are older, white, married, and well-educated females. Sales of diet drinks are also declining in America as a result of concerns about their slightly bitter aftertaste and unnatural sweeteners. On a worldwide basis, diet drinks comprise 12 percent of soda sales, but the percentages vary widely, from 3 percent or below in Asian countries to as much as 35 percent in Australia.

Are Sodas Addictive?

Soft drinks include caffeine as well as sugars. Addiction researchers note that even small amounts of caffeine make people feel more alert, energetic, and cheerful and can induce symptoms of dependence in susceptible individuals. In laboratory animals and in some people, caffeine and sugars independently encourage habitual daily use and induce symptoms of dependence and withdrawal. It remains an open question whether sugars and caffeine, alone or together, are addictive in the usual sense—inducing cravings, an inability to stop the craving, and intense discomfort when the craved substance is unavailable. Addictive or not, health advice to consume sodas only in moderation makes good sense. See ADDICTION.

See also SODA FOUNTAIN.

Basu, Sanjay, Martin McKee, Gauden Galea, and David Stuckler. "Relationship of Soft Drink Consumption to Global Overweight, Obesity, and Diabetes: A Cross-National Analysis of 75 Countries." *American Journal of Public Health* 103, no. 11 (2013): 2071–2077.

Beverage Marketing Corp. *Carbonated Soft Drinks in the U.S.* New York: Beverage Marketing Corp., 2013.

Credit Suisse Research Institute. *Sugar at a Crossroads.* Zurich, Switzerland: Credit Suisse AG, September 2013. https://publications.credit-suisse.com/tasks/render/file/index.cfm?fileid=780BF4A8-B3D1-13A0-D2514E21EFFB0479 (accessed 9 October 2014).

Jacobson, Michael F. *Liquid Candy: How Soft Drinks Are Harming Americans' Health.* Washington, D.C.: Center for Science in the Public Interest, 2005. http://www.cspinet.org/new/pdf/liquid_candy_final_w_new_supplement.pdf (accessed 9 October 2014).

U.S. Department of Agriculture, and U.S. Department of Health and Human Services. *Dietary Guidelines for Americans, 2010.* Washington, D.C.: U.S. Department of Agriculture, 2010. http://www.cnpp.usda.gov/DietaryGuidelines-2010 (accessed 9 October 2014).

Marion Nestle

The **soda fountain**, which began as a simple utilitarian device to dispense carbonated soda water, evolved into an inviting public space where consumers enjoyed beverages, ice cream, and light meals. Completing a circle, in the fast-food era the soda fountain returned to its roots as an uninteresting machine that dispenses fizzy liquids.

Primitive societies ascribed magical powers to the effervescent waters bubbling up from underground sources. Many people believed these special waters could cure diseases. Scientists studied the effervescent waters, hoping to replicate them and make their curative powers available to everyone. Around 1766 Henry Cavendish, an Englishman, designed an apparatus for making aerated water. In Sweden, chemist Torbern Bergman produced effervescent waters in his lab and promulgated his method in the 1770s. The noted British scientist Joseph Priestly conducted simple experiments to infuse water with gas expelled from fermentation vats in a brewery. He built a device to impregnate distilled water with carbon dioxide, and John Mervin Nooth improved on his design. In the early 1800s, British entrepreneurs sold bottled water infused with carbon dioxide, which was commonly called soda or carbonated water.

Benjamin Silliman, a chemistry professor at Yale, took the lead in popularizing soda water in the United States. After buying an apparatus from Nooth in 1806, he carbonated and bottled water in New Haven, Connecticut. Silliman found a ready market for his soda water, but a shortage of bottles limited his output. To sidestep this problem, he set up a pump room where the customers drank from glasses. To expand his business, he recruited partners and opened shops in Baltimore and New York City. Other entrepreneurs launched pump rooms in Philadelphia and New York.

Pump rooms and drugstores produced their own soda water. Typically, the carbonating apparatus was located in the cellar, and the soda water was pumped upstairs via a metal tube, which protruded through a countertop. To fill a glass, the server turned a stopcock at the top of the tube. For decorative purposes, the tube was often hidden inside an attractive urn or column.

In the mid-nineteen century, physicians generally agreed that carbonated water had no significant merit as a medication. Yet soda water sales were strong: consumers liked the bubbly, refreshing drink even if it didn't cure their ills. In 1832 John Matthews

Students at Cranbrook, an elite boarding school in Bloomfield Hills, Michigan, enjoy a soda fountain right on campus in 1955. Soda fountains were most popular in the United States in the 1940s and 1950s. HISTORIC PHOTOGRAPH COLLECTION, CRANBROOK ARCHIVES

began manufacturing soda fountains in New York City, and John Lippincott opened a similar business in Philadelphia. The two men were innovators who greatly improved the equipment for making and dispensing carbonated water.

Matthews, Lippincott, and other manufacturers built equipment that dispensed both unflavored soda water and carbonated water flavored with syrups, such as chocolate or strawberry. They encased the equipment in marble boxes with multiple spigots to dispense the different syrups. To catch the consumer's eye, they added fanciful, showy decorations to the boxes. Towers or onion-shaped domes sat atop some box fountains; others had intricate metallic scrollwork and shiny metal ornaments. In general, box soda fountains were placed against a wall, and the server worked with his back to his customers. During the early 1900s the counter-service fountain replaced the marble boxes. In the new arrangement, the drafts and syrup pumps were attached to one side of the counter, and the customers sat on stools on the other side.

Before mechanical refrigeration, soda fountains relied on large blocks of ice to keep beverages and ice cream cold. In the early 1900s, technological advances led to "iceless" fountains, which used brine as the coolant, and to "50 percent fountains," which combined ice and mechanical refrigeration. In the 1920s, many stores installed soda fountains with ammonia refrigeration. The Liquid Carbonic Company, Bishop and Babcock, the Bastian-Blessing Company, and L. A. Becker led the charge to modernize the industry. See REFRIGERATION.

The soda fountain flourished in drugstores, department stores, ice cream parlors, and train stations. It seemed to be a permanent part of the American landscape. But an array of trends caused the fountain's gradual decline. Americans fell in love with automobiles and ate in their cars at drive-in restaurants. Drugstores cut costs by switching to self-service and eliminating the labor-intensive soda fountain. Supermarkets sold a dazzling variety of ice cream products at affordable prices. Vending machines sold ice-cold soft drinks in cans and bottles.

To avoid extinction, the soda fountain morphed into an insipid, boxy fixture that dispenses carbonated drinks in fast-food outlets and convenience stores. Perhaps more transformations await the soda fountain in the future.

See also ICE CREAM and SODA.

Brown, Chandros Michael. *Benjamin Silliman: A Life in the Young Republic*. Princeton, N.J.: Princeton University Press, 1989.

Chester, Thomas. *Carbonated Beverages: The Art of Making, Dispensing, and Bottling Soda-Water, Mineral-Waters, Ginger-Ale, and Sparkling-Liquors.* New York: P. H. Reilly, 1882.

Funderburg, Anne Cooper. *Sundae Best: A History of Soda Fountains*. Bowling Green, Ohio: Bowling Green State University Popular Press, 2002.

Anne Cooper Funderburg

sonker

See FRUIT DESSERTS, BAKED.

sorbet

See SHERBET.

sorbitol is a sugar alcohol employed as a sugar substitute. A French chemist discovered it in 1872 in berries, and the substance was later detected in a wide range of fruits. Although found in nature, sorbitol has been prepared synthetically since the 1960s from sugar, glucose syrup, or starch, with the most common sources for the starch being corn and cassava.

Sorbitol is sold in liquid and crystalline forms. It is metabolized more slowly than glucose or fructose, so it can be used by diabetics, since it does not increase blood glucose levels when consumed. Sorbitol also contains fewer calories than table sugar (sucrose), and it is used in many diet foods as a bulk sweetener. In the food industry it is mainly used in fruit preserves, cake mixes, ice cream, cookies, chocolates, pastries, and sugar-free candy and gum. Its main nonfood applications are in toothpaste, mouthwash, cosmetics, and laxatives.

At high doses, sorbitol can cause gastrointestinal problems—diarrhea, abdominal cramps, bloating, and flatulence. Of particular concern is the amount of sorbitol in fruit juices and chewing gum consumed by children. Despite potential problems, it is on the U.S. Food and Drug Administration's Generally Recognized as Safe (GRAS) list and is approved by most other countries when used for sweetening. The Center for Science in the Public Interest, however, has argued for labeling indicating potential problems when sorbitol is consumed in high doses.

See also ARTIFICIAL SWEETENERS; GLUCOSE; FRUCTOSE; and STARCH.

Branen, A. Larry, P. Michael Davidson, and Seppo Salminen, eds. *Food Additives*. 2d ed. New York: M. Dekker, 2002.

O'Donnell, Kay, and Malcolm Kearsley, eds. *Sweeteners and Sugar Alternatives in Food Technology*. 2d ed. Chichester, U.K.: Wiley-Blackwell, 2012.

Andrew F. Smith

sorghum syrup is a natural sweetener made from the juice of sorghum cane, a tropical grass brought to the United States from Africa and Asia in the mid-1800s. Sorghum cane resembles corn without the ears. The plant can grow to a height of 12 to 14 feet; when the cane is almost mature, it produces a seed head on top. These heads are cut off and usually saved for seed for the following season, while the leaves are stripped with a machete or small handsaw. The stalks are cut off and the juice squeezed from them by means of revolving rollers. Traditionally, a horse or mule turned the cane mill, but today tractors pull modern machinery that cuts the cane off at the ground, while large rollers squeeze the juice right in the field. The juice is then pumped into a tank that is pulled behind the machine. The juice is next transported to a mill, where it is preheated overnight before being boiled down the next day. While the juice boils, the chlorophyll (impurities) is skimmed off to achieve a thick, amber syrup in a ratio of 10 to 1—ten gallons of sorghum juice are needed to produce one gallon of sorghum syrup.

Sorghum syrup has long been mistaken for molasses. See MOLASSES. In truth, sorghum syrup is made from sorghum cane, and molasses is a byproduct of sugarcane and sugar beet refining. See SUGAR BEET; SUGARCANE; and SUGAR REFINING. There are several differences between sorghum cane and sugarcane. Sorghum cane is an annual grass, whereas sugarcane is a perennial. Sorghum cane produces a sweet syrup, but sugarcane produces sugar and the thick, dark syrup byproduct called molasses. A further difference is that sorghum cane can tolerate a colder climate than sugarcane. Sorghum also has a shorter growing season, around three to four months, while sugarcane takes from ten months and up to two years until it is ready to harvest.

Sorghum syrup has a mild caramel taste that many describe as earthy and fruity. It is rich in antioxidants and is high in protein, potassium, iron, calcium, and other nutrients. The syrup is delicious on a hot buttered biscuit or even a piece of toast. It makes an excellent addition to baked beans, barbecue sauce, gingerbread, sorghum cookies, apple stack cake, pecan pie, and many other cakes, pies, and cookies. See APPALACHIAN STACK CAKE. Sorghum syrup is also good for glazing ham, marinating steaks, and as an addition to green beans or sweet and sour sauce.

Sorghum syrup gained popularity in the early 1860s during the Civil War, when the North found a way to make syrup out of sorghum cane, which grew well in their colder climate. The North also didn't like the idea of slave labor being used in the production of sugar; if they could make their own substitute sweetener, so much the better, and they were eager to grow an acre or two of sorghum cane to boil down into syrup. By the 1870s, when the North could once again obtain sugar from the South, sorghum syrup production in the North slowed down. And because sorghum cane will not boil down into solid sugar, it lost even more popularity.

During the Great Depression, beginning in 1929, family farms grew sorghum cane and made sorghum syrup for their own use. Sugar was rationed and expensive and considered a luxury, so farmers grew an acre of sorghum cane, squeezed the juice out of the stalks, and boiled it down to a rich syrup. Many older people still remember syrup making at their homes and the candy or other desserts their mothers created out of the sorghum. They also remember the taste of sorghum syrup mixed with butter and eaten on a cathead biscuit—a misshapen and rough biscuit the size of a cat's head.

At the end of World War II many families in the United States migrated to cities, and sorghum syrup production declined. By the 1970s it had reached an all-time low. Today, sorghum syrup is still not made on a commercial basis, but production has increased slightly. More and more chefs are using sorghum in their cooking—it is not just for eating on biscuits anymore. The majority of sorghum syrup produced today is in North Carolina, Kentucky, and Tennessee, some other southern states, and some northeastern states.

The National Sweet Sorghum Producers and Processors Association (NSSPPA) was formed in 1985. The Association's main goal is to promote sweet sorghum syrup. Since the U.S. Department of Agriculture does not even recognize sorghum syrup production in their crop reporting statistics, many of the 332 members of the NSSPPA are hobbyists, who make only a few gallons of sorghum for family and friends and are trying to keep a bygone culture alive. A few members of the association produce a large amount of sorghum and make it available to stores and through Internet sales.

See also MAPLE SYRUP and SUGAR RATIONING.

Lee, Matt, and Ted Lee. *The Lee Bros. Southern Cookbook*. New York: Norton, 2006.

Sohn, Mark F. "Sorghum." In *The New Encyclopedia of Southern Culture*, Vol. 7: *Foodways*, edited by John T. Edge, pp. 537–538. Chapel Hill: University of North Carolina Press, 2007.

Mark and Sherry Guenther

soufflé has been part of the French dessert repertoire since at least the time of Vincent La Chapelle's *Cuisinier moderne* (1733–1735). A soufflé is made of stiffly beaten egg whites that are gently folded into a sauce base and baked. The heat of the oven expands the air bubbles trapped in the beaten egg whites, causing the mixture to puff up above the sides of the baking dish. The name derives from the French word *souffle*, meaning breath. This delicate confection must be served as soon as it comes out of the oven, as it will collapse when it begins to cool. The necessary precision in timing is why restaurants ask that a dessert soufflé be ordered at the beginning of the meal. Dessert soufflés can have either a cream or a fruit purée base, for which there are many possible formulas, with the choice of flavorings being almost endless. Chocolate and lemon are two of the most common flavors. The top is dusted with confectioner's sugar as the soufflé comes out of the oven, and the dessert is often served with a sauce, such as crème anglaise. Any kind of macerated or cooked fruit (e.g., peaches, raspberries, apricots, oranges) works well, as do various nuts (almonds, hazelnuts, or a mixture of roasted chopped nuts). Other typical flavorings include liqueur, vanilla, crushed pralines, and macarons. See MACARONS.

Soufflés are baked in individual ramekins or in a single large mold. The traditional soufflé mold, either small or large, is made of porcelain, with straight sides above which the mixture rises as it cooks. The design on the outside of the mold is fluted in imitation of the folded paper container (*caisse* or *papillote*) used for soufflés, as shown in Favre's *Dictionnaire universel de cuisine pratique* (1905). In classical French cuisine, a cylindrical metal charlotte mold, which has higher sides, is also used.

See also CUSTARD.

McGee, Harold. *On Food and Cooking: The Science and Lore of the Kitchen*. New York: Scribner, 2004.

Wheaton, Barbara Ketcham. *Savoring the Past: The French Kitchen and Table from 1300 to 1789*. Philadelphia: University of Pennsylvania Press, 1983.

Kyri W. Claflin

sound is rarely considered when food is discussed, yet using all available cues from our five senses to decide what to eat is essential to our survival. From sight—the appearance of the food, or even its packaging—we gain a lot of information. Thus it is not surprising that we tend to associate the color red with sweetness and yellow with sourness, as a ripe fruit is more likely to be red. Sweets manufacturers have long been aware of this color association, and consequently they produce sweets in all kinds of colors and shapes. Sometimes the change of color indicates a change in flavor, but sometimes it does not. As for smell, after examining a given food, we will usually smell it before putting it into our mouth, especially if we have doubts about its freshness. See OLFACTION. Once we are chewing a given food, our sense of touch, which is very developed in the mouth, will further inform us about some of its characteristics. Finally, the sounds heard when biting into a given food can tell us a lot about its texture and can influence our perception of its freshness. For example, it has been shown that modifying the sound heard when biting into chips will change their perceived crispiness and freshness.

There are, however, associations between the senses that are more difficult to explain. Does it make sense to ask what the taste of sweetness sounds like? Participants in an experiment at the Crossmodal Research Laboratory at Oxford University were asked to match tastes and flavors with musical notes. Most of them chose high-pitched notes for sweetness and sourness, while low-pitched notes were preferred for bitterness. This association extends to smell, with fruity odors being matched more often to high-pitched notes. Moreover, the timbre could also be matched with the tastes: piano for sweetness, brass instruments for bitterness or sourness. The tastes do not even have to be completely different. Similar foods can be associated with distinctive sounds: chips of different flavors or different types of chocolate lead to a different choice of sounds. For example, milk chocolate is associated with higher-pitched notes than dark chocolate is.

One factor underlying these associations seems to be the pleasantness of the tastes. In the experiment using dark chocolate, the lovers of the stuff tended to pick the piano, while those who hated it preferred to match it with notes played by brass instruments that were also less pleasant to hear. However, both lovers and haters seemed to agree that dark chocolate should be matched to a low-pitched note, suggesting that the role of pleasantness is not sufficient to explain the associations between tastes and pitch. The reason behind these associations is thus still a bit of a mystery. One suggestion is a link with the faces made when tasting, as these are innate. Newborns, for example, will lick their lips and suck when given a sweet solution, while a bitter taste will lead to mouth gaping and frowning. The sounds that can be produced while making such faces vary in pitch, so that different tastes could end up being associated in the mind with different pitches. These associations could also be part of a complex network of associations or correspondences among the senses. For example, sourness is associated with lemons, lemons are yellow, and brighter colors are associated with higher pitches. Thus, sourness would be associated with a high pitch.

Pitch and timbre are not the only musical elements that can be matched to tastes. In an experiment conducted in Argentina, musicians were asked to improvise based on taste words. Their compositions on the same taste had some similitudes not only in pitch but also in articulation, loudness, or length of the notes: "sweet" pieces tended to be consonant and use long notes, played legato, for example. Moreover, naïve listeners were able to guess with rather good accuracy whether the pieces were inspired by the word "bitter," "salty," "sour," or "sweet."

Wherever they come from, these associations can affect our perception of food. When listening to a "sweet" soundtrack, participants in a laboratory experiment rated cinder toffee to be sweeter than they did when listening to a "bitter" soundtrack. The type of music also affected their pleasantness ratings. The same has been demonstrated for wine: "zingy and refreshing" or "powerful and heavy" music listened to while tasting increased the ratings of the same description for the taste of the wine. Researchers and chefs are starting to team up to create events where tasting is combined with the whole atmosphere of a room (colors, decoration, music, etc.), leading to a truly multisensory experience. One can easily try this at home: gather some favorite sweets and favorite musical recordings and try different combinations with food, and see whether your overall perception changes. As new studies are conducted, the number of elements shown to influence our perception of food keeps increasing. For example, don't hesitate to play with the weight, shape, and color of plates and cutlery, as well as the general atmosphere of the room. It is surprising what a difference all these factors can make.

See also NEUROSCIENCE and SUGARPLUMS.

Crisinel, Anne-Sylvie, Stefan Cosser, Scott King, Russ Jones, James Petrie, and Charles Spence. "A Bittersweet Symphony: Systematically Modulating the Taste of Food by Changing the Sonic Properties of the Soundtrack Playing in the Background." *Food Quality and Preference* 24, no. 1 (September 2012): 201–204.

Crisinel, Anne-Sylvie, and Charles Spence. "As Bitter as a Trombone: Synesthetic Correspondences in Nonsynesthetes between Tastes/Flavors and Musical Notes." *Attention, Perception, & Psychophysics* 72, no. 7 (2010): 1994–2002.

Crisinel, Anne-Sylvie, and Charles Spence. "The Impact of Pleasantness Ratings on Crossmodal Associations between Food Samples and Musical Notes." *Food Quality and Preference* 24, no. 1 (2012): 136–140.

Mesz, Bruno, Marcos A Trevisan, and Mariano Sigman. "The Taste of Music." *Perception* 40, no. 2 (2011): 209–219.

North, Adrian C. "The Effect of Background Music on the Taste of Wine." *British Journal of Psychology* 103, no. 3 (August 2012): 293–301.

Zampini, Massimiliano, and Charles Spence. "The Role of Auditory Cues in Modulating the Perceived Crispness and Staleness of Potato Chips." *Journal of Sensory Studies* 19, no. 5 (October 2004): 347–363.

Anne-Sylvie Crisinel

soup with a sweet taste is generally made from berries and other fruits. Traditionally, such soups were prepared mostly by poor people, who used what they harvested in their small gardens or collected in nearby woods. They even dried the ingredients in order to make soup throughout the year (as in Scandinavian rose hip soup). Sweet soups were often prepared for invalids as a light yet nutritious meal. Only the wealthy could afford to season sweet soups with sugar; otherwise the soups relied on the intrinsic sweetness of the fruits, or sometimes the addition of honey.

As an umbrella term, "sweet soup" can cover a broad spectrum of dishes ranging from liquid to solid. Liquid compote (fruit, often dried, and stewed with sugar) is served in Central Europe as either a dessert or as a side dish to accompany roasts, cordon bleu (breaded and fried meat with cheese), and, especially in Austria, various *Schmarren* (a type of eggy fried pancake). In Russia, kissel (or *kisel'*)—fruit juice thickened with potato starch—ranges from a pourable mixture to a slightly jelled one. Solid dishes include the various cold fruit porridges of Scandinavia and Germany that were originally made with grain, such as Denmark's *rødgrød* and Germany's *rote Grütze*. Nowadays these beloved dishes are made with red berries mixed with potato starch or cornstarch.

Sweet soups in Central Europe were generally made from milk, cream, beer, wine, or, later, chocolate, egg yolk, and roasted white bread. They were popular breakfast soups, very substantial and mostly eaten with a thick slice of brown bread. Milk and cream soups could also be afforded by peasants, who ate their soup with black bread and always served hot; the use of sour milk meant that some of these soups were neither very sweet nor salty. Members of aristocratic families ate their morning soups with white bread or sponge cake. Over the course of the eighteenth century, breakfast soups were gradually replaced by tea, chocolate (i.e., a beverage made from chocolate boiled in milk and sweetened with sugar), and coffee—which were luxury beverages at the time, initially introduced at princely courts and in other noble households. In the nineteenth century, as sugar became more affordable, the affluent middle classes were able to afford tea, coffee, or chocolate for breakfast. In some rural areas, however, people had sweet soups for breakfast as late as the 1930s.

In northern and eastern Europe, sweet soups became a more common dish that was eaten not only for breakfast. Fruit soups in particular were, and still are, served hot during the winter and cold in summer, such as *Sotsuppe*, a Scandinavian sweet soup made from raisins or currants, dried apricots, and prunes. In these regions, cold fruit soups appear either at the beginning of a summertime meal or as dessert. Many of the Scandinavian and Baltic sweet soups contain dried fruit or berries, collected in the summer and preserved for the winter. Water-based pear soups are characteristic of Sweden and northern Germany, as are soups made from bilberries or cranberries.

Kalte Schale, or *Kaltschale* (cold bowl), is a genuinely German dish mentioned as a common meal as early as 1836. It consists of beer, breadcrumbs, sugar, lemon peel, various domestic fruits, and small raisins. Cold bowls are also made from apricots, melons, yogurt, and *Liebesperlen* (pomegranate seeds). They are served as cold instead of hot soups in summer, and nowadays mostly as a dessert. Other cold soups include cherry soup, made from cherry juice, water, sugar, cinnamon, wine, and potato starch, and served with slices of white bread.

A specialty of the northern and eastern regions of Germany is fruit soups and sweet soups based on meat stock, to which sliced fresh fruit is added. Sometimes the cooked meat is sliced and added to the soup as a garnish. Thickened with eggs, cream, and flour, or flour fried in butter and sweetened with sugar, such soups provide a hearty main course. These special soups can also be found in Transylvania, where settlers from northern Germany and Saxony brought along their traditional dishes and defended them against Hungarian and Romanian influences. The soups, called *Kächen*, were sweetened with sugar; fruits (apples, pears, berries) were added 20 minutes before the soup was done.

Asian cuisines also have various traditional soups based on meat or fish broth with vegetables, which range from sweet, to sweet and sour, to hot, sweet, and sour. Often seasoned with sweet soy sauce, they are served at the beginning of a meal or between mealtimes. Many soups in this category are closely linked to theories of traditional Chinese medicine, and thus are considered restorative. An example is Korean *naing kuk*.

Black, Maggie. *Medieval Cookery: Recipes and History*. Swindon, U.K.: English Heritage, 2003.

Egenolff, Christian. *Von Speisen, Natürlichen und Kreuter Wein, aller verstandt*. Frankfurt am Main: Egenolff, 1531.

Hagger, Conrad. *Neues Saltzburgisches Kochbuch 1719.* Munich: Heyne, 1979.
Haslinger, Ingrid. *Dampf stieg aus dem Topf hervor: Eine Kulturgeschichte der Suppen aus aller Welt.* Vienna: Mandelbaum, 2010.

Ingrid Haslinger

sour cream today, in usual commercial packaged versions, only vaguely resembles cream that happens to have naturally gone sour. Before universal pasteurization, cream and milk spontaneously soured by the action of certain lactic acid bacteria that were ubiquitous in most of northern Europe and the British Isles. Loosely labeled "mesophilic," or adapted to temperatures between about 70° and 90°F (21° to 32°C), these organisms ferment part of the original lactose (milk sugar) to lactic acid, thickening the cream to a gel and lending it a noticeable but discreet sourness.

When cream was skimmed from milk on the farm or at home, sour cream was infinitely variable. See CREAM and MILK. The richness of the original cream, along with conditions such as ambient temperature and a shorter or longer ripening period, determined both texture and flavor. Increasing nineteenth-century urbanization meant a corresponding decrease in the number of consumers familiar with simple changes in milk or cream between milking pail and table. But around the turn of the twentieth century, immigrants who had grown up with sour milk and sour cream in Eastern Europe and the Jewish Pale of Settlement flooded into American cities. Small businesses sprang up to address this market, just as modern science was starting to impose more system and uniformity on the dairy industry. Commercial brands using pasteurized cream and laboratory cultures soon arrived.

Jewish and other cooks from Eastern Europe prized sour cream that was nearly as thick as a set custard, with a delicately flowery, buttery quality. In its own right, it was an excellent dessert topping or sauce. It was also useful in baking, where its slight acidity helped weaken gluten development and prevent toughness in cakes and pastries. In some pastry doughs it could substitute for part of the butter and milk or other liquid.

Commercial sour cream gradually moved beyond a restricted ethnic clientele, though its acceptance by other cooks proceeded quite unevenly. By the mid-1940s, *The Boston Cooking-School Cook Book,* formerly geared to cautious New England sensibilities, called for sour cream in more than half a dozen recipes ranging from gingerbread to fudge. But even in the late 1950s, requests for sour cream in many American grocery stores might have been met with bewilderment.

A dramatic expansion of the industry during the 1950s and 1960s coincided with aggressive public health advocacy of low-fat diets. Major sour-cream manufacturers already seemed to have abandoned the use of rich cream, trying instead to mimic richness by adding stabilizers or thickeners to cream standardized at less than 20 percent milk fat, or lightly setting it with a small amount of rennet. Some adopted a double-homogenization technique developed in the late 1950s, which eliminated some leakage of whey (viewed as a defect by uninformed consumers) and created a very fine, smooth body. Many tried to cater to the low-fat market by further reducing milk-fat content and throwing in still more additives or aiming for "fat-free sour cream," which is unrelated to sour cream.

Several decades ago, commercial sour cream began encountering competition from American attempts to reproduce a similar French cultured cream unhelpfully known as *crème fraiche* (fresh cream) or, a little more intelligibly, *crème fraîche épaisse* (thick fresh cream). Chiefly associated with Normandy, thick crème fraîche was formerly made from raw milk colonized by natural mesophilic bacteria. The old method has been almost wholly replaced by laboratory inoculation of pasteurized milk with chosen mesophilic strains.

Today, several commercial American brands of crème fraîche are available. They are expensive, but their advantage over the major sour cream brands is twofold. First, they usually contain more than 30 percent butterfat, just slightly less than U.S. heavy cream. (There is, however, no official standard of identity.) Crême fraîche as rich as this does not curdle on heating, so it can easily be used in either savory or dessert sauces. It also works well in short or yeast-raised pastry doughs and cake batters.

Second, crème fraîche manufacturers generally take pains in selecting the different mesophilic bacteria used to culture the cream, in order to balance a mild acidity against the aromatic flowery quality mentioned earlier. This fragrant effect had also been prized in sour cream made for the old clientele of

Eastern European shtetl refugees, but it is less noticeable in today's commercial product. This aroma chiefly depends on a compound called diacetyl, produced through the action of *Leuconostoc meserentoides* and certain subspecies of *Lactococcus lactis*.

To some extent, the American success of crème fraîche has encouraged home cooks to try ripening heavy cream at home to obtain something richer and fuller-flavored than today's rather weak-bodied commercial sour cream. Some cooks have also experimented with making yogurt from cream. See YOGURT. In both cases, success depends on creating a delicate balance of crucial organisms, not easy to duplicate without either firsthand experience or access to laboratory cultures.

Kosikowski, Frank V. and Vikram V. Mistry. *Cheese and Fermented Milk Foods*. 3d ed. 2 vols. Westport, Conn.: F. V. Kosikowski, 1997.

Mendelson, Anne. *Milk: The Surprising Story of Milk through the Ages*. New York: Alfred A. Knopf, 2008.

Selitzer, Ralph. *The Dairy Industry in America*. New York: Dairy & Ice Cream Field and Books for Industry, 1976.

Anne Mendelson

The **South (U.S.)** is said to have the finest bakers in the United States, directly attributable to the reputed Southern sweet tooth. Things are a bit more complicated than that. The desserts of the American South vary through geography, the economics of class and status, poverty, the legacy of slavery, and, in the twentieth century, electricity and the rise of air conditioning. Geographically as large as Western Europe, the South stretches down the eastern seaboard from Maryland to Florida and across to Texas. The region is usually defined by the 11 states of the Confederacy, plus the so-called border or slave holding states that did not secede: Kentucky, Maryland, Delaware, and Missouri, plus West Virginia, which seceded from Virginia after Virginia seceded from the United States. Florida, Texas, and especially Louisiana have developed their own cuisines, and their cooking is no longer classically Southern, although it certainly overlaps.

Early desserts reflected the influences of each cook's country of origin, of the foodstuffs available in the region, and of course economics and status. The early influences on Southern desserts were primarily transatlantic, with the dominant techniques and recipes derived from England and France, followed by Germany and Spain. The availability of soft-wheat flour contributed to the prevalence of cakes, pies, and biscuits, and cane sugar was more available than beet sugar, both due to importation and a small amount of cultivation in the Deep South. See SUGARCANE and SUGARCANE AGRICULTURE.

A symbiotic relationship developed between African slaves and their primarily white owners when blacks became the cooks in homes and on plantations. Primarily female slaves, they learned the techniques and recipes for cakes, pies, candies, and other confections by heart. Few were allowed to learn to read. They gradually excelled in their execution and became known and valued for their skill. When the importation of slaves ended in 1808, the expanding domestic slave trade dispersed many skilled of these slave cooks throughout the Deep South states. This movement helped create the common basis for desserts throughout the slave-owning South. See SLAVERY.

The dominant Southern ports also brought in foodstuffs that became known as "Southern." Pineapple was considered so fashionable that having one on a dinner table in places such as Charleston, South Carolina, denoted wealth and status. Coconut, brought from Cuba, became a "Southern" ingredient, even though coconut was hardly grown in the South. Other ingredients, such as benne seeds, were primarily imported from Africa and India. Benne seed wafers are still popular in Charleston, although there is no benne seed production of note. See BENNE SEED WAFERS. New Orleans, whose slaves and Free Persons of Color primarily came from the French West Indies after the Haitian revolution, brought skills for beignets and other sweets that reflected those origins. Pralines and tea, each sweet enough to "set one's teeth on edge," are claimed by both Charleston and New Orleans. See NEW ORLEANS and PRALINE. Rice, extensively cultivated by African slaves in the hot coastal regions, was used in rice pudding, the rice fritters called calas, and other sweets. Ingredients such as pecans were indigenous to the Americas and provided roulades, soufflés, pecan ice cream, and more. These ingredients were also incorporated into European recipes for sweets. Strawberries were plentiful, and in the nineteenth century Charleston was the strawberry capital of the United States. Peanuts were featured prominently in desserts from brittles to chocolate pies.

Puddings, both French and English, were quickly adapted to the South. Classic boiled puddings, baked puddings, mousses, and other puddings coddled children and adults alike during the cooler months from fall to spring. See HUGUENOT TORTE and PUDDING.

Cakes

Cakes were primarily English and French in origin. Historic cookbooks feature pound cake, sponge cake, angel food cake, and other cakes that remain popular. See ANGEL FOOD CAKE; POUND CAKE; and SPONGE CAKE. Lady Baltimore cake, described in the 1906 Owen Wister novel *Lady Baltimore*, is a favorite. Batter cakes became popular as soon as baking soda was developed, offering a much faster and easier way to utilize fruits, and their popularity increased during the mid-twentieth century. Peach cobbler is more likely to be a batter cake than a pie in the warmest areas of the Deep South, particularly for church suppers and community gatherings, although the further north one goes in the Southern states, the more prominent crisps and peach pies are. See FRUIT DESSERTS, BAKED. Few cookies were made until the twentieth century.

A table covered with cakes was once common at annual barbecues. Sweet cakes like caramel cake and sweets such as divinity fudge came to the South from elsewhere and stayed until they were considered "native." The story goes that "a Southerner is not sure he is loved unless multilayered caramel cake and coconut cake are on the table at holiday times."

Temperature affected chocolate usage, enabling Virginia and other northernmost Southern states to use it more readily than states further south. Even so, as late as the 1879 *Housekeeping in Old Virginia* cookbook, recipes using chocolate were scarce. In the southernmost states it was primarily used in the colder months, if at all, until air conditioning became common and stabilizers added.

Pastry and pies were less common than puddings until the mid-twentieth century and electric ovens, because they had to be made in the rare cool morning hours, or during the winter months in the lower South. Peach pie was made from stewed peaches rather than fresh slices, as we know it now, the filling having to be "at the ready" to expedite the process once the pastry was made. Although puff pastry is referred to in early cookbooks, with its high butter content, it is difficult to imagine anyone making it except in the coolest of situations. Fresh lard, much easier to work with all year long than butter, was widely available, as well as less expensive. Pecans, harvested in late fall, dominated the winter holidays in the form of pecan pies, tassies, and other tarts. Fried pies were developed into a staple because they were easy to make from reconstituted dried fruit, especially apples and peaches. Cooks simply tucked the filling into biscuit dough, folded it over, and pan-fried the pies. Custard pies such as buttermilk pie and chess pie remain favorites.

Electricity and air conditioning changed everything. Pies could be made any time of year, with butter, lard, or shortening. Cakes were baked in more easily regulated ovens. Cookies were now easier for the home cook to deal with and became the norm. Chocolate could be safely stored in a cupboard without melting.

The development of Florida into a major East Coast growing area for fruits and vegetables, and the lower South's many growing seasons, keep fruit desserts at the top of the list. Today, mangos and other subtropical fruits are incorporated into batter cobblers and pies. Florida and Texas have introduced Spanish influences, and flan now rivals standard crème caramel. Although home baking is on the decline, bakeries satisfy the Southern sweet tooth. Grocery stores offer mixes and prepared cream cakes and other popular cakes year round. But no matter who is doing the cooking, batter cobblers, ice cream, holiday cakes, and pies still appear without fail on the table.

See also APPALACHIAN STACK CAKE; CAKE; COCONUT; FLAN; FLOUR; PASTRY, PUFF; and PIE.

Dull, Mrs. S. R. *Southern Cooking*. Atlanta: Ruralist Press, 1928.

Fowler, Damon Lee. *Damon Lee Fowler's New Southern Baking: Classic Flavors for Today's Cook*. New York: Simon & Schuster, 2005a.

Fowler, Damon Lee. *Dining at Monticello: In Good Taste and Abundance*. Charlottesville, Va.: Thomas Jefferson Foundation, 2005b.

A Lady of Charleston and Sarah Rutledge. *The Carolina Housewife or, House and Home*. Charleston, S.C.: W. R. Babcock, 1851.

Rhett, Blanche Salley, and Lettie Gay. *200 Years of Charleston Cooking*. New York: H. Smith & R. Haas, 1934.

Smith, E. *The Compleat Housewife, or, Accomplish'd Gentlewoman's Companion*. London: Printed for J. Pemberton, 1729.

Nathalie Dupree

South Asia is a term applied to countries on the Indian subcontinent: the Republic of India and the Islamic Republic of Pakistan, both created in 1947; the People's Republic of Bangladesh, formed in 1971; the Federal Democratic Republic of Nepal; and the Democratic Socialist Republic of Sri Lanka (formerly Ceylon). India is a secular state with a Hindu majority; Pakistan and Bangladesh have largely Muslim populations; while the main religions in Nepal and Sri Lanka are Hinduism and Buddhism. See BUDDHISM; HINDUISM; and ISLAM.

Food, like language, is not conterminous with political boundaries, and Indian sweets such as laddu, peda, rice puddings, jalebis, barfi, kulfi, and halwa are universally popular throughout South Asia. See BARFI; INDIA; and LADDU. However, other sweets are more local, especially those associated with festivals, religious events, and family celebrations.

Pakistan

Pakistan is an ethnically diverse country, consisting of four provinces and four federal territories. The cuisine and sweets of Punjabis and Muhajirs (descendants of immigrants from India during Partition in 1947) are very similar to those in India: halwa, jalebi, and rice pudding are especially popular. See HALVAH. Sweets are always part of an iftar, the meal that breaks the daily fast during the fasting month Ramadan. See RAMADAN. The end of Ramadan, called Eid al-Fitr, is celebrated with such desserts as *sewian* (vermicelli pudding) and the similar *sheer khurma*, vermicelli cooked in thickened, sweetened milk with nuts and raisins. Another traditional festive dish is *zarda*, a sweet, saffron-colored rice pilaf made with rice, thickened milk (*khoya*), sugar, and nuts, and flavored with rosewater. See FLOWER WATERS.

The Pakistani province of Sindh was settled by Arabs in the eighth century. The Arabs brought many kinds of halwa to Sindh, the most popular of which is made from sesame paste and studded with fruit and nuts. *Mazoon* is another halwa made from ground nuts, *khoya*, and poppy seeds. *Penhon* is a typical Sindhi dessert of crushed rice cooked in sugar water; it is often served at breakfast, especially the day after a wedding. *Tahiri* is a dish of cooked rice, sugar, ghee, cardamom, saffron, and nuts served during the rainy season.

Bangladesh

In Bangladesh, which shares a common language and cuisine with neighboring West Bengal, sandesh, pithas, ros malai, and rosogolla are as popular as they are across the border. See SANDESH and ROSOGOLLA. Dhaka is as famous as Kolkata for its sweet makers (*moira*). See KOLKATA. Pithas (or *pithes*) are especially popular and are often made at home. These are little cakes made from rice flour, thickened milk (*khoya*), and jaggery or sugar; they can be fried or steamed. For Ramadan and Eid, *Shahi Jilapi* is very popular; this is a large round disk made of flour and yogurt that is poured into hot fat in the shape of a spiral, and then soaked in sugar syrup. It is a variation of jalebi, although unlike jalebi, the spirals stick together. It is also a popular street food, sometimes served with *zarda*.

Nepal

The mountainous country of Nepal has 100 ethnic groups, many with their own distinctive cuisines and dishes. Indian sweets are popular, especially in the capital, Kathmandu. Most indigenous Nepali sweets are far less likely to be milk-based and are less sugary than Indian sweets. Local sweets include *sel-roti*, crisp deep-fried rounds of ground rice and bananas that are made during family celebrations and religious festivals, especially Tihar Bhai Tika (the equivalent of Diwali); *malpuwa*, wheat pancakes soaked in sugar syrup; and *khajuri*, flaky cookies made from flour, sugar, and clarified butter pressed into molds and then fried in clarified butter. Sweets made of sugar and molasses from various sources (including palm and sugarcane) and sesame seeds are also popular. See PALM SUGAR.

The Newaris, a large ethnic group, have many distinctive dishes. *Laakha-mari* is a ceremonial sweet bread that is sent to people with a wedding invitation. To make it, rice flour dough is pressed into molds of various shapes and sizes, then deep fried and glazed with sugar to give it a satiny finish. *Yomari* is a steamed rice-flour conch-shaped "dumpling" stuffed with roasted sesame seeds and brown sugar. *Juju dhau*, a sweetened yogurt made from buffalo milk and flavored with cardamom, pistachios, and saffron, is a highlight of festivals.

Sri Lanka

An island of many ethnicities and influences, Sri Lanka was colonized successively by the Portuguese, the Dutch, and the British, all of whom left their mark on the local South Asian cuisine. See PORTUGAL'S INFLUENCE IN ASIA. Baked goods made with wheat flour, sugar, and eggs, such as cakes, tarts, and cookies, reflect the European influence. One Portuguese legacy is love cake, made from flour, eggs, spices, crystallized fruit, and nuts, and baked so that the center remains moist. *Broeder* is of Dutch origin, a round, rich, yeasty cake made of white flour and raisins and cooked in a pan resembling a Gugelhupf pan. See GUGELHUPF.

The use of coconut, rice, and palm as ingredients in many sweet dishes reflects an older, precolonial tradition. *Kalu dodol* is made by heating a mixture of rice flour, coconut milk, and palm sugar until it thickens, then adding cashew nuts and cardamoms. The most traditional Sri Lankan sweet dish, sold at roadside stands throughout the country, is *kiri pani*, buffalo milk yogurt with a layer of cream, which is served with palm syrup.

See also BREADS, SWEET; COCONUT; DIWALI; FESTIVALS; and YOGURT.

Deutrom, Hilda, ed. *Ceylon Daily News Cookery Book*. 4th ed. London: Associated Newspapers of Ceylon, 1956.

Pathak, Jyoti. "The Traditional Sweets of Nepal." *Taste of Nepal* (blog) 4 September 2012. http://tasteofnepal.blogspot.com/2012/09/the-traditional-sweets-of-nepal-part-1.html (accessed 10 October 2014).

Ramzi, Shanaz. *Food Prints: An Epicurean Voyage through Pakistan*. Karachi: Oxford University Press, 2012.

Colleen Taylor Sen

Southeast Asia, a region of subtropical and tropical environments, includes the Philippines, Indonesia, East Timor, Brunei, Malaysia, Singapore, Vietnam, Laos, Cambodia, Thailand, and Burma (also known as Myanmar). In addition, some of the peoples living in China's Yunnan province near the border with Burma and Laos have closer cultural and culinary connections to Southeast Asia than to the rest of China. In most of the region, fruit is the main sweet treat. Prepared sweets, mostly the preserve of specialized cooks rather than made by home cooks, are eaten as a snack or treat rather than as the last sweet course in a meal.

Before the arrival of European powers in the sixteenth century, Southeast Asian sweets relied on local ingredients, primarily coconut, palm sugar and cane sugar, sweet rice, also known as sticky rice or glutinous rice, taro, bananas, and other sweet fruits. See COCONUT; PALM SUGAR; and STICKY RICE SWEETS. Trade, immigration, and colonial conquest resulted in the introduction of new ingredients that found their way into the sweets of the region: tapioca (manioc), wheat flour, butter, milk products, sweet corn, sweet potato, and other New World and temperate-climate foods. See TAPIOCA. Foreign cooking techniques and dishes from Europe, China, and India became adapted once they reached Southeast Asia, including deep-frying in oil, egg custard (from Portugal and Spain), roti (sweetened fried wheat-flour flatbreads from the Indian subcontinent), ice cream and other cooked milk dishes, *lumpia* (fried "eggrolls"), tarts and pastry, and leavened cakes and bread.

Thailand and Laos

In Thailand, as in the rest of Southeast Asia, sweets are most popular as afternoon snacks, though sweet sticky rice treats also sell well in the morning markets. See THAILAND. Thai sweets are inventive and often combine sweet and savory in unexpected ways. For example, *sankaya*, classic Thai coconut milk custard, comes topped with fried shallots and is often steamed in a small kabocha-like squash. Minced garlic and a few coriander leaves, or shrimp and shredded coconut, flavor the sweet meringue topping on the Thai tuiles called *kanom beuang*. As in much of Southeast Asia, pandanus leaves (also known as "screwpine," which give a delicate scent and green color) perfume some sweets and tint them a pale green. See PANDANUS. Sticky rice, both black and white, is sweetened with palm sugar and coconut milk, then served with tart-sweet fruit, most commonly sliced mango. In neighboring Laos, this treat is called *khao nio mamuang* as it is in Thailand; versions of some of the other simple Thai sweets such as deep-fried baban and taro are also made in Laos. A Southeast Asia–wide approach to bananas includes grilling (*gluay bing*) or deep-frying in a simple sweetened rice or wheat-flour batter (*gluay kaek*); taro is also deep-fried. Cubes of taro are sometimes cooked in sweetened coconut milk to make a soupy comfort food snack called *pua gaeng buad*; the banana equivalent, *gluay bua chi*, often topped with sesame seeds or chopped roasted peanuts, is found in Laos, Cambodia, and Vietnam as well as Thailand.

Burma

In Burma (formally known as Myanmar), people may eat a sweet snack in the morning, but more frequently indulge in mid- or late afternoon. Confections range from the sweet street-side coconut cream and rice-flour crepes called *ah-boh* to rice-flour dumplings known as *moun yon lei bo*, the large ones filled with palm sugar and the small ones served in a light sugar syrup. Home cooks and teashops make a two-layer pudding of tapioca topped with creamy coconut milk custard, the tapioca often dyed with pandanus. Sticky rice is the basis of the cake called *htamanei*, which is flavored with peanuts, sesame seeds, and palm sugar and may also include coconut shavings and ginger. The Shan people make deep-fried sticky-rice doughnuts that are drizzled with melted palm sugar. The delicate Indian-inflected sweetmeat called *shwe gyi mont* is a version of halvah and is made from semolina flour cooked with butter and sugar, enriched with coconut milk and sometimes eggs, and then baked. See HALVAH.

China

In the areas of China's Yunnan province that border Laos and Burma, as in Laos and the northern hill areas of Burma, the primary sweet is fruit (bananas, papayas, litchis, etc.). In addition, sticky rice sweetened with crude cane sugar or white sugar, or pounded to a paste, grilled, and drizzled with liquid sugar, is a favorite sweet treat, especially in the morning. Fritters made of wheat flour or rice flour, sugar, and often sweet corn are a common mid-afternoon sweet sold by street vendors.

Cambodia

Cambodian (Khmer) sweets overlap with those of neighboring Thailand and Vietnam, but often with a slight twist. Examples are *sankya lapoh*, custard steamed in squash or pumpkin; *bobo samdaik ankoy*, sticky rice and black bean pudding with coconut milk; and *vavee*, known as golden threads or angel hair. *Kralan* resembles the bamboo-steamed rice dishes of Laos and northeast Thailand: rice, red beans, coconut, coconut milk, and palm sugar are mixed and then stuffed into a hollow bamboo and steamed over a fire. *Num treap* is a cousin of the Burmese *htamanei*, cooked sticky rice flavored with sweetened coconut milk and topped with sesame seeds.

Vietnam

Vietnam's geography and history have resulted in sweets that vary greatly from the temperate north near the Chinese border to the tropical south. Northern sweets make extensive use of mung beans and black-eyed peas. Rice dumplings called *banh troi nuoc*, cousins to the Khmer *num treap*, are filled with a sweetened mung bean mixture and served in a ginger syrup that evokes Chinese sweets. *Che hot sen that tranh* is an iced agar jelly sweet that combines lotus seeds, scented water, sugar, and mung beans and is topped with coconut milk. The same combination is found in the familiar "bubble tea" made with large tapioca pearls and a variety of colorings and flavorings. See BUBBLE TEA. For *che dau trang*, a sweet similar to the Khmer *bobo samdaik ankoy*, cooked black-eyed peas are combined with glutinous rice, sugar, and coconut milk. Vietnamese make tamarind candy and candied coconut, *mut dua*. There is a whole repertoire of sweet soups made of fruits, coconut, noodles, sweet beans, and more, such as *che chuo* (banana and tapioca cooked in coconut milk, like the Khmer *chaek katih*). See SOUP. And *ansom chaek*, the Khmer dish of bananas wrapped in rice and then banana leaves before grilling, is a favorite that the Vietnamese call *chuoi nuong*. A range of sweetmeats known as *mut* also exists that includes candied ginger, star fruit, coconut, and orange peels. See CANDIED FRUIT.

Indonesia

In Indonesia, with its multitude of islands and tropical climate, there are distinctive local sweets as well as more generally available treats such as *pisang goring*, fried bananas. A number of them, like the sesame-coated, deep-fried rice balls filled with bean paste found in Java, are inherited from Chinese tradition. Mochi is made of rice-flour dough filled with chopped sweetened peanuts; similar rice-flour treats, called *cendil*, are colored, so they look a little like Turkish Delight and are served topped with grated coconut. See MOCHI. The glutinous rice-flour dumplings called *klepon*, or *onde-onde*, filled with palm sugar and boiled, are prepared like the *moun lon yei bo* of Burma but are often colored pale green with pandanus. The spicy fruit salad named *rojak manis*, served either as a dessert or a snack, combines powdered dried red chilies and palm sugar with chopped mixed fruit and vegetables such as pineapple, green mango, starfruit, jicama, green apple, and cucumber. Yucca is cooked, sweetened, and mashed, then shaped into disks and coated with fresh grated coconut to make the sweet snack *getuk lindrii*. Agar agar is used to thicken puddings and cake fillings, such as the coconut pudding called *agar degan* made with coconut milk and young coconut flesh, eggs, and palm sugar. Agar is also used to make the rice-flour jelly noodles that are an important ingredient in *cedol*, the layered shaved ice treat that has become popular across Southeast Asia. See SHAVE ICE. *Cedol* (Burmese *mont let saung*; Thai *lot chong*; Vietnamese *banh lot*) layers colorful jelly rice noodles, shaved ice, green dye (originally pandanus coloring), sweet corn, coconut cream, and sometimes red beans.

Malaysia and Brunei

Sweets in Malaysia and in Brunei, the small sultanate on the north coast of the island of Borneo, are very like those of Indonesia, with similar names. Thus, one encounters there *goreng pisang*, bananas coated in a rice-flour batter and deep-fried (yams and sweet potatoes are cooked the same way); tapioca pudding called *kuih benkah*; and *kolak*, also called *pengat pisang*, plantains cooked in coconut milk and palm sugar, a treat eaten at the feast that ends Ramadan. There are a number of thick, porridge-like dishes sweetened with sugar and coconut, and often made richer with coconut milk. They include *pulut hitam*, made of black sticky rice, and *lek tau tang*, created with green mung beans and colored and flavored with pandanus. The popular tall shaved ice treat known as *ais kacang*, a version of *cedol*, includes peanuts, basil seeds, and red beans.

Singapore

Sweets in the city-state of Singapore reflect its mixed Chinese, South Asian, and Malay heritage, with a huge dose of cosmopolitan modernity thrown in. Hawker stalls sell the Malay classics, along with sweetened roti topped with sweetened condensed milk, Chinese-style sweetened bean dishes, silken tofu in sweet ginger syrup, and shaved ice combos. Western-style cakes and pastries, available at all hours, include custard tarts, coconut tarts, and tapioca puddings.

Philippines

The Philippines arguably has the largest repertoire of sweets in the region. See PHILIPPINES. Apart from the usual tropical ingredients such as coconut, sweet rice, and banana, Philippine sweets make inventive use of purple yam (*dioscorea alata*); avocado; *kalamansi* (a distinctive local lime); wheat flour (for little doughnuts called *bunuelos*, and for bread pudding—*pan de sal*—and cakes); silken tofu (called *taho*); sweetened red beans; sago and tapioca (in *helo-helo*, shaved ice sweet drinks); and milk and cream. The latter are used to make flan, leche, and ice cream, a big favorite that comes in a wide range of flavors, including cheese and avocado. See FLAN (PUDÍM) and ICE CREAM.

See also CHINA; INDIA; and RAMADAN.

Alford, Jeffrey, and Naomi Duguid. *Hot, Sour, Salty, Sweet: A Culinary Journey through Southeast Asia.* New York: Artisan, 2000.
Besa, Amy, and Romy Dorotan. *Memories of Philippine Kitchens.* New York: Stewart Tabori, & Chang, 2006.
Duguid, Naomi. *Burma: Rivers of Flavor.* New York: Artisan, 2012.
Nguyen, Andrea. *Into the Vietnamese Kitchen.* Berkeley, Calif.: Ten Speed, 2006.
Oseland, James. *Cradle of Flavor.* New York: Norton, 2006.
Thompson, David. *Thai Street Food.* Berkeley, Calif.: Ten Speed, 2009.

Naomi Duguid

The **Southwest (U.S.)** has a repertoire of native sweets that entwine with those of the former Spanish empire like stripes on a candy cane. The original foray into the American Southwest, into what is now northern New Mexico, was led by the Spanish conquistador Juan de Oñate in 1598. Unlike many European colonists on the Atlantic coast, the pioneers who settled in this region remained intensely loyal to their homeland, including its culinary traditions, and they immediately planted their familiar wheat upon arrival. *Panocha*, a porridge or pudding made from wheat and little else, was likely the first sweet prepared on the frontier. Wheat kernels were rinsed with water, bagged, and set near a fire or other warm place until the grain sprouted. This germinated grain was dried (malted) before being ground into flour (also called *panocha*), which had a subtle natural sweetness. Spanish settlers had access to some honey, and they grew a little sugarcane and sorghum in areas as unlikely as the New Mexican foothills.

However, sugar was in short supply until the railroad came to the region in the latter half of the nineteenth century. Today, cooks flavor their *panocha* with cinnamon and brown sugar, caramelized white sugar, or *piloncillo*, a cone-shaped raw sugar dissolved in hot water. See SUGAR. This dish, cooked on the stovetop and then oven-baked, resembles a lustrous Indian pudding. It is most often served in northern New Mexico and southern Colorado during Lent.

Corn is the basis of several sweet Southwestern beverages. *Atole* is a hot drink sometimes made of blue corn; *champurrado* blends masa harina or other corn flour with chocolate for a hot beverage. Other corn-based sweets include the fruity tamales—similar to their Mexican counterparts—that are especially popular in southern Arizona and the El Paso region. See MEXICO. The *masa* corn flour batter might be flavored with preserves or crushed pineapple, or even stained nearly red from strawberries.

Spanish nuns from convents in the Andalusia sherry region of Spain brought the tradition of egg- and dairy-rich sweets to Mexico and the American Southwest. Sherry producers clarified their wines with egg whites and gave the yolks to the sisters, who devised ways to use them in desserts and other confections. See CONVENT SWEETS. Flan, the baked caramel-topped custard, is one of the many sweets from the frontier period that still dominate southwestern dessert cooking. The use of canned evaporated milk or sweetened condensed milk became common by the nineteenth century. Today, many southwestern cooks still make flan with canned milk because the taste resembles their grandmother's version. See FLAN (PUDÍM); MILK; and SWEETENED CONDENSED MILK.

Another offspring of this egg- and dairy heritage, still popular in New Mexican home kitchens today, is *natillas*. Similar to the Spanish classic, this stovetop vanilla custard or pudding has beaten egg whites folded into the custard in "floating island" style. See CUSTARD. Susan Shelby Magoffin, the bride of an early trader, described in her *Down the Santa Fe Trail and into Mexico* (a diary from 1846–1847, first published in 1926) a dessert that was likely *natillas* as a part of her "first entire Mexican dinner" in Santa Fe. In another entry, Magoffin describes a dessert "made of boiled milk and seasoned with cinnamon and nutmeg" as "very good, the recipe I should like." She was talking about dulce de leche, most often made with cow's milk. See DULCE DE LECHE. *Cajeta*, a goat's milk caramel, is made in a similar style, and sometimes cooked down to candy. Simple homemade goat cheeses, often eaten for breakfast in the past, were usually covered in molasses, honey, or sorghum. See HONEY; MOLASSES; and SORGHUM SYRUP.

Syrupy sweets include *dulce de calabaza*, pumpkin candied with sugar syrup and cinnamon. In *Early California Hospitality* (1952), Ana Bégué Packman notes that the confection "was to California what pumpkin pie was to New England." A caramel syrup forms the base of bread pudding called *capirotada* or *sopa*, most popular in New Mexico and Arizona. White bread is combined with raisins, nuts, mild cheese, and the syrup. The pudding has an association with Lent and Easter because of the religious significance of breaking bread. See CARAMEL.

Other sweet breads are *buñuelos*, *sopaipillas*, and frybread. All are most often made with a baking-powder dough that rises high when dunked in hot oil. See DOUGHNUT. Discus-like buñuelos, most often eaten as snacks in Texas and Arizona, are frequently drizzled with a piloncillo syrup. New Mexican sopaipillas, slathered in honey, may serve as bread or dessert. Frybread, a tradition of the Diné, Pueblo, and other Native Americans, was first created out of adversity, with rancid flour offered by the U.S. Army. It has become a hallmark of skilled Native American cooking. See NATIVE AMERICAN. With a shower of confectioner's sugar, frybread can be snack, bread, or dessert.

Both *empanadas* and *empanaditas*, fruit-filled half-moon pastries, have Spanish antecedents. Baked or fried, the sweets might have a filling of stewed dried apples or apricots, or fresh pumpkin with raisins and pine nuts, or mincemeat. *Pastelitos* comprise a fruit filling sandwiched on a baking sheet between two crusts, and then cut into squares.

Not many states have an official cookie, but New Mexico's legislature recognized the *bizcochito*, or *biscochito*, decades go. This shortbread-like molded cookie is flavored with cinnamon, anise, and often brandy.

One of the few Anglo-American sweets with any degree of history is cowboy Dutch-oven-cooked fruit cobbler. See FRUIT DESSERTS, BAKED. Chuckwagon historian Tom Perini, author of *Texas Cowboy Cooking* (2001), emphasizes that cobblers were not common on long trail drives but were wildly popular as special-occasion treats.

Today's hottest sweets often include chili in some playful way. Chocolate truffles and brownies are enhanced with New Mexican red or smoky chipotle, while ice cream might be fired up from a tiny chiltepin or a hefty New Mexican green pod.

See also BREADS, SWEET; BROWNIES; CANDIED FRUIT; ICE CREAM; PUDDING; SHORTBREAD; TURNOVERS; and TRUFFLES.

Dunmire, William W., and Evangeline Dunmire. *Gardens of New Spain: How Mediterranean Plants and Foods Changed America.* Austin: University of Texas Press, 2004.

Jamison, Cheryl Alters, and Bill Jamison. *The Border Cookbook: Authentic Home Cooking of the American Southwest and Northern Mexico.* Boston: Harvard Common Press, 1995.

Rozin, Elisabeth. *Blue Corn and Chocolate.* New York: Knopf, 1992.

Cheryl Alters Jamison and Bill Jamison

Spain is a peninsula with marked regional, geoclimatic, and cultural differences that yield an impressive array of sweet dishes. Along the lush northern Cantabrian coast and extending to the Atlantic Ocean in the northwest, regional specialties such as *arroz con leche* (rice pudding), *natillas* (custard), *tocino de cielo* (milkless flan), *casadielles* (fried pastries made with butter and anise liqueur, stuffed with a paste of ground walnuts, butter, lemon peel, sherry, and cinnamon), and *filloas* (very thin crepes served with cinnamon and honey) make good use of the local dairy products, eggs, wheat, and fresh and dried fruits. Roman and Arabic traditions—the original Mediterranean diet—marry along the eastern Mediterranean coast, where *mel y mató* (whey similar to cottage cheese), *menjar blanc* (milk pudding with ground almonds), and *flaó* (cheese tart with mint) are inspired by the local dairy products. There are also baked doughs such as *cocas* (thin, crisp bread with dried fruit), *pan quemado* (round cake made without eggs), and a wide range of *turrones* (nougats). In the central Meseta extending to the west, as well as in Extremadura, lard, wheat, and eggs are used to bake simple, exquisite cakes like *bizcochos* and *magdalenas,* or the fried doughnut-like *rosquillas.* In Andalusia, which borders the Mediterranean and Atlantic coasts in the south, the art of frying in olive oil was inherited from the Semitic populations and led to a panoply of sweets of different shapes and textures, collectively described as *frutas de sarten* (frying pan fruits). See FRIED DOUGH. Examples include *pestiños* and the complex *alajú,* flat, round baked dough made with aniseed, cinnamon, coriander, sesame seeds, and cloves. In the Canary Islands, roasted corn flour, called *gofio,* is used to make the local version of nougat.

Over the centuries this immensely contrasting scenery saw a changing population of many different peoples. Native Tartessians and Iberians witnessed the successive arrivals of Celts, Greeks, Romans, Jews, Visigoths, Moors, other Europeans, and Americans. These various influxes resulted in a dynamic exchange of material culture, including ingredients, culinary tools, and cooking techniques.

Spaniards still enjoy sweets handed down from classical antiquity made with honey, wheat flour, olive oil, eggs, and wine, such as *hojuelas de aceite y vino,* thin, fried pastries in the shape of leaves or ears (*orejas*), as well as thick, round, fried *rosquillas de anis* and thin, flat baked *tortas de aceite* with sesame seeds. From the Visigoths, they inherited a passion for fruits, as can be seen in *arropes* (mixed fresh fruits boiled with honey and juices) and *compotas* (compotes of boiled dried figs and chestnuts), as well as in the general preference for oleaginous fruits, such as the almonds and walnuts native to the peninsula.

Spain also enjoys a rich Arabic-Andalusian legacy that includes sweets such as *alajú* (flat, round, baked dough made with almonds, walnuts, pine nuts, toasted breadcrumbs, orange peel, cinnamon, and honey), *talvina* (a kind of porridge made with pistachios, almond milk, and milk), and *almojábanas* (a mixture of flour, olive oil, milk, and cheese that is baked and soaked in honey with cinnamon and pepper). This culinary inheritance includes the Arabic method of making fried, flour-based desserts sweetened with syrups and honey, like *alfajores* (a complex mixture of toasted breadcrumbs, orange and lemon peels, cinnamon, and nutmeg, boiled in honey with cloves) and *pan de Alá* (bread of Allah), which has similar ingredients but is shaped into a loaf. The most emblematic of all sweets handed down from this period are the *turrones* (almond nougat made with egg whites and honey) and *mazapanes* (marzipan), both typical Christmas fare. See MARZIPAN and NOUGAT. The most traditional *turrones* (*turrón de Jijona* and *turrón de Alicante*) date from the thirteenth century. In the sixteenth century, during the reign of Phillip II, *turrones* became renowned in the Far East and were eaten throughout Europe. A wider variety emerged, including hard and soft versions, those using whole or ground almonds, and those with egg yolk and candied fruit. Today, chocolate *turrón* is becoming popular. Unlike the marzipan of other European countries, Spanish marzipan does not contain bitter almonds, so it is sweeter. Marzipan comes in several shapes and sizes, from tiny *figuritas de mazapan* (3D representations of all sorts of animals) to the large, extravagant, and most expensive *anguila*. Typical of Toledo, this eel-shaped loaf is filled with pumpkin jam, sweet potato, and egg yolk and is decorated with sugar lace and candied fruit.

Spaniards developed a taste for the small scale from the Arabic-Andalusian tradition of edible artistry, and so *pasteles* (assorted small cakes) are preferred over *tartas* (large cakes); an overflowing tray is considered more tempting than a single dessert that can be divided. There are many types of tiny sweets, from *huesos de santo* (realistic-looking marzipan "bones" filled with "marrow" made of chestnut, sweet potato, coffee, or egg yolk paste) to *buñuelos de viento* (airy spheres stuffed with *cabello de angel*, a sweet that looks like fairy hair made from a fibrous variety of pumpkin).

Spanish *tartas* are mostly flat and more ceremonial than their European counterparts; they are conceived more to delight than to nourish. The star ingredients are egg yolks, as in the aristocratic *tarta Capuchina*; almonds, as in the *tortada de almendras*; and the combination of both, as in the popular and now commercial *tarta de Santiago*. The *tarta de manzana* (apple tart) is less interesting than in other countries; by contrast, the *tarta helada* (a frozen cake with layers of custard covered in cream and chocolate) was the first quirky application of technology to pastry making and represents each pastry chef's signature work of art. It is an appealing choice for special occasions.

Although Spain's consumption of ice cream is relatively low outside of summer compared to that of other countries, it is enjoyed in the hottest months. The best ice cream comes from the Balearic Islands and Jijona, Alicante, such as the delicious *helado de turrón* (nougat), *helado de avellana* (hazelnut), *helado de almendra* (almond), and *helado de leche merengada* (made from chilled sweetened milk flavored with lemon rind and cinnamon). In the summer vendors throughout the country also sell the refreshing beverages *horchata de chufa* (tiger nut milk), *granizado de limón*, and *granizado de café* (lemon and coffee granitas).

Christopher Columbus's return from the Americas also had sweet consequences for Spain. *Frutas de Aragón* (dark-chocolate-covered candied fruit) are a perfect marriage of the newly arrived chocolate with the ancient inclination to experiment with orange peel and other candied fruits. They are beautifully wrapped in cellophane and sold in wooden boxes. *Bombones* (chocolates) are mostly sold by weight, rather than in boxes, whereas children prefer *chocolatinas*, small chocolate bars.

As a country of *lamineros*—people with a sweet tooth—Spain has a daily timetable for eating sweets. In the morning, *bollería* (pastries) like *ensaimadas* (pastry coils dusted with confectioner's sugar), *suizos* (sweet buns), *trenzas* (pastry braids), and *churros* (long, thin strips of fried dough sprinkled with sugar) are dunked into thick hot chocolate (*chocolate a la Española*) right up to the fingers until dark moustaches tattoo the indulger's face. In the early hours of New Year's Day, Spaniards everywhere eat *churros* with family and friends, and *churrerías* throughout Spain are packed with people very late at night. Dessert after lunch may be *queso con membrillo* (manchego cheese with quince paste), *macedonia de frutas* (fresh fruit salad), *pasteles*, or *tartas*. *Merienda* (afternoon tea) often involves local specialties such as *bizcochos* (cakes), *bizcochos borrachos* (cakes soaked in sugar syrup and wine), or some of the enormous array of *pastas* (biscuits) with evocative names like *feos* (ugly things), *mostachones* (moustaches), and *estacazos* (thrusts), or the popular jelly-roll-like *brazo de Gitano* (Gypsy arm).

Julio Camba, author of *The House of Lucullus or The Art of Eating*, wrote that the Spanish kitchen is full of garlic and religion. In this regard, many votive sweets devoted to each locality's patron saint are now baked beyond convent walls: *coca de San Juan* (an oval or rectangular cake made of flour, eggs, sugar, and lard, decorated with candied fruit), *huesos de San Expedito* (finger- or cylinder-shaped and made from a dough of flour, sugar, and egg yolk fried in aniseed-perfumed olive oil), *panecillos de San Antón* (sweet buns), and *rosquillas de Santa Clara* (fried anise-flavored doughnuts topped with meringue). *Yemas de Santa Teresa* and *yemas de San Leandro* are considered special. Both are made of egg yolk fondant, the latter with a center of *huevo hilado*, thin threads of egg yolk boiled in syrup. See EGG YOLK SWEETS.

Industrious nuns in cloistered convents still maintain local pastry traditions. See CONVENT SWEETS. Originally, making these pastries was their humble and authentic way to thank and honor their donors. Today, the income from baking allows the convents to survive. Although local religious festivities are respected, the classic repertoire consists mainly of fried and baked sweets made with natural ingredients like flour, eggs, milk, almonds, lard, butter or olive oil and lemon peel, cinnamon, and sesame seeds. Most convents produce *pastas caseras* (homemade biscuits), whether *mantecadas* (egg, sugar, and butter cupcakes), *sobadillos* (anise and lard cookies), *almendrados* (almond cookies), *galletas de nata* (cream crackers), or *pastas de té* (tea biscuits or teacakes). The ritual of buying these cookies from the *torno* (turntable through which the sweets are passed) adds a spiritual dimension.

The sweets calendar begins in December with *turrones* and *mazapanes*, as well as *polvorones* (shortbread made of flour, sugar, milk, and nuts), *peladillas* (bite-sized dragées), and the solemn *roscón de reyes* (three kings cake in the shape of a wheel, containing a tiny surprise). Lent and Easter high teas are celebrated with *torrijas* (slices of bread soaked in milk or wine with honey, then dipped in egg and fried); *pestiños* (deep-fried pieces of dough glazed with honey and sesame seeds); *buñuelos de viento* (fried dumplings made with wheat flour, shortening, and eggs, with an array of fillings); and *cocas* or *monas de Pascua* (round cakes with a boiled egg in the middle), often consumed on Easter day along with *longaniza de Pascua* (cured sausage) and soaked in thick, hot chocolate *a la española*. Summer is marked by *coca de San Juan* and autumn by *buñuelos* and *huesos de santo* for All Saints Day and the Day of the Dead. See DAY OF THE DEAD. People in Spain never miss the tiniest occasion to celebrate with ecstatic immersions into the earthly paradise of sweets.

See also CANDIED FRUIT; FLAN (PUDÍM); MIDDLE EAST; and TWELFTH NIGHT CAKE.

Casas, Penélope. *The Foods and Wines of Spain*. New York: Knopf, 1984.

Díaz Viñas, Flor. *La España dulce*. Madrid: Ciclo Editorial, 1989.

Pérez, Dionisio (pseudonym Post-Thebussem). *Guía del buen comer español: Inventario y loa de la cocina clásica de España y sus regiones*. Madrid: Ediciones Velázquez, 1976.

Ríos, Alicia, and Lourdes March. *The Heritage of Spanish Cooking*. New York: Random House, 1992.

Roden, Claudia. *The Food of Spain: A Celebration*. London: Penguin, 2012.

Alicia Rios

The **Spanish-American War** (1898) revolved around the Spanish Caribbean colonies of Puerto Rico and Cuba, as well as around Guam and the Philippines. Economic and political conditions in Cuba triggered the war. At the encouragement of American owners of sugar plantations in Cuba, the U.S. Congress passed the McKinley Tariff Act (1890), which eliminated tariffs on imported refined sugar from Cuba, then a Spanish dependency. See LEGISLATION, HISTORICAL; PLANTATIONS, SUGAR; and SUGAR BARONS. The Cuban sugar industry was more efficient than its counterpart in the United States, and with an open market, Cuban sugar-plantation owners ramped up production, and exports to America soared. Under pressure from American sugar producers, Congress reversed direction in 1894 and passed the Wilson-Gorman Tariff Act, which levied a 40 percent tariff on imported sugar from Cuba, making Cuban sugar more expensive than sugar produced in the United States.

Sugar exports from Cuba rapidly declined, as did the price of Cuban raw sugar, which had no other major market. Workers on Cuban sugar plantations were laid off, and many joined Cuban guerilla groups fighting for independence from Spain. Guerillas destroyed sugar refineries as well as cane fields. Spanish colonial authorities responded with harsh measures to put down the revolt. The resulting atrocities were covered by many newspapers in the United States; the inflammatory articles, called "yellow journalism," eventually swayed American public opinion to support the guerillas.

In February 1898, two months after the U.S.S. *Maine*, an American battleship, blew up in Havana harbor (the cause was never determined), the United States declared war on Spain. Five months later the American military occupied Cuba, Puerto Rico, Guam, and the Philippines. During the war the United States also annexed Hawaii, then controlled by American sugar interests.

After the war, sugar output in Puerto Rico, Hawaii, and the Philippines increased to some extent, but Cuban production skyrocketed thanks to low American tariffs and the advent of new milling methods, such as the use of water mills, enclosed furnaces, steam engines, and improved vacuum pans. See SUGAR REFINERIES and SUGAR REFINING. American investments in Cuban sugar also soared. By 1919 Americans were estimated to control about 40 percent of the Cuban sugar industry. Cuban sugar production reached 3.5 million tons by 1925. When Fidel Castro took control of Cuba in 1959, the United States drastically reduced purchases of Cuban sugar. In retaliation, Castro nationalized Cuba's sugar operations, many of which were owned by Americans. The United States responded by halting all imports of Cuban sugar in 1961.

Ayala, César J. *American Sugar Kingdom: The Plantation Economy of the Spanish Caribbean, 1898–1934.* Chapel Hill: University of North Carolina Press, 1999.

Weigle, Richard Daniel. "The Sugar Interests and American Diplomacy in Hawaii and Cuba, 1893–1903." Ph.D. diss., Yale University, 1939.

Andrew F. Smith

speculaas are thin, crisp, light-brown spice cookies, usually with a raised design imprinted on the top. Speculaas are thought to have originated in the Netherlands several centuries ago, and their popularity soon spread to other regions near the Rhine River, including Belgium (*speculoos*), northern Germany (*Spekulatius*), and northeastern France (*spéculos*), where they are a traditional holiday treat for St. Nicholas Eve (5 December) and St. Nicholas Day (6 December).

The cookie dough is made of flour, butter, brown or white sugar, and sometimes milk or eggs, with seasonings such as cinnamon, nutmeg, ginger, cloves, cardamom, coriander seed, white pepper, mace, anise, and grated lemon zest. The chilled, stiff dough is pressed into an elaborately carved wooden mold that shapes the outline of the cookie and imprints a raised design on the top. See COOKIE MOLDS AND STAMPS. Before the dough is baked, flaked almonds are often pressed onto the back of it. A rich variation is "filled speculaas," with a layer of marzipan baked between two layers of the spicy dough. See MARZIPAN.

Speculaas molds range in size from a few inches to three feet tall. Early molds were carved to produce cookies in the form of St. Nicholas. Other popular motifs are men and women in traditional folk costumes, animals, ships, farmhouses, and windmills. (In the United States, speculaas are often known as "windmill cookies.") The origin of the cookie's name is uncertain: perhaps from the Latin *speculator* (overseer or bishop), referring to the fourth-century bishop of Myra in Turkey, source of the St. Nicholas legend; or the Latin *speculum* (mirror) because the imprinted designs are the mirror image of the motifs in the carved molds; or simply the Latin *species* (spice).

A recent speculaas spin-off is Belgian speculoos cookie butter, a thick, sweet, caramel-and-gingerbread-flavored paste made from crushed speculoos cookies, sugar, and vegetable oils, which is used as a spread like peanut butter.

See also BELGIUM; NETHERLANDS; and SPICES.

House on the Hill: Cookie Molds for Baking, Crafting, Decorating. http://www.houseonthehill.net/ (accessed 9 September 2013).

Lingen, Helmut. *Leckere Weihnachts-Bäckerei.* Cologne: Lingen Verlag, 1979.

Sharon Hudgins

spices are easy to identify, but they are complicated to define. All are aromatic, nearly all are plant products, most have medicinal effects, they generally contribute strong flavors to food, and the great majority originate in the tropics. Many spices have been traded over great distances for many centuries—this is their truly salient property. People far from spices' points of origin craved them and were prepared to pay dearly for them. They wanted spices for their health benefits at least as much as for their flavors and aromas.

Spices are used in all kinds of foods, and in quite different ways from one culture to another, but it is easy to forget how important they are in sweets. Sugar, long considered a spice, almost defines what is meant by "sweets." Physicians once prescribed this sweet "spice" to their wealthy patients just as enthusiastically as they now forbid it. See MEDICINAL USES OF SUGAR.

The point of origin of sugarcane (*Saccharum officinarum*) is said to be central New Guinea, on the eastern edge of modern Indonesia, where it emerged in early farming as the result of hybridization of three or more preexisting species. See SUGARCANE. Several other spices originate not far away. Cloves (*Syzygium aromaticum*) came from the eastern Moluccas, particularly the little islands of Ternate and Tidore, whose rulers had grown rich on the spice trade before the arrival of the greedy Europeans in the late sixteenth century. Nutmeg and mace, the nut and husk of a single tree (*Myristica fragrans*), came from the Banda islands a few hundred miles to the south.

Black pepper (*Piper nigrum*), long pepper, cubebs, and other relatives—members of the Piperaceae family—originate in southern India and Indonesia. Pepper vines are not as difficult to propagate as nutmeg and clove trees, but they, too, demand a tropical climate. Although not common in sweets, black pepper occasionally shows up in spiced cookies, as the names of Venetian *pevarini*, Dutch *pepernoten*, and Swedish *pepparkakor* illustrate.

Cinnamon (*Cinnamomum verum*), the aromatic inner bark of a small tree related to bay (laurel), is at its best in Sri Lanka. It has relatives in Southeast Asia with thicker bark and coarser flavor, and the cheaper aromatic from these other species—sometimes called cassia (*Cinnamomum cassia*) but often not distinguished from true cinnamon—is widely used in confectionery.

Ginger (*Zingiber officinale*) and cardamom (*Elettaria cardamomum*), along with their less well-known relative galanga, belong to the Zingiberaceae family of flowering plants, native to India, southern China, and Southeast Asia, whose fruits, shoots, and rhizomes are the sources of many natural aromas. They, too, are tropical plants, but ginger is relatively easy to grow: it is propagated by dividing the rhizome, and it is this fleshy, root-like part that is valuable. Not only is it the essential ingredient in gingerbread and other spiced desserts, the rhizome itself is commonly candied. See CANDIED FRUIT and GINGERBREAD.

It means little now to say that a food product comes from the other side of the world. Chilled and frozen foods from distant continents reach us with astonishing speed, at negligible cost to us, and taste nearly as good as when fresh. Long before any other foods belonged to a global economy, spices were in demand far from their places of origin, but long-distance trade was then very different. It is true that the real producers, then as now, were rewarded with only a small proportion of the final sale price. There was, though, a good reason for the price differential. Whether they were on their way to China or to Europe, the spices of tropical Asia, once picked and brought to market, had a long and difficult journey ahead of them.

Trade Routes

The usual stages of this journey—the Spice Route—can be set out briefly. Indonesian spices came, in successive local steps, to one or another of the early ports neighboring the Straits of Malacca. From there, if going west, they crossed the Bay of Bengal, with the monsoon, to the neighborhood of Madras in southeastern India; the Indian peninsula itself, relatively narrow at this point, was then often crossed by land. The South Indian spices, if going east, followed the return route of the same ships.

From the Straits of Malacca, the China trade took spices northward by sea, skirting the coast of Indochina, to Canton, and from there either by land or by coastal shipping to the great cities of northern China. Meanwhile, from the neighborhood of Cochin in southwestern India, spices destined for Europe crossed the Indian Ocean, again with the monsoon, to Somalia or southern Yemen, where they were often trans-shipped for the northward journey along the Red Sea and then onward by land to Alexandria. The next leg was by sea across the Mediterranean to a European port such as Venice. A less-used route from India was to Basra, at the head of the Persian Gulf, then by barge up the Euphrates, by land to Antioch or Aleppo, and thence, again, across the Mediterranean.

This traditional route began to flourish when the use of the monsoon to facilitate direct crossings of the Indian Ocean in both directions was discovered. Rightly or wrongly, Greeks and Romans credited the second-century B.C. navigator Hippalos with this crucial discovery. Earlier than that, only the tiniest quantities of tropical Asian spices had reached China or Europe, and some were quite unknown.

The end of the Spice Route was foreshadowed by Vasco da Gama's opening of the seaway from Europe around Africa to India. This discovery was quickly followed by European conquests in the East and by bitter competition to create and control spice monopolies, all of which eventually came to nothing as ingenious botanists and gardeners (including the well-named Pierre Poivre) learned to grow the desirable species elsewhere.

Other Spices

Apart from the tropical Asian spices, a half dozen others have been important for their use in sweets: one from central Asia, one from Africa, two from the Mediterranean, and two from the Americas.

Licorice root was chewed by the ancient Greeks, to whom it came from the steppes north and east of the Black Sea. That was where English explorers found it again in the sixteenth century while traversing Russia in search of the Silk Road. The origins of licorice are far from tropical, but it is one more of the spices that are of equal interest in China and Europe. See LICORICE.

Grains of paradise are the seeds of a cardamom-like plant (*Aframomum melegueta*) native to West

Africa. They first came to medieval Europe by way of camel caravans across the Sahara, then more cheaply by sea in the sixteenth century as a side effect of the direct sailings to India. Although now almost forgotten, grains of paradise were a regular ingredient in the sweet, spiced medicinal wine hippocras (or hypocras). See HIPPOCRAS.

Saffron, the most expensive of spices today, consists of the flower stigmas of the saffron crocus (*Crocus sativus*). After at least 3,300 years of cultivation, it is no longer known in the wild and its origin is uncertain, though southern Turkey is a strong possibility. The high cost of saffron results not from its rarity—it is now grown in many countries—but from the intense labor of harvesting the tiny stigmas.

Mastic comes even today from one geographical location. See MASTIC. The Greek island of Chios is the only place where the mastic tree (*Pistacia lentiscus* var. *Chia*) flourishes. The resin that is gathered by slashing the bark of this tree was a significant source of the wealth of Genoa in medieval times: mastic was among the spices that Columbus, a Genoese familiar with the trade, was most eager to find in the Indies.

Vanilla is the unripe, fermented pod of a vine (*Vanilla fragrans*) that grew in the forests of Mexico. It was used by the Maya and Aztecs, and by the Spanish after them, to flavor chocolate. More recently it has been cultivated in Madagascar, the Indian Ocean islands, and Indonesia. More recently still, synthetic vanillin has replaced it in many sweets, but nothing matches real vanilla. See VANILLA.

From a little farther south, in Central America, came chocolate: From sugar to chocolate, we begin and end with everyday foods that were once prized as medicinal and traded as spices. See CHOCOLATE.

Uses of Spices

Specific uses of spices vary infinitely. Americans love the flavor of cinnamon in cakes; Scandinavians prefer cardamom. Romans flavored cakes and custards with pepper, where others might choose nutmeg. The English like ginger biscuits and ginger wine. The Chinese chewed cloves to freshen their breath, but medieval Europeans chewed mastic. Galanga was reputed to be an aphrodisiac, grains of paradise were believed to make alcoholic drinks seem stronger than they are, and both were frequently included in hippocras. South Asians not only include a wide variety of spices in savory cooking but also add them to sweets; cardamom is an especial favorite. Candied spices are consumed as well, both as a palate cleanser and as an ingredient in sweet paan recipes. See COMFITS.

Ancient and medieval peoples paid high prices for many centuries for exotic spice imports. Having acquired them, they reveled in them, dreamed of them, and were cured of all ills by them. The thirteenth-century French *Roman de la Rose* features a dream of a garden in which all the spices grow. It is at the same time a vision of Paradise, where every spice must surely have flourished, and a mirror of the banquet tables of premodern Europe, laden with cakes, sweets, and spiced wines, each individually healthy, invigorating, and irresistible.

Dalby, Andrew. *Dangerous Tastes: The Story of Spices.* London: British Museum Press, 2000.

Freedman, Paul. *Out of the East: Spices and the Medieval Imagination*. New Haven, Conn.: Yale University Press, 2008.

Keay, John. *The Spice Route: A History*. Berkeley: University of California Press, 2006.

Laurioux, Bruno. "Spices in the Medieval Diet: A New Approach." *Food and Foodways* 1, no. 1–2 (1985): 43–75.

Walker, Harlan, ed. *Spicing up the Palate: Proceedings of the Oxford Symposium on Food and Cookery 1992.* Totnes, U.K.: Prospect, 1993.

Andrew Dalby

spirituality, a heightened emotional state traditionally achieved by perceived unity with the divine through mortification of the flesh, including meditation under stress, finds its physical equivalent in the pleasure delivered by sweetness. Whatever the source—biblical manna from heaven, sweet dates eaten at sunset after the daylong fast of Ramadan, honey used to sweeten the Aztec emperor's sacred cup—sweetness delivers an intense feeling of happiness, however brief. This experience, when shared, enters the collective memory on which all belief systems depend. The seemingly magical ability of sweetness to transform unpalatable foodstuffs—whether sour, bitter, or even poisonous—must surely have increased the feeling of mystery.

Moments of spiritual importance when sweets are eaten include rites of passage—funerals and days of the dead as well as weddings, harvests, and the advent of spring. See FUNERALS and WEDDING. The association of sweetness with religious festivals is particularly evident in Mediterranean lands where Arab culinary influence was strong and the secrets of the pastry cooks of the seraglio passed to the convents. Nuns prepared delicious sweetmeats for sale on the great feast days of the church, providing them with erotic names such as "virgin's breasts" and "nuns' sighs." See CONVENT SWEETS. Even in the mid-twentieth century, as described by Maria Grammatico in *Bitter Almonds* (1994), the San Carlo orphanage in Erice, Sicily, prepared almond confections for important holy days: almond pastry hearts were baked for Christmas, cannoli for Carnival, paschal lambs at Easter, and *ossi di morti* (bones of the dead) for All Saints. See CARNIVAL; CHRISTMAS; DAY OF THE DEAD; and EASTER. Marzipan fruits, beautifully molded and realistically painted, were once taken to the churchyard on All Souls Day, and the orphanage also prepared them to order at Christmas and Easter. They are now sold in every Sicilian *pasticceria* throughout the year. The transition of sacred to secular, facilitated by the arrival of cheap beet sugar, has simply increased the availability of these treats. Sweet confections—the focus of near-spiritual longing—remain more desirable than any other foodstuff.

Wedding rituals involving the sharing of sweets, such as cutting or breaking apart a rich cake or the distribution of sugared almonds or sweetened grains, have a practical purpose in guaranteeing the community's support for a young couple about to embark on the dangerous business of bearing children. Even the strictest of nonconformist puritans permit the eating of sweets at a marriage feast. Edna Staebler, writing at the end of the last century, described the good things served at a Mennonite wedding celebrated in Ontario, Canada: "After the chiffon cakes had been consumed by two hundred guests . . . the bride passed around a tray with little packages of hard candies wrapped in cellophane . . . the groom followed her, carrying a tray full of chocolate bars distributed to all." More casual tokens of friendship are the syrup-soaked fruit preserves offered to welcome guests in the Middle Eastern tradition, a gesture also implicit in the bowl of sweets at a restaurant till, and in the wrapped piece of chocolate placed on the pillow in a hotel bedroom.

If sweetness lies at the heart of our emotional response to one another at moments of celebration, it features equally strongly in our relationship with death. While not all belief systems look toward the life everlasting, faith in resurrection is expressed in Christian rituals through the sharing of sweetened porridges made with unmilled grains, among them frumenty, a whole-grain porridge once eaten in Britain on All Hallows Eve, the night when the dead revisit the living. See HALLOWEEN. The Turkish food historian Mary Işın points out that sweetened wheatberry dishes such as *aşure* and *anus abur* eaten in memory of the dead are always made with unmilled grains, since milling a seed, which holds within it the possibility of resurrection, destroys its spiritual significance. See WHEAT BERRIES. Among similar preparations is *koliva*, a dish of whole-grain porridge decorated with almonds, raisins, and brightly colored sugar crystals distributed among mourners at Eastern Orthodox funerals in Greece and the Balkans, and also eaten on the eve of All Souls. In China at the midwinter festival of Dong Zhi, writes Deh-Ta Hsiung in *The Festive Food of China* (1991), "a lavish feast is laid out before the ancestral altar, empty chairs for the spirits are set at the head of the table," and the main dish offered, traditionally made by the new bride in the family, is Eight-Treasure Rice, a variable dish of sweetened rice with red beans prettily layered with dried fruits and nuts finished with sugar syrup. In the Jewish tradition, an important element of the Seder plate set on the table at the thanksgiving feast of Passover, or Pesach—from which many of the rituals of the Christian Easter are derived—is *haroset*, a pounded paste of nuts and grains sweetened with honey. See PASSOVER.

Ancestral memory as expressed through spirituality shapes the rules by which we live, whatever the circumstances or belief systems to which we may or may not subscribe. Sweetness, even when delivered in the form of a chemical copy rather than from sources provided by nature, remains a powerful weapon in humanity's spiritual armory.

See also BUDDHISM; CHRISTIANITY; ISLAM; JUDAISM; MANNA; and WEDDING CAKE.

Grammatico, Maria, and Mary Taylor Simeti. *Bitter Almonds: Recollections and Recipes from a Sicilian Girlhood.* New York: William Morrow, 1994.

Hsiung, Deh-Ta. *The Festive Food of China.* London: Kyle Cathie, 1991.

Işın, Mary. *Sherbet and Spice: The Complete Story of Turkish Sweets and Desserts.* London and New York: I. B. Taurus 2013.

Powers, Jo Marie, and Anita Stewart, eds. *Northern Bounty: A Celebration of Canadian Cuisine.* Toronto: Random House Canada, 1995.

Elisabeth Luard

sponge cake, once a special cake using only eggs, sugar, and flour baked in an attractive mold or shaped as a biscuit, is now encountered in tiramisù, Twinkies, and store-bought strawberry shortcake shells. Beating air into eggs for long periods, particularly when the eggs are separated, causes the whites to form a mountain of foam, forcing the batter to rise when heated, which results in a lighter texture than the centuries-old yeast, pound, and fruit cakes. See FRUITCAKE and POUND CAKE. Recent sponge cakes may contain oil, butter, and even baking powder.

The earliest sponges were "biskets" or small cakes (cookies). The "Prince-bisket" recipe in Sir Hugh Plat's *Delightes for Ladies* (1602), probably the first in an English cookbook, contained the same proportions as some later sponge biscuits and nineteenth-century ladyfingers. See PLAT, SIR HUGH and SMALL CAKES. The bisket had made its way to England from Italy via France, thus the names Naples Biscuits and Savoy Biscuits, or Savoyardi. In 1913 the French writer Marcel Proust memorialized the madeleine, a shell-shaped sponge biscuit made by the genoise method of stirring the ingredients over heat. See MADELEINE. Larger cakes, such as the Savoy, were baked in elaborate molds, buttered, and then sprinkled with sugar to form a sweet, crisp crust.

Angel food cake is an American sponge cake using only the beaten whites of eggs, sugar, flour, flavoring, cream of tartar, and, later, cornstarch; the last two ingredients affect the cake's lightness and whiteness. Lacking butter, the angel food cake is not derived from Silver, Lady, or other white butter cakes, but rather the White Sponge Cake that first appeared in the 1839 *Kentucky Housewife.* Most likely the first angel food recipe in a cookbook was in Isabella Stewart's *The Home Messenger Book of Tested Receipts* of 1878. This cake quickly became popular, with ten recipes appearing in *My Favorite Receipt* cookbook, from 1886. See ANGEL FOOD CAKE.

Early cookbook authors acknowledged that the sponge was the hardest type of cake to perfect. Thus, when the recipe for chiffon cake was made public in 1948, it called for a novel ingredient—vegetable oil—as well as for baking powder, which made it more reliable. A green chiffon cake in Southeast Asia, the pandan, is colored by using pandanus leaves. See CHIFFON CAKE and PANDANUS.

Jelly and cream rolls are made from malleable sponge cake to form the French bûche de Noël (Christmas Yule log), the British Swiss roll, and the Spanish *brazo de gitano* (Gypsy's arm). Commercial American snack cakes like Yodels and Ho Hos are also based on sponge cake. For all of these rolled cakes, the batter is baked in a shallow, rectangular pan, removed, spread with jelly, jam, custard, or cream, then rolled while still warm.

The versatile sponge has also been used for layer cakes. It is spread with custard and a chocolate glaze for Boston cream pie and forms the dome of the Swedish marzipan-draped *Prinsesstårta* (princess cake); it creates the espresso-soaked almond layers for the elegant layered opera cake. Since the classic sponge cake contains no butter or cream, it is perfect for observant Jews who must not follow a dinner that includes meat with desserts containing dairy products. An unusual sponge, the Ma Lai Go, is steamed and often served as part of the Chinese dim sum spread.

Like any good absorbent sponge, the sponge cake makes an ideal base to soak up liquors and custard, with the added benefit of not getting soggy or disintegrating as butter cakes would. Sponge or Savoy cakes were used as the base for trifles, charlottes, and tipsy puddings—the Squire, the Parson, and Hedgehog—and now is encountered in the ubiquitous tiramisù. This Italian trifle of ladyfingers dipped in coffee with mascarpone has gained in popularity, as has the tres leches cake, which usually uses a sponge base for soaking up three types of milk. See TIRAMISÙ and TRES LECHES CAKE. Thus the sponge cake survives, having taken on new forms through the centuries.

See also BOSTON CREAM PIE; BÛCHE DE NOËL; CHARLOTTE; TRIFLE; and TWINKIE.

Bryan, Lettice. *Kentucky Housewife.* Cincinnati, Ohio: Shepard & Stearns, 1839.

Plat, Hugh. *Delightes for Ladies.* London, 1602. Reprint, Herrin, Ill.: Trovillion Private Press, 1939.

Stewart, Isabella. *The Home Messenger Book of Tested Receipts.* Detroit: E. B. Smith, 1878.

Patricia Bixler Reber

spoon sweet is a soft, toffee-like confection made of boiled sugar syrup, which is then stirred until it becomes opaque. A variety of flavorings can be added, such as fruit juice, mastic, or nuts. See MASTIC. Spoon sweet originated as an Islamic medicinal preparation called *lâ'ûk,* made palatable with sugar or honey; it subsequently evolved in fifteenth-century Turkey into a sweetmeat called *lohuk* or *çevirme.* The term *çevirme,* which means "turning," refers to the long process of stirring in one direction that causes the sugar to form tiny crystals and yields a smooth, viscous texture.

In the seventeenth century this sweetmeat was incorporated into Ottoman hospitality rituals as a refreshment offered to guests before coffee. Each guest took a spoonful of the sweet paste, hence the Greek name *glykokoutaliou* (spoon sweet). Wealthy families used special sets of spoons for this ceremony. Although this custom has virtually died out in Turkey, it is still widespread in Greece. Lord Charlemont was offered spoon sweet when received by Ottoman minister of the Interior Nailî Efendi in Istanbul in June 1749: "He called for coffee, and his servants presented me with a silver vessel, filled with a sort of perfumed marmalade with a large gold or gilt spoon.... I put into my mouth a spoonful, which served instead of sugar to the coffee, which was then brought in."

Traditional flavors included fruits, nuts, spices, and flowers such as violets, roses, and jasmine. In Istanbul today, only mastic and bergamot are available, whereas in Greece spoon sweet is still produced in a wide range of flavors.

Apart from the long stirring, spoon sweet is identical to fondant, which almost certainly originated from it, since fondant made a sudden appearance in France in the 1860s, not long after the Bavarian royal confectioner Friedrich Unger published numerous *lohuk-scherbet* (spoon sweet) recipes in his book on oriental confectionery. See FONDANT.

See also FLOWER WATERS; GREECE; and TURKEY.

Işın, Mary. "*Çevirme*–Fondant." In *Sherbet and Spice: The Complete Story of Turkish Sweets and Desserts*, pp. 91–100. London and New York: I. B. Tauris, 2013.

Priscilla Mary Işın

sports nicknames with sweet references may seem surprising, given the brutal image of sports like boxing and football. But in fact boxing was termed "the Sweet Science of Bruising" as early as 1813, in English journalist Pierce Egan's volumes of *Boxiana*.

The most famous athlete with a sweet name is Sugar Ray Robinson (1921–1989), a boxer whose actual name was Walker Smith Jr. As a fledgling fighter in the late 1930s, Smith borrowed the Amateur Athletic Union card of an older friend named Ray Robinson. Watching the agile fourteen-year-old, George Sainford, later Robinson's manager, called him "Sugar Ray" for his ease and élan, a style as "sweet as sugar." Smith never used his real name again. Although boxing is a violent sport, Sugar Ray's fans never associated him with the sport's brutality, perhaps because of his nickname.

Other boxers adopted the sobriquet "Sugar" to convey the sweetness of their styles and similarity to Sugar Ray Robinson. Probably no one came closer to that identification than Ray Charles Leonard (b. 1956). In the 1972 U.S. Olympic Trials, a coach watching Leonard's smooth approach muttered, "That kid you got is sweeter than sugar." From then on, throughout his championship years in five different divisions, Leonard was known as "Sugar Ray" Leonard, both in homage to the first, most famous, Sugar Ray and in praise of his artful, dance-like style.

Among the tender sobriquets in other sports, the best was assigned to the Chicago Bears' Walter Payton (1954–1999), one of football's greatest running backs, who carried the affectionate nickname "Sweetness."

Boxing great Sugar Ray Robinson at the height of his fame. His toughest rival, Jake LaMotta, once quipped, "I fought Sugar Ray so often, I almost got diabetes."

At 5 feet 10 inches and 200 pounds, Payton was small for professional football, but he compensated with speed and grace, characteristics that sports fans associate with the quality of sweet.

Baseball players speak of the "sweet spot," the part of the bat most likely to produce a hit, and few hitters enjoyed a sweeter spot than George Herman Ruth Jr. (1985–1948), known as "Babe," whose association with sweetness extends beyond the bat to a candy bar. The "Baby Ruth" bar, produced by the Curtiss Candy Company, was a triumph of advertising and good luck, as its sales soared along with Babe Ruth's career. From the first, Otto Schnering, the candy visionary who named and marketed the Baby Ruth in 1920, maintained that the bar was named for President Grover Cleveland's daughter, Ruth, born in the White House in 1891. Baseball fans remained skeptical, as did lawyers working for Babe Ruth, but Schnering was adamant in all of his court depositions, not wanting to share profits with the baseball great. He didn't have to worry about Ruth Cleveland, who had died of diphtheria in 1904.

See also CANDY BAR and SUGAR BOWL.

Kawash, Samira. *Candy: A Century of Panic and Pleasure.* London: Faber & Faber, 2013.
Robinson, Sugar Ray, and Dave Anderson. *Sugar Ray.* New York: Viking, 1970.

Dean Crawford and Marty Mulé

springerle are white- or ivory-colored cookies made from flour, sugar, and eggs, leavened with hartshorn salt (ammonium carbonate) or baking powder, and flavored with anise seeds and sometimes grated lemon zest. The dough is rolled out flat and firmly pressed with a special springerle rolling pin or cookie mold to imprint one or more designs on top. See COOKIE MOLDS AND STAMPS. After the mold is removed, the dough is cut into shapes—squares, rectangles, circles, hearts, stars, human or animal figures—that frame the embossed designs. The dough cutouts are transferred to a baking sheet sprinkled with anise seeds and left to dry overnight before baking. After they have cooled, the hard, dry cookies are kept in a tightly closed container for three to four weeks to soften a bit and allow their flavor to develop.

The history of springerle dates back at least 500 years, to the southern German region of Swabia, where these cookies probably originated. From Swabia their popularity spread to Bavaria, Bohemia, Switzerland, Austria, and Alsace. These pretty "picture cookies" belong to a larger family of northern European shaped-and-stamped cookies made from a variety of doughs, including gingerbread, shortbread, and almond-paste cookies.

The word *springerle* translates literally as "little springer" or "little jumper," but its exact origin is unknown. It might refer to the popular motif of a jumping horse carved on cookie molds in the Renaissance era, or just to the rising, or springing up, of the dough as it bakes, to form a pale golden base on the underside of the cookie, a result of the dough having dried overnight.

Many springerle molds are small works of folk art. Although the molds have been made from stone, ceramics, metals, plaster, wax, and even leather, they are most commonly carved from wood, especially fruit woods. The earliest surviving wooden molds are intricately carved flat boards dating from the sixteenth century. Later, rolling pins were also carved with designs for imprinting springerle cookies.

The motifs on historical springerle molds range from religious figures and scenes to secular designs such as knights on horses, ladies in fancy dresses, and fairy-tale characters; and from domestic animals such as horses, sheep, cats, and dogs to mythical figures like mermaids and unicorns. Modern springerle molds often have simpler depictions of birds, flowers, fruits, and holiday motifs, some of them hand carved, others machine made. Reproductions of historical molds are sometimes made from a composite of powdered wood and resin, stained to look like wood.

Although historical molds show that springerle were baked for religious holidays and secular occasions throughout the year, today these cookies are most often associated with the Christmas season. Usually eaten in the afternoon with coffee or tea, springerle can also be accompanied by a glass of chilled white wine. Sometimes the white cookies are also painted with food coloring or other paints, for use as holiday decorations. An old custom was to hang springerle cookies, painted or unpainted, as ornaments on Christmas trees. When the trees were finally taken down after Epiphany, the children were allowed to eat the cookies.

See also GERMANY; GINGERBREAD; and SHORTBREAD.

Handbuch für de Weihnachtsbäckerei: Von Advent bis Silvester. Cologne: Pfeifer & Langen, 1977.

House on the Hill: Cookie Molds for Baking, Crafting, Decorating. http://www.houseonthehill.net/ (accessed 9 September 2013).
Hudgins, Sharon. "Edible Art: *Springerle* Cookies." *Gastronomica: The Journal of Food and Culture* 4, no. 4 (2004): 66–71.
Iaia, Sarah Kelly. *Festive Baking: Holiday Classics in the Swiss, German, and Austrian Traditions*. New York: Doubleday, 1988.

Sharon Hudgins

sprinkles, to state the obvious before getting into the curious, suggests the act of scattering or dispersing, and yet when used in confectionery parlance the term is actually quite broad. Decorative sprinkles can refer to sanding sugar, slightly coarser than table sugar, whose clear, multicolored crystals lend sparkle to cookies or pastries. It might also reference French *decoratifs* called nonpareils ("without equal"), tiny balls made of sugar and starch that provide flourish to elaborate desserts, or dragées, the inedible spheres of sugar with metallic outer shells used primarily for the formal adornment of wedding cakes. But, most commonly, sprinkles are the cylindrical bits of candy toppings that add color and texture to a range of sweets, generally requiring frosting, ice cream, or other surfaces onto which to adhere. See ICE CREAM and ICING.

Historical mentions of sprinkles date to the early 1920s, and in 1927 the Loose-Wiles Biscuit Company of Kansas City introduced a product called "chocolate sprinkle cookies" under its Sunshine brand. However, the ascendance of sprinkles in the dessert kitchen is most notably credited to the efforts of a Russian immigrant by the name of Samuel Born.

In 1916, only six years after arriving in America, Born invented a machine to mechanically insert sticks into lollipops. In 1923 he established the Just Born Candy Company in New York City, its logo featuring a baby resting in a candy measuring scale. See LOLLIPOPS. After moving operations to Bethlehem, Pennsylvania, in 1932, he began producing rod-shaped bits of candy, first offered as "chocolate grains" and later trademarked as "jimmies," the name inspired, according to company history, by Jimmy Bartholomew, a Just Born candy maker.

Over the years, Americans have named the treats toppettes, trimettes, shots, fancies, hundreds-and-thousands, and mice. While jimmies has remained the term of choice in New England, throughout most of the country they are simply called sprinkles.

Multicolored rainbow sprinkles are made of sugar, cornstarch, vegetable oil, and food coloring; chocolate sprinkles contain chocolate, cocoa, and sugar. Ingredients are combined into a doughy paste and forced through an extruder in much the same way pasta is made. The "noodles" are cut to the right size and shape, then dried and tumbled to make them uniform in appearance. Finally, a confectioner's glaze is applied, creating those tiny cylinders of garnishing magic.

It was at his family's chocolate factory in the Netherlands in 1936 that Gerard de Vries developed a machine to produce the Dutch version of sprinkles. They were named *hagelslag* (the Dutch word for hail) after their resemblance to the pellets of a hailstorm. Fruit-flavored *vruchtenhagel* and anise-flavored *anijshagel* followed the success of *chocolade hagelslag* onto the Dutch breakfast table, where sprinkling over lightly buttered bread has become a national ritual.

Hartel, Richard W., and AnnaKate Hartel. *Food Bites: The Science of the Foods We Eat*. New York: Copernicus, 2008.
Just Born, Inc. "Our History." http://www.justborn.com/get-to-know-us/our-history (accessed 5 August 2013).
Venz Hagelslag. "Historie." http://www.venz.nl/historie.php (accessed 5 August 2013).

Michael Turback

spun sugar

See SUGAR SCULPTURE.

Sri Ramakrishna was a nineteenth-century spiritual leader whose influence on the sociocultural life of Bengal extends to the respect he enjoyed among Kolkata's confectioners and literati. See KOLKATA. Ramakrishna came to prominence after taking over as head priest of the Dakshineshwar Temple dedicated to the goddess Kali following the death of his brother Ramakumar, the temple's first head priest. Like Sri Chaitanya, another religious figure whose arrival marked the advent and spread of Vaishnavism in sixteenth-century Bengal, Ramakrishna and his teachings influenced the daily life of Bengal. Followers and nonfollowers alike embraced both of these spiritual figures by naming stores after them and hanging their portraits in sweetshops.

In addition, their biographies provide a valuable source of information for food historians, because they describe two distinct traditions of sweet making in Bengal that indicate the shift from sweets based on kheer (thickened milk) to *chhana* (fresh curd cheese). In *Sri Sri Ramkrishna Kathamrita*, Mahendranath Gupta writes of Ramakrishna's fondness for sandesh and jalebi, which he shared with his disciples. See SANDESH. Rani Rashmoni, the founder of the temple, bought tons of sandesh from Bhimchandra Nag, a famous Kolkata sweetshop, for the temple's inauguration. Ramakrishna was known to be partial to this sweet.

Unlike kheer-based products, which predominate in Chaitanya's biography, *chhana*-based products appear throughout Sri Ramakrishna's biography, often in reference to rituals. *Chhana* is prepared from milk that is considered to be ritually pure; however, in *A Historical Dictionary of Indian Food*, K. T. Achaya mentions a taboo against using curdled milk for ritual use. Nevertheless, *chhana*-based sweets became common in ritual offerings, as Ramakrishna's autobiography makes clear.

According to confectioners in Kamarpukur, Ramakrishna's birthplace, he was particularly fond of *sada bonde* (white bonde), a confectionery made of tiny granules prepared by grinding a special pulse called *barbati kalai* into flour. Today, this sweet is available in a few shops in Kamarpukur and Jairambati, the birthplace of Sri Ma Saradamani, Sri Ramakrishna's wife.

See also HINDUISM; INDIA; LADDU; MITHAI; and ROSOGOLLA.

Gupta, Mahendranath. *Sri Sri Ramkrishna Kathamrita*. Vols. 1–5. 1902. Translated into English, http://www.kathamrita.org/kathamrita (accessed 12 December 2014).

Krondl, Michael. *Sweet Invention: A History of Dessert*. Chicago: Chicago Review Press, 2011.

Ishita Dey

stages of sugar syrup describe the transformations that sugar and water undergo when heated together. From thin syrup the mixture thickens, bubbles, becomes malleable, and then cracks when dropped into cold water before it finally caramelizes and turns brown. The unique physical properties of each stage lend themselves to particular candying techniques. The rather thin thread stage, for example, is used for candying fruit and making jellies, while the hard ball stage is employed for various soft candies.

Stages of Sugar Syrup

Name	*French*	*Description*	°C *	°F *
coated	*nappé* (alternatively, *lissé*)	The syrup appears transparent and just coats the spoon. Escoffier (1846–1935) and previous authors never mentioned this modern, French stage. Used for fruits in syrup.	100	212
small thread (or gloss)	*petit filé* (historically, *lissé*)	Modern English and some French cooks consolidate the thread stage into a single unit. Gilliers instructed readers to stick their index finger into the pot, press a small glob of syrup against their thumb, and then pull finger and thumb apart. The small thread stage has been reached if an almost imperceptible thread (3 mm, or ⅛ in.) forms and quickly collapses. Used for jellies, confitures, and almond paste.	103–105	217–221
large thread (or gloss); also referred to as syrup	*grand filé* (historically, *lissé*)	A longer, firmer thread (5 mm, or ¼ in.) can be made. Used for candied fruits, buttercreams, and icings.	106–110	223–230

Name	*French*	*Description*	*°C **	*°F **
small pearl	*petit perlé*	Historically important but rare today. Using the previous test, one can fully separate one's fingers and the thread doesn't break. Sometimes described as synonymous with the *soufflé* (blow) stage, which historically constituted its own category. Used for jelly, jams, candy, fruit liqueurs, and some icings.	110–112	230–234
large pearl (sometimes called *soufflé*—see below)	*grand perlé* (sometimes *grand soufflé*)	The thread reaches up to 2 cm, or ¾ in. Used for jams, candied fruits, and *marrons glacés.*	113–115	235–239
blow	*soufflé*	Used by chefs through Carême's generation but rare today. If one dips a skimmer, into the syrup and blows on it, bubbles fly out of its holes.		
small feather	*petit plume*	Historical. When syrup is shaken off a skimmer, it forms a fanning, feather-like pattern.		
large feather	*grand plume*	Historical. A greater quantity of even larger bubbles fly off the skimmer if one blows on it.		
soft (or small) ball	*petit boulé* (or *petit boulet*)	When a small amount of syrup is rolled between the fingers, it forms a squishy ball. Escoffier described this as synonymous with the feather and blow stages that earlier chefs held to be distinct. Used for jams, jellies, soft caramel, and nougat.	116–118	241–244
hard (or large) ball	*grand boulé* (or *gros boulé, grand boulet*)	The ball keeps its shape more easily and has the texture of soft caramel candy. Used for sugar decorations, Italian meringue, fondant, and caramels.	121–124	250–255
soft crack (or light or small crack)	*petit cassé*	A drop of the sugar mixture plunged into cold water cracks slightly but is flexible and sticks to the teeth. Used for toffee.	129–135	264–275
hard crack	*grand cassé*	A drop of the sugar plunged in cold water cracks like glass. Used for boiled sweets, sugar flowers, icings, and spun sugar.	149–150	300–302
light caramel	*caramel clair*	The mixture takes on a pale coloring; early authors frowned on this and elided it with the crack stage. Used for crème caramel, puddings, cakes, etc.	151–160	304–320
brown or dark caramel	*caramel foncé*	The mixture takes on a deep, golden color. Used for sauces and cakes.	166–175	331–374

*Temperatures are approximate due to the variable effects of humidity, altitude, and sugar purity.

Modern home confectioners rely heavily upon candy thermometers to help them determine when the syrup reaches the increasingly cooked stages of thread, soft ball, hard (or firm) ball, soft (or small) crack, hard crack, and caramel. However, factors such as altitude, humidity, and sugar purity also affect the rate at which these phenomena occur, and thus the temperatures at which they are achieved. Professional kitchens since at least the 1820s have therefore utilized refractometers to measure degrees Brix (°Bx), which is the percentage of sucrose in an aqueous solution. See BRIX.

Before the technologies of the thermometer or Brix meter came into widespread use, many confectioners had gradually codified the basic stages of boiled sugar through direct observation. Eighteenth-century confectioners, especially those working in France, inherited, elucidated, and published details of various terms. Joseph Gilliers's *Le cannameliste français* (1751) disseminated a list that includes all of the major stages currently in use. It also included the blow stage, which appears only rarely on contemporary charts, and the feather stage, which dropped entirely out of use after the generation of Antonin Carême (1784–1833). See CARÊME, MARIE-ANTOINE and GILLIERS, JOSEPH.

Gilliers felt it necessary to warn confectioners to have a bowl of chilled water handy before sticking a finger into the boiling mixture to test it. This is still good advice, and reflects the fact that, in spite of antecedents, Gilliers did not assume that his readers had previous knowledge of sugar boiling techniques. That subsequent authors gradually cribbed his directives into shorthand bears witness to the degree to which they had become codified and accepted as a fundamental building block of Western confectionery, as evolved from French techniques. The simplification in the number of stages began in the early nineteenth century and continued under Auguste Escoffier (1846–1935) and later authors, attesting to the overall modification of French culinary techniques that resulted from a reduction in staff due to increasingly high labor costs. See ESCOFFIER, GEORGES AUGUSTE. Instructions also shortened over time because of the increased reliance on scientific instruments, which reduced the role of the old-fashioned directives to a back-up position. By contrast, Gilliers's inclusion of phenomena that later chefs glossed over speaks to the meticulous precision with which the *office* of a grand French kitchen operated prior to the 1789 Revolution.

Elisions to Gilliers's system have occurred with a degree of overlap, especially with the finer, lower-temperature stages, which are rarely used in contemporary recipes. For example, the thin syrup that the French now call *nappé* (coated) can, confusingly, also appear as *lissé* (smooth), although historically that was the French name given to the thread stage, which later came to be known as *filé*.

Even in the heyday of the ancien régime, authors introduced idiosyncratic stages to describe their personal observations in terms that they felt their readers would comprehend. The eighteenth-century author Menon, who in 1746 published *La Cuisinière bourgeoise,* included a *queue-de-cochon* (pig's tail) stage, which takes its name from the fact that at that stage of cooking, a drizzle of the syrup from a skimmer resembles its eponym. Some contemporary French sources also include a *morvé* (mucus-like) stage to lump together many of the subtler stages described by Gilliers that occur between the thread and soft ball stages. Nevertheless, despite overlaps and inconsistencies of nomenclature, the observable phenomena that occur when sugar boils remain unchanged since Gilliers's day.

More significantly, the deep caramel color and flavor now so greatly admired was considered "burnt" by Gilliers's generation and simply thrown away. It was only in Carême's era that this state became appreciated in its own right, and it later became, especially for Anglophones, the preferred one.

On the other hand, new research demonstrates that it is possible to caramelize sugar without boiling it at all. In 2012 Shelley Schmidt and colleagues at the University of Illinois showed that sucrose breaks down and transforms in hitherto misunderstood ways. As opposed to water, for example, which has a defined melting point of 32°F (0°C), sugar in water, if heated over time, transforms into caramel due to two overlapping phenomena. There is a range of temperatures at which sucrose molecules get jittery and break loose. However, they attach themselves to their neighbors at a separate range, which turns out to start much sooner than previously thought. Early experiments with this discovery have led the food-science writer Harold McGee to produce caramel-center crystals and roasted sugar, among other inventions.

Boiling sugar, however, remains the norm. Whether measured using eighteenth-century techniques, home thermometers, or professional refractometers, the stages of cooked sugar continue to underpin candy making today.

See also CONFECTIONERY EQUIPMENT; MEASUREMENT; and SACCHARIMETER.

Carême, Antonin. *Le pâtissier royal parisien*. Paris: Dépôt des Moulins, 1854.
Escoffier, Auguste. *Le guide culinaire*. 3d ed. Paris: Flammarion, 1921.
Gilliers, Joseph. *Le cannameliste français*. Nancy, France: J. B. H. Leclerc, 1751.
Menon. *La cuisinière bourgeoise*. New ed. Saint-Malo, France: L.-H. Hovius, 1802.
Robuchon, Joël, and the Gastronomic Committee, eds. *Larousse Gastronomique*. New ed. London: Hamlyn, 2001.

Carolin C. Young

starch is a digestible carbohydrate made by chaining together hundreds or thousands of glucose molecules. Plants produce starches from carbon dioxide and water through photosynthesis. The linkages between glucose units are readily broken, enabling plants, as well as organisms that consume plant material, to rapidly reclaim the individual simple sugar units to use as an energy source. In the kitchen, starches are used to thicken sweet and savory sauces, and to help puddings and fillings set.

Starch molecules can be classified by their three-dimensional molecular structure. Amylopectins are highly branched and fold into sheet-like structures, while amyloses are smaller, helically shaped molecules with minimal branching. Roughly three-quarters of the starches in plants are amylopectins. The spiral units of amyloses pack tightly together, making them substantially less soluble than amylopectins. Starch molecules pack into larger granules, ranging in size from 1 micron to over 0.1 millimeters in diameter.

Culinary starches are derived from a wide variety of plants, including wheat, tapioca, corn, and arrowroot. Starch is the major component of flour, by mass making up 85 percent of corn flour and 70 percent of wheat flour. Pure starches are most often used as a thickening agent. Each plant starch has slightly different properties, depending on the size of the starch granules and the relative proportions of amylopectins and amyloses. Arrowroot cannot be used with dairy products, for example, and cornstarch-based sauces will refuse to thicken if they are too acidic. The texture of confections made with cornstarch will suffer upon freezing, while tapioca-thickened mixtures are cold tolerant.

Arrowroot effectively thickens citrus glazes, and the starch in wheat flour thickens the base of sweet and savory soufflés. Under certain conditions, starch mixtures will form a gel. The filling in Boston cream pie is a cornstarch-based gel, while tapioca is often added to fruit-pie fillings, where it combines with the juice exuded by the fruit to produce a clear gel that sets as the pie cools. See BOSTON CREAM PIE and PIE. When starches are heated in the presence of water, the water insinuates itself into the granules, breaking up their ordered structure and causing them to swell to many times their original size. As they swell, some of the smaller amylose molecules move out of the granules entirely and into the surrounding solution. These amylose molecules, along with the granules and fragments of the granules, gradually become dispersed throughout the water, thickening it in much the same way that water trapped in a web of protein molecules becomes gelatin. The resulting dispersion can gelatinize if the concentration of material becomes high enough. Acid-modified starches are more likely to form gels, and are thus used to make the popular gummy candies and Turkish delight. See GUMMIES and LOKUM.

The ability of starches to temporarily trap water helps to keep baked goods moist. As baked goods age, the starches expel the water and return to a more ordered structure, resulting in a drier, tougher texture.

Since proteins coagulate above about 180°F (82°C), well below the boiling point of water, starches can be added to interfere with protein coagulation, reducing the formation of undesirable clumps of coagulated protein—particularly in egg-based sauces and custards—and increasing the temperature at which coagulation will occur. Addition of too much starch, however, can trap too much water and result in custard with a rubbery, gel-like consistency.

The enzyme alpha-amylase quickly breaks down starches into glucose. See GLUCOSE. Human saliva contains alpha-amylase, as do egg yolks. While the presence of this enzyme in cake batters is of no consequence, since prolonged heating above 180°F will destroy the enzyme, care must be taken to see that sauces or custards that contain egg yolk are heated long enough to completely inactivate the amylase. Introducing saliva into a custard or sauce (for example, by eating half of a dessert and reserving the rest until the next day) can also lead to the degradation of the starches. The water trapped by the starches is released and the dessert may separate unappetizingly.

Dispersions of amylose in solution tend to clump when cooled close to or below the freezing point of water, resulting in custards that weep or sauces that separate when frozen. Starches that have a higher proportion of amylopectin, such as rice starch, are less likely to undergo this retrogradation process.

Cornstarch is the feedstock for production of the sweetener high-fructose corn syrup. See CORN SYRUP and FRUCTOSE. The cornstarch is broken down into individual glucose units using the enzymes alpha-amylase and glucoamylase. Another enzyme, xylose isomerase, then converts some of the glucose molecules into fructose (which has the same molecular formula, but a different arrangement of atoms).

See also CUSTARD and EGGS.

Corriher, Shirley. *BakeWise: The Hows and Whys of Successful Baking, with over 200 Magnificent Recipes.* New York: Scribner, 2008.

Whistler, Roy L., and James R. Daniel. "Starch." In *Kirk-Othmer Encyclopedia of Chemical Technology*, 4th ed., edited by Raymond E. Kirk and Donald F. Othmer. New York: Wiley, 2000.

Michelle M. Francl

state desserts are part of the official symbolism decreed by state legislatures to represent the various traditions and natural resources of the 50 U.S. states. These symbols range from official state poems and state toys to state firearms and state dinosaurs. Nearly half of America's states have some sort of official state dessert, treat, or sweet snack, reflecting the country's well-known sweet tooth.

Pie, that classic American dessert, is by far the most common official state sweet. See PIE. Delaware, a leading producer of peaches in the nineteenth century, represents itself with a warm, perfumed wedge of peach pie, while Florida's pick is Key lime pie, a creamy, sweet-tart mix of condensed milk and eggs flavored with the tiny, yellow-skinned Key limes indigenous to the islands off the South Florida coast. Citizens of Indiana adore sugar cream pie, in particular the "Hoosier pie" ("Hoosier" is a nickname for an Indianan), a custard pie combining sugar, butter, and cream that originated with the state's Amish and Quaker communities. See CREAM PIE. In summer the fields of Maine are overgrown with wild blueberries, which are smaller and tarter than their domesticated cousins, and they become the key ingredient in wild blueberry pie, Maine's official state pie. Oklahoma and Texas go nuts for pecan pie, made from the fruit of a species of hickory tree native to both states. Traditional pecan pie combines pecans and corn syrup (either light or dark). See CORN SYRUP. Texas also has an official cobbler—peach cobbler—to honor the state's love of sweet, juicy peaches. More rustic than pie, cobbler consists of fruit baked in a pan with a biscuit or batter topping. See FRUIT DESSERTS, BAKED. It is a popular dessert throughout the American South. The chilly New England state of Vermont is famous for its apples, making apple pie appropriate as its state symbol, even though the pie is beloved throughout the United States. See UNITED STATES.

Far fewer cakes than pies appear on the list of official desserts. Despite its name, Massachusetts's state dessert of Boston cream pie is actually a cake comprising sponge layers filled with vanilla custard and topped with a chocolate glaze. See BOSTON CREAM PIE. The Boston cream doughnut, essentially a miniature version of the pie, is the state doughnut. Even though it is also called a pie, Maine's state treat, the whoopie pie, is actually a cake-cookie hybrid consisting of two individual-sized cake rounds filled with marshmallow cream. See WHOOPIE PIE. One actual cake on the list is Maryland's Smith Island Cake, a specialty of Smith Island, a fishing community in the Chesapeake Bay accessible only by boat. This tall cake alternates at least eight thin layers of yellow cake with chocolate frosting.

After pies, pastries are the second-largest category of official state desserts. Louisiana's state doughnut is the beignet, a nod to the state's Creole heritage. Beignets are fritters of hot fried dough, usually served with powdered sugar. They were introduced by French immigrants who settled in the region in the 1700s and are a popular item at coffee shops in New Orleans's French Quarter. See FRIED DOUGH. South Dakota's state dessert is kuchen, a traditional German cake of sweet, yeasted dough filled or topped with custard or fruit—no surprise for a state where nearly half of the residents claim German heritage. See KUCHEN. Proving that everything really is bigger in Texas, the Lone Star State has two official pastries in addition to their official pecan pie and peach cobbler—sopaipillas and strudel. Sopaipillas are fried dough topped with powdered sugar or honey, while strudel is a flaky layered pastry typically filled with fruit. See STRUDEL. These pastries honor both the Hispanic and the German heritage of the Lone Star State. Wisconsin, with its rich Danish heritage, has the kringle, a classic Scandinavian flaky pastry ring.

Two states have given cookies the official stamp of approval. Massachusetts honors the chocolate chip cookie, the classic American drop-style cookie, which was invented in 1930 by Ruth Wakefield, owner of the Toll House Inn in Whitman, Massachusetts, when she ran out of baker's chocolate and used a chopped-up semisweet chocolate bar instead. New Mexico reflects its Spanish and Hispanic heritage with the bizcochito, a crisp rolled cookie made with lard or butter and flavored with anise, traditionally served around Christmas.

Missouri bucks the pie-pastry question with its state dessert, the ice cream cone. Though the original inventor of the ice cream cone is unknown, the cone was popularized at the 1904 St. Louis World's Fair, where vendors rolled waffle cookies into cones to serve the hungry crowds. See ICE CREAM CONES.

Utah's state snack is Jell-O. See GELATIN DESSERTS. This jiggly, sweet gelatin dessert is wildly popular in the state, and residents of Salt Lake City are said to eat more Jell-O than the inhabitants of any other city. Jell-O's popularity might be attributable to Utah's high percentage of children—due to the traditional Mormon preference for large families, Utah has more children per family than any other state.

See also MIDWEST (U.S.); NEW ENGLAND (U.S.); PACIFIC NORTHWEST (U.S.); SOUTH (U.S.); SOUTHWEST (U.S.); and WEST (U.S.).

Hawkins, Nancy, and Arthur Hawkins. *The American Regional Cookbook: Recipes from Yesterday and Today for the Modern Cook*. Englewood Cliffs, N.J.: Prentice-Hall, 1976.

McDonald, Barbara. *The Fifty States Cookbook*. Chicago: Culinary Arts Institute, 1977.

Paddleford, Clementine. *How America Eats*. New York: Scribner, 1960.

Emily Matchar

stevia refers to a large genus of American plants. The name honors Petrus Jacobus Stevus (in Spanish, Pedro Jaime Esteve), a sixteenth-century professor of anatomy and medical botany at the University of Valencia. The word "stevia" was introduced in 1797 by Antonio José Cavanilles, a taxonomic botanist from Valencia who was one of the first Spanish scientists to use the Linnaean classification system.

Stevia rebaudiana is a species native to Paraguay, where it is known locally as *ka'a he'hê* and used for sweetening and medicinal purposes. Moisés Santiago Bertoni, a Swiss botanist of Italian descent who worked in Paraguay, learned about this plant from a local guide in 1887. He obtained leaves in 1899, and an actual plant soon thereafter, and named it in honor of Ovidio Rebaudi, a Paraguayan chemist who published the first analysis of its sweet constituent. Paraguayan farmers began growing *Stevia rebaudiana* around 1902. Cultivation later moved to the Far East, with China becoming the largest producer.

Cecil Gosling, the British Consul at Asunción, sent samples of *Stevia rebaudiana* to the British Royal Botanical Gardens at Kew in 1901. The United States Department of Agriculture got some leaves and seeds in 1919. European scientists isolated the glycosides that give the plant its sweet taste in 1931, and in 1971 Morita Kagaku Kogyo Co., Ltd., in Japan, began producing a sweetener based on this purified substance. Truvia, a stevia-based sweetener developed by Cargill and the Coca-Cola Company, came on the market in 2008. PureVia is a similar product developed by PepsiCo and the Whole Earth Sweetener Company.

Stevia rebaudiana is substantially sweeter than sucrose and is a suitable sweetener for people who are diabetic or obese. However, since some of the compounds in the plant may be toxic, the U.S. Food and Drug Administration allows the commercial distribution of products containing purified stevia extracts, but not stevia leaves and stevia extracts. The European Food Safety Authority has given approval to stevia but suggests that daily intake be limited.

See also ARTIFICIAL SWEETENERS.

Lewis, Walter H. "Early Uses of *Stevia rebaudiana* (Asteraceae) Leaves as a Sweetener in Paraguay." *Economic Botany* 46 (1992): 336–337.

Deborah Jean Warner

sticky rice sweets, which have as their main ingredient white, black, or purple varietals of glutinous or sweet rice, comprise hundreds of Asian desserts and sweet snacks. Low in amylose starch, opaque and waxy when uncooked and moist, glossy and tacky when steamed, sticky rice yields two basic types of sweets: those that incorporate the whole grain, and those based on a smooth or nearly smooth dough made with either sticky rice flour or steamed sticky rice that has been pounded, mashed, or otherwise transformed into a paste. Across Asia, sticky rice sweets of all kinds are often made or purchased to celebrate holidays like New Year's, to recognize special occasions such as weddings, and to serve as offerings on religiously significant days.

"Whole-grain" sticky rice sweets range from simple combinations of rice with various accompaniments and toppings, to those formed into cakes or dumplings of varying degrees of intricacy. Of the former, *khao niaow mamuang*, sweetened sticky rice with lightly salted coconut cream and fresh mango (Thailand and Laos), is probably the most well known, but the Vietnamese eat a similar sweet for breakfast called *xoi*, sticky rice that may be topped with (among other ingredients both sweet and savory) crushed peanuts, sugar mixed with salt, and grated fresh coconut. Sweet rice cakes are found from China (*ba bao fan*, or Eight Treasure Rice, is a cake steamed with lard and sugar and studded with dried fruits and nuts) to Indonesia (*wajik*, variously shaped and tinted cakes boiled with palm sugar), India, and Japan. Malaysia is especially rich in sticky rice *kuih* (Malay for "cake"); among the most beautiful are *pulut tai tai*, slabs of sticky rice tinted blue with dried butterfly-pea flowers (*Clitoria ternatea*) and smeared with coconut milk and egg jam; and *seri muka*, diamond-shaped cakes of rice cooked in coconut milk, topped with a layer of coconut milk rice flour custard tinted green from pandan leaf extract.

Lao *khao lam*—black or white sticky rice cooked with coconut milk, sugar, and salt, and sometimes mixed with dried legumes, sweet potato and yam, or sesame seeds—is stuffed into a bamboo tube and cooked over an open fire. Thais and Cambodians make a similar snack. More often sticky rice, cooked with coconut milk and sugar and formed into logs, squares, and other shapes, is steamed in banana, lotus, and other leaves. Filipino *suman* are a large subset of steamed sticky rice dumplings, both sweetened and plain but eaten with sweet accompaniments. In northern Thailand, banana-leaf-wrapped sticky rice logs enclose a variety of banana that turns pink when cooked and tastes like strawberries; in Malaysia, banana-leaf-wrapped triangles of sweetened coconut sticky rice are crowned with a point of grated coconut cooked with pandan leaf and palm sugar. See PALM SUGAR and PANDANUS. The Malaysian Nyonya specialty *rempah udang*, banana-wrapped and steamed sticky rice logs filled with coconut and palm sugar, get a savory kick from dried prawns and a bit of ground chili.

Of all dough-based sticky rice sweets, Japan's mochi—pounded sticky rice cakes traditionally filled with azuki bean paste (but these days hiding everything from green-tea-flavored pastry cream to ice cream)—are probably the most widely known around the world. See MOCHI. Mochi's Chinese equivalent is *zi ba*, plain or filled sticky rice confections that may or may not be rolled in sweetened soybean or peanut powder. *Migu* are Taiwan's version of *zi ba*, filled with sweet bean paste and colored red for religious offerings. The Nyonya of Malaysia and Singapore make a similar sticky rice sweet filled with mung bean paste called *angkoo*. Asia's spherical sticky rice dumplings include China's *tang yuan*, filled with ground sesame or peanuts and floating in warm, sometimes ginger-flavored sugar syrup; and Malaysian *onde-onde*, which are colored green with pandan juice, coated with grated coconut, and filled with semiliquid palm sugar.

See also CHINA; INDIA; JAPAN; PHILIPPINES; SOUTHEAST ASIA; and THAILAND.

Phillips, Carolyn. *All Under Heaven: Recipes from the 35 Cuisines of China*. San Francisco: McSweeney's, September 2015.

Schiller, J. M., M. B. Chanphengay, B. Linquist, and S. Appa Rao, eds. *Rice in Laos*. Los Baños, The Philippines: International Rice Research Institute, 2006.

Robyn Eckhardt

sticky toffee pudding is a light, baked sponge studded with chopped dates and topped with a butterscotch sauce. See DATES and BUTTERSCOTCH. It was made popular in Britain after it became a standby on the menu of the Sharrow Bay Country House hotel in Ullswater, Cumbria, in the early 1970s. Coincidentally, there was a rising affection for traditional puddings and desserts among the British dining classes, which was stimulated and encouraged by restaurant kitchens (which were more prepared to do the work than were private cooks). The two most significant examples of this tendency were sticky toffee pudding and Banoffee pie (a tart of caramelized condensed milk with sliced banana and an instant-coffee-cream topping) created by the Hungry Monk restaurant in Jevington, Sussex. Neither was traditional; both were excessively sweet.

While there is little doubt that Sharrow Bay's adoption of the dish contributed greatly to its popularity in Britain (the hotel was among the most celebrated of that era), whether the chef and co-proprietor Francis Coulson (1919–1998) actually invented the recipe (as was claimed) is more debatable. Many have asserted otherwise. The most credible of these alternatives was admitted by Francis Coulson himself to the British chef and food writer Simon Hopkinson. Coulson had, in fact, taken the recipe from Mrs. Martin, a cook at the Old Rectory restaurant in Claughton, Lancashire (and it was first published by her in the *Good Food Guide Dinner Party Book* of 1971). She, in turn, had picked the recipe up from a friend in Canada (which may explain the muffin-like composition of the sponge batter).

See also DULCE DE LECHE; PUDDING; and UNITED KINGDOM.

Fawcett, Hilary, and Jeanne Strang. *The "Good Food Guide" Dinner Party Book*. London: Hodder & Stoughton, 1971.
Kent, Elizabeth. *Country Cuisine*. London: Sidgewick & Jackson, 1980.

Tom Jaine

Stohrer, Nicolas (1706–ca. 1781), was born to a modest family in Wissembourg, Alsace. He became an apprentice in the kitchen of King Stanisław of Poland, who had been exiled in Wissembourg, sometime around 1720. Stohrer then followed Stanisław's daughter Marie Leszczyńska to Versailles as her pâtissier in 1725, when she married King Louis XV. In 1730 he opened Pâtisserie Stohrer, now Paris's oldest pastry shop, at 51 Rue Montorgueil (then called Rue du Mont Orgueilleux).

The shop has long been associated with the classic French baba, a sweet, yeasty cake similar to a Gugelhupf, with a colorful mythology linking it to King Stanisław and Stohrer. See BABA AU RHUM and GUGELHUPF. Stohrer may have played some part in introducing the cake, common for centuries in the German-speaking world, to the French court of Louis XV. The baba is depicted in a wall mural of a sylph-like woman holding pastries, painted for the shop in 1864 by Paul Baudry.

Tourists still flock to Rue Montorgueil to sample the shop's various babas: one rum-soaked, another filled with pastry cream, a third with whipped cream. A saffron-tinted version is available by special order. Stohrer is also renowned for its old-fashioned *puits d'amour* (wells of love), tarts filled with caramelized vanilla cream that are popular for Valentine's Day; macarons; and *religieuse*, a confection of éclairs and cream that is meant to resemble a nun's habit.

See also MACARONS and VALENTINE'S DAY.

Krondl, Michael. *Sweet Invention: A History of Dessert*. Chicago: Chicago Review Press, 2011.

Elizabeth Field

stollen is Germany's most traditional Christmas cake. Its history encompasses the entire debate about the religious dietary rules, sins, and indulgences of medieval times. Looking at today's recipe heavy with butter, almonds, and dried fruit, it is hard to believe that stollen originated as a cake for the Advent period of fasting before Christmas. The cake's shape is meant to symbolize the infant Jesus wrapped in swaddling.

The first recorded mention of stollen dates back to 1329 in the city of Naumburg an der Saale, near Leipzig. Back then, strict Catholic regulations allowed the loaf to be made only from water, oats, and the local rapeseed oil. However, from the mid-fifteenth century on, dispensation from fasting laws in general became more common, since people were less and less inclined, for reasons of costs or taste, to replace butter or lard with local or imported oil. In the second edition of his *Traité des jeûnes de l'église* (1693), Père Louis Thomassin wrote that in 1475 Pope Sixtus IV authorized the use of butter in Germany, Hungary, and Bohemia during Advent for the next five years. However, most sources cite a dispensing *Butterbrief* or "butter letter" sent by Pope Innocent VIII to the duke of Saxony in 1491. This allowance was not exceptional but part of the regular sale of indulgences, which were often linked to the financing of building projects, including the construction of St. Peter's Basilica in Rome. Some historians believe that the papal letter simply gave official approval to a practice that was widespread anyway. Whatever the case, stollen developed into the now familiar treat rich with fruit and almonds and, in some modern industrial versions, overloaded with marzipan.

Although a regional variation, *Bremer Klaben*, is popular in northern Germany, the most famous recipe is undoubtedly the yeasted stollen from Dresden in Saxony, which was given a European Union Protected

Geographical Indication designation in 1996. It is traditionally made several weeks before Christmas to give it time to mature.

See also BREADS, SWEET and GERMANY.

Heinzelmann, Ursula. *Food Culture in Germany*. Newport, Conn.: Greenwood, 2008.

Ursula Heinzelmann

street food, ancient. Street food dominated the daily lives of the lower- and middle-income groups in ancient urban societies, such as those of Athens and Rome. Because the lower classes may have had no more than a sleeping space and certainly no kitchen, many of their daily food needs were met on the street, in the form of both sweet and savory pastries and other dough products. Honey boiled into syrup provided the sweetener for the many forms of deep-fried fritters that seem to have been common. See FRIED DOUGH and FRITTERS. One particular type (*encytum*) was pressed through a perforated bowl into hot oil and shaped into a spiral that was then smothered in honey, a technique still widely used in the Middle East today. *Globi* were round balls of semolina and cheese deep-fried in lard and covered in honey and poppy seed. Fritters like these are still found in many parts of the Mediterranean, from the *churros* of Spain and *struffoli* of Italy to the *loukoumades* of Greece.

It is quite certain that an early filo-like pastry, called *itria* in Greek and *tracta* in Latin, was utilized in ancient societies, and although no direct archaeological or literary evidence exists, it is almost certain that parcels or pies with both sweet and savory fillings were made and sold on the street. We know that deep-fried pastries called *enkrides* were sold on the streets of Athens because Aristophanes refers to "enkrides vendors" (*Danaids* Fr 269), and a character in *Small Change*, a play written by Pherecrates in the mid-fifth century B.C.E., is accused of snatching them hot from the stall! In Rome, food stalls called *popinae* were allowed to sell all manner of sweet and savory (vegetarian) snacks but were prevented, it seems, from selling meat products by the Emperor Nero.

Honey was also boiled down into toffee and mixed with nuts, fruit, and sesame seeds to make brittle or soft toffee-like sweets known as *gastris* in Greece. See BRITTLE; GASTRIS; and TOFFEE. There were also thin and crisp biscuits called *itrion and lagana*, made either of flour or crushed sesame. The hard biscuit (in its original "twice-baked" context) also has a parallel in ancient food; *dipyros*, from the Greek *di* meaning "twice" and *pyr* meaning "fire," was a product literally put to the fire twice. The *buccellatum* was a twice-baked small piece of bread used as a military ration on campaigns; something similar was quite likely consumed by the rest of the population, too. Both could be eaten only after soaking in wine or water. We also know that pancakes, both thick and thin, were eaten, and their shape is clearly suited to street eating. See PANCAKES. Although numerous references to cakes and sourdough-enriched breads are made in Greek drama, we have no information about them beyond the fact of their names. It is quite likely that they would have resembled simple forms of brioche.

See also ANCIENT WORLD; ATHENAEUS; FILO; GREECE; ITALY; and SPAIN.

Athenaeus. *The Deipnosophists*, 645e, 647f. Edited by S. D. Olson. Loeb Classic Library 235. Cambridge, Mass.: Harvard University Press, 2008.
Cato the Elder. *De Agricultura* 80, 79. Translated by W. D. Hooper; revised by H. Boyd Ash. Loeb Classical Library 283. Cambridge, Mass.: Harvard University Press, 1935.
Dalby, Andrew. *Food in the Ancient World*, pp. 53–54, 251. London: Routledge, 2003.
Grant, Mark. *Roman Cookery: Ancient Recipes for a Modern Kitchen*. London: Serif, 2008.
Grocock, Christopher, and Sally Grainger. *Apicius*, pp. 25, 253. Totnes, U.K.: Prospect, 2006. A critical edition with an introduction and English translation of the Latin recipe text.

Sally Grainger

streusel (from a German word meaning "to strew" or "to scatter") is a popular, easy-to-make, sweet crumbly topping for many kinds of baked goods and desserts. The basic ingredients are flour, sugar, and fat, which are combined to form a dry, somewhat lumpy mixture that is usually sprinkled in an even layer on top of a cake batter or yeast dough before baking. In a few modern recipes the flour is replaced by Bisquick (a commercial baking mix of flour, baking powder, salt, and oil), Grape-Nuts cereal, or raw rolled oats. Granulated white sugar is the most common sweetener, but brown sugar and confectioner's sugar are also used. The fat is usually cold butter, although some recipes use melted butter, vegetable oil, or vegetable shortening. Additional ingredients can include breadcrumbs, chopped nuts, poppy seeds, grated orange and lemon zest, cocoa powder, nut extracts, and spices such as cinnamon, nutmeg, cloves, ginger, allspice, vanilla, and salt. Occasionally a beaten egg is added to help hold the dry mixture together.

When baked, the streusel mixture forms a slightly crunchy, light- to golden-brown topping. Usually baked on top of sheet cakes, coffee cakes, and sweet breads, streusel can also be a topping for muffins, pancakes, shortbreads, cookies, cheesecakes, and French toast. Sometimes it is marbled through the batter for cakes and quick breads. Streusel is the classic topping for shoo-fly pie, and it can form the top crust of pumpkin pies, fruit pies, and tarts, as well as baked fruit puddings and fruit "crumbles." Baked on its own, crisp streusel is also used as a filling between cake layers, and it is sometimes crumbled over ice cream, puddings, mousses, and yogurt.

Streusel is especially popular in Central European cooking, where it probably originated, with German *Streuselkuchen* (streusel cake) the most traditional recipe.

See also COFFEE CAKE; FRUIT DESSERTS, BAKED; and GERMANY.

Bloom, Carole. *The International Dictionary of Desserts, Pastries, and Confections*. New York: Hearst, 1995.

Krümel, Streusel & Brötchen Kuchen. Bielefeld, Germany: Dr. Oetker Verlag, 2005.

Sharon Hudgins

strudel is a Central European pastry made by rolling paper-thin dough around a fruit filling with the aid of a cloth. The filling is frequently but not exclusively made from apples. The dough is an *ausgezogener Strudelteig* made from wheat flour, warm water, and oil, which is stretched in a manner similar to pizza dough to make it as thin and translucent as possible. It is impressive to see bakers in the several lands contiguous to the Danube stretching the dough. For those who are not adept, commercially available filo pastry or even puff pastry can be used. See FILO and PASTRY, PUFF. Although strudel's origins are often thought to be oriental, there is evidence from as early as the fourteenth century of a Hungarian pastry layered with very thin dough. This derivation is also suggested by Marx Rumpolt's *Ein new Kochbuch* (1581), which offers a recipe for a "Hungarian Turte" that consists of 20 or 30 sheets of pastry made from flour and water, "thin as a veil," each spread with butter or lard and placed over an apple filling. See TORTE. The first extant recipe for an Austrian curd-cheese strudel is to be found in the manuscript "Koch Puech" from 1696, now in the State Library in Vienna. This *Milchrahm* or *Topfenstrudel* is still a popular alternative to apple strudel today. Cherries, pears, and poppy seeds are other favorite fillings; there are also savory versions (particularly in Burgenland) filled with beans, cabbage, potatoes, or black pudding. Savory strudels are more likely to use potato flour than wheat flour. One of the most popular apple strudels in Vienna is made at Café Korb in the Brandstätte. The filling combines cooking apples, breadcrumbs fried in butter, raisins soaked in lemon juice, sugar, and cinnamon. Others recipes replace the raisins with walnuts.

See also AUSTRIA-HUNGARY; CAFÉ; and MIDDLE EAST.

Maier-Bruck, Franz. *Das große Sacher-Kochbuch*. Munich: Schuler Verlag, 1975. See pp. 491–494.

Giles MacDonogh

sub-Saharan Africa has never been known globally for its sweets. Meals traditionally include a filling starch served with a relish, sauce, stew, or soup. Ending meals with a dessert is still largely considered superfluous. One or two main meals a day are supplemented by snacking on fruits, nuts, and seeds, or on starchy foods like plantain or corn that have been roasted, boiled, or fried.

Honey

Initially, honey, berries, and other fruits were the main sources of sweetness in sub-Saharan Africa. See HONEY. The honeybee likely originated in Africa, and honey has always been prized; it is used medicinally as well as for food. In many places honey is still a part of the bride price a man provides to his future in-laws. Besides being consumed raw, honey is used to coat fruit and nuts and as the base for drinks such as Ethiopia's alcoholic *tej* or nonalcoholic *birz*. It is also added to beverages and made into candy.

Refined Sugar

Today, refined sugar has replaced honey in urban areas. Sugarcane was introduced to sub-Saharan

Africa by Asian and Arab traders, who brought it in the 640s, along with production know-how, to the Mediterranean and Middle East. Between the seventh and tenth centuries, Arabs and Islamic expansion helped carry sugarcane southward along the Swahili Coast of eastern Africa as far as Zanzibar. Portuguese explorers carried sugarcane to Africa's northwest coast, where it arrived in West Africa in the fifteenth century. See SUGARCANE.

Ironically, although enslaved West and Central Africans provided most of the labor on sugarcane plantations in the New World, sugarcane cultivation was not initially significant in sub-Saharan Africa. See PLANTATIONS, SUGAR. Throughout the twentieth century, heavy investment in sugarcane or beet sugar plantations and refineries in places like Sudan and southern Africa encouraged the development of a "sweet tooth." Immigrants and traders also helped broaden the defining ingredients of some sub-Saharan African cuisines to make a modest place for sugary foods.

In the fifteenth through twentieth centuries, European colonial administrators, traders, teachers, and missionaries, as well as new immigrant populations, imported elite and high-status foods into sub-Saharan Africa. These included desserts made with imported ingredients like wheat flour, tinned milk, sugar, and butter. In the twentieth and early twenty-first centuries, as urbanization and industrialization spread, sugar became increasingly accessible. Today, as a preference among urban populations for sweet drinks, snacks, and frozen treats continues to grow, sub-Saharan Africa is a growing and eagerly sought-after market by both domestic and international sugar and sweets producers. Sweets are both consumed as snacks and shared on special occasions like birthdays or holidays.

Flavors, Popular Sweets, and Ingredients

Some common elements to traditionally popular sweets can be identified, such as a preference for fresh tropical fruits. Fruits also flavor desserts like fruit salads, fritters, cakes, and puddings. Fresh peeled sugarcane is chewed as a treat.

Fried doughnuts, dropped, twisted, or rolled and cut, are beloved in the region. See DOUGHNUTS. They are flavored with different spices and ingredients, such as coconut milk, cardamom, cinnamon, nutmeg, sugar, orange, and vanilla, and go by many names: *maandazi, koeksisters, puff puff, togbei, mikaté, gbofloto, botokoin, malasadas,* and *mofo baolina.* Leavening agents include yeast, baking powder, baobab powder, palm wine, and beer.

Candies often combine ingredients such as peanuts, sesame, or coconut with sugar or honey, sometimes including a starch. Eastern Africa has *kashata na nazi* (coconut and peanut candy); Ghana has groundnut, coconut, or sesame (benne) "cakes," which are similar in texture to peanut brittle. Sugar is melted in liquid, cooked without stirring, combined with crushed peanuts (or freshly grated coconut meat, or sesame seeds), pressed into a pan to harden, or shaped into balls or cones. For Sierra Leone's *kanya,* peanuts are pounded into a paste, mixed with sugar or honey and browned pounded rice or rice flour, then rolled out and cut into shapes.

Fresh ginger is a popular seasoning. In Ghana overripe plantains are pounded and combined with ginger, chili pepper, red palm oil, and other seasonings to create a rich, sweet-spicy baked loaf known as *ofam. Tombi* (Mende for "tamarind") is a Sierra Leonean treat combining sugar, chili pepper, tamarind, and seasoning cubes, thus blending sweet, spicy, savory, and salty tastes.

Areas with dairy products use yogurt or milk or cream in puddings, fools, custards, and dessert porridges, which often include fruits such as mango or papaya, eggs, coconut, and sugar. Senegal's *ngalakh* is made from millet or wheat couscous, milk, yogurt, juice from the fruit of the baobab tree, peanut butter, sugar, and other seasonings. Sub-Saharan Africa's *caakiri* is a pudding originally made with fonio or millet, but now commonly prepared from wheat-based couscous. Sometimes toffees are made from canned sweetened condensed milk. See TOFFEE. Desserts are also made with nondairy ingredients, such as Ghana's tiger nut pudding, made from chufa tubers and rice ground together.

In places like South Africa, with a significant number of European, Indian, or Asian immigrants, preserves, conserves, pastries, puddings, and other sweet preparations abound.

Sweetened beverages, including thin drinkable porridges, are popular throughout sub-Saharan Africa. These include beloved ginger juice or beer; hibiscus, tamarind, or baobab drinks; other juices and drinks made from fruit or corn; bottled non-alcoholic malted beverages (e.g., Nestle's Milo or Guinness's Malta); and soft drinks such as Coca-Cola, Fanta, and Sprite.

Teas and coffee are often sweetened. A popular instant porridge or beverage in South Africa called Morvite is sorghum-based. Sweetened beverages are sometimes frozen and sold as icy treats.

In parts of West Africa, especially Ghana and Nigeria, sweetness is sometimes simulated by chewing the fresh, red, grape-sized berries of the indigenous plant *Synsepalum dulcificum*, whose juice coats the tongue for about an hour and tricks the brain into thinking sour or bitter foods are sweet. See MIRACLE BERRY.

See also BENNE SEED WAFERS and HORCHATA.

Dinham, Barbara, and Colin Hines. "Sugar." In *Agribusiness in Africa*, pp. 71–90. London: Earth Resources Research, 1983.
Harris, Jessica B. "Desserts: Makroud and Mangoes." In *The Africa Cookbbook: Tastes of a Continent*, pp. 295–354. New York: Simon & Schuster, 1998.
Himes, Douglas. The Congo Cookbook. http://www.congocookbook.com/ (accessed 30 September 2013.
Osseo-Asare, Fran. *Food Culture in Sub-Saharan Africa.* Westport, Conn.: Greenwood, 2005.
Ponting, Clive. *World History: A New Perspective.* London: Chatto & Windus, 2000.

Fran Osseo-Asare

Sucanat, a word derived from the French *sucre de canne naturel* (natural cane sugar), is an expensive and flavorful cane sugar that retains most of its original minerals. It was the first product of Pronatec AG, a company established in Switzerland in 1976 by Albert Yersin. Yersin had been influenced by Max-Henri Béguin (1918–2000), a Swiss pediatrician and pacifist who promoted organic, unprocessed foods.

Early advertising in the United States claimed that Sucanat "has more calcium than broccoli; more Vitamin A than Brussels sprouts; more iron than raisins; more potassium than potatoes; and about the same Vitamin C as fresh tangerines." But, following a complaint by the Center for Science in the Public Interest, the National Advertising Division of the Council of Better Business Bureaus prodded Pronatec to tone down its rhetoric.

Nevertheless, Pronatec still claims that Sucanat is "the world's first organic whole cane sugar," made by "evaporating organically grown 100 percent cane juice." The company does not, however, explain how Sucanat differs from traditional raw sugar, or how the method used to evaporate the water from Sucanat differs from that used elsewhere. See SUGAR. Because the cane for Sucanat is grown under "Fair Trade" conditions in Costa Rica, and the sugar itself is labeled "organic," Sucanat appeals to a demographic of affluent consumers. Ethical vegetarians like the fact that no animal charcoal (bone black) is used in its processing.

Deborah Jean Warner

sucket fork is a utensil for eating sweetmeats that was used in the sixteenth, seventeenth, and early eighteenth centuries, with fork tines at one end and sometimes a spoon bowl at the other end of a common stem.

Sucket forks have an ancient history as a method of spearing and consuming sticky delicacies—succade—and are recorded at least a century and a half before table forks became widely adopted for eating savory foods. Smaller and more delicate in form than the typical late-seventeenth-century place setting (*couvert*) of knife, fork, and spoon, sucket forks were gradually replaced by sets of gilded sweetmeat knives, forks, and spoons. The design of these new tools for dessert matched the main course flatware, although they were smaller and more decorative. Late-seventeenth-century examples are often engraved.

The decline of the sucket fork was largely due to a switch in the ingredients of desserts. From the mid-seventeenth century on, sugar-based sticky

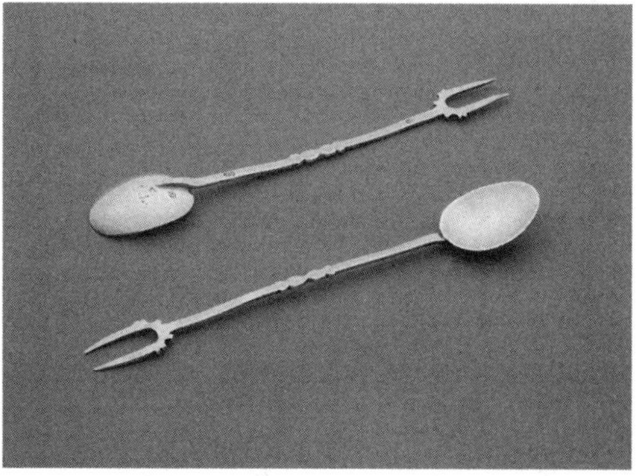

Sucket forks, with tines on one end and often a spoon bowl on the other, were used to spear and consume sticky delicacies, or succade. They are recorded at least a century and a half before table forks became widely adopted for savory foods. This pair of silver sucket forks was made in Boston in 1677 by William Rouse. MUSEUM OF FINE ARTS, BOSTON. GIFT OF JOHN AND MARY COOLIDGE candied fruit or ginger gave way to fresh fruit and flavored creams, and finally to ice cream, each of which called for a different type of tool. See CANDIED FRUIT and ICE CREAM. Delicate pastry and meringues, popular in the eighteenth century, also required distinctive implements. See MERINGUE.

Although most surviving sucket forks are made of silver, examples are known with agate or rock crystal, or even enamel, handles. At the New Year celebration in 1587, Queen Elizabeth was given a little gold fork and spoon, trimmed with coral and diamonds, which was a very grand set for eating succade.

See also SERVERS, ICE CREAM; SERVING PIECES; and SUCKETS.

Coffin, Sarah D., et al. *Feeding Desire: Design and the Tools of the Table, 1500–2005*. New York: Cooper-Hewitt National Design Museum/Assouline, 2006.

Philippa Glanville

suckets were forerunners of modern candied and sugar-preserved fruits. The English term "sucket" (from the French *succade*, and Italian *succata*) was first used for candied peels of citrus fruits. See CANDIED FRUIT. From the mid-sixteenth century on, the term had a wider meaning—almost anything could be made into suckets—not only pieces of fruits but also vegetables, roots, and nuts. A recipe from the *Good Huswives Jewell* (1597) mentions lemons, oranges, peaches, apples, and green walnuts. Pears and plums, stalks from angelica and marshmallow plants, roots from alisanders, borage, elecampane, sea holly, fennel, and ginger could also be used.

There were two principal types of suckets: wet and dry. Wet suckets were first cooked in a sugary liquid and then stored in jars, covered with the cooking syrup. Dry suckets were cooked until the sugary solution was incorporated into them; then they were dried (in fresh air, in an oven, or near the fire) and sometimes rolled in additional sugar. The recipe for dry suckets in *The Arte of Perseruing, Delightes for Ladies* (1609) is easy: orange peels are first boiled in sugared rosewater and then dried in an oven.

Similar recipes have survived from previous centuries. In the Middle Ages, dried, candied, glazed, and sugar-preserved fruits and pieces of ginger were already popular. Regularly enjoyed at the beginning, during, and at the end of meals in wealthy households, they were also used to flavor various sweet bakery products, pancakes, crepes, and cakes. *Le ménagier de Paris* from the late fourteenth century contains a recipe for "Orengat": in a nine-day process, orange peels are first cooked in water and then in honey and finally stored for a month before eating. An Italian recipe collection (*Liber per Cuoco*) from the same period records a method for preparing "Ranciata": the orange peels are first soaked for two weeks, then boiled in water, next dried for three days, then boiled in honey and spices, and finally left to air-dry for several days.

Because storing fresh fruit was difficult in the past, fruits were often processed in one way or another. Medical experts thought that fresh, unprocessed fruits were hard to digest and potentially detrimental to the human body. Sugar and honey were believed to neutralize harmful properties in fruits, and so methods such as poaching fruit in a sugar-sweetened solution and making jams were highly recommended. See FRUIT PRESERVES and MEDICINAL USES OF SUGAR.

A special "sucket fork" was developed after the Middle Ages. Usually made of silver, the small utensil had a two- or three-pronged fork at one end for picking up fruit from syrup, and a spoon bowl at the other, for conveying the syrup to the mouth. See SUCKET FORK.

The word "sucket" went out of use after the early modern period, but dry and wet sugar-preserved fruits continued to be made, and eighteenth-century cookery books contain numerous recipes for them, usually under the titles of "preserves" and "conserves." Today, the tradition of old-fashioned, heavily sugared wet suckets lives on in ginger-root preserves.

See also FRUIT and HONEY.

Paston-Williams, Sara. *The Art of Dining: A History of Cooking and Eating*. London: The National Trust, 1993.

Redon, Odile, Françoise Sabban, and Silvano Serventi. *The Medieval Kitchen: Recipes from France and Italy*. Translated by Edward Schneider. Chicago: University of Chicago Press, 1998.

Hannele Klemettilä

sucrose

See SUGAR.

sugar, as it is commonly understood, is simply sucrose, even if food chemists recognize many other sorts of sugars, including fructose (fruit sugar), lactose (milk sugar), maltose (malt sugar), and dextrose (corn sugar), to name some the most common types. While many of these sugars are widely used in the food industry, home cooks and pastry chefs depend on cane- or beet-derived sugar for flavoring almost all of their recipes.

Sugar is widely used to sweeten both desserts and candy, but it is also used to add a sweet note to many savory foods. Its chemical characteristics allow it to be dissolved, melted, caramelized, and turned into a multitude of candy textures, from barely chewy to hard and brittle. In dessert making, sugar affects moisture retention, texture, browning, and freezing, as well as taste. In many cases the lack of any discernable taste other than sweet is desirable, since refined sugar does not mask other flavors. Nevertheless, partially refined sugars can offer a panoply of other tastes, including butterscotch, toffee, caramel, wine, molasses, spice, and even bitterness. Understanding the different types and textures of sugar, and how best to use them, can add complexity, drama, and flair to cooking as well as to candy making and baking.

Sugar Production

The sucrose molecule is a disaccharide consisting of the monosaccharides glucose and fructose. See FRUCTOSE and GLUCOSE. In general it is crystalline in form, though when a controlled amount of acid is added, sugar will partially break down into its constituent parts, resulting in a syrup, or "invert sugar." Sucrose can be extracted from many plants, including certain varieties of palms, maple trees, and sorghum, but the overwhelming majority (about 75 percent in 2003) of the world's sugar comes from sugarcane, with sugar beets making up almost all the remainder. See SORGHUM SYRUP; SUGAR BEET; and SUGARCANE.

Sugarcane was first converted to a solid form in India as early as the sixth century B.C.E. Originally the cane juice was simply boiled to remove the water, resulting in a semi-crystalline raw sugar now called jaggery. By 500 B.C.E., documents mention granular, more highly refined crystals called *sarkara*, from which Indo-European languages derive the many variants of the word "sugar."

Today, the milling process begins with harvesting the raw product. The cane or beets are shredded and pressed to remove the juices, then boiled in large steam evaporators. Eventually sugar crystals precipitate out of the syrup and are separated in a centrifuge. This process is repeated several times, with the sugar retaining more molasses each time. Often this darker sugar is reprocessed, so that eventually all the crystals, referred to as raw sugar, are 97 to 99 percent pure sucrose; the centrifuged liquid is molasses. In some cases, not all of the molasses is spun off, resulting in naturally brown sugars of varying intensities. Most raw sugar is refined further by dissolving it once again in water, chemically precipitating out any remaining impurities, then bleaching, filtering, and recrystallizing it, producing a substance that is 99.8 percent or more sucrose. See SUGAR REFINING. Although there are numerous culinary uses for this virtually pure refined sugar—such as in meringues, fondants, and syrups—the less-refined varieties, due to their more complex flavor, are often a better choice in many recipes ranging from cakes to stews. Also, in addition to removing impurities and color, the refining process can at times produce an undesirable element of slight bitterness not present in sugar that still retains a trace amount of natural molasses.

Refined Sugar

Once sugar has been refined, it is passed through sieves with a specific hole size that determines the largest grain in any given batch. Some sugars are also sieved to remove smaller crystals. All refined sugar has equal sweetening power (by weight), regardless of the degree of granulation. The one exception is confectioner's sugar, because it contains a modicum of starch.

Loaf or *cube sugar* is granulated sugar that has been pressed into molds while still moist. It is subsequently dried to retain its shape. Most sugar was sold in this form prior to the late nineteenth century; consequently, old recipes sometimes call for it. See SUGAR CUBES.

Rock sugar or *rock candy* is a confection of transparent colorless or amber crystals, sometimes sold on a string or as swizzle sticks for stirring coffee or tea.

Medium coarse, coarse pearl sugar, or *sanding sugar* consists of crystals approximately 600 to 800μm (microns) in size. It is sometimes referred to as "strong" sugar because large-grained sugars are usually crystalized from the highest-purity sugar solutions; consequently, this sugar resists color changes and inversion, making it ideal for preparing caramel, as well as for other uses in which a confectioner needs to avoid crystallization. The large granules, sometimes tinted, can also be sprinkled on finished baked goods, such as cookies, to give them a sparkling appearance.

Regular granulated or *fine granulated* (<1200µm) is the all-purpose sugar found in most sugar bowls and supermarkets. It is often not sifted, resulting in a wide range of crystal sizes. Regular granulated sugar is suitable for making syrups, but for most other baking a smaller crystal size is preferable.

Extra-fine sugar (200–600µm) is also called *fruit sugar* because it is used in fruit preserves. See FRUIT PRESERVES. Many professional bakers like to use it as their all-purpose sugar when baker's special (see below) is unavailable. When used in cakes, it yields a fine crumb and lighter texture because its smaller crystals provide more surface area to trap air. This is especially the case when creaming together sugar and fat. Cookies made with extra-fine sugar are smoother and have fewer cracks. A more finely granulated sugar also dissolves more readily, resulting in lighter, more delicate meringues. See MERINGUE.

Baker's special splits the difference between extra-fine and superfine, making it the perfect compromise for just about all baking. Home bakers can approximate it by grinding a coarser sugar in a food processor for a few minutes, even though the crystals won't be as uniform as the commercially processed version. British "caster sugar" is similar.

Superfine, or *ultrafine* (<500µm) refers to the finest granulation of sugar. It is sometimes called *bar sugar* because bartenders use it to make drinks that require fast-dissolving sugar. Its ability to dissolve quickly also makes it ideal for meringues and cake fillings.

Powdered, confectioner's, or *icing sugar* (<250µm) is made by crushing granulated sugar into powder. In the process, the sugar loses its granular shape, making it more hydrophilic. To prevent it from becoming lumpy, an anticaking agent is added; in the United States about 3 percent cornstarch is typical. The starch adds what is perceived as a floury taste and makes powdered sugar less suitable than granulated sugar for use with ingredients that are not to be cooked. Powdered sugar comes in various particle sizes, the most common being (in increasing fineness) 4X, 6X, and 10X, although 3X, 12X, and 14X also exist.

Nonmelting powdered sugar is coated with a fat to prevent it from melting when sprinkled on top of cakes or fruit. It gives off a slight, unpleasant mouth-coating sensation.

Vanilla sugar is made by flavoring granulated sugar with vanilla. In Europe it is widely used instead of vanilla extract. To make vanilla sugar at home, bury two to three vanilla beans in a pound of sugar, cover and let stand for at least one week. See VANILLA.

Brown Sugar

Before the invention of centrifuges, molasses was removed from sugar crystals by packing them into inverted cones and allowing the molasses to drip out the bottom. See MOLASSES. The color within these sugar cones would range from pale golden to brown, depending on the residual molasses. Different names came to be assigned to these different colored sugars, most originating with the Portuguese or Dutch, pioneers of the transatlantic sugar trade. See SUGAR TRADE. Today, the color of centrifuged sugar varies, depending on whether it is from the first, second, or third crystallization. However, the great majority of brown sugar is not made this way; instead, a small amount of molasses (and sometimes coloring) is added to partially or even fully refined sucrose. Home cooks can approximate the process by adding 3.5 percent molasses to white sugar to make light brown sugar, and 6.5 percent for dark brown. Recipes that call for brown sugar usually require the light version, unless otherwise specified. By volume, brown sugar has the same sweetening power as white sugar, but it weighs more due to the additional molasses. The added molasses also adds some moisture.

Because brown sugars derived from sugarcane and beets are made somewhat differently, there is a difference in taste and appeal. The former is made with partially refined sugar that retains some of its natural molasses. Since sugar-beet molasses is not fit for human consumption, brown sugar from beets is made with fully refined sugar to which either sorghum or cane molasses is added to achieve the requisite flavor and color. As a result, the molasses merely coats the grains. A simple test to determine if the sugar has only been coated is to stir a spoonful into a glass of water. After just a few minutes, the water in the beet sugar will turn a pale brown and the sugar crystals will be clear. With partially refined cane sugar that still contains its natural molasses, the water will remain clearer and the sugar crystals remain somewhat brown.

Sugar that still contains some of its molasses and isn't clarified is often referred to as "unrefined," which is not to say it hasn't undergone a great deal of initial processing necessary to obtain crystals (boiling, centrifuging, and washing). Unlike refined, virtually pure white sugar, and even commercially produced brown sugars, batches of "unrefined" sugars may vary in color, flavor, and intensity.

Turbinado (from the Portuguese *turbinar*, "to spin") mostly comes from the first batch of sugar to be crystalized and centrifuged. The sugar is washed to remove the surface molasses. Turbinado ranges from pale golden to a richer amber and retains a pleasant trace of molasses flavor. Sugar marketed as raw sugar can be turbinado or demerara. This same "raw" sugar is also made into cubes or crystals intended for sweetening hot beverages. Although turbinado sugar closely resembles refined white sugar in sweetening ability and composition, it can't always be substituted for it in recipes because of the presence of impurities and a slightly higher moisture content. In the United Kingdom, finely granulated turbinado is referred to as "golden caster sugar."

Demerara, named after a region of Guyana where the Dutch used to raise sugarcane, is a somewhat darker crystalline sugar that may come from the first or second centrifuge, depending on the producer. French *cassonade* is typically demerara, although other brown sugars are also occasionally called by this name.

Muscovado (from the sixteenth-century Portuguese *mascavado*, or "unrefined") is generally a moist brown sugar produced in the second or third crystallization. Light muscovado has approximately the same molasses flavor as North American dark brown sugar, while dark muscovado is a little more intense and complex in flavor than dark brown sugar. In the United Kingdom, a *molasses sugar* is also sold that has an even greater molasses concentration. It is best used in gingerbread, fruitcakes, mincemeat, and barbecue sauces to add extra moisture or stickiness and flavor. See FRUITCAKE; GINGERBREAD; and MINCE PIES.

Jaggery (derived from the Sanskrit *sarkara* by way of the Portuguese) is simply cane juice boiled down to the point where it will harden. It is widely used throughout South Asia to flavor sweet and savory dishes. Jaggery has a rich, earthy, and almost mineral taste. A similar product is made in Latin America under the name of *panela* (*pilloncillo* in Mexico and *rapadura* in Brazil). Jaggery can also be made from certain palm saps.

Wasanbon is an artisanally produced Japanese unrefined sugar made from a variety of locally grown sugarcane called *chikuto*. The processing is still done by hand and involves a multiday procedure in which the cane syrup is boiled down, the sugar crystals are kneaded several times, and the resulting sugar is drained in wooden tubs weighed down with stones. Wasanbon is highly sought after by local confectioners. See WASANBON.

Sugar from Other Sources

Palm sugar is made from either the sap or flower bud nectar of several palm tree varieties, including the palmyra, toddy, coconut, and nipa palms. The sweet liquid is boiled down to a thick fudge consistency and used widely in both South and Southeast Asia in sweet and savory preparations. Palm sugar has a milder and somewhat more vegetal flavor than raw cane sugar. See PALM SUGAR.

Date sugar is produced from the sweet fruit of the date palm, which contains as much as 81 percent sucrose in its solids. It retains the date's mineral complexity. See DATES.

Maple sugar is made by boiling away virtually all the water from maple sap, resulting in a crystalline sugar that can be anywhere from 88 to 99 percent sucrose. It has a pleasing maple flavor and can be substituted pound for pound for raw cane sugar in most baked goods. See MAPLE SUGARING and MAPLE SYRUP.

Liquid Sugar

Cane syrup is made from partially evaporated cane juice, resulting in a dark syrup with a noticeable but not overwhelming molasses flavor. It is widely used in Louisiana in recipes that elsewhere might call for molasses or dark corn syrup. See CORN SYRUP.

Invert sugar syrup is made from regular refined sugar by chemically breaking apart the sucrose molecule into its constituent parts, fructose and glucose. It may be made commercially or as part of the candy-making process by adding an acid, such as cream of tartar, to a sugar syrup. The resulting liquid sugar is added to fondant creams, fudge, and other candies to ensure a smooth texture and discourage crystallization. See FONDANT and FUDGE. Because it is hydroscopic it ensures that chewy candies won't dry out or become overly brittle.

Refiner's syrup, called *golden syrup* in the United Kingdom, is made by combining sugar syrup and invert sugar syrup. The processing gives it a very mild caramel flavor, and the high ratio of monosaccharides makes it somewhat sweeter by weight than sugar. The syrup contains 15 to 18 percent water. In most recipes it can be used interchangeably with light corn syrup, offering a mellow, intriguing flavor. See GOLDEN SYRUP.

Molasses, traditionally the byproduct of sugar processing, is not only used for culinary purposes but also for animal feed and to make ethanol. Today, food-grade molasses, sometimes referred to as unsulfured, is generally made by boiling down sugarcane juice to about 80 percent Brix (20 percent water content). See BRIX. Consequently, it is sweet and complex in flavor, with notes of rum and earth. Blackstrap molasses, on the other hand, is the residual molasses spun off from the third sugar crystallization, which yields a darker, less sweet, and noticeably bitter syrup. Similar to molasses in both flavor and water content is the *black treacle* produced by British sugar refineries by repeatedly heating a molasses-rich, partially inverted sugar syrup. The syrup is valued by the British for baking and confectionery when rich flavor, dark color, and moist texture are required, as in gingerbread, fruitcakes, and licorice.

Making Sugar Syrups

Confectioners, bakers, and even mixologists use a wide variety of sugar syrups in their respective crafts. The sugar and water solution varies in concentration, depending on the use. Bartenders often use a "simple syrup" of one part sugar and one part water to flavor drinks. On the other hand, to make an Italian meringue or classic French buttercream, most of the water is boiled away to form a supersaturated sugar solution. As the density increases, the temperature of the solution rises. Confectioners can gauge the concentration by the temperature. Concentration can also be measured by density using a saccharimeter or the Baumé sugar weight scale. See SACCHARIMETER and STAGES OF SUGAR SYRUP.

Because supersaturated sugar solutions are unstable, the use of an "interfering agent" such as invert sugar (a little more than one-fourth the weight of the granulated sugar), butter, cream of tartar, or citric acid helps keep the solution stable by interfering with the crystallization. This technique is helpful when the syrup will be repeatedly dipped into, as when making spun sugar.

Caramel is made by cooking melted sugar to a temperature at which it begins to brown. At this point it begins to break down into complex compounds that contribute to a richer flavor; caramel is less sweet than white sugar and is pleasantly bitter. One-half cup sugar makes about a quarter cup of caramel (plus any residue that clings to the pot). If made in a nonstick pan and then pulverized, caramel returns to its approximate original volume.

General Uses of Sugar

Sugar, in one form or another, is utilized in just about every cuisine, not to mention its use in cosmetics, pharmaceuticals, and even energy production. See COSMETICS, SUGAR IN; PHARMACOLOGY; and SUGAR, UNUSUAL USES OF. In preparations both sweet and savory, its applications are manifold. Besides contributing to sweetness, viscosity, and body, sugar enhances the flavor, appearance, and texture of many foods.

How sugar affects texture in baking is especially apparent in cakes. In addition to facilitating the incorporation of air during the creaming of the sugar and the fat, sugar creates tenderness, because during baking it raises the temperature at which egg protein coagulates and starch granules gelatinize, allowing the gas cells to expand more before the batter has a chance to set. The result is a more open texture that weakens the cake's structure so that it melts faster in the mouth. However, even though a cake high in sugar is more tender—that is, it falls apart more easily—it won't have as soft a mouthfeel.

But cakes are just the beginning. In baked goods, sugar aids moisture retention; in custards, it raises the boiling point; and in frozen desserts, it lowers the freezing point. Sugar assists in the emulsification in chocolate, baked goods, and ice creams, and in fermentation in bread and beer. Sugar gives stability to beaten eggs. It delays staling in baked goods, discoloration in fresh fruit, and coagulation in egg cookery. It slows down mold growth in preserves and tenderizes baked goods by combining with the gluten-forming proteins in flour to reduce gluten formation. See FLOUR. Cooks find sugar handy for savory dishes, too. It brings out and softens the flavor of starch-containing vegetables like peas and carrots and lends them sheen; it moderates the acidity in foods like tomatoes and enhances the caramelization of the natural sugar present in onions.

Although there are many substitutes and alternatives to sugar, when it comes to baking, confectionery, and even cooking, sugar is a sweet wonder.

See also ARTIFICIAL SWEETENERS; CARAMELS; HARD CANDY; MEDICINAL USES OF SUGAR; PULLED SUGAR; POPPING SUGAR; SAP; STEVIA; and SERVERS, SUGAR.

Asadi, Mosen. *Beet-Sugar Handbook.* Hoboken, N.J.: Wiley-Interscience, 2007.

Belitz, H.-D., W. Grosch, and P. Schieberle. *Food Chemistry.* 4th rev. ed. Berlin: Springer, 2009.

Beranbaum, Rose Levy. "Rose's Sugar Bible." *Food Arts* (April 2000). http://foodarts.com/news/classics/20964/roses-sugar-bible (accessed 10 October 2014).

McGee, Harold. "Sugars, Chocolate, and Confectionery." In *On Food and Cooking: The Science and Lore of the Kitchen*, pp. 645–712. New York: Scribner, 2004.

Paul, Pauline C., and Helen H. Palmer. *Food Theory and Applications.* New York: Wiley, 1972.

Pennington, Neil L., and Charles W. Baker. *Sugar, a User's Guide to Sucrose.* New York: Van Nostrand Reinhold, 1990.

Rose Levy Beranbaum and Michael Krondl

sugar, biochemistry of. Sugar, to a chemist, refers not to a single compound, but to any one of a class of molecules called the saccharides. Many saccharides, though not all, taste sweet. Sucrose, common table sugar, is a crystalline white solid at room temperature. Its chemical formula is $C_{12}H_{22}O_{11}$ and its formal chemical name is α-D-glucopyranosyl-β-D-fructofuranoside. Sucrose is a disaccharide, comprising two simple sugars, glucose and fructose, linked through an oxygen atom. See GLUCOSE and FRUCTOSE. Glucose has five carbon atoms and a single oxygen atom arranged in a six-membered ring that is folded up like a lounge chair. Fructose is based on a not-quite planar five-membered ring, made up of four carbons and a single oxygen atom.

Sucrose is a naturally occurring chemical compound; in many plants it is the principal source of carbon used for growth. Table sugar is produced commercially by extracting and purifying sucrose from plant sources, particularly sugarcane and sugar beets. See SUGARCANE and SUGAR BEET. Like many biologically active molecules, sugars are chiral (from the Greek *kheir* [χειρ], for "hand"). Chiral objects cannot be superimposed on their mirror image, like a pair of hands. The biological activity of two mirror-image molecules can be quite different; spearmint oil is the exact mirror image of caraway oil, but it tastes and smells unmistakably different. Simple sugars have two types of chiral forms, D and L. Sucrose links a D form of glucose to a D form of fructose. Humans (and other terrestrial organisms) selectively metabolize the D forms of sugars. Since both the L and D forms of many simple sugars, including glucose and fructose, taste sweet, the L forms are essentially low-calorie versions of their mirror images.

In addition to its sweet taste, sucrose has a number of physical and chemical properties that make it particularly useful to cooks and bakers. It is hygroscopic: in solid form sucrose readily absorbs water from its surroundings. Water trapped by sucrose in baked goods helps makes them moist. Water also binds preferentially with the sucrose, preventing starches from swelling and producing an undesirably coarse texture. Unlike many other molecular compounds, pure table sugar doesn't melt at a precise temperature, but, fortunately for cooks, when table sugar is heated above 302°F (150°C) it undergoes a complex series of decomposition reactions that result in caramelization. See CARAMEL and STAGES OF SUGAR SYRUP. The decomposition process produces a rich array of compounds, including the buttery flavored molecule diacetyl, which contributes to the rummy, butterscotchy flavor characteristic of caramelized sucrose.

Sucrose is extraordinarily water soluble, due in part to the plethora of hydroxyl (OH) groups with which it is adorned. At room temperature, roughly 2 grams of table sugar will dissolve in 1 milliliter of water, and nearly 5 grams will dissolve in a milliliter of boiling water. By comparison, only about ⅓ of a gram of common table salt (sodium chloride) can be dissolved in a milliliter of room-temperature water. The ability to achieve such highly concentrated solutions makes sucrose a potent and inexpensive natural antimicrobial; simple syrup, a 1:1 table sugar to water solution, will kill *E. coli*. Bacteria that come into contact with such concentrated solutions undergo plasmolysis. The difference in osmotic pressure between the concentrated solution and the interior of the cell causes water to drain out of the cell's interior, leading the cell wall to degrade and collapse. Makers of jellies and jams capitalize on the resulting antimicrobial activity. Pure granulated sugar has even proved effective in treating severely infected wounds.

Table sugar that is wet, even slightly, is sticky. Adhesion, or stickiness, requires that a material be able to bind to another substance at the molecular level, but also that it be able to bind to itself, like links in a stretchy chain between two gateposts. Viscous materials that can flow into all the submicroscopic crevices of a substrate also tend to be sticky. They make contact with a larger surface area of the substrate, increasing friction. The forces between molecules in a sucrose-water mix are strong and do not depend heavily on the relative orientation of the molecules, making these solutions more likely to be viscoelastic—thick and stretchy—and hence sticky.

Metabolism of Sugar

The metabolism of sugars is a complex process that eventually produces energy to run the body—carbon dioxide and water, the same products that result from incinerating sugar at high temperatures. Sucrose is essentially a biological fuel.

When humans consume sugars, the sugars are rapidly broken down into monosaccharides—simple sugars such as glucose, fructose, and galactose. Acid secreted in the stomach can catalyze the breaking of the covalent bond between sugar units; sucrose is exceptionally susceptible to this cracking reaction. The resulting glucose and fructose, along with any remaining undigested sucrose, are passed to the small intestine, where enzymes complete the digestion. Each enzyme is targeted to break down a specific complex sugar. Lactase is the enzyme specific for the digestion of lactose, found in milk, into the simple sugars galactose and glucose, while sucrase plays the same role for table sugar. Molecular chaperones then actively escort individual glucose molecules across the intestinal membranes into the bloodstream, while fructose is left to diffuse through the membranes on its own, through a slower process.

Once glucose makes it to the bloodstream, about one-third of it is stored in the liver as glycogen, a polymerized form of glucose. Another third is stored in muscle cells, and the remainder is immediately metabolized by cells for fuel. Cells first pull glucose into their interiors. Once the glucose is inside, an elaborate cascade of enzyme-catalyzed reactions turns it into two 3-carbon fragments (pyruvates). In aerobic metabolism, driven by the presence of oxygen, the pyruvates are moved into the mitochondria, where the citric acid cycle (which may be more familiar as the Krebs cycle often memorized in high school biology) further degrades the pyruvates into carbon dioxide and water. Side products of the citric acid cycle also go on to play a role in the synthesis of amino acids, which are the building blocks of proteins. Carbon dioxide is returned via the bloodstream to the lungs, where it is disposed of into the atmosphere. Water is used ubiquitously throughout the body.

Fructose meets a similar fate to glucose, albeit by a different route. About 60 percent of the fructose eaten (from any source, including the pure fructose in fruits, or fructose that results from the digestion of more complex sugars, such as sucrose) is enzymatically converted to glucose, feeding into the glucose metabolic pathway. The bulk of the remaining fructose is broken down into the same simple 3-carbon pyruvate molecules as glucose, by a mechanism that is distinct from, but interlaced into, the glucose pathway.

The Sugar Rush

When the levels of circulating glucose begin to drop, the body signals for the reserves of glycogen to be converted back to glucose. Two small proteins, glucagon and insulin, have key roles in the regulation of this process, which works to keep the levels of glucose in the blood within a tight range around a concentration between 100 and 150 mg/dL, roughly equivalent to that of half a teaspoon of sugar dissolved in a liter of water. Within 30 minutes of consuming pure sucrose or glucose on an empty stomach, blood sugar levels rise to a peak, the so-called sugar rush. Over the next two to four hours, glucose levels will slowly fall back to their starting values, or even below, serving as one of many triggers for the complex behavior of hunger.

All along the way, this complicated ballet of small molecules and enormous enzymes produces energy, which is used to drive the cellular reactions that synthesize molecular structures and machinery, and to keep the body at a normal operating temperature.

The energy contained in the chemical bonds of glucose that are broken when it is metabolized is "stored" in a high-energy molecule, ATP (adenosine triphosphate). Cells can later draw on the energy stockpiled in ATP as they construct new molecules. The consumption of sugar charges our cellular batteries.

See also SUGAR; SUGAR REFINING; and SUGAR AND HEALTH.

Chirife, J., L. Herszage, A. Joseph, and E. S. Kohn. "In Vitro Study of Bacterial Growth Inhibition in Concentrated Sugar Solutions: Microbiological Basis for the Use of Sugar in Treating Infected Wounds." *Antimicrobial Agents and Chemotherapy* 23, no 5 (1983): 766–773.

Voet, Donald, Judith G. Voet, and Charlotte W. Pratt. *Fundamentals of Biochemistry*. New York: Wiley, 1999.

Wolever T. M., and J. B. Miller. "Sugars and Blood Glucose Control." *American Journal of Clinical Nutrition* 62, 1 suppl. (1995): 212S–227S.

Michelle M. Francl

sugar, unusual uses of, include applications ranging from medieval art to warfare to Hollywood special effects and 3-D printing. One of the more creative uses is to preserve waterlogged ancient timbers, and even leather, by soaking them in a 67 percent sugar solution. This preservation method, in which the high concentration of sugar effectively ties up the water so that it is unavailable to microorganisms, has been used in Eastern Europe for many years, and it was recently used in the United Kingdom to preserve the remains of three medieval bridges found near Leicester.

The sugar in our daily lives normally comes in crystalline form, with its molecules of linked glucose and fructose packed perfectly into tiny, sharp-edged boxes in a shape called "monoclinic hemihedral" by crystallographers. Even in this commonly found form it can have unusual uses, especially in times of war, because within the boxes lies a hidden power. Because sugar burns to produce a large volume of gas (carbon dioxide and water vapor), it can be used as a component of explosives when mixed with an oxidizing agent and ignited. It can also be tipped surreptitiously into the petrol tank of an enemy vehicle, where some of the crystals in a bouncing vehicle may be carried in suspension to the spark plug, melting in the heat of the spark to stop the plug firing, although this effect is apparently much rarer than urban legend would have it.

The most unusual uses of sugar, though, require it to be transformed from its crystalline form to a glassy state, in which the molecules are disorganized, the sharp edges disappear, and the material becomes clear, hard, smooth, and transparent. This transformation can be accomplished either by melting the sugar or by adding a little water, as teenage girls learned to do in the 1950s when they soaked their petticoats in concentrated sugar solutions and then allowed them to dry. Most of the water evaporated,

In 2014 the Sugar Lab, a Los Angeles micro-design firm, launched a unique 3D printing system for edibles. Sugar sculptures are created by applying a mixture of water and alcohol to a sugar substrate, which hardens on contact with moisture. THE SUGAR LAB

but in fact a tiny amount remained bound to the sugar, which maintained it in a glassy state that held the petticoats rigidly in shape.

Long before this, medieval monks used sugar in the glassy state to impart a gloss to their illuminated manuscripts. More recently, Pablo Picasso used it in the *sugar-lift* etching technique, in which the artist draws or paints directly on a copper plate with a thick sugar syrup to which black ink (and sometimes gum arabic) has been added. The plate is then allowed to dry. As with petticoats, some water remains bound to the sugar, setting it into a hard glassy state that retains the structure of the pen or brush marks. The plate is then covered with acid-resistant resin before being dipped in warm water, which removes the sugar to expose the areas where the artist has drawn, which can then be etched with acid.

Sugar in the glassy state has also found a use in Hollywood films, where its brittle nature and transparent appearance once made it an ideal substitute for window glass in stunts where an actor had to be defenestrated. Sugar has now been replaced for this purpose by synthetic resins such as Piccotex, which have the advantage of not gradually becoming cloudy in damp weather. Beer glasses made from glassy sugar are still available, however, and will actually hold beer for a limited time. They smash very satisfactorily when clinked together during comedy routines.

The most unusual use of glassy sugar must surely be as a substrate in three-dimensional printing, in which successive layers of material are used to build up a three-dimensional structure from a series of cross-sections, with the printing head moving in raster fashion to either lay down the material (via a syringe-like tip) or cut holes in it (via a focused laser beam, for example).

One of the earliest examples of 3-D printing using sugar was called CandyFab. In this method, a modified hot air gun is used as the printer head to melt different areas in successive layers of sugar crystals, with the unmelted sugar being cleared away between passes. In this way, complicated shapes such as a trefoil knot (i.e., a pretzel) could be constructed.

The CandyFab project stalled in 2009, but others have taken up the challenge. The Sugar Lab, a Los Angeles startup "micro-design firm" bought in 2013 by the printing giant 3D Systems, developed a system in which a syringe-like printing head applies precisely monitored mounts of an alcohol-water mixture to successive granular sugar layers, with the alcohol evaporating to leave just the right amount of water to convert the sugar to a glassy state. This technique allows even more elaborate shapes to be constructed than was possible with the CandyFab approach.

Both of the aforementioned projects are designed to produce unusual sugar confections, but 3-D printing with sugar has gone much further than that. It has even found application in the biomedical field to help build artificial organs such as livers. The technique, described in the September 2012 issue of *Nature*, uses 3-D printing to construct an interconnected network of glassy sugar fibers that mimics the network of blood vessels found in the real organ. Appropriate living cells are then allowed to grow on the fibers. Once the cells have filled the spaces between them, the sugar (actually a mixture of sucrose and one of its polymers called dextran) is dissolved away, leaving a network of vascular channels within the newly created "organ." It may thus transpire that the sugar we eat will also be used to create the organs that help us digest it.

Sugar is also an excellent nutrient for microorganisms. In this form it has recently found its way back into the world of fashion in the form of *biocouture*, where bacteria are allowed to grow and multiply as a tough skin on the surface of a weak nutrient broth of sugar in green tea. After several weeks the skin can be harvested, dried, cut, sewn, and dyed to produce a most unusual line of clothing. The places of sugar in our lives are indeed manifold.

"How to Make Sugar Glass." WikiHow. http://www.wikihow.com/Make-Sugar-Glass (accessed 10 October 2014).

Miller, Jordan S., Kelly R. Stevens, Michael T. Yang, et al. "Rapid Casting of Patterned Vascular Networks for Perfusable Engineered Three-Dimensional Tissues." *Nature Materials* 11 (September 2012): 768–774.

Weber, Urs M., and Kurt J. Rosenthaler. "Wet Archaeological Wood Treated with Sucrose: Preliminary Test Series." *Zeitschrift für Schweizerische Archäologie und Kunstgeschichte* 51, no. 1 (1994) 1–8.

Len Fisher

sugar and health have shared a connection from the earliest times. Originally considered the ultimate medicine to cure stomach ailments, fever, and the plague, sugar is now considered complicit

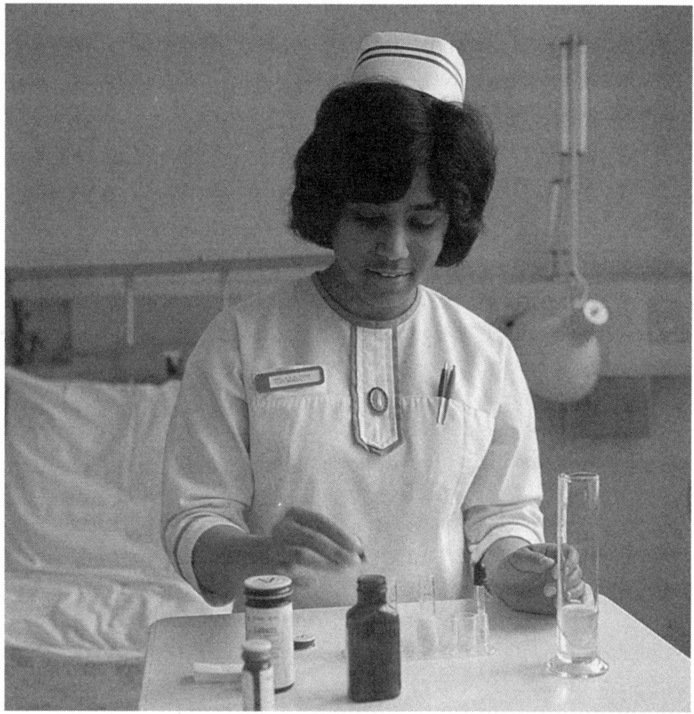

A nurse tests a patient's urine using dipsticks that change color according to the presence of sugar in the specimen. ANTHEA SIEVEKING, WELLCOME IMAGES

in many chronic diseases. As early as 500 B.C.E., North Indian Sanskrit texts documented the processes of extracting sugar from sugarcane, with accompanying information on the medicinal uses of sugar and recipes for fermented drinks and rice pudding. Later Greek and Roman writings cited India as the source of sugar in Hellenic and Roman cultures. The Roman physician Dioscorides (40–90 C.E.) wrote that sugar "has the consistence of salt" and was good for the stomach, bladder, and kidneys. See MEDICINAL USES OF SUGAR.

Between 600 and 800 C.E., the Indian sugarcane refining techniques began to spread toward China to the east and to the Mediterranean cultures to the west. The Venetians and the Genoese controlled the sugar trade northward into continental Europe. As sugar became available to wealthy Europeans in the eleventh and twelfth centuries, physicians began to prescribe it. The Arab medical scholar Constantinus Africanus (ca. 1020–1087 C.E.) prescribed sugar to quell a cough, relieve chapped lips, and cure stomach diseases, while the Byzantine emperor Manuel Comnenus (1143–1180) recommended it for breaking a fever. In the thirteenth century, the Dominican friar Albertus Magnus (ca. 1200–1280) mentioned sugar's humoral qualities as moist and warm, and therefore "good for the stomach." In the thirteenth to eighteenth centuries, the saying "like an apothecary without sugar," describing a state of desperation, speaks to the role that sugar played in medical practice: it healed, it was a common curative, and it was considered good for one's health.

Sugar in the Modern Age

In the sixteenth and seventeenth centuries, a few dissenting voices to the "sugar-as-nostrum" appeared, along with the spread of a new milling technique that eliminated the need to chop the sugarcane before pressing. The German physician Hieronymus Bock described sugar as "more an extravagance for the rich than as a remedy" (1539), and he and others noted sugar's reprobate role in tooth decay, especially among the wealthy. See DENTAL CARIES. By the mid-seventeenth century, European medical professionals had largely changed their position on sugar.

James Hart's *The Diet of Diseases* (London, 1633) described sugar as having dangerous effects on the body, causing hot blood, wasting, blackened teeth, and "a loathsome stinking breath." Although Dr. Frederick Slare considered sugar to have curative powers, he noted in 1715 in one of his *Experiments and Observations* publications that it was "very high a Nourisher" and may make women "fatter than they desire to be." Slare was one of the first physicians to link sugar to corpulence.

By the nineteenth century, sugar was no longer used as a pharmaceutical ingredient, and with the rise of commercial canning, it was consumed in ever-greater amounts as a preservative. The late nineteenth century saw the formal creation of the academic discipline of nutrition through newly established research laboratories and university departments of home economics and food chemistry. In the 1890s, the Seventh-day Adventist John Harvey Kellogg advocated for abstention from sugar as part of his regimen against "Americanitis," his term for the national dyspepsia. Kellogg was so convinced of the unhealthiness of sugar that he went to court to protest the addition of sugar to his own toasted corn flakes cereal. See BREAKFAST CEREAL. However, American medical professionals remained agnostic about sugar, which official early-twentieth-century food guides recognized as a concentrated source of carbohydrates. By 1920 annual sugar consumption in the United States had reached 100 pounds per capita; nevertheless, sugar was not considered in American nutrition policies as deleterious to health until after World War II.

Sugar, Sweet Substitutes, and Health

In the late nineteenth century, Constantin Fahlberg, a chemist at Johns Hopkins University, accidentally discovered the first chemical replacement for sugar: saccharin. See ARTIFICIAL SWEETENERS. Its use was widespread in Europe during World War I due to sugar rationing, and it remained a popular sugar substitute in the interwar period. However, in the United States, saccharin's use was limited to diabetics until after World War II. By the late 1960s, bench chemists had discovered the sugar substitutes cyclamate, acesulfame K, and aspartame, but until 1982—when aspartame was approved for wider use in Europe and the Americas—only saccharin was government-approved as a sugar replacement. Chemical companies and food and beverage manufacturers promoted calorie-free sweeteners as healthier alternatives to sugar. Public demand for these replacements was so high that the threat of a saccharin ban by the U.S. Food and Drug Administration in 1977—spurred by a study linking cancer and saccharin consumption—caused one million consumers to protest.

While this protest illustrates the modern American desire for the taste of sweet, it also shows that public perception of sugar was shifting. In the case of the "saccharin rebellion," many American women saw sugar as bad for their figure, while saccharin allowed them to savor the taste of sweet without worrying about calories. In 1972 Robert Atkins published *Dr. Atkins' Diet Revolution*, which promised weight loss by eschewing all carbohydrates, sugars in particular. However, the Atkins diet did allow, and even encourage, the use of artificial sweeteners. This vilification of sugar may have been more cosmetic and cultural than purely health related, but as the century progressed and "sugar" in the form of high-fructose corn syrup (HFCS), dextrose, maltose, cane syrup, and juice concentrates was added to virtually all industrial food products, doctors, dieticians, and nutritionists became concerned with the role of sugar consumption in diabetes, obesity, and "metabolic syndrome."

First described as "Syndrome X" by Gerald Reaven in 1988, "metabolic syndrome" refers to the unhealthy profile of high insulin, high blood sugar, elevated triglycerides, and low levels of HDL cholesterol. While popular medical opinion at the time continued to attribute heart disease to a high intake of red meat and saturated fat, Reaven pointed to the perils of excess sugar and high glycemic-indexed carbohydrates. Between 2004 and 2006 the ubiquity of HFCS in soda and processed snack foods became fodder for both research scientists and science journalists, who drew links between the widespread consumption of HFCS and the so-called obesity epidemic. See CORN SYRUP; FRUCTOSE; and SODA. In 2009, the pediatric endocrinologist Robert Lustig released a YouTube video titled "Sugar: The Bitter Truth," in which he stated that sugar is a leading cause of obesity, a toxin that upsets both endocrine and metabolic function in the body, and the cause of chronic diseases like diabetes and cardiovascular disease. Lustig published his findings in 2013, citing evidence that the consumption of refined sugar causes metabolic syndrome, illustrated by the enormous increase in the incidence of obesity and diabetes in the Western world.

Sugar is, and will continue to be, closely linked to human health. Diet experts will continue to study the amount of sugar we can eat while still remaining healthy, and academics will continue to research and debate the topic. Meanwhile, sugar consumption continues to rise worldwide. Delicious or deleterious? The jury is still out.

See also SUGAR, BIOCHEMISTRY OF; SUGAR REFINING; and SUGAR TRADE.

de la Peña, Carolyn. *Empty Pleasures: The Story of Artificial Sweeteners from Saccharin to Splenda.* Durham: University of North Carolina Press, 2010.

Lustig, Robert H., Laura A. Schmidt, and Claire D. Brindis. "Public Health: The Toxic Truth about Sugar." *Nature* 482 (2012), 27–29.

Mintz, Sidney. *Sweetness and Power: The Place of Sugar in Modern History.* New York: Penguin, 1986.

Jessica Mudry

sugar barons were the owners of extensive plantations in the Caribbean. From the mid-seventeenth century to the beginning of the nineteenth century, they made huge fortunes growing and processing sugar.

Around 1642, after years of struggle, the tiny English colony of Barbados suddenly found itself the richest spot of land in the British Empire. James Drax, one of the original 50 settlers in 1627, had successfully grown sugarcane and processed sugar. See SUGARCANE and SUGARCANE AGRICULTURE. According to Richard Ligon, who spent three years in Barbados, from 1647 to 1650, there had been costly failures along the way, but with advice from Dutch planters in Brazil, and thanks to the "thriving genius of James Drax," the difficult processes had been mastered. Drax's first shipment of sugar arrived in London at a time of scarcity, largely caused by disturbances and crop failures in Brazil, and he made a fortune. Within half a dozen years, almost the entire island was planted with cane.

Drax established a 700-acre plantation in St. George parish and built himself a Jacobean-style mansion where he advertised his newfound wealth by giving the island's most extravagant parties. See PLANTATIONS, SUGAR. At one dinner, Richard Ligon counted at least five courses, each with up to 20 different dishes, washed down with gallons of wine, beer, sherry, and brandy.

Drax also led the way in changing the island's labor force. The initial colonial concept had been for the West Indian islands to be white settler communities powered by indentured servants: poor whites from the British Isles who sold their labor (and, effectively, freedom) for five to seven years in return for passage, subsistence, and a plot of land at the end of the tenure. See COLONIALISM. The islands were also seen as an outlet for surplus population and troublemakers, and thousands of prisoners of war, vagrants, felons, and prostitutes were shipped to the Caribbean. But the arrivals proved rebellious, drunken, and feeble, with about a third dying within three years, mostly from yellow fever. So Drax looked elsewhere, buying enslaved Africans from Dutch traders. See SLAVERY. Slaves cost about twice the price of a white servant, but they were bound for life, and their offspring would be born as slaves of their mother's owner. By 1654 Drax had about 200 enslaved Africans. According to Ligon, he "kept them in such good order, as there are no mutinies amongst them."

Other planters followed Drax's lead, and by 1660 there were some 20,000 enslaved Africans in Barbados, while the white population had declined from a high of 30,000 to 24,000. It took considerable capital to establish a sugar operation, and land prices increased dramatically. Few indentured servants who survived to reach the end of their tenure had the means to produce sugar; some continued in the north of the island, eking out a living growing cotton or tobacco, but many emigrated to less congested colonies nearby or to North America. Combined with the fearsome mortality rate, this led to a dwindling of the "middling" whites—by 1690 there were less than 20,000, while the enslaved population had risen to 60,000.

For the sugar barons—the small number of families who now owned most of the best land and controlled the top positions in the island's government, judiciary, and militia—this numerical inferiority in a newly racialized system brought constant fear of rebellion and overthrow. See RACE. Indeed, there were a string of slave plots in Barbados during the last decades of the seventeenth century. The planters responded by building their homes as forts and using sadistic brutality against the blacks.

Drax invested his sugar profits in land and urban property in England and diversified into commerce and shipping, including shares in slave-trading vessels. In 1654 he left Barbados, saluted by the militia, and settled in London, from where he controlled his Atlantic network. He was knighted by Cromwell, and after the Restoration he was given a baronetcy by Charles II, which gives an indication of his political dexterity.

Drax's eldest son's health proved unequal to the climate of Barbados, so the Barbados estate was taken over by his second son, Henry. Henry lacked the drive and energy of his father, but his careful stewardship of Drax Hall and his relatively humane treatment of his slaves saw his wealth rise to match that of the grandest landed families in England. He reluctantly left Barbados in 1679 after his wife had suffered three infant deaths, and the family became absentee owners, as they remain to this day, still owning and running the Barbados plantation where James Drax pioneered sugar production.

The Codringtons

The profitable, though cruel and unstable, sugar plantation model was exported around the region, driven by a handful of families who often intermarried. James Drax's sister married Christopher Codrington, a royalist refugee who arrived in Barbados around 1640. Their son, also named Christopher, consolidated his father's estates in St. John's parish and at the age of only 29 became deputy governor of Barbados, lauded as a young man of "liberal, debonaire humour." He introduced measures to restrict alcohol consumption, increase the white population, build schools and hospitals, and attack widespread smuggling.

But Codrington's youthful optimism foundered on planter inertia and self-interest, and was corrupted by the materialistic, cruel, and licentious culture of the sugar empire. In 1669 he was accused of murdering the nephew of the governor in a dispute over ownership of a plantation and expelled from the governing council. He responded by throwing himself into illegal trading, and he started moving his capital off the island. In 1683 he relocated to Antigua, where he was key in introducing Barbados-style plantations; he soon became the most powerful sugar baron and governor general of the Leewards, leading English forces in their constant battles with the French. The position provided Codrington with excellent opportunities for embezzlement, and he died in 1698 only just ahead of disgrace.

His son, Christopher Codrington III, had, like most sons of the sugar barons, been educated in England, where he became one of Oxford's most accomplished scholars. He was also devout, a gifted lawyer and a decorated soldier. He inherited his father's governorship and sailed to the Leewards determined to reform the chaotic legal system, curtail the despotic power of the biggest planters, and, above all, improve the brutal treatment of the enslaved workforce.

But within a few years, with all these hopes unfulfilled and with his health in ruins, Christopher III, like his father, was being accused of embezzlement, of siring a host of mulatto children, and of conspiracy to murder. He died in 1710, leaving the majority of his slaves and estates in Barbados, St. Kitts, and Antigua to his nephew William, who soon returned to England to enjoy the life of an absentee owner.

The Beckfords

By 1720, Jamaica, captured from the Spanish by a Cromwellian force in 1655 and having 10 times the combined area of all the other English sugar islands, had become the key sugar producer, helped as elsewhere by an influx of major planters from Barbados. For a hundred years it would remain the most important possession in the British Empire, its primacy for defense contributing to the loss by Britain of the North American colonies. But because of Jamaica's mountainous interior, which gave hope to rebellious slaves, it was also the most savagely brutal of England's slave colonies, with uprisings and their vengeful aftermath occurring almost every year.

For most of the eighteenth century the leading slave-owning family was the Beckfords, a dynasty started by a cattle rustler in the 1660s. Colonel Peter Beckford, as he became known, was energetic, physically fit, and utterly ruthless—all essential attributes for the successful sugar baron. His son, also named Peter, shrugged off murder charges and built a huge sugar empire, worth at his death in 1735 more than £300,000, at a time when the average income in Britain was around £15 a year. His main inheritor, William, further increased the fortune, before returning to England to build a lavish, stately home in Wiltshire called Fonthill Splendens, and to enter politics. Other sugar barons were by now doing the same, and by midcentury there was a substantial "West India Interest" in the House of Commons, able to steer imperial policy to their own advantage. William Beckford became a close confidant of William

Pitt the Elder, and he was twice made lord mayor of London.

A generation later, however, the Beckford fortune was gone. Part of the Beckford family assets went to William's brother's son, William of Somerley, an artistic idealist far too soft to make a success of the brutal plantation business. By 1788 he was back in England, confined in Fleet Prison for debt. William's main inheritor, becoming in 1770 the richest commoner in Europe, was a Gothic novelist and pampered aesthete who never visited Jamaica, where his attorneys were busy siphoning off his money. What was left was wasted in an orgy of eccentric and spectacular spending.

Other sugar baron families follow this pattern from entrepreneur to grandee to hapless inheritor. At the same time, growing competition from other sugar producers, particularly French and Dutch, and popular revulsion at the violence, rape, and drunken sadism of the slave system, saw the eclipse of the West Indian nabobs and the abolition of slavery in the British Empire in 1833. With damage from hurricanes, the cutting off of vital supplies after the American Revolution, and the long-term effects of constant disease, war, and corruption in the West Indies, abolition was the end of the primacy of the Caribbean empire, and of the power of the sugar barons.

See also HAVEMEYER, HENRY OSBORNE; SUGAR; SUGAR REFINING; and TATE & LYLE.

Blome, Richard. *A Description of the Island of Jamaica.* London: T. Milbourn, 1672.

Brown, Vincent. *The Reaper's Garden: Death and Power in the World of Atlantic Slavery.* Cambridge, Mass.: Harvard University Press, 2008.

Burnard, Trevor. *Mastery, Tyranny, and Desire: Thomas Thistlewood and His Slaves in the Anglo-Jamaican World.* Chapel Hill: University of North Carolina Press, 2004.

Dunn, Richard S. *Sugar and Slaves: The Rise of the Planter Class in the English West Indies, 1624–1713.* Chapel Hill: University of North Carolina Press, 1972.

Ligon, Richard. *A True and Exact History of the Island of Barbados.* London, 1657.

Oliver, Vere Langford. *Caribbeana: Being Miscellaneous Papers Relating to the History, Genealogy, Topography, and Antiquities of the British West Indies.* 6 vols. London: Mitchell & Hughes, 1894–1899.

Sheridan, Richard B. *Sugar and Slavery: An Economic History of the British West Indies, 1623–1775.* Baltimore: Johns Hopkins University Press, 1974.

University College London. Legacies of British Slave-Ownership. http://www.ucl.ac.uk/lbs/ (accessed 27 November 2014).

Matthew Parker

sugar beet (*Beta vulgaris*), which, unlike sugarcane, thrives in temperate climates, has since the mid-nineteenth century been a commercially important alternative source of sucrose. At the time, it was an especially important source for northern nations lacking tropical colonies, or for those unwilling to purchase sugar produced by slaves.

The recognition of the beet's industrial potential as a sweetener dates back to the beginning of the seventeenth century. In 1600, Olivier de Serres, a French agronomist, documented similarities between boiled beet juice and sugar syrup, thus making a scientific fact out of a phenomenon that had long been known in kitchens around the world. Andreas Sigismund Marggraf, a German chemist, reported in 1747 that he had extracted sugar from beets. In 1801, Frederick William III of Prussia provided funds so that Marggraf's student, Franz Karl Achard, could establish a sugar beet farm and a beet sugar factory in Silesia. In 1811, facing complaints from cooks and consumers who could not get sugar from cane grown on British plantations in the Caribbean—there was a British blockade of Continental Europe and a Napoleonic ban on commerce with the enemy—Napoleon decreed that sugar beets be planted in France, that factories be established, and that schools provide instruction in the business. By midcentury, beet sugar was a major industry in Europe and competitive with cane sugar on the world market. Sales of beet sugar outpaced those of cane sugar in the 1880s. Beet sugar today accounts for about 20 percent of the world's sugar production.

Many scientists provided support for the industry in the nineteenth century. Among them was Augustin Pierre Dubrunfaut, who wrote *Art de fabriquer le sucre de betteraves* (The Art of Manufacturing Beet Sugar, 1825), gave courses in the subject in France, and developed techniques for testing sugar quality. With funding from the Association of the German Beet Sugar Industry, Carl Scheibler established the Laboratory for Sugar Chemistry and Technology in Berlin. Harvey Wiley of the U.S. Department of Agriculture (USDA) prepared a publication that allegedly "formed the basis of most of the

A worker shovels beets at a sugar beet plant in Szczebrzeszyn, Poland, in 1974. Today about 20 percent of the world's sugar supply comes from beets. FORUM / UIG / BRIDGEMAN IMAGES

work undertaken by private enterprise in this important industry." He also sent USDA agents to inspect sugar beet farms and factories across the country.

The techniques used for processing beet sugar are similar to those used for cane sugar, but with several important differences. Juice is pressed from cane, but it is extracted from beets by the diffusion method, which involves cutting the beets into thin slices and soaking the resulting "cossettes" in a series of warm-water tubs. The impurities are removed from cane sugar by washing the raw sugar in a refinery. With beet sugar, the impurities are removed from the juice by means of carbonatation, a process that involves the addition of such chemicals as calcium hydroxide, carbon dioxide, and calcium carbonate.

The next step of the production process for both beet and cane sugar involves evaporating the water from the sugar juice. The vacuum pan was the first important solution to this problem. Devised by the English chemist Edward Charles Howard, the vacuum pan made use of the well-known principle that a liquid placed in a partial vacuum will boil at a lower temperature than at atmospheric pressure. The multiple-effect apparatus joined several vacuum pans together in such a way that vapor released from the liquid in one pan was used to boil the liquid in the next, with each pan at successively lower pressure and temperature. Norbert Rillieux, a free person of color who was born in New Orleans and educated in France, imagined an energy-efficient apparatus of this sort in 1830 and oversaw its implementation on sugarcane plantations in Louisiana in the 1840s. The technology was introduced to beet sugar factories in Europe in the 1850s, and it is still used today.

The work of planting, cultivating, and harvesting sugar beets is arduous, and historically it was mostly done by poor people, many of them immigrants, women, and children who were willing to work for pathetically low wages. This practice was as true in the United States as it was elsewhere in the world. In 1933, *Fortune* magazine described beet sugar as an American industry with un-American working conditions, noting that the cultivation of sugar beets required vastly more labor than any other common crop. The trade journal *Sugar* agreed that the industry had been "shackled to 'stoop' labor, hired in battalions to work on hands and knees or stooped doubled all day long at thinning, weeding, topping and loading sugar beets," and acknowledged that it "was almost the last American form of agriculture to leave the age old peasant level of farming." Mechanization replaced much of this hand labor around the mid-twentieth century.

American farmers depended on European beet seed. Fearing that European farmers got the best seed, Americans pushed for a domestic source, and by the 1930s researchers had succeeded in creating a monogerm seed that produced one beet root rather than several, thus eliminating the need to thin plants in the field. Another new seed produced beets that were resistant to the curly top virus that devastated many fields.

A marketing study in the 1940s found that industrial users knew that sucrose was sucrose, whatever the source, but many domestic consumers thought beet sugar had an unpleasant odor. The problem was that cane sugar refineries operated continuously and consistently; beet sugar operations, on the other hand, were seasonal, and so the product was less consistent. Despite a massive ad campaign arguing that beet sugar was as good as cane sugar, this perception of difference lingers today, and probably explains why many beet sugar packages are now labeled "pure sugar" while cane sugar packages are labeled "pure cane sugar." Today, some 80 percent of the world's supply of sugar comes from cane, and 20 percent from beet. Russia is the largest producer of beet sugar.

While bagasse—the dried cane stalks left over from producing sugar—can be used as fuel, beet pulp and molasses are valued as animal feed. And in Iran and Turkey, cooked sugar beets are a favorite street food. Vendors sell the ruby-red beets by the piece, deliciously caramelized in a simmering, sweet broth.

See also SUGARCANE AGRICULTURE and SUGARCANE.

Asadi, Mosen. *The Beet Sugar Handbook*. Hoboken, N.J.: Wiley, 2006.

Poggi, E. M. "The German Beet Sugar Industry." *Economic Geography* 6 (1930): 81–93.

Deborah Jean Warner

The **Sugar Bowl** is an aptly named college football game that was first played in January 1935, during the depths of the American Depression. For 40 years the game took place at the old Tulane Stadium in New Orleans, near the site of the sugar plantation of Étienne de Boré (1740–1820), where cane sugar was first successfully granulated in 1795. To make sugar syrup crystallize, de Boré combined a vacuum-pan process with Spanish molasses-making methods. But he did not invent this process; de Boré's accomplishment was making sugar profitable as a commodity crop, and his entrepreneurial success made him famous.

Fred Digby (1912–1958), the sports editor of the *New Orleans Item*, is credited with being the driving force behind the annual football exhibition, and with calling it the Sugar Bowl. Although American "bowl" games take their name from the bowl-shaped stadium first designed at Yale University, the Sugar Bowl literalizes its name by using a sugar bowl as its logo. The irony of staging the Sugar Bowl at the site of a sugar plantation that utilized slaves may not be lost on the football players, most of whom are now African American, according to statistics compiled by the television sports network ESPN.

Ever since the Sugar Bowl was moved to the Superdome (now the Mercedes-Benz Superdome) in 1975, the Sugar Bowl has attracted ever-larger crowds, topping 70,000 in 2012. Now 80 years old, the Sugar Bowl has showcased 23 national championship teams—more than any other college bowl—and has distributed more than half a billion dollars to college athletic departments over the course of its history. Perhaps the greatest Sugar Bowl game was the wild offensive match in 2006 between West Virginia (the underdog) and Georgia, won 38–35 by West Virginia, which gained 502 yards to Georgia's 501.

In a city renowned for its pralines and sweet blues and jazz, the Sugar Bowl remains a sweet spot in the New Orleans economy, as it is a most profitable enterprise.

See also NEW ORLEANS; PLANTATIONS, SUGAR; SPORTS NICKNAMES; and SUGAR REFINING.

This postcard, printed by the E. C. Kropp Company between 1935 and 1960, shows an aerial view of Tulane University football stadium in New Orleans, Louisiana, where the Sugar Bowl football game is played annually. LIBRARY OF CONGRESS

Mulé, Marty. *Sugar Bowl Classic: A History*. Clearwater, Fla.: Mainstream Media International, 2008.

Stacey, Truman. "Etienne de Boré." In *Notable Men and Women of SWLA*. http://www.calcasieupreservation.com/index.php?option=com_content&view=category&layout=blog&id=133&Itemid=178 (accessed 10 October 2014).

Dean Crawford and Marty Mulé

sugar cubes were first made in the early 1840s by Jakub Kryštof Rad, director of a sugar-beet refinery in Dačice, Moravia (now in the Czech Republic). Sugar cones, though beautiful, were hard to break into handy pieces, and lumps cut with sugar nips varied considerably in size and shape. See SERVERS, SUGAR. Rad experimented with pressing moist, grated sugar into something resembling a modern ice-cube tray: once completely dry, the cubes were ready for use. His innovation was so successful that he obtained a five-year patent for it in 1843. However, a few years later he moved to another enterprise, and his technique was gradually forgotten.

Development of the Sugar Cube

The next sugar-cube breakthrough occurred in Cologne, Germany, at the Pfeifer & Langen sugar company, founded in 1870 and still flourishing today. In 1872 Eugen Langen developed his own technique for making sugar cubes, which relied on a centrifuge to create blocks of sugar that were then sawn into cubes. Patented in 1874, the method proved so effective that the British sugar giant Henry Tate bought exclusive rights for British production and introduced sugar cubes to the British public on a large scale. See TATE & LYLE. In 1894 Tate switched to another technique that had been invented in Belgium in late 1880. This process used special cylindrical turbines to manufacture tablets from powdered sugar that were then sawn into regular cubes, initially called "dominoes." In 1902 the Tienen Sugar Refinery, Belgium's largest sugar maker, adopted the technique, which it uses to this day to produce an extremely hard cube known as *morceau dur*, or Adant cube, after its inventor.

While this type of hard cube is still favored in Belgium, France, and some Arab countries, softer

This carved sugar sculpture, called *Sir Henry Tate's Mausoleum*, was created by the artist Brendan Jamison in 2012. Henry Tate, the owner of the British sugar giant Henry Tate & Sons (later Tate & Lyle), bought exclusive British rights to a sugar cube manufacturing patent and introduced the British public to sugar cubes in the 1870s. COURTESY OF BRENDAN JAMISON SCULPTURE STUDIO

cubes molded from loose sugar are preferred in most other countries. The three predominant techniques for manufacturing softer cubes are the compression-based Chambon process (developed in France in 1949), the vibration-based Vibro process (invented in Sweden in the late 1950s), and the compression-based Elba process (invented in the Netherlands in 1970s; this process also produces tablets for hard sugar cubes). Other processes exist, including the still-used Hersey drum, patented in 1879 by Boston's Charles H. Hersey. This was the first popular device to mold sugar cubes that do not require subsequent sawing. Originally called a molding sugar machine, it was perfected in 1929 to mold sugar into fancy irregular shapes.

The first wrapped sugar cubes appeared before World War I, although they proliferated only in the 1950s with the success of the Chambon process. Wrapped sugar cubes are still very popular in France and Belgium, and collectors avidly seek out the wrappers.

Uses of Sugar Cubes

Although the first sugar cubes created by Rad were sold in Vienna, Europe's great center of coffee culture, they were labled "tea-sugar," indicating that from the start sugar cubes were intended for use with tea. This may have been due to the old tea habit, especially popular in Russia and Persia, of drinking tea while holding a lump of sugar between one's teeth and sucking the tea through it (the Russian term is *vprikusku*). A precisely cut sugar cube served this purpose even better than an irregular lump. The tradition, though gradually disappearing, still exists; Mosen Asadi, author of *The Beet Sugar Handbook*, mentions it as key to the continuing popularity of hard sugar cubes in modern times: "In most countries, people put a cube of sugar into a cup to sweeten their tea, so they want a cube that dissolves quickly. In some countries, however, people put sugar into their mouth where it slowly dissolves while they drink tea, so they want a hard cube" (2006, p. 455). Sugar cubes were fashionable at aristocratic tea parties, such as English afternoon tea; in the United States they were manufactured in the shapes of playing-card suits—diamonds, hearts, clubs, and spades—to be served at bridge parties.

During the American cocktail boom in the 1920s, sugar cubes were used for such classics as the Old Fashioned, for which a sugar cube is infused with Angostura bitters. In Europe, especially in France, the cubes became de rigueur for serving absinthe: a sugar cube was set on a slotted spoon over a glass, then cold water was poured over the cube to dissolve it. As the sugar dripped, it turned the green absinthe milky white. At midcentury the cubes became a vehicle for delivering the polio vaccine, and later for delivering LSD (indeed, "cube" or "sugar cube" is slang for LSD). See PHARMACOLOGY and SLANG.

Today, when people tend to sweeten their drinks with artificial sweeteners, sugar cubes are essentially a niche product found mainly in bars and at proper afternoon teas. Tiny, multicolored and multi-themed sugar cubes (shaped into flowers, sea creatures, cats, elephants, etc.) are very popular in Japan, while in the West the dazzling white sugar-cube architecture by the Irish sculptor Brendan Jamison is featured in many art galleries.

See also ARTIFICIAL SWEETENERS; SUGAR; and SUGAR REFINING.

Asadi, Mosen. *The Beet Sugar Handbook.* Hoboken, N.J.: Wiley, 2006.

Centre d'Études et de Documentation du Sucre (CEDUS). http://www.lesucre.com (accessed 15 October 2014).

Chalmin Philippe. *The Making of a Sugar Giant: Tate and Lyle, 1859–1989.* Translated by Erica E. Long-Michalke. London: Harwood Academic, 1990.

Chen, James C. P., and Chung Chi Chou. *Cane Sugar Handbook: A Manual for Cane Sugar Manufacturers and Their Chemists.* 12th ed. New York: Wiley, 1993.

Sugar Cane: A Monthly Magazine, Devoted to the Interests of the Sugar Cane Industry 12 (January–December 1880).

Alexandra Grigorieva

sugar in experimental cuisine—the movement in which chefs seek to understand the underlying science of their craft in order to control the various elements with which they work—is the basis of much investigation, notably to produce desserts that are less sweet than traditional ones. For many chefs, such "modernist" desserts not only harmonize with the savory side of the menu, they can also be more healthful, since their minimalism relies on intensified flavors rather than on abundant amounts of sugar and fat.

Will Goldfarb, one of the world's leading pastry chefs and cofounder of the Experimental Cuisine Collective, identifies the evolution of nougatine as a key development related to sugar in experimental cuisine. In the 1990s the acclaimed French chef Michel Bras made nougatine (typically, a caramelized mixture of sliced or chopped nuts and sugar) by mixing crumbled *pâte sablée* dough into caramel; he then rolled it into a sheet as thin as filo dough to make nougatine with the crackling consistency of a crème brûlée crust. See CRÈME BRÛLÉE. Working at Spain's famed restaurant elBulli, Albert Adrià, the most advanced experimental pastry chef in the world, built on Bras's recipe by substituting fondant and glucose for the sugar; he then went a step further, replacing the fondant and glucose with isomalt, a sugar alcohol. See FONDANT; GLUCOSE; and ISOMALT. Bras had played with the sugar in nougatine to make it easier to control; Adrià built on Bras's work by attempting to control the confection's hygroscopic properties and keep it a neutral color. With isomalt, Adrià was finally able to control nougatine's texture as well as its sweetness, allowing him to play with flavors and shapes in multi-component desserts to evoke imagery such as landscapes. By revealing how various ingredients behave in baking and confectionery, Bras's and Adrià's experiments led to further developments in the experimental pastry kitchen.

For instance, isomalt, which is manufactured from sucrose in a two-stage process, is less sweet than other sweeteners, and it does not take on color until heated above 356°F (180°C). The fact that isomalt and other sugar alcohols like sorbitol don't turn golden or brown means that pastry chefs can incorporate them into recipes in which a bit of sweetness is needed, but not a caramel color or flavor. At Mugaritz in Spain, chef Andoni Aduriz and his team spent five years developing "the Broken Egg, the Frozen Yolk, and the White Flowers," a dessert featuring what looked like a real egg shell in both appearance and texture but was edible because it had been made of mannitol, a sugar alcohol. The dish also includes egg yolks cured in a mixture of sugar and salt that essentially cooks them.

Experimental pastry chefs often use sugar alternatives to sweeten their desserts, such as coconut nectar, palm sugar, birch sap, Stevia, granulated honey (prized for the texture it adds), and natural milk sugars. The natural sugars in parsnips, beets, and carrots have also made these vegetables popular in desserts in recent years. The experimental pastry kitchen is currently a hotbed of research, partly because the tasting-menu format of many high-end restaurants guarantees that pastry chefs have a role in the meal. Thus they can experiment with less risk than at traditional restaurants, where diners might reject an unusual dessert or choose not to order dessert at all.

See also PASTRY CHEF; PLATED DESSERTS; and POPPING SUGAR.

Figoni, Paula. *How Baking Works: Exploring the Fundamentals of Baking Science.* 3d ed. Hoboken, N.J.: Wiley, 2011.

Anne E. McBride

sugar lobbies, made up of individuals or firms employed by the sugarcane and sugar-beet industries, act on behalf of these industries to influence government policies and actions that might affect sugar production, transport, labor, or sales and, therefore, profits. The U.S. government generally requires most lobbyists to register, to disclose who pays them and how much, and to list the matters they discuss with officials. The history of sugar lobbying in the United States can be traced back to the late eighteenth century, when Congress first imposed a tariff on imported sugar to generate revenue. Because tariffs are also protectionist, domestic sugar producers lobbied to maintain them and have done so consistently ever since. In the 1930s they also lobbied successfully for acreage allotments and support prices. That such policies remain in place today despite the higher cost of sugar to consumers can be attributed to the steadfast work and consequent political power of sugar-industry lobbying groups, and the obscurity and complexity of agriculture policy to the average American.

In 2013, 44 companies, trade associations, and organizations specifically mentioned the word "sugar" in their lobbying disclosure forms. These included sugar producers and processors such as the American Crystal Sugar Company and the Fanjul Corporation, and their trade associations, such as the American Sugar Cane League. Collectively, these politically powerful groups are known as Big Sugar. Others lobbying on sugar issues are international companies and associations that sell, transport, or trade sugar itself or foods and beverages that contain it. Public-interest groups concerned about the health effects of excessive sugar consumption also lobby on sugar issues. See SUGAR AND HEALTH. These groups, however, are not equally influential. As commonly used, the term "sugar lobby" refers to Big Sugar.

Although lobbyists do not have to disclose their opinions on issues, it is easy to make educated guesses about what sugar lobbyists want from government officials, based on the primary elements of current sugar policies: price supports, marketing allotments, and tariff-rate quotas. These decades-old and seemingly immutable policies maintain the price of domestic sugar at levels higher than those on the world market. Big Sugar wants to keep protectionist policies in place and so far has succeeded in doing so.

Big Sugar gets its way through another mechanism: campaign contributions through political action committees (PACs). To cite just one example, the Florida Sugar Cane League's PAC disclosed $155,000 in campaign contributions during the 2011–2012 election cycle. According to OpenSecrets.org, a site that tracks such expenditures, these funds supported politicians in Florida and 38 other states, with 44 percent of the contributions going to Democrats, 54 percent to Republicans, and 1 percent to an Independent. This PAC contributed to the campaigns of every congressional leader of the House and Senate Agriculture Committees. Other Big Sugar PACs followed similar contribution patterns.

The opponents of current U.S. sugar policies, whose efforts have proved unsuccessful to date, include companies such as Hershey's and Kraft Foods that buy large amounts of sugar to use in their products and wish it were cheaper; food trade associations, such as the American Beverage Association; and business groups like the U.S. Chamber of Commerce that favor a free market in agriculture.

The strongest public argument for reform of current policies is the higher cost of sugar to consumers. In 2000 the Government Accountability Office estimated that elimination of sugar quotas and tariffs would save $1.9 billion annually. Passed along to consumers, this savings would come to only $6 per American, an amount too small to generate much outrage by elected officials or by the public.

Interest in sugar policy also comes from public-health groups such as the American Dental Association, the American Diabetes Association, and the Center for Science in the Public Interest. During negotiations over the 2014 farm bill, these groups lobbied for a government-funded study of the health consequences of sugar-sweetened beverages, but failed to get it. See SODA.

Because lobbying takes place in secret, it is difficult to know precisely how Big Sugar exerts its influence, but occasional examples surface. In 1998 the Starr Report revealed that sugar producers have unusual access to the highest levels of government. When President Bill Clinton entertained Monica Lewinsky on a national holiday, he interrupted their tryst by accepting a telephone call from Florida sugar tycoon Alfonso Fanjul. Fanjul was objecting to a proposed tax on Florida sugar growers for cleaning up the pollution his company's sugar production was causing to the Everglades. The tax was not enacted.

Another example occurred in 2003, when the World Health Organization (WHO) recommended that added sugars comprise no more than 10 percent of daily calories. Sugar lobbies induced two senators to demand that the United States withdraw funding from the WHO if it did not rescind the proposal. International sugar lobbies visited the governments of sugar-growing nations, warning them of the dire consequences of such advice. The WHO withdrew the proposal.

Early in 2014 the WHO reintroduced the 10 percent recommendation and suggested that consuming added sugars at 5 percent of calories would be even better for public health. Sugar lobbies expressed immediate displeasure, but times had changed and the recommendation held.

Nevertheless, Big Sugar has a long history of getting what it wants. Its work has ensured that no reform of sugar policy is imminent. The 2014 farm bill left the U.S. sugar program virtually unchanged, and sugar policies will not be reconsidered for another five years. But it is safe to assume that lobbyists on all sides of sugar policy issues are already working to influence the outcome of the next farm bill.

See also SUGAR BARONS and SUGAR REFINERIES.

Alvarez, José. "Sweetening the U.S. Legislature: The Remarkable Success of the Sugar Lobby." *Political Quarterly* 76, no. 1 (2005): 92–99.

Bartlett D. L., and J. B. Steele. "Sweet Deal: Why Are These Men Smiling? The Reason Is in Your Sugar Bowl." *Time Magazine*, 23 November 1998.

USDA. "Sugar & Sweeteners Policy." http://www.ers.usda.gov/topics/crops/sugar-sweeteners/policy.aspx.

Waxman, Amalia. "The WHO Global Strategy on Diet, Physical Activity and Health: The Controversy on Sugar." *Development* 47, no. 2 (2004): 75–82.

Daniel Bowman Simon and Marion Nestle

sugar painting is a Chinese folk art involving the creation of real and fantastic animals such as horses and dragons, as well as birds, flowers, and, more recently, bicycles, out of caramelized rock sugar. Practitioners trickle the hot caramelized liquid from a metal ladle onto a marble board or slab, working fast and with a sure hand because of temperature constraints that make it impossible to conceal or correct mistakes. Generally found in urban settings at markets and in parks, as well as at temple fairs, sugar painting is especially popular with children, who sometimes spin a wheel to select their model.

Sugar use in religious rituals is ancient; actual records of molded sugar animals and figures exist from the late Ming dynasty (1368–1644), when sugar was also used medicinally and became a luxury item. See MEDICINAL USES OF SUGAR. By no later than 1700, weddings of rich and poor alike included molded sugar animals, people, and even buildings said to enhance the experience of women when they later—with luck—gave birth.

Sugar painting was especially fashionable in Beijing, Tianjin, Shandong, the Huai river basin, and Jiangnan, encompassing the great cities of Nanjing, Suzhou, and Hangzhou; it was also popular in Guangdong Province. However, the art largely disappeared after the 1911 revolution, except in Sichuan Province, where high levels of sugar production and relatively peaceful conditions enabled it to flourish. Folk artists adopted designs for sugar painting that drew on the arts of paper-cutting and shadow puppets. Efforts to preserve sugar painting include competitions, classes, and official recognition as part of local cultural heritage.

See also CHINA; STAGES OF SUGAR SYRUP; SUGAR; and SUGAR SCULPTURE.

Pomeranz, Kenneth L. *The Great Divergence: China, Europe, and the Making of the Modern World Economy.* Princeton, N.J.: Princeton University Press, 2000. See chapter 3, especially pp. 119–120.

"A Sweet Art—Sugar Painting." Cultural China. http://kaleidoscope.cultural-china.com/en/8Kaleidoscope7248.html (accessed 10 October 2014).

"糖画 (Tang Hua, Sugar Painting)." http://xiaoooo.lofter.com/post/f2ad1_254914 (accessed 10 October 2014).

Joanna Waley-Cohen

sugar rationing is the national mandatory allotment and distribution of sugar, particularly in wartime. Instituted by the state, sugar rationing, accompanied by institutional price controls, is designed to ensure an equitable distribution to all civilians. As a major commodity in the modern world, sugar has frequently been rationed by governments during times of war and food scarcity.

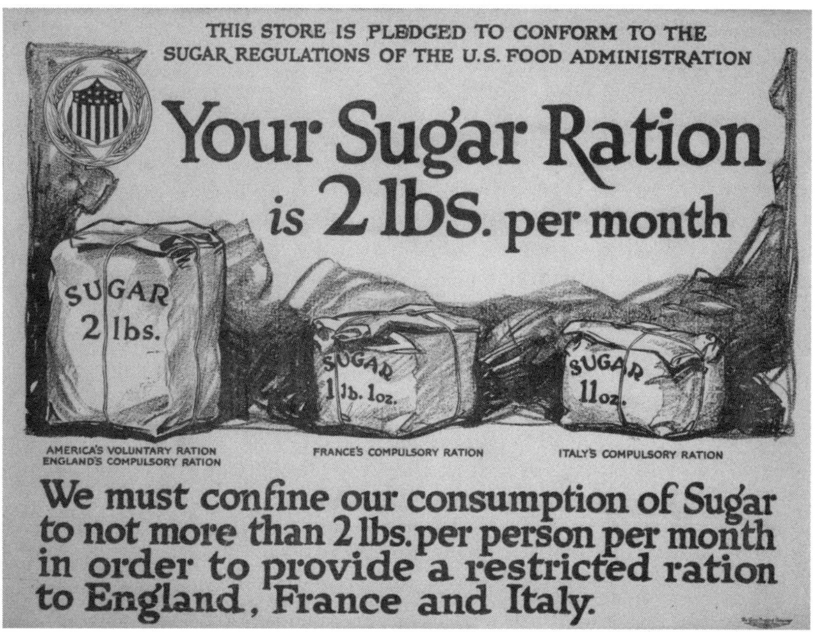

THIS STORE IS PLEDGED TO CONFORM TO THE
SUGAR REGULATIONS OF THE U.S. FOOD ADMINISTRATION
Your Sugar Ration
is 2 lbs. per month
SUGAR
2 lbs.
SUGAR
1 lb. 1oz.
SUGAR
11oz.
AMERICA'S VOLUNTARY RATION
ENGLAND'S COMPULSORY RATION
FRANCE'S COMPULSORY RATION
ITALY'S COMPULSORY RATION
We must confine our consumption of Sugar to not more than 2 lbs. per person per month in order to provide a restricted ration to England, France and Italy.

This 1917 poster compares America's voluntary sugar rations during World War I to the compulsory rations of two pounds in England, just over a pound in France, and less than a pound in Italy. LIBRARY OF CONGRESS

The term "food rations" originally referred to a day's worth of foodstuffs allotted to soldiers in the military. Although military rations existed in ancient civilizations, sugar, a rare luxury of the time, was not included. Government rationing of sugar for civilians began in the early twentieth century as modern warfare wreaked havoc on national economies. By then, industrialization had allowed citizens of all classes to consume sizeable amounts of sugar. In World War I, Great Britain and Germany instigated rationing in general, and sugar rationing in particular, to stave off dire food shortages, rampant inflation, and black markets that severely hampered citizens' ability to procure sufficient supplies. While the United States placed controls on sugar manufacturers and wholesalers during World War I, it did not implement mandatory consumer rationing, opting instead for campaigns urging citizens to voluntarily reduce their sugar intake, an approach that was only minimally effective.

With the advent of the World War II, however, both Allied and Axis powers instituted government rationing of food and other vital goods such as rubber, shoes, and clothing. Sugar rationing began in 1940 in Great Britain and was not lifted until 1953, years after the war's end. To maintain morale, Britain allotted each citizen between 8 and 16 ounces per week, depending on availability, regardless of the individual's size or caloric needs. The Soviet Union implemented rationing in 1941, mainly for metropolitan areas. Rationing was not deemed necessary for rural peasants, who were closer to food supplies, though in reality they suffered severe food shortages. In the United States, sugar was among the first items to be rationed, beginning just months after the bombing of Pearl Harbor, and among the last to be lifted, in 1947. Sugar rationing in Australia began in 1943. In contrast to the Allied practice, Germany's allotments of rationed sugar differed according to citizens' caloric needs. Worried about maintaining a strong output of agriculture and manufacturing, the government allocated greater quantities of food in general, and sugar in particular, to manual laborers than to office workers and children. Rations also differed according to ethnic heritage, especially for German Jews, whose rations approached starvation levels.

Rationing accompanied by price controls was designed to combat high inflation and ensure an equitable distribution of scarce resources, which governments regarded as vital to citizens' wartime morale. In the case of the United States during World War II, government officials viewed rationing as a way to ensure an equitable distribution of food regionally and also across socioeconomic boundaries. The rationing of sugar in particular helped maintain a needed check on citizens' consumption, and it assisted in muting the resentment that would occur if the more affluent received greater quantities than those of more humble means.

Most people at midcentury regarded sugar positively. Sugar was not just a pleasurable treat used in baked goods and beverages, but it was also deemed a reliable source of calories and energy. Although health professionals were aware that sugar was devoid of nutrients, they did not condemn it as a dietary evil. Moreover, sugar, as well as meat, was psychologically important, functioning as a symbol of abundance and cultural well-being. U.S. wartime sugar stocks were much greater than Europe's, averaging 24 pounds per person annually, but Americans still found it difficult to satisfy their collective sweet tooth.

During World War II, and in the United States in particular, there was a common assumption, reinforced by the media, that women consumed more sugar than men. See GENDER. Women were therefore told to cut down on their sugar intake for the good of the war. Although it is difficult to determine whether women actually consumed more sugar, evidence indicates that women did seem to feel the impact of sugar rationing more than men. For women, sugar carried implicit notions of femaleness that pervaded the culture, and the sense of deprivation regarding sugar was largely a result of the highly symbolic and important domestic activity of home baking being curtailed by wartime rationing. The symbolic importance of baking as part of women's contribution to the household economy, and the felt absence of this important ritual of domestic nurture during the war, heightened American women's sense of what they were sacrificing. Housewives reported that sugar was the item they missed most and found the hardest to do without.

While most countries have instituted sugar rationing only during wartime, some countries experiencing chronic food shortages, such as Cuba, maintain a system of government rationing, including of sugar.

See also POLITICS OF SUGAR.

Bentley, Amy. *Eating for Victory: Food Rationing and the Politics of Domesticity.* Urbana: University of Illinois Press, 1998.

Collingham, Lizzie. *The Taste of War: World War II and the Battle for Food.* New York: Penguin, 2011.

Amy Bentley

sugar refineries create very pure white sugar from the raw cane sugar produced in sugar mills. Raw sugar varies in color from a deep brown to a light tan, depending on its purity. Although various grades of refined sugar are produced, they differ only in purity and color; usually, refined sugar is sparkling white and colorless in solution. See SUGAR.

Most refined sugar is produced in stand-alone refineries, so-called destination refineries, located close to major markets. Raw sugar is generally transported in large bulk carrying ships, and conveyed to and from the ships at a high rate, typically 1,000 tons per hour. In some cases, refined sugar is produced at small refineries attached to a raw sugar mill. The costs of production for the latter are lower, particularly because they have the benefit of using steam and electric power produced at the sugar mill, using sugarcane bagasse as fuel. In order to be cost competitive, the very large stand-alone refineries need to make use of economies of scale. The disadvantage of refineries at raw mills is usually their distance from markets, since transporting refined sugar in packs or closed bags or containers that prevent contamination tends to be much more costly than transporting bulk raw sugar. In addition, raw sugar mills do not process sugarcane all year round, but have season lengths of between three and ten months, so that the storage of the refined sugar can be a major issue.

The number of refineries declined during the last century, with the smaller refineries closing down and the remaining refineries expanding. New refineries need to produce about 1 million tons of sugar annually to be profitable, although most existing refineries are smaller. In the late 1990s, the European Union ended subsidies for exports of white sugar from beet sugar producers. As a result, over two dozen new refineries have been built outside of the European Union in the last 20 years to replace the exports and provide for the ever-increasing demand for sugar. Most of these new refineries have been built in the Middle East, close to available markets. The new refineries are generally much larger than average size, with two refineries in the Middle East each producing more than 2 million tons of refined sugar yearly.

The largest sugar refining company is now American Sugar Refining, Inc., which owns six refineries in North America, including a back-end refinery in Florida, as well as the Tate & Lyle refinery in London and a refinery in Portugal. See AMERICAN SUGAR REFINING COMPANY and TATE & LYLE.

White sugar is produced to specifications laid down by the European Union and by major consumers, particularly soft-drink manufacturers. Differences in specification relate largely to color, but in most cases the grades of refined sugar all appear identical to the human eye. Sugars are also produced in different size ranges to suit customers. These include cube sugar, castor sugar, icing sugar, and large decorative, and sometimes colored, sugar crystals. See SUGAR CUBES.

In addition to white sugar, most refineries produce various grades of specialty sugars. These are mainly brown sugars, often carefully prepared by the refiners to meet niche markets and command a premium price in retail consumer packs. Various grades include soft brown sugar, caramel sugar, yellow sugar, and treacle sugar. All are boiled from low-purity syrups as a product of the refining process, or blended by coating fine sugar with a refiner's syrup to produce unique flavors and colors. These sugars offer the ability to sell non-sucrose components with the products and reduce the amount of low-value molasses produced. See MOLASSES.

Some refineries also produce liquid sugars, usually solutions of white sugar. This is the preferred form of refined sugar for some industrial customers. The advantages of this form include less labor, no handling of bags, elimination of dust, enhanced cleanliness, and reliable quality control. Liquid sugar is usually produced at a concentration of 67 grams of sucrose per 100 grams of solution—low enough to ensure that crystallization does not occur and high enough to reduce the transport of water in the product. An alternative product is invert syrup, which has some of the sucrose inverted to glucose and fructose, the advantage being the increased solubility of these invert sugars, enabling the production of a solution of 77 grams of sugar per 100 grams of product. See FRUCTOSE and GLUCOSE.

No discussion of refineries would be complete without reference to golden syrup. This is an invert syrup made by a special process to provide an appealing taste. Made famous by Tate & Lyle in England, it has been produced for well over 120 years and is well known for its logo of a lion and the slogan "Out of the strong came forth sweetness," a reference to Samson's biblical exploits.

See also SUGAR REFINING.

Clarke, Margaret, and Mary An Godshall, eds. *Chemistry and Processing of Sugarbeet and Sugarcane: Proceedings of the Symposium on the Chemistry and Processing of Sugarbeet, Denver, Colorado, April 6, 1987, and the Symposium on the Chemistry and Processing of Sugarcane, New Orleans, Louisiana, September 3–4, 1987.* Amsterdam: Elsevier, 1988.

Lyle, Oliver. *Technology for Sugar Refinery Workers.* 3d ed. London, Chapman & Hall, 1957.

Peter W. Rein

sugar refining is the process of converting raw sugar into a high-purity white sugar. Raw sugar is a fairly pure product, normally varying between 98 and 99.5 percent pure sucrose. The refining process is largely dictated by the need to remove color and the other non-sucrose components. Refining is essentially a separation process rather than a bleaching operation.

Non-sucrose components from the raw sugar end up in the molasses stream. The lower the purity of the raw sugar, the higher the quantity of molasses produced. Since some sugar is present in the molasses, the yield of white refined sugar is usually between 95 and 99 percent, depending on the raw sugar. One of the major aims of the refiner is to minimize the loss of sugar in the molasses. See MOLASSES.

The Refining Process

About half of the non-sucrose components, including color bodies, are contained in the thin molasses film around the raw sugar crystals. The affination process involves mingling the raw sugar with a syrup, and centrifuging off the liquid in high-speed batch centrifuges. This is an important step when processing lower-purity raw sugars, but it requires more equipment and energy. Therefore, this step is usually omitted when higher-purity raw sugars are processed.

The sugar is dissolved in water to give a solution of about 66 grams of sugar per 100 grams of liquor.

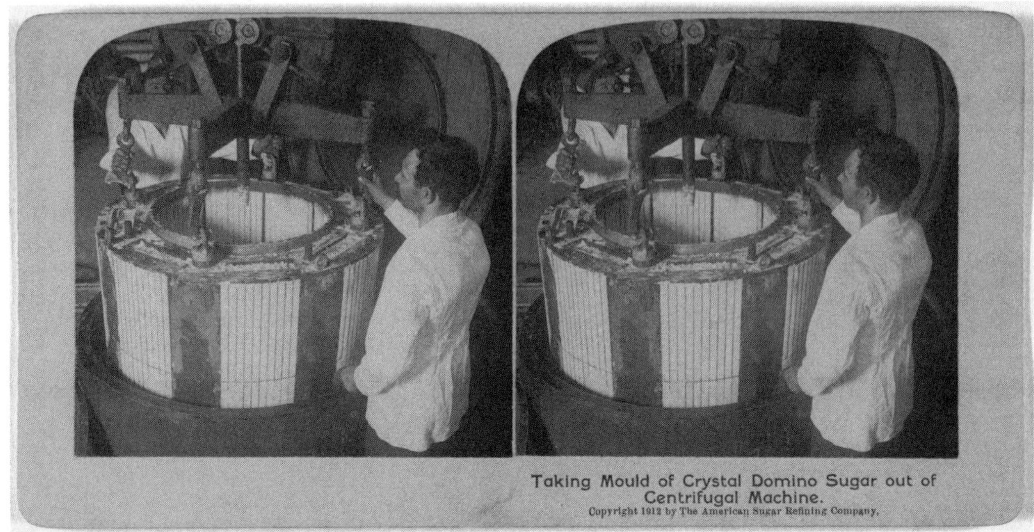

Taking Mould of Crystal Domino Sugar out of
Centrifugal Machine.
Copyright 1912 by The American Sugar Refining Company.

This stereograph from 1912 shows how high-speed centrifuges spun off all the uncrystallized sugar, or liquor, leaving the crystallized sugar behind in a mold. LIBRARY OF CONGRESS

The next step in the process involves clarification and filtration of this liquor. In most refineries, this is achieved by one of two processes:

- *Carbonatation*, where lime is added to the liquor and a gas containing carbon dioxide (usually boiler flue gas) is sparged into the liquor in vessels called saturators to create a chalky precipitate of calcium carbonate, which occludes impurities as it is formed, facilitating the subsequent filtration process.
- *Phosphatation*, where lime is added as well as phosphoric acid, forming a precipitate of calcium phosphate. A flocculant (a high molecular mass polyelectrolyte) is added that causes the precipitated material to agglomerate into clumps called flocs, capturing some of the non-sucrose components in the process. This flocculated material is removed by dissolved air flotation, and the scum removed is treated to recover sugar before being discarded.

Both clarification processes remove between 30 and 60 percent of the color, depending on the dosage of chemicals and whether additional decolorizing chemical additives are used.

Bone char was traditionally used to decolorize the liquor. It was very efficient but had numerous disadvantages related to the sizeable and expensive plant required, as well as the large inventory of char needed. Decolorizing is now almost universally accomplished by pumping the liquor through columns of either ion exchange resins or granulated activated carbon (GAC).

- *Ion exchange* is a cheaper process, requiring less capital and with low operating costs. The resin has to be regenerated periodically with a salt solution, and it creates a highly colored effluent stream with a high concentration of salt. In most cases a membrane separation system is employed to recover a large proportion of the salt for reuse, reducing the quantity of effluent by about 80 percent. However, problems associated with disposing of the effluent can sometimes rule out the use of this option.
- *Decolorizing with GAC* is a somewhat more expensive process. But carbon is an excellent adsorbent, enabling the removal of color and other non-sucrose components, including flavorants. GAC requires periodic regeneration in a high-temperature kiln, which uses additional energy, since high temperatures up to 1,800°F (1,000°C) are required. The advantage is no effluent production.

The decolorized liquor is concentrated to a level close to saturation (about 74 g sugar/100 g liquor) before the crystallization process to reduce steam usage. Crystallization is accomplished under vacuum to minimize the formation of color and reactions involving losses of sugar, which are enhanced at high temperature. The process is usually carried out in batch vacuum pans, producing between 20 and 50 metric tons of sugar in each cycle of about two hours.

The liquor is concentrated in the pan until it becomes slightly supersaturated. It is then seeded with very fine crystals of sugar to initiate crystallization, and growth of the crystals proceeds rapidly. When the pan is full and the crystals have grown to the required size, the mixture of sugar crystals and liquor (termed massecuite) is run from the pan and subsequently fed to banks of high-speed centrifuges. The sugar is retained on perforated screens, while the mother liquor is spun off under centrifugal forces about 1,000 times the force of gravity. A little over half of the massecuite consists of solid crystals. Any higher crystal content would cause the massecuite to be too viscous to flow out of the vacuum pan. However, there is still enough sugar in the run-off liquor from the centrifuges to subject it to a second crystallization step. In fact, this is repeated, usually four times, before the color of the crystal produced is no longer low enough to be included in the product white sugar and still meet the quality specification. The run-off from the fourth boiling is sent to the recovery house, where additional sugar is removed. This recovered sugar is recycled to the beginning of the process to be reprocessed. The liquor from the final boiling in the recovery house is a molasses, which contains some sugar, but it can no longer be economically removed.

The white sugar product is dried before being sent for packaging or dispatch. However, sugar has a great propensity to cake, forming lumps and in extreme cases creating "tombstones" in bagged products, due to a small amount of moisture on the crystal surfaces that causes partial recrystallization as conditions change. At points of contact between crystals, this surface crystallization causes intercrystalline bridging. The sugar ceases to be free flowing and is said to be caked. Even though the dried sugar has a very low moisture content (about 0.04 g/100 g sugar), the sugar usually has to be conditioned in large silos to reduce its moisture content by about half. The sugar is contacted by warm, low-humidity air in the silos over a period of 24 to 72 hours, during which time the small amount of water within the crystal slowly migrates through the crystal and out into the air stream.

Profitable Refining

The major cost in refining, apart from the raw sugar, is energy. Stand-alone refineries generate their own steam and in most cases their own power as well. For this reason, all refiners attempt to be as thermally efficient as possible. On average refineries use about one ton of steam for every ton of sugar processed. This ratio depends to a large extent on the quality of raw sugar being processed. Older refineries tend to be less energy efficient. Some of the newer refineries get well below the average steam requirement by process integration involving a somewhat greater capital investment. Refiners with access to cheap forms of fuel are at a big advantage. Historically, due to the relative paucity of fuel and capital in the cane-growing colonies, most final refining was done close to the eventual consumers.

Refineries in Venice, Lisbon, and Antwerp, and later in London and New York, would reboil the sugar and clarify it, in many cases using blood or egg whites to absorb the impurities. With industrialization came steam power and advances in chemistry that made sugar refining ever more efficient, dramatically decreasing the cost and availability of refined sugar to the masses in the developed world. See SUGAR REFINERIES.

The energy used is also the major contributor to the carbon footprint of refined sugar. The carbon footprint is largely dependent on the carbon footprint of raw sugar, which can in fact be close to zero if significant amounts of power are exported by the sugar mill. On average, the greenhouse gas emission from producing white refined cane sugar is on the order of 600 grams of CO_2 equivalent per 1 kilogram of sugar. This is much lower than that of many other foodstuffs.

The cost of labor is also an important factor, particularly in a packing station. Most refineries are now automated to improve efficiencies and to reduce labor complements.

Another important aspect in refining is the management of sugar losses. Raw sugar is accurately weighed into the refinery, and the amount of sugar produced is carefully recorded, so that the overall loss can be established with confidence. The task of the refinery operator is to reduce the losses of sugar in molasses, filter cake, packaging processes, and in any effluents. It is also important to control process temperatures and pH values to minimize losses of sucrose due to degradation reactions. Loss of sugar in molasses can be reduced by utilizing some of the non-sucrose components, which would otherwise contribute to the molasses quantity, in the production of direct consumer specialty sugars. This can be an additional profitable revenue stream.

There has been a trend over the last few decades for the average quality of raw sugar to improve. Historically, 96 grams sucrose per 100 grams raw sugar was the raw sugar standard, and some producers still convert production back to this reference point. Refiners realize that better raw sugar contributes greatly to both sugar recovery and energy usage, and they are now prepared to pay more for higher-purity raw sugar. As a result, the average quality of raw sugar traded has substantially improved.

See also BOSTON MOLASSES DISASTER; SUGAR; and SUGARS, UNREFINED.

Chou, Chung Chi, ed. *Handbook of Sugar Refining.* New York: Wiley, 2000.

Lyle, Oliver. *Technology for Sugar Refinery Workers.* 3d ed. London: Chapman & Hall, 1957.

Rein, Peter W. *Cane Sugar Engineering.* Berlin: Bartens, 2007.

Rein, Peter W. "Sustainable Production of Raw and Refined Cane Sugar." *Sugar Industry* 136, no. 11 (2011): 734–741.

Peter W. Rein

sugar riots refers to a series of consumer protests during the French Revolution. In the winter of 1792, as the growing threat of European war prompted panic and stockpiling, ordinary Parisians took matters into their own hands. Much as other consumers had done over the past century, they attacked any merchant who charged more than a "fair" amount for goods and refused to pay more than the "customary" price. Their rhetoric—the demand that merchants think not about maximizing profits but about meeting their neighbors' needs—was itself traditional. Nonetheless, their demands were new, for protesters in 1792 (and again the following year) extended the idea of a "moral economy" to sugar.

Over the course of the eighteenth century, roughly six and a half million enslaved Africans were forcibly shipped across the Atlantic. See SLAVERY. Their labor made sugar into one of the first imports of truly mass consumption: between 1700 and 1790, more than 13 million tons went from the Caribbean to Europe. See SUGAR TRADE. Used in jams, jellies, bonbons, cakes, pastries, and (perhaps most important of all) added to coffee, tea, and chocolate to make those bitter stimulants palatable, sugar became an increasingly central item in all urban diets. While France's sugar consumption overall grew more slowly than Britain's, the situation in Paris was different—by the 1780s, average consumption may well have been twice what it was in Britain, perhaps as high as a pound of sugar per person per week. Louis-Sébastien Mercier did not exaggerate when he described the city's breakfasts as global commerce in miniature: "China or Japan supplies the porcelain . . . the tea comes from Asia . . . and with a silver spoon dug from the mines of Peru, you serve the sugar that unfortunate Negroes, transplanted from Africa, have made grow in America."

The 1789 French Revolution severely disrupted these international commodity flows. In 1791, slave rebellions swept across the plantations of France's richest colony, Saint Domingue (modern-day Haiti). The radical journalist Jean-Paul Marat responded in his *L'ami du peuple* (The People's Friend, 29 November 1791) by asserting that no one really knew what was happening in the faraway Caribbean: tales of arson and murder were just rumors spread by grocers as excuses for raising their prices. In the eyes of Parisian consumers, the high price of sugar was as much a political crime as an economic hardship. Expanding the well-established belief in a "famine plot" (the widely shared idea that grain shortages were never accidental) to the case of sugar, consumers charged wholesalers with price-gouging and with depriving patriotic citizens of necessary goods.

In calling the protests of winter 1792 "sugar riots," members of the political elite attempted to invalidate consumers' demands. Sugar and coffee, legislators said, were merely "fictional needs," no more truly necessary than handkerchiefs or pocket watches. Yet the social developments that did so much to make the French Revolution possible—the fortunes made trading sugar and slaves, the popularity of café culture, the growth of mass consumption—had also introduced new necessities. In the autumn of 1793, when they yielded to popular pressure and imposed price controls on "necessary goods," officials included white, brown, and crystallized sugar in that category.

See also CAFÉ and LEGISLATION, HISTORICAL.

Austen, Ralph A., and Woodruff D. Smith. "Private Tooth Decay as Public Economic Virtue: The Slave-Sugar Triangle, Consumerism, and European Industrialization." In *The Atlantic Slave Trade: Effects on Economies, Societies, and Peoples in Africa, the Americas, and Europe*, edited by Joseph E. Inikori and Stanley L. Engerman, pp. 183–203. Durham, N.C.: Duke University Press, 1992.

Burstin, Haim. *Une révolution à l'oeuvre, le faubourg Saint-Marcel (1789–1794)*. Seyssel, France: Champ Vallon, 2005.

Jones, Colin, and Rebecca Spang. "Sans-culottes, *sans café, sans tabac*: Shifting Realms of Necessity and Luxury in Eighteenth-Century France." In *Consumers and Luxury: Consumer Culture in Europe, 1650–1850*, edited by Maxine Berg and Helen Clifford, pp. 37–62. Manchester, U.K.: Manchester University Press, 1999.

Mathiez, Albert. *La Vie chère et le mouvement social sous la Terreur.* Paris: Payot, 1927.

Mercier, Louis Sébastien. *Le tableau de Paris.* Hambourg: Virchaux, 1781. For a partial translation into English, see Jeremy Popkin, ed., *Panorama of Paris* (University Park: Pennsylvania State University Press, 1999).

Rebecca Spang

sugar sculpture, the practice of molding and modeling sugar into dramatic forms, has delighted diners for centuries. Few materials are more transitory in nature than sugar. Despite its ephemeral qualities, this substance has been used for at least a thousand years to create edible art and miniature architecture for the table, often as an expression of status, power, and extravagance. Though short-lived, these works were often significant features of prestigious events such as coronation banquets, sacred feasts, and military triumphs. No historical sugar sculptures have survived, but enough archival material, in the form of written descriptions, illustrations, and tools, exists for us to gain at least a fragmentary understanding of their magnificence.

In medieval and early modern Europe, sugar was a luxury product, and confectionery table ornaments were confined to royal or ducal entertainments. These extravagant examples of luxurious consumption had their origins in the Islamic world three centuries before sugar became readily available in Europe. Early confectioners in the Middle East and North Africa, who were responsible for developing sugar's roles as a preservative and a medicine, also pioneered the use of this unlikely material as an artistic medium. In 1040 the Persian philosopher Nasir-i Husrau (or Khusraw, 1004–ca. 1074) visited the Cairo court of the Fatimid caliph Alī az-Zāhir (1005–1036). In his travelogue *Safarnāme*, Husrau explains how he attended a lavish banquet hosted by the caliph for the entire population of Cairo. Nearly 160,000 pounds of sugar were used to create sweetmeats and table ornaments for the feast, including a massive orange tree, 157 statues, and seven tabletop palaces, all crafted from sugar.

The culinary historian Meryle Evans describes a much later Ottoman festival in Istanbul in 1582, at which confectioners known as *sukker nakkasarli* provided several hundred cast-sugar figures for a spectacular parade commemorating the circumcision of the son of the culture-loving Sultan Murad III (1546–1595). The figurines included giraffes, elephants, lions, fountains, and castles, some of which were so large that they had to be carried by four people. This tradition seems to have been very well established in the city and may predate the Ottoman invasion of 1453, as the *sucker nakkarsali* were from the ancient Byzantine Jewish community. The strong sugar trading links enjoyed by the Middle East with Venice almost certainly acted as the vector that brought the art of sugar sculpture to Europe. It is likely that knowledge of the techniques used for constructing edible art works of this kind spread from the Levantine centers of sugar production to Venice and then on to the European courts.

To create figurines and other sugar novelties, these early workers used two methods, both of Middle-Eastern origin. The first, sugar casting, exploited the ability of hot syrup to crystalize, or "grain," as it cooled in wooden, plaster, ceramic, or metal molds. It was best suited to simple subjects. The second technique was to freely model or mold a pliable paste made from a mixture of powdered sugar, gum tragacanth, and water. A recipe for this material, known variously as pastillage, sugar plate, or gum paste, first appeared in print in Girolamo Ruscelli's *De' secreti del reuerendo donno Alessio Piemontese* in 1552, though it had almost certainly been in use for a number of centuries before this. Its

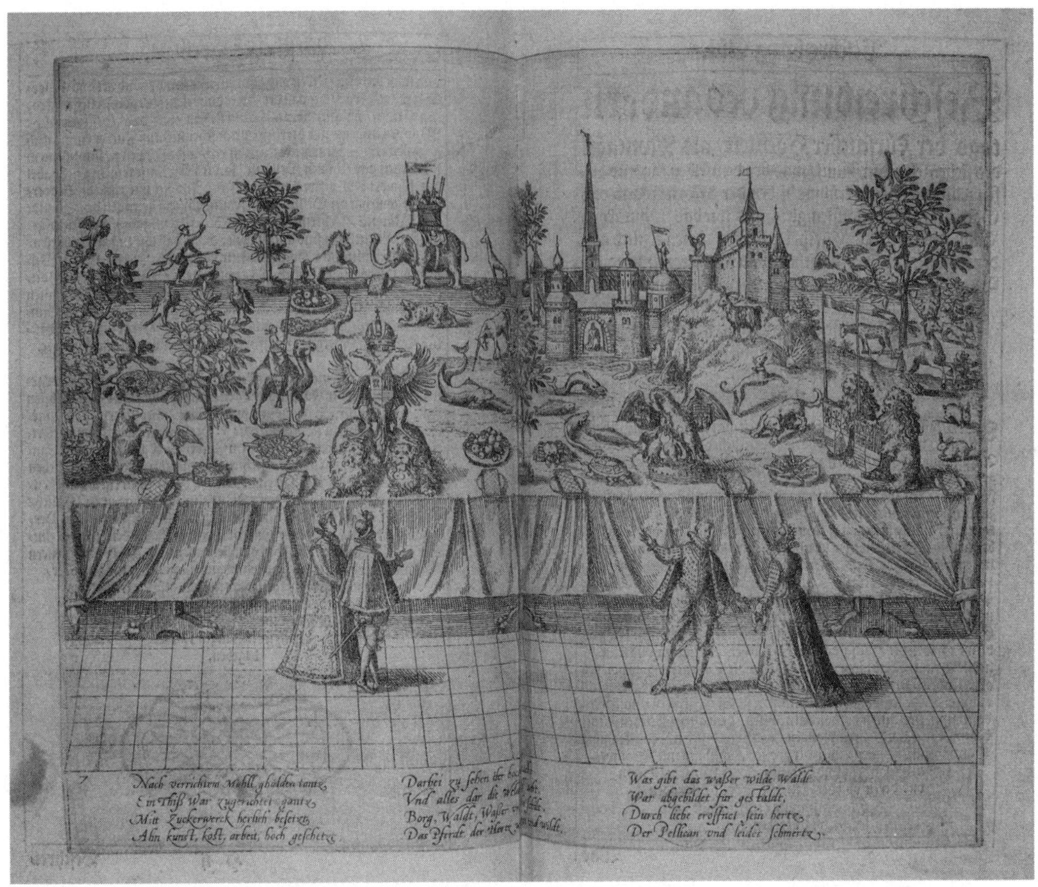

Sugar sculptures of mythic, natural, and heraldic animals serve as ornaments for the banquet table at the lavish wedding of Princess Jakobea of Baden and Duke Johann Wilhelm of Jülich-Cleves, held in the great hall of the castle at Düsseldorf, Germany. Theodor Graminaeus (1530–1590?) made this etching in 1587. GETTY RESEARCH INSTITUTE

ability to be freely modeled and printed with very fine surface detail made it a much more flexible medium than grained sugar. See PASTILLAGE and TRAGACANTH.

The first detailed accounts in Europe of table ornaments made from food materials are in descriptions of fifteenth-century court feasts. These sweet novelties frequently shared their place on the table with other decorative elements, such as ornamental pastry, elaborately folded napkins, and intricately carved fruit. Allegorical devices wrought from wax, almond paste, and sugar were frequently displayed between the courses of royal or ducal entertainments, often in the context of dramatic and musical performances. In France these table emblems were known as *entremets*, literally meaning "between courses." See ENTREMETS. Although they were constructed from sugar or other foodstuffs, they were not necessarily intended to be eaten, as many were gilded and painted with inedible and sometimes toxic pigments. The most spectacular were frequently reserved for the finale of the meal. Pierre Jean-Baptiste Le Grand d'Aussy (1737–1800) describes a seven-course feast in 1458 given by Gaston de Foix (1422–1472) to Charles VII of France (1403–1461), at which the final course culminated in a spectacular display of entremets in the form of stags, lions, and other beasts, all embellished with the king's arms.

In England, where the most common term to describe a device of this kind was a sotelte, such table ornaments were presented at table with the other dishes of each course. Related to the sotelte was a variation known as a warner, though like the French entremet, it was presented in the intervals between courses rather than with the food itself. Presumably warners were given their name because they alerted the diners that the next course was about to commence. Both warners and soteltes frequently incorporated texts or mottoes relevant to the occasion. In *Appendicis ad Joannis Lelandi Antiquarii Collectanea Pars Secunda* (1770) John Leland cites a great feast on Passion Sunday in 1504 to celebrate the enthronization of the scholar William Warham as archbishop of Canterbury. A warner was conveyed into the hall on a portable round table before the feast commenced. The board was divided up into eight sections, with eight embattled towers made of flowers, representing the Oxford colleges, with "the Kyngg sytting in the Parliament with Lordes about hym in their robes, and Saint Wylliam lyke an Archbishop sytting on the right hande of the Kyng; Then the Chaunceler of Oxforde, with other Doctors about hym, presented the said Lord Wylliam, kneelying in a Doctor's habite, unto the Kyng." Texts in Latin issued from the mouths of the figurines of Saint William and King Henry VII, extolling the archbishop's virtues. After this initial allegorical display, the first course of 14 dishes of fish was served, followed by "a subtyltie, as the last dyshe served at the same course."

By the sixteenth century these elaborate creations were frequently mounted upon disks of almond paste known as marchpanes. The scholar J. S. Brewer in 1875 transcribed a set of accounts listing the expenses of a royal sugar banquet given by Henry VIII at Greenwich in 1526. We are told: "Wages of 7 cooks, 4 days at 20*d*., for making a subtilty, with a dungeon and a manor place, set upon 2 marchpanes, garnished with swans and cygnets swimming about the manor, 13*s*. 4*d*." and "to Hugh, master cook to the Princess, for cutting of a tower set on a marchpane, and 2 chess boards and chessmen, garnished with 100 fine gold, 5*s*."

Other royal kitchen accounts from the reign of Henry tell us that court heralds were also involved in the construction and decoration of these works. Carved wooden molds were frequently used in their construction. A probate inventory of 1551 of the goods belonging to a deceased York cook called William Thornton lists an impressive array of these prints: "A print called Sampson; print with Fleurdelice; small leache print; print with Lion and Unicorn; standing print with hart and hind; print with one knot; close print with birds; . . . print with other arms on it; small print; print with wheatsheaf; print with dolfinge."

Similar molds from this period made from wood and pewter survive in German and Portuguese collections. The quality of workmanship is usually exceptionally high. Subject matters include heraldic devices, biblical scenes, mythological figures, and animals. Some German examples even depict erotic scenes in bathhouses. The English antiquarian Richard Warner (1791) discusses some indecent table ornaments from this period, including "representations of the *membra virilia, pudenaque muliebria*, which were formed of pastry, or sugar, and placed before the guests at entertainments."

In Italy sugar sculptures were known as *trionfi di tavola*. At the wedding of Costanzo Sforza and Camilla Marzano D'Aragona in Pesaro in 1475, they were used as edible props in a complex allegorical performance that took place during a 12-course feast. See WEDDING. Costumed performers playing the role of the messengers of the gods announced the dishes of each course, some bearing emblematic *trionfi* to the table. One, for instance, dressed as a figure representing "the influence of fortune," carried a painted sugar pail filled with gilded sugar money on which was coiled a sugar snake. Each coin was printed with portraits of the bride and groom.

A remarkable manuscript with detailed miniatures of the entertainments at this feast, with some of the *trionfi* clearly illustrated, has survived in the Vatican Library (MS Vat. Urb. Lat. 899). This manuscript is exceptional, as very few images of these objects, other than a few hazy sketches, survive from this early period. It was not until the seventeenth century that detailed drawings and prints of sugar sculpture began to appear in any quantity. The evidence of these remarkable images indicates that these fleetingly ephemeral art works were made with the same consummate skill as sculpture in more orthodox materials.

In addition to professional confectioners, important artists were frequently involved in the creation of *trionfi*. The historian Rocco Benedetti (1574) gives a detailed account of a visit of Henry III of France to the Doge's Palace in Venice, at which the king was presented with an assemblage of sugar statuettes made from old designs by the deceased artists Jacobo Sansovino (1486–1570) and Danese Catteneo (ca. 1512–1572). Sugar figurines at some feasts appear to have been identical to bronze miniatures cast by other mannerist masters, such as Giambologna (1529–1608) and Pietro Tacca (1577–1640).

The art historians K. J. Watson and Bruce Boucher suspect that molds for casting these figures in grained sugar could have been made from the original bronzes. In 1600, artists in Giambologna's workshop were involved in a project to create sugar statuettes from his designs for the wedding banquet of Maria de Medici to Henry IV of France. Michelangelo Buonorroti il Giovane gives a detailed account of the banquet, held in the Palazzo Vecchio in Florence, where "among the constant changing table ornaments were sugar figures of the Labours of Hercules, the slaughter of lions and bulls, Nessus and Deinara and before the queen an equestrian statue of the king." Since Henry was not present at the occasion (the couple were married by proxy), this sugar figure, created by Pietro Tacca, was the closest that Maria got to her groom on their wedding day. It was probably identical to Tacca's miniature bronze of Henry mounted on a horse, which survives at the Musée des Beaux-Arts in Dijon.

Some of the finest images of baroque sugar sculpture are to be found in some albums of sketches by Pierre Paul Sévin (1650–1710), a French artist who lived in Rome between 1666 and 1688. A number of Sévin's drawings, which are in the National Museum in Sweden, illustrate papal table settings laid out with *trionfi* of an intensely religious character. A feast for Maundy Thursday given by Clement IX in the Vatican in 1667 shows a table decorated with angels carrying the instruments of Christ's Passion, all executed in a lively baroque style. However, some even more detailed images of Italian sugar sculpture from this period are shown in a series of engravings included in John Michael Wright's *Ragvaglio della solenne comparsa,* which gives a detailed account of an ambassadorial banquet held in the Palazzo Pamphilli in Rome in 1686.

Wright's book contains a folding plate nearly four feet long that shows 12 large trionfi in the style of Bernini, ranged down a long table, with vases of sugar flowers and smaller figurines of heraldic lions, unicorns, and eagles scattered in the spaces. Wright, a Scottish portrait painter who organized the event, describes the table: "Thro' the middle of it, from one end to the other, ran a Range of Historical Figures (some almost half as big as the Life) which the *Italians,* call *Trionfi*: They are made of a kind of Sugar-Paste, but modelled, to the utmost skill of a Statuary; So that they are afterwards, sent as Presents to the greatest Ladies; and their use at Entertainments, is to gratifie the Eye, as the Meat, Musique, and Perfumes, do the other Senses." His observation that these complex and highly articulated figures were modeled from sugar paste, rather than cast from hot sugar syrup, is not surprising.

The emergence of porcelain figures and ornaments for the table during the course of the eighteenth century failed to eclipse these grand sugar tableaux. The new ceramic decorations merely came to share the table with their sugar prototypes. Numerous designs for dessert tables featuring garden plateaux laid out with sugar parterres, sculpture courts, and edible flowers were published in most European countries. A gradual fall in the price of the sugar resulted in a fashion for cheap, mass-produced sugar table ornaments among the merchant class. Richard Warner describes this downward percolation of what had formerly been a phenomenon exclusive to the royal courts: "It seems probable that the splendid desert [*sic*] frames of our days, ornamented with quaint and heterogeneous combinations of Chinese architecture, Arcadian swains, fowl, fish, beasts, and fanciful representations drawn from Heathen mythology, are only the remains of, or, if more agreeable to the modern ear, refinements on, the Old English Sotiltees."

After the French Revolution, the French pâtissier Marie-Antonin Carême (1784–1833) published many eclectic designs for table ornaments, or *pièces montées,* to be constructed in pastry, spun sugar, nougat, and other edible materials. See CARÊME, MARIE-ANTOINE. His hugely influential drawings ranged across a wide spectrum of styles and included designs for ruined classical temples, neo-Gothic spires, Russian churches, and even Swiss cottages. However, his chief influence was to combine the formerly separate roles of confectioner and pastry cook. Many see Carême's work as the start of something new, but in terms of sugar sculpture, it was also the end of something very old. In addition to using pastillage and grained sugar constructions, Carême popularized spun sugar techniques, though it was left up to a number of his followers to develop the related techniques of sugar pulling and blowing. As the nineteenth century advanced, the genre declined into sentimental kitsch, its chief expression being the iced Twelfth Night and wedding cakes of the Victorian period. See TWELFTH NIGHT CAKE and WEDDING CAKE. The privations of the two world wars initiated enormous cultural changes, and the sugary excesses of the patrician table became sociably unacceptable.

In the 1960s a resurgence of interest in old confectioner's skills, chiefly among amateur cake decorators, initiated the modern sugar craft movement, which has now burgeoned into a global phenomenon with its own major support industry providing instruction manuals, classes, raw materials, and equipment. More recently, professional pâtissiers such as Ewald Notter and Jacquy Pfeiffer have developed the use of isomalt (hydrogenated isomaltulose) as an additive to cane sugar to produce impressively clear blown and pulled sugar constructions. See ISOMALT. This aspect of the craft has become increasingly popular in China, where it is frequently practiced in public by street vendors. A number of serious artists have also been attracted to the genre, most notably Belfast-born Brendan Jamison, who constructs architectural caprices from carved sugar cubes. See SUGAR CUBES.

See also CAKE DECORATING; COMPETITIONS; STAGES OF SUGAR SYRUP; SUGAR PAINTING; and VENICE.

Benedetti, Rocco. *Le Feste et trionfi fatti dalla Sereniss: Signoria di Venetia nella felice venuta di Henrico III. christianiss. re di Francia et di Polonia*. Venice, 1574.

Evans, Meryle. "The Splendid Processions of Trade Guilds at Ottoman Festivals." In *Food in the Arts: Proceedings of the Oxford Symposium on Food and Cookery, 1998*, edited by Harlan Walker, pp. 67–72. Totnes, U.K.: Prospect, 1999.

Husrau, Nasir-i. *Safarnāme: Das Reisetagebuch des persischen Dichters Nāṣir-i Ḫusrau.* Edited by Manfred Mayrhofer. Translated by Uto von Melzer. Graz, Austria: Leykam, 1993.

Probate Register Folio 13b/826r, Borthwick Institute of Historical Research, York.

Ruscelli, Girolamo. *De' Secreti del reuerendo donno Alessio Piemontese*. Venice, 1552.

Warham, William. "The Inthronization of Archbishop Warham." In *J. Lelandi antiquarii de rebus Britannicis collectanea*, Vol. 6. London, 1770.

Wright, John Michael. *Ragvaglio della solenne comparsa*. Rome, 1687. An English version (not an exact translation) was published as *An Account of His Excellence Roger, Earl of Castlemaine's Embassy* (London, 1688).

Ivan Day

sugar trade, which arose from the increasing demand for sugar that began in the early sixteenth century and has continued unabated ever since, parallels the political, economic, and cultural ascendance of European and Euro-American nation-states on the global stage since 1500. It is perfectly accurate to associate the growing global importance of sugar with the "rise of the West," as the astronomical success of the transatlantic European trade in semi-refined cane sugar produced by slave labor in the Caribbean and Brazil that began in the sixteenth century provided the economic motor for the expansion of European empires in the early modern era and, as some have argued, for the Industrial Revolution that followed. Moreover, a direct link exists between the entrenchment of cane sugar in culinary habits across social and economic divides of Western Europe in the eighteenth century and the modern culture of sweetness.

In 1961, describing the transcendent place of sugar in the American diet, French critic Roland Barthes wrote, "Sugar is a time, a category of the world" (p. 28). Although he was concerned with characterizing something of the uniqueness of the mid-twentieth-century American diet, sugar consumption today is on the rise across the globe. The sugar trades that supply global demand in the twenty-first century are diverse and complex, at least in part because sugar, in its purest form as sucrose, can be derived from many plant sources, of which the two most common are sugarcane and the sugar beet. See SUGARCANE and SUGAR BEET. The refining of sugar is pivotal to its history and to its worldwide spread, as it has permitted sugar to take on the transportable and marketable crystalline form that we recognize today. Although other refined sweeteners such as saccharine and high-fructose corn syrup have largely replaced beet- or cane-derived sugar in soft drinks, processed baked goods, and other pillars of contemporary Western food culture, sugar, nonetheless, is exceptional.

Beginnings

Although the origin of sugarcane is in the South Pacific, the first general indication of the appearance of a form of sugar that was transportable long distances, and thus susceptible to being widely traded, was in northern India before 500 B.C.E. The earliest Sanskrit reference to manufactured refined sugar (as opposed to other forms of cane sugar, such as cane juice) occurred sometime between the seventh and fourth centuries B.C.E., with the earliest datable reference appearing in a manual on statesmanship written between 324 and 300 B.C.E. There are multiple references in Sanskrit after that date that testify to the widespread cultivation, refinement, and consumption of sugar, as much for medical uses as for culinary ones. See MEDICINAL USES OF SUGAR; SUGAR REFINING; and SUGARCANE AGRICULTURE.

Both the knowledge of sugarcane and sugar products themselves diffused from India to China via the Indo-Chinese trade. Sugarcane was grown in northern Vietnam (Tonkin and Annam) during the period of the Indian Mauryan Empire (322–185 B.C.E.) when trade connections between India and China were being strengthened. Sugarcane was also cultivated elsewhere on the Malaysian Peninsula and traded into southern China from these locations from the third century B.C.E. By the third or fourth century C.E. loaf cane sugar was a commodity that was both imported and produced in Szechuan and elsewhere in southern China, with the first concrete reference to sugar manufacture within China appearing during the later years of the Han dynasty (206 B.C.E.–220 C.E.). By the Tang dynasty (618–906), the cultivation of sugarcane was well established in several locales in China; by the earlier period of this same dynasty, it was firmly entrenched in Chinese culinary practices, alongside other sweeteners such as palm sugar and honey. See HONEY and PALM SUGAR. During the latter part of the Tang, loaf cane sugar was also imported from Iran into China via the Silk Road. By the medieval period widespread evidence exists for the exchange of cane sugar and agricultural knowledge of sugarcane cultivation between centers in the Middle East, North Africa, and China. For example, the travel accounts of Marco Polo (1254–1324) and Ibn Baṭṭūṭah (1304–1378) attest to the extensive culinary uses of sugar at the Chinese court and the knowledge Chinese cane growers gained from as far away as Egypt.

Medieval Islamic Sugar Trade

How did the Middle East emerge to be a center of sugarcane cultivation, and how did vibrant medieval trades in sugar develop concurrently in the Middle East and in both Islamic and Christian Europe? These trades depended on the diffusion of sugar westward from Asia, from India in particular, a process that occurred in gradual steps; the development of sugar industries and of export trades in sugar represented only the final stage. Knowledge of the sugarcane plant in Europe and the Middle East greatly preceded the commercial production of sugarcane and cane products in those places, which occurred only many centuries after commercial sugarcane production had been established in India.

The first wave of diffusion from India was to Persia in the sixth century. Once established in Persia, sugarcane spread with alacrity throughout the Middle East and further west, in waves that corresponded to Arab expeditions of conquest after the death of Muhammad around 632. Sugarcane was one of the most profitable of a broad array of crops, which included citrus fruit, eggplant, and spinach, dispersing from India through the Middle East to the Mediterranean and North Africa via Islamic conquests in the so-called Arab Agricultural Revolution.

There is evidence that a minor sugar industry existed in Mesopotamia in the decades before Muhammad's death, but only in the tenth century do records point to sugar being a major industry in important Muslim areas of the former Persian Empire such as Hormuz, the valleys of the Tigris and the Euphrates, and south of the Caspian Sea. Sugar was also introduced to the Arabian Peninsula, Eastern Africa, and Zanzibar in the ninth and tenth centuries. Although it was being produced in Abyssinia by the twelfth century, a sugar industry did not develop further inland in sub-Saharan Africa. In North Africa, references to sugar export industries existed in Morocco and Tunisia as of the tenth century; while in Egypt, which became a center of sugar production and export, cultivation began in the tenth century, although large-scale sugar plantations did not develop in Upper Egypt until the eleventh and twelfth centuries.

The diffusion of sugar making to Islamic and Christian Europe, the strengthening of sugar trades bringing sugar into northwestern Europe, and the development of European culinary practices using sugar took two broad paths, one in the west and the other in the east of the continent. On the Iberian Peninsula in the west, sugarcane arrived in Spain soon after the Muslim conquest in 711, although the first references to a Spanish sugar industry date only to the ninth and tenth centuries. Southern Spain—Granada up to Valencia, in particular—became a hub of sugar production. In the eastern Mediterranean, the Norman conquest of Sicily in the twelfth century was responsible for spreading knowledge of sugar making and sugar consumption practices northward into Continental Europe, as sugar had been cultivated in Sicily in small amounts after the Arab invasion of 655, and in larger amounts after the growth of an export trade in the tenth century. The expansion of the northwestern European demand for sugar led to greater sugar cultivation in the Middle East and eastern Mediterranean (in Palestine, Cyprus, Rhodes, and Crete, for instance).

The Mediterranean sugar trades were largely in the hands of Italian merchants. Venetians dominated the eastern Mediterranean, whereas Genoese merchants controlled the Spanish sugar trade in the western Mediterranean, encouraging the expansion of production, even into the Algarve in Portugal in the early fifteenth century. In the sugar centers of the eastern Mediterranean, sugar often made up the same cargoes as the spices that Venetian merchants were bringing into Europe. See VENICE. Although of the two groups of commodities, sugar was of significantly less value than spices, even the relatively lower-valued crystalline form of cane sugar remained an elite good in Europe and the Middle East, consumed, as in China, in an array of culinary and medicinal ways. Venetian merchants shipped crystalline sugar by sea from the ports of Beirut, Alexandria, and Tripoli westward to Italy, Marseilles, and Aigues-Mortes in southern France, Catalonia, and England. Maritime trade networks taking sugar into Europe were connected to land-based distribution systems leading inland into Provence, Lyons up to Flanders from port cities in southern France, and into the Alps and Germany from Italy. Land-based networks also took Sicilian, Egyptian, and Cypriot sugar east to Baghdad, the Arabian Peninsula, and Yemen.

Decline of Mediterranean Sugar and the Rise of Atlantic Sugar

The decline of the Mediterranean sugar industry between the fourteenth and sixteenth centuries was paralleled by the concomitant rise of the Atlantic sugar industry, which, nonetheless, was not the principal cause of the waning of the trade in Mediterranean sugar. The temperate climate of the Mediterranean, as well as other impediments of geography such as a lack of rainfall, had always constituted obstacles to the successful development of large-scale production in Europe of what is essentially a tropical crop. But the key causes of this decline were European and Middle Eastern warfare, recurrent waves of the bubonic plague, the stagnation of technological development, and restrictive production and trade policies in certain important centers such as Egypt. In addition to these factors weakening the trade in Mediterranean sugar, the Portuguese, who had newly colonized the island of Madeira, began to cultivate sugar there in 1433 and by midcentury were exporting it back to Portugal. The production of sugarcane on the islands off the western coasts of Africa, colonized by the Portuguese and Spanish with the goal of exporting sugar to Europe, continued apace in the fifteenth and early sixteenth centuries, as Portuguese overseas expansion intensified. After Madeira, the Spanish introduced sugar production to the Canary Islands, and the Portuguese to the islands of São Tomé and Príncipe in the Gulf of Guinea, where a subtropical climate ideally suited to sugarcane production and an enslaved African workforce were, for the first time, associated with the plantation model that had been developed in the Mediterranean. See PLANTATIONS, SUGAR and SLAVERY. By the first decade of the sixteenth century, São Tomé sugar was being exported to Antwerp that, with Bruges and Lisbon, was the most vibrant hub of sugar refining and international sale in Western Europe, reflecting the dominance of the Spanish sugar trade in the sixteenth century, when the Netherlands were politically integrated into the sprawling Habsburg Spanish Empire. The southern provinces of the Netherlands, which contained Antwerp, remained under the control of Spain after confederation of the northern United Provinces in 1580. After this date Amsterdam, the new vibrant capital city of the United Provinces, began to compete with Antwerp in sugar refining and the sugar trade. See SUGAR REFINERIES.

By this time sugarcane production had been established in the new Iberian Atlantic world, transported by both the Portuguese and Spanish across the Atlantic Ocean almost from the beginning of their transatlantic expeditions. Christopher Columbus, a Genoese navigator with sugar-trading experience in Madeira, sailed under the Spanish flag and brought sugarcane to the island of Hispaniola in the

Caribbean on his second voyage (1493), while the Portuguese colony of Brazil was home to sugar plantations before 1516. See BRAZIL. By the mid-sixteenth century Caribbean sugar made up 10 percent of the sugar imported into the Antwerp sugar market, whereas 50 percent was still from São Tomé; by the end of the century, though, Brazilian sugar had overtaken all competitors and furnished 85 percent of Antwerp's sugar. By this time the crowns of Spain and Portugal were united, thereby greatly facilitating the integration of Brazilian sugar into Spanish sugar markets across Europe. More important, Brazil, with its capacity for plantations of a scale heretofore unseen in Mediterranean and Atlantic island settings, and with a propitious climate, provided the model that would successfully diffuse outward. Two other factors played key roles in the success of this Brazilian model: first, after initially depending on enslaved Amerindian peoples to make up the labor force on sugar plantations, the Portuguese turned in greater numbers after the 1570s to imported enslaved Africans, thereby hugely expanding the Portuguese transatlantic slave trade and rendering the trade in sugar more profitable. Second, technical innovations in milling in the first quarter of the seventeenth century improved the efficiency of sugarcane processing on plantations.

Sugar production on the Spanish Caribbean possessions of Hispaniola, Cuba, and Puerto Rico developed slowly in the sixteenth century and could not seriously compete in European markets with Brazilian sugar. Nevertheless, by the eighteenth century it was the British and French island possessions in the Caribbean which, by far outstripping Brazil, had become the locus of the Atlantic production of sugar, as well as of the burgeoning global empires of Britain and France. This process began with the diffusion northward of the Brazilian model of sugar plantations and its slow and erratic establishment in the Lesser Antilles in the second half of the seventeenth century, aided in no small part by the arrival on Barbados, Martinique, and Guadeloupe of Dutch refugees from Brazil in 1656, who had been ousted by the Portuguese from their 30-year occupation of Brazil. Dutch refugees were vectors for both European and African knowledge of sugarcane cultivation and sugar processing according to the "Brazilian model." By the late eighteenth century British and French Caribbean sugar production had exploded and reached its peak, largely due to increasing British investment in the transatlantic trade in enslaved Africans and to the attribution in the early eighteenth century to sugarcane cultivation of vast tracts of land in the Greater Antilles: the two most productive sugar islands were British Jamaica and French Saint-Domingue (the western third of the island of Hispaniola). Expanding sugar production in the Caribbean led to the global transformations that defined European empires in the eighteenth century. It fueled the triangular transatlantic trades linking sugar production in the Caribbean with the African sources of slave labor that ensured sugar could be profitably produced, and with European consumers via complex merchant networks that also shipped textiles and other manufactured goods, foodstuffs, and naval stores, as well as sugar byproducts and other tropical commodities, around the Atlantic world.

By this period sugar consumption had become deeply entrenched in Western Europe and in European colonies in the Atlantic world and across the globe. The lowering of the price of sugar that slave labor permitted meant that sugar was no longer exclusively an elite good, but one that had begun to permeate all social classes. Expanded sugar consumption entailed not only an increased direct consumption of the many grades and qualities of sugar and sugar byproducts now available (including treacle, molasses, and other sugar syrups, as well as rum), but also the creation of new forms of sugar consumption (such as in the new dessert course, in baked goods and preserves, and with tea) that were widely shared among social classes. See MOLASSES and RUM. Cane sugar consumption also stimulated the production and sale of a whole array of manufactured goods that accompanied these new culinary forms (such as sugar tongs, sifters, spoons, and bowls), reflecting the depth of its widespread adoption in European culinary cultures. See SERVERS, SUGAR.

Emergence of the Sugar Beet

The depth of the cultural absorption of sugar explains why the wars, revolutions, and transformations to the institution of plantation slavery that occurred over 40 years at the end of the eighteenth century and into the nineteenth century, disrupting the transatlantic trades in cane sugar and cane sugar byproducts, did not stem the overall consumption of sugar, but instead profoundly altered the way it was produced. The first of these events was the 1791 Haitian Revolution, when the enslaved plantation labor force of the French colony of Saint-Domingue successfully overturned the social, political, and economic structures of power—including slavery—and, almost overnight, upset the supply of cane sugar in the single most productive sugar colony in the world. Concurrently, rising abolitionism in Western Europe eventually led to the end of the slave trade and the emancipation of slaves by the 1830s in the British colonies and 15 years later in the French ones. The new types of Asian and Indian immigration that were devised by colonial authorities after the collapse of slavery were not, however, profitable labor alternatives when it came to sugar production. Eventually, both these phenomena led to an overall decline in the cane sugar productivity of the traditional sugar colonies. While cane sugar production continued in Spanish and Portuguese colonies of the Atlantic world, especially in Cuba in the late nineteenth century and in British Guiana, these regions did not completely fill the vacuum left by the British and French Caribbean colonies, which were also facing competition in global sugar markets by colonies located in tropical Asia and Asia Pacific, where European empires were extending themselves in new ways and with renewed vigor in the nineteenth century.

However, the competition to cane sugar that would have the longest-lasting impact on global sugar markets occurred with the emergence of the sugar beet during the Napoleonic Wars (1799–1815). The ability to extract and refine sucrose from the common sugar beet (*Beta vulgaris*)—grown in Europe since at least the end of the fifteenth century—had been developed in Germany in the mid-eighteenth century, launching a fledgling industry there. But it was the British blockade of Continental Europe, cutting French transatlantic access to its remaining sugar colonies in the Caribbean, which prompted Napoleon to initiate a French sugar beet industry. By 1813 France was producing 7.7 million pounds of sugar from sugar beets. The resumption of transatlantic shipping in 1815 temporarily brought the growth of this French industry to a halt, but it quickly picked up in the postwar years, due chiefly to its competitive advantages compared to cane sugar in this period. From being a largely French industry within Europe, sugar beet production grew slowly in Austria, Hungary, and Russia.

Unlike sugarcane, which required a tropical climate and was primarily grown in monocultural plantation settings, sugar beets could be comprehensively incorporated into preexisting European agricultural systems: leaves and roots were used as cattle feed, and the crop was used in rotation with other crops, which increased yields overall. For these reasons, the European sugar beet industry—again unlike sugarcane—became inextricably bound up with the globalization of agriculture in the nineteenth century, in which free trade was the political economic watchword of the new imperial superpowers. While Britain had emerged as the largest global consumer of sugar in the eighteenth century—due in no small part to the fact that France controlled the lucrative re-export trades in sugar within Europe, leaving Britain to consume its own colonial production—the country's sugar consumption only increased in the nineteenth century, thanks to cheap European beet sugar imports. By the end of the century sugar beets provided just over 50 percent of the world's refined sugar, and sugarcane just under 50 percent.

Modern Sugar Trade

The proportions of cane sugar and beet sugar reversed in the early twentieth century as a result of changes in the system of agricultural tariffs; however, the real challenge to the growing dominance of beet sugar was posed by the rising power of the American market for sugar, which had been gathering strength since the late nineteenth century. In this period of American expansionism, U.S. investors and imperialists, who (often in tandem) maintained active political and commercial interests in Caribbean and Latin American territories as well as in Hawaii, promoted the expansion and intensification of cane sugar cultivation in these territories to profit from this domestic market. They also lobbied for the removal of import tariffs on cane sugar. See SUGAR BARONS and SUGAR LOBBIES. Nowhere was this pattern more fully and successfully put into practice than in Cuba, which, by 1918, had grown to be the world's largest sugar producer, based entirely on sugarcane. The global context for Cuba's rise was the devastation of Europe's sugar beet production during World War I.

The first half of the twentieth century saw the extension of both the sugar beet and sugarcane industries within the continental United States (according to geographic variability). Fledgling sugar beet industries similarly developed in Britain, across the British Commonwealth (including Canada), Brazil, and elsewhere. In all these cases, production was intended for domestic consumption, with Commonwealth countries also supplying Britain. Steeply rising rates of sugar consumption across the globe in the nineteenth and twentieth centuries had the effect of multiplying the countries that grew sugarcane or sugar beets for domestic consumption, as well as increasing the demand on external markets for sugar. For instance, China began growing sugar beets in the early twentieth century. Nevertheless, by the end of the century, Europe alone dominated the global sugar beet industry, producing four-fifths of the world's supply. India and Brazil, on the other hand, currently dominate sugarcane production, whereas Cuba is still the biggest Caribbean producer, despite the post-1989 loss of its markets after the disintegration of Communist-bloc countries in Eastern Europe. While cane sugar today dominates the world's sugar supply, almost two-thirds of all sugar is now consumed in the country where it is produced, testifying to vigorous demand across the globe and to the national sugar industries that have been developed to meet it. The global sugar trade, which once had stimulated the world's appetite for sugar, no longer supplies it.

See also BELGIUM; CHINA; LEGISLATION, HISTORICAL; MIDDLE EAST; NETHERLANDS; NORTH AFRICA; PORTUGAL; SPAIN; SPANISH-AMERICAN WAR; and SUGAR.

Barthes, Ronald. "Towards a Psychosociology of Contemporary Food Consumption." In *Food and Culture: A Reader*, 3d ed., edited by Carole Counihan and Penny Van Esterik, pp. 28–34. London: Routledge, 2013. Essay originally published 1961.

Deerr, Noël. *The History of Sugar*. 2 vols. London: Chapman and Hall, 1949.

Galloway, J. H. *The Sugar Cane Industry: A Historical Geography from Its Origins to 1914*. Cambridge, U.K., and New York: Cambridge University Press, 1989.

Higman, B. W. "The Sugar Revolution." *Economic History Review* 53 (2000): 213–236.

International Sugar Organization. *Sugar Yearbook*. Annual periodical.

McGillivray, Gillian. *Blazing Cane: Sugar, Communities, Class, and State Formation in Cuba, 1868–1959*. Durham, N.C.: Duke University Press, 2009.

Mintz, Sidney. *Sweetness and Power: The Place of Sugar in Modern History*. New York: Viking, 1985.

Schwartz, Stuart B., ed. *Tropical Babylons: Sugar and the Making of the Atlantic World, 1450–1680*. Durham, N.C.: University of North Carolina Press, 2004.

Stein, Robert Louis. *The French Sugar Business in the Eighteenth Century*. Baton Rouge: Louisiana State University Press, 1988.

Bertie Mandelblatt

Sugar Trust was the popular name for the American Sugar Refining Company (ASRC), a powerful conglomeration of sugar manufacturers that dominated the U.S. sugar industry from the 1880s onward. Although the ASRC was technically a trust for only a few short years, the popular press continued to refer to the company as the "Sugar Trust" for many decades. Like John D. Rockefeller's famous Standard Oil Trust, the Sugar Trust symbolized ruthless corporate competition for a generation of muckraking journalists and populist politicians. Opponents were especially worried that the Sugar Trust's actions raised sugar prices for consumers, and political cartoons sometimes personified the Trust as a bloated bully cruelly stealing penny candies from innocent children. Concerns about the Sugar Trust came up in debates over tariffs, corporate regulation, and even U.S. expansion into the Caribbean and Pacific at the turn of the twentieth century.

The Sugar Trust originated in a period when U.S. business leaders were experimenting with new ways to maximize profits and minimize the economic booms and busts that had characterized the nineteenth century. Before the late 1880s, no single firm dominated the sugar refining industry. Multiple independent firms—some corporations and some private partnerships—competed to sell their sugar. But a few large companies, mostly on the eastern seaboard, had made large capital investments in modern refinery equipment that they hoped to protect by limiting competition. Headed by the sugar magnate Henry Havemeyer, the largest refiners explored legal ways to consolidate their control over the competition. See HAVEMEYER, HENRY OSBORNE. In 1887, under Havemeyer's leadership, 17 of the nation's 23 sugar refining companies combined into a trust. The new organization, the Sugar Refineries Company (SRC), controlled 75 percent of the sugar refining business in the United States. A board of trustees managed all of the participating companies, and they issued inflated stock certificates in exchange for the original capital stock. The new company reorganized the entire industry and closed a number of refineries, so that by 1891 only four of the original refineries remained in operation.

Just three years later Congress prohibited this type of merger through the Sherman Antitrust Act (1890). The "Sugar Trust" quickly regrouped as the American Sugar Refining Company (ASRC), making use of a brand-new provision of New Jersey incorporation law that authorized "holding companies." The holding company, like the trust, enabled the board of directors to control prices, allocate market shares, and otherwise coordinate the industry. The ASRC hastily acquired a number of the remaining independent refineries on the East Coast, which prompted the Department of Justice to begin an investigation. This inquiry led directly to the Supreme Court case *United States v. E.C. Knight,* which was decided in favor of the ASRC in 1895. This ruling set an important precedent, making it difficult for the federal government to regulate corporate mergers for the next several decades. For this reason, the "Sugar Trust" continued to symbolize lax antitrust enforcement among muckrakers and reformers.

Throughout the 1890s, the Havemeyer-controlled ASRC engaged in ruthless price wars with its main competitors, especially those operating on the West Coast. One competitor, the German-born Claus Spreckels, imported duty-free raw sugar from Hawaii to refine in his California factories. Spreckels had invested heavily in Hawaiian plantations, developing an irrigation system and recruiting laborers from Asia to work the fields. The conflict with Spreckels was neither the first nor the last turf battle for the Sugar Trust, although the major sugar refiners periodically reached agreements about dividing the market among themselves and setting prices. After Havemeyer's death in 1907, the ASRC began a process of vertical integration, through which they gained control not only of their competitors, but also of resources at every stage of sugar production from seed to table. Especially after World War I, the ASRC expanded its control of Caribbean sugar plantations with help from New York investment bankers. The ASRC continued to be a powerful player throughout the twentieth century, eventually acquiring a controlling interest in Spreckels's operations. In the early 1970s ASRC changed its name to Amstar and began investing heavily in the high-fructose corn syrup industry. See CORN SYRUP. The company changed hands and went through a number of reorganizations, and since the early 2000s the company, with a diverse investment portfolio, has been called Domino Foods. Even though the phrase "Sugar Trust" has steadily fallen out of use since the 1910s, the company has repeatedly faced federal antitrust lawsuits at nearly every stage of its history.

See also AMERICAN SUGAR REFINING COMPANY; SUGAR REFINING; and SUGAR REFINERIES.

Ayala, César J. *American Sugar Kingdom: The Plantation Economy of the Spanish Caribbean, 1898–1934.* Chapel Hill: University of North Carolina Press, 1999.

Eichner, Alfred S. *The Emergence of Oligopoly: Sugar Refining as a Case Study.* Baltimore: Johns Hopkins University Press, 1969.

April Merleaux

sugarcane looks very much like any other grass in the savanna. Some variants of it still grow wild in the fields, waving in the tropical winds of its native New Guinea. Tall and segmented like bamboo, with its reed-like stalk filled with sweet sap, *Saccharum officinarum* is at the origin of the main cultivated sugarcane species known today, all of which are hybrids. Cane has been known for at least 2,200 years and is a curiously adaptable plant. A perennial with a deep root system, it can flourish and grow upwards of 15 feet tall. Cane likes a climate where temperatures are above 70°F (21°C) and thrives in places where temperatures register above 81°F (27°C). When temperatures fall below 52–55°F (11–13°C), cane dies. It requires water but will do well when properly irrigated. It is tolerant of a wide range of soil conditions and can grow on both hillsides and on flat land.

No one knows whether cane moved by man, by weather, or by spontaneous generation, but cane was growing in India by about 550 B.C.E., and possibly in China by approximately 200 B.C.E. It was in India, though, that the sugar-bearing reed gained importance and became one of the first plants to inspire humans to technology. It was discovered that crushing and then boiling it could concentrate the sweetness of the plant. Sugarcane presses were used like oil presses. Cane was crushed, the juice was boiled, and a catalyst was added to precipitate out impurities. The sugar mills and the basics of processing sugar

History was changed forever by the introduction of sugarcane to the New World in 1493. Demand for the sweet substance produced by this perennial grass led directly to plantation slavery and its terrible abuses. MISSOURI BOTANICAL GARDEN

from cane juice remained virtually the same for millennia; however, as the process became more refined, so did the sugar, ultimately yielding the white crystals that we know today. See SUGAR and SUGAR REFINING. Early texts suggest that the cane was transformed into many different grades of sugar, with special medicinal effects attributed to each. See MEDICINAL USES OF SUGAR. Rock sugar called *khand* (thus, our word "candy") was first described for the West in 326 or 327 B.C.E. by those in the retinue of Alexander the Great as "stones the color of frankincense, sweeter than figs or honey."

Sugarcane's Travels

Sugarcane's voyage to the western Mediterranean was a slow one that would take more than a millennium. Cane took 700 years to make its way from the Indian subcontinent to Persia by 600 C.E., and from there to the Middle East—notably, Egypt, Syria, and the Holy Land, where it arrived by the eighth century. There, cane and the technology of processing it into sugar became known by the Crusaders, who produced sugar in small quantities. By the thirteenth century, cane had progressed from the Holy Land into the Mediterranean, brought under Islam's star and crescent. Monopolies rose and fell as Venetians, Genoese, and others vied for control of the increasingly lucrative trade. By the mid-fifteenth century, sugar had crossed the Mediterranean, leaving refineries in Crete, Cyprus, and other outposts, and had reached the Atlantic islands. By 1432 it was being refined in Madeira, around 1480 it was being established in the Canary Islands, and in the last decades of the fifteenth century it was being grown and processed on São Tomé. By then slave labor had been added into the deadly equation, and the die was cast for sugar's conquest of the New World tropics. See SLAVERY.

The Four Curses of Sugar

Throughout its march around the world, sugarcane brought with it what the historian Peter Macinnis has called the four curses of sugar:

1. Sugarcane is capital intensive and it requires large amounts of money to establish large sugarcane plantations.
2. Sugarcane requires immediate processing when ready for harvest, as it deteriorates rapidly. Generally, cane juice needs to be processed by boiling within 16 to 24 hours of harvest in order to destroy enzymes and maintain sucrose.
3. Sugar production consumes enormous amounts of fuel, resulting in deforestation.
4. Sugar production is labor intensive, and therefore the growth of sugar meant the growth of enslavement.

Sugarcane and the slavery that it brought would soon transform the Western Hemisphere.

New World Sugar

Sugarcane was brought to the Western Hemisphere from La Gomera in the Canary Islands by Columbus on his second voyage in 1493. Columbus was familiar with the plant because his mother-in-law owned a sugarcane plantation in Madeira. Cane flourished on Hispaniola, and in his diaries Columbus remarks on the abundance of the harvest, although at that time there seems to have been no attempt made to cultivate it on a large scale. Small backyard plots were established in numerous locations—so many that when future colonists arrived, they thought the plant was native to the region.

Brazil would transform New World sugar and turn it into a commodity that would change the way that sugar was grown, and thus change the complexion of the Western Hemisphere. See BRAZIL. The Dutch, who were at war with the Portuguese in northeastern Brazil, perfected the plantation system there, using enslaved African labor and large land holdings. See PLANTATIONS, SUGAR. In the mid-seventeenth century, they were instrumental in creating the Sugar Revolution that transformed the Lesser Antilles to the monoculture of sugar.

The Sugar Revolution

The Dutch plantation system was brought to Barbados in the 1640s. Within two decades, what came to be known as the Sugar Revolution had begun in the Caribbean, transforming the region from a backwater of colonists trying to survive growing tobacco, cotton, indigo, and other crops to a haven for those in search of riches.

Richard Ligon was among those who set out for the region in 1647. His *True and Exact History of The Island of Barbados,* published in 1650, details early sugar production on the island. It may also be the first work in the English language to describe rum and its effects. The process of refining sugar was simple and remained relatively unchanged since ancient times. The raw cane was crushed in wind- or water-driven mills, and the resulting liquid—the trash called *bagasse*—was removed and used to fire the burners that heated the cane juice. The heated juice was clarified with a small amount of lime, and then ladled into copper boiling pans of successively smaller size, each over increasingly higher heat. Once the syrup reached the last boiling pan, it was allowed to evaporate until reduced to a thick syrup. This syrup was allowed to cool and was then further cooled in troughs before being poured into large casks or hogsheads that were perforated in the bottom to allow the molasses to drip out. This process was called the Jamaica Train method. Byproducts of sugar production were molasses, which could be reboiled after having dripped from the hogshead, and rum, which was prepared from the first skimmings of the copper pans or made from molasses. Both became valuable commodities in themselves. See MOLASSES and RUM. The raw sugar and molasses were shipped off to the mother countries in Europe, where the raw sugar was further refined, thus guaranteeing economic and political control over the colonies that produced the sugar.

Sugar created great fortunes in the Caribbean, and in the seventeenth and eighteenth centuries the expression "as rich as a Barbados planter" became a term for extreme wealth; the period was one of lavish excess on the part of the plantocracy, and of abject misery for the enslaved. See SUGAR BARONS. The Sugar Revolution marched through the Caribbean from south to north, first conquering the Lesser Antilles, then moving northward through the French and then Spanish islands until the Caribbean region was virtually given over to the monoculture of sugar. The eighteenth century was characterized by the model of large slave holdings and offered little change in technology. The nineteenth century added innovations such as the use of horizontal rollers, evaporating pans, and steam engines to turn the mills. By the early nineteenth century the discovery of beet sugar and its subsequent production heralded major competition for cane sugar. See SUGAR BEET. The elimination of the transatlantic slave trade and the gradual abolition of enslavement in the British and then the French, Dutch, and eventually Spanish and Brazilian colonies also contributed to the end of the sugar epochs in the Caribbean.

The Continuity of Cane

Although sugar has never again been as transformational as it was during its early years in the Caribbean, it remains a major commodity. In Louisiana, where cane had been grown since colonization, it became an important crop in the early nineteenth century following an exodus of planters from Saint Domingue, and in the mid-nineteenth century the sugar industry began to take off in the state. Technological innovations like the vacuum pan evaporator, patented by Norbert Rillieux in 1843, replaced the Jamaica Train method and made Louisiana sugar profitable. Today, southern Louisiana remains sugar's capital in the United States, and sugar from cane remains one of that state's major industrial crops. In the 2010–2011 crop year, Brazil was the world's largest producer of sugarcane, followed by India, China, Thailand, the United States, Mexico, and Pakistan.

Sugarcane continues to be one of the world's most important crops. Although cane's four curses have changed somewhat in the twenty-first century, they still apply. Having transformed the destinies of two hemispheres, sugar contributes to the world's economy, and to its health, in ways that are still being determined.

See also COLONIALISM; SUGARCANE AGRICULTURE; and SUGAR TRADE.

Abbott, Elizabeth. *Sugar: A Bittersweet History*. New York: Overlook, 2011.

Kiple, Kenneth F., and Kriemhild Coneé Ornelas, eds. *The Cambridge World History of Food*. Cambridge, U.K.: Cambridge University Press, 2000.

Ligon, Richard. *A True and Exact History of the Island of Barbados*. London, 1657. E-text available at http://www.davidchansmith.net/#!the-richard-ligon-project/c1fc1.

Macinnis, Peter. *Bittersweet: The Story of Sugar*. Crows Nest, Australia: Allen & Unwin, 2002.

Mintz, Sidney W. *Sweetness and Power: The Place of Sugar in Modern History*. New York: Viking, 1985.

Taussig, Charles William. *Some Notes on Sugar and Molasses: Being the Story of an American Industry by Charles William Taussig, with Many Illustrations, and a Foreword by J. T. Winterich*. New York: Charles Wiliam Taussig, 1940.

Jessica B. Harris

sugarcane agriculture likely originated in India and New Guinea. It is difficult to determine when cane sugar first became the principal cultivated sweetener, although evidence exists that it achieved dominance on the subcontinent of India more than 2,500 years ago, and it was in that country and China that commercial sugar was first produced from sugarcane. It was not until the early eighteenth century, however, that sugar began to be used by the general population in Western Europe. Sugarcane was unknown in the New World until Columbus introduced it on his second voyage in 1493. Today, it is highly adapted to a wide range of tropical and subtropical climates, soils, and cultural conditions and is propagated in over 100 countries, occupying more than 20 million hectares of land worldwide. There can be little doubt that as a source of food and renewable energy, and as a supplier of income to millions of people, sugarcane ranks among the top agricultural crops in the world.

Sugarcane is a tall perennial tropical grass with tillers—shoots that arise from the base of the plant to produce unbranched stems (stalks) from 2 to 4 meters or taller, and around 5 centimeters in diameter. The grass is cultivated for these stalks or canes, from which the sugar containing juice is extracted. The plant is described as a strongly growing grass with a C_4 carbon cycle photosynthetic pathway and a high chromosome number exceeding 125.

Sugarcane Improvement and Variety Development

The first improvements in sugarcane resulted from the selection of sweeter, less fibrous types suitable for

Harvesting sugarcane is highly labor intensive, as crops ready for harvesting deteriorate rapidly. This 1938 photograph, taken by Russell Lee as part of a U.S. government project to create a pictorial record of American life, shows a Louisiana sugarcane worker at a rare moment of rest. LIBRARY OF CONGRESS

chewing. Sugarcane breeding is widely acknowledged as the principal method for improving productivity and lowering costs. Sugarcane varieties are the lifeblood of most major sugarcane industries. Further, variety diversification is essential to the survival of most sugar industries worldwide. The modern varieties, such as HoCP 96-540, HoCP 00-950, and L 01-299, have many different and often specific traits, such as high cane or sugar yield, good ratooning or stubbling ability, low fiber, and good sucrose extraction, which give them an advantage over the older varieties, such as CP 65-357, CP 70-321, and LCP 85-384. The variety must also have tolerance to disease and insect pests, be adapted to the local climate and soil environment, and fit into the management system in use. A variety might start out well but suddenly give way to a change in insect pests or disease pressure or to a new introduced pest or disease. Six to twelve or more years are generally required to develop a new variety using conventional breeding and selection techniques from the year the cross is made until its release as a commercial variety. Through the application of biotechnology and the use of genetic transformation and molecular markers, the industry is on the threshold of a potential revolution in sugarcane improvement.

The ultimate goal of any effective sugarcane breeding and selection program is the development of new varieties capable of producing high sugar and other products of economic importance (such as ethanol) at a lower cost than can be attained with existing varieties.

How Sugarcane Is Propagated

Sugarcane is propagated vegetative, usually from setts (pieces of stalk that can be planted as single setts, multiple bud or eye setts, or as a whole stalk). Labor permitting, whole stalks are typically cut into shorter segments, containing three-budded setts, in the planting furrow. Approximately 5 to 10 centimeters of packed soil is placed over the setts. Sett germination varies with the season, variety, and treatment. Germination can be expected to be about 80 percent under normal conditions. However, with cool temperature, that is, below 61°F (16°C), germination and emergence of the setts can be drastically reduced.

Factors Affecting Sugarcane Cultivation

Sugarcane agricultural practices are influenced by many factors, including climate, soil composition and structure, irrigation and drainage requirements, varieties, pests and diseases, management, and availability of skilled labor and harvesting methods. Growers need to carefully consider such factors as variety, quality of the seed cane, row spacing, planting depth, fertilizer placement, sett treatment with fungicides and insecticides, planting time, and availability of water either from rainfall or irrigation. The main requirements for a high-yielding sugarcane crop are water, heat, sunlight, and adequate nutrition. The performance of a variety depends on its genetic potential, the quality and cleanliness of the planting material (pest- and disease-free), climate suitability for growth, time of milling, and, most important, the level of management provided. Varieties must be selected on the basis of proven performance (whether for sugar, fiber, or ethanol). Priority must be given to selecting the variety with the required agronomic and milling characteristics and with pest and disease resistance or tolerance. For the subtropics, where freezing temperatures occur, stalk freeze tolerance has to be taken into account. Sugarcane should be planted into well-drained and prepared soil corrected with lime as required. Cane should be planted when rains are reliable to conserve moisture for rain-fed cane; where irrigated, it should be planted only after irrigation has been installed.

Sugarcane Crop Cycle

The sugarcane production cycle typically lasts five to six years in most countries, during which time four to five annual harvests are made, but under irrigation and with the right variety, the cycle can be extended to over 30 harvests. The sugarcane's life cycle begins in year one with the plow-out of old stubble from the previous crop cycle, followed by a period of fallow to prepare seed bed for a new planting. This fallow period can be as little as one to two weeks in the tropics to approximately one year in the subtropics. After the variety has been selected for planting, seed cane of that variety is machine- or hand-planted either as setts or whole stalks. After the plant crop has been harvested, it is normal to allow the crop to regrow once or several times so that two or more harvests are taken from the original planting, a procedure known as ratooning or stubbling. At the end of the cycle, the crop is ploughed out, and the field is replanted with sugarcane or another crop either more or less immediately, or after the period of fallow.

Sucrose Accumulation and Maturity

In the stalk, starch formation and storage occupy a greatly reduced role, presumably due to breeding and selection for varieties with enhanced stored sucrose levels. Sucrose, therefore, dominates as an accumulating end product and is transported from the leaves to the stalk via the phloem. Sucrose accumulation can be increased by factors such as environmental stress (incident sunlight, water, nutrients, and temperature), application of chemical ripeners, and planting density or arrangement. The phenomenon of ripening occurs when growth or stalk elongation ceases or slows, along with the accumulation of sucrose in tissues developed during the growth phase. Therefore, conditions that promote growth are not conducive for sucrose accumulation. Plant maturity also has a role in the relative rate of sucrose accumulation since, in the early stage of growth, plant tissues contain high levels of nitrogen, moisture, invert sugars, and enzymes, while operating with enhanced nitrogen metabolism and respiration rates. The process of aging eventually produces conditions where there is a gradual exhaustion of nitrogen and water with lowered reducing sugars, namely glucose and fructose, and reduced activities of the enzymes, resulting in the accumulation of sucrose. Thus, cane maturity is a function of variety and nitrogen and moisture status, but it is unpredictably complicated by climatic parameters such as light, temperature, rainfall, and humidity. Adding to this complexity is the fact that different varieties of sugarcane possess different sensitivities to the stresses that alter the rates of photosynthesis, structural growth, and sucrose accumulation. In some sugarcane-growing regions of the world, normal ripening does not occur for whatever reason, and interest is widespread in developing chemical methods to induce or increase ripening, or to enable its synchronization with harvest. Most chemical ripeners are growth regulators or herbicides that are applied in sublethal doses, which induce ripening by chemically restricting growth, allowing the plant to accumulate sucrose.

Harvest Management

One of the most important (and expensive) aspects of sugarcane production is the harvesting and the cane's transport to the mill for processing. Hand cutting is still practiced in many parts of the world, particularly when cane is burned before harvesting. The move to green cane harvesting has brought with it a move to combine (chopper) harvesting, which is increasingly practiced by larger growers. Whole-stalk harvesters are still used in some areas but have been largely phased out in favor of chopper harvesters. Good harvest management is crucial to the profitability of both the cane grower and the miller. The grower invests significant time and money to produce the crop, but poor harvesting and transport operations can result in dramatic losses of recoverable sugar, both from physical losses of cane in the field and deterioration in cane quality before milling, especially if the cane is burned before harvesting and cut into short billets by the chopper harvester. Yield in the subsequent ratoon or stubble crop can also be depressed by poor harvesting practices. The harvesting and transport costs form a large proportion of the overall cost of cane production. Very careful consideration must therefore be given to both the selection and management of the harvesting and transport systems.

Environmental Management

Today, environmental management is a key priority at local, national, and international levels. The selection of suitable land for growing sugarcane and many aspects of farm management must be suitably managed to minimize adverse environmental impacts. The adaption of appropriate farming practices will ensure the long-term sustainability of soil and water resources, minimize impacts on downstream environments, protect or enhance regional biodiversity, and develop positive community relations. Most industries, particularly intensive agricultural industries like the sugar industry, must address a range of environmental concerns. Many of the environmental issues faced by the sugar industry are shared with other intensive agricultural industries. Some environmental issues arise from practices specific to the sugarcane industry, most notably, the practice of burning fields prior to harvesting to reduce the quantity of extraneous material delivered to the mills with the cane. Others, such as mill effluents and boiler emissions, arise from the nature of sugar as an industrial crop and the fact that, because of the costs of transporting cane, processing must be performed close to the point of harvest. All industries are required to follow local environmental legislation, which is different in each country. Essentially, they focus on management of emissions into the air, water use, liquid effluents, and solid wastes.

See also SUGAR and SUGAR REFINING.

Heinz, D. J., ed. *Sugarcane Improvement through Breeding.* Developments in Crop Science 11. Amsterdam: Elsevier, 1987.

Hogarth, D. M., and P. G. Allsopp, eds. *Manual of Cane Growing, Brisbane.* Bureau of Sugar Experiment Stations. Brisbane, Australia: Fergies, 2000.

Hunsigi, G., ed. *Production of Sugarcane: Theory and Practice.* Advanced Series in Agricultural Sciences 21. Berlin: Springer-Verlag, 1993.

James, Glyn, ed. *Sugarcane.* World Agriculture Series. Oxford: Blackwell, 2004.

Keating, B. A., and J. R. Wilson, eds. *Intensive Sugar Production: Meeting the Challenges beyond 2000.* Wallingford, U.K.: CAB International, 1997.

Meyer, Jan, Peter Rein, Peter Turner, and Kathryn Mathias, eds. *Good Management Practices for the Cane Sugar Industry.* Berlin: Bartens, 2013.

Benjamin L. Legendre

sugarplums, in their traditional form, are sweetmeats made of dried fruits—not necessarily plums (prunes), but also figs, apricots, dates, and cherries in any combination—formed into an oval or round shape and rolled in sugar. Chopped almonds, honey, and spices such as aniseed, cardamom, fennel seeds, and caraway were sometimes included, further varying the basic recipe.

The association of sugared fruits with goodness has a long history. Fresh fruits preserved in honey were eaten for pleasure in ancient China and India, and throughout the Middle East, ancient Egypt, and classical Greece. In Europe, during the rise of the Roman Empire, sweetness in the form of preserved fruits became a metaphor for civilization and the virtues of the rule of law, a concept as much philosophical as practical. See ANCIENT WORLD.

The historian Maguelonne Toussaint-Samat writes that in France, as early as 1344, "candied fruits of many colours" were served as the eighth and final course at the coronation banquet of Pope Clement VI in Avignon. Arab hospitality has included similar offerings as "part and parcel of Ottoman hospitality rituals from the seventeenth century onwards." The food historian Mary Işın notes that in *The Book of Ceremonies* prepared for Emperor Constantine VII in ninth-century Byzantium, mention is made of preserves and jellies prepared with plums, quince, citron, apple, and pear. At her marriage feast in seventeenth-century Istanbul, Mehmed IV's daughter received from the groom "30 mules laden with sugar plums and sweet-meats."

Meanwhile, the fabulous courts of medieval Italy—particularly those of Mantua and Florence—were setting new standards in luxurious feasting, exporting a taste for extravagant sugar fantasies using confectionery skills learned from the Arabs along with expertise in candying fruits. Candied fruits begin to appear as emblems of luxury in romantic literature as cane sugar replaced honey in the preparation of fruit-based sweetmeats, gaining popularity in northern Europe on the tables of the rich through supplies of loaf sugar exported through Venice and Genoa. See CANDIED FRUIT.

Throughout non-temperate Europe, recipes for fruit preserves published in cookbooks increased the interest in the use of sugar as far north as Scandinavia and Russia, where native fruits—hedgerow berries as well as orchard fruits—were available to the poor as well as the rich. See FRUIT PRESERVES. In Britain, techniques for preserving fruit appeared in books such as Mary Eales's *Receipts*, but the name "sugarplum" was also in general use from the seventeenth to the nineteenth century to denote a comfit or dragée, a preparation of dried fruit or nuts given a hard shell by panning, a labor-intensive process of coating in layers of sugar to produce a luxurious sweetmeat. See COMFIT and PANNING. The word "sugarplum" also came to be a synonym for a bribe. By the 1830s, mechanization of the sugaring process brought "sugarplum candy" in manufactured form within the means of the general public while keeping the original (spurious) association with the fruit.

Sugarplums entered popular culture thereafter as a symbol of goodness and kindness, while sour plums can be taken as symbols of discontent. As bringers of joy, sugarplums wrapped in silver foil are hung on the tree at Christmas and given as presents; the Sugar Plum Fairy appears as the spirit of goodness in Tchaikovsky's ballet *The Nutcracker*; and good children in Clement Moore's poem "A Visit from St. Nicholas" (best known from the first line, " 'Twas the Night before Christmas") have "visions of sugarplums" dancing in their heads.

The original concept of the sugarplum as luxury pleasure-giver continues in the form of real candied plums—particularly those of Carlsberg—wrapped and boxed for Christmas. At the popular (cheap) end of the confectionery business, the idea of the original sugar-rolled, chopped-fruit sugarplum survives in Britain in the form of fruit pastilles—sugar-dusted, plum-shaped, fruit-flavored, chewable sweeties. In Scotland, never a land to follow the English lead, "soor plums" is the name given to hard candy with a very sour flavor, known south of the Scottish border as "acid drops." Scottish confectioners claim that the name commemorates an incident when plum-thieving English soldiers were worsted by the Scots—'twas ever thus. Meanwhile, in the United States, confectionery manufacturers jumped on the sugarplum bandwagon with plum-shaped, plum-flavored candies marketed as "sugarplum candy."

See also CHRISTMAS; SPICES; and VENICE.

Eales, Mary. *Mary Eales's Receipts.* London: Prospect, 1985. Facsimile of 1733 reprint edition.

Işın, Mary. *Sherbet and Spice: The Complete Story of Turkish Sweets and Desserts.* London and New York: I. B. Taurus, 2013.

Mason, Laura. *Sugar Plums and Sherbet: The Prehistory of Sweets.* Totnes, U.K.: Prospect, 2004.

Toussaint-Samat, Maguelonne. *A History of Food.* Translated by Anthea Bell. Cambridge, Mass.: Blackwell, 1992.

Elisabeth Luard

sugars, unrefined—sometimes called raw sugars—are produced by boiling the juice from sugarcane, sugar beet, sorghum, maple, or palm sap to the point of crystallization. See STAGES OF SUGAR SYRUP. Once cooled and solidified, the resulting sugar is usually brown, because molasses adheres to the crystals. See MOLASSES. However, depending on the manufacturing process, the sugar may be lighter or almost white in color. Modern sugarcane mills produce an off-white raw sugar—sometimes called turbinado, muscovado, demerara, or rapadura sugar—while more rudimentary techniques result in a wider range of colors because they are less efficient at removing molasses and impurities. See SUGAR and SUGAR REFINING. Refining refers to the process by which the remaining molasses particles are removed from the sugar crystals in order to make a perfectly white sugar. During the nineteenth century, sugar was refined by remelting the raw sugar, mixing it with lime, skimming off impurities, and finally filtering it through charcoal, sometimes of animal origin. In the twentieth century, non-animal forms of charcoal have become increasingly common. Soft brown sugars commonly used in cooking are not necessarily unrefined but may in fact be refined sugar with molasses added for color, flavor, and to increase the moisture content.

Until recently, consumers have placed a premium on whiter sugars, assuming that they were both sweeter and more pure. Refined sugar prices have fallen steadily since the nineteenth century, when advances in milling and refining brought economies of scale. Cheaper prices for refined white sugar have also helped to make it a popular choice. However, raw sugars now enjoy a growing niche market, selling at a premium price. Contemporary consumers sometimes prefer the unrefined product because it retains a mild molasses flavor, is less likely to have been processed using animal byproducts, or is perceived to be more natural or healthy.

For a variety of political and cultural reasons, people have continued to make and eat brown, unrefined sugars, despite the predominance of the refined product. Farmers and small-scale manufacturers in Asia, Latin America, and Africa have continued to make unrefined sugar from cane, sorghum, or palm sap on a small scale, using what might be called handicraft techniques. See PALM SUGAR and SORGHUM SYRUP. The juice is extracted using small mills, which might be animal, water, or motor powered. The juice is then boiled in open pans, often with lime or other ingredients to help remove plant matter and impurities. After skimming, the juice is left to cool in cones, loaves, or other shaped molds, or is sometimes formed into balls or cakes. The process requires experience and skill, but it is not particularly capital intensive. The resulting sugars typically have a distinctive flavor and may be somewhat more healthful than refined sugar because they retain more mineral nutrients.

Consumers sometimes prefer unrefined sugars because they hold symbolic, religious, or nostalgic meanings. *Gur* and *khand* are unrefined sugars that continue to be eaten in India, even after the colonial government began to promote the refined sugar industry in the 1930s. See INDIA. Mahatma Gandhi called for Indians to refuse factory-made sugar, suggesting that villages could resist British colonialism by making their own gur. Hindu consumers preferred khand and gur for religious reasons, since refined sugar might have been processed with animal bones. And cane farmers and millers preferred making unrefined sugars because they did not have to pay excise taxes, and their products were not subject to price controls. In the Philippines, unrefined sugar of this variety is called *panocha*, and during the period of U.S. colonial administration in the early twentieth century it continued to be popular despite colonial efforts to encourage modern sugar production. As in India, farmers made panocha in part because it was exempt from excise taxes. In Japan this type of sugar is called *kuro zatō* and *kokutō*. *Panela*, a cake-shaped version of unrefined brown sugar, is common throughout Latin America. *Piloncillo* is formed into a cone shape and is used in Mexico. Mexican merchants began importing piloncillo into the United States in the 1910s and 1920s to sell to Mexicans, many of whom had, ironically, arrived to work in the beet sugar fields. Mexican workers in the United States ate piloncillo, which sold for nearly three times more than refined beet sugar in the 1920s, mainly for religious and patriotic celebrations, and because its unique flavor reminded them of home. For example, piloncillo is an important ingredient in *capirotada*, a bread pudding traditionally made for Lent in Mexican and Mexican American cookery. See LATIN AMERICA. A variety of other plants besides cane have been used to produce unrefined sugar. *Jaggery*, an unrefined sugar made from palm sap, is common across Asia and Africa, for example. Most of these unrefined sugars can be purchased in ethnic grocery stores.

See also MAPLE SYRUP; SUGAR BEET; and SUGARCANE.

Bosma, Ulbe. *The Sugar Plantation in India and Indonesia: Industrial Production, 1770–2010.* Cambridge, U.K.: Cambridge University Press, 2013.

Fergusson, Erna. *Mexican Cookbook.* Albuquerque: University of New Mexico Press, 1969.

Knight, G. Roger. *Commodities and Colonialism: The Story of Big Sugar in Indonesia, 1880–1942.* Leiden, The Netherlands: Brill, 2013.

Niall, Mani. *Sweet! From Agave to Turbinado, Home Baking with Every Kind of Natural Sugar and Sweetener.* Cambridge, Mass.: Da Capo, 2008.

April Merleaux

summer pudding is one of Britain's best puddings. It uses bread and fruit and is made in a pudding basin, but only the fruit is lightly cooked, which makes it unlike other British puddings. This dessert was customarily made with raspberries and red currants, which give a pleasing, slightly sharp taste; now white currants, strawberries, blackberries, mulberries, and sometimes pitted cherries are used. The fruit is briefly cooked with a little sugar until the juices begin to run and the sugar has dissolved. The basin is tightly lined on the bottom and sides with slices of day-old white bread; when cool, the fruit is added and covered with a layer of bread to enclose it completely. The pudding is chilled overnight with a weight on top to compact it. To serve, summer pudding is unmolded onto a dish, cut into wedges, and served alone or with cream. The fruit juices soak into the bread, turning it a deep red, making the domed pudding truly spectacular and inviting. See PUDDING and UNITED KINGDOM.

It is difficult to discover when recipes for summer pudding first appeared, and when this name was first used. *Cassell's New Universal Cookery Book* (1896) includes a recipe called Hydropathic Pudding, but the author notes that this pudding goes by many names. She adds plums to the fruits that may be used, and also gives an alternative preparation that calls for filling the bowl with layers of thinly sliced bread and fruit. She concludes that the pudding is "useful for those who cannot take pastry or rich puddings, or for children," a view echoed by Alan Davidson, who found it was served in health resorts where pastry was forbidden (giving rise to the name "hydropathic pudding").

Davidson, Alan. *The Oxford Companion to Food*. Oxford: Oxford University Press, 1999.
Heritage, Lizzie. *Cassell's New Universal Cookery Book*. London: Cassell, 1896.

Jill Norman

A **sundae** is a luscious, cold dessert made of ice cream covered with toppings, such as syrup, whipped cream, berries, nuts, sprinkles, or chunks of candy. A sundae is a rhapsody of taste that is both complex and amazingly simple. Although a sundae may contain many ingredients, making this dessert requires minimal cooking skills. A little imagination is the most important ingredient, and a homemade sundae can taste even better than one served in a restaurant.

Soda fountains and ice cream parlors served sundaes in the 1890s, but historians cannot pinpoint the treat's origins. See SODA FOUNTAIN. In 1897 a soda fountain manual contained a peach sundae recipe and noted that other fruits and fruit-flavored syrups could be used to make the dessert. In 1900 a trade paper included eight sundaes in a list of treats every soda fountain should serve.

Over the years, sources have identified the sundae's birthplace as Buffalo, New York; Evanston, Illinois; Two Rivers, Wisconsin; Norfolk, Virginia; Plainfield, Illinois; Ithaca, New York; Cleveland, Ohio; New Orleans, Louisiana; or New York City. A persistent legend attributes the sundae's creation to blue laws that forbade the sale of soda, but not ice cream, on Sundays. However, there is no firm evidence to support this thesis. Two Rivers, Wisconsin, and Ithaca, New York, have been identified most often as the sundae's birthplace, and blue laws were not a factor in either city.

In Two Rivers, Wisconsin, Edward C. Berners owned a popular ice cream parlor. One night a customer named George Hallauer ordered a dish of vanilla ice cream. Craving something more than ice cream, Hallauer impulsively asked Berners to pour chocolate syrup over it. Berners thought the combination was a bad idea, but he deferred to his customer. Hallauer liked the dish so much that he ordered another. Other customers tried the new treat, and word of the sensational dessert spread like wildfire through Two Rivers and nearby towns.

In Ithaca, New York, a young minister habitually stopped at Platt and Colt's soda fountain for a dish of ice cream after his Sunday sermon. One Sabbath the pastor, yearning for a new taste treat, ordered a dish of ice cream with cherry syrup on top. On 5 April 1892, an ad in the *Ithaca Daily Journal* hawked the

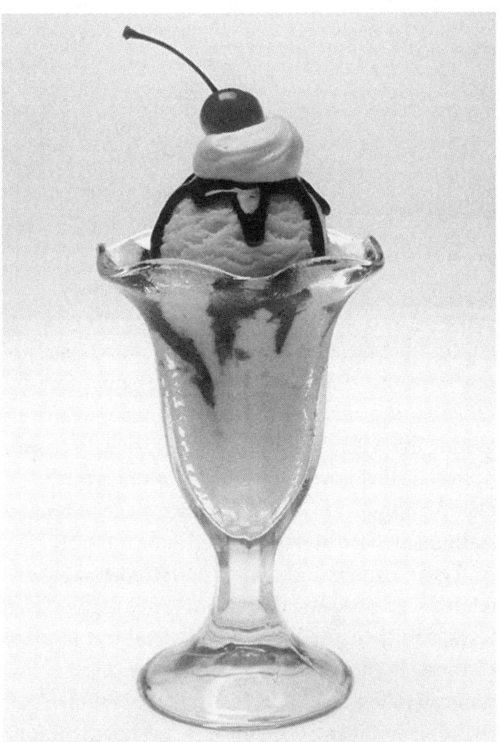

Soda fountains and ice cream parlors were serving sundaes as early as the 1890s. This classic fountain-style glass is filled with an ice cream sundae—ice cream topped with hot fudge sauce, whipped cream, and a cherry. RENEE COMET

"Cherry Sunday, A New Ten-Cent Ice Cream Specialty Served Only at Platt and Colt's." A few days later the paper described the Cherry Sunday as "ice cream served in a champagne glass with cherry juice syrup and candied French cherries on top." Although these newspaper items do not conclusively prove that Ithaca was the birthplace of the sundae, they offer more evidence than other towns have produced.

The Ithaca newspaper called the treat a Sunday, but other printed sources used sundaye, sondie, sundi, sundhi, or sundae. According to ice cream lore, religious leaders objected to the use of "Sunday" because they felt that the Sabbath should not be commercialized as the name of a soda fountain treat. Hence, sundae became the standard spelling.

The ice cream sundae is a delightful dish loved by millions. Chocolate, hot fudge, caramel, butterscotch, strawberry, and marshmallow syrup are popular sundae toppings, but they are only the tip of the flavor iceberg. Sundaes are most often built on a foundation of vanilla ice cream, but any flavor can be used. Sundae lovers are not bound by rigid recipes. They can choose their ingredients and experiment until they find just the right combination to satisfy their taste.

See also BUTTERSCOTCH; CARAMEL; ICE CREAM; MARSHMALLOWS; and SPRINKLES.

"An Important Decision: The Sale of Soda Water on Sunday Is Not Illegal." *The Pharmaceutical Era* (26 September 1895): 401.

"Stop Me if You've Heard This One Before." *Ice Cream Trade Journal* (July 1927): 68.

Anne Cooper Funderburg

Swedish Fish

See GUMMIES.

sweet and sour is a combination of two basic flavors found in many food cultures. The culinary equivalent of guerilla warfare, it is a gastronomic ambush so pleasurable it makes even seemingly unpalatable foodstuffs taste good. Proof is provided by the food writer Mary Taylor Simeti, who recorded her friend Maria Grammitico's memories of a dish—veal tripe *in agrodolce*—served at the conclusion of a wedding feast in Sicily: "Towards midnight you'd eat again... first you make a sauté of garlic, onions and celery... [then] you put in the innards, and then you added a bit of sugar, and when it was time to take it off the fire, you added vinegar."

While sweet-sour flavors please the adult palate, the infant palate rejects sourness, even when sweetened, as nature's warning of toxicity. As a digestive, the combination of sweet and sour bestows a feeling of well-being, real or imagined. The true value of a balsamic, the sweet-sour grape-must vinegar of Modena that provided duchesses with dowries, lay in medicinal rather than culinary use, though spiciness and complexity of flavor enhanced its primary purpose. In France and Germany, the digestive properties of sweet and sour are particularly appreciated in combination with mustard seeds, a palate-stimulator also found in Italy in the honey-sweetened, vinegar-sharpened fruit mustards of Cremona. See GRAPE MUST and MOSTARDA.

Further evidence of the pleasure-giving properties of sweet-sour can be found in the effect of lemon juice in creamy desserts, in vinegar taffy, in the Nordic taste for sweet-sharp dressings with salt-cured herrings, in China's sour-sweet saucings for pork and duck, in America's liking for sweet-sharp dressings on salads, and in the spiced chutneys and sweet-sour fruit sauces of British tradition.

Grammatico, Maria, and Mary Taylor Simeti. *Bitter Almonds: Recollections and Recipes from a Sicilian Girlhood.* New York: William Morrow, 1994.

Elisabeth Luard

sweet meals, occasions when the majority of the dishes are sweet, are highly culture specific, both in terms of the time of day when they are eaten and the foods served. Some are little more than snacks, while others are full-blown meals. Americans will happily make a meal of Cocoa Puffs cereal or French toast early in the day, but a sweet supper is considered peculiar. To most East Asians, a sugary repast isn't a meal at all, an attitude they share with the French. An Austrian, on the other hand, wouldn't think it odd to indulge in a slice of Gugelhupf for breakfast, a main dish of fruit dumplings for lunch, or pancakes for dinner (although probably not all in the same day). See GUGELHUPF and PANCAKES.

In the elite kitchens of medieval and renaissance Europe, the distinction between sweet and savory was nebulous; sprinkling just about any food with sugar was commonplace. See DESSERT. There were, however, events where most, if not all, of the food was something we would call "dessert" or "confectionery." Pompeo Molmenti documents many of these sorts of meals in the sugar-refining capital of Venice. As early as 1493, Beatrice d'Este, visiting from Milan, describes a meal "composed of diverse things all made with gilded sugar, which numbered three hundred; with infinite plates of confectionery." In the sixteenth century, meetings at the Doge's Palace were accompanied by "*storti, buzolai pignocadi, confetti pasterelli* [probably cakes or tarts, ring-shaped cakes, and candied spices], and other confections." Perhaps the most famous sweet meal was served to the French king Henry III in 1574 during his Venice sojourn. Molmenti notes that the fête featured some 1,260 sweetmeats, and even the tablecloth and napkins were made of sugar paste. See VENICE.

In seventeenth-century France, as coffee, tea, and chocolate made inroads into aristocratic foodways, it was up to the confectioners and pastry chefs to come up with a snack to accompany the sugar-laced beverages. According to Nicolas de Blegny's 1691 guidebook to Paris, visitors to the city's cafés could expect *biscuits*, marzipan, and *craquelins* (a large cracker) as well as sweet wafers and waffles on the menu. See CAFÉ. Depending on the occasion and the status of the host, these snacks could turn into elaborate spreads, referred to as a *colation* by the titled set, according to Pierre Richelet, in his 1728 *Dictionnaire de la langue françoise ancienne et moderne* (he adds that they are called *gouté* by the commoners and the bourgeoisie). Somewhat earlier, in his *L'art de bien traiter* (1674), the cookbook author known only as L. S. R. gives a menu for a late-night *colation* that includes fresh and dried fruit, marzipan, and biscuits, but also venison paté, tongue, sausages, and cheese (*colation* also encompassed the meaning of "meal," as it does in English). As late as the nineteenth century, these sorts of sweet meals could be quite elaborate. *Le glacier royal* (1844) gives menus for balls and soirées that might include five kinds of pastry, another five of ice cream, a selection of creamy desserts, and various soft drinks, as well as spiked punch. See ICE CREAM and PUNCH. For those on a diet there is consommé; for the rest, ham and tongue "sandwichs."

In eighteenth-century England, mostly sweet meals began to form around the habit of serving tea, a beverage that had generally usurped the role of coffee in English society. See TEA. By the 1750s afternoon tea had become an institution, with cookbooks suggesting a variety of tea wafers, tea cakes, crumpets, and buttery buns to serve for the occasion. Tea gardens and tea rooms proliferated along with the pleasure gardens then popular. In the nineteenth century, mass-manufactured biscuits, such as the "sponge tea cakes" manufactured as early as the 1830s by Huntley & Palmers and others, came to play a significant role in the afternoon ritual. See BISCUITS, BRITISH. By the Edwardian era (1901–1910), our current idea of afternoon tea had become institutionalized. The American magazine *Good Housekeeping* noted that, in 1906, London's Cottage tea rooms offered a tea-time menu of "homemade cakes, scones and various sandwiches, not forgetting the proverbial English ices and iced coffee," which, putting aside the ices, is not so different from what London's Claridge's Hotel serves today.

In the late eighteenth century, the French, in one of their periodic bouts of Anglophilia, briefly adopted the English habit of taking tea, although with a twist. According to the Irish novelist Sydney Morgan, who visited France a little after Waterloo, "The most usual, and indeed the most fashionable evening collation [in Paris] is 'le *thé*,' which, without being strictly the English tea, or the French *goûter*, formerly taken between dinner and supper, combines much of what is *best* in both—the exhilarating beverage of souchong and hyson, with confectionary and ices, found only in France." Apparently *le thé* was often served a little before midnight. Later in the century, the petit bourgeoisie transposed the sweet snack into the afternoon hours, and it eventually moved into the public realm when *salons de thé* began to open in the late 1800s. See SALON DE THÉ. Today, this mid-afternoon pause (*goûter* in French) of coffee and pastry is still relatively common.

In Central Europe, as in France, English tea was in vogue around the dawn of both the nineteenth and twentieth centuries. That said, there seem to have been a lot more pastries and coffee served than actual tea. François Le Goullon, the French chef to Anna Amalia, duchess of Saxe-Weimar-Eisenach in the late 1700s, includes a wide variety of both Central European and French sweetmeat recipes in *Der elegante Theetisch*, but not much information on tea. The popular little volume, first published around 1800, was still in print three decades later. The English tea revival in the Edwardian era filled German-

and Czech-language cookbooks with dozens of recipes for *Theegebäck* (tea cakes) as well as *Kaffeegebäck* for the afternoon get-together or *Jause*. As perhaps nowhere else, the afternoon snack of coffee and cake remains an Austrian institution and is best savored at one of the country's Café-Konditerei (café-pastry shops). See AUSTRIA-HUNGARY and VIENNA.

Sweet foods are hardly limited to the *Jause* in the former domains of the Habsburg Empire. A typical Austrian hotel breakfast buffet will include cold cuts and cheese, but also a variety of sweetened breads, Gugelhupf, and even tarts and cakes. But that's just the beginning. A unique aspect of Central European cuisine is its long history of serving a sweet main course for either lunch or supper. This practice dates from an era when a variety of flour- or grain-based dishes were served on the many meatless days prescribed by the Catholic calendar. See MEHLSPEISE. Though less common than it once was, a meal of soup followed by sweetened dumplings, strudel, pancakes, noodle pudding, or similarly filling dishes is considered normal.

In the United States, as in most cultures, there was and continues to be a strict division between foods considered appropriate for dessert and those served as the primary course in a meal. This distinction shifted as the country became more industrialized and urbanized. Today, few would consider a piece of apple pie and a hunk of cheese sufficient for supper, or mutton chops, tripe, and minced codfish appropriate for breakfast, as was common in the mid-nineteenth century. By the twentieth century, American suppers were supposed to be savory, even as breakfast became increasingly sweet, with sugary cereal, pancakes, waffles, doughnuts, and the like highlighting the morning meal. See BREAKFAST CEREAL. Brunch, essentially a substantial sit-down breakfast eaten either late morning or in the middle of the day, is made up of both sweet and savory main dishes featuring eggs in one form or another, whether whole, as in Eggs Benedict, or incorporated into the batter of French toast or pancakes. Though early brunch menus of the 1960s emphasized savory dishes, it is now quite normal to eat only sweet foods at brunch. Other than these variations on breakfast, Americans frown upon a wholly sweet meal, even though manufacturers have made a valiant effort to convince dieters to forgo lunch and dinner in favor of "meal replacement shakes" and "bars." Admittedly, given how much sugar is consumed in "savory" foods in the United States, the distinction between sweet and savory meals may be as irrelevant as it was in the Italian Renaissance. See UNITED STATES.

See also BANQUETING HOUSE; BREADS, SWEET; FRANCE; ITALY; and SUGAR SCULPTURE.

Bernardi, T. *Le glacier royal, ou, L'art de donner des bals et soirées*. Paris: G. Barba, 1844.
Blégny, Nicolas de. *Les Adresses de la ville de Paris, avec le trésor des almanachs: Livre commode en tous lieux, en tous temps & en toutes conditions*. Paris: Chez la Veuve de Denis Nion, 1691.
Le Goullon, François. *Der elegante Theetisch oder Die Kunst, einen glänzenden Zirkel auf eine geschmackvolle und anständige Art ohne großen Aufwand zu bewirthen*. Weimar, 1800.
Krondl, Michael. *Sweet Invention: A History of Dessert*. Chicago: Chicago Review Press, 2011.
L. S. R., Pierre de Lune, and Audiger. *L'art de la cuisine française au XVIIe siècle*. Paris: Payot, 1995.
Molmenti, Pompeo, and Horatio F. Brown. *Venice: Its Individual Growth from the Earliest Beginnings to the Fall of the Republic*. Chicago: A. C. McClurg, 1906.
Morgan, Lady (Sydney). *France in 1816*. Paris: Londres, 1817.

Michael Krondl

sweet wine has a history that goes back to before the production of the first cane sugar. Then, as now, it required propitious conditions and specialized techniques, making it scarce. From the Middle Ages in Europe until very recently in the West, sweet wines conferred high status upon those who consumed them. Legends ascribe curative powers to sweet wines and declare them appropriate for the deathbeds of kings, thereby increasing their aura of the miraculous.

There is something genuinely miraculous about sweet wines, because yeast tends to convert all the sugar in grape juice into alcohol (and various fermentation byproducts), resulting in dry wines. Despite all the advances in winemaking technology during the last century, sweet wines still sometimes come about by accident when yeast fails to do its job properly. However, it is not by chance that many low-priced red and white wines on supermarket shelves that seem to be dry are actually slightly sweet. The sweetness in these wines has been added, usually in the form of grape juice concentrate, to make them taste more immediately appealing. Here we find a parallel to "savory" convenience foods with added sweetness.

When people speak of sweet or dessert wines, they are usually referring to white wines that have a much greater sweetness, at least 10 percent (a sweetness comparable to cola), if not 20 percent or more. Sweet wines are every bit as diverse as dry wines, thanks to three basic factors: the grape varieties used; the vineyard location, or "terroir"; and the harvesting and winemaking techniques used. A very particular combination of these three factors underlies each of the classic sweet wines.

Straw Wine

Excluding sweet fortified wines, three main methods are used to produce sweet wines. See FORTIFIED WINE. Straw wine is made by drying the grapes on straw mats for a couple of weeks outdoors, or over several months indoors, until desiccation has concentrated the sugar content of their juice to the point where the yeast cannot convert it all into alcohol. Hesiod described this technique around 700 B.C.E., and it is still widely used in the Mediterranean Basin, most importantly in various regions of Italy for Vin Santo, but also for Recioto di Soave and the red Recioto della Valpolicella in Veneto, and for Vinsanto on the Greek island of Santorini. From farther north come the rare Austrian Schilfwein and Vin de Paille of the French Jura and Hermitage on the Rhône. Locally prevalent grape varieties are usually used for their production. Malvasia delle Lipari from the Aeolian Islands off Sicily is a rare example made from an ancient grape variety (Malvasia) and is the closest among contemporary wines to what Hesiod described. Straw wines tend to have a high alcohol content of 13 to 16 percent and a raisin-like flavor, and are often amber in color from deliberate oxidation.

Desiccation on the vine is a rare variation on this theme, most importantly as the main method for the production of sweet *Moëlleux* white wines from the Chenin Blanc grape in the Vouvray and Coteaux du Layon appellations of the Loire Valley in France (noble rot also plays a role in many top vintages). These wines tend to have around 11 to 13 percent alcohol, pronounced acidity and freshness, and aromas reminiscent of candied citrus and caramel.

The most famous sweet wines were produced by this method in Constantia, South Africa, between about 1700 and 1865. Arguably, Constantia was the first global wine, since it was exported not only to Europe during that period, but also to the Far East. In the early 1980s the Klein Constantia estate recommenced production under the name Vin de Constance, using the Muscat grape and closely imitating production methods described in the eighteenth century.

Noble Rot

The second method for producing sweet wines is to allow noble rot—the fungus *Botrytis cinerea*—to accelerate desiccation of the grapes by perforating their skin. Simultaneously, an enzyme released by the fungus oxidizes many substances in the grapes. A wine utterly different in aroma results, one that is also richer in flavor and body to that made from similar grapes unaffected by noble rot. A little bit goes a long way, hence the common practice of marketing these wines in half bottles.

Château d'Yquem in Sauternes, Bordeaux, is often cited as the classic example of a wine made from nobly rotten grapes. Its claim as the best such wine is hotly debated (Château Climens is the most obvious challenger in Sauternes, and they are legion in other regions). Like the dry white wines of Bordeaux, Sauternes is also produced primarily from a blend of Sauvignon Blanc and Semillon grapes. It does not have nearly as long a history as is commonly supposed, the method of harvesting Sauternes by pickers making successive passes through the vineyards removing only the nobly rotten grapes having been developed only at the beginning of the nineteenth century at Château d'Yquem. Because making wine from rotten grapes was counterintuitive, European winemakers discovered the possibilities opened up by noble rot comparatively late in the history of winemaking.

After fermentation in small new-oak *barrique* casks, Sauternes has an alcoholic content of 13 to 15 percent. The alcohol and the tannins extracted by the wine from the oak cask during up to four years of maturation balance the sweetness of the wines, which have a rather low acidity content. Sauternes from top vintages can age for decades, the aromas changing during this process from fruit compote, marzipan, and vanilla to dried fruits and orange marmalade. As with all high-quality sweet wines, although the analytical sweetness level doesn't change during the aging process, the level of sweetness one perceives reduces with time.

In recent years numerous attempts to copy this style have been undertaken, with varying degrees of success, in regions from California's Napa Valley to Australia's Riverina. The most widely acclaimed wines of this kind are made in the Neusiedlersee region on the eastern bank of the eponymous steppe lake in Burgenland, Austria, where Alois Kracher perfected this style during the 1990s. Humidity from the Neusiedlersee and many smaller nearby lakes encourages the rapid spread of noble rot, and given ideal autumn conditions, large quantities of lush sweet wines can be produced here with ease, as in Sauternes.

Confusingly, most sweet wines from this region are marketed under the designations *Beerenauslese* or *Trockenbeerenauslese*, which in their German homeland refer to wines in which the high grape sweetness content is balanced by high natural acidity, but there is no oak flavor, and the alcoholic content is low (usually below 8 percent, but often close to the EU's legal lower limit of 5.5 percent). There is thus a totally different flavor profile in the majority of sweet wines from the Neusiedlersee, with their higher alcoholic content and moderate acidity.

This confusion doesn't afflict the Neusiedlersee-Hügelland region on the western bank of the lake, which developed its own distinctive sweet wine, Ruster Ausbruch, in the early seventeenth century. Today, these wines are made from grape varieties ranging from the Hungarian Furmint to the French Chardonnay. Traditionally, they were made in barrels of neutral oak or acacia, and fermentation was encouraged to continue until a fairly high alcoholic content was formed. However, during the quality renaissance of the 1990s, producers like Feiler-Artinger pioneered Ausbruch, with a lower alcoholic content and new oak flavors.

A similar stylistic diversity can be found in contemporary wines from the Tokaj region in eastern Hungary's Bodrog Valley. That wine industry experienced radical change following the end of communism in 1989, due both to foreign investment and homegrown pioneers like Istvan Szepsy. Traditional-style Tokaji *Aszu* wines tend to be amber in color with a higher alcoholic content (12 to 14 percent) than modern-style wines, which are invariably paler and are sometimes marked by oak aromas from ageing in *barrique* casks. Today, the Furmint and Hárslevelü grapes dominate, but in earlier centuries many others were also used.

Cellar techniques are also crucial for the wines' distinctive style. Today, as when Máté Sepsy Laczko first described their production in 1630, Tokaji *Aszu* from top producers is made by fermenting the grape juice together with the skins and pulp, as in red winemaking. This intensifies the spicy aromas and increases the textural complexity of the wine. Today the designations 5 and 6 *Puttonyos* on the label are used for Aszu wines of ascending richness and sweetness, with a 6 *Puttonyos* wine (minimum 15 percent unfermented sugar) being sweeter than Sauternes. In March 2014 the designations 3 and 4 *Puttonyos* were abolished and the minimum sweetness of 5 *Puttonyos* raised from 12 to 13 percent—a rare example of standards being raised.

The very rare Tokaji *Essencia* is once again among the most sought-after sweet wines in the world, as it was for three centuries, until about 1950, when the effect of the communist economic system began to undermine the winemakers' hitherto strong commitment to quality, a situation that became much worse after the crushing of the uprising of 1956. A minimum of 45 percent unfermented grape sweetness in the finished wine is required for this category. At this sugar concentration, fermentation is very slow and difficult. The result is a wine of overwhelming intensity, the dried fruits, honey, and spice flavors lingering long after it has been swallowed. The texture is also close to that of liquid honey.

The entire category of sweet wine is now in a paradoxical state. The golden age of sweet wines in the West ended roughly half a century ago due to changing culinary habits (notably nouvelle cuisine) and wine fashion, yet the world's most expensive white wine remains a sweet wine. It is the very rare and enormously concentrated Riesling Trockenbeerenauslese from Egon Müller-Scharzhof in Germany's Mosel. Systematic production of sweet Riesling wines of this kind began in Germany at Schloss Johannisberg in the Rheingau when the accidental delaying of the 1775 harvest resulted in the entire crop being infected with noble rot, leading to wines of a hitherto unfamiliar type. This method spread rapidly through Germany following the international sales breakthrough the Rheingau achieved with its wines of the 1811 vintage.

These wines, in ascending order of richness and sweetness designated Spätlese, Auslese, Beerenauslese, and Trockenbeerenauslese (often abbreviated to BA and TBA), tend to be low in alcohol with an interplay of grape sweetness, acidity, and aromas that is either exciting or tense, depending upon your taste. The spectrum of their aromas is arguably wider than for any other sweet wines, spanning the entire range of flowers, dried and fresh fruits, honey, and spices. Balsamic notes and aromas like beeswax, marzipan, and toast develop after bottle aging, and the finest of these wines will age for 30 (Spätlese) to more than 100 years (TBA).

Nowhere in the world did new winemaking technology more profoundly change sweet wine production than in Germany, not least because sterile filtration technology was developed there during World War I. Its later use in the wine industry enabled the addition of *Süßreserve*, or clarified grape juice, to "improve" simple wines, finally leading to the boom in cheap and sweet *Liebfraumilch* during the 1970s and early 1980s. Sweetness went from being an attribute exclusive to Germany's finest wines to something they shared with the nation's cheapest, a development that was fatal for the reputation of sweet German wine, which began recovering only at the turn of the twenty-first century. More recently, this method of popularizing simple wines has been applied to everything from Californian Chardonnay to red Australian Shiraz.

Ice Wine

The last method of sweet wine production is also a German invention. Ice wine is made by harvesting and pressing frozen grapes so that much of the water they contain remains in the press as ice. This results in juice too syrupy for the yeast to ferment to dryness. It took two centuries from the first recorded chance production of such wines until widespread systematic production of *Eiswein* began in Germany with the 1961 vintage. Ice wines can be as rich as BA and TBA, but they lack the honey and spice character of those wines (which come from noble rot). However, they are even higher in acidity, and this characteristic, combined with their high sweetness and tropical fruit aromas, makes them spectacular or extreme wines, depending upon your viewpoint.

Ontario, Canada, began ice wine production during the early 1980s, and when the 1989 Ice Wine from Inniskillin winery won the Grand Prix d'Honneur at the VINEXPO wine trade fair in Bordeaux in 1991, it was a breakthrough not only for that style of wine from Ontario but for Canadian wine as a whole. Today, Canada has slightly higher legal minimum standards for ice wine than Germany, and Ontario is the biggest producer of ice wine in the world. Recently, China also began ice wine production by employing Canadian experts, and like everything else new in China, it is being done on a major scale.

Brook, Stephen. *Liquid Gold: Dessert Wines of the World.* London: Constable, 1987.

Brook, Stephen. *Sauternes and Other Sweet Wines of Bordeaux.* London: Faber & Faber, 1995.

Reinhardt, Stephan. *The Finest Wines of Germany: A Regional Guide to the Best Producers and Their Wines.* Berkeley: University of California Press, 2012.

Stuart Pigott

sweetened condensed milk is the product obtained by partly evaporating the water from milk and adding a sweetener, usually sugar. The condensed milk created by modern canning technology was long preceded by Indian sweets made from milk boiled down to a thick concentrate, sometimes with sugar added partway through the cooking. The same idea may have independently given rise to the Norman *confiture de lait* and some Iberian precursor of today's Latin American *dulce de leche*, but documentation is sparse.

The industrial product arose not as a delicacy in its own right but in response to the importance placed by nineteenth-century dietary advisors on the single most perishable form of milk: fluid milk for drinking. In 1856 the American inventor Gail Borden Jr. devised a method of slowly evaporating the water from milk in a vacuum pan and pumping the thickened milk into large open cans. See EVAPORATED MILK. His invention arrived in time to benefit from lurid 1858 journalistic exposés of the filthy "swill dairies" then providing milk to many New York City consumers. In 1861 Borden unveiled a more sterile and transportable version that used sugar as a preservative and could be sold in hermetically sealed cans. This heavy, syrupy sweetened form, which earned him a lucrative contract to supply milk to the Union Army during the Civil War, is what has been known as "condensed milk" ever since. Like its predecessor, it was meant to be heavily diluted in order to approximate the milk's original water content.

Within a few decades, other innovators were selling unsweetened evaporated milk and uncondensed fluid milk produced and distributed by improved sanitary methods. Both appealed much more to people who liked the taste of fresh milk. Sweetened condensed milk might have shrunk to the status of a rare emergency ration. Instead, it eventually reached a market for its own sake, precisely because of qualities *not* found in fresh milk.

At least some consumers in the industrialized temperate-zone world came to see the powerful sweetness and viscous body of condensed milk as pleasures, not drawbacks. It could be spread on bread or toast like honey, spooned onto hotcakes or biscuits like maple syrup, or used as a ready-made, endlessly adaptable dessert sauce. See HONEY; MAPLE SYRUP; and SAUCE. As early as 1866, *Jennie June's American Cookery Book* suggested serving it with fresh strawberries as an alternative to cream. By the early twentieth century, both home cooks and professionals working for food manufacturers were experimenting with other uses, turning condensed milk into various kinds of puddings or pie fillings. Purists denounced such shortcuts. In 1932 the food writer Sheila Hibben mocked expedients such as an uncooked filling made from "Screech Owl Condensed Milk"—a clear reference to Borden's "Eagle" brand—mixed with lemon juice and poured into a graham cracker crust. Already, however, these shortcuts were indispensable in many kitchens. Many Florida Key lime pie recipes today are only marginally more elaborate than the "Screech Owl" version.

For generations, milk seldom reached most English or European colonies of the tropics and subtropics in anything but canned form. Sweetened condensed milk thus acquired many popular uses. In (and beyond) Latin America, cooks learned to place unopened cans in boiling water for several hours until the already thick milk condensed further into a close reproduction of dulce de leche. Condensed milk, sometimes mixed with evaporated or fresh milk, also became a popular base for flans. It usually figures in fillings for the Mexican version of American-style cheesecake, *pay de queso*. Throughout the Caribbean it appears in eggnog-like holiday punches, such as the Puerto Rican *coquito*. See DULCE DE LECHE; EGG DRINKS; and FLAN (PUDÍM).

English colonists in Africa and Southeast Asia relied on condensed milk in sweet sauces (e.g., the custard sauce for trifles) and desserts resembling cornstarch puddings that involved Bird's custard powder mixed with condensed milk. See CUSTARD. It also went into resoundingly popular versions of coffee and tea, hot or iced, in Thailand and several neighboring countries. The famous Malaysian and Singaporean *teh tarik*, or "pulled tea," often sold by *mamak* (Muslim Tamil) street vendors, is made by adding condensed milk to freshly brewed tea and rapidly pouring the combination between two containers to raise a froth.

Condensed milk was a well-known standby among the British in Hong Kong, Shanghai, and other treaty ports of the late Qing Empire. Both in China and abroad, cooks still favor it for a few uses. Condensed milk is an almost invariable sauce for some versions of *mantou*, small steamed or fried yeast buns that originated in northern China, and it sometimes sweetens the formerly salty egg filling in modern reworkings of *lai wong bao*, another kind of steamed bun. See CHINA.

The French brought sweetened condensed milk to Vietnam, along with avocado trees and yogurt. Today avocado and condensed milk are a familiar pairing, with the milk used as a sauce for avocado halves or blended in an extravagantly rich milkshake. Meanwhile, Vietnamese-style yogurt made by inoculating a combination of fresh and thinned condensed milk with yogurt cultures has come to the United States with immigrant Vietnamese communities. See YOGURT.

See also INDIA; SOUTHEAST ASIA; and THAILAND.

Laudan, Rachel. "Fresh from the Cow's Nest: Condensed Milk and Culinary Innovation." In *Milk: Beyond the Dairy; Proceedings of the Oxford Symposium on Food and Cookery 1999*, edited by Harlan Walker, pp. 216–224. Totnes, UK: Prospect, 2000.

Mendelson, Anne. *Milk: The Surprising Story of Milk through the Ages*. New York: Knopf, 2008.

Selitzer, Ralph. *The Dairy Industry in America*. New York: Dairy & Ice Cream Field and Books for Industry, 1976.

Anne Mendelson

sweetness preference refers to the predilection for sweet tastes observed in numerous species, including humans, from infancy on. Our sense of taste is unlike any of our other senses, in that we are born with established likes and dislikes for its fundamental qualities. This fact reveals that there is something quite crucial about taste that cannot wait for the normal processes of postnatal experience and learning. From an evolutionary standpoint, sensitivities to sweetness (as a signal for *calories*), bitterness (*toxins*), and saltiness (*sodium*) are likely to have important roles in regulating the intake of nutrients and avoidance of toxins. This interpretation is supported by findings in rats of strong *inverse* associations between degree of toxicity of taste compounds and their palatability.

Most taste qualities—sweetness, sourness, bitterness, and *umami* (glutamate taste)—can also be shown to elicit stereotyped hedonic responses (facial expressions, suckling responses) very shortly after birth in humans. In particular, unambiguously positive facial expressions are observed when sugar is placed on the tongue of human newborns. This contrasts with the similarly obvious dislike shown to bitter or strongly sour tastes. Moreover, the same positive facial responses to sweetness may be observed in both rodents and apes. Infants also find sweet tastes pacifying in the face of painful hospital procedures such as drawing blood. Cross-cultural studies indicate that sweetness per se evokes nearly identical patterns of largely positive responses in adults—in this case, in the form of ratings of liking over increasing sucrose concentrations—even when their diets are substantially different. All these findings strongly suggest that our responses to sweetness as a quality are innate, with minimal input from our experiences with foods.

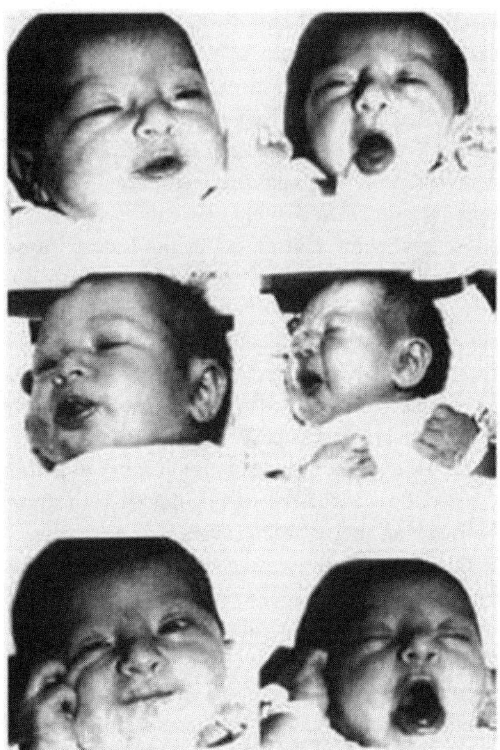

Jacob Steiner, an Israeli scientist interested in the physiology of the senses, observed unambiguously positive facial expressions when he placed sugar on the tongue of human newborns, suggesting that our responses to sweetness are largely innate. © JACOB STEINER

Sweetness Preferences and Evolution

The evolutionary explanation is that our survival depends on our ability to take in energy from our diet, and one of the major sources of such energy is carbohydrates, which include sugars. See SWEETS IN HUMAN EVOLUTION. Sweetness, therefore, is an excellent signal for the presence of energy. In order to maximize energy intake, preferences generally rise with sweetness intensity. Human newborns not only respond positively to sugars, they also discriminate among different sugars, consuming more if given free access to those that are more sweet (sucrose and fructose), as compared to less sweet glucose and lactose. Moreover, the fact that sweetness preferences can be observed in very many species across diverse animal classes argues strongly for the importance of sweetness as a nutritive signal. In mammals, the only species that do not respond positively to sweetness are obligate carnivores such as cats. See ANIMALS AND SWEETNESS. Any mammal species that consumes plants is thought to show sweet preferences—signaling the adaptive importance of plant-derived carbohydrates.

Food Preferences Determined by Sweetness

One reason why both children and adults prefer so many sweet foods is that sweetness is a major factor in the development of food preferences. Thus, repeatedly experiencing a novel food flavor with a sweet taste leads to an increase in liking for that flavor, over and above pairing the flavor with just water. This observation remains true even when the flavor is tasted afterward without the sweet taste being present. The interpretation of this effect is that sweetness in intrinsically positive, and the flavor becomes—by association—also positive. In addition, though, a sensation of sweetness may be a signal to the body that energy is being provided, something most clearly shown when flavors are paired with a caloric sweetener. Again, liking for the flavor increases, but only when the sweetener provides energy—that is, the increase does not occur with nonnutritive sweeteners such as aspartame or saccharin. Similarly, such *conditioned flavor preferences* do not operate in the absence of hunger, so that need for energy determines whether or not additional energy from a sweetener is sufficiently positive to generate a preference for an associated flavor. For the same reason, the reverse is also true: the pleasantness of a sweet taste relies on our metabolic needs, and ingesting calories to meet those needs reduces the pleasantness of a subsequently experienced sweet taste.

Sweetness remains generally positive into adulthood, even in the form of sugar dissolved in water. On average, we tend to prefer sucrose in water at 10–12 percent (by weight), which corresponds to approximately the concentration of sugar in many ripe fruits. This equivalence has fed the argument for the evolutionary significance of sweet preferences. However, it is clear that this average preference value hides considerable person-to-person variation. The scientific data actually support the existence of a "sweet tooth" in perhaps half of the population, as well as of substantial numbers of people who increasingly reject sweetness as it becomes more and more intense, even if weaker levels remain liked.

How such differences arise out of the newborn's universal acceptance of sweet tastes is not known. Evidence exists that greater liking for sweetness is linked to the higher consumption of both added sugars and sweet foods, suggesting the importance of experience and learning. Thus, among African Americans, higher rates of sweet liking have been reported, and one interesting habit in such populations is for mothers to feed their infants sweetened water. In both adults and children, the experience of a highly sweet version of a product produces an increased preference for that version. Variations in sweet liking act to influence the degree to which we develop liking for foods. For sweet likers, the pairing of a flavor with a sweet taste will result in a liking for that flavor; for those who show relative sweetness dislike, the result may be no increased liking or even a learned dislike for the flavor.

Sweetness plays an important role, too, in aiding the acceptance of foods or drinks that are initially too sour or bitter or spicy to consume. Adding cream or milk, plus sugar, a common combination for novice coffee drinkers, not only reduces the bitterness, but also provides the necessary positive tastes to produce liking for the coffee flavor itself. This is why, even if you drink your coffee white and sweetened, the smell of black coffee brewing is so appealing. This also explains why the transition in coffee drinking is overwhelmingly from sweetened coffee to unsweetened coffee, rather than vice versa. Other prominent examples of this kind of positive association are beer and wine, where consumers typically commence drinking sweeter versions and then graduate to drier (less sweet) wines or more bitter ales.

Genetic factors are also important in determining to what extent we prefer sweet tastes. Sensitivity to sweetness, as measured by the threshold at which we can detect it, shows unremarkable variation across individuals for either sucrose or saccharin. However, the pleasantness of very sweet solutions of sugar has been found to be partly heritable, as have the pleasantness and frequency of consumption of selected sweet foods. This finding is consistent with the fact that the sweet liker/disliker distinction is not associated with different degrees of *sensitivity* to sweetness, but rather seems to be confined to how much we liked increasing sweetness. Craving for sweet foods such as chocolates, while apparently not related to bodily needs, does, however, also seem to be partly heritable.

Sweetness in Food Contexts

Although overall most people highly like foods that are dominated by sweetness, our diets do not consist of foods that are overtly and predominantly sweet. Nor do we like unlimited amounts of sweetness—for each food, there is a "just right" level. From infancy onward, our experience of sweetness is usually within foods or drinks that have a characteristic sweetness level. Hence, our response to sweetness in foods becomes highly context-dependent. We are less likely to hear the complaint from children that a food is too sweet, but as we become more familiar with a particular level of sweetness within a food or drink, that level becomes the preferred one. Most tea or coffee drinkers will have an opinion about how much sweetener to add. If you take no sweetener, then any is too much. If you take two spoonsful, then any variation up or down will leave you dissatisfied. In other words, "appropriate" sweetness levels are learned.

More generally, preferred sweetness in foods is often linked to other food ingredients, such as the acids in fruit and the fat in desserts, cakes, and all things creamy. We tend to prefer our sweetness in balance with these other qualities. Indeed, there appears to be a genetic determinant to whether or not a particular degree of combined sweetness and creaminess is preferred. Whereas sweet, creamy sensations are generally liked, how much sugar or fat is required for greatest preferences varies, due to genetic markers of overall taste intensity.

As noted above, when sweet tastes are paired with odors and flavors, they become more liked, at least if you are not someone who dislikes sweets. This process of association also produces the interesting, commonplace phenomenon of odors that smell sweet, such as caramel, vanilla, and strawberry. See AROMA. It is thought that sniffing an odor that has been previously paired with a sweet taste evokes that taste from memory, thus providing the experience of sweetness. The relevance of this phenomenon is twofold. First, it demonstrates that the sweetness experience consists of more than just "sugar on the tongue"—our past experiences are also crucial. Second, these odors can work in much the same way as "real" sweetness by, for example, making a sweet beverage or food more sweet, or a sour one less sour.

Sweet Preferences and Overall Diet

What effects do our preferences for sweetness have on our diet? When asked to eat until they are comfortably full, most people will consume much greater quantities of sweet foods than savory or salty ones. This phenomenon appears to have more to do with the taste, rather than a need for the energy that a sweetener might provide, since it occurs even if we use sweeteners that do not provide calories. In fact, in modern Western diets, sweet taste and energy consumption have been increasingly decoupled. Because it is so innately rewarding, sweetness does not always need to be accompanied by calories for it to be pleasurable or influence food consumption. It is the quality of sweetness itself that our bodies respond to, since its meaning has previously been unambiguous. Hence, sweet tastes can exert effects on palatability and consumption in the absence of any effect sweetness has on our metabolism. This fact has an upside in terms of its effects on calories consumed. Dieters who eat foods that are sweet—but without calories (for example, sweetened with aspartame)—are better able to comply with their diets and lose weight.

It is not difficult to think about the universal pleasure derived from sweetness in terms of drug like properties. It is known that sweetness palatability is mediated by the same opioid (morphine-like) biochemical systems in the brain that are believed to be the basis for all highly rewarding activities. Drugs that block the activity in brain opioid systems to eliminate the effects of heroin and other opioid drugs will also reduce food palatability and intake, especially of sweet foods.

Such parallels, however, merely illustrate that sweet tastes are rewarding. That the majority of foods self-selected by children in Western societies are primarily sweet reflects the innate pleasure that sweetness provides; of course, this choice may also indicate just how available and promoted sweet foods are. In terms of the body's needs, a high preference for sugars makes sense when energy needs are high. However, very little evidence exists that strong preferences for sweet foods in childhood necessarily lead to adult obesity, or even to continued high consumption of sweet foods beyond puberty, as they often are consumed (or at least traditionally have been) in childhood.

See also ADDICTION and SUGAR AND HEALTH.

Kim, J-Y., et al. "Patterns of Sweet Liking in Sucrose Solutions and Beverages." *Food Quality and Preference* 36 (2014): 96–103.

Prescott, J. *Taste Matters: Why We Like the Foods We Do.* London: Reaktion, 2012.

Scott, T. R., and G. P. Mark. "The Taste System Encodes Stimulus Toxicity." *Brain Research* 414 (1987): 197–203.

Steiner, J. E., et al. "Comparative Expression of Hedonic Impact: Affective Reactions to Taste by Human Infants and Other Primates." *Neuroscience & Biobehavioral Reviews* 25, no. 1 (2001): 53–74.

Zellner, D. A., et al. "Conditioned Enhancement of Human's Liking for Flavor by Pairing with Sweetness." *Learning and Motivation* 14 (1983): 338–350.

John Prescott and Paul Rozin

sweets in human evolution are a subject of considerable study among scientists ranging from molecular biologists to cultural anthropologists. Our mammalian and primate heritage predisposes us to liking sweet taste for a number of reasons. See SWEETNESS PREFERENCE. Mammalian milk contains the sweet-tasting disaccharide lactose (glucose linked to galactose in β1-4 glycosidic linkage). The higher lactose and much higher oligosaccharide content of primate milk makes it even sweeter than cow's milk or the milk of other dairy animals. We belong to a lineage with a long history of frugivory, defined by a taste for ripe fruit, and like our closely related ape cousins the chimpanzees and bonobos, we tend to love honey. Even early in our evolution our ancestors sought out ripe fruit, favoring the sweetness that develops as plants accumulate sugars in their maturing fruit to entice consumption by seed dispersers. The sweet taste of fruit is mostly due to glucose, the disaccharide sucrose (glucose linked to fructose in α1-2 linkage), and the monosaccharide fructose, which tastes even sweeter than sucrose. See FRUCTOSE; FRUIT; and GLUCOSE. Most primates exhibit the hedonic "gusto-facial reflex" when tasting soluble sugars. Interestingly, larger primates appear to have lower detection thresholds for sugar.

Honey

Chimpanzees love to eat honey from a variety of bee species, including African honeybees (*Apis mellifera*) and stingless bees (*Melipona, Meliponina, Meliplebeia,* and *Trigona* spec.). Chimpanzees use stick tools to dip into the honey of stingless bees, but they raid the much larger hives of honeybees by rapidly reaching into the nest to rip out a comb before fleeing. African honeybees will fiercely defend their hives by stinging any intruder, including large apes. Humans use fire and smoke to gain access to both wild and domestic beehives. It is unknown when humans started using fire. The oldest evidence from Wonderwerk Cave in South Africa is dated at 1 million years ago, though it is conceivable that the use of fire is as old as the genus *Homo* (2 million years). Honeybees react to smoke by engorging themselves with honey, and the smoke severely limits pheromone communication among the bees. Thus, approaching a beehive with an ember wrapped in dry grass or leaves to generate continuous smoke allows humans to harvest large quantities of honeycomb and brood comb (for extra protein and fat). Humans are the only species capable of harvesting honey in such quantities. It has recently been proposed that humans have been raiding honeybee hives for possibly more than a million years. This hypothesis is supported by the phylogenetic analysis of two distinct lineages of the African greater honeyguide (*Indicator indicatoer*), a bird that lives symbiotically with humans. The greater honeyguide points out the location of beehives so that humans can raid the hives and make wax comb available to the bird, the only vertebrate capable of digesting wax. Living hunter-gatherers in Africa and Asia report that honey is among their most favored foods. See HONEY.

Plants and Sugars

Most plants use photosynthesis to fix carbon dioxide from the atmosphere into sugars. Plants build their rigid cell walls out of cellulose (long polymers of β1-4 linked glucose). Cellulose is difficult to digest, but animals such as ruminants and primates with specially adapted fermenting guts (leaf monkeys and gorillas) can extract substantial energy from cellulose with the help of cellulose-digesting microorganisms. Humans can digest disaccharide sucrose and poly-glucose starch (which, unlike cellulose, consists of glucose in α1-4 glycosidic linkages). See STARCH. Grasses such as rice, wheat, barley, millet, and corn also store sugars as starch in the endosperm of their seeds. The mere act of chewing starch introduces salivary amylase enzymes, which cleave starch into shorter and sweet-tasting oligosaccharides (malt). There is genetic evidence for human adaptation to the consumption of starch, as human populations with longer histories of grain agriculture have larger copy numbers of functional amylase genes in their genomes. (All humans have higher amylase gene copy numbers than any of the great apes.) Grain seeds themselves contain amylases (hydrolases). Germinating the seeds serves to activate the amylase enzymes; when the crushed seeds are mashed in warm water, sweet-tasting malt is generated. However, the human love for sugars and sweet taste can be a liability, as it favors a taste for one of the major byproducts of sugar fermentation: the ethanol found in alcoholic drinks. See FERMENTATION.

"Human-Made Honey"

Fire can also be used to cook and concentrate sugar-rich plant juices into syrups or solid crystalline sugar. Many different plants are used to these ends, but most famously, the ancient people of Papua New Guinea domesticated the sugarcane plant, which spread to India, China, and North Africa and was much later named *Saccharum officinarum* by

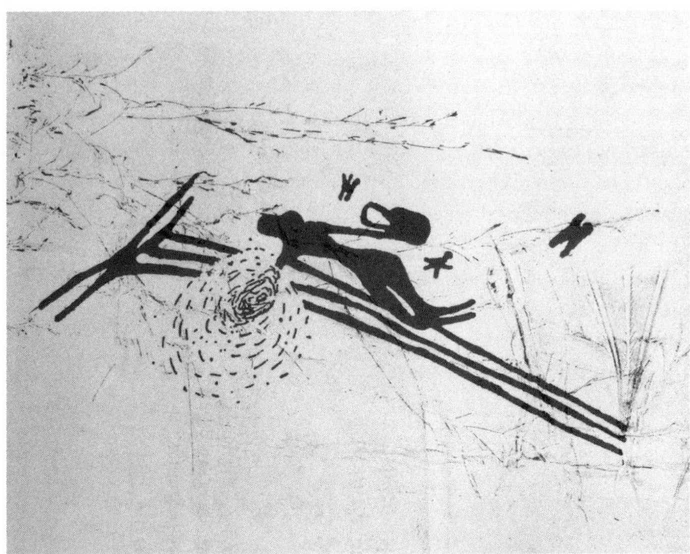

Prehistoric honey hunters risked multiple stings to track down wild beehives in rock crevices and tree hollows. This image of a honey gatherer being attacked by a swarm of bees, found in the Cuevas de la Araña caves in Valencia, Spain, is believed to be 8,000 years old. INTERFOTO / ALAMY

Europeans. See SUGARCANE. Other plants used for sugar extraction include various species of palm trees, agave, and beets (the sugar beet was specifically bred for its high sucrose content). See AGAVE NECTAR; PALM SUGAR; and SUGAR BEET. Boiled-down plant juices provide raw sugars that usually have a brownish color. This raw sugar can then be further refined. See SUGAR REFINING and SUGAR, UNREFINED. In the twentieth century, the production of sugar has shifted from natural sucrose to enzymatically treated cornstarch generated in wet mills that turn starches into pure glucose syrup, which can then be enzymatically transformed into fructose. Industrial food companies mix glucose and fructose in a 50:50 ratio to generate high-fructose corn syrup. See CORN SYRUP. This product represents an ironic convergence with honey, which also consists mostly of 1:1 free glucose and fructose. Honeybees cleave the nectar sugars with their salivary enzymes as they chew nectar into mature honey; this process allows honey to be 80 percent sugar, a concentration not achievable with the disaccharide sucrose found in nectar alone.

An Evolutionary Liability

People in Cameroon use a plant they call "forget" (*oubli*). This African vine (*Pentadiplandra brazzeana*) makes a small protein that mimics the taste of sugar. Legend has it that children given berries from this plant forget the milk of their mother. Several other African tropical plants have evolved powerful peptide mimics of sugar. Similarly, leaves of the South American stevia plant are added to *mate dulce*, traditionally made by the Guarani Indians of Paraguay, and they have also become the basis for a popular low-calorie sweetener. See STEVIA. Modern synthetic chemistry has tried out a variety of artificial sweeteners with mixed results. See ARTIFICIAL SWEETNERS. Ironically, the tsunami of artificially sweetened drinks and foods seems only to have accelerated obesity trends. Furthermore, concerns have been raised that dissociating sweet taste from energy may, as University of Washington epidemiologist Adam Drewnowski and colleagues put it, "disrupt the balance between taste response, appetite and consumption, especially during development."

Our profound love of sweetness has given rise to the many ways in which we obtain sugars from plants. As we live surrounded by ever more readily available sugar, we are paying a steep price for our sensory bias. Rates of obesity and acquired insulin resistance (type 2 diabetes) are skyrocketing around the world. Humans will have to learn how to live with and love sugar and sweetness responsibly. Some health advocates go so far as to demand that sucrose be labeled a dangerous drug. See ADDICTION and SUGAR AND HEALTH.

Crittenden, Alyssa N. "The Importance of Honey Consumption in Human Evolution." *Food and Foodways: Explorations in the History and Culture of Human Nourishment* 19, no. 4 (2011): 257–273.

Drewnowski Adam, Julie A. Mennella, Susan L. Johnson, and France Bellisle. "Sweetness and Food Preference." *Journal of Nutrition* 142, no. 6 (2012): 1142S–1148S.

Dudley Robert. "Ethanol, Fruit Ripening, and the Historical Origins of Human Alcoholism in Primate Frugivory." *Integrative & Comparative Biology* 44, no. 4 (2004): 315–323.

Hladik, Claude Marcel, and Bruno Simmen. "Taste Perception and Feeding Behavior in Nonhuman Primates and Human Populations." *Evolutionary Anthropology* 5, no. 2 (1996): 58–71.

Lustig, Robert H., Laura A. Schmidt, and Claire D. Brindis. "Public Health: The Toxic Truth about Sugar." *Nature:* 482 (2012): 27–29.

Perry, George H., Nathaniel J. Dominy, Katrina G. Claw, et al. 2007. "Diet and the Evolution of Human Amylase Gene Copy Number Variation." *Nature Genetics* 39, no. 10 (2007): 1256–1260.

Pascal Gagneux

sweetshop is a British English term for shops selling mostly, though not exclusively, sugar- and chocolate-based confectionery. The word has mildly childish overtones, and the color, sparkle, and glitter of hard candies and foil wrappers, as well as the seemingly endless choice of fruit drops, toffee, licorice, and other sugar-based items, are intensely attractive to children. In practice, such establishments may also sell a range of other items, including ice cream, newspapers, and tobacco. The North American candy store and the French *confiserie* also display the enchantment of boiled sugar in massed form, as do Turkish shops specializing in *lokum*, or Turkish delight.

Although many items also found in sweetshops—such as comfits, pulled sugar, and marzipan—have long histories, it is unlikely that anything remotely equivalent to the modern British sweetshop existed until about 400 years ago. The various confections developed along multiple routes, including fruit preserving, and sweets were also associated with apothecary shops, as druggists regularly coated their herbal and medicinal compounds with sugary shells or distilled them in syrupy concoctions. See FRUIT PRESERVES and PHARMACOLOGY. Making items from sugar and other ingredients was also affected by guild regulations in some locations, notably France and Central Europe, where sugar confectioners were not allowed to work with flour. Thus, some types of confectionery were more highly valued than others. See GUILDS.

The sweetshop, as it is known in England—and, by extension, in the rest of the British Isles—developed from shops kept by confectioners in the early modern period, at a time when sugar was still expensive and had medicinal overtones but was becoming more popular and available. The antecedents of the traditional sweetshops so magical in modern memory lie in eighteenth-century Western Europe and Great Britain. Lavish architectural appointments, including cabinetry, mirrors, and lighting, defined the fancy confectioner's shop from early on.

These shops, which catered to a well-heeled clientele, displayed candied fruits, nuts, dragées, and delicate chocolate confections like jewels upon fine porcelain plates and cut-glass pedestals. In Britain, in addition to candies, early sweetshops often featured baked goods such as cookies, cakes, pies, and other pastries. Cheaper sugar led to backstreet sugar-boiling establishments and inexpensive candy from street barrows or little shops for the poor. The nineteenth century saw the American invention of the soda fountain at the local pharmacy, extending the link between confectionery and apothecary and setting the precedent for the wide candy aisles found in chain drug stores today. See SODA FOUNTAIN. Ironically, the advent of these chains and the factory-made candies purveyed within them caused the demise of many local candy shops in the twentieth century.

Self-sustaining sweetshops, in their purest form, are now rare in the United Kingdom and depend largely on purchased stock. Elsewhere in Western Europe, they usually involve some specialty confections made onsite. Chocolate truffles in Paris, glacéed fruit in Florence, and shops dedicated to sculptured marzipan in Vienna turn regional confections into destinations. See CANDIED FRUIT and TRUFFLES. Often these establishments feature some part of the production on view, so that customers can watch bonbons being dipped in chocolate or taffy being pulled on a hook. Sweetshops often contain these house specialties alongside an array of boxed chocolates, panned fruits and nuts, jellies, ice cream, licorice, and caramels, with dizzying variety. These are places of childhood delight beyond the realm of reality, where all of the possible dreams of youth may be fulfilled for a few coins at the penny-candy counter. See PENNY CANDY. It is no wonder that the common aphorism for ultimate human pleasure remains as constant "as a kid in a candy store."

See also CHILDREN'S CANDY; CHOCOLATE, BOXED; COMFIT; HARD CANDY; LICORICE; LOZENGE; MARZIPAN; MEDICINAL USES OF SUGAR; PULLED SUGAR; and TOFFEE.

Mason, Laura. *Sugar Plums and Sherbet: The Prehistory of Sweets.* Totnes, U.K.: Prospect, 1998.

Richardson, Tim. *Sweets: A History of Candy.* London: Bantam, 2002.

Woloson, Wendy A. *Refined Tastes: Sugar, Confectionery, and Consumers in Nineteenth-Century America.* Baltimore: Johns Hopkins University Press, 2002.

Ryan Berley and Laura Mason

Switzerland is a place where one is never far from a bakery or pastry shop, even in rural towns and mountain villages, a fact that reflects the country's sweet tooth. Most meals finish on a sweet note, even if that means only fruit, yogurt, or a square of chocolate. But the Swiss do not have a taste for extreme sweetness; fruit- and dairy-based desserts are popular, and local specialties continue to reflect the country's poor, mostly agrarian roots. Breads, cakes, tarts, pies, and other baked goods make frequent appearances on Swiss tables. Whether a croissant in the morning or pastry with coffee during an afternoon work break, sweet things occupy a special place in the rhythm of Swiss life. The baked goods sold at pastry shops—mille-feuilles, baba au rhum, fruit tartlets, and chocolate slices—generally reveal a strong French influence. See BABA AU RHUM and PASTRY, PUFF. Most shops also sell petits fours; more sophisticated ones add chocolate bonbons to their offerings. See BONBONS and SMALL CAKES.

Special occasions (which can be merely having friends or family over for lunch) call for store-bought products that are more elaborate than one might make at home, but Swiss home cooks are proud bakers, too, and over the centuries rich and distinctive traditions have developed from canton to canton. Common elements typically found throughout the country include the use of nut flours, particularly almond and hazelnut; jams and other fruit fillings or toppings; and spices, including cloves, anise, and cinnamon. Homemade cakes tend to be one-layer affairs that might be topped with a dusting of confectioner's sugar or light lemon icing; elaborate icings and ganaches are more of the domain of pastry chefs. See ICING. Loaf cakes (called "cake" in both the French and German sides of the country) are among the most popular home-baked goods, since they can be served as an after-school snack or as dessert, and an individually wrapped slice fits well in a lunch bag. Popular flavors include chocolate, lemon, marble, and almond (*financier*).

The names of many pastries and cakes reflect the city or canton where they originated, even if they are enjoyed equally throughout Switzerland. *Brunsli*, or *bruns de Bâle*, made with egg whites, chocolate, almonds, and sugar formed into a rough dough, is one such specialty, originally from Basel but now consumed throughout Switzerland during the Christmas

The Swiss chocolatier Daniel Peter invented milk chocolate in the mid-1870s, when he mixed dried milk powder with chocolate. Seventy percent of the chocolate consumed in Switzerland remains milk chocolate. The Swiss company Suchard trademarked their milk chocolate Milka bar in 1901. The brand's well-known symbol, a purple cow, is not visible in this 1950s poster.

holidays (alongside cinnamon stars, anise cookies, and *Mailänderli/milanais*, a simple butter, flour, and sugar cookie cut into shapes). *Appenzeller Biberli*, a lightly spiced dough shaped as a round or a rectangle and filled with almond paste, originated in Appenzell but now enjoys country-wide popularity. It is available in supermarkets year-round but is most prevalent at the holiday season, when pastry shops use a special mold to impress an image of St. Nicholas or other seasonal design on the cookie's top. The treat bags that children receive for St. Nicholas Day or Christmas might contain a *biberli* or its unfilled cousin, a type of gingerbread, either soft or hard, that is often formed into traditional holiday shapes. See GINGERBREAD.

Carrot cake (*Rüeblitorte*) is a specialty from Aargau, while Zug is known for its Kirsch-flavored cake (*Kirschtorte*). Walnut tart (*Engadiner Nusstorte*), from the Grisons, is widely popular throughout the country, sold as tartlets or full-size tarts in both pastry shops and supermarkets. A close cousin of the American pecan pie, its *pâte sablée* shell is filled with a cooked mixture of honey and walnuts. Open faced or covered with another layer of dough, *Engadiner Nusstorte* is rarely made at home. Pear bread (*Birnbrot*) from Glaris has also made its way to the rest of the country; its filling includes dried pears, Kirsch, nuts, and spices, encased in a thin layer of yeasted dough. *Basler Leckerli*, originally from Basel, is a hard cookie that incorporates honey, candied citrus peels, and spices into the dough.

Dairy products are common, and nearly every dessert menu offers the possibility of adding a side of lightly sweetened whipped cream to ice creams or tarts. Seré, a fresh cheese, is commonly used in mousses and cakes made at home. *Meringues à la crème de Gruyère* originated in the canton of Fribourg, where the town and eponymous cheese of Gruyère are located, but this dessert is popular well beyond the canton's borders. Meringue shells are served with a double cream so thick that it will not drip if the bowl is turned upside down, along with a sprinkle of sugar. In the summer, raspberries are often added. See MERINGUE.

The Swiss chocolatier Daniel Peter invented milk chocolate in 1875, when he mixed evaporated milk powder with chocolate. While dark chocolate, from bonbons to bars, is widely available, 70 percent of the chocolate consumed in Switzerland remains milk chocolate. See CHOCOLATE, POST-COLUMBIAN and PETER, DANIEL. With a per capita consumption of about 12 kilos, or 26 pounds, Switzerland ranks first in the world (although this statistic is a little misleading, as it includes purchases made by tourists, which are considerable). The *carac*, a ganache tartlet typical of the French part of Switzerland, covered in green fondant and adorned with a chocolate pastille, is a prime example of a chocolate pastry-shop treat. Beautiful chocolate sculptures adorn the windows of urban pastry shops, and sophisticated bonbons are popular as gifts. However, the everyday chocolate of the Swiss is most often a piece of a supermarket-bought chocolate bar, eaten on its own after a meal, or as a snack, with bread.

See also BLACK FOREST CAKE; CHRISTMAS; FRANCE; HOLIDAY SWEETS; and PIE DOUGH.

Bossi, Betty. *Desserts de Choix: Délicieux & Irrésistibles.* Zurich, Switzerland: Editions Betty Bossi, 2003.
Bossi, Betty. *Cuisine Suisse.* Zurich, Switzerland: Editions Betty Bossi, 2009.
Hazelton, Nika Standen. *The Swiss Cookbook.* New York: Hippocrene, 1998. First published 1967.
McBride, Anne E. "Switzerland." In *Food Cultures of the World Encyclopedia.* Vol. 4: *Europe*, edited by Ken Albala. Santa Barbara, Calif.: ABC-Clio/Greenwood, 2011.
Patrimoine Culinaire Suisse. http://www.patrimoineculinaire.ch (accessed 15 October 2014).

Anne E. McBride

syllabub is an English sweet milk or cream dish containing wine or cider and served as a light froth or curd. It was one of the wet sweetmeats of the banquet or dessert course. See DESSERT. Although syllabub is first mentioned in literature in 1537, recipes do not appear in print until the following century; some of them indicate that it was occasionally made in the field by milking a cow into a bowl of cider or wine. More often, however, the cream and other ingredients were agitated with a whisk, or shaken in a bottle, to create an aerated curd. In the early versions of the dish the mixture was left to rest overnight and allowed to separate into a clear liquid below, with froth above. In the late seventeenth century, glass pots with spouts were used to serve this sort of syllabub. The alcoholic whey at the bottom was sucked through the spout and the froth eaten with a spoon. One popular variation known as whip syllabub was made by spooning off the bubbles created by whisking and laying them on a sieve to drain. The resulting froth was extremely delicate and was floated on top of sweet wine or whey. Syllabub glasses, with bell tops to support this topping of foam, evolved during the course of the eighteenth century, replacing the older spout pots. A later development was the everlasting or solid syllabub, really an alcoholic whipped cream, made with a higher ratio of cream to wine. It was also favored as the topping for layered trifles. See TRIFLE.

Syringes known as "wooden cows" were sometimes used to squirt the milk or cream into the wine and lemon juice mixture. The botanist Stephen Hales (1677–1761) is credited with inventing a labor-saving syllabub engine, which, "with the help of a pair of bellows, blows up cream into syllabub with great expedition."

Syllabub went out of fashion during the course of the nineteenth century, but the everlasting variety, at least, was revived in the 1960s by the food writers Elizabeth David and Jane Grigson, and the dish is now frequently encountered on restaurant menus.

See also CREAM; MILK; and WHISKS AND BEATERS.

Day, Ivan. "Syllabubs and Jellies." In *Eighteenth Century Glasses for the Dessert: The Tim Udall Collection.* Chippenham, U.K.: Delomesne and Son, 2011.

Ivan Day

symbolic meanings of the sweet are many-layered. Foods can accrue symbolic meanings through being shaped into representational forms, through association with their history of use, or through the semantic content ascribed to their characteristic flavors. Sweet substances achieve symbolic meanings in all of these ways, and the content of those meanings manifests some notable consistencies throughout history. One can consider the symbolism of sweet substances in terms of the significance of the taste itself, the meanings attached to the substance that yields the taste, and the uses of sweet foodstuffs in decorative or commemorative shapes.

Honey provides the oldest sweet, having been collected and consumed both in earliest recorded history and probably in prehistory as well. (There are Neolithic rock paintings of honey gathering in areas as far-flung as India, Spain, and southern Africa.) See HONEY. This intensely sweet substance has a distinctive property that invites attribution of significance beyond its flavor, for it is virtually unique in being a foodstuff that does not decay. (It will crystallize, but the crystals can be redissolved.) This is probably one reason that many ancient peoples—in South Asia, Europe, and the Americas—considered honey food for the gods, since it seemed, like the gods themselves, to be eternal. To the ancient Hebrews, honey—pure, incorruptible, untainted by human manufacture—also symbolized truth. See JUDAISM.

Human beings, and indeed mammals generally, naturally like sweet flavors. See SWEETNESS PREFERENCE. Perhaps this is because mother's milk is sweet, or perhaps it indicates an adaptive disposition, since sweetness in nature is often a sign of edibility, in contrast to bitterness, which is often, though not always, an indicator of poison. Whatever its origins in nature, the tendency to like sweet things has resulted in a set of closely related symbolic meanings that circulate throughout the globe. The meanings of sweetness cluster in the pleasant range: good luck, prosperity, and social harmony. This sort of symbolic meaning is manifest in various traditional practices, such as placing honey on the lips of newborns (parts of Africa) and uniting newly married couples with a dose of honey (Central Europe). It endures in religious rituals such as eating honey at Rosh Hashanah, the Jewish New Year. See ROSH HASHANAH. Such symbolic attributions of honey—signifying divinity, purity, good fortune—emerge from the actual properties of the substance, including the fact that it lasts a remarkably long time, and that it is immediately pleasant to taste for creatures like us. See WINNIE-THE-POOH. This kind of symbolism is sometimes termed "exemplification," where objects call attention to properties that they literally possess.

Sweetness is also easily extended to metaphoric usage, for something that tastes sweet is comparable to other things that are good and pleasant, as in the phrase "sweets to the sweet." Sweet foods symbolize goodness, luck, and happiness in widely distributed cultures, though this does not mean that the same foods are preferred. Sweetness comes in many forms and intensities, so particular foods that carry shared meanings often differ. Nonetheless, in its various forms, sweetness retains consistent symbolic meanings, and the practice of eating sweet things at celebratory festivals is widespread and enduring. At the Chinese New Year, sweets betoken prosperity and luck for the future, for example. See CHINESE

NEW YEAR. The Hindu festival of Diwali, during which numerous traditional sweets are both offered to the gods and consumed by participants, celebrates the triumph of good over evil. See DIWALI. Sweetness also signals benevolence and hospitality, and hence sweet foods are served as gestures of welcome to visitors. While such usage is common enough to have become culinary social habit, eating sweets at celebrations continues to seem appropriate because of the expressive uses of sweetness to signify happiness and good things generally.

Sweetness in the form of refined sugar extracted from sugarcane was, for a substantial period of time, a luxury available only to those of means outside the areas where the cane flourished (originally South Asia). See SUGAR and SUGARCANE. Under circumstances of scarcity, the sweetness provided by crystallized sugar connoted wealth and privilege, a significance achieved by association of the substance with those who consumed it. This symbolic meaning diminished as sugar became cheaper and more widely distributed; and indeed, at present, refined sugar has the opposite association, with cheap and unhealthy food—a marked contrast with the ancient notions that sweet things connoted health (they were often even ascribed medicinal properties). See MEDICINAL USES OF SUGAR.

Sugars readily combine with other foodstuffs, such as butter, flour, cocoa, or ground nuts, and as such they are easily molded into representational shapes, thereby expanding the potential range of symbolism. Where the sweetness of the substance is appropriate for the occasion, the symbolism of the representation converges with the symbolism of the taste. With the candy hearts made for Valentine's Day, for example, the symbolic meaning of sweetness unites with the symbolic meaning of the heart that signifies love. See VALENTINE'S DAY. Wedding cakes are common celebratory dishes for which a confection may be decorated with images that signal fond wishes to a newly married couple; when shared with company, they distribute good wishes to those assembled. See WEDDING and WEDDING CAKE.

The malleability of confectionery permits the formation of substances with sweet flavors into virtually any representation, as with chocolates molded to resemble insects, buildings, fruits, or flowers. Sometimes the shapes are consistent with traditional meanings of the sweet: luck and happiness. Other times they achieve a more complicated meaning, such as the sugar skulls produced for the Day of the Dead in Mexico, during which meals are prepared to welcome the spirits of the recently departed. See DAY OF DEAD and MEXICO. Such traditions indicate the complexity with which a taste functions within a symbolic practice. At the same time, the representational possibilities of easily molded foods can depart radically from traditional meanings and become ironic, comic, interesting, or merely weird, as with the manufacture of a chocolate spider. The symbolism of sweet things can therefore progress from deeply rooted traditions to transient representational whims, but it is the former that endure with the symbolic uses of sweetness to signify prosperity, welcome, happiness, and good fortune.

See also BUDDHISM; CHRISTIANITY; HINDUISM; ISLAM; and SPIRITUALITY.

Elkort, Martin. *The Secret Life of Food: A Feast of Food and Drink History, Folklore, and Fact.* Los Angeles: Jeremy P. Tarcher, 1991.

Goodman, Nelson. *Languages of Art: An Approach to a Theory of Symbols.* Indianapolis, Ind.: Bobbs-Merrill, 1968.

Mintz, Sidney W. *Sweetness and Power: The Place of Sugar in Modern History.* New York: Viking, 1985.

Outram, Alan K. "Hunter-Gatherers and the First Farmers: The Evolution of Taste in Prehistory." in *Food: The History of Taste,* edited by Paul Freedman, pp. 35–61. Berkeley: University of California Press, 2007.

Toussaint-Samat, Maguelonne. *A History of Food.* Translated by Anthea Bell. Oxford: Blackwell, 1992.

Carolyn Korsmeyer

taffy is a category of chewy candy whose definition is somewhat elastic. What differentiates a taffy from a toffee from a caramel varies from country to country and even from maker to maker. See CARAMEL and TOFFEE. Two criteria are most consistently used to define taffy. One is the absence of dairy ingredients. Whereas toffee and caramel include milk or cream and/or butter, taffy is typically composed primarily of sugar, corn syrup, water, and a stabilizer of some kind, such as starch or gelatin (though, to confuse matters, that stabilizer might be a dairy product). The other, more salient distinguishing characteristic of taffy is the fact that once the ingredients have been combined and cooked, the resulting sweet, sticky mass is pulled repeatedly in order to incorporate air, producing a candy that is lighter in both color and texture, as well as soft and chewy. Taffy also comes with a wider array of ingredients added for flavor and color; popular varieties range from peppermint to chocolate, cherry, lemon and licorice, in assorted pastel shades.

Part of the confusion is etymological. The origins of the words "taffy" and "toffee" are murky. The latter word is a variant of the former, and there is evidence that the harder, richer, creamier sweet we now know as English-style toffee evolved out of a softer, pulled, sugar-and-molasses-based sweet much closer to what is now known in the United States as taffy. By the early nineteenth century in the British Isles, sugar was available to all social classes, and confections such as taffy were made at home. In Wales, where taffy is also called taffi, toffee, and *cyflaith*, there was the Christmas Eve tradition of the *Noson Gyflaith* (Toffee Evening), in which hot sugar syrup was poured onto a buttered surface, and guests with buttered hands took turns pulling the stuff to make a kind of taffy. In Cumberland, England, there are records of a winter pastime called a "taffy join," in which youngsters would pull a mixture of butter, sugar, and treacle, playfully flicking each other with the pliable strands. Immigrants to the United States brought their taffy-making traditions with them, instituting the candy-making party known to Americans as the taffy pull.

By the late nineteenth century in the United States, taffy making had become a commercial enterprise as well. It was associated in particular with seaside resorts, where taffy pulls were a common boardwalk attraction, and taffy a popular vacation souvenir. See BOARDWALKS. Sometime in the 1880s, the candy began to be marketed as "saltwater taffy." There are a few competing origin stories. One centers on an Atlantic City, New Jersey, shop owned by John Ross Edmiston. One stormy night, so the story goes, the tide washed over the shop, drenching it and its stock of taffy with seawater. Finding that the taffy was still edible, Edmiston, it is said, spun the event into a bit of marketing magic, thereafter labeling his product saltwater taffy. Other accounts maintain that the alleged baptism of the taffy in saltwater was mythical and, in fact, various sellers—notable among them Atlantic City's Joseph Fralinger and Enoch James—simply liked the sound of the name and its association with seaside pleasures, and began using it to sell their taffy around the same time. In the early 1920s, Edmiston obtained a trademark for the name "saltwater taffy," but he lost a lawsuit brought by his competitors, with the U.S. Supreme Court ruling that saltwater taffy "is born of the ocean and summer resorts and other ingredients that are the common property of all men everywhere." In a 2013 survey of 2,000 adults from all 50 states conducted by the online retailer Candy Crate, one-fourth of respondents named saltwater taffy as their favorite summertime candy. To this day, no seawater is used in the making of saltwater taffy; it differs from other taffies in name only.

Over the course of the twentieth century, many new taffy products entered the U.S. candy market, including Mary Jane, rectangles of peanut butter-filled molasses taffy; Bit-O-Honey, honey-flavored taffy flecked with bits of toasted almond; Abba-Zaba, a taffy candy bar with a peanut butter center; Tangy Taffy, long, fruit-flavored slabs; and Laffy Taffy, originally sold as squares of fruity taffy in wrappers printed with jokes, and later repackaged under the Nestlé company's Wonka brand as long, narrow bars. Though chocolate candies currently dominate the U.S. market, chewy candies claim more than 39 percent market share among non-chocolate confectionery sales. Candy companies continue to create new taffy products. Recent innovations include Wazoo, a taffy bar with a creamy, tangy coating covered in sprinkles, launched in Blue Razz and Wild Berriez flavors by the Topps Company in 2009, and Juicy Drop Taffy, individual pieces of taffy that come in a pouch along with an applicator filled with sour gel, debuted by Bazooka Candy Brands in 2012.

Still, nostalgia remains a powerful selling point among taffy consumers. In 2010, Bonomo Turkish Taffy, a beloved brand launched in Coney Island in 1912 but discontinued in the 1980s, returned to the market. The relaunch came thanks to the efforts of Kenneth Wiesen and Jerry Sweeney, two diehard fans who acquired the intellectual property rights in 2002 and embarked on a years-long quest to resurrect the original formula, tracking down former Bonomo cooks, building specialty equipment, and finally debuting at the National Confectionery Association Sweets and Snack Show in Chicago. Today, Bonomo Turkish Taffy is made in York, Pennsylvania, and packaged with the vintage Bonomo logo and directive to "Smack It, Crack It!" on the wrapper—a testament to the candy's enduring appeal.

See also CANDY; CHILDREN'S CANDY; CORN SYRUP; GELATIN; and STARCH.

Almond, Steve. *Candyfreak: A Journey through the Chocolate Underbelly of America.* Chapel Hill, N.C.: Algonquin, 2004.

Kawash, Samira. *Candy: A Century of Panic and Pleasure.* New York: Faber and Faber, 2013.

Kimmerle, Beth. *Candy: The Sweet History.* Portland, Ore.: Collectors Press, 2003.

Lilliefors, Jim. *America's Boardwalks: From Coney Island to California.* New Brunswick, N.J.: Rutgers University Press, 2006.

Beth Kracklauer

tapioca is a starch extracted from the cassava root (*Manihot esculenta*). It is used as a thickener and to make puddings and other sweets. Tapioca "pearls" are obtained by heating the moist starch that remains in the water after cassava roots have been washed and pressed to produce flour. The pearls can be heated a second time to pop like corn, or they can be rolled into different sizes. See CASSAVA.

In the sixteenth century tapioca spread from Brazil to Africa, the Philippines, and throughout Southeast Asia, but it was introduced into Europe as a commercial instant thickener only in the mid-nineteenth century. Professional and household kitchens alike soon adopted this novelty food item, which allowed cooks to make custards without eggs. In 1854 Henriette Davidis, Germany's most important cookbook writer, published a recipe for tapioca for invalids in her *Praktisches Kochbuch* (Practical Cookbook). Europeans considered tapioca a light, easily digestible food, although the sticky pudding resulting from boiling its grains with sugar, milk, and a pinch of cinnamon owed its soothing effect more to the ingestion of the sweetened carbohydrates than to any medical virtue.

In Latin American and in Asia, tapioca mixed with sugar remains a luxurious dessert. It may be combined with coconut, spices, and eggs to make cakes, ice creams, and puddings, which are often covered with golden caramel. There is also a traditional Brazilian dessert—*sagu*—made with pearl tapioca cooked in red wine. In Asia, tapioca is also transformed into colorful jellies, flavored with pandan (*Pandanus amaryllifolius*) and tossed with grated coconut. See PANDANUS.

See also BRAZIL; BUBBLE TEA; and PUDDING.

Cars, Jean des. *Tapioca, cet inconnu.* Paris: Éditions Perrin, 2008.

Davidis, Henriette. *Praktisches Kochbuch für die gewöhnliche und feinere Küche.* 6th ed. Bielefeld, Germany: Verlag Velhagen & Klasing, 1854.

Freyre, Gilberto. *Açúcar, algumas receitas de bolos e doces do Nordeste.* Rio de Janeiro, Brazil: José Olympio Editora, 1938.

Marcia Zoladz

tart in its sweet version is a subset of the sweet pie. The Anglo-American tart can be traced to late medieval European innovations in pie pastry formulations, which made the crust tender through the addition of fat. In contrast to the tough, leak-proof flour and water crusts that dominated pie cookery at the time, these softer crusts were enticingly bitable and chewable. See PIE and PIE DOUGH. They encouraged pies in which the diner simultaneously took in filling and crust to create complex combinations of taste and texture in the mouth.

Tart entered written English from France around the cusp of the fifteenth century; the British dropped the "e" from *la tarte* and, as is common when dishes cross borders, modified the concept to fit their own cultural preferences. What differentiates sweet tarts from pies in the British tradition is not ingredients or the placement of the filling in relation to the crust. It is the tart's relative refinement, particularly its thinness. Gervase Markham, the author of *The English Huswife* (1615), the most important early-seventeenth-century British cookbook, explicitly specifies the depth of his pippin tart as 2.5 centimeters (approximately 1 inch), the height of manufactured tart pans today. In addition to providing a closer balance between filling and crust than is experienced with a pie, the tart's thinness means that it satiates the eye and mouth more that it satisfies hunger. The tart is a dessert for the connoisseur, not the glutton; when hungry, you do not tuck into a slice of tart.

The sweet tart's basic form is that of a disk approximately 9 inches in diameter and 1 inch high; the tart pan is often fluted. See PANS. When baked freeform on a sheet with the edges of dough folded in toward the center, the tart is frequently referred to as a "rustic tart." Today, in the Anglo-American tradition, tarts are usually completely open-faced, the form most closely associated with tarts in France. The open tart is sometimes ornamented with cross-hatching or pastry leaves or stars, radical simplifications of a previous tradition associated with high-status tables. Elaborate patterns in cut pastry characterized the pippin and pear tarts sketched by Robert May in his seminal cookbook *The Accomplisht Cook* (1685). However, until the late nineteenth century British fruit tarts tended to be covered, with a lightly glazed top; such glazed, covered tarts are now rare.

Fillings common to both tarts and pies include fruit purées, stewed fruits, and halved, quartered, or sliced fresh fruits. See FRUIT. The open tart's halved fruits, because they cannot hide, are always the most perfect available. Physical perfection might not be required of halved fruits in closed tarts, but peak ripeness is assumed in all tarts, as a comparatively small amount of fruit must communicate the dessert's character and clarity of flavor. The tart's tender, thin crust also means that an open tart can be spread with nothing more than a little jam or pastry cream, as a layer of intense or clean flavor epitomizes the tart's focus on the distillation of taste experience over quantity. As a dessert intended to be savored, tarts are often produced in individual serving sizes, a disk no more than a few inches in diameter. Small tarts may be referred to as "tartelettes." Historically, small British pies were referred to as "tarts."

Different tart traditions handle identical fruits differently. For example, in the French culinary tradition, apple and pear tarts are made with slices of precisely sliced fruits laid down in perfect circles and then glazed. In Anglo-centric culinary cultures, this style of tart is now often explicitly referred to as a French apple (or pear) tart. Conversely, the nineteenth-century French *tourte* tradition did not encompass fruit pies, so cookbooks such as Fouret's *Le cuisinier royale* (1820) offered recipes for the English covered fruit tart under the name of Tourte à l'Anglaise, à la Bourgeoise.

While historically the British and early American tart was clearly defined as a closed, thin fruit pie, today many English-language dictionaries restrict "tart" to the French meaning of a thin, open pie. Based on cookbook language, the shift in taste from what can be thought of as the British tradition of closed tarts to the French open tart took place in the first decades of the nineteenth century, initially in the United States. While Susannah Carter's *Frugal Housewife* (1803) specifies a lid for the apple tart, by 1830 Lydia Child's *American Frugal Housewife* makes clear that her cranberry tart has "no upper crust." Webster's *An American Dictionary of the English Language* (1830), perhaps in its attempt to define an American as opposed to British lexicon, explicitly places tart fillings "on" the crust, rather than "in."

In her best-selling mid-nineteenth-century British cookbook *The Book of Household Management* (1861), Mrs. Beeton indexes her strawberry tart as an "open tart," which implies that, unmodified, the word "tart" was too ambiguous to use. See BEETON, ISABELLA. Beeton specifies the open tart as always appropriate for jam tarts and thus offers a period source for understanding the nature of the tarts that created such a ruckus in Lewis Carroll's *Alice in Wonderland* (1865). Mrs. Beeton's apricot tart is covered, and as late as the 1880s, British cooks still readily conceived of tarts as either open or covered, as the *Handbook of Domestic Cookery*'s (1882) language makes clear: "Ice the covered tart, and send the open one without any addition to the table." Nineteenth-century cookbooks were used well into the twentieth century, but eventually the long-standing British covered tart tradition died out in the face of expanding French culinary influence.

Given the easy accessibility the Internet offers to historic and international recipes, the Anglo-American tart may once again change its form, and the dictionaries their definitions of "tart" to keep up with changing cultural practice.

Beeton, Isabella M. *The Book of Household Management [etc.]*. London: S. O. Beeton, 1861.
Carter, Susannah. *The Frugal Housewife, or, Complete Woman Cook; Wherein the Art of Dressing All Sorts of Viands Is Explained in Upwards of Five Hundred Approved Receipts, in Gravies, Sauces, Roasting [Etc.] Also the Making of English Wines*. New York: G. & R. Waite, 1803.
Heine, Mrs. *Handbook of Domestic Cookery, Adapted to the Requirements of Every Household [etc.]*. London: William Collins, 1882.
Markham, Gervase. *Country Contentments: or, The Husbandsmans Recreations [etc.]*. 4th ed. London: Printed by Nicholas Okes, for John Harison, 1631. Originally published as *The English Huswife*, 1615.
Santich, B. "The Evolution of Culinary Techniques in Medieval Era." In *Food in the Middle Ages: A Book of Essays*, edited by Melitta W. Adamson, pp. 61–81. New York and London: Garland, 1995.

William Rubel

tarte Tatin is an upside-down apple tart made by putting butter and sugar in the bottom of a tin-lined copper pan, baking dish, or ordinary pie pan about two and a half inches deep, adding a layer of peeled and quartered (or sliced) apples, then adding more butter and sugar to the apple layer. The whole is covered by a layer of pastry—which can be short crust, sweet short crust, or puff pastry—and baked in a hot oven until the pastry is browned and the apples are deep golden and nicely caramelized. Julia Child points out that judging the right amount of caramelization is greatly aided by the use of a Pyrex baking dish. Once the tart is cooked, it is unmolded upside down so that the crust is on the bottom and the apples are on the top, a move that may take some practice.

Tarte Tatin is served with whipped cream or ice cream while still warm. It is a rustic dessert with origins in the French provinces. The name "Tatin" belonged to two sisters who ran an inn in the Orléanais village of Lamotte-Beuvron. Whether these women invented the upside-down tart, or simply wrote down the recipe for this regional specialty, their name is famously attached to one of the most beloved desserts in France.

See also PASTRY, PUFF and UPSIDE-DOWN CAKE.

Child, Julia. *Mastering the Art of French Cooking*. New York: Knopf, 1979.
Croze, Austin de. *Les plats régionaux de France*. Paris: Editions Montaigne, 1928.

Kyri W. Claflin

Tate & Lyle is well known around the world as a sugar refiner and manufacturer of sweeteners and other products. Tate & Lyle PLC is also one of the hundred largest companies in Britain. It dates from 1921, when the two biggest British refiners amalgamated, though their founders, Henry Tate and Abram Lyle, were by that time long dead. Indeed, they never met.

Henry Tate (1819–1899) began in sugar refining in 1859, originally in Liverpool. Abram Lyle (1820–1891) was from Greenock in Scotland, where he bought a refinery in 1865. Both companies also opened refineries in London. They refined imported raw cane sugar and, in later years, faced stiff competition from imports of beet sugar, many of which were subsidized, from Continental Europe, especially Germany. See SUGAR BEET. When sugar prices collapsed in the early 1880s, the two companies responded by innovating and specializing. Lyle began to make Golden Syrup, using a secret formula, and this became the company's most profitable product. See GOLDEN SYRUP. In 2006 it was recognized as the world's oldest extant product brand. Tate invested in new production processes to improve efficiency, and he bought patents (from Germany in 1875 and Belgium in 1892) to make sugar cubes. Sugar had previously been sold in lumps or "loaves" which had to be broken, so small cubes were a major convenience. See SUGAR CUBE. While the two companies

Tate & Lyle formed from the 1921 merger of the two biggest British sugar refiners, Henry Tate & Sons and Abram Lyle & Sons. Here, the company advertises various kinds of sugar in packets, although it was better known for sugar cubes and Golden Syrup. HIP / ART RESOURCE, N.Y.

were competitors, they also made complementary products.

Henry Tate was a great, though discreet, benefactor, making donations to Liverpool University and other educational and medical institutions. He had been a keen collector of contemporary art, especially pre-Raphaelite paintings, and wished to donate the greater part of his collection of pictures and sculptures to the nation. To do so, he financed the construction of a new gallery at Millbank in London, opened in 1897, as the National Gallery of British Art; this museum has always been known as the Tate Gallery, after its founder.

The Tate & Lyle Company

Both businesses continued to be family run, and they overcame difficulties with supplies in World War I. By 1918 they together accounted for a third of British sugar production. Although competitors, the two companies chose to amalgamate in order to maintain their power in the market, and the government sanctioned the merger even though it gave the company such a dominant position. The new company extended operations by taking over a number of smaller producers in subsequent years. In 1923 Tate & Lyle accounted for half of the refined sugar in Britain; by 1938 business acquisitions meant that it controlled three-quarters of British refining capacity. The new company also took an interest in producing its own sugar for refining by investing in a beet sugar factory in 1925. In 1937, following the establishment of the British Sugar Corporation that had a monopoly in beet production, Tate & Lyle bought cane plantations in Jamaica and Trinidad. Thus, on the eve of World War II, the company had a virtual monopoly in refining and was a major supplier of raw cane sugar.

In the years following World War II, however, refining in Britain declined slightly and accounted for a falling share of Tate & Lyle's profits. Production of raw sugar and refining abroad became more important, although the company also began to diversify into new products, including high-fructose corn syrup as a sweetener for drinks. See CORN SYRUP. In 1950 the company began to make Black Treacle—a variant on Golden Syrup. Britain's entry into the European Common Market in 1973 exposed the oversupply of sugar, and the company moved further into diversification with industrial materials and artificial sweeteners. See ARTIFICIAL SWEETENERS. In response to the growing demand for low-calorie sweeteners, in 1976 the company developed sucralose, which they marketed as Splenda in partnership with the American company MacNeil Nutritionals, a subsidiary of Johnson & Johnson. Unlike other synthetic sweeteners, Splenda has the great advantage of being not only a substitute table sweetener, but also being useful in manufacturing. This product has become the company's most important.

Industrial products like Splenda, including some with no connection to the food industry, became so vital to the company that it began concentrating on producing goods as inputs for industrial processes rather than for retail consumption; for instance, MacNeil supplied Splenda to the retail market, while Tate & Lyle concentrated on industrial production. In 2010 Tate & Lyle PLC sold their sugar and syrup making interests to American Sugar Holdings. Under the name "Tate & Lyle Sugars," the new company continues to be the largest cane sugar refiner in Europe, using only "Fair Trade" materials. So the name has remained, and the new company still produces the two products that made the founding companies famous: sugar cubes and Golden Syrup.

See also SUGAR; SUGARCANE; PLANTATIONS, SUGAR; SUGAR REFINERIES; and SUGAR REFINING.

Chalmin, Philippe. "Lyle, Charles Ernest Leonard." In *Dictionary of Business Biography*, edited by David Jeremy, Vol. 3, pp. 884–888. London: Butterworths, 1985.

Chalmin, Philippe. *The Making of a Sugar Giant: Tate and Lyle, 1859–1989.* Chur, Switzerland: Harwood Academic, 1990.

Freedman, Michael. "Sweet Stuff: Iain Ferguson Has British Icon Tate & Lyle Growing Again." *Forbes* 175, no. 3 (2005): 98–100.

Jeremy, David. "Sir Henry Tate." In *Dictionary of Business Biography*, edited by David Jeremy, Vol. 5, pp. 438–443. London: Butterworths, 1986.

Munting, Roger, "Lyle, Leonard, First Baron Lyle of Westbourne." In *Oxford Dictionary of National Biography*, edited by H. C. G. Matthew and Brian Harrison, Vol. 34, pp. 865–866. Oxford: Oxford University Press, 2004a.

Munting, Roger. "Tate, Sir Henry, First Baronet." In *Oxford Dictionary of National Biography*, edited by H. C. G. Matthew and Brian Harrison, Vol. 53, pp. 805–807. Oxford: Oxford University Press, 2004b.

Munting, Roger. "Lyle, Abram." In *Oxford Dictionary of National Biography* online edition. May 2005. http://www.oxforddnb.com/view/article/88654.

Roger Munting

tea is a beverage made from the dried leaves of the evergreen plant *Camellia sinensis.* From its legendary beginnings in China to the present day, it has become the second most popular drink in the world, after water, and is enjoyed by millions across the globe. The Chinese drink fragrant teas from delicate bowls, the Japanese whisk it, Tibetans churn it with butter, Russians serve it with lemon, and North Africans add mint. Indians boil tea with condensed milk, the British and Irish drink it strong with milk, while Americans prefer it iced. Tea is very often sweetened with sugar or honey.

There are six types, determined by the method of treating the leaves. White, yellow, and green teas are unfermented, oolong is semi-fermented, and black and puerh (compressed teas) are fermented. These types are all processed in different ways to produce a huge variety in the color and shape of the leaf, and in the flavor and aroma of the beverage.

When green tea first arrived in the West in the seventeenth century, it was expensive, and only the rich could afford to drink it. This tea was quite bitter and was often taken for medicinal purposes. Quite early on, sugar (which was by now a familiar ingredient) was added as a sweetener. Milk was sometimes added, but its use became widespread only with the introduction of black tea.

In Central Asia, along the Silk Road from China to Turkey, tea prepared fairly weak, steaming hot, and without milk is often served with plenty of sugar, especially for guests as a sign of hospitality: the more sugar, the more honor. It is sometimes the custom to serve something sweet with the tea, rather than sweetening the tea itself. Sugar lumps are sometimes placed on the tongue and the tea is drawn through them. See SUGAR CUBE. Sweets and sweetmeats such as sugared almonds are popular accompaniments; in Russia, jam is served in a little dish and eaten by the spoonful alternately with sips of tea. In Japan, delicate and beautiful small confections or sweetmeats called *wagashi* are served with green tea, especially during the Tea Ceremony, to offset the tea's bitterness. See WAGASHI.

"Tea" can also mean a meal or a social occasion such as afternoon tea, which became fashionable in Britain in the nineteenth century. As the evening meal came to be served later, the hungry gap in the afternoon was filled by a light meal, at about 4 or 5 o'clock, of dainty savory or sweet items such as cucumber, jam, or honey sandwiches, cakes, pastries, or biscuits. Cream tea include cones with strawberry jam and cream.

During the nineteenth century the tradition of high tea was finding a place in lower- and middle-class homes, as the tax was reduced in 1784 and

Tearooms sprang up in many cities of Britain and North America at the end of the nineteenth century. Ladies tired from shopping could enjoy a refreshing cup of tea with their friends and sustain themselves until dinner time with a slice of cake or sweet pastry. Here, two little girls have dressed up for their own tea party, circa 1909. LIBRARY OF CONGRESS

cheaper black tea was now being imported from India. Working-class families could now afford to drink tea as their main beverage (rather than gin or beer), and after work they welcomed a hearty meal at about 6 o'clock, served with a pot of black tea with milk and sugar. Hot dishes were eaten; sometimes there were cold meats and pies accompanied by bread, butter and jam, cakes, fruit loaves, and biscuits.

Meanwhile, in the United States, ladies were gathering in their parlors or on their verandas for "low tea" (so-called because the tea and cakes were served on low tables, in contrast to "high tea," when a more substantial meal was eaten at a high dining table). Tea parties, with homemade specialties such as strawberry shortcake, pecan pie, or angel cake, were held to raise funds for churches or charities.

Tea rooms sprang up in many cities of Britain and North America at the end of the nineteenth century. Ladies tired from shopping could enjoy a refreshing cup of tea with their friends and sustain themselves until dinner time with a slice of cake or sweet pastry. Taking afternoon tea out has again become fashionable, especially in large hotels, where the fare is sumptuous and elegant. In France, salons de thé, which became popular in the early twentieth century, still thrive. See SALONS DE THÉ. Exquisite gateaux, tarts, and biscuits such as macarons, palmiers, and madeleines are served. The French have devised new blends of teas flavored with fruits and spices, and have also developed a tea-based cuisine, including tea-scented jellies.

During the nineteenth century, British women in India adapted afternoon tea to local traditions. A typical Anglo-Indian afternoon tea would consist of sandwiches (often with spicy fillings), Indian savories such as pakora and samosas served with English cakes, kul kuls (a type of fried cake), or sweetmeats such as barfi. See INDIA.

In Australia, where tea is still an important evening meal, teatime sweet specialties include lamingtons and Anzac biscuits. A pavlova might be served for special occasions. See PAVLOVA.

Tea is also an important flavoring in food, especially in sweet dishes, and is becoming increasingly popular, partly because of the variety of teas available. The flavor of teas can be strikingly different depending on how the tea is produced. Japanese green teas, which are steamed, have grassy, seaweed flavors, while Chinese green teas, which are pan-fried, produce savory toasted flavors. Oolongs lend a floral or fruity taste; black teas are richer and stronger, sometimes adding a hint of bitterness. Flavoring with *matcha* (powdered green tea) not only gives a vibrant color, because of its high caffeine content it also adds a little kick. Teas scented with flowers, fruits, or aromatic oils are particularly good for flavoring sweet dishes.

Pettigrew, Jane, and Bruce Richardson. *The Tealover's Companion: A Guide to Teas around the World.* London: National Trust, 2005.
Saberi, Helen. *Tea: A Global History.* London, Reaktion, 2010.

Helen Saberi

temple sweets are confections offered to gods and goddesses at their temples' altars throughout India. Food (cooked or raw) that is offered to the deities is called *bhog.* After the priest has presided over the gift-giving ceremony and presented the offering, the blessed food comes back to the devotees as *prasad.* This practice of sharing foods with the immortals has long been the central idea of communal kitchens in temple complexes. Hindu gods and goddesses are known for their sweet tooth and fondness for milk products. See HINDUISM. Lord Krishna in his childhood often stole butter, and his disciple in Bengal, Chaityana, shared his tastes, particularly when it came to kheer (milk pudding). Another Hindu god with a fondness for sweets is Lord Ganesha. Lord Ganesha, the elephant god, is renowned for his prodigious appetite for modaka and laddu. See LADDU and MODAKA.

To facilitate such sweet encounters between devotees and the objects of their worship, special care is taken to maintain the purity of the food offered. Thus, temples sometimes hire cooks who are Brahmin (the priestly caste), or sometimes specially trained men are employed in the sacred ritual of preparing temple sweets. For instance, the Siddhivinayak Temple in central Mumbai, which is devoted to Ganesha, sells devotees *mahaprasad* (blessed food) of specially prepared laddus (here made with *chhana dal,* ghee, sugar, peanuts, and cardamom). The holy treats are made by 36 trained cooks in the sacred kitchen. Each location has its own rules regarding the preparation of sacred sweets offered and shared with devotees. At the Sikh Golden Temple (Harmandir Sahib) in Amritsar, for example, the person cooking the *kadaprasad* (a creamy grain-based dessert made with equal amounts of wheat flour, sugar, and ghee) in the holy site's kitchens has to recite scriptures while preparing the sweet offering.

Perhaps the best known of the pilgrimage sites is the Jagannath Temple in Puri, Odisha. There, 500 cooks and 300 helpers prepare and offer the *mahaprasad* to Lord Jagannath six times a day, feeding around 100,000 devotees daily. Mainly the sweets are prepared from one of the following combinations: flour, ghee and sugar; rice or wheat flour, milk, and sugar; or sugar cooked with various forms of milk. Of all the sweets, *khaja*—an oval, layered, fried sweetmeat prepared from flour, sugar, and clarified butter—is perhaps the most popular item in *mahaprasad* parcels. It is just one of Odisha's contributions to the map of the temple sweets of India.

Lastly, *peda,* a round sweet prepared from khoa (thickened milk), sugar, and a good dose of cardamom, is found in the Kashi Viswanath Temple in Benaras and the Baidyanath Temple in Deogarh. There is a dedicated lane in the temple town of Deogarh that goes by the name Peda Galli, with sweetshops selling this famous sweet.

See also INDIA and MITHAI.

Krondl, Michael. *Sweet Invention: A History of Dessert.* Chicago: Chicago Review Press, 2011.
Mahias, Marie-Claude. "Milk and Its Transmutations in Indian Society." Translated by Mary Hyman. *Food and Foodways* 2, no. 1 (1988): 265–288.
O' Brien, Charmaine. "Odisha Feeding the Divine." In *The Penguin Food Guide to India,* pp. 138–148. New Delhi: Penguin, 2013.
Sinha, Anil Kishore. *Anthropology of Sweetmeats.* New Delhi: Gyan, 2000.
Singh, Rocky and Mayur Sharma."Ganapati Peda Bhandar." In *Apollo Highway on My Plate: The Indian Guide to Roadside Eating.* Noida: Random House India, 2010.

Ishita Dey

Thailand, a nation in the Indochina peninsula in Southeast Asia, has a sweets culture that has evolved dramatically since its origins in the thirteenth century. Historically, Thai sweets were sacred and precious, reserved for divinity—monks and royalty. Today, sweets are abundant and accessible to people of all stations.

Origin of Thai Sweets

Centuries before the founding of the first Thai kingdom of Sukhothai, sometime in the thirteenth century, Thais migrated from southern China to Southeast Asia, where they settled among inhabitants of the Dvaravati and Angkor kingdoms. They embraced the Buddhism and Hinduism taught by Indian and Ceylon priests, adapting and assimilating new religious rituals into their traditional cultural beliefs and customs. See BUDDHISM and HINDUISM.

Sweets were originally introduced as religious and ceremonial offerings. Since they were considered sacred foods, only celestial beings, including mortals with royal lineage and monks, were allowed to eat them.

Religious fables contain many stories of ancient Thai sweets. The earliest sources reveal that Thai sweets were named for the main ingredient, appearance, technique, or vessel used in their making. The first sweets were predominately Indian in origin and made from staples with religious significance, such as rice, coconut, beans, honey, seeds, and jaggery made from coconut sap, palm sap, or cane sugar, which would remain the staples used in the creation of Thai sweets for many centuries. See INDIA and PALM SUGAR. Cooking methods were limited to slow boiling, steaming, or grilling, because the early cooking wares were made from fragile terra cotta that could not handle high temperatures.

Rice was the ingredient held in the highest esteem. The Thai word for sweet is *khanom*, a combination of *khao* and *nom*, meaning "food with sweet taste." *Khao* means "food or rice," and *nom*, a Khmer word, implies "food made with rice flour." Some historians interpret the word *nom* as milk or, in particular, rice milk or a milky batter made from milling rice grains and water together with a stone grinder. Most Thai sweets were made with *nom*.

However, ancient sweets made with whole-grain glutinous rice were not called *khanom* but were given names starting with *khao* (rice). *Khao nieo daeng* is a good example. Garnished with sesame seeds, it is made with cooked glutinous rice and a mixture of coconut cream and palm jaggery, which colors the rice red.

Another example illustrates an ingenious cooking method that uses leaves to wrap the ingredients. *Khao tom phat*, a mandatory sweet for alms and religious rituals, is made with partially cooked glutinous rice sweetened with coconut cream and palm jaggery, wrapped in banana leaves and stirred while boiling.

Sweets made with rice dough have names starting with *khanom*, such as *khanom tom daeng* (boiled red) and *khanom tom khao* (boiled white). Rice-dough sweets were presented as offerings to the Rice Goddess during rice planting and harvesting. Glutinous rice dough perfumed with flower-scented water and jaggery are shaped into small balls and boiled. A portion of each ball is dressed with grated coconut cooked with reddish jaggery, while the rest is coated with fresh grated coconut, salt, and sesame seeds.

Khanom bueng (terracotta tile) is a sweet named after the cooking vessel it resembles. A light batter of rice and mung bean flour, coconut cream, and jaggery is spread paper-thin over a heated flat terracotta pan. The result is small, round, sweet crisps resembling tiles.

Ayutthaya Kingdom (1351–1767)

Toward the latter period of the Ayutthaya Kingdom, Maria Guimard (or Maria Gimard, or Maria Guyomar de Pinha), a woman with Portuguese, Japanese, and Bengalese ancestry, is credited with inventing countless Thai sweets. She lived some time during the seventeenth century and inherited her skill from her mother's Japanese Catholic family, who in turn had acquired most of their culinary experience from Catholic missionaries before fleeing Japan to escape religious persecution.

Guimard had a very dramatic life. Her Greek husband, a colorful advisor to King Narai (1656–1688), was executed for treason, landing her in jail, from which she escaped. She was recaptured, however, and subsequently became a slave in the royal kitchen. Cooking for two kings over several decades, she was eventually honored for her culinary contributions.

Guimard created egg-based desserts from Portuguese recipes by using refined sugar, a rare commodity that became available due to the demands of Europeans who preferred their tea sweetened. See PORTUGAL and PORTUGAL'S INFLUENCE IN ASIA. Metal cookware, available in the royal kitchen, enabled her to employ new cooking techniques, such as baking and glacé, the process of coating sweets with a sugary syrup. In addition, serving sweets as desserts, a foreign custom, was introduced to the royal table.

Guimard's most famous confections are *phoi thong* (golden fluff, originally Portuguese *fios de ovos*), *thong yip* (pick-up gold), *thong yod* (gold droplets), and *med khanun*, which resembles jackfruit seed. These golden delicacies came to symbolize prosperity and auspicious blessings, and are presented as religious and ceremonial offerings to this day.

Guimard substituted coconut milk for cow's milk to make Portuguese *pudim fla*, inventing a steamed Thai flan, *sangkhya*. See FLAN (PUDÍM). She also recreated caramel custard, but Thais later changed her recipe, using whole eggs instead of egg whites and baking the dessert in ordinary terracotta pots instead of rare metal pans, calling it *khanom moh kang* (pot for making curry).

Guimard also recreated Japanese-European sponge cake, or *kasutera*, which the Thais called *khanom foo* (light and airy). Her Bengalese background liberated her to invent sweets using tropical ingredients. One magnificent creation was *luk chob*, originally *doces finos* from Portugal. Using sweetened mung bean paste as a substitute for the Portuguese almond paste filling, she shaped the mixture into exquisite miniature fruits and flowers encased in thin floury paste, sweetened with sugar and coconut milk, and scented with jasmine water. They were painted with natural dyes to resemble the real flowers and fruit.

Maria Guimard's innovations created a sensation among her assistants, who duplicated her recipes at home, even though it was forbidden and considered a sacrilege. The temptation not to eat them was too great. Eventually, sweets were made in larger quantities as offerings during special ceremonies. Afterward, in order to not waste them, they would be served to guests and family members. And by the eighteenth century, Bangkok had many sweet markets selling confections made not only by Thais, but by Chinese, Indians, and European settlers as well.

Chakri Kingdom (1782 to Present)

By the beginning of the Chakri dynasty in the eighteenth century, countless new sweets had been invented, mostly in the royal courts. Each day the king was served a dessert tray with at least five kinds of exquisitely shaped sweets, selected for their complementary tastes and appearances. A profusion of delicacies was swathed in aromatic infusions and natural colorings that incorporated perfumed blossoms, herbs, barks, and smoke from scented candles. See AROMA and FOOD COLORINGS. Ice shipped from Singapore for the first time during the reign of Rama IV (1851–1868) was used to cool the perfumed syrups, creating new sweets for the king's table.

Commoners also created sweets, using regional ingredients. Some reinvented royal recipes by substituting ordinary ingredients for rare and expensive ones. A good example is sweet and creamy sticky rice. Imaginative toppings invented by commoners—including one made with sweet-savory dried shrimp perfumed with kaffir lime threads—garnished this adaptation of a court confection. And yet, for the Thais, sweets remained precious, gracing the tables of the king and wealthy aristocrats. Fruits remained the commoners' choice, served at the end of the meal to cleanse the palate. See FRUITS.

In the twentieth century, prosperity and Westernization revolutionized the culture of sweets. While traditional and ancient Thai sweets continue to be imbued with symbolic and religious meanings and served at rituals and ceremonies, they are no longer considered sacred. Instead, sweets are meant to be enjoyed by everyone and for all occasions. Today the Thais display savoir-faire and a taste for a modern lifestyle by emulating the latest fads from America and Europe. Specialty shops selling expensive and exquisitely baked pastries, such as chocolate and Japanese cakes with a Western twist, are popular. Sweets are not eaten merely as desserts but are identified by trendsetters who can afford the latest imported delicacies. In twenty-first-century Thailand, sweets have become the symbol of fashionable taste.

See also EGG YOLK SWEETS and NANBANGASHI.

Hada, Reiko. "Madame Marie Guimard: Under the Ayudha Dynasty of the Seventeenth Century." *Journal of the Siam Society* 80, no. 1 (1992): 71–74.

Hamilton, Alexander. *A Scottish Sea Captain in Southeast Asia, 1689–1723.* Edited by Michael Smithies. Chiang Mai, Thailand: Silkworm, 1997.

Muntarbhorn, Kanit. *Thai Food History and Transliterations.* Gastronomy in Asia 3. Bangkok: M. T. Press, 2007.

Pramoteshe, Lady Usana, and Chantanee Santabutra, eds. *Tamrub Khanom Thai Kong Sapasattri Hang Chad Nai Prabaromrachinupathom 2514 (Sa Nguyen Li Kasit)/ Thai Dessert Recipes by the National Women's Council of Thailand under the Royal Patronage of H.M. the Queen.*

Promsao, Kannikar, and Nanta Benjasilarak. *Sumrab Thai.* Chiang Mai, Thailand: Wanrak, 1999.

Samransuk, Mongkol, ed. *Regional Thai Wisdom and Technology.* Bangkok: Fruscale, 1999.

Su-Mei Yu

tiramisù is a dessert made of coffee-soaked ladyfinger cookies (*savoiardi*) with mascarpone cheese, cocoa powder, eggs, liqueur, and sugar. Its name, *tiramisù* (*tira mi sù*), means "pick-me-up," perhaps a reference to the effect of the caffeine in the espresso and cocoa powder used in the recipe. The dessert is made in nearly a hundred variations, and although it is a kind of zuppa inglese, an old dish related to the trifle, in its present form tiramisù is a relatively recent invention—the first written mention by name in any language dates only to the 1980s. See ZUPPA INGLESE.

Tiramisù is thought by many to have been invented in the Veneto region of Italy in the 1960s. The *Washington Post* writer Jane Black attributes its invention there in 1969 to Carminantonio Iannaccone, a baker who worked as a chef in Treviso (Veneto). Gino Santin, in his *La Cucina Veneziana* (1988), attributes the dessert's invention to Alfredo Beltrame, the owner of El Toulá restaurant in Treviso. But there are additional claims, one of the best supported being that of another Treviso restaurant, Le Beccherie (now closed), where owners Aldo and Ada Campeol and their pastry chef Roberto Linguanotto are said to have invented the dessert in 1970. Tiramisù's original creation is also claimed by regions outside the Veneto, the most important being Friuli Venezia-Giulia, where the heirs to the restaurant Il Roma di Tomezzo (also now closed) have initiated a lawsuit to prove that their tiramisù predates all others.

However, most culinary invention stories are apocryphal, as dishes tend to evolve rather than be invented. Legend has it that the antecedent of tiramisù may be the sweet known as *dolce del principe*, found in Lombardy, Emilia, Tuscany, and the Veneto, born perhaps as part of the banquet celebrating the visit of the grand duke of Tuscany, Cosimo III de' Medici, to the city of Siena in the 1570s. The present-day popularity of tiramisù may be due to the relative ease of its preparation, which increased in the early 1980s with the availability of commercial mascarpone cheese and its subsequent export to the United States.

See also ITALY and TRIFLE.

Black, Jane. "The Trail of Tiramisu." *Washington Post*, 11 July 2007. http://www.washingtonpost.com/wp-dyn/content/article/2007/07/10/AR2007071000327.html (accessed 17 October 2014).

Santin, Gino, and Anthony Blake. *La Cucina Veneziana: The Food and Cooking of Venice*. New York: Prentice Hall, 1988.

Clifford A. Wright

toffee, in Britain, denotes confections based on sugar, often brown, boiled with golden syrup or molasses-dark black treacle, and with milk, butter, or cream, to between 284° and 309°F, or 140° to 154°C (soft to hard crack). See STAGES OF SUGAR SYRUP and SUGAR. Its color varies from medium to dark brown, and its texture is hard. Toffee boiled to higher temperatures is brittle enough to break but still chewy when eaten. Closely related to caramels and butterscotch, toffee provides a flavoring for sweet sauces or sticky toffee pudding, and small pieces add interest to ice creams. See BUTTER; CARAMEL; and STICKY TOFFEE PUDDING. Chewy varieties are included in chocolate bars. The toasty flavor that characterizes toffee is produced by the Maillard reaction, which occurs when sugars and proteins (from the dairy products) are heated together at high temperatures. See MAILLARD, HENRI. Graining (recrystallization of the sugar) is discouraged, often by the addition of tartaric or other acid, except in a handful of recipes associated with Scotland and closely related to fudge or tablet. See FUDGE. Tablet is similar to fudge but has a harder texture and snaps satisfyingly; however, it still has the grained texture of fudge.

Toffee is made both at home and commercially. Glucose, corn syrup, and vegetable fats such as palm oil find their way into recipes used in industry, as do flavorings such as lemon, mint, vanilla, rum, and banana. See CORN SYRUP and GLUCOSE. Nuts, especially almonds, Brazil nuts, or coconut, can be stirred in. See COCONUT and NUTS. Homemade toffee is poured into trays to set. Commercially produced toffee used to be presented this way in Britain and was broken in the shop using a special hammer, but hygiene regulations now discourage this practice. Industrially produced varieties are frequently cut into small pieces and individually wrapped for sale as toffees.

Toffee remains popular in the United Kingdom, Ireland, Australia, and New Zealand. In North America a hard, buttery candy with almonds is known specifically as English toffee (just as chewy milk and sugar confections used to be known as "American caramels" in Britain). As a class of confectionery, it is less general in the non-Anglophone world, although some items, such as Dutch hopjies, are similar.

Cinder toffee or honeycomb toffee (known as hokey pokey in New Zealand) is a special type, made by boiling sugar to the crack stage and adding vinegar and bicarbonate of soda immediately before pouring. This addition makes the mixture foam, creating a distinctive airy texture. Honeycomb toffee is used commercially as the filling for a popular chocolate bar known as a Crunchie in the United Kingdom and Violet Crumble in Australia. It has a special association with the Ould Lammas Fair at Ballycastle in Ireland, where it is known as "yellowman."

Taffy is recorded as an earlier version of the word "toffee"; dictionary definitions suggest a possible link to a sugar-refining term, "tafia," indicating the point at which boiling molasses would set to a hard cake. See TAFFY. Taffy survived as a name in Wales, and in the United States, sometimes in reference to a pulled version of the sweet; in both countries a taffy pull was a form of evening entertainment into the twentieth century.

Everton toffee (once associated with Everton, now a suburb of Liverpool) is claimed to have originated in the late eighteenth century with a family recipe originally belonging to one Molly Bushell. The cookbook author Eliza Acton included recipes for it in her *Modern Cookery* of 1847, showing it as similar to modern butterscotch and flavored with lemon or ginger. Nearly 40 years later, in the *Confectioner's Hand-Book* (ca. 1881), E. Skuse wrote, "I do not think I could select a better, older, or more popular sweet than Everton toffee to commence my recipes, because it is a toffee which is known all over the world; it is a great favorite with young and old." Only the presentation distinguished this type of toffee from butterscotch. See BUTTERSCOTCH.

Other than these mentions, the history of toffee remains obscure. Recipes for it are notable by their absence from printed confectionery books prior to the mid-nineteenth century. A hard texture seems to have been the most consistent feature. Among Skuse's recipes are rose or lemon toffee, based on white sugar. Neither involves dairy products, a usage suggesting that the term "toffee" had a wider application relating to sugar boiled at a high temperature (the term "toffee apple" for a fresh apple dipped in sugar boiled to hard crack may reflect this). Perhaps other names were used for toffee-type confections. Skuse also mentions "stickjaw" (toffees are notorious for welding one's teeth together), made from boiled sugar and coconut and popular among London children; "hardbake," a hard sweet including almonds, possibly the ancestor of North American "English toffee"; and "tom trot," made from boiled molasses. See MOLASSES. Tim Richardson, in *Sweets: A History of Temptation* (2002), quotes a confectioner from 1864 who remarked that the latter two treats were popular everywhere in England. Although toffee became an everyday sweet, in northern England hard toffee made with black treacle or molasses had, until a few decades ago, a distinct association with the time around Guy Fawkes Night (5 November); and an early nineteenth-century Scottish source refers to "taffie" as treacle and flour boiled together and eaten at Halloween. See HALLOWEEN.

Toffees packed in brightly colored tins were enormously popular in early- and mid-twentieth-century Britain, as they were an inexpensive luxury. They were produced by the ton by several large companies, such as Sharp's, Bluebird, and Mackintosh (later part of Rowntree-Mackintosh, a brand now subsumed into Nestlé). The tins were often treasured by their owners long after the contents were consumed, and many survive as collectors' items.

See also HARD CANDY.

Mason, Laura. *Sugar Plums and Sherbet: The Prehistory of Sweets*. Totnes, U.K.: Prospect, 2004.
Richardson, Tim. *Sweets: A History of Temptation*. London: Bantam, 2002.
Skuse, E. *The Confectioner's Hand-Book and Practical Guide*. 3d ed. London: E. Skuse, 1881.

Laura Mason

Tootsie Roll is a classic, grainy, cocoa-flavored taffy. It is widely believed that Tootsie Roll was invented in 1896 by the Austrian-born immigrant Leo Hirschfeld, who sold the candies in his Brooklyn candy shop, and later merged with a larger candy company to expand his business. However, contemporary records, trademark filings, and advertising suggest that this account is not entirely accurate.

Stern & Saalberg, a midsized New York candy manufacturer, trademarked the name "Tootsie Roll" in 1909; the filing specifies the first use in commerce in 1908. The company marketed the candy heavily beginning in 1910. At that time, Hirschfeld was the head candy maker for Stern & Saalberg, where he had worked since at least 1894. Stern & Saalberg was reorganized in 1917 as The Sweets Company of America; Hirschfeld, who had risen to the position of vice president, left in 1922 and committed suicide in 1924.

Although Tootsie Roll today is considered a children's candy, in the early decades it was marketed to and enjoyed by both adults and children. Traditionally, chocolate could only be sold in the cooler months. Toostie Roll was appealing as a year-round chocolate alternative. In World War II and later conflicts, Tootsie Rolls were a popular choice for military rations due to their sturdy durability—so much so that some battalions were said to use "Tootsie Roll" as a code name for bullets.

The Tootsie Pop, a hard candy surrounding a soft Tootsie center, was introduced in 1931. It was the first lollipop to contain a candy "prize." See LOLLIPOPS. Today, Tootsie Pops and Tootsie Rolls are the flagship products of Chicago-based Tootsie Roll Industries, the direct descendent of Stern & Saalberg.

See also MILITARY and TAFFY.

"From Steerage to Fortune." *Pittsburgh Press*, 13 April 1913.
Tootsie Roll Industries. http://www.tootsie.com (accessed 17 October 2014).
"Wealthy Candy Man Kills Self in Hotel Room." *New York Tribune*, 14 January 1922.

Samira Kawash

torrone

See NOUGAT.

torte, the German word for gâteau or cake, typically designates a festive, fancy, round concoction, usually multilayered and filled. It thus stands in contrast to the French *tarte* (thin and mostly involving fruit of some kind) and German *Kuchen*, a simpler affair. See KUCHEN and TART. In Germany today, *Torten* are often composed of several sponge cake layers (sometimes sitting on a thin shortcrust base) spread with buttercream or whipped cream, or some variation of them. See CREAM and SPONGE CAKE. Glazed with cream or jam (or both), or coated with a thin sheet of marzipan, they are typically garnished with chocolate sprinkles, fruit, nuts, or small marzipan figures. See MARZIPAN and SPRINKLES. Comparable American-style cakes typically involve much more sweet icing or frosting. See ICING. Some French gâteaux, for example the Opéra, bear some similarity to *Torten*; however, the French term is much looser in meaning and may refer to a wide variety of pastries. The most popular and best-known tortes are arguably the Hungarian Dobos torte (multiple thin sponge cake layers alternating with chocolate buttercream and topped with caramel) and German Black Forest cake. The Austrian Linzer torte is somewhat atypical, resembling a tart more than a cake, and the Viennese Sachertorte consists of a chocolate cake spread with apricot jam and glazed with chocolate icing. See BLACK FOREST CAKE; DOBOS TORTE; LINZER TORTE; and SACHERTORTE.

The late Latin word *torta* stood for a flat, round bread, which spawned many variations throughout Europe, such as the French *tarte* and *tourte* (meat or fish pie, pastry with fruit or jam) and the Italian *torta*. Today, the latter designates a simple open or covered pie, usually with a savory filling (the open sweet version is generally called a *crostata*). But during the Renaissance these sorts of baked goods were often very elaborate.

In Germany, the patrician Sabina Welserin from Augsburg showed herself to be a real *Torten* specialist in her 1553 *Kochbuch*. For her, as well as for Marx Rumpolt in his *Ein New Kochbuch* (1581), *Turte* [*sic*] tended to be a covered pie, with a savory or sweet filling, often involving fruit and vegetables, but also with cheese or almond paste. See PIE. It was baked in a special pan, typically round and with straight sides. Rumpolt's Hungarian *Turte* differs from these, however. Based on a fourteenth-century Italian recipe for a *torta ungaresca*, it consists of 20 or 30 sheets of pastry made from flour and water, each "thin as a veil," spread with butter or lard, and sitting on top of an apple filling: a kind of apple strudel, in fact. See STRUDEL.

Conrad Hagger offers another rich source on the subject of tortes. His 1718 *Neues saltzburgisches Koch-Buch* includes over forty recipes (and engravings) for richly, colorfully decorated sweet and savory cakes (among them the first German-language recipes using chocolate). These cakes were clearly also intended to decorate the table along with sugar sculptures, which in turn came to be replaced by porcelain, allowing the pastry makers to concentrate on *Torten*. See SUGAR SCULPTURE. As sponge cake became fashionable in the seventeenth century under the guise of the French *biscuit*, elaborate constructions took the place of the medieval pies of old, with bright, flashy icings or edible lace—styles of decoration that led to the richness of contemporary tortes.

See also CAKE; CAKE DECORATING; and LAYER CAKE.

Hagger, Conrad. *Neues saltzburgisches Koch-Buch.* Augsburg, 1718.
Welserin, Sabina. *Das Kochbuch der Sabina Welserin.* Augsburg, 1553: http://www.uni-giessen.de/gloning/tx/sawe.htm

Ursula Heinzelmann

tragacanth is a gum exudate obtained from various species of wild goat thorn (*Astragalus* spp.) native to the Mediterranean and Middle East. It is most commonly harvested from the Mediterranean species *A. massiliensis* (Miller) Lam. and from the Asiatic *A. brachycalyx* Fisch., which grows in Lebanon, Iran, and Syria. Both are dense, thorny shrubs that favor rocky hillsides. The sap exudes naturally from the lower branches in June, and in the heat of the day it coagulates into irregular ribbons and long vermicular strands of dry white gum. In commercial culture, both the lower branches and upper roots are slashed to encourage the release of the sap. Most of the world's supply currently comes from Iran. It usually appears in commerce as a fine, cream-colored powder. It has also been referred to in culinary literature as Syrian tragacanth, adragant, and gum dragon.

Tragacanth has been used since antiquity in medicine and as a binding agent for making pills, incense, and pomander beads. When the gum is put into water, it swells into a gelatinous mass. Its principal use in confectionery is as a binding ingredient of gum paste and other edible modeling materials. Printed recipes for preparing sugar pastes of this kind first appeared in books of secrets published in the second half of the sixteenth century. Early practitioners usually soaked the gum in rosewater until it formed a thick mucilaginous mass, kneading in powdered sugar to make a thick, pliable paste. William Jarrin (1784–1848), a late Georgian confectioner, invented a specialized press for producing very large quantities of the paste. See JARRIN, WILLIAM ALEXIS. Tragacanth was also employed to bind modeling pastes made with starch, marble dust, plaster, and alabaster for making more durable table ornaments.

For making very fine gum paste ornaments for *pièces montées* and cake decorations, confectioners formerly used intricately carved wooden boards. The intaglio motifs were dusted with starch before the paste was pressed in, the excess trimmed off with a knife, and the ornament knocked out by banging the mold on the work surface. Gum pastes used for this purpose needed a high degree of strength and elasticity. A generous proportion of tragacanth to sugar, often as high as one ounce of gum to one pound of sugar powder, was required. See SUGAR SCULPTURE.

Tragacanth is still an important ingredient of commercial confectioners' preparations such as petal paste and pastillage, but its high price in recent years has meant that it is commonly substituted with carboxymethyl cellulose (commercially sold as tylose powder, or CMC), which has similar thickening and binding properties.

In the early modern period, tragacanth was also occasionally used as an ingredient in a few specialized baked goods and biscuits, as in this 1699 recipe from the manuscript receipt book of Elizabeth Birkett:

> To bake jumbals all of sugar
>
> Take one pound of refined sugar, beat it and searce it finely, put to it a graine of muske and as much ambergrease, and put it into a marble or wooden mortar, and as much Gum Dragon; that hath been steeped all night in rose water, and of the white of an egg well beaten, of them both as much as will wet it. See that you may beat it to a paste, work them up with a little fine sugar, and rowl them, make them into what fashion you please, lay them on a wafer and bake them in a soft oven.

See also CAKE DECORATING; PASTILLAGE; and SAP.

Day, Ivan. *Royal Sugar Sculpture.* Barnard Castle, U.K.: Bowes Museum: 2003.
Jarrin, William. *The Italian Confectioner.* London: John Harding, 1820.

Ivan Day

treacle

See GOLDEN SYRUP.

tres leches cake (*pastel de tres leches* in Spanish) is a sponge cake soaked in three milks (*tres leches*), usually condensed milk, evaporated milk, and cream. The immediate origin is almost certainly a recipe developed or at least disseminated by Nestlé in the 1970s or 1980s in cookbooks and on the backs of labels on cans of La Lechera (the milkmaid) condensed milk. The technique of soaking cakes and tortes in liquids goes back several centuries and is found in English trifle and Italian tiramisù. In the Spanish world, *antes* (starters) were often liquid-soaked cakes and tortes that bridged the sweet-savory boundary.

By the 1990s, tres leches cake had spread across Latin America. Although most closely associated with Mexico, almost every Latin American country has a version. It is called *torta genovesa* (torta from Genoa) in Colombia, is cakey rather than sodden in Argentina, is offered at weddings in Panama, and is served direct from the pan in Costa Rica. By the first decade of the twenty-first century, tres leches cake was to be found in the United States, Canada, Australasia, Britain, Germany, and India, in forms varying from cupcakes to ice cream, with and without fruits, and dressed up with frostings of meringue or whipped cream. Supermarkets offered tres leches cake mixes and cans of ready-mixed tres leches.

See also EVAPORATED MILK; SWEETENED CONDENSED MILK; TRIFLE; TIRAMISÙ; and TORTE.

Pack, M. M. "Got Milk?™: On the Trail of Pastel de Tres Leches." *Austin Chronicle* 13 February 2004. http://www.austinchronicle.com/food/2004-02-13/196888/ (accessed 30 August 2013).

Rachel Laudan

trifle is a traditional British dessert consisting of layers of cake or sponge biscuits (often laced with sherry or other alcohol), jam or fruit, crushed macarons or ratafia biscuits, thick rich custard, and a frothy cream or a syllabub topping, often decorated with slivered almonds, angelica, glacé cherries, or the like. There are many variations on this theme. Trifle is best made in a glass bowl so that the decorative layers can be seen. It is often served at parties, celebrations, or festive occasions such as Christmas.

The word "trifle" comes from the Middle English *trufle*, which in turn came from the Old French *trufe* (or *trufle*), meaning something of little importance, a fit subject for mockery, or an idle tale. Originally the culinary meaning of the word trifle was "a dish composed of cream, boiled with various ingredients," or not far removed from what we call today a fool. See FOOLS. In fact, the words "fool" and "trifle" were used interchangeably for a period, and Florio, in *A Worlde of Words*, his Italian–English dictionary of 1598, bracketed the two terms when he wrote: "a kind of clouted cream called a foole or a trifle."

The first known recipe titled "trifle" appeared in Thomas Dawson's *The Good Huswife's Iewell* in 1596. It was made of thick cream, sweetened with sugar, and flavored with ginger and rosewater, more like a fool. This theme continued throughout the seventeenth century, with slight variations in flavorings. However, in 1654, Jos Cooper, cook to Charles I, gave a recipe "To make a Foole," which bears a closer resemblance to the modern trifle: slices of bread soaked in sack (sherry) at the bottom of the dish, with a custard perfumed with mace and rosewater and sweetened with sugar poured over.

It was not until the mid-eighteenth century that trifle became the complex dessert known today. The first printed recipes for a trifle similar to the modern version appeared in 1751. One was given by Hannah Glasse in the fourth edition of *The Art of Cookery Made Plain and Easy*, and two appeared in *The Lady's Companion*. All three recipes called for Naples biscuits soaked in sack or red wine, layered with custard and topped with syllabub or cream. Glasse garnished her trifle with ratafias, currant jelly, and flowers, while one of the recipes from *The Lady's Companion* was garnished with apples, walnuts, or fruit.

After this appearance of the "modern" trifle, other "trifling relations" appeared on the scene, such as whim wham, The Dean's cream, Swiss Cream, Tipsy cake, Hedgehog cake, and Wassail Bowl. In Victorian times, trifles became even grander and were given imposing titles such an "An Excellent," "An Elegant," "A Grand," and "Queen of Trifles."

Trifle was enthusiastically welcomed in the United States and was often called by endearing names such as tipsy squire, gipsy squire, or tipsy parson, and it was an American writer, Oliver Wendell Holmes, who in 1861 wrote of "that most wonderful object of domestic art called trifle... with its charming confusion of cream and cake and almonds and jam and jelly and wine and cinnamon and froth."

See also BISCUITS, BRITISH; CUSTARD; FLOWER WATERS; MACARONS; and SYLLABUB.

Saberi, Helen, and Alan Davidson. *Trifle*. Totnes, U.K.: Prospect, 2001.

Helen Saberi

trompe l'oeil (French for "that which deceives the eye") had its origin in classical Greece and Rome and refers to the depiction of people, objects, or scenes rendered with such meticulous, three-dimensional exactitude that they appear to be real. Simultaneously witty, amusing, and intellectual, trompe l'oeil engages spectators, raising philosophical questions about the very definitions of art and perception. And it embraces not only painting, sculpture, architecture, and the decorative arts, but the culinary arts as well—reaching far above and beyond the mock apple pie recipe on the back of a Ritz Cracker box, a "dirt cake" made from crushed chocolate cookies and presented in a flowerpot (gummy worms optional), or a fondant-swathed custom creation that is more performance piece than dessert.

Culinary deception has had a long, distinguished history, and sophisticated examples continue to surprise and delight the senses. In Japan, which is home to two ancient, interlinked examples of edible trompe l'oeil—*mukimono* (decorative vegetable sculpting) and *modoki*, playful-poetic evocations of dishes based in the Buddhist avoidance of meat and fish products out of respect for animal life—sweets are generally eaten as a snack or during tea ceremonies, or presented as gifts. Inspiration has always been taken from the fields, forests, oceans, and seasons, and, according to the Japanese food authority Elizabeth Andoh, the maker must discern how best to convey the essence of the food he or she is preparing. In turn, the recipient provides a vivid imagination and a sense of humor, as well as a full measure of *kando* (awe) and *kansha* (appreciation). A number of the steamed rice-and-bean confections called *wagashi*, which were greatly influenced by foreign trade and the introduction of sugar during the late Muromachi era (1336–1573), imitate something from nature—a baked sweet potato, say, or a chestnut. See WAGASHI. A more modern (ca. 1909) snack, sold at street stands and food courts, is the beguiling fish-shaped pastry called *taiyaki* (baked sea bream), molded and cooked in what is basically a waffle iron. Although red bean paste is the traditional filling, other sweet options include custard, fruit, chocolate, and hazelnut spread. (Chinese sausage, bacon, pizza, and cheeseburger are among the savory choices.) One theory as to the enduring appeal of *taiyaki* stems from the fact that sea bream is an expensive fish. Eating *taiyaki*, which are cheap to make and buy, is a way for a penny-pinching student or humble salaryman to feel wealthy.

The qualities of awe and appreciation, along with religion, also played an integral part in the trompe l'oeil foods of Europe during the Middle Ages, when dishes disguised as something else relieved the tedium of a Christian church calendar packed with meatless fasting days. Eggs and dairy products were among the foods abstained from, and fast-day recipes in early cookery books might substitute, for instance, almond milk, made from expensive almonds ground and steeped in water, for butter and eggs in cakes and pies.

Edible objects modeled from march-pane (marzipan) and similar pastes, then hardened in an oven, were in evidence at royal feasts in France during the thirteenth century. See MARZIPAN. As the Renaissance took hold, so did the decorative possibilities of sugar, which had spread throughout Europe from North Africa—Egypt, in particular. Sugar's great popularity could be attributed to three factors: a preference for the whitest (i.e., most processed, thus most expensive) sugar, which was derived both from the Arab style and an age-old association between whiteness and purity; the durability of refined sugar under optimal circumstances; and the ease with which it could be combined with ingredients such as almonds. In *Charlemagne's Tablecloth: A Piquant History of Feasting* (2004), Nicola Fletcher takes note of an account of a wedding in Pesaro in 1475: "The entire table service was made out of sugar: plates, cutlery, and even wineglasses that remained waterproof for the duration of the feast (they were broken and eaten afterward), as well as imitation fruit, nuts, and berries for decoration." Sugar plate, which resembled translucent porcelain, was made by dissolving gum tragacanth in rosewater and lemon juice and pounding the mixture together with egg white and fine sugar to create a smooth, malleable paste, which was then rolled into sheets. See TRAGACANTH. Not only was sugar sweet, Fletcher observes, "it provided endless scope for showing off. The medieval voidee, or final course, became so elaborate that it evolved into an event in its own right. Whereas the words banquet and feast used to mean the same thing, now a feast meant the meat and fish courses and a banquet meant just the sweetmeats."

Taking pride of place at a banquet (which could be offered any time of day, with or without a preceding feast) was an extravagant edible centerpiece, which ranged from an allegorical representation of a classical figure, say, to one that reflected purported aphrodisiac properties—a gingerbread bull or ram, for instance. See SUGAR SCULPTURE. Both animals were symbols of lust, and spicy ginger was said to provoke Venus. The sculpted sugar displays, or "subleties," which marked the courses of a banquet, were often anything but. The sly, winking reference points came in a great variety of forms, including animals, objects, castles, mounted knights, and what the Reverend Richard Warner described in *Antiquitates culinarie* (1791) as "an extraordinary species of ornament, in use both among the English and the French ... representations of the *membra virilia, pudendaque muliebira*, which were formed of *pastry* or *sugar*, and placed before the guests at entertainments, doubtless for the purpose of causing jokes and conversations among them." The playfulness of the tradition lives on in the gingerbread houses, candy hearts, molded chocolate bunnies and eggs, and wares of erotic bakeshops today.

Another relic is the French bûche de Noël (Yule log cake), a sponge roulade with buttercream "bark," marzipan holly sprigs, and cunning little mushrooms made of meringue and dappled with cocoa powder. See BUCHE DE NOËL and MERINGUE. Its antecedent is found in the winter solstice celebrations of the Iron Age, when the Celts burned enormous logs decorated with holly, pine cones, or ivy; the pagan ritual was one of many woven into later Christmas celebrations across Europe. The first known recipe for bûche de Noël was published in 1898, in *Le mémorial historique et géographique de la pâtisserie*, by the Parisian pastry chef Pierre Lacam.

Trompe l'oeil foods are not necessarily about preference, dietary restrictions, wealth, or craftsmanship. American mock foods, for instance, were created by cooks well versed in Old World traditions who had to punt with ingredients more readily to hand. Take apple pie, for instance. Even though recipes for apple pie—not to mention the apples themselves—came to the colonies very early, thrifty cooks in the mid-nineteenth century substituted soda crackers when fresh apples were out of season or when they ran out of their supplies of dried or storage apples. Soda crackers (improved versions of ship's or soldier's biscuit) were sturdy and absorbed liquids and flavors well; in addition to being used in apple and mince pies, they were used in all manner of shore dishes, such as hashes, crab or griddle cakes, puddings, and chowders. An "Apple Pie without Apples" appeared in the *Confederate Receipt Book* of 1863 (in which it appears above "Artificial Oysters," made with green, or sweet, corn); and in *How We Cook in Los Angeles* (1894), Mrs. B. C. Whiting referred to it as "California Pioneer Apple Pie, 1852," noting that "the deception was most complete and readily accepted. Apples at this early date were a dollar a pound, and we young people all craved a piece of Mother's apple pie to appease our homesick feelings."

In 1934 the National Biscuit Company (Nabisco) introduced a richer, more delicate cracker called "Ritz" to its Philadelphia and Baltimore markets. Although the name conjured the elite sensibilities of César Ritz, the "king of hoteliers and hotelier to kings," at 19 cents a box it was advertised as one of life's most affordable luxuries during the Great Depression. Nabisco's recipe for mock apple pie, which first appeared on the box in 1935, was an immediate sensation, and the company soon distributed the upscale buttery cracker nationwide. In 1991, after a 10-year hiatus, the recipe was reinstated on the box in response to consumer demand.

The faux filling in a mock apple pie is helped along by cream of tartar (potassium hydrogen tartrate), a white, odorless powder that is a natural by-product of winemaking. It comes from the tartaric acid found in grapes and other fruits, including apples. But the pie's enduring appeal is also due in large part to the brain's effect on culinary perceptions: If it has a golden crust and is sweet and fragrant with cinnamon and lemon, it must be an apple pie. The brain is essentially filling in the blanks—such as true apple flavor and aroma. This phenomenon of how our various senses are stimulated is called "multisensory perception." See NEUROSCIENCE. Extremely important to flavor, it has sparked the scientific curiosity of restless, innovative chefs the world over. For almost 40 years there has always been more to a meal than meets the eye at the restaurants (in Los Angeles; Washington, D.C.; Las Vegas; and New York City) of Michel Richard. A former pastry chef with a classical foundation—and arguably the best French chef in the United States—Richard is known for witty, artistic (and often fat-free) presentations that look one way and taste another. One dessert on the dinner menu at Citronelle (now closed) in Washington, D.C., that always elicited gasps of delight was a wake-up call for the eyes and palate: It consisted of chocolate and puff-pastry "bacon"; a "fried egg" made of apricot paste (the yolk) and cream-cheese sauce (the white); slices of lemon pound-cake "toast" with vanilla ice cream "butter"; "hash browns" with caramelized apple standing in for the potato, and raspberry sauce "ketchup"; and, served in a coffee cup, a "cappuccino" of coffee mousse topped with cream and grated chocolate.

In recent years, modernist wizards such as Ferran and Albert Adrià, Andoni Luis Aduriz, Wylie Dufresne, and René Redzepi have embraced the concept of trompe l'oeil. Their transformative offerings may trick the eye, such as Dufresne's carrot-and-coconut "sunnyside-up egg"; turn a preconceived idea on its head, such as Aduriz's "carpaccio" of dehydrated watermelon; or create an edible illusion that explores the boundaries between sweet and savory, like Albert Adrià's "dessert of frozen time," which he describes as "a dirt road" in autumn. "The dessert, as it was eventually plated, included cherry sorbet, salted honey yogurt, frozen chocolate powder, and spice bread, all evoking one fall moment" (Gopnik, 2011, p. 54). Who is to say they're not real?

See also BANQUETING HOUSES; PLATED DESSERTS; and SWEETNESS PREFERENCE.

Andoh, Elizabeth. "Mukimono & Modoki: Japan's Culinary Trompe L'oeil." In *Vegetables: Proceedings of the Oxford Symposium on Food and Cookery 2008*, edited by Susan Friedland. Totnes, U.K.: Prospect, 2009.

Anderson, Jean. *The American Century Cookbook: The Most Popular Recipes of the 20th Century.* New York: Clarkson Potter, 1997.

Fletcher, Nichola. *Charlemagne's Tablecloth: A Piquant History of Feasting.* New York: St. Martin's, 2004.

Gopnik, Adam. "Sweet Revolution: The Power of the Pastry Chef." *New Yorker*, 3 January 2011. http://www.newyorker.com/magazine/2011/01/03/sweet-revolution (accessed 17 October 2014).

Jane Lear

truffles, named after the precious subterranean fungus, are orbed confections made from chocolate ganache, usually enrobed with couverture chocolate. The contrast between the creamy center and the crisp chocolate shell reflects the contrast between the artisanal and the industrial, and between tradition and modernity. Home cooks often simply roll the ganache in unsweetened cocoa powder. See COCOA.

There is documentation that a small amount of *pastel trufado*, or chocolate truffle, was shipped from Hamburg, Germany, to Guaymas, Mexico, in 1883. As with many well-loved confections, however, truffles have their own origin legends. The most common story credits a certain French confectioner, N. Petruccelli, with creating the first truffle, in Chambéry, France, in 1895. After he ran low on chocolate for the holiday season, he stretched what little he had by mixing small balls of cream, sugar, and powdered chocolate, then dipping them in chocolate. Antoine Dufour popularized the treat when he began selling truffles in a luxury London shop, Prestat, by 1902. Their popularity was established by 1908, when they appeared in the textbook *Revised American Candy Maker*, and surged again with the introduction of Lindt's Lindor melting chocolate in 1949. The iconic round shape of Lindt truffles dates to 1967.

Part of the reason for the popularity of truffles is that, while they are a fashionable product, they are flexible enough to allow modifications. Cultural preferences cause American, Swiss, French, and Belgian truffles to vary in size and purity of ingredients. Truffles easily adapt to trends, incorporating new flavors and exotic spices, including curry powder–coconut, matcha green tea, and raspberry–salted licorice. They can be made inexpensively for the mass market by machines that produce 500 pounds of truffles an hour, or carefully shaped by hand to retain a luxurious, artisanal appeal.

See also CHOCOLATE, LUXURY and LINDT, RODOLPHE.

Terrio, Susan. *Crafting the Culture and History of French Chocolate.* Berkeley: University of California Press, 2000.

Beth M. Forrest

Turkey has been a melting pot of peoples and cultures for thousands of years, from the first farmers of the Neolithic Age to the Hittites, Lydians, and Byzantines. Turkish people from Iran and Central Asia arrived in large numbers after the Iranian Seljuks, a Turkish dynasty, spawned the Anatolian Seljuk state in 1077. The Seljuks were followed by centuries of Ottoman rule (1299–1922), when a sophisticated cuisine evolved that exerted widespread influence across western Asia and eastern Europe. The diversity of Turkish sweets and desserts reflects both the varied roots of the cuisine, ranging from Central Asia and Persia to the Middle East and the Balkans, and the innovative character of Ottoman cuisine. Particularly from the fifteenth century onward, the palace and upper echelons of society could afford fine ingredients and skilled

A Turkish street vendor sells lollipops in the form of birds and flowers in Istanbul in the mid-seventeenth century. The lollipop sticks have been inserted into a bottle gourd attached to a long pole. The Dutch caption reads, "Sweets seller, little birds made of sugar." Dated 1660.

cooks to prepare dishes for those who appreciated good food.

Symbolic significance is attached to sugar in Islamic culture, as shown by two apocryphal sayings ascribed to the Prophet Muhammad: "The love of sweets springs from faith" and "True believers are sweet." See ISLAM. Mevlana Jalaladdin Rumi, an Islamic mystic who lived in Konya during the Seljuk period, frequently used sugar as a metaphor for God's love, as in, for example, "I am a mine of sugar, I am the sugarcane." The Turks gave this spiritual significance a fresh twist by renaming the three-day festival of Eid al-Fitr following Ramadan the Şeker Bayram (Sugar Feast). All over Turkey, sweet foods symbolize happiness and goodwill, so no rite of passage or religious festival is complete without the sweets associated with it. *Zerde* (saffron pudding) is traditionally served at circumcision feasts, *lokma* (doughnuts) or *irmik helvası* (semolina helva) at funerals, sweets such as *akide* (hard boiled sweets), *lokum* (Turkish delight) and sugared almonds at *mevlits* (memorial ceremonies), and *aşure* (a pudding made of whole-wheat grains, dried fruits, pulses, and rosewater) during the month of Muharrem (especially the tenth day). *Nevruz macunu,* a sweet paste made of 40 or more spices mixed with sugar, has been distributed in the city of Manisa on Nevruz, the first day of the ancient Persian New Year, since the sixteenth century. Ramadan is not complete without *güllaç* (a milk pudding made from layers of transparent starch wafers) and baklava, which is also a favorite on just about every festive occasion. Some traditions have lapsed in the twentieth century, such as preparing a crumbly type of flour helva called *gaziler helvası* (warriors' helva) for the souls of dead soldiers after battles. See HALVAH.

Origins

The most ancient Turkish pudding is *aşure* (related to the English flummery, frumenty, or fluffin; the Greek and Romanian *koliva;* Armenian *anuş abur;* Russian *kutya;* Sephardic Jewish *kofyas;* and Chinese *ba bao zou*), whose roots go back to harvest rituals in the Neolithic period when wheat was first domesticated at Karacadağ in eastern Turkey. See WHEAT BERRIES.

Sweet dishes with a Central Asian stamp are *güllaç* ("rose food," the pudding made of transparent starch wafers soaked in syrup or sweetened milk) and sweet pastries like baklava made with layers of thin pastry that were a staple of nomadic Turcoman cuisine. See FILO. Pastries soaked in honey or sugar syrup originate in medieval Arab cuisine, itself rooted in earlier Sasanian (224–651) Persian cuisine. In Ottoman Turkish cuisine, some of these pastries, such as *yassı kadayıf* (a yeast-risen griddle cake soaked in syrup), continued almost unchanged after the medieval period, while new types such as baklava emerged in the early fifteenth century. See BAKLAVA. Other contributions of the Persian or Arab cuisines to Turkish confectionery are the earliest sweets—sugar candy, *peynir şekeri* (pulled sugar), *koz helvası* (nougat), and sugared almonds—as well as puddings like flour helva, *muhallebi* (milk pudding made with rice flour), and saffron-scented *zerde. Tavukgöğüsü* (milk pudding thickened with shredded chicken breast), another dish of Arab origin that later spread to Western European cuisines, survives today only in Turkey, where it is also made in a caramelized version known as *kazandibi,* an innovation of the nineteenth century. See BLANCMANGE.

Keten helva or *pişmaniye* (from the Persian *pashmak*), a confection in the form of fine silky threads made of roasted flour and boiled sugar or honey, was introduced from Persia to Turkey in the Anatolian Seljuk era (eleventh to thirteenth centuries). This texture inspired the Turkish name *keten helva* (linen helva), the Greek *molia tis grias* (old woman's hair), and the Chinese "dragon's beard." Although *keten helva* is sometimes likened to candy floss, the ingredients, flavor, and method are very different. *Keten helva* is made by repeatedly twisting and stretching a ring of pulled sugar or honey in flour roasted in butter, a process requiring a high degree of expertise. The ring should be twisted between 15 to 45 times, each additional twist producing finer strands. *Keten helva* used to be made at home for winter gatherings of friends and neighbors called *helva sohbeti* (helva conversation) in towns and villages throughout most of Turkey, but today this custom is dying out, and the sweetmeat is now produced mainly by commercial confectioners.

Provincial specialties include *peynirli helva* ("cheese helva," made with semolina and fresh cheese, sometimes then baked); *kar helvası* (snow helva), made by mixing *pekmez,* honey or fruit syrup, with crunchy compacted snow; hot baklava with a cheese filling; lollipops in the form of hollow animal figures; *demir tatlısı* (fritters made with decoratively shaped irons, known as *nan-i panjara* in Iran and rosettes in the United States); and ice cream thickened with salep (orchid root). The latter, a specialty associated with the city of Kahramanmaraş in southeastern Turkey, is called *dövme dondurma* (beaten ice cream) because it is beaten with a wooden implement to produce a chewy consistency. It can be stretched into long ropes that take nearly an hour to melt, even in direct sunlight.

Confectionery of many kinds used to be sold by street vendors, but few of these varieties remain today. Among the survivors are *macun,* a soft toffee in bright colors wrapped around a stick, and *kağıt helva* (paper helva), consisting of wafers sandwiched together with soft nougat. See NOUGAT and TOFFEE.

Unraveling the origin of sweetmeats is not always possible, since the peoples of many faiths and ethnicities who lived in Turkey shared and exchanged foodways. Even dishes with known origins were often reshaped by Ottoman Turkish tastes. *Zırva,* a feast-day pudding, derives from a medieval Arab stew called *zirbaj,* made of mutton, chickpeas, spices, and honey. The Turks substituted dried fruits for the meat and chickpeas, omitted the spices, and used starch to thicken the juice, creating a pudding linked by nothing but name to its ancestor. *Zırva* used to be made in Turkey's *imarets* (public kitchens providing food for students, travelers, mosque staff, and the poor), but it died out in the early twentieth century with the closure of these institutions. The Arab pudding *ma'mûniyya* (Turkish *memuniye*) underwent a similar transformation, while *kadayıf*, which originated as a griddle cake, metamorphosed into threads of batter cooked on a griddle in early Ottoman times. See QAṬĀ'IF. This new type, known in Turkish as *tel kadayıf* ("strand kadayıf") and in Arabic as *kunâfa*, was first recorded in the first half of the fifteenth century and became so popular that it spread throughout the Middle East.

Helva made with tahini (sesame paste) was similarly unknown in pre-Ottoman times, yet today it is the main type of helva commercially produced throughout Turkey and the Middle East. In Ottoman times, tahini helva for the well-off was prepared with tahini, egg whites, white honey, rosewater, and lemon or white mulberry juice; the cheaper version for ordinary people was made by substituting extract of gypsophila root for egg whites and *pekmez* (grape molasses) for honey. See PEKMEZ. Today tahini helva is made by large manufacturers as well as by many small-scale confectioners in towns throughout Turkey.

In the Ottoman period, sweet courses were served at intervals throughout grand meals, a custom that still survives for special meals in some provincial areas of Turkey. In the early nineteenth century, Helmuth von Moltke, a German army officer who served in the Turkish army, described a banquet given for foreign diplomats to celebrate the circumcision of Sultan Mahmud II's sons: "The first dish was a roasted lamb stuffed with rice and raisins . . . Then came halwa, a sweet dish made with flour and honey, then again a roast, again a pudding, some hot, some cold, some sour, some sweet, each dish superb; but the manner in which they were combined was hard for a European stomach to comprehend and nor was there any wine. Ice cream was served in the middle of the repast."

Influence on Europe

From the early sixteenth century onward, Ottoman cuisine exerted an influence on Europe. Rice pudding, described as "Turkish-style rice" and made with milk, sugar, butter, and rosewater, was introduced into Italy, where it was served, for instance, at Ercole d'Este's wedding in 1529. Sherbet, a sweetened drink made with fruit juices, ground nuts, or spices, also spread first to Italy; in 1577 Francesco I de' Medici requested recipes for preparing "Turkish sorbette." See SHERBET. Flavored syrups still common in Italy and Central Europe today are likely descended from the Turkish original. After Italy, sherbet spread via France to England, where in the seventeenth century it was made from crunchy slabs of flavored sugar (*sert şerbet*) imported from Turkey. This preparation was replaced in the nineteenth century by a cheap substitute made of sugar, bicarbonate of soda, and citric acid, the fizzy sherbet powder that is still popular with English children today. See SHERBET POWDER.

Koz helvası (nougat), although originating in Arab cuisine, was introduced from Turkey into Central Europe and became known in Hungary as *törökmez* (Turkish honey) and in southern Germany and Austria as *Türkischer Honig*, the names still used today for the nougat on sticks sold to children at fairs and festivals in those countries. Baklava followed the same route, inspiring the famous *Apfelstrudel* (apple strudel). Described as "Hungarian tarts" in Marx Rumpolt's *New Kochbuch* (1581), the strudel was made with a chopped apple filling and 20 or 30 layers of dough stretched in the hands until "as thin as a veil." See STRUDEL. Finally, in the mid-nineteenth century, a soft sweetmeat called *çevirme* flavored with fruits or spices was introduced to Europe and became known in France as fondant. See FONDANT and SPOON SWEET.

European Influence on Turkish Confectionery

Since the nineteenth century, Western influence on Turkish confectionery has increased rapidly, so that apart from lokum and pastries soaked in syrup such as baklava and *tel kadayıf*, traditional Turkish sweets struggle to compete with caramels, chocolates, biscuits, and cakes, which now have a lion's share of the market. In the first half of the twentieth century, French cuisine was not just fashionable but a symbol of modernization. A Turkish book on confectionery written in 1939 is filled with crèmes, marmalades, gateaux, biscuits, cakes, tartelettes, mille-feuilles, and petits fours, with just a sprinkling of Turkish recipes. Although home cooks, especially in the provinces, have largely remained faithful to traditional sweets and puddings, most hotel and restaurant chefs ignored them until the 1990s, preferring instead to churn out imitations of French pâtisserie. But then the tide began to turn, and traditional sweet pastries and other desserts returned to both menus and cookery school curricula that had focused almost entirely on French *cordon bleu*. People are increasingly aware of the need to preserve Turkey's diverse sweets and desserts, many of which are unknown elsewhere, such as *güllaç, tavukgöğüsü, peynir helvası, ayva tatlısı* (quince halves stewed in clove-flavored syrup), *su muhallebisi* (unsweetened starch jelly served with rosewater and powdered sugar), *kazandibi*, and *ekmek kadayıf* (a kind of bread pudding in syrup served with clotted cream).

See also FUNERALS; ISTANBUL; PERSIA; and RAMADAN.

Algar, Ayla Esen. *The Complete Book of Turkish Cooking.* London: Kegan Paul, 1995.
İlkin, Nur, and Sheilah Kaufman. *A Taste of Turkish Cuisine.* New York: Hippocrene, 2013.
Pekin, Ersu, and Ayşe Sümer, eds. *Timeless Tastes: Turkish Culinary Culture.* Istanbul: Vehbi Koç Vakfı, 1996.
Roden, Claudia. *Arabesque: A Taste of Morocco, Turkey and Lebanon.* London: Michael Joseph, 2005.
Yerasimos, Marianna. *Evliya Çelebi Seyahatnâmesi'nde yemek kültürü* [Food Culture in Evliya Çelebi's Book of Travels]. 2d ed. Istanbul: Kitap Yayınevi, 2011.

Priscilla Mary Işın

turnovers are, as the name suggests, a type of pastry in which the filling is placed on one half of the rolled-out dough, and the other half is then turned over to enclose the contents. Their appeal to both cooks and consumers is based on their convenience and adaptability. Turnovers are eminently portable, individually sized snacks or meals in the hand. Any form of pastry may be used, from bread dough to puff pastry and Mediterranean filo. Turnovers may be baked or fried, and the filling may be sweet or savory.

The word "turnover," in its culinary context, is first attested in England's *Sporting Magazine* in 1798, in the phrase "an old woman was employed in heating her oven, and preparing her turnovers, commonly called apple-pies." The concept itself, however, is much older. A turnover is essentially a pasty, and under this name has been around since at least the thirteenth century, and in all likelihood a great deal longer. In recipes from various times, regions, and sources it is also called a "pie" or a "puff." See PIE. In John Ray's *A Collection of English Words Not Generally Used* (1674), Ray refers to the Suffolk word "*Stuckling*: an Apple-pasty or Pye." The English agriculturalist William Ellis, in his *The Modern Husbandman* (1742), mentions "two-cornered turnover pasties" filled with a type of pear, and particularly relished by harvest-workers.

Published recipes routinely postdate the actual use of a dish, often by a very long period of time, especially in the case of common, rustic foods. The first recipe found to date for what is clearly a turnover is for "Apple Pasties to Fry," in *The Whole Duty of a Woman* (London, 1737):

> Pare and quarter Apples, and boil them in Sugar and Water, and a stick of Cinnamon, and when tender, put in a little White Wine, the Juice of a Lemon, a piece of fresh Butter, and a little Ambergrease or Orange-Flower-Water; stir all together, and when cold, put it in a Puff-past and fry them.

In America, dried apples were a nineteenth-century staple, so it is not surprising that they commonly found their way into turnovers. In the second half of the nineteenth century, these handy pies formed part of the regular fare offered to railroad passengers, and in 1917 dried apple turnover pies were referred to as "an old fashioned favorite" in the *Bulletin of the Agricultural and Mechanical College of Texas.*

Turnovers were also a popular nineteenth-century method of using up and eking out leftover cold meat in both Britain and America. Catherine Beecher's *Domestic Receipt Book* (New York, 1848) gives the following recipe:

> Roll out wheat dough very thin, and put in it, like a *turnover*, cold meat chopped fine, and seasoned with pepper, salt, catsup, and sweet herbs. Make small ones, and fry them in lard till the dough is well cooked.

Historically, in most times and regions, in spite of the great adaptability of the basic concept, the most common and iconic form is the apple turnover. That these small pies remain enormously popular in the United States is evidenced by the annual National Apple Turnover Day on 5 July, a holiday that, like all special observance days, required Presidential approval.

See also FILO and PASTRY, PUFF.

Smith, Andrew F., ed. *Oxford Encyclopedia of Food and Drink in America.* 2d ed. New York: Oxford University Press, 2012.
"Turnovers." http://www.foodtimeline.org/foodpies.html#turnovers (accessed 17 October 2014).

Janet Clarkson

tutti frutti (also tutti-frutti), a term in popular use in a wide number of languages and countries around the world, designates a variety of confections that involve mixtures of fruits or fruit flavors. The term is derived from the Italian words for "all fruits." In Italy itself "tutti frutti" is not a traditional, fixed culinary term, though the combination of words, especially with the definite article—*tutti i frutti*—naturally occurs with its literal meaning.

A likely place where "tutti frutti" was first coined as a culinary term is New York, whence the earliest attestation (1834) in connection with ice cream. See ICE CREAM. Given the central role played by Italians in the development of ice cream and its subsequent spread into and around English-speaking lands, it is possible that the term was actually coined by an Italian. Italians were prominent ice cream makers in New York, London, and elsewhere as early as the latter part of the eighteenth century.

Early on, tutti frutti was primarily used to designate mixtures of fruit pieces that had been candied or macerated with sugar in alcoholic beverages, in particular brandy—an Anglo-American adaptation of the Italian use of candied or macerated fruits, especially citrus peels, in the making of ices and ice creams to mixtures that included other fruits already used in traditional English confections, such as fruitcakes and fruit puddings. See FRUITCAKE. Also noteworthy is the resemblance of Anglo-American tutti frutti to German *Rumtopf* and Danish *romkrukke*, a fruit mixture macerated in rum with sugar that is enjoyed in northern Europe with ice cream, as well as in other applications. The *Rumtopf* became widely known in the United States from its use in the once numerous German-owned confectioneries. Secondary to this use of the term "tutti frutti" to designate mixtures of fruits is its meaning as a multi-fruit flavoring, attested in the United States as early as 1885 as a brand name of chewing gum. See CHEWING GUM.

The resemblance of tutti frutti as an element in frozen desserts to the fruit mixtures employed in making English-style fruitcakes lies behind the name of the "tutti frutti cake" popular in India, which is made with a mix of candied fruit pieces. See CANDIED FRUIT. In the Netherlands, the term "tuttifrutti" (attested in Dutch since the late nineteeth century) is applied to a mixture of dried fruits (apricots, pears, apples, plums, etc.) and also to a dish made from those fruits, in which the mixture is soaked or cooked in water or apple juice, sweetened, and spiced (e.g., with cinnamon). Elsewhere, this sort of dish is called compote.

See also PUDDING.

Furiassi, Cristiano. "False Italianisms in British and American English: A Meta-Lexicographic Analysis." In *Proceedings of the 15th EURALEX International Congress, Oslo, 7th–11th August 2012*, edited by Ruth Vatvedt Fjeld and Julie Matilde Torjusen , pp. 771–777. Oslo: Department of Linguistics and Scandinavian Studies, University of Oslo, 2012.

Quinzio, Geraldine M. *Of Sugar and Snow: A History of Ice Cream Making.* Berkeley: University of California Press.

Anthony F. Buccini

Twelfth Night cakes celebrate Epiphany, the bringing of gifts by the Magi to the Christ child, twelve days after his birth. These cakes are most popular in Roman Catholic countries, especially France and Spain, although England, Germany, Switzerland, and Greece all have their own versions.

To mark the winter solstice, pagans named a king for a single day. Ancient Romans baked a bean into pastry to celebrate their version of 21 December, Saturnalia. Both traditions eventually merged with the Christian holiday, featuring a special cake whose hidden bean designates a king for a day. The medieval French called this cake *gastel a feve orroriz* (now the *galette* or *gâteau des rois*). The Spanish call it *roscón de reyes*; the Portuguese, *bolo rei*; the southern Germans and Swiss, *Dreikönigskuchen*; the Greeks, *vasilopita*; and the English, King Cake. Whoever finds the hidden token in their slice is named king for the day, a figure representing the Magi who is granted specific rights and responsibilities and sometimes gets to wear a paper crown—although, in the aftermath of the French Revolution, the cake was briefly called a *galette de l'égalité*.

In Paris and northern France, *frangipane*—an almond-paste-filled puff pastry—is the preferred Twelfth Night cake, while southern France favors a brioche-like cake containing dried fruit. See FRANGIPANE. The Spanish and Latin American versions are topped with candied fruit to imitate the jewels of a crown. In New Orleans—where Creoles adapted the French tradition of marking the end of the period after Epiphany—a round, twisted brioche King Cake

During Twelfth Night festivities celebrating the Christian Epiphany, whoever finds a token in their slice of cake is named king for the day. Originally the tokens were edible, but over time they took more permanent forms, as in this assortment of twentieth-century ceramic Twelfth Night charms from France. PRIVATE COLLECTION / ARCHIVES CHARMET / BRIDGEMAN IMAGES

is iced in purple, green, and gold, the colors of Mardi Gras. See NEW ORLEANS. In England, color is less important than location: since 1796, a cake has been cut every twelfth night by the cast of the currently running play *Twelth Night* at London's Theatre Royal, thanks to a bequest by actor Robert Baddeley (1733–1794).

The hidden bean—known as a *fève* in French and *monito* or *sorpresa* in Spanish—can vary as much as the cake. The original broad bean, its form symbolic of a human embryo, was sometimes superseded by an almond. Either might be swallowed on purpose as part of the ritual. This practice changed once charms were made of more permanent materials, such as porcelain and metal. Babies, representing the Christ child, and depictions of the Three Wise Men, were the most common. In seventeenth-century England, printed-paper tokens became popular. When King Cake tokens morphed into lucky charms for English birthday, wedding, and Halloween cakes, they were often made of lead or silver. American Mardi Gras cakes increasingly used plastic babies, which are the most common today.

Ironically, it is the French, who had all but abandoned the Twelfth Night cake by the 1950s, who have become the twenty-first-century's *fève* fanatics (*fabophiles*), supporting a Musée de la Fève near Nantes with 20,000 examples of beans and charms, annual collectors' fairs in both Paris and Blain, and the last manufacturer of china tokens, Les Fèves de Clamecy, in Burgundy. Only one French citizen is barred from receiving a fève in his cake: the nation's president. So his *galette des rois* is baked *sans fève*.

See also BREADS, SWEET and CHRISTIANITY.

Boyer, Marie France. "Bean Fest." *World of Interiors*, January 2010, pp. 34–39.

Karp, Marilynn Gelfman. *In Flagrante Collecto*. New York: Harry N. Abrams, 2006.

Francine Kirsch

Twinkies, officially Hostess Twinkies, the small, mass-marketed, extra-sweet, oily, packaged snack cakes, have one of the most recognizable brand names in American consumer product history. Infamous for their 45-day shelf life, and for the long list of artificial ingredients making that shelf life possible, Twinkies are known to many as the epitome of processed food. Fittingly, the Twinkies label touts color and texture, not flavor or taste, with a banner proclaiming "Golden sponge cake with creamy filling."

Foodies may deride them, but Twinkies sell by the hundreds of millions every year, as they have for generations.

If the president of the United States decides a sweet snack cake is important, then it must be so: President Bill Clinton included a Twinkie in the millennium time capsule in 1999. When Twinkies' longtime corporate owners, Interstate Bakeries Corporation, went bankrupt in 2012, almost every major media outlet featured the story. It was big, national news. And when private equity firms Apollo Global Management and C. Dean Metropoulos and Company paid $410 million for the rights to Twinkies (and their chocolate siblings Ding Dongs and Ho Hos, among others), and then brought the snack cakes back to life in July 2013 with a nostalgia-based marketing campaign, that comeback story once again garnered headlines in every major media outlet around the country. Money talks. Twinkies matter. No other snack cake is as significant, well known, beloved, hated, or celebrated both as a cultural icon and symbol of everything wrong with our food habits as Hostess Twinkies.

Other snack cakes, such as Little Debbie Golden Cremes, may sell in larger numbers, use pretty much the same ingredients, and strive for a similarly long shelf life, but rival confections somehow lack Twinkie's aura. See LITTLE DEBBIE. Is it because they are so famous? The men's magazine *Maxim* once ran an article on five tough guys in movies who eat and love Twinkies, including a monster, a cop, a ghost buster, a zombie killer, and Genghis Khan, despite his having been dead for about 800 years. No other snack cake can make that claim. And let us not forget that tough guy Archie Bunker, the main character in *All In The Family*, one of the longest-running, most popular TV shows in history, had a Twinkie in his lunch bag every day. More recently, Twinkies gained notoriety in the successful "Twinkie defense" of Dan White, accused in 1978 of murdering San Francisco mayor George Moscone and fellow city supervisor Harvey Milk. White's lawyer successfully argued for White's temporary insanity based on his overconsumption of junk food, convincing the jury to charge him on the lesser count of manslaughter.

Despite frequently negative press, Twinkies remain uniquely iconic and beloved among American snack cakes. Not too bad for a Midwestern confection, invented in the Chicago suburb of Schiller Park in 1930 by James A. Dewar, manager of the Continental Baking Company. Hoping to find a year-round use for the shortcake pans used only during strawberry season, Dewar injected banana cream into the shortcake batter, and Twinkies were born. During World War II, when bananas were in short supply, the company substituted vanilla cream, which has remained the filling ever since.

Twinkies became popular thanks to two forces: television advertising and post–World War II chemistry. In the 1950s, ubiquitous TV ads promoted Twinkies as a proper dessert and even as a healthy snack, "full of protein to grow on." Twinkies were a major sponsor of the first widely viewed and influential children's TV show, *The Howdy Doody Show*, which prompted mothers to include the snack cakes in just about every daily lunch box in America. Many baby boomers today look back at that show as their introduction to Twinkies and TV. At the same time, there was increasing consumer demand for more processed, convenient foods. Food product manufacturers responded by using new chemicals and finding new uses for the older chemicals widely available after World War II as the chemical industry ceased its high level of wartime production. The TV advertising tag line "Better living through chemistry" was a familiar household phrase in the early 1950s, and the concept of a non-spoiling, cheap dessert cake appealed greatly to Americans.

This convenience food trend translated into the development and availability of low-cost ingredients that reduced the cost of processed foods while creating the possibility of food types that had not existed before, such as TV dinners. Twinkies are typical of highly processed foods that rely on artificial ingredients for their shelf life and low cost. Cakes stored at room temperature are fertile ground for microorganisms, mainly because of the dairy products in their frosting and fillings. And while we don't know the exact recipe for the original, 1930s-era Twinkies, they were notable for two things the contemporary version lacks: they incorporated fresh ingredients (cream, butter, and eggs), and they spoiled after only a few days on the shelf. Until the introduction of artificial ingredients, salesmen had to remove unsold Twinkies every few days.

That drive for longer shelf life led to a reliance on alternatives to dairy products and eggs. By the early 2000s, Twinkies included such ingredients as polysorbate 60 (a gooey egg-yolk substitute), cellulose gum (a moisture binder and fat substitute), sodium stearoyl lactylate/mono and diglycerides (cream substitutes), and sorbic acid (the lone preservative in Twinkies)—among an impressive 39 ingredients and sub-ingredients. Some of those sub-ingredients are surprisingly artificial: the vitamins in the enriched flour are made primarily from Chinese petroleum or in Chinese fermentation labs, not, as one might expect, from ground-up berries, roots, or bark. In the future, we can perhaps expect to see the inverse in a new breed of Twinkies, as the new marketers might add fiber, go gluten free, or create low-sugar options in what has previously been beloved for being a decadent treat. For now, the little Twinkie stands as a symbolic dividing line between those who prefer fresh and whole and those who simply want their sweets sweet and cheap.

See also HOSTESS; SMALL CAKES; and UNITED STATES.

Ettlinger, Steve. *Twinkie, Deconstructed.* New York: Hudson Street, 2007.

Newman, Kara. "Twinkies." In *The Oxford Companion to American Food and Drink,* edited by Andrew F. Smith. New York: Oxford University Press, 2007.

Steve Ettlinger

The **United Kingdom** comprises Great Britain and Northern Ireland. Many, perhaps most, of its people associate the word "sweets" with the confectionery lining supermarket shelves or displayed in jars in small local shops. Confusingly, the term also covers a wider array of sweet foods eaten at the end of a meal, which may be called "sweet," "dessert," or "pudding," depending on linguistic usage as well as social and geographic position. The word "afters" has now entered the culinary lexicon to refer to all three, in an attempt to avoid arguments about which word to use.

Sugar first came to Britain in the eleventh century, along with spices. It was a high-value rarity, a status symbol, and was recorded in the spice accounts. Sugar's earliest use was as a medicine, and this link with the work of the apothecary continued into the seventeenth century. See MEDICINAL USES OF SUGAR. Similar to its use on the European continent, sugar was also a valued sculptural medium. These uses of sugar were largely developed by men. Imported confections, especially preserved fruit and fruit pastes such as marmelada, were also sought after. See FRUIT PASTES and FRUIT PRESERVES. By the Elizabethan age—the second half of the sixteenth century—sugar was cheaper and more widely available; increasingly, it replaced honey as the usual sweetener, not only for the gentry but also for the rising yeoman class. The German traveler Paul Hentzner noted that the English had a taste for sugar, and that their teeth suffered in consequence. See DENTAL CARIES.

Sugar work became a fashionable pastime for ladies in their own homes, as illustrated by Sir Hugh Plat's *Delightes for Ladies* (1602), which provided instructions for "preserving, conserving and candying." See PLAT, SIR HUGH. Over the next two centuries, several women wrote books for domestic use, with instructions for fruit preserving and other sugary recipes, but men remained predominant in the public sphere and as confectioners in wealthy households. The elegant shops of professional confectioners glittered with fruit pastes, ices, biscuits and cakes, comfits, drops, and lozenges for the gentry and bourgeoisie. The most influential also published their recipes for their apprentices and for home cooks. Their names—Negri, Gunter, Jarrin—guaranteed quality because they sold goods made on the premises. See JARRIN, WILLIAM ALEXIS.

Confectionery

West Indian sugar produced by the plantation system was ever more available, a source of revenue for the government and the foundation of many British personal fortunes. See PLANTATIONS, SUGAR. By the mid-nineteenth century, sugar, no longer taxed, had become a vital food for the workers in the industrial cities that were developing in many parts of the British Isles. In the damp and chilly climate, the desperate poor could buy calories, comfort, and a brief glimpse into a refined world of sweetness and light from the cheap confectionery that developed from the older aristocratic tradition. But they could not afford to buy from reputable shops; in *London Labour and the London Poor* (1851), Henry Mayhew recorded the large variety of sweet goods and confectionery made by sweet-stuff makers to "tempt the street eaters." Garish colors were achieved using lead, mercury, or copper-based dyes, and public concerns were raised about cases of (sometimes fatal) poisoning. See ADULTERATION. Gaudy stalls and shops sold dragées, lozenges, mints, and sweets molded into highly colored shapes to appeal to children. Fantasy was, and is, more important than taste when it comes to sweets. See CHILDREN'S CANDY.

Nineteenth-century industrialization moved the production of sweets from retailers to factories, and from midcentury onward, advances were made in mechanization. Factory brands became important, especially in chocolate manufacture, and subsequently for toffees and other boiled sweets. The great variety of sweets on sale today has come about in the last hundred or so years, although many are simply reinterpretations of techniques and formulae known for centuries. Britain is now one of the biggest producers and consumers of confectionery in the world. Sweets may have little nutritional value beyond providing energy, but they have a social role when given as a reward, as consolation or comfort, or as an encouragement. Among children, they can be items to barter. On a wider level, sweet foods of many types are important in the United Kingdom—jams and preserves, desserts, pastries, cakes, biscuits, and sweetened dairy products.

Fanciful forms of confectionery are still popular: fruits, hearts, animals, licorice allsorts "sandwiches," and lollipops on sticks. See LICORICE and LOLLIPOPS. Transparent fruit drops and barley sugars, chewy caramels and toffee, fudge, marshmallows, jelly beans, gumballs, and gobstoppers all have their enthusiasts. See BARLEY SUGAR; CHEWING GUM; FUDGE; JELLY BEANS and MARSHMALLOWS. Some sweets are traditional to season or place: eggs at Easter and candy floss (cotton candy) at fairgrounds. Hard sugar molded into joke shapes and sticks of rock with letters running through them and a vivid pink coating are an essential purchase on any seaside holiday. See ROCK. Sweets, once elegant morsels for adults, are now largely designed to appeal to, and be consumed by, children.

Chocolate was known as a drink, and it only become a significant item in confectionery in the nineteenth century. See CHOCOLATE, POST-COLUMBIAN. Mechanization was well suited to processing cacao, and the first chocolate bars appeared in the 1860s. Initially, they were sold unwrapped from large boxes and distributed to shops across the country by railway. Production became concentrated in the hands of a few firms—Fry, Cadbury, Rowntree, Terry—names still found on chocolate today. See CADBURY. Growth in the production of boxed chocolates and bars increased hugely as prices of chocolate fell in the early years of the twentieth century. Production and consumption have continued to rise, slowed only by the rationing imposed for 10 years during and after World War II. See CHOCOLATES, BOXED.

Recent years have seen the emergence of artisan chocolatiers working with single varieties of cocoa beans from specified estates or countries. They have become the smart confectioners of the twenty-first century, commanding high prices for their "grand cru" chocolates. See CHOCOLATE, SINGLE ORIGIN.

Banquets and Desserts

The Forme of Cury (the first British cookery book), compiled in the late fourteenth century, was written for informed, sophisticated palates. It makes clear that some savory and sweet dishes were served together. Small game birds appeared on the table with tarts, fritters, preserved fruits, and the sweet wafers introduced by the Normans.

This pattern of dining remained until the sixteenth century, when sweet dishes could also become a banquet laid out in a separate room or a special building. See BANQUETING HOUSE. As a show of wealth, the table was decorated with sugar-paste sculptures and spread with candied fruits and nuts, quince paste, marchpanes (marzipan), jellies, almond cakes, fruits made from sugar, and even tableware of sugar paste that could be eaten. See MARZIPAN and SUGAR SCULPTURE. The Elizabethans called these dishes and the sweet, spiced wines that accompanied them "banketting stuffe."

Elinor Fettiplace's Receipt Book (1604) reflects the shift from medieval dishes to the more modern; the spicing of earlier times was much reduced, although rosewater remained as a flavoring for desserts. Almond milk, a mainstay of earlier cooking, was little used, as religious changes led to the relaxation of the Catholic notion of fasting; cream and milk took its place. A "creame" might be cooked, clotted, raw, or whipped into a syllabub. See CREAM. Lightly spiced warm custard poured into a precooked pastry "coffin" was baked to make a tart. Curds were made into cheesecakes and tarts. See CHEESECAKE and TART.

Milk products became increasingly important. Baked milk "puddings" of rice, sago, bread, and oatmeal, spiced and sweetened with sugar, became popular. Cabbage cream, made with the skins that formed over a bowl of thick cream layered with rosewater and sugar and carefully built up to resemble a cabbage, remained in vogue until late in the seventeenth century.

When the banquet went out of fashion in the eighteenth century, sweet dishes such as cakes, creams, ice creams, jellies, puddings, and pies were called "dessert" after the French model. Sugar also sweetened drinks such as chocolate, coffee, and the tea that became inextricably entwined in social life throughout Great Britain and Ireland, and it was increasingly used in cakes. Following the building of ice houses on country estates, ice creams based on fruits and nuts or flavors we think of as modern, such as jasmine or Parmesan, became fashionable. See ICE CREAM.

The present-day trifle came into being at this time; Hannah Glasse provided one of the first recipes in *The Gentle Art of Cookery* (6th edition, 1758). It calls for Naples biscuits, macaroons, and ratafia cakes soaked in sack (fortified wine), covered with a "good boiled custard," topped with a syllabub, then decorated with more ratafia cakes, currant jelly, and flowers. Syllabubs remained a dessert, served in glasses to show the clear wine below the thick cream. However, trifle eventually replaced the syllabub as the British party pudding, and whipped cream was used to top the trifle instead of syllabub. See SYLLABUB and TRIFLE.

Other items from the Elizabethan banquet that survived and prospered included "biscuit bread," or Savoy Biscuit, the ancestor of modern sponge cakes, and various types of sweet pastry. See SPONGE CAKE. These have been much enriched by the influence of pastry cooks of Continental European origin, supplementing the home-grown tradition of fruit cakes and other sweet baked goods. The British sweet tooth was further indulged by the development of the biscuit industry in the nineteenth century, providing mass-produced alternatives to the fine almond macarons and more robust shortbreads of earlier times. In Britain, biscuit became a catch-all term for small flat baked goods, roughly equivalent to the American "cookie." See BISCUITS, BRITISH.

Puddings

The British also developed a wide range of sweet puddings from originally savory recipes. Pudding is an ambiguous word in English, now referring both to frivolous dessert items and to more substantial sweet dishes counted as staple foods. History only partially explains this usage.

In the sixteenth century, currants, dates, and sugar were added to the mixtures of meat or blood—spices and fat that hitherto had been used to stuff the animal guts that made the original sausage-like puddings. Shortly afterward, a more convenient alternative, the pudding cloth, came into use, which meant boiled puddings could be made at any time. It was cited in a contemporary recipe for Cambridge pudding—breadcrumbs, flour, dried fruits, suet, eggs, sugar, milk, and butter, wrapped in a cloth and boiled, ancestor to the plum pudding. Suet was the last link to the original meat pudding. In his *Dictionary* (1755) Dr. Johnson defined pudding as "a kind of food very variously compounded but generally made of meal, milk and eggs." Later flavorings included ginger, treacle, syrup, or jam. See PUDDING.

Baked milk puddings became commonplace, and batter puddings were baked in the oven or cooked under the spit in the dripping from a roasting joint. Since Victorian times, steamed puddings have usually been made in pudding basins standing in a large pan of simmering water.

Puddings were enthusiastically adopted across British society. Steamed, boiled, or baked, with imaginative names—plum duff, spotted dick, apple hat, Sussex pond—they were eaten daily in many households, yet another source of comfort and calories, especially for the less well off. Fruit puddings, particularly pies baked in deep dishes with a pastry crust; bread puddings like summer pudding; and bread and butter pudding remain favorites. See SUMMER PUDDING. The notion expanded to include dishes of foreign origin such as apple charlotte. See CHARLOTTE. Puddings are usually served with a sauce, custard being the most common, or with cream.

Recent years have seen a resurgence of enthusiasm for traditional British desserts and puddings. Forgotten dishes have been revived, and new ones invented. Sticky toffee pudding, Bakewell tart, gypsy tart, queen of puddings, Eton mess, and banoffee pie, to name just a few, are popular at home and in restaurants. See ETON MESS. Sweetened yogurt and packaged desserts continue the dairy tradition, and even the notion of the old-fashioned sweetshop lined with jars shows a certain resurgence. The British, long known for their passion for sweet things, have not lost their sweet tooth in the twenty-first century.

See also BOARDWALKS; CANDY; CANDY BAR; COMFIT; CUSTARD; FLOWER WATERS; FOOLS; HIPPOCRAS; and SWEETSHOP.

Davidson, Alan. *The Oxford Companion to Food.* Oxford: Oxford University Press, 1999.

Mason, Laura. *Sugar Plums and Sherbet: The Prehistory of Sweets.* Totnes, U.K.: Prospect, 1998.

Mason, Laura, and Catherine Brown. *The Taste of Britain* London: Harper, 2006.

Pullar, Phillippa. *Consuming Passions: Being an Historic Inquiry into Certain English Appetites.* Boston: Little, Brown, 1970.
Richardson, Tim. *Sweets: A History of Temptation.* London: Bantam, 2002.
Spurling, Hilary. *Elinor Fettiplace's Receipt Book.* New York: Viking Penguin, 1986.
Wilson, C. Anne. *Food and Drink in Britain: From the Stone Age to the 19th Century.* Harmondsworth, U.K.: Penguin, 1973.

Jill Norman

The **United States** has a culinary culture permeated by sweetened foods and beverages. Many Americans begin their day with a bowl of sugary cereal, doughnut, muffin, pancakes, or other sweet food, typically accompanied by sweet orange juice, sweetened coffee, or a soft drink. For lunch, dinner, or snacks, sugary ingredients are ubiquitous as well, not only in obviously sweet foods but also in savory ones. Most processed foods—from tomato sauce to ketchup, bread to bagels, hot dogs to bacon—contain varying quantities of sugary ingredients, often derived from corn. Other than water, almost all bottled beverages, whether flat or carbonated, contain a hefty dose of corn syrup, sugar, fruit concentrate, or synthetic sweetener. See CORN SYRUP. Given the American predilection for the sweet, it is hardly surprising that even desserts in the United States are often noticeably sweeter than their European counterparts. Ever since the late nineteenth century, Americans have reliably been among the top five per-capita consumers of sweeteners in the world.

The Colonial Period

It is difficult to reconstruct the eating habits of the varied native populations before European contact, but given the foods available, it is likely that Native Americans limited their sweet indulgences to certain corn products, maple syrup, and both fresh and dried wild fruits. See NATIVE AMERICAN. Apart from the use of certain ingredients (maple sugar, corn, pecans, and the like), today's culture of sweetness inherited little from the continent's first inhabitants. Instead, America's sweet tooth was largely passed down from the English colonists who first settled New England and Virginia. As early as the Elizabethan period, the English elite were notorious for their penchant for sweet food. As sugar became somewhat more affordable during the late colonial period, this predilection moved down the social ranks. Imports from the Caribbean assured British North America a continuous supply of both sugar and molasses. See SUGAR TRADE. The Molasses Act, passed by the British government in 1733, sought to limit imports of the sweetener from British possessions, but the law was widely flouted by the colonists. The similar Sugar Act of 1764 was one of several triggers of the American Revolution. See LEGISLATION, HISTORICAL.

The American population, predominantly of English extraction and refreshed by wave after wave of British immigrants, baked, fried, and boiled the desserts they had grown up with. English cookbooks, such as Hannah Glasse's *The Art of Cookery, Made Plain and Easy* (1747) and Susanna Carter's *Frugal Housewife* (ca. 1765), were both imported and republished in eighteenth- and early-nineteenth-century America. As specifically American desserts were developed, some publishers simply inserted an addendum to the English texts. Both Glasse's and Carter's books were published (in 1805 and 1803, respectively) with an identical appendix of "new receipts adapted to the American mode of cooking." Among the new desserts were such New England staples as Indian pudding, pumpkin pie, dough nuts [*sic*], cranberry tarts (pies), maple sugar, and maple molasses, as well as Dutch-influenced recipes for crullers and whaffles [*sic*]. The first purely American-written cookbook, Amelia Simmons's *American Cookery* (1796), includes a similar selection of unfussy American sweets embedded in a text of mostly English desserts such as puddings, custards, and syllabubs, as well as old-world confections such as quince and red currant preserves. See UNITED KINGDOM and NEW ENGLAND (U.S.).

Outside of New England, the future landmass of the United States was far less homogenous. In the South and West, the Spanish arrived with their own cookies, cakes, and the predecessors to churros. In Louisiana, the French settlers maintained contacts with Paris long after the Louisiana Purchase of 1804, importing French confectioners as well as sending their cooks to France to train. Throughout the South, ethnically African cooks improvised to create such African-inflected sweets as calas (rice fritters), benne wafers, and others. See BENNE SEED WAFERS. In Pennsylvania and elsewhere, German settlers brought a tradition of sweetened yeast breads, doughnuts, and funnel cakes, as well as candy making. The Dutch left a lasting influence on the language, if less so on the cuisine, giving us such words as waffle, cruller, and, most notably, cookie. Even Amelia Simmons includes a recipe for cookies, which take the form of rather dry, coriander-scented biscuits. See NEW ORLEANS; PENNSYLVANIA DUTCH; SOUTH (U.S.); and SOUTHWEST (U.S.).

Home Baking

With the coming of independence from Britain, American sweet making increasingly began to branch out from its English roots. In England, pies tended to be savory, whereas tarts were sweet. In the United States, pies were not only invariably sweetened, but their varieties proliferated. Hitherto obscure regional specialties such as Hertfordshire's "dough nuts" multiplied in shape, variety, and technique. Cakes became noticeably daintier than the heavy, fruitcake-type confections of the past—though this was, admittedly, happening across the Atlantic as well. Distinctly American drop cookies, made with oats, peanut butter, and chocolate chips, were developed around the turn of the twentieth century. See DROP COOKIES. Ice cream became relatively commonplace, at least if we are to believe Frederick Marryat, a captain in the British Royal Navy, who, while visiting St. Louis in 1837, noted the universal availability of ice with the consequence that "ice-creams [were] universal and very cheap." See DOUGHNUTS; ICE CREAM; and PIE.

Unlike in Europe, food and fuel, as well as ice, were relatively cheap; labor, however, was dear. This circumstance, combined with the spread-out nature of frontier settlements, meant that even middle-income Americans had to rely much more on mothers and wives to do the baking than did their European counterparts, who could patronize professional pastry cooks or have recourse to servants. In the absence of affordable helpers, American women sought to simplify their lives in the kitchen, looking to recipes that used quick-rising artificial leaveners instead of yeast or beaten eggs to aerate their cakes, cookies, and doughnuts, and adopting labor-saving devices whenever possible. See CHEMICAL LEAVENERS. In the second half of the nineteenth century, high levels of female literacy, relatively weak bonds to tradition, urbanization, and social mobility created a growing market for cookbooks both aspirational and practical.

Like the home cooks, most of the professional advice givers were female (though they too styled themselves homemakers despite their successful careers). Among the most influential were Eliza Leslie and Lydia Maria Francis Child in the mid-nineteenth century, Fannie Farmer at the century's end, and Irma Rombauer in the twentieth century. See FARMER, FANNIE and ROMBAUER, IRMA STARKLOFF. When suburban women of the 1960s sought to learn how to make French cream puffs, they looked to Julia Child rather than to some male chef with a foreign accent.

Sweet Industry

Some of the professional cookbook writers found jobs with large corporations, which were busy pitching the idea that becoming a virtuous, efficient, and loving wife and mother was impossible without newfangled devices such as hand-cranked ice cream makers and rotary beaters, or modern innovations such as Royal Baking Powder, Crisco, Jell-O, and, eventually, Duncan Hines. See CAKE MIX; GELATIN DESSERTS; HINES, DUNCAN; ICE CREAM MAKERS; and SHORTENING. American corporations used premium cookbooks, packaging, advertising, and product placement to distribute and popularize recipes such as chocolate chip cookies, Rice Krispies treats, and Jell-O salads. By the mid-twentieth century, the recipes published in magazines such as *Family Circle*—with a circulation of 4 million—often involved little more than assembling mass-produced convenience foods. A typical 1955 recipe for Marshmallow Brownie Pudding is "home-made" from canned chocolate-flavor syrup, marshmallows, and devil's food cake mix.

Certainly today, most of the sweet food consumed in the United States is not homemade, however contorted that term has become. Many of America's favorite sweet snacks have long been made by corporations, whether in the form of candy (M&M's, Reese's Pieces, and Hershey's Bar were the nation's top three in 2009, according to *Businessweek*), "snack cakes" (Twinkies, Ring Dings, and others), or cookies (most especially the Oreo). See HERSHEY'S; HOSTESS; M&M'S; OREOS; REESE'S PIECES; and TWINKIE. Other foods, particularly doughnuts but also ice cream and milkshakes, are eaten, or bought, at franchised outlets such as Dunkin' Donuts, Baskin-Robbins, and Dairy Queen.

Millions start their day with breakfast cereal, a trend that only went mainstream when Will Kellogg added sugar to his brother's Corn Flakes recipe in 1906, an innovation that eventually led to the likes of Fruit Loops, Count Chocula, and Honey Smacks. According to a 2011 report by the Harvard School of Public Health, some cereals are more than 40 percent sugar. See BREAKFAST CEREAL. In the twenty-first century, cereals have been losing market share to such things as the even sweeter breakfast bar and yogurt. See YOGURT.

Subsequent to the American Revolution, hot sweetened tea was gradually replaced by sweetened coffee as the nonalcoholic beverage of choice. In the twentieth century the role of these hot caffeinated beverages was mostly usurped by cold, caffeinated drinks, most notably Coca-Cola and Pepsi-Cola but also, in the last 50 years, a vast panoply of iced teas, sports drinks, and fruit-flavored beverages. See SODA. Even coffee has seen a sweet makeover, whether as syrup-laced coffee at Starbucks or in the form of Dunkin' Donuts' Caramel Coffee Coolatta.

Ideas of health and morality have been a recurring theme throughout the country's history. A tasty dessert is described as "sinful" or "indulgent." At various points, "heavy" foods such as pies and doughnuts were considered objectionable; white sugar was considered healthier than brown, and then vice versa; synthetic sweeteners were sold as a panacea for weight loss until, in the 1970s, studies indicated a link between saccharin and cancer—at least in rats. See ARTIFICIAL SWEETENERS. More recently sugar has been demonized for being as addictive as cocaine and heroin. See SUGAR AND HEALTH.

America Now

In the twenty-first century, America's populace has become increasingly Balkanized into niche markets based on income, education, lifestyle, ethnicity, age, and gender. Both televised food shows and social media have created a dedicated minority obsessed with food trends. A small but visible reaction to mass-produced desserts has produced artisanal cupcakes, gourmet ice cream shops, four-dollar doughnuts, and ultra-premium versions of Ring Dings and Mars Bars. As this list indicates, many of these sweets pay homage to the industrially formed tastes of American children. For the overwhelming majority, the American sweet tooth continues to be defined by the likes of corporations such as Unilever, General Foods, and Coca-Cola.

See also BASKIN-ROBBINS; CUPCAKES; DAIRY QUEEN; DUNKIN' DONUTS; KRISPY KREME; and MARS.

Carter, Susannah. *The Frugal Housewife, or, Complete Woman Cook*. New York: G. & R. Waite, 1803. http://digital.lib.msu.edu/projects/cookbooks/html/books/book_02.cfm (accessed 18 October 2014).

Krondl, Michael. *Sweet Invention: A History of Dessert*. Chicago: Chicago Review Press, 2011.

Levenstein, Harvey A. *Paradox of Plenty: A Social History of Eating in Modern America*. New York: Oxford University Press, 1993.

Shapiro, Laura. *Perfection Salad: Women and Cooking at the Turn of the Century*. New York: Farrar, Straus and Giroux, 1986.

Simmons, Amelia. *American Cookery, or the Art of Dressing Viands, Fish, Poultry, and Vegetables, and the Best Modes of Making Pastes, Puffs, Pies, Tarts, Puddings, Custards, and Preserves, and All Kinds of Cakes, from the Imperial Plum to Plain Cake: Adapted to This Country, and All Grades of Life*. Hartford, Conn: Printed for Simeon Butler, 1798. http://digital.lib.msu.edu/projects/cookbooks/html/books/book_01.cfm (accessed 18 October 2014).

Smith, Andrew F. *The Oxford Encyclopedia of Food and Drink in America*. 2d ed. Oxford: Oxford University Press, 2012.

Michael Krondl

upside-down cake is an American dessert made by candying slices of fruit in a butter and brown sugar mixture, then pouring a batter over them, and baking. To serve, the cake is turned upside down.

Throughout the colonial period in America, and into the nineteenth century, cooks without ovens often prepared cakes in cast-iron skillets on their stovetops. Even as late as 1943, *The Joy of Cooking* included a recipe for an upside-down cake made entirely in a skillet.

Upside-down cake's antecedents were likely the cake-like puddings or cobblers that became popular toward the end of the nineteenth century. They had fruit on the bottom and a very plain yellow cake—often called "cottage pudding"—on the top; some were inverted for serving. Early-twentieth-century cookbooks featured recipes for upside-down cakes using apples, cherries, and other stone fruits, but the cake surged in popularity in the 1920s, when canned pineapple became chic, thanks in no small part to aggressive marketing by the Hawaiian Pineapple Company. Pineapple rings were placed in the butter and sugar mixture to caramelize over heat, with a maraschino cherry—another newly fashionable ingredient—set in the center of each ring. After baking, the cake was carefully inverted onto a serving platter to reveal the decorative pattern on top.

Pineapple upside-down cake appears in Jean Anderson's *American Century Cookbook: The Most Popular Recipes of the 20th Century.* In Great Britain and the Commonwealth countries, upside-down cake is sometimes known as "upside-down pudding." French cuisine's tarte Tatin, made of caramelized apples and pastry dough, is similarly inverted for serving. See TARTE TATIN.

See also FRUIT DESSERTS, BAKED.

"Pineapple Upside-Down Cake." http://www.foodtimeline.org/foodcakes.html#pineapple.

Rombauer, Irma, and Marion Rombauer Becker. *The Joy of Cooking.* Indianapolis, Ind. and New York: Bobbs-Merrill, 1975.

Darra Goldstein

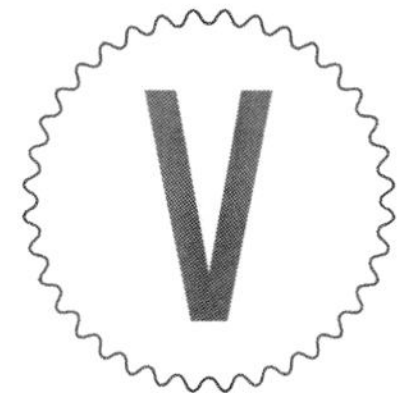

vacherin is a French dessert consisting of an elaborately decorated meringue shell filled with whipped cream, fruit, ice cream, or sorbet. It is not to be confused with the cow's milk cheese of the same name that is made in the French and Swiss Alps.

The sweet vacherin is formed by piping a meringue base onto a baking sheet and then building the circumference with rings of meringue, which are then baked at low heat for several hours, until the meringue becomes solid and no moisture is left. See MERINGUE. A variation, *vacherin avec couronne en pâte d'amandes,* uses rounds of lightly baked almond paste instead of meringue.

The precise origins of the vacherin are unclear. The great nineteenth-century French chef Marie-Antoine Carême is generally credited with the creation of vacherin, as the layering of the piped meringue disks and the dessert's adaptability to lavish decoration fit his style. See CARÊME, MARIE-ANTOINE. Since then, many pastry chefs have made the vacherin their signature dessert, creatively imagining new shapes and forms, including rectangles and spheres, and replacing the traditional strawberries or raspberries with exotic fruits and sorbets. The pavlova, a meringue cake with fruit that dates to the early twentieth century, may be seen as a later iteration of the original vacherin. See PAVLOVA.

Montagné, Prosper. *Larousse gastronomique: The Encyclopedia of Food, Wine and Cookery.* Edited by Charlotte Turgeon and Nina Froud. New York: Crown, 1961.

Bill Yosses

Valentine's Day, legends say, metamorphosed from a pagan fertility ritual to a commemoration of Christian martyrs named Valentine, and then to a saint's day. Today, Valentine's Day is an international lovers' celebration and a candy sellers' delight.

Possibly because of its hypothetical erotic origin, 14 February became associated with love by such writers as Chaucer and Shakespeare. By the eighteenth century, English sweethearts were exchanging handwritten Valentine's Day love notes. By the nineteenth century, mass-produced paper-lace cards were fashionable in England and in the United States.

Late in the nineteenth century, chocolates, long believed to be an aphrodisiac, became a favored Valentine's Day gift. The finest were boxed in red or pink heart-shaped containers boasting all the frills, lace, and ribbons of Valentine cards. The English confectioner Richard Cadbury is credited with creating the first heart-shaped chocolate box in 1868. See CADBURY and CHOCOLATES, BOXED.

Other candy makers also profited from the holiday. In the United States in 1902, the New England Confectionery Company (NECCO) began stamping out inexpensive sugary conversation hearts called "Sweethearts." Still popular today, the tiny candies bear messages such as "Marry Me" or "True Love." See NECCO.

Valentine's Day is celebrated in many countries, with everything from roses to heart-shaped cakes and cookies. But candy, especially chocolates, is among the most popular gifts. Typically, men give candy to women, though in Japan women give candy to men on 14 February, and the men reciprocate in March. See JAPAN.

Tireless promotion of the holiday has led to sweet success for candy makers and retailers. According to the National Confectioners Association, U.S. confectionery sales for Valentine's Day currently add up to more than a billion dollars a year, 75 percent of which is for chocolate.

See APHRODISIACS and GENDER.

Chivers, Tom. "History of Valentine's Day." *Telegraph*, 14 February 2010. http://www.telegraph.co.uk/women/sex/valentines-day/7187784/History-of-Valentines-Day.html (accessed 15 October 2014).

Woloson, Wendy A. *Refined Tastes: Sugar, Confectionery, and Consumers in Nineteenth-Century America.* Baltimore: Johns Hopkins University Press, 2002.

Jeri Quinzio

Valrhona is a high-end French chocolate producer founded in 1922 by pastry chef Albéric Guironnet. The company is headquartered in Tain l'Hermitage, in the heart of Rhône Valley wine country; its name derives from the words "valley" and "Rhône." Valrhona began exporting to the United States in 1984, and since then it has played an important role in the still-unfolding American chocolate revolution. Prior to the 1980s, little heed had been paid to cacao percentages or origins, and chocolate invariably meant milk chocolate of poor quality.

With the rise in status of American chefs in the 1980s, many restaurants began to hire pastry chefs. Once dessert mattered, so did the quality of the chocolate used for the increasingly complex plated desserts these chefs sought to produce. See PLATED DESSERTS. Many pastry professionals turned to Valrhona, in part because of its French pedigree, but mainly because of its superior flavor and consistency.

The development of an artisanal food industry, including winemaking, bread baking, and cheese making, also fueled an interest in quality handmade chocolate, both bars and bonbons. See BONBON. The perception that chocolate was merely candy was changing. Chefs and consumers began to realize that chocolate could have different taste profiles depending on where the beans were grown and how they were handled after being harvested. While pastry chefs and chocolatiers in the United States did have other options for base chocolate, many deemed Valrhona the most desirable, and by the late 1980s and early 1990s, Valrhona could be found on the dessert menus of better restaurants throughout the United States.

Part of the company's success may lie in the support services it provides to its professional customers: pastry chefs and chocolatiers are invited to attend classes at any of several École du Grand Chocolat locations as a way of becoming more familiar with the Valrhona product line, as well as more proficient at their craft. The schools are located in Tain l'Hermitage, Versailles, Tokyo, and Brooklyn, New York. Valrhona is also known for its innovation, especially in regard to white and milk chocolate, and new flavors are regularly launched in both the professional and nonprofessional sectors. Lesser known are Valrhona's Vintage and Estate-Grown dark chocolate bars from Madagascar, Venezuela, Trinidad, and the Dominican Republic. These bars showcase terroir in chocolate and are fine examples of bean-to-bar single-origin bars. See CHOCOLATE, SINGLE ORIGIN.

Over the last decade, both consumers and producers have begun to consider issues of sustainability surrounding cacao. Fair Trade practices and the reality of child labor are of utmost concern. See CHILD LABOR. As a company policy, Valrhona does not source beans from Ivory Coast, where bean quality tends to be poor and where a significant number of children are engaged in the cultivation and harvest of cacao.

See also COCOA and CHOCOLATE, POST-COLUMBIAN.

Terrio, Susan J. *Crafting the Culture and History of French Chocolate.* Berkeley: University of California Press, 2000.

Alexandra Leaf

van Houten, Coenraad Johannes (1801–1887), developed a superior form of drinking chocolate by devising a process that removed substantial amounts of fatty cocoa butter from the cocoa mass, thus creating a more homogenized finished product. In the seventeenth and eighteenth centuries in Europe, chocolate was used almost exclusively as a beverage. Chunks of unsweetened chocolate were dissolved in hot water or milk, sometimes with the addition of sugar. But the beverage was oily and heavy because of the cocoa bean's high cocoa butter content; wooden sticks called *moulinets* were used to whip the drink into a froth, partly an attempt to disperse the fat evenly throughout the liquid. See CHOCOLATE POTS AND CUPS.

Coenraad van Houten's father, Casparus (Senior), ran a chocolate business in Amsterdam, Holland,

and developed a screw press that could separate cocoa powder from cocoa butter. See COCOA. He patented the process in 1828. The leftover cocoa butter could be added to ordinary ground cocoa beans to make the paste smoother and more tolerant of added sugar—a boon for modern candy making. Cocoa powder itself transformed "hot chocolate" into the drink we know today, rather than the oily brew of yesteryear.

Coenraad himself was an innovator. He improved on his father's work by inventing a process called "dutching" (a.k.a. Dutch-process), which involves washing cocoa beans in an alkaline solution, usually potassium carbonate, to reduce their acidity. Dutching cocoa powder results in a darker color and milder flavor and improves its ability to dissolve in liquid. Although natural cocoa powder can be substituted for Dutch-process cocoa in most recipes (though not vice versa), it is best to follow specific recipe instructions to achieve the desired flavor and texture of the finished product.

McGee, Harold. *On Food and Cooking: The Science and Lore of the Kitchen*. New York: Scribner, 1984.

Elizabeth Field

vanilla, a flavor that in American usage has become synonymous with "ordinary" and "plain," is actually exotic, intoxicating, and vastly underutilized. It shines on its own and enhances other flavors. Vanilla is equally useful in desserts, confections, beverages, entrees, and side dishes, and it stars in such beloved dishes as vanilla crème brûlée, vanilla milkshakes, chocolate chip cookies, and white and yellow cakes. It has medicinal value, adds aromatic notes to perfumes, and is a proven aphrodisiac. See APHRODISIACS; CRÈME BRÛLÉE; and SODA FOUNTAIN.

A native of the Americas, *Vanilla planifolia* is the only edible fruit of the orchid family, the largest and oldest family of flowering plants in the world. Vanilla is indigenous to coastal Mexico, Central and South America, and the Caribbean. It is a tropical rainforest plant, both an epiphyte and root-producing vine. Its delicate yellow-white flowers bloom once a year, opening early in the morning, wilting by midday, and dying by mid-afternoon unless they are (rarely) pollinated by bees or hand-pollinated, a process known worldwide as "the marriage of vanilla."

Vanilla is the world's most labor-intensive agricultural crop. It cannot be grown commercially on massive plantations; most plantations are only a hectare or two in size. After pollination, vanilla beans remain on the vines for nine months and are picked individually. They require a four-to-six-week curing, drying, and conditioning process. They are then sorted and placed on racks to rest for at least a month before coming to market. Throughout this process, each bean is handled dozens of times.

To the early Mesoamericans, vanilla was second only to cacao in value and was treasured for its sacred properties. Its flowers were carried in amulets, as protection against the "evil eye," and its perfumed beans adorned altars. Vanilla played a supporting role to cacao in *xocolatl* (chocolatl), the beverage of the elite, drunk by the Olmec and Maya long before Moctezuma served it to Cortés in 1519. See COCOA and CHOCOLATE, PRE-COLUMBIAN. The indigenous people of Mesoamerica used vanilla medicinally, as documented by Fray Bernardino de Sahagún, who came to New Spain in 1529. Of vanilla he wrote, "It is perfumed, fragrant, precious, good, and a medicine."

Cortés introduced cacao and vanilla to the Spanish court as a beverage. The Spaniards substituted cane sugar, cinnamon, and black pepper for the native wild honey, chili peppers, red clay, and ear flowers the Central Americans had used, and they served their chocolate hot. See CHOCOLATE, POST-COLUMBIAN and CHOCOLATE POTS AND CUPS. Until the beginning of the seventeenth century, vanilla in Europe was considered only a flavoring for chocolate, but this perception changed as vanilla's popularity among the affluent quickly spread. Queen Elizabeth I adored sweets laden with sugar and flavored with vanilla. The elite of France and Italy couldn't get enough of vanilla, whether as a flavor, a fragrance, a medicine, or an aphrodisiac.

Until the seventeenth century, the Spanish controlled the world's supply of chocolate and vanilla, making a tidy profit. When the Dutch chartered the Dutch West India Company in 1621, they dramatically expanded the sugar trade to meet demand for sweetening chocolate, coffee, and tea. See SUGAR TRADE. Sephardic Jews who had fled the Inquisition traveled to Brazil and the Caribbean with the Dutch, working as sugar refiners and merchants, then expanding to the cacao and vanilla trade. They secured the monopoly over vanilla, sending the much-desired pods to their merchant friends and families in Europe.

Vanilla's intoxicating flavor won over Thomas Jefferson during his time in France. Unable to find any pods upon his return to the United States, he requested that some be sent to him in Philadelphia. Soon Jefferson became known for his refined vanilla ice cream (a handwritten recipe is now in the Library of Congress). See ICE CREAM. In the midst of the French Revolution vanilla actually traveled on sailing ships from Mexico to France, and then back to the United States.

As demand for vanilla continued to grow, plantations were established in tropical colonies around the world. The plant flourished but did not produce fruits, confounding both botanists and gentlemen farmers alike. The Totonacas in the Misantla Valley of southeastern Mexico are credited as being the first to domesticate vanilla. It appears that domestication actually occurred between the mid-1600s and mid-1700s, from as far south as coastal Guatemala north to the Misantla Valley. However, although each vine produced 30 to 40 beans annually—more than the 8 to 10 beans of wild vanilla—it was not enough to meet the rising demand for vanilla in both New Spain and Europe.

It wasn't until twelve-year-old Edmund Albius, a slave boy in Réunion, hand-pollinated some vanilla orchids in 1851, that the code for producing vanilla in volume was broken. Orchids need pollinators. As the flowers survive only a day, natural pollination rarely occurs, even in its native habitat. This vital information secured the Indian Ocean's place in vanilla production, first in Réunion, and later in Madagascar and the Comoro Islands. Vanilla finally became more accessible as a flavor and fragrance.

In the mid-1800s, French and Italian immigrants came to the Gulf Coast of Mexico, where some became vanilla producers. They developed more effective methods of curing and drying the beans, thus improving quality. In the early 1870s, three French immigrants went to France on business and learned about hand-pollination. Upon returning to Mexico, they charged for their welcomed information, and within two decades vanilla production grew to over 300 tons a year. The Mexican industry thrived until the early twentieth century, when the demand for oil and the Mexican Revolution triggered its decline. Madagascar soon surpassed Mexico in vanilla production, and Mexico never recovered. Vanilla is now grown in tropical regions worldwide, but Madagascar continues to lead the industry.

People in Europe have always used vanilla beans in cooking, but in the United States extracts are generally used. It is easy to adulterate pure extracts with imitation vanilla, or to substitute imitation vanilla and label it as pure—a serious problem in the first half of the twentieth century. See ADULTERATION. In the 1960s the U.S. Food and Drug Administration established a Standard of Identity in an effort to guarantee pure vanilla in manufactured products. Nevertheless, the battle over the regulations continues, as the powerful Flavor and Extract Manufacturers Association (FEMA) lobby represents traders who sell pure vanilla as well as manufacturers who produce both pure *and* imitation flavors. FEMA's advocacy for both sides has made it difficult to enforce the label laws for pure vanilla, thereby undercutting its use.

Supply and demand control the cost of vanilla. When prices are low, pure vanilla is used; when vanilla is scarce, prices go up, the laws are ignored, and "natural flavors or "other natural flavors" (a euphemism for imitation vanilla) are substituted for pure, thus undercutting the farmers. Increasingly, vanilla farmers are switching to other crops in order to survive.

While pure vanilla may never completely disappear, the industry continues to decline. It is up to consumers to demand pure vanilla in purchased products, and to use it in cooking to keep pure vanilla a viable crop. Certainly the world would be considerably more plain and ordinary without it.

Coe, Sophie D., and Michael D. Coe. *The True History of Chocolate.* New York: Thames and Hudson, 1996.

Rain, Patricia. *Vanilla: The Cultural History of the World's Favorite Flavor and Fragrance.* New York: J. P. Tarcher, 2004.

Patricia Rain

varenyky

See DUMPLINGS.

vegetables and herbs, the leaves, stems, roots, and nonsweet fruits of any edible plant, can be sweetened to deliver what our ancestors valued as happiness—the taste of the sun and the promise of ripeness. Candidates most suited to this transformation from everyday foodstuff to pleasure giver are those vegetables and herbs whose stems or fruits or leaves are sufficiently fleshy and bland to allow them to absorb and retain the effect of applying sweetness in whatever form is most appropriate.

Among plant foods of Eurasian or African origin, the fruits of nonsweet melons and gourds, aubergines (eggplants), and the fleshy stems of chard, lovage, celery, artichoke, angelica, fennel, and celery are traditionally sugared, candied, or preserved in syrup. See CANDIED FRUIT and FRUIT PRESERVES. Among roots and tubers similarly available for sugar-treatment are ginger, dandelion, parsnip, turnip, carrot, yam, and eryngo, while seaweed is also eaten sugared in Eastern traditions. Herbs and seeds traditionally sugared or candied (rather than used for flavoring) are usually those with digestive properties, such as mint, cumin, and aniseed. See COMFIT and CONFETTI.

Plant foods of New World descent suitable for sugaring—a treatment unavailable until after the Columbian exchange—include sweet cassava, both savory and sweet potatoes, tomatoes, cactus paddles, and all of the squashes, particularly pumpkin and marrow. Ingredients and recipes traveled in both directions. Jean Anderson, in *The Food of Portugal*, describes *doce de chila* or *gila*, a sweet preserve made from *Cucurbita ficifolia*, "a gourd with strings like spaghetti-squash," as a popular stuffing in Portuguese egg sweets, including a version of the ever-popular caramel custard, *toucinho do céo*, to replace the more labor-intensive *fios de ovos*, egg-yolk threads trickled into hot sugar-syrup. See EGG YOLK SWEETS and PORTUGAL.

The process by which any foodstuff, including bitter medicinal herbs, can be made more palatable through sweetening was simple and primitive when honey or cane syrup served as the transforming agent; it has become complicated and open to commercialization with the arrival of cheap, manufactured beet sugar, corn syrup, and the like. Stems and leaves have little if any natural sweetness, though their roots can sometimes be providers, making them an excellent vehicle for the juice of sugarcane, a giant grass native to the delta of the Ganges that traveled east to China and west through Persia and the Middle East. A taste for sugar eventually spread into Europe through the Arab ascendancy at both ends of the Mediterranean. See SUGARCANE. In *The Legendary Cuisine of Persia,* the food historian Margaret Shaida provides a recipe for carrot jam cooked with its own weight of sugar flavored with orange zest, rosewater, and cardamom, and another for cucumber jam similarly prepared. In her book *Sherbet & Spice*, the Turkish food writer Mary Işın underlines the high regard for sweet foods in Islamic culture and provides instructions for making an aubergine preserve that has been popular throughout the Ottoman Empire since the sixteenth century.

The virtues of sugared vegetables, particularly those with established medicinal properties, are well recognized in literature. In sixteenth-century France, says historian Maguelonne Toussaint-Samat, Nostrodamus suggested that candied eryngoes, the roots of sea holly prepared in imitation of ginger root, "have all the virtues, goodness and qualities of green ginger." See NOSTRADAMUS. French confectioners who had learned their skills from the extravagant courts of Italy prepared "candied ribs of lettuce leaves in syrup like angelica," calling them angels' lips (*bouches d'ange*) to encourage licentious behavior in ladies of the aristocracy. Similar preserves prepared with celery, considered an aphrodisiac, could be considered appropriate for gentlemen. Identical hopes are expressed when Shakespeare has his comic character Falstaff, in *The Merry Wives of Windsor*, mention eryngo root (presumably candied) as an aphrodisiac: "Let it hail . . . kissing confits, and snow eringoes." See APHRODISIACS.

Meanwhile, traditional recipes that make use of the natural sweetness in roots and tubers continued in parallel with sugar-based confections, particularly in northern lands. Even after they had fallen out of favor, they reappeared at times of shortage, as in poverty or wartime, when trade routes were cut. Parsnip and carrot have long been the poor man's sweetener in cakes, puddings, and dumplings, and they continue to feature in contemporary recipes for festival foods, such as the English Christmas pudding. The tradition for home-grown sweetness in celebration foods is maintained in the pumpkin pie (with or without maple syrup) of America's Thanksgiving dinner, while sweet potato pie is eaten by African Americans as a reminder of their African heritage at the more recently established winter festival of Kwanzaa.

In everyday eating, cheap sugar has transformed what was an occasional treat into a daily necessity. Relishes, chutneys, sweet pickles, and ketchups—sole survivors of that ancient tribe of vegetable pleasure-givers—add interest to fast food, whose taste would otherwise be bland.

See also CANE SYRUP; CORN SYRUP; HONEY; and SUGAR BEET.

Anderson, Jean. *The Food of Portugal.* London: Hale, 1986.
Işın, Mary. *Sherbet and Spice: The Complete Story of Turkish Sweets and Desserts.* New York: I. B. Taurus, 2013.
Shaida, Margaret. *The Legendary Cuisine of Persia.* London: Grub Street, 2000.

Elisabeth Luard

Venice, Italy, "the Floating City," is a UNESCO World Heritage Site whose birth in the sea, dominion over it, and genius for commerce spawned a great trading empire, the world's largest in its day. Over the centuries, the city created merchant princes and provided the Republic of Venice with inestimable wealth. One chronicler, writing in 1267, described the scene in the metropolis: "Merchandise flows through this noble city like water through fountains."

Evidence of that mercantile history can still be seen along her thoroughfares: Calle dello Zucchero, Corte della Raffineria, and the Ruga dei Speziali. All are place names typical of Venice, yet they are rarely mentioned in guidebooks. But stumble on Sugar Street, the Court of the Refinery, or the Street of the Spice Merchants, and you are encountering the city's Golden Age. These, and other related names, come largely from a time when, as a result of her vast power in the marketplace and seafaring might, Venice was dubbed Queen of the Adriatic and sugar was central to her livelihood. Here it was sold wholesale, here retail; here it was refined, here made into sweets, here purveyed as medicine. Picture ships in the harbors listing under sugar's weight, the large warehouses heaped with it along the Zattere (begun as a loading dock in 1519), the merchants bidding for it in Rialto, once the city's chief marketplace. Travelers commented on sugar's presence in much the same way that Marco Polo, one of Venice's most famous citizens, commented on the enormous quantities of sugar he saw in Hangzhou, China, during his travels.

Although *il sale dolce*, or "sweet salt," as sugar was once called, had already made an appearance in Venice by the time the Crusades began in 1095, its fame grew after Crusaders found it under cultivation in the East and spread the word. They referred to sugar as a "spice," a category in which it remained for centuries. Thus, when Venice was the spice capital of Europe and the eastern Mediterranean, sugar was included among her wares, along with cardamom, mace, pepper, cloves, nutmeg, turmeric, ginger, and cinnamon. See SPICES.

Sugar, once called "sweet salt," was central to Venice's fortunes, and Venetians acquired great skill in refining it. This pen, ink, and watercolor drawing by Jan van Grevenbroeck (1731–1807) shows workers at a Venetian sugar refinery. MUSEO CORRER, VENICE, ITALY / ROGER-VIOLLET, PARIS / BRIDGEMAN IMAGES

Long a producer and seller of salt, and an important trading center from the eighth century, with burgeoning connections around the Mediterranean, the Republic of Venice had moved naturally and determinedly into dealing in spices. Of these, sugar had begun to enter the Republic around 1000 C.E. By 1150, Venice is said to have been the chief port for it in the world, and from her domains sugar was distributed broadly. Sources for it changed and overlapped through the centuries. Egypt, the Levant, and Asia Minor were primary. Then, with the Fourth Crusade and the sacking of Constantinople in 1204, more avenues opened.

Sugar also came from the Stato da Mar, Venice's "State of the Sea," her maritime and overseas colonial possessions. One was Tyre in present-day Lebanon, where a number of Venetians had traded sugar and cultivated it on land grants, but there were also the islands of Crete (then known as Candia) and Cyprus. Our primary associations with sugar and slavery are in the Caribbean. But an early link between the two was forged earlier, largely (though not only) in colonial Venice, and particularly in those very islands. Indeed, Cyprus and Crete are often cited as the model for what was to come. There the Republic and her entrepreneurial citizens created plantation agriculture and processing facilities run at least in part by slave labor. See PLANTATIONS, SUGAR; SLAVERY; and SUGARCANE AGRICULTURE. When war and plague decimated the local agricultural workers, slaves from Arabia and Syria, sometimes prisoners of war from Greece, Bulgaria, and Turkey, were brought in to do the work alongside serfs or other members of the native population. The price of sugar was set at Rialto, the city's chief marketplace, but the considerable human cost was not part of the calculation.

As sugar increased in importance, the estates devoted to it increased in size. Of particular note was that of the great Venetian Cornaro family on Cyprus. In 1494, Canon Pietro Casola, a pilgrim who stopped in Venice on his way to Jerusalem, wrote of his visit there, "I can only speak of a great farm . . . which belongs to a certain Don Federico Cornaro, a patrician of Venice . . . where they make so much sugar, that, in my judgment, it should suffice for all the world."

At first, refined sugar was transported to Venice from the point of origin. But, eventually, toward the end of the 1400s, unrefined sugar began to be imported, and processing and manufacture were undertaken in the city and her possessions. Over time, Venetians perfected the refining process, producing a higher-quality product that was whiter as well as purer. As a result of their success, in the sixteenth century the republic published the first manuals on how to refine sugar and make sweets.

Of course, Venice herself used the sugar that was manufactured and bought and sold there. Treasured by the patricians of the city (the only ones who could afford it), sugar was an ingredient in their cuisine, a flavor enhancer, and a condiment. In the Renaissance the separation between sweet and savory did not yet exist. Therefore, sugar was used in cooking many dishes with which we would not associate it today, such as eggs, pasta, meat, and fish. A few of these recipes still remain, like Veneto's famous *sarde in saor*, a dish of sardines in a sweet and sour sauce made with vinegar, onions, and raisins or sugar that could delight a Renaissance appetite, and probably did.

However, things are different where the sweet course or desserts are concerned. Dishes keep being invented—one of the most famous, tiramisù, believed to have been devised in the 1960s, is thought to come from Treviso, Veneto, the region of which Venice is the chief city. See TIRAMISÙ. But the origin of other sweets, especially certain typically Venetian biscuits or cookies, goes back centuries. *Favette,* little fried dough balls sometimes flavored with anise liquor, have sugar sprinkled on top and are among the typical sweets prepared for Venice's celebrated Carnival. See CARNIVAL and FRIED DOUGH. They appear in a plain version in *100 Ricette di Cucina Veneziana,* published in 1908, considered the first cookbook specifically dedicated to Venetian cuisine. (A fourteenth-century manuscript, *Anonimo Veneziano,* is often cited as the first, but its recipes are not exclusively, or even primarily, Venetian.) *Fritole,* fried balls of yeast-raised dough, often mixed with pine nuts, are also one of the beloved sweets most associated with Carnival in La Serenissma. Once made on the spot by *fritoleri,* whose carts were stationed throughout the city, they are now found in pastry shops. *Baicoli,* a simple, but beloved, oval-shaped biscuit that goes back centuries, takes its name from a resemblance to tiny branzino (*baicoli* in Venetian), a common fish of the lagoon. *Baicoli* are often served with the light custard zabaglione. See ZABAGLIONE. *Azzime dolci* (sweet matzah) are biscuits sometimes enriched with fennel seeds or aniseed, mentioned by the famous Venetian rabbi,

Leone di Modena, in a work published in 1637, where he recommends the addition of sugar for the weak or unwell. *Zaeti* are very sweet, yellowish biscuits made with polenta flour that date from the sixteenth century and frequently include raisins soaked in grappa or water. Such biscuits or cookies were often dunked in sweetened hot chocolate or coffee.

Culinary applications were not sugar's only attraction. Equally important to its popularity in the era of humoral medicine were its medicinal uses. Spices were considered salutary and were prescribed for a variety of conditions; pharmacopeias of the day identified the properties of each. See MEDICINAL USES OF SUGAR and PHARMACOLOGY. Sugar, almost a miracle drug, was often recommended for the healing of wounds, to relieve childbirth pains, to cure ulcers and respiratory ailments, to relieve the pain of headaches, to cleanse the blood, and as a tonic for general health. Sugar was even sometimes used in an attempt to combat the plague.

Spices revolutionized the practice of medicine because they greatly increased products available for treating health problems. That also made them the province of apothecaries, often called *spezieri* (spice sellers). At first, spice sellers and "pharmacists" overlapped, but in the middle of the 1300s, two separate groups, both of which dealt with sugar, were established. The *spezieri da medicina* sold spices, syrups, electuaries, and tonics, and became so expert in this art that they were renowned throughout Italy and beyond for their skills. (*Lo Speziale* [The Apothecary], an opera by Joseph Haydn with a libretto by the eighteenth-century Venetian playwright Carlo Goldoni, turns on making the title character believe that the sultan of Turkey has summoned him for his skills.) The second group, the *spezieri da grosso*, sold spices and sugar, but not for therapeutic use. They were also the purveyors of candles, soap, cosmetics, ink, paper, marzipan, confetti (sugared spices), sweetmeats, almonds and other nuts, dried fruits, and more. See CONFETTI; DRIED FRUIT; MARZIPAN; and NUTS. Nor were they simply retailers. They fabricated many of their products and were involved in import and export and the wholesale trade. Thus, it was the *spezieri da grosso* who became the most heavily involved with the sugar refineries in the city, as well as with the business of sugar in general.

Sugar had one last major use, the building of sugar sculptures, pieces known as *trionfi di zucchero*, *trionfi di tavola*, or, in Venice, *spongade*. See SUGAR SCULPTURE. Famous for her love of spectacle and hospitality to visitors, Venice was highly skilled in this art. In 1493, Beatrice d'Este, on a state visit representing her husband, Ludovico del Moro, the duke of Milan, wrote to him of a banquet in the Ducal Palace in which the different dishes and confetti were carried in to the sound of trumpets, and of "sugar figures of the Pope, the Doge, and the Duke of Milan, with their armorial bearings and those of your Highness; then St. Mark plus many other objects." They were, she continued, of "colored and gilded sugar, making as many as three hundred in all, together with every variety of cakes and confectionery." However, the most famous such occasion was a collation in 1574 when King Henry III, the new ruler of France, passed through Venice. Designs by the great architect and sculptor Jacopo Sansovino were executed by the apothecary Niccolo Cavallieri. In addition to every kind of statuette, bread, plates, knives, forks, tablecloth, furniture, fruit, flowers, and trees were all said to be so lifelike that it was only when a napkin broke in his hand that the astonished king realized that the settings were an illusion, there to dazzle him with works in sweet salt that spoke to Venice's great power.

See also ITALY; SUGAR REFINING; and SUGAR TRADE.

Brown, Patricia Fortini. *Art and Life in Renaissance Venice.* New York: Harry N. Abrams, 1997.

Da Mosto, Francesco. *Francesco's Kitchen: An Intimate Guide to the Authentic Flavours of Venice.* London: Ebury, 2007.

Galloway, J. H. *The Sugar Cane Industry: An Historical Geography from Its Origins to 1914.* New York: Cambridge University Press, 1989.

Lane, Frederic C. *Venice, A Maritime Republic.* Baltimore: Johns Hopkins University Press, 1973.

Maffioli, Giuseppe. *La cucina veneziana.* Padua, Italy: Franco Muzzio, 1995.

Molmenti, Pompeo. *Venice, Its Individual Growth from the Earliest Beginnings to the Fall of the Republic.* Translated by Horatio F. Brown. London: John Murray, 1906.

Cara De Silva

verrine is a term coined by the Paris patissier Philippe Conticini in 1994, when he began stylishly layering ingredients with contrasting or complementary flavors, textures, and colors in small, clear glasses. It is derived from the French word *verre* (glass). Heading up the kitchen at Petrossian in

Paris a few years later, Conticini served individual courses throughout entire meals the same way, with long-handled flatware with which to savor each bite. "What creates synergy in a dish," he explained in the *New York Times* in 2001, "is not just the combination of flavors, but how they are combined. And often with a dessert, a plate simply won't do. Because it's flat, it does not allow the components to mingle as they are eaten. I played around with different dishes and bowls and finally decided on a glass...the flavors are like neighbors in a small community. They bump into one another, they interact and they are concentrated."

With their element of surprise, stunning visual appeal, and make-ahead assembly, verrines have since sparked the imagination of other patissiers, who showcase them in chic shops from Paris to New York City and Tokyo. In France, sweet and savory verrines are served at bistros and cafés, as well as at Michelin-starred restaurants. Their presence in that country's supermarket frozen-food cases is arguably evidence of the inevitable slide from culinary trend to cliché.

The verrine has been slow to catch on in the United States. For Americans, it is perhaps less an artful concept than a very modern, delicate, clean-tasting parfait—and, more important, a reminder of flavors that go together. Even a simple combination, such as the components of a Greek salad layered in a jam jar (à la *Gourmet* magazine, August 2008), can transform lunch into *un pique-nique*.

See also PLATED DESSERTS.

Librairie Larousse. *Larousse Gastronomique: The World's Greatest Culinary Encyclopedia.* Rev. ed. New York: Clarkson Potter, 2009.

Méjanès, Stéphane. "Philippe Conticini/Rencontre avec un Survivant." *Le Nouvelle Observateur,* 31 August 2012. http://obsession.nouvelobs.com/portraits/20120831.OBS0892/philippe-conticini-rencontre-avec-un-survivant.html (accessed 17 November 2014).

Jane Lear

Vienna, the capital of Austria, was the residence of the Habsburg monarchs for several centuries and the center of an empire that around 1900 had more than 50 million inhabitants. See AUSTRIA-HUNGARY. The various nationalities in this multinational empire, among them Austrians, Slavs, Italians, and Hungarians, all contributed to what are today known as Viennese cuisine and Viennese sweets. While Vienna is nowadays widely known as *the* capital of cakes, confections, ice cream, and coffeehouses, it took quite some time for the city to establish this reputation.

Until the sixteenth century, sugar was very expensive. Honey was the main sweetening agent used, and gingerbread and mead were widely appreciated. See GINGERBREAD; HONEY; and MEAD. By the thirteenth century, Vienna had become a center of fine pastry. Subsequent centuries saw the development of various other trades dealing in sweet pastry, including bakers of flat wafers (*Oblaten*) and hollow wafers (*Hohlhippen*), as well as fritters (*Krapfen*). See FRITTER and WAFERS.

Initially, only apothecaries—also called *confectionarii*—had the right to make and sell sugar. It was traded either in a pure form, as a medicine, or in the form of candied fruit, herbs, blossoms, spices, or roots, which were considered to be "healthy" food. See CANDIED FRUIT and SPICES. Many products of this sort came to Vienna via Italy. Duke Albert III (1349–1395) decided that only apothecaries were allowed to produce and sell candied items; all imports from Venice were forbidden. See VENICE. Only around the middle of the sixteenth century did the apothecaries lose their monopoly in producing and selling sugar and candied products. Others were now allowed to call themselves *Zuckermacher* (producers of sugar) or *Zuckerbacher* (producers of candied fruit, stewed fruit, jams, etc.). It is assumed that the German term *bacher,* as in *Zuckerbacher,* has nothing to do with baking. The word seems to come from *zusammenpacken*—packing things together like sugar and fruit, nuts, and herbs. *Zuckerbäcker* did not *bake* anything for a long time. In any case, sixteenth-century guild regulations forbade confectioners from using ordinary flour for their work—they were allowed to use only expensive rice flour—and compliance with this rule was closely monitored by the urban bakers. See GUILDS.

It is said that Emperor Ferdinand I (1503–1564) brought confectioners from the Netherlands to Vienna. The earliest document mentioning a court confectioner in Vienna dates from the year 1566, when Matthias de Vos(s), from the Netherlands, was employed at court. From that time onward, confectioners worked at the Habsburg court, until the collapse of the empire in 1918.

The new trade, with its tempting products, did not remain restricted to the court. Soon independent confectioners opened their own shops in Vienna—Hanns Eysengrein, Georg Thurner, and Georg Diersch were the first, around 1568. Diersch's daughter Catharina also became a confectioner in Vienna. But the number of independent confectioners grew slowly, because the raw materials for their work were very expensive, and the number of wealthy people who could afford their costly products was limited. Confectioners were allowed to use a narrow range of raw materials: rice flour, almonds, pine nuts, sweet chestnuts, raisins, pistachios, and fruit. They produced sugar bars, delicate breads made from ground almonds and pistachios, sugar-bretzels, marchpane (marzipan), candied fruit, jams, almond milk, ice cream, and lemonades.

The Vienna Guild of Confectioners was founded in 1744. Eighteen confectioners were accepted as members; each was allowed to employ a single apprentice. The confectioners were entitled to sell their products either within the city walls or outside the city. At that time the city center (today Vienna's first district) was still walled in. The city walls were separated from the suburbs by a large green area where the Viennese frequently took their Sunday walks. Afterward they would enjoy some delicacies at a confectioner's shop. But the range of confectionery products was still limited: biscuits, zwieback, almond and sugar pastry, white and colored sweetmeats, marzipan, candied fruit, fruit preserved in sugar, ice cream, fresh jellies, and all kinds of refreshments were offered to the public by the city's independent confectioners.

Confectioners' Shops and Coffeehouses in Vienna

Confectioners' shops—*Konditoreien* in German—were not technically cafés. See CAFÉ. Coffeehouses had sprung up in Vienna in the seventeenth and eighteenth centuries. The Viennese appreciated the new drink and the parlors that offered it, where men could smoke and read newspapers. Only the owners of coffeehouses were allowed to sell coffee, and they sold little that could be characterized as dessert. In turn, confectioners were not allowed to sell coffee, a regulation that changed only at the turn of the twentieth century, when confectioners were allowed for the first time to sell savory products like sandwiches, salads, ham rolls, toasts, and Prague eggs (hard-boiled eggs filled with a mixture of yolk and mayonnaise and decorated with fish, ham, etc.). Originally, confectioners' shops were mainly visited by ladies—but ladies were mostly accompanied by gentlemen, and therefore, around 1900, the confectioners' guild thought that the shops should also offer something more substantial.

In addition to being served at small confectionery shops, delicacies were offered in lemonade huts and refreshment tents, which were especially set up for the summer. The eighteenth century brought an ice-cream boom to Vienna; the most fashionable confectioners in the second half of the eighteenth century were Milano and Taroni in the elegant Graben (today a fashionable shopping street linking Kohlmarkt and St. Stephen's Square)—another indication of Italy's important influence on the production of sweets, candy, and ice cream. See ICE CREAM and ITALY.

In the eighteenth century, too, Vienna's sweet makers began to expand their repertoire. An advertisement by the city confectioner Ulrich Schmidt in *Wiener Zeitung* from 1748 shows that confectioners had finally won the fight against restrictions to their production. Schmidt was evidently now able to use wheat flour, and his shop offered butter pies and various types of cake, including bread cake, butter cake, Linzer Torte, almond cake, biscuit and French cake. See LINZER TORTE. Around 1800, Konrad Höfelmeyer ran an elegant confectioner's shop at Tuchlauben, where he sold jams and cakes alongside edible table centerpieces such as tragacanth figures. See SUGAR SCULPTURE and TRAGACANTH. Ludwig Dehne from Württemberg established a fashionable ice-cream parlor on Michaelerplatz, opposite the Imperial palace, around 1785. Under the direction of Dehne's widow, the shop later became famous for its *crèmes*, pink vanilla jelly, cakes, sugar-coated pills and fruit, sweets, candy, sorbets, liqueurs, and ice cream. In 1857, Dehne's was taken over by Christoph Demel, the chief confectioner of Dehne. Demel successfully continued what Dehne had begun.

Sweets for a Broader Public

Once domestic sugar refined from beets came onto the Austrian market in the mid-nineteenth century, sweets became less expensive and more accessible to a broader public. Thus, more confectioners were able to set up their own businesses. Among them were Ludwig Heiner, who opened his shop on Wollzeile in 1840; Louis Lehmann, whose establishment on Singerstrasse was well known for stewed and sugar-coated fruit (Lehmann's shop moved to Graben after 1945 and closed in 2008); Anton Gerstner, whose shop at Stock-im-Eisen (now Kärntner Strasse) opened in 1847 and became famous for ice cream and Christmas decorations; and Joseph Sluka in Rathausstrasse. All of these confectioners—including Demel—became purveyors to the imperial and royal court. The list of their sweet inventions was almost endless: strudels, cakes, biscuit-rolls filled with jam, doughnuts, sweet slices, *Marmorkuchen* (a cake made to look like marble by combining dark and light batters), and many others. See DOUGHNUTS and STRUDEL.

For a long time chocolate was little used by confectioners. It was very hard and crumbled easily. Chocolate was primarily made into a hot drink, although in Austria it might be ground and added to cake batters. It was only after Swiss innovations in the mid-nineteenth century that chocolate could easily be melted and added to batters and made into chocolate icing. The popularity of Joseph Dobos's eponymous torte in the 1890s led to a wide assortment of chocolate-based cakes, such as *Esterházy Torte, Alpenmilchtorte,* and *Panamatorte,* to name just a few. See DOBOS TORTE.

Ice cream was made not only by Viennese confectioners. From the second half of the nineteenth century, a number of Italian families came to Vienna to open ice-cream parlors. They stayed during the warm months and returned to Italy in winter. Many of these families still have their shops in Vienna and sell their ice cream from April to October.

In the twentieth century an ever-larger number of people could afford confectionery products. Josef Prousek had come to Vienna in 1896 from Gablonz (today in the Czech Republic). He worked as a confectioner, and in 1913 he took over a confectioner's shop and chocolate manufactory in Vienna's second district. Prousek was able to expand his business quickly, adding a large number of shops to his network all over Vienna. Today his chain of confectionery shops, now run under the name Aida, offers a wide range of cakes, sweet snacks, bonbons, and savory snacks.

See also BONBON; CAKE; FRUIT PRESERVES; LEMONADE; MARZIPAN; NUTS; and TORTE.

Haslinger, Ingrid. *Die ehemalige Hofsilber—und Tafelkammer, Sammlungskatalog.* Vol. 2. Vienna: Anton Schroll, 1997.

Haslinger, Ingrid, Erika Patka, and Maria Luise Jesch. *Der süße Luxus.* Vienna: Kulturkreis Looshaus, 1996.

Leitich, Ann Tizia. *Wiener Zuckerbäcker, Eine süße Kulturgeschichte.* Vienna: Amalthea, 1980.

Ingrid Haslinger

vinarterta is a strictly Icelandic cake, even though its name means "Viennese cake" and its origins are most likely Viennese by way of Denmark. Traditionally served with coffee at weddings and Christmas since around 1860, the festive, rectangular delicacy comprised five to nine layers of fruit jam and shortbread pastry, although contemporary versions incorporate baking powder–leavened bread in order to achieve a lighter consistency. It is frequently iced with a simple sugar glaze that can be laced with vodka or bourbon. The dough is often flavored with almonds, and the fruit filling spiked with cardamom, vanilla, or red wine. In the late nineteenth century, prunes, once a luxury item in Iceland, were gradually replaced in many households by less expensive fruits, such as the rhubarb that proliferates in the countryside. Because vinarterta has a long shelf life, it can last for several months when well wrapped.

Vinarterta's many layers have led to its nickname of *randalín,* which means "striped lady." The torte is perhaps more beloved today by Iceland's expatriate community, particularly in Canada, than in its own country. This fact is not surprising if one considers that vinarterta was at the height of its popularity when the Icelandic fishing industry collapsed in the late 1800s, and ash-fall from the explosion of the volcano Askja in eastern Iceland in 1875 poisoned much of the nation's vegetation and livestock. As a result of these natural disasters, nearly 25 percent of Iceland's population relocated to find work abroad. They took with them their beloved vinarterta recipe, and the dessert soon became (and remains to this day) a powerful symbol of national identity for Iceland's displaced people, even as their use of the Icelandic language declined and they anglicized their names.

Rögnvaldardóttir, Nanna. *Icelandic Food and Cookery.* New York: Hippocrene, 2002. See pp. 166–167.

Jody Eddy

The **Vipeholm experiment** sought to determine the role of carbohydrates in dental cavity formation through a series of tests carried out in a Swedish mental institution in the 1940s. In the 1930s, dental health in Sweden was exceptionally poor, with 99.9 percent of the population suffering from cavities. Thus, in 1938, the Swedish Parliament passed a costly resolution to provide all citizens with dental care (the Public Dental Service). The National Medical Board was asked to conduct a preventative clinical study at Vipeholm, an institution for the mentally disabled in Lund whose isolation would allow for the kind of controlled conditions the experiment required.

The investigation began in 1945 as a vitamin study but was refocused in 1947 to examine the correlation between dental caries and the consumption of carbohydrates. See DENTAL CARIES. The patients in the test sample were forced to consume unnatural quantities of carbohydrates. For two years they were served sugar in the form of liquids, as bread at meals or between meals, and in as many as 24 sticky toffees a day. The outcomes revealed high levels of lactobacilli in the patients, and their consumption of sticky carbohydrate-dense products between meals led to high rates of caries activity. The publication of the results in 1953, and the controversy it engendered, caused the Swedish government to refuse all subsequent grants to the institution that conducted the Vipeholm study. Nonetheless, the findings prompted the replacement of sugar with sugar substitutes in commercial products such as chewing gum that were frequently consumed between meals.

Saturday Candy

The results also prompted the Swedish government to introduce "Saturday candy," which remains a Swedish custom. National marketing campaigns encouraged parents to allow children to consume candy once a week, rather than spreading their consumption out over several days. As a result, Swedes eat 17.9 kilograms of candy per capita each year, an amount second only to the Danes. The Swedes' excessive sweet tooth for candy is particularly noticeable among the younger generation: the average teenager today consumes candy three to five times a week, and among the general population candy constitutes an estimated quarter of the average weekend energy intake. In light of these statistics, and with the intention to improve overall population health, the Swedish government is considering reinforcing the Saturday candy tradition to prevent the current harmful consumption of candy several times a week. Critics are skeptical of this approach and find the pervasive "eat as much as you like, once a week" mantra harmful to public health. Instead, they suggest a 10 kronor ceiling on the amount of candy that can be consumed once a week, a constraint that would place Sweden at the average candy consumption level of the European Union—7.5 kilograms per capita per year.

Gustafsson, B. E., C. E. Quensel, L. S. Lanke, et al. "The Vipeholm Dental Caries Study: The Effect of Different Levels of Carbohydrate Intake on Caries Activity in 436 Individuals Observed for Five Years." *Acta Odontologica Scandinavica* 11, no. 3–4 (1954): 232–264.

Livsmedelsverket. "Barn och Ungdomar." http://www.slv.se/sv/grupp1/Mat-och-naring/Matvanor---undersokningar/Barn-och-ungdomar/ (accessed 18 May 2013).

Elinor Samuelsson

vision, or visual cues—especially color—influence how we perceive what we eat. Even before our first bite, we anticipate what we will taste based upon how the food looks, and this anticipation can influence how we then experience the flavor. Darker-colored chocolate is perceived to have a more intense chocolate flavor than lighter-colored chocolate, and orange-colored chocolates can seem to have an orange flavor—but only if the person eating it thinks that the orange ones should taste orange. A green macaron might be pistachio, lime, or green tea-flavored, depending on the shade, but it is probably not infused with salted caramel or vanilla. In this case, the color creates an expectation about the flavor of the macaron. When the actual flavor is similar to the expectation, assimilation often occurs; people taste what they expect to taste, and an orange-flavored macaron that is colored green could easily be perceived as lime by many people. But when there is a larger discrepancy, such as with a green-colored but coffee-flavored macaron, contrast occurs and the mismatch is more often detected, to the delight or dismay of the consumer.

At least some color-flavor associations are learned over time. They can vary across cultures as well as within a culture. As different cultures consume different sweets (pumpkin, blackcurrant, and red bean all can be used in sweets but are popular in different regions), the expectation elicited by a particular color will depend hugely on context. The color of a gummi bear can indicate its flavor, but whether green means apple, lime, or strawberry depends on both the manufacturer and country of purchase. As with the macaron, the color creates an expectation about the specific identity of the flavor of the gummi bear. Some expectations about intensity, however, might exist without the need for experience. In the case of dark chocolate, the richer color creates an expectation that the chocolate will be more intense, and it may be that the brain naturally expects flavors that look more intense to taste more intense. But even these sorts of associations can change as a result of experience; adding red food coloring tends to lead to foods tasting sweeter, but adding green can actually reduce the perceived sweetness. Some scientists have speculated that this particular association has to do with fruit becoming both redder and sweeter as it ripens. Fans of red velvet cake might think about how much the red color might be enhancing their flavor experience. Moreover, even the color of the plate on which a dessert is served can matter; people eating strawberry mousse on a white plate perceived the mousse as more intense and sweeter, and liked it more, than when it was served on a black plate. Food manufacturers are aware of these effects, and many have experimented with adjusting the color of both actual food items and food packaging.

While the role of color has been explored for many years, other cues may be important as well. Glossiness can provide information about oiliness or wetness, and can potentially influence expectations about flavor. Recent studies have shown that shape can also influence taste. For instance, people are better at detecting low levels of sugar in water when looking at curved shapes than when looking at sharp-edged shapes. This could be because the curved shapes evoke pleasantness, which is in turn associated with sweetness. However, at least for sweets, the mapping between shape and identity may be less consistent than that between color and identity. Various chocolatiers make heart-shaped chocolates with raspberry, praline, or even chili and cinnamon ganache. While shape can influence the eating experience directly by changing the rate at which chocolate melts in the mouth, shape also likely influences perception by providing visual information that sets expectations, and perhaps even by eliciting particular flavor memories. In the United Kingdom, after Cadbury changed their Dairy Milk bar to a more curved shape, some consumers believed that the taste had changed as well, though the recipe remained the same. See SHAPE.

Further evidence for the role of vision comes from restaurants in which people "dine in the dark." At these restaurants, which now exist in cities around the world, blind waiters serve patrons an entire meal in complete darkness. The restaurants vary in how much information patrons are given about what they will eat; some keep the entire menu a surprise, whereas others allow particular dishes to be selected. When people do not know what to expect and lack visual information, they often are unable to identify what they are eating. Although people in other settings may sometimes close their eyes to enhance the perceptual sensitivity of their other senses, there is no evidence that removing visual cues entirely sharpens flavor sensitivity. Much of the appeal of these restaurants may be due to the novelty of the experience rather than to actual heightened taste experiences.

Some chefs use visual cues in a playful way, to create dishes in which visual expectations add drama to the dining experience. Heston Blumenthal has created a dessert that looks like a traditional British Christmas fruitcake but tastes like a chocolate brownie. Ferran Adrià has developed an "apple caviar" dish that has the appearance of caviar but tastes sweet rather than savory. At Manresa, near San Francisco, a meal starts with a brown-colored olive madeleine and a red bell pepper jelly, and ends with a chocolate madeleine and a strawberry jelly colored so that they look identical to the starter. The scientific evidence shows that visual presentation matters, so the next time you serve sweets, remember that your eyes can also feast upon a delicious dessert.

See also FOOD COLORINGS and NEUROSCIENCE.

Delwiche, Jeannine F. "You Eat With Your Eyes First." *Physiology & Behavior* 107, no. 5 (2012): 502–504.

Liang, Pei, Soumyajit Roy, Meng-Ling Chen, and Gen-Hua Zhang. "Visual Influence of Shapes and Semantic Familiarity on Human Sweet Sensitivity." *Behavioural Brain Research* 253 (2013): 42–47.

Piqueras-Fiszman, Betina, Jorge Alcaide, Elena Roura, and Charles Spence. "Is It the Plate or Is It the Food? Assessing the Influence of the Color (Black or White) and Shape of the Plate on the Perception of the Food Placed on It." *Food Quality and Preference* 24, no. 1 (2012): 205–208.

Spence, Charles, Carmel A. Levitan, Maya U. Shankar, and Massimiliano Zampini. "Does Food Color Influence Taste and Flavor Perception in Humans?" *Chemosensory Perception* 3 (2010): 68–84.

Carmel A. Levitan

wafers are thin, crisp sheets made by cooking batter between flat metal plates. The traditional wafer iron resembles a pair of scissors with plates where the blades would be.

In a sense, wafers are descended from the Jewish matzah, since they originated as the bread (the Communion wafer) used in the Catholic mass, which has always been unleavened because the Last Supper took place during Passover. See PASSOVER. This bread (called *oblata,* "that which is offered," by the sixth century) was regularly marked with a religious design before baking. The first wafer irons appeared in the ninth century, probably so that a religious establishment could make an unlimited number of wafers with a standard design over an ordinary fire without having to heat up an oven.

By the twelfth century laypeople had developed a taste for *oblatas* and were eating them for pleasure. Secular wafers were cooked in irons with nonreligious patterns, the most common being hexagons resembling the cells of a honeycomb. As a result, they were often called by names derived from *wafel,* a Germanic word for honeycomb. (In French, this was pronounced *walfre* and eventually became *gaufre* or *gaufrette.*)

However, the religious name *oblata* (French *oublie,* English obley) long continued to be used for secular wafers. The late-thirteenth-century Anglo-Norman "Treatise of Walter of Bibbesworth" includes an enthusiastic description of a banquet ending with sweet spices *e oubleie a fuisoun* (and plenty of wafers), and the word survives in Spanish and Czech.

In the Middle Ages, wafers still usually kept company with wine, specifically the spiced wine hippocras. See HIPPOCRAS. In the manuscript known as *Le ménagier de Paris* (ca. 1390), 6 out of 20 model menus ended with hippocras and wafers known as *mestiers.* By this time, wafers were often enriched with eggs, wine, and other ingredients; *Le ménagier* describes wafers made with cheese. Although the manuscript gives recipes for *gaufres,* it also recommends buying them from pastry makers.

Occasionally, though, wafers were used in cooking, in ways we might not expect. *The Forme of Cury* (also ca. 1390) gives an English recipe for stewed hare, which instructs, "Take obleys oþer wafrouns in defaute of loseyns and cowche in dishes" (take oblatas or wafers in place of broad noodles and lay in dishes).

In more recent times, although plain wafers still sometimes appear with wine, they are nearly always sweetened and typically accompany coffee or ice cream. The crisp texture and versatile shape of the wafer have inspired many uses, which we would today consider sweet biscuits or cookies. In the early seventeenth century they were rolled up into cylinders while still warm, as depicted in Lubin Baugin's painting *Le Dessert de gaufrettes* (1630–1635). Such wafers may be filled, frequently with chocolate, as in the Dutch New Year's treat *knieppertjies,* and in commercially made Piroulines, which originated in Belgium in 1860. Wafers could also be formed into cones, which were occasionally used for serving ice cream in the nineteenth century. The craze for ice cream cones in the United States, the most ice-cream-crazed country, dates from the 1904 Columbian Exposition. See ICE CREAM CONES.

The obvious way to elaborate wafers is to stack them. The spa wafers (*oplatky*) that originated in the health resorts of the Czech Republic and Slovakia in the nineteenth century consist of two thin wafers

Wafers lend themselves to being rolled up while still warm, as we see in Lubin Baugin's painting *Le Dessert de gaufrettes* (Still Life with Wafers, 1630–1635). The goblet of wine suggests the original use of wafers as Communion bread, though by the twelfth century they were being enjoyed in secular settings as well. THE YORCK PROJECT, DISTRIBUTED BY DIRECTMEDIA PUBLISHING GMBH

sandwiched together, usually with a filling of chocolate and hazelnut. In Mexico and Central America, an *oblea* is two wafers sandwiched with dulce de leche. A particularly remarkable wafer is the Dutch *stroopwafel*, which consists of a slightly leavened wafer split in half while hot and filled with a thick caramel syrup (*stroop* being Dutch for "syrup"). Unfortunately, it loses its delightful crispness after a few days.

But why stop with two wafers? Thicker products, such as the Neapolitan wafer (actually of Austrian origin), can be made with three to five layers and perhaps covered with chocolate or another coating, as with the Kit Kat bar.

The word "wafer" has come to refer to any thinnish sheet—hence the name of the American vanilla cookie Nilla Wafers, which are baked rather than cooked between irons. The ultimate development of the wafer is cooked in an iron that creates a deep pattern of square indentations. There are several local varieties in Belgium, where caramelized waffles are a yeast-raised snack or street food. In the United States, the Belgian waffle is a breakfast treat—a fancy-dress pancake, as it were—raised with baking powder.

See also BISCUITS, BRITISH; CANDY BAR; COOKING IRONS; DULCE DE LECHE; NETHERLANDS; ROLLED COOKIES; and ZALABIYA.

Anonymous. *The Goodman of Paris (Le ménagier de Paris): A Treatise on Moral and Domestic Economy by a Citizen of Paris*. Translated by Eileen Power. Woodbridge, U.K., and Rochester, N.Y.: Boydell, 2006. Originally published 1928.

Hieatt, Constance B., and Sharon Butler, eds. *Curye on Inglysch: English Culinary Manuscripts of the Fourteenth Century (Including the "Forme of Cury")*. New York and Toronto: Oxford University Press, 1985.

Charles Perry

wagashi, which means "Japanese confectionery," signifies a broad category of sweets that includes mochi and dumplings (*dango*) made in Japan from the prehistoric era; Chinese imports such as stuffed buns (*manjū*) and *yōkan*, initially introduced as vegetarian foods in the Kamakura period (1185–1333) but transformed into confectionery in the early modern period (1600–1868); and "southern barbarian sweets," sixteenth-century adaptations of Portuguese recipes. See AZUKI BEANS; DANGO; MANJŪ; MOCHI; and NANBANGASHI. The term *wagashi* was coined at the end of the 1800s to contrast Japanese confectionery with "Western sweets" (*yōgashi*)—cakes and other baked goods that had entered the Japanese diet through later European and American introductions. See JAPANESE BAKED GOODS.

However, wagashi did not become the standard term for Japanese confectionery until after World War II.

Wagashi combines the referent for Japan (*wa*) with *kashi* (which becomes *gashi* in compound words). *Kashi* refers to any type of sweet today, but the word's literal meaning is "fruit and nuts," which were Japan's earliest snacks; these included dried persimmons, chestnuts, and Japanese nutmeg (*kaya*). These snacks were eaten between meals in the ancient period and served as "sweets" for the tea ceremony in the 1500s. Sugar, known in Japan since the 700s, was considered a rare medicine; in its place, the Japanese made limited use of honey, rice glucose (*mizu ame*), and a decoction from the sweet arrowroot vine (*amazura*). Besides popularizing sugar in Japan, the Portuguese disseminated knowledge of its use in confectionery, allowing for sweetened versions of previously savory snacks like manjū and mochi. In the 1600s tea practitioners began using sugar-sweetened confectionery purchased from confectioners, who were the major buyers of imported sugar. Apart from their reliance on refined sugar, wagashi are distinguished by the use of highly milled rice flour, and by *an*, a paste made from sweetened azuki beans. In addition to aficionados of the tea ceremony, the consumers of wagashi in the early modern period were wealthy merchants, court aristocrats, and the warrior elite. Commoners enjoyed "inexpensive sweets" (*dagashi*), penny candies and other treats made from domestic brown sugar and less highly refined flours.

Among the many varieties of wagashi are "moist sweets" (*namagashi*) and "dry sweets" (*higashi*). Moist sweets derive their soft texture from *an*. Sometimes the *an* is combined with sugar and rice flour to make a dough called *konashi* that is shaped into sweets. In other instances, the *an* is a topping or filling, or it can serve as the primary ingredient, as in *yōkan*. Dry sweets such as *rakugan* have little water content and are made from rice flour and refined sugar molded into various shapes. *Senbei*, savory crackers made from rice flour, are sometimes included in the category of *higashi*. The sweet called *monaka* was invented in the early 1800s as a *senbei* stuffed with *an*; the crisp shell offsets the soft filling in a marriage of moist and dry sweets.

Wagashi use similar ingredients, but by changing their colors and shapes, confectioners in the early modern period developed hundreds of varieties, as evidenced by culinary texts and sample books of the period. See JAPAN. Handmade wagashi are works of art, rivaling in their craftsmanship and beauty the jewelry of Fabergé or Tiffany. Connoisseurs appreciate the taste, odor, texture, appearance, and even sound of the wagashi when they are eaten. The artistic names (*mei*) given to the many varieties of traditional sweets add to their appeal. These names can suggest a particular region or reference famous people, local scenery, flowers, and animals; they can also evoke phrases from ancient poems. Because most varieties of wagashi are available only during certain times of the year, their names are associated with holidays and the seasons, as by suggesting the flowers that will soon be in bloom. February is the time for plum blossom motifs, March for peach, and April for cherry blossoms. October sweets reference chrysanthemums, persimmons, chestnuts, rice plants, or geese. Appreciating the artful name of the sweet is an important part of enjoying wagashi, especially in the tea ceremony.

Traditional sweets are available at confectioners, many of which also market to customers in the gigantic food emporiums in department-store basements. Since confectionery is often given as gifts, wagashi are beautifully packaged and available at tourist destinations, airports, and train stations. The confectioner Toraya operates a wagashi museum in Tokyo; in Kyoto there is another museum, opened by the confectioner Tawaraya Yoshitomi. June 16 is Wagashi Day in Japan, a holiday that originated with the early-modern warrior government and imperial court, which distributed sweets to retainers as a way of promoting health.

See also PORTUGAL'S INFLUENCE IN ASIA.

Akai Tatsurō. *Kashi no bunkashi*. Kyoto: Kawara Shoten, 2005.

Aoki Naomi. *Zusetsu wagashi no konjaku*. Kyoto: Tankōsha, 2000.

Nakayama Keiko. *Wagashi monogatari*. Tokyo: Asahi Shinbunsha, 1993.

Rath, Eric C. *Food and Fantasy in Early Modern Japan*. Berkeley: University of California Press, 2010.

Eric C. Rath

wasanbon is the most famous sugar used in traditional Japanese confectionery. See SUGAR. Faintly yellow in color, it has fine crystals and a subtle bouquet. The derivation of the word is uncertain. The referent *wa* indicates domestic Japanese manufacture; *sanbon* could be the Japanese version of the name of the Chinese person who disseminated the sugar-making process to Japan, or it could refer to "three bowls" (*sanbon*) used in the production process.

While sugar was known as an expensive medicine in the 700s, Japanese cooking did not make much use of sweeteners until the Portuguese and Chinese reintroduced sugar in the late 1500s, and Japanese consumers quickly developed a taste for the product. See JAPAN. In an effort to improve Japan's balance of trade, Shogun Tokugawa Yoshimune (1684–1751) sought to stem purchases of imported sugar by encouraging the domestic production of sugarcane. Although Yoshimune directed that sugar be planted throughout Japan, today sugarcane for *wasanbon* is grown only in Kagawa and Tokushima prefectures in Shikoku, where the artisanal techniques used to make *wasanbon* developed in the late 1700s. Farmers plant a thin variety of Chinese sugarcane called *Saccharum sinense*. The cane is harvested in December and crushed to extract the juice, which is then boiled to evaporate the water. The cooled liquid is pressed in a cloth bag and kneaded by hand in four changes of water to remove the molasses before the sugar is dried. *Wasanbon* is mainly used to make dry confectionery (*higashi*), for which it is mixed with refined rice flour and formed into molded shapes. See WAGASHI.

Hosking, Richard. *A Dictionary of Japanese Food: Ingredients and Culture.* Rutland Vt.: Charles E. Tuttle, 1996.

Eric C. Rath

Weber, Johannes Martin Erich (1885–1961), was arguably the premier publisher of confectionery trade manuals in their golden age between the two world wars. He established his baking school and publishing and supply houses in Dresden, Germany, in 1911, moving them in the early 1920s to Dresden's suburb, Radebeul, where they remained until being closed by the Communist government in 1948.

While the creations Weber presented in his books, and the books themselves, were as lavish as those of his competitors, what really set his volumes apart was their breadth of readership. From 1913 to 1929, Weber marketed his works to an international audience by publishing the texts in multiple languages rather than in separate supplements. For example, his first publication, *Practical Confectionery Art* (*Praktische Konditorei-Kunst*), appeared in at least eight editions, including one in German, Danish, Czech, and Dutch; another in German, Swedish, Spanish, and English; and an all-English version intended exclusively for American readers. To make his typically long German titles easier to remember, he abbreviated some of them into snappy nicknames, such as *Pra-Ko-Ku* for *Praktische Konditorei-Kunst*.

He also often included teaching aids with his more expensive volumes: cardboard or celluloid stencils, perforated paper patterns, separate how-to-pipe plates, recipe booklets, and even an enormous foldout pattern sheet for sugar temples. Always the savvy promoter, Weber would either print his supply catalog on a book's final pages or glue one inside the back cover.

After Hitler's rise to power, Weber published only in German, employing Gothic type and geometric designs that could be interpreted as either modernist or fascist. Most of his work during the 1930s emphasized practical information, but his final publication, in 1939, *Webers bildlicher Fachunterricht zu Hochstleistungen in moderner Konditorei* (Weber's Illustrated Textbook in Advanced Modern Confectionery) contained 600 pages and 1,000 illustrations.

After World War II, Weber was interned by the Soviets for several years. On his release he returned to Radebeul and lived there until his death.

See also BLACK FOREST CAKE; CONFECTIONERY MANUALS; and GERMANY.

Kirsch, Francine. "Over the Top: The Extravagant Confectionery of J. M. Erich Weber." *Gastronomica* 4, no. 2 (May 2004): 28–34.

Francine Kirsch

wedding celebrations have historically provided an opportunity for lavish displays of wealth, and ever since the late medieval period, sugar confectionery has been an important feature of European weddings. Like so many other cultural phenomena, sugar's close relations to nuptial celebrations appears to have originated in Italy at the humanist courts. Important patrician wedding feasts in the early Renaissance were more like complicated theatrical performances than dinners. Costly confections, sweetmeats, and sugar sculpture often played their role in expressing power and status at more straightforward civic banquets, but when two powerful dynastic houses were joined in marriage, no expense was spared. See SUGAR SCULPTURE.

In *A Renaissance Wedding*, Jane Bridgeman describes a truly remarkable wedding feast held in Pesaro in 1475 celebrating the marriage of Costanzo Szorza and Camilla Marzano d'Aragona. Compared to most modern wedding receptions, this was a truly lavish affair. It included many sweet elements that have survived into modern times, so it is worth giving a fairly full account of the occasion here.

A banquet consisting of twelve courses was served in the great hall of the ducal palace in Pesaro, its ceiling decorated with stars and astrological blessings. The first six courses were presided over by the sun, and the second six by the moon. Each course was presented to the table by a god or goddess. This epic meal lasted over seven hours, and sugar confections and fantasies were featured throughout. At one point youths performing a ballet offered the guests items of sugar jewelry from elaborate sugar caskets. During another interval, 80 young men danced before the table with baskets of confectionery and sugar sculptures of castles, birds, and animals. Beautifully decorated majolica bowls, tazze, and goblets were offered to the bride and groom, but these also turned out to be made of sugar. After this brief amusement, an "Ethiopian," mounted on a large model of a camel, scattered comfits into the hall from two heavily laden basket panniers. This was followed by the entrance of a large triumphal carriage drawn by two white oxen representing *The Triumph of Chastity*, entirely made from sugar and offered as a gift by one of the leading apothecaries of Pesaro. At the end of the feast the couple were presented with a sugar sculpture of Mount Parnassus, while 20 actors dressed as Greek and Latin poets read from books made out of sugar painted to look like real illuminated manuscripts.

In addition to all the allegorical sugar floats and figures that appeared during the intervals of the meal, the first, sixth, seventh, and twelfth courses consisted entirely of sweets. Among the nine dishes of the first course were lilies modeled out of pine-nut marzipan, sugar garlic cloves (a joke), gilded bread for the high table, and silvered bread for everyone else. The sixth course featured junkets ornamented with the Svorza armorials, and clary wafers in the form of clouds. See JUNKET. The final *servizio* consisted of spiced wine, comfits of every kind, twisted wafers, and quince paste. See COMFIT and WAFERS.

This type of Italian humanist model set the style for high-status weddings throughout Europe. Although fish, flesh, and fowl were important elements at these feasts, sugar and confectionery were served in just as much abundance and in extraordinary variety. In the early days, sugar was a very costly item in Europe, so offering it in considerable abundance to the guests was an impressive expression of largesse and conviviality.

The custom of comfit throwing, which was carried out from the back of a fake camel at the Pesaro wedding, featured at most other weddings in fifteenth- and sixteenth-century Europe. It was derived from the ancient Judaic ritual of scattering the bride and groom with grains of wheat to presage worldly wealth and sexual fecundity. This age-old tradition, one of the most durable of wedding customs, is still with us today. The throwing of rice, sugared seeds, and paper confetti have all evolved from this practice. European colonists took the tradition all over the world. A 1748 text by Louis de Gaya describes a Portuguese wedding in Goa: "When they are married they are brought home in some Order, with the sound of Trumpets, Cornets, and other musical Instruments, every one as they pass by throwing Flowers, sweet Waters and Confits upon them, which are gathered up by the servants." Confetti, the Italian name for a sugar-encrusted seed, spice, or nut, was transferred to the now-familiar tiny paper cutouts in France at the end of the nineteenth century. These were sold as a safe alternative to sugared almonds, which had caused eye injuries when thrown by overly enthusiastic revelers. See CONFETTI.

The counterfeit sugar jewelry (there were also gilded coins printed with the happy couple's portraits) offered to guests at the Sforza wedding are early instances of wedding favors, edible gifts designed to take home as mementos. The oldest and most durable example of these were sugared almonds, which were always on offer in abundance during the final course of Renaissance wedding banquets for the guests to fill their purses and pockets. From Europe to the United States, these are still popular today. Favors molded into figurative devices were also important, such as the musk comfits printed with armorials in the last course of the Sforza wedding.

An anonymous English cookery book called *The Whole Duty of a Woman* (London, 1704) explains how they were made: "Your small Toys made of Sugar, in the Shape of Birds, Beasts, Flowers &c are made of melted Sugar in Rose-water cast in Moulds, and Gilded or Painted afterwards at Discretion." In the late nineteenth century, when chocolate tempering had become fully understood, molded chocolate novelties suddenly became very popular. The mold manufacturers' catalogues of the period are full of chocolate bridal bouquets, horseshoes, doves, and all the other sentimental emblems of marital bliss. See PUBLICATIONS, TRADE.

Pretzel-like cookies known as *gemelli, gimblette,* or *jumbals,* tied up in the form of true lovers' knots, appear to have been an important element in early modern weddings, particularly in the Low Countries. Early seventeenth-century Antwerp school artists such as Clara Peeters and Osias Beert frequently depicted these intricately knotted symbols of fidelity in paintings of wedding banquets. Quince paste, considered an aphrodisiac, and iced marchpanes scattered with comfits and embellished with sprigs of gilded rosemary also feature in these works.

See also CAKE DECORATING; FRUIT PASTES; HARD CANDY; HIPPOCRAS; MARZIPAN; and WEDDING CAKE.

Bridgeman, Jane. *A Renaissance Wedding. The Celebrations at Pesaro for the Marriage of Costanzo Sforza and Camilla Marzano d'Aragona.* London: Harvey Miller, 2013.

Gaya, Louis de. *Matrimonial Ceremonies Display'd.* London: W. Reeve, 1748.

Ivan Day

wedding cake may have its origins in the ancient Roman practice of breaking a cake of wheat or barley (*mustaceum*) over the bride's head as a symbol of good fortune, but many centuries would pass before a special cake became a focal point at weddings. As was the custom with other important celebrations, the hosts served the finest food they could afford; for the wealthy and nobility this included dishes containing dried fruits, spices, and sugar, luxuries imported from exotic lands. Enormously expensive, they became fashionable status symbols for the affluent elite. See DRIED FRUITS and SPICES.

Medieval European bakers made lavishly spiced fruit cakes for special occasions, adding dried fruits, spices, and sugar to bread dough, although the cakes were not covered with icing. See FRUITCAKE.

British Wedding Cakes

Rich, spicy fruitcakes were served at splendid medieval feasts, and for centuries afterward at important occasions and celebrations such as Easter, Christmas, weddings, and christenings.

The first published recipe for a cake made specifically for a wedding appeared in 1655, in *The Queen's Closet Open'd.* This was "the Countess of Rutland's receipt for making the rare Banbury cake." It was actually enriched bread dough containing yeast, eggs, butter, dried fruits, spices, rosewater, ambergris, and musk; the dough was encased in pastry before baking. See AMBERGIS; BREADS, SWEET; and FLOWER WATERS. The enormous cake, which weighed more than 30 pounds, was carried by an usher and shown off to the wedding guests for them to admire.

A cake made expressly for a wedding became known as "Bride Cake." The less prosperous would have had much smaller and less costly bride cakes. One example consisted of two large rounds of shortcrust pastry sandwiched together with currants and sprinkled with sugar on top. See PIE DOUGH. Very few homes at the time had an oven, but this type of pastry cake could easily be cooked on a bakestone on the hearth or on an iron griddle.

Another British recipe expressly noted for a wedding is Bride Pye, recorded by Robert May in the 1685 edition of *The Accomplisht Cook.* Bride Pye, served at the wedding feast of Oliver Cromwell's daughter in 1657, was an extraordinary feature of seventeenth-century wedding banquets. The large round pie had an ornately embellished pastry crust that concealed a filling of oysters, pine kernels, cockscombs, lambstones (testicles), sweetbreads, and spices. The less affluent had cheaper versions containing minced meat, suet, and sometimes dried fruits and spices. Bride pie was still being served at weddings in some parts of England as late as the nineteenth century. See MINCE PIES and PIE.

Bride cake covered with white icing first appeared in the seventeenth century. It was frosted with the forerunner of royal icing; a meringue mixture of whisked egg whites and sugar was applied to the hot cake straight from the oven and then returned to the oven to set. Constant vigilance was required to ensure that it didn't color. See ICING and MERINGUE.

Sugar had been imported to England since the Middle Ages, but by the 1540s it was more readily available and affordable in cones of varying quality. "Double refined" sugar was twice-refined white sugar; powdered icing or confectioner's sugar was unknown. References to "powdered sugar" refer to granulated sugar that had been pounded fine and sifted. See SUGAR. A pure white icing was much sought after, as it meant that only the finest refined sugar (the most expensive) had been used. Thus, a pure white cake was a status symbol, a display of the family's wealth. The Victorians put forward the concept that the white icing symbolized purity.

The earliest printed recipe for a Bride Cake with icing appeared in Elizabeth Raffald's book *The Experienced English Housekeeper* (1769). It was the first to unite bride cake, almond paste, and icing. Raffald's recipe used eggs as a raising agent, and the batter was cooked in a wooden hoop, not enclosed in pastry. After baking, the cake was spread with a layer of almond paste, then covered with white icing made with double-refined sugar, fine starch (possibly corn starch), and egg whites. Commercial icing sugar began to be produced in the mid-nineteenth century.

At Queen Victoria's wedding to Prince Albert in 1840, white icing decorated the cake; this icing has been known as "royal icing" ever since. The elaborately decorated, multi-tier cake measured more than nine feet in circumference and was the first wedding cake to depict sugar sculptures of the bride and groom—a feature that was quickly copied by wedding-cake makers everywhere. Illustrations of the royal wedding cake appeared in publications throughout the world, and those who could afford it wanted a similar cake.

The multi-tiered British wedding cake—an impressive edifice of heavily fruited cake layers decorated with royal icing and embellished with sugar flowers, doves, horseshoes, and bells—had its origins in the wedding cake made for the marriage of Prince Leopold in 1882. Unlike Queen Victoria's cake, where only the base consisted of cake and the upper tiers were entirely of sugar, Prince Leopold's wedding cake had three tiers, and each tier was an iced cake. For the first time guests could enjoy a wedding cake made entirely of cake. The iced cakes were placed one on top of the other to form a stack, rather like hatboxes. The icing in between was hardened to prevent the upper tiers from sinking into the lower layers. It would be another twenty years before the tiers would be separated by columns (often disguised pieces of broom handle), and it was not until the beginning of the twentieth century that the tiers were separated and supported by columns of hardened icing. The British wedding cake influenced wedding cakes throughout the British Empire and beyond, with wealthy families vying to outshine one another by the height and weight of their wedding cake.

By the nineteenth century, Bride Cake had gradually acquired the name "wedding cake," although Alexis Soyer's *A Shilling Cookery for the People* (1854) carried an illustrated baker's advertisement for "Bride and Wedding Cakes."

British wedding cakes remained virtually unchanged from the elaborate Victorian creations until the 1980s, when the intricately piped royal icing began to be replaced by softer fondant icing, which could be rolled out, draped, frilled, and modeled into flowers, bells, and other ornaments. At the same time, simpler, American-style layer cakes, such as carrot cake with cream cheese filling or Key lime coconut cake, came into vogue. See CAKE DECORATING.

Other Wedding Cakes

The rest of Europe regarded the traditional tiered iced fruitcake as peculiarly English and preferred less heavy confections, with many regional specialties taking pride of place on the wedding table.

French weddings are traditionally celebrated with a *croquembouche* (literally "crunch in the mouth"), a conical construction of choux balls on a nougatine base filled with whipped cream, held together with caramel and decorated with rosettes of whipped cream, candied fruits, sugared almonds, and spun sugar. See CARAMEL and CROQUEMBOUCHE. Croquembouche is a descendant of the *pièce montée*, a large, ornamental item of patisserie that had its heyday in the nineteenth century when the great French chef Carême reigned supreme. See CARÊME, MARIE-ANTOINE and SUGAR SCULPTURE.

Traditional Italian wedding cakes are simpler. *Crostata di frutta* (fresh fruit tart), *millefoglie* (mille feuilles), or *pan di spagna* (sponge cake) filled with cream and covered in icing or whipped cream are typical, although, as with all Italian cooking, there are many regional specialties; Sardinian weddings serve *caschettas*, small pastries shaped like white roses ("as thin as the veil of a bride") and typically filled with honey, hazelnuts, cinnamon, and orange peel. See SPONGE CAKE.

Spanish wedding cakes resemble a flan and are typically filled with nuts and fruits and occasionally custard. Another type consists of several sponge cakes with a caramel topping and fresh cream, which may be filled, layered, tiered, or stacked in a hatbox fashion.

In Salamanca, *bollo Maimón* is a ring-shaped cake made with flour, sugar, eggs, and yeast; nowadays it is usually covered in chocolate.

Sourdough wedding bread decorated with beads and blossoms was traditional at Greek weddings. These days many Greek couples favor a flourless almond cake filled with vanilla custard and fruit and covered in sliced almonds.

In Germany the traditional *Baumkuchen* or "tree cake" is a tower of irregular cake rings with a coating of white or dark chocolate icing. It is not baked in a tin but built up with over fifteen layers of batter, which are spooned over a revolving hardwood roller in front of an open flame. When the cake is cut into wedges, it resembles the rings of a tree trunk. See BAUMKUCHEN. In northern Germany, *Butterkuchen* (butter cake) and *Zuckerkuchen* (sugar cake) are sweet yeast dough cakes; the topping is created by pressing holes into the dough, spreading butter over the top, then sprinkling with sugar and almonds. Modern German wedding cakes tend to be rich nut or sponge cakes laced with liqueur or syrup and filled with jam, marzipan, or nougat covered in fondant or ganache. See FONDANT; MARZIPAN; and NOUGAT.

The Scandinavian and Icelandic wedding cake *kransekake* comes in two forms. The traditional wedding cake is conical in shape, baked in ring tins of varying sizes and decorated with white icing. Sometimes the same dough is used to make a cornucopia (*overflødighedshorn*) so that the open end of the horn can be stuffed with chocolates and other sweets.

Enriched breads like babka, a rich, buttery, yeasted dough, are popular in eastern Europe. See BREADS, SWEET. The sweet dough is decorated with symbols of family and fertility, such as birds and trees. The round Polish wedding bread has a hole cut into it which is filled with salt for good luck. In Slovenia the wedding bread is usually a beautifully decorated braided dough.

Many of today's brides throughout the world opt for British- and American-style cakes with multiple layers, fondant icing, piped frosting, and decorations, although contemporary wedding cakes can be of any color, flavor, or shape. From a tower of colorful cupcakes or individual desserts to a plain sponge cake simply iced and decorated with fresh or sugar flowers, wedding cakes, like the bride's dress, are subject to the vagaries of fashion, with celebrity weddings and cake designers continually striving to create new trends.

See also CAKE.

Charsley, Simon. *Wedding Cakes and Cultural History.* London: Routledge, 1992.

May, John. *The Accomplisht Cook, or the Art & Mystery of Cookery.* London: Printed for Obadiah Blagrave, 1685. Reprint, Totnes, U.K.: Prospect, 2000.

Raffald, Elizabeth. *The Experienced English Housekeeper.* Manchester, U.K.: J. Harrop, 1769. Reprint, East Sussex, U.K.: Southover, 1997.

Carol Wilson

The **West (U.S.),** with its moderate climate and fertile land, particularly along the coast and inland valleys, features desserts that decidedly focus on the fruits and nuts that flourish in the region. A favorite dessert flavor is lemon—often the sweet Meyer, followed by other fruits and nuts, with apples possibly in the lead. Chocolate is also very popular. Recently cultivated with success in Hawaii, chocolate also has a long history of quality production in the West.

Even before the arrival of European explorers, the West was a land of plenty, and it was more densely populated by indigenous peoples than other regions of North America. Many native ingredients, favored for desserts today, are now grown commercially, such as blueberries, cranberries, raspberries, blackberries, currants, and hazelnuts (filberts). Foragers in the Northwest harvest, as the Native peoples did, salmonberries, cloudberries, thimbleberries, huckleberries (red and blue), and wild strawberries. See NATIVE AMERICAN and PACIFIC NORTHWEST (U.S.). The Lewis and Clark expedition of 1804 opened the Northwest to overland pioneers who brought their traditional American pies, cakes, cobblers, and puddings. Later, Scandinavian immigrants introduced their pastries and sweets.

The southern half of the West was Spanish territory from the sixteenth century. Spanish missionaries settled California in the eighteenth century and immediately planted grapes, fruit and nut trees, and much more. In 1821, Mexico took over, with its legendary *ranchero* hospitality. The flavors of Spain and Mexico linger in Western desserts—flans, *polvorones* (Mexican wedding cookies), cookies, and tres leches cake (incorporating cream and two kinds of canned milk). See TRES LECHES CAKE and SOUTHWEST (U.S.).

California gained independence in 1846 and was annexed as a state in 1850 during the frenzy of the Gold Rush. San Francisco, the port of entry for the flood of gold seekers, predominately male, from all over the world—Europe, Russia, Africa, the Far East, Mexico, and Latin America—became the epitome of a boomtown. The demand for the best by those who struck it rich set off a food and wine frenzy that has never really slowed in the city. French food and wines were the standard, and elegant French desserts became and remain a part of the West's repertoire.

Many who sought gold found it, not in "them thar hills," but in San Francisco and mining towns catering to tastes for high living. Ghirardelli and Guittard, two chocolate manufacturers who settled in San Francisco around this time, are still present. See GHIRARDELLI and GUITTARD. Contemporary producers include Sharffen Berger and TCHO in the San Francisco Bay area, and Theo Chocolate in Seattle.

In the early 1900s, San Francisco's St. Francis Hotel brought aboard Victor Hirtzler, a French chef who had literally cooked for kings. His book *The 1910 Hotel St. Francis Cook Book* (reissued in 1988) reinforced appreciation for all that was French—crêpes, savarin, pound cake, crème caramel, and bavarois. See DESSERTS, CHILLED; FLAN (PUDÍM); PANCAKES; and POUND CAKE.

Santa Clara Valley, today dubbed Silicon Valley, was known in post–Gold Rush years as the Valley of the Heart's Delight because, until the 1960s, it was the largest fruit-producing region in the world. Apricots, peaches, pears, plums, cherries, and more grew abundantly. These farms have shifted locations, largely to the Central Valley, where California continues to harvest more than half of all U.S. production of non-citrus fruits and nuts, and over 30 percent of the U.S. citrus crop. Washington State ranks third.

Sunset, a West-centric lifestyle magazine founded in 1898 and featuring articles on home, garden, food, and travel, has long celebrated the regional bounty and was instrumental in popularizing the use of locally grown persimmons, pomegranates, Asian pears, avocados, citrus varietals, macadamias, English walnuts, papaya, passion fruit, mangoes, kiwifruit, Meyer lemons, Rangpur limes, boysenberries, and marionberries—often with grow-it-yourself instructions.

In a July 1930 *Sunset* article titled "Eating Up and Down the Coast," Genevieve Callahan and Lou Richardson reported on crêpes for dessert, *zabaione* (zabaglione) with sherry or port, mangoes, and coconut dainties. See ZABAGLIONE. The editors raved about baked oranges at Mission Inn in Riverside, California, and praised frango, a flaky frozen dessert at Frederick and Nelson's tearoom in Seattle. But they complained that they couldn't get fresh local peaches, pears, oranges, apricots, cherries, or apples, since the best produce was not sold in the areas where it was grown. That issue has since been resolved with the explosion of farmers' markets, thanks to the California Direct Marketing Act of 1977, which made available locally wonderful produce varieties, many old, some new, that were considered too perishable or not productive enough for commercial use.

Helen Evans Brown wrote in her *West Coast Cook Book* (1956) that by the 1860s and 1870s, sugar was available, as trading vessels were stopping at Western ports, and early cookbooks had multiple recipes for cakes and pies, as well as chocolate soufflés, caramels, éclairs, meringues with fruit, ices, and blancmange. See BLANCMANGE; CARAMELS; ICE CREAM; MERINGUE; and SOUFFLÉ. Brown's recipes included burnt almond cream, avocado mousse, crêpes, sour cream date pie, filbert torte, lemon butter, deep-dish apple pie, and Chinese almond cookies.

The Italian immigrant element is well represented in popular desserts like zabaglione, cannoli, tiramisù, zuppa inglese, panna cotta, biscotti, fried cream, and crostatas. See BISCOTTI; TIRAMISÙ; and ZUPPA INGLESE.

Like the tides of the Pacific, favored desserts roll in and out. Flavors persist; ingredients persist and expand, as do old-fashioned names, but the presentations and combinations are ever changing—with "fresh" as the magic word that characterizes the desserts of the West.

Callahan, Genevieve. A. *Sunset All-Western Cook Book.* 3d ed. San Francisco: Lane, 1936. See pp. 40–120.

Kamp, David. *The United States of Arugula, How We Became a Gourmet Nation.* New York: Broadway Books, 2006. See pp. 29, 123, 126, 157, 133–134, 161, 252.

Soule, Frank, John H. Gihon, and James Nisbet. *The Annals of San Francisco: A Complete Facsimile Edition of the Original Work Published in 1855 by D. Appleton & Company*. Berkeley, Calif.: Berkeley Hills Books, 1998. See Part 1: chapters 1, 3, 6, 7, 11; Part 2: chapters 1, 5, 6, 9, 18, 23; and pp 639–652, 665–674.

Jerry Anne Di Vecchio

wheat berries are the raw kernels of the cereal plant wheat. Native to Anatolia and the Fertile Crescent, wheat was first domesticated in Neolithic times. Since then it has been a staple nourishment as well as a symbol of fertility, prosperity, birth, and rebirth for cultures throughout the world. As the cultivation of wheat spread, so did its cultural significance. Because wheat has long been associated with deities, it is not surprising that both the early Christian and Islamic traditions in Anatolia adopted it. See CHRISTIANITY and ISLAM. In earlier cultures the Greek goddess Demeter is depicted with a wheat stalk in hand, as are many other fertility goddesses, including Hittite Kubaba and Roman Ceres, the mother of agriculture and of all grain crops.

In Anatolia, the Balkans, Eastern Europe, Russia, and the Middle East, celebratory wheat dishes mark seasonal changes, rites of passage, religious holidays, and other important occasions. Sweets made with boiled whole-wheat berries are indispensable for certain occasions: the first month of the Islamic calendar is marked by *aşure* in Turkey; Christmas and New Year are welcomed by Armenians with *anush abur*; Sephardic Jews celebrate the flowering of fruit trees and the awakening of nature with *kofyas* or *trigo koço* at Tu b'Shevat; the appearance of the first baby tooth is shared with tooth wheat under a variety of names in Turkey, Lebanon, and Syria; and the same sweet (*berbara, burbara*) gives hope to unmarried girls on St. Barbara's (or Varvara's) Day on 4 December. All these dishes represent hope for the future.

Yet wheat berries also signify mourning: the dead are bid farewell with Greek *koliva* or *kólliva*. The dish appears throughout the Balkans under similar names. Although some suggest that the term *koliva* derives from *helva*, another funeral sweet in Turkey, it comes from the Greek *kollybos*—the smallest coin, whose name relates to a Semitic word meaning "to exchange." Similar, too, is Georgia's honey-sweetened *gorgot* or *korkoti* for funerals and commemorations. Commemorative wheat-berry sweets also include Chinese longevity grain porridge, *ba bao zou* or *laba zhou*, "eight-jewel rice pudding." All these wheat-berry sweets are linked to the concept of sharing. They are always made in huge quantities and distributed to the community, neighbors, friends, and relatives, even to strangers and the poor.

Some of these sweets are of pudding consistency; others are dry, the boiled grains like little pellets. Turkish *aşure* and its Balkan and Armenian equivalents are soupy puddings. Abundant with dried fruits, raisins, sultanas, dried apricots, figs, and nuts, they are flavored with rosewater and cinnamon and decorated with more nuts and pomegranates to represent plenty. See FLOWER WATERS. The funeral or commemoration wheat-berry sweets are generally dry. They are mixed with toasted flour to absorb moisture, then buried under a blanket of sugar, as if to anticipate that they will symbolically rise from the grave like Jesus. Sometimes wheat berries are mixed with other seeds to emphasize fertility. Cypriot Turks make *golifa* with various mixed seeds, pomegranates, and nuts for the New Year. Russian Christmas and New Year are marked with *sochivo*, whereas the similar *kutya* or *kutia* is traditional in Ukraine, Belarus, and some parts of Poland. Both incorporate poppy seeds as a symbol of abundance. See POPPY SEED.

A legend attributes the origin of Turkish *aşure* to Noah's Ark. The sweet is believed to have been created with whatever food remained on board once the ark finally reached shore after the flood, which explains why in rural Anatolia the dish is also referred to as *şükran çorbası* (thanksgiving soup). *Aşure*'s name derives from the word *ʿāshūrāʾ*, which means "tenth" in Arabic, indicating the date on which it is traditionally prepared, the tenth day of Muharram, the first month of the Islamic lunar calendar. This date also marks the tragedy of Kerbela, when the Prophet's grandsons were killed, making it a day of lamentation for Turkey's Alevi Muslims. A different wheat-berry legend may be found in Sicily, where *cuccìa di Santa Lucia* is prepared to honor the Festa di Santa Lucia on 13 December, when ships loaded with grain suddenly appeared in the harbor after the long famine of 1582.

Sprouting wheat for Christmas, St. Lucia's Day, St. Barbara's Day, and Nowruz (the Persian New Year) is customary to symbolize the rebirth of nature. The sprouted berries adorn the table along with dried fruits and nuts. For Nowruz, a potent brown paste called *sümenek* (*semeni, samani, samanak*) is prepared by boiling down freshly pounded sprouted wheat.

See also BIRTH; FUNERALS; and JUDAISM.

Kaneva-Johnson, Maria. *The Melting Pot-Balkan Food and Cookery*. Totnes, U.K.: Prospect, 1999.

Tan, Aylin Öney. "Be Merry Around a Wheat Berry! The Significance of Wheat in Anatolian Rituals and Celebrations." In *Proceedings of the Oxford Symposium on Food and Cookery, 2011*, edited by Mark McWilliams, pp. 346–355. Totnes, U.K.: Prospect, 2012.

Aylin Öney Tan

whisks and beaters are implements used to incorporate air into batters, eggs, and cream. Until the first decades of the nineteenth century, a bundle of twigs, a wooden spoon, or a knife blade was the traditional kitchen tool used for the arduous chore of beating eggs "to a raging foam" or whipping cream to firm peaks. An illustration in the *Opera* of Bartolomeo Scappi (1580) depicts a kitchen worker using a large whisk, while the patisserie equipment plate in Diderot and Alembert's *Encyclopedie* (1765) resembles a miniature broom. A recipe for a cake baked annually in nineteenth-century American Shaker communities to commemorate the birthday of the sect's founder, Ann Lee, instructs the cook to "Cut a handful of peach twigs which are filled with sap at this season of the year. Clip the ends and bruise them and beat the cake batter with them. This will impart a delicate peach flavor to the cake."

The "Dover" eggbeater, first manufactured by the Dover Stamping Company in the 1870s, won the hearts of generations of American cooks with its double-geared cast-iron wheels and tin-plated blades that revolved in opposite directions. LEVI SZEKERES

Early cookbooks describe the beating procedure. In a recipe titled "To Ice a Large Cake" in *The American Domestic Cookery* (1823), Maria Eliza Rundell advised beating the whites of 20 fresh eggs, adding sugar, orange flower water, and lemon peel, and whisking the flavored egg whites "for three hours till the mixture is thick and white, then with a thin, broad bit of board spread it all over the top and sides." Frederick Nutt, in *The Complete Confectioner* (1807), recommended beating egg yolks and sugar with a wooden spoon until "they blow up in bladders of wind," then whisking the whites in a copper pan "till they are almost strong enough to bear an [unshelled] egg," while Amelia Simmons, in *American Cookery* (1796), pronounced the whites ready when a silver 25-cent piece remained on top.

The Philadelphia cookbook writer Eliza Leslie thought "there is nothing so good" for beating as willow rods, and in *Miss Leslie's New Receipts for Cooking* (1854) she offered helpful hints for reducing fatigue: "Do not use your elbow, but keep it close to your side. Move only your hand at the wrist, and let the stroke be quick, short, and horizontal...persist till after the foaming has ceased... continue until the surface is smooth as a mirror."

As the nineteenth century progressed, sturdy wire whisks and ingenious mechanical labor-saving devices appeared in ever-increasing numbers in England and America. Tinsmiths produced flat and balloon-shaped wire whisks, and designs for revolving, oscillating, and agitating beaters began to flow into the patent office. "The present is truly the age of invention," wrote one newspaper editor in a testimonial praising the new Hale Aerating eggbeater, patented in 1866. "It so readily performs the operation... that one half the eggs generally required is saved." The Hale beater was a tin cylinder with a plunger in which the eggs were churned, the action filling them with tiny globules of air. Other manufacturers introduced box-like tin beaters with a crank handle, as well as revolving wire beaters encased in a glass jar, but the breakthrough design was a revolving interlacing beater that cut through the glazy albumen of the egg rather than literally beating it.

Although there were several patents granted in the 1860s, the Dover Stamping Company in the 1870s was the first to manufacture on a large scale the new-style beater with double geared cast-iron wheels and tin-plated blades that revolved in opposite directions. Leading culinary experts eagerly endorsed the "Dover." Marion Harland, who devoted a whole chapter of her book *Breakfast, Luncheon and Tea* (1875) to eggbeaters, praised the Dover, writing, "If I could not get another I would not sell mine for fifty dollars or a hundred." In *The Home Cookbook,* compiled by Chicago Ladies for the benefit of a home for the friendless in 1875, a latter-day Patrick Henry declared, "As long as there are eggs to beat, give me Dover or give me death." Although it inspired dozens of imitations, like Baby Bingo, the Merry Whirl, and the Cyclone, it was the Dover that won the hearts of generations of American cooks.

However, not everyone endorsed the Dover. A century before Julia Child brandished a whisk during a television interview promoting her book *Mastering the Art of French Cooking* (1961), professional cooks were extolling the whisk's merits. Pierre Blot, the transplanted French chef who came to the United States in the mid-nineteenth century and founded the first French cooking school in America, wrote in *Handbook of Practical Cookery* (1867) that he had tried five different kinds of beaters before a large audience in Boston, but "not one could beat eggs as well as a common hand beater," meaning the wire whisk, illustrated in his book.

When the twentieth century ushered in the age of electricity, both the whisk and the Dover lay forgotten in kitchen drawers. The first patent for a power mixer was granted in 1885, but it was not until after World War I that the Hobart Company marketed the KitchenAid mixer with a bowl on its own stand. The mixer worked on the principle of planetary action: a single beater traveled around the bowl in one direction while the bowl rotated on its axis in the opposite direction.

Today, even with a vast array of electric aids, many cooks, like Blot and Julia Child before them, prefer the hand-held whisk. Contemporary designs, often in a rainbow of colors, with easy-to-clean silicone wires, appeal to energetic cooks as an alternative to the whirring motor of a mixer. The basic configuration is a long stainless-steel or wooden handle holding flexible wire loops.

Variations abound; the balloon is a favorite, a shape that easily conforms to the concave sides of a mixing bowl. Also popular are the French, an elongated version of the balloon; the double-looped butterfly; and the ball, with individual straight wires with tiny balls at the tip attached to the handle. Now it is no longer "Give me Dover. . . ." Cooks can select from a world of whisks to whip up a glossy meringue or beat eggs to a raging foam.

Blot, Pierre. *Handbook of Practical Cookery.* New York: D. Appleton, 1867.

Dover Stamping and Manufacturing Company. *Catalog 34.* Cambridge, Mass., n.d.

Harland, Marion. *Breakfast, Luncheon and Tea.* New York: Scribner, Armstrong & Co., 1875.

Thornton, Don. *Beat This: The Eggbeater Chronicles.* Sunnyvale, Calif.: Off Beat Books, 1999.

Meryle Evans

whoopie pie is formed from two palm-sized rounds of chocolate sponge cake filled with a white frosting, made either of confectioner's sugar, which is beaten with shortening, or marshmallow frosting. Associated strongly with Maine and Pennsylvania, where they are sometimes called "gobs," whoopie pies first gained popularity in early-twentieth-century Maine as a bakery-made treat. They were later adopted by home cooks.

Competing claims for the invention of whoopie pies clutter their history. Early-twentieth-century cocoa or baking chocolate manufacturers popularized so-called Devil's food cakes, the very opposite of the then-stylish, egg-white raised angel food cake. Devil's food was the obvious source for the name Devil Dog, the white-frosting-filled, chocolate hot dog–shaped cake treat trademarked by New Jersey–based Drake's Cakes in 1926. Probably desiring a competitive product, and possibly inspired by the Amish gobs, the Berwick Baking Company, based in Roxbury, Massachusetts, apparently developed whoopie pies to avoid infringing Drake's trademark, and by 1931 it was advertising them throughout New England by that name.

In the 1930s the Durkee-Mower Company, manufacturer of Marshmallow Fluff, issued a cookbook titled *The Yummy Book,* which contained a whoopie pie recipe attributed to the Amish. The recipe caught on, and home cooks make whoopie pies to this day. The treat is also sold in bakeries, mom-and-pop stores, gas stations, and convenience stores all over Maine and the New England region.

Whoopie pies are the official Maine treat, and the town of Dover-Foxcroft, Maine, celebrates an annual Maine Whoopie Pie Festival on Whoopie

Pie Day, the fourth Saturday in June. Whoopie pies now vary widely in the type of cake and the flavors of filling they use.

See also ANGEL FOOD CAKE; MARSHMALLOW FLUFF; SMALL CAKES; and SPONGE CAKE.

Sandra L. Oliver

Winnie-the-Pooh, a loveable bear from children's literature, climbed stickily into posterity in 1926 as he headed for a buzzing noise that he knew would yield honey. See HONEY. Inspired by a London Zoo bear from Canada named Winnie, who had a taste for sweetened condensed milk, Winnie-the-Pooh was created by the author A. A. Milne and illustrator Ernest H. Shepard. In a series of books the two portrayed Pooh not only as Christopher Robin's cherished toy, but also as the embodiment of childhood delights. The bear's exploits, translated into over 50 languages, including Latin, spawned a Disney character and adult works like *The Tao of Pooh*.

For Pooh, "the only reason for making honey is so as I can eat it." His search for sweets is a universally comforting quest, his plumpness evidence of a honey obsession. Pooh's proclivity for honey would have been familiar to British children, who knew the substance as a teatime sweetener and sickroom remedy. It is not surprising that Pooh's adventures to satisfy his taste for a "goloptious full-up pot" of HUNNY should have stuck with generations of children, and their parents, like honey on a spoon. Honey, to Pooh, symbolizes life's sweetness: "A day without a friend is like a pot without a single drop of honey left inside." Pooh is never satiated, anticipating the happiness promised by his favorite sweet even more than he does the ultimate licking of "a little smackerel" of honey from his paws. For it turns out that Pooh is a philosopher whose worldview coincides with the Taoist idea that awareness of the process is as fulfilling as the reward: "Because, although Eating Honey was a very good thing to do, there was a moment just before you began to eat it which was better than when you were."

Milne, A. A., and E. H. Shepard. *The Christopher Robin Story Book: From When We Were Very Young, Now We Are Six, Winnie-the-Pooh, The House at Pooh Corner.* New York: E. P. Dutton, 1929.

Ardath Weaver

xylitol is a monosaccharide sugar alcohol found in small quantities in mushrooms, fruits, and vegetables, and in the fiber of various trees, such as birch. It was discovered in 1890, but it did not become an important sweetener until after World War II, when Finnish scientists began to promote "birch sugar" as a substitute for table sugar (sucrose). Finnish food manufacturers popularized xylitol as a sugar substitute in chewing gums and lozenges in the 1960s.

Xylitol has a number of unusual characteristics. It has the same appearance and sweet taste as sucrose, but the human body absorbs it more slowly and incompletely. Compared to sucrose, xylitol has fewer calories, and it does not spike blood sugar or raise insulin levels. Because it has a very low glycemic index, it is a useful sweetener for diabetics. In addition, oral bacteria do not metabolize xylitol, so it does not promote tooth decay; some studies suggest that it may facilitate remineralization of teeth. See DENTAL CARIES. Xylitol also produces a cooling sensation in the mouth, which adds to the refreshing qualities of chewing gum and pastilles.

The U.S. Food and Drug Administration approved xylitol for human consumption as a sweetener and gave it the status of "Generally Recognized as Safe" (GRAS). Xylitol is considered by many authorities to be a healthful substitute for sugar, although when consumed in large quantities it can produce intestinal gas and cause diarrhea. It is also toxic to dogs.

Historically, xylitol was used mainly as a sweetener in medications, foods for diabetic diets, and chewing gum. See CHEWING GUM. In the twenty-first century, it has been touted as a weight-loss panacea in numerous articles and cookbooks, such as Fran Gare's *The Sweet Miracle of Xylitol* (2002). World production has recently exploded, as new facilities in China, Korea, and Taiwan began producing synthetic xylitol. In 2010, world production reached 200,000 tons, of which the European Union produced about half and the United States about 20 percent; the remainder was produced in India, China, Taiwan, and Korea. Production is expected to rapidly expand in the future as new facilities come online.

See also ARTIFICIAL SWEETENERS and SUGAR AND HEALTH.

Gare, Fran. *The Sweet Miracle of Xylitol: The All-Natural Sugar Substitute Approved by the FDA*. North Bergen, N.J.: Basic Health Publications, 2002.

Prakasham, R. S., R. S. Rao, and P. J. Hobbs. "Current Trends in Biotechnological Production of Xylitol and Future Prospects." *Current Trends in Biotechnology and Pharmacy* 3, no. 1 (January 2009): 8–36.

Andrew F. Smith

yeast is a living microorganism, a single-celled fungus. While there are more than 1,000 known species of yeast, bakers use domesticated strains of the species *Saccharomyces cerevisiae*—the name roughly translates to "the sugar fungus found on beer." Baker's yeast, also called brewer's yeast, is a microscopic rod-shaped organism. In the wild, *Saccharomyces cerevisiae* is principally found on fruit skins, including grapes. A mature yeast cell is about 4 micrometers in length; a grain of salt is about a thousand times larger, and even skin cells are nearly 10 times the size of a typical baker's yeast cell.

Yeast is added to a wide variety of baked goods as a biological leavening agent. Leaven has its roots in the Latin *levare*, meaning "to lighten" or "to lift." Leavening makes a baked good less dense by incorporating many gas pockets into the structure. The 400 grams of wheat flour in a loaf of bread already contain about 120,000 wild yeast cells before any additional yeast is added; however, not all of these belong to strains that would raise a wheat-flour dough, and in any case, this amount is not enough to lift the weight of flour to make an acceptable loaf of bread. It requires billions of yeast cells to leaven a dough made with a kilogram of wheat flour.

In the past, households brewed not only in order to have alcoholic beverages on hand, but also to produce the barm that rose to the top of a fermenting mash, which would be used to make bread rise. Bakers and brewers were experienced microbiologists, carefully (and sometimes jealously) cultivating their yeast colonies. Yeast's mechanism of action was a mystery for millennia, finally solved by the invention of the microscope, which allowed the living yeasts in barm to be seen, and by Louis Pasteur's work, which firmly established that yeast is the organism responsible for fermentation in both baked goods and alcoholic beverages.

Yeast is a saprophyte, which means it is an organism that feeds on decomposing plant or animal matter. The mechanism by which yeast leavens baked goods is anaerobic, requiring no oxygen. Dormant when dry, yeast becomes active when wet. Yeast converts the simple sugars glucose and fructose into ethanol and carbon dioxide (CO_2). See FRUCTOSE and GLUCOSE. The carbon dioxide produced by the decomposition of the sugars remains trapped within the tangles of proteins (gluten) that give structure to bread and other baked goods, forming small pockets of gas. The resulting porous material is much less dense than it would be otherwise.

The process of fermentation has two basic steps: (1) the breakdown of carbohydrates to simple one-unit sugars, and (2) the conversion of these monosaccharides to gaseous carbon dioxide and ethanol. Yeasts in a wet flour mixture feed first on the simple sugars sucrose, glucose, fructose, and maltose that are naturally present in small amounts in wheat. (About 1 percent of the total weight of wheat flour is actually sugars.) Once these sugars are consumed, the yeasts feed in earnest on the starches. See STARCH. Enzymes in the flour, released when the wheat is ground, cut apart the starches in the wheat into smaller sugar units, which can then be digested by the yeast. Enzymes in the yeast, principally invertase and maltase, break down the resulting sucrose and maltose into their component sugars, glucose and fructose—the feed stocks for fermentation.

The fermentation reaction enzymatically converts glucose (or fructose) to ethanol, a process that provides energy for the yeast and produces carbon dioxide and ethanol as waste products. The rate of fermentation, and thus the production of carbon dioxide, increases with temperature—much as the respiration rates of humans go up when they have a fever—so warm dough will rise faster. The heat of baking causes the trapped gas to expand, further lightening the texture of the material, and also sets the structure around the bubbles. The alcohol (a scant tenth of a milliliter total in a loaf of bread) evaporates during baking, but technically this is the same fermentation process that produces beer or ale, just in a different matrix and stopped at a much earlier stage. The high heat also kills off most of the yeast cells, which do not tolerate temperatures much above 130°F (54°C).

Yeast-leavened sweet doughs have difficulty rising, not because the sugar inactivates the yeast, but because the sugar reacts chemically with precursors to gluten, limiting the amount of gluten that can be formed. See BREADS, SWEET. Without the structure provided by gluten, sweet doughs are fragile and require longer rise times. Strains of yeast have been developed that produce more carbon dioxide than the regular strains and are more suited to use with low-gluten doughs. Adding spices to the dough, such as cinnamon, cardamom, nutmeg, or ginger, has the same effect, doubling or more the amount of carbon dioxide produced. Fats in the dough also reduce the formation of gluten by coating the individual protein strands before they can interact.

Yeast for baking can be obtained in many forms. Cream yeast, the fresh yeast once begged from local bakers or brewers or, as the name suggests, skimmed like cream from milk off the household's own fermenting alcohol, is a suspension of live yeast cells. Yeast is a natural product, and it was often difficult to gauge how much of a yeast suspension to use. Recipes routinely called for "proofing" yeast; that is, giving it some flour and water to feed on to check its viability.

It is only in the last hundred years or so that reliable, shelf-stable forms of yeast have been available. Billions of kilograms of yeast are now grown commercially every year. Pressed cakes of fresh yeast can be kept for one to two weeks in the refrigerator. Dried granules of yeast will keep for months on the shelf. Two forms are popular: the coarsely granulated active dry yeast, which must be rehydrated before using; and the more finely granulated instant yeasts, which do not require hydration before incorporation into a dough. And, of course, many bakers keep on hand their own culture, usually as poolish—a starter dough.

See also CHEMICAL LEAVENERS.

Corriher, Shirley O. *BakeWise: The Hows and Whys of Successful Baking, with Over 200 Magnificent Recipes.* New York: Scribner, 2008.

David, Elizabeth. *English Bread and Yeast Cookery.* New American ed. Newton, Mass.: Biscuit Books, 1994. First published 1977.

Michelle M. Francl

yogurt is a fermented milk product obtained through the action of certain bacteria. The prehistoric spread of dairying across an area extending from the Balkans to the Indian subcontinent and the western fringes of China went hand in hand with the spread of milk soured to produce what we now call by the Turkish name *yogurt.* Throughout these regions, hot temperatures during summer milking season have favored the action of particular lactic acid bacteria known as "thermophilic" because they act best at warm temperatures (between about 105° and 115°F, or 40° to 46°C). Such organisms rapidly colonize milk exposed to the open air, fermenting most of the lactose (milk sugar) to lactic acid and other flavorful byproducts. The result is a creamy, refreshingly tart substance useful for both sweet and savory purposes.

In the absence of commercial laboratory cultures, unstandardized clusters of wild lactic acid bacteria figure in the process, to varying effect. Historically speaking, nobody expected fixed uniformity in yogurt from different regions, or indeed from different households. The situation changed after 1900, when the two budding fields of dairy microbiology and gastroenterology began to intersect.

Partly drawing on earlier researchers' work and partly following his own erratic opinions, the Russian-born Nobel Prize winner Elie Metchnikoff—not himself a bacteriologist—announced in 1907 that yogurt contained certain beneficial organisms able to destroy pathogens in the colon and greatly prolong the human life span. Though his idea that yogurt bacteria could survive in the gut would be substantially disproved, his claims rapidly raised yogurt to the popular status of edible medicine.

Other researchers (especially Stamen Grigorov and Felix Lohnis) had already done pioneering work with lactic acid bacteria. Microbiologists soon were able to isolate and identify two organisms chiefly responsible for the characteristic flavor and texture of yogurt. Industrial laboratories began propagating and selling pure strains of both. Today they are usually known as *Streptococcus thermophilus* and *Lactobacillus bulgaricus*. When they are used together to inoculate milk, *S. thermophilus* rapidly initiates lactic acid production at a temperature of about 110° to 115°F (43° to 46°C) before *L. bulgaricus* kicks in to produce more noticeable acidity at a slightly lower temperature over several hours. Their joint action converts the casein in milk to a fragile, slightly tart gel that never becomes a fully formed curd.

Yogurt remained a minor specialty until a dramatic marketing makeover after World War II. U.S. manufacturers began masking its natural tartness—unpalatable to American consumers—with sweetened fruit preserves or syrup, and selling it in disposable individual containers from which it was meant to be directly eaten. They also claimed a new health-benefit angle by replacing whole milk with reduced-fat or nonfat milk, in line with the latest low-fat dietary agendas. To offset the loss of body, they often added dried nonfat milk, along with starch, pectin, and/or gelatin.

In effect, promoters had turned an ancient form of cultured milk into a pre-packaged sweet—advertised, however, not as a sweet but as a healthful dieters' snack or small meal. The two main forms were "Swiss-style," with sweetening and other flavorings mixed through the whole, and "sundae-style," with fruit preserves on the bottom to be stirred into the rest of the yogurt by consumers. Both were resounding triumphs. American domestic production of yogurt—virtually all sweetened—went from less than 300 million pounds in 1950 to about 6 billion pounds in 2010, with the most spectacular gains occurring between 1960 and 1990.

Another avenue opened up in the 1970s: frozen yogurt, marketed as a low-fat alternative to ice cream or frozen custard. After some fluctuations in popularity, several highly publicized new retail franchises (Pinkberry, Menchies, the Korean-based Red Mango, and more) featuring self-serve machines and choices of toppings kicked it into a growth spurt around 2005.

Meanwhile, plain unflavored yogurt is enjoying a modest renaissance after long neglect. Small producers using milk from small dairy herds (sheep or goats as well as cows) have begun making yogurt for an informed clientele. The market has expanded with increased immigration from India, Turkey, the Caucasus, Iran, Central Asia, Greece, Russia, and the Balkans. In those regions, plain yogurt has long been served together with honey, jaggery-type sugar, or poached dried fruit (especially apricots). India has produced the most inspired yogurt-sugar marriages: sweetened versions of the drink called lassi (sometimes with pureed fruit); the saffron-perfumed Gujarati dessert *shrikhand*; and combinations of yogurt with sweetened concentrated milk in the Bengali *bhapa doi* and *mishti doi*. Some of these specialties have become known to other American cooks in recent decades.

In the last few years, two new developments have galvanized the mainstream commercial yogurt market.

Shortly before Metchnikoff's pro-yogurt efforts, the gastroenterologist Ernst Moro had isolated an organism that naturally occurs not in food but in the human colon, where it seems to have some of the pathogen-fighting properties that Metchnikoff had wrongly ascribed to yogurt. It was eventually named *Lactobacillus acidophilus*, for its resistance to acidity strong enough to kill other lactic acid bacteria. By about 1920 it was being experimentally added to milk, to create a harshly sour second cousin of yogurt. "Acidophilus milk" was eaten by only a small fan club of health-food zealots until the late 1990s. At that point many natural-foods adherents became convinced that foods inoculated with "probiotics," or "good" bacteria capable of colonizing the colon, could rid the body of pathogens and bacterial toxins. A huge market emerged for yogurt containing not just the usual organisms but *L. acidophilus* along with clusters of other reportedly therapeutic bacteria. Today, it is impossible to buy yogurt manufactured without *L. acidophilus* and four or five other supposedly probiotic organisms. Consequently, formerly mellow versions of yogurt—even from artisanal producers—have acquired a sharper acidity that may require adjustments by cooks.

At about the same time, manufacturers in Greece began exploring the U.S. market for yogurt that is pre-thickened by draining off most of the whey. Unaware that this is the normal manner in which most people eat yogurt from Central Asia to the Balkans, American consumers greeted this "Greek yogurt" as an exciting new discovery. No federal standard of identity covers the term. Other manufacturers both here and abroad were thus free to exploit its rising popularity by producing supposed "Greek" versions of what various immigrant groups already knew as *labne* (Arabic) or *suzme* (Turkish) yogurt. Drained whole-milk yogurt is far better for cooking purposes—including most sweets—than previous mass-market U.S. versions. However, producers here soon reinvented "Greek yogurt" in a multitude of low-fat and nonfat forms with the sugar, flavorings, and added thickeners that Americans have come to associate with yogurt.

Katz, Sandor Ellix. *The Art of Fermentation: An In-Depth Exploration of Essential Concepts and Processes from Around the World.* White River Junction, Vt.: Chelsea Green, 2012.

Kosikowski, Frank V., and Vikram V. Mistry. *Cheese and Fermented Milk Foods.* 3d ed. 2 vols. Westport, Conn.: F. V. Kosikowski, 1997.

Mendelson, Anne. *Milk: The Surprising Story of Milk through the Ages.* New York: Knopf, 2008.

Anne Mendelson

zabaglione (*zabaione,* or *sabayon* in French) is a rich, frothy dessert or thick beverage made with well-beaten egg yolks and sugar slowly thickened by cooking in a bain-marie. Depending on the region, sweet Marsala wine (Sicily, Calabria, and Campania), Moscato d'Asti (Piedmont), or Vin Santo (Tuscany) is added to the egg mixture. The secret of zabaglione lies in the freshness of the eggs and the incorporation of large amounts of air to make the foam light as a feather.

Like blancmange, zabaglione began as a dish that we would no longer classify as dessert: it was made with beaten eggs enriched with Malvasia wine and chicken broth. See BLANCMANGE. The first recipe for this dessert can be found in Bartolomeo Scappi's *Opera* (1570), where *zambaglione* is savory and contains no sugar. However, a similar one for *genestrata* (broom-colored dessert) does contain sugar, which was a widely used ingredient in the Renaissance. In *Lo scalco alla moderna* (1694), Antonio Latini refers to *zambaglione* flavored with perfumed waters, cinnamon, and pistachio nuts. See LATINI, ANTONIO. An early Italian recipe for home cooks calls for the eggs to be left whole in the wine until the shell disintegrates completely, providing an additional source of calcium.

When made with fresh raw yolks, zabaglione was considered an excellent tonic for ailing children or for the elderly, while men readily imbibed it for its supposed ability to increase their sexual prowess. Latini considered *zabaglione* so uplifting that no other food would be required for the whole day. The secret was supposed to be a pinch of nutmeg to improve the flavor. See NUTMEG. Today, zabaglione, often prepared in special glasses, can be enjoyed both as a warm drink in winter or as cold refreshment in summer. The creamy dessert version of zabaglione is often served with berries, fresh or stewed fruits, or plain cakes.

Sambayòn is particularly appreciated in Argentina, Uruguay, and Venezuela, thanks to their substantial Italian populations. As an ice cream flavor it is exceedingly popular in many countries. Zabaglione is also a well-known bottled liqueur with a characteristic bright yellow color; it is drunk neat or poured as a topping onto desserts.

Gosetti della Salda, Anna. *Le ricette regionali italiane. 16th ed.* Milan: Solares, 2005.

Scappi, Bartolomeo. *Opera di Bartolomeo Scappi.* Venice: Tramezzino, 1570.

June di Schino

zalabiya is an ancient pastry that has been spelled in a number of ways in Iran and neighboring regions: *zalībiyā, zolūbiyā, zolbiyā, zulābiyyah,* and, in India, *jalebi* or *jilebi.* Its meaning has drifted in several directions as well.

The oldest recipes appear in a tenth-century Baghdad recipe collection called *Kitāb al-Ṭabīkh.* See BAGHDAD. Some are for frying shaped pieces of leavened dough, and one is for a leavened cake baked in a tandoor oven. But the chief variety, also known as *mushabbak* (lattice), has been one of the most popular Middle Eastern and Indian pastries ever since. See INDIA and MIDDLE EAST. It remains one of the favorite sweets served at Eid al-Fitr, the feast that ends the Muslim fasting month of Ramadan. See ISLAM and RAMADAN.

Mushabbak is made by dribbling a leavened batter into boiling oil from a special utensil with a hole bored in the bottom (in the medieval books, often a coconut shell). A typical medieval instruction goes as follows: "Put your finger over the hole; then raise your hand over the frying pan and quickly remove your finger. The batter will run out through the hole into the frying-pan as you turn your hand in circles, forming rings, lattices and so on." All varieties of *zulābiyā* were soaked with honey or sugar syrup after cooking, and *mushabbak* might be colored red or green with food coloring during the Middle Ages, as it still often is.

In thirteenth-century Arab cookbooks, the *mushabbak* variety predominates, but there are also recipes for stuffed *zulābiyā*, which was a piece of firmly kneaded dough stuffed with nuts, shaped in a mold, dipped in *zulābiyā* batter, and then in sesame oil. A pastry called *qāhiriyya* consisted of rings of pistachio paste dipped in *zulābiyā* batter and then fried. See NUTS.

In the modern world, the most widespread shape is a round lattice of overlapping loops, but in Algeria the lattice takes the form of parallel lines that can be separated into batons after frying. In Palestinian cuisine, this sort of shape can come out as a big flat cake. In Egypt, Syria, and Yemen, *zulābiyā* often means walnut-sized balls of dough (sometimes stretched a few inches in length before frying), which can be a little hard to distinguish from *luqam al-qāḍī* or the similar leavened fritters called *'awwāmāt* (swimmers). See FRITTERS and FRIED DOUGH. In these places the lattice shape is called always *mushabbak*.

Although the *mushabbak* version might seem to have triumphed over its rivals, the shaped *zulābiyā* seems to have survived in Syria down to modern times, and it may also have played a role in the creation of one of the best-known Western sweets. According to a well-known story, the ice cream cone was invented at the 1904 Columbian Exposition in St. Louis when an ice cream seller ran out of bowls. A neighboring stall operated by Ernest Hamwy was selling a sort of *zulābiyā*, which took the form of a wafer cooked between heated metal sheets. Hamwy helped his neighbor out by rolling up his wafers, while still hot and pliable, into cones that could hold a scoop of ice cream. See ICE CREAM CONES. Like European wafers (and waffles), they had a waffle pattern to distinguish them as a secular food from the Communion wafers used for Christian sacramental purposes. Other Syrian immigrants named Abe Doumar, Nick Kabbaz, and David Avayu also claimed to have invented the ice cream cone, making it clear that the wafer *zulābiyā* was known in Syria, despite having rarely if ever been recorded in cookbooks. See WAFERS.

See also HONEY.

Perry, Charles, trans. "The Description of Familiar Foods (*Kitāb Waṣf al-Aṭ'ima al-Mu'tāda*)." In *Medieval Arab Cookery*, pp. 273–450. Totnes, U.K.: Prospect, 2000.

Charles Perry

zeppole

See FRIED DOUGH.

zuppa inglese, an Italian version of English trifle, is a typical Italian holiday dessert for Christmas, New Year's, or Easter. Found in a number of regions of Italy, its name means "English soup," in recognition of its similarity to trifle. The dessert belongs to a category of sweets known as a *dolce al cucchiaio*, or a "spoon sweet," meaning that it is soft and eaten with a spoon. Zuppa inglese consists of génoise cake (*pan de Spagna*, or sponge cake) soaked with liqueur, pastry cream, jam, and chocolate.

The origin of zuppa inglese is debatable. The food writer Arthur Schwartz argues for Naples, for which there is some evidence, as this dessert was served at a banquet given by King Ferdinand and Maria Carolina to honor the English admiral Horatio Nelson. Other writers, such as the famous Roman cookbook author Ada Boni (1881–1973), argue for Lazio, and still others for Tuscany. The Italian historian and archivist of the Archivio di Stato di Siena, Alessandro Lisini (1851–1945), suggested that the dish, once known as *zuppa del duca*, was introduced by the sizable and flourishing Anglo-Saxon community of expatriates in Florence in the late nineteenth century. Others contend that zuppa inglese originated in Siena, since it uses *pan di Spagna*, a sponge cake offered by the Florentine ambassador Ippolito da Corregio to that city in acknowledgment of the agreement between Siena and the Spaniards who were besieged there in July 1552. Yet another conjecture is that Charles V's (1500–1558) minister in Siena, the duke of Amalfi, preferred this dessert to all others.

See also ITALY; SPONGE CAKE; and TRIFLE.

Boni, Ada. *La cucina romana*. Rome: Newton Compton, 2010.

Parenti, Giovanni Righi. *La cucina toscana*. 2d ed. Rome: Newton Compton, 1999.

Schwartz, Arthur. *Naples at Table: Cooking in Campania*. New York: HarperCollins, 1998.

Clifford A. Wright

APPENDIXES

FILMS

In the movie *Mary Poppins*, the nanny of the title instructs her young charges with a song, telling them, "A spoonful of sugar helps the medicine go down." In fact, Mary Poppins was on to more than just medicine. Sweets in film carry messages, too, bringing a key plot point, theme, or character into healthier view. Sweets elicit sympathy, expressing love, healing, and togetherness, as well as heartbreak, sadness, and sickness. They can also foster antipathy and signal danger or death. Sugar is so facile in films that it can function as the sticky nectar that binds characters to each other or as a poison powder that dries relations to a crumble. Or it can be a trophy, a sign of triumph among competing pastry chefs, for example, or a destructive ingredient in a personal or professional downfall.

The following list of films that employ sweets to tell their stories is by no means comprehensive. Instead, it provides a mere peek into the pantry, showing different ways that sweets can be used to heighten the flavor of a film's narrative fiction or feed the premise of a documentary. But make no mistake, sweet foods enlighten us about people and cultures beyond the frame as well. When looking at film through the dessert lens, it quickly becomes clear that no sweet or sweet-as-metaphor is as American as pie or as French as *chocolat*.

***A Lot of Chocolate* (d. Peter Brogna, 2009)**
The accurate and wry synopsis of this 2-minute, 27-second black-and-white short is "A man eats a lot of chocolate." As one actor systematically eats his way through a fridge packed with chocolate foods, the audience is taken on a hypoglycemic journey, experiencing excitement, elation, and then a crash of disgust after witnessing the overindulgence.

***Amadeus* (d. Milos Forman, 1984)**
Among the array of tarts and sweet treats on display in this rich tale of rivalry, hubris, and musical virtuosity, *capezzoli di Venere* (nipples of Venus) are the most seductive, betraying the composer Salieri's ruthlessness when he uses the titillating chestnut treats to tempt Mozart's wife into revealing secrets about the mad genius.

***American Pie* (d. Paul Weitz, 1999)**
In this above-average teen sex comedy, four male friends make a pact to lose their virginity by prom night. A warm apple pie—the main character Jim's "favorite," says his mom—serves as both a metaphor and hilarious practice ground for the young men's conquest.

***Because I Said So* (d. Michael Lehmann, 2007)**
A mother and daughter run a catering company and explore their relationship with each other and the men in their lives while creating enormous, elaborate, and untraditional ceremonial cakes. The film's cakes were provided by Cake Divas, a Beverly Hills bakery started by two Food Network Challenge contestants best known for making one-of-a kind cakes for popular television shows.

***The Belly of an Architect* (d. Peter Greenaway, 1986)**
A successful Chicago architect becomes obsessed with Étienne-Louis Boullée, an eighteenth-century French architect who designed magnificent buildings and tombs for Rome despite never having visited the city. When the American arrives in Rome, his welcome reception includes a cake molded in the shape of Boullée's spherical tomb for Isaac Newton. The cake gives the architect stomach pains that grow increasingly worse, leading to an obsession with bellies, poisoning, and greed-induced paranoia.

***Bugsy Malone* (d. Alan Parker, 1976)**
Child stars Scott Baio and Jodie Foster are among the kids playing mobsters and molls in this musical

underworld where whipped cream "splurge" guns are the weapons of choice—and a sly reminder to kids that indulging in sweets will have negative consequences.

***Candyman: The David Klein Story* (d. Costa Botes, 2010)**
A documentary about the eccentric inventor of the Jelly Belly—the candy that defined the Reagan era—who innovatively created a demand for an "upmarket" jelly bean with its super-smooth texture, an unusual array of flavors, and considerable marketing savvy. But as business boomed, so did strife within the company as well as within Klein's heart of gold, leading him to give away his ownership and fortune and claim that the little bean "ruined his life."

***Chocolat* (d. Lasse Hallström, 2000)**
A beguiling chocolatier and her daughter open a chocolate shop and turn an uptight French village into Love Central. Juliet Binoche is the pharmacist in this aphrodisiacal apothecary; Johnny Depp unconvincingly plays her own object of affection.

***The Chocolate War* (d. Keith Gordon, 1988)**
When Jerry, a new enrollee at an exclusive Catholic prep school, attempts to fit in by joining the football team, he quickly learns that selling chocolate bars for a school fundraiser—or rather, agreeing not to—is the real secret to peer acceptance.

***Comfort and Joy* (d. Bill Forsyth, 1984)**
Inspired by real events that took place in Glasgow, this quirky comedy follows a heartbroken radio DJ into the middle of the town's ice cream mafia war, through which he comes to appreciate anew the sweetness of a simple life.

***Drag Me to Hell* (d. Sam Raimi, 2009)**
When a gypsy puts a curse on a mortgage broker for failing to extend a mortgage request, the "Lamia" demon wreaks havoc on the snobbish young woman, causing her nightmares and extreme nosebleeds, and turning a cake into a maggoty, evil-eyeball confection that spurts blood when touched with the tines of a fork.

***Eating* (d. Henry Jaglom, 1990)**
A fiction film made in a documentary style about a group of unhappy women who gather for a birthday party, and in their discussions about food (and commonly, throwing it up) reveal the complexity of their relationships with men, women, work, and themselves—all while, unsurprisingly, declining to eat the cake.

***El Bulli: Cooking in Progress* (d. Gereon Wetzel, 2011)**
This documentary about the now-shuttered Catalonian restaurant focuses on master chef Ferran Adrià and his team of cooks, who recombined familiar ingredients into tastes completely new. Their inventiveness included creating new courses, such as "pre-desserts," which were small dishes served after the *tapas* and before the desserts to ease diners from savory to sweet flavors, and "morphs," which replaced petits fours at the conclusion of the meal.

***Elf* (d. Jon Favreau, 2003)**
An endearing Christmas comedy about a 6′3″ man raised by Santa's elves. With an elf suit, guileless charm, and childlike naïveté, Buddy seeks out his real (and really reluctant) father in New York City, all the while subsisting on elves' four main food groups: candy, candy corn, candy canes, and syrup.

***A Feast at Midnight* (d. Justin Hardy, 1994)**
A British comedy about a bullied son of a top chef who decides to create a gourmet club, "the Scoffers" (named after Escoffier), at his new boarding school. With indulgent delicacies made from his father's recipes providing an alternative to the school's grim meals, the boy wins over his classmates, causing some mischief with alcohol-laced chocolate cake along the way.

***The Five Senses* (d. Jeremy Podeswa, 1999)**
In this drama about human relationships and urban alienation, five characters' emotional journeys correlate with the five senses, including a loveless baker who creates visually stunning cakes that are horrible to eat because she herself has no sense of taste.

***The Fly* (d. David Cronenberg, 1986)**
In this head-buzzing remake of the 1956 sci-fi thriller, a scientist develops matter-transporting "telepods" and accidentally takes a housefly along for a test ride. With the insect now part of the scientist's DNA, among the more grotesque changes he begins to experience is an insatiable, frantic, and chaotic appetite for sugar.

***Food Will Win the War* (d. Hamilton Luske, 1942)**
An animated wartime propaganda short created by Walt Disney Studios to give encouragement to underfed allies, assert the United States' lead in a new international food economy, reassure farmers that their work was needed, and tell Americans not to panic about food shortages. Among the impressively illustrated statistics: an annual amount of U.S.-grown fruit at the time would fill a pie 25 miles in diameter.

***Forrest Gump* (d. Robert Zemeckis, 1994)**
When the affable and egoless title character utters, "My momma always said, 'Life is like a box of chocolates. You never know what you're gonna get,'" he sets in motion the film's key metaphor, as Forrest finds himself a part of

the major American cultural events of the second half of the twentieth century, in contrast with the less charmed life of the girl he has loved since boyhood.

***La Grand Bouffe* (d. Marco Ferreri, 1973)**
Italian comic opera ("opera buffa") meets the French *bouffer* (slang for excessive eating) in this legendary film about four middle-aged male friends who embark on a suicidal bacchanal—eating, drinking, and sexing themselves to death, with diabetic Philippe the last to die after eating a cake shaped like a pair of breasts.

***Grease* (d. Randal Kleiser, 1978)**
This kitschy teen dream of a musical about love between a good girl and a bad boy includes many misguided attempts at sophistication among the young characters, including drinking wine with Twinkies. "It says right here it is a dessert wine," says Jan, the chubby compulsive eater in the Pink Ladies.

***Haute Cuisine* (d. Christian Vincent, 2012)**
Based on the true story of a provincial cook and truffle specialist who became the private chef of French president François Mitterand when he expressed a preference for simple, country-style cooking, a Gâteau Saint Honoré with "Granny's cream" is the film's signature, emotionally rich dessert offering.

***Heartburn* (d. Mike Nichols, 1986)**
This comedic drama about a food writer, her tumultuous relationship with another journalist, and all the dinner parties in between is based on a novel by Nora Ephron and includes a well-tossed key lime pie that initiates the tossing out of an unfaithful husband.

***The Help* (d. Tate Taylor, 2011)**
In this story about a young female journalist who, in writing about 1960s Mississippi housemaids' experiences, encourages the women to claim their voice and demand respect, Minny, a housemaid, exacts revenge by serving her nasty employer an extra-special chocolate pie.

***Inglourious Basterds* (d. Quentin Tarantino, 2009)**
Tarantino's penchant for cinematic violence extends even to sweets when, in this film, a Nazi colonel interrogates a woman whose family he murdered years before about using her theater to show a propaganda film—all while attacking, with flourish, a piece of strudel indulgently layered with extra cream.

***Julie and Julia* (d. Nora Ephron, 2009)**
Seeking solace from her workday doldrums, a young woman passes a chocolate shop and spontaneously decides to make a chocolate cream pie—and then challenges herself to a one-year goal of mastering Julia Child's *Mastering the Art of French Cooking*. Her advancement from that first pie to the lightly underbaked chocolate and almond Reine de Saba cake becomes a major marker of her achievements.

***Keystone Cops films* (Mack Sennett Studios, 1912–1917)**
Ah, sweet anarchy! Sennett's silent Keystone Cop films critique institutional law and order in the form of incompetent policemen, literally giving them a cream pie in the face.

***King Corn* (d. Aaron Wolf, 2007)**
Americans' addiction to high-fructose corn syrup is explored in this documentary, which follows two best friends who discover through laboratory hair analysis that their bodies are primarily made out of corn. With the omnipresent syrup the likely culprit, they decide to test their theory by growing and tracking the processing of an acre of corn.

***Kings of Pastry* (d. Chris Hegedus and D. A. Pennebaker, 2009)**
A documentary about the Meillieurs Ouvriers de France (Best Craftsmen of France) competition, held every four years, and 16 pastry chefs challenged to create, in the three-day contest period, elaborate and perfectly executed confections in order to win the supremely exclusive title.

***Knock on Any Door* (d. Nicholas Ray, 1949)**
In this social problem film, a man's criminal behavior is allegedly the consequence of having grown up in city slums. His misfortune extends past his legal punishments to romantic ones, represented in varying degrees by food, such as a wedding dinner scene with crêpes flambées foretelling his new marriage going up in flames.

***La petite chocolatière* (d. Marc Allégret, 1932)**
Based on a popular play by Paul Gavault and featuring one of the earliest film appearances of Simone Simon, the film tells the class-conscious story of a daughter of a wealthy candy manufacturer who, when her car breaks down in front of the home of a blue-collar family, ends up spending the night with them and falling in love with a government clerk.

***Like Water for Chocolate* (d. Alfonso Arau, 1992)**
Based on the romantic and recipe-laden novel by Laura Esquivel, a woman woos her intended loved one with her cooking. The magical realism of this Mexican feature gloriously seduces the audience as well.

***Marie Antoinette* (d. Sophia Coppola, 2006)**
Set against a modern soundtrack and decorated with Ladurée pastel macaron pyramids to demonstrate Marie

Antoinette's love of all things stylish, pretty, and decorative, this amped-up story of the legendary queen of Versailles is a lavish, decadent affair, regardless of whether she actually uttered the phrase "Let them eat cake."

Merci pour le chocolat **(d. Claude Chabrol, 2000)**
A French crime drama in which an heiress to a chocolate company fortune serves hot chocolate at bedtime to all of her guests, although who gets the drugged version, and why, eludes the audience until the film's end.

Mildred Pierce **(d. Michael Curtiz, 1945)**
Noir meets women's melodrama in this classic film based on James M. Cain's novel about a woman who, upon splitting from her cheating husband, starts obsessively making pies, opens her own restaurant, and finds herself in a sweet-turning-very-sour relationship with a conniving playboy. In Todd Haynes's 2011 HBO miniseries update of the film, the baking becomes more sensual and masterful, offering a modern sensibility of female strength, competency, and sexuality.

Monty Python's The Meaning of Life **(d. Terry Jones and Terry Gilliam, 1983)**
From birth to middle age to death, no life stage goes without crude or comedic comment here, but it's the over-indulgent critique of the obese that really explodes audience expectations. Beware the thin mint.

Nothing Like Chocolate **(d. Kum-Kum Bhavnani, 2012)**
Susan Sarandon narrates this documentary on the history of chocolate and its manufacture, from the food's various cultural currencies to the wealth it currently provides industrial giants, especially those willing to use and exploit child labor. An anarchist chocolate maker and independent cocoa farmer are among those shown providing ethical alternatives.

Once Upon a Time in America **(d. Sergio Leone, 1984)**
Following a group of Jewish male hoodlums growing up in New York in the 1920s through the 1960s, the film shows one boy's coming-of-age moment that occurs when he sits outside the apartment of a young whore, mustering the courage to ask for her services. He carries with him a small Charlotte Russe with lots of whipped cream, just the way she likes it, and in his anticipatory excitement, he devours the pastry himself, first by gently licking the sides, then voraciously eating the mammary-like creation before dashing off fulfilled and relieved.

Peeping Tom **(d. Michael Powell, 1960)**
Everyone likes cake, so why wouldn't the murderer upstairs? In this grim psychological thriller, a man's childhood traumas lead him to kill women, including his neighbor Helen, who fatefully decides to be nice to the odd bird by bringing him a slice of her birthday cake.

The Price of Sugar **(d. Bill Haney, 2007)**
Narrated by Paul Newman, this documentary exposes the thousands of dispossessed Haitians in the Dominican Republic working under armed guard on sugarcane plantations to meet U.S. market demands. A Spanish priest, Father Christopher Hartley, is shown organizing the extremely poor and abused laborers and challenging those profiting from their work, including the common consumer.

Pulp Fiction **(d. Quentin Tarantino, 1994)**
This off-kilter crime treasure is so packed with sweet foods it almost induces a coma, including noteworthy scenes with Pop-Tarts, doughnuts, blueberry pie, and a "five-dollar shake" that eases the chill between Mia and Vince, eventually leading them onto the dance floor together.

Singin' in the Rain **(d. Stanley Donen and Gene Kelly, 1952)**
Among the delights of this classic musical is its self-referentiality toward Hollywood moviemaking, such as when Kathy, besotted with and humiliated by movie star Don Lockwood, cries, "Here's one thing I've learned in the movies!" She then hurls a cake at him, accidentally—and hilariously—hitting his amorous female costar instead.

Stand by Me **(d. Rob Reiner, 1986)**
Based on the novella *The Body* by Stephen King, the film tells the story of a group of nearly adolescent boys who spend a strange, tragic, and wonderful summer together contemplating life through events real and imagined, including a spectacular yarn about the town's fat kid ("Lardass"), who becomes a local hero when he turns a pie-eating contest into "a complete and total barf-o-rama."

Steel Magnolias **(d. Herbert Ross, 1989)**
Sugar is pernicious in this filmed version of the Robert Harling play about the bond of six Louisiana women, one of whom dies from diabetes, as did Harling's own sister. Absurd, humorous, grotesque, and slightly macabre, then, is an enormous groom's cake devoured early on that, with red velvet cake and gray-colored cream cheese, resembles a bleeding armadillo.

Sugar Shack **(*a.k.a. Sucrerie de la Montagne*) (d. James Boo and Ian Parker, 2012)**
A documentary short about a restaurant in Quebec where traditional Canadian maple syrup is the star of the

kitchen, while an array of characters who work in the sugar bush make sure the pure, unadulterated sweet treat remains up to the nation's highest standards.

***Sweet Movie* (d. Dusan Makavejev, 1974)**
Makavejev's disquieting film about human urges, behavior, and biological necessities includes characters having sex in pounds of sugar and squirming in a vat of chocolate, overloading the audience with sensual signifiers.

***Toast* (d. S. J. Clarkson, 2010)**
When an insecure teenager and future food writer (Nigel Slater, on whose memoir the film is based) bakes a ridiculously tall lemon meringue pie, the teen finally surpasses his unpleasant stepmother in winning his widowed father's affections.

***Vatel* (d. Roland Joffe, 2000)**
Shot primarily on location at the sumptuous Château de Chantilly in France, this film stars Gérard Depardieu as the real-life seventeenth-century innovative chef and royal party planner credited for creating Chantilly (whipped) cream—a fact that is disputed—before becoming desperately disillusioned with the nobility he was trained to revere.

***Who Is Killing the Great Chefs of Europe?* (d. Ted Kotcheff, 1978)**
When the great chefs of Europe start being murdered off, an American chef and her ex-husband solve the caper and fall back in love. This comedy's tension culminates in a dessert contest featuring a monstrous chocolate creation called—and possibly containing—"La Bomba."

***Willy Wonka and the Chocolate Factory* (d. Mel Stuart, 1971)**
A musical fable about five children who win a chance to visit a magical candy factory, where, when faced with sweet temptations, they reveal their selfishness and suffer an array of confectionery punishments. The 2005 remake, *Charlie and the Chocolate Factory*, by director Tim Burton, decreases the sugar and ups the Grand Guignol.

Rebecca L. Epstein

SONGS

As raw material, sweets have proven irresistible to lyricists. Sweet things can stand metaphorically for so many larger ideas, including love, sex, and longing. They can also be used as pet names, compliments, condescension, and terms of endearment, charging an inert phrase with nostalgia or imbuing familiar words with new meaning. Musicians have cast the words "sugar" and "sweet" and seemingly every dessert, juice, and candy in unexpected ways, creating a unique catalog of songs both meaningful and memorable, if sometimes more catchy than profound.

In the Western musical canon, songs about sweets are a subset of a larger food-themed body of work. With subjects ranging from tacos to chop suey, chitlins to turtle soup, the American songbook alone draws from a range of cultural traditions as varied as the nation's diverse population. It isn't limited to solid foods: innumerable songs involve coffee, tea, beer, wine, or whiskey. But the sheer volume and diversity of sweets songs warrant a distinct designation, something akin to but far more creative than a "Sweets Songs Tradition," and one that captures the way sweets even influence band names, having inspired the 1980s hip-hop group "Sugar Hill Gang," the 1990s punks the "Candy Snatchers," and the modern garage rockers the "Thick Shakes."

What follows is a selection of fifty largely American songs that, in some way, construct themselves around sweets. Whether a sentimental sensory allusion or an ode to a favorite confection, the songbook incorporates everything from cupcakes to fortune cookies, gingerbread to ginger ale, marshmallows to marmalade, banana pudding to Doublemint gum. This list offers a variety of noteworthy titles in a highly subjective list whose breadth and playful eclecticism should make up for its inherent limitations (there are so many great songs and only so many pages). Rather than seeing this list as incomplete, consider it open-ended, more of a mixtape than a collection of greatest hits.

"Blueberry Hill" (Fats Domino)
Fats Domino's biggest hit takes place on a hill where two people make love before drifting apart, though we never learn if the hill was named Blueberry because it was under cultivation, or if "berry" is a euphemism for virginity. We only know that the memory hits the narrator as both bitter and sweet.

"Brown Sugar" (The Rolling Stones)
With controversial lyrics involving a "Gold Coast slave ship bound for cotton fields" and "black girls" who "taste so good," this 1969 song's central metaphor suggests everything from slave owners who raped their slaves, to Mexican tar heroin, to the way modern white upper-class men eroticize what they consider "exotic," although some listeners claim "brown sugar" simply refers to attractive ebony females.

"Butterscotch" (Freddy King)
This 1961 song by the influential instrumental bluesman draws its name from one of the least utilized sweets in the American music canon, though with no lyrics to examine, we'll never know why King chose this over other hard candies.

"Candy" (Iggy Pop)
The Stooges' punk frontman scored his biggest mainstream hit with this nostalgic 1990 song about lost love. A duet with B-52's singer Kate Pierson, "Candy" reached 28 on the *Billboard* charts and proved that the wild, convulsing Iggy was as tender a musician as he was versatile.

"Candy Girl" (New Edition)
A teenage boy band's 1983 tribute to a girl who looks "so sweet" she's a "special treat," this song features rhyming lyrics so charmingly innocent that you almost forget how formulaic they are.

"Candy Man" (Mississippi John Hurt)
"All heard what sister Johnson said / She always takes a candy stick to bed / Don't stand close to the candy man / He'll leave a big candy stick in your hand." The blues are filled with sexual innuendo, but these rank as some of the spiciest.

"Candy Says" (The Velvet Underground)
Named for Candy Darling, an actress in some of Andy Warhol's films. Darling identified as a woman and traded her birth name James for Candy, partly because she loved sweets, and partly because, as the song said, she'd come to hate her body, and her new identity's elegant femininity suited her better.

"Cheese Cake" (Dexter Gordon)
Gordon's 1962 classic contains one of midcentury jazz's most memorable melodies and most literal titles. As the saxophonist himself put it during a concert at Carnegie Hall, "And this one is about something very, very good to eat: cheese cake." Sometimes it's as simple as that.

"Cherry Bomb" (The Runaways)
A car in cherry condition, virginity as a cherry to lose—this all-female rock band used the often patronizing euphemism for purity and goodness to write a catchy anthem to explosive womanhood, in which there is no shame in desire and nothing bad about being sexual; there is only a group of women singing "Hello world, I'm your wild girl," and demanding that the world deal with it.

"Cherry Pie" (Warrant)
This top-ten hit was written in 15 minutes on a pizza box under record label pressure. The pizza box is on display at the Hard Rock Cafe in Destin, Florida, and the central metaphor is even more prominent: cherry pie as a euphemism for a woman's vagina, which, in this simplistic conception, resembles a triangular piece of pie.

"Cotton Candy Land" (Elvis Presley)
The song Elvis sings in the 1963 film *It Happened at the World's Fair* portrays a children's fantasy world where "every star is a candy bar, and the moon is a marshmallow dream," offering a psychedelic precursor to Roald Dahl's novel about Willa Wonka's candy factory, which came out the following year.

"C.R.E.A.M." (Wu-Tang Clan)
Although not a dessert in and of itself, cream factors in many decadent treats, from ice cream to crème brûlée. On the metaphor menu, cream represents money, the best of the best or most desirable, and in this timeless hip-hop anthem, it's an acronym for "Cash Rules Everything Around Me," which describes the mindset that leads many people out of urban poverty, as well as the central mechanism that drives the bulk of human affairs: the "dollar, dollar bill y'all."

"Goodnite, Sweetheart, Goodnite" (The Spaniels)
This 1954 doo-wop song hit number five on *Billboard*'s R&B chart during a time when Bermuda shorts and poodle skirts were popular, but, as a term of endearment, "sweetheart" has never gone out of style.

"Honey Bee" (Muddy Waters)
In the sexual metaphor of human propagation, women often feature as the colorful flowers who emit seductive scents and wait, petals open, for fertilization, while men are the pollinators who buzz flower to flower, bumbling their way to fatherhood, and whose polygamous nature must supposedly be forgiven. The bluesman Muddy Waters turns this metaphor around and makes a particular woman the bee, because even though she's "been all around the world making honey," she sweetens his life enough that he accepts her polyamory—as long as she "don't sail so long."

"Honey Hush" (Albert Collins)
Like "sugar" and "sweetheart," the pet name "honey" often exudes warmth and intimacy, but it's a double-edged sword. Playing off the old unfortunate stereotype that women talk a lot, this blues uses "honey" not as a term of endearment but as a demeaning power play, an assertion of rank in the gender hierarchy, where the narrator belittles his companion and says her constant "conversation is just about to separate us."

"The Honeydripper" (Roosevelt Sykes)
Coupled with the word "honey," this blues uses the sexually charged verb "drip" to refer not only to a woman's feminine allure, but the physical embodiment of her sexuality: her fluids. A musician who names himself "The Honeydripper" boasts of his cocky virility and attractiveness to women.

"I Want a Little Sugar in My Bowl" (Nina Simone)
The phrase "gimme some sugar" can be a request for a kiss, for sex, or something as simple as your partner's hand. The great singer-pianist Nina Simone wants some love in her life, though "bowl" here suggests she's looking for more than a kiss.

"I Want Candy" (Bow Wow Wow)
Pop music is often more playful than cerebral, and this new wave band's bubblegum cover of a 1960s rock-and-roll tune transforms the emotional strain and complexity of desire into a contagious ode to the singer's desire for a

boy so sweet that he makes her mouth water. See? Nothing complicated about that.

"Ice Cream" (Raekwon)
Raekwon and other Wu-Tang associates liken women to ice cream in this 1995 hip-hop track, representing different skin tones with different flavors, from French vanilla, butter pecan, caramel Sunday, and chocolate deluxe, which the men hope to "scoop" in their ice cream truck. If that isn't metaphorical brilliance, it is, sexually speaking, the mark of an equal opportunity scooper.

"Jelly Roll Blues" (Jelly Roll Morton)
In early blues and jazz circles, the term "jelly roll" alternately meant "sex," "spouse," and "a loving woman," and it was also slang for a man's penis—their shared cylindrical shapes—and for the female genitalia—partly because some thought the rolled dessert cake's folds vaguely resembled labia, and partly because people compared the jelly filling to semen (I'm gonna put some jelly in your roll). Whatever the meaning, the cocky New Orleans jazz pianist Ferdinand Joseph LaMothe earned the boastful nickname "Jelly Roll," and this became one of his signature songs.

"Juicy" (The Notorious B.I.G.)
Widely considered one of the greatest hip-hop songs of all time, this rags-to-riches story uses the word "juice" to mean wealth, power, influence, and vitality. Although B.I.G. never mentions sugar or sweets, being juicy here means living a sweet life of abundance and ability, because when you're juicy, you're flourishing.

"Just Like Honey" (The Jesus and Mary Chain)
Some listeners think this lyrically opaque shoegaze classic is a straightforward reference to the 1958 British play *A Taste of Honey*; some think it's about oral sex or vertical mobility, while others believe it describes a man's undying love for a woman he can't put out of his mind and how, upon returning to her, he accepts all the flack and condemnation that accompany his decision—his willingness to eat "up the scum," as the lyrics say, to taste the honey.

"Lollipop Guild" (*Wizard of Oz*)
In one of American cinema's most iconic musical sequences, Dorothy arrives in Munchkinland, and a group of little people who represent a guild named after lollipops comes out to sing her this 23-second ditty.

"Milkshake" (Kelis)
In this 2003 international pop hit, Kelis's milkshake "brings all the boys to the yard," though rather than a specific body part, milkshake is, in Kelis's words, a metaphor for "the thing that makes women special. It's what gives us our confidence and what makes us exciting."

"Money Honey" (The Drifters)
In this 1953 doo-wop hit, money is a force that binds and dissolves relationships and that, in the process, reduces people's value to their economic usefulness—you need "money, honey, if you want to get along with me."

"My Boy Lollipop" (Millie Small)
With its phallic shape and all the licking required of it, a lollipop may seem an overly sexual metaphor for a teenage girl to sing about, but the song's authors might have intended nothing more than to symbolize a boy who's "sweet as candy" and a "sugar dandy," rather than fellatio.

"Orange Crush" (R.E.M.)
In this slyly political song, singer Michael Stipe uses "Orange Crush" to refer not to the sweet American citrus soda or the corrosive cultural influence that outsiders can have; he refers to Agent Orange, the toxic chemical defoliant sprayed on the Vietnamese countryside during the Vietnam War, offering a surprising lyrical twist that reveals how a simple nickname can sugarcoat unspeakable acts and mask the ugliness of battle.

"Peaches" (R. L. Burnside)
A cover of an older blues song by the farmer Yank Rachell, the yellow peaches hanging "way up in" the woman's tree could represent her breasts suspended on her frame, or the rounded shape of her bottom, though they seem just as likely to symbolize the way the woman's overwhelming femininity makes Burnside want to fetch a stepladder in order to climb up on her "top limb" to "get up there among" her sweet fruit.

"Peaches" (The Presidents of the United States of America)
With its comic, catchy lead about "moving to the country, gonna eat me a lot of peaches," it's tempting to interpret this as an anthem to gluttony, and peaches as a symbol of rural simplicity, summer bounty, and relaxation—the sweet life away from consumer culture—but the central metaphor is no metaphor at all: singer Chris Ballew wrote the song after sitting under a peach tree in the yard of a woman he had a crush on, while on LSD. "I really did squish peaches in my fist," he told me.

"Peppermint Man" (Dick Dale)
Unlike most of his songs, which are instrumental, the surf music superstar Dick Dale wrote this vocal number about callousness and emotional inaccessibility, where a

type of man he calls Mr. Peppermint has a heart so icy that he hurts every woman who tries to love him.

"Pour Some Sugar on Me" (Def Leppard)
The recognizable rock lyrics "Pour some sugar on me, in the name of love" may mean that the singer wants to be graced by a woman's touch, or they may be total nonsense, but what's clear is that the singer is sexually aroused and covered in enough sugar to literally and figuratively be, as he says, "hot, sticky sweet, from my head to my feet, yeah."

"Rolling in My Sweet Baby's Arms" (Roy Acuff)
In a genre known for cheating and heartbreak, the country singer Roy Acuff offers this relatively upbeat number, where "sweet" means "adored" and "rolling" means "sex."

"Savoy Truffle" (The Beatles)
In this tribute to the chocolate habit of his friend Eric Clapton, George Harrison plucked many of the lyrics directly from a box of Mackintosh's Good News chocolates, and he offered an honest chorus about the dental effects of sweets: "But you'll have to have them all pulled out after the Savoy truffle."

"Sour Grapes" (John Prine)
The phrase "sour grapes" originates in Aesop's fable "The Fox and the Grapes," where a fox derides the same fruit he covets because he can't reach it: "Oh, you aren't even ripe yet! I don't need any sour grapes." In this 1972 country song, John Prine sings about his cognitive dissonance concerning the weather, friends, jobs, and peoples' opinions, and he copes with his feelings about the woman who left him by saying, "I was gonna leave her anyway."

"Strawberry Fields Forever" (The Beatles)
Fans have spent decades trying to figure out what The Beatles were singing about in "Lucy in the Sky with Diamonds," but this song is easier to interpret: it's a literal reference to the name of a Salvation Army children's home where John Lennon played as a kid. Although strawberries play only an indirect role in this 1967 classic, this small red berry has never enjoyed a more visible position in popular music.

"Sugar Magnolia" (Grateful Dead)
One of the Dead's old concert staples, this song uses a nonexistent, though poetically charged, flowering hardwood to celebrate a woman and the wondrous necessity of nature.

"Sugar, Sugar" (The Archies)
Legend has it that when the pop band The Monkees declined to record this tune, the songwriters gave it to The Archies, a fictional band from *The Archie Show*; unfortunately, the part about The Monkees never happened. What did happen was that the songwriters and session musicians who played the cartoon Archies scored a huge hit in the United States, United Kingdom, and Canada in 1969, and the song is about nothing more than one boy's love for his "candy girl."

"Sweet Child o' Mine" (Guns N' Roses)
The same Los Angeles metal heads who penned such anthems to hedonistic self-destruction as "Welcome to the Jungle" and "Mr. Brownstone" gave us this tender, nostalgic ballad about longing for simplicity, one of the most memorable in hard rock. Here "sweet" means "precious" or "dear," and Axl Rose sings not about a child but a woman whose appearance reminds him of the innocence and purity of childhood, which he equates with "a warm safe place," and the thought of which is strong enough to make him "break down and cry."

"Sweet Dreams (Are Made of This)" (The Eurythmics)
Dark and mysterious, the chorus "Sweet dreams are made of this / Who am I to disagree / I travel the world and the seven seas / Everybody's looking for something" suggests ancient wisdom and ranks as one of pop music's most memorable lyrics.

"Sweet Georgia Brown" (miscellaneous artists)
Performed by everyone from Ella Fitzgerald to Ray Charles, the lyrics to this 1925 jazz standard were cleaned up over time, but the original race-based version concerned a dark-skinned prostitute named Sweet Georgia Brown who was so attractive that the only "fellers she can't get are fellers she ain't met."

"Sweet Home Chicago" (Robert Johnson)
In a genre defined by so much covering, borrowing, and re-appropriation that a song's authorship can remain hazy, this blues song became a standard about longing and displacement, telling a powerful, elusive tale of homesickness, migration, and the hunger for release, either in a mythical home free of racism and trouble, as some listeners interpret it, or in the shelter of a literal Chicago. Here "sweet" means "beloved" rather than "lovely," a reference to a place that the singer "wants to go," though surely any itinerant twentieth-century bluesman could appreciate Johnson's feeling no matter where he hailed from.

"Sweet Jane" (The Velvet Underground)
This Lou Reed original appeared on the Velvet's 1970 studio album *Loaded*, and its soft, haunting chorus is one of the most iconic in underground rock history.

"Sweet Leaf" (Black Sabbath)
Either the band took poetic license, or they failed to recognize that the marijuana they cherish in this song is composed not of leaves, but of clustered flowers.

"Sweet Little Angel" (B. B. King)
Rather than comparing his beloved to fruit or candy, King compares her to an angel who brings "joy in everything," yet he couldn't resist amplifying his expression of affection by adding the word "sweet," which only goes to show that even biblical metaphors benefit from confectionery enhancement.

"Sweet Little Sixteen" (Chuck Berry)
Berry's ode to the 1950s archetypal teenage rock fan, the darling, innocent kind who had to have "about half a million framed autographs," and wore lipstick and tight dresses to dance at rock shows, but also had to ask her parents' permission: "Please may I go?"

"Sweet Potato Pie" (Domino)
Much like Warrant's "Cherry Pie," this 1993 hip-hop song compares the female anatomy to a triangular wedge of dessert, though the ultra-macho rapper chooses a dark, sugary tuber more closely associated with black America than cherries: the sweet potato.

"Sweet Surrender" (John Denver)
The country singer John Denver's introspective lyrics show him wrestling with his sense of meaning, purpose, and direction in life, and trying to embrace the seemingly pleasant freedom of being unmoored, "like a fish in the water, like a bird in the air."

"Sweet Talking Guy" (The Chiffons)
To "sweet-talk" means to manipulate through flattery, and the narrator of this 1966 pop song questions why she's fallen for a player who sends flowers while he cruises town for other women; in the process, she offers a warning: "Don't give him love today, tomorrow he's on his way."

"Sweet Virginia" (The Rolling Stones)
From pills (red, greens, and blues) to heroin ("the desert in my toenail") and "the speed [hid] inside my old shoe," Mick Jagger and Keith Richards's country ballad doesn't endorse or glorify drugs as "sweet" so much as it features a narrator struggling with some sort of internal "stormy weather" that has him calling "Come on, come on down, sweet Virginia / Come on, honey child, I beg of you."

"Sweet Young Thing Ain't Sweet No More" (Mudhoney)
A mordant 1988 rock song about a vague every-girl character who passes out on the toilet full of pills; here the word "sweet" sarcastically refers to the purity, virtue, and inexperience that supposedly define youth, qualities this "sweet young thing" has lost.

"Sweets" (Ty Segall)
With lyrics like "I heard you got lollipops in your backyard / Oh, lollipop, lollipop, lollipop, lollipop / Sweets are good, sweets are bad, you're the sweetest thing I've ever had," this 2008 song seems a fitting one from a musician whose recording engineer described him as "a big sugar head . . . a kid when it comes to candy."

"Tangerine" (Led Zeppelin)
Often described as one of the few Zeppelin songs whose lyrics Jimmy Page penned, "Tangerine" actually originated as an uncopyrighted Yardbirds composition called "My Baby," of which Page later took ownership. No matter the song's origins, a tangerine's sweet, tart taste provides a suitable title for a song about mourning the loss of a woman named Tangerine, and the painful way time and memories slip "away to grey" from bright citrus hues.

"Tutti Fruiti" (Little Richard)
Although they amused small club audiences, the original lyrics to Little Richard's 1955 masterpiece were too sexually charged for the record label, so it changed "Tutti Frutti, good booty / If it don't fit, don't force it / You can grease it, make it easy," into the vague, phonetic "Tutti Frutti, Aw-Rootie."

Aaron Gilbreath

PASTRY SHOPS

From the grand patisseries and Konditoreien of Paris and Vienna, graced with gilded ceilings and velvet chairs, to corner boutiques tucked away in quiet neighborhoods, pastry shops are places of pilgrimage and ritual. Wide-eyed children beg parents for treats, friends gather to chat over sweet delicacies, and solitary shoppers buy goods to cart home. Buttery aromas waft from the ovens, blending with those of melted chocolate and caramelized fruits, and glass cases hold heaping trays of cookies and elaborate displays of macarons, meringues, and marzipan. Pastry shops sell specialties for holiday celebrations and special occasions, but mostly they cater to the indulgences of the quotidian—the croissants and fruit tarts that mark the break of day, the elegant petits fours and spiced cakes that accompany afternoon tea, and the decadent chocolate tortes that close an evening meal.

Loyal customers proclaim the unrivaled talent of their favorite pastry chefs and bakers, making it impossible to compile an exhaustive list of the world's greatest pastry shops. Moreover, in many countries the best sweets are found outside dedicated stores. In Korea, for instance, prized confection sets are sold in high-end department stores; Argentina's best *alfajores* (dulce de leche sandwich cookies) are easily bought from supermarkets; Mexican markets offer some of the country's most authentic and delicious baked goods; and in much of Africa, sweet snacks are made exclusively for domestic consumption, traded informally or sold from impermanent roadside stalls. Thus, the list that follows is not meant to be comprehensive, but rather to highlight a few dozen of the most notable and beloved independent pastry shops, Konditoreien, and patisseries around the world. While delightful in their own right, candy stores, chocolatiers, fudge makers, gelaterias, and ice cream parlors are not included here. Attention is paid instead to the shops that offer varieties of sweet baked goods, most with traditional European roots, but many bearing signs of local adaptation and creative interpretation.

The shops on this list range in scale and style from companies with multiple outlets, some spanning continents, to small, single stores hidden in hard-to-find corners of a city. Some offer table service in extravagant spaces, where patrons may sip coffees or cordials while delighting in signature sweets, while others sell goods exclusively for takeout. Many are well over a century old, steeped in history and known for their famous clientele, while others are more recent ventures, labors of love built by entrepreneurial bakers. A few offer online ordering and international delivery, but all deserve a visit. Only in person can one fully appreciate the ingenuity of the chefs, the elegant displays, and the pleasure of biting into a freshly baked pastry.

EUROPE

Pastéis de Belém
www.pasteisdebelem.pt
Rua de Belém no. 84 a 92, Lisbon, Portugal
Tel.: +351 21 3637423

Legend has it that the small egg tarts known as "Pastéis de Belém" were invented in the early 1800s in the parish of Belém, now part of Lisbon. Following the closing of a monastery in the aftermath of the Liberal Revolution of 1820, a former monk began selling little tarts in a nearby shop for survival. Today, these tarts are made in the eponymous factory and sold to hordes of visitors for takeout or delivered to customers seated in the simple blue-and-white tiled café. Cookies, cakes made with nuts and candied fruits, marmalades, and jellies are also available.

Bettys
www.bettys.co.uk
Six locations in Harrogate, York, Ilkley, and Northallerton, England
Tel.: +44 1423 814008

Frederick Belmont, a Swiss patissier, first opened a Bettys café in 1919. Today, the family-run business consists of six cafés across Yorkshire, offering a winning combination of Swiss confectionery, cakes, and pastries along with irresistible local specialties such as Yorkshire curd tart, tea loaf, and Fat Rascals (cookies packed with dried fruit and almonds and topped with glacé cherries), plus coffees and teas sourced by the sister company Taylors of Harrogate. Online shopping is available.

Caelum

www.caelumbarcelona.com
Carrer de la Palla 8, Barcelona, Spain
Tel.: +34 93 302 69 93

Spain's convents have a long history of producing excellent cakes and confections, which they sell to the public to help support their institutions. Caelum, an elegant café and shop in Barcelona's Gothic Quarter, offers local specialties from more than a dozen convents all over Spain, including a Santiago's tart from Galicia and a cider cake from Seville. The boutique sits on street level, but it is in the rooms below, framed by hauntingly beautiful stone arches said to have once been home to medieval Jewish baths, that customers linger over pastries while sipping coffee and wine.

Café-Konditorei Buchwald

www.konditorei-buchwald.de
Bartningallee 29, Berlin, Germany
Tel.: +49 30 3915931

Maker of excellent Baumkuchen (round layered cakes made on a rotating spit) since 1852 and former purveyor to the royal court, Café-Konditorei Buchwald remains wonderfully old-fashioned. The menu is refreshingly limited, offering a selection of coffee, cakes, and tortes. During warmer months, outdoor seating is available overlooking the banks of the Spree.

Demel

www.demel.at
Kohlmarkt 14, Vienna, Austria
Tel.: +43 1 535 17170
A second branch is in New York City

A refined café-pastry shop with roots dating back to 1786, Demel has been supplying fancy pastries and confections to the Austrian court and nobility for two centuries. Today, it is widely considered Vienna's premier Konditorei. Elaborate displays of cakes and other Austrian desserts complement the Old World décor and rich wood paneling, making dining there feel like a glimpse into Vienna's majestic history. Seating spills onto the sidewalk with a view of the Hofburg Palace. Online shopping is available.

Dosnon Doumiel

www.dosnondoumiel.fr
10, Rue du College, Villeneuve-Sur-Yonne, Burgundy, France
Tel.: +33 3 86 871764

Founded in 1920, this artisan baker makes some of the best spice bread in northern Burgundy, a region justly famous for these dark, aromatic loaves. Dosnon Doumiel also sells honey products, meringues, and confectionery from its charming storefront located in the center of the riverside town of Villeneuve-sur-Yonne.

Forno Boccione

Via del Portico D'Ottavia 1, Rome, Italy
Tel.: +39 06 687 8637

Also known as Il Forno del Ghetto, this corner Jewish bakery offers only takeout, but the quality of the baked goods fully justifies the lines of eager customers. Not to be missed are the *crostata di ricotta e viscole*, a ricotta cherry pie baked until blackened on top, and the *pizza ebraica*, a sweet bread made with almonds, pine nuts, raisins, and candied fruit. Hours are limited, so call ahead.

Gerbeaud

www.gerbeaud.hu
1051 Vörösmarty tér 7-8, Budapest, Hungary
Tel.: +36 1 429 9000

Established in 1858, Budapest's grandest patisserie once counted many members of the Habsburg family as regulars. Located on the most central square in Budapest, Gerbeaud played an important role in the development of baking and desserts in Budapest and Hungary. Today the café offers savory plates along with a wide range of pastries, candies, and other sweets. The extravagant décor from eras past has been subdued, and today the ambience is one of utter refinement.

Giovanni Scaturchio

www.scaturchio.it
Piazza San Domenico Maggiore 19, Naples, Italy
Tel.: +39 081 551 7031

This café is a wonderful respite from the bustle of central Naples, where patrons sip coffee over masterfully crafted *sfogliatella*—flaky pastries filled with soft ricotta and candied fruit and lightly dusted with sugar—or drink aperitifs accompanied by exquisite *babà*, small yeast cakes soaked in rum that are a specialty of Naples. In addition to a range of sweet pastries, the café serves savory bites, and the boutique offers packaged pantone, torrone, chocolates, and cookies for those unable to eat there.

Conditori La Glace

www.laglace.dk
Skoubogade 3, Copenhagen, Denmark
Tel.: +45 33 144646

Established in 1870, this is the oldest Konditori in Copenhagen, and its longevity is well deserved. Cakes by the slice and traditional Danish butter cookies along with hot chocolate or the house fruit tea are served indoors and, during fine weather, on café tables that line the street. Little details, like the addition of a tiny macaron to a slice of cake, vault the pastries to a level above most. The setting is polished and inviting, and every morsel tastes like Old World luxury.

Kleinblatt

www.kleinblatt.be
Provinciestraat 206, Antwerp, Belgium
Tel.: +32 3 233 75 13

While offering decorative cakes, Kleinblatt is celebrated for its exceptional kosher baked goods, including Eastern European specialty breads, Viennese Sachertorte, butter cakes, and other masterful pastries. It also sells ice cream and fresh pasta. The bakery's current managers include the great-grandchildren of a baker who opened a shop in Poland in 1903, and the goods produced at Kleinblatt reflect the family's adoption of both Eastern and Western European baking traditions.

Konditori Vete-Katten

www.vetekatten.se
Kungsgatan 55, Stockholm, Sweden
Tel.: +46 8 20 84 05

A beloved Konditori since 1928, Vete-Katten is a warren of small rooms where the pastries were once served on Royal Copenhagen china. Although the plates are now more pedestrian, the baked goods remain spectacular. This is the place to go for a classic Swedish *fika*, or coffee break. Don't miss the *kanelbullar* (soft cinnamon buns), *semlor* (tender cardamom-flavored yeast buns filled with marzipan and whipped cream for Fat Tuesday), or the lavish *prinsesstårta* (a sponge cake layered with pastry cream, raspberry jam, and whipped cream mounded into a dome and draped with a sheet of pale green marzipan).

Café Maldaner

www.cafe-maldaner.de
Café Maldaner GmbH, Marktstraße 34, Wiesbaden, Germany
Tel.: +49 611 305214

Claiming to be the "Original Wiener Kaffeehaus Deutschlands," this elegant Old World café has been a Wiesbaden institution since 1859. It is well known for its handmade chocolates and creamy-rich cakes and tortes, which are available for takeout and also can be savored over coffee or tea in the elegant wood-paneled dining room. Café Maldaner is considered the finest Konditorei in Wiesbaden.

Café Niederegger

www.niederegger.de
Breite Straße 89, Lübeck, Germany
Tel.: +49 451 5301126

The confectionery and pastry shop of the Niederegger Company has been one of Germany's most famous producers of marzipan confections since the nineteenth century. It offers 300 kinds of marzipan confections for sale, as well as more than two dozen cakes and tortes, including their specialty, Niederegger Nusstorte, a rich hazelnut cake covered with a layer of marzipan, and served with a little glass of Cuandolé marzipan liqueur. The four-story café also features two plush salons and a small marzipan museum.

The Original Maids of Honour

www.theoriginalmaidsofhonour.co.uk
288 Kew Road, Richmond, Surrey, United Kingdom
Tel.: +44 20 8940 2752

This lovely pastry shop-cum-restaurant, in business since 1887, is located just a few steps from the main entrance to Kew Gardens. The star product is "maids of honour," luscious tarts made from puff pastry and cheese curds according to a secret family recipe that is believed to hail back to Tudor times and King Henry VIII's unfortunate infatuation with Anne Boleyn. Other English cakes and pastries, both savory and sweet, are equally delicious. The restaurant serves lovely spreads for breakfasts, traditional luncheons, and cream teas in the quaint, pink dining room.

Pierre Hermé

www.pierreherme.com
72 Rue de Bonaparte, Paris, France
Tel.: +33 1 43 544777
Multiple locations in France, England, Japan, United Arab Emirates, Hong Kong, and Qatar

High among France's best patissiers, Pierre Hermé makes sweets that are inventive, cleverly flavored, and glorious to behold, including impeccable macarons and a croissant that tastes of roses. Shops vary in scale and décor, but the central boutique in Paris's Sixth Arrondissement is not to be missed. It is a most exquisite shop dominated by a long, minimalist display case, reminiscent of a jeweler's, in which each item is celebrated as a visual and gustatory gem. There are no tables for eating on premises. Online shopping is available.

Rivoire
www.rivoire.it
Piazza della Signoria Angolo Via Vacchereccia 4R, Florence, Italy
Tel.: +39 055 214412

Established in 1872 on the historic Piazza del Signoria, Rivoire is the classic European sweet shop, with beautiful signature pastries, digestifs, and rich hot chocolate. The decor is dripping with Beaux-Arts detailing that mirrors the jewel-like qualities of the chocolate bonbons on display, for which Rivoire is famous. Table service is available, and outdoor seating offers an extraordinary view of Florence's Palazzo Vecchio.

Café Sacher
www.sacher.com/sacher-cafes
Philharmonikerstraße 4, Vienna, Austria
Tel.: +43 1 514 560
Additional locations in Salzburg, Innsbruck, and Graz

This elegant Café-Konditorei is said to be the original home of the famous Sachertorte, but it also offers a variety of spiced and layered cakes. A favorite destination for an evening stroll, Café Sacher's ornate red and ivory rooms swell with patrons who descend on the space after a concert at the nearby Mozarteum. As an accompaniment to the sweets, try an Einspänner (espresso topped with whipped cream) or one of thirty specialty coffees available.

Pâtisserie Sadaharu Aoki
www.sadaharuaoki.com
Boutique Vaugirard, 35 Rue de Vaugirard, Paris, France
Tel.: +33 1 45 444890

Multiple locations in Paris, Tokyo, and Taipei, and one in Nagoya, Japan

The brilliant colors and minimalist beauty of Japanese-born patissier Sadaharu Aoki's creations, arranged neatly in stark white cases like precious gems, will take your breath away. Petite cakes reveal layers of contrasting flavors and textures—pastry creams infused with green tea, chocolate ganache, mousse and buttercream, bean paste, and dustings of cocoa or matcha (powdered green tea). The unexpected flavorings—wasabi, red bean, matcha, and black sesame—of the macarons, mille-feuilles, and the perfectly plump bonbons are subtle and compelling. The creative, cool aesthetic culminates in the signature "bonbon maquillage," rows of intensely colored chocolates resembling pots of eye shadow.

NORTH AMERICA

Brown Sugar Bakery
www.brownsugarbakerychicago.com
328 East 75th Street, Chicago, Illinois, United States
Tel.: +1 773 224 6262

Brown Sugar Bakery promises to make cakes that are "dangerously delicious," and it lives up to its word. Owner and baker Stephanie Hart specializes in decadent cakes, drawing customers from near and far, but also offers a range of pies—including sweet potato pie—bread pudding, banana pudding, cookies, brownies, and cupcakes. The Brown Sugar Bakery was a best-kept secret within Chicago for nearly a decade, until media coverage and awards launched it to fame.

Dahlia Bakery
www.tomdouglas.com/restaurants/dahlia-bakery
2001 4th Avenue, Seattle, Washington, United States
Tel.: +1 206 441 4540

Dahlia Bakery is renowned for its triple coconut cream pie, an ethereal concoction of flaky crust made with shredded coconut, filled with a creamy coconut pastry cream, and topped with whipped cream, toasted coconut, and white chocolate curls. Fans also return for the peanut-butter sandwich cookies with their creamy peanut center, and for the caramel apple brioche. Lunch patrons rave about the artisanal sandwiches, soups, and salads.

Dominique Ansel Bakery
www.dominiqueansel.com
189 Spring Street, New York, New York, United States
Tel.: +1 212 219 2773

Opened by the former executive pastry chef of Daniel, this new bakery stole the city's spotlight with the introduction of the Cronut, a pastry made of croissant-like dough that is shaped and fried like a doughnut. Lines for this treat, which every month bears a different flavor, begin long before the store opens and last for hours. Separate registers are available for purchasing rich cannelés of Bordeaux, mini apple tarte tatin, berry pavlova, ethereal *gâteau battu*, a variety of miniature cakes and tarts, and a range of savory sandwiches.

Au Kouign Amann Boulangerie Patisserie
322 Avenue du Mont-Royal Est, Montreal, Canada
Tel.: +1 514 845 8813

This patisserie is widely praised for its croissants, but do not miss the exquisite kouign-amann, a layered pastry with Breton roots. This sticky golden treat tastes of butter and caramelized sugar—pure contentment. With the shop's limited seating, most patrons opt for takeout.

Manny Randazzo King Cakes
www.randazzokingcake.com
3515 North Hullen Street, Metairie, Louisiana, United States
Tel.: +1 504 456 1476

Since it opened in 1965, fans have flocked to Manny Randazzo for what is arguably the region's best traditional-style King Cakes. Ever popular, especially around Mardi Gras, these cakes are made with a Danish-style dough, braided and twisted into a ring, baked, and topped with icing and bright sprinkles. It is considered auspicious to be the one to find the small plastic baby buried inside the cake.

Pasteleria la Gran Vía
http://pastelerialagranvia.com
Matriz Amsterdam 288-A, Colonia Hipódromo Condesa, Mexico City, Mexico
Tel.: +52 5574 4008

This small bakery offers a variety of sweets, from layer cakes to doughnuts and snow-white meringues. But it is best known for its sweet breads, which include *conchas*, or seashells, made from an egg-based dough and plenty of butter and topped with a crusty, sugary topping in a shell-like pattern (also available in chocolate); and *cuernitos*, made with a similar base but shaped into a crescent. Fresh out of the oven midmorning, both go wonderfully with a cup of coffee.

Pastelería Ideal
Avenida 16 de Septiembre 18, Colonia Centro, Mexico City, Mexico
Tel.: +52 5130 2970
Two other locations in Mexico City

One of Mexico City's biggest and best bakeries, Pastelería Ideal first opened its doors in 1927. Tables piled with *bolillos* (French rolls with pointed ends), dozens of varieties of *pan dulce* (sweet breads and rolls), cookies and biscuits extend across the ground floor. Upstairs, the mammoth bakery is packed with towering cakes offered on special order for weddings, quinceañero parties, anniversaries, and birthdays.

Tartine Bakery & Cafe
www.tartinebakery.com
600 Guerrero Street San Francisco, California, United States
Tel.: +1 415 487 2600

The baking at Tartine Bakery & Café is impeccable, from perfectly crusty breads to delicious croissants, scones, tarts, and cakes. The pastry is French in orientation, with richer caramelization and darker flavors than are found at most American bakeries, but the ambience is strikingly casual and strictly Californian. Customers order at the counter but can use window counters and tables for eating on site.

Veniero's
www.venierospastry.com
342 East 11th Street, New York, New York, United States
Tel.: +1 212 674 7070

Founded in 1894, this pasticceria sells cakes, cannoli, biscotti, cookies, and pastries, mostly by the pound. The café offers a marvelous atmosphere of stained glass, stamped copper ceilings, and Italian marble floors. While located in a different neighborhood from New York's famous Little Italy, Veniero, in both its products and ambience, beautifully preserves the Italian spirit of old New York. Online shopping is available for delivery within the United States.

SOUTH AMERICA

Candelle
www.pasteleriacandelle.com
Avenida Francisco Bilbao 2526, Providencia, Santiago, Chile
Tel.: +56 2 2225 3628

Fanciful and refined, strikingly colored or subdued, the wedding cakes for which Candella is renowned—such as the signature "Torta Candella" made of rum, raspberries, and nuts—are all meticulously executed, with superb flavors worthy of Santiago's elite clientele. While custom orders are the norm, the charming shop, located in an upscale corner of the city, offers smaller, individual cakes to walk-in customers. In addition to the ever-popular layer cakes in flavors ranging from *tres leches* to strawberry yogurt, customers can find *torta cuchufli* (a cake made of rolled wafer cookies filled with dulce de leche) and *torta saint honores* (a cake of French origin made from cream puffs).

Confeitaria Colombo
www.confeitariacolombo.com.br
Saint Gonçalves Dias 32, Centro, Rio de Janeiro, Brazil
Tel.: +55 21 2505 1500

This mesmerizing combination café, bar, and restaurant occupies a grand hall with soaring ceilings, walls bedecked with mirrors, a breathtaking stained-glass skylight, and ornate tiled floors. The pastries rival the magnificent space. Specialties include *casdinhos* (cookies filled with caramel and fruit), *rivadávia* (sponge cake with dulce de leche), petits fours made with cashew nuts instead of flour, custard tarts, and other traditional Brazilian and Portuguese delicacies. A sister café at the Copacabana Fort offers al fresco dining.

Dos Escudos Café
www.dosescudos.net
Juncal 905, Buenos Aires, Argentina
Tel.: +54 43270135
Second location in Montevideo 1690, Buenos Aires, Argentina

Located in a charming historical corner of Buenos Aires, this bakery offers a lovely array of pastries, including *Berlinesas* (hole-less doughnuts) filled with dulce de leche and cream; churros and palmeras; cakes and traditional sweet breads. Fresh croissants and sandwiches make the adjacent café a popular stop for breakfast and lunch.

Pastelería Mila
www.mila.com.co/mila-pasteleria
Calle de la Iglesia, No. 35-76, Cartagena, Colombia
Tel.: +57 5 6644607

In seaside Cartegena, visitors and locals alike descend upon this cheery café in the city center to relax over coffee and sweets. Specialties include dense brownies covered in dulce de leche, crisp churros, cupcakes, and homemade *alfajores*. Scrambled eggs and pancakes topped with bacon make breakfasts here wildly popular.

Pastelería San Antonio
www.pasteleriasanantonio.com
De La Roca De Vergallo 201, Lima, Peru
Tel.: +51 1 7058885
Four additional locations across the city

Since it opened in 1959, Pastelería San Antonio has risen to become one of the city's most bustling places to meet, where couples and chatty groups linger throughout the morning and afternoon, sampling various sweet and savory offerings and sipping coffee in the glassed interior or under umbrellas on the patio. Additional branches have opened across the city, offering the same bright interiors, refined décor and service, and sumptuous arrays of éclairs, tarts, and other pastries crowned with whipped cream, chocolate, and glistening fruits.

Smeterling
www.smeterling.com
Uruguay 1308, Recoleta, Buenos Aires, Argentina
Tel.: + 54 11 5294 6070

Tucked away in an elegant neighborhood, this refined boutique has an open kitchen where customers can watch the pastry chefs at work mixing dough, baking, and decorating their beautiful cakes. Argentina's favorite dessert ingredient—dulce de leche—is incorporated into many of the sweets. Refreshingly simple cupcakes and rich cheesecakes topped with fresh berries are favorites, but the "smeterling," a chocolate cookie covered in mousse with a white chocolate center, steals the show. Very limited seating is available.

MIDDLE EAST AND NORTH AFRICA

Ahmad Makhrum
www.mahroum-baklawa.com
Paulos 6 Street, Nazareth, Israel
Tel.: +972 4 6554470

The Arab town of Nazareth is famous for its sweet shops, of which there are many, specializing particularly in *knafeh*, made with shredded filo pastry and sweet goat's cheese. Locals choose their preferred sweet shop on the basis of the kind of *samneh* (clarified butter) used to make the goods. One of the most popular shops is Ahmad Makhrum, on the main square. This Arab bakery is kosher, and also has branches in Jerusalem, and in Hebron and Ramallah in the West Bank.

Conditoria Albert
36 Matalon Street, Levinsky Market, Tel Aviv, Israel
Tel.: +972 3 6823863

This family-owned shop first opened in the 1930s and moved to its present site in the Levinsky market in southern Tel Aviv in the 1960s. It has scarcely changed since, and it is now one of the last survivors of the Sephardic baking traditions of the Jews of Salonica. It specializes in marzipan, *maronchinos* (almond biscuits), and *bezeh* (filled meringues), which are available for takeout only.

Ali Muhiddin Hacı Bekir
www.hacibekir.com.tr
İstiklal Caddesi No. 83A, Beyoğlu, Istanbul, Turkey
Tel.: +90 212 244 2804
Three additional locations in Istanbul

Founded in the last quarter of the eighteenth century, and still operating on the same premises, the shop is run by descendants of the founder, Hacı Bekir, thought to be the first person to export Turkish delight to Europe. It sells Turkish delight, halvah, and other traditional sweets, including *mastic çevirme*, the origin of fondant.

Amal Bohsali
www.abohsali.com.lb
Alfred Nobel Street, Hamra, Beirut, Lebanon
Tel.: +961 1 354400
Two other locations in Beirut and one in Montreal, Canada (www.amalbohsali.ca)

The origins of Amal Bohsali date to 1878, when the ancestors of the current owners opened a small shop on the bustling Union Square, now known as Martyrs' Square. Today the shop sells beautiful Arab pastries, including varieties of flaky and delicious baklava and *ma'amoul* (shortbread cookies filled with dates, pistachio, or walnuts and covered with powdered sugar). Worldwide delivery is available, but the Beirut shops are well worth a visit in person for their tempting displays of sweets.

Pâtisserie Bennis Habous
Habous Palais Royal, 2 Rue Fkih El Gabbas, Casablanca, Morocco
Tel.: +212 5223 03025

No visit to Casablanca is complete without a stop at Pâtisserie Bennis, in the Habous district, the area that encompasses the royal palace. Founded in 1930 and still family-run, Pâtisserie Bennis is the place to pick up a kilo or two of traditional Moroccan pastries, such as honey-coated *briouats* (filo triangles filled with almond paste), gazelle horns coated with powdered sugar, miniature glistening *shbakiya* sprinkled with sesame seeds, *m'hencha* ("the snake"—a baked coil of almond paste), or even *bestila,* Morocco's culinary gem of sweet shredded chicken and fresh herbs.

Karakoy Güllüoglu

www.karakoygulluoglu.com
Rıhtım Cad. No. 3-4, Karaköy, Istanbul, Turkey
Tel.: +90 212 2930910

Founded in 1820, this company makes some of the best baklava and other filo-based, syrup-sweetened treats in Turkey. They come in various sizes and shapes with different nut fillings, but all are flaky, sweet, and delicious. Although the products are made in centralized facilities, Karakoy Güllüoglu's commercial success and fame have not caused its quality to deteriorate. Locals sing its praises and continue to frequent its many shops across Istanbul. The products are also available in specialty stores within Turkey and internationally.

Lord Café and Confectionary

Nejatollahi Street, Tehran, Iran
Tel.: +98 21 8890 0833

Lord Café specializes in Armenian pastries but also offers a range of Iranian sweets. The elegant cakes, made with a Russian-Armenian influence, are exquisite, as are the fruit tarts. Customers can savor these delicacies over sips of rich Turkish coffee in the bright store or have them neatly packed for takeout.

Semiramis Pastries

www.semiramispastries.com
Outlets in the United Arab Emirates and Qatar

One of the best Middle Eastern sweets-makers anywhere, Semiramis produces exquisite baklava, *ma'amoul, ballorieh* (sweetened pistachios surrounded by fine threads of baked knafeh), pine nut *assabe* (filo rolls filled with nuts), and a variety of rose- and citrus-flavored cookies. The original shop was located in Damascus, Syria. While production recently moved to Egypt, ownership and oversight remain under the founding family's control. A series of high-end outlets have opened in Doha, Qatar, and in Sharjah and Abu Dhabi in the United Arab Emirates, but the bustling original shop remains sorely missed.

ASIA AND AUSTRALIA

Adriano Zumbo

www.adrianozumbo.com
296 Darling Street, Balmain, Sydney, Australia
Tel.: +61 2 9810 7318
Three other locations in Australia

Locals and tourists alike line up outside this sliver of a Sydney bakery, where celebrity patissier Adriano Zumbo sells macarons in imaginative Aussie-fusion flavors: Vegemite, musk, pandan sticky rice, and Milo. While the flavors may sound strange, the execution is superb, and the deliciousness of the results confirms that the shop deserves its fame. In addition to macarons, Zumbo sells stunning cakes in fanciful colors and shapes. The displays alone make visiting the shops a must.

Bengawan Solo

www.bengawansolo.com.sg
Twenty-five outlets across Singapore
Tel.: +65 6756 9088

This small chain of shops specializes in traditional Indonesian cakes and confections and *nonya kueh,* the delicacies produced by the Peranakan communities of Malacca and Penang. The *kueh* and *lapis,* or layered cakes, come in a stunning array of flavors, colors, and shapes. Although it is a commercial operation with several storefronts, many items are still made by hand, using traditional ingredients. Orders must be placed in advance for certain specialty items. No seating is available.

Au Bon Vieux Temps

2-1-14 Todoroki, Setagaya-ku, Tokyo, Japan
Tel.: +81 3 3703 8428

Located in the residential district of Oyamadai, Au Bon Vieux Temps is among the most famous cake shops in Tokyo, and customers flock from across the city to buy the exquisite traditional French confections. Parisian-trained patisserier Kawada turns out delicious cakes and tarts, mille-feuille, and a variety of other classic pastries, along with chocolates, fruit gelées, and caramels. Limited seating is available.

Girish Chandra Dey & Nakur Chandra Nandy

www.girishnakur.com
56 Ramdulal Sarkar Street, Kolkata, India
Tel.: +91 94 3249 4423

This shop is one of the best for traditional Bengali milk-based sweets delicately topped with ground nuts and flower petals. Varieties include *kancha golla,* sweetened balls made with fresh cheese; *sarpuriya,* square treats cut from a mass of condensed *malai* (the creamy layer that forms at the top of boiled milk) and dusted with ground pistachios; and *gurer monohora,* soft creamy balls covered in a thick, golden syrup. Locals typically buy various items from the small shop to take home.

K.C. Das

www.kcdas.co.in
11A & B Esplanade East, Kolkata, India
Tel.: +91 33 2248 5920
Multiple outlets in Kolkata and Bangalore

A beloved chain of shops in northern India, K.C. Das is famous for its *rossogolla,* balls of fresh milk curd soaked in sugar syrup. According to company lore, they were invented by the founder, Nobin Chandra, in his small shop in Bagbazar in northern Kolkata in 1868. The company bears the initials of Chandra's son, Krishna Chandra Das, who carried on the tradition of making these sweets and is himself credited with inventing the popular *rossomalai* (cheese balls soaked in cardamom-scented *malai,* or clotted cream). Today, the company feeds a global market with traditional Indian sweets, including canned *rossogolla.* Many agree that despite its success, the shop has retained its excellent quality.

Leong Chee Kee

8-C People's Court, Campbell Street, Penang, Malaysia
Tel.: +60 4 263 9487

Leong How Keng learned to bake under the tutelage of his Cantonese immigrant father and now makes some of the best coconut tarts in all of Asia. They are made with a layered, flaky pastry and a not-too-sweet filling packed with coconut shreds. The 30-year-old bakery is also famous for its *hor chio pia,* thin rectangular biscuits with a delicious swirl of spices, heavy with black pepper. The shop is little more than a shed in one corner of a parking lot, but its delicacies are worth the effort it takes to find it.

SunnyHills

www.sunnyhills.com.tw
No. 1, Alley 4, Lane 36, Section 5, Minsheng East Road, Taipei, Taiwan
Tel.: + 886 2 2760 0508
Additional outlets in Singapore, Shanghai, and Tokyo

Many agree that SunnyHills makes Taiwan's best pineapple cakes, which are the country's defining dessert. This bakery uses only pure pineapple for the fillings, refusing to substitute cheap winter melon, as many other bakeries do. The result is a rich, buttery crust encircling a soft, chewy center with layers of flavor, including the dark tang and floral notes of pineapple—a perfect accompaniment for tea when dining in the gorgeous, minimalist space of the original Taipei branch. Online ordering is available.

Tai Cheong Bakery

35 Lyndhurst Terrace, Central, Hong Kong, China
Tel.: +852 2544 3475
Multiple locations throughout Hong Kong

Among the dozens of shops offering egg tarts across Hong Kong, Tai Cheong Bakery is widely considered to offer the best of these sunflower-yellow pastries. Tai Cheong's tarts are perfectly balanced between a tender, lard-based shortcrust and a yolky, custardy filling. The shop also sells dense, creamy doughnuts that should not be overlooked. Sales are for takeout only, with no seating available.

Sierra B. Clark

MUSEUMS

Only rarely do we stop to consider the history and traditions behind the sweets that bring smiles to our faces. Numerous small museums throughout the world help visitors learn about the history, ingredients, and manufacturing processes that give rise to the candies and confections people love. Wide-ranging exhibitions focus on particular companies or different genres of sweets. The museums on this list offer a glimpse of highly local culture even as they explore larger issues, such as the cultural significance of sugar and the societal costs of its production. From the exhibitions, visitors can discover the art of confectionery from chocolate to baked goods to Gummi Bears, while museum cafés and shops often offer a taste of the sweet things on display.

EUROPE

Carpigiani Gelato Museum
http://gelatomuseum.com/en
Via Emilia, 45, Anzola Emilia, Bologna, Italy
Tel.: +39 051 6505306

"Gelato is an emotional reward at any age," states the museum's website. The museum traces the history and culture of gelato making in Italy and has a gelato school for children and young adults.

Gorrotxategi Museum of Confectionery
www.museodelchocolate.com
Xaxueta, S. L. B-20593257, Plaza Zarra 7, Tolosa, Spain
Tel.: +34 943 651 226

Managed by the Gorrotxategi family and company, this museum has exhibits dedicated to chocolate, honey, turrón, marzipan, and regional sweets, including *xaxus* (marzipan cakes), *tejas* (crisp almond cookies), and *cigarillos* (rolled butter wafers).

Kalev Marzipan Museum Room
www.kalev.ee/en/maiasmokk-cafe/kalev-marzipan-museum-room
Tallinn, Pikk tn 16, the Maiasmokk Café House, Tallinn, Estonia
Tel.: +372 64 64 192

This museum in Estonia's capital documents the long history of marzipan and houses a collection of antique marzipan molds and figures. Marzipan-decorated cakes are also part of the museum's collection.

Laima Chocolate Museum
www.laima.lv/en/tours/laima-chocolate-museum
Miera Street 22, Riga, Latvia
Tel.: +371 67080301

Opened in 2013 by the Laima Chocolate Company, this museum traces the history of chocolate production in Latvia as it follows the trajectory of cacao beans from their origins in West Africa to the company's factory, which was founded in 1870.

Linzer Torte Exhibition, Oberösterreichisches Landesmuseum
www.landesmuseum.at/sammlungen/kultur/bibliothek/linzer-torte
Museumstraße 14, Linz, Austria
Tel.: +43 732 7720 52200

This small exhibition pays tribute to the Linzer torte, with models of different varieties. It is connected to library collections containing early recipes for the dessert.

Musée de la Confiture (Preserves Museum)
www.francis-miot.com/confitures-confiseries/pc/LE-MUSEE-d2.htm

Rond Point d'Uzos—D37, Uzos, France
Tel.: +33 5 59 06 89 13

Antique pots, jars, and other utensils used in preparing preserves are on display at this museum. Vintage posters highlighting various brands of French preserves are included in the collection, which also documents the history and techniques of jam, jelly, and preserve making.

Le Musée du Bonbon Haribo (Haribo Candy Museum)
www.haribomuseum.com
Pont des Charrettes Uzès, France
Tel.: +33 4 66 22 74 39

The Haribo Museum follows the history and production of Haribo candies, which were first made in 1920. Visitors can see posters, advertisements, and displays of the various flavors the company has produced over the years. Machinery is also on display.

Le Musée du Miel (The Honey Museum)
http://musee-du-miel.com
A Moure, Gramont, France
Tel.: +33 5 63 94 00 20

A visit to this museum provides an in-depth exploration of the history of honey and beekeeping, and of honey-based food traditions in the Midi-Pyrénées region of France.

Museo del Turrón (Nougat Museum)
www.museodelturron.com
Polígono Industrial Espartal II, Xixona, Alicante, Spain
Tel.: +34 96 56 10 712

The rich heritage of *turrón* (nougat) in Xixona (Jijona), Spain, is detailed in numerous displays devoted to the ingredients, manufacture, and marketing of this region's best-known confection.

Museu de la Xocolata (Chocolate Museum)
www.museuxocolata.cat/museu.php
Carrer Comerç, 36, Barcelona, Spain
Tel.: +34 93 268 78 78

The history of chocolate, and of Catalan chocolate confectionery in particular, is the focus of this museum, which also offers classes for children and adults.

Museum of Chocolate and Cocoa History
http://www.chokomuseum.ru
7 Ul. Malaya Krasnoselskaya, Moscow, Russia
Tel.: +7 495 982 57 97 or +7 915 027 65 77

In the heart of Moscow, this museum offers a comprehensive look at the global history of chocolate, from the Maya to the present, including exhibitions relating to some of Russia's most popular confectioners, Krasny Oktyabr (Red October) and Babaevsky, which document the story of the chocolate industry in Russia from the early nineteenth century up to the present.

Österreichisches Gebäckmuseum (Austrian Museum of Baking)
www.wels.at/Kultur-und-Bildung/Museen-der-Stadt-Wels/Burg-Wels/Gebaeckmuseum.html
Stadtplatz 1, Wels, Austria
Tel.: +43 7242 235 0

Part of a cultural complex in the town of Wels, this museum displays examples of celebratory and symbolic baked goods from the collection of Professor Ernst Burgstaller, arranged according to the progression of holidays throughout the year.

Pain d'Épices Museum (Gingerbread Museum)
www.paindepices-lips.com/musee
110 rue Principale, Gertwiller, France
Tel.: +33 3 88 08 93 52

This museum devoted to gingerbread has an extensive collection of antique pans, molds, cutters, and transfers used for decorating gingerbread cookies and cakes. Visitors also learn about the history and importance of gingerbread in Alsatian food culture and can see a reconstruction of a traditional eighteenth-century kitchen.

Palais des Bonbons et du Nougat
www.palais-bonbons.com
100 Route de Valence, Montélimar, France
Tel.: +33 4 75 50 62 66

Candy, nougat, and even toys are the highlights of this museum. Permanent exhibits explore sugar, chocolate, and nougat production. A living honeycomb is on display, as is the world's largest block of nougat, which set a Guinness World Record, and other sculptures crafted of nougat and chocolate.

Sally Lunn's Kitchen Museum
www.sallylunns.co.uk/kitchen-museum
4 North Parade Passage, Bath, United Kingdom
Tel.: +44 1225 461 634

Part of Sally Lunn's historic eating house, this museum features a replica of a seventeenth-century kitchen, as well as tools dating back to medieval times. The house and kitchen are thought to be the site of the first Bath bun ever baked. The "eating house" menu includes Bath buns and sweet or savory Sally Lunn loaves.

Szamos Marzipan Museum and Confectionery

www.szamosmarcipan.hu/en/shops
Dumtsa Jenő utca 12, Szentendre, Hungary
Tel.: +36 26 310 545

Szamos, one of Hungary's leading confectionery companies, is behind this Marzipan Museum, where visitors can see a life-sized marzipan replica of the Hungarian Parliament, learn about the company's history, and taste its products in the museum café.

NORTH AMERICA

Alexander and Baldwin Sugar Museum

www.sugarmuseum.com
P.O. Box 125, Puunene, Hawaii, United States
Tel.: +1 808 871 8058

The brutal conditions of plantation life for immigrant workers are sugar coated in this museum devoted to the rise of the sugar industry on Maui, and to its role in creating Hawaii's multiethnic society.

Ice Cream Capital of the World Visitor's Center

16 5th Ave NW, LeMars, Iowa, United States
Tel.: +1 712 546 4090

LeMars, Iowa, is the home of Blue Bunny Ice Cream. The town's welcome center shares the company's history with visitors, who can also experience a reconstructed ice cream parlor from the 1920s and taste 37 different varieties of ice cream.

The Jell-O Gallery

www.jellogallery.org
23 East Main Street, Le Roy, New York, United States
Tel.: +1 585 768 7433

Operated by the Le Roy Historical Society in the town where the iconic jiggly gelatin dessert was born, this museum collection includes material from Jell-O advertising campaigns, recipes and recipe books, and a large collection of Jell-O molds.

Kuyper Cake Collection, formerly The Cake Lady's Mini Cake Museum

http://southernfood.org/kuyper-cake-collection
http://holpalms.com/minicakemuseum.html
1609 Oretha C. Haley Boulevard, New Orleans, Louisiana, United States
Tel.: +1 504 569 0405

Frances Kuyper, a former vaudevillian turned cake decorator, maintained this collection of preserved decorated cakes, along with over 500 cake-decorating manuals, at her home in Pasadena, California, until 1999, when she moved to a retirement home, where she stored the collection in the basement until her death in 2010. Today Mrs. Kuyper's collection is part of the permanent collection of the Southern Food and Beverage Museum in New Orleans, Louisiana.

Life Is Sweet Museum

http://candyality.com/life-is-sweet-candy-museum
520 North Michigan Avenue, Chicago, Illinois, United States
Tel.: +1 312 527 1010
3737 North Southport Avenue, Chicago, Illinois, United States
Tel.: +1 773 472 7800

Run by Candyality, a store specializing in a wide variety of commercial sweets from gummi-style candies to chocolates, this museum features candy art and candy-related artifacts.

El Museo del Dulce de la Calle Real (The Royal Road Candy Museum)

http://delacallereal.com
Avenida Madero #440, Colonia Centro, Morelia, Michoacán, Mexico
Tel.: +52 443 312 8157

De la Calle Real, the oldest candy maker in Mexico, runs this museum from the site of its old candy shop. The shop now displays old photos, letters, family recipes, and candy-making equipment as part of the museum's exhibits. In the demonstration kitchen, visitors can watch centuries-old candy-making techniques and taste the finished products.

Schimpff's Candy Museum

www.schimpffs.com/museum.html
347 Spring Street, Jeffersonville, Indiana, United States
Tel.: +1 812 283 8367

This museum is an arm of Schimpff's Candy, a company known for old-fashioned hard candies such as horehound, lemon, and clove drops, as well as a regional favorite known as the Modjeska. It features American candy equipment, memorabilia, and other artifacts.

Spangler Candy Museum

www.spanglercandy.com/about-us/tour-store-museum
400 North Portland Street, Bryan, Ohio, United States
Tel.: +1 888 636 4221 or +1 419 633 6439

Spangler Candy makes Dum Dums (lollipops), Jolly Rancher hard candies, Saf-T-Pops, and old-fashioned Circus Peanuts. The museum shares historical information and realia from the Spangler Company's 108 years in business. A tour is available.

Wilbur Chocolate Candy Americana Store and Museum
www.wilburbuds.com/docs/museum.html
48 North Broad Street, Lititz, Pennsylvania, United States
Tel.: +1 888 294 5287

Located deep in Pennsylvania's Amish country, this museum has an extensive collection of antique candy tins and candy-related novelties, as well as old advertisements, candy-making equipment, and artwork from around the world.

ASIA

Dessert Kitchen, Topkapı Palace Museum
www.topkapisarayi.gov.tr
Sultanahmet, Fatih, Istanbul, Turkey
Tel.: +90 212 512 04 80

This enormous kitchen was dedicated to the preparation of sweets during the Ottoman Empire. On display are utensils, copperware, and other tools used to prepare traditional halvah and other Turkish confections.

Kuo Yuan Ye Museum of Cake and Pastry
www.kuos.com/museum
Man Lam Road, Shihlin District, Taipei City 546, 4th Floor, Taipei, Taiwan
9 Bayberry Lane County, Taoyuan City Youth Cubs Industrial Area Road 1, Yangmei City, Taiwan
Tel.: +886 2 2831 3422

Traditional Taiwanese pastry making, pastry history, and culture are the subjects of exhibitions at both branches of this museum, which also offers classes in the art of Taiwanese pastry. Visitors can take tours of the Kuo Yuan Ye pastry factory at the Yangmei City location.

Kyōgashi Shiryōkan
www.kyogashi.co.jp/shiryokan
Yanagizushichō 331-2, Kamidachiuri Agaru, Karasuma Dōri, Kamigyōku, Kyoto, Japan
Tel.: +81 75 432 3101

This museum, devoted to the art of traditional Japanese sweet making in Kyoto, is operated by and adjacent to the confectioner Tawaraya. It has a small exhibition hall and sweet-making workshops, and offers samples of Kyoto confectionery.

Thai Dessert Museum
Amphawa Municipality City Hall 75110 Amphawa, Samut Songkhram, Thailand
Tel.: +66 3 475 1359

The history of *khanom*, meaning "dessert" in Thai, is the focus of this museum on the Mae Klong River. On display are colorful resin replicas of over 100 different desserts.

Tsujiguchi Hironobu Confectionery Art Museum
www.kagaya.co.jp/le_musee_de_h
65-1 Wa, Wakura-machi, Nanao, Ishikawa Prefecture, Japan
Tel.: +81 767 62 4000

Pâtissier Tsujiguchi Hironobu designed the Confectionery Art Museum to showcase his sugar art, which is on display. In the museum café, visitors can enjoy his original confections.

Yao Museum
www.konpeitou-kingdom.com/info_museum/index.html#yao
2-88 Wakabayashicho, Yao, Osaka Prefecture, Japan
Tel.: +81 72 948 1339

This museum is part of a network that includes the Sakai Petit and Fukuoka museums. All three focus on the history and culture surrounding the production and consumption of *konpeitō*, a traditional Japanese rock candy brought to the island by the Portuguese in the sixteenth century. Factory tours are given at each location.

Rachel Finn

DIRECTORY OF CONTRIBUTORS

Elizabeth Abbott
Senior Research Associate, Trinity College, University of Toronto, Author of *Sugar: A Bittersweet History*, Toronto, Canada

Rachel Adams
Writer and Professor of English and American Studies, Columbia University, New York, New York

Bill Addison
Restaurant Editor, *Eater*, New York, New York

Pal Ahluwalia
Pro Vice Chancellor, University of Portsmouth, Portsmouth, United Kingdom

Ken Albala
Director of Food Studies and Professor of History, University of the Pacific, Stockton, California

Gary Allen
Empire State College, Saratoga Springs, New York

Steve Almond
Author of *Candyfreak: A Journey through the Chocolate Underbelly of America*, Arlington, Massachusetts

Micah Auerback
Assistant Professor of Japanese Religion, University of Michigan, Ann Arbor, Michigan

Frances Baca
Creative Director, San Francisco, California

Elizabeth Baird
Cookbook Author (*Classic Canadian Cooking*), Former Food Editor of *Canadian Living Magazine*, and Columnist, *Toronto Star* and *Toronto Sun*, Toronto, Canada

Deirdre F. Baker
Children's Book Reviewer, *Toronto Star*, and Assistant Professor, Department of English, University of Toronto, Toronto, Canada

Adam Balic
Independent Scholar, Edinburgh, Scotland, United Kingdom

Chitrita Banerji
Author of *Eating India* and *Bengali Cooking: Seasons and Festivals*, Cambridge, Massachusetts

Carolyn Bánfalvi
Food and Travel Journalist, Author of *Food Wine Budapest*, Budapest, Hungary

Marc Bekoff
Author of *Rewilding Our Hearts*, Professor Emeritus of Ecology and Evolutionary Biology, University of Colorado Boulder, Boulder, Colorado

Ron Ben-Israel
Chef/Owner of Ron Ben-Israel Cakes, New York, New York

Amy Bentley
Department of Nutrition, Food Studies, and Public Health, New York University, New York, New York

Rose Levy Beranbaum
Cordon Rose LLC, Hope, New Jersey

Ryan Berley
Owner, The Franklin Fountain & Shane Confectionery, Philadelphia, Pennsylvania

Amy Besa
Owner, Purple Yam Restaurant (New York, New York and Malate, Manila), Co-author, *Memoirs of Philippine Kitchens*, Brooklyn, New York

Carole Bloom
Pastry Chef, Confectioner, and Author of *Caramel* and *Truffles, Candies, and Confections: Techniques and Recipes for Candymaking*, Carlsbad, California

Janet Boileau
Publisher, *Taste & Travel Magazine*, Ottawa, Canada

John Bradley
Author of *Cadbury's Purple Reign: The Story behind Chocolate's Best-Loved Brand*, Oakville, Canada

Joël Glenn Brenner
Author of *The Emperors of Chocolate: Inside the Secret World of Hershey and Mars*, New York, New York

Catherine Brown
Food Historian, Author of *Broths to Bannocks: Scottish Cookery*, Perthshire, Scotland, United Kingdom

Anthony F. Buccini
Associate, Department of Linguistics, University of Chicago, Chicago, Illinois

Norma E. Cantú
Professor, Latina/Latino Studies Program, and Department of English, University of Missouri, Kansas City, Missouri

Joseph M. Carlin
Author of *Cocktails: A Global History* and Adjunct Professor, Simmons College School of Nursing and Health Sciences, Boston, Massachusetts

Julie A. Cassiday
Department of German and Russian, Williams College, Williamstown, Massachusetts

Maureen Cassidy-Geiger
Independent Scholar, Hudson, New York

Carmel Cedro
Writer and Historian, Melbourne, Australia

Kyri W. Claflin
Gastronomy Lecturer, Boston University Metropolitan College, and Co-editor of *Writing Food History: A Global Perspective*, Boston, Massachusetts

Sierra B. Clark
Department of Nutrition, Food Studies, and Public Health, New York University, New York, New York

Janet Clarkson
Food Historian, Author of *Food History Almanac: Over 1,300 Years of World Culinary History, Culture, and Social Influence*, New Farm, Australia

Andrew Coe
Independent Scholar and Author of *Chop Suey: A Cultural History of Chinese Food in the United States*, Brooklyn, New York

Sarah D. Coffin
Head of the Product Design and Decorative Arts Department and Curator of Seventeenth- and Eighteenth-Century Decorative Arts, Cooper-Hewitt, Smithsonian Design Museum, New York, New York

Caroline Conran
Author of *Sud de France: The Food & Cooking of Languedoc*, London, United Kingdom

Dean Crawford
English Department, Vassar College, Poughkeepsie, New York

Leila Crawford
Independent Scholar, Williamstown, Massachusetts

Anne-Sylvie Crisinel
Independent Researcher, Renens, Switzerland

Andrew Dalby
Linguist, Translator, and Historian, Author of *The Classical Cookbook*, Saint-Coutant, France

Ivan Day
Food Historian, Professional Chef, and Confectioner, Cumbria, United Kingdom

Edan Dekel
Chair of Jewish Studies Program, Department of Classics, Williams College, Williamstown, Massachusetts

Abigail Dennis
Department of English, University of Toronto, Toronto, Canada

Daphne Derven
Curator of Education, The Historic New Orleans Collection, New Orleans, Louisiana

Cara De Silva
Writer, Editor, and Food Historian, New York, New York

Ishita Dey
Department of Sociology, Delhi School of Economics, University of Delhi, New Delhi, India

June di Schino
Food Historian, Senior Researcher, Università Roma Tre, Rome, Italy

Jerry Anne Di Vecchio
Author, Writer, Retired Food and Wine Editor, *Sunset Magazine*, San Francisco, California

Jim Dodge
Director of Specialty Culinary Programs, Bon Appétit Management Company, Author, *Baking with Jim Dodge*, Palo Alto, California

Naomi Duguid
Food Writer and Photographer, Author of *Burma: Rivers of Flavor* and Co-author of *Hot Sour Salty Sweet: A Culinary Journey through Southeast Asia*, Toronto, Canada

Fuchsia Dunlop
Cook and Writer Specializing in Chinese Cuisine, Author of *Every Grain of Rice, Sichuan Cookery*, and *Shark's Fin and Sichuan Pepper*, London, United Kingdom

Nathalie Dupree
Author, Chef, and Cooking Show Host, Charleston, South Carolina

Robyn Eckhardt
Food Journalist and Cookbook Author, Penang, Malaysia

Jody Eddy
Cookbook Author, County Mayo, Ireland

Anastasia Edwards
Writer and Food Historian, London, United Kingdom

Hattie Ellis
Food Writer, Author of *Sweetness and Light: The Mysterious History of the Honey Bee* and *Spoonfuls of Honey*, London, United Kingdom

Rebecca L. Epstein
Director of Communications and Academic Programs, UCLA Chicano Studies Research Center, Los Angeles, California

Steve Ettlinger
Author of *Twinkie, Deconstructed*, New York, New York

Meryle Evans
Culinary Historian, Contributing Editor, *Dessert Professional* magazine, New York, New York

Waltraud Faissner
Former Librarian of Upper Austrian Provincial Museum, Linz, Grünbach, Austria

Gillian Feeley-Harnik
Department of Anthropology, University of Michigan, Ann Arbor, Michigan

Rien Fertel
Writer, Author of *Imagining the Creole City*, New Orleans, Louisiana

Elizabeth Field
Food Writer, Author of *Marmalade: Sweet and Savory Spreads for a Sophisticated Taste*, Canaan, New York

Michael Finlay
Freelance Publisher and Author of *Western Writing Implements, English Decorated Bronze Mortars* and *Pastry Jiggers and Pastry Prints*, Cumbria, United Kingdom

John E. Finn
Professor of Government, Government Department, Wesleyan University, Middletown, Connecticut

Rachel Finn
Writer, Librarian, Food Historian, New York, New York

Len Fisher
Visiting Research Fellow, School of Physics, University of Bristol, and Author of *How to Dunk a Doughnut: The Science of Everyday Life*, Bristol, United Kingdom

Kathleen Fitzgerald
Independent Scholar and Co-author of *Northern Hospitality: Cooking by the Book in New England* and *America's Founding Food: The Story of New England Cooking*, Jamestown, Rhode Island

Ken Forkish
Owner, Ken's Artisan Bakery, Ken's Artisan Pizza, and Trifecta Tavern & Bakery, and Author of *Flour Water Salt Yeast: The Fundamentals of Artisan Bread and Pizza*, Portland, Oregon

Beth M. Forrest
Associate Professor of Liberal Arts, Culinary Institute of America, Hyde Park, New York

Richard Foss
Board Member, Culinary Historians of Southern California, California Curator for the Museum of the American Cocktail, and Author of *Rum: A Global History*, Manhattan Beach, California

Ove Fosså
President of the Norwegian Slow Food Ark of Taste Commission, Sandnes, Norway

Michelle M. Francl
Professor of Chemistry, Department of Chemistry, Bryn Mawr College, Bryn Mawr, Pennsylvania

Sara B. Franklin
Department of Nutrition, Food Studies, and Public Health, NYU Steinhardt, Brooklyn, New York

Anne Cooper Funderburg
Author of *Sundae Best: A History of Soda Fountains*, Concord, California

Elizabeth Gabay
Master of Wine, Independent Scholar, Saint-Martin-Vésubie, France

Pascal Gagneux
Associate Professor, Biomedical Sciences, University of California, San Diego, San Diego, California

Ashley Gearhardt
Department of Psychology, University of Michigan, Ann Arbor, Michigan

Aaron Gilbreath
Essayist and Journalist, Portland, Oregon

Philippa Glanville
Social Historian and Author of *Silver in England*, *Elegant Eating*, and *The Art of Drink*, Richmond, United Kingdom

Anna P. Goldstein
Independent Scholar, South Hadley, Massachusetts

Darra Goldstein
Willcox and Harriet Adsit Professor of Russian, Williams College, and Founding Editor of *Gastronomica: The Journal of Food and Culture*, Williamstown, Massachusetts

David B. Goldstein
Associate Professor, Department of English, York University, Toronto, Canada

Sally Grainger
Reconstructionist Cook and Author of *Cooking Apicius: Roman Recipes for Today*, London, United Kingdom

Cynthia Graubart
Former Cooking Show Television Producer and James Beard Award-Winning Co-author of *Mastering the Art of Southern Cooking*, Atlanta, Georgia

Jonathon Green
Lexicographer, Author of *Green's Dictionary of Slang*, London, United Kingdom

Amy Butler Greenfield
Writer and Historian, Oxford, United Kingdom

Alexandra Grigorieva
Classics and Food History, Helsinki Collegium for Advanced Studies, University of Helsinki, Helsinki, Finland

William Grimes
New York Times, Astoria, New York

Mark Guenther
Muddy Pond Sorghum Mill, Monterey, Tennessee

Sherry Guenther
Muddy Pond Sorghum Mill, Monterey, Tennessee

Katie Guthorn
Former Singer in ZaSu Pitts Memorial Orchestra (1983–1986), San Francisco, California

Kevin A. Guze
Department of Oral Medicine, Infection & Immunity, Division of Periodontology, Harvard School of Dental Medicine, Boston, Massachusetts

Martin Hablesreiter
Co-author of *Food Design XL* and *Eat Design*, Vienna, Austria

Trine Hahnemann
Chef and Author of *The Scandinavian Cookbook*, *The Nordic Diet*, *Scandinavian Christmas*, and *Scandinavian Baking*, Copenhagen, Denmark

Jessica B. Harris
Professor, Queens College – CUNY, and Author of *High on the Hog: A Culinary Journey from Africa to America*, New York, New York

Ingrid Haslinger
Historian, Author of *Tafelspitz und Fledermaus*, Deutsch-Wagram, Austria

Judith Hausman
Writer, Co-author of *Over the Rainbeau: Living the Dream of Sustainable Farming*, South Salem, New York

Ursula Heinzelmann
Food and Wine Writer and Author of *Beyond Bratwurst: A History of Food in Germany*, Berlin, Germany

Mimi Hellman
Associate Professor of Art History, Art History Department, Skidmore College, Saratoga Springs, New York

Anissa Helou
Cookbook Author, Teacher, Consultant, and Chef, London, United Kingdom

Paula Henderson
Architectural and Garden Historian, Gloucestershire, United Kingdom, and Nantucket, Massachusetts

Janie Hibler
Past President of the International Association of Culinary Professionals, Author of *The Berry Bible*, Portland, Oregon

Emily Hilliard
Writer, Folklorist, and Media Producer, Washington, D.C.

Geraldene Holt
Food Writer, Visiting Fellow, Oxford Brookes University, Oxford, United Kingdom

John-Bryan Hopkins
Owner, Foodimentary, Birmingham, Alabama

Miriam Kasin Hospodar
Author of *Heaven's Banquet: Vegetarian Cooking for Lifelong Health the Ayurveda Way*, Santa Barbara, California

Sharon Hudgins
Independent Scholar, Cookbook Author, and Culinary Journalist, McKinney, Texas

Phil Iddison
Civil Engineer, Food Historian, and Oxford Symposiast, London, United Kingdom

Priscilla Mary Işın
Food Historian, Author of *Sherbet and Spice: The Complete Story of Turkish Sweets and Desserts*, Istanbul, Turkey

Tom Jaine
Former Restaurateur, Food Writer, and Proprietor of Prospect Books, Devon, United Kingdom

Bill Jamison
Cookbook Author, Co-author of *The Border Cookbook: Authentic Home Cooking of the American Southwest and Northern Mexico*, Santa Fe, New Mexico

Cheryl Alters Jamison
Cookbook Author, Co-author of *The Border Cookbook: Authentic Home Cooking of the American Southwest and Northern Mexico*, Santa Fe, New Mexico

Stefanie S. Jandl
Independent Scholar and Museum Professional, Acton, Massachusetts

Kaare H. Jensen
Assistant Professor, Department of Physics, Technical University of Denmark, Kongens Lyngby, Denmark

Sandor Ellix Katz
DIY Food Activist and Author of *The Art of Fermentation*, Liberty, Tennessee

Cathy K. Kaufman
Independent Scholar, Author of *Cooking in Ancient Civilizations*, New York, New York

Samira Kawash
Independent Scholar, Author of *Candy: A Century of Panic and Pleasure*, Brooklyn, New York

Ian Kelly
Actor, Historical Biographer, and Playwright, Author of *Cooking for Kings: The Life of the First Celebrity Chef Antonin Carême*, London, United Kingdom

Francine Kirsch
Freelance Writer Specializing in Cultural History, Portland, Oregon

Hannele Klemettilä
Cultural Historian, Author of *The Medieval Kitchen: A Social History with Recipes*, Sonning-on-Thames, United Kingdom

Carolyn Korsmeyer
Professor of Philosophy, Department of Philosophy, University at Buffalo, Buffalo, New York

Beth Kracklauer
Food and Drinks Editor at *The Wall Street Journal*, New York, New York

Aglaia Kremezi
Journalist, Author of *Mediterranean Vegetarian Feasts* and *The Foods of the Greek Islands*, Kea, Greece

Michael Krondl
Food Historian, Author of *Sweet Invention: A History of Dessert*, New York, New York

Corby Kummer
Senior Editor, *The Atlantic*, Boston, Massachusetts

Rachel Laudan
Food Historian, Author of *Cuisine and Empire: Cooking in World History*, Austin, Texas

Helen M. Leach
Emeritus Professor, Department of Anthropology and Archaeology, University of Otago, Dunedin, New Zealand

Alexandra Leaf
Culinary Historian, Author of *The Impressionists' Table*, New York, New York

Jane Lear
Food and Travel Writer, New York, New York

Jennifer 8. Lee
Journalist, Author of *The Fortune Cookie Chronicles*, New York, New York

Benjamin L. Legendre
Professor and Department Head, Audubon Sugar Institute, LSU Agricultural Center, Saint Gabriel, Louisiana

Eric LeMay
Assistant Professor, Department of English, Ohio University, Athens, Ohio

Jane Levi
Silphium Consulting, London, United Kingdom

Carmel A. Levitan
Assistant Professor, Cognitive Science, Occidental College, Los Angeles, California

Katie Liesener
Journalist, Chicago, Illinois

Elisabeth Luard
Food Writer, Journalist, and Broadcaster, Trustee Director of the Oxford Symposium on Food and Cookery, Ceredigion, Wales, United Kingdom

Giles MacDonogh
Writer, Historian, and Translator, Author of *Brillat-Savarin: The Judge and His Stomach*, London, United Kingdom

Glenn R. Mack
President, Le Cordon Bleu College of Culinary Arts, Atlanta, Georgia

Nick Malgieri
Director, Baking Programs, Institute of Culinary Education, New York, New York

Bertie Mandelblatt
Assistant Professor, Department of History and Program in Caribbean Studies, University of Toronto, Toronto, Canada

M. M. Manring
Department of Orthopaedics, The Ohio State University, Columbus, Ohio

Lawrence E. Marks
John B. Pierce Laboratory, Yale University, New Haven, Connecticut

Susan Marks
Author of *Finding Betty Crocker: The Secret Life of America's First Lady of Food*, Minneapolis, Minnesota

Tasha Marks
Guest Lecturer at the Victoria and Albert Museum, London, United Kingdom

Laura Mason
Food Historian, Author of *Sugar-Plums and Sherbet: The Prehistory of Sweets*, Yorkshire, United Kingdom

Emily Matchar
Freelance Writer, Author of *Homeward Bound: Why Women Are Embracing the New Domesticity*, Chapel Hill, North Carolina

Anne E. McBride
Director of the Experimental Cuisine Collective, Co-author of *Les Petits Macarons: Colorful French Confections to Make at Home*, New York, New York

Anne Mendelson
Food Historian, Co-founder of the Culinary Historians of New York, and Author of *Milk: The Surprising Story of Milk through the Ages*, New York, New York

April Merleaux
Author of *Sugar and Civilization: American Empire and the Cultural Politics of Sweetness*, Department of History, Florida International University, Miami, Florida

Sidney Mintz
William L. Straus Jr. Professor of Anthropology Emeritus and Research Professor, Department of Anthropology, John Hopkins University, Baltimore, Maryland

Mark Morton
Centre for Teaching Excellence, University of Waterloo, Waterloo, Canada

Lisa Morton
Horror Author and Screenwriter, North Hollywood, California

Alexia Moyer
Postdoctoral Fellow, McGill Institute for the Study of Canada and the Department of English, McGill University, Montreal, Canada

Jessica Mudry
Department of Professional Communication, Faculty of Communication & Design, Ryerson University, Toronto, Canada

Marty Mulé
Freelance Sportswriter, Author of *Game Changers: The Rousing Legacy of Louisiana Sports*, Covington, Louisiana

Roger Munting
School of History, University of East Anglia, Norwich, United Kingdom

Nawal Nasrallah
Independent Scholar, Author of *Delights from the Garden of Eden: A Cookbook and History of the Iraqi Cuisine*, Salem, New Hampshire

Joan Nathan
Author of *Jewish Cooking in America*, Washington, D.C.

Marion Nestle
Paulette Goddard Professor of Nutrition, Food Studies, and Public Health, New York University, New York, New York

Jacqueline M. Newman
Editor-in-Chief, *Flavor and Fortune*, Kings Park, New York

Jill Norman
Former Editor of the Penguin Food and Wine List, Author of *Herbs and Spices: The Cook's Reference* and *The New Penguin Cookery Book*, Editor of *The Cook's Book*, and Literary Trustee of the Elizabeth David Estate, London, United Kingdom

Sandra L. Oliver
Food Historian and Writer, Author of *Maine Home Cooking*, Islesboro, Maine

S. Douglas Olson
Department of Classical and Near Eastern Studies, University of Minnesota, Minneapolis, Minnesota

Lynne M. Olver
The Food Timeline, Randolph, New Jersey

Fran Osseo-Asare
BETUMI: The African Culinary Network, State College, Pennsylvania

Tom C. Pagonis
Department of Restorative Dentistry and Biomaterials Sciences, Division of Endodontics, Harvard School of Dental Medicine, Boston, Massachusetts

Fabio Parasecoli
Associate Professor and Director of Food Studies Initiatives, The New School, New York, New York

Matthew Parker
Author of *The Sugar Barons: Family, Corruption, Empire, and War in the West Indies*, London, United Kingdom

Greg Patent
Cookbook Author, Baker, and Radio Show Host, Author of *Baking in America*, Missoula, Montana

Karen Pepper
Writing, Rhetoric, and Professional Communication, Massachusetts Institute of Technology, Cambridge, Massachusetts

Charles Perry
Independent Scholar, Author of *A Baghdad Cookery Book*, Sylmar, California

Michael J. Pettid
Professor of Premodern Korean Studies, Department of Asian and Asian American Studies, Binghamton University, Binghamton, New York

Stuart Pigott
Wine Critic and Author, Berlin, Germany, and New York, New York

John Prescott
TasteMatters Research & Consulting, Author of *Taste Matters: Why We Like the Foods We Do*, Sydney, Australia

Maricel E. Presilla
Culinary Historian, Restaurant Owner, and Author of *The New Taste of Chocolate: A Cultural and Natural History of Cacao with Recipes*, Hoboken, New Jersey

Susan G. Purdy
Cookbook Author, Culinary Journalist, Teacher, and Author of *Pie in the Sky*, Roxbury, Connecticut

Jeri Quinzio
Author of *Food on the Rails: The Golden Era of Railroad Dining*, *Pudding: A Global History*, and *Of Sugar and Snow: A History of Ice Cream Making*, Boston, Massachusetts

Patricia Rain
Vanilla Queen, Food Historian, Owner of The Vanilla Company (www.vanillaqueen.com), and Author of *Vanilla: The Cultural History of the World's Favorite Flavor and Fragrance*, Santa Cruz, California

Denise Ramzy
Cornell University, Ithaca, New York; Parsons The New School for Design, New York, New York

Eric C. Rath
Author of *Food and Fantasy in Early Modern Japan*, Professor, History Department, University of Kansas, Lawrence, Kansas

Patricia Bixler Reber
Independent Culinary Historian, Ellicott City, Maryland

LaDonna Redmond
Campaign for Food Justice Now, Minneapolis, Minnesota

Matt Reid
PWR Wines: The People's Wine Revolution, Calistoga, California

Peter W. Rein
Emeritus Professor, Louisiana State University, Stone, United Kingdom

Peter Reinhart
Founder of Brother Juniper's Bakery, Charlotte, North Carolina

Elizabeth Gawthrop Riely
Independent Scholar, Author of *The Chef's Companion*, Brookline, Massachusetts

Neide Rigo
Founder and Author of "Come-Se" (come-se.blogspot .com), São Paulo, Brazil

Gillian Riley
Author of *The Oxford Companion to Italian Food*, London, United Kingdom

Alicia Rios
Food Historian and Food Artist, Author of *Heritage of Spanish Cooking*, Madrid, Spain

Toni Risson
University of Queensland, Brisbane, Australia

Joe Roberts
Travel Writer and Contributor to *The Oxford Companion to Food*, Bath, United Kingdom

Andrea Rocco
Journalist and Food Writer, Genoa, Italy

Frank Rosillo-Calle
Honorary Senior Research Fellow, Faculty of Natural Sciences, Centre for Environmental Policy, Imperial College London, London, United Kingdom

Alice Ross
Historical Food Consultant, Co-founder of the Culinary Historians of New York, and Director of Alice Ross Hearth Studios, Smithtown, New York

Susan M. Rossi-Wilcox
Botanical Museum, Harvard University (Retired), Author of *Dinner for Dickens: The Culinary History of Mrs. Charles Dickens's Menu Books*, Independent Scholar, Niles, Ohio

Noah Rothbaum
Cocktails and Spirits Expert and Author of *The Business of Spirits* and *The Art of American Whiskey*, New York, New York

Leyla Rouhi
John T. McCoy and John B. McCoy Professor of Romance Languages, Williams College, Williamstown, Massachusetts

Paul Rozin
Professor, Psychology Department, University of Pennsylvania, Philadelphia, Pennsylvania

William Rubel
Author of *Bread: A Global History*, Santa Cruz, California

Helen Saberi
Food Historian and Co-author of *Trifle*, London, United Kingdom

Elinor Samuelsson
Parsons The New School for Design, New York, New York

Barbara Santich
Professor Emeritus, University of Adelaide, Adelaide, Australia

Fred Sauceman
Center for Appalachian Studies and Services, East Tennessee State University, Johnson City, Tennessee

Jill Sauceman
Center for Appalachian Studies and Services, East Tennessee State University, Johnson City, Tennessee

Jeanne Schinto
Independent Writer, Andover, Massachusetts

Doreen Schmid
Independent Curator, Writer, and Editor, www.doreenschmid.com, Napa, California

Stephen Schmidt
Principal Writer and Researcher for the Manuscript Cookbooks Survey, New York, New York

Peter Scholliers
History Department, Vrije Universiteit Brussel, Brussels, Belgium

Mindy Segal
Chef and Owner of Mindy's HotChocolate Restaurant and Dessert Bar, Chicago, Illinois

Francine Segan
Food Historian, Public Speaker, and Author of *Dolci: Italy's Sweets*, New York, New York

Colleen Taylor Sen
Independent Scholar, Chicago, Illinois

Laura Shapiro
Journalist and Culinary Historian, Author of *Julia Child: A Life*, New York, New York

Mimi Sheraton
Food Critic, New York, New York

Robert Sietsema
Food Critic, *Eater*, New York, New York

Daniel Bowman Simon
Department of Nutrition, Food Studies, and Public Health, New York University, New York, New York

Nina Simonds
SpicesofLife.com, Author of *Spices of Life: Simple and Delicious Recipes for Great Health* and *A Spoonful of Ginger*, Salem, Massachusetts

Max P. Sinsheimer
Editor, Oxford University Press, New York, New York

Juliann Sivulka
Professor, American Studies, Waseda University, and Author of *Soap, Sex, and Cigarettes: A Cultural History of American Advertising*, Tokyo, Japan

Andrew F. Smith
Food Studies Department, The New School, New York, New York

Hannah Smith-Drelich
Doctoral Candidate, Department of English, Stanford University, Stanford, California

Rodney Snyder
Chocolate History Research Director, Mars Chocolate, Elizabethtown, Pennsylvania

Raymond Sokolov
Former Food Editor of the *New York Times* and Restaurant Critic for *The Wall Street Journal*, Author of *Steal the Menu: A Memoir of Forty Years in Food*, Gardiner, New York

Toby Sonneman
Author of *Lemon: A Global History*, Bellingham, Washington

Rebecca Spang
Director, Center for Eighteenth-Century Studies, Indiana University, Bloomington, Indiana

Charles Spence
Department of Experimental Psychology, University of Oxford, United Kingdom

Harley Spiller
Museum Educator, New York, New York

Zona Spray Starks
Independent Food Researcher and Writer, Nokomis, Florida

Keith Stavely
Independent Scholar and Co-author of *Northern Hospitality: Cooking by the Book in New England* and *America's Founding Food: The Story of New England Cooking*, Jamestown, Rhode Island

Sonja Stummerer
Honey & Bunny Productions, Co-author of *Eat Design*, Vienna, Austria

Damon Talbott
American Studies, University of Kansas, Lawrence, Kansas

Aylin Öney Tan
Food Journalist, Researcher, and Author of *A Taste of Sun & Fire: Gaziantep Cookery*, Ankara, Turkey

John Martin Taylor
Culinary Historian and Food Writer, Author of *Hoppin' John's Lowcountry Cooking: Recipes and Ruminations from Charleston and the Carolina Coastal Plain*, Savannah, Georgia

Malcolm Thick
Historian, Author of *Sir Hugh Plat: The Search for Useful Knowledge in Early Modern England*, Harwell, United Kingdom

Carolyn Thomas
Professor, American Studies, University of California, Davis, Davis, California

Bret Thorn
Senior Food Editor at *Nation's Restaurant News*, New York, New York

Rebecca Tolley-Stokes
Associate Professor and Librarian, East Tennessee State University, Johnson City, Tennessee

Poppy Tooker
Producer and Host of *Louisiana Eats!*, New Orleans, Louisiana

Roy C. Towlen
Retired Financial Writer and Outdoors Editor, Underhill Center, Vermont

Amy B. Trubek
Associate Professor, Nutrition and Food Science Department, University of Vermont, Burlington, Vermont

Michael Turback
Restaurateur, Author of *Ice Cream Sundae: 100 Greatest Fountain Formulas*, Ithaca, New York

Nicoline van der Sijs
Professor of Dutch Historical Linguistics at Radboud University Nijmegen, and Senior Researcher at Meertens Institute, Amsterdam, the Netherlands

Joanna Waley-Cohen
Silver Professor of History, New York University, New York, New York, and Provost, New York University Shanghai, Shanghai, China

Emily Wallace
Deputy Editor, *Southern Cultures*, Chapel Hill, North Carolina

Carole Walter
Past President of the New York Association of Cooking Teachers, Winner of the James Beard Award, Author of *Great Cakes, Great Pies & Tarts, Great Cookies*, and *Great Coffeecakes*, West Orange, New Jersey

Deborah Jean Warner
National Museum of American History, Smithsonian Institution, Washington, D.C.

Ardath Weaver
Research Director at North Carolina Arts Council, Raleigh, North Carolina

William Woys Weaver
Author of *As American as Shoofly Pie: The Foodlore and Fakelore of Pennsylvania Dutch Cuisine*, Devon, Pennsylvania

Robin Weir
Co-author of *Ice Creams, Sorbets and Gelati*, London, United Kingdom

Laura B. Weiss
Journalist and Author of *Ice Cream: A Global History*, New York, New York

Ken Wells
Journalist and Novelist, New York, New York

Robert Wemischner
Pastry Chef and Culinary Educator, Author of *The Dessert Architect*, Los Angeles, California

Barbara Wheaton
Honorary Curator of the Culinary Collection at the Schlesinger Library, Radcliffe College, Cambridge, Massachusetts

Anne Willan
Founder of La Varenne Cooking School and Author of *The Cookbook Library*, Burgundy, France, and Santa Monica, California

Psyche Williams-Forson
Associate Professor, American Studies, University of Maryland, College Park, Maryland

Carol Wilson
Food Writer, Cookbook Author, Wirral, United Kingdom

Clifford A. Wright
Cook, Independent Research Scholar, and Author of *A Mediterranean Feast*, Santa Monica, California

Bill Yosses
Former White House Executive Pastry Chef and Co-author of *Desserts for Dummies* and *The Perfect Finish: Special Desserts for Every Occasion*, New York, New York

Carolin C. Young
Dining Historian and Author of *Apples of Gold in Settings of Silver: Stories of Dinner as a Work of Art*, Paris, France

Sera Lewise Young
Author of *Craving Earth: Understanding Pica—the Urge to Eat Clay, Starch, Ice, and Chalk*, Division of Nutritional Sciences, Cornell University, Ithaca, New York

Su-Mei Yu
Owner, Saffron, and Author of *Cracking the Coconut: Classic Thai Home Cooking*, *Asian Grilling*, and *The Elements of Life: A Contemporary Guide to Thai Recipes and Traditions for Healthier Living*, La Jolla, California

Nancy Zaslavsky
Author of *A Cook's Tour of Mexico: Authentic Recipes from the Country's Best Open-Air Markets, City Fondas, and Home Kitchens*, Los Angeles, California

Melissa Ziobro
Monmouth University, Department of History and Anthropology, West Long Branch, New Jersey

Marcia Zoladz
Chef, Journalist, and Food Historian, Rio de Janeiro, Brazil

INDEX

Page numbers in boldface refer to the main discussion on the subject. Page numbers in italics refer to illustrations and tables.

H

Q